SÜDOSTEUROPA-HANDBUCH
Band VI

V&R

HANDBOOK ON SOUTH EASTERN EUROPE
Volume VI

BULGARIA

Edited by
Klaus-Detlev Grothusen

With 151 Tables, Diagrams and Maps
and one Coloured Map

VANDENHOECK & RUPRECHT IN GÖTTINGEN

SÜDOSTEUROPA-HANDBUCH
Band VI

BULGARIEN

Herausgegeben von
Klaus-Detlev Grothusen

Mit 151 Tabellen, Schaubildern und Karten
und einer farbigen Übersichtskarte

VANDENHOECK & RUPRECHT IN GÖTTINGEN

Gedruckt mit Unterstützung
des Förderungs- und Beihilfefonds Wissenschaft der VG Wort

CIP-Titelaufnahme der Deutschen Bibliothek

Südosteuropa-Handbuch / hrsg. von Klaus-Detlev Grothusen. –
Göttingen : Vandenhoeck u. Ruprecht.
Parallelt.: Handbook on South Eastern Europe
NE: Grothusen, Klaus-Detlev [Hrsg.]; PT
6. Bulgarien. – 1990
ISBN 3-525-36206-4

© Vandenhoeck & Ruprecht, Göttingen 1990
Printed in Germany. – Das Werk einschließlich aller seiner Teile
ist urheberrechtlich geschützt. Jede Verwertung außerhalb
der engen Grenzen des Urheberrechtsgesetzes ist ohne
Zustimmung des Verlages unzulässig und strafbar.
Das gilt insbesondere für Vervielfältigungen, Übersetzungen,
Mikroverfilmung und die Einspeicherung und Verarbeitung
in elektronischen Systemen.
Satz: Tutte Druckerei GmbH., Salzweg-Passau
Druck und Einband: Hubert & Co., Göttingen

Inhaltsverzeichnis

Vorwort 1
Klaus-Detlev Grothusen, Hamburg

VORAUSSETZUNGEN

Geographical Foundations 7
Ian M. Matley, East Lansing/Michigan

Historical Foundations 27
Richard J. Crampton, Canterbury/Kent

DIE POLITISCHE ENTWICKLUNG SEIT DEM ZWEITEN WELTKRIEG

Domestic Politics 56
John D. Bell, Baltimore/Maryland

Außenpolitik 84
Klaus-Detlev Grothusen, Hamburg

POLITISCHES UND RECHTSSYSTEM

Regierungssystem 136
Otto Luchterhandt, Köln

Politisches System 173
Wolfgang Höpken, München

Rechtssystem 224
Christa Jessel-Holst, Hamburg

Landesverteidigung 262
Wilhelm Nolte, Hamburg

WIRTSCHAFT

Wirtschaftssystem 277
Werner Gumpel, München

Industry and Handicrafts 304
Marvin R. Jackson, Tempe/Arizona

Land- und Forstwirtschaft 333
Ilse Grosser, Wien

Bergbau und Energiewirtschaft 355
Jochen Bethkenhagen, Berlin

Handel, Versorgung und Verkehr 371
Franz-Lothar Altmann, München

Tourismus 388
Magarditsch A. Hatschikjan, St. Augustin

Außenwirtschaft 394
Roland Schönfeld, München

GESELLSCHAFT

Raumplanung und Umweltschutz 419
Wolf Oschlies, Köln

Population Structure 433
Robert N. Taaffe, Bloomington/Indiana

Social Structure 458
Roger Whitaker, Boston/Massachusetts

Nationale Minderheiten 474
Stefan Troebst, Berlin

Schulsystem 490
Peter Bachmaier, Wien-Klosterneuburg

Hochschulen und Wissenschaft 518
Milan Beneš, Berlin

Churches and Religious Communities 543
Marin Pundeff, Northridge/California

Massenmedien und Sprachkultur 567
Wolf Oschlies, Köln

KULTUR

Volkskultur 590
Klaus Roth, München

Inhaltsverzeichnis VII

Literatur 605
Reinhard Lauer, Göttingen

Theater 632
Gunnar Hille, Bonn

Film 644
Klaus Eder, München

Bildende Kunst 656
Friedbert Ficker, München

Music 666
Barbara Krader, West Berlin,
unter Mitarbeit von *Gerald F. Messner,* Geelong/Victoria

Sport und Körperkultur 677
Hans-Joachim Hoppe, Köln

DOKUMENTARISCHER ANHANG

Zeittafel 688
Lutz Häfner, Hamburg

Oberste Organe 704
Götz Mavius † und *Michael Schmidt-Neke,* Hamburg

Verträge 718
Christa Jessel-Holst, Hamburg

Biographies of Prominent Public Figures 728
Stephen Ashley, München

Bibliographie 739
Jozo Džambo, München

VERZEICHNISSE

Ortsnamenkonkordanz 777

Abkürzungsverzeichnis 778

Verzeichnis der Tabellen, Schaubilder und Karten 780

Verzeichnis der Autoren 783

Register 786

Vorwort

Mit dem Erscheinen des sechsten Bandes des Südosteuropa-Handbuchs beginnt sich das Ende eines Planes abzuzeichnen, der 1972 von dem damals noch bestehenden Südosteuropa-Arbeitskreis der Deutschen Forschungsgemeinschaft konzipiert worden ist. Inhalt dieses Planes war es, auf der Grundlage einer möglichst umfassenden, internationalen wie interdisziplinären Zusammenarbeit erstmals in der internationalen Südosteuropa-Forschung ein wissenschaftliches Informationsinstrument für alle Länder Südosteuropas in ihrer Entwicklung seit dem II. Weltkrieg zu erarbeiten. Dieser Konzeption lag ein geographischer Südosteuropa-Begriff zugrunde, wie er in der deutschen Südosteuropa-Forschung ebenso wie in der UNESCO – vertreten durch ihre regional zuständige NGO, die *Association Internationale d'Études du Sud-Est Européen* – üblich ist, d. h. als Oberbegriff für acht Länder: Albanien, Bulgarien, Griechenland, Jugoslawien, Rumänien, Türkei, Ungarn und Zypern. Als möglicher Bearbeitungszeitraum für einen Band wurden drei Jahre angesetzt, als finanzielle Förderorganisation die Deutsche Forschungsgemeinschaft vorgeschlagen.

Damit war der Rahmen abgesteckt, an den sich die Bearbeitung bis heute gehalten hat und der auch für den Abschluß des Werkes mit den noch ausstehenden Bänden VII: Albanien und VIII: Zypern gelten soll. Am Ende des ersten Dreijahreszeitraums ist 1975 als Band I: Jugoslawien erschienen, planmäßig folgten 1977 als Band II: Rumänien und 1980 Griechenland als Band III. Nur scheinbar ergab sich bei Band IV: Türkei mit dem Erscheinungsjahr 1985 eine Verzögerung, da der Band V: Ungarn schon 1987 folgte, an den sich ganz im Sinne der Gesamtplanung von 1972 nunmehr 1989 Bulgarien als Band VI anschließt. Die Verschiebung im Erscheinungsjahr des Türkei-Handbuchs hatte seinen Grund nicht in Schwierigkeiten auf seiten der Redaktion, sondern in der innenpolitischen Entwicklung der Türkei, deren neues politisches System der Jahre 1982 und 1983 auf jeden Fall noch miterfaßt werden sollte. Falls es gelingt, auch noch die Bände VII: Albanien und VIII: Zypern pünktlich, d. h. Ende 1992 bzw. 1995 zu veröffentlichen, wäre der Plan von 1972 ohne Rückstand verwirklicht.

Über die methodischen wie inhaltlichen Erfahrungen mit der Bearbeitung eines derart langfristigen und umfangreichen Forschungsprojektes sollte zum jetzigen Zeitpunkt noch nicht abschließend gesprochen werden. Nur zwei Gesichtspunkte seien genannt. Der erste betrifft die Internationalität und Interdisziplinarität der Arbeit, die sich augenfällig in dem für jeden Band neu zusammenzustellenden Team der Autoren zeigt. Als Durchschnittszahlen können 33 Wissenschaftler aus 6 Ländern gelten: Türkei 37 Autoren aus 5 Ländern, Ungarn 30 Autoren aus 7 Ländern, Bulgarien 35 Autoren aus 5 Ländern. Daß die damit verbundenen Koordinationsprobleme nicht gering sind, liegt auf der Hand. Der zweite Gesichtspunkt betrifft die inhaltliche Gliederung der Bände. Hier hat sich eine echte Güterabwägung ergeben: Auf der einen Seite kann der Benutzer zu Recht erwarten, daß die Gesamtgliederung aller Bände einem einheitlichen Schema folgt, das es ihm erlaubt, sich ohne Schwierigkeiten von Band zu Band zurechtzufinden. Auf der anderen Seite müssen Länderspezifika berücksichtigt werden, die sich allein schon aus der stets von Neuem so überaus reizvollen Mannigfaltigkeit Südosteuropas ergeben. Es sei nur darauf verwiesen, daß die Zugehörigkeit zur NATO oder zum Warschauer Pakt, zur EG oder zum RGW, zum System westlich-parlamentarischer Demokratie, zum (bis 1989 gültigen) kommunistischen Einparteiensystem oder zum Bereich blockfreier Länder a priori unterschiedliche Gliederungsgesichtspunkte erfordert. Der Leser wird das Bemühen bemerken, einen nachvollziehbaren Kompromiß von Band zu Band zu finden.

Wenn damit die Besonderheiten des nunmehr vorzulegenden Bandes VI: Bulgarien angesprochen sind, so folgt seine Gliederung natürlich im wesentlichen derjenigen des Bandes V: Ungarn, handelt es sich doch in beiden Fällen um RGW- und WP-Länder. Hingewiesen sei speziell aber z. B. auf das Kapitel Volkskultur, das bewußt an den Anfang des Hauptteils Kultur gestellt worden ist. Die typisch balkanische Bedeutung der Volkskultur, zudem im eindringlichen Verständnis des Verfassers, ließ diese Änderung sinnvoll erscheinen.

Eine Besonderheit ganz anderer Art ergab sich daraus, daß sich im Falle Bulgariens ebenso wie bei Griechenland und – teilweise – bei Jugoslawien das Problem der Transliteration eines nicht-lateinischen Alphabets stellte. Für alle deutschen Autoren ließ sich dieses relativ leicht lösen: Es ist die in der Slawistik eingeführte, sog. wissenschaftliche Transliteration gewählt worden, die folgendes Bild ergibt:

Kyrillischer Buchstabe		Transliteration	Kyrillischer Buchstabe		Transliteration
Bulgarisch					
А	а	a	П	п	p
Б	б	b	Р	р	r
В	в	v	С	с	s
Г	г	g	Т	т	t
Д	д	d	У	у	u
Е	е	e	Ф	ф	f
Ж	ж	ž	Х	х	ch
З	з	z	Ц	ц	c
И	и	i	Ч	ч	č
Й	й	j	Ш	ш	š
К	к	k	Щ	щ	št
Л	л	l	Ъ	ъ	ă
М	м	m		ь	´
Н	н	n	Ю	ю	ju
О	о	o	Я	я	ja

Wesentlich schwieriger war es, die Wahl für die englischsprachigen Autoren zu treffen, da im angelsächsischen Bereich mehrere wissenschaftliche Transliterationen gebraucht werden. Die Wahl ist auf das zumindest im großen amerikanischen Bibliothekswesen eingeführte System der Library of Congress in Washington gefallen:

Vorwort

Bulgarian Letter		Transliteration	Bulgarian Letter		Transliteration
А	а	a	П	п	p
Б	б	b	Р	р	r
В	в	v	С	с	s
Г	г	g	Т	т	t
Д	д	d	У	у	u
Е	е	e	Ф	ф	f
Ж	ж	zh	Х	х	kh
З	з	z	Ц	ц	ts
И	и	i	Ч	ч	ch
Й	й	ĭ	Ш	ш	sh
К	к	k	Щ	щ	sht
Л	л	l	Ъ	ъ	ŭ
М	м	m	Ь	ь	ʹ
Н	н	n	Ю	ю	i͡u
О	о	o	Я	я	i͡a

Eine gewisse Parallele zum Ungarn-Band ergab sich bei den Orts- und sonstigen geographischen Namen. Zwar fehlt in Bulgarien die Fülle für Ungarn typischer doppelter und sogar dreifacher Bezeichnungen, wohl war aber eine nicht ganz kleine Zahl von Ortsumbenennungen zu berücksichtigen (Dobrič → Tolbuchin) und im Einzelfall sogar auch die Aufhebung solcher Umbenennungen (Šumen → Kolarovgrad → Šumen). Wie im Falle Ungarns gilt, daß im laufenden Text die heute gültigen Bezeichnungen verwandt werden, von im Deutschen üblichen Formen wie Sofia, Donau usw. abgesehen. Eine Ortsnamenkonkordanz gibt die nötigen Erläuterungen.

Als günstig hat sich weiterhin im Verlauf der Bearbeitung des Handbuchs erwiesen, Institutionen im laufenden Text überwiegend mit den im Lande üblichen Abkürzungen zu zitieren, da nur so Mißverständnisse ausgeschlossen werden können. Auch hier gibt eine Konkordanz die nötigen Hinweise.

Und wie bei allen bisherigen Bänden sei der Leser auch dieses Mal nachdrücklich auf den Dokumentarischen Anhang hingewiesen. Er enthält eine Fülle an zusätzlichen Informationen, die das Ziel unterstützen, auch diesen Band des Südosteuropa-Handbuchs als ein wissenschaftliches Ganzes vorzulegen und nicht als Addition unverbundener Teile. Dahinter stand auch dieses Mal das Bemühen um wissenschaftliche Objektivität bei der Analyse und Interpretation des Weges, den ein südosteuropäisches Land seit dem II. Weltkrieg gegangen ist und der eine unerschöpliche Fülle an Besonderheiten aufweist, was allein schon an dem eben nicht nur lexikalischen Unterschied zwischen russisch *perestrojka* und bulgarisch *preustrojstvo* deutlich gemacht werden kann. Der Herausgeber hat dankbar zur Kenntnis genommen, daß sich die zahlreichen Besprechungen, die das Südosteuropa-Handbuch bis jetzt mit erfreulich positiver Tendenz erhalten hat, gerade auch auf diesem für jede Wissenschaft besonders schwierigen Feld zustimmend über das bisher Erreichte ausgesprochen haben.

Die Nennung von *perestrojka* und *preustrojstvo* führt im übrigen als Letztes, was inhaltliche Probleme des Bulgarien-Bandes betrifft, zum Ende der Ära Živkov und dem damit verbundenen Übergreifen der Kettenreaktion ostmittel- und südosteuropäischer Umstürze des Jahres 1989 als Ergebnis der *perestrojka* Gorbačevs vom 10.11.1989 an auch auf Bulgarien. Bis zu diesem Datum, das ohne Zweifel zu den „historischen", d.h. tatsächlich Geschichte bewirkenden, in der Nachkriegsentwicklung Bulgariens gehört, war unter der retardierenden Führung Živkovs noch kaum von einer Übernahme des sowjetischen *perestrojka*-Vorbildes durch Bulgarien die Rede gewesen, wie die einschlägigen Analysen aller Kapitel des Handbuchs deutlich machen. Erstmals in der Nachkriegsgeschichte Ostmittel- und Südosteuropas verlor Bulgarien damit die Position des „treuesten Gefolgsmanns" der Sowjetunion.

Der Umsturz vom 10.11.1989 an ließ Bulgarien dann wieder Tritt fassen, was für die Arbeit am Handbuch nicht geringe Probleme mit sich brachte: Als die große innenpolitische Bewegung auch Bulgarien erfaßte, lag der fertige Umbruch des Bandes vor, und auch das Register war als letzter Arbeitsabschnitt praktisch abgeschlossen. Aufgrund großen Entgegenkommens des Verlages Vandenhoeck & Ruprecht sowie der Einsatzbereitschaft vor allem der Herren Prof. Dr. J.D. Bell und Dr. W. Höpken sowie des Hamburger Mitarbeiterteams konnten die wesentlichen Weichenstellungen in Bulgarien bis Anfang 1990 sowie die Absichtserklärungen für 1990 – Parteitag der BKP, Wahlen, neue Verfassung – dann aber doch noch aufgenommen werden. Der Leser wird die Ergebnisse des Umsturzes vom 10.11.1989 an daher mit allen notwendigen Einzelheiten in den Kapiteln „Domestic Politics" und „Politisches System" sowie im „Dokumentarischen Anhang" bei den „Obersten Organen", den „Biographien" und in der „Zeittafel", dazu in einschlägigen Kapiteln wie der „Außenpolitik" und natürlich im Register finden. Die Brücke zur weiteren Entwicklung in Bulgarien ist damit geschlagen. Es sollte in diesem Zusammenhang aber ohnehin nicht vergessen werden, daß alle Bände des Handbuchs zeitlich zwischen den beiden Eckpfeilern „Beginn der Nachkriegsentwicklung" 1944/45 und dem Erscheinungsdatum des jeweiligen Bandes stehen. Der Umsturz in Bulgarien macht so, ebenso wie der weitaus heftigere in Rumänien vom Dezember 1989 einschließlich der Hinrichtung Ceauşescus, nur erneut deutlich, daß nach Abschluß des Gesamtwerkes mit dem Band VIII: Zypern, eine 2. Auflage zu erarbeiten sein wird, die neben Berichtigungen der vorliegenden Darstellungen vor allem der jüngsten Entwicklung in den verschiedenen Ländern zu widmen sein wird.

So bleibt denn auch dieses Mal, am Ende des Vorworts Worte des Dankes zu sagen. Im Gegensatz zu den früheren Bänden sei mit dem auf Menschen bezogenen Dank begonnen, dem dann erst die fördernden Institutionen folgen. Der Grund ist, daß zum ersten Mal in der Geschichte des Südosteuropa-Handbuchs einer der verdientesten jüngeren Mitarbeiter, Herr Dr. G. Mavius, während der Bearbeitung eines Bandes aufgrund einer heimtückischen Krankheit verstorben ist. Sein Andenken bleibt ehrenvoll mit der Geschichte des Südosteuropa-Handbuchs verbunden. Aus dem Hamburger Mitarbeiterkreis sind für den vorliegenden Band außerdem besonders zu nennen: Frau B. Scholz sowie die Herren Dr. M. Schmidt-Neke, A. Lewandowski M.A. und T.M. Bohn. Der Dank an die Autoren schließt sich an, die alle mit nicht enden wollender Geduld Einsicht in die Notwendigkeiten redaktioneller Handbucharbeit gehabt haben.

Was Institutionen betrifft, denen es zu danken gilt, so seien auch dieses Mal aus der Vielzahl von Namen aus vielen Ländern, die genannt werden könnten, zunächst wie gewohnt nur die beiden kontinuierlich für das ganze Südosteuropa-Handbuch entscheidenden hervorgehoben: der Verlag Vandenhoeck & Ruprecht in Göttingen, dessen über Jahrhunderte gewachsenem Verständnis für wissenschaftliche Forschungsvorhaben nicht nachlassender Dank gebührt, und dann die Deutsche Forschungsgemeinschaft, die vom Band I: Jugoslawien an stets die Grundförderung des Handbuchs getragen hat und dies für die verbleibenden zwei Bände hoffentlich weiterhin tun wird. Einen wesentlichen Kostenfaktor hat die DFG allerdings bis jetzt nicht zu übernehmen brauchen: die Druckkosten. Insofern ist an dieser Stelle erstmals der Förderungs- und Beihilfefonds Wissenschaft der VG Wort dankbar zu nennen, der auf Wunsch des Verlages großzügig zur Finanzierung beigetragen hat.

Hamburg, im Dezember 1989   K.-D. Grothusen

Geographical Foundations

Ian M. Matley, East Lansing/Michigan

I. General Geography: 1. Area and Administrative Divisions – 2. Location and Neighbouring States – II. Physical Geography: 1. Basic Relief and Hydrography – 2. Climate – 3. Vegetation and Soils – 4. Mineral and Energy Resources – III. Human Geography: Rural and Urban Settlements – IV. Regional Geography: 1. Western Region – 2. North-eastern Region – 3. South-eastern Region

I. General Geography

Bulgaria is a country with considerable physical diversity. Although it is traversed by mountain ranges, only about one-third of the country's area is above 500 m above sea level. The remaining areas of plains, tablelands, and valleys form a suitable basis for farming and other human activities. Climate and soils are in general favourable. Although the mountain regions contain deposits of metallic minerals, Bulgaria has limited domestic supplies of energy and must rely on imports of coal, oil, and natural gas.

1. Area and Administrative Divisions

The area of the People's Republic of Bulgaria (*Narodna Republika Bŭlgariĩa*) is 110,994 km², making it slightly larger than the GDR or the state of Ohio. Its total population at the end of 1987 was 8,976,255, giving a population density of 80.9 persons per km², compared with the neighbouring countries of Romania (96), Yugoslavia (90), and Greece (75).

The number and type of administrative divisions have varied considerably in recent times. In 1949 the largest unit, the region (*oblast*), was abolished, and an older unit, the province or department (*okrŭg*, pl. *okrŭzi*), was reintroduced, named after its principal town. In that year there were 15 *okrŭzi*, including the city of Sofia, subdivided into 95 districts (*okoliĩa*) and 2,074 communes (*obshtina*). The number of *obshtini* has changed virtually from year to year.

In 1959 the *okoliĩa* was abolished and 30 *okrŭzi* were created, including the cities of Sofia, Plovdiv and Varna. The number of *obshtini* was reduced to 979. In 1985 there were 28 *okrŭzi*, and the number of *obshtini* was reduced to 300. In 1987 a major reorganization of administrative regions took place. The *oblast* (region) was reintroduced as the largest administrative division and the *okrŭg* abolished. There are 9 *oblasti*, namely Mikhaĭlovgrad, Lovech, Razgrad, Varna, Plovdiv, Khaskovo, Burgas, Sofia, and Sofia city. There are 299 *obshtini*, with an additional 12 in the city of Sofia[1]).

2. Location and Neighbouring States

Bulgaria lies between the latitude of 44°13′ and 41°14′N and the longitudes of 22°21′ and 28°36′E. The total length of its boundaries amounts to 2,245 km. The northern boundary with Romania extends for 609 km, of which 470 km is clearly defined by the River Danube. The remaining 139 km crosses the Dobrudja region in the north-east and follows no distinguishing features. The eastern border consists of 378 km of Black Sea coast. The western border with Yugoslavia is 506 km in length. In general it follows the heights of several mountain ranges which form the watersheds between the valley of the Struma River and the tributaries of the Danube on the Bulgarian side and the valleys of the Morava and Vardar Rivers on the Yugoslav side. The southern border runs for 752 km, of which 493 km is shared with Greece and 259 km with Turkey. It follows the ranges of the southern Pirin and Rodopi Mountains. East of the Mesta River the boundary in general follows the watershed between the tributaries of the Maritsa River and the rivers flowing to the Aegean Sea. It curves northwards to the Maritsa River, and crosses the Tundzha River to the Black Sea.

There are few features which constitute clearly defined natural boundaries and during the last century a number of boundary changes have occurred[2]).

The present boundaries with Yugoslavia and Greece were demarcated between 1919 and 1922 and ratified by the Treaty of Lausanne on 24 July 1923. During the Second World War the boundary between Bulgaria and Romania was fixed by the Treaty of Craiova of 7 September 1940 which gave the districts of Silistra and Dobrich (now Tolbukhin), in the southern Dobrudja to Bulgaria.

II. Physical Geography

1. Basic Relief and Hydrography

The relief of Bulgaria is complex and reflects a complicated geological structure[3]). In general a zone of mountains extends across the country from east to west, separating an area of plains in the north from a smaller lowland region to the south. The southern part of the country consists of large blocks of mountains penetrated by north-south valleys.

---

[1]) See also the chapter on Regierungssystem by O. Luchterhandt, pp. 158/59.
[2]) See maps of boundary changes in K.-D. Grothusen's chapter on Außenpolitik, pp. 104/05.
[3]) See map 1 for major physical regions. Information on physical geography comes mainly from Gŭlŭbov, Zh.: Fizicheska geografiîa na Bŭlgariîa (Physical Geography of Bulgaria). Sofia 1977; Atlas na Narodna Republika Bŭlgariîa (Atlas of the People's Republic of Bulgaria). Sofia 1973; SG. 1988; Maruszczak, H.: Bulgaria. Warsaw 1971.

The central mountain zones consist of three major components, the Stara Planina, the Stara Planina foothills, and the Sredna Gora (see map 1). The Stara Planina (sometimes called the Balkan Mountains) extends for about 600 km. It is a continuation of the Carpathian system and was formed in the same geological period as the Carpathians and the Alps. Most of its rocks are of the Triassic and Jurassic periods, and are limestones, intermingled with some older crystalline schists and granite. The ranges are in general not high and tend to have rounded summits. The highest mountain in the Stara Planina is Mt. Botev in the centre of the zone at 2,376 m. There are ten summits over 2,000 m, all in the central and western part of the ranges. The eastern ranges are considerably lower due to weak folding, with few summits over 1,100 m. They divide into a number of outlying branches of the main ranges, one of which reaches the Black Sea to form Cape Emine.

Map 1: Major Physiographic Regions.

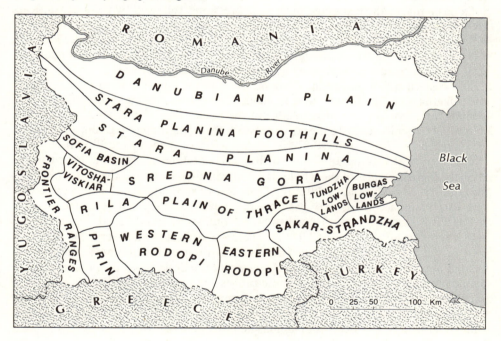

The Stara Planina does not form a major barrier to movement between the north and south of the country. Its greatest width is not more than about 50 km and it averages in general about 30 km in width. It is penetrated by a number of passes, the most notable being the Iskŭr Gorge and the Shipka Pass in the west and centre of the zone. The summit of the Shipka Pass is 1,200 m above sea level. Among the highest passes is the Ribarishki Pass (1,570 m) and the lowest is the Prokhod na Republikata (680 m). They lie to the west and east of the Shipka Pass respectively.

The Stara Planina foothills lie to the north and run parallel with the main mountain ranges. These foothills are rarely higher than 600 m and are separated in places from the Stara Planina by river valleys and basins, such as the Botevgrad, Mezdra, Sevlievo, and Elena basins.

South of the Stara Planina there is a second zone of lower and discontinuous mountains known as the Sredna Gora or the Anti-Balkan Mountains. *Gora* in modern Bulgarian means a forest, but in Old Bulgarian it meant a mountain, as in most other Slavic languages. The Sredna Gora extends over 220 km from the Iskŭr valley eastwards and is divided into three parts by the Topolnitsa and Strĭama rivers. The central part is the highest and contains Mt. Bogdan (1,604 m). It is known as the Sŭshtinska (True) Sredna Gora. Although there are 13 summits over 1,000 m in the Sredna Gora, most of the ranges are below that height. They are formed from igneous and metamorphic rocks, with some areas of limestone.

The Sredna Gora is separated from the Stara Planina by a number of valleys and basins created by erosion in the west and by faulting in the east. The eastern end of the Sofia basin marks the beginning of these depressions, followed by the Zlatitsa, Karlovo, Kazanlŭk, Tvŭrditsa and Sliven basins. The last three are located in the upper valley of the Tundzha River. The Sliven basin marks the end of the Sredna Gora and merges with the Tundzha Lowlands to the south. These depressions form a relatively easy west-east route between the two parallel mountain chains.

The western end of the Sredna Gora merges into the ranges of the Vitosha-Viskĭar and Rila massifs. The former zone includes the Vitosha Planina (mountains) which extends for 27 km at the southern edge of the Sofia basin. It reaches 2,290 m at the summit of Cherni Vrŭkh. To the north-west are the lower ranges of Lĭulin and Viskĭar which reach 1,077 m. To the south the large massifs of the Rila and Pirin mountains stretch southwards to the boundary of Bulgaria and Greece. The Rila Planina contains the highest ranges of the whole Balkan Peninsula, including the highest peak in the country, Mt. Musala, at 2,925 m. There are 12 summits over 2,500 m in height. The Rila Planina consists mainly of granite, gneiss, and crystalline schists.

The Pirin massif follows a north-west to south-west trend for about 60 km. Its highest point is Mt. Vikhren at 2,914 m. There are seven summits over 2,000 m. To the west of the valley of the Struma River several ranges of mountains and hills are located along the border with Yugoslavia, from the Sofia basin in the north to the boundary with Greece. Several of these ranges run in a west-east direction and are partly on Yugoslav territory. They consist mainly of schists and limestones. The highest range is the Osogovska Planina where Mt. Ruen reaches 2,251 m. The Vlakhina, Ograzhden and Belasitsa Planinas all have summits over 1,500 m. There are a number of passes which link the Struma valley with the Vardar valley in Yugoslavia, of which the most important is the Strumitsa valley in the south-west.

The largest mountain massif in southern Bulgaria is formed by the ranges of the Rodopi Mountains. They extend from the Mesta River for about 220 km to the Turkish frontier. The Rodopi, along with the Rila, Pirin and the frontier ranges, form part of a large block of old, hard crystalline rocks which occupies much of the regions of Macedonia and Thrace. It was around this block that the younger mountain systems of the Balkan Peninsula were formed. The Rodopi are divided into a higher western zone and a lower eastern zone. The highest summit is Golĭam Perelik at

2,191 m, but there are seven more over 2,000 m, and a large number over 1,500 m. The eastern zone consists of hills with few summits over 800 m. Movement through the wide massif of the Rodopi is difficult. Routes follow the Mesta valley (between the Rila-Pirin massifs and the Rodopi), the Vŭcha valley, which connects to the upper Arda valley, and the Chepelarska valley, from which the Arda valley is reached by crossing the watershed at Rozhen at over 1,400 m. The Arda valley cuts across the eastern Rodopi from west to east.

North of the confluence of the Maritsa and Tundzha Rivers the Sakar hills rise to a maximum height of 856 m, while east of the Tundzha the northern ranges of the Strandzha uplands form part of the border with Turkey. Both of these uplands with their associated ranges, such as the Derventski, Manastirski, and Kara Tepe hills, are outliers of the Rodopi and consist mainly of crystalline rocks.

About 31 percent of the country lies below 200 m above sea level. The largest area of lowlands, the Danubian Plain, forms a wide zone in the north extending from the Yugoslav border to the Black Sea. This zone is not strictly speaking a plain, but rather a platform. It slopes from the foothills of the Stara Planina northwards to the Danube River and contains small areas of hills, such as the heights north of Pleven, and the Popovski, Razgradski, and Samuilovski heights east of the Iantra River, which in places reach over 440 m. North of these ranges of hills there is the lower Ludogorie plateau and to the east, the Dobrudjan plateau. Between the latter and the Black Sea there is a broad coastal plain. Much of the Danubian Plain consists of limestone and clay of Cretaceous and Tertiary age with a covering of loess, especially west of the Tantra. Much of the Bulgarian bank of the Danube River has high cliffs of loess.

The second largest area of lowlands is the Plain of Thrace, located in the south-central part of the country, south of the Sredna Gora. This plain is part of a depression which forms the upper valley of the Maritsa River. Much of it is covered with Quaternary deposits, mainly of alluvial origin. To the east, the Plain of Thrace is separated from the Tundzha Lowlands by the low range of hills forming the watershed between the Maritsa and Tundzha river basins. In turn, the Tundzha Lowlands are separated by the Bakadzhitsite hills from the Burgas Lowlands. Although these hills are not higher than 400–500 m, the main route from the Plain of Thrace to the Black Sea coast avoids them by turning north-eastwards to follow the southern edge of the Sredna Gora.

In the west the Sofia Basin forms a minor but important area of lowlands. It is some 80 km in length and up to 25 km in breadth, and averages about 550 m above sea level. It is crossed by the Iskŭr and several of its tributaries. It is covered largely by Quartenary deposits. To the west the Sofia Basin has relatively easy access to the Morava valley in Yugoslavia via the Nishava River valley. The route to the east is less easy and must cross the watershed of the Topolnitsa and Strîama Rivers or follow the more southerly route through the Momina gorge of the upper Maritsa River to the Plain of Thrace.

Bulgaria's longest river is the Danube which flows for 471 km along the northern border. Its maximum flow is in April–May, when it has received snow-melt from the plains and hills via its tributaries. The lowest level of flow is in September–October. The difference in water level between high and low periods averages between 6 and 8 m.

There are few lagoons on the Bulgarian bank of the Danube compared with the large number on the flatter Romanian side. There are more than 90 islands in the river, of which some are Romanian territory. The largest Bulgarian island is Belene island, between the mouths of the Osŭm and Îantra Rivers.

About 57 percent of the discharge of water from the rivers of Bulgaria ends in the Black Sea, much of it via the Danube. Most of the tributaries of the Danube rise in the Stara Planina, of which the most important are, from west to east, the Timok, Lom, Ogosta, Vit, Osŭm (314 km), Îantra (286 km) and its tributary, the Rositsa, and the Rusenski Lom with its tributaries. The largest tributary of the Danube and the longest river wholly on Bulgarian territory is the Iskŭr (368 km). It has a basin of 8,846 km². It rises in the Rila Planina and flows northwards through the Samokov depression and the Sofia Basin to cross the Stara Planina through a deep gorge. It then reaches the Danube via the Mezdra basin and a valley through the foothills of the Stara Planina.

The longest river, apart from the Danube, flowing directly to the Black Sea is the Kamchiîa (245 km). It rises in the eastern Stara Planina and its southern branch, the Luda Kamchiîa, has cut a long west-east valley in the eastern end of the massif. A number of smaller rivers flow in a fan-shaped pattern across the Burgas Lowlands to the Gulf of Burgas. Other rivers flowing to the Black Sea include the Provadiĭska in the north and the Veleka and Rezovska in the south.

About 43 percent of the discharge of Bulgaria's rivers reaches the Aegean Sea. The longest river of this group is the Maritsa (322 km on Bulgarian territory). Its basin covers 21,084 km² and is the largest in Bulgaria, apart from the Danube. The Maritsa rises on the slopes of Mt. Musala in the Rila massif and flows through the Momina gorge across the Plain of Thrace to the junction of the borders with Greece and Turkey. Its major tributaries, from west to east, are the Topolnitsa, Chepinska, Vŭcha, Chepelarska, Strîama, Sazliĭka, and Tundzha Rivers. The Tundzha is the longest (350 km) and has a basin with an area of 7,884 km². Another tributary of the Maritsa is the Arda River, which flows eastwards for 241 km from its source in the Rodopi to the Greek border.

The Struma River flows directly to the Aegean Sea from its source on the Vitosha Planina. Its basin covers 10,797 km². Along its 290 km course to the Greek border it passes through the Kresnenska Gorge. The Mesta River (126 km) reaches the Aegean from its source in the Rila Planina via the Momina Gorge.

Bulgaria has few natural lakes. The largest are the lagoons and estuaries found along the Black Sea Coast. The largest estuary is on the Provadiĭska River at Varna, while the Burgas Lowlands contain three lagoons, Lakes Atanasov, Burgas, and Mandra. The last is used as a reservoir. They were formed on the flood plains of rivers and separated from the sea by sand spits. There are several other small coastal lakes. Lakes of tectonic origin are found in the mountain regions, while others of glacial and karst origin also occur. None are of any significant size.

A number of artificial reservoirs have been formed, mainly for the production of electric power and for irrigation. The largest is on the Iskŭr, south-east of Sofia. There are others on the Arda, Tundzha, and rivers in the western Rodopi.

2. Climate

Bulgaria is located in a transitional area between the zones of Mediterranean and continental climates. The Stara Planina forms a divide between the region of continental climate to the north and Mediterranean influences to the south. The Danubian Plain and the foothills of the Stara Planina lie in a zone of temperate continental climate. Winters are cold, averaging − 1 to − 2 °C, while summers are warm, with average temperatures of 23–24 °C. Winds from the north-east can bring winter temperatures as low as − 36 °C. Snow cover lasts on the average for 50–60 days. Maximum precipitation occurs in summer and the minimum in winter, with annual averages of 580–600 mm. The rain in summer often falls in heavy showers and the passage of cold fronts is sometimes accompanied by strong winds. The Sofia Basin, because of its altitude (550 m), shows climatic characteristics similar to those of the northern zone (see Table 1).

Table 1: Selected Climatic Data (Temperatures in °C and Precipitation in mm)

Climatic Region	January Average	July Average	Annual Average Precipitation
Temperate Continental			
Sofia	−1.8	20.4	640
Shumen	−1.2	21.6	605
Pleven	−1.8	23.5	563
Transitional Continental			
Îambol	0.5	23.4	513
Plovdiv	0.0	24.0	539
Pazardzhik	0.2	23.4	515
Transitional Mediterranean (max. precipitation in winter)			
Kŭrdzhali	1.8	23.4	640
Petrich	1.6	25.1	670
Ivaĭlovgrad	2.0	23.5	652
Black Sea Coast			
Varna	1.4	22.6	474
Burgas	0.8	23.6	558
Michurin	3.2	23.1	657
Mountain (Rila Planina)			
Mt. Musala (at 2,390 m)	−7.2	5.1	1,071
Borovets (at 1,340 m)	−4.4	15.3	932

Sources: Gŭlŭbov, Zh.: Fizicheska geografiîa na Bŭlgariîa. Sofia 1977; Maruszczak, H.: Bulgaria. Warsaw 1971.

South of the Stara Planina there is a transitional zone with predominantly continental characteristics. This zone includes the Plain of Thrace and the Tundzha Lowlands, the depressions between the Stara Planina and the Sredna Gora, and the upper Struma valley. Winter temperatures average over 0 °C, the period of snow cover is shorter and the growing season longer than in the north. However, winter temperatures can fall as low as − 33°C. Summer temperatures average between 24° and 25°C, but can reach a maximum of over 40°C. The amounts of precipitation falling in winter and summer tend to be more equal than in the north, with totals averaging over 500 mm per annum.

Further south a transitional zone with some Mediterranean characteristics is found. It consists of the lower Struma valley, the Mesta valley, the eastern Rodopi, especially the valleys of the Arda river and its tributaries, and the valleys and foothills of the Sakar-Strandzha region, especially the middle Maritsa and lower Tundzha valleys. The Mediterranean characteristics are most noticeable in the form of higher winter temperatures and a concentration of precipitation in November and December, with annual average totals over 650 mm. Summer temperatures average between 23° and 26°C, with highest temperatures in the west of the region. Winter temperatures are generally over 1°C, with averages of over 2° and 3°C in the southern extremities of the country. Snow cover lasts on the average between 15 and 30 days, often with several periods of thawing during the winter. However, temperatures can on occasions drop as low as − 15°C to − 20°C, which prevents this climatic zone from being classed as purely Mediterranean in type.

A zone of Black Sea climate with a width of 20–40 km extends along the coast. Maritime influence is most noticeable in the moderation of temperatures which in summer average under 23°C in the north and between 23° and 24°C in the south, and in winter from 1° to 3°C from north to south. Mediterranean influences are most noticeable in the south of the zone. Precipitation totals are low, especially in the north where they average around 400 mm annually. The nearness to the sea is reflected in higher levels of relative humidity than further inland.

Mountain regions over 1,000 feet above sea level, which constitute about 10 percent of the country's total area, have their own climatic characteristics. They experience lower temperatures and higher precipitation levels than the neighbouring lowland regions. On the highest summits over 1,000 mm of precipitation falls yearly on the average, much in the form of snow. In some years snow lies in places in the summer.

3. Vegetation and Soils

Vegetation zones are closely related to climatic patterns. There are three major forms of vegetation: mid-latitude forests, steppe, and Mediterranean woodlands.

The northern zone includes most of the Danubian Plain. Originally much of its area was covered by steppe and forest steppe, but human action has removed most of the original vegetation. Patches of oak and elm remain. The banks and islands of the Danube support some willow, alder, and poplar. In upland areas, such as the Ludogorie plateau, forests of oak scrub occur.

To the south, deciduous forests, predominantly oak with some beech, ash, lime, elm, chestnut, and maple, are found in the Stara Planina, and Sredna Gora, Vitosha, and western frontier mountains. At higher altitudes beech is more evident. Similar forests are found on the lower slopes of the Pirin, Rila, and western Rodopi, up to about 1,000 m. Above that altitude coniferous forests predominate, consisting of various species of fir, pine, and spruce, intermingled with birch and beech. About 32 percent of the country is forested, and of this area about 75 percent consists of deciduous trees and 25 percent of coniferous.

The Plain of Thrace and the Tundzha Lowlands have vegetation which exhibits a transition from Central European to Mediterranean type. Scrub varieties of oak, hornbeam, and plane tree occur with evergreen shrubs. A similar vegetation occurs in the Struma and Mesta valleys. The Strandzha uplands support beech forests and deciduous evergreen shrubs, including rhododendron.

The upper slopes of mountains over 2,200 m have areas of mountain pine and alpine meadows.

The major soil zones correspond closely to those of climate and vegetation. Most of the Danubian Plain is covered by chernozem (black earth) soils, with areas of alluvium along the Danube and its tributaries. These fertile soils have been formed on a base of loess. About 23 percent of the country's total area is covered by chernozem soils.

In the foothills of the Stara Planina and the hillier parts of the east Danubian Plain grey forest soils are predominant, while in the mountain areas of the Stara Planina, Sredna Gora, the western border ranges, Rila, and western Rodopi, brown forest and cinnamon forest soils form the major types. Cinnamon soils also occur in the eastern Rodopi and the Sakar-Strandzha region. Brown and cinnamon forest soils have developed mainly on slopes which are well-drained and dry, while in wetter areas in the Plain of Thrace, the Tundzha Lowlands, the Burgas Lowlands, and the Sofia Basin a type of chernozem soil known as smolnitsa (pitch) is found. It is formed mainly on andesite bedrock. On these plains and basins, as well as in the valleys of rivers such as Struma and Mesta, areas of alluvial soils are found.

Over half the country's area is covered by soils suitable for cultivation, although at present about 38 percent of the total area is under cultivation. The most fertile soils are the chernozem and smolnitsa soils, followed by brown and grey forest soils. However, some of these soils have a poor structure for cultivation and problems of erosion, swampiness, and salinization affect considerable areas.

4. Mineral and Energy Resources

Bulgaria is not particularly rich in either mineral or energy resources and reserves of coal, oil, and natural gas are small[4]). Bituminous coal is in particularly short

---

[4]) See map 2 for major mineral and energy resources. Information on energy and mineral deposits comes mainly from: Penkov, I., Khristov, T.: Ikonomicheska geografiiă na Bŭlgariiă (Economic Geography of Bulgaria). Sofia 1978; Ikonomicheska geografiiă (Economic Geography). 3 vols. Ed. by T. Iordanov. Sofia 1981; Information Bulgaria. A Short Encyclopaedia of the People's Republic of Bulgaria. Ed. by The Bulgarian Academy of Science. Oxford 1985; Atlas na Narodna Republika Bŭlgariiă (Atlas of the People's Republic of Bulgaria). Sofia 1973; Steblez, W.: The Mineral Industry of Bulgaria, in: Bureau of Mines Minerals Yearbook. Washington D.C. 1985; East European Economic Handbook. London 1985, pp. 58–59. Further information on minerals and energy is contained in the chapter on Bergbau und Energiewirtschaft by J. Bethkenhagen.

supply. Over 90 percent of reserves is found in the Balkanbas field, located in the upper Tundzha valley near Sliven. This coal is of medium calorific value (80–85 percent carbon) with a high ash content and occurs in thin seams at depths up to 700 m. The field consists of a number of deposits. All these factors make exploitation of the coal difficult and costly. Besides, the coal needs enrichment for coking purposes. There are smaller deposits of bituminous coal in the north-west and south. A basin of good quality coal is located near Kavarna in the Dobrudja region at a depth of 1,375 to 1,950 m. Seams are up to 11 m thick. Exploitation is difficult because of the great depth of the deposits and the complex tectonic structure of the region.

Map 2: Major Energy and Metallic Mineral Resources.

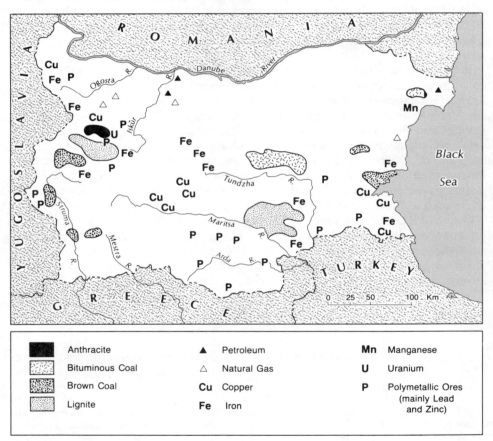

By far the largest coal reserves consist of lignite, comprising 77 percent of total deposits of all types of coal. About 70 percent of all lignite reserves are found in the Marbas-Iztok (east) and Marbas-Zapad (west) fields in the eastern Plain of Thrace, north of Dimitrovgrad. Marbas-Iztok is by far the largest of all the coalfields in the country and accounts for about half of all coal mined. The lignite has a low calorific value and a high moisture and ash content. Compact seams at shallow depths of 5–120 m make open-cast mining possible. The Marbas-Zapad reserves are located at a depth of 250–290 m and require shaft mining. With enrichment the lignite is suitable for electric power production and is also made into briquettes for heating purposes. Other smaller deposits are found in the Sofia Basin and in the surrounding area. Of these, the Sofia Basin deposits are the most important and are partly mined by open-cast methods.

Brown coal has a higher calorific value than lignite (about 70 percent carbon) but is in short supply. About three quarters of reserves are located at Bobovdol and Pernik in the upper Struma valley. Another field is located near Burgas on the Black Sea coast, and some smaller ones elsewhere. Deposits are in general quite deep and range from 150–200 m at Pernik to 700 m at Bobovdol and 800–1,000 m at the small Pirin field in the lower Struma valley.

Anthracite of high calorific value (over 90 percent carbon) occurs in small quantities at Svoge, north of Sofia. Narrow seams at a depth up to 600 m are covered by strongly folded rocks and extraction is difficult. Anthracite is used in several industrial processes, including glass-making and the production of carbide.

Production of bituminous coal and anthracite amounts to about 2 percent of total annual coal output. About two-thirds of the coal produced in Bulgaria ranks among the lowest-grade mined anywhere in Europe.

Domestic supplies of oil and natural gas are very limited. Most deposits are found in areas with complex geological structures and in general are deep below the surface. The main industrial deposits were first developed between 1951 and 1963. The main areas of oil production are at Tiulenovo, near Shabla in the eastern Dobrudja, and at Dolni Dŭbnik, Gorni Dŭbnik and Dolni Lukovit, near Pleven. The Gorni and Dolni Dŭbnik deposits lie at 3,100 to 3,400 m below the ground, and are of easily processed highgrade paraffin-based oil. The Tiulenovo deposits are 140 m below the surface, but have a high asphaltic and weak paraffin base. Oil was found in 1967 at Gigen, north of Pleven near the Danube, at a depth of 900–1,000 m. It has a high asphaltic base and is difficult to process. Natural gas is also found at most of these locations. The main natural gas deposits are at Chiren and Mramoren, north of Vratsa, in the Kamchiia valley near Staro Oriakhovo, south of Varna, and at Devetaki and Aleksandrovo, south-west of Pleven. The Devetaki deposits are located at 4,000 m below the surface.

Limited supplies of coking coal are matched by relatively meagre reserves of other raw materials for the iron and steel industry. Iron ore deposits occur in a number of locations, of which the most important is Kremikovtsi at the base of the south slopes of the Stara Planina near Sofia. It contains about 93 percent of all the country's reserves. Deposits are not deep and can be mined by open-cast methods, but the iron content is low (31 percent) and the ore contains considerable quantities of barites (18 percent), lead, copper, manganese, zinc, silver and other metals, which makes its use difficult. The iron ore consists of limonite, siderite and hematite. Other deposits are found near Mikhaĭlovgrad (Martinovo and Chiprovtsi), Iambol (Krumovo), Burgas, Troian (Shipkovo, Neshkovtsi, and Chiflik), and Sofia (Gradets). The Martinovo and Krumovo ores are magnetites with about 40 percent iron content. Most of these deposits are small and difficult to exploit. About 60 percent of total iron ore reserves consist of limonites (hydrated oxides of iron), similar to the Jurassic ore fields of Western Europe. The low iron content of these ores and the complex technology required for extraction of the metal is partially compensated for by the compactness of the deposits and their relatively shallow depth. The greatest promise for future ore supplies lies in the Kremikovtsi, Krumovo, and Martinovo deposits, but reserves are limited. Deposits of ore with a relatively high iron content have been located in the Blagoevgrad area and there is a possibility of further discoveries in the Burgas area.

Bulgaria is more fortunate with its supplies of manganese of which it is one of the major producers in Europe. The largest deposits are at Obrochishte, north of Varna, and in the Varna area. Metal content is about 28 percent. The iron ores of Kremikovtsi contain about 6 percent manganese. The low metal content of Bulgaria's manganese ores is compensated for by their large reserves. Chromite is found in about 120 separate small bodies, some of them not worth exploitation. The metal content is low (18 percent) and supplies are limited. The largest deposit is near Kŭrdzhali.

Supplies of non-ferrous metals are good, especially of copper, lead, and zinc. Most of these metals are found in mountainous regions with Palaeozoic structures associated with vulcanism. Copper and copper pyrites are mainly found in the western areas of the Sredna Gora. The most important deposits are at Medet, Chelopech, Krasen, Radka, and Elshitsa, in the Panagĭurishte area. The Medet deposits have a low copper content, but have large reserves and can be mined by open-cast methods. Medet is one of the largest open-cast copper mines in South-East Europe. In 1975 copper mines with considerable reserves were opened at Elatsite at a high altitude in the Stara Planina near Etropole. Copper is also mined at Rosen and other localities near Burgas, and at Gorni Lom in the north-west. Some of these ores also contain pyrites, molybdenite, and hematite.

There are a large number of deposits of polymetallic ores. These ores are of particular importance as supplies of lead and zinc. The eastern Rodopi region contains about half of the reserves of these ores. The Gorubso mines at Madan, south-east of Smolĭan, are the richest, and produce lead, zinc, galenite, sphalerite, and pyrites. Other similar ores are located further east at Momchilgrad, Kŭrdzhali, and Madzharovo, and to the north at Davidkovo and Lŭki. These mines are located at heights from 250 to 1,250 m above sea level. The ranges of the Stara Planina south of Vratsa contain a mixture of ores, at Izdremets and at Sedmochislenitsi, where an important deposit contains a low percentage of copper but a high content of silver. These ores also contain other metals such as galenite, sphalerite, and pyrites. To the north-west, mines at Chiprovtsi and Martinovo produce lead, zinc, galenite, sphalerite, pyrites, and silver. These ores are associated with the magnetite and siderite ores mined there for the iron and steel industry. The Chiprovtsi ores have been mined since ancient times and in the Middle Ages miners from Saxony were brought in to work them. Some of the deposits in the Vratsa region have been exhausted.

Other polymetallic ores are found in the western border range of the Osogovska Planina, at Ruen and Lebnitsa, near Kĭustendil, where lead, zinc, copper, and pyrites are mined. In the Sakar-Strandzha region polymetallic ores are mined at Golĭamo Krushevo, near Bolĭarovo, and near Malko Tŭrnovo, where copper, iron ore, pyrites and other metals are found. Some uranium is mined in the western Stara Planina and processed near Sofia.

Bulgaria has a variety of more than 60 types of non-ore minerals of which about 40 are used in industry and construction. They include kaolin, ceramic clays, quartz sands, gypsum, asbestos, barytes, perlite, phosphorite, feldspar, mica, rock salt, marble, limestone, dolomite, marl, and chalk. These minerals are distributed widely across the country, but there are certain concentrations of the most important which are worth noting. Kaolin is found mainly in the north-east, especially in the area between Ruse, Tolbukhin, and Shumen. Gypsum is located mainly near the Danube, at Vidin and Oriakhovo in the north-west, and in the Plain of Thrace, south-east of Stara Zagora. The largest deposits of barytes are on the south slopes of the Sredna Gora near Stara Zagora, while supplies also come from the Kremikovtsi iron ores. Fluorite occurs in the Ograzhden Planina in the extreme south-west and in the west and central Rodopi. Perlite and asbestos are found in the Kŭrdzhali area. Large supplies of rock salt are mined from the single deposit near Provadiia, between Shumen and Varna. Sea salt is obtained from the Black Sea.

There are many medicinal springs, most of which are warm or hot (35–60 °C). They are located predominantly in the Sredna Gora and the Rila and Rodopi mountains and in the region of Sofia.

III. Human Geography: Rural and Urban Settlements

Bulgarian rural settlements have much in common with those in other regions of the Balkan Peninsula[5]). They consist of three major types: villages, hamlets, and farmsteads, and may be clustered or dispersed. Dispersed settlements are found almost exclusively in mountain areas, as are isolated farmsteads. They may have originated as the old South Slav communal family hamlet or *zadruga*. Some dispersed farms and hamlets were also established in the foothills of the mountain areas as people left the lowlands during the period of Turkish occupation. Others left lowland villages to establish sheepfolds (*koshari*) in the mountains, which sometimes developed into permanent settlements. Today these mountain settlements usually take the form of hamlets with 200 to 500 inhabitants. These hamlets are known as *kolibi* or *makhali*. Although they are similar in form, the *koliba* is of Slav and the *makhala* of Turkish origin. Their houses may be clustered or dispersed quite widely and there is no standard pattern. In 1987 about 60 percent of rural settlements were under 500 inhabitants in size, but contained only 18.6 percent of the total rural population.

In 1987 about 56 percent of the rural population lived in villages with more than 1,000 inhabitants. Such villages are generally clustered with an irregular plan. The degree of dispersion of the houses also varies and some villages can be described as

---

[5]) Information on rural and urban settlements comes from: Vakarelski, Kh.: Etnografiia na Bŭlgariia (Ethnography of Bulgaria). Sofia 1977, pp. 250–259; Hoffman, G.: Transformation of Rural Settlement in Bulgaria, in: Geographical Review. 54 (1964), pp. 45–64; SG. 1988.

semi-clustered. A clustered village, known as a *kŭpno selo*, generally contains a church and a *khorishte* or *igrishte*, an open space for dancing or games. A *selo* is found predominantly in the plains, with relatively few in mountain regions. In the Danubian Plain some villages have over 5,000 inhabitants. Street villages, common in many regions of Europe, are rare. Most villages are of Slav origin, but in the north-east some were the result of Turkish settlement.

After the First World War villages were more regularly planned and new types of houses began to replace the traditional small wood and plaster houses with their clay or wood tiled roofs. This modernization trend was accelerated after 1945. Mountain villages in many areas still remain relatively primitive and remain limited in size due to restricted natural conditions for farming.

A type of village transitional between a rural village and a town, known as a *palanka*, is occasionally found. They generally have between 3,000 and 8,000 inhabitants. They formerly had a fort, as the Turkish name suggests, and also had the role of service centres for surrounding villages. Many of them today have lost this function.

Urban settlements are of ancient origin, although urbanization is a recent phenomenon[6]). Until after the Second World War cities remained few and small. The three largest cities, Sofia, Plovdiv, and Varna are among the oldest in the country. Sofia was the Roman Serdica and was later renamed Sredets by the Slavs due to its central location in the Balkan Peninsula. It lay on the main route from the Maritsa valley to Nish in Serbia, at its junction with the route from the Sofia Basin to the Struma valley and the Aegean Sea. To the north the Danubian Plain could be reached by the gorge of the Iskŭr River. In spite of its location on important routes, Sofia was situated on the fringe of the medieval Bulgarian Empire, and the more centrally located Tŭrnovo became the capital with Sofia as the second city. In 1382 it was captured by the Turks and became the administrative center of part of Rumelia. When it became the capital of liberated Bulgaria in 1879 it had only some 18,000 inhabitants. It grew rapidly in population and area and lost much of its Turkish appearance. Severe damage from Allied air raids in 1944 resulted in reconstruction and further development. It has become not only the administrative and cultural centre of the country but also its chief industrial city. At the end of 1987 the population of Sofia was 1,128,859 or 12.6 percent of the country's total population.

Plovdiv was originally the Thracian settlement of Eumolpias. In the 4th century B. C. Philip of Macedonia converted the village into the city of Philippopolis. As the Roman city of Trimontium it saw further development, but suffered later from Bulgar and Slav attacks. Captured by the Turks in 1364, it became a commercial centre with a cosmopolitan population under the Turkish name of Filibe. It received its present name in the 19th century, when it began to emerge as the second city of Bulgaria with a number of important trade, transport, and industrial functions. Its population in 1987 was 356,596.

Varna, with a 1987 population of 305,891, is the third largest city and a major port. It was founded by the Greeks in the 6th century B. C. as Odessos. It was named Varna by the Slavs and in the Middle Ages it became a fortified town and trading centre for

---

[6]) See map 3 for urban settlements.

the Bulgarian Empire. At the time of liberation from the Turks, Varna had 24,600 inhabitants and was the third largest city after Plovdiv and Ruse. A rail link with Sofia in 1899 resulted in further expansion of the port. Since 1945 it has also become an important industrial centre. It was called "Stalin" 1949–56.

The other urban settlements are considerably smaller, and of the seven with a population between 100,000 and 250,000 inhabitants in 1987 only two, Ruse and Burgas, had over 180,000 inhabitants. Ruse, along with Vidin, Svishtov, and Silistra, were fortified Roman ports on the Danube. By the 19th century Ruse had become the main Turkish city on the Danube. In 1865 it was joined to Varna by rail and became Bulgaria's largest Danube port and a manufacturing centre. Ruse is linked to Giurgiu in Romania by a bridge built in 1952–54.

Burgas is one of the younger cities of Bulgaria. Although it was the site of a Roman town and a Byzantine fishing village, it had only about 3,000 inhabitants in 1878. The construction of port facilities in 1906 and of the railway from Sofia via Plovdiv and Stara Zagora made Burgas the chief port for southern Bulgaria and for Sofia.

Most of the other cities with over 100,000 inhabitants, such as Pleven, Sliven, Stara Zagora, Tolbukhin, and Shumen are manufacturing centres, although some are of ancient origin and had other earlier functions. Of the 18 towns with populations in 1987 between 50,000 and 100,000, some such as Pernik, Gabrovo, Kazanlŭk, Îambol, Dimitrovgrad, and Pazardzhik, are predominantly industrial centres. Most became industrialized only after 1945. Other cities in this group, such as Vidin, Silistra, Kfustendil, Veliko Tŭrnovo, Mikhaĭlovgrad, and Khaskovo have both industrial and service functions.

IV. Regional Geography

There have been several systems devised for the economic regionalization of Bulgaria, most of them for planning purposes. The regional divisions adopted here for descriptive purposes are based on those outlined by I. Zakhariev and others (1962) and further developed by I. Penkov and T. Khristov (1978) (see Map 3). The subdivisions of these regions as delineated by Penkov and Khristov agree very closely with the administrative regions (*oblasti*) adopted in the 1987 reform[7]).

1. Western Region

The western region includes the Sofia and Mikhaĭlovgrad *oblasti*[8]). It comprises about 28 percent of the area of the country and is its most important economic region. The region stretches across the physical grain of the country and includes, from north

---

[7]) See also the chapter on Regierungssystem by O. Luchterhandt, pp. 158/59.
[8]) Information on the economic regions comes mainly from the sources given in footnote 2 with the addition of: The People's Republic of Bulgaria, in: Economic Geography of the Socialist Countries of Europe. Ed. by N. Alisov, E. Valev. Moscow 1985, pp. 175–199.

Map 3: Urban Settlements with over 50,000 Inhabitants.

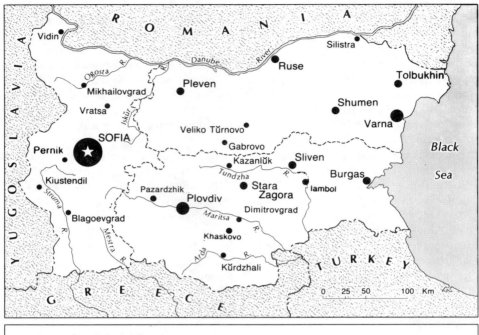

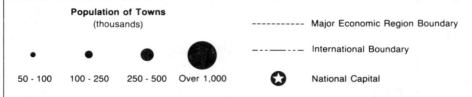

to south, the western parts of the Danubian Plain and of the Stara Planina, the Sofia Basin, the Vitosha-Viskîar region, the frontier ranges, the Rila and the Pirin mountains.

Agricultural conditions and types of farming activities in the region vary greatly. The northern lowlands produce wheat and corn, along with sunflowers and sugar beet. Vineyards are found along the Danube. Further south the mountain regions are largely forested with areas of herding of cattle and sheep, along with some flax and potato growing. The Sofia Basin produces some grain. The upper valley of the Struma produces fruit, especially apples, with horticulture and livestock herding, while in the lower valley, fruit, grapes, vegetables, and tobacco, are grown. The lower Mesta valley specializes in tobacco growing[9]).

---

[9]) For further information on agriculture see the chapter on Land- und Forstwirtschaft by I. Grosser.

Industry is the most important branch of the regional economy. Its focus is the city of Sofia, which accounts for about 16 percent of total national industrial output. Apart from the iron and steel plant in adjacent Kremikovtsi, there is an important engineering industry, including the manufacture of radio electronic equipment and machine-tools, and also chemicals, including rubber, textiles, and others. Nearby Pernik has an iron and steel plant, engineering, and glass industries, as well as coal mining. Other smaller towns around Sofia have non-ferrous metallurgy, and chemical and engineering industries. The western region contains over 90 percent of Bulgaria's brown coal reserves and all its anthracite. Coal is used for the production of electric power with major power stations at Sofia, Pernik, and Vratsa, and at the mines at Bobovdol. A nuclear power station with an planned capacity of 3.7 million kw is located at Kozloduĭ on the Danube. It began operating in 1974 and in 1985 supplied about 28 percent of national electric power production.

Apart from Sofia and Pernik, other industrial centres are Vratsa (chemicals, wood-working, textiles), Vidin (engineering, synthetic fibres, tyres, tobacco), and Sredna Gora (copper refining, chemicals). In Lom, Mikhaĭlovgrad, Stanke Dimitrov, Blagoevgrad, and Kfustendil, engineering, textiles, and food and tobacco processing are the dominant industries. Razlog has wood-working and cellulose industries[10].

The western region has good transportation links both internally and externally. A railway line runs from Sofia to Pernik and then south to Stanke Dimitrov, Blagoevgrad, and the Greek border, with branches to Kfustendil and Petrich. A line runs north from Sofia to Vratsa and Vidin, with branches to Mikhaĭlovgrad and Lom. The international line linking Belgrade with Istanbul reaches Sofia via Nish and the Nishava valley and continues eastwards through the Sredna Gora. The roads of the region in general follow the same routes as the railways and, like them, radiate from Sofia. In spite of its westerly location, Sofia has in general good communications with other parts of the country[11].

2. *North-eastern Region*

The north-eastern region contains the *oblasti* of Lovech, Razgrad, and Varna. It comprises the largest part of the Danubian Plain and the foothills of the Stara Planina and occupies about 34 percent of the country's area. It is the most important agricultural region, due to its favourable landforms and soils. The Danubian Plain is the country's major producer of wheat, maize, and barley, along with sunflowers, sugar beet, and some soya beans. Viticulture is found along the Danube and near Pleven, Shumen, and Varna. A large area of viticulture and horticulture (especially tomatoes, onions, and peppers) is located around the Ĭantra and Rositsa basins north of Veliko Tŭrnovo, where sugar beet, cotton, and tobacco are also grown. Livestock, especially dairy and beef cattle and pigs, are also important. In the north-east, tobacco-growing and sheep-herding are also found.

---

[10] Further information on industry is contained in the chapter on Industry and Handicraft by M. Jackson.

[11] The development of the national transport net is discussed in the chapter on Handel, Versorgung und Verkehr by F. Altmann.

The region has several industries of a specialized nature, of which the most important are shipbuilding, heavy machinery, chemicals, porcelain and ceramics, textiles, leather goods, and food processing. The most important industrial centre is Varna, which has shipbuilding, and the manufacture of diesel engines. A chemical industry is located in nearby Devnĭa, based on rock salt and other minerals. Devnĭa is linked by canal to the Black Sea.

The north-eastern region has many of the major deposits of non-ore minerals. It contains most of the deposits of the country's small oil and natural gas reserves. An oil refinery is located at Dolni Dŭbnik. Other industrial centres are Ruse (ships, railway rolling stock, farm machinery, electronics, oil refining, chemicals, and textiles), Pleven (farm machinery, food-processing, textiles, oil refining, and chemicals), and Gabrovo (woolen and cotton textiles, textile machinery, and footwear). The industrial region of the upper Îantra valley, comprising Gabrovo, Gorna Orĭakhovitsa, Veliko Tŭrnovo, and smaller towns, such as Drĭanovo, Debelets, and Trĭavna, is being developed with a specialization in engineering, textiles, and footwear. Other smaller centres are Shumen (truck factory), Lovech (food-processing, engineering), Troĭan (engineering, wood-working), Tolbukhin (textiles, food-processing), Svishtov (artificial fibres), and Silistra (woodworking). Sugar refining is carried out in large refineries at Ruse, Gorna Orĭakhovitsa, and Dolna Mitropolĭa, near Pleven.

Electric power production is mainly by thermal power stations, with the largest being at Varna, Devnĭa and Ruse. Work on a nuclear power station began at Belene on the Danube in 1982. A hydro-electric power complex is under construction on the Danube at Nikopol, opposite Turnu Măgurele in Romania. This joint Bulgarian-Romanian project will give a generating capacity of 400,000 kw on the Bulgarian side. A railway bridge over the Danube is also under construction at the site of the dam.

The Black Sea coast north of Varna has been developed for tourism with major resorts at Druzhba, Zlatni Pĭasŭtsi, Chaĭka, and Albena.

The major railway links within the region are the lines from Pleven to Varna via Shumen, with connections south to Gabrovo and Stara Zagora, and north to Ruse. A line runs from Ruse to Varna, with a branch line to Silistra. Rail connections with Romania and the Soviet Union are via the bridge at Ruse and by a line from west of Varna via Tolbukhin. Varna is an important port, especially for trade with the Soviet Union, and a large rail ferry operates between the new port of Varna-Zapad and Il'ichevsk, near Odessa. The river ports of Ruse, Silistra, Svishtov, and Lom on the Danube also play a significant role in trade with the Soviet Union, of which about 90 percent moves by water.

3. South-eastern Region

The south-eastern region contains Plovdiv, Khaskovo, and Burgas *oblasti* and comprises some 38 percent of the total area of the country. Its major physical features are the ranges of the Stara Planina and the Sredna Gora, the Plain of Thrace and the Tundzha and Burgas Lowlands, the Rodopi massif, and the Sakar-Strandzha hills.

This diversity of landforms leads to a great variety of conditions for agriculture. The most productive areas are the Plain of Thrace and the basins between the Stara Planina and the Sredna Gora. Both of these areas have horticulture (with a specialization in growing tomatoes, melons, strawberries and peppers) and viticulture as major activities. A large complex of greenhouses is located near Pazardzhik. The cultivation of industrial crops such as cotton, tobacco, hemp, sugar beet, and oil crops, and of fruit crops, such as apples, apricots, and peaches, is also important. The eastern Plain of Thrace is the main cotton-growing area of the country. About 60 percent of the farmland in the Plain of Thrace is irrigated and conditions are suitable for rice cultivation. The basins of Kazanlŭk and Karlovo specialize in the growing of roses for the production of attar of roses for export for the perfume industry. The Tundzha and Burgas Lowlands produce mainly maize, wheat, and sunflowers.

The mountain ranges of the Stara Planina, Sredna Gora, Rodopi, and Sakar-Strandzha regions support some livestock herding. In the south the hills of the Arda river basin have been important tobacco-growing areas since the 19th century.

The industrial economy of the region is dominated by non-ferrous metallurgy and mining. The region contains most of the deposits of copper and polymetallic ores. It also has the lignite fields of the Maritsa basis as well as the Balkanbas bituminous coalfield in the Sliven area. Several large thermal power stations located on the Marbas-Iztok field supply electric power not only to the region, but also to other regions and to Turkey. About 30 percent of national electric power production comes from these stations. Hydroelectric stations on the rivers of the Rodopi, such as the Dospat, Mŭtnitsa, Vŭcha, Arda, and Krichim, and also the Tundzha, supply further power. The largest hydro-complex consists of the Belmeken-Sestrimo stations with a capacity of 755 million kw and the nearby Chaira pumped-storage station with a capacity of 864 million kw. Most hydro-power stations in the region are peak-power stations with reservoirs, which are also used for irrigation and water storage. Part of this large production of electric power is used in the production of non-ferrous metals. Plovdiv, Kŭrdzhali, and Rudozem are major centres of lead and zinc metallurgy.

The major industrial area of the region consists of Plovdiv, Pazardzhik and Asenovgrad. They have engineering, food and tobacco processing, and chemical industries. Plovdiv and Pazardzhik have textile manufacturing, and Pazardzhik has wood-working and pulp and paper manufacture. The other industrial concentration comprises the towns of Dimitrovgrad (fertilizer, chemical engineering, and textile industries), Stara Zagora (food products, computers, textiles, and chemicals), and Khaskovo (tobacco processing).

Further east, Îambol has a large synthetic fibre factory, flour-milling, and the manufacture of farm machinery. Sliven has the country's largest wool combine along with engineering factories. Burgas on the Black Sea coast is not only a major port, but is also the most important industrial centre of the south-east region. It has a large oil-refining and petro-chemical complex linked to an oil port on the south shore of the Gulf of Burgas. Other industries are shipbuilding, engineering, and food-processing, especially fish canning. Burgas is also a centre for fishing. Nearby Sozopol has a large fishing fleet and fish canning industry, and Pomorie has fishing, food-processing, and a large distillery. Both towns attract tourists as does the old town of Nesebŭr to the north. The latter is visited mainly by tourists from the adjacent resort of Slŭnchev Briāg.

The main railway line of the region runs from Sofia via Plovdiv, Stara Zagora, and Îambol to Burgas. There are several branch lines, of which the most important are Plovdiv-Karlovo, Plovdiv-Panagîurishte, and Karnobat-Varna. A second major line follows the Maritsa river from Plovdiv via Dimitrovgrad and Svilengrad to Edirne in Turkey. A third line runs from Stara Zagora south to Dimitrovgrad, Khaskovo, Kŭrdzhali, Momchilgrad, and Podkova. The road network in general follows the alignment of the railways. Svilengrad is an important border-crossing point for truck traffic from Western Europe to Turkey and the Middle East.

Historical Foundations

Richard J. Crampton, Canterbury/Kent

I. Bulgaria before 1878 – II. The Reign of Alexander Battenberg, 1879–1886 – III. Stefan Stambolov and Prince Ferdinand, 1886–1894 – IV. Ferdinand's Personal Rule, 1894–1908 – V. War and the Failure of Territorial Expansionism, 1908–1918 – VI. Post-War Radicalism and the Government of Stamboliĭski, 1918–1923 – VII. The Failure of the Traditional and the New Right, 1923–1935 – VIII. Boris's Personal Régime, 1935–1941 – IX. Bulgaria in the Second World War, 1941–1944 – X. Social and Economic Factors in Bulgarian History, 1878–1944 – XI. Conclusions

I. Bulgaria before 1878

The Bulgarians arrived in the Balkan peninsula in the first half of the seventh century. By 681 they had established a state based upon the city of Preslav. The Bulgarians themselves were of mixed racial origin and although they soon adopted many of the customs of the Slavs whom they had overrun a true merging of Bulgar and Slav was possible only after Prince Boris adopted Christianity as the state religion in 864. The conversion also brought literacy to the Bulgarians and the fact that it was the new religion which brought literacy firmly established the church as a dominant factor in Bulgarian cultural development. Christianity did not, however, mean easier relations between the Bulgarian state and its chief rival for power, Byzantium. In 1014/18 the first Bulgarian empire was broken by the Emperor Basileios II Boulgaroktonos (the „Bulgar-slayer")[1].

A second Bulgarian empire was established in 1185, centred this time upon the religious capital, Tŭrnovo. This empire reached the height of its power under Tsar Kaloîan (1197–1207) who ruled lands stretching from the Dnieper to the Aegean, and from the Adriatic to the Black sea and who drove the Magyars out of Bulgaria and prevented their movement further south. In cultural terms the second empire produced the great riches but it rarely enjoyed political stability. It was involved in numerous wars whilst at home its nobles feuded and its population took refuge in Bogomilism which allowed, if it did not encourage, a disdain for worldly phenomena and temporal power[2]. Bulgaria therefore fell easy prey to the Sultan's armies in 1393/96.

The Bulgarian state was dismantled, its nobility dispossessed and its cultural identity driven into the small villages. There it survived in a non-political form, kept alive

---

[1] Zlatarski, V.N.: Istoriĭa na bŭlgarskata dŭrzhava prez srednite vekove (History of the Bulgarian State during the Middle Ages). 3 vols. Sofia 1918–40.
[2] Obolensky, D.: The Bogomils. Cambridge 1948.

by the Bulgarian variety of Orthodox Christianity, by folk-tales and by the fact that most purely Bulgarian communities were remote and largely self-contained. Some Bulgarians, the *Pomaks*, converted to Islam but even they retained their native Bulgarian language and folk-customs.

There were occasional outbursts, spawned by social discontent and foreign, frequently Catholic, intrigue[3]), but it was not until the second half of the eighteenth century that cultural stirrings began, the most notable achievement being the work of the monk Paisiĭ of Khilendar. Paisiĭ, anxious at the extension of Greek influence, wrote a history of the long-dead Bulgarian kings and empires in which he called upon his fellow Bulgarians „to know your nation and language and study in your own tongue". To give encouragement in this direction Paisiĭ wrote in a mixture of formal Old Church Slavonic and contemporary Bulgarian. He influenced a number of contemporaries but their importance was retrospective rather than formulative, because they and the Bulgarian „pre-renaissance" were submerged in the political and social confusion which ravaged the Ottoman empire in the late eighteenth and early nineteenth centuries[4]).

Only when those upheavals had been stilled could order return to the Bulgarian lands. With order came prosperity. A number of towns, in many of which the Bulgarian element had increased considerably in the preceding century, grew rich through the provision of cloth, lace and other commodities to the Ottoman market. Some of the profits made by the Bulgarian guilds went to encourage urban renewal but money was also spent in educating Bulgarian youths and in financing Bulgarian religious foundations. It was here that the nationalist nerve first began to throb. The extension of Greek influence had not been contained and Greek influence in the episcopate was enormous. But ecclesiastical preferment was a costly process and each bishop recouped what he had had to pay for his office from those beneath him. Greek bishops were therefore inceasingly associated with corruption. By 1851 the leaders of the powerful Bulgarian community in Bucharest could declare that „Without a national church there is no salvation"[5]). Support for this view grew steadily in the following decade and on Easter Sunday 1860 bishop Ilarion Makariopolski in Istanbul declared the Bulgarian church virtually independent of the patriarchate. The Porte, glad to leave its Christian subjects to feud with each other, did not recognise the separate Bulgarian exarchate until 1870. The patriarch remained unreconciled and in 1872 excommunicated the Bulgarian church.

The establishment of the exarchate was the greatest achievement of pre-liberation Bulgarian nationalism. The achievement was primarily that of the Bulgarians themselves for foreign powers were uninterested or hostile.

---

[3]) Duĭchev, I.: Chiprovets i Vŭstanieto prez 1688 g. (Chiprovets and the Rising of 1688). Sofia 1938.

[4]) Gandev, Kh.: Ranno Vŭzrazhdane (The Early Renaissance). Sofia 1939; Angelov, B.: Sŭvremenitsi na Paisiĭ (Contemporaries of Paisiĭ). 2 vols. Sofia 1963/64.

[5]) Nikov, P.: Vŭzrazhdane na bŭlgarskiĭa narod: Tsŭrkovno-natsionalni borbi i postizheniĭa (Renaissance of the Bulgarian Nation: National Struggles and Efforts in the Church). Sofia no date, p. 66.

The religious movement had taken much of its strength from the cultural and educational renaissance which began in the mid-1830s. The first Bulgarian school was founded in Gabrovo in 1835 and thereafter the number of schools grew steadily. Initially Bulgarian education was often seen as an adjunct rather than an alternative to schooling in Greek, but by the 1850s education was purely Bulgarian and had been extended into the secondary sector. The first school for girls was opened in 1840 in Pleven[6]).

Along with education came the birth of Bulgarian publishing. The new schools needed textbooks whilst the emergence of a new, literate element encouraged the publication of a wide range of reading materials. Between 1806 and 1830 only seventeen original Bulgarian books were published but between 1830 and 1854 264 appeared. An integral element in the cultural renaissance was the *chitalishte* which provided reading rooms, newspapers, books, and a venue for plays, lectures and meetings[7]).

Whatever the achievements of the religious and cultural revivals, however, there emerged a small group for whom no national movement could be complete without political concessions. This group was eventually to precipitate the greatest of all changes, political separation from the Ottoman empire, but that change was not, as the Bulgarian church had been, the work of the Bulgarians alone. The political activists initiated a process eventually completed by European diplomacy and the Tsar's armies.

There had been sporadic outbursts of disorder and rebellion in the Bulgarian lands since 1800 but there had been neither organisation nor political reason to such revolts. After the Crimean War Ivan Kishelski, a Bulgarian serving in the Russian army, had talked of Bulgaria's liberation[8]) but few had listened and it was not until the 1860s that serious schemes for a redrawing of the Balkan political map were devised. Inspired by the union of the Rumanian principalities and by events in Italy, a small group of Bulgarians began to argue for a Balkan revolution. The leading Bulgarian advocate of this dream was Georgi Rakovski whose goal was a Balkan federal republic; his methodology was that of the small armed band or *cheta*. In Belgrade he founded a small Bulgarian Legion which took part in the Serbian action against the Ottoman garrison in that city but he did not send *cheti* into Bulgaria until the mid-1860s. They failed utterly. With Rakovski's death in 1867 leadership of the revolutionary cause passed to the triumvirate of Lîuben Karavelov, Vasil Levski and Khristo Botev which established the Bulgarian Revolutionary Central Committee in Bucharest in 1869. The leading ideologue was Karavelov. Like Rakovski, he was a federalist but his republicanism was less pronounced and he was even willing to consider a Bulgaro-Ottoman *Ausgleich* to ensure self-government for the Bulgarians. Revolutionary methods also changed, the more so after the abysmal failure of a

---

[6]) Dorosiev, L.: Materiali za izuchavaneto na uchebnoto delo v Bŭlgariîa (Material for the Study of Educational Activity in Bulgaria). Sofia 1925.

[7]) Chilingirov, S.: Bŭlgarskite chitalishta predi Osvobozhdenieto (Bulgarian Reading Rooms before the Liberation). Sofia 1930.

[8]) Shashko, P.: General Ivan Kishelski's Program for the Liberation of Bulgaria, in: Bulgaria Past and Present. Ed. by Butler, T. Columbus, Ohio 1976.

number of *cheti* in 1868. Karavelov continued to aspire towards complete liberation but knew now that the *cheti* could not achieve that goal; it could be secured only by a national uprising. Karavelov, who had been influenced by the Russian Populists, argued that such a national uprising should be prepared by small groups of „apostles". Levski agreed and by 1869 was inside Bulgaria organising a network of revolutionary committees. In 1872, however, he was betrayed and in the following February went to a martyr's death. Botev's political inclinations were to a romantic socialism, but his chief contribution to the movement lay not in his ideology but in his verse which inspired his followers and enriched Bulgarian literature.

The failure of the *cheti* and the death of Levski convinced Karavelov and Botev that if they were to succeed they must find foreign support. That was most likely to come from the other Balkan states. In 1875, with the region in a state of great tension following the Bosnian revolt, a new Bulgarian Revolutionary Central Committee was founded. In the following year Serbia went to war with the Ottoman empire and the Bulgarian conspirators seized what they believed was their chance. A new revolt was prepared, this time under the direction of Georgi Benkovski. The revolt was planned for May 1876 but broke out prematurely in Koprivshtitsa in April.

The April Uprising was a turning point in Bulgarian history, but not, perhaps, in the way its architects had intended. The popular response was lethargic or even hostile, yet the consequences were horrendous. Ottoman irregulars, many of them *Pomaks*, exacted a revenge so fearful that the conscience of Europe was stirred and the passions of Russia aroused. In April 1877 Russia began military operations against the Ottoman empire. After being delayed by the siege of Pleven and in the Shipka Pass, where it was helped by Bulgarian volunteers, the Russian army descended into the Thracian plains to make steady progress almost to the walls of Istanbul. At San Stefano, in March 1878, Russia drafted a preliminary peace which envisaged a huge new Bulgarian state including Thrace, southern Dobrudja and all of Macedonia. It was everything the Bulgarians had desired, and all that the British feared. (For the territorial revisions of the Bulgarian state, see maps in Professor Grothusen's chapter; for the general physical geography of the country, see the four-colour map at the end of the volume.) Terrified that new Bulgaria would be a huge Russian stalking horse within easy ride of the Straits, Disraeli insisted that Macedonia and Thrace be returned to Ottoman rule, that much of the Dobrudja be handed to Rumania, and that the Morava valley was handed to Serbia. In the treaty of Berlin of July 1878 he had his way. The new Bulgaria was confined to the small area between the Danube and the Balkan mountains, whilst that between Bulgaria and the Ottoman frontier was to form the new autonomous Ottoman province of Eastern Rumelia. All Bulgarians could unite in denunciation of the new settlement. And hatred at such supposed injustice would continue to unite the nation even when it was riven by other, internal divisions[9]).

---

[9]) For the political movement, the April rising and the Russo-Turkish war, see Arnaudov, M.: Georgi Stoĭkov Rakovski. Zhivot-Delo-Idei (Georgi Stoĭkov Rakovski. Life-Action-Ideas). 3rd ed. Sofia 1969; Kosev, K. *et al*: Istoriia na Aprilskoto Vŭstanie 1876 (History of the April Uprising 1876). Sofia 1986.

Table 1: Population by Mother Tongue, 1880–1934

Year	1880/84*		1887		1892		1900		1905		1910		1920		1926		1934	
	Number	%age	Number	%age	Number	%age	Number	%age	Number	%age	Number	%age	Number	%age	Number	%age	Number	%age
Bulgarian	1,909,027	67.84	2,326,250	74.60	2,505,326	75.67	2,887,869	77.13	3,205,019	79.41	3,523,311	81.23	4,041,276	83.36	4,585,620	83.70	5,274,854	86.79
Turkish	701,984	24.95	607,331	19.45	569,728	17.21	539,656	14.41	497,820	12.35	504,560	11.63	542,904	11.20	607,763	11.09	618,268	10.17
Greek	42,659	1.52	58,326	1.87	58,518	1.77	70,887	1.89	69,761	1.73	50,866	1.17	46,759	0.97	12,782	0.23	9,601	0.16
Gypsy			50,291	1.61	52,132	1.57	89,549	2.39	94,649	2.35	121,573	2.80	61,555	1.27	81,996	1.50	80,532	1.32
Jewish**			23,541	0.75	27,531	0.82	32,573	0.87	36,455	0.90	38,554	0.89	41,927	0.88	41,563	0.76	28,026	0.46
Others	160,518	5.69	52,636	1.69	97,478	2.95	123,758	3.31	131,942	3.26	98,649	2.28	112,550	2.32	148,954	2.72	66,658	1.10
Total	2,813,868	100.00	3,118,375	100.00	3,310,713	100.00	3,744,283	100.00	4,035,646	100.00	4,337,513	100.00	4,846,971	100.00	5,478,741	100.00	6,077,939	100.00

* The first census in the Bulgarian principality was held in 1880, the first in Eastern Rumelia in 1884.
** Includes speakers of both Hebrew and Ladino.

Sources: Battenberg, F.J. Prinz von: Die volkswirthschaftliche Entwicklung Bulgariens von 1879 bis zur Gegenwart. Leipzig 1891, p. 6; Statistichesko Bjuro (Statistical Buro): Naselenieto v Bŭlgariĭa spored prebroĭavanĭata na 1 Ianuariĭ 1888, 1 Ianuariĭ 1893 i 31 Dekemvriĭ 1900 (The Population of Bulgaria according to the Censuses of 1 January 1888, 1 January 1893 and 32 December 1900), Sofia 1907; ibid, Obsht rezultat ot prebroĭavanieto na Naselenieto v Tsarstvo Bŭlgariĭa na 31 Dekemvriĭ 1910 (General Result of the Census in the Kingdom of Bulgaria, 31 December 1910). Sofia 1911; the same agency with the same titles *mutatis mutandis* published the other census results in 1927, 1931 and 1937.

Such division appeared as soon as the Constituent Assembly, a mixture of elected, nominated and *ex officio* members, convened in Tŭrnovo in 1879. The assembly contained two main factions, the Liberals and the Conservatives. The decisive clash was over the question of the legislature. The Conservatives argued that the peasant nation, long subjected to foreign and autocratic rule, could not be entrusted to legislate wisely; a second chamber was therefore necessary to allow the small Bulgarian intellectual and economic élite to restrain the untutored masses. The Liberals rejected such patronising attitudes. The Bulgarian peasantry, they said, had exercised political responsibility in managing the affairs of its villages; besides which the Bulgarian élite was negligeable and so homogeneous a society as that of Bulgaria had no need of gradations in political rights, for these would only create class division where none had existed before. The Liberals won an overwhelming victory. Not only was the NSb to be unicameral but the constitution finally enacted at Tŭrnovo was, on paper at least, one of the most advanced yet seen in Europe[10]).

II. The Reign of Alexander Battenberg, 1879–1886[11])

The Liberal triumph at the Constituent Assembly was not the end of Bulgaria's political teething troubles. As prince the powers had chosen Alexander of Battenberg, a young officer who had fought with the Russians in the recent war. Unfortunately Alexander's experience of the Russian army had not endeared him to that country and, of more immediate consequence, his political views chimed precisely with those of Bulgaria's defeated Conservatives. Continuing conflicts between the Russians and the Bulgarians and between the Prince and the Liberals condemned the infant state to years of political instability.

Alexander wished, like the Conservatives, to create a paternalist system but neither had a sufficiently strong political base to enforce their views. Furthermore, Alexander wished to import into Bulgaria, and especially into its fledgling army, German rather than Russian practices. The Russians, who retained a large number of advisers and army officers in Bulgaria, were determined to prevent the Germanisation of the country which they had liberated. The Russian feeling that they deserved a privileged status in Bulgaria led to further complications which were to drive a wedge between them and their natural allies against Alexander, the Liberals.

Alexander began his reign by appointing a Conservative ministry but this could not command the confidence of the Liberal-dominated NSb and by March 1880 the young Prince had been forced to appoint Dragan Tsankov, a prominent Liberal, as prime minister. Tsankov's first concern was to build up the apparatus of the new state and he had neither time nor inclination to contain the more extreme members of his

---

[10]) Dimitrov, I.: Knîaz, konstitutsiîa i narodŭt (Prince, Constitution and the Nation). Sofia 1972; Radev, S.: Stroitelite na sŭvremenna Bŭlgariîa (Builders of Contemporary Bulgaria). 2 vols. Sofia 1911, reprinted 1973.

[11]) For a biography of Battenberg see Corti, E.: Alexander of Battenberg. London 1954.

party. Nor was the Prince over-inclined towards compromise. He angered the Liberals by affecting titles which the constitution denied him, by dissolving the municipal council of Sofia, and by intriguing secretly with the Bulgarians in Eastern Rumelia, a development which disturbed the Russians whose preoccupations in Central Asia made any threat to the Balkan *status quo* unwelcome.

Alexander's preferred solution to Bulgaria's political problems, a change in the constitution, was initially ruled out by the Russians. That view changed in 1881 with the murder of Alexander II and the accession of the more conservative Alexander III. In May 1881 Alexander Battenberg carried out a virtual coup d'état. The amendments to the constitution produced a much-reduced NSb, an indirect franchise and a State Council which was to perform the restraining functions the Conservatives had hoped to invest in a second chamber. Alexander seemed to have created the system which he had always wanted. He was soon to be disappointed. The Conservatives with whom he now hoped to share power were not acceptable to the politically-conscious section of the nation; the nation's preferred candidates, the Liberals, were unacceptable to Alexander who therefore turned to the Russians, importing generals Leonid Sobolev and Aleksandr Kaulbars as his senior ministers. This solution was short-lived. The generals embarrassed him by hoping that the Liberals might be gradually reintegrated into the political process, and they angered all Bulgarians, Liberals included, by pressing too hard on two sensitive nerves: the case for Russian involvement in the new state bank, and the Russian suggestion that a railway be built to link Sofia to the Danube, a line which would have obvious strategic significance in any Russian advance through the Balkans. Ultimately Russian insensitivity united almost all Bulgarian factions and in September 1883 an ill-defined pact between Alexander, the Conservatives and Tsankov forced Kaulbars and Sobolev to return to Russia and brought the Liberal leader back to office. The core of the agreement was that the Prince would restore the Tŭrnovo constitution and promised that any further revision of it would be carried out only by constitutional means. For their part the Liberals accepted the four-power convention on the construction of an international trunk railway from Vienna to Istanbul, an obligation laid upon the new state by the treaty of Berlin but bitterly resented by the Russians.

In December 1883 constitutional amendments were enacted but many Liberals felt that the manner in which they had been forced through the NSb was itself unconstitutional. This was the beginning of a rapid division in the ranks of the LP and by the summer of 1884 the Liberals were openly operating as two factions and as such they contested the general election held in June. The more extreme faction won and a new administration was formed under Petko Karavelov, brother of Lĭuben.

Karavelov's government was a watershed in Bulgaria's political topography. It disposed of the major problems which had hitherto preoccupied the nation's rulers, yet it also saw the reemergence of another which would plague and perplex future leaders. Karavelov's first priority was to abolish the amendments of the previous December and in so doing he laid to rest the constitutional problem which had dominated Bulgarian politics since 1879. He then nationalised both the bank and the country's railways, present and future, thus putting an end to Russian dreams of a privileged position in Bulgaria. At the same time, however, Karavelov was forced to face the dangers inherent in the divided Bulgaria created at Berlin.

Nationalist passions had been overshadowed since 1879 by the constitutional debate but now that was stilled former preoccupations reappeared. In 1885 two *cheti* crossed into Macedonia from Bulgaria. The bands were soon dispersed but it was clear that they had been helped by officials in Bulgaria. Karavelov, who subscribed to the Liberal notion that Bulgarian foreign but not domestic policy should be made dependent upon Russia's wishes, was highly embarrassed because complications in the Balkans were still most unwelcome in St. Petersburg. But it was not Macedonia but Eastern Rumelia which saw the most important developments on the nationalist front.

Eastern Rumelia had been given a political structure intended by its devisors to guarantee a place in public life for the three major national groups in the province: Bulgarians, Turks and Greeks. This had not come about. The Bulgarians had rapidly established complete domination of the political and administrative systems and Rumelian public affairs had settled into a mild contest between two oligarchies. The Bulgarian coup of 1881 gingered Rumelian politics for Karavelov and other Liberal exiles took refuge south of the Balkans. By 1885 the movement for unification had built up a powerful head of steam and on 18 September a bloodless revolution took place in Plovdiv and union with Bulgaria was proclaimed[12].

The Russians were furious but Alexander Battenberg could scarcely turn his back on what was an overwhelmingly popular event, even though it was to throw Bulgaria into deep crisis. Karavelov had no heart for something of which the Russians disapproved and the reactions of the Sultan, whose sovereignty had been infringed, could not be foreseen. The Ottoman empire did not contest the Union but Serbia did and in November declared war on Bulgaria. Bulgaria's forces seemed hopelessly outmatched. Their senior officers, all of them Russian, had been withdrawn as a mark of the Tsar's displeasure, and most of the army was concentrated in the south in anticipation of Ottoman intervention. The troops had to march from one end of the country to the other with no organised commissariat and little in the way of modern transportation, yet when they confronted the Serbs at Slivnitsa on 14–19 November they won a resounding victory[13].

The campaign of 1885 was a magnificent achievement which cemented the Union with Rumelia but it did not bring lasting political peace to Bulgaria. The Russians let it be known that they would never be reconciled to a Bulgaria led by Battenberg and this was too much for the stalwart pro-Russians in the LP. They soon linked up with army officers slighted at being denied promotion and in August 1886 Battenberg was abducted. He returned a few weeks later but announced that he would not resume his duties unless the Tsar gave his blessing. Alexander III did not, and Battenberg finally left Bulgaria on 7 September 1886[14].

---

[12] For Rumelia between 1878 and 1885 see Madzharov, M. I.: Iztochna Rumeliĭa. Istoricheski Pregled (Eastern Rumelia. Historical Review). Sofia 1929.

[13] Istoriĭa na srŭbsko-bŭlgarskata voĭna, 1885 (History of the Serbo-Bulgarian War, 1885). Ed. by Mitev, Ĭ. Sofia 1971.

[14] Radev (note 10) remains the best source for the events of 1886.

III. Stefan Stambolov and Prince Ferdinand, 1886–1894

The political convulsions of 1886 had a profound effect upon Bulgarian politics. In the first place they underlined the critical importance of the army. It had been one faction of the officer corps which deposed Battenberg, and it was to be another which enabled order to be maintained in subsequent years. 1886 was also important in party political terms. The previous dividing lines between Liberal and Conservative and between one Liberal group and the other had been basically constitutional. The constitutional issue was now decided or submerged by that of relations with Russia. One faction of the LP, and some Conservatives, retained the belief that Bulgarian foreign policy must be subservient to Russia's; others insisted upon independence in this as in other sectors. The division between Russophile and Russophobe was to be profound and damaging, particularly in the next decade[15]).

In the short term 1886 produced a new strong-man in Bulgarian politics. Stefan Stambolov, the son of an inn-keeper from near Tŭrnovo, had been active in the nationalist movement and after 1878 had stood on the left of the LP[16]). By 1886 he held the influential position of president of the NSb and this post, together with his links with the army through his brother-in-law, colonel Sava Mutkurov, enabled him to dominate domestic affairs after the departure of Alexander Battenberg. Stambolov thwarted Russian attempts to intervene in elections in 1886 and so enraged were the Russians that they cut all official links with Bulgaria. They continued, however, to back intrigues and even unofficial armed intervention in Bulgaria, some of it encouraged by the leading and exiled Russophile, Tsankov.

Stambolov's first priority was to find a new prince whose installation, he believed, would make subversion and destabilisation more difficult. The search was long and arduous. It ended in Vienna in the summer of 1887 when Ferdinand of Saxe-Coburg-Gotha agreed to take the vacant throne. This was not the end of Stambolov's travails. Because of a Russian veto neither the great powers nor the Porte would recognise Ferdinand as the legitimate prince, and an unrecognised ruler was a more easy target for subversion than a legitimate one. Stambolov, the natural choice as Ferdinand's prime minister, set out to prove that even if the Prince were unrecognised outside Bulgaria he was nevertheless firmly in control within the country[17]).

This was no easy task. The Orthodox church remained suspicious of a Catholic ruler, there was rumbling discontent in the army, and the state was short of funds for railway construction and other obligations. Stambolov adopted two basic strategies. The first was ruthless repression of opposition. The second was to seek agreements abroad which, if they did not bring recognition, would at least signify that Bulgaria

---

[15]) Panaĭotov, I.: Rusiĭa, velikite sili i bŭlgarskiĭat vŭpros sled izbora na Kniaz Ferdinanda (1888–1896 g.) (Russia, the Great Powers and the Bulgarian Question after the Election of Prince Ferdinand (1888–1896)). Sofia 1941.

[16]) Marinov, D.: Stefan Stambolov i novata ni istoriĭa (Stefan Stambolov and our Recent History). Sofia 1909 is the best biography of Stambolov.

[17]) For Ferdinand's reign up to 1896 see Königslöw, J. von: König Ferdinand von Bulgarien. Munich 1970; for a modern biography see Constant, S.: Foxy Ferdinand, Tsar of Bulgaria. London 1979.

was not entirely an international pariah; in 1888 and 1889 loans and trading agreements were therefore concluded with Austria, Germany, Britain and a number of other states. More significant than these agreements were the concessions granted by the Porte in 1890 for nominating exarchate bishops to three Macedonian dioceses. These concessions were vitally important. In 1890 Stambolov and Ferdinand faced the most serious threat to their régime in the form of a wide-ranging conspiracy led by major Kosta Panitsa, a close friend of Alexander Battenberg. Stambolov persuaded the Porte that if he and Ferdinand were removed their successors would be expansionists who would threaten Ottoman power in Macedonia; concessions in that area, on the other hand, would short-circuit that danger and increase Ferdinand's credibility as the defender of Bulgarian national interests. This in fact proved to be the case. The granting of the bishoprics won over the church in Bulgaria and greatly enhanced the prestige of the régime in Sofia.

The success of 1890 did not prevent attempts to assassinate Stambolov, but it did encourage the prime minister to press ahead with further efforts to consolidate Ferdinand's position. A bride was sought and found in Princess Marie Louise of Bourbon-Parma. As a Catholic she insisted that the Bulgarian constitution be amended to allow the heir to the throne to profess his parents' religion and, this being accomplished, the betrothal was announced. The wedding took place in April 1893 and nine months later, in January 1894, a son and heir, Boris, was born[18].

That Stambolov had persuaded the nation and its church to accept a Catholic heir to the throne was a measure of his power, but the more Stambolov entrenched Ferdinand the more expendable he, Stambolov, became. By 1893 the Prince was becoming ever more restless at his minister's power and at his increasing arbitrariness. Furthermore, Stambolov had secured Ferdinand upon his princely throne but he had not brought about international recognition and it was generally assumed that the Russians would never grant that recognition whilst Stambolov was still in office. Stambolov, by 1894, had served his purpose and Ferdinand therefore began to apply his considerable abilities as an intriguer to bring about his downfall. The Prince flirted with the opposition which coalesced in 1893 around the journal *Svobodno Slovo* (Free Speech), a paper which thereafter pursued a consistent campaign against Stambolov and his NLP. Far more important was Ferdinand's success in appointing a dependent who served as both chief of the general staff and minister of war. The army was in the Prince's hands by 1894 and in May of that year Stambolov resigned; in July 1895 he was hacked almost to pieces near his home and died a few days later.

---

[18] For the consolidation of Ferdinand's power, see Crampton, R.J.: Bulgaria 1878–1918: A History. Boulder, Co. and New York 1983, chapter 6.

IV. Ferdinand's Personal Rule, 1894–1908

Stambolov's successor, Konstantin Stoilov, was a weak man. His political legitimacy rested upon his claim to be the alternative to the harsh and arbitrary Stambolov, but the new premier lost moral credit by arbitrarily replacing hostile officials and indulging in electoral management. A further sign of his weakness was the freedom allowed to the Macedonian lobby. This was not popular in Russia and Russian favour had to be won if Bulgaria were to achieve its major immediate objective, recognition of Ferdinand. Stoilov was not prepared to make abject concessions to St. Petersburg but he did agree to relax restrictions on Russophile politicians and even to allow some exiled army officers to return[19]. For their part the Russians eventually made it known that recognition depended on one further concession from Bulgaria: that Prince Boris be converted to Orthodoxy. This was a difficult decision for Ferdinand whose wife's family were implacably opposed to conversion. Finally Ferdinand bowed to political necessity. Boris was received into the Orthodox church in February 1896 and shortly afterwards Ferdinand was recognised as Prince of Bulgaria.

Recognition was primarily Ferdinand's success and it did little to help Stoilov whose administration was running into financial heavy water. The core of the problem was the railway system in southern Bulgaria, formerly Eastern Rumelia. The railways there had been built by the Oriental Railway Company (ORC) and had not become part of the BDZh system. The ORC charged higher freight duties than the other companies which formed the international line from Vienna to Istanbul, and refused to levy the concessionary rates which BDZh charged to Bulgarian industrial producers as part of Stoilov's attempts to promote native manufacturing. Not least because Stoilov's NP relied upon south Bulgarian votes in the NSb the government decided to build a parallel line to by-pass that of the ORC. It was a disastrous decision. Bulgaria could not afford such a luxury. The project had to be abandoned and Stoilov resigned early in 1899, but not before large sums had been borrowed from foreign banks[20].

There was worse to come. In an effort to augment internal revenues it was announced in November 1899 that for the years 1900–1904 the land tax, introduced in 1894 as a modern alternative to the tithe, would once again be collected in kind. The peasants, already suffering from exploitation by the usurer and from increasing taxation, were furious. For the first time in the history of the Principality there was widespread social unrest from which emerged, after some metamorphosis, the BZNS, the most important native Bulgarian political organism[21].

BZNS was not yet to play a major role in Bulgarian politics and from 1900 to 1903 public attention was concentrated upon the problem of Macedonia. Greece and

---

[19] Popov, R.: Bŭlgariiâ i Rusiiâ (1894–1898) (Bulgaria and Russia (1894–1898)). Sofia 1985, p. 160–237.

[20] Todorova, Ts.: Diplomaticheska istoriiâ na vŭnshnite zaemi na Bŭlgariiâ, 1888–1912 (The Diplomatic History of Bulgaria's Foreign Loans, 1888–1912). Sofia 1971, p. 172–256.

[21] Bell, J.D.: Peasants in Power. Princeton 1977, p. 22–54; Slavov, G.: Selskoto dvizhenie v Bŭlgariiâ i sŭzdavaneto na BZNS (The Peasant Movement in Bulgaria and the Creation of BZNS). Sofia 1976.

Serbia were building up claims to part of the Ottoman inheritance and there also emerged a powerful, indigenous Macedonian movement, the VMRO, which demanded autonomy for the area rather than incorporation into a neighbouring state. This produced tension between VMRO and the Supremacists, a Sofia-based organisation aiming for the incorporation of Macedonia into Bulgaria. In 1903 VMRO, partly to head off Supremacist intervention, staged a full-scale rising on 2 August or Ilinden, St. Elijah's Day. It was a hopeless venture. The rising was suppressed and although reforms backed by the great powers were enacted for Macedonia both the autonomist and the Bulgarian cause there had suffered an irreparable blow. After 1903 neither VMRO nor the Supremacists had the strength to defeat Hellenist or Serbian designs on European Turkey; Macedonia, the most important portion of *Bulgaria irredenta*, was now unobtainable without war[22].

The years following the fall of Stambolov witnessed a steady rise in Ferdinand's power. By the end of the century his personal rule was well-established[23]. This was based upon the victory of the executive over the legislature. Ferdinand had secured control of the army via the ministry of war and he dominated foreign affairs. He was also able to exercise considerable pressure on his ministers by using his secret archives which listed politicians' peccadilloes in considerable detail. Whilst the executive grew stronger the legislature weakened. The original party division of 1879 over constitutional issues had been settled; the divisions of 1886–1894 over foreign affairs and the relationship to Russia ceased to be a real issue because Ferdinand now dominated diplomacy so completely. And without serious social divisions there were no questions of principle around which factions might group. Political parties therefore became mechanisms for securing personal advantage through the patronage which an incumbent ministry could exercise. With but a few exceptions Ferdinand would decide when a ministry should fall and a new one be formed. After that a stage-managed election would be held to provide the new administration with a NSb majority and once in power the new ruling party would reward its supporters with office. The system was relatively simple, reasonably efficient and totally corrupt. Its great weakness was that should it fail it could expect no mercy from a disillusioned public.

V. War and the Failure of Territorial Expansionism, 1908–1918

The Berlin settlement had left Bulgaria technically a vassal of the Sultan. This status initially limited Bulgarian freedom of action in tariff and other policies but by the turn of the century such restrictions were largely ignored. When the Young Turk government attempted to reactivate all the Sultan's legal rights Sofia became alarmed and on 5 October 1908 Bulgaria declared itself fully independent, Ferdinand taking the title of „Tsar of the Bulgarians"[24].

---

[22] On Macedonia the best source is Adanir, F.: Die Makedonische Frage. Wiesbaden 1979.

[23] Crampton (note 18), p. 172/73, 325–28.

[24] Todorova, Ts.: Obiaviavaneto nezavisimostta na Bŭlgariia prez 1908 g. (Bulgaria's Declaration of Independence, 1908). Sofia 1960.

The Tŭrnovo constitution required that any constitutional change be endorsed by a VNSb, a body twice as large as an ordinary NSb. Such an assembly did not meet to legalise the changes of 1908 until 1911 and when it did convene the meeting could not but reflect the growing strength of the BZNS (Table 2). Its rise owed much to the genius of Aleksandŭr Stamboliĭski who emerged as the dominant figure in the Agrarian movement but not even his skills could defeat the 1911 constitutional amendments which, in addition to the changes of 1908, included experiments in proportional representation.

The 1911 VNSb also increased the Tsar's power to negotiate foreign agreements. In the context of the Balkans in 1911 this was a most significant development. Young Turk reforming and modernising enthusiasms had not been entirely welcome in the peninsula. They required that the Albanians submit to the twin curses of the modern state, taxation and conscription, and in 1911 the Albanians again revolted. For the other Christian states the Albanian action posed the danger that Istanbul would rush to establish tighter control over its Balkan possessions or that, if this failed, the great powers would impose their own solution. In either case the road to territorial expansion for the Balkan states would be closed. The answer was for those states to act together. They were encouraged in this direction by Russia which mistakenly assumed she would have control of the chicken she was hatching. By early 1912, with past disagreements in Macedonia temporarily set aside, Bulgaria had concluded an agreement with Serbia. Montenegro later gave a verbal commitment to act with the allies and by the summer Greece too had joined the Balkan alliance[25]).

The alliance had an offensive purpose: to assert the territorial claims of the Balkan states upon Turkey-in-Europe. Its direct result was to unleash the Balkan wars. In October the alliance took to the field and initially it prospered mightily. By the middle of November the Ottoman armies had been driven back to their capital and the Porte had asked for an armistice. The Bulgarians at first refused, chosing to press home an attack upon Istanbul itself. That attack failed and an armistice was then signed. Early in 1913 renewed fighting enabled the Bulgarians to capture Edirne. But the spoils were more easily acquired than apportioned.

The great powers' insistence that an Albanian state be created denied Serbia its planned westward expansion. It demanded compensation in Macedonia which Bulgaria resisted. At the same time the Rumanians were pressing for southern Dobrudja as compensation for Bulgarian territorial gains, whilst the Greeks were aligning secretly with Serbia to preserve their acquisitions in Macedonia, principally Salonika. In June an exasperated Bulgaria attacked its erstwhile allies. It was a disastrous move. The Rumanian and the Ottoman armies invaded, taking advantage of Bulgaria's commitments in the west. In August the treaty of Bucharest deprived Bulgaria of most of its gains from the first war and also transferred southern Dobrudja to Rumania. A localised, Balkan war had failed to recreate San Stefano Bulgaria; the

---

[25]) The latest writings on the Balkan alliance and the Balkan wars include Crampton, R.J.: The Hollow Detente. Anglo-German Relations in the Balkans, 1911–1914. London no date; Rossos, A.: Russia and the Balkans. Inter-Balkan Rivalries and Russian Foreign Policy, 1908–1914. Toronto 1981. See also the historical maps in the chapter „Außenpolitik" by K.-D. Grothusen.

Table 2: Votes Cast in Bulgarian Elections, 1908–1923

Parties	1908 Number	1908 %age	1911 Number	1911 %age	1913 Number	1913 %age	1914 Number	1914 %age	1919 Number	1919 %age	1920 Number	1920 %age	April 1923 Number	April 1923 %age	November 1923 Number	November 1923 %age
Liberal groupings	52,079	4.61	131,723	7.08	207,763	38.23	345,730	44.92	8,994	1.37	19,215	2.10	56,102	5.20	124,509	11.35
			19,145	1.03												
National Liberals	54,944	4.86	121,145	6.52					27,674	4.22	39,537	4.32				
			25,167	1.35												
Democrats	595,385	52.69	112,726	6.06	42,971	7.91	86,611	11.25	66,953	10.20	91,177	9.96				
											8,242	0.90				
National	112,234	9.93	22,470	1.21	24,344	4.48	39,005	5.07	57,907	8.02	61,647	6.74				
			945,652	50.86							8,065	0.88				
Progressive Liberals	68,993	6.11	18,844	1.01	11,863	2.18	23,307	3.03	37,178	5.66	46,478	5.08				
Radical Democrats	15,530	1.37	52,403	2.82	24,007	4.42	27,353	3.55	33,861	5.16	41,930	4.58				
Young Liberals	8,786	0.78	20,976	1.13					4,093	0.62						
BZNS	168,186	14.88	256,791	13.81	113,761	20.93	147,143	19.12	203,630	31.02	349,212	38.16	571,907	53.00	144,406	13.17
															68,934	6.29
															8,437	0.77
BKP/BRP			48,889	2.63	54,217	9.98	43,251	5.62	119,395	18.20	184,616	20.17	203,972	18.90		
Socialists, Broad/SDP	17,334	1.53	52,331	2.81	55,157	10.15	45,235	5.88	84,185	12.83	55,452	6.06	27,816	2.58		
Constitutional Bloc													31,768	2.95		
Democratic Alliance													166,909	15.47	645,252	58.85
Others & Spoilt Ballots	36,447	3.24	31,157	1.68	9,367	1.72	12,077	1.56	12,484	1.90	9,601	1.05	20,534	1.90	104,939*	9.57
Total	1,129,918	100.00	1,859,419	100.00	543,450	100.00	769,712	100.00	656,354	100.00	915,172	100.00	1,079,008	100.00	1,096,477	100.00

*Includes 92,964 spoilt ballots.

Source: Glavna Direktsiiá na Statistika (Chief Directorate of Statistics): Statisticheski Godishnik na Bŭlgarskoto Tsarstvo (Statistical Yearbook of the Bulgarian Kingdom). 17 (1927), p. 414-5.

only hope for the weakened Bulgaria now lay in a larger, European conflict in which it must be careful to align itself with the ultimate victor.

At the beginning of the first world war Bulgaria's prime minister, Vasil Radoslavov, declared neutrality until, in September 1915, it seemed a German victory was assured. Bulgaria joined the central powers in October. Both sides to the conflict had courted Bulgaria whose strategic importance lay primarily in its ability to close the supply lines between Germany and the Ottoman empire. Radoslavov had always been a supporter of the Triple Alliance and in 1914 Bulgaria had taken out a large loan in Berlin, but these considerations, though influential, were not decisive. The decisive factors were the central powers' ability to promise all of Macedonia to Bulgaria, and those powers' military successes on the eastern front and in Gallipoli.

Bulgarian commitment to the central powers was by no means a popular decision; Stamboliĭski's vehement opposition to it earned him three years in a prison cell, although his party did vote for war credits. Bulgaria's war aims, said Radoslavov, were to unite the Bulgarian nation in its historic and ethnographic borders. By the end of 1915 the Bulgarians occupied much of Macedonia together with the Morava valley, and in the following year they advanced into Thrace, northern Greece and Rumania. There were some setbacks in late 1916 but it was not until September 1918 that the Bulgarian army began to suffer serious defeat. By then the soldiers had become demoralised through inadequate supplies and by the knowledge that at home their families were suffering great privation. The army in fact buckled under the impact of an allied attack and Bulgaria became the first of the central powers to collapse.

Failure in war had robbed the political establishment of all respect. The stage was set for radical change[26]).

VI. Post-War Radicalism and the Government of Stamboliĭski, 1918–1923

With the military collapse came unrest in the Bulgarian army. Mutinous troops congregated at Radomir and, rejecting appeals from political leaders, including the recently-released Stamboliĭski, declared for a Republic and began to march upon Sofia. But by then the Radomir rebellion had lost its momentum. The signing of an armistice in Salonika on 29 September meant that the major objective of the mutineers, peace, had been gained, and a few days later the abdication of Ferdinand in favour of his son, Boris III, further decreased revolutionary zeal.

In October 1918 an interim cabinet was formed pending a general election. This took place in August 1919 (Table 2) but it took until October to negotiate a coalition of BZNS and a number of groups on the non-socialist left. The delay was lengthened by the fact the Stamboliĭski had to remain in Paris until details of the Bulgarian peace treaty had been determined. The treaty of Neuilly-sur-Seine, signed on 27 November

---

[26]) For internal political affairs, 1915–1918, see Crampton (note 18), chapter 23; Khristov, Kh.: Voĭnishkoto vŭstanie, 1918 (The Soldiers' Revolt, 1918). Sofia 1961.

1919, deprived Bulgaria of some 5,500 square miles along its western border and confirmed Rumanian possession of the Dobrudja. The settlement also required that Bulgaria pay reparations amounting to 2,250 million gold francs to the allies and hand over specified quantities of raw materials and livestock to Yugoslavia. The Bulgarian army was to be limited to 20,000 men. These terms were harsh but not crippling and article 48 guaranteed Bulgaria an economic outlet on the Aegean. Stamboliĭski signed without serious protest because he believed that this treaty, like that of Berlin, would soon be revised.

With the signing of the treaty the way was cleared for the major domestic political confrontation which had been incipient ever since the end of the war: the struggle for the succession. The war had discredited the ruling parties and correspondingly strengthened the two main factions on the left of Bulgarian politics, the Agrarians and the Socialists. The BRSDP had been founded in 1891 and in 1903 had split into „Broad" and „Narrow" factions, the latter rejecting cooperation with non-Marxist parties[27]. In 1915 the Narrows were the only group to vote against war credits and their strength increased further with the Bolshevik coup in Russia in 1917; in 1919 the Narrows formed the BKP, the Broads retaining the title of Workers' Social Democratic Party, usually abbreviated to Social Democratic Party (SDP). The Communists seemed to Stamboliĭski to be natural allies in the building of a new Bulgaria but his offer was spurned. The Communists had never cooperated with other parties and were not prepared now, when the old order was so weak, to join with one whom they saw as the Bulgarian Kerensky.

Communist confidence was boosted by the 1919 election which showed their vote 176% above its 1914 level (Table 2) and which made them the second largest party after the Agrarians. Their power was increasing also in the trade union movement and amongst the urban *nouveaux pauvres* of the inflation-hit civil service and professions. At the end of the year full confrontation came between the Communists and the Stamboliĭski government. On 28 December, with the Communists and the SDP acting together for the first time since 1903, a general strike began. Stamboliĭski declared martial law and used all the force at his disposal, including the BZNS armed body, the Orange Guard. The all-out stoppage lasted only until 5 January 1920 but some workers in communications and the mines remained out for weeks. Having broken the strike Stamboliĭski consolidated his victory in a general election on 28 March 1920 which was primarily a contest between the Communists and BZNS (Table 2). The Communists put up a strong fight and denied the Agrarians an absolute majority. To secure this Stamboliĭski resorted to the discredited methods of the old system and annulled the election of thirteen deputies, nine of them Communists[28].

With the defeat of the Communists Stamboliĭski set out to enact a radical, Agrarian programme. The BZNS had not in fact drawn up a party programme until 1918 but when published it enshrined the classic agrarian/populist notions of social

---

[27] Rothschild, J.: The Communist Party of Bulgaria. New York 1959; Bell, J. D.: The Communist Party of Bulgaria from Blagoev to Zhivkov. Stanford 1986.
[28] Bell (note 21), p. 122–53; Kazasov, D.: Burni godini (Stormy Years). Sofia 1949.

justice and egalitarianism based upon an independent producer made economically efficient by the cooperatives. These had already established themselves as an important factor in the Bulgarian countryside, most notably in protecting the peasant against the usurer, and Stamboliĭski saw them as a vehicle for modernising the economy and educating the peasant politically. Stamboliĭski's vision was of a Bulgaria of small, clean villages in which the cooperatives and the BZNS provided the peasant proprietors with the benefits of modern civilisation – health services, libraries, cinemas, post-offices, schools etc.

Stamboliĭski and his government did not enjoy complete freedom of action. The reparations payments, particularly those in kind, hampered economic development, and the national exchequer was burdened by having to maintain large numbers of penniless refugees from the lost territories. In political terms the old parties, the Communists and the throne were all potential opponents of the régime. The allies also watched carefully what the Bulgarian government was doing, insisting, for example, on the disbandment of a state grain-purchasing agency because it was deemed in restraint of trade.

Despite these restrictions the Agrarian government of 1920–1923 enacted a number of important reforms. Like all agrarian régimes it was anxious to redistribute landed property. A maximum holding of 30 hectares for each family was decreed with provision for extra land for families with more than four members. Excess land from individual owners and from institutions such as the church was to go into a state land fund before being redistributed. Bulgaria had less need of land redistribution than many other states and this in part accounts for the fact that although the régime hoped to reallocate some 230,000 hectares by 1923 only 82,000 hectares had changed hands by then. In addition to promoting land redistribution the Stamboliĭski government also encouraged crop diversification, commassation, the extension of the cooperatives, and the expansion of agricultural education. Much of this legislation, including that for the redistribution of landed property, remained in force, albeit in modified form, after the fall of the Stamboliĭski government[29].

One of the most enduring reforms of that government was the introduction of the Compulsory Labour Service (*Trudovata povinnost*), a forerunner of the present brigade system. In June 1920 it was enacted that all males between eighteen and forty and all unmarried females between sixteen and thirty were liable respectively to twelve and six months labour service[30]. Those working under the scheme, the *trudovatsi*, were involved in building projects, usually to expand social overhead capital. The Labour Service was intended to inculcate a sense of agrarian patriotism amongst the *trudovatsi* but the latter were organised into units which to the western allies had a suspiciously military appearance. The Labour Service was not, as they feared, an attempt to evade the military restrictions of the treaty of Neuilly, but the allies nevertheless intervened and insisted upon some alterations in the system.

Education had long formed an important plank in Agrarian propaganda and it was in this sector that Stamboliĭski's government secured perhaps its most enduring

---

[29] For Agrarian policies see Bell (note 21), chapter 6; Gentizon, P.: Le Drame Bulgare. Paris 1924.
[30] For the CLS see Lazard, M.: Compulsory Labour Service in Bulgaria. Geneva 1922.

success. Education had played an important part in the national revival of the nineteenth century but after liberation Bulgarian teachers had frequently preached either jingoistic nationalism or destructive socialism. The Agrarians banned both from the classroom and at the same time reduced the role of religion to make more time available for lessons on agricultural techniques. It was also the Agrarian ministry which made secondary education compulsory and to cope with the increased demand constructed some 1,100 new schools[31]).

Stamboliĭski's administration was equally innovatory in foreign policy. He rejected the concept of territorial expansion, his desired solution to external problems being an agrarian-based internationalism, the first step towards which would be the formation of a Balkan federation of peasantist governments. Until this ideal appeared he wanted peace and cooperation between the Balkan states with the key to this peace being, he believed, good relations between Bulgaria and Yugoslavia. These were not easily achieved, primarily because of the Macedonian question. After the war discontented Macedonian extremists had established a virtual state within the state at Petrich where the Bulgarian, Greek and Yugoslav borders meet, and from here the dissidents conducted raids into Yugoslav and Greek Macedonia and harried the Bulgarian government in Sofia. Stamboliĭski defied the Macedonian extremists and by November 1922 even a doubting Yugoslav government had become convinced of his sincerity and in March 1923 the two countries signed the Nish agreement to combat terrorist activity. It was a declaration of war by Stamboliĭski on the Macedonians.

The Macedonians took up the challenge and occupied Kn̂ustendil in protest; in February 1923 they made an attempt on the prime minister's life. The Macedonians, however, were but one of a number of groups now deeply wary of Stamboliĭski. He had never been loved by the army. By 1922 a Military League (*Voenen Sŭûz*) had been formed to protect its interests. A new factor in Bulgarian public life, and one equally opposed to Stamboliĭski, was constituted by the White Russian refugees, 36,000 of whom entered the country after the end of the Russian civil war. Many of them retained their weapons and until Stamboliĭski moved against them in the spring of 1922 they formed the largest armed force in the country.

The BZNS had always concentrated its attention upon the countryside and it was not surprising that this earned it the hostility of many urban Bulgarians. The small working-class and the artisanate looked towards the Communists, not least because the Agrarians were unable to check an inflation which meant that by 1923 the leva was only a seventh of its 1919 value. In the local elections of February 1923 the Communists performed well and the discovery of arms on a Soviet merchantman bound for Varna in June heightened tension between the government and its chief opponent on the left. But it was not only the workers who riled at Agrarian rule. The depressed civil servants, the lawyers who were a particular object of Agrarian suspicion, left-wing teachers who had lost their jobs, journalists who resented censorship, all were discontented and looked not to the Communists but rather to the old NSb parties, especially the left-leaning Democrats.

---

[31]) Bell (note 21), p.177.

These traditional parties formed a Constitutional Bloc (*Konstitutsionen Blok*) which itself established links with the Military League through the National Alliance (*Naroden Sgovor*). In September 1922 the leaders of the Constitutional Bloc were detained „for their own protection". In February 1923 Stamboliĭski abolished proportional representation and reinstituted single-member constituencies in advance of the general election due in April. Many now genuinely feared that Stamboliĭski was about to create a one-party republic and after BZNS's crushing victory in the April election (Table 2) it seemed that legal opposition was pointless. After the elections, therefore, a conspiracy was hatched by the Military League, the Macedonians, the National Alliance and even some members of the BRSDP. On 9 June 1923 they acted and toppled the Agrarian government. Many died on that and subsequent days, the most notable victim being Stamboliĭski himself who, like Stambolov, was hacked to pieces[32]).

The 1923 coup shattered BZNS. It was never again to form a ministry on its own. It fell to feuding and splintered, recapturing its honour only in a brief, heroic stand against the Communists in 1947. The ruination of BZNS meant that never again did the government of Bulgaria command the full allegiance and support of the peasants who formed the majority of the nation until the 1960s. The government was now divorced from the mass of the nation. The political arena was left to the Communists, the traditional parties, the Macedonians, the army and the Tsar. Like characters in an Agatha Christie story, they were to fall one by one.

VII. The Failure of the Traditional and the New Right, 1923–1935

After the 1923 coup a government was formed under Professor Aleksandŭr Tsankov. It was backed by the Democratic Alliance (*Demokraticheski Sgovor*), a combination of the National Alliance and factions from some of the parties not in that grouping. It was to remain in office until 1931.

Initially the Democratic Alliance set out to conciliate the nation. Much Agrarian legislation remained in force and other groups were courted with concessions such as the relaxation of censorship, the release of some detainees, and the reinstatement of many of those who had lost their jobs through taking part in the strike of 1919/1920. This period of conciliation ended abruptly in September 1923.

In Moscow the Comintern had reacted angrily to the passivity of the BKP in June and an immediate about face was ordered. On 23 September Bulgaria's Communists therefore staged a rising. It ended disastrously. The Communists were hopelessly ill-prepared and they received no significant support from either the army or the other socialist groups. Furthermore, many Communists found it difficult to see the Agrarians, who until recently had been derided as the rural petite bourgeoisie, as martyred comrades who had to be redeemed by revolt[33]).

---

[32]) For the conspiracy and the coup see Kazasov (note 28), p. 136–73.
[33]) Kosev, D.: Septemvriĭskoto vŭstanie 1923 g. (The September Revolt, 1923). Sofia 1954.

The September rising was used by Tsankov as an excuse to shackle the Bulgarian nation. In November 1923 a Defence of the Realm Act gave the government greatly enhanced powers and an election in the same month provided it with a firm NSb majority. In April 1924 the BKP was banned, its trade union and youth organisations broken up, its property confiscated and its deputies expelled from parliament. Leadership of the party passed to Vasil Kolarov and Georgi Dimitrov in Moscow but inside Bulgaria extreme elements pushed the party towards acts of terrorism. The greatest of these was the bombing of Sofia's Sveta Nedelîa cathedral on 16 April 1925 during a funeral service due to be attended by the Tsar and the government. The Tsar was late and his ministers survived, but over one hundred and twenty of the congregation did not. The outrage unleashed a savage wave of terror in which over six thousand people were arrested, many of them to disappear for ever[34]).

The September rising and the Cathedral outrage, together with the repression which they occasioned, gravely weakened the BKP. It retained a good deal of popular support but its organisation was dislocated and its political effectiveness correspondingly depreciated.

If the power of the Communists declined after 1923 that of the Macedonians did not, though much of it was dissipated in feuding between the various Macedonian factions[35]). Nevertheless, the Macedonian lobby could not be neglected and it exerted a constant if not always an obvious influence in the political life of Bulgaria.

The excesses of the Tsankov régime were such that the western powers, above all Britain, refused to lend money to Bulgaria as long as he remained at the head of its affairs. With a loan being desperately needed Tsankov therefore gave way to Andreĭ Lîapchev in January 1926[36]).

Lîapchev was to remain in office until 1931. He relaxed the Tsankovist terror. He allowed the Communists to reappear as the BRP, but he did nothing to check the activities of the Macedonians who offended many important persons and institutions, not least the army which was angered by the persecution of allegedly anti-Macedonian officers. For much of Lîapchev's period in office Bulgaria enjoyed a moderate prosperity and stability, despite a decline in world tobacco prices. At the same time, however, Lîapchev was losing his grip on the Democratic Alliance upon which he relied for support in the NSb. It was not entirely his own fault. The parties in the assembly tended to splinter so that the nineteen groups identified in 1926 had become twenty-nine by 1934[37]).

In the elections of 1931, for which proportional representation was reintroduced, Lîapchev paid the price for his lack of control when the Democratic Alliance was defeated by a new grouping, the People's Bloc (*Naroden Blok*), a combination of non-Alliance bourgeois parties and leftist Agrarians. The election of 1931 was singular in

---

[34]) Kazasov (note 28), p. 270–8; Peshev, P.: Istoricheskite sŭbitîa i deîateli (Historical Events and Figures). Sofia 1929, p. 811–28.

[35]) Swire, J.: Bulgarian Conspiracy. London 1939; Troebst, S.: Mussolini, Makedonien und die Mächte, 1922–1930. Köln 1987, p. 103–20.

[36]) Mitev, D.: The Refugee Loan of 1926 and Britain, in: Études Historiques. 12 (1984), p. 175–97.

[37]) Crampton, R.J.: A Short History of Modern Bulgaria. Cambridge 1987, p. 104–7.

that it produced a genuine conflict and determined the composition of the succeeding ministry. Because of the inclusion of the Agrarians, the People's Bloc raised the hope that the peasant masses might once more be reconciled to those who ruled them. It was not to be. The depression produced great suffering which radicalised the towns with the BRP securing notable victories in local elections and even taking control of Sofia city council in February 1932; the council was dissolved a year later. The government, in an effort to shelter the peasant from the worst effects of the economic storm, eased debt burdens and created Khranoiznos, a state purchasing agency which guaranteed grain producers a market at a fixed price. For this the peasants were grateful but they took exception to other aspects of the People's Bloc rule, above all to the manner in which ministers, and especially the Agrarians, squabbled over office and filled their own pockets from the already depleted public purse.

By 1934 it was clear the People's Bloc had squandered public goodwill. It was also clear that Bulgaria faced serious dangers, both internal and external. At home a noisy, but in fact rather weak, pseudo-Nazi movement, Tsankov's National Social Movement (*Narodno-Sotsialno Dvizhenie*), swaggered onto the political stage, but more threatening were developments abroad. In February 1934 Yugoslavia, Rumania, Greece and Turkey signed the Balkan entente, a repetition of the baleful anti-Bulgarian grouping of 1913. The state would need internal cohesion if it were successfully to resist pressure from such a combination. But who was to provide such cohesion? The left, both Agrarian and Communist, was divided and discredited; the bourgeois parties had failed in the 1920s as they had before 1918; the extreme right had produced a variety of new formations none of which had sufficient strength to seize power. The time was ripe for experimentation and the organisation which seized the initiative was *Zveno* (Link).

Zveno had been formed in 1927. It argued that all Bulgaria's public ills derived from the party-political system; like the Piłsudskiites in Poland Bulgaria's *Zvenari* wanted to cleanse the political system and rescue the nation from corrupt party politicians. *Zveno* advocated a rationalising and centralising of the administration. Small and élitist, it had a considerable following amongst the intelligentsia and, more importantly, it had connections with factions inside the army. On 19 May 1934 the latter acted and in an efficient, bloodless coup colonels Damian Velchev and Kimon Georgiev seized power[38]).

The 19 May régime accomplished a good deal in its short spell of power. It established relations with the Soviet Union and courted Yugoslavia. At home it abolished the political parties, closed their newspapers and confiscated their properties. It dissolved the NSb which was to be reconstructed on the basis of „estates" on the Italian model, and it reformed the system of local government, depriving elected councils of much of their power. Centralisation was also the motive behind the reorganisation of the government ministries and state institutions such as the banks. In 1935 a huge Bulgarian Workers' Union (*Bŭlgarski Rabotnicheski Sŭiuz*) was estab-

---

[38]) Swire (note 35), chapter 11; Migev, V.: Utvŭrzhdavane na monarkho-fashistkata diktatura v Bŭlgariia, 1934–1936 (The Consolidation of the Monarcho-Fascist Dictatorship in Bulgaria, 1934–1936). Sofia 1977, p. 25–75.

lished to replace the trade unions which had been abolished along with the political parties.

So absorbed were Velchev and Georgiev in their restructurings that they neglected to defend themselves against intrigue. In January 1935 Georgiev was replaced as prime minister by general Pencho Zlatev who was much closer than his predecessor to the Tsar. Zlatev remained in office only until April and his successor, Andreĭ Toshev, lasted little longer, resigning in November to hand the premiership to the Tsar's dependent, Georgi K'oseivanov. The Tsar had also increased his power in 1935 by moving against the Macedonians. The army too came under much firmer royal control. In the autumn of 1935 the exiled Velchev had been arrested whilst attempting a clandestine return to Bulgaria. In March 1936 he was tried, sentenced to death and reprieved, but the trial gave Boris the chance he needed to disband the Military League. All other factors had been eliminated and Boris, who had stood so long in the wings, now walked, albeit reluctantly, to the centre of the political stage[39]).

VIII. Boris's Personal Régime, 1935–1941

In April 1935 Boris had issued a manifesto promising a return to constitutional rule when an appropriate constitution could be devised. A good deal of time was devoted to the study of possible systems but none seemed entirely suitable and Bulgaria evolved a form of „controlled democracy" in which there was just as much control as democracy[40]). Political opposition was, however, allowed and in 1936 it crystallised around an enlarged. Constitutional Bloc (*Konstitutsionen Blok*), a wide-ranging coalition which included even the Communists, and whose platform was basically a return to the Tŭrnovo system. In 1937 the government entered upon a gradual modification of the constitution by reforming the local government franchise; voting was to be spread over three Sundays to enable the authorities to concentrate police where they were needed, voters had to have educational qualifications, and Communists were not allowed to stand as candidates, but on the other hand married women and widows were given the vote for the first time. These ideas were applied at a national level in the general election of March 1938 in which proportional representation was once again abolished and which returned a much smaller NSb. Nevertheless, despite a good deal of government pressure the opposition secured over sixty of the 160 seats. K'oseivanov dissolved the assembly after little more than a year and in December 1939 and January 1940 held fresh elections to secure a more amenable parliament.

In the second half of the 1930s in internal affairs Bulgaria had joined the other Balkan states in moving towards authoritarianism. It had also shared their preoccupation with foreign affairs. After 1923 Bulgaria had made its first foreign policy objective the implementation of article 48 of the treaty of Neuilly and in its

---

[39]) For a stimulating recent biography see Groueff, S.: Crown of Thorns. Lanham, New York 1987.
[40]) Migev (note 38), p. 76–167.

campaign had looked to the League of Nations and to Italy for support. In the early 1930s Italy was less well-disposed towards Bulgaria and after 1933 the League was in a state of terminal decline, a fact which sharpened the sense of isolation created by the Balkan entente of 1934.

Boris, whose command of foreign affairs was uncontested after 1935, certainly wanted to escape from this isolation but he was also anxious to keep out of any entanglement with a great power. He found a partner in Yugoslavia which also wished to avoid too close an association with the great powers and which had been disturbed at Bulgaria's exclusion from the Balkan entente. In January 1937 Sofia and Belgrade signed a pact of eternal friendship.

By 1938 all states were being affected by the momentous events in central Europe. After Munich Bulgaria was the only European state defeated in 1918 not to have had some lost territory returned to it. Each German diplomatic success increased Berlin's powers of attraction, in addition to which Germany had established complete domination over Bulgaria's foreign trade (Table 4). At the same time the western powers seemed too enfeebled to be of any value whilst to the east the purges had placed a huge question mark over the military effectiveness of the Soviet Union. In 1939 the Nazi-Soviet pact at least made cooperation with Germany more acceptable to Bulgaria's Russophile peasantry. Yet neither Boris nor his political associates wished to make an out-and-out commitment to Germany and when the European war began in September 1939 Bulgaria immediately declared its neutrality.

That neutrality was maintained for a year and a half. In 1939 Boris brushed aside offers of cooperation with the Soviet Union and the Balkan entente but by early 1940 he was making conciliatory gestures towards Berlin. These included the replacement in February 1940 of the pro-western K'oseivanov with Bogdan Filov, an ardent Germanophile. At the same time the powerful masonic lodges in Bulgaria were closed and one of the country's few anti-semites made minister of the interior. The German victories of May-June 1940, like those of 1915, had a profound effect upon Bulgaria. A Defence of the Realm Act was passed giving the government greatly increased powers, and preparations were made for the mobilisation of the economy. On 7 September 1940 came Bulgaria's first reward when the treaty of Craiova returned the southern Dobrudja to Bulgarian ownership. Yet Boris would still not commit his country definitely to the Axis or any other cause. In September 1940 he rejected a Turkish proposal for an alliance, in October he spurned Italian offers of access to the Aegean in return for cooperation in the attack upon Greece, and in November, much to the anger of pro-Soviet elements in Bulgaria, he turned down a mutual assistance pact offered by Moscow.

By the end of 1940 Hitler's patience was running out and German plans for the east placed Boris under ever greater pressure. The German army began to congregate in Rumania and when Hitler decided to eliminate Greece Bulgaria became of critical importance. Boris eventually capitulated and on 1 March 1941 Filov went to Vienna to sign the Tripartite pact. The following day the German army began to cross the Danube *en route* to Greece. Although war was not declared on Britain and the USA until after Pearl Harbour, Bulgaria had become in effect a partner in the Axis. Boris's motives, however, remained mixed. Clearly Bulgaria had territorial desires which only Germany could gratify but at the same time the Tsar hoped that by becoming part of the New Europe he might at least preserve something of the old Bulgaria and its independence[41]).

IX. Bulgaria in the Second World War, 1941–1944[42])

As its reward for joining the Tripartite pact Bulgaria was allowed to occupy a large portion of Macedonia and inland Thrace. Full ownership was not to be confirmed until after the war, lest the Bulgarians take their booty and quit. In Thrace Bulgarian rule was tough and uncompromising but in Macedonia it brought educational benefits, including a university in Skopje. Increasing centralisation from Sofia and the imposition of non-Macedonian officials and bishops, however, dissipated the goodwill with which the Bulgarians had originally been greeted.

Association with the Tripartite pact had brought the welcome entry into Macedonia but the German attack upon the Soviet Union brought great political complications. In the first place the local Communists were released from the embarrassments which the Nazi-Soviet pact had placed upon them. With Soviet backing they moved immediately to the offensive but, as in 1923, this brought upon them savage repression. By early 1942 they had lost most of their leaders to the secret police and the concentration camps which expanded vigorously after June 1941.

The German attack posed the question of whether Bulgaria should commit itself to the new war. The extreme right naturally supported the call for a crusade against Bolshevism. The government did not and rejected even the proposal for a volunteer legion, Boris fearing that such a legion, returning from a successful campaign, might seize power and remould Bulgaria on fascist lines. To parry German pressure Boris also argued, with some justification, that the Bulgarian army had not been sufficiently modernised to fight effectively in a mobile campaign. Furthermore, said the Tsar, it would be prudent to retain his army in the Balkans where a substantial force was needed to counter any forward move by hostile forces such as the partisans, the Turks or, after their victories in North Africa, the allies.

Boris succeeded in fending off German pressure and Bulgaria did not declare war on the Soviet Union. Boris was also successful in resisting Nazi pressures on the Jewish question. Anti-semitic legislation was introduced into Bulgaria. Jews were required to wear the yellow star and their entry into education and the professions was subjected to a *numerus clausus*[43]). In March 1942 Jews were denied the protection of the law and in March of the following year plans were far advanced for their deportation to the death camps. As soon as rumours of the impending deportations were abroad there were protests in the NSb, in the press, in the pulpits and in the streets. The Tsar willingly complied with public pressure. Rather than sending Jews

---

[41]) Toshkova, V.: Bŭlgariiã v balkanskata politika na SASHT, 1939/1944 (Bulgaria and the Balkan Policy of the USA, 1939–1944). Sofia 1985; Hoppe, H.-J.: Bulgarien – Hitlers eigenwilliger Verbündeter. Stuttgart 1979.

[42]) Miller, M.L.: Bulgaria during the Second World War. Stanford 1975.

[43]) Chary, F.B.: The Bulgarian Jews and the Final Solution. Pittsburgh 1972.

to the „resettlement" camps in Poland he ordered that they should be sent to camps in the Bulgarian countryside where they would be required to serve as labourers on roads and other public works. This was not an easy life, but it was life. The Jews of the areas under Bulgarian occupation in Macedonia and Thrace did not benefit from these measures and they suffered the horror of the Final Solution in its awful plenitude.

By the summer of 1943 Boris and his associates were increasingly anxious to escape from their commitment to the Axis. Not only were they wearied by the arguments over the eastern front and the Jewish question but it was becoming more apparent that the Germans could not win the war. Stalingrad and the Axis defeat in Italy stiffened Boris's resolve to resist German pressure even for more Bulgarian troops for occupation duties in Yugoslavia. This was the subject of stormy debate when Boris visited Hitler early in August 1943. On 28 August the Tsar died, aged only forty-nine. Mystery has surrounded the death ever since and recent research has strengthened the case for suspecting foul play[44]).

Boris was succeeded by six-year old Tsar Simeon with a regency formed by Filov, Boris's brother Kiril, and general Nikola Mikhov. A new prime minister, Dobri Bozhilov, was appointed. From the summer of 1943 the war moved ever closer to Bulgaria. The Red Army began its gradual roll to the west and in January 1944 the RAF and the USAAF launched a massive strike on Sofia. Thousands fled the city throwing the administration of the country into disarray; civil servants had to be ordered back to their posts. Many city-dwellers, especially women and children, remained in the countryside where housing was scarce and where, more pressingly, there were serious food shortages.

The growing crisis produced two results. Bozhilov intensified efforts begun under his predecessor to sound out the allies on possible peace terms. The response was far from encouraging; Bulgaria would be required to relinquish all the territory she had acquired since 1939 and to surrender unconditionally. Even if the Bulgarians had considered negotiating on such terms the Germans would not have allowed Bulgaria to defect and would have occupied the country, as they had Italy.

The second result of the crisis was the growth of the anti-government OF and the resistance[45]). The growth of the OF and partisan activity gave greater urgency to the government's search for an accommodation with the western allies. That search became yet more frenetic in the spring of 1944. On 18 May the Soviets issued a virtual ultimatum to Bulgaria, demanding that all Axis equipment and personnel be removed from Bulgaria's Black Sea ports, that Bulgaria declare strict neutrality and that it break off diplomatic relations with Germany. Such terms were unacceptable because to have acceded to them would have invited a German occupation as had happened in March in Hungary. On the other hand if Bulgaria did not negotiate a peace the Soviets might arrive and occupy the country on the pretext of wishing to drive out the Germans. In June Bulgaria suffered a further blow with the allied invasion of France. The landings in Normandy and the percentage agreements of

---

[44]) Groueff (note 39), p. 362–84.
[45]) Details in J. D. Bell's chapter „Domestic Politics".

October ended Bulgarian dreams that the western powers might descend upon the Balkans in which case they would desperately need Bulgarian cooperation. Bulgaria passed into the Soviet zone of influence and the local Communists made their dispositions accordingly.

X. Social and Economic Factors in Bulgarian History, 1878–1944

The ethnic composition of the Bulgarian state underwent notable changes in its early years. Before the April Uprising approximately a quarter of the population of what was to become Bulgaria was Muslim, much of it Turkish. After the liberation many Turks were unable to adapt to life in a Christian state. They left in considerable numbers in 1877/78 and their decline continued at a less intense rate in subsequent years (Table 1). Early in the twentieth century hostility towards the Greeks caused many of them to emigrate, a process which intensified after 1918. Whilst Greeks and Turks left Jews and Armenians arrived, confident of finding greater security in Bulgaria than in Russia, Rumania or the Ottoman empire. Bulgarians also came into the country after the territorial losses of 1913 and 1918 and with the reacquisition of the southern Dobrudja in 1940.

Changes in the ethnic composition of the country were not accompanied by changes in its social structure. Even before the liberation most Bulgarian peasants were in effect independent peasant proprietors. Despite steady population growth (Table 1) most Bulgarians remained independent producers, a fertile soil for BZNS. The urban population was 18 % of the total in 1880, 19 % in 1910 and a maximum of 19.7 % in 1934; in 1937 the independent proprietor and his family outnumbered the landless, agricultural labourer by 924 to one[46]).

The reasons for the persistence of the independent proprietor were various. Immediately after the liberation the exodus of Muslims left large areas of land available for purchase[47]). When that supply began to run dry there were still tracts of communal property and woodland which could be put under the plough and therefore until the 1920s the supply of land generally kept pace with demand, although there were increasing problems of the shrinkage of average holdings, parcellisation and rural overpopulation[48]). Such a system could not be efficient. Shortly after the Second

---

[46]) Clark, C.: The Conditions of Economic Progress. London 1951, p. 437.

[47]) Todorov, G.T.: Deinostta na vremennoto rusko upravlenie po urezhdane na agrarniâ i bezhanskiâ vŭpros prez 1877–1879 g. (The Activity of the Provisional Russian Administration in the Settlement of the Agrarian and Refugee Questions, 1877–1879), in: Istoricheski Pregled. 11 (1955) 6, p. 27–59; Khristov, Kh.: Niâkoi problemi na prekhoda ot feodalizma kŭm kapitalizma v istoriâta na Bŭlgariâ (Some Problems in the Transfer from Feudalism to Capitalism in the History of Bulgaria), in: Istoricheski Pregled. 17 (1961) 3, p. 83–107.

[48]) The average holding contracted from 5.72 hectares in 1926 to 4.31 hectares in 1946, and the average number of strips per holding rose from eleven in 1908 to seventeen by 1926. Mateev, B.: The Establishment of the Cooperative System in Agriculture in Bulgaria, in: Études Historiques. 5 (1970), p. 616–46.

World War it was estimated that the cultivation of one acre of maize in Bulgaria required 305 man-hours compared to 28 in the USA[49]).

Some relief from the inefficiences of small-scale agriculture had been provided by the cooperatives. These had emerged in the 1900s to protect the Bulgarian peasants against the money lender and thereafter had grown rapidly in size and spheres of operation and had established close links with BZNS. Their expansion continued after 1918 until by 1937 sixty percent of the total population had dealings with them[50]). Further relief to the farmers came with crop diversification. Until the first world war wheat had been the predominant export crop but the acquisition by Bulgaria of tobacco-growing areas in Macedonia in 1913 followed by the disruption of the established European trading patterns after 1914 gave Bulgaria a virtual monopoly in the central European market[51]). After the crash of 1929 the Bulgarian government encouraged further diversification into soft fruit, sugar beet, sunflower seeds, cotton, vegetables, vines and other crops which could be processed by home manufacturers and then sold in European markets. In the worst years of the depression an important role was also played by Khranoiznos which acquired control over the sale as well as the purchase of grain and was soon exercising similar powers over other products. Together with the civilian and military bodies established in both world wars to regulate the domestic economy, Khranoiznos provided a pattern for state control in the economic sector.

If the Bulgarian countryside underwent little structural change between 1878 and 1944 urban modernisation could not be avoided. Some settlements declined, primarily those textile towns along the Balkan foothills, but others expanded. Sofia, as the new capital and the centre of a burgeoning bureaucracy, grew most rapidly, increasing from 20,000 in 1880 to 102,000 in 1910 when one in four of its working population were civil servants[52]).

The growth of Sofia was as much the result of the building of the new state machine as of industrial development. That development did, however, occur. The state was anxious that it should. The early Liberal governments nationalised the railways and the major bank but the first systematic attempt to promote Bulgarian manufacturing came in 1894 with Stoilov's Encouragement of Industry Act. The act gave Bulgarian producers cheaper freight rates on BDZh, free grants of land, tax concessions and other incentives[53]). Later governments extended the 1894 act and it was not until the 1930s that the number of industries enjoying state encouragement began to decline. In addition to the 1894 act the Stoilov administration also introduced protective tariffs designed to stimulate home manufacturing and these too became a permanent feature of Bulgarian policy.

---

[49]) Clark (note 46), p. 223/4.
[50]) For the cooperatives and for a general economic history see Lampe, J. R.: The Bulgarian Economy in the Twentieth Century. London 1986.
[51]) Lampe (note 50), p. 53.
[52]) Lampe, J. R.: Modernization and Social Structure: The Case of the Pre-1914 Balkan Capitals, in: Southeastern Europe. 5 (1979) 2, p. 11–32.
[53]) Crampton (note 18), p. 372–75.

Table 3: Growth of State-Encouraged Enterprises, 1894–1937

Year	No. of Enterprises	No. of Workers
1894	72	3,027
1900	103	4,716
1904	166	6,149
1907	206	7,646
1909	266	12,943
1911	345	15,886
1921	454	17,293
1924	552	20,763
1937	854	44,408

Sources: Natan, Zh. *et al.*: Ikonomikata na Bŭlgariiă (The Economy of Bulgaria). Sofia 1969, vol. 1, p. 372, 486; Lampe, J.R.: The Bulgarian Economy in the Twentieth Century. London 1986, p. 69.

Efforts to promote industrial development met with some success. The number of concerns enjoying state encouragement grew (Table 3) and even between 1929 and 1939 Bulgaria managed an annual increase in industrial production of 4.8%, when the European average was 1.1%, but modern industrial production contributed no more than 5.6% of the total national income during the 1930s and the units of production remained small with an average workforce of only 31 in 1937[54]. There were, however, significant shifts in the pattern of Bulgarian trade with Germany rising inexorably to a position of total dominance (Table 4).

Table 4: Main Trading Partners 1896–1939, %age of total external trade

	1896–1900		1911		1929		1934		1939	
	Import	Export	Import	Export	Import	Export	Import	Export	Import	Export
Austria-Hungary	8.1	7.5	24.2	5.7						
Britain	23.1	22.3	15.1	13.1	8.8	1.5	6.4	2.1	2.8	3.1
Germany	12.5	13.1	20.0	11.9	22.2	29.8	40.1	42.7	65.5	67.8
France	5.3	11.5	12.5	6.0	8.1	5.1	3.8	2.1	1.2	0.9
Italy	4.3	2.1	4.6	2.1	10.6	10.4	7.8	9.2	6.9	6.1
Turkey	11.1	24.9	8.0	15.8	Not Listed Separately					

Source: Natan, Zh. et al.: Ikonomikata na Bŭlgariiă, vol. 1, pp. 398, 544, 590.

---

[54] Lampe (note 50), p. 94–96.

XI. Conclusions

Bulgaria began its modern existence as a small, backward yet extremely liberal state still technically paying allegiance to an external monarch, the Sultan. In 1944 it retained, in theory at least, the constitution of 1879 but it still found itself tied more closely than it wished to a larger power, this time Nazi Germany. The political evolution of the country had seen the elimination of all powerful internal factors. The Liberals who had dominated the Tŭrnovo assembly, having defeated Alexander Battenberg over constitutional questions, had split over their attitude to Russia and had thereafter been outwitted and cowed by his successor. The disasters of the second Balkan war and the first world war ruined Ferdinand and gravely damaged all but the left-leaning of the traditional NSb parties. Into the vacuum stepped the Agrarians, the largest but the least coordinated political force on the left. They could not survive the tragic indifference of the Communists and the seething hostility of the traditional and populist right. After the Agrarians were broken in June 1923 the Communists put their own heads on the block with the September uprising and the Sveta Nedelia bombing of April 1925. The right wing parties of the Democratic Alliance discredited themselves by their lack of cohesion, their inability to discipline the Macedonians and by their powerlessness in the face of the great depression. In 1934 the élitist intelligentsia of *Zveno* seized power with the backing of the army. *Zveno* was incapable of countering the intrigues of the Tsar who elbowed it aside in 1935 and neutralised the army in the following year. The Tsar was virtually unchallengeable. When he died in 1943 Bulgaria was left rulerless. The peasant majority for the large part remained loyal to the Agrarians; the increasingly confident Communists looked to an ever more powerful Soviet Union; and the NSb parties, to whom the weak commercial and industrial bourgeoisie looked, thrashed around in a fruitless search for an escape from a war which was to doom them.

Domestic Politics

John D. Bell, Baltimore/Maryland

I. The Establishment of the Communist Regime (1944–1947): 1. Background – 2. Party Reorganization and Expansion – 3. The Instruments of Power – 4. The Defeat of the Opposition – II. The Period of Stalinism (1948–1953): 1. The Suppression of Pluralism: a) Parties – b) Unions – c) Churches – 2. The Expropriation of Property – 3. The Trial of Traĭcho Kostov – 4. The Chervenkov Regime – III. Destalinization (1953–1962): 1. Stalin's Death and the „New Course" – 2. The April Plenum – 3. The Period of Collective Leadership – IV. Bulgaria under Zhivkov (1962–1980): 1. The „April Conspiracy" – 2. Political Development – V. Domestic Politics in the 1980s: 1. New Initiatives: a) Overview – b) The New Economic Mechanism – c) Liûdmila Zhivkova's Cultural Reforms – d) Demographic Policy – 2. The Impact of *glasnost'* and *perestroĭka*

I. The Establishment of the Communist Regime (1944–1947)

1. Background

Among the factors that shaped Bulgaria's politics in the postwar period were important developments during the war itself. The movement of armed resistance, though of small military significance, brought the Communists a degree of legitimacy they had not previously enjoyed[1]). The formation of the OF coalition with *Zveno*, the BRSDP, and the *Pladne* wing of the BZNS linked the party with influential or popular political groups and created the embryo of the postwar government[2]). On the other hand, right-wing political formations along with the parties and individuals who supported the Tsar's royal-military dictatorship and German orientation were discredited and open to persecution. The wishful thinking of the „legal opposition" led it to be overwhelmed by rapidly developing events. Men such as Nikola Mushanov, leader of the DP, Dimitŭr Gichev of the conservative wing (*Vrabcha – 1*) of the BZNS, or Atanas Burov of the NP had in varying degrees opposed Bulgaria's commitment to Nazi Germany and might have strongly reinforced the political center. But they had rejected appeals to join the OF, preferring to place their faith in the Tsar's acumen, expecting that Boris would know when to switch sides and that at the appropriate moment he would call on them to „save Bulgaria". The sudden death of Boris in August 1943 deprived them of that hope, but they clung to the belief that since

---

[1]) A careful assessment of the size and significance of the resistance movement is found in Oren, N.: Bulgarian Communsim: The Road to Power, 1934–1944. New York, London 1971, pp. 214–20.
[2]) The most important source on the formation of the OF coalition is Dragoĭcheva, Ts.: Povelîa na dŭlga (The Call of Duty). Vol. 3 Sofia 1980. See also Bell, J. D.: The Bulgarian Communist Party from Blagoev to Zhivkov. Stanford, California 1986, pp. 66–76 (Cit. as: Bell).

Bulgaria had not declared war on the USSR the government would find a way to negotiate with the British and Americans for an orderly, relatively painless withdrawal from the war.

The sudden collapse of Rumania ended this hope, for it brought the Red Army to the shores of the Danube months before it had been expected, and the Soviet declaration of war (5 September) set off a wave of internal upheavals. The members of the OF were prepared to seize the moment and agreed on a distribution of power assigning four ministries each to the BKP, *Pladne*, and *Zveno*, two to the BRSDP, and two to independents. The experienced hand of *Zveno* was apparent in the efficient *coup d'état* that began at 2:15 AM on the morning of 9 September. The „legal opposition" was now open to the charge that its desultory tactics amounted to collaboration, while actual control of the government passed to the Front.

Although the Communists held key positions in the new government, including the justice and interior ministries, and Soviet forces were in the process of occupying the country, the OF regime was not a Communist dictatorship. Its initial program was moderate, resembling most of all the program of Aleksandŭr Stamboliĭski's Agrarian government after World War I. From Moscow Georgi Dimitrov warned the party not to alienate the population by hasty moves against the Church, the monarchy, or private property[3]. Party leaders spoke of a long period in which state, cooperative, and private enterprises would develop in harmony[4]. The process through which the BKP[5] would achieve complete power extended over a three-year period that coincided with the completion of the peace treaty with the Allies and with the presence of Soviet occupation forces. It would involve an immediate assault on the remnants of the Old Regime that could reasonably be branded as collaborationist, the building of an effective party organization, and the slow strangulation of the BKP's erstwhile allies in the Front. The pace of Bulgaria's „revolutionary transformation" would be affected by the strength of the opposition and by the international environment.

2. Party Reorganization and Expansion

Immediately after 9 September Bulgaria's Communists moved to adapt the party to the new situation in the country. At the top level the Politburo was reorganized. Traĭcho Kostov, liberated from prison on the eve of the *coup* became CC secretary and head of its agitation and propaganda section. Georgi Chankov was placed in charge of organizational affairs, and Tsola Dragoĭcheva, Dimitŭr Ganev, and Raĭko Damĭanov were made the party's links with the OF, mass organizations, and trade

---

[3] Isusov, M.: Sŭzdavane na legalnite rŭkovodni organi na BRP(k) (Formation of the Legal Governing Organs of the BRP(k), in: Vekove. (1982) 1–2, p. 49 (Cit. as: Isusov, Sŭzdavane).

[4] Ludzhev, D.: Drebnata burzhoaziĭa v Bŭlgariĭa 1944–1958 (The Petite Bourgeoisie in Bulgaria, 1944–1958). Sofia 1985, pp. 123/24 (Cit. as: Ludzhev).

[5] The BKP had changed its name in 1927 when it attempted to avoid the government's anticommunist legislation. At the time of the 9 September coup it was called the Bulgarian Workers' Party (Communists) (*Bŭlgarska rabotnicheska partiĭa [komunisti]*), but since the original BKP designation was restored in 1948 that term is used here throughout to avoid confusion.

unions respectively. Petko Kunin became head of the party's commission on administration. The famous exiles Georgi Dimitrov and Vasil Kolarov remained in Moscow until November 1945, presumably because Stalin thought their return might complicate relations with his Western Allies, but the Foreign Bureau of the party was dissolved, with Dimitrov and Kolarov becoming full members of the Politburo and Vŭlko Chervenkov and Georgi Damianov candidate members. Anton Iugov and Dobri Terpeshev, as ministers in the OF government, were not formally included in the Politburo although they usually attended its meetings as did Todor Pavlov, the Communist member of the Regency Council.

Kostov flew to Moscow early in 1945 for consultations with Dimitrov, Molotov, and Stalin. Following his return, the Eighth Enlarged Plenum of the CC (27 February–1 March) formalized the new party structure, expanding the CC to 39 full and 11 candidate members by coopting a number of younger leaders who had distinguished themselves in the resistance. Dimitrov was named president of the CC and a three-man secretariat was established including Chankov and Chervenkov with Kostov as First Secretary[6]).

Three days after the seizure of power, the CC issued its first directive to local party units with instructions for transforming the illegal, underground organization into a „mighty, mass party of industrial workers and laborers in town and country"[7]). Party committees for the nine regions (*oblasti*) were in place by late September. They in turn oversaw the formation of approximately 90 district (*okoliia*) committees during the next six weeks. The party newspaper, *Rabotnichesko delo* (Workers' Cause), began to appear on 18 September and, with its advantage in access to printing facilities and newsprint, quickly developed the widest circulation of any Bulgarian newspaper (60,000 copies, rising to 250,000 by March 1945). A theoretical journal, *Sŭvremennik* (Contemporary), also began to appear in January 1945, and a Central Party School for the training of cadres opened the same month[8]).

On the eve of 9 September the party numbered approximately 13,700. By mid-January 1945 it had acquired over 250,000 members, an expansion paralleled by the growth of the party youth organization from 15,000 to 225,000. This growth, however, was achieved at the cost of quality. While some party committees refused to admit even industrial workers who lacked the proper political consciousness, more often party organizers threw open the gates, recruiting door-to-door or staging mass enrollments[9]).

---

[6]) Isusov, Sŭzdavane, pp. 43–52.

[7]) Isusov, M.: Politicheskite partii v Bŭlgariia, 1944–1948 (The Political Parties in Bulgaria, 1944–1948). Sofia 1978, p. 36 (Cit. as: Isusov, Politicheskite partii).

[8]) Avramov, P.: Organizatsionno izgrazhdane na BKP sled izlizaneto i ot nelegalnost, 9 septemvri 1944 g.–fevruari 1945 g. (Organizational Structuring of the BKP after Its Emergence from Illegality, 9 September 1944–February 1945), in: Istoricheski pregled. 21 (1965) 2, pp. 3–31; Ostoich, P.: BKP i izgrazhdaneto na narodno-demokraticheskata dŭrzhava, 9 septemvri 1944–dekemvri 1947 (The BKP and the Construction of the People's Democratic State). Sofia 1967 (Cit. as: Ostoich).

[9]) Genchev, N.: Razgromŭt na burzhoaznata opozitsiia v Bŭlgariia prez 1947–1948 godina (The Utter Defeat of the Bourgeois Opposition in Bulgaria during 1947–1948), in: Godishnik na Sofiskiia universitet (ideologichni katedri). 56 (1962), p. 235 (Cit. as: Genchev).

Coinciding with the rapid expansion of party membership was the mushrooming of local OF Committees, which stood outside the formal apparatus of government. They were predominantly Communist. According to the government's statistics, by the end of 1944 there were 7,292 committees with 26,255 members, of which 54 percent were Communists, 33 percent Agrarians, 3 percent Socialists, and 2 percent *Zveno*. Some historians have seen these committees as „Bulgaria's soviets", a principal engine for securing Communist power on the local level. More recent investigations indicate that this view is highly romanticized. Despite the Communists' preponderance, there were many committees that were not under their control, and the local cadres were often too inexperienced and undisciplined to carry out a coordinated policy. It could hardly have been otherwise, one Bulgarian historian has written, when 95 percent of the party had joined only after 9 September. The OF Committees sometimes terrorized the local priest, schoolteacher or other representative of the „old order," but such conduct as often as not alienated the local population. The BKP itself recognized this, and by the end of the year Minister of the Interior Iugov issued orders curbing their activity and preventing their interference with legal authority[10].

3. The Instruments of Power

Of far greater importance to the Bulgarian Communists was their control of the interior and justice ministries and the authority of General Sergeĭ Biriuzov, the chairman of the ACC[11]. Within weeks after 9 September the Ministry of the Interior discharged nearly 30,000 officials. The police were replaced by a state militia, composed mainly of „partisans, former political prisoners, members of the party and the party youth organization"[12]. The new militia received the arms and authority of the old police and used them to settle scores with their old enemies or any „reactionaries" who got in their way. Within the Interior Ministry Dimo Dichev was given the assignment of organizing a network of security police with the aid of advisers furnished by the NKVD.

The Interior Ministry abolished the educational requirements for officeholders that had existed in the past and set up training schools to provide crash courses in administrative law and accounting for its new functionaries. By the end of 1944 Iugov had effected an almost complete turnover in local government[13].

---

[10] Ostoich, pp. 39–65. Kopylov, A.: K voprosu o funktsiiakh komitetov otechestvennogo fronta neposredstvenno posle 9 sentiabria 1944 goda (On the Question of the Functions of the Committees of the OF Immediately after 9 September 1944), in: Todorova, Ts.; Isusov, M. (eds.): Bŭlgarskata dŭrzhava prez vekovete (The Bulgarian State through the Centuries). Vol. 2. Sofia 1982, pp. 383–88.

[11] On the place of Bulgaria in Allied diplomacy see Bell, pp. 77–79. Biriuzov's rather uninformative memoirs are available in Biriuzov, S.: Sovetskiĭ soldat na Balkanakh (A Soviet Soldier in the Balkans). Moscow 1963.

[12] Ostoich, pp. 71, 76/77.

[13] Ostoich, p. 70; Peĭkov, I.: Razgrom na svalenata ot vlast monarkho-fashistka burzhoaziia v Bŭlgariia 9.IX.1944–IX.1945 (The Utter Defeat of the Monarcho-fascist Bourgeoisie that had fallen from Power in Bulgaria 9 September 1944–September 1945). Sofia 1982, pp. 17–38 (Cit. as: Peĭkov, Razgrom).

The need for expertise forced the Ministry of Justice to retain a larger proportion of its personnel, but by the end of 1944 it had replaced 200 of its 628 officials, including 121 judges and prosecutors in the district courts[14]). But the main work of the Justice Ministry lay in the establishment of people's courts outside the normal judicial system. The concept of special courts to try war criminals was not new to Bulgaria. After World War I the Agrarian government had set up people's courts to try 22 former ministers and military leaders held to be „responsible for the national catastrophe". Moreover, punishment of fascists was part of the original OF program and was also required by the terms of Bulgaria's armistice with the Allies. But it quickly became apparent that the Communists intended to define „fascist" and „war criminal" as broadly as possible.

The work of the people's courts got under way with the mass trial of former political leaders held in Sofia from 20 December 1944 to 1 February 1945. The defendants included the three former regents, the ministers of the five wartime cabinets, 130 NSb deputies, and other high officials. The court went beyond even the demands of the prosecution, handing down an even 100 death sentences. The former regents, 28 former ministers, 68 deputies, and an adviser to the tsar were all executed the next day. Even the members of the anti-German Muraviev government received lengthy prison sentences combined with the confiscation of their possessions. The people's courts in the provinces followed the example of the Sofia trial. By the time they completed their work in April 1945 they had tried 11,122 people. Of these 2,730 were condemned to death, 1,305 to life imprisonment, 5,119 to terms up to twenty years, and 1,516 were acquitted[15]).

A purge of the military was slower to develop because the Soviet Union wanted to use the Bulgarian army against Germany and because War Minister Damîan Velchev of *Zveno* waged a skillful campaign to protect the old officer corps. Taking advantage of the absence of Communist ministers from a cabinet meeting on 23 November, Velchev persuaded his colleagues to issue a decree providing for a blanket amnesty for all military personnel who served with honor in the war against Germany. The Communists, however, appealed to General Birûzov who intervened to demand that the decree be withdrawn. By the end of the year approximately 1,100 officers were expelled from the army. At the same time 718 Communists with military or partisan experience were given commissions and more than 300 others were enrolled in the military academy. Upon graduation in 1945 they were appointed to ranks as high as colonel. Communists were also appointed to the newly created post of deputy commander at the army and divisional levels, where they functioned as political commissars responsible to Georgi Damîanov, head of the BKP's military department.

After the German surrender Velchev sought to reduce the influence of the Communists in the army by ordering the demobilization of officers who did not meet minimal educational qualifications. The Communists responded by transferring control of

---

[14]) Ostoich, p. 91.
[15]) Peĭkov, I.: Podgotovka, provezhdane i znachenie na narodniiâ sŭd prez 1944–1945 g. (The Preparation, Conduct, and Significance of the People's Court during 1944–1945), in: Istoricheski pregled. 20 (1964) 2–3, pp. 151–70. The fates of 452 defendants could not be determined.

military personnel from the Ministry of War to the full Ministerial Council. This permitted a hastily organized investigating committee to purge 1,940 officers. The political police also „unmasked" a number of clandestine organizations with ties to the military, providing grounds for further arrests and intimidation. Communist control of the army was fully secured by September 1946 when Velchev was replaced as war minister by Georgi Damīanov[16]).

While some of the noncommunist ministers packed their ministries with their own supporters and sought to limit Communist influence, they had only limited success. Communist-led unions fought for „fair play" in the branches of government not under Communist control, and in any case these were far less important than the critical ministries in Communist hands.

4. The Defeat of the Opposition

In the months immediately following 9 September, political activity was permitted only to the members of the OF. In adapting to the new conditions in the country *Zveno*, the BRSDP, and the BZNS remained remarkably true to their traditions[17]). A national conference of *Zveno* in October formally converted the organization into a political party, the National Alliance *Zveno* (*Naroden sŭīuz Zveno*). But despite the fact that it attracted some support from members of the middle class who had belonged to the now illegal „bourgeois" parties, its membership remained small. As the product of an antidemocratic tradition, it consisted of a corps of élite, often highly capable individuals, who conceived of politics in terms of putschism and behind-the-scenes maneuvers. With their ties to the military severed, *Zveno*'s leaders lost their traditional power base and became dependent on the Communists. With the exception of Damīan Velchev and a few others, *Zveno*'s leadership followed the example of Prime Minister Kimon Georgiev, who chose the path of collaboration and was well rewarded. Similarly, Propaganda Minister Dimo Kazasov, who had broken with *Zveno* before the war, demonstrated his uncanny instinct for survival by placing control of the press and radio in the hands of Communist functionaries.

The constituency of the BRSDP was also narrow, since the party had traditionally drawn its support from teachers, civil servants, and a small segment of the working class that belonged to the socialist trade unions. Moreover, from the beginning it was split over the issue of cooperation with the Communists. On the right, party doyen Krŭstîu Pastukhov advocated open opposition to the Communists. On the left, Dimitŭr Neĭkov called for the closest collaboration between Bulgaria's „two working-class parties". Grigor Cheshmedzhiev and Kosta Lulchev sought a middle ground that would preserve the party's independence.

The core of the democratic opposition was the *Pladne* wing of the BZNS, whose growth after 9 September probably exceeded that of the Communists and was

---

[16]) Khristov, F.: Deveti septemvri i bŭlgarskata narodna armiîa (9 September and the Bulgarian People's Army), in: Istoricheski pregled. 25 (1969) 2–3, pp. 172–93; Ostoich, pp. 85–90.

[17]) The detailed study of M. Isusov in his „Politicheskite partii" is the best Bulgarian account of the noncommunist parties after 9 September.

achieved under far less favorable conditions[18]). On 23 September Dr. Georgi M. Dimitrov returned from exile, and his progress by train from the Turkish border to Sofia was met by mass demonstrations all along the route. At the BZNS's national conference on 14–15 October he was acclaimed as the Union's general secretary[19]). From the beginning Dr. Dimitrov was convinced that the Communists planned to take full control of the country and his belief was reinforced by Nikola Petkov, who confessed to him that he had misread the Communists' intentions and had blundered in agreeing to their control of the police and judiciary. Further warnings came from the two noncommunists on the Regency Council. Dr. Dimitrov consequently rejected proposals that he join the OF government, even though Traĭcho Kostov held open the possibility of his becoming prime minister. Instead, he chose to devote his full efforts to preparing the BZNS for an independent struggle.

Inspired by Dr. Dimitrov's firmness, the Agrarians began to move away from the official OF positions. They revived the traditional Agrarian slogan „Bread, Peace, and Democracy", which implied criticism not only of the OF government's economic and political policies but also of the continued participation of the Bulgarian army in the war. In meetings with the Communists and other leaders of the OF, Dr. Dimitrov protested the conduct of the people's militia and the sweeping powers of the people's courts, and he was backed by the Agrarian ministers, who threatened to leave the government.

From Moscow Georgi Dimitrov sent radiograms ordering Kostov to take measures against the growth of Agrarian strength in the countryside, and he apparently coordinated a plan of action with the Soviets to strike directly at the Agrarian leader. The first move came from General Birĭuzov, who seized on the Agrarian call for peace to charge Dr. Dimitrov with defeatism. He threatened to use his authority as head of the ACC to dissolve the entire BZNS if Dr. Dimitrov did not step down from the leadership. Faced with this pressure and ill with pneumonia, Dr. Dimitrov resigned as general secretary in January 1945, yielding his place to Nikola Petkov. Later in the month the Communists pushed through the Council of Ministers a Law for the Defense of the People's Authority, prohibiting acts that contributed to the demoralization of the army or that were injurious to Bulgaria's international prestige[20]). It provided the grounds for Dr. Dimitrov's arrest in April.

Nikola Petkov had willingly cooperated with the Communists in the past, but by this time he had lost any illusions about their intentions and began to offer firm and courageous resistance. The immediate area of conflict was the organization of NSb elections, which according to the Yalta Declaration on Liberated Europe (11 February) were to be „free elections of governments responsible to the will of the people." At the BKP's eighth plenum, Traĭcho Kostov proposed that the four OF parties present a single list of candidates with the distribution of power among them

---

[18]) Zarchev, Ĭ.: Bŭlgarskiĭat zemedelski naroden sŭĭuz, 9 septemvri 1944–1948 g. (The Bulgarian Agrarian National Union, 9 September 1944–1948), in: Izvestiĭa na Instituta po istoriĭa na BKP. 32 (1975), pp. 120/21.

[19]) The career of Dr. G. M. Dimitrov is the subject of Moser, C.: Dimitrov of Bulgaria. Ottawa, Illinois 1979.

[20]) Peĭkov, Razgrom, p. 153.

decided before the election. No party outside the OF would be allowed to organize, so that opposition candidates would have to run as individuals, not as party representatives. Since this would have the effect of perpetuating the existing OF government, Petkov objected and appealed to the Western Powers.

Finding Petkov harder to deal with than expected, the Communists decided to „render friendly assistance to the healthy forces in the BZNS"[21]). This assistance took the form of support for Aleksandŭr Obbov, a former Agrarian leader who was convinced that the BZNS could survive only through cooperation with the BKP. In May Obbov's supporters staged a national conference that expelled Petkov from the Union and named Obbov general secretary. Minister of the Interior Ĭugov recognized Obbov's faction as the official BZNS and decreed that the party's newspaper and other assets belonged to it. Petkov was forced to make his own home the headquarters for a rival Agrarian Union. Later in the year, the same tactics were used to capture the BRSDP for Dimitŭr Neĭkov. Cheshmedzhiev and Lulchev formed their own BRSDP (*obedinena*) (united) and moved to join hands with Petkov.

Ultimately, the hopes of the opposition rested on the influence that the Western democracies could or would bring to bear on the Bulgarian government and the USSR, and the threat to withhold recognition of the Bulgarian government or to delay the signing of a peace treaty with it were significant weapons in the Western diplomatic arsenal. In May Dr. Dimitrov escaped from house arrest and found refuge in the residence of Maynard Barnes, head of the American diplomatic mission. At the same time, the British intervention in Greece created the impression that the Western powers were prepared to take a harder line on the question of Soviet influence in Eastern Europe. On August 23, three days before the NSb elections were scheduled to be held, the British and American ministers carried the complaints of the opposition to General Birĭuzov and pressed for a postponement and for measures that would eventually make Bulgarian elections more genuinely democratic. Birĭuzov promised to consult Moscow, and on the following day the OF government did in fact announce that the elections would be postponed[22]).

Further concessions to the opposition followed. The Bulgarian government stated that it would not hinder Dr. Dimitrov's departure from the country, and the former Agrarian leader was permitted to go into exile. Petkov's Agrarians were recognized as a legal opposition party, the BZNS-NP (for Nikola Petkov), as was the BRSDP (*obedinena*) of Cheshmedzhiev and Lulchev. Both were permitted to publish newspapers, although access to the radio remained a monopoly of the OF.

The Communists also amnestied approximately 1,000 prisoners who had been convicted by the people's courts – Atanas Burov, Nikola Mushanov, and Dimitŭr Gichev among them. Mushanov was allowed to reorganize his DP, and the government also recognized the small RP of Stoĭan Kosturkov. These measures were inten-

---

[21]) Avramov, P.: Borbata na BKP protiv gemetovshtinata i restavratorskata opozitsiĭa, za krepŭk rabotnichesko-selski sŭĭuz, 1944–1947 g. (The Struggle of the BKP against Dr.-Dimitrovism and the Restoring Opposition, for a Firm Worker-Peasant Alliance, 1944–1947), in: Izvestie na visshata partiĭna shkola „Stanke Dimitrov" pri ts. k. na BKP: Otdel istoriĭa. 4 (1959), p. 111.

[22]) Black, C. E.: The View from Bulgaria, in: Witnesses to the Origins of the Cold War. Ed. T. Hammond. Seattle, Washington 1982, pp. 60–97.

ded both to impress the Western powers and to fractionalize the opposition. In this respect Gichev played a useful role as an opponent of what he called Petkov's „dictatorship" of the opposition BZNS.

These changes did not alter the political situation in any fundamental way. Opposition candidates were harassed and intimidated, and the Communist-dominated printers' unions frequently interfered with the printing or distribution of the opposition press[23]). As a result, the opposition decided to boycott the NSb elections now scheduled for November 18. In September Vasil Kolarov returned to Bulgaria to rally the Communist forces, and on 4 November Georgi Dimitrov returned after 22 years in exile. His first public speech was a brutal denunciation of the opposition, which left no doubts about the regime's intentions.

The elections produced the expected majority for the OF list, which took 88.18 percent of the 3,853,097 votes cast. There were 455,425 blank ballots, an impressive statement in view of the Communist control of the election machinery[24]). The opposition again counted on British and American support, but the West's concern for developments in Bulgaria was waning. At the Moscow conference of foreign ministers in December, Secretary of State Byrnes settled for Stalin's agreement to „advise" the Bulgarian government to add two members of the opposition. As a result Petkov's Agrarians and Lulchev's Socialists (Cheshmedzhiev had died in the fall of 1945) were asked to enter the government. They refused to do so unless the Communists relinquished control of the Interior and Justice ministries and respected the right of the opposition to criticize government policies. Andreĭ Vyshinskiĭ, who was dispatched from Moscow to confer with the opposition, told them bluntly that it was not for them to set conditions. Petkov and Lulchev rejected the offer[25]).

A reorganization of the government in March 1946 increased the number of Communist ministers at the expense of the party's allies in the front. Socialist Krŭstiŭ Pastukhov was arrested, charged with writing articles intended to demoralize the army, and sentenced to five years' penal servitude. War Minister Velchev, who testified in Pastukhov's defense, was ejected from the cabinet in September, and in the same month Dr. Dimitrov was tried *in absentia* for treason and sentenced to death. State Security also publicized the „unmasking" of secret, counterrevolutionary, terrorist organizations that supposedly had links to the opposition.

Dimitrov, Kolarov, and Kostov met with Stalin and Molotov on 6 June in Moscow to discuss „measures to strengthen the people's democratic power in Bulgaria"[26]). Following their return the Politburo announced that a referendum would be held on the future of the monarchy, after which elections would be held for a VNSb to alter the constitution. Prime Minister Georgiev „was informed of this decision"[27]). No party defended the institution of the monarchy, and in the referendum held on

---

[23]) K'oseva, Ts.: Izpolzuvane na oktomvriĭskiia opit v borbata sreshtu burzhoazniia pechat v Bŭlgariia (1944–1948 g.) (The Application of the October Experience in the Struggle against the Bourgeois Press in Bulgaria (1944–1948)), in: Istoricheski pregled. 43 (1987) 11, pp. 54/55.
[24]) Isusov, Politicheskite partii, p. 230.
[25]) Isusov, Politicheskite partii, pp. 243–65.
[26]) Isusov, Politicheskite partii, p. 288.
[27]) Isusov, Politicheskite partii, p. 289.

8 September 93 percent of the voters favored its abolition. Bulgaria was proclaimed a republic one week later, and the nine-year-old Simeon and other members of the royal family left the country. The Regency Council was dissolved and Vasil Kolarov named president of a provisional presidency.

In preparation for the VNSb elections scheduled for 27 October, the Communists announced that instead of being presented with a preselected OF list, voters would be allowed to vote for the Front with different colored ballots indicating a preference for one of the Front parties. Seats in the Assembly and ministerial posts would then be apportioned among the OF parties in accordance with the result. Since Neĭkov's Socialists and *Zveno* had almost no popular following, and Obbov's Agrarians only an insignificant one, the effect of this measure was to deprive the noncommunist Front parties of any significance.

The major opposition parties – Petkov's Agrarians, Lulchev's Socialists, and a group of „independent intellectuals" – joined forces on the eve of the elections and bitterly protested the lack of democratic freedoms[28]). They gained some support from defectors from *Zveno* and Obbov's Agrarians. The opposition polled over one million votes, 28 percent of the total, a considerable achievement considering the conditions prevailing in the country[29]).

After the elections the role of the noncommunist parties in the government was downgraded. Georgi Dimitrov became prime minister; Kimon Georgiev dropped to minister of foreign affairs. The Communists took half the ministries, leaving the less significant ones to be divided among their partners.

The noncommunist parties in the OF reacted in different ways. Neĭkov's Socialists were ready for whatever role the Communists assigned them. Some members of *Zveno*, however, saw themselves victimized by a Communist doublecross. The Communists dealt with them by naming several prominent *Zveno* figures as ambassadors and sending them out of the country. Damĭan Velchev became ambassador to Switzerland and probably saved his life later by refusing orders to return home. Obbov moved toward the opposition, secretly laying plans with Petkov to purge the BZNS of Communist agents and sympathizers. As a result, the Communists engineered an internal coup that replaced Obbov with Georgi Traĭkov.

The hope that Western pressure would restrain the regime was fast fading. By 1947 whatever interest had existed in promoting Bulgarian democracy had given way to an impatience to conclude the peacemaking process and get on to other concerns. The treaty with Bulgaria was signed on 10 February. Soon afterward, the BKP CC ordered the printers' unions to refuse to publish the newspapers of the opposition. The State Department issued a protest for the record, but its actual response was to try to hasten the ratification of the treaty and recognition of the Bulgarian government before the situation became so much worse that it might cause embarrassment.

Deprived of all other forums, the opposition made its last stand in the VNSb. Despite Georgi Dimitrov's threat that it would cost him his head, Nikola Petkov continued to defy the government and to call for a restoration of genuine democracy.

---

[28]) Genchev, pp. 201–10.
[29]) Genchev, p. 206.

On 4 June the state prosecutor reported to the VNSb that he possessed evidence linking Petkov to underground terrorist organizations. On the next day, the same day the US Senate ratified the peace treaty with Bulgaria, the VNSb voted to deprive Petkov of his parliamentary immunity. Five days later, another 23 Agrarian deputies were expelled. Petkov's trial for treason took place on 5–16 August, accompanied by staged demonstrations demanding his blood. The court complied by handing down a death sentence, and the VNSb outlawed the entire opposition BZNS. Western protests against Petkov's trial came from both private citizens and governments, but Western diplomats were primarily concerned that it not impede the normalization of relations. Petkov was hanged like a common criminal, rather than shot, and denied both final sacraments and a religious burial. One week later the USA extended Bulgaria formal diplomatic recognition.

II. The Period of Stalinism (1948–1953)

1. The Suppression of Pluralism

a) Parties

The defeat of Petkov's opposition was followed by an assault on nearly all the elements of pluralism in Bulgarian society, the impetus for which came from the Soviet Union[30]). At the founding congress of the Cominform in September 1947 Zhdanov and Malenkov stressed the necessity for the more rapid transformation of the socialist camp. The Bulgarian delegates to the congress, Vŭlko Chervenkov and Vladimir Poptomov, went directly to Moscow for more detailed instructions. Upon returning to Sofia, Chervenkov delivered a report critical of the party for not having fully realized that 9 September marked the beginning of a socialist revolution and for moving too slowly to institutionalize the BKP's leading role.

The party's response was to move quickly to mop up the last vestiges of the opposition and to establish a monopoly of power over the country's political and social institutions. Neĭkov's Socialists applied to join the BKP and were submerged in its ranks. At the same time Lulchev and most of the opposition Socialist deputies were arrested and condemned as traitors. Lulchev was sentenced to fifteen years' penal servitude, and his party was disbanded[31]). Georgi Traĭkov formally repudiated traditional Agrarian ideology at a congress of the official BZNS, and defined the Union's new role as loyal ally and helpmeet of the BKP. *Zveno*, the DP and the RP announced their „self-liquidation" and dissolved into the OF, which itself was converted into a broad patriotic organization under Communist control[32]).

---

[30]) Bogdanova, R.: Overcoming the Ideological and Political Pluralism in Bulgarian Society (September 1947 – beginning of 1949), in: Bulgarian Historical Review. 14 (1986) 3, pp. 3–22.
[31]) Isusov, Politicheskite partii, pp. 429/30.
[32]) Zarchev, Razgromŭt, pp. 55–66; Isusov, Politicheskite partii, pp. 387–90.

b) Unions

The Communists had long dominated some of Bulgaria's trade unions, and they quickly moved to take over the rest. The party created the General Workers' Trade Union (*Obsht rabotnicheski profesionalen sŭiuz* – ORPS) as a blanket labor organization and applied increasing pressure on the noncommunist unions to join. With the collapse of the political opposition, their labor affiliates were quickly absorbed into ORPS[33]. Similarly, the youth organizations of the various parties were incorporated into the DKMS.

c) Churches

Exarch Stefan, leader of the Orthodox Church in Bulgaria, tried to coexist with the Communist regime, accepting the separation of church and state and the exclusion of religious education from the schools. But he resisted the Communists' attempts to control internal church affairs with the same courage he had earlier demonstrated in opposing the Tsar's pro-German policies and in his fight to prevent the extermination of Bulgaria's Jews. In 1948, when the government's director of religious denominations ordered the church to halt all criticism of the state, preach love for the Communist leadership from the pulpit, defend the USSR, and display portraits of party leaders, Stefan rejected the order as „unsent, unreceived, and invalid"[34]. Few details of what followed are known, but in September Stefan suddenly resigned his office and retired to a monastery. He was replaced by the more compliant Paisiĭ, who was himself dismissed in 1950 in favor of Kiril, who created no difficulties for the authorities[35].

On 1 March 1949 the government enacted a Law on Religious Denominations that subjected all religious orders to direct state control. At the same time, fifteen pastors from evangelical Protestant churches were arrested and tried for treason, espionage on behalf of the United States and England, currency speculation, and conspiracy to restore capitalism. During 1952 approximately 30 Catholic priests, nuns, and laymen were tried for spying for the Vatican and conducting anticommunist propaganda. The bishop of Nikopol and three others were executed and the rest sentenced to penal servitude[36].

The nearly 50,000 Jews who remained in Bulgaria at the war's end sought, but were not permitted to retain, their traditional cultural autonomy. During 1948/49 the government permitted mass emigration to Israel in return for „large sums" of hard

---

[33]) Georgiev, V.: Sŭzdavane i ukrepvane na obshtiĭa rabotnicheski profesionalen sŭiuz prez perioda ot 9 septemvri do dekemvri 1947 g. (The Establishment and Strengthening of the General Workers' Trade Union during the Period from 9 September to December 1947), in: Profsŭiuzni letopisi. (1963) 2, pp. 8–56.

[34]) Tsŭrkoven vestnik. 19 July 1948.

[35]) Tobias, R.: Communist-Christian Encounter in Eastern Europe. Indianapolis, Indiana 1956 (School of Religion Press), pp. 352–79; Pundeff, M.: Church-State Relations in Bulgaria under Communism, in: Bociurkiw, B. and Strong, J. (eds.): Religion and Atheism in the USSR and Eastern Europe. Toronto 1975, pp. 328–36. See also the chapter of M. Pundeff in this volume.

[36]) Pundeff, pp. 337–40.

currency. By the end of 1949 only about 6,000 Jews remained in the country. The government also resorted to resettlement in an attempt to reduce Bulgaria's Muslim population. More than 150,000 ethnic Turks were forced across the Turkish border before Ankara closed the frontier[37]).

2. *The Expropriation of Property*

In the VNSb, Bulgarian constitutional experts were advised by a team of Soviet jurists, and the resulting Dimitrov Constitution, adopted on 4 December 1947, was modeled closely on the 1936 Soviet constitution[38]). The principle of checks and balances was rejected in favor of the „unity of state power", which gave ultimate control of all state bodies to a presidium named by the NSb. Although the constitution promised Bulgarian citizens freedom of religion, speech, and assembly and the right to hold private property, it also contained qualifications stating that these privileges could not be exercised „to the detriment of public good".

In fact the BKP had begun an assault on private property almost immediately after 9 September, employing a variety of measures aimed at confiscating the wealth of „fascists" or „speculators". By 1946, 11.8 percent of the country's industrial capital was already in government hands, and the Dimitrov Constitution provided for the large-scale nationalization of industry that soon followed its enactment[39]). Punitive taxation and direct „administrative measures" were used to force Bulgaria's artisans, shopkeepers, and independent transport workers either out of business or into state-controlled enterprises[40]).

In the countryside, the peasantry had been given permission to form collective farms (TKZS) as early as April 1945. Before the defeat of the opposition, the government stressed the voluntary nature of collectivization, and indeed by the end of 1948 only six percent of the country's arable land belonged to TKZSs. But the independent farmer was clearly living on borrowed time. In 1950 the government decreed that the day had come to root out capitalism in the countryside as it had been destroyed in the cities, and a major drive for collectivization was begun. Nearly 45 percent of the land was collectivized by the end of the year, but peasant resistance, including the burning of crops and the slaughter of livestock, produced a disastrous harvest, causing the program to be temporarily halted. After a brief respite, the drive for collectivization was resumed in 1952 and was substantially completed by 1959[41]).

---

[37]) Oren, N.: Revolution Administered: Agrarianism and Communism in Bulgaria. Baltimore 1973, pp. 122–25. See also the chapters of K.-D. Grothusen and S. Troebst in this volume.

[38]) Isusov, Politicheskite partii, p. 390.

[39]) Petkov, P.: Obshtoto i spetsifichnoto v likvidiraneto na kapitalisticheskata sobstvennost v promishlenostta v Bŭlgariâ (The General and the Particular in the Liquidation of Capitalist Property in Industry in Bulgaria), in: Izvestiâ na Instituta po istoriâ na BKP. 20 (1969), pp. 10–28.

[40]) Ludzhev, pp. 80–200.

[41]) Migev, V.: Za etapite na kooperiraneto na selskoto stopanstvo v Bŭlgariâ, 1944–1959 g. (On the Stages of the Cooperatizing of Agriculture in Bulgaria, 1944–1959), in: Vekove. 13 (1984) 1, pp. 52–57; Lampe, J. R.: The Bulgarian Economy in the Twentieth Century. New York 1986, pp. 146–49 (Cit. as: Lampe).

3. The Trial of Traĭcho Kostov

Traĭcho Kostov had been the key figure in the BKP's drive to power. Although less well known than the „legendary heroes" of Bulgarian Communism, Dimitrov and Kolarov, he had long been an effective force in the party and had guided the formation of the Communist regime since 9 September. He had never shown himself to be anything other than a dedicated party leader of the Stalinist type, nor had he ever indicated less than complete faith in Communism, the Soviet Union, or its great leader. Why, then, was he made into an archetype of heretic and traitor[42])? Two factors were probably of primary importance. Tito's disaffection from the Soviet camp heightened Stalin's fear of potential disloyalty among his East European allies, and Kostov incurred Stalin's personal animosity by refusing to reveal the prices commanded by certain goods on the world market during trade negotiations with the USSR. Even this limited display of independence was probably sufficient to provoke Stalin, who at one meeting in Moscow called Kostov a „swindler" and stormed from the room cursing. The second factor was the struggle for power that was shaping up in the Bulgarian party as the health of Georgi Dimitrov declined. Although the distinction between „home" and „Muscovite" Communists was less clear in Bulgaria than in the other Communist Parties of Eastern Europe, Kostov had spent far less time in the USSR than either Vasil Kolarov or Vŭlko Chervenkov, the other obvious candidates for the succession.

The first outward sign that Kostov was in trouble came at the party's V congress (1948), when the party was restructured to bring it into conformity with the model of the CPSU. Dimitrov assumed the newly created post of general secretary, while Kostov's old position as political secretary was abolished. He retained his membership in the Politburo, but was not included in the new party secretariat. In January 1949 Dimitrov asked the Politburo to discuss „mistakes" made by Kostov, charging him with nationalism and „intellectual individualism". Kostov denied the charges, but was isolated from the rest of the Politburo.

Soon after leveling the accusations against Kostov, Dimitrov left Bulgaria for the last time, dying in a sanitarium near Moscow on 2 July. After his departure Kolarov and Chervenkov continued to pursue the case. On 26–27 March Kolarov delivered a report to a plenum of the CC on „The Crude Political and Antiparty Errors of Traĭcho Kostov" based on „evidence" supplied by Kiril Slavov, an economic official who had died during police interrogation. The plenum responded by removing Kostov from the Politburo and his government posts. It concluded, however, that Kostov was not an enemy and that he could retain his membership in the CC. Surprisingly, the provincial party organizations in Sofia and Plovdiv protested the CC's decision, maintaining that Kostov was in fact a dangerous enemy, deserving severe punish-

---

[42]) The most detailed analysis of Traĭcho Kostov's career and trial is: Semerjeev, P.: Sudebnyĭ protsess Traĭcho Kostova v Bolgarii, 7–12 dekabrîa 1949 (The Trial of Traĭcho Kostov in Bulgaria, 7–12 December 1949). Jerusalem 1980 (Cit. as: Semerjeev). The official Bulgarian account appears in: The Trial of Traĭcho Kostov and his Group. Sofia 1949. See also Isusov, M.: Trajčo Kostov – Public Figure and Statesman, in: Bulgarian Historical Review. 16 (1988) 1, pp. 3–15.

ment. This was undoubtedly part of a prearranged intrigue, since protests against CC decisions were hardly common. Moreover, the two provincial party secretaries, Todor Zhivkov of Sofia and Demir Ianev of Plovdiv, both would advance rapidly in the coming Chervenkov era. Zhivkov's involvement probably explains why, despite Kostov's partial rehabilitation in 1956 and more extensive one in 1963, no full account of the case has ever appeared in Bulgaria.

The Politburo reopened the investigation, and in June Kolarov addressed a new CC plenum charging that Kostov had long been a partisan of „left sectarianism", a heresy that he linked to Trotskyism[43]. Kolarov also read a letter, supposedly sent by the dying Dimitrov, calling Kostov an „accomplished scoundrel"[44]. The plenum expelled him from the party. He had already been placed under house arrest when the plenum opened and he was now turned over to State Security.

After Dimitrov's death, Kolarov became both prime minister and head of the Politburo. But because his health was failing, Chervenkov actually held power. Under his direction, a large number of state and party officials were arrested during the fall. They included Politburo member Petko Kunin, several members of the CC, and a number of ministers and vice ministers. By and large they were home Communists, and they were replaced by men whose careers had primarily been in Soviet emigration.

The organization of the trial as well as the interrogation of Kostov and his codefendants was supervised by Lavrenty Beria's chief aide V. S. Abakumov, who made frequent visits to Bulgaria at this time, and by the Soviet ambassador. Their methods succeeded in extracting Kostov's signed confession but did not entirely break his will to resist. Kostov was charged with having been a police agent during the Second World War, working with British and American intelligence services, conducting economic sabotage, and forming a conspiracy with „Tito and his clique" to overthrow the government. His ten codefendants, including former party functionaries, officials of the economic ministries, and three party officials of Macedonian origin, were selected to substantiate the various parts of the indictment. They and 44 witnesses followed the prosecution's script, but in court Kostov admitted only that he had tried to keep the prices of certain Bulgarian goods from Soviet officials, and he repudiated the rest of his confession. Even after the guilty verdict was pronounced, he continued to assert his innocence.

Kostov was shot on 9 December; his codefendants received prison sentences ranging from life to fifteen years, but their lives were spared. Chervenkov later told the CC that this was because they had shown how to behave during a trial.

4. The Chervenkov Regime

Vasil Kolarov died less than a month after Kostov's execution. Thus, within six months the triumvirate that had dominated Bulgarian Communism and led it to

---

[43] Semerjeev, pp. 56–58.
[44] Semerjeev, p. 59.

power, had all passed from the scene. Their successor, Vŭlko Chervenkov, had spent most of his career in the Soviet Union, where he had held various positions in the KI. His rise was facilitated by his marriage to Dimitrov's sister, by his own considerable intelligence, and, according to party lore, by his ties to the Soviet secret police[45]). He was well suited to reshape the Bulgarian party in the Stalinist mode.

Chervenkov was named prime minister in February 1950, chairman of the National Council of the OF in March, and general secretary of the party in November. As he consolidated his power, major figures who had led the party at home during the war were demoted or purged to be replaced by men who had spent many years in Soviet exile. By April 1951 more than 100,000 individuals had been expelled from the party, many being sent to labor camps. Among the victims were thirteen members of the CC, six members of the Politburo, and ten ministers.

Within the Politburo Vladimir Poptomov and Mincho Neĭchev sought to curb the terror, but Chervenkov led a Politburo delegation to Moscow, where Stalin told the Bulgarians that they stood at a crossroads, one path leading to Titoism, the other the path of loyalty to the USSR. After this meeting the terror resumed and continued until Stalin's death[46]).

Chervenkov brought the cult of Stalin's personality to Bulgaria and bathed in its reflected light. Known as „Little Stalin," he was greeted by prolonged, rhythmic applause and chants of „Cher-ven-kov" at his public appearances. His pronouncements were treated as holy writ, and his portrait was on view everywhere. The Soviet *nomenklatura* system with its rigid hierarchies was introduced for the distribution of posts and was an important tool for imposing conformity. During the period of his dominance, Bulgaria closed itself off from the outside world and even, in some senses, from itself. National heroes and cultural figures from the past were written off as relics of the country's bourgeois heritage, and all things Soviet or Russian were exalted. Literature and the arts were forced into the straitjacket of socialist realism as defined by Stalin and Zhdanov, and many of the prewar leaders of cultural life fell silent[47]).

III. Destalinization (1953–1962)

1. Stalin's Death and the „New Course"

The immediate impact of Stalin's death was not dramatic, but there were some indications of change. Police terror was somewhat diminished and the eighth anniversary of 9 September saw the amnesty of a considerable number of political prisoners. In his speech on the occasion of the anniversary of 9 September Chervenkov cautiously embraced the policies of the „New Course", promising greater efforts to raise the standard of living. The government reduced the prices of a number of

---

[45]) Semerjeev, p. 106.
[46]) Semerjeev, pp. 110–14.
[47]) Markov, G.: Zadochni reportazhi za Bŭlgariia (*In Absentia* Reportings on Bulgaria). Zurich 1980 (The Georgi Markov Fund), vol. 1, pp. 45–51.

basic goods, particularly foodstuffs, and the goals set for the second five-year plan (1953–1957) reduced the pace of industrialization in favor of the development of consumer industry and housing[48]).

Among the intelligentsia, limited signs of a „thaw" in cultural life preceded Stalin's death. This was signaled by Chervenkov's intervention in the debate that followed the publication of Dimitŭr Dimov's novel *Tiutiun* (Tobacco) in 1951. Having as its theme the revolutionary movement among the tobacco workers before and during the Second World War, the book was attacked by party critics because its characters showed signs of multidimensionality, that is, the party organizers were not sufficiently heroic and the workers were portrayed as having lives, ideas, and emotions outside their involvement in the revolutionary struggle. Chervenkov, however, praised the novel and accused the critics of dogmatism. Bulgarian cultural leaders immediately responded. Lîudmil Stoîanov, head of the SBP called for an antidogmatic approach to literature, and a younger group of critics and poets began an extended discussion of „craftsmanship" in poetry that ignored the standard of party consciousness. In December 1953 Chervenkov wrote an open letter to the poetess Elisaveta Bagrîana on the occasion of her sixtieth birthday that called for a redefinition of socialist realism. At the same time many prewar bourgeois writers were „reevaluated" and restored to their places in Bulgarian cultural history, their works reappearing in the country's bookstores[49]).

Stalin's death underlined the political vulnerability of Chervenkov, who despite his emulation of the Soviet dictator had not achieved a comparable monopoly of power. Influential home Communists, such as Anton Îugov and Dobri Terpeshev, had been downgraded, but not completely eliminated. Îugov, especially, remained both a minister and a member of the Politburo. In May 1953 he was sent to the Plovdiv region to deal with a strike among the tobacco workers who were protesting the introduction of more onerous work rules. Îugov himself had once labored in those fields, and he handled the strike by recognizing the justice of the workers' grievances and promising significant changes[50]). Several concessions were indeed made to the peasantry, including a sizable reduction in compulsory deliveries from the TKZSs and the cancellation of some back debts and taxes. The BZNS, which had seemed destined for extinction, was given a new lease on life as the BKP's „little brother". A number of Agrarians, including Stamboliĭski's son Asen and several associates of Nikola Petkov, were released from prison in return for their agreement to tour the countryside speaking in favor of the regime's agrarian policies. During the following year those architects of the overthrow of the Stamboliĭski government who were still alive were placed on public trial as a further demonstration of the regime's concern for peasant interests[51]).

---

[48]) Todorov, N. *et al*.: Stopanska istoriîa na Bŭlgariîa (Economic History of Bulgaria). Sofia 1981, p. 451. Brown, J. F.: Bulgaria under Communist Rule. London 1970, pp. 39–52 (Cit. as: Brown).

[49]) The most detailed work on the Bulgarian cultural thaw is: Slavov, A.: The „Thaw" in Bulgarian Literature. New York 1981 (East European Monographs). Further information is found throughout the two volumes of Markov's Zadochni reportazhi (*In Absentia* Reportings).

[50]) Brown, pp. 25/26.

[51]) Zarchev, Î.: Bŭlgarskiîat zemedelski naroden sŭîuz i sotsializmŭt, 1944–1971 (The BZNS and Socialism, 1944–1971), in: Istoricheski pregled. 35 (1979) 4–5, pp. 65–72.

Chervenkov was caught in the trap that held many East European Stalinists. Having built his career on slavish imitation of the Soviet model, he was committed to following the Soviet example even though he found the changes proceeding in the USSR uncongenial and even threatening. At the BKP's VI Congress (25 February–3 March 1954) he emulated Malenkov by accepting the principle of „collective leadership" and yielding his post as party general secretary. This position was downgraded to that of „first secretary" and given to the lightly regarded Todor Zhivkov. The congress also saw the comeback of a number of figures who had suffered in the Kostovite purges. Dobri Terpeshev, Slavcho Trŭnski, Boĭan Bŭlgaranov, and Kiril Dramaliev were restored to an enlarged CC. Îugov remained on the Politburo and soon became first deputy premier. The new Politburo included four „Muscovites", Chervenkov, Raĭko and Georgi Damĭanov, and Ivan Mikhaĭlov, and five home Communists, Zhivkov, Îugov, Georgi Chankov, Georgi Tsankov, and Encho Staĭkov, although the latter group was not homogeneous since Îugov and Staĭkov belonged to the prewar generation of leaders while Zhivkov, Chankov, and Tsankov had only recently come to the forefront. Chervenkov still remained the party's dominant figure, and the congress recognized him as „responsible for the work of the Politburo"[52]). During the following year the release of political prisoners continued, with more than 10,000 returning home by the summer of 1955. Soviet advisors, who had occupied prominent posts in many Bulgarian institutions, were withdrawn, and in October 1954 the transfer of joint Soviet-Bulgarian companies to Bulgarian ownership was begun[53]).

2. The April Plenum

The controlled pace of the amelioration of Stalinist policies and Chervenkov's hold on power were both upset by Khrushchev. First, the Soviet leader's *rapprochement* with Tito, marked by his visit to Yugoslavia in the summer of 1955, undermined Chervenkov, who had branded Kostov as a Titoist and who in his numerous purges had always used alleged sympathy towards Yugoslavia as a weapon against his enemies. Still, the Bulgarian leader seemed secure enough to lead the Bulgarian delegation to the XX Congress of the CPSU (1956) while Zhivkov, the little-known first secretary, remained at home. Khrushchev's sudden, direct attack on Stalin and the „cult of personality" brought the issue of party reform to the forefront and made Chervenkov's position untenable.

Bulgaria's response to the XX CPSU Congress was the CC plenum of 2–6 April at which Zhivkov delivered the principal address and reaped the greatest benefits. The resolutions of the plenum emphasized the importance of Soviet experience as a guide for combatting the cult of personality and the „violations of Leninist norms". Chervenkov was explicitly criticized for having fostered his own personality cult and for undermining party legality and the principle of collective leadership. The persecution

---

[52]) Istoriĭa na BKP (History of the BKP). Sofia 1981, p. 490.
[53]) Brown, pp. 53–58.

of Traĭcho Kostov was not directly mentioned, but in an address to Sofia party activists on 11 April Zhivkov admitted that innocent comrades had been unjustly condemned and promised that they would be rehabilitated[54]).

The plenum's focus on socialist legality required a short delay so that the proper forms could be observed, and on 16–18 April the NSb convened to accept Chervenkov's resignation as prime minister, his place being taken by Ĭugov. But Chervenkov was not entirely out. Demoted rather than purged, he became a deputy prime minister and retained his membership in the Politburo, although he lost his leading role there to Zhivkov[55]). His political survival was probably intended to reassure the apparatus that a wholesale purge of Stalinists was not contemplated, a message reinforced by the appointment of Ĭugov, who as postwar minister of the interior had a number of „violations of legality" on his own record.

The April plenum gave rise to the expectation of major liberalization. Within the BKP itself, at meetings of party activists voices were raised criticizing the plenum as insufficient and calling for a party congress to take decisive measures to eliminate the consequences of the personality cult and to punish those responsible for it[56]). In the press, Vladimir Topencharov emerged as a major spokesman for liberalization. Topencharov, who was editor of the OF newspaper, president of the Union of Journalists, and brother-in-law of Traĭcho Kostov, published a series of editorials accusing the party leadership of having divorced itself from the people. In literature many younger writers and some of the older generation sought greater freedom of expression. Novelist Emil Manov published *Nedostoveren sluchaĭ* (An Unauthentic Case), which contrasted idealistic communism with some of the realities of the Stalinist past. Todor Genov made the same point with his play *Strakh* (Fear). A new literary journal, *Plamŭk* (The Flame), pledged to support „new forms, ... new styles, new currents". The young poet Georgi Dzhagarov published in it his influential poem, „*Predprolet*" (The Pre-spring), in which, with fairly obvious symbolism, he called for the young birds to find their voices and hasten the approach of a true spring.

This ferment did not long survive under the conditions that set in after the Hungarian revolution, which shook the confidence of the Bulgarian leadership. Thousands of Bulgarians, some only recently freed by political amnesty, were placed under preventive detention by State Security[57]). Because the regime was convinced that dissident intellectuals had been responsible for the events in Hungary, it determined to crack down on the intelligentsia. For this purpose, Chervenkov was appointed Minister of Education and Culture and given broad control over the country's intellectual life, and the dogmatist philosopher Todor Pavlov, who had headed the BAN since 1949, was given increased authority and was named to the BKP CC. During the July 1957 meeting of the SBP, Manov, Genov and others were severely criticized. By the end of the year most of them were removed from respon-

---

[54]) Brown, pp. 66–69.
[55]) Istoriĭa na BKP, p. 505.
[56]) Migev, V.: Aprilskiĭat plenum na TsK na BKP i organizatsionnoto razvitie na partiĭata (1956–1958) (The April Plenum of the CC of the BKP and the Organizational Development of the Party (1956–1958)), in: Istoricheski pregled. 42 (1986) 3, pp. 6/7 (Cit. as: Migev, Aprilskiĭat plenum).
[57]) Markov, Zadochni reportazhi, vol. 1, p. 253; Migev, Aprilskiĭat plenum, pp. 9/10.

sible positions, and the staffs of *Plamŭk*, the academic journal *Filosofska misŭl* (Philosophical Thought), and the OF newspaper, where liberal voices had been loudest, were dismissed, Topencharov being sent as a correspondent to Cairo. In April 1958 almost the entire leadership of the SBP was replaced, not to encourage reform but to impose a firmer hand.

In the wake of the Hungarian revolution, the party leadership was also purged to create a greater degree of uniformity. In July 1957, only days after the purge of the „antiparty group" in the USSR, a plenum of the BKP CC dismissed Dobri Terpeshev, Ianko Panov, and Georgi Chankov. Terpeshev and Panov, a partisan general during the Second World War and more recently a deputy minister of defense, were known to have favored more extensive liberalization. Chankov, however, was accused of „unhealthy ambition", a charge that may have had some foundation, since he was a natural rival to Zhivkov[58]).

Although the hopes that the April plenum would be followed by extensive liberalization were disappointed, the plenum was not without effect. The worst abuses of the earlier period were curbed, cultural life became a little freer, and real progress was made in improving the living standards of industrial workers and collective farmers. Moreover, the April plenum set out ideals that could be appealed to against the immediate conservative reaction. In time the „April line" set out at the plenum came in party tradition to symbolize the beginning of a new era marked by the overcoming of past mistakes, the acceptance of a greater measure of legality, internal democracy, and cultural liberalization[59]). It would be regularly invoked to justify and legitimize future reform programs.

3. The Period of Collective Leadership

The upheavals of 1956–1958 were followed by a period of genuine collective leadership based on the fact that no faction was strong enough to achieve complete dominance. The most striking development of this period was the so-called „Great Leap Forward" aimed at drastically accelerating the pace of economic development. In January 1959 a CC plenum approved the so-called „Zhivkov Theses", which called for industrial production by the end of 1962 to double that of 1957. Agricultural production was to double in one year and to achieve three times the 1958 output by 1960. To achieve these goals „Chinese methods" were used, and all the party's resources and experience in agitation and propaganda were employed to mobilize the population to a frenzy of effort the chief result of which was economic disruption and slowdown[60]). By 1961 the results had become obvious, and the regime reverted to the economic goals of the third five-year plan (1958–1960) that had supposedly been superseded by the „Great Leap".

---

[58]) Brown, pp. 78–80.
[59]) Ognianov, L.: Istoricheskite zavoevaniia na sotsialisticheska Bŭlgariia sled aprilskiia plenum na TsK na BKP, 1956 g. (The Historic Achievements of Socialist Bulgaria after the April Plenum of the CC of the BKP, 1956), in: Istoricheski pregled. 37 (1981) 2, p. 20.
[60]) Lampe, pp. 149–53.

Because the Bulgarian press borrowed Chinese terminology to describe the campaign, and because Chervenkov had visited China shortly before it began, there was speculation that Bulgaria's „Little Stalin" was pulling the party in a Maoist, anti-Khrushchev direction. In fact, Zhivkov was the architect of the „Great Leap", which in its fundamentals was based on Khrushchev's economic experiments in the USSR. As far as can be determined, neither Îugov nor Chervenkov had favored it, and this would be a factor in the coming leadership struggle.

Zhivkov enjoyed two advantages vis-à-vis Îugov and Chervenkov. The first was the power of patronage he wielded as first secretary, which allowed him to build and advance a core of supporters. At the VII Party Congress (1958), Zhivkov added Mitko Grigorov and Pencho Kubadinski to the secretariat, where they joined Stanko Todorov, appointed a year earlier, and guaranteed the first secretary a consistent majority. During the following year, Todorov moved up to candidate membership on the Politburo and became chairman of the State Planning Commission, where he could make inroads into Îugov's domain of state administration. At the same time, Boris Velchev and Tano Tsolov, who also proved to be long-term Zhivkov supporters, were added to the secretariat. At lower levels, Zhivkov's experience in organizational work and his power of appointment steadily eroded the bases of support for the Chervenkov and Îugov factions.

The second factor operating in Zhivkov's favor was Khrushchev's ascendancy in the Soviet Union and the beginning of a new wave of reform at the XXII CPSU Congress (1961). Khrushchev and Zhivkov were remarkably similar in their origins and background, and it is likely that a rapport developed between them. Certainly Khrushchev sheltered his younger counterpart under his wing during the coming party struggle, and Zhivkov consistently echoed Khrushchev's positions in Bulgaria, at least until the Soviet leader was removed. But by then Zhivkov's preeminence was secure.

One month after the XXII CPSU Congress that began a new round of destalinization and that condemned the Chinese Communists for dogmatism, a plenum of the BKP CC expelled Chervenkov from the Politburo and his government posts. According to Zhivkov's report, Chervenkov was guilty of a host of errors and abuses of power. And Zhivkov added that the party still contained many who shared Chervenkov's outlook and opposed the policies of the CPSU Congress. Zhivkov's position was further strengthened by the addition of Stanko Todorov and Mitko Grigorov to the Politburo. In March 1962 Georgi Tsankov, who had run the Interior Ministry since 1951, was „promoted" to an honorific post, and the ministry taken over by General Diko Dikov, who in turn appointed Zhivkovites to key positions.

During May 1962 Khrushchev spent a week in Bulgaria, exuberantly lauding Zhivkov for the „normalization" of party life that had taken place under his leadership. His praise of Zhivkov's „personal qualities" made it clear that Zhivkov was his chosen instrument to rule Bulgaria. Still, the following summer was full of difficulties, since the country faced a major food crisis that was due at least in part to the agricultural policies imposed during the „Great Leap". The government was forced to ration a number of basic commodities, to import grain from Canada, and to request the urban population to accept further „temporary sacrifices". Îugov apparently tried to use this crisis to rally support on the CC, for Zhivkov cut short a plenum at the end of October to fly to Moscow for direct consultations with Khrushchev. Days after his return, at the opening of the party's VIII Congress (1962), he announced the expulsion of Îugov and his supporters from their offices and from the CC. Chervenkov was expelled from the party altogether[61]).

Zhivkov assumed the post of prime minister, combining party and state leadership as Khrushchev and János Kádár in Hungary had already done. Two of his supporters, Boris Velchev and Zhivko Zhivkov (no relation), were added to the Politburo, giving the first secretary a solid majority. Twenty-eight full members and fourteen candidates were dropped from the CC, including a number of prominent figures from both the Îugov and Chervenkov factions. They were replaced by a group of younger men whose careers Zhivkov had shaped[62]).

IV. Bulgaria under Zhivkov (1962–1980)

1. The „April Conspiracy"

Despite his victory over Chervenkov and Îugov, Zhivkov still faced formidable political problems. The sudden fall of Khrushchev in 1964 both removed his most influential patron and demonstrated that even an entrenched, powerful leader was vulnerable to a palace revolution. The uncertainties in Bulgarian political life after Khrushchev's removal were almost certainly a factor in the so-called „April Conspiracy" that attempted to remove the First Secretary in 1965. Its leader was General Ivan Todorov-Gorunîa, who killed himself to avoid arrest. Todorov-Gorunîa had been political commissar of the Gavril Genov Partisan Detachment during the war, secretary of the Vratsa Provincial Party Committee until 1961, and then a deputy minister for agriculture. He was joined by a number of high-ranking military officers, many of whom had past associations with the Genov Detachment. According to the official version of the case, the conspirators were Maoist sympathizers, but rumors suggested that they were opposed to Zhivkov's extreme subservience to the USSR or that they resented the favoritism he displayed toward veterans of his own Chavdar Brigade of partisans. Ten men were brought to trial, receiving remarkably light sentences that ranged from three to fifteen years penal servitude. Others thought to have been involved were not immediately punished, although during the next two years several high-ranking military figures were transferred from their positions to posts in foreign embassies, and an unusually large number of district party secretaries were replaced. Zhivkov waited three years before suddenly purging the Vratsa party organization amid charges that it harbored sympathy for Todorov-Gorunîa's Chinese line. The purge saw 359 individuals expelled from the party[63]).

---

[61]) Zhivkov was not brutal toward his former opponents. When Chervenkov died in at the age of eighty in 1981, the press reported that he had been quietly rehabilitated and readmitted to the party in 1969. In 1984 the press reported that Îugov was awarded the decoration „Hero of Socialist Labor" on the occasion of his eightieth birthday, and his wartime record was especially commended.
[62]) Brown, pp. 126–42.
[63]) Little information regarding the „April Conspiracy" appeared in the Bulgarian press. The best account is Brown, pp. 173–87.

2. Political Development

In the years that followed the collapse of the April Conspiracy Bulgaria experienced a long period of relative political stability. In part this was due to the emergence of an international environment that was favorable to the country's steady economic development. Particularly in the era of *détente* Bulgaria was able to expand its cultural and economic contacts with the West without creating difficulties for its traditionally close relationship with the USSR. The high rates of economic growth achieved in this period undoubtedly contributed to social stability.

But Bulgaria's political stability also owed much to the political skill that the First Secretary was able to bring to bear on the internal situation. Zhivkov demonstrated considerable circumspection in dealing with the older generation in the party, as indicated by the light sentences given to the April conspirators and the long delay in cleaning out their Vratsa nest. One means he used to retain the good will of the Old Guard was direct material support in the form of large monthly stipends to the wartime „Active Fighters Against Fascism and Capitalism". Various state awards, usually given party functionaries for long service, also carried with them a range of privileges, including access to coveted educational programs for their children. Zhivkov also made sure that they continued to be represented at the highest levels. At the party's IX Congress (1966), the two oldest members of the Politburo, Boris Bŭlgaranov (70) and Ivan Mikhaĭlov (69), who had been expected to retire, kept their positions and were joined by Tsola Dragoĭcheva (68) and Todor Pavlov (76). Bŭlgaranov remained in the Politburo until his death in 1972; Pavlov retired at the XI Congress (1976); Mikhaĭlov stayed on until the XII Congress (1981); and Dragoĭcheva finally retired in 1984[64]).

Despite his solicitude for the generation of „tested revolutionaries", Zhivkov seemed also convinced that the future lay with younger, better-trained, and more professional cadres. He favored the careers of a number of younger leaders and entrusted them with serious responsibilities. These included Stanko Todorov and Aleksandŭr Lilov in administration and ideology, Ognîan Doĭnov and Todor Bozhinov in economic policy, Ivan Bashev and Petŭr Mladenov in foreign policy, and Zhivkov's daughter Lîudmila and Georgi Ĭordanov in cultural affairs. At the same time he did not allow any of his rising younger supporters to become serious rivals for power. Mitko Grigorov was dropped unexpectedly from the Politburo and party secretariat at the party's IX Congress (1966). Politburo-member Boris Velchev was purged suddenly in 1977.

Zhivkov did not introduce a personality cult like those of Chervenkov or his northern neighbor, Nicolae Ceauşescu. On the contrary, he cultivated a common touch and a reputation for accessibility. The importance of personal relationships is magnified in a small country with a relatively narrow elite. Zhivkov developed friendships with individuals outside party ranks – with the writer Georgi Dzhagarov, for example – who established „Zhivkov factions" in many areas of public life.

Zhivkov presided over a substantial structural reform of the Bulgarian government

---

[64]) Bell, pp. 126/27.

in 1971. A new constitution, proposed at the X BKP Congress (1971) and approved in a national referendum, replaced the 1947 Dimitrov Constitution. It explicitly recognized the Communist Party at the „governing force" in society. Its most innovative feature was the creation of a DS to which the Council of Ministers was subordinated. Its chairman was the official head of state. When the constitution went into effect, Zhivkov assumed this office, yielding the post of prime minister to Stanko Todorov. The constitution also recognized the „fraternal cooperation" of the BZNS in governing the country[65]). Membership in the Agrarian Union has remained stable at 120,000 for nearly two decades, and Agrarians usually held a quarter of the seats in the NSb, a fifth of the positions on local soviets, and a few ministries. The post of first deputy chairman of the DS, whose occupant is the formal successor to the head of state, has also been held by an Agrarian, permitting Zhivkov to avoid designating an official heir from the BKP. Until his death in 1974 the BZNS was led by Georgi Traĭkov, who developed a close relationship with Zhivkov and became one of the publicized men in the country. He was succeeded by Petŭr Tanchev. The BZNS has been useful to the regime in implementing its policies in the countryside and in maintaining contacts with noncommunist agrarian parties around the world.

The X BKP Congress also updated the program of the BKP to adapt it to a newly defined stage of „mature socialism", which was described as „the highest and concluding development of socialism as a phase in the building of communism". The new program recognized the importance of the April plenum for guiding the party's conduct, but focused primarily on the party's role in construction, emphasizing the necessity of mastering science and technology for the improvement of production.

V. Domestic Politics in the 1980s

1. New Initiatives

a) Overview

Although the influence of *glasnost'* and *perestroĭka* in the USSR would have a major impact on Bulgaria in the late 1980s, the regime had already begun to experiment with new methods and policies in several areas of national life. This did not involve any weakening of the party's grip on the country or of Zhivkov's grip on the party. Despite occasional rumors that age or illness would force him to step down, Zhivkov continued to demonstrate physical vigor and to act as the initiator and chief spokesman of new policies. His control of the party apparatus was demonstrated by his thorough purge of the Varna party organization in 1981, by his demotion of longtime ally Stanko Todorov from the post of prime minister to the less prestigious presidency of the NSb in 1982, and by the purge of Aleksandŭr Lilov in 1983. As he approached his seventieth birthday, the XII BKP Congress (1981) recreated for him the title of General Secretary.

---

[65]) Spasov, B.: Bŭlgarskite konstitutsii (The Constitutions of Bulgaria), in: Bŭlgarskata dŭrzhava prez vekovete. Ed. V. Gîuzelev. Sofia 1982, vol. 1, pp. 486–90.

In the early 1980s two factors of growing importance impelled Zhivkov toward reform. One was the slowing of economic growth that became apparent in the late 1970s. The declining competitiveness of Bulgarian industrial goods combined with severe setbacks in agriculture due primarily to drought spurred the regime to search for methods to improve productivity. The second factor was the continued decline of population growth, which created immediate labor shortages and a sense of pessimism about the future. A factor that also probably weighed on the minds of Bulgaria's leaders was the example of the unrest in Poland. Late in 1980 or early in 1981 Zhivkov circulated a letter to party officials warning that while Bulgaria faced no immediate danger of succumbing to the Polish infection, poor economic performance and official abuses of power were having a bad effect on the population[66]).

b) The New Economic Mechanism

In 1979 a CC plenum introduced the so-called NIM in agriculture. The NIM, whose principles and implementation are described below in Professor Gumpel's chapter on the economic system, was extended to industry in 1980, but fell far short of effecting a major economic transformation[67]). In the Spring of 1983 Zhivkov condemned the continuing low quality of Bulgarian products and complained that even when advanced Western technology was employed the output was „Bulgarized" by low standards of labor discipline and inefficient management[68]). Todor Bozhinov and Ognîan Doĭnov, reportedly the chief architects of NIM suffered because of its poor results. Bozhinov was removed from the Politburo on the eve of the party's XIII Congress (1986) and Doĭnov, although retaining Politburo membership, was relegated to increasingly less influential posts in economic administration.

c) Lîudmila Zhivkova's Cultural Reforms

In the late 1970s and early 1980s Bulgaria's cultural life was greatly affected by the influence of Zhivkov's daughter Lîudmila. Born in 1942, she was broadly educated, specializing in history and spending a year as a graduate student at St. Anthony's College, Oxford. Following the death of her mother in 1971, she became more active in politics, often playing the role of Bulgaria's „first lady" and rising through the country's cultural bureaucracy. By 1976 the Committee on Science and Culture (*Komitet za izkustvo i kultura*), which she headed, had authority over education, publishing, international cultural relations, and the media as well as the traditional cultural fields. In 1979 she became a full member of the Politburo, where she headed a Politburo commission on science, culture, and education.

A devotee of Eastern religions and some native Bulgarian forms of mysticism, Zhivkova paid little more than lip service to party dogmatism in the arts. She encouraged both the avant-garde and the exploration of traditional nationalist themes.

---

[66]) Staar, R. F. (ed.): Yearbook on International Communist Affairs, 1982. Stanford, California 1982, p. 381 (Cit. as: YICA).
[67]) Lampe, pp. 215–19.
[68]) YICA. 1984, p. 305.

Without any sign of overt anti-Sovietism, she stressed Bulgaria's separate cultural identity and historic achievements. She removed Sofia's lawyers to the suburbs and converted the Palace of Justice into a national historical museum. Her agents went on around-the-world buying sprees to find works of art for new Bulgarian cultural centers, of which the crowning jewel was the imposing Palace of Culture which now bears her name. Vast sums were spent to finance international exhibitions or to bring foreign specialists to Bulgaria, and during 1981 under her direction the country engaged in a year-long celebration of the 1300th anniversary of the founding of the first Bulgarian state. Her creation, the International Children's Assembly, put Bulgaria on the circuit of international cultural events. Zhivkova also favored the careers of a number of protégés, most notably the poet Liûbomir Levchev and the historian Aleksandŭr Fol, who became minister of education, and gained an enthusiastic following particularly among the younger intelligentsia, which was genuinely saddened by her untimely death in 1981[69]. Even though her death was followed by a swing toward cultural conservatism, many of the developments she set in motion continued to affect Bulgaria's cultural life for the rest of the decade.

d) Demographic Policy

During the 1980s the low birthrate of the ethnic Bulgarian population increasingly became a focus of political attention. The dimensions of Bulgaria's demographic problems, which are discussed more fully below in the chapters by Professors R. Taaffe and S. Troebst, led Bulgarian leaders to express apprehension regarding the future need for labor and military manpower, and even for longterm national survival[70]. To encourage Bulgarians to have larger families, the government adopted a broad range of measures including raising the level of child support, imposing higher fees for abortion and divorce, discrimination against childless couples through taxation and the allocation of housing, and mandating three years of marriage before a legal separation could be recognized.

Demographic concern also prompted the measures of unusual brutality directed against the Turkish minority that attracted international attention beginning late in 1984[71].

2. *The Impact of glasnost' and perestroĭka*

Zhivkov has always made much of the close relationship between Bulgaria and the USSR, stating that the two countries share „a single circulatory system" and that the

---

[69] Zhivkova's ideas may be examined in a collection of her most important speeches: Zhivkova, L.: Za usŭvŭrshenstvuvane na choveka i obshtestvoto (On the Improvement of Man and Society). Sofia 1980.

[70] A most detailed examination of the problem by the politically well-connected writer Georgi Dzhagarov appeared in the army newspaper Narodna armiiâ (People's Army), 1–2 September 1982.

[71] Amnesty International: Bulgaria: Imprisonment of Ethnic Turks. New York 1986, and Amnesty International: Bulgaria: Continuing Human Rights Abuses against Ethnic Turks. New York 1987.

Bulgarian watch runs on Moscow time. Inevitably, Soviet *glasnost', perestroĭka*, and „new thinking" had a powerful impact on both the government and society. Initially, Bulgaria responded in a predominantly mechanical way, imitating Soviet campaigns against alcoholism, corruption, and bureaucratic formalism[72]). But at a CC plenum in July 1987, Zhivkov clearly seemed to position himself at the head of a reform movement and advanced a set of proposals far more radical than any the country had yet seen. While boasting of the past accomplishments of Bulgarian socialism, he added that the present system had exhausted itself and that the time had come for a 180 degree change of course. Announcing that Bulgaria had entered a period of transition from „power on behalf of the people to power through the people", he called for sweeping changes in economic and political administration and structural reforms, including the fusion of the State and Ministerial Councils into a single governing body and the adoption of multiple candidacies for elective office[73]).

Two months later the government abolished the system of economic administration that had been set up only one year before and consolidated a number of ministries. The most surprising step was the creation of a new Ministry of the Economy and Planning (*Ministerstvo na ikonomikata i planiraneto*), which was given to Stoĭan Ovcharov, a forty-five-year-old specialist in biotechnology who was not even a candidate member of the CC. His appointment seemed to indicate Zhivkov's preference for young professionals over senior party bureaucrats. At the end of August, the NSb approved a major reform of territorial organization, replacing the twenty-eight district governments with nine *oblasti*. Although the consolidation of district governments was supposed to take place gradually over the course of the year, in what amounted to a virtual *coup d'état* directed against the district leaderships the Politburo decided to implement the reform at once and immediately appointed „temporary" *oblast* party committees and people's councils. Only about one-third of the local government officials received appointments on the *oblast* level, and the rest were directed to find work on lower administrative levels or in economic enterprises. Zhivkov justified this reform by charging that the old district governments had pursued „feudal" policies, aiming at economic self-sufficiency without regard to national needs, and building entrenched, conservative bureaucracies that stifled initiative.

The July plenum represented the highpoint of Zhivkov's commitment to *perestroĭka* as he and a core of conservatives in the leadership grew alarmed at the emergence of spontaneous, popular reform movements. Exposures of official corruption in the press, and above all, the organization of an independent committee containing prominent intellectuals and some political figures that called attention to the pollution of the air of Ruse by a Romanian chemical combine, provoked a sharp backlash. At a National Party Conference in January 1988, Zhivkov announced that consideration of fundamental reforms would be deferred until the BKP's XIV Congress (1991)[74]). In elections for regional and municipal councils in March 1988, more than one candidate was allowed on the ballot in only one-fifth of the races[75]). Several

---

[72]) YICA. 1987, p. 278.
[73]) RD. 29 July 1987.
[74]) Sofia News. 3 February 1988.
[75]) Sofia News. 2 March 1988.

intellectuals prominent in the call for reforms were dismissed from their positions for their „negativism", and pro-reform political figures were purged from the government and party leadership. Chudomir Aleksandrov, believed to have been the architect of the territorial reform, and Stanko Todorov, whose wife was an outspoken supporter of liberalization, were forced off the Politburo in July 1988, and Stoîan Mikhaïlov was fired as a CC Secretary amid charges that he had been too lax in managing the party's dealings with the intelligentsia[76]).

Bulgaria's intellectuals were not so easily cowed, and continued to denounce government repression in spite of arrests, harassment, and exile. Protests grew as well among the ethnic Turks, leading to violent clashes with the authorities during the spring of 1989. Zhivkov denied the existence of this problem and dared Turkey to open its borders to ethnic Turks wishing to leave Bulgaria. When Turkey accepted the challenge, the Bulgarian government launched a reign of terror against the ethnic Turks that resulted in bloodshed, the expulsion of thousands, and the flight of many more. Before Turkey again imposed visa requirements, more than 300,000 ethnic Turks left Bulgaria. This exodus both disrupted the Bulgarian economy, particularly in agriculture, and focused worldwide attention on Bulgaria's human rights abuses. Zhivkov also alienated powerful party figures by his efforts to force his son, Vladimir, into the top leadership.

Zhivkov was removed from office on 10 November in a move that was apparently organized by Foreign Minister Petŭr Mladenov and Defense Minister Dobri Dzhurov. Mladenov became head of both the BKP and the Bulgarian state, and launched a purge of Zhivkov's cronies. Zhivkov, himself, quickly became the target of charges of corruption and abuse of power and was expelled from the party along with his son. The new BKP leadership pledged to work for genuine democratization. Figures persecuted by Zhivkov were amnestied and restored to their positions and Mladenov announced that the constitution would be amended to remove the article guaranteeing the BKP a monopoly of power. Meanwhile, dissident groups, now free to organize and speak out, formed a United Opposition, which looked forward to the creation of a multi-party system[77]).

---

[76]) YICA. 1989, pp. 298/99.

[77]) The events surrounding Zhivkov's fall are more fully discussed by Dr. Höpken in his chapter „Political System".

Außenpolitik

Klaus-Detlev Grothusen, Hamburg

I. Systematischer Teil: 1. Die bulgarische Außenpolitik zwischen Souveränität und Sozialistischem Internationalismus – 2. Die bulgarische Außenpolitik als Regionalpolitik – 3. Quellen und Forschung – 4. Periodisierung – II. Darstellender Teil: 1. Voraussetzungen – 2. Die „Sowjetisierung" (1944–1947/49) – 3. Die Stalin-Zeit (1947/49–1953/56) – 4. Die Übergangszeit (1953/56–1964/68) – 5. Zwischen Sozialistischem Internationalismus und Friedlicher Koexistenz: Die Živkov-Ära (1964/68–1989) – 6. Der Umsturz des 10.11.1989 und seine Folgen

I. Systematischer Teil

1. Die bulgarische Außenpolitik zwischen Souveränität und Sozialistischem Internationalismus

Nicht anders als in den Kapiteln „Außenpolitik" der vorhergehenden Bände des „Südosteuropa-Handbuchs" soll auch an dieser Stelle versucht werden, anhand systematischer Überlegungen Kriterien für die Beurteilung von Außenpolitik als Ereignisgeschichte zu gewinnen, deren Darstellung Aufgabe des zweiten Hauptteils sein soll. Wenn damit einerseits eine Verbindung von politikwissenschaftlichen und zeithistorischen Fragestellungen angestrebt wird, so soll andererseits mit Blick auf das weitere Voranschreiten des „Südosteuropa-Handbuchs" auch ein zweites Ziel nicht außer acht bleiben: das Bemühen, außenpolitische Strukturen in Südosteuropa zu erkennen. Der Reiz einer solchen Zielsetzung speziell in einem Raum wie Südosteuropa liegt auf der Hand, wo nacheinander NATO- bzw. EG-Länder – Griechenland und die Türkei –, WP- bzw. RGW-Länder – Rumänien, Ungarn, Bulgarien – und blockfreie Länder – Jugoslawien, Albanien und Zypern – zu behandeln sind. Es ist nicht zuviel gesagt, daß es keinen anderen Teil der Erde gibt, der sich mit dieser Vielfalt auch nur entfernt messen könnte. Den theoretischen Rahmen derartiger Bemühungen hat G. Brunner vorbildhaft abgesteckt, wenn er eindringlich den Nutzen von Strukturmodellen unterstreicht und zugleich vor der Gefahr von Verlaufsmodellen warnt[1]).

Die Doppelschichtigkeit der Aufgabe im Falle Bulgariens liegt auf der Hand: einmal die Einordnung der bulgarischen Außenpolitik in eine Typologie der Außenpolitik aller Ostblockstaaten und dann deren Vergleich mit der Außenpolitik der Westblock- bzw. blockfreien Staaten. Was als erstes eine Typologie der Außenpolitik der

---

[1]) Brunner, G.: Über Sinn und Unsinn von Verfassungs- und Herrschaftsmodellen in der Osteuropaforschung, in: Sowjetsystem und Ostrecht. Festschrift für Boris Meissner zum 70. Geburtstag. Berlin 1985, S. 43/44.

Außenpolitik

Ostblockstaaten betrifft, so kann hier, beginnend mit terminologischen Fragen wie „Ostblock" oder „Sozialistische Gemeinschaft", ohne weiteres an die Überlegungen angeknüpft werden, die an den Anfang des Kapitels über die ungarische Außenpolitik gestellt worden sind[2]). Das Ergebnis war, daß auf der Basis einer beeindruckend reichhaltigen Forschung allein schon in der Bundesrepublik Deutschland, die in den letzten Jahren ständig weitergeführt worden ist[3]), sowie nicht außer acht zu lassender Veröffentlichungen in Osteuropa[4]) ein relativ klares modelltheoretisches Bild von den außen- (und innen-) politischen Rahmenbedingungen der osteuropäischen Länder besteht. Eingebunden ist dieses in eine Analyse der historischen Entwicklung Osteuropas seit 1944/45: Den Ausgangspunkt bildet die Phase des Aufbaus eines Kranzes von „Satelliten" im westlichen Vorfeld der Sowjetunion, von 1944/45 bis 1947/49, deren außenpolitischer Spielraum bis zu Stalins Tod auf Null absank. Erst seitdem hat sich allmählich und mit höchst unterschiedlichen Nuancierungen im Einzelfall jenes System des „Sowjetblocks zwischen Vormachtkontrolle und Autonomie" herausgebildet, wie R. Löwenthal und B. Meissner es eindringlich bezeichnet und beschrieben haben[5]), dessen weitere Entwicklung aufgrund der Impulse durch die *perestrojka* Gorbačevs seit 1985 und der umstürzenden Ereignisse des Jahres 1989 heute in allen Konsequenzen zwar noch nicht abzuschätzen ist, wo aber zumindest das endgültige Ende des Sowjetblocks Stalinscher Prägung unbezweifelbar erscheint.

In diesen Rahmen ist nun Bulgarien einzuordnen. Kein Argument gegen das Interesse, das an der bulgarischen Außenpolitik genommen werden könnte, ist dabei, daß Bulgarien geographisch das kleinste Land des Sowjetblocks ist. Wichtig ist dagegen, daß die bulgarische Außenpolitik von ganz wenigen und zudem nicht einmal sicheren Ausnahmen abgesehen von der westlichen Forschung immer wieder unter das Verdikt des „treuesten Satelliten" der Sowjetunion, des „loyalsten Bündnispartners", von „Servilität" oder „subjugation" gestellt worden ist, in welches Bild dann auch Živkov als „zuverlässigster Gefolgsmann" oder – in einer albanischen Variante – als

---

[2]) Grothusen, K.-D.: Außenpolitik, in: Südosteuropa-Handbuch. Bd. V: Ungarn. Göttingen 1987, S. 107–14.

[3]) Grothusen (Anm. 2), S. 108, Anm. 2; ferner: Sowjetunion '86. Bilanz und Ausblick aus Anlaß des XXVII. Parteitags der KPdSU, in: Osteuropa. Zeitschrift für Gegenwartsfragen des Ostens. 36 (1986), S. 579–821; Simon, G. (Hrsg.): Weltmacht Sowjetunion. Umbrüche, Kontinuitäten, Perspektiven. Köln 1987; Uschakow, A.; Frenzke, D.: Der Warschauer Pakt und seine bilateralen Bündnisverträge. Analyse und Texte. Berlin 1987.

[4]) Für die ältere Literatur s. Anm. 2, darüber hinaus: Kritika buržuaznych fal'sifikacij istorii Socialističeskogo sodružestva v Evrope (Kritik der bürgerlichen Verfälschungen der Geschichte der Sozialistischen Gemeinschaft in Europa). Otv. red. V. K. Volkov. Moskau 1986; Organizacija Varšavskogo dogovora 1955–1985. Dokumenty i materialy (Die Organisation des Warschauer Paktes 1955–1985. Dokumente und Materialien). V. F. Mal'cev (otv. red.). Moskau 1986; Fel'dman, D. M.: Socialističeskie meždunarodnye otnošenija – obščestvennye otnošenija novogo tipa (Die sozialistischen internationalen Beziehungen – gesellschaftliche Beziehungen eines neuen Typs), in: Naučnyj kommunizm. (1987) 5, S. 69–76; Istorija meždunarodnych otnošenij i vnešnej politiki SSSR (Geschichte der internationalen Beziehungen und der Außenpolitik der UdSSR). T. 2: 1945–1970. T. 3: 1970–1987. Red. G. V. Fokeev. Moskau 1987.

[5]) Löwenthal, R.; Meissner, B. (Hrsg.): Der Sowjetblock zwischen Vormachtkontrolle und Autonomie. Köln 1984.

„blindes Werkzeug der sowjetischen Zaren"⁶) nahtlos hineinpaßte. Anlaß zu solchen Beurteilungen, die wenig Hoffnung auf außenpolitische Freiräume ließen, gaben dabei nicht zuletzt die unzählbaren Bekundungen besonderer Liebe und aufrichtigster Hinneigung zur Sowjetunion durch die bulgarischen Führer selbst und sämtliche Parteitage der BKP. Immer wieder zitiertes und auch ins Parteiprogramm von 1971 aufgenommenes Leitmotiv war die Formulierung Dimitrovs von 1943, die Freundschaft mit der Sowjetunion sei für Bulgarien „nicht weniger notwendig als die Sonne und die Luft für jedes Lebewesen"⁷). Živkov hatte dieses Bild noch dadurch gesteigert, daß er 1974 davon gesprochen hat, die Annäherung beider Länder werde soweit entwickelt werden, „daß beide Staaten und Systeme einen einzigen Organismus bilden, von einem gemeinsamen Blutkreislauf durchpulst werden"⁸). Die von Živkov angesprochene „Annäherung" (sbližavane) an die „große Sowjetunion" findet sich auch im Parteiprogramm von 1971⁹) und hatte neben vielen anderen vergleichbaren Äußerungen seit den 40er Jahren immer wieder der Vermutung Vorschub geleistet, die Sowjetunion werde Bulgarien als 16. Republik in ihren Staatsverband aufnehmen. Auch wenn hieran schon längst nicht mehr zu denken ist, bleibt doch unbestreitbar, daß nicht nur das Bekenntnis zur Sowjetunion, sondern auch zur Sozialistischen Gemeinschaft und ihrem Leitprinzip des Sozialistischen Internationalismus in Bulgarien ungewöhnliche Ausmaße erreichte. Nachdem Brežnev schon 1967 das Verhältnis zwischen der Sowjetunion und Bulgarien als Musterbeispiel für „Sozialistischen Internationalismus in Aktion" bezeichnet hatte, gehörte auch diese Formulierung lange Zeit zum bulgarischen Standardwortschatz, und der Sozialistische Internationalismus als solcher hat in einer auch für den Sowjetblock ganz ungewöhnlichen Weise 1971 sogar Verfassungsrang erhalten¹⁰). Um den Kreis zu schließen, sei aus dem Rechenschaftsbericht des ZK der BKP an den XIII. Parteitag von 1986 zitiert: „Die Grundlage unserer Außenpolitik ist der Kurs auf brüderliches Zusammenwirken, Freundschaft und allseitige Annäherung mit der KPdSU und der Sowjetunion"¹¹).

Richtig ist sicherlich aber auch, daß die bulgarische Führung mit ihrer verbalen Hinneigung zur Sowjetunion nicht allein gestanden hat, worauf bereits im Zusammenhang der ungarischen Außenpolitik hingewiesen werden konnte, zusammen mit

---

⁶) Beispiele aus der westlichen Forschung finden sich ohne Zahl. Herausgegriffen seien: Brown, J. F.: Bulgaria Under Communist Rule. London 1970, S. 263, 304; Osteuropa-Handbuch. Begründet von W. Markert. Sowjetunion. Außenpolitik 1955–1973. Hrsg. v. D. Geyer. Köln, Wien 1976, S. 340, 398; Hoensch, J. K.: Sowjetische Osteuropa-Politik 1945–1975. Kronberg/Ts. 1977, S. 468/9; Hakker, J.: Der Ostblock. Entstehung, Entwicklung und Struktur 1939–1980. Baden-Baden 1980, S. 610, 737; Crampton, R. J.: A Short History of Modern Bulgaria. Cambridge u. a. 1987, S. 189; für Albanien s. Zëri i Popullit (Die Stimme des Volkes). 9.9.1969.
⁷) Dimitroff, G.: Ausgewählte Schriften. Bd. 3: 1935–1948. Berlin 1958, S. 239; Programm der Bulgarischen Kommunistischen Partei, einmütig angenommen auf dem X. Parteitag der BKP am 24. April 1971. Sofia 1971, S. 88/89.
⁸) RD. 21.3.1974.
⁹) Parteiprogramm (Anm. 7), S. 9.
¹⁰) Für Brežnev s. RD. 13.5.1967; für die Verfassung: Verfassung der Volksrepublik Bulgarien vom 18. Mai 1971, in: Brunner, G.; Meissner, B.: Verfassungen der kommunistischen Staaten. Paderborn u. a. 1979, Art. 5, S. 51.
¹¹) Rechenschaftsbericht des Zentralkomitees der Bulgarischen Kommunistischen Partei an den XIII. Parteitag. Bestätigt vom XIII. Parteitag am 5. April 1986. Sofia 1986, S. 25/26.

der Warnung W. Leonhards, daß derartige Lippenbekenntnisse die Sowjetunion kaum getäuscht haben[12]). Einen Schritt weiter geht W. Oschlies, der einem leicht zusammenzustellenden „Kompendium roter Balkanrhetorik" keine allzu hohe Bedeutung beimessen will, obwohl auch er zumindest im Bereich der Wirtschaft von einer „Baumschulen-Funktion" Bulgariens für die Sowjetunion spricht[13]). Und gerade die Außenwirtschaft Bulgariens mit ihrer im Vergleich zur Vorkriegszeit ungewöhnlich hohen Ostorientierung – heute ca. 80% RGW, ca. 60% allein die Sowjetunion[14]) – beweist in eindrucksvoller Weise, daß es sich bei den Aussagen der bulgarischen Führer eben nicht nur um Balkanrhetorik gehandelt hat. Stattdessen muß das Ergebnis von Überlegungen zur typologischen Einordnung Bulgariens in den Sowjetblock sein, daß es tatsächlich das einzige Land gewesen ist, das kontinuierlich und stabil von 1944 an zur Sowjetunion gestanden hat: Ein Blick auf das nähere Balkanumfeld weist sofort Extreme des „Antisowjetismus" aus, der nicht zufällig einen hohen Stellenwert bei den negativ besetzten Termini in Bulgarien hat: Jugoslawien und Albanien haben den Bereich sowjetischer Hegemonie schon längst verlassen; aber auch die beiden zum Block gehörenden südosteuropäischen Nachbarn – Ungarn und Rumänien – haben in ihrer Geschichte der letzten Jahrzehnte aufs Deutlichste bewiesen, was Antisowjetismus bedeuten kann. Ähnliches gilt für die DDR (1953), die Tschechoslowakei (1968) und Polen seit 1956 zu wiederholten Malen. Nur Bulgarien ist das Land innenpolitischer Stabilität und außenpolitischer Zuverlässigkeit gewesen, jedenfalls was die wesentlichen Leitlinien der internationalen Politik angeht. Ausnahmen gibt es nur im Bereich des geographisch engeren Feldes des Balkans, wo Eigeninteressen im Sinne von Regionalpolitik festzustellen sind (vgl. I,2).

Daß der Umsturz vom 10.11.1989 an in Bulgarien ebenso wie in den anderen ostmittel- und südosteuropäischen Ländern aufgrund der Ereignisse des Jahres 1989 bis dahin ungeahnte Möglichkeiten zu neuen Entwicklungen gebracht hat, steht außer Frage. Deutlich ist allerdings auch, daß bis zum Jahresende 1989 nur die Innenpolitik Bulgariens real und programmatisch wesentliche Änderungen aufzuweisen hat, noch nicht jedoch die Außenpolitik.

Wenn Bulgarien auf diese Weise deutlich eine Sonderstellung im Sowjetblock einnimmt, so ergibt sich natürlich als nächstes die Frage, ob es Gründe für diese ebenso unbestreitbare wie kontinuierliche Sowjetuniontreue gibt? Auszugehen ist dabei von der Tatsache, daß dieses Phänomen nicht nur ein Theorem der westlichen Forschung ist, sondern mit größtem Nachdruck auch innerhalb Bulgariens betont wird. Aus dem Rechenschaftsbericht des ZK der BKP an den XIII. Parteitag von 1986 als zeitlich letzter parteioffizieller Äußerung ist bereits zitiert worden, und von hier aus läßt sich ohne weiteres über die Verfassung von 1971 eine Linie zurück bis zur ersten Regierungserklärung der ersten Regierung der OF vom 17.9.1944 ziehen, wo sofort im ersten Punkt herzliche Freundschaft mit der Sowjetunion und ewige Brüderschaft

---

[12]) Grothusen (Anm. 2), S. 109/10; Leonhard, W.: Am Vorabend einer neuen Revolution? Die Zukunft des Sowjetkommunismus. München u.a. 1975, S. 239.
[13]) Oschlies, W.: Bulgarien – nahe der Sowjetunion, fern dem Westen?, in: Löwenthal, R.; Meissner, B. (Anm. 5), S. 252 u. 282.
[14]) Vgl. das Kapitel „Außenwirtschaft" von R. Schönfeld im vorliegenden Handbuch.

mit dem russischen Volk gefordert wird[15]). Was nun die Erklärung dieses innerhalb des Sowjetblockes so einzigartigen Phänomens betrifft, so ist in der Forschung keine Einmütigkeit festzustellen, sondern die jeweils unterschiedliche Gewichtung eines Bündels von Faktoren: Diese reichen von einer kulturell und ethnisch begründeten, den Bulgaren immanenten Russophilie unter Einschluß nicht nachlassender Dankbarkeit für die Befreiung 1877/78 über die Einsicht, daß ein kleiner Balkanstaat ohne einen mächtigen äußeren Patron schutzlos allen außenpolitischen Gefahren ausgeliefert sei, bis zu handfesten wirtschaftspolitischen Interessen, die Bulgarien seit 1944 oder zumindest seit Beginn der 60er Jahre nur Vorteile gebracht hätten[16]). Abgesehen davon, daß in Bulgarien tatsächlich wohl nur gegenüber Russen und Deutschen eine historisch gewachsene, echte Sympathie nachweisbar ist, führt die Frage der Interessen noch einen Schritt weiter: zum imperialen Interesse Rußlands im 18. und 19. Jh. am Balkan im allgemeinen und an Bulgarien im besonderen – verbunden mit echter Sympathie für das Los der slawischen Glaubensbrüder unter türkischer Herrschaft –, das seine Fortsetzung allerdings auch in Molotovs Verhandlungen mit Hitler in Berlin am 12./13.11.1940 hatte und nahtlos zum berüchtigten „Prozentabkommen" Churchills und Stalins vom 9.10.1944 führt. Sowjetischem Interesse an Vormachtkontrolle über Bulgarien steht damit schon zu Beginn der bulgarischen Nachkriegsgeschichte englisches Desinteresse gegenüber sowie, wenn der Vorwurf zutrifft, amerikanische „Non-Policy"[17]). Dieses russische bzw. sowjetische Interesse an Bulgarien, das durchaus politisch für Bulgarien verwertbar war, existiert bis heute weiter und erklärt sich leicht mit Blick auf alle anderen südosteuropäischen Länder.

Wenn sich auf diese Weise im Rahmen von Bemühungen um eine außenpolitische Typologie Südosteuropas durchaus nachdenkenswerte Gesichtspunkte auch im Falle Bulgariens finden lassen, so bleibt noch, auf ein für Bulgarien wie für Ungarn und Rumänien höchst charakteristisches Moment hinzuweisen, das der neueren westlichen Geschichtstheorie durchaus zuwiderläuft: die Bedeutung der großen historischen Persönlichkeit. Es handelt sich um dieselbe Fragestellung, die im Zusammenhang der ungarischen Außenpolitik anhand von Rákosi und Kádár diskutiert worden ist[18]) und die sich im Falle Bulgariens mit den Namen von Dimitrov, Červenkov und Živkov verbindet. Auch die bulgarische Außenpolitik ist dementsprechend im gesamten Verlauf seit 1944 ganz wesentlich von den Führern der Partei bestimmt worden. Das Besondere an der bulgarischen Entwicklung ist nur, daß nach dem

---

[15]) Verfassung von 1971 (Anm. 10), Präambel, S. 50; Iz programata na pravitelstvoto na Otečestvennija front, 17 septemvri 1944 g. (Aus dem Programm der Regierung der OF. 17. September 1944), in: Vănšna politika na Narodna Republika Bălgarija (Die Außenpolitik der NRB) (zit. als VPB). T. 1: 1944–1962. Sofia 1970, S. 9.

[16]) Keine westliche Untersuchung der bulgarischen Außen- oder Innenpolitik kommt an diesen Fragen vorbei. Vgl. die in den Anm. 6 u. 13 genannte Literatur als Beispiele.

[17]) Churchill, W.S.: Der Zweite Weltkrieg. Bd. 6, 1. Stuttgart 1954, S. 269–73; Resis, A.: The Churchill-Stalin Secret „Percentages" Agreement on the Balkans, Moscow, October 1944, in: The American Historical Review. 83 (1978), S. 368–87; Lundestad, G.: The American Non-Policy towards Eastern Europe 1943–1947. New York 1978; Boll, M.M.: U.S. Plans for a Postwar Pro-Western Bulgaria. A little known Wartime Initiative in Eastern Europe, in: Diplomatic History. 7 (1983) 2, S. 117–38; Harbutt, F.J.: The Iron Curtain. Churchill, America and the Origin of the Cold War. New York, Oxford 1986. – Für die Einzelheiten vgl. im übrigen II,2.

[18]) Grothusen (Anm. 2), S. 113.

unbezweifelbar bedeutenden, wenn auch unbedingt moskautreuen Dimitrov sowie Červenkov, der zu den typischen Führern des Hochstalinismus in Osteuropa gehört, mit Živkov einer der farblosesten osteuropäischen Parteiführer an die Macht gekommen ist, der sie vielleicht aber gerade deswegen länger als je ein anderer innegehabt hat und gegen den erst nach seinem Sturz am 10. 11. 1989 in Bulgarien selbst schwere Vorwürfe der verschiedensten Art erhoben worden sind[19]). Auch an seiner Moskautreue ist nie gezweifelt worden, die ihn persönlich speziell mit Chruščev und Brežnev verband und als Garant der Prinzipien des Sozialistischen Internationalismus erscheinen ließ. Daß sich auch bei ihm im Einzelfall die Frage nach außenpolitischer Selbständigkeit stellte, zeigte sich vor allem im engeren und eigentlichen Bereich bulgarischer Außenpolitik, der Regionalpolitik auf dem Balkan.

2. Die bulgarische Außenpolitik als Regionalpolitik

Daß Außenpolitik im Sinne eigenständiger bulgarischer Interessen Balkanpolitik bedeutet, zieht sich wie ein roter Faden von der endgültigen Wiedererrichtung des Staates durch den Berliner Kongreß 1878 über die Zeit der Balkan- und Weltkriege bis in die Gegenwart des Jahres 1989[20]). Es ist das Verhältnis zu den unmittelbaren territorialen Nachbarn – Serbien/Jugoslawien, Griechenland, Rumänien, Osmanisches Reich/Türkei –, das allein nationale Emotionen zu wecken vermag. Richtig ist allerdings auch, daß Bulgarien mehr noch als seine Nachbarn eines „Patrons" zu bedürfen scheint, welche Rolle nacheinander Rußland, Deutschland und die Sowjetunion übernahmen. Das Ergebnis für die Entwicklung der bulgarischen Außenpolitik von 1944 bis in die jüngste Zeit ist im Sinne des im vorigen Abschnitt Gesagten, daß zumindest programmatisch die Balkananliegen durchweg auf den zweiten Platz hinter den Bereich Sowjetunion und Sozialistische Gemeinschaft zurückfielen[21]). Dies ändert trotzdem nichts an der Bedeutung, die das Verhältnis zu den Nachbarn während dieser ganzen Zeit für das bulgarische Selbstverständnis gehabt hat, von der weiteren Entwicklung in der Zukunft ganz abgesehen. Offen erscheint in der Forschung nur, ob Bulgarien sich durch Wohlverhalten gegenüber der Sowjetunion in Fragen der internationalen Politik bewußt einen Freiraum für seine Balkanpolitik schaffen wollte[22]).

Daß diese Frage schwer zu beantworten ist, zeigt ein Blick auf die beiden Problemfelder, die mit Abstand die wichtigsten in der bulgarischen Balkanpolitik sind: das

---

[19]) Zur Person Živkovs vgl. J. F. B.: Todor Zhivkov. Twenty Years as Bulgarian Party Leader, in: RFE. Research. B/2. 5. III. 1974; Oschlies, W.: Bulgariens Staats- und Parteichef – 75 Jahre alt. Skizzen zu einem Porträt Todor Shiwkows, in: Osteuropa. 36 (1986), S. 1015–21.

[20]) Für die Zeit bis 1944 vgl. das Kapitel „Historical Foundations" von R. J. Crampton in diesem Handbuch.

[21]) Vgl. als letztes: Rechenschaftsbericht des ZK der BKP an den XIII. Parteitag (Anm. 11), S. 31/32.

[22]) Oschlies (Anm. 19), . 1017; Höpken, W.: Die bulgarisch-türkischen Beziehungen, in: Südosteuropa. 36 (1987), S. 76; für den bulgarischen Standpunkt vgl. Gančev, T.: Družba i sătrudničestvo săs SSSR – osnova na vănšnata politika na NR Bălgarija (Freundschaft und Zusammenarbeit mit der UdSSR – die Grundlage der Außenpolitik der NRB), in: Socialističeskata vănšna politika na Narodna Republika Bălgarija 1944/1974 (Die sozialistische Außenpolitik der NRB 1944/1974). Sofia 1974, S. 49–60.

Makedonien-Problem praktisch ohne Unterbrechung von 1944 an und das Verhältnis zur Türkei seit dem Beginn der Assimilationspolitik gegenüber der über 10% der Gesamtbevölkerung umfassenden türkischen Minderheit seit Ende 1984 bis hin zu der völlig überraschenden Erlaubnis zum Massenexodus „muslimischer Bulgaren" von Ende Mai 1989 an[23]). In bezug auf Makedonien und überhaupt Jugoslawien mit den großen Krisen 1948, 1958, 1968 und 1978 mag eine Koinzidenz mit der Sowjetunion noch überwiegend nachweisbar sein, für den offenen Streit mit der Türkei seit 1984 erscheint dies dafür eher unwahrscheinlich.

Deutlich in Übereinstimmung mit der sowjetischen Balkanpolitik befindet sich Bulgarien dafür mit seinem regionalpolitischen Grundanliegen seit 1957: dem Balkan als Zone des Friedens und der Freundschaft bzw. auch als atom- und chemiewaffenfreie Zone. Diese Forderung, die sich natürlich bewußt und vorteilhaft von dem alten Verruf des Balkans als „Pulverfaß Europas" unterscheidet, ist zuerst als sog. Stoica-Plan von Rumänien 1957 vorgetragen worden, anschließend 1959 von Rumänien, der Sowjetunion und Bulgarien gemeinsam, und gehört seitdem zu den „ceterum censeo"-Formulierungen bulgarischer Balkanpolitik[24]). Speziell sowjetische Wünsche scheinen sich nur in dem einen Punkt bemerkbar zu machen, daß Bulgarien über weite Strecken den bilateralen Verhandlungen den Vorzug vor multilateralen gegeben hat. Interessenidentität von Sowjetunion und Bulgarien liegt ohnehin z. B. mit Blick auf die Atomwaffen der NATO in Griechenland und der Türkei auf der Hand, da Bulgarien aufgrund des Friedensvertrages von 1947 keine derartigen Waffen auf seinem Territorium haben darf.

Was die einzelnen Länder der Region betrifft, so erweist sich das Verhältnis zu Jugoslawien im ganzen als das komplizierteste: von den Föderationsplänen bis zum Kominformbruch 1944–1948, dazu das makedonische Dauerproblem. Was das letztere betrifft, so hat Živkov vor langer Zeit schon und besonders nachdrücklich 1978 eine Lösung vorgeschlagen, die allerdings von Jugoslawien abgelehnt worden ist: Anerkennung des territorialen status quo (Grenzgarantie), jedoch ohne Verzicht auf eine bulgarisch-makedonische Geschichte und mit ausdrücklicher Betonung des bulgarischen Charakters von Pirin-Makedonien[25]). Was das Verhältnis zu Griechenland angeht, so hat es sich nach Überwindung der Phase des Bürgerkrieges (1944–1949) ungewöhnlich positiv entwickelt. Seit 1964 können die gegenseitigen Beziehungen fast durchweg als gut, zum Teil sogar als sehr gut bezeichnet werden, wofür in den letzten Jahren vor allem der Name Andreas Papandreous zu nennen ist. Allerdings haben die griechischen Wahlen vom 18.6.1989 hier möglicherweise für eine Zäsur gesorgt, deren Auswirkungen zum Zeitpunkt der Drucklegung dieses Bandes noch nicht abzuschätzen sind. Dasselbe könnte für die Türkei gelten, wenn hier nicht das genannte Problem der Assimilation der türkischen Minderheit seit 1984 zu einem ungewöhnlich schweren Konflikt geführt hätte, der sich im Gefolge der Novel-

---

[23]) Für Einzelheiten vgl. Teil II dieses Kapitels. Zur Einführung für Makedonien: Troebst, S.: Die bulgarisch-jugoslawische Kontroverse um Makedonien 1967–1982. München 1983 (Untersuchungen zur Gegenwartskunde Südosteuropas. 23). Für die bulgarisch-türkischen Beziehungen: Höpken (Anm. 22).
[24]) Vgl. als letztes die bulgarische Haltung auf der Belgrader Balkan-Konferenz vom 24.–26.2.1988, s. u. S. 133 mit Anm. 195.
[25]) RD. 16.6.1978.

Außenpolitik

le zum Paßgesetz vom 19. 5. 1989, Živkovs Fernsehrede vom 26. 5. 1989 und dem sich anschließenden Massenexodus von Angehörigen der türkischen Minderheit in die Türkei und der Schließung der Grenze seitens der Türkei am 21. 8. 1989 nur noch steigerte[25a]). Obwohl P. Mladenov Živkov nach dem 10. 11. 1989 für diese Entwicklung die persönliche Schuld zugesprochen hat, hat sich seitdem noch keine grundsätzliche Änderung abgezeichnet. Ebenfalls auf die persönliche Entscheidung Živkovs ist das erstaunlich ungetrübte Verhältnis zu Rumänien zurückzuführen, das sich in immer wiederkehrenden Treffen mit Ceaușescu manifestierte. Die sowjetisch-rumänischen Spannungen machten sich praktisch nicht bemerkbar. Der Sturz beider Männer im November/Dezember 1989 läßt die Schaffung einer neuen Vertrauensbasis denkbar werden. Anders verhält sich Bulgarien dafür seit 1959 gegenüber Albanien im Zusammenhang des sowjetisch-chinesischen Gegensatzes. Das Abrücken Albaniens von China 1978 ließ umgehend bulgarische Annäherungsversuche folgen. Immerhin hatte Albanien seit 1971 regelmäßig Handelsprotokolle mit Bulgarien unterzeichnet.

3. Quellen und Forschung

Ein eingehender Literaturbericht kann aus Platzgründen an dieser Stelle nicht gegeben werden. Für spezielle Literaturangaben muß daher auf die Anmerkungen dieses Kapitels sowie auf den Außenpolitikteil der Allgemeinen Bibliographie des Handbuchs verwiesen werden. Was stattdessen aber an dieser Stelle als sinnvoll erscheint, sind Hinweise methodischer Art, die sich aus der Beschäftigung mit einem Thema wie der bulgarischen Außenpolitik in den letzten Jahrzehnten ergeben haben.

a) Quellen

Daß Archivbenutzung in Bulgarien allein schon wegen der Sperrfrist nicht die Grundlage der Arbeit sein konnte, versteht sich von selbst. Von westlichen Archiven abgesehen mußten daher veröffentlichte Quellen in möglichst großem Umfang herangezogen werden. Unter methodischen Gesichtspunkten erweisen sich dabei zwei Aspekte als besonders interessant: Einmal die Möglichkeit, Quellen unterschiedlicher Provenienz zu gleichen Sachthemen heranzuziehen, was zu eindrucksvollen Unterschieden führte. Als Beispiele seien genannt: die Konferenzen von Jalta und Potsdam im Licht der älteren amerikanischen und neueren sowjetischen Editionen[26]); die kritische Phase der bulgarisch-jugoslawischen Beziehungen 1944–1948/49 im Spiegel

---

[25a]) Für Živkovs Rede s. Otečestven Front. 31. 5. 1989; für die Einzelheiten s. u. S. 136/37; für die Gesetzesnovelle s. DV (1989) 38.
[26]) Foreign Relations of the United States. Diplomatic Papers (zitiert als: FRUS): The Conferences of Malta and Yalta 1945; The Conference of Berlin (The Potsdam Conference) 1945. Vol. 1.2. Washington 1955.1960; Die Krim(Jalta)konferenz der höchsten Repräsentanten der drei alliierten Mächte – UdSSR, USA und Großbritannien (4.–11. Februar 1945). Dokumentensammlung; Die Potsdamer (Berliner) Konferenz der höchsten Repräsentanten der drei alliierten Mächte – UdSSR, USA und Großbritannien (17. Juli–2. August 1945). Dokumentensammlung. Moskau, Berlin 1986.

bulgarischer und jugoslawischer Quellenveröffentlichungen[27]); oder schließlich die Auseinandersetzungen in der „Allied Control Commission" (ACC) für Bulgarien 1944–1947 anhand amerikanischer und sowjetischer Quellen[28]). Und zweitens Einzelbeispiele aus der bulgarischen Geschichtswissenschaft, wichtige Quellen im Rahmen umfangreicher und respektabler Editionen zu übergehen, wodurch Lücken entstehen. Das beste Beispiel hierfür betrifft G. Dimitrov, dessen Rolle als international berühmter und anerkannter Führer der BKP im Prinzip selbstverständlich nicht im Geringsten angezweifelt wird. Dennoch sind die auf Jugoslawien bezogenen Passagen seines Rechenschaftsberichtes im Namen des ZK an den V. Parteitag der BKP vom 19.12.1948 – „Die Föderation der Südslawen und die makedonische Frage" – in der bulgarischen Ausgabe seiner Werke weggelassen worden[29]). Die DDR hat dies in ihrer Ausgabe der Werke Dimitrovs übernommen, und die neuere bulgarische Forschung stützt sich selbstverständlich nur auf diese Version[30]). Auffällig ist weiterhin z.B., daß in einer in allen sozialistischen Ländern gepflegten Ausgabe der Quellen zu den jeweiligen Beziehungen zur Sowjetunion im Band über die Stalinzeit die Aufnahme aller – wie stets zeitgeschichtlich höchst interessanten – Adressen und Stellungnahmen zum 70. Geburtstag Stalins (21.12.1949) und zu seinem Tod (5.3.1953) unterblieben ist[31]). Oder es sei als letztes darauf hingewiesen, daß in der Standardquellenedition zur bulgarischen Außenpolitik die Erörterung der bulgarisch-türkischen Spannungen von 1950–1953 ebenso fehlt wie die Texte der 12 wichtigen Verträge zwischen Bulgarien und Griechenland vom 9.7.1964 oder der Text des bulgarisch-türkischen Emigrationsvertrags vom 22.3.1968[32]).

b) Forschung

Vergleichbares gilt für die Forschung: Es ist eine Fülle an Veröffentlichungen zum Sowjetblock im allgemeinen und zur bulgarischen Außenpolitik im besonderen erschienen, so daß zunächst einmal von der Quantität her keine Schwierigkeiten einer Bearbeitung entgegenstehen. Methodisch ergeben sich dieselben Probleme wie bei den Quellen: Es ist zwischen der bulgarischen und der eng mit ihr verbundenen sowje-

---

[27]) VPB. 1. 1944–1962. 1970; Petranović, B.; Zečević, M.: Jugoslavija 1918–1984. Zbirka dokumenata (Jugoslawien 1918–1984. Dokumentensammlung). Belgrad 1985; From recognition to repudiation (Bulgarian attitude on the Macedonian question). Articles, speeches, documents. Sel. and red. V. Čašule. Skopje 1972.

[28]) Boll, M.M.: The American Military Mission in the Allied Control Commission for Bulgaria, 1944–1947: History and Transcripts. Boulder, Co., New York 1985; Birjuzov, S.S.: Sovetskij soldat na Balkanach (Als sowjetischer Soldat auf dem Balkan). Moskau 1963.

[29]) Peti kongres na Bălgarskata komunističeskata partija. 18–25 dekemvri 1948 g. Stenografski protokol, č.1. (V. Parteitag der BKP. 18.–25.12.1948. Stenographisches Protokoll, Teil 1). Sofia 1949, S. 184/85 und 187–196; Dimitrov, G.: Săčinenija (Werke). T. 14. Sofia 1955, S. 221–340.

[30]) Dimitroff (Anm. 7), S. 525–642; Dobrinov, D.: Jugoslavskata istoriografija za Georgi Dimitrov, makedonski văpros i bălgaro-jugoslavskite otnošenija (1944–1948 g.) (Die jugoslawische Historiographie über Georgi Dimitrov, die makedonische Frage und die bulgarisch-jugoslawischen Beziehungen (1944–1948)), in: Istoričeski pregled. 39 (1983) 5, S. 105–16.

[31]) Sovetsko-bolgarskie otnošenija 1948–1970. Dokumenty i materialy (Die sowjetisch-bulgarischen Beziehungen 1948–1970. Dokumente und Materialien). Moskau 1970. (Parallelausgabe auf bulgarisch).

[32]) VPB. 1.2. Sofia 1970/71.

tischen sowie der übrigen Ostblockforschung auf der einen Seite sowie der westlichen auf der anderen zu unterscheiden. Interessante Aspekte kommen auch hier durch die jugoslawische Forschung hinzu. Was Standardwerke der westlichen Forschung betrifft, so sei zusätzlich zu den schon genannten (Anm. 6) noch auf L. A. D. Dellin, Zb. K. Brzezinski, P. Lendvai, R. L. Wolff, H. Hartl, B. Jelavich und H. Seton-Watson[33]) verwiesen. Unersetzlich sind ferner die laufend veröffentlichten Analysen durch *Radio Free Europe* sowie in den beiden Zeitschriften *Südosteuropa* und *Südosteuropa-Mitteilungen*[34]). Als Beispiel für eindringende Einzeluntersuchungen sei neben der bereits zitierten Arbeit von S. Troebst über den Makedonien-Konflikt nur je eine amerikanische und eine deutsche erwähnt, beide über die Außenpolitik der ersten Nachkriegsjahre[35]). Bulgarische, jugoslawische und sowjetische Veröffentlichungen kommen hinzu, um speziell diesen Zeitraum methodisch besonders interessant zu machen[36]). Mit unterschiedlicher Intensität gilt Ähnliches für die sich anschließenden Perioden der bulgarischen Nachkriegsaußenpolitik, wobei an dieser Stelle nur auf den folgenden Hauptteil II mit seinen Literaturangaben verwiesen werden kann. Eine grundsätzliche Schwäche der bulgarischen wie der amerikanischen Forschung ist, daß sie die Ergebnisse der westeuropäischen Forschung zu wenig zur Kenntnis nimmt[37]). Unter systematischen Gesichtspunkten ist zunächst aber noch die Frage der Periodisierung der bulgarischen Außenpolitik ebenso wie bei der Darstellung in den bisherigen Bänden des „Südosteuropa-Handbuchs" zu beantworten.

---

[33]) Bulgaria. L. A. D. Dellin, Ed. New York 1957 (East-Central Europe under the Communists); Brzezinski, Z. K.: The Soviet Block. Unity and Conflict. Rev. and enlarg. ed. Cambridge, Mass. 1967; Lendvai, P.: Der Rote Balkan zwischen Nationalismus und Kommunismus. Frankfurt a. M. 1969; Wolff, R. L.: The Balkans in our time. Cambridge, Mass. 1974; Hartl, H.: Der „einige" und „unabhängige" Balkan. Zur Geschichte einer politischen Vision. München 1977; Jelavich, B.: History of the Balkans. Twentieth Century. Vol. 2. Cambridge u. a. 1984; Seton-Watson, H.: The East European Revolution. Boulder and London 1985.

[34]) Südosteuropa (früher: Wissenschaftlicher Dienst Südosteuropa). Monatsschrift der Abteilung Gegenwartsforschung des Südost-Instituts (München). 1 (1952) ff; Südosteuropa-Mitteilungen. Vierteljahresschrift der Südosteuropa-Gesellschaft (München). 1 (1961) ff.

[35]) Boll, M. M.: Cold War in the Balkans. American Foreign Policy and the Emergence of Communist Bulgaria, 1943–1947. Lexington, Ken. 1984; Hatschikjan, M. A.: Tradition und Neuorientierung in der bulgarischen Außenpolitik 1944–1948 – Die „nationale" Außenpolitik der Bulgarischen Arbeiterpartei (Kommunisten). München 1988.

[36]) Meždunarodni otnošenija i vănšna politika na Bălgarija sled Vtorata svetovna vojna (Internationale Beziehungen und Außenpolitik Bulgariens nach dem II. Weltkrieg). Sofia 1982; Balkanite i meždunarodni otnošenija 1944–1948 (Der Balkan und die internationalen Beziehungen 1944–1948). Sofia 1984; Jugoslovensko-bugarski odnosi u XX veku (Die jugoslawisch-bulgarischen Beziehungen im 20. Jh.). T. 1, Belgrad 1980 ff. (dazu eine Besprechung von bulgarischer Seite in: Istoričeski pregled. 43 (1987) 8, S. 99–103); Razvoj na SR Makedonija 1945–1984 (Die Entwicklung der Sozialistischen Republik Makedonien 1945–1984). Skopje 1986; Žignja, K. L.: Imperialističeskaja politika SŠA i Velikobritanii v otnošenii Bolgarii i Rumynii (1944–1947 gg.) (Die imperialistische Politik der USA und Großbritanniens gegenüber Bulgarien und Rumänien (1944–1947). Kišinev 1987.

[37]) Vgl. z. B. das wissenschaftlich anspruchsvolle Werk von Grigorova, Z.: Balkanskata politika na socialističeska Bălgarija 1944–1970 (Die Balkanpolitik des sozialistischen Bulgarien 1944–1970). Sofia 1985.

4. Periodisierung

Die Frage der Periodisierung ist aus drei Gründen im Rahmen systematischer Vorüberlegungen wichtig. Zunächst gibt die Periodisierung den Schlüssel an die Hand, um einen gegebenen ereignisgeschichtlichen Zusammenhang wie die bulgarische Außenpolitik seit dem Ende des II. Weltkrieges in Sinnzusammenhänge zu teilen, wodurch der Gesamtverlauf leichter verständlich werden sollte. Zweitens kann auf diese Weise die in Politik- wie Geschichtswissenschaft diskutierte Frage nach dem Verhältnis von Außen- und Innenpolitik[38] anhand eines Beispieles aus der Praxis erneut überprüft werden, und zwar nicht nur für Bulgarien allein, sondern nach Möglichkeit erneut mit Blick auf die anderen Länder Südosteuropas, wie sie bislang bereits im Rahmen des „Südosteuropa-Handbuchs" behandelt worden sind. Verbunden sollte dies wie schon früher mit der Frage sein, ob eine Typologie der Zuordnung zu gewinnen ist. Und schließlich sollte das Augenmerk darauf gerichtet werden, ob es ein Schema für die außenpolitische Entwicklung der Länder des Sowjetblocks seit 1944/45 gibt, in das dann auch die bulgarische Außenpolitik eingeordnet werden könnte.

Um mit dem letzteren, einer allgemeinen Periodisierung der Geschichte des Sowjetblocks, zu beginnen, so ist in der westlichen Forschung in nicht überraschender Weise Übereinstimmung, aber auch Unterschiedlichkeit festzustellen. Übereinstimmung herrscht für die drei ersten Perioden: erstens die Phase der „Sowjetisierung"[39], d. h. der Errichtung volksdemokratischer Regime unter Einschluß der Außenpolitik. Als zeitlicher Beginn gilt das Ende des II. Weltkrieges und die Ansätze der neuen politischen Systeme, also 1944/45, als Ende innenpolitisch in der Regel die endgültige Beseitigung von Opposition sowie der Erlaß einer neuen Verfassung, außenpolitisch die Ablehnung der Teilnahme am Marshallplan (Juli 1947), die Gründung des Kominform (September 1947), der Abschluß der „ersten Generation" bilateraler Verträge zwischen den Blockstaaten 1947–1949[40] und schließlich die Gründung des RGW am 25.1.1949[41]). Auch über die zweite Phase herrscht Einigkeit: Es ist die sich anschließende Zeit uneingeschränkter Herrschaft Stalins über sein Imperium 1949–1953. Und auch für die folgende dritte Phase des sog. Neuen Kurses oder des Tauwetters besteht kein Zweifel. Gemeint sind die Jahre bis zum XX. Parteitag der KPdSU (14.–25.2.1956) und den sich daraus ergebenden dramatischen Ereignissen des Jahres 1956 bis zum ungarischen Volksaufstand (23.10.–4.11.1956), die mit der

---

[38]) Krippendorf, E.: Ist Außenpolitik Außenpolitik?, in: Politische Vierteljahresschrift. 4 (1963), S. 243–66; Czempiel, E.O.: Das Primat der auswärtigen Politik. Kritische Würdigung einer Staatsmaxime, ebenda, S. 266–87.

[39]) Außer der in den Anm. 6 u. 33 genannten Literatur s. Grothusen, K.-D.: Zur „Sowjetisierung" der bulgarischen Außenpolitik nach dem Zweiten Weltkrieg, in: Kulturelle Traditionen in Bulgarien. Hrsg. v. R. Lauer. Göttingen 1989, S. 317–331. Außerdem von seiten der DDR: Entscheidungen in Europa zur Zeit der volksdemokratischen Revolutionen 1943–1948. Berlin (Ost) 1984 (Jahrbuch für Geschichte. 30); Befreiung und Beginn der revolutionären Umgestaltung in Mittel- und Südosteuropa. Hrsg. v. E. Donnert. Halle (Saale) 1987 (Beiträge zur Geschichte der UdSSR. 15).

[40]) Für die Vertragstexte s. Meissner, B.: Das Ostpakt-System. Dokumentensammlung. Frankfurt a.M., Berlin 1955; sowie: Uschakow (Anm. 3).

[41]) Meissner (Anm. 40), S. 108/09.

Erklärung der Sowjetregierung vom 30.10.1956 – einem Vorgriff auf die Brežnev-Doktrin von 1968 – und der Niederschlagung des Volksaufstandes ihren Abschluß fanden[42]. Von da an gehen die Periodisierungsbemühungen der westlichen Forschung verständlicherweise auseinander, weil jedes Land des Sowjetblocks innerhalb des Sozialistischen Internationalismus unterschiedliche Wege gegangen ist. Einigkeit besteht erst wieder in der Bewertung der *perestrojka* von 1985 an als einschneidender Zäsur mit dem Epochenjahr 1989 als vorläufiger Akme, hinter die es kein Zurück mehr geben kann. Aus dem Rahmen dieser Überlegungen fällt G. Stökl, der speziell die sowjetische Entwicklung nach den leitenden Staatsmännern gliedert – Stalin, Chruščev, Brežnev[43] –, was insofern erwähnenswert ist, weil auch im Falle Bulgariens die Versuchung nahe liegen könnte, ebenso zu verfahren und von drei personengebundenen Phasen auszugehen: Dimitrov (1944–1949), Červenkov (1950–1954/56), Živkov (1954/56–1989)[44].

Die östliche Forschung hat es hier einfacher, wobei jedoch etwas anderes auffällig ist: Nach der ebenfalls vorbehaltlos akzeptierten Phase der Jahre 1944/45–1947/49 ist lange Zeit vermieden worden, die Stalinzeit als eigene Phase anzuerkennen (es wird allenfalls von der „Phase des Personenkults" gesprochen). Stattdessen fällt die nächste Zäsur gleich in die Jahre 1956/58[45]. Eine zögernde Neueinschätzung läßt sich weiterhin mit dem Beginn der *perestrojka* in der Sowjetunion, also von 1985 an, feststellen. Nennenswertes für die Zeit seit dem Sturz Živkovs am 10.11.1989 liegt in scharfem Gegensatz zur Innenpolitik für den Bereich der Außenpolitik noch nicht vor.

Für die westliche Forschung dürfte es auch im Falle Bulgariens richtig sein, von typologischen Überlegungen auszugehen. Das Ergebnis sind fünf Phasen der bulgarischen Nachkriegsaußenpolitik, von denen die beiden ersten problemlos im Sinne des oben Gesagten abgrenzbar sind: die Phase der „Sowjetisierung" und die Stalinzeit. Was die Phase der „Sowjetisierung" betrifft, so sind sich westliche wie bulgarische Forschung in ihrer Abgrenzung einig[46]: Ausgangspunkt für die bulgarische Außen- wie Innenpolitik hat der Staatsstreich vom 9.9.1944 zu sein. Für die Außenpolitik sind weiter zu nennen: die Kriegserklärung der Sowjetunion an Bulgarien vom 5.9.1944, die Kriegserklärung Bulgariens an Deutschland vom 8.9.1944 und das „Prozentabkommen" Churchill – Stalin vom 9.10.1944, in dem die Sowjetunion ein Einflußrecht von 75% auf Bulgarien erhielt. Einigkeit besteht auch darin, daß sich

---

[42]) Für die Erklärung vom 30.10.1956 s. Pravda. 30.10.1956; für die Brežnev-Doktrin: Meissner, B.: Die „Breshnew-Doktrin". Dokumentation. Köln 1969; für den ungarischen Volksaufstand: Südosteuropa-Handbuch. Bd. V: Ungarn. Göttingen 1987, S. 90–93 u. 129–34.

[43]) Stökl, G.: Russische Geschichte von den Anfängen bis zur Gegenwart. 4., erw. Aufl. Stuttgart 1983, S. 704–832.

[44]) Ansätze bei: Bell, J.D.: The Bulgarian Communist Party from Blagoev to Zhivkov. Stanford, Calif. 1986, S. 125–148; Crampton (Anm. 6), S. 166–99.

[45]) Außer den beiden bereits genannten Werken aus der DDR (Anm. 39) vgl.: Geschichte der sozialistischen Gemeinschaft. Von einem Autorenkollektiv unter Leitung v. E. Kalbe. Berlin (Ost) 1981, S. 195–290; Geschichte der Bulgarischen Kommunistischen Partei. Sofia 1986, S. 204–69.

[46]) Vgl. die Literatur in den Anm. 33, 35 u. 39 sowie auch: Nakov, A.: Etapi v razvitieto na vănšnopolitičeskite otnošenija meždu Bălgarija i Săvetskija săjuz (Die Etappen in der Entwicklung der außenpolitischen Beziehungen zwischen Bulgarien und der Sowjetunion), in: Istoričeski pregled. 43 (1987) 11, S. 17–28.

das Ende dieser Phase über einen längeren Zeitraum hinzieht: von der Unterzeichnung des Pariser Friedensvertrages (10.2.1947) über die Absage an die Pariser Marshall-Plan-Konferenz (8.7.1947), die Teilnahme an der Gründung des Kominform (22.–27.9.1947) und am Kominformbruch 1948 mit Jugoslawien samt der damit verbundenen Beendigung der wichtigen Föderationspläne bis zum Abschluß der bilateralen Verträge über Freundschaft, Kooperation und gegenseitigen Beistand mit den anderen Ländern des Sowjetblocks 1948 (vor allem mit der Sowjetunion am 18.3.1948) und als multilateraler Abschluß die Teilnahme an der Gründung des RGW (25.1.1949).

Es folgt als zweite Phase die Stalinzeit von 1947/49 bis 1953, die sich für die bulgarische Außenpolitik nicht zufällig als besonders ereignislos erweist. Ungleich interessanter ist dafür die sich anschließende dritte Phase des Neuen Kurses, dessen Beginn wie in den anderen Ländern des Sowjetblocks in die Jahre 1953–1956 fällt. Schwieriger ist es jedoch, ein Ende in außenpolitischer Hinsicht zu finden. Wenn es richtig ist, die Überwindung des Kalten Krieges bzw. die Normalisierung eingefrorener Beziehungen als Maßstab zu nehmen, muß diese Phase bis 1964/68 gerechnet werden: am 6.3.1964 Abkommen über Waren- und Zahlungsverkehr sowie die Errichtung von Handelsvertretungen mit der Bundesrepublik Deutschland, am 9.7.1964 der schon erwähnte Abschluß von 12 Verträgen mit Griechenland, vom 22.–27.9.1965 der erste Besuch Titos in Bulgarien seit 1947 und schließlich das Repatriierungsabkommen mit der Türkei vom 22.3.1968 (ratifiziert am 19.8.1969). Die bulgarische Geschichtswissenschaft ergänzt diese Eingrenzung noch durch den besonderen Hinweis auf den Vertrag mit der Sowjetunion vom 12.5.1967, nach westlicher Zählung also mit dem Beginn der zweiten Etappe im Paktsystem[47]). Wie jedoch gerade das Beispiel Jugoslawiens zeigt, wo es 1968 zur nächsten großen Krise in den Beziehungen kam, fällt es schwer, hier zu allgemeingültigen Aussagen zu kommen. Immerhin erscheint es möglich, vom Abschluß des Prozesses der außenpolitischen Normalisierung Mitte der 60er Jahre an von einer vierten Phase zu sprechen, die unter den allgemeinen Vorzeichen von Sozialistischem Internationalismus für den Bereich der sozialistischen Länder und Friedlicher Koexistenz für den Westen steht. Ausgehend vom Beginn der *perestrojka* in der Sowjetunion 1985, bildet der Umsturz in Bulgarien vom 10.11.1989 an dann ohne Zweifel den Beginn einer fünften und letzten Phase, auch wenn diese im Bereich der Außenpolitik in deutlichem Gegensatz zur Innenpolitik bis Ende 1989 weder praktisch oder auch nur programmatisch für die nähere Zukunft eine klar faßbare Gestalt gewonnen hätte.

Was als letztes die Frage einer Zuordnung von Außen- und Innenpolitik angeht, so kann als Ergebnis der früheren Bände des „Südosteuropa-Handbuchs" festgestellt werden, daß diese im Falle der Türkei unmöglich, für Griechenland und Ungarn dagegen durchaus möglich war[48]). Was Bulgarien betrifft, so zeigt ein Vergleich der Kapitel über Außen- und Innenpolitik, daß auch hier die Vergleichsmöglichkeiten

---

[47]) Nakov (Anm. 46), S. 21; Meissner, B.: Die zwei Kreise des sowjetischen Bündnissystems, in: Löwenthal, R.; Meissner, B. (Anm. 5), S. 59–61.

[48]) Vgl. die Kapitel „Außen-" und „Innenpolitik" in den Bänden III–V des „Südosteuropa-Handbuchs". Göttingen 1980–1987.

durchaus überwiegen⁴⁹). Die Idee, zu einer Typologie zu kommen, erscheint demnach nicht ohne Hoffnung.

II. Darstellender Teil

1. Voraussetzungen

Um die bulgarische Außenpolitik vom 9.9.1944 an bis heute in ihrem eigensten Umfeld, als Regionalpolitik auf dem Balkan, aber auch darüber hinaus im weiteren Bereich der internationalen Politik zu verstehen, sind in Anwendung der im vorangehenden Teil vorgetragenen systematischen Überlegungen zwei Aspekte seit der Wiedererrichtung des bulgarischen Staates durch die Verträge von San Stefano (3.3.1878) und Berlin (13.7.1878)⁵⁰) von Bedeutung: einmal das allen jungen europäischen Nationalstaaten des 19. Jh. gemeinsame Ziel der Vereinigung aller Angehörigen der Nation im eigenen Staat und dann die Einsicht in die Notwendigkeit, daß die kleineren der neuen Staaten gerade dieses Ziel nicht ohne die Hilfe einer der Großmächte zu erreichen imstande waren. Die Begründung hierfür ist, daß das nationale Ziel der Vereinigung aller Nationsangehörigen unausweichlich zu territorialen Auseinandersetzungen mit den Nachbarn führen mußte, die dasselbe Ziel, nur in umgekehrter Richtung, verfolgten. Wenn dann noch hinzukommt, daß der Begriff „Nation" noch bis ins 20. Jh. hinein oftmals nur schwer in der politischen Realität zu definieren war⁵¹), ist die Grundlage für ein Verständnis auch der Balkangeschichte jener Zeit gegeben, die gerade deswegen sehr zu Unrecht die Bezeichnung des „Pulverfasses Europas" erhalten hat.

Für die außenpolitischen Probleme Bulgariens sind auch heute noch an erster Stelle drei geographische Begriffe unabdingbar: Makedonien, Thrakien und die Dobrudscha (vgl. die beigefügten Karten S. 98 und 99). Erwerb oder Verlust dieser Gebiete mußten identisch sein mit dem politischen Verhältnis zum westlichen Nachbarn Serbien (bis 1918) bzw. Jugoslawien (ab 1918), zum südlichen Nachbarn Griechenland und zum nördlichen Rumänien. Außenpolitische Wünsche und durch die Großmächte diktierte Realität verbinden sich aus bulgarischer Sicht dabei nach wie vor mit den Grenzen von San Stefano und Berlin mit dem Ergebnis, daß im wesentlichen nur die „kleinbulgarische" Lösung hat erzielt werden können. Von Makedonien, das durch den Frieden von Bukarest (10.8.1913)⁵²) in die drei ungleichen Teile Vardar-, Ägäisch- und Pirin-Makedonien geteilt wurde, konnte Bulgarien nur das kleine Pirin-Makedonien erwerben, ohne den Anspruch auf das ganze Gebiet aufzu-

---

⁴⁹) Vgl. das Kapitel „Domestic Politics" von J.D. Bell.
⁵⁰) Ausgewählte diplomatische Aktenstücke zur orientalischen Frage. Zsgest. u. erl. v. K. Strupp. Gotha 1916, S. 118–26 u. 139–61.
⁵¹) Reiter, N.: Gruppe, Sprache, Nation. Wiesbaden 1984 (Balkanologische Veröffentlichungen. 9.); Winkler, H.A.: Nationalismus. 2. Aufl. Königstein/Ts. 1985.
⁵²) Strupp (Anm. 50), S. 281–85.

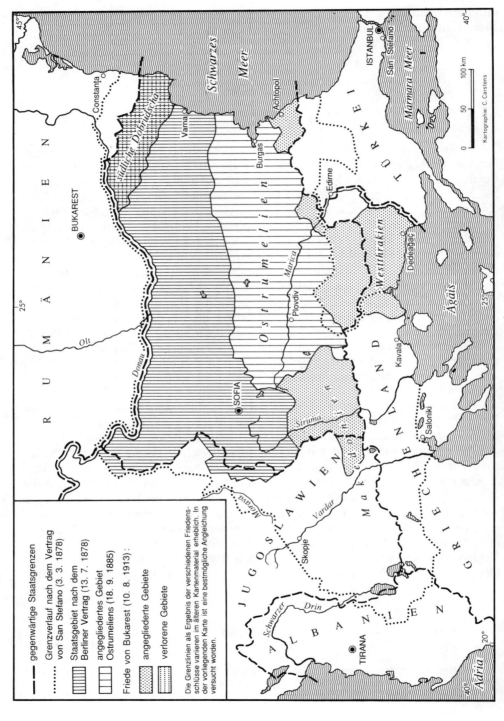

Karte I: Bulgariens territoriale Entwicklung 1878–1913.

Außenpolitik

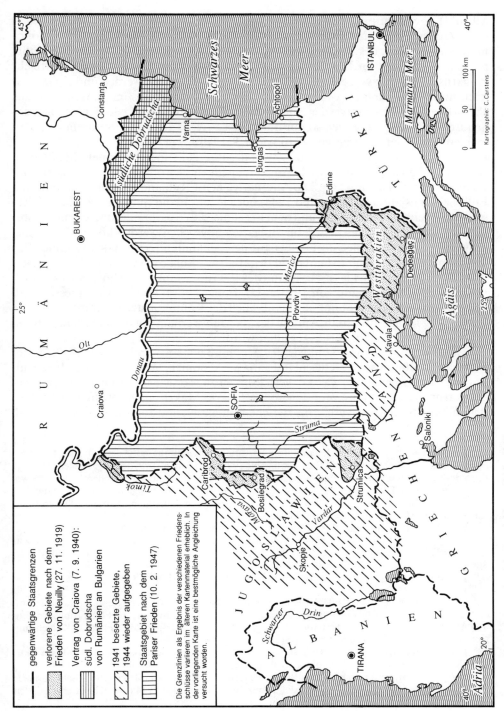

Karte II: Bulgariens territoriale Entwicklung 1919–1947.

geben[53]). Wenn im Falle Makedoniens bis heute Grundfragen der mittelalterlichen bulgarischen Geschichte mit angesprochen sind, so war mit Thrakien auch das ökonomische Problem des Zugangs zur Ägäis stets mitbestimmend. Dieses Ziel mußte mit der Niederlage im I. Weltkrieg als Verbündeter Deutschlands und Österreich-Ungarns im Vertrag von Neuilly (27.11.1919)[54]) aufgegeben werden und erwies sich auch im zweiten Anlauf, wiederum im Gefolge Deutschlands im II. Weltkrieg, als ebenso wenig erreichbar wie der erneute Zugriff auf Vardar-Makedonien[55]). Bleibenden Erfolg konnte Bulgarien so nur durch den Erwerb der Süddobrudscha von Rumänien durch den Vertrag von Craiova (7.9.1940)[56]) erzielen.

Auch der andere grundsätzliche Aspekt der Politik kleinerer europäischer Staaten ist damit schon angesprochen: die Anlehnung an eine Großmacht. Das Ergebnis im Falle Bulgariens ist eindeutig: Die Alternative heißt Rußland/Sowjetunion (mit den Entscheidungsjahren 1877/78 und 1944) oder Deutschland (mit der „Waffenbrüderschaft" in beiden Weltkriegen) und dem Ergebnis, daß Russophilie und Germanophilie nach wie vor als Konstanten für Bulgarien angesehen werden können[57]). Umso schwieriger gestaltete sich dafür stets aus den genannten territorialen Gründen das Verhältnis zu den Nachbarstaaten auf dem Balkan: Bulgarien war wie Ungarn in der Zwischenkriegszeit ein klassisches Land des Revisionismus und gehörte so denn auch nicht der Kleinen Entente von 1933 an[58]). Immerhin sei aber nicht vergessen, daß sowohl von der Seite A. Stambolijskis als auch der Kommunisten unter maßgeblicher Beteiligung Dimitrovs bereits Anfang der 20er Jahre erneut auf die alten Balkanföderationspläne des 19. Jh. zurückgegriffen wurde[59]).

Der II. Weltkrieg wirkt dann wie der Abschluß der Entwicklung seit 1877/78: der Versuch, im Bündnis mit Deutschland ganz Makedonien, Westthrakien und die Süddobrudscha zu gewinnen, was das Verhältnis zu Jugoslawien, Griechenland und Rumänien notwendigerweise vergiften mußte[60]). Was Makedonien betrifft, so ist außerdem für das Nachkriegsverhältnis zwischen Bulgarien und Jugoslawien wichtig, daß

---

[53]) Außer dem Kapitel von R.J. Crampton: Historical Foundations vgl. Adanir, F.: Die Makedonische Frage. Ihre Entstehung und Entwicklung bis 1908. Wiesbaden 1979; de Jong, J.: Der nationale Kern des makedonischen Problems. Ansätze und Grundlagen einer makedonischen Nationalbewegung (1890–1903). Frankfurt a.M., Bern 1982; oder sehr typisch von jugoslawischer Seite: Stefanović, M.; Krstić M.; Apostolski, M.: Velikobugarske pretenzije od San Stefana do danas (Die großbulgarischen Ansprüche von San Stefano bis heute). Belgrad 1978.

[54]) Nouveau Recueil Général de Traités. Troisième ser. 12. Leipzig 1924, S. 323–423.

[55]) Hoppe, H.J.: Bulgarien – Hitlers eigenwilliger Verbündeter. Eine Fallstudie zur nationalsozialistischen Südosteuropapolitik. Stuttgart 1979; Miller, M.L.: Bulgaria during the Second World War. Stanford, Calif. 1975.

[56]) Bruns, U. (Hrsg.): Politische Verträge. 3,2. Berlin 1942, S. 1247–76.

[57]) s.o. S. 87/88.

[58]) Sundhaussen, H.: Die Rolle der Kleinen Entente bei der Stabilisierung und Destabilisierung des Friedens im Donau-Balkan-Raum, in: Friedenssicherung in Südosteuropa. Föderationsprojekte und Allianzen seit dem Beginn der nationalen Eigenstaatlichkeit. Hrsg. v. M. Bernath u. K. Nehring. Neuried 1985, S. 139–54 (Südosteuropa-Studien 34.).

[59]) Außer Hartl (Anm. 33) s.a. Helmstaedt, A.: Die kommunistische Balkanföderation im Rahmen der sowjetrussischen Balkanpolitik zu Beginn der zwanziger Jahre. Bd. 1. Berlin 1976.

[60]) Vgl. z.B. Mitrovski, B. u.a.: Das Bulgarische Heer in Jugoslawien 1941–1945. Belgrad 1971; Živković, N.: Ratna šteta koju je Bugarska učinila Jugoslaviji 1941–1944 (Der Kriegsschaden, den Bulgarien Jugoslawien 1941–1944 verursacht hat). Belgrad 1985.

es auch zwischen BKP und KPJ zu scharfen Auseinandersetzungen kam, die erst nach Anrufung der Komintern und Stalins zugunsten der Jugoslawen entschieden wurden[61]). Bezeichnend ist ferner, daß Zar Boris durchaus bemüht war, im Gegensatz zu Ungarn und Rumänien zumindest den Krieg mit der Sowjetunion zu vermeiden. Nachdem Bulgarien England und den USA bereits am 13.12.1941 den Krieg erklärt hatte, folgte mit der Kriegserklärung der Sowjetunion an Bulgarien vom 5.9.1944 und Bulgariens an Deutschland vom 8.9.1944 kurz vor dem Staatsstreich vom 9.9.1944 noch die absurde Situation, daß sich Bulgarien im Gefolge einer ohnehin chancenlosen Außenpolitik mit beiden kriegführenden Seiten im Kriege befand.

2. Die „Sowjetisierung" (1944–1947/49)

Wie bereits im Zusammenhang des allgemeinen Periodisierungsproblems ausgeführt (I, 4), besteht in der westlichen wie der östlichen Forschung Einigkeit darüber, daß die Jahre von 1944–1947/49 für Ostmittel- und Südosteuropa als deutlich abgrenzbare eigene Phase zu verstehen sind. Zeitlich ist für Bulgarien von dem relativ engen zeitlichen Umfeld vom 5.9.1944 (Kriegserklärung der Sowjetunion), 8.9. (Kriegserklärung an Deutschland), 9.9. (Staatsstreich), 9.10. (Prozentabkommen Churchill – Stalin) bis zum 28.10. (Moskauer Waffenstillstandsvertrag) auszugehen. Den Abschluß bildet wie im Falle Ungarns und Rumäniens ein längerer Zeitraum: vom Pariser Friedensvertrag (10.2.1947) über die Absage an die Pariser Marshallplan-Konferenz (8.7.1947), die Gründung des Kominform (22.–27.9.1947), den Kominformbruch mit Jugoslawien 1948 bis zur ersten Etappe bilateraler Verträge zwischen den Staaten des sich bildenden „Sozialistischen Weltsystems" ebenfalls 1948 und der Gründung des RGW (25.1.1949).

Inhaltlich ist diese Phase die wichtigste in der bulgarischen Nachkriegsaußenpolitik: Ob „Sowjetisierung" genannt oder Aufbau des Sozialistischen Weltsystems[62]), unbestritten ist, daß hier mit dem abrupten Wechsel der Hegemonialmacht von Deutschland zur Sowjetunion eine bis heute unvermindert fortbestehende, grundsätzliche außen- (und innen-) politische Umorientierung eingetreten ist. Zwei Aspekte haben dabei grundsätzliche Bedeutung: einmal, daß der Primat der Außenpolitik[63]) für diese Jahre unbestreitbar ist, und dann ein für alle der „Sowjetisierung" verfallenden Länder erstaunlicher Gegensatz zwischen formaler und realer außenpolitischer Souveränität. Formal gab es bis zum Friedensvertrag nur eine stark eingeschränkte Souveränität, real hörte diese gerade danach in der Hochzeit des stalinistischen Imperial- und Satellitensystems auf[64]). Hatschikjan spricht so für diese Jahre mit einigem Recht für Bulgarien von der Zeit „nationaler Außenpolitik"[65]).

Was die Rangfolge der außenpolitischen Probleme betrifft, so ist zunächst auf das Verhältnis zu den Großmächten Sowjetunion, England und USA einzugehen sowie

---
[61]) Petranović, B.; Zečević, M. (Anm. 27), S. 513–561 passim.
[62]) Vgl. die Literatur in Anm. 39.
[63]) s.o. S. 96.
[64]) Für den Gesamtzusammenhang von „Sowjetisierung" und Stalinzeit vgl. die Literatur in den Anm. 5 u. 6.
[65]) Hatschikjan (Anm. 35).

auf den Pariser Friedensvertrag, dann als hervorragende Problemfelder der Regionalpolitik auf die Beziehungen zu Jugoslawien und Griechenland.

Weitaus an erster Stelle steht dabei selbstverständlich das Verhältnis zur *Sowjetunion*, denn diese war es, die direkt und unmittelbar die Ursache für die völlige Umorientierung der bulgarischen Außen- und Innenpolitik bildete. Ein Blick auf die sowjetische Seite ist insofern erforderlich, der lehrt, daß eine erstaunliche Linie der Kontinuität von San Stefano über die Molotov-Gespräche in Berlin (12./13.11.1940) und das Prozentabkommen Churchill – Stalin (9.10.1944), in dem die Sowjetunion 75% des Einflusses auf Bulgarien erhielt, bis zur Gründung des RGW (25.1.1949) führt und deren Ergebnis die vollständige Einbindung Bulgariens in den sowjetischen Einflußbereich war. Es ist beeindruckend zu sehen, mit welcher Konsequenz die Sowjetunion vor allem in Potsdam und auf den folgenden Außenministerkonferenzen die Anerkennung ihres neuen Besitzstandes zu verteidigen wußte, dessen abschließende Anerkennung durch die Pariser Friedensverträge (10.2.1947) erfolgte[66].

Für unseren Zusammenhang ist dann allerdings als nächstes zu fragen, wie diese radikale Umstellung von bulgarischer Seite aus zu bewerten ist, ob ausgehend von dem Grundfaktum der Besetzung Bulgariens durch die Rote Armee (September 1944 – Dezember 1947) und der radikalen Umgestaltung der Innenpolitik jener Jahre[67] für die Außenpolitik von einer negativen Entwicklung zu sprechen ist. Bezeichnend für die bulgarische Bewertung ist, daß sich Dimitrovs zitierte Formulierung von 1943, daß die Freundschaft zur Sowjetunion für Bulgarien „nicht weniger notwendig [sei] als die Sonne und die Luft für jedes Lebewesen"[68], als Leitmotiv für sämtliche außenpolitischen Stellungnahmen von Partei und Regierung vom 9.9.1944 an erweist: Immer wird die Freundschaft zur Sowjetunion an die Spitze außenpolitischer Zielvorstellungen gestellt[69]. Auch von außen betrachtet ergibt sich dabei, daß die außenpolitische Hilfe der Sowjetunion gegen England und die USA im vehement ausbrechenden Kalten Krieg für Dimitrov nur willkommen sein konnte. Nicht nur die Verhandlungen der großen Konferenzen, sondern vor allem auch die Geschichte der ACC zeigt eindringlich, wie Interessen der bulgarischen Kommunisten ebenso wie eigene sowjetische von der Sowjetunion widerspruchsfrei vertreten werden konnten. Ein Beispiel für bulgarische Interessen ist die noch näher zu behandelnde Reparationsfrage, die schon im Waffenstillstandsvertrag angesprochen war, wenn auch ohne Festlegung von Summen[70]. Daß aber auch bei dieser Art der Interessenvertre-

---

[66] Für Quellen zu Potsdam s. Anm. 26; für die Außenministerkonferenzen: Byrnes, J.F.: Speaking Frankly. New York, London 1947; für die Friedensverträge: European Peace Treaties After World War II. Ed. by A.C. Leiss in coop. with R. Dennett. Worcester, Mass. 1954.

[67] Vgl. das Kapitel „Domestic Politics" von J.D. Bell, S. 56–66.

[68] s. Anm. 7.

[69] Proklamation der Regierung der OF vom 9.9.1944, Regierungsprogramm vom 17.9.1944 (VPB. 1.1970, S. 7–11), Rechenschaftsbericht Dimitrovs auf dem V. Parteitag der BKP (18.–25.12.1948) (Anm. 29, S. 176 und passim). – Daß die bulgarische Geschichtswissenschaft dieser Leitlinie folgt, ist selbstverständlich. Vgl. außer der Literatur in den Anm. 36 u. 37 z.B.: Emanuilov, E.G.: Potsdamskata konferencija 1945 g. i zaštita na nacionalnata nezavisimost na Bălgarija ot Săvetskija Săjuz (Die Potsdamer Konferenz des Jahres 1945 und die Verteidigung der nationalen Unabhängigkeit Bulgariens durch die Sowjetunion), in: Istoričeski pregled. 41 (1985) 12, S. 19–33.

[70] Für Quellen zur ACC vgl. Anm. 28, als Darstellungen: Boll (Anm. 35) u. Žignja (Anm. 36). Der Text des Waffenstillstandsvertrages findet sich bei Boll (Anm. 28), S. 323–28, für die Reparationen dort Art. 9.

tung keineswegs nur Erfolge erzielt wurden, beweist der Rückzug der bulgarischen Truppen aus Westthrakien ebenso wie das Scheitern der Föderationspläne mit Jugoslawien im Winter 1944/45. Und nicht zu übersehen ist schließlich auch, daß vom Standpunkt der BKP aus damals im Einzelfall Entscheidungen der Sowjetunion zu akzeptieren waren, die gegen bulgarische Interessen verstießen: ob es die verspätete Rückkehr Dimitrovs erst am 4.11.1945 oder vor allem die Ablehnung von Dimitrovs weitgespannten Föderationsplänen durch Stalin (18.1.1948) war[71]).

Davon abgesehen ist jedoch deutlich, daß Bulgarien vom 9.9.1944 an konsequent den Weg der Annäherung an die Sowjetunion gegangen ist. Hierher gehört auch die von beiden Seiten betriebene Teilnahme an der Schlußphase des II. Weltkrieges. Rund 340000 Mann bulgarischer Truppen haben auf diese Weise unter sowjetischem Kommando in Jugoslawien, Ungarn und Österreich gekämpft. Es ist fester Bestandteil des heutigen bulgarischen Geschichtsbildes, daß diese nach sowjetischem Vorbild „Vaterländischer Krieg" genannten Kämpfe mit der Zahl von 31910 Toten und Verwundeten für das Selbstverständnis der bulgarischen Außenpolitik außerordentlich bedeutsam sind[72]). Zu erwähnen ist allerdings auch, daß England und die USA sich trotzdem weigerten, Bulgarien als Alliierten anzuerkennen und daß vor allem bis heute scharfe Auseinandersetzungen mit Jugoslawien darüber bestehen, in welcher Funktion die bulgarischen Truppen damals in Jugoslawien kämpften: ob Jugoslawien die bulgarische Hilfe brauchte, um sich von den Deutschen zu befreien, oder ob Jugoslawien Bulgarien die Teilnahme an den Kämpfen als Beweis innerer Umkehr erlaubte, ohne selbst auf Hilfe angewiesen zu sein[73]).

Vom Kriegsende führt der Weg der Anbindung an die Sowjetunion über die Wiederaufnahme diplomatischer Beziehungen (16.8.1945) zum Vertrag über Freundschaft, Zusammenarbeit und gegenseitigen Beistand (18.3.1948), der das wichtigste Glied in der Kette bilateraler Verträge mit den anderen Staaten der sich bildenden Sozialistischen Gemeinschaft ist: Albanien (16.12.1947), Tschechoslowakei (23.4.1948), Polen (29.5.1948) und Ungarn (16.7.1948)[74]). Wenn es sich hierbei bewußt um bilaterale Verträge handelte, so brachten die Gründung des Kominform (22.–27.9.1947), die allgemeine Ablehnung der Teilnahme am Marshall-Plan (durch Bulgarien am 8.7.1947) mit dem sich anschließenden Weg zur Gründung des RGW (25.1.1949)[75]) auch multilaterale Bindungen. Und schließlich sollte in diesem Zu-

---

[71]) Für die Einzelheiten s.u. S. 107/08.

[72]) Aus der zahlreichen Literatur vgl. nur: Otečestvenata vojna na Bălgarija 1944–1945. Dokumenti, materiali (Der Vaterländische Krieg Bulgariens 1944–1945. Dokumente, Materialien). Bd. 1–. Sofia 1978 ff.

[73]) Für die bulgarische Auffassung außer Anm. 72 z. B. Borisov, G.: Bălgarskata narodna armija v Belgradskata operacija prez 1944 g. (Die bulgarische Volksarmee in der Belgrader Operation 1944), in: Istoričeski pregled. 43 (1987) 4, S. 44–53; für die jugoslawische Auffassung s. Mitrovski (Anm. 60), außerdem als gemeinschaftliche sowjetisch-jugoslawische Arbeit: Beogradska operacija (Die Operation Belgrad). Belgrad 1964.

[74]) Alle Vertragstexte bei Meissner (Anm. 40).

[75]) Texte zu Kominform und RGW bei Meissner (Anm. 40). Zum Kominform s. Artikel „Kominform", in: Sowjetsystem und demokratische Gesellschaft. Eine vergleichende Enzyklopädie. Bd. 3. Freiburg/Br. 1969, Sp. 709–14; Timmermann, H.: Das Kominform und seine Folgen in den sowjetischen Außenbeziehungen. Köln 1984 (Berichte des Bundesinstituts für ostwissenschaftliche und in-

sammenhang die Belgrader Donauschiffahrts-Konvention (18.8.1948) nicht vergessen werden, die die Konvention von 1921 ablöste und das Donauregime allein den Anrainern überantwortete, unter denen selbstverständlich auch die Sowjetunion (und die Ukraine) war[76]).

Wenn wir uns damit dem Verhältnis Bulgariens zu den *USA* und *England* zuwenden, so mutet es wie die Kehrseite ein und derselben Medaille an. Am Anfang, in den Regierungserklärungen vom 9. und 17.9.1944, werden die „großen westlichen Demokratien" und vor allem die „große amerikanische Republik" noch fast in einem Atemzug nach der „ewigen Freundschaft mit dem brüderlichen russischen Volk" genannt; im Dezember 1948, auf dem V. Parteitag der BKP, greift Dimitrov den US-amerikanischen Imperialismus gnadenlos an und wirft ihm vor, als direkter Nachfolger des Hitler-Regimes die imperialistische Weltherrschaft anzustreben, wofür Marshall-Plan und Truman-Doktrin nur äußere Zeichen seien[77]). Dazwischen liegt nicht nur die geschilderte Phase der außenpolitischen „Sowjetisierung" Bulgariens, sondern auch der vollen Entfaltung des Kalten Krieges in Südosteuropa. Und wenn von Griechenland abgesehen sei, wo der Kalte Krieg zum „heißen" Bürgerkrieg wurde, so kann kein Zweifel sein, daß Bulgarien hier weit z.B. vor Ungarn zu nennen ist. Ein gutes Merkzeichen ist, daß die USA die diplomatischen Beziehungen zu Ungarn schon im September 1945 wieder aufnahmen, zu Bulgarien dagegen erst am 1.10.1947.

Die bulgarische Politik dieser Jahre ist in diesem Zusammenhang allerdings weitaus weniger interessant als die amerikanische (sowie in geringerem Umfang die englische). Der Grund ist, daß nach dem Prozentabkommen Churchills mit Stalin mit seinem 75%-Anteil für die Sowjetunion auch durch den Waffenstillstandsvertrag vom 28.10.1944 der sowjetische Einfluß als Grundlage der weiteren Entwicklung eindeutig abgesteckt war. Artikel 18 des Vertrages legte – ebenso wie im ungarischen und rumänischen Vertrag – fest, daß für die ganze Periode des Waffenstillstandes die ACC „under the chairmanship of the representative of the Allied (Soviet) High Command" arbeiten solle[78]). Die Folge war, daß sich ein vollkommenes Zusammenspiel zwischen dem Vorsitzenden der ACC und Leiter der sowjetischen Mission, Generalmajor S.S. Birjuzov[79]), und der bulgarischen Regierung ergab, gegen das die amerikanischen und englischen Vertreter praktisch machtlos waren. Trotz dieser faktischen Machtlosigkeit haben sich die USA aber dennoch in erstaunlicher Weise bemüht, die rasch fortschreitende „Sowjetisierung" Bulgariens aufzuhalten. Lundestads These von der amerikanischen „Non-Policy"[80]) muß daher zumindest im Falle Bulgariens widersprochen werden, wofür eine Fülle aufschlußreichen Quellenmaterials vorliegt:

---

ternationale Studien (zitiert als BOIS) 8–1984); zum Marshallplan: Brabant, J.M.v.: Entstehung und Aufgabe des Rates für Gegenseitige Wirtschaftshilfe, in: Der Marshall-Plan und die europäische Linke. Hrsg. v. O.N. Haberl u. L. Niethammer. Frankfurt a.M. 1986, S. 552–74; sowie Kritika (Anm. 4).

[76]) United Nations Treaty Series (zit. als UNTS). 33 (1949), S. 182–225.
[77]) Für die Quellen s. Anm. 69.
[78]) Boll (Anm. 28), S. 328.
[79]) Für die verschiedenen Memoirenbände Birjuzovs vgl. z.B. Anm. 28.
[80]) Anm. 17.

von der Potsdamer Konferenz und den sich anschließenden Außenministerkonferenzen über die tägliche Arbeit in der ACC bis zu einer großen Zahl von Protestnoten[81]). Die Ablösung des englischen Engagements durch die USA läßt sich für Bulgarien in diesen Jahren damit ebenso feststellen wie im Falle Griechenlands und der Türkei. Nicht zufällig wird Bulgarien so denn auch in der Truman-Doktrin (12.3.1947) ausdrücklich als Land genannt, in dem das Jalta-Abkommen verletzt worden sei[82]).

Richtig ist allerdings auch, daß im perfekten Zusammenspiel zwischen bulgarischer und sowjetischer Regierung alle Bemühungen der USA zunichte gemacht wurden, Einfluß auf die bulgarische Entwicklung zu nehmen. Die diplomatische Anerkennung vom 1.10.1947, eine Woche nach der Hinrichtung N. Petkovs, bedeutet so die Kapitulation der USA gegenüber der bulgarischen Innenpolitik. Außenpolitisch setzten die USA ihren Widerstand jedoch fort, durchaus von England unterstützt. Das beste Beispiel hierfür ist, daß beide Länder nicht nur den von der Sowjetunion unterstützten Antrag Bulgariens auf Aufnahme in die UNO (26.7.1947) vom Oktober 1947 an bis 1955 nicht weniger als fünfmal ablehnen lassen konnten, sondern am 22.10.1949 auch über die UNO beim Internationalen Gerichtshof im Haag ein Verfahren gegen Bulgarien, Ungarn und Rumänien wegen Verletzung der Friedensverträge im Zusammenhang der Kominform-Prozesse und der Kirchenverfolgung anstrengten[83]). Im Falle Bulgariens konnte die internationale Aufmerksamkeit dadurch vor allem auf die Hinrichtung T. Kostovs (17.12.1949) gelenkt werden. Der Preis, den die USA zahlen mußten, war allerdings der Abbruch der diplomatischen Beziehungen zwischen dem 19.1. und dem 21.2.1950[84]). Am Ende der Phase der „Sowjetisierung" waren die Beziehungen zwischen Bulgarien und den USA damit auf dem Nullpunkt angekommen.

Davor lag aber noch als letztes wichtiges Ereignis nicht nur der bulgarischen Außen-, sondern auch Innenpolitik die Unterzeichnung des Pariser Friedensvertrages, der am selben 10.2.1947 unterzeichnet wurde wie die Friedensverträge für Italien, Ungarn, Rumänien und Finnland. Da er von allen drei Großmächten unterzeichnet wurde, liegt der Gedanke nahe, daß zumindest hier Einhelligkeit bestanden habe. Dies ist jedoch nur formal richtig. Wichtiger und richtiger ist die „tiefste Dankbarkeit", die Dimitrov auf dem II. Kongreß der OF (2./3.2.1948) in diesem Zusammenhang der Sowjetunion – „unserer zweifachen Befreierin und Beschützerin" – sowie im besonderen auch Jugoslawien aussprach[85]). Dies entspricht der einhelligen Meinung der heutigen bulgarischen Geschichtswissenschaft, die das günstige Ergebnis der Pa-

---

[81]) Die Quellenlage kann so nur als ungewöhnlich gut bezeichnet werden. Als Beispiele vgl. Anm. 26, 28 u. 66. Außerdem weiterführend Boll (Anm. 35).

[82]) Europa-Archiv. 2 (1947), S. 820.

[83]) Cour Internationale de Justice. Recueil des Arrêts, Avis Consultatifs et Ordonances. Compètence de l'Assemblée Générale pour l'admission d'un état aux Nations Unies. Avis consultatif du 3 mars 1950. Leyde 1950; Cour Internationale de Justice. Mémoire, plaidoiries et documents. Interpretation de traités de paix conclus avec Bulgarie, la Hongrie et la Roumanie. Avis consultatifs des 30 mars et 18 juillet 1950. Leyde 1950. – Vgl. auch das Kapitel von M. Pundeff: Churches and Religious Communities.

[84]) Alle Einzelheiten in: FRUS. 1950, 4. Washington 1980, S. 503–25.

[85]) Dimitroff (Anm. 7). Bd. 3, S. 449.

riser Verhandlungen ausschließlich der Sowjetunion zuschreibt[86]). Und auch die westliche Wissenschaft stimmt zu: Der Pariser Vertrag für Bulgarien ist günstiger als diejenigen für Ungarn und Rumänien und nur durch die Hilfe der Sowjetunion möglich gewesen[87]).

Dieses günstige Ergebnis – auch im Vergleich etwa mit Neuilly – läßt sich an mehreren Punkten des Vertrages verdeutlichen. Als erstes ist Artikel 1 zu nennen, der die Grenzen Bulgariens auf den 1.1.1941 festlegte, während es für Ungarn und Rumänien der 1.1.1938 war[88]). Der Grund war, daß Bulgarien auf diese Weise die Süddobrudscha im Sinne des Vertrages von Craiova (7.9.1940) behalten konnte. Daß weder Makedonien noch Westthrakien bzw. ein Ägäiszugang (letzterer trotz der Unterstützung durch die Sowjetunion und Bemühungen Dimitrovs) zu halten war, war dafür klar. Immerhin konnte sich Griechenland seinerseits nicht mit heftigen Forderungen nach Grenzkorrekturen durchsetzen. Als zweites ist Artikel 21 zu nennen, der die bulgarischen Reparationszahlungen auf 70 Mio. Dollar begrenzte (45 Mio. für Griechenland, 25 Mio. für Jugoslawien). Ungarn und Rumänien wurden zu je 300 Mio. Dollar verpflichtet. Wichtig für die spätere Entwicklung bis heute ist weiterhin Artikel 13, der Bulgarien den Besitz von Atomwaffen und Raketen verbot. Eingehalten wurde auch Artikel 20, der den Abzug aller fremden Truppen, d.h. der Roten Armee, innerhalb von 90 Tagen vorsah, während Artikel 9, der die Größe der bulgarischen Armee begrenzte, zum steten Ärger Griechenlands nicht eingehalten worden ist. Und schließlich erhielt Bulgarien durch den Pariser Vertrag seine volle Souveränität zurück, obwohl es für den Schwebezustand der Jahre davor spricht, daß die diplomatischen Beziehungen mit einer Reihe von Ländern schon vorher wieder aufgenommen worden waren, darunter Frankreich (19.10.1944) und Italien (3.1.1945).

Wenn mit dem Pariser Friedensvertrag ohne Zweifel ein wichtiger Markstein im Rahmen der Überwindung der Folgen des II. Weltkrieges und des Einbaus Bulgariens in den sowjetischen Herrschaftsverband erreicht ist, so bildet das Verhältnis zu *Jugoslawien* schon in jenen Jahren einen Sonderfall. Die unter I, 2 behandelte These, daß bulgarische Außenpolitik im Prinzip nur als Regionalpolitik eigene Akzente setze und darüber hinaus weit vor allen anderen Ländern des Sowjetblocks durch stabile und zuverlässige Zusammenarbeit mit der Sowjetunion gekennzeichnet sei, findet hier zum ersten Mal ihre Bestätigung. Ein bis heute in der Forschung umstrittenes Problem ist allerdings, inwieweit auch im Rahmen der Regionalpolitik die sowjetische Richtlinienkompetenz von Bulgarien bereitwillig anerkannt wird oder ob auch eigene politische Ziele verfolgt werden[89]).

---

[86]) Außer schon zitierter Literatur (Anm. 36. 46. 72) vgl. Nikolov, C.: Roljata na SSSR za sključ-vane na mirnija dogovor s Bălgarija (Die Rolle der UdSSR für den Abschluß des Friedensvertrages mit Bulgarien), in: Velikite sili i Balkanite v novo i naj-novo vreme (Die Großmächte und der Balkan in neuer und neuester Zeit). Sofia 1985, S. 282–89.

[87]) Hatschikjan (Anm. 35), S. 185, 225 und passim.

[88]) Für die Texte der Friedensverträge s. Anm. 66.

[89]) Grundsätzliche Überlegungen bei Lendvai, P.: Nationalismus in Ost- und Südosteuropa – Nicht nur Gefahr, sondern auch Stütze für die sowjetische Hegemonie, in: Nationalitätenprobleme in Südosteuropa. Hrsg. v. R. Schönfeld. München 1987, S. 33–38.

Unbestreitbar ist zunächst, daß von allen Balkanländern Jugoslawien seit dem Ende des II. Weltkriegs mit weitem Abstand am problematischsten für die bulgarische Außenpolitik gewesen ist, wenn von den Spannungen zur Türkei seit 1984 abgesehen wird. Dies ergibt sich zunächst aus dem zeitlichen Aspekt: Die Makedonien-Frage ist ohne Unterbrechung relevant geblieben. Hinzu kommt für die Jahre 1944 bis 1948 das Föderationsproblem mit Jugoslawien und seit dem Kominformkonflikt von 1948/49 für Bulgarien viel mehr als für Ungarn oder Rumänien die Aufgabe der „Vorhut" gegenüber dem „Spalter" der sozialistischen Einheit.

Auf die Voraussetzungen ist hingewiesen worden (I, 2 und II, 1): Gegensätze und Einheitsstreben sind für das bulgarisch-serbisch/jugoslawische Verhältnis seit 1877/78 charakteristisch. Im Zentrum der Probleme standen dabei stets die Föderationsfrage und das Schicksal Makedoniens (sowie der sog. bulgarischen Westgebiete, kleiner Enklaven im Grenzgebiet zu Serbien). Auf der Grundlage von Dimitrovs Föderationsplänen der 20er Jahre und Titos klarer Entscheidung für eine eigene makedonische Republik im Rahmen des föderativen Staatsaufbaus des neuen Jugoslawien (II. AVNOJ-Konferenz 29./30.11.1943) waren die Weichen für die Nachkriegszeit gestellt: Föderation von Bulgarien und Jugoslawien (wobei als Frage nur auftauchte, ob als Föderation von zwei Staaten oder mit Bulgarien nur als 7. Teilrepublik Jugoslawiens neben den 6 anderen) und Anerkennung der politischen, ethnischen und historischen Eigenständigkeit Makedoniens durch Bulgarien, einschließlich der Abtretung Pirin-Makedoniens an (Vardar-)Makedonien.

Es kann trotz teilweise anderer Interpretation durch die bulgarische Geschichtswissenschaft[90]) kein Zweifel sein, daß Dimitrov, die BKP und die Regierungen der OF von 1944 bis Anfang 1948 diesen Plänen zugestimmt haben: Von der Regierungserklärung der OF vom 17.9.1944 über den Regierungsvorschlag vom Dezember 1944, das 10. Plenum des ZK der BKP (9.8.1946) bis zu Dimitrovs berühmtem Interview vom 18.1.1948, das den Kominformkonflikt auslöste, und zu seinem Rechenschaftsbericht auf dem V. Parteitag der BKP (18.–25.12.1948) reicht eine lückenlose Kette der Beweise[91]). Hinzu kommen andere Symptome einer ungewöhnlichen Hinwendung zu Jugoslawien: am 5.10.1944 in Craiova der erste völkerrechtliche Vertrag Bulgariens nach dem 9.9.1944, vom 27.7. bis 3.8.1947 ein ausgedehntes Treffen zwischen Dimitrov und Tito in Bled, wo der erste bilaterale Vertrag über Freundschaft, Zusammenarbeit und gegenseitigen Beistand mit einem sozialistischen Land, den Bulgarien abgeschlossen hat, zusammen mit einer Reihe von Zusatzvereinbarungen ausgearbeitet wurde. Jugoslawien verzichtete in Bled auf die ihm aufgrund des Pariser Vertrages zustehenden 25 Mio. Dollar. Der Freundschaftsvertrag wurde anläßlich eines Gegenbesuches Titos in Bulgarien am 27.11.1947 unterzeichnet[92]). Der Zusammenbruch dieser Pläne, die das politische Kräftegewicht in Südosteuropa al-

---

[90]) Typisch: Dobrinov (Anm. 30).
[91]) Regierungserklärung (Anm. 69), Regierungsvorschlag und 10. ZK-Plenum: Petranović (Anm. 27), S. 603–05, 671/72 (dort eine Fülle weiterer in Bulgarien nicht veröffentlichter Dokumente und Literaturhinweise!); Interview: RD. 20.1.1948 (zur immer wieder variierenden Datierung von Dimitrov-Interview und Pravda-Artikel: Hatschikjan (Anm. 35), S. 347; Rechenschaftsbericht (Anm. 29).
[92]) Craiova: Petranović (Anm. 27), S. 601/02; Bled und Vertrag vom 27.11.1947: Meissner (Anm. 40), S. 30–32; Nešović, S.: Bledski sporazumi (Die Vereinbarungen von Bled). Zagreb 1979.

lerdings bleibend verändert hätten, geht nicht zu Lasten Bulgariens. Stalin hat den Föderationsplänen in ihrer ursprünglichen Form bis zum Kominformbruch stets zugestimmt und sich nur gegen Dimitrovs weitergehende Überlegungen vom 18.1.1948 gewandt[93]). Es war insofern England, das vor und während der Konferenz von Jalta (8.–11.2.1945) sein Veto einlegte und bis zum Sommer 1946 für eine Pause sorgte[94]). Und vom 18.1.1948 bzw. den Verhandlungen in Moskau am 10.2.1948 an war es Tito, der durch seine Unnachgiebigkeit den Bruch mit dem Sowjetblock heraufbeschwor[95]). Für die Frage nach Eigenständigkeit oder Blocktreue der bulgarischen Außenpolitik ist es dabei bezeichnend, daß Dimitrov bis zu den zitierten Passagen seiner Rede auf dem V. Parteitag hin zwar noch Zeichen der Sympathie für Tito zu erkennen gab, dennoch aber vorbehaltlos die Kominformresolution vom 28.6.1948 über die Lage in der KPJ mittrug, die voll sind von Wendungen wie „für einen Kommunisten unwürdige Haltung", „antisowjetische Einstellung der Führer der KPJ, die mit dem Marxismus-Leninismus unvereinbar ist" oder „Weg der Kulakenpartei der ‚Narodniki'"[96]). Hier sind Weichen gestellt worden, die bis heute Bedeutung behalten haben, nicht zuletzt auch durch die damit einhergehende strategische Aufwertung Bulgariens aus sowjetischer Sicht. Am Ende der Phase der „Sowjetisierung" konnte Bulgarien anders als die anderen Länder der Sozialistischen Gemeinschaft daher durchaus auch positive Ansatzpunkte in seinem Verhältnis zur Sowjetunion sehen. Nicht zu verkennen ist allerdings auch, daß sich der Hinweis auf Bulgariens besondere Hinwendung zur Sowjetunion deutlich auf die Dimitrov-Zeit zurückverfolgen läßt.

Nicht ganz so spektakulär, dennoch aber auch charakteristisch genug ist das Verhältnis Bulgariens damals zu *Griechenland* und damit zu einem anderen kontinuierlichen Partner bulgarischer Regionalpolitik gewesen. Zwei Problemkreise gab es, die sich nicht nur zeitlich überschnitten, wobei für beide die damalige Beurteilung durch Dimitrov und die BKP unverändert durch die heutige bulgarische Geschichtswissenschaft weiter vertreten wird. Der erste Problemkreis betrifft die Kriegsfolgen, die von seiten Griechenlands zu der extrem hohen Forderung von 985 Mio. Dollar Reparationen führten, außerdem zu vor allem strategisch begründeten Wünschen nach Grenzkorrekturen[97]). In bezug auf die letzteren sprach Dimitrov von „Befriedigung der räuberischen Ansprüche der großgriechischen Chauvinisten und ihrer hohen Patrone" (gemeint waren England und die USA)[98]) und setzte sich seinerseits mit Unterstützung der Sowjetunion bei den Pariser Verhandlungen für einen bulgarischen Ägäiszugang ein. Und gegenüber den hohen griechischen Reparationsforderungen wartete die bulgarische Delegation mit der noch heute wiederholten Behauptung auf,

---

[93]) Unersetzlich nach wie vor: Djilas, M.: Gespräche mit Stalin. Frankfurt a. M. 1962, S. 217–36; ferner: Dedijer, V.: Dokumenti 1948. Bde. 1–3. Belgrad 1980.
[94]) FRUS. The Conferences at Malta and Yalta. Washington 1955, S. 890/91.
[95]) Quellen vgl. Anm. 93 sowie Meissner (Anm. 40), S. 87–107; Literatur Anm. 75.
[96]) Meissner (Anm. 40), S. 99–102.
[97]) Grothusen, K.-D.: Außenpolitik, in: Südosteuropa-Handbuch. Bd. III: Griechenland. Göttingen 1980, S. 159–163.
[98]) Dimitroff (Anm. 7). Bd. 3, S. 448.

Bulgarien habe bei seiner Besetzung Westthrakiens und Ägäisch-Makedoniens selbst investiert und dieses Kapital durch das Kriegsende verloren[99]).

Der zweite Problemkreis ergab sich aus dem griechischen Bürgerkrieg, den Bulgarien nicht anders als Jugoslawien und Albanien durch Öffnung seiner Grenzen logistisch nachdrücklich unterstützt hat. Dimitrov gab dies auch offen zu, wenn er sagte: „Ebenso ist es natürlich, daß das bulgarische Volk mit dem Kampf des griechischen Volkes sympathisiert und bereit ist, den Opfern des in Griechenland herrschenden terroristischen Regimes, sollten sie in unserem Land Zuflucht suchen, zu helfen"[100]). Tatsächlich wird damit gerechnet, daß von den ca. 80 000 Flüchtlingen Anfang der 60er Jahre allein in Bulgarien noch fast 16 000 waren. Die im Oktober 1946 gegen 5 sowjetische Vetos gegründete Untersuchungskommission der UNO (UNSCOB) hat in ihren detaillierten Berichten keinen Zweifel an den bulgarischen Hilfeleistungen gelassen. Zu erwähnen ist allerdings auch, daß von der Regierungserklärung des 17.9.1944 an auch damals schon wiederholt als Ziel bulgarischer Regionalpolitik der Balkan als Zone des Friedens postuliert worden ist, was vom Ende der 50er Jahre an zur Hauptforderung bulgarischer Balkanpolitik erhoben wurde.

Fast erstaunlich ruhig entwickelte sich demgegenüber bis 1948 und eigentlich sogar bis 1950 hin das *bulgarisch-türkische Verhältnis*. Erstaunlich ist dies deswegen, weil schon 1945 der Kalte Krieg durch die Sowjetunion auch auf die Türkei ausgedehnt worden war[101]). Bulgarien beteiligte sich erst 1948 durch Abstufung der Botschaften zu Gesandtschaften und erste Hinweise auf die türkische Minderheit in Bulgarien, die von 1950 an dann zum großen Streitpunkt werden sollte.

Nicht vergessen sei als letztes später problematisches Land der Region *Albanien*. Hier kam es schon früh, am 16.12.1947, zum Abschluß des typischen bilateralen Freundschaftsvertrages[102]). Erwähnt sei wegen der späteren Entwicklung auch, daß *Rotchina* bzw. seine Vorstufen sich damals noch der größten Hochachtung in Bulgarien erfreuten[103]).

Abschließend ist aus dieser ersten Phase bulgarischer Nachkriegsaußenpolitik noch wichtig, daß 1948/49 aus dem „Land ohne Antisemitismus", in dem fast alle Juden – 1946 44 209 – den II. Weltkrieg hatten überleben können, nicht weniger als 32 781 mit Genehmigung der Regierung nach Israel auswanderten[104]). Zusammen mit einer weiteren Emigration in den 50er Jahren bedeutete dies das faktische Ende des bulgarischen Judentums.

---

[99]) BAN, Institute of History: Problems of the Transition from Capitalism to Socialism in Bulgaria. Sofia 1975, S. 259.
[100]) Dimitroff (Anm. 7), Bd. 3, S. 452.
[101]) Grothusen, K.-D.: Außenpolitik, in: Südosteuropa-Handbuch, Bd. IV: Türkei. Göttingen 1985, S. 107–09; Höpken (Anm. 22), S. 75–95.
[102]) Für den Text s. Meissner (Anm. 40), S. 33/34.
[103]) Vgl. die massiven Hochrufe etc. auf dem V. Parteitag der BKP: Anm. 29, S. 181.
[104]) Oschlies, W.: Bulgarien – Land ohne Antisemitismus. Erlangen 1976, S. 90/91.

3. Die Stalin-Zeit (1947/49–1953/56)

Die Stalin-Zeit im engeren Sinn, d. h. vom Abschluß der „Sowjetisierung" bis zu Stalins Tod (5.3.1953), gilt in der westlichen Forschung zurecht als diejenige des absoluten Tiefpunkts außen- wie innenpolitischer Selbständigkeit in der Geschichte der sozialistischen Länder Ostmittel- und Südosteuropas. Ob von der „Phase der totalen Konformität", „Die Ära Stalin: Von der Autonomie zur Uniformität" oder von „Stalinism: Institutional and Ideological Uniformity" gesprochen wird[105]), gemeint ist dasselbe: Im vollen Gegensatz zu der durch die Pariser Verträge vom 10.2.1947 erlangten theoretisch vollen außenpolitischen Souveränität verstand es Stalin, in der Praxis die volle Abhängigkeit von der Sowjetunion und den Verzicht auf Selbständigkeit durchzusetzen. Auch in den Augen Bulgarien aufgeschlossen gegenüberstehender Beobachter bleibt für diese Zeit keine andere Bezeichnung als „Mustersatellit"[106]). Verbunden ist diese Entwicklung in allen drei südosteuropäischen Fällen mit dem Namen des jeweiligen Parteiführers: in Bulgarien V. Červenkov, in Ungarn M. Rákosi und in Rumänien Gh. Gheorghiu-Dej, was besonders nachdrücklich auf die unter I, 1 angesprochene Problematik der Wirksamkeit der historischen Einzelpersönlichkeit zurückverweist. Dies gilt auch für das Ende dieser Phase mit dem Tode Stalins. Gewiß wurde die „Ratifizierung der Blockbildung" endgültig erst am 14.5.1955 mit dem Warschauer Vertrag erreicht[107]), dennoch fällt dieser schon so sehr in den Bereich des *Neuen Kurses*, daß er zunächst außer acht gelassen werden kann. Wichtiger ist zur Charakterisierung der Stalin-Zeit dafür, daß Stalin formal deutlich wesentlich mehr im Sinne der ersten Generation der Sowjetblock-Verträge auf bilaterale Beziehungen Wert legte als auf multilaterale – trotz der Existenz von Kominform und RGW.

Und innerhalb dieser bilateralen Beziehungen waren es wieder wesentlich mehr die persönlichen zwischen den Parteiführern bzw. zwischen den Parteispitzen als die formale Außenpolitik, die auf diese Weise in jenen Jahren ihren absoluten Tiefpunkt in der Nachkriegsentwicklung erlebte[108]). Bezeichnend für die erst in der jüngsten Phase der *perestrojka* einsetzende Diskussion um diese Problematik ist schließlich, daß bis dahin nur eine Phase von 1944 bis 1956 bzw. von 1949 bis 1956 abgegrenzt wurde und daß eine inhaltliche Auseinandersetzung mit Stalin auch nur auf außenpolitischem Gebiet nicht stattfand[109]). Dies braucht u.a. aber auch deswegen nicht zu verwundern, weil die Verbindung nationaler außenpolitischer bulgarischer Interessen mit Stalins Politik in den ersten Nachkriegsjahren in der unter II,2 dargestellten Phase oft durchaus vorhanden war. Daß in den einschlägigen Quellenveröffentli-

---

[105]) Hacker (Anm. 6), S. 303; Löwenthal; Meissner (Anm. 5), S. 13; Brzezinski (Anm. 33), S. 65.

[106]) Oschlies (Anm. 13), S. 276; zum Vergleich mit Ungarn und Rumänien vgl. die entsprechenden Kapitel in den Südosteuropa-Handbüchern Bd. II und V.

[107]) Für die „Ratifizierung der Blockbildung" s. Loth, W.: Die Teilung der Welt. Geschichte des Kalten Krieges 1941–1955. München 1980, S. 309; für den Warschauer Vertrag: Meissner (Anm. 40), S. 203–208.

[108]) Osteuropa-Handbuch. Begründet v. W. Markert. Sowjetunion. Außenpolitik 1917–1955. Hrsg. v. D. Geyer. Köln, Wien 1972, S. 427.

[109]) Vgl. Grigorova (Anm. 37) oder Nakov (Anm. 46); ferner: Geschichte der BKP (Anm. 45), S. 204–45.

chungen wichtige Ereignisse wie Stalins 70. Geburtstag (21.12.1949) oder sein Tod (5.3.1953) bis jetzt z.T. fehlen, ist gesagt worden[110]).

Ohne bulgarische Besonderheiten verliefen diese Jahre denn auch im Verhältnis zum *Westblock*: Der Kalte Krieg beherrschte im Prinzip die Beziehungen. Die Anfang 1950 abgebrochenen Beziehungen mit den USA wurden so auch in jenen Jahren nicht wieder aufgenommen, ebensowenig wie der Westen die Blockade der Aufnahme Bulgariens in die UNO aufgab. Die sich allgemein zwischen den Blöcken entwickelnden Außenhandelsbeziehungen konnten hiergegen kein echtes Gegengewicht schaffen. Immerhin ist erwähnenswert, daß es von 1950 an auch zwischen der Bundesrepublik Deutschland und Bulgarien auf dem Weg über regelmäßig erneuerte Warenlisten zur Wiederaufnahme des Außenhandels kam, der sich rasch positiv entwickelte.

In diesen Gesamtzusammenhang paßt auch der *Balkan* als das Feld der bulgarischen Regionalpolitik. An erster Stelle gilt dies selbstverständlich für *Jugoslawien*, wo Bulgarien bis 1953 in vollem Umfang an der Fortsetzung der Politik des Kominformbruchs teilnahm. Argumentativ unterstützt wurde diese Haltung allerdings auch durch den – zeitlich späten – Abschluß des Balkanpakts zwischen Jugoslawien, Griechenland und der Türkei durch die Verträge von Ankara (28.2.1953) und Bled (9.8.1954)[111]).

Was damit als letztes Griechenland und die Türkei betrifft, so ist ohne Zweifel richtig, daß aufgrund der oben dargestellten Entwicklung das Verhältnis Bulgariens zu *Griechenland* zunächst weitaus belasteter war: Die Grenzfrage ist ebenso zu nennen wie die Reparationen – Bulgarien weigerte sich standhaft, die vertraglich festgelegten 45 Mio. Dollar zu zahlen, so daß es 1952 fast zum Krieg kam[112]) – und das Fortwirken der Gegensätze aus der Zeit des griechischen Bürgerkrieges mit dem Flüchtlingsproblem und den Auseinandersetzungen im Rahmen der UNO. Es bestanden so auch keine diplomatischen Beziehungen zwischen den beiden Ländern. Brown mag insofern recht haben, wenn er den Eisernen Vorhang zwischen Bulgarien und Griechenland als den dichtesten überhaupt bezeichnet[113]).

Dennoch ist es aber so, daß sich nachhaltig das Verhältnis zur *Türkei* als noch schlechter erweisen sollte. Dies ist umso erstaunlicher, als die Ausgangsbedingungen von 1944 an, wie oben dargestellt, zunächst günstig waren. Dies änderte sich jedoch schlagartig, als Bulgarien mit einer Note vom 10.8.1950 die Aussiedlung von 250000 Angehörigen der türkischen Minderheit – ein knappes Drittel der Gesamtzahl nach der Volkszählung von 1946 – innerhalb von drei Monaten ankündigte[114]). Die westliche Forschung ist sich darüber einig, daß der Grund für diese spektakuläre Maßnahme nicht in einer subversiven Tätigkeit der Türkei in Bulgarien zu suchen ist oder auch nur in Unruhen innerhalb der türkischen Minderheit, sondern in einer Teilnahme Bulgariens an den erwähnten, seit 1945 laufenden Aktionen der Sowjetunion im

---

[110]) Živkov, T.: Izbrani săčinenija (Ausgewählte Werke). Bd. 1.2. Sofia 1975; VPB 1. 1970.

[111]) Vgl. außer den Kapiteln „Außenpolitik" in den Bänden I, III u. IV des Südosteuropa-Handbuchs: Grothusen, K.-D.: Der Balkanpakt als Instrument der Friedenssicherung für Südosteuropa nach dem Zweiten Weltkrieg, in: Friedenssicherung (Anm. 58), S. 179–90.

[112]) Tönnes, B.: Bulgarische Griechenlandpolitik, in: Südosteuropa. 33 (1984), S. 418.

[113]) Brown (Anm. 6), S. 274.

[114]) Was die Größe der türkischen Minderheiten angeht, vgl. das Kapitel v. S. Troebst, Nationale Minderheiten, für die bulgarisch-türkischen Spannungen: Höpken (Anm. 22), S. 75–95.

Rahmen des Kalten Krieges gegen die Türkei. Warum Bulgarien mit dieser Teilnahme gerade im August 1950 begann, ist ungeklärt, da die Archive nicht zugänglich sind. Das Ergebnis ist jedenfalls deutlich: 1950/51 verließen rund 154000 Türken Bulgarien[115]), deren Aufnahme und Integration durch die Türkei eine große Leistung darstellt. Außenpolitisch war das Ergebnis, daß das Verhältnis zwischen beiden Ländern nachhaltig belastet wurde.

4. Die Übergangszeit (1953/56–1964/68)

Die Eingrenzung der auf die klar faßbare Stalin-Phase folgenden Periode ist nicht ganz einfach. Innenpolitisch steht sie im Zeichen der Machtübernahme durch Živkov vom VI. Parteitag 1954 bis zum VIII. Parteitag 1962[116]). Von bulgarischer Seite gilt allerdings nicht dieser personenbezogene Gesichtspunkt als vorrangig, sondern stets das Plenum des ZK der BKP vom 2.–6.4.1956 – das sogenannte Aprilplenum –, und zwar auch für die Außenpolitik[117]). Konkrete Auswirkungen zumindest für die letztere lassen sich allerdings nicht nachweisen, ebenso wenig wie der Funke des XX. Parteitags der KPdSU (14.–25.2.1956) im Sinne Polens und vor allem Ungarns auf Bulgarien übergesprungen wäre. Im Gegenteil: Für Bulgarien hat sich bis zur Teilnahme am Einmarsch in die Tschechoslowakei (21.8.1968) stets die sowjetische außenpolitische Linie als die maßgebliche erwiesen: von der Erklärung der Sowjetregierung vom 30.10.1956 über die 12-Parteien-Erklärung 1957 und die 81-Parteien-Erklärung 1960 bis zur Erklärung von Bratislava vom 3.8.1968 und die 75-Parteien-Erklärung 1969, d.h. der Weg zur Brežnev-Doktrin bzw. zum Sozialistischen Internationalismus als Leitprinzip der Sozialistischen Gemeinschaft[118]). Als Symbol hierfür kann gelten, daß die enge Bindung an die Sowjetunion in der neuen bulgarischen Verfassung von 1971 nicht weniger als dreimal genannt wird und der Sozialistische Internationalismus Verfassungsrang erhalten hat (Artikel 5)[119]). Die enge, auch persönliche Beziehung Živkovs zu Chruščev sowie von 1964 an auch zu Brežnev kommt hinzu, die für diese Zeit zum Vorwurf besonderer Anlehnung führt[120]).

Dennoch wäre es falsch, diese Periode allein unter dem Aspekt des Gegenbeispiels gegen Ungarn und auch Rumänien – Machtübernahme durch Ceauşescu am 22.3.1965 – zu sehen. Auf dem eigentlichen Feld bulgarischer Außenpolitik, der regionalen Balkanpolitik, lassen sich durchaus Entwicklungen feststellen, die wichtig sind, obschon sicherlich auf der Basis von Koordination mit der Sowjetunion: der Aussöhnungsprozeß mit Griechenland, der mit 12 Verträgen am 9.7.1964 abgeschlossen wurde, und der Familienzusammenführungsvertrag mit der Türkei vom

---

[115]) Eine statistische Aufrechnung bei Höpken (Anm. 22), S. 95.
[116]) Vgl. das Kapitel v. J.D. Bell: Domestic Politics, S. 71–77.
[117]) Mladenow, P.: Vier Jahrzehnte eine Außenpolitik des Friedens, in: Bulgarien – 40 Jahre auf dem Weg des Sozialismus. Sofia 1985, S. 165.
[118]) Meissner (Anm. 42); Frenzke, D.: Die Prinzipien des sozialistischen Internationalismus als Völkerrechtsproblem, in: Sowjetsystem (Anm. 1), S. 617–38.
[119]) Verfassung (Anm. 10), S. 50/51.
[120]) Costello, M.: Bulgarien, in: Die kommunistischen Parteien der Welt. Hrsg. v. C.D. Kernig. Freiburg u.a. 1969, Sp. 115.

22.3.1968[121]). Hierzu paßt, daß Bulgarien von 1959 an die ursprünglich rumänische Idee des Balkans als Zone des Friedens (Stoica-Plan vom 9.9.1957) aufnahm, während sich nur das Verhältnis zu Jugoslawien als dauernd schwankend und nicht in dieses Bild passend erweist. Im ganzen läßt sich jedoch sagen, daß die blockinterne Entwicklung seit Stalins Tod 1953 ebenso wie die Détente in den Beziehungen zum Westen deutlich auf die bulgarische Außenpolitik eingewirkt haben. Die Teilnahme Bulgariens an der Gründung des WP (14.5.1955) paßt insofern ebenso hierher wie die Aufnahme in die UNO (14.12.1955) zusammen mit Ungarn und Rumänien.

Was damit als erstes das Verhältnis zur *Sowjetunion* in jenen Jahren betrifft, so kann tatsächlich kein Zweifel daran sein, daß die Metapher von der Freundschaft zur Sowjetunion als „Eckstein der bulgarischen Außenpolitik", wie sie Živkov, von vielen anderen Anlässen abgesehen, auf dem VII. Parteitag der BKP (2.–7.6.1958) verwandte[122]), für diesen ganzen Zeitraum zutrifft. Auch wenn es richtig sein sollte, daß Živkov zweimal von Chruščev nicht gebilligte Maßnahmen getroffen haben sollte – dabei außenpolitisch die Annäherung an Griechenland[123]) –, so kann dies im Vergleich zur realen und nicht nur rhetorischen außenpolitischen Ausrichtung auf die Sowjetunion nicht ins Gewicht fallen. Es kommen die Aussagen der sowjetischen Führer hinzu, die diesen Sachverhalt vollauf bestätigen. So hat sich Chruščev dem jugoslawischen Botschafter Mićunović gegenüber im Februar 1957 anläßlich eines bulgarischen Staatsbesuches nachdrücklich dahingehend geäußert, daß zwischen der Sowjetunion und Bulgarien „vollstes Vertrauen" bestehe, während in der bilateralen Deklaration Dimitrovs Vergleich von 1943 von der Notwendigkeit der Freundschaft zur Sowjetunion wie von Sonne und Luft für jedes Lebewesen wiederholt wird[124]). Nicht minder berühmt geworden ist Brežnevs Formulierung von 1967, wo er auf die Frage, was Sozialistischer Internationalismus sei, antwortete, das Verhältnis zwischen Sowjetunion und Bulgarien sei „Sozialistischer Internationalismus in der Praxis"[125]). Und auf den Boden konkreten Völkerrechts führt schließlich im Rahmen der Bündnisverträge der zweiten Generation die Präambel des „Vertrages über Freundschaft, Zusammenarbeit und gegenseitigen Beistand" zwischen der Sowjetunion und Bulgarien vom 12.5.1967, wo ebenso von der „ewigen, unverbrüchlichen Freundschaft" wie von „unerschütterlichen Prinzipien des sozialistischen Internationalismus" die Rede ist[126]).

Es ergibt sich, daß die Anbindung der bulgarischen Außenpolitik an die Sowjetunion ebenso verbal wie im persönlichen Verhältnis der Parteiführer, im Völkerrecht wie in konkreten ökonomischen Interessen Bulgariens zu finden ist: Allein bis 1961

---

[121]) Für die Verträge mit Griechenland s. RD. 10.7.1964 sowie DV. (1964) 87 u. 88 (sie fehlen in VPB. 2.1971!); für den Vertrag mit der Türkei s. UNTS. 759 (1970), S. 223–239.
[122]) VII Kongres na Bălgarskata Komunističeska partija, 2 juni–7 juni 1958 g. Stenografski protokol (VII. Parteitag der BKP, 2.–7. Juni 1958. Stenographisches Protokoll). Sofia 1958, S. 31.
[123]) Oschlies (Anm. 13), S. 257.
[124]) Mićunović, V.: Moskauer Tagebücher 1956–1958. Hrsg. v. W. Höpken. Stuttgart 1977, S. 265; VPB. 1.1970, S. 260.
[125]) RD. 13.5.1967. Vgl. auch King, R.R.: Bulgarian-Soviet Relations: „Socialist Internationalism in Action". München 1975 (RAD Background Report. 89. RFE Research. 26.5.1975).
[126]) Uschakow; Frenzke (Anm. 3).

hat Bulgarien Wirtschaftshilfe von 1,29 Mrd. Rubel erhalten[127]). Und schließlich ist auf manifeste außenpolitische Interessen beider Seiten hinzuweisen, dabei an erster Stelle im Rahmen des Sowjetbocks und der Balkanpolitik.

Was den *Sowjetblock* bzw. die Länder der Sozialistischen Gemeinschaft angeht, so handelt es sich vom sowjetischen Standpunkt aus um ungewöhnlich schwere Jahre, deren Probleme von der DDR (1953), Ungarn und Polen (1956), Albanien und China (ab 1959/61) und Rumänien (ab 1965) bis zur Tschechoslowakei (1968) sämtliche Mitgliedsländer mit einer Ausnahme erfaßten: Bulgarien. Allein Bulgarien hat in seiner Außenpolitik damals die Grenze, die der Sozialistische Internationalismus bzw. die Brežnev-Doktrin dem eigenen Bewegungsspielraum setzte[128]), nie überschritten und an seiner Treue gegenüber der Sowjetunion keinen Zweifel aufkommen lassen. Živkovs Rede vom 10.6.1969 auf der Moskauer Parteienkonferenz kann hier in allen außenpolitischen Fragen als Musterbeispiel gelten[129]). Parallel dazu ging der reibungslose Abschluß der zweiten Generation der Freundschaftsverträge durch Bulgarien mit allen verbliebenen Blockstaaten von 1967–1970[130]).

Und als nicht minder zuverlässig erwies sich Bulgarien bei der Unterstützung der Sowjetunion in den einzelnen Krisenfällen. Für den *ungarischen Volksaufstand* (23.10.–4.11.1956) gibt eine Rede Živkovs vom 28.11.1956 eine verläßliche Wiederholung der sowjetischen Interpretation: ausgehend von der Verurteilung des imperialistischen Angriffs auf Ägypten (Suezkrise) bis zum Lob für die brüderliche Hilfe, die die Rote Armee gegen die Verbindung von NATO-Subversion von außen und chauvinistisch-reaktionären Kräften im Innern Ungarns geleistet habe[131]). Und dasselbe wiederholt sich 1968 noch verstärkt im Fall der Tschechoslowakei: Hier geht es nicht nur um die verbale Einzelunterstützung der Sowjetunion oder die Teilnahme an kollektiven Erklärungen[132]), sondern vor allem auch um die Teilnahme am Einmarsch in die Tschechoslowakei. Der Vergleich mit Ungarn und Rumänien ist bezeichnend: Rumänien nahm an der Invasion überhaupt nicht teil, Ungarn tat es zwar, doch wissen wir, wie verzweifelt Kádár sich bis zur letzten Minute um eine friedliche Lösung bemüht hat[133]).

Und als letztes ist in diesem Zusammenhang auf die Linientreue der bulgarischen Außenpolitik gegenüber *Albanien* und *China* hinzuweisen. Nachdem es mit Albanien zunächst sehr früh – am 16.12.1947 – zum Abschluß eines Vertrages über Freundschaft, Zusammenarbeit und gegenseitigen Beistand gekommen war[134]) und Živkov in seinem Rechenschaftsbericht auf dem VII. Parteitag der BKP (2.–7.6.1958) unter dem anhaltenden Beifall der Delegierten Albanien wie China die ewige Freundschaft

---

[127]) Osteuropa-Handbuch (Anm. 6), S. 371; ferner das Kapitel „Außenwirtschaft" von R. Schönfeld.
[128]) Für Quellen und Interpretation s. Anm. 118.
[129]) Živkov (Anm. 110). 16.1976, S. 188–227.
[130]) Polen (6.4.1967), Sowjetunion (12.5.1967), Ungarn (10.7.1969), Rumänien (19.11.1970), Tschechoslowakei (26.10.1968), DDR (7.9.1967). Alle Texte bei Uschakow (Anm. 3).
[131]) Živkov (Anm. 110). 3.1975, S. 5–27.
[132]) Für die Einzelunterstützung vgl. Rede vom 12.11.1968: Živkov (Anm. 110). 15.1976, S. 382–390, für die kollektiven Erklärungen s. Meissner (Anm. 42).
[133]) Für Kádárs Bemühungen s. Grothusen (Anm. 2), S. 137.
[134]) Meissner (Anm. 40), S. 33/34; für Albanien vgl. Anm. 6.

Bulgariens versichert hatte[135]), folgte Bulgarien von 1959/60 an dem sowjetischen Vorbild der rapide schlechter werdenden Beziehungen. Der bulgarische Botschafter wurde aus Tirana abgerufen, und 1967 waren die diplomatischen Beziehungen zu beiden Ländern auf Geschäftsträgerebene reduziert. Auf der 75-Parteien-Konferenz in Moskau 1969 war Živkov einer der schärfsten Wortführer gegen China („Die heutigen chinesischen Führer wollen China in eine Kraft verwandeln, die der sozialistischen Gemeinschaft, der Sicherheit der Völker unverhohlen feindlich ist"), wogegen Albanien mit der Formulierung von Bulgarien als „dem blinden Werkzeug der sowjetischen Zaren" aufwartete[136]).

Im Verhältnis zu den *westlichen Ländern* gilt ebenfalls das Leitbild der sowjetischen Außenpolitik. Den Gegenpol zum Sozialistischen Internationalismus und der ewigen Freundschaft mit der Sowjetunion bildet hier das Nachlassen des Kalten Krieges und der Weg in die Détente. Als zeitliche Eckdaten können als Ausklang des Kalten Krieges die Gründung des WP (14.5.1955) ebenso wie die Aufnahme Bulgariens in die UNO (14.12.1955) gelten, als Abschluß der sog. Budapester Appell (17.3.1969) als Beginn des Dialogs über die KSZE von seiten des Sowjetblocks[137]), in den Bulgarien selbstverständlich von Anfang an eingeschaltet war.

Auch an allen anderen gemeinsamen Aktionen war Bulgarien stets beteiligt. Es sei nur der Abbruch der diplomatischen Beziehungen zu *Israel* zusammen mit Polen, der Tschechoslowakei und Ungarn (aber ohne Rumänien!) (11.–13.6.1967) im Gefolge der Sowjetunion (10.6.1967) als Reaktion auf den Junikrieg 1967 genannt oder die Unterstützung der *Vietnam*-Politik der Sowjetunion (Abschluß eines Wirtschafts- und Militärvertrages mit Nordvietnam am 30.6.1968). Was bilaterale Beziehungen betrifft, so ist als erstes die Wiederaufnahme der diplomatischen Beziehungen zu den *USA* (15.1.1960) und der kontinuierliche Ausbau der Wirtschaftsbeziehungen zu allen westlichen Ländern zu erwähnen. Darüber hinaus wurden politische und kulturelle Beziehungen mit einer zunehmenden Zahl von Ländern der *Dritten Welt* gesucht, von denen für jene Jahre besonders Tunesien, Ghana, Guinea, Mali, aber auch Indien Gewicht zukommt.

Als besonders instruktives Einzelbeispiel sei schließlich auf die *Bundesrepublik Deutschland* eingegangen. Für die 50er Jahre ist einerseits der Ausbau noch inoffizieller Handelsbeziehungen wichtig, andererseits die volle Unterstützung der DDR im Kampf gegen den „westdeutschen Revisionismus", „Revanchismus" und „Militarismus", allerdings auch in der Forderung nach friedlicher Wiedervereinigung Deutschlands[138]). Der große Umschwung kam mit dem Abschluß eines langfristigen Abkommens über den Waren- und Zahlungsverkehr und vor allem der Errichtung von Handelsvertretungen (6.3.1964), von wo an die Bundesrepublik Deutschland der wichtigste westliche Handels- und Tourismuspartner Bulgariens wurde, nur gelegent-

---

[135]) VII Kongres na BKP (Anm. 122), S. 32–34.
[136]) Živkov (Anm. 110). 16.1976, S. 200; Zëri i Popullit. 9.9.1969.
[137]) Sicherheit und Zusammenarbeit in Europa (KSZE). Analyse und Dokumentation. Hrsg. v. H.-A. Jacobsen u.a. Köln 1973–1978, S. 120–22 (Dok. 13) (Dokumente zur Außenpolitik. 2).
[138]) Vgl. z. B. die Rede D. Ganevs auf dem V. Parteitag der SED: Protokoll der Verhandlungen des V. Parteitages der Sozialistischen Einheitspartei Deutschlands. 10.–16. Juli 1958. 1.–5. Verhandlungstag. Berlin 1959, S. 518–21.

lich im Handel von Italien überflügelt[139]). Was fehlte, war die Aufnahme voller diplomatischer Beziehungen. Eine Möglichkeit hierzu hätten die Initiativen der Regierungen Erhard und Kiesinger 1966/1969 gegeben[140]). Und fast schien es so, als ob Bulgarien dem Beispiel Rumäniens (Aufnahme der diplomatischen Beziehungen am 31.1.1967) zu folgen bereit wäre, als die Karlsbader Konferenz einen Riegel vorschob und Živkov mit seiner Rede dort (25.4.1967) auf den noch ablehnenden Kurs der Sowjetunion einschwenkte[141]). Nur eine Wiederholung findet sich anläßlich der Unterzeichnung des neuen Vertrages über Freundschaft, Zusammenarbeit und gegenseitigen Beistand mit der DDR (7.9.1967)[142]).

Was schließlich als letztes den *Balkan* als Feld bulgarischer Regionalpolitik angeht, so macht sich auch hier der Einfluß der Détente bzw. des Abflauens des Kalten Krieges deutlich bemerkbar, und zwar sowohl multilateral auf beiden Seiten als auch im Bemühen um bilaterale Kontakte. Was multilaterale Bemühungen betrifft, so ist für die Türkei, Griechenland und Jugoslawien an erster Stelle das Einschlafen des Balkanpaktes zwischen 1959 und 1962 zu nennen[143]). Von seiten des Sowjetblocks lassen sich von 1957 an kontinuierlich Vorschläge finden, Balkangipfelkonferenzen einzuberufen und den Balkan in eine Zone des Friedens zu verwandeln. Von 1959 an trat die Forderung nach Verwandlung des Balkans in eine atomwaffenfreie Zone hinzu. Verbunden sind diese Pläne vor allem mit dem Namen des rumänischen Ministerpräsidenten Ch. Stoica (9.9.1957 und 7.6.1959), doch schloß sich auch Bulgarien rasch an und unterstützte diese Pläne, wie denn ein fast ohne Unterbrechung sehr gutes persönliches Verhältnis zwischen Živkov und Ceauşescu typisch für das Verhältnis beider Länder zueinander ist. Die Reihe der bulgarischen Initiativen beginnt mit einer Note vom 18.9.1957 und führt über den VII. Parteitag (2.–7.6.1958), eine UNO-Rede Živkovs (28.9.1960) bis zum IX. Parteitag (14.–19.11.1966)[144]). Nicht zu vergessen ist auch die 1959 ins Leben gerufene „Bewegung für Frieden und Zusammenarbeit auf dem Balkan", die von Bulgarien etwa durch die Ausrichtung von Kongressen nachdrücklich unterstützt wurde[145]).

Wenn damit ein neuer Ton in die bulgarische Balkanpolitik hineingekommen ist, der bis heute unvermindert fortwirkt, so ist allerdings auch nicht zu übersehen, daß konkrete Ergebnisse nicht auf diesem Feld multilateraler Pläne erzielt worden sind, sondern nur im engeren Bereich bilateraler Bemühungen. Hier ist an erster Stelle

---

[139]) Mitteilungen des Auswärtigen Amtes über die deutsch-bulgarischen Verhandlungen vom 7. März 1964, in: Die deutsche Ostpolitik 1961–1970. Kontinuität und Wandel. Dokumentation. Hrsg. v. B. Meissner. Köln 1970, S. 75/76 (Dok. 31). Für den Außenhandel vgl. das Kapitel von R. Schönfeld, für den Tourismus das Kapitel von M. A. Hatschikjan.
[140]) Beginnend mit der Regierungserklärung vom 13.12.1966. Für alle Texte vgl. Deutsche Ostpolitik (Anm. 139), S. 161–379.
[141]) Živkov (Anm. 110). 14.1976, S. 81 ff. passim.
[142]) Wie Anm. 141, S. 272–76.
[143]) Grothusen (Anm. 111), S. 187/188.
[144]) VPB. 1.1970, S. 299–301; VII Kongres na BKP (Anm. 122), S. 33/34; Živkov (Anm. 110). 6.1975, S. 94/95; IX Kongres na BKP, 14 noemvri – 19 noemvri 1966 g. Stenografski protokol (IX. Parteitag der BKP, 14.–19. November 1966. Stenographisches Protokoll). Sofia 1967, S. 28/29. Vgl. außerdem Tönnes, B.: Bulgariens balkanpolitisches Konzept, in: Südosteuropa. 33 (1984), S. 313–26.
[145]) RD. 20.4.1961; VPB. 1.1970, S. 584/85; VPB. 2.1971, S. 229–32.

Griechenland zu nennen, wenn davon ausgegangen wird, daß der Eiserne Vorhang bis 1953 nirgendwo in Europa so undurchlässig war wie zwischen Bulgarien und Griechenland[146]). Am 5.12.1953 kam es dann aber schon zum Abschluß eines Handelsvertrages, und am 22.5.1954 wurden die diplomatischen Beziehungen wieder aufgenommen. Offen blieb vor allem die Zahlung der 45 Mio. Dollar Reparationen aufgrund des Pariser Friedensvertrages. Bulgarische Annäherungsversuche in der zweiten Hälfte der 50er Jahre führten so noch zu keinem Ergebnis. Erst am 9.7.1964 wurde der große Durchbruch erzielt: Es kam zum Abschluß von nicht weniger als 12 Verträgen, wozu die Regelung der Reparationsfrage gehörte – Bulgarien zahlte im Endeffekt 7 Mio. Dollar –, die Aufwertung der diplomatischen Vertretungen auf Botschafterebene, verschiedene Wirtschaftsabkommen sowie ein Kulturabkommen[147]). Es mag dabei dahingestellt bleiben, ob Živkov sich in diesem Fall mit einer eigenen Außenpolitik gegen die Sowjetunion gestellt hat[148]), sicher ist, daß hier eine wichtige Weiche in der bulgarischen Nachkriegsaußenpolitik gestellt worden ist.

Im Prinzip ähnlich entwickelte sich das Verhältnis zur *Türkei*. Hier war es allerdings nicht die Reparationsfrage, sondern das Problem der türkischen Minderheit, das als Erbe aus der Zeit des Kalten Krieges übernommen und durch die minderheitspolitischen Beschlüsse des Aprilplenums von 1956 nicht beseitigt wurde[149]). Davon abgesehen finden sich aber auch der Türkei gegenüber in der zweiten Hälfte der 50er Jahre dieselben Annäherungsversuche wie gegenüber Griechenland. Bis zum Durchbruch dauerte es allerdings vier Jahre länger, obwohl die Gesandtschaften schon 1966 zu Botschaften aufgewertet wurden. Erst mit dem Besuch Živkovs bei Demirel (20.–26.3.1968) und der dabei erfolgten Unterzeichnung eines Anschlußvertrages über die Auswanderung von Familienangehörigen der Auswanderer von 1950/51 (22.3.1968)[150]) wurden jedoch die letzten Mißhelligkeiten beseitigt. Es wird geschätzt, daß daraufhin in den folgenden 10 Jahren ca. 130000 Türken Bulgarien verlassen haben[151]). Obwohl andere Bereiche sonst kaum entwickelt wurden – etwa die Wirtschaftsbeziehungen – galt das bulgarisch-türkische Verhältnis von da an für längere Zeit als besonders gut.

Deutlich komplizierter liegen die Verhältnisse schließlich in bezug auf *Jugoslawien*. Hier kann nicht einfach von einer Phase der Wiederannäherung nach dem Tiefpunkt des Kominformbruches die Rede sein, die zu einem definitiven Ergebnis geführt hätte. Stattdessen fügt sich die bulgarische Außenpolitik gegenüber Jugoslawien einerseits nahtlos in das bezeichnend wellenförmige Verhältnis Jugoslawiens zum ganzen Sowjetblock ein, ist andererseits aber auch durch die beiden Sonderprobleme „makedonische" Minderheit in Pirin-Makedonien und die jugoslawische Sozialistische Republik Makedonien bestimmt. Der generellen Tendenz der bulgarischen Außenpolitik, der Linie der Sowjetunion im Ganzen zu folgen, mag es entsprechen, wenn Brown daraufhin auch im makedonischen Sonderproblem nur einen Indikator für das Ver-

---

[146]) Brown (Anm. 6), S. 274.
[147]) Für die Verträge s. Anm. 121; außerdem Tönnes (Anm. 112), S. 418/19.
[148]) Oschlies (Anm. 13), S. 257.
[149]) Vgl. die Kapitel von J.D. Bell, Domestic Politics, S. 73–75, und S. Troebst, Nationale Minderheiten, S. 488.
[150]) Vgl. Anm. 121.
[151]) Für die Einzelheiten sowie Quellen und Literaturangaben s.u. S. 129–132.

hältnis zwischen der Sowjetunion und Jugoslawien sieht[152]). Dennoch ist deutlich, daß gerade hier in der Phase von 1953 bis 1968 mehr bulgarische Eigenprobleme sichtbar werden als bei allen anderen außenpolitischen Fragen.

Auszugehen ist allerdings von den übergeordneten Blockinteressen, die auch vom jugoslawischen Standpunkt aus in jenen Jahren höchste Bedeutung hatten[153]). Es folgten aufeinander: Bemühungen der Sowjetunion um eine Bereinigung des Kominformbruches, die in den Belgrader und Moskauer Erklärungen (2.6.1955 und 20.6.1956) ihren vorläufigen Höhepunkt erreichten. Schon mit dem ungarischen Volksaufstand (23.10.–4.11.1956) schlug die Entwicklung jedoch wieder um, wofür vor allem auch der VII. Parteitag des SKJ in Ljubljana wichtig ist (22.–26.4.1958) bzw. Chruščevs Stellungnahme dazu auf dem VII. Parteitag der BKP (2.–7.6.1958), wo er Jugoslawien eine „Art trojanisches Pferd" des „zeitgenössischen Revisionismus" nannte[154]). Von 1962 bis 1967 war es dann wieder soweit, daß die Frage auftauchen konnte, ob der „Soldat" (Jugoslawien) „in seine Kompanie zurückkehre". 1968, mit der Invasion in die Tschechoslowakei, fand diese Phase ihr abruptes Ende.

Dieser generellen Linie ist die bulgarische Außenpolitik durchaus gefolgt, wenn auch deutlich zögernd und ohne besonderen Nachdruck. Erklärlich wird dies nicht nur aus der unnachgiebigen Haltung Jugoslawiens gegenüber dem makedonischen Sonderproblem, sondern auch wegen der jugoslawischen Forderung nach Rehabilitierung T. Kostovs und Entmachtung Červenkovs als Zeichen des Schlußstriches unter den Kominformkonflikt. Daß beides 1956 bzw. 1962 tatsächlich geschah, hat ohne Zweifel primär innenpolitische Gründe, die mit Živkovs Machtübernahme zusammenhängen, doch wurden damit zugleich auch die jugoslawischen Forderungen erfüllt. Der ausgiebige Besuch Živkovs in Jugoslawien (22.9.–8.10.1956) stellt den Höhepunkt dieser Phase dar, die 1958 dann aber rasch in schärfste gegenseitige Polemik zurückschlug[155]). Und nicht anders verhält es sich mit der nächsten Welle von Annäherung und Abstoßung: Titos erster Besuch in Bulgarien nach 1947 fand vom 22.–27.9.1965 statt, und im November 1968 erschien jene Broschüre der BAN *Makedonskijat văpros. Istoriko-političeska spravka* (Die makedonische Frage. Eine historisch-politische Untersuchung), die den Höhepunkt einer neuen, eindeutig durch das Makedonienproblem bestimmten Auseinandersetzung zwischen beiden Ländern markiert[156]).

Mit Blick auf Bulgarien kann dabei durchaus von einer doppelten Strategie gesprochen werden: Wenn der Zensus von 1956 noch 187 789 Makedonier in Bulgarien, d. h. vornehmlich im Pirin-Gebiet, ausgewiesen hatte, so waren davon 1965 noch 9632 übriggeblieben, so daß von jugoslawischer Seite von einem „statistischen Genozid"

---

[152]) Brown (Anm. 6), S. 282.

[153]) Für die Einzelheiten vgl. Grothusen, K.-D.: Außenpolitik, in: Südosteuropa-Handbuch. Bd. I: Jugoslawien. Göttingen 1975, S. 155–78.

[154]) Pravda. 4.6.1958. Weitere Quellen in: Die feindlichen Brüder. Jugoslawiens neuer Konflikt mit dem Ostblock 1958. Ein Dokumentenband red. u. eingel. v. C. Gasteyger. Bern 1960.

[155]) Zum Živkov-Besuch s. Živkov (Anm. 110). 2.1975, S. 509–41; für die Quellen s. From Recognition to Repudiation (Anm. 27), S. 131–82; als Darstellung King, R. R.: Minorities under Communism. Cambridge, Mass. 1973, S. 197–99.

[156]) Sofia 1968. Für den Text in englischer Übersetzung s. auch: From Recognition to Repudiation (Anm. 27), S. 183–212 sowie als Darstellung Troebst (Anm. 23).

gesprochen wurde[157]). Andererseits hat Bulgarien – und zwar gerade auch in der sonst unerbittlich den bulgarischen Standpunkt vertretenden Broschüre von 1968 – immer wieder erklärt, daß es zwar auf die Geschichte Makedoniens Anspruch erhebe, aber keine territorialen Forderungen gegenüber Jugoslawien in Hinsicht auf die SR Makedonien habe. Im ganzen ist festzustellen, daß am Ende der hier zu behandelnden Periode wohl das Verhältnis Bulgariens zu Griechenland und der Türkei nachhaltig entspannt war, nicht jedoch dasjenige zu Jugoslawien.

5. Zwischen Sozialistischem Internationalismus und Friedlicher Koexistenz: Die Živkov-Ära (1964/68–1989)

Auch für die letzte Phase bulgarischer Nachkriegsaußenpolitik bis heute gilt, daß Kontinuität und Stabilität weit eher als in allen anderen Ländern des Sowjetblocks als erstes Charakteristikum zu nennen sind. Die Person Živkovs als des inzwischen mit Abstand dienstältesten Parteichefs, an dessen Loyalität zur Sowjetunion niemals ein Zweifel aufgekommen ist, spielt hier sicherlich ebenso eine Rolle wie die Gesamtentwicklung des Sowjetblocks, wo gerade in der Außenpolitik bis zu Gorbačev die „Vormachtkontrolle" stets stärker im Vordergrund gestanden hat als die „Autonomie"[158]). Und zumindest gilt dies für Bulgarien, wo die gegenseitigen Interessen – von der Außenwirtschaft Bulgariens bis zu den strategischen Interessen der Sowjetunion in der Balkanregion[159]) – in erfreulicher Weise zusammengekommen sind, um die allgemeine Tendenz zu mehr Handlungsspielraum für die einzelnen Länder des Blocks mit der überkommenen Treue zur Sowjetunion im beiderseitigen Interesse zu verbinden. Es ist so durchaus möglich, von den zentralen eigenen Quellen Bulgariens auszugehen: vor allem von den außenpolitischen Teilen der Rechenschaftsberichte der Parteitage dieser Jahre, d. h. vom X. Parteitag (20.–25. 4. 1971) bis zum bis heute letzten XIII. Parteitag (2.–5. 4. 1986), von der Verfassung vom 18. 5. 1971 und vom neuen Parteiprogramm vom 24. 4. 1971, wo das schon zitierte Dimitrov-Zitat vom 27. 12. 1943 ohne Quellenangabe wieder aufgenommen worden ist: „Für die BKP und das bulgarische Volk ist die bulgarisch-sowjetische Freundschaft wie die Sonne und die Luft für jedes Lebewesen, sie ist eine Freundschaft seit Jahrhunderten und für Jahrhunderte, eine der Haupttriebkräfte unserer Entwicklung, Bedingung und Garantie für den künftigen Aufstieg unseres sozialistischen Vaterlandes, für seinen morgigen Tag."[160]) Sicher ist es richtig, daß speziell seit der Machtübernahme Gorbačevs

---

[157]) Außer Troebst (Anm. 23) vgl. das Kapitel „Nationale Minderheiten" (S. 480/81) von demselben Autor.

[158]) Von Löwenthal, R.; Meissner, B. (Anm. 5) und dem dort gedruckten Beitrag von Oschlies (Anm. 13) abgesehen vgl. Höpken, W.: Bulgarisch-sowjetische Beziehungen seit Gorbačev, in: Südosteuropa. 35 (1986), S. 611–30, sowie ders.: Sofia und Gorbačevs Reformen (Dokumentation), ebenda. 36 (1987), S. 146–56.

[159]) Vgl. die Kapitel von R. Schönfeld, Außenwirtschaft, und von W. Nolte, Landesverteidigung.

[160]) Für den Rechenschaftsbericht an den X. Parteitag s. Živkov (Anm. 110). 18.1978, S. 335–78; für den XIII. Parteitag: Otčet na Centralnija Komitet na BKP pred XIII partien kongres (Bericht des ZK der BKP vor dem XIII. Parteitag), in: XIII kongres na Bălgarskata Komunističeska Partija. Stenografski protokol (XIII. Parteitag der BKP. Stenographisches Protokoll), 3. Sofia 1987, S. 267–85.

in der Sowjetunion einzelne Mißtöne, speziell im wirtschaftlichen Bereich unüberhörbar geworden sind[161]), dennoch ändert dies im ganzen an der Zuverlässigkeit Bulgariens in den grundsätzlichen Fragen der Blockaußenpolitik nichts, wofür Bulgariens Teilnahme an allen KSZE-Verhandlungen seit 1975 nur ein besonders gutes Beispiel ist[162]). Auch die im Rahmen der deutsch-bulgarischen Beziehungen wichtige, obschon späte Wiederaufnahme der diplomatischen Beziehungen mit der Bundesrepublik (21.12.1973) gehört hierher.

Die einzig denkbare Ausnahme bildet jener Bereich, wo von bulgarischen außenpolitischen Eigeninitiativen gesprochen werden kann: die Balkanpolitik. Und hier haben die letzten Jahre allerdings mit der Assimilierungspolitik gegenüber der großen türkischen Minderheit in Bulgarien seit Ende 1984 sowie dem Exodus von 1989 nicht nur negative Akzente gesetzt, sondern auch solche, wo erstmals die Frage nach dem Konsens mit der Sowjetunion fraglich erscheinen mußte[163]). Andere Probleme wie vor allem dasjenige der angeblichen bulgarischen Verantwortung für das Attentat auf Papst Johannes Paul II. (13.5.1981)[164]) oder Bulgariens Rolle im internationalen Rauschgift- und Waffenhandel mußten demgegenüber zurückstehen, obwohl sie auch dazu beitrugen, das internationale Renommee Bulgariens zu schädigen. Im allgemeinen überwiegt jedoch nach wie vor ohne Zweifel das Bild desjenigen Landes, dessen Außenpolitik auch heute noch im ganzen Sowjetblock den Leitlinien der Sowjetunion am engsten folgt.

Was damit als erstes die Einzelheiten des Verhältnisses zum mit Abstand wichtigsten außenpolitischen Partner Bulgariens auch in dieser bis jetzt letzten Phase betrifft, zur *Sowjetunion*, so lassen sich in der Theorie wie in der Praxis zwei Linien unterscheiden: die große Hauptlinie verbaler wie realer Unterstützung der Weltpolitik der Sowjetunion in allen relevanten Bereichen und daneben gelegentliche Differenzen, die die Hauptlinie aber nie ernsthaft gestört haben, speziell seit dem Amtsantritt Gorbačevs aber auch nicht übersehen werden können.

Bezüglich der Hauptlinie ist erneut festzustellen, daß die kontinuierlichen verbalen Treue- und Zuneigungsbekundungen zur Sowjetunion nicht einfach als „Balkanrhetorik" abgetan werden können. In keinem anderen Land des Sowjetblocks ist die Tendenz zu derartigen Bekundungen so ausgeprägt. Zusätzlich zu den eben schon gegebenen Beispielen sei auf die ständige Wiederholung der Antwort Brežnevs auf die Frage hingewiesen, was denn Sozialistischer Internationalismus sei („das Verhältnis von Sowjetunion und Bulgarien zueinander ist sozialistischer Internationalismus in der Praxis")[165]), auf Živkovs Formulierung von dem „einzigen Organismus" und „einem gemeinsamen Blutkreislauf", und vor allem schließlich auf die „Annähe-

---

[161]) Vgl. Höpken (Anm. 158). Ganz anders von bulgarischer Seite Palaveev, Č.: Za preustrojstvo na meždunarodnite otnošenija (Für die *preustrojstvo* der internationalen Beziehungen). Sofia 1988.

[162]) Vgl. Sicherheit und Zusammenarbeit in Europa (Anm. 137). Die Entwicklung bis 1974 sowie überhaupt eine Zusammenfassung der bulgarischen Außenpolitik von 1944 bis 1974 aus bulgarischer Sicht gibt: Socialističeskata vănšna politika na Narodna Republika Bălgarija (Anm. 22); für den sowjetischen Standpunkt s. Istorija... (Anm. 4), t. 3.1987.

[163]) s.u. S. 129–132 und das Kapitel von S. Troebst, Nationale Minderheiten, S. 478–480.

[164]) Henze, P.B.: The Plot to kill the Pope. New York 1980.

[165]) Parteiprogramm (Anm. 7), S. 9; Shiwkow, T.: Rechenschaftsbericht des ZK der BKP an den XII. Parteitag und die nächsten Aufgaben der Partei. Sofia 1981, S. 120.

rung", ja die „allseitige Annäherung" (*vsestranno sbližavane*) als eigentlichem Kern der Beziehungen zwischen beiden Ländern[166]). Im persönlichen Bereich ist vor allem das enge Verhältnis Živkovs zu Brežnev zu nennen, den „Freund und Bruder", den „größten und verehrtesten Führer und Staatsmann unserer Zeit"[167]). Parallel dazu ist während der ganzen letzten Periode bulgarischer Außenpolitik die Unterstützung der zentralen Anliegen der internationalen Politik der Sowjetunion verlaufen: ob blockintern von der Verankerung der Brežnev-Doktrin des Sozialistischen Internationalismus als Leitprinzip im Gefolge der Tschechoslowakei-Intervention, in der strikten Verurteilung der Vorgänge in Polen von 1980 oder außerhalb des Blocks im Verhältnis zur NATO, in der Frage der KSZE, Afghanistans, Chinas oder im Nahen Osten und schließlich auch in der Perestrojka Gorbačevs als außenpolitischem Prinzip[168]). Zwei charakteristische Einzelbeispiele sind die Teilnahme am Boykott der Olympischen Sommerspiele 1984 und die Absage des Živkov-Besuches in Bonn im Zusammenhang des NATO-Doppelbeschlusses im Herbst desselben Jahres. Von allen anderen Erklärungsmöglichkeiten dieser Gefolgstreue abgesehen ist dabei sicherlich nicht zuletzt auf die über Jahrzehnte gewachsene, intensive außenwirtschaftliche Verflechtung der beiden Länder hinzuweisen: 60 % des bulgarischen Außenhandels werden heute mit der Sowjetunion abgewickelt[169]).

Gerade die Außenwirtschaft gehört nun aber seit der Machtübernahme Gorbačevs zu den Bereichen, wo Reibungspunkte zwischen beiden Ländern deutlich geworden sind, „scharfe Ecken", wie es Gorbačev selbst in einer für die Beziehungen zwischen beiden Ländern ganz ungewöhnlichen Weise genannt hat[170]). Die Sowjetunion kritisiert die Qualität der bulgarischen Exporte sowie überhaupt die Unausgewogenheit der gegenseitigen Wirtschaftsbeziehungen. Schon lange vorher, noch zur Zeit Brežnevs, wurde aber z. B. während des X. Parteitages 1971 deutlich, daß die Sowjetunion von Bulgarien die Rücknahme einer multilateralen Balkanpolitik zugunsten bilateraler Beziehungen wünschte[171]). In der kurzen Amtszeit Andropovs soll es zu Mißhelligkeiten wegen sowjetischer Pläne gekommen sein, Atomraketen auf bulgarischem Boden zu stationieren. Und schließlich ist zumindest ungeklärt, wie die Haltung der Sowjetunion zum Verdacht der Teilnahme Bulgariens am Papstattentat und vor allem zur Assimilierung der türkischen Minderheit ist. Bei den protokollarisch stets überlegten Russen ist es kaum ein Zufall, daß Gorbačev 1986 wohl zum XI. Parteitag der SED, nicht aber zum XIII. Parteitag der BKP gefahren ist. Wie stark diese Differenzen im einzelnen aber auch gewesen sein mögen, es fehlt im allgemeinen wie für die Außenpolitik im besonderen bis heute jeder Hinweis, daß der Sturz Živkovs am 10.11.1989 durch Gorbačev initiiert worden sei.

---

[166]) RD. 21. 3. 1974; Otčet...pred XIII partien kongres (Anm. 160), S. 273.
[167]) Shiwkow: Rechenschaftsbericht (Anm. 165), S. 121; Edinadeseti kongres na BKP, 29 mart–2 april 1976 g. Stenografski protokol (XI. Parteitag der BKP, 29. März–2. April 1976. Stenographisches Protokoll). Sofia 1976, S. 31.
[168]) Palaveev (Anm. 161).
[169]) Vgl. das Kapitel von R. Schönfeld, Außenwirtschaft, S. 405.
[170]) Pravda. 25. 10. 1985. – Für das eher zurückhaltende Verhältnis zur Perestrojka vgl. die Dokumentation Anm. 158.
[171]) Kerr, J. L.: Bulgaria and its Neighbours: A Hundred Years After Independence. RAD Background Report. 1 (Bulgaria). 2 January 1978, S. 4.

Andererseits dürfen derartige Differenzen auf keinen Fall überbewertet werden: Die wechselseitigen Interessen sind hierfür viel zu evident und stark. Ein unübersehbares Beispiel stellt in diesem Zusammenhang auch Bulgariens generelles Verhalten innerhalb des *Sowjetblocks* seit 1964/68 dar. Keines der anderen Länder kann sich in Hinsicht auf Blockloyalität mit Bulgarien messen: Ungarn und die DDR nicht, und die Tschechoslowakei erst seit Abschluß des Prozesses der „Normalisierung", wobei auch besonders auf den ungewöhnlich hohen Beitrag Bulgariens im Rahmen der Militärausgaben des WP hingewiesen werden kann[172]). Živkovs gleichbleibende Aussagen bei allen relevanten Anlässen dürfen hier ohne Verdacht des „Lippenbekenntnisses" herangezogen werden: von der „Internationalen Beratung der kommunistischen und Arbeiterparteien" in Moskau (5.–17.6.1969) über die 29-Parteien-Konferenz in Ostberlin (29./30.6.1976) bis zum XIII. Parteitag der BKP (2.–5.4.1986), wo er unter Berufung auf den Sozialistischen Internationalismus ausführte: „Die Grundrichtung in der internationalen Tätigkeit von Partei und Staat bildete die Festigung der Einheit und Geschlossenheit, die Vertiefung der Zusammenarbeit mit unseren engsten Verbündeten, den Ländern der sozialistischen Staatengemeinschaft... Die Volksrepublik Bulgarien beteiligt sich unmittelbar an der Gestaltung und Realisierung der abgestimmten Außenpolitik."[173]) Es ist insofern auch nur logisch, daß Bulgarien in der Zusammenfassung von R. L. Hutchings für die Jahre 1968–1980 mit Abstand die geringste Rolle spielt[174]).

Einige Beispiele können dies verdeutlichen. Als erstes sei der bulgarische Außenhandel genannt, wo der RGW-Anteil inzwischen die 80 %-Grenze erreicht hat (unter Einschluß des Handels mit der Sowjetunion)[175]). Nicht weniger aussagekräftig ist die Unterstützung der von der Sowjetunion den Blockländern vorgegebenen Haltung gegenüber Polen 1980: Die bulgarischen Aussagen reichen von der „Todesgefahr", in der sich Polen befunden habe, über das unmißverständliche Angebot „brüderlicher Hilfe" bis zu der laut Protokoll von Beifall begleiteten Aussage Živkovs auf dem XXVI. Parteitag der KPdSU: „Polen war, ist und wird immer ein Mitglied der Familie sozialistischer Länder sein"[176]). Nicht minder typisch ist der „Vertrag über Freundschaft, Zusammenarbeit und gegenseitigen Beistand" zwischen Bulgarien und der DDR vom 14.9.1977, der zu den bis jetzt noch ganz wenigen Verträgen der letzten Generation im Sowjetblock gehört und alle Merkmale einer möglichst engen Blockbindung der Sozialistischen Gemeinschaft auf der Grundlage des Sozialisti-

---

[172]) Für Ungarn und die DDR s. Grothusen (Anm. 2), S. 142/43: für den WP s. Nelson, D. N.: Alliance behavior in the Warsaw Pact. Boulder and London 1986 und das Kapitel „Landesverteidigung" von W. Nolte, S. 266.

[173]) XIII kongres (Anm. 160), S. 271.

[174]) Hutchings, R. L.: Soviet-East European Relations. Consolidation and Conflict 1968–1980. London 1983.

[175]) Vgl. das Kapitel von R. Schönfeld, Außenwirtschaft, S. 405.

[176]) IX. Außerordentlicher Parteitag der Polnischen Vereinigten Arbeiterpartei, 14.–20. Juli 1981. Dokumente und Materialien. Warschau 1981, S. 620; Shiwkow (Anm. 165), S. 119; XXVI s-ezd Kommunističeskoj Partii Sovetskogo Sojuza. 23 fevralja – 3 marta 1981 goda. Stenografičeskij otčet (XXVI. Parteitag der KPdSU, 23. Februar–3. März. Stenographisches Protokoll), 1. Moskau 1981, S. 204. – Vgl. auch: Die Reaktionen auf die Ereignisse in Polen, in: Südosteuropa. 31 (1982), S. 112–15.

Außenpolitik 123

schen Internationalismus aufweist[177]). Nicht vergessen werden sollte auch das Vertragspaket, das anläßlich eines Partei- und Staatsbesuches in Sofia (16.–23.12.1981) zwischen Bulgarien und Afghanistan abgeschlossen wurde und Ausdruck von Blocksolidarität mit der sowjetischen Afghanistan-Politik ist[178]).

Und als letztes und wohl bestes Beispiel ist die bulgarische Haltung gegenüber *China* und *Albanien* zu nennen. Eine bessere Unterstützung der sowjetischen Anliegen gegenüber China von 1969 an läßt sich kaum finden als diejenige durch Bulgarien. Ob Živkov 1969 auf der Moskauer Konferenz von „Verrat an den revolutionären Kämpfen der Kommunisten" durch die chinesische Führung sprach, „die eine antisowjetische Politik betreibt und durch ihre Taten die internationale kommunistische Bewegung zersetzt", 1976 auf dem IX. Parteitag der SED vom „gemeinsamen Chor antisowjetischer Psalmen", die er als „entweder dreist und boshaft oder schmeichelnd-heuchlerisch" charakterisierte, bis zum XXVI. Parteitag der KPdSU 1981, wo von einer durch China geschaffenen „konterrevolutionären Weltfront" die Rede ist – die Blocktreue ist unüberhörbar. Dies gilt auch für den inzwischen eingeleiteten Prozeß der Wiederannäherung, der als letztes auf dem XIII. Parteitag der BKP 1986 ausdrücklich begrüßt wurde[179]). Und auch das Verhalten gegenüber Albanien paßte sich diesem Muster an, obwohl als Variante die damals fast unbegrenzte Bereitschaft Albaniens zumindest zum verbalen Gegenschlag hervorzuheben ist. Nachdem von 1968 bis 1970 die diplomatischen Beziehungen sogar noch über das chinesische Maß hinaus vollständig unterbrochen gewesen waren, hat sich Bulgarien von 1971 an deutlich und wiederholt um einen Ausgleich bemüht. Die albanische Reaktion bestand jedoch zunächst darin, daß Enver Hoxha Bulgarien als „eine wahre Kolonie der sowjetischen Sozialimperialisten" bezeichnete, als „Aufmarschgebiet gegen unsere Länder" und das bulgarische Volk als „Kanonenfutter"[180]). Auch der Bruch zwischen Albanien und China von 1978 brachte noch wenig Bewegung in das erstarrte Verhältnis. Erst mit dem Abschluß eines Handelsvertrages im Gefolge mehrerer Handelsprotokolle seit 1971 für die Zeit von Ende 1985 bis 1990 wurde eine deutliche Auflockerung erzielt[181]). Es entsprach so denn auch durchaus den Zielen bulgarischer Balkanpolitik, daß Albanien an der Belgrader Außenministerkonferenz (24.–26.2.1988) teilgenommen hat, wobei der stellvertretende Außenminister I. Ganev in diesem Zusammenhang Albanien einen ersten Besuch abgestattet hat.

---

[177]) Uschakow; Frenzke (Anm. 3), S. 357–61 (Text) sowie für die Analyse passim; Die Oststaaten, das sowjetische Bündnissystem und die KSZE vor und nach Helsinki. Bearb. v. D. Frenzke u. A. Uschakow. Köln 1983 (Internationales Recht und Diplomatie. Jg. 1977–1980); aus DDR-Sicht: DDR-VRB. Freundschaft und Zusammenarbeit. Berlin, Sofia 1979; Dokumente und Materialien der Zusammenarbeit zwischen der Sozialistischen Einheitspartei Deutschlands und der Bulgarischen Kommunistischen Partei 1977 bis 1984. Berlin, Sofia 1984.
[178]) Tönnes, B.: Der bulgarisch-afghanische Freundschaftsvertrag. Im Dienste der sowjetischen „Friedenspolitik", in: Südosteuropa. 31 (1982), S. 78–81 (Text und Kommentar); zur Invasion in Afghanistan s. Wissenschaftlicher Dienst Südosteuropa. 29 (1980) 1/2, S. 1.
[179]) Živkov (Anm. 110). 16.1976, S. 199/200; Protokoll der Verhandlungen des IX. Parteitages der Sozialistischen Einheitspartei Deutschlands im Palast der Republik in Berlin, 18. bis 22. Mai 1976, Bd. 1. Berlin 1976, S. 231; XXVI s-ezd (Anm. 176), S. 205.; XIII. kongres (Anm. 160), S. 274.
[180]) Zëri i Popullit. 5.10.1974. Vgl. außerdem Topp, H. D.: Sofioter Gesprächsofferten an Tirana, in: Wissenschaftlicher Dienst Südosteuropa. 27 (1968), S. 256–58.
[181]) Otečestven front. 5.12.1985; vgl. auch Höpken (Anm. 158), S. 617/618; Historia e Shqipërisë (Geschichte Albaniens). Bd. 4. Tiranë 1983, S. 433.

Hervorzuheben ist schließlich, daß erstmals seit dem Bruch zwischen Albanien und dem Sowjetblock eine Freundschaftsgesellschaft mit Albanien gegründet worden ist, nämlich eine „Gesellschaft für bulgarisch-albanische Freundschaft" (Mai 1989)[181a].

Eine gewisse Sonderstellung nimmt höchstens Bulgariens Haltung gegenüber Rumänien ein, und zwar deswegen, weil diese, von einer Phase der Abkühlung 1968/69 wegen der Nichtteilnahme Rumäniens an der Intervention gegen die Tschechoslowakei sowie einer leichten Irritation wegen der Norddobrudscha 1984[182]) abgesehen, stets besonders positiv gewesen ist. Das deutlichste Zeichen hierfür sind die ständigen Treffen zwischen Živkov und Ceaușescu, von denen bis zum Sturz beider Ende 1989 rund 40 stattgefunden haben. Und wenn der Block, geführt von der Sowjetunion, Rumänien sein Mißfallen hat merken lassen – etwa wegen der Chinapolitik –, hat sich Bulgarien stets auffällig zurückgehalten. Eine zureichende Begründung hierfür ist nicht bekannt, doch kann damit gerechnet werden, daß im Zuge der weiteren Abkehr vom Regime Živkovs speziell durch P. Mladenov in Zukunft hier weitere Erklärungen zu erwarten sind, die ebenso wie im Falle der von der Weltöffentlichkeit überwiegend negativ aufgenommenen Türkei-Politik Bulgariens der letzten Jahre in einer persönlichen Schuldzuweisung an Živkov bestehen werden.

Im Verhältnis Bulgariens zu den *westlichen Ländern* ist als erstes ebenso charakteristisch wie selbstverständlich, daß die große Linie vollständig der „abgestimmten Außenpolitik" des Sowjetblocks entspricht und daß sich Bulgarien im speziellen auch hier seit Jahren neben der Tschechoslowakei als der zuverlässigste Verbündete der Sowjetunion erweist. Ständige Beweise hierfür erbringt das Abstimmungsverhalten Bulgariens in den verschiedenen Organen der UNO – wobei Bulgarien bereits zweimal, 1966 und 1985, zum Nichtständigen Mitglied des Weltsicherheitsrates gewählt worden ist – und die Mitarbeit in internationalen Gremien wie der KSZE mit ihren Folgekonferenzen oder der KVAE[183]). Ein gewisser Widerspruch hierzu ergibt sich allerdings daraus, daß Bulgarien aus mehreren Gründen wie kein anderes Land des Sowjetblocks in den letzten Jahren Schädigungen seines guten Rufes im Westen hat hinnehmen müssen. Zu nennen ist als erstes die angebliche Verantwortung für das Attentat auf Papst Johannes Paul II. (13.5.1981)[184]). Nachdem sich Živkov selbst in den Jahren davor um eine Verbesserung der Beziehungen zum Vatikan bemüht hatte – etwa durch einen Besuch bei Papst Paul VI. im Zusammenhang seines ersten Besuches in Italien (23.–27.6.1975) –, kam der Verdacht überraschend, deswegen aber nicht weniger unangenehm, daß Bulgarien als Organisator hinter dem eigentlichen Attentäter, dem Türken Mehmed Ali Agça, gestanden habe. Am 25.11.1982 wurde der Leiter des römischen Büros von Balkan Airlines, S.I. Antonov, verhaftet. Auch wenn er ebenso wie zwei mitangeklagte Bulgaren am 31.3.1986 mangels Beweisen freigesprochen wurde, blieb der Verdacht gegen Bulgarien bestehen. Und nicht min-

---

[181a]) Zëri i Popullit. 23.5.1989.

[182]) Ghermani, D.: Rumänisch-bulgarische Zwistigkeiten, in: Südosteuropa. 35 (1986), S. 127–31.

[183]) Für die Mitarbeit an der UNO s. Information Bulgaria. A short encyclopedia of the People's Republic of Bulgaria. Oxford u. a. 1985, S. 909–15; für KSZE und KVAE: Oschlies, W.: Bulgariens Stellung zur KSZE. Köln 1973 (BOIS. 24–1973); Fesefeldt, J.: Der Warschauer Pakt auf dem Madrider KSZE-Folgetreffen und auf der KVAE (ohne Rumänien). Köln 1984 (BOIS. 40–1984).

[184]) Vgl. Henze (Anm. 164).

der schädlich für das bulgarische Ansehen war es, daß immer wieder im Westen Vorwürfe laut wurden, Bulgarien spiele eine maßgebliche Rolle im internationalen Drogen- und Waffenhandel sowie im Terrorismus. Besonders empfindlich reagierten die USA, die 1983 die Zusammenarbeit in der Bekämpfung des Drogenhandels mit Bulgarien einstellten, weil konkret behauptet wurde, daß 30 % des illegalen amerikanischen Drogenimports aus Bulgarien stammten. Erst durch zwei Besuche von Vizeaußenminister J. Whitehead in Sofia – zuletzt am 18./19. 10. 1988 – konnte das Klima deutlich verbessert werden[185]).

Wenn der Westen im Rahmen der gesamten Außenpolitik des Sowjetblocks und damit selbstverständlich auch für Bulgarien politisch eine zentrale Rolle spielt, so kann dies nach wie vor gerade im Falle Bulgariens nicht für die Außenwirtschaft gelten. Knapp 17 % ist hier der höchste Anteil gewesen, den der Westen bis jetzt hat erreichen können, wobei vom deutschen Standpunkt aus wichtig ist, daß die Bundesrepublik Deutschland von wenigen Jahren abgesehen, wo Italien Platz 1 einnahm, stets mit großem Abstand der wichtigste westliche Handelspartner ist[186]).

Was damit die *Bundesrepublik Deutschland* betrifft, so sind zwei Dinge charakteristisch: einmal, daß Bulgarien die diplomatischen Beziehungen als letztes Land des gesamten Sowjetblocks aufgenommen hat (21. 12. 1973)[187]), und dann, daß dieses Faktum allein auf Blockdisziplin zurückzuführen ist, während unabhängig davon die Problemlosigkeit, ja Herzlichkeit der gegenseitigen Beziehungen, die allerdings auch nicht durch Fragen wie Reparationszahlungen, Minderheiten usw. belastet sind, charakteristisch ist. Die alten wechselseitigen Kulturbeziehungen haben sich als gute Basis für das heutige Verhältnis erwiesen. Nach vorbereitenden Gesprächen über die Aufnahme der diplomatischen Beziehungen am Rande der KSZE-Verhandlungen in Helsinki 1973 besuchte Außenminister W. Scheel am 25./26. 3. 1974 als erster Minister der Bundesrepublik Deutschland Bulgarien, und vom 24.–28. 11. 1975 fand der erste Besuch Živkovs in Bonn statt. Daß der zweite, für den September 1984 geplante Besuch – ebenso wie derjenige Honeckers – kurzfristig abgesagt wurde, lag nicht an den bilateralen Beziehungen, sondern ergab sich als Folge von Spannungen zwischen der Sowjetunion und dem Westen wegen Nachrüstungsfragen. Als Živkov seinen Besuch vom 2.–5. 6. 1987 nachholte, konnte Bundeskanzler Kohl feststellen, daß sich die Beziehungen zwischen beiden Ländern „in allen Bereichen erfreulich" entwickelten[188]). Ein Indikator hierfür ist der deutsche Touristenstrom, wo die Bundesrepublik unter den westlichen Ländern auf Platz 1 liegt[189]). Den positiven Schlußpunkt hat bis jetzt der erste Staatsbesuch eines Bundespräsidenten gebildet, den Richard

---

[185]) FAZ. 10. 2. 1985 und 30. 1. 1988; Sofioter Nachrichten. 19. 10. 1988.

[186]) Vgl. das Kapitel von R. Schönfeld, Außenwirtschaft.

[187]) Oschlies, W.: Bonn – Sofia. Vor und nach Aufnahme diplomatischer Beziehungen, in: Osteuropa. 24 (1974), S. 586–98; Dokumente zur Entwicklung der Beziehungen zwischen der Bundesrepublik Deutschland und Bulgarien 1971–1974, ebenda, S. A. 548–55; Höpken, W.: Unproblematisches Verhältnis ohne förmliche Beziehungen – Sofia in Wartestellung in Richtung Bonn, in: Unfertige Nachbarschaften. Hrsg. O. N. Haberl u. H. Hecker. Essen 1989, S. 91–116.

[188]) Offizieller Besuch des Vorsitzenden des Staatsrates der Volksrepublik Bulgarien vom 2. bis 5. Juni 1987, in: Presse- und Informationsamt der Bundesregierung. Bulletin Nr. 53, 4. 6. 1987, S. 460–73.

[189]) Vgl. das Kapitel „Tourismus" von M. A. Hatschikjan, S. 391.

von Weizsäcker vom 21.–24.11.1988 Bulgarien abstattete. Bei dieser Gelegenheit konnte Bundesaußenminister Genscher außer einem Doppelbesteuerungsabkommen endlich auch das lange angestrebte Abkommen über die Errichtung von Kulturinstituten in beiden Ländern (Sitz des bulgarischen wird München sein) unterzeichnen. Bulgarien folgte damit mit großem Abstand dem Vorbild Ungarns und Rumäniens, was auf hinhaltenden Widerstand der DDR zurückzuführen sein dürfte. Aus der weiteren Entwicklung der bilateralen Beziehungen ist der Abschluß eines Abkommens über die Zusammenarbeit im Umweltschutz (Luftreinhaltung, Gewässerschutz, Abfallwirtschaft) am 14.4.1989 in Bonn zu nennen sowie der Besuch von Bundesumweltminister Klaus Töpfer in Sofia am 4.7.1989, bei dem es vorrangig um den gemeinsamen Schutz der Donau ging.

Betrachtet man als letztes vor dem speziellen Bereich der Balkanpolitik die *Dritte Welt*, so hält sich die bulgarische Außenpolitik auch hier an die durch den Sozialistischen Internationalismus und die Sowjetunion vorgegebenen Normen. Vorrang hat der „Kampf um die Beseitigung der Überreste des Kolonialismus, gegen Neo-Kolonialismus, Rassismus und Apartheid, gegen diktatorische und volksfeindliche Regime"[190]). Dies schließt die direkte Unterstützung der sozialistischen Länder in Afrika durch Wirtschafts- wie vor allem auch durch Ausbildungshilfe ebenso ein wie Assistenz für die Sowjetunion in der Nahostpolitik. Für die besondere Verbundenheit Bulgariens mit der Sowjetunion spricht es z.B., daß Živkov im April 1980 als erstes Staatsoberhaupt eines Sowjetblock-Staates in Syrien mit Y. Arafat zusammengetroffen ist und sich dabei nachdrücklich für einen Palästinenserstaat ausgesprochen hat. Die logische Fortsetzung dieser Politik ist es gewesen, daß Bulgarien am 25.11.1988 den nunmehr auf der 19. Sondertagung des Palästinensischen Nationalrates gegründeten Staat – nicht anders als z.B. auch die DDR und Rumänien – anerkannt hat. Aber auch der Besuch Živkovs in Indien (22.–27.1.1969) diente übergeordneten Zwecken, war es doch der erste Versuch der Interventionsmächte, nach der Tschechoslowakeikrise von 1968 bei den blockfreien Ländern wieder Ansehen zu gewinnen. Nicht zufällig wurde so denn auch auf dem XIII. Parteitag der BKP den Blockfreien besondere Anerkennung gezollt[191]).

Was damit als letzten Bereich den *Balkan* als das Feld abgrenzbarer bulgarischer Regionalpolitik betrifft, so ist davon auszugehen, daß hier in den letzten Jahren einerseits deutlich neue Entwicklungen von teilweise großer Tragweite in Gang gekommen sind, daß sich an der Grundstruktur bulgarischer Außenpolitik aber auch hier nichts geändert hat, abgesehen allerdings von der Kehrtwendung in der Haltung gegenüber der Emigrationsmöglichkeit der türkischen Minderheit von der Fernsehrede Živkovs am 29.5.1989 an[191a]). Der Balkan bleibt der einzige außenpolitische Bereich, wo Bulgarien deutlich Eigeninteressen hat, was im Einzelfall – obschon nur schwer nachweisbar – zu Interessenkollisionen mit der Sowjetunion führen kann. Auf ein Beispiel – die Rücknahme multilateraler Initiativen auf dem X. Parteitag von 1971 – wurde bereits hingewiesen[192]). Viel wichtiger ist aber, daß auch in der Balkan-

---

[190]) XIII kongres (Anm. 160), S. 277/78.
[191]) Ebenda, S. 278.
[191a]) Otečestven front. 31.5.1989.
[192]) s.o. S. 121f.

politik vorrangig von Interessenidentität von Bulgarien und Sowjetunion ausgegangen werden kann. Bulgarien ist seit langem der einzige zuverlässige Partner der Sowjetunion in diesem strategisch so überaus wichtigen Schnittbereich von WP, NATO und Blockfreien, was seine Stellung im Binnenverhältnis zur Sowjetunion mit Sicherheit nachhaltig stärkt. Zwei grundsätzlich verschiedene Zielrichtungen der bulgarischen Außenpolitik lassen sich dabei auch in dieser bis heute letzten Phase unterscheiden: die multilaterale, auf den ganzen Balkan gerichtete und die bilaterale, d. h. das Einzelverhältnis zu den verschiedenen Ländern. Was das letztere betrifft, so sind an dieser Stelle, nachdem auf Rumänien und Albanien bereits eingegangen worden ist, nur noch Griechenland, die Türkei unter Einschluß des Zypernproblems und Jugoslawien zu behandeln.

Die multilaterale Balkanpolitik ist von Bulgarien aus gesehen deutlich derjenige Bereich, dem verbal die Priorität zukommt, handelt es sich doch um Fragen wie die Verwandlung des Balkans in eine Zone des Friedens, eine atomwaffen- und neuerdings auch chemiewaffenfreie Zone. Die bulgarische Außenpolitik knüpft hier an die dargestellten Bemühungen seit dem Stoica-Plan von 1957 an[193]). Vom X. Parteitag 1971 abgesehen ziehen sich Bemühungen in dieser Richtung durch den gesamten Zeitraum bis heute, wobei ihnen der Abschluß des KSZE-Vertrages 1975 neuen Auftrieb gegeben hat. Es ist nur bedingt richtig, wenn von bulgarischer Seite immer wieder auf eine Rede Živkovs vom 20.10.1981 als Ausgangspunkt dieser Bemühungen hingewiesen wird[194]). Stattdessen lassen sich die Aufforderungen Bulgariens an seine regionalen Partnerländer durch alle maßgeblichen Verlautbarungen seit 1957 hindurch verfolgen, von denen diejenigen anläßlich des XIII. Parteitages von 1986 und der Belgrader Balkankonferenz vom 24.–26.2.1988 nur die letzten sind[195]). Etwas anderes ist dafür, inwieweit diesen kontinuierlichen Vorschlägen ein Realitätsbezug zugesprochen werden kann: Da Bulgarien aufgrund des Pariser Friedensvertrages von 1947 ohnehin nicht über Kernwaffen und Raketen verfügen darf[196]), würde in diesem Bereich eine gravierende Vorleistung der NATO-Staaten Griechenland und Türkei erforderlich sein. Und auch sonst erweist es sich bis jetzt, daß nur wenig echte Fortschritte erzielt worden sind, und wenn, dann ohne Zutun Bulgariens.

Was das letztere betrifft, so sind die Balkankonferenzen gemeint, die es in den letzten beiden Jahrzehnten durchaus mehrfach gegeben hat: in Athen (26.1.–5.2.1976), in Sofia (15.–18.6.1981), wieder in Athen (16.1.–13.2.1984) und

---

[193]) s. o. S. 113. Mit einer Fülle oft populärer Veröffentlichungen unterstützt die bulgarische Regierung ihren Standpunkt. Vgl. Sachariewa, J.; Ljubenov, I.: Bulgarien kämpft für einen kernwaffenfreien Balkan. Sofia 1984; Dejanow, R.: Der kernwaffenfreie Balkan und das Streben nach allgemeiner Sicherheit. Sofia 1987; Bulgarien und der Frieden auf dem Balkan. Sofia 1987. – Eine seriöse westliche Analyse gibt Tönnes, B.: Bulgariens balkanpolitisches Konzept, in: Südosteuropa. 35 (1984), S. 313–26.

[194]) Živkov (Anm. 110). 32. 1984, S. 244.

[195]) XIII kongres (Anm. 160), S. 275–77; Außenministerkonferenz der Balkanländer. Belgrad, 24.–26. Februar 1988, in: Internationale Politik. H. 910. 5. März 1988, S. 9–33; Reuter, J.: Die Außenministerkonferenz der Balkanländer in Belgrad, in: Südosteuropa. 37 (1988), S. 128–41; Ashley, S.: Bulgaria and the Balkan Foreign Ministers' Conference, in: RFE Research. Bulgaria/3. 8 March 1988. Situation Report, S. 3–8; Neue Entwicklungen auf dem Balkan. Die Belgrader Außenministerkonferenz und weitere bilaterale Treffen, in: Europa-Archiv. 43 (1988) 9, S. D 233–44.

[196]) European Peace Treaties (Anm. 66), Art. 9 und 13, S. 254.

vor allem in Belgrad (24.–26.2.1988)[197]). Größere Bedeutung hat von diesen nur die Belgrader Konferenz von 1988 gehabt, weil hier im Kreis der Außenminister – und zudem vollständig, d.h. zum ersten Mal unter Teilnahme Albaniens – eine Grundsatzdiskussion geführt und eine weiterführende Kooperation beschlossen wurde, nachdem es vorher eher um zweitrangige Fragen – wie den Güterverkehr – gegangen war. Verwirklicht worden sind bis heute Nachfolgetreffen unterhalb der Ministerebene (Sofia 21.–23.6.1988 und Tirana 18.–20.1.1989)[197a]), wobei sich speziell in Tirana Albanien bemüht haben soll, die festgefahrenen bulgarisch-türkischen Gespräche wieder in Gang zu setzen. Größere bulgarische Aktivität ist damit nur 1981 in Sofia festzustellen sowie in der weiteren Unterstützung der „Bewegung für Frieden und Zusammenarbeit auf dem Balkan".

Als sehr viel konkreter und oft auch überraschender erweisen sich insofern die bilateralen Beziehungen. Dies gilt als erstes bereits für das Verhältnis zu *Griechenland*. Mit keinem Balkannachbarn Bulgariens sind, wie dargestellt, die Ausgangsbedingungen für ein gutnachbarliches Verhältnis nach 1944 zunächst so schlecht gewesen wie im Falle Griechenlands[198]). Umso erstaunlicher ist es, wie positiv sich die Beziehungen seit den Verträgen von 1964 entwickelt haben. Der Rechenschaftsbericht des ZK für den XIII. Parteitag vermerkt zu Recht, daß die wechselseitigen Beziehungen „ein gutes Beispiel für friedliche Koexistenz von Staaten unterschiedlicher Gesellschaftsordnung" und „ein Beitrag zur politischen Stabilität auf dem Balkan" seien, was z. B. durch den stellvertretenden Außenminister I. Ganev dadurch ergänzt worden ist, daß er die „Deklaration über Freundschaft, gute Nachbarschaft und Zusammenarbeit zwischen der Volksrepublik Bulgarien und der Republik Griechenland" vom 11.9.1986 als „einmaliges Dokument von Staaten unterschiedlicher Gesellschaftsordnung" bezeichnet hat[199]).

Tatsächlich ist festzustellen, daß sich die Beziehungen zwischen beiden Ländern seit 1964 ohne Bruch bis heute positiv entwickelt haben, was umso bemerkenswerter ist, als Griechenland seitdem drei höchst unterschiedliche Phasen seiner Entwicklung durchgemacht hat: die Junta (1967–1974), die Zeit Karamanlis' (1974–1981) und 1981–1989 A. Papandreous[200]). Nicht einmal die Junta-Zeit hat Bulgarien von seinem Kurs der Annäherung abbringen können: Am 8./9.5.1970 ist I. Bašev als erster bulgarischer Außenminister seit dem II. Weltkrieg nach Athen gefahren, und am

---

[197]) Zur Athener Konferenz von 1976 ausführlich Hartl (Anm. 33), S. 75–93; zur Belgrader Konferenz 1988 Anm. 195.

[197a]) Ivanova, A.: Continuing Efforts in Inter-Balkan Diplomacy, in: RFE Research. Vol. 13, No. 30 Part II of 2 Parts. 29 July 1988, S. 13–17; Zanga, L.: A „new spirit" in the Balkans, in: RFE Research. RAD Background Report. 16 (East-West Relations). 1.2.1989, S. 1–4; Jelić, V.: Die Kontinuität der balkanischen Zusammenarbeit, in: Internationale Politik. H. 918/19. 5.–20.7.1988, S. 7–9; Vučković, C.: Zusammenarbeit auf dem Balkan. Außenministerkonferenz der Balkanstaaten in Tirana, ebd., H. 932. 5.2.1989, S. 10/11.

[198]) S. o. S.117.

[199]) XIII kongres (Anm. 160), 276/77; Interview des stellvertretenden Außenministers I. Ganev, 2. und 5.10.1987, in: Die Umgestaltung. Bulletin der Agentur Sofia Press. 3. Oktober 1987, S. 4; für den Text der Deklaration vom 11.9.1986 s. Bulgarisch-griechische Freundschaftserklärung, in: Südosteuropa. 35 (1986), S. 600–03; als Analyse Tönnes (Anm. 112), S. 417–28.

[200]) Für die Einzelheiten vgl. Südosteuropa-Handbuch. Bd. III: Griechenland. Hrsg. v. K.-D. Grothusen. Göttingen 1980, passim.

31.5.1973 wurde eine erste „Deklaration über die Prinzipien der guten Nachbarschaft, der gegenseitigen Verständigung und der Zusammenarbeit" unterschrieben, die allerdings noch nicht den Grad der Intensität hatte wie die Deklaration von 1986[201]). Und erst mit dem Regierungsantritt von Karamanlis entwickelten sich auch persönlich ungewöhnlich gute Beziehungen zu Živkov, die ihren Ausdruck in regelmäßigen wechselseitigen Besuchen fanden und damit ein Vorspiel für das erst recht enge Verhältnis von Živkov und Papandreou bildeten. Wichtig für die Annäherung der beiden Länder ist dabei speziell seit der türkischen Landung auf Zypern (20.7.1974), daß Griechenland auf diese Weise versucht, Unterstützung im Ägäis- und Zypernstreit mit der Türkei zu gewinnen. Noch unabsehbar sind zum heutigen Zeitpunkt die Konsequenzen des nach den griechischen Parlamentswahlen vom 18.6.1989 erfolgten Regierungswechsels für die Beziehungen beider Länder. Immerhin ist in einer für Griechenland sehr typischen Weise bereits deutlich geworden, daß es gegen jeden Gedanken Protest eingelegt hat, Nordzypern als Auffanggebiet für die türkische Fluchtbewegung aus Bulgarien seit dem Mai 1989 zu benutzen[201a]).

Bulgariens Haltung im *Zypernkonflikt* entspricht dabei im Ganzen durchaus mehr der sowjetischen als der griechischen: Von vereinzelten starken Worten abgesehen, daß es der „destabilisierenden Rolle der Türkei in der Region" entspreche, wenn die Türkei hier „die einzige militärische Aggression in der Nachkriegsgeschichte Europas" durchgeführt habe, wiederholt Bulgarien bis heute den bekannten Standpunkt der Sowjetunion: Rückzug der türkischen Truppen im Sinne der UNO-Resolutionen von 1974, Wiederherstellung der Einheit, Unabhängigkeit und Blockfreiheit Zyperns und gegebenenfalls zur Herbeiführung dieser Ziele eine internationale Konferenz[202]). Die bulgarische Reaktion war so denn auch matt, als der griechische Außenminister Papoulias am 27.3.1987 überstürzt nach Sofia flog, um aufgrund der Konsultationsklausel der Deklaration von 1986 wegen einer erneuten Verschärfung des Ägäiskonflikts mehr bulgarische Unterstützung zu gewinnen.

Das bulgarische Interesse an Griechenland geht stattdessen – nicht anders als das sowjetische – dahin, seine Blockzugehörigkeit und vor allem die NATO-Bindungen nach Möglichkeit aufzuweichen. Nach acht Jahren Regierungszeit Papandreous muß allerdings im Sommer 1989 festgestellt werden, daß Bulgarien diesem Ziel noch keineswegs nähergekommen ist. Davon abgesehen bleibt es aber dabei, daß das Verhältnis zu Griechenland neben demjenigen zu Rumänien heute mit Abstand das beste zu einem Balkanland ist. Einen Hinweis darauf lieferte Živkovs Grußbotschaft zu Papandreous 70. Geburtstag (5.2.1989), die von den bulgarischen Medien nachdrücklich in den Vordergrund geschoben worden ist.

Im Gegensatz dazu liegen im *bulgarisch-türkischen Verhältnis* vom Winter 1984/85 an Jahre der offenen Gegensätzlichkeiten zurück, die an die Zeiten des Kalten Kriegs auf dem Balkan erinnern. Die Ursache hierfür ist die radikale Bulgarisierungspolitik der bulgarischen Regierung gegenüber der ca. 10 % der Gesamtbevölkerung des Lan-

---

[201]) RD. 2.6.1973.   [201a]) FAZ. 21.6.1989.
[202]) Für die „starken Worte": Bulgarien und der Frieden auf dem Balkan (Anm. 193), S. 11; zurückhaltender: XIII kongres (Anm. 160), S. 277; für den sowjetischen Standpunkt s. Anisimov, L.N.: Problema Kipra. Istoričeskij i meždunarodnopravovoj aspekty (Das Zypernproblem. Historische und völkerrechtliche Aspekte). Moskau 1986; vom westlichen Standpunkt: Grothusen, K.-D.: Außenpolitik (Anm. 101), S. 131 ff. passim.

des oder etwa 1 Mio. Menschen umfassenden türkisch-islamischen Minderheit – oder, nach der bulgarischen Formulierung, gegenüber den „muslimischen Bulgaren" –, die Ende 1984 ihren Anfang nahm und ihren hervorstechendsten Ausdruck in dem zwangsweisen Oktroi bulgarisch-slawischer Namen fand[203]. Es konnte nicht ausbleiben, daß die türkische Regierung, je länger und je schärfer die Kampagne lief, mit desto nachdrücklicheren Mitteln ihren bedrängten Landsleuten zu Hilfe kommen mußte. Hier von „anachronistischen pan-türkischen Ambitionen" und „Schürung einer antibulgarischen Psychose" oder zumindest von grundlosen Versuchen zu sprechen, sich in die inneren Angelegenheiten Bulgariens einzumischen, konnte nur auf türkischen Protest stoßen[204]. Wichtiger ist aber noch die Frage, wo die Begründung zu dieser für das internationale Renommee Bulgariens nach den Vorwürfen wegen des Papstattentates, des Drogen- und Waffenhandels sowie der Unterstützung des internationalen Terrorismus negativen Vorgehensweise liegt. Am wahrscheinlichsten ist es, den Grund in dem seit Anfang der 70er Jahre nachweislichen Streben nach einer „einheitlichen sozialistischen Nation" in Bulgarien zu suchen.

Der Schaden, der auf diese Weise und erst recht seit dem Mai 1989 durch die plötzliche Erlaubnis zum Massenexodus türkischer Bulgaren dem bulgarisch-türkischen Verhältnis zugefügt worden ist, kam völlig überraschend. Vom Familienzusammenführungsvertrag vom 22.3.1968 an hatten sich die wechselseitigen Beziehungen an sich fast so gut entwickelt wie die bulgarisch-griechischen, auch wenn der türkische Anteil am bulgarischen Außenhandel minimal war und blieb[205]. Eine ganze Reihe verschiedener Verträge wurde jedoch abgeschlossen, darunter vor allem am 3.12.1975 ebenfalls eine „Deklaration über die Prinzipien guter Nachbarschaft und Zusammenarbeit"[206]. Zahlreiche Besuche auf höchster Ebene wurden ausgetauscht, wobei es für die komplizierte Lage der Türkei im westlichen Bündnis nach der Militärintervention vom 12.9.1980 bezeichnend ist, daß General K. Evrens erster Staatsbesuch in Europa im Februar 1982 Bulgarien galt. Nicht zu vergessen ist schließlich, daß Bulgarien kontinuierlich für die Türkei als Durchreiseland für die in Westeuropa tätigen Gastarbeiter eine wichtige Funktion erfüllt (2 Mio. Durchreisende im Jahr), daß andererseits aber auch die Türkei für die stark ausgebaute Lastzugflotte Bulgariens den einzig möglichen Durchreiseweg in den Nahen Osten bietet.

Umso unerklärlicher müssen die Ereignisse vom Winter 1984/85 an sein. Nicht nur, daß die Türkei auf allen Ebenen – durch Besuche ihrer führenden Staatsmänner in fast allen Ländern des Sowjetblocks, durch Aktivierung des Europarates, der NATO, der UNO und der Islamischen Konferenz sowie selbstverständlich durch direkte diplomatische Noten – tätig wurde, deutlich wurde binnen kurzem auch, daß

---

[203] Für die Einzelheiten vgl. das Kapitel über die Nationalen Minderheiten von S. Troebst, S. 479/80.

[204] RD. 18.7.1986; XIII kongres (Anm. 160), S. 277. Von westlichen Quellen und Analysen vgl. Troebst, S.: Von bulgarischen Türken und „getürkten" Bulgaren, in: Südosteuropa. 34 (1985), S. 359–67; Höpken, W.: Außenpolitische Aspekte der bulgarischen „Türken-Politik", ebenda. 34 (1985), S. 477–85; ders.: Die bulgarisch-türkischen Beziehungen, ebenda. 36 (1987), S. 178–94; ders.: Bulgarien – Türkei: Der schwierige Dialog (Dokumentation), ebenda. 38 (1989), S. 54–59.

[205] Vgl. das Kapitel „Außenwirtschaft" von R. Schönfeld.

[206] VPB. 3,2. 1983, S. 555–57.

der außenpolitische Schaden für Bulgarien außerordentlich war, wenn etwa auch Amnesty International umfangreich und sehr scharf Stellung bezog[207]).

Ungeklärt ist dabei schließlich die im Gesamtzusammenhang der bulgarischen Außenpolitik wichtige Frage, ob dies alles ohne Wissen der UdSSR, gegen ihren Willen oder aber auf ihre Weisung hin geschehen ist. Die beiden ersten Erklärungen wollen in das gewohnte Bild bulgarischer Außenpolitik nicht hineinpassen, die dritte widerspricht dem westlichen Verständnis sowjetischer Außenpolitik zumindest seit dem Amtsantritt Gorbačevs im Frühjahr 1985, so daß die – etwaige – Schuld für den Beginn der Kampagne Černenko träfe.

An diesem unerfreulichen Stand der Dinge hatte sich bis zum Mai 1989 nichts geändert, als es zu schweren Unruhen der türkischen Minderheit kam, die auch nach offiziellen bulgarischen Angaben Tote und Verletzte forderten und die Türkei zu massiven Protesten veranlaßten[207a]). Wohl hatten sich die Außenminister P. Mladenov und M. Yılmaz am Rande der Belgrader Balkankonferenz zweimal getroffen und die Schaffung von zwei Kommissionen zur Normalisierung der Beziehungen beschlossen[208]), die erstmals im Mai 1988 in Sofia getagt haben, doch hatte dies ebensowenig zu greifbaren Ergebnissen geführt wie der erwähnte albanische Vermittlungsversuch in Tirana im Januar 1989. Stattdessen hatte die türkische Regierung die 40. Wiederkehr der Verabschiedung der UN-Menschenrechtsdeklaration (10.12.1988) benutzt, um über ihre Auslandsvertretungen scharfe Verurteilungen der Haltung Bulgariens zu veröffentlichen, und auch dafür gesorgt, daß Bulgarien von der 18. Versammlung der Außenminister der Islamischen Konferenz in Riad (13.–16.3.1989) in besonders nachdrücklicher Weise zu einer Änderung seiner Haltung aufgefordert wurde.

Eine ebenso radikale wie trotz des Umsturzes vom 10.11.1989 an unerklärte Bewegung kam im Mai 1989 in diese Lage, beginnend mit einer Novelle zum bulgarischen Paßgesetz (19.5.), die allen Bulgaren das Recht auf einen Paß und Ausreisevisa in Aussicht stellte, den erwähnten schweren Unruhen (20.–27.5.) und einer Fernsehrede Živkovs (29.5.), in der er die Türkei aufforderte, ihre Grenzen für auswanderungswillige „bulgarische Muslime" zu öffnen[208a]). Von da an folgte jener weltweit Aufsehen erregende Massenexodus von Angehörigen der türkischen Minderheit, der bis Ende August 1989 bereits ca. 300000 der ca. 1 Mio. umfassenden Minorität in die Türkei strömen ließ. Die Türkei versuchte, den Emigrantenstrom in kontrollierte Bahnen zu lenken, indem sie am 21.8.1989 die Grenze zu Bulgarien schloß. Auch wenn seine Beschreibung als „Vertreibung" wohl unzutreffend ist, so war zumindest

---

[207]) Die Zahl der Quellen ist fast unübersehbar geworden. Es seien nur genannt: die nützliche Zusammenstellung von türkischer Seite: Turkish Minority in Bulgaria – Foreign Press Coverage. Ankara 1985; Summary Record of the Debates Concerning the Turkish Minority in Bulgaria during the 761st and 762nd Meetings of the U.N. Committee on the Elimination of Racial Discrimination. New York, March 11, 1986; Amnesty International. Bulgaria. Imprisonment of ethnic Turks. Human rights abuses during the forced assimilation of the ethnic Turkish minority. London 1986.
[207a]) Vgl. Erklärung von Außenminister Yılmaz vom 23.5.1989, verbreitet über alle Botschaften der Türkei.
[208]) Ashley, S.: A Move Toward Reconciliation with Turkey, in: RFE Research. Bulgaria/3. 8 March 1988 (Situation Report), S. 9–14.
[208a]) Für das Paßgesetz s. DV. (1989) 38, S. 1 f.; für Živkovs Rede s. Anm. 191a. – Zur Entwicklung des Exodus s. RFE-Situation Report Bulgaria 6/89 vom 7.7.1989.

die weithin geübte Kritik an seiner Form (Mitnahme nur eines Minimums an transportablem Eigentum) ohne Zweifel berechtigt. Unklar blieb bis zur Drucklegung außerdem die politische Zielsetzung der Aktion, da Bulgarien allein schon aus ökonomischen Gründen kaum an einer vollständigen Beseitigung dieser Minderheit interessiert sein kann. Sicher ist dafür, daß die Türkei damit 1989 mehr denn je neben Jugoslawien das zweite Nachbarland Bulgariens ist, zu dem die außenpolitischen Beziehungen aufgrund von Minderheitenfragen aufs schwerste belastet sind, wobei P. Mladenov nach dem 10.11.1989 immerhin soviel hat verlauten lassen, daß er die Schuld für die in der Weltöffentlichkeit überwiegend negativ beurteilte Entwicklung Živkov persönlich anlastete und als Außenminister nicht mehr bereit gewesen sei, die Verantwortung hierfür stellvertretend länger zu tragen. Die Außenpolitik scheint damit zumindest partiell als Ursache für den Sturz Živkovs mitgespielt zu haben. Andererseits hat sie aber offenbar nicht insoweit im Vordergrund gestanden, daß sich bis zum Jahresende 1989 auch nur programmatisch von seiten Mladenovs eine neue Türkei-Politik Bulgariens abzeichnen würde. Nicht einmal der unbestrittene Rückstrom von Türken nach Bulgarien – im Oktober 1989 allein sollen 40–50000 Rückkehrer gezählt worden sein – kann hier genannt werden, da er deutlich vor dem 10.11.1989 eingesetzt hat.

Was damit als letztes die Beziehungen Bulgariens zu Jugoslawien betrifft, so verließen wir diese im Unterschied zu allen anderen Balkannachbarn mit Ausnahme Albaniens 1964/68 in einer erneuten Phase vollkommener Abkühlung. Und tatsächlich erweist sich heute in der Rückschau des Jahres 1989, daß die Beziehungen zu Jugoslawien von Bulgarien aus gesehen nicht nur im ganzen seit 1944 die kompliziertesten gewesen sind, sondern zudem noch in einem historisch nicht zu erklärenden Rhythmus alle zehn Jahre durch ein neues Tief bestimmt werden. Auf die Doppelbelastung des Verhältnisses wegen Makedonien und der Intervention in der ČSSR 1968 ist so nach einer zögernd einsetzenden Phase der Entspannung im Gefolge des Versöhnungsbesuchs Brežnevs vom 22.–25.9.1971 1978/79 erneut eine Phase von ungewöhnlich scharfen Gegensätzlichkeiten gefolgt – beginnend mit einer Rede Živkovs in Blagoevgrad am 15.6.1978[209]) –, die Anfang der 80er Jahre abklang, bis heute aber auch nur wieder zu dem Ergebnis einer relativen Beruhigung geführt hat. Die vorsichtige Formulierung des XIII. Parteitages – „wir blicken der Zukunft der bulgarisch-jugoslawischen Beziehungen trotz mancher noch nicht überwundener Schwierigkeiten und Differenzen mit Optimismus entgegen"[210]) – dürfte so tatsächlich das Maximum heute möglicher Prognosen darstellen, während Vizeaußenminister Ganevs Formulierung vom Oktober 1987, die bulgarisch-jugoslawischen Beziehungen seien „so gut wie nie zuvor", kaum hilfreich ist[211]).

De facto erweist es sich, daß nach wie vor das Makedonienproblem in seiner mehrfachen Bedeutung zwischen Bulgarien und Jugoslawien steht, wozu dann noch die Bewertung der bulgarischen „Hilfe für die Befreiung Jugoslawiens" am Ende des

---

[209]) Živkov (Anm. 110). 27. 1980, S. 397–416, speziell S. 408–12. – Für die Einzelheiten vgl. Reuter, J.: Zur Verschärfung des Mazedonienkonflikts, in: Wissenschaftlicher Dienst Südosteuropa. 27 (1978), S. 179–82.
[210]) XIII kongres (Anm. 160), S. 276.
[211]) Ganev (Anm. 199), S. 4.

II. Weltkrieges kommt und die Beurteilung der Politik des bulgarischen Nationalsymbols Dimitrov im Zusammenhang der bulgarisch-jugoslawischen Föderationsprojekte 1944–1948. Was dabei zunächst Makedonien betrifft, so war es auch 1978/79 wieder eben diese Frage, die den bis heute letzten großen Konflikt auslöste. In seiner Rede vom 15.6.1978 hatte Živkov eine sofortige Grenzgarantie angeboten, ohne jedoch das Wort Makedonien zu erwähnen. Die jugoslawische Reaktion war nicht nur auf dem unmittelbar folgenden XI. Parteitag des SKJ (20.–23.6.1978), sondern auch durch Dokumentenveröffentlichungen des jugoslawischen Außenministeriums vernichtend ablehnend[212].

Von da an entwickelte sich eine äußerst heftige Kontroverse, die die gegensätzlichen Standpunkte vollkommen deutlich gemacht hat: Bulgarien war – und ist bis heute – bereit, die Grenze zu Jugoslawien zu garantieren und auf alle territorialen Forderungen zu verzichten. Dafür verlangt es von Jugoslawien die Anerkennung der Tatsache, daß in Pirin-Makedonien keine Makedonier, sondern nur Bulgaren leben. Und außerdem besteht Bulgarien darauf, wie es die führende Altkommunistin C. Dragojčeva in einem als Sonderbroschüre 1979 erschienenen Vorabdruck aus Band III ihrer Memoiren eindeutig formuliert hat, daß „jedem nur einigermaßen gebildeten Menschen in der Welt bekannt (ist), daß das Vardar-Makedonien und der größere Teil seiner Bevölkerung seit eh und je Fleisch vom Fleisch und Blut vom Blut der bulgarischen Erde und des bulgarischen Volkes sind"[213]. Einschließlich der Grenzen des Vertrages von San Stefano, dessen 100. Jahrestag 1978 in Bulgarien nachdrücklich gefeiert wurde, gibt es hier bis heute keine Möglichkeit der Verständigung[214]. Es nimmt so auch nicht wunder, daß Jugoslawien die Haltung der Türkei in der Frage der Bulgarisierung der türkischen Minderheit seit 1984 massiv unterstützt und dabei vor Formulierungen wie „KZs" in Bulgarien oder „Genozid, Assimilation, Entnationalisierung" nicht zurückschreckt[215].

Vergleichbares gilt für die beiden anderen strittigen Problemkreise: Bulgariens „Hilfe" zur Befreiung Jugoslawiens am Ende des II. Weltkrieges und die Beurteilung der Rolle Dimitrovs bei den Föderationsplänen von 1944 bis zum V. Parteitag der BKP vom 18.–25.12.1948. Was das erstere betrifft, so besteht Bulgarien nach wie vor auf seiner „Hilfe", während die jugoslawische Alternative nach wie vor lautet: „Das Nationale Komitee der Befreiung Jugoslawiens gibt die Erlaubnis für die Beteiligung

---

[212] Für die offizielle bulgarische Seite vgl. außer der Živkov-Rede vom 15.6.1978 noch diejenige vom 27.4.1979 (Anm. 110), Bd. 29. 1983, S. 30–38, und die Erklärung des bulgarischen Außenministeriums vom 24.7.1978: Za vsestranno razvitie na bălgaro-jugoslavskite otnošenija (Für die allseitige Entwicklung der bulgarisch-jugoslawischen Beziehungen). Sofia 1978. Für die jugoslawische Seite vgl. Politika. 30.6.1978.

[213] Dragoitschewa, Z.: Makedonien – kein Zankapfel, sondern Faktor der guten Nachbarschaft und der Zusammenarbeit. Erinnerungen und Gedanken. Sofia 1979, S. 103.

[214] Vgl. hier vor allem auch das 1978 erschienene Buch von M. Stefanović u.a. (Anm. 53).

[215] Reuter, J.: Die Entnationalisierung der Türken in Bulgarien. Sofias Politik der Zwangsbulgarisierung aus jugoslawischer Sicht, in: Südosteuropa. 34 (1985), S. 169–77; Tupurkovski, V.: Wir wollen möglichst gute Beziehungen zu unseren Nachbarn. Aus diesem Kontext kann die Frage der Minderheiten in den Nachbarländern nicht ausgeklammert werden, in: Internationale Politik. H. 909. 20.2.1988, S. 7.

der Einheiten der BVA an den Kämpfen auf dem Boden Jugoslawiens"[216]). In bezug auf Dimitrov muß die bulgarische Position teilweise als defensiv im Lichte des in Teil II,2 Ausgeführten erscheinen[217]).

Als Ergebnis ist festzustellen, daß deutlich zwei Phasen der Wiederannäherung vorhanden sind – von 1971 bis 1978 und von 1980 bis heute –, daß dabei aber auch nicht entfernt eine Intensität der Beziehungen wie etwa gegenüber Rumänien oder Griechenland erreicht worden ist. Es mag der Hinweis genügen, daß Tito zwischen seinem Besuch im Jahre 1965 und seinem Tode 1980 nicht mehr nach Bulgarien gefahren ist und daß sich auch die sonstigen diplomatischen Begegnungen in engen Grenzen halten. Stattdessen gehen die Auseinandersetzungen auf wissenschaftlicher Ebene fast unvermindert weiter[218]).

Was im Bereich der bulgarisch-jugoslawischen Beziehungen ebenso wie als Grundfaktor bulgarischer Außenpolitik seit 1944 und seit Mai/Juni 1989 auch mit Blick auf die bulgarisch-türkischen Beziehungen bleibt, ist eine Bewertung des „sowjetischen Faktors"[219]), d. h. die Frage, wie autonom die bulgarische Führung in ihren außen- (und natürlich auch innen-)politischen Entscheidungen gewesen ist. Mangels Archivzugang divergieren die Meinungen in der westlichen Forschung hier gerade mit Blick auf Bulgarien und seiner im Sowjetblock kontinuierlich besonders engen Beziehung zur Sowjetunion deutlich, wie auch die Beurteilung der letzten Phase der Beziehungen zu Jugoslawien erneut beweist: Geht die Wiederannäherung von 1971 an auf ein direktes Eingreifen Brežnevs zurück, ist die bulgarische Jugoslawienpolitik ein „Regulativ gegen die totale Fixierung auf die Sowjetunion", handelt es sich nur um einen „Stellvertreterkrieg", den Bulgarien im Auftrag der Sowjetunion führt, oder steht die Sowjetunion gerade umgekehrt auf seiten Jugoslawiens – so lauten die Fragen[220])? Sicher ist auf jeden Fall nur, daß der Balkan am Ende der Ära Živkov wie stets seit 1944 der einzige Bereich gewesen ist, wo Bulgarien eigene außenpolitische Interessen gehabt hat, auch wenn es 1989 mit 120 Ländern diplomatische Beziehungen unterhielt[221]).

---

[216]) Mitrovski u. a. (Anm. 60), S. 247–315; Neshkovich, S.: Through My Investigations I Present the Truth About Macedonia, in: Macedonian Review. 18 (1988), S. 134–140; von bulgarischer Seite neuerdings Dimitrov, D.: Narodnoosvoboditelnite vojski na Makedonija, vzaimodejstvuvašti s Bălgarskata narodna armija (septemvri–noemvri 1944 g.) (Die makedonischen Volksbefreiungstruppen, die mit der bulgarischen Volksarmee zusammengearbeitet haben (September–November 1944)), in: Istoričeski pregled. 44 (1988) 2, S. 41–53.

[217]) Dobrinov (Anm. 30).

[218]) Als Beispiele sei nur auf die folgenden umfangreichen Veröffentlichungen verwiesen: Institut d'Histoire Nationale. Macedoine (Articles d'histoire). Skopje 1981; Bulgarische Akademie der Wissenschaften. Makedonien. Eine Dokumentensammlung. Sofia 1982; Petranović (Anm. 27).

[219]) Troebst (Anm. 23), S. 88–92.

[220]) Troebst (Anm. 23), S. 14/15; Oschlies (Anm. 183), S. 12; Schönfeld, R.: Außen- und sicherheitspolitische Konzepte Bulgariens, in: Reform und Wandel in Südosteuropa. Hrsg. v. R. Schönfeld. München 1985, S. 77 (Untersuchungen zur Gegenwartskunde Südosteuropas. 26).

[221]) Information Bulgaria (Anm. 183), S. 884.

Außenpolitik

6. Der Umsturz des 10. 11. 1989 und seine Folgen

An dieser Feststellung wird sich auch im Gefolge des eindeutig primär innenpolitisch orientierten Umsturzes vom 10. 11. 1989 an für Bulgarien nichts ändern. Als Prognose bietet sich mit Blick auf die anderen Länder des ehemaligen Sowjetblocks zwar die Vermutung an, daß der Grad auch der außenpolitischen Unabhängigkeit Bulgariens von der Sowjetunion wachsen wird, doch sind dafür bis zum Jahresende 1989 nicht einmal Überlegungen von seiten der neuen bulgarischen Führung bekannt geworden, ganz zu schweigen von konkreten Handlungen, obwohl – oder eben gerade weil! – mit P. Mladenov ein erfahrener Außenpolitiker zumindest vorläufig die Macht übernommen hat. Nichts spricht daher vorerst dafür, daß sich Bulgarien nach dem Umsturz des alten Regimes außenpolitischen Ideen zum Austritt aus dem RGW oder WP anschließen würde, wie sie in Ungarn und Polen diskutiert werden. Stattdessen deuten die Zeichen bis jetzt eher darauf hin, daß die Landmarken bulgarischer Außenpolitik seit Jahrzehnten – Kontinuität bei den eigenen Zielen und Anlehnung an die Sowjetunion soweit wie möglich – auch vorerst Gültigkeit haben werden.

Regierungssystem

Otto Luchterhandt, Köln

I. Strukturprinzipien der Staatsordnung: 1. Parteisouveränität – 2. Gewalteneinheit – 3. „Demokratischer Zentralismus" – 4. Gesellschafts- und Wirtschaftsplanung – 5. „Sozialistische Gesetzlichkeit" – 6. „Sozialistischer Internationalismus" – II. Die staatlichen Repräsentations- und Leitungsorgane: 1. Die Volksversammlung (NSb) – 2. Der Staatsrat (DS) – 3. Der Ministerrat (Ministerski săvet) – 4. Probleme der zentralen Rechtsetzung – III. Die Staatsverwaltung: 1. Die Zentralbehörden: a) Ministerien – b) Sonderbehörden – 2. Die nachgeordneten allgemeinen Verwaltungsbehörden: a) Territoriale Gliederung und Kompetenzen – b) Die Organisationsstruktur der territorialen Verwaltungseinheiten – 3. Sonderverwaltungsbereiche – 4. Das Verwaltungsverfahren – 5. Die Verwaltungskontrolle – IV. Die Rechtspflege: 1. Die Gerichte – 2. Die Staatsanwaltschaft – V. Die Rechtsstellung des Einzelnen: 1. Die Staatsbürgerschaft – 2. Die Grundrechte – 3. Die Grundpflichten – 4. Der Verwaltungsrechtsschutz

I. Strukturprinzipien der Staatsordnung

Mit „Regierungssystem" bezeichnet man jenes institutionelle Sinngefüge, dessen Tätigkeit auf die Gewinnung solcher politischen Entscheidungen gerichtet ist, die für das gesamte Gemeinwesen verbindlich sein sollen. Sein Begriff ist enger als der des „Politischen Systems", der auch Eigentümlichkeiten der politischen Kultur und Institutionen erfaßt, die in nur mittelbarer Beziehung zur Funktion der „Regierung" stehen (vgl. das Kapitel von W. Höpken, Politisches System). Während freilich im liberaldemokratischen Verfassungsstaat das Regierungssystem eine spezifische Form der Organisation der Staatsgewalt meint und seinen Schwerpunkt folglich in den Staatsorganen besitzt, liegt im kommunistischen Staatswesen sowjetischer Prägung der institutionelle Kern des Regierungssystems regelmäßig im Organisationsbereich der „Partei". Die Parteiführungsorgane (Politbüro; Sekretariat des ZK) sind das dirigierende Aktionszentrum; sie besitzen eine politische Richtliniengewalt und lenken jenes Ensemble von Staatsorganen, die nach der geschriebenen Verfassung des Landes das Regierungssystem ausmachen.

Der folgende Überblick beschränkt sich auf den staatlichen Teil des Regierungssystems, auf die vom Staats- und Verwaltungsrecht förmlich geregelten Elemente des staatlichen Entscheidungsmechanismus. Er stützt sich wesentlich auf die (geltende) Verfassung vom 18.5.1971. Sie löste die an der UdSSR-Verfassung von 1936 und der Verfassung Jugoslawiens von 1946 orientierte, „volksdemokratisch" geprägte Verfassung vom 4.12.1947 ab[1]).

---

[1]) Das frühere Verfassungsrecht wird dargestellt von Spasov, B.; Angelov, A.: Dăržavno pravo na Narodna Republika Bălgarija (Staatsrecht der NRB). 2. Auflage. Sofia 1968 (zit. als: Spasov/Angelov); aus westlicher Sicht: Schultz, L.: Die Verfassungsentwicklung der VR Bulgarien seit 1944, in:

Die Verfassung stellt das von ihr geordnete Gemeinwesen in den alles durchdringenden weltanschaulichen Sinnzusammenhang des Marxismus-Leninismus[2]). Die NRB versteht sich als „sozialistischer Staat" (Art. 1 Abs. 1 Verf.); Zwischenziel ihres politischen Weges soll der Aufbau der „entwickelten sozialistischen Gesellschaft" (Präambel; Art. 1 Abs. 3; Art. 4 Verf.), Fern- und Endziel „die kommunistische Gesellschaft" (Art. 4 Abs. 2 Verf.) sein[3]). Aufgrund dieser ideologischen Voraussetzungen wird die Staatsordnung von Leit- und Strukturprinzipien beherrscht, die denen der Sowjetverfassung vom 7.10.1977 gleichen[4]).

1. Parteisouveränität

Das wichtigste Leitprinzip ist die Souveränität der BKP (vgl. den Beitrag von W. Höpken, Politisches System). Sie ist die „leitende Kraft in der Gesellschaft und im Staat" (Art. 1 Abs. 2 Verf.). Die Partei leitet ihre Führungskompetenz nicht aus einem Zustimmungsakt des Volkes (Wahlen) ab; sie bezieht die Legitimität ihrer Herrschaft aus dem Marxismus-Leninismus, der als angeblich einzige wahre Gesellschaftswissenschaft der Partei die richtige Einsicht in die Gesetzmäßigkeiten sozialer bzw. geschichtlicher Prozesse verschafft und dadurch eine zuverlässige Orientierung für den „Weg des Sozialismus und Kommunismus" vermittelt (vgl. Präambel des Parteistatuts).

Der weltanschauliche Wahrheits- und politische Richtigkeitsanspruch macht die Partei zur präkonstitutionellen Quelle des Rechts und stellt sie über das (positive) Gesetzesrecht. Art. 29 Parteistatut drückt diesen Umstand von fundamentaler Bedeutung mit der Formulierung aus, daß das ZK der BKP „die Arbeit der zentralen Organe des Staates leitet". Im Hinblick auf die „Gesellschaft" äußert sich die Parteisouveränität in dem Recht zur Leitung der Massenorganisationen (Art. 29; 36 lit. f. Parteistatut), das diese in ihren Statuten ausdrücklich anerkannt haben.

Die wichtigsten organisatorischen Instrumente zur Durchsetzung der Parteisouveränität in Staat und Gesellschaft sind die Direktiven der Parteiführungsorgane, die „Auswahl und Verteilung der leitenden Kader" (Art. 29 Parteistatut), also die Perso-

---

Jahrbuch des öffentlichen Rechts der Gegenwart. N. F. Bd. 22 (1973), S. 203 ff. Einen Überblick über die Verfassungsentwicklung seit 1879 gibt Luchterhandt, O.: Bulgarien, in: Verfassungen der kommunistischen Staaten. Hrsg. v. G. Brunner; B. Meissner. Paderborn 1979, S. 45–49; seit 1971: Jessel, Ch.: Die neuere Verfassungsentwicklung in Bulgarien, in: Verfassungs- und Verwaltungsreformen in den sozialistischen Staaten. Hrsg. v. F.-C. Schroeder; B. Meissner. Berlin (-West) 1978, S. 221–256.

[2]) Zum geltenden Staatsrecht siehe Spasov, B.; Želev, G.: Dăržavno pravo na Narodna Republika Bălgarija (Staatsrecht der NRB), Teil I und II. Sofia 1974 (zit. als: Spasov/Želev); Übersetzungen wichtiger Teile des Staatsrechts ins Deutsche finden sich in: Volksrepublik Bulgarien. Staat, Demokratie, Leitung. Dokumente. Hrsg. von W. Lungwitz. Berlin (-Ost) 1979.

[3]) Vgl. auch die Präambel des Statuts der BPS vom 10.3.1972; Präambel des Statuts des DKMS vom 13.1.1968; Präambel des Statuts der OF vom 3.2.1948; Sipkov, I.: The Bulgarian Communist Party under the Law, in: The Party Statutes of the Communist World. Hrsg. von W. B. Simons; S. White. The Hague, Boston, Lancaster 1984, S. 197–206.

[4]) Text: Vedomosti Verchovnogo Soveta SSSR (Amtsblatt des Obersten Sowjet der UdSSR). 1977, Nr. 41, Art. 616.

nalhoheit der Partei, und die Kontrolle über die Durchführung der Parteibeschlüsse (Art. 33; 36 lit. a; 51 Abs. 1; 58 Abs. 2 Parteistatut). Es ist stehende Praxis, daß sich die Partei auch unmittelbar in die Rechtsetzung einschaltet, indem sie in Gestalt des ZK zusammen mit dem DS oder mit dem Ministerrat „gemeinsame Verordnungen" erläßt. Sie wählt diesen Weg dann, wenn sie ihre Autorität besonders nachdrücklich bei der operativen Lösung staatspolitischer Aufgaben zur Geltung bringen will[5]).

Die Parteisouveränität überlagert das in Art. 2 Abs. 1 Verfassung in klassischer Formulierung verankerte Prinzip der Volkssouveränität: „In der Volksrepublik Bulgarien geht alle Macht vom Volke aus und gehört dem Volk." Der Begriff des „Volkes" wird von der Verfassung (Präambel) auf der Grundlage der marxistisch-leninistischen Klassentheorie ideologisch-normativ bestimmt und umfaßt „die Arbeiterklasse, die werktätigen Bauern und Volksintelligenz". Seine Macht übt „das Volk" durch die staatlichen Vertretungskörperschaften aus (Art. 2 Abs. 2 Verf.); folglich teilt es deren Machtlosigkeit.

2. Gewalteneinheit

Die Verfassung (Art. 5) bekennt sich zur „Gewalteneinheit"; sie verleiht ihr dadurch Ausdruck, daß die Volksvertretungen die Fülle der staatlichen Gewalt innehaben und ausüben: „Die Volksversammlung vereinigt die gesetzgebende und die vollziehende Tätigkeit des Staates und übt die oberste Kontrolle aus" (Art. 67). Entsprechendes gilt für die örtlichen Volksräte (Art. 113 Verf.). Die Folge dieser Konzeption ist die förmliche Überordnung (Suprematie) der NSb über alle anderen Staatsorgane[6]).

Das Prinzip der Gewalteneinheit schließt eine gewisse Aufteilung der selbstverständlich auch im kommunistischen Staatswesen vorhandenen Rechtsfunktionen der Gesetzgebung, des Gesetzesvollzuges, der Rechtsprechung, der Planung und Kontrolle unter mehreren Staatsorganen nicht aus; sie erweist sich im Interesse eines Mindestmaßes an rationeller Funktionsfähigkeit vielmehr als unumgänglich. Eine solche Funktions- und Arbeitsteilung ist in Bulgarien verschieden stark ausgeprägt: Am stärksten tritt eine institutionelle Selbständigkeit bei der Kontrolle über den Gesetzesvollzug (Staatsanwaltschaft; Gerichte) in Erscheinung. Eine Tendenz zur rechtsstaatlichen Gewaltenteilung zeichnet sich – trotz der unter sowjetischem Einfluß angelaufenen Reformdiskussion – vorläufig nicht ab.

3. „Demokratischer Zentralismus"

Der Demokratische Zentralismus (Art. 5 Verf.) ist das bestimmende Organisationsprinzip innerhalb des politischen Systems, das gleichermaßen die Partei (Art. 14 Parteistatut), die Massenorganisationen (vgl. Art. 6 Statut der OF) und den Staats-

---

[5]) Spasov/Želev (Anm. 2) I, S. 92f.
[6]) A.a.O., S. 71 (vărchovenstvo).

aufbau strukturiert. Die Verfassung verzichtet auf seine Definition, da der Inhalt des Prinzips seit langem in der kommunistischen bzw. bulgarischen Staatsrechtslehre feststeht. Theoretisch verbindet der Demokratische Zentralismus in sich die gegenläufigen Elemente der vollen Entscheidungsgewalt von oben und der größtmöglichen Demokratie von unten. Der demokratische Aspekt bedeutet, daß 1. die Vertretungskörperschaften von unten gewählt und alle sonstigen Staatsorgane von ihnen bestellt werden, 2. die Staatsorgane gegenüber den Vertretungskörperschaften rechenschaftspflichtig sind; der zentralistische Aspekt bedeutet, daß 1. die Beschlüsse der übergeordneten Organe für die untergeordneten unbedingt verbindlich sind, 2. die höheren Organe die unteren kontrollieren und deren Akte aufheben dürfen[7]). In der Praxis haben die zentralistischen Elemente seit Begründung des kommunistischen Herrschaftssystems in Bulgarien die beherrschende Rolle gespielt und die demokratischen Mechanismen mehr oder weniger zu formalen Prozeduren ohne politisches Gewicht degradiert.

Zwar spricht die Verfassung (Art. 110) in bezug auf die örtlichen Gebietseinheiten von „Selbstverwaltung", ein Wort, das neuerdings unter dem Eindruck der Reformpolitik Gorbačevs stark in den Vordergrund gerückt wird (vgl. dazu unten III.2.), aber eine echte Dezentralisierung, d. h. eine verfassungsrechtlich garantierte gemeindliche Autonomie, ist damit nicht gemeint.

4. Gesellschafts- und Wirtschaftsplanung

Durch die Zielsetzung der Partei, auf wissenschaftlicher Grundlage die kommunistische Gesellschaft zu schaffen, wird die Planung zwangsläufig zum Prinzip. Die Verfassung bekennt sich zu einer „planmäßigen" Entwicklung nicht nur der Wirtschaft, sondern der Gesellschaft insgesamt (Art. 3 Abs. 1; 22 Abs. 1, Abs. 3, Abs. 4). Zwar sagt sie nichts Näheres über die Struktur und Wirkungsweise der „einheitlichen Pläne der gesellschaftlichen und wirtschaftlichen Entwicklung des Landes" (Art. 78 Nr. 6; 103 Nr. 3 Verf.), doch ist Bulgarien bisher dem sowjetischen Modell einer imperativen Zentralplanung gefolgt, die keinen relevanten Bereich des Gemeinwesens ausklammert[8]); ihre aufgeschlüsselten Aufgabenstellungen sind für alle Wirtschaftsbetriebe, Staatsorgane und gesellschaftlichen Organisationen verbindlich. Die „Richtlinien über die Wirtschaftstätigkeit" vom Dezember 1986 sehen allerdings eine Vertiefung der Wirtschaftsreform vor, die auch zu einer Umgestaltung des Planungssystems führen, nämlich den Übergang zu einer indikativen Planung einleiten soll (vgl. das Kapitel von W. Gumpel, Wirtschaftssystem).

5. „Sozialistische Gesetzlichkeit"

Das Konzept der „Sozialistischen Gesetzlichkeit" (Art. 5, 8, 125 Abs. 2 Verf.), das in seiner stalinistischen Ursprungsform zwei konträre Elemente in sich vereinigt,

---

[7]) A. a. O., II, S. 27/28.
[8]) Art. 12 der Planungsordnung vom 23.12.1975 (DV. (1975) 101).

nämlich die strikte Anwendung des positiven Rechts einerseits und die Beachtung der Parteilichkeit, d. h. der ideologisch-politischen Opportunität andererseits, wird von der bulgarischen Rechtswissenschaft seit den 60er Jahren zunehmend in einem normativen, tendenziell rechtsstaatlichen Sinne verstanden[9]. Freilich, in dem Maße, wie sich die neue sozialistische Rechtsordnung etablierte, mußte das außergesetzliche Moment der Parteilichkeit in den Hintergrund treten; verschwunden ist es aber keineswegs. Heute versteht man unter „Sozialistischer Gesetzlichkeit" in Anlehnung an Art. 8 Verf. 1. das juristische Formprinzip staatlicher Organisation und Kompetenzbestimmung, 2. eine Methode staatlicher Herrschaftsausübung und 3. die strikte Bindung aller staatlichen Institutionen, gesellschaftlichen Organisationen und Bürger an die Gesetze[10].

Ein Schlüsselproblem der Wahrung der Gesetzlichkeit bildet die Gesetzestreue der Staatsorgane bei der Rechtsanwendung bzw. -auslegung. § 46 des Gesetzes über die Normativakte vom 29. 3. 1973[11] bestimmt, unklare Rechtsvorschriften so auszulegen, daß sie 1. vergleichbaren (analogen) Vorschriften, 2. dem Ziel des betreffenden Rechtsaktes, 3. den Grundprinzipien des bulgarischen Rechts oder 4. den Regeln der sozialistischen Moral maximal entsprechen[12]. Hier kommt nun die „Parteilichkeit" zur Geltung, und zwar vor allem dadurch, daß die Parteibeschlüsse und -direktiven regelmäßig mehr oder weniger detailliert die politischen Ziele der Rechtsetzung bestimmen, womit sie zwangsläufig zur wichtigsten Interpretationsgrundlage für Verwaltung und Justiz werden.

In institutioneller Hinsicht soll sich die „sozialistische Gesetzlichkeit" vor allem in dem Monopol der NSb zum Erlaß von (förmlichen) Gesetzen und in der Gesetzlichkeitsaufsicht von Staatsanwaltschaft und Gerichten verkörpern.

6. „Sozialistischer Internationalismus"

Das Selbstverständnis Bulgariens als „sozialistischer" Staat bestimmt auch seine Beziehungen nach außen gemäß der sowjetischen Doktrin des „sozialistischen Internationalismus", den Art. 5 Verf. zum Prinzip erklärt (vgl. das Kapitel von K.-D. Grothusen, Außenpolitik). Das Land ist militärisch und ökonomisch fest in den sowjetischen Hegemonialbereich eingebunden. Es hat allerdings – im Unterschied zur DDR und ČSSR – mit der UdSSR weder einen Beistandsvertrag abgeschlossen, der den Schutz der „sozialistischen Errungenschaften" zum Gegenstand hat, noch sind in Bulgarien sowjetische Truppen stationiert. Juristische Anhaltspunkte, die sich im Sinne einer förmlichen Anerkennung einer sowjetischen Interventionsbefugnis im

---

[9] Petkov, A.; Tanev, T.: Problemi na socialističeskata zakonnost (Probleme der sozialistischen Gesetzlichkeit). Sofia 1973, S. 43 ff.

[10] Spasov/Želev (Anm. 2) II, S. 34 ff. Narodnaja Respublika Bolgarija. Osnovy gosudarstvennogo stroja (Die NRB. Grundlagen der Staatsaufbaus). Izd. Ja. C. Radev; B. N. Topornin. Moskau 1974, S. 354 ff. (zit. als: Radev/Topornin).

[11] DV. (1973) 27.

[12] Dazu ausführlich Spasov, B.: Tălkovatelnata dejnost na Dăržavnija săvet (Die Auslegungspraxis des DS). Sofia 1978, S. 69 ff. (zit. als: Spasov, Tălkovatelnata dejnost).

Falle der Gefährdung der sowjetloyalen Einparteiherrschaft bzw. der sowjetischen Hegemoniestellung, d.h. als „völkerrechtlich-staatsrechtliche Gemengelage" (D. Frenzke)[13]) im Verhältnis UdSSR-NRB interpretieren ließen, liegen nicht vor.

II. Die staatlichen Repräsentations- und Leitungsorgane
(vgl. das Kapitel „Oberste Organe" im Anhang)

1. Die Volksversammlung (NSb)

Dem Konzept der identitären Demokratie verhaftet, erklärt die Verfassung die NSb zur Verkörperung des Willens des Volkes und seiner Souveränität (Art. 66) und folgerichtig zum „obersten" Organ der Staatsgewalt (Art. 67), von welchem alle weiteren Staatsorgane ihre Macht entweder direkt ableiten (DS, Ministerrat usw.) oder welcher sie – so die örtlichen Staatsorgane – untergeordnet sind (vgl. auch das Kapitel W. Höpken, Politisches System). Die Konstituierung mehrerer rechtlich im Prinzip gleichgeordneter Verfassungsorgane als Träger verschiedener Staatsfunktionen oder Ausschnitte der Staatsgewalt ist dadurch ausgeschlossen.

Die Wahlperiode dauert (seit 1971) 5 Jahre (Art. 6 Abs. 2 Verf.); durch Mehrheitsbeschluß kann sie bei Eintreten „außergewöhnlicher Umstände" aber auf unbestimmte Zeit (Art. 69 Abs. 3), bei „wichtigen Gründen" um 1 Jahr verlängert werden (Art. 69 Abs. 4). Die Periodizität ist bisher eingehalten worden; sie stimmt mit der Laufzeit der Fünfjahrespläne überein.

Alle Staatsangehörigen sind mit der Vollendung des 18. Lebensjahres sowohl aktiv als auch passiv wahlberechtigt, unabhängig insbesondere davon, wie lange sie am Wohnort wohnen. Ausgenommen sind nur die zu Freiheitsentzug Verurteilten (Art. 6 Abs. 3 Verf.; Art. 16 Abs. 4 WahlG).

Es gibt 400 Mandate (Art. 68 Verf.), die in einer gleichen Zahl von Einmannwahlkreisen nach absolutem Mehrheitswahlrecht verteilt werden (Art. 74, 77 WahlG). Obwohl Art. 43 WahlG vom 30. 6. 1973[14]) ausdrücklich die Nominierung einer „unbegrenzten Zahl" von Kandidaten in jedem Wahlkreis zuließ, wurde in der Praxis bis in die jüngste Vergangenheit an der Aufstellung nur *eines* Wahlkreiskandidaten festgehalten. Das Wahlgesetz legitimierte freilich selbst diese Praxis mit der Bestimmung (Art. 46), daß lediglich 1 Kandidat aufgestellt werden dürfe, wenn sich die in der OF unter Führung der BKP zusammengeschlossenen gesellschaftlichen Kräfte auf eine Person geeinigt hätten. Gerade das aber war schon unter dem früheren Wahlrecht (1949; 1953) eiserne Praxis gewesen[15]) und entsprach auch ganz der systempolitischen Funktion der OF (Art. 2 lit. a Statut von 1948 in der geltenden Fassung).

Nachdem Ungarn, Polen und sogar Rumänien schon seit längerem von dieser Praxis Abschied genommen hatten, hat sich im Dezember 1987 auch die bulgarische

---

[13]) Frenzke, D.: Die Rechtsnatur des Sowjetblocks. Eine juristische Entschleierung. Berlin (-West) 1981, S. 217ff. (214).
[14]) DV. (1973) 58.
[15]) Spasov/Angelov (Anm. 1), S. 114f.

Führung zu einem solchen Schritt entschlossen[16]). Zwar hält man an der Gleichschaltungsfunktion der OF grundsätzlich fest, sieht jetzt aber im Gegenteil die Möglichkeit vor, daß „eine unbegrenzte Zahl von gemeinsamen Kandidaten aufgestellt und registriert wird" (Art. 46 n. F. WahlG). Die Wahlen zu den örtlichen Volksräten vom 28. 2. 1988 boten die erste Gelegenheit, das neue Verfahren zu praktizieren. In den 55 539 Wahlkreisen waren 66 048 Kandidaten registriert worden[17]). Durchschnittlich jeder Fünfte hatte somit einen Gegenkandidaten. Bei einer Wahlbeteiligung von 99,15 %[18]) stimmten 89,06 % für die Gebiets-, 89,10 % für die Gemeinde- und 89,80 % für die Bürgermeistereikandidaten. In 302 Wahlkreisen (ca. 0,5 %) erhielt keiner der Kandidaten die erforderliche absolute Mehrheit[19]). Dies ist ein zwar kleiner, aber durchaus bedeutsamer Schritt zu einer demokratischeren Willensbildung des Volkes.

Die statisch verstandene politisch-moralische Einheit des Volkes spiegelt sich auf der Ebene der NSb in einem weitgehend zementierten Vertretungsschlüssel wider: Während der BZNS rund 100 Mandate (25 %) besitzt, liegt der Anteil der Kommunisten – BKP und DKMS – bei 70 % der Sitze (285–290 Mandate). Der Anteil der Frauen schwankt zwischen 15 und 20 %; der Anteil junger Abgeordneter (bis 30) liegt bei gut 10 %[20]).

Die Volksvertreter besitzen zwar einige traditionelle Statusrechte, die ihrer persönlichen Unabhängigkeit dienen (Immunität, Indemnität – Art. 88, 89 Verf.; Urlaub und Lohnfortzahlung während der Sitzungszeiten; kostenlose Benutzung öffentlicher Verkehrsmittel usw.)[21]), aber ein freies Mandat besitzen sie nicht, vielmehr ein abgemildertes imperatives Mandat. Art. 86 Verf. läßt diese Frage in einer gewissen Schwebe, indem er bestimmt, daß sich die Volksvertreter „in ihrer Tätigkeit von den Interessen des ganzen Volkes und von den Interessen ihrer Wähler leiten lassen" sollen. Letztere finden in den „Wähleraufträgen"[22]) ihren Niederschlag, für deren Verwirklichung sich die Abgeordneten einzusetzen haben. Kümmern sie sich darum nicht, verletzen sie ihre Pflichten und können von den Wählern abberufen werden[23]). Dies ist das Grundmuster des imperativen Mandats[24]).

Tatsächlich wird die Durchschlagskraft des Wählerwillens jedoch dadurch wesentlich abgeschwächt, daß die neugewählte Volksvertretung die Wähleraufgabe unter

---

[16]) Gesetz über die Änderung und Ergänzung des WahlG vom 11. 12. 1987 (DV. (1987) 98). – Zu Ungarn vgl. Brunner, G.: Das Regierungssystem, in: Südeusteuropa-Handbuch. Bd. V: Ungarn. Göttingen 1987, S. 213–249.

[17]) Vgl. RD. 1. 3. 1988. Gewählt wurden 8 Gebietsräte, der Rat der Hauptstadt, 273 Gemeinderäte und 3985 Bürgermeistereien. Zur Wahl ausführlich Höpken, W.: Demokratisierung in kleinen Schritten: Die Kommunalwahlen in Bulgarien, in: SOE. (1988), S. 208–218.

[18]) Wahlberechtigt waren 6 652 792, gewählt hatten 6 595 981.

[19]) Es handelt sich um 13 Gebietswahlkreise, 157 Gemeindewahlkreise und 132 Bürgermeistereien. In 31 Bürgermeistereien kam keine Wahl zustande.

[20]) Radev/Topornin (Anm. 10), S. 238f.

[21]) Art. 44ff. Gesetz über die Volksvertreter und Volksrätemitglieder vom 13. 4. 1977 (DV. (1977) 32).

[22]) Dekret über die Wähleraufträge vom 3. 2. 1978 (DV. (1978) 12).

[23]) Art. 10 Abs. 1 Gesetz über die Volksvertreter; Art. 81ff. WahlG.

[24]) In diesem Sinne Načeva, S.: Dăržavnopravni procesualni normi (Staatsrechtliche Verfahrensnormen). Sofia 1983, S. 70. (zit. als: Načeva).

Berücksichtigung der gesamtstaatlichen Interessen, d. h. der zentralen Planvorgaben zu einem realisierbaren Programm verarbeitet und so zum Beschluß erhebt. Erst darauf bezieht sich die Bindung des Abgeordneten. In der Praxis ist für eine Abberufung ohnehin nicht der Wählerwille entscheidend, sondern allein der der zuständigen Parteiorganisation.

Das bulgarische Staatsrecht geht nicht von dem Bild des Berufsparlamentariers aus; die Volksvertreter setzen ihre Berufstätigkeit fort; sie erhalten keine Diäten, was angesichts der geringen Sitzungsbelastung auch konsequent ist.

Soweit die Abgeordneten Mitglieder der BKP bzw. des BZNS sind, werden sie zu „Parlamentsgruppen" (*parlamentarni grupi*) zusammengefaßt, die zwar von der Geschäftsordnung mit gewissen Rechten ausgestattet, im Unterschied zu den Ausschüssen jedoch keine förmlichen Gliederungen der NSb sind[25].

Die NSb soll mindestens dreimal im Jahr einberufen werden (Art. 71 Abs. 2 Verf.); tatsächlich tritt sie etwa vierteljährlich, in der Regel für die Dauer eines Tages zusammen. Das Einberufungsrecht steht dem DS zu (Art. 71, 93 Nr. 3 Verf.); ein Fünftel der Abgeordneten kann ihn dazu zwingen.

Pro forma gebietet die NSb über die Fülle der Staatsgewalt, doch tatsächlich werden die für das politische Leben des Landes entscheidenden Kompetenzen und Funktionen weitgehend vom DS wahrgenommen, während ihr nur wenige staatsleitende Aufgaben von der Verfassung vorbehalten sind[26]: Änderung und verbindliche Auslegung der Verfassung; Annahme von (förmlichen) Gesetzen unter Einschluß des Staatshaushaltsplanes; institutionelle Ausgestaltung des DS und Ministerrates; personelle Besetzung des DS und des Obersten Gerichts; Wahl des Generalstaatsanwalts und des Ministerpräsidenten; Änderung der Landesgrenzen. Der Schwerpunkt ihrer Tätigkeit, die nach einem jährlichen Arbeitsplan abgewickelt wird, liegt in der Gesetzgebung. Mit ca. sieben Gesetzen im Jahr, bei denen es sich zumeist um Novellierungen handelt (vgl. Tabelle 1), besitzt sie – verglichen mit liberaldemokratischen Parlamenten – nur geringen Umfang. Eine weitere Hauptaufgabe, dessen praktische Bedeutung sich nur schwer abschätzen läßt, ist die Kontrolle der Ministerialbürokratie.

Die praktische Arbeit der NSb geschieht – wie in allen Körperschaften solcher Größenordnung – vor allem in den acht ständigen Fachausschüssen, die für übergreifende Politik- und Funktionsbereiche bestehen[27]: gesellschaftliche und ökonomische Entwicklung; Sozialpolitik; geistige Entwicklung; Schutz und Reproduktion der natürlichen Umwelt; Außenpolitik; Volksräte und lokale Selbstverwaltung; Gesetzgebung; Schutz der gesellschaftlichen Interessen und Bürgerrechte. Parallel zu diesen Fachausschüssen arbeiten beim DS mit gleichem Aufgabenbereich „Räte" (*săveti*), denen im Unterschied zu den Ausschüssen auch externe Fachleute insbesondere aus Wissenschaft und gesellschaftlichen Organisationen (z. B. Gewerkschaften) angehören (dürfen). Beide Gremien arbeiten bei sich überschneidenden Projekten zusam-

---

[25] Zu ihnen Spasov/Želev (Anm. 2) II, S. 72 f. Die dem DKMS und den anderen gesellschaftlichen Organisationen angehörenden Abgeordneten bilden keine „Fraktion". Vgl. Art. 16; 17; 52 Geschäftsordnung (GO) der NSb vom 14. 4. 1977 (DV. (1977) 32).

[26] Vgl. für 1987: DV. (1987) 101.

[27] Art. 76 Verf. i. V. m. Art 16 ff. GO NSb; vgl. auch DV. (1986) 50.

Tabelle 1: Rechtsetzungstätigkeit der obersten Staatsorgane im Vergleich

Jahr	NSb	DS	Ministerrat
1976	11 Gesetze	32 Dekrete, davon: 14 Internat. Vertr. 4 Gesetzesänderg.	99 Verordnungen, davon: 36 unveröffentlicht
1977	12 Gesetze	32 Dekrete, davon: 13 Internat. Vertr. 9 Gesetzesänderg.	83 Verordnungen, davon: 35 unveröffentlicht
1978	12 Gesetze	32 Dekrete, davon: 15 Internat. Vertr. 7 Gesetzesänderg.	61 Verordnungen, davon: 17 unveröffentlicht
1979	15 Gesetze	28 Dekrete, davon: 17 Internat. Vertr. 4 Gesetzesänderg.	59 Verordnungen, davon: 8 unveröffentlicht
1980	10 Gesetze	18 Dekrete, davon: 10 Internat. Vertr. 2 Gesetzesänderg.	82 Verordnungen, davon: 23 unveröffentlicht
1981	9 Gesetze	23 Dekrete, davon: 10 Internat. Vertr. 6 Gesetzesänderg.	54 Verordnungen, davon: 19 unveröffentlicht
1982	11 Gesetze	22 Dekrete, davon: 15 Internat. Vertr. 2 Gesetzesänderg.	52 Verordnungen, davon: 11 unveröffentlicht
1983	11 Gesetze	21 Dekrete, davon: 8 Internat. Vertr. 3 Gesetzesänderg.	58 Verordnungen, davon: 13 unveröffentlicht
1984	11 Gesetze	28 Dekrete, davon: 12 Internat. Vertr. 7 Gesetzesänderg.	70 Verordnungen, davon: 21 unveröffentlicht
1985	12 Gesetze	15 Dekrete, davon: 5 Internat. Vertr. 6 Gesetzesänderg.	81 Verordnungen, davon: 15 unveröffentlicht
1986	10 Gesetze	28 Dekrete, davon: 13 Internat. Vertr. 6 Gesetzesänderg.	73 Verordnungen, davon: 23 unveröffentlicht
1987	12 Gesetze	33 Dekrete, davon: 14 Internat. Vertr. 9 Gesetzesänderg.	69 Verordnungen, davon: 13 unveröffentlicht

Quelle: DV. 1976–1988.

men und werden dabei vom „operativen Büro des Staatsrates" unter Hinzuziehung des Vorsitzenden der NSb koordiniert[28]).

Die ständigen Ausschüsse haben zur Erfüllung ihrer Kontrollfunktion eine Reihe bedeutsamer Rechte gegenüber den staatlichen Verwaltungsorganen, die in der Praxis freilich nur sehr unvollkommen ausgeübt werden[29]). Generell sind sie berechtigt, von den Behördenchefs aller Verwaltungsstufen vom Minister abwärts Berichte, Informationen und Erklärungen anzufordern. Wollen sie bestimmte Vorgänge einer genaueren Prüfung unterwerfen, können sie nach Ermessen Arbeitsgruppen unter Hinzuziehung externer Fachleute bilden; sie dürfen in den staatlichen Behörden unmittelbar Untersuchungen vornehmen, zu diesem Zweck insbesondere die Herausgabe von Akten verlangen und Vertreter zu den Sitzungen der leitenden Verwaltungskonferenzen (Ministerien; Exekutivkomitees) entsenden. In neuerer Zeit sind die Ausschüsse auch zur Durchführung öffentlicher Anhörungen übergegangen[30]).

Die Aufgabe der Verfassungskontrolle, d. h. der Überprüfung der Verfassungsmäßigkeit von Gesetzen, wird vom Ausschuß für Gesetzgebung im Zuge des Gesetzgebungsverfahrens wahrgenommen (Art. 40 Abs. 2 GeschäftsO); praktisch geschieht dies allem Anschein nach in Abstimmung mit dem „Rat für Gesetzgebung" beim DS und mit den Rechtsabteilungen (*otdel praven*) von DS und Ministerrat[31]). Über eventuell bestehende Bedenken der Verfassungswidrigkeit entscheidet die NSb selbst (Art. 85 Verf.).

Der *Gesetzgebungsprozeß* ist ziemlich ausführlich geregelt[32]). Das Recht zur Gesetzesinitiative ist breit gestreut. Entwürfe zu allen Fragen können der DS, der Ministerrat, die ständigen Ausschüsse, die Abgeordneten, das Oberste Gericht und der Generalstaatsanwalt einbringen. Die Zentralorgane der gesellschaftlichen Organisationen (OF, Gewerkschaften, DKMS usw.) dürfen im Rahmen ihrer Verbandsaufgaben initiativ werden. In der Praxis kommen 80–90% der Gesetzesentwürfe aus dem Ministerrat[33]). Bevor sie bei der NSb eingebracht werden, leitet der Ministerpräsident sie dem DS mit der Bitte um Stellungnahme zu. Noch einmal im Ministerrat beraten und eventuell überarbeitet, wird der Entwurf mit Begründung der NSb zugeleitet. Begleitet von einem Gutachten (meist) des Gesetzgebungsausschusses geht der Entwurf in die erste Lesung, in welcher nicht beraten, sondern nur im Prinzip über die Annahme entschieden wird. Erst darauf folgen die mehr oder weniger ausführlichen Beratungen in den Fachausschüssen und im mitberatenden Gesetzgebungsausschuß,

---

[28]) Art. 20 i. V. m. Art. 8 GO NSb; Živkov, V.: Struktura i organizacija raboty Gosudarstvennogo soveta NRB (Struktur und Organisation des DS der NRB), in: Sovetskoe gosudarstvo i pravo (Sowjetstaat und -recht) – künftig: SGiP. (1984) 12, S. 68–71 (70) (zit. als: Živkov, Struktura).

[29]) Zum folgenden vgl. Art. 24ff. GO NSb.

[30]) Spasov, B.: Razvitie gosudarstvennogo prava NRB na sovremennom ètape (Die Entwicklung des Staatsrechts der NRB in der gegenwärtigen Etappe), in: SGiP. (1985) 11, S. 36–43 (40f.).

[31]) Načeva (Anm. 24), S. 58.

[32]) Grundlage sind Art. 80, 83, 84 Verf., das Gesetz über die Normativakte vom 29. 3. 1973 (DV. (1973) 27) und Art. 70–78 GO NSb vom 14. 4. 1977 (DV. (1977) 32).

[33]) 1971–1981 (d.h. VI. und VII. NSb) gingen bei der NSb 79 Entwürfe ein, davon 64 vom Ministerrat, 8 vom DS. Nur 1 Entwurf kam aus der Mitte der NSb selbst (Ausschuß). Vgl. Načeva (Anm. 24), S. 54.

der die Hauptlast der Arbeit trägt[34]). Die zweite Lesung beginnt mit dem Bericht des zuständigen Ausschusses zum Entwurf und endet mit der endgültigen Annahme (oder Ablehnung) in offener Abstimmung bei einfacher Stimmenmehrheit.

Das beschlossene Gesetz wird spätestens 15 Tage danach vom DS im DV verkündet und veröffentlicht und tritt grundsätzlich drei Tage später in Kraft (Art. 84 Verf.).

Die Änderung der Verfassung ist der NSb vorbehalten (Art. 78 Nr. 2 Verf.); ein entsprechender Entwurf muß förmlich als solcher in bestimmten Fristen eingebracht werden und bedarf zur Annahme einer qualifizierten Mehrheit von zwei Dritteln der gesetzlichen Mitglieder (Art. 143 Verf.). In der Praxis werden diese Formen beachtet[35]).

2. Der Staatsrat (DS)

Der DS ist ein Verfassungsorgan, das über weit gespannte Kompetenzen verfügt und dabei mehrere Rechtsfunktionen in sich vereinigt: die Vollmachten eines gesetzgebenden Ersatz- und – gegebenenfalls – Notparlaments, die traditionellen, vorwiegend repräsentativen Aufgaben eines Staatsoberhauptes und die staatslenkende Regierungsfunktion, die Gubernative, durch deren Ausübung der Ministerrat innerhalb der Exekutivgewalt auf die Administrative beschränkt wird. Die 1968 auf dem Juli-Plenum des ZK der BKP beschlossene, 1971 erfolgte Einführung des DS hatte augenscheinlich den Zweck, dem Parteichef (Todor Živkov) auch innerhalb der Staatsorganisation eine herausgehobene Stellung mit präsidialen Zügen einzuräumen (vgl. auch den Beitrag von W. Höpken, Politisches System).

Der DS besteht aus dem Vorsitzenden, vier bis sechs stellvertretenden Vorsitzenden, ca. 20 Mitgliedern und dem Sekretär (Art. 92 Abs. 1 Verf.). Während die Mitglieder bisher mit jeder neuen Amtsperiode mindestens zur Hälfte ausgetauscht worden sind, ist die Besetzung der herausgehobenen Positionen nahezu stabil geblieben. Die Angehörigen des DS müssen – im Unterschied zu gleichnamigen historischen Vorläufern – durchweg Mitglieder der NSb sein.

Der Vorsitzende wird nach der bisherigen Praxis aufgrund eines gemeinsamen Vorschlages der (beiden) Parlamentsgruppen (siehe oben), die sonstigen Mitglieder werden auf seinen Vorschlag hin gewählt (Art. 12 Abs. 1 GeschäftsO). Eventuelle Änderungen durch die NSb kann der Vorsitzende ablehnen und dem notfalls mit seiner Rücktrittsdrohung Nachdruck verleihen[36]). Die DS-Mitglieder sind demnach bis zu einem gewissen Grade vom Vertrauen des Vorsitzenden abhängig. Diese Ab-

---

[34]) Von den insgesamt 63 Ausschußsitzungen der 6 Ausschüsse in der VII. Legislaturperiode (1976–1981) entfielen auf den Gesetzgebungsausschuß allein oder mitberatend 32 Sitzungen. Načeva (Anm. 24), S. 58. Die Sitzungsfrequenzen scheinen starken Schwankungen zu unterliegen, z. B. 1973: 42, 1978: 19.

[35]) Die 1987 erfolgte Abschaffung der „Kreise" und ihre Ersetzung durch „Gebiete" änderte zwar faktisch die Art. 109 Abs. 1, Art. 110, Art. 111, Art. 116, Art. 124 Abs. 4 Verf., doch bedurfte es in diesem Falle keiner (förmlichen) Verfassungsänderung, da gemäß Art. 109 Abs. 2 die territoriale Verwaltungsgliederung auch durch ein einfaches Gesetz geändert werden darf.

[36]) Art. 11 Abs. 2 GO. Vorschlagsberechtigt ist theoretisch auch jeder einzelne Abgeordnete. Vgl. Živkov, Struktura (Anm. 28), S. 69.

hängigkeit zeigt sich auch im Geschäftsablauf des DS: Der Vorsitzende „organisiert und leitet die Arbeit" (Art. 96 Abs. 1 Ziff. 1 Verf.), d. h. er beruft die Sitzungen ein, stellt die Tagesordnung auf und verteilt die Arbeit nach seinem Ermessen unter den Stellvertretern und Mitgliedern mit Hilfe des Sekretärs; er kann von ihnen Berichte verlangen und ihnen in organisatorischer Hinsicht Weisungen erteilen. Auch wenn der Vorsitzende in Pattsituationen kein ausschlaggebendes Stimmrecht haben sollte[37]), verleihen ihm diese organisatorischen Vorrechte mehr als nur die Stellung eines primus inter pares. Unter Berücksichtigung der Tatsache, daß der Vorsitzende zugleich der Parteichef ist, nähert sie sich faktisch der eines „Präsidenten" der NRB an.

Protokollarisch zeigt sich die herausgehobene Stellung des Vorsitzenden vor allem darin, daß er den DS nach außen sowohl innerstaatlich wie zwischenstaatlich repräsentiert und dabei einen Teil der dem DS von Art. 93 der Verfassung zugewiesenen traditionellen Funktionen des Staatsoberhauptes in eigener Person selbständig ausübt (Vertretung des Staates nach außen; Ernennung der Vertreter Bulgariens im Ausland; Ausübung des Begnadigungsrechts; Verleihung von Orden, Medaillen und Ehrenzeichen; Verkündung der Gesetze; Ratifikation und Kündigung internationaler Abkommen; Ernennung der Behördenchefs unterhalb der Ministerebene). Diese Delegationsmöglichkeit wird durch Art. 96 Abs. 2 Verf. eröffnet und durch das Recht, die Beglaubigungs- und Abberufungsschreiben der ausländischen Diplomaten entgegenzunehmen (Art. 96 Abs. 1 Nr. 2), bereits konkretisiert.

Ein förmliches Vorschlagsrecht für die Besetzung des Amtes des Ministerpräsidenten besitzt der DS-Vorsitzende nicht; Ministerpräsident und Regierung sind ihm, hier liegt ein wesentlicher Unterschied zu einem Präsidialregime, nicht verantwortlich.

Die administrativen Entscheidungen des DS und seines Vorsitzenden werden von (sechs) „Kommissionen" vorbereitet (Begnadigung; Schuldenerlaß; Auszeichnung; Asylrechtsverleihung; Namengebung; Ordensverleihungen).

Die Funktion des DS als *Ersatzparlament* äußert sich darin, daß er zwischen den Tagungen der NSb (also fast immer) die meisten ihrer in Art. 78 Verf. genannten Kompetenzen stellvertretend ausübt (Art. 94). Der DS ist befugt, Dekrete (*ukazi*) zu erlassen, und zwar 1. in dringenden Fällen zur Änderung formeller Gesetze und 2. in grundlegenden Fragen der Staatsverwaltung[38]); sie müssen der NSb auf ihrer nächsten Tagung zur Bestätigung vorgelegt werden (Art. 94 Nr. 2 Verf.). Die Bestätigung ist eine Formsache; jedenfalls treten die Dekrete schon vorher in Kraft[39]). Der DS darf ferner Gesetze und Beschlüsse der NSb „in grundsätzlichen Fragen" durch bestätigungsfreie Dekrete ausgestalten (Art. 93 Nr. 7 Verf.). Allerdings ist deren Anteil an seiner Rechtsetzung nicht sehr umfangreich. Insgesamt ist die Rechtsetzung des DS gegenüber der der NSb wesentlich umfangreicher (vgl. Tabelle 1). Die Ermächti-

---

[37]) Grundsätzlich entscheidet der DS als Kollegialorgan mit Stimmenmehrheit, in welchem Verfahren, bleibt seiner autonomen Regelungskompetenz überlassen. Seine (nichtveröffentlichte) Geschäftsordnung sieht drei Formen vor: Plenarentscheidungen; Entscheidungen im (schriftlichen) Umlaufverfahren und Büroentscheidungen. Vgl. Živkov, Struktura (Anm. 28), S. 70.
[38]) Spasov/Želev (Anm. 2) II, S. 174. Ausgeschlossen sollen der gesamte Justizbereich und die allgemeine Staatsleitung sein.
[39]) Sollte die Bestätigung wider Erwarten einmal verweigert werden, würde dies eine Aufhebung des Dekrets mit Wirkung ex nunc bedeuten. Vgl. Spasov/Želev (Anm. 2) II, S. 177 f.

gung zu staatsleitenden Regierungsakten umfaßt sehr verschiedene Befugnisse, die Art. 94 Nr. 1 in der Generalermächtigung zur „allgemeinen Leitung der Innen- und Außenpolitik des Staates" zusammenfaßt. Im einzelnen rechnen hierzu die Leitung und Kontrolle der örtlichen Staatsorgane, die Kontrolle der Staatsanwaltschaft, die Leitungsbefugnisse gegenüber dem Ministerrat (Art. 94 Nr. 3) und die Vornahme von Notstandshandlungen (Anordnung von Verteidigungsmaßnahmen und der Mobilmachung; Erklärung des Kriegs- oder Ausnahmezustandes); im Kriegsfall darf der DS auch die der NSb vorbehaltenen Rechtsetzungs- und Organisationsbefugnisse ausüben (Art. 95 Verf.).

Unabhängig vom Zusammentreten der NSb ist der DS im übrigen für die allgemeine Leitung der Verteidigung und Sicherheit des Landes zuständig, bestimmt die Mitglieder des Staatlichen Verteidigungskomitees (*Dăržaven komitet na otbranata*) und die obersten Kommandostellen der Streitkräfte (Art. 93 Nr. 9–11 Verf.), kann Behörden im Rang unter den Ministerien errichten (Art. 93 Nr. 16), kontrolliert den Ministerrat, die Ministerien und anderen Zentralbehörden (Nr. 17), kann den Bestand und die Grenzen der örtlichen Verwaltungseinheiten ändern (Nr. 25).

Abgesehen von den erwähnten parlamentsrechtlichen Befugnissen (Ausschreibung von Wahlen; Einberufung der NSb; Gesetzesinitiative; Referendum; Volksdiskussion) hat der DS ferner die Aufgabe, die Einhaltung der Gesetze durch die Staatsverwaltung zu kontrollieren (Art. 93 Nr. 18). Er darf die Gesetze verbindlich auslegen (Art. 93 Nr. 8) und gesetzeswidrige nachgeordnete Rechtsakte der Zentral- und Lokalbehörden aufheben (Nr. 19; 20).

Der DS und die NSb verfügen über einen gemeinsamen Verwaltungsapparat. Ein 8 Personen zählendes „operatives Büro" (stellvertretende Vorsitzende, Sekretär, Vorsitzende der Räte beim DS) koordiniert die laufende Arbeit. Neben den für die wichtigsten politischen Ressorts eingerichteten „Räten" arbeiten funktionale „Abteilungen beim DS" (Recht; Wirtschaft und Finanzen; ständige Ausschüsse; Orden; Kanzlei; Petitionen). Die Rechtsabteilung ist für die Herausgabe des DV zuständig.

3. Der Ministerrat (Ministerski săvet)

Der Ministerrat wird von der Verfassung „Regierung" (*pravitelstvo*) genannt (Art. 98), aber gerade dies ist er nicht, da die Gubernative, wie bemerkt, beim DS liegt. Indem Art. 98 den Ministerrat als das „höchste vollziehende und verfügende Organ im Staat" bezeichnet, das „die Durchführung der Innen- und Außenpolitik des Staates organisiert" (Art. 103 Nr. 1, Nr. 13 Verf.), definiert er ihn direkt als die Spitze der (staatlichen) Administrative. Die Notwendigkeit eines herausgehobenen zentralen Organs der Verwaltungskoordination ergibt sich aufgrund der für das kommunistische System generell typischen Ausweitung des „Staates" auf Kosten der „Gesellschaft" und der Bevorzugung der Exekutive unter den Staatsfunktionen.

Der Ministerrat steht unter der Leitung und Kontrolle von NSb und DS; er ist ihnen verantwortlich und rechenschaftspflichtig (Art. 102 Verf.), wobei die Unterordnung unter den DS der entscheidende Faktor ist. Die machtpolitische Bedeutung des Ministerrats wird dadurch nicht eliminiert. Sie ist beträchtlich, denn er ist das Schlüsselinstrument, durch welches die leitenden Parteiorgane ihren politischen Willen in erster Linie konkret verwirklichen. Dem Ministerrat fällt die mehr oder weniger schwierige Aufgabe zu, die meist allgemein gehaltenen Direktiven der Partei und die Normativakte von NSb und DS durch praktische Detailregelungen zu realisieren.

Die wichtigsten Aufgaben des Ministerrates sind: 1. die Aufstellung der Volkswirtschaftspläne unter Einschluß der Sozial- und Kulturplanung sowie des jährlichen Staatshaushaltes (Art. 103 Nr. 4 und 5 Verf.); 2. die allgemeine Leitung der Streitkräfte des Landes (Art. 103 Nr. 8); 3. die Beteiligung an der Gestaltung und Abwicklung der auswärtigen Beziehungen insbesondere durch die Ausarbeitung von Verträgen und den Abschluß von Regierungsabkommen (Art. 103 Nr. 9, 10); 4. die Sorge für die Einhaltung der öffentlichen Sicherheit und Ordnung und für den Rechtsschutz der Bürger (Art. 103 Nr. 6, 7); 5. die Wahrnehmung der Zweckmäßigkeits- und Rechtmäßigkeitskontrolle über die Ministerien und nachgeordneten Staatsbehörden (Art. 103 Nr. 11–16).

Zur Erfüllung dieser Aufgaben besitzt er eine Reihe funktionaler Befugnisse, zu denen insbesondere die Gesetzesinitiative (Art. 103 Nr. 2), der Erlaß von Verordnungen (*postanovlenija*), Verfügungen (*razporeždanija*) und Beschlüsse (*rešenija*) und eine begrenzte selbständige Organisationsgewalt in bezug auf den zentralen Regierungsapparat gehören (Art. 104 Abs. 1; 105 Verf.).

Der Ministerrat besteht aus dem Ministerpräsidenten, seinen Stellvertretern und sonstigen Mitgliedern; er wird von der NSb gebildet, die zunächst nach Nominierung durch die Parlamentsgruppen der beiden Parteien den Ministerpräsidenten wählt und auf dessen Vorschlag die Stellvertreter und einfachen Mitglieder (Art. 99; 101 Verf.)[40]. Gegen den Willen des Ministerpräsidenten kann die NSb also eine andere personelle Zusammensetzung nicht herbeiführen, es sei denn, sie entscheidet sich für einen anderen Vorsitzenden. Die Mitglieder des Ministerrats brauchen keine Abgeordneten und auch nicht unbedingt Mitglieder der BKP zu sein; in der Praxis hat diese in engen Grenzen auch Angehörige des BZNS und Parteilose bei der Vergabe der Posten beteiligt.

Beim Zusammentreten einer neuen NSb erklärt der Ministerrat seinen Rücktritt (Art. 13 GeschäftsO); jene ist frei, ob sie ihn annimmt oder die „Regierung" im Amt bestätigt. Tatsächlich wird sie in jeder Legislaturperiode neu gebildet. Der Ministerrat kann von der NSb vorzeitig abberufen werden (Art. 78 Nr. 16 Verf.); gleiches gilt für einzelne seiner Mitglieder, was insbesondere im Zuge von Auflösungen bzw. Fusionen von Ministerien laufend geschieht; zu letzterem ist auf Vorschlag des Ministerpräsidenten auch der DS ermächtigt (Art. 94 Nr. 4 Verf.).

Den Kern der „Regierung" bildet das „Büro des Ministerrates". Dem Präsidium des Ministerrats der UdSSR vergleichbar, wurde es am 8.7.1971[41], d.h. mit Annahme der neuen Verfassung, geschaffen. Das Büro setzt sich aus dem Ministerpräsidenten, seinen Stellvertretern und 3–4 weiteren Ministern zusammen; es bereitet die Entscheidungen des Ministerrats vor, tritt unter Umständen aber auch an dessen Stelle, wobei die Beschlüsse des Büros als Ministerratsbeschlüsse gelten[42]. Der Mini-

---

[40] s. das Kapitel „Oberste Organe".
[41] RD. 9.7.1971. Ausführlich Spasov/Želev (Anm. 2) II, S. 198 f.
[42] Radev/Topornin (Anm. 10), S. 304; Spasov/Želev (Anm. 2) II, S. 200 f.

sterpräsident nimmt als Repräsentant der Administrative nach außen, als leitender Koordinator der Geschäfte im Ministerrat (Büro) und als Vorgesetzer des für den Ministerrat arbeitenden Fachapparates eine herausgehobene Stellung ein.

1986/1987 hat die Partei- und Staatsführung wieder einmal einschneidende Änderungen in der Organisationsstruktur der Zentralbehörden vorgenommen. Im Zuge dessen wurden zunächst zahlreiche Fach- und Branchenministerien aufgelöst, später jedoch zum Teil wieder hergestellt (III.1.).

Die *normative Tätigkeit* des Ministerrates übertrifft die von NSb und DS quantitativ bei weitem (vgl. Tabelle 1). Die Zahl der Verordnungen schwankt seit 1975 zwischen ca. 60 und 100 im Jahr, von denen allerdings unter Umständen über 1 Drittel nicht veröffentlicht wird. Neben den (selbständigen) Verordnungen erläßt der Ministerrat noch Durchführungsverordnungen zu Gesetzen meist in Form von Organisations- und Verfahrensregelungen (*pravilnici*), Durchführungsbestimmungen zu einzelnen Gesetzesvorschriften (*naredbi*) und Erlasse (*instrukcii*) an die nachgeordneten Verwaltungsbehörden zur Erläuterung und Anwendung von Rechtsvorschriften.

4. Probleme der zentralen Rechtsetzung

Die bulgarische Rechtsordnung und ihr folgend die Staatsrechtslehre kennen zwar eine Hierarchie der Rechtsquellen – von der Verfassung über Gesetz, Dekret und Verordnung zu Anordnung, Instruktion und Befehl (*zapoved*) – und damit den Vorrang von Verfassung und Gesetz gegenüber allen nachgeordneten Rechtsakten, aber unklar ist, *wann* eine Sachfrage durch (förmliches) „Gesetz" (*zakon*) geregelt, wann also die NSb tätig werden muß. Das Gesetz über die Normativakte vom 29.3.1973 (Art. 3) läßt diese Frage bewußt offen. Die Rechtslehre versteht zwar unter einem „Normativakt" (im Unterschied zum Individual- oder Verwaltungsakt) eine abstrakt-generelle rechtliche Regelung menschlichen Verhaltens[43]), aber sie verbindet diesen klassischen materiellen Gesetzesbegriff nicht mit der Forderung, die Anordnung solcher Regelungen grundsätzlich der Volksvertretung vorzubehalten („Gesetzesvorbehalt"), ihren Erlaß durch die Exekutive hingegen nur mit förmlich-gesetzlicher, also parlamentarischer Ermächtigung zuzulassen.

Ausnahmsweise ordnet allerdings Art. 4 des Gesetzes über die Normativakte die Herausgabe von „Gesetzbüchern" (*kodeks*) für zusammenhängende Rechtszweige (z. B. Zivilrecht; Arbeitsrecht; Strafrecht) oder für abgesonderte wichtige Teile von ihnen an, und Art. 3 bestimmt ergänzend, daß, *wenn* man zur Form des „Gesetzes" greife, es „alle hauptsächlichen gesellschaftlichen Beziehungen vollständig (selbst) regeln müsse", während es die weniger bedeutsamen Fragen einem „nachgeordneten Akt" überlassen dürfe. Hierin liegt der Ansatz zu einem Gesetzesvorbehalt. Bedeutung hat dieser Umstand vor allem für das Verordnungsrecht des Ministerrates, das teils unselbständigen Durchführungscharakter *secundum legem* (Art. 6 Nr. 1; 7 Gesetz über die Normativakte), teils selbständigen Normsetzungscharakter *praeter le-*

---

[43]) Spasov, B.: Vǎprosi na novata konstitucija (Fragen der neuen Verfassung). Sofia 1973, S. 216 ff. (zit. als: Vǎprosi).

gem besitzt (Art. 6 Nr. 2 Gesetz über die Normaktivakte). Das selbständige Verordnungsrecht soll nach Meinung V. Vălkanovs die Ausnahme darstellen[44]); tatsächlich findet es aber in den von Gesetzen relativ wenig berührten Bereichen der Wirtschaft, des Sozial- und Gesundheitswesens sowie der Kultur breite Anwendung.

Zwischen dem selbständigen und dem unselbständigen Verordnungsrecht des Ministerrats besteht praktisch freilich nur ein gradueller Unterschied, da in Bulgarien keine Verfassungsgerichtsbarkeit zur Prüfung der Vereinbarkeit von Verordnungen mit Gesetzen und Verfassung existiert. Zwar übt der DS die Funktion der abstrakten Normenkontrolle aus (Art. 93 Nr. 8 Verf.), und zwar bei Anerkennung der Auslegungsbedürftigkeit durch ein zu veröffentlichendes Dekret, aber praktisch ist dies bedeutungslos[45]).

Das Verordnungsrecht besitzt eine hohe *politische* Bedeutung, denn es bildet die juristische Grundlage für die „Gemeinsamen Verordnungen" von ZK der BKP und Ministerrat, die seit 1949, sowjetischem Vorbild folgend, in Bulgarien zur Praxis wurden. Durch sie bestimmt die Partei- und Staatsführung die langfristige politische Zielperspektive in den wichtigsten Fragen der Staatsverwaltung[46]). Gemeinsame Verordnungen erläßt der Ministerrat ferner mit dem Zentralrat der Gewerkschaften und gelegentlich auch mit den Zentralorganen der anderen Massenorganisationen.

Im zentralen Normsetzungsprozeß nimmt der Ministerrat faktisch die stärkste Position ein, und zwar nicht nur quantitativ, sondern auch qualitativ, da die meisten Gesetzesentwürfe von ihm eingebracht werden (vgl. oben II.1.).

Während die Gesetze und sonstigen Entscheidungen der NSb spätestens 15 Tage nach ihrer Verabschiedung im DV verkündet werden müssen (Art. 84 Abs. 1 Verf.), ist eine Veröffentlichung der Dekrete des DS (Art. 97 Abs. 2 Verf.) und der Verordnungen des Ministerrates (Art. 104 Abs. 2 Verf.) nicht zwingend[47]). Unklar ist, ob alle Dekrete veröffentlicht werden; die Ministerratsverordnungen werden jedenfalls nur teilweise veröffentlicht.

Insgesamt weist das bulgarische Staatsrecht nicht unbeträchtliche gesetzliche Lücken auf.

---

[44]) Eingehend Vălkanov, V. Normativnite aktove na ministerskija săvet (Die Normativakte des Ministerrats). Sofia 1979, S. 39 ff; 63 ff. (zit. als: Vălkanov, Normativnite aktove).
[45]) Vgl. Art. 49 ff Gesetz über die Normativakte; ausführlich Spasov, Tălkovatelnata dejnost (Anm. 12), S. 28 ff; 102 ff. Zwischen 1976 und 1987 wurde 1 Dekret veröffentlicht, das zudem das völlig nebensächliche Ordensrecht betraf.
[46]) Vălkanov, Normativnite aktove (Anm. 44), S. 80 ff. (82/83).
[47]) Art. 37 Gesetz über die Normativakte.

III. Die Staatsverwaltung

1. Die Zentralbehörden

Nach ihrem rechtlichen Verhältnis zum Ministerrat lassen sich in Bulgarien – ebenso wie in der UdSSR und anderen sozialistischen Staaten – zwei Kategorien von Zentralbehörden unterscheiden[48]): 1. Ministerien und ihnen rangmäßig gleichgestellte Zentralorgane; sie werden von der NSb bestimmt (Art. 100 Verf.); 2. Sonderbehörden ohne Sitz im Ministerrat, die vom DS (Art. 93 Nr. 16) oder Ministerrat (Art. 105) eingerichtet werden. In beiderlei Hinsicht hat es in neuester Zeit verwirrend viele Änderungen gegeben.

a) Ministerien

Im Zusammenhang mit der Wirtschaftsreform war im Januar 1986 eine Reihe von Ministerien aufgelöst oder umgestaltet worden[49]). Ein Teil der Verwaltungsapparate wurde vier neugeschaffenen sogenannten „Räten beim Ministerrat" zugeordnet[50]): Wirtschaftsrat; Sozialrat; Rat für Wissenschaft, Kultur und Bildung (später: Rat für Geistesentwicklung); Rat für Land- und Forstwirtschaft. Relativ verselbständigte Fachkabinette des Ministerrats und Superressorts zugleich, waren sie damit betraut, die in ihrem Kompetenzbereich tätigen, ihnen unterstellten Staatsorgane, Wirtschaftsbetriebe, aber auch gesellschaftlichen Organisationen zur Verwirklichung der gesetzten Planaufgaben zu lenken. Die Beschlüsse der „Räte" galten als solche des Ministerrats.

Die Aufgliederung des Ministerrats in eine Vielzahl komplizierter Subsysteme bewährte sich offensichtlich nicht, denn schon im August 1987 wurden die „Räte" wieder aufgelöst; man kehrte namentlich in der Wirtschaft zum klassischen Modell der Fachministerien zurück[51]). Heute bestehen Ministerien für Innere Angelegenheiten und Staatssicherheit; für Rechtspflege; für Wirtschaft und Planung; für Land- und Forstwirtschaft; für Außenwirtschaftsbeziehungen; für Transportwesen; für Volksgesundheit und Sozialfürsorge; für Kultur, Wissenschaft und Aufklärung; für

---

[48]) Einen guten Einblick in den Dschungel der Zentralbehörden gibt das enzyklopädische Handbuch: Bălgarskite dăržavni institucii (Die bulgarischen Staatsinstitutionen) 1879–1986. Sofia 1987, (zit. als: Bălgarskite institucii). S. außerdem die Übersicht über die „Obersten Organe" im Anhang.

[49]) Es handelte sich um die Ministerien für Bauwesen und Städtebau, Außenhandel, Versorgung, Produktion und Handel von Konsumgütern, ferner um die Staatskomitees für Wissenschaft und technischen Fortschritt sowie für Planung (DV. (1986) 9). An ihre Stelle traten: das Staatskomitee für Handel, die Staatliche Plankommission, das Staatskomitee für Forschung und Technologie (a.a.O.), die jedoch mit Wirkung vom 1.1.1988 wieder aufgelöst wurden (DV. (1987) 65).

[50]) Beschlüsse vom 27.1.1986 (DV. (1986) 9) bzw. 25.12.1986 (DV. (1986) 101). Die „Räte" waren ebenso wie der Ministerrat organisiert. Sie bestanden aus dem von der NSb gewählten Vorsitzenden, seinen Stellvertretern und dem Sekretär, die vom DS, und aus Mitgliedern, die vom Ministerrat bestimmt worden waren. Vgl. die Reglements der „Räte" (DV. (1986) 66; (1987) 12).

[51]) Beschluß der NSb vom 18.8.1987 (DV. (1987) 65). Zugleich wurden zum 1.1.1988 die Ministerien für Bildung, Finanzen und Handel, die Staatliche Plankommission und das Staatskomitee für Forschung und Technologie aufgelöst.

Volksverteidigung; für Auswärtige Angelegenheiten. Hinzu kommen die Komitees für Staats- und Volkskontrolle (vgl. unten III.5.) sowie für Territorial- und Stadtentwicklung.

Aufgrund einer eigenartigen konzeptionellen Verbindung einer verstärkten Gleichschaltung von oben mit einer gewissen Partizipation von unten wurden seit den späten 60er Jahren wichtige nationale Lebensbereiche zu „Komplexen" erklärt und gemischten staatlich-gesellschaftlichen/gesellschaftlich-staatlichen Verwaltungsapparaten (meist) im Range von Ministerien unterstellt (vgl. auch Art. 78 Nr. 14 Verf.). Man wollte damit die von Staatsorganen und gesellschaftlichen Organisationen wahrgenommenen Aufgaben enger koordinieren und zugleich kollegiale, demokratische Mechanismen der „Gesellschaft" auf den „Staat" einwirken lassen[52]). So bildete man z. B. einen sog. Nationalen Komplex „Künstlerisches Schaffen, Kulturelle Tätigkeit und Masseninformationsmittel". Sein (formell) höchstes Organ ist der „Kongreß der Bulgarischen Kultur", der auf der Grundlage der Kulturpolitik der BKP die Hauptrichtungen der Kulturarbeit im Lande formuliert und als Exekutivorgan das aus ca. 185 Mitgliedern bestehende Komitee für Kultur wählt. Dessen Organe sind das Büro, der Vorstand (Vorsitzender, Stellvertreter, Generalsekretär) und der Vorsitzende. Es verfügt über einen territorialen Unterbau in Form von „Räten"[53]).

Der tatsächliche Erfolg dieser Konzeption läßt sich nur schwer einschätzen, da die kurzatmigen Reorganisationen die Sammlung gesicherter Erfahrungen nicht begünstigt haben.

Die Ministerien, Staatskomitees und die ihnen gleichgestellten Zentralbehörden werden grundsätzlich monokratisch, d. h. durch den verantwortlichen Minister (Vorsitzenden) geleitet (Art. 106 Verf.). Sie sind befugt, in den Grenzen ihrer Zuständigkeit Verfahrensregelungen, Anordnungen, Instruktionen und Befehle zu erlassen, die auch für die anderen Staatsorgane und die gesellschaftlichen Organisationen verbindlich sind (Art. 108 Abs. 1 Verf.), ferner den nachgeordneten Fachbehörden der territorialen Volksräte Weisungen zu erteilen, deren rechtwidrige Verwaltungsakte aufzuheben (Art. 107 Abs. 1 Verf.) und die von ihnen für rechtswidrig gehaltenen Normativakte der Exekutivkomitees der Volksräte zu suspendieren und vom Ministerrat überprüfen zu lassen (Art. 107 Abs. 2).

Das monokratische Prinzip wird in einem gewissen Maße durch kollegiale Leitungsformen aufgelockert: Dem Minister steht zur Beratung ein „Kollegium" zur Seite, dem er selbst, sein Stellvertreter sowie angesehene Fachleute und Vertreter externer Institutionen, namentlich aus Wissenschaft und Massenorganisationen, angehören. Ob der hiermit erstrebte Zweck – eine Stärkung der Sachlichkeit bzw. Qualität der Leitung und zugleich ein gewisser Interessenausgleich – auch tatsächlich er-

---

[52]) Kostadinov, G.: Razvitie administrativnogo prava v NRB (Die Entwicklung des Verwaltungsrechts in der NRB), in: SGiP. (1985) 11, S. 52–60 (54f.) (zit. als Kostadinov, Razvitie).

[53]) Zur Entwicklung vgl. DV. (1977) 101 (Bildung des Komitees); DV. (1978) 75 (Statut des Komitees); DV. (1986) 9; 25; 66 (Unterordnung unter den „Rat für Geistesentwicklung"); DV. (1987) 65 (Unterstellung unter das Ministerium für Kultur, Wissenschaft und Aufklärung). Vgl. auch Bălgarskite institucii (Anm. 48), S. 103 ff.

reicht wurde (wird), läßt sich angesichts der Schweigsamkeit der bulgarischen Staatsrechtsliteratur zu diesem Problem nicht sicher beurteilen.

Stärker kommt das Kollegialprinzip in den Staatskomitees zur Geltung, da hier das Komitee als Kollegialorgan neben seinem Vorsitzenden (als Minister) auch eigene Entscheidungsbefugnisse besitzt.

Während die Ernennung der Minister der NSb vorbehalten ist, werden die Stellvertreter und die Sekretäre der Komitees (im Rang von Ministerien) und die Leiter der sonstigen Zentralbehörden vom DS, die übrigen Behördenleiter vom Ministerrat ernannt.

b) Sonderbehörden

Die Zentralbehörden ohne Sitz im Ministerrat erfüllen zwar ebenfalls ressortübergreifende funktionelle Aufgaben, sind aber enger spezialisiert. Sie sind dem Ministerrat unmittelbar zugeordnet; ihre Leiter können ausnahmsweise Ministerrang haben.

Derartige nachgeordnete Zentralbehörden sind insbesondere die BNB, die Komitees für Qualitätsstandards, zum Schutze der natürlichen Umwelt, für Informatik, für die Nutzung der Atomenergie für friedliche Zwecke, für Geologie sowie die Zentrale Statistische Verwaltung[54]).

Die Zentralbehörden dieser Kategorie dürfen nicht mit jenen „Komitees", „Hauptverwaltungen", „Räten" usw. verwechselt werden, die im Verantwortungsbereich von Ministerien als Untergliederungen spezielle Aufgaben erfüllen wie z. B. das (1981 aufgelöste) Komitee für Pressewesen oder das Komitee für Kultur.

2. Die nachgeordneten allgemeinen Verwaltungsbehörden

a) Territoriale Gliederung und Kompetenzen

Die Gestalt der Territorialverwaltung hat sich gegenüber den Verhältnissen vor der kommunistischen Machtergreifung wesentlich geändert. Zwar gab es auch schon im Vorkriegsbulgarien „Räte" (*săveti*) als Vertretungskörperschaften der Bevölkerung in den Gemeinden und Kreisen[55]), aber sie waren Organe einer echten lokalen Selbstverwaltung der Bürger aufgrund eigener, dem Eingriff der Zentralorgane entzogener Sachaufgaben. Das durch die „volksdemokratische" Verfassung vom 4.12.1947 übernommene sowjetische Rätesystem unterscheidet sich hiervon grundlegend, da es gemäß den Prinzipien der Gewalteneinheit und des Demokratischen Zentralismus (vgl. oben I.2. und 3.) eine dezentralisierte Eigenständigkeit der Staatsgewalt ausschließt. Eine gewisse Kontinuität weist demgegenüber die territoriale Verwaltungseinteilung auf. Die Gebietsreform von 1959 löste den dreistufigen Verwaltungsaufbau der Vorkriegszeit aus Gemeinden (*obštini*), Bezirken (*okolii*) und Kreisen (*okrăzi*) durch einen zweistufigen Aufbau ab: die (95) Bezirke wurden abgeschafft, stattdessen zum einen die Zahl der Gemeinden durch Zusammenlegungen halbiert, zum anderen

---

[54]) Dekret des DS vom 21.2.1986 (DV. (1986) 16).

[55]) Vgl. dazu den Überblick von Handjieff, N.: Organisation der Staats- und Selbstverwaltung in Bulgarien. München 1931, S. 53 ff.

die Zahl der neben der Hauptstadt Sofia bestehenden 12 Kreise auf 29 erhöht[56]). Den Hauptgrund dieser Maßnahmen bildete die sowjetischem Vorbild folgende Territorialisierung der Wirtschaftsverwaltung, die anstelle der schwerfälligen zentralistischen Branchenministerien nun auf die örtlichen Räte übergehen sollte. Von der bald wieder einsetzenden Rezentralisierung wurde die territoriale Gliederung der Verwaltung als solche allerdings nicht berührt.

Der 1973 unternommene Schritt zu einer strafferen integrierten Raumordnung, Infrastruktur- und Bauplanung[57]) auf der Grundlage sog. Siedlungssysteme (*selištni sistemi*) als territoriale Hauptplanungseinheiten[58]) kündigte eine neue Gebietsreform an. Sie wurde 1978 durch die Zusammenlegung der Gemeinden mit den 291 Siedlungssystemen vollzogen[59]). Der Übergang zu diesen Großgemeinden wurde nicht nur mit dem allgemeinen Erfordernis einer größerräumigen Infrastrukturplanung, sondern insbesondere auch damit begründet, daß der Zusammenhang von landwirtschaftlicher Erzeugung und industrieller Weiterverarbeitung wesentlich enger geworden sei; die Verbesserung der Sozialversorgung und des Verkehrswesens hätten im übrigen größere Grundeinheiten der Territorialverwaltung erforderlich gemacht[60]). Die hierdurch drohende Entfernung der Verwaltungsdienststellen von der (Land-)Bevölkerung versuchte man aufzufangen, indem man gleichzeitig unterhalb der Gemeinden „Bürgermeistereien" (*kmetstva*) in Dörfern (Siedlungen) mit mindestens 100 Einwohnern schuf[61]).

Im Zuge der von Gorbačevs Reformpolitik in Bulgarien ausgelösten Reorganisationen schritt man im August 1987 erneut zu einschneidenden Veränderungen in der Territorialverwaltung, deren rechtliche Ausgestaltung zur Zeit noch nicht abgeschlossen ist: Die nunmehr 28 Kreise wurden durch 9 „Gebiete" (*oblasti*) ersetzt (vgl. Tabelle 2); zugleich wertete man die Großgemeinden auf[62]).

Die Auflösung der Kreise rechtfertigte man mit einem Bündel sehr verschiedener Gründe: Beseitigung der eingetretenen regionalen Disproportionen; Schaffung etwa gleichgroßer und gleichstarker Verwaltungsgebiete; Aufwertung und Förderung zweitrangiger Provinzzentren durch ihre Bevorzugung als Sitz der Gebietsverwaltung

---

[56]) Dekret über die neue Verwaltungseinteilung des Landes vom 23.1.1959 (Izvestija. (1959) 7). Die Zahl der Landgemeinden sank von 1883 auf 867, die der Stadtgemeinden stieg von 112 auf 120. Zur Entwicklung der Territorialräte vgl. Janev, J.; Kolev, Ž.: Văznikvanie i razvitie na narodnite săveti v Narodna Republika Bălgarija (Die Entstehung und Entwicklung der Volksräte in der NRB), in: Godišnik na Sofijskija universitet (Jahrbuch der Sofioter Universität). 70 (1977). Sofia 1979, S. 23–34.

[57]) Gesetz über die Territorial- und Siedlungsstrukturentwicklung vom 29.3.1973 (DV. (1973) 29) mit den wichtigsten Änderungen von 1977 (DV. (1977) 102).

[58]) Art. 34 Gesetz i. d. F. von 1977.

[59]) Art. 3 Gesetz vom 1.12.1978 über die Änderung und Ergänzung des Gesetzes über die Volksräte (DV. (1978) 97). Bereits durch Gesetz vom 22.12.1977 (DV. (1977) 102) waren für die Siedlungssysteme Vertretungskörperschaften eingerichtet worden. Es wurde 1 Jahr später aufgehoben.

[60]) Kostadinov, Razvitie (Anm. 52), S. 54.

[61]) Vgl. die Art. 66ff., die am 1.12.1978 dem Gesetz über die Volksräte angefügt wurden. Die Mindestgröße von 100 Einwohnern galt schon im Gemeinderecht der Vorkriegszeit.

[62]) Gesetz von 18.8.1987 (DV. (1987) 65). Zugrunde lag der Plenarbeschluß des ZK der BKP vom 28.7.1987; vgl. dazu Höpken, W.: „Perestrojka auf Bulgarisch": Sofia und die Reformpolitik Gorbačevs, in: SOE. (1987), S. 616–646 (637f.).

Tabelle 2: Neue territoriale Gliederung Bulgariens

Bezirk	gebildet aus den früheren Kreisen:	Größe absolut	in %	Bevölkerung absolut	in %	Anteil der städt. Bevölk. in %	Ø Bevölk. pro Siedl.einheit	National-einkommen	Anteil an: Ind.prod. (in %)	Landwirt.
Burgas	Burgas, Jambol, Sliven	14664	13,2	872487	9,7	64,7	1779	12,5	13,7	11,6
Chaskovo	Chaskovo, Stara Zagora, Kărdžali	13864	12,6	1042810	11,5	54,1	1101	10,2	10,6	11,5
Loveč	Loveč, Pleven, Gabrovo, Vel. Tărnovo	15182	13,7	1074810	12,0	62,1	1128	14,4	13,6	14,8
Michajlovgrad	Michajlovgrad, Vraca, Vidin	10570	9,5	674438	7,5	53,8	1712	6,4	7,4	10,0
Plovdiv	Plovdiv, Smoljan Pazardžik	13617	12,3	1252695	13,9	63,2	2194	14,5	13,0	11,9
Razgrad	Razgrad, Silistra, Tărgovište, Ruse	10812	9,7	849384	9,5	54,5	1723	8,3	8,7	14,7
Sofia-Land	Sofia-Land, Pernik, Kjustendil, Blagoevgrad	19087	17,2	1018748	11,4	57,8	1115	9,7	10,6	9,6
Sofia-Stadt	(unverändert)	1194	1,1	1204273	13,4	95,1	31542	13,8	13,2	1,2
Varna	Varna, Šumen, Tolbuchin	11918	10,7	978551	10,9	67,6	1872	10,2	8,4	14,5

übernommen von Höpken, W.: Sofia und die Reformpolitik Gorbačevs, in: SOE. (1987), S. 645.

(Michajlovgrad, Chaskovo, Loveč, Razgrad); Verkleinerung der staatlichen Verwaltungsapparate; Bekämpfung regionaler Selbstherrlichkeit; Beseitigung der Bevormundung der Betriebe und Gemeinden durch die Kreisbürokratie.

Natürlich hat man auch und gerade diese Verwaltungsreform als Beitrag zur Stärkung der „Selbstverwaltung" hingestellt, denn abweichend vom Gesetz über die Volksräte sollen die Gebiete und Gemeinden nicht mehr „örtliche Organe der Staatsmacht", sondern nur noch „Selbstverwaltungsgemeinschaften der Bevölkerung" (*samoupravljavašta se obštnost na naselenieto*) sein[63]). Ob mit dieser verbalen Akzentverschiebung sich auch tatsächlich der Entscheidungsspielraum der Gemeinden erweitern wird, muß sich erst noch erweisen; die bisherigen Erfahrungen zwingen zur Skepsis.

Zusammengefaßt bietet die Territorialverwaltung heute folgendes Bild:

Auf der *mittleren* Ebene bestehen acht Gebiete sowie die einem Gebiet gleichgestellte Hauptstadt Sofia[64]). Ihre Kompetenzen sind erst vorläufig und auch nur ziemlich allgemein festgelegt worden[65]). Sie erstrecken sich zwar grundsätzlich auf alle von der Verfassung (Art. 114) anerkannten Bereiche der örtlichen Verwaltung, nämlich Wirtschaft, Sozialwesen, Versorgung, Kultur, Wahrung von öffentlicher Sicherheit und Ordnung, sollen sich aber funktional auf allgemeine Planungs- und Leitungsaufgaben, auf die Koordination der Gemeinden zur Erfüllung regionaler und gesamtstaatlicher Ziele, auf die Förderung und Unterstützung der Gemeinden bei ihrer Tätigkeit sowie auf ihre Kontrolle konzentrieren. Daß die Gebietsräte sich auch in der Praxis künftig auf diese allgemeine Leitungsfunktion beschränken, könnte dadurch begünstigt werden, daß der den Ministerien unterstellte Fachapparat im Unterschied zu früher ausschließlich auf der Gemeindeebene angesiedelt sein soll, die Verwaltung der Gebietsräte also – im Vergleich zu der der Kreise – deutlich kleiner ausfallen wird. Freilich werden dadurch die ministeriellen Einflüsse auf die Gemeinden umso stärker und die Chancen für eine echte Selbstverwaltung entsprechend geringer.

Eine herausgehobene Stellung nimmt die Stadtverwaltung von Sofia ein, die dem Ministerrat direkt untergeordnet und daher faktisch eher den Ministerien gleichgestellt ist[66]).

Die *untere* Verwaltungsebene bilden die 299 gebietsangehörigen „Gemeinden" (*obština*)[67]). Ihnen sind die 12 (Stadt-)Gemeinden von Sofia gleichgestellt[68]). Das „Vor-

---

[63]) Vgl. die Deklaration der NSb vom 7.7.1987 über die Umwandlung der Gemeinden in sich selbst verwaltende Gemeinschaften der Bevölkerung (DV. (1987) 54).

[64]) Dekret über die Bestimmung der Zahl und Grenzen der Gebiete und der in sie einbezogenen Gemeinden sowie ihrer Verwaltungszentren vom 26.8.1987 (DV. (1987) 67).

[65]) Eine erste Kompetenzbeschreibung liefert das Gesetz vom 18.8.1987. Die Verordnung des Ministerrats vom 18.12.1987 setzte ein „Vorläufiges Reglement über die Selbstverwaltung der territorialen Gemeinschaften" in Kraft (DV. (1988) 3), das ohne Bezug auf den 11 Punkte umfassenden Kompetenzkatalog des Gesetzes eine eigene Aufgabenbeschreibung vornimmt (Art. 16–21).

[66]) Vgl. Spasov/Želev (Anm. 2) II, S. 221 (Anm. 1).

[67]) Mit Ausnahme der Gebiete von Burgas (26 Gemeinden) und Sofia (52) sind die Zahlen ziemlich ausgewogen: Varna: 30; Loveč: 38; Michajlovgrad: 38; Plovdiv: 40; Razgrad: 39; Chaskovo: 36. Vgl. die Aufzählung im Dekret vom 26.8.1987 (DV. (1987) 67).

[68]) Früher „Rayone" (*rajoni*) genannt, heißen sie nun „Gemeinden" (*obštini*). Vgl. das Gesetz vom 10.12.1987 (DV. (1987) 97).

läufige Reglement" vom Dezember 1987 nennt sie die „grundlegende administrativterritoriale Einheit... der Bevölkerung" (Art. 9 Abs. 1). Die neue basisdemokratische Rhetorik setzt sich in der feierlichen Formel fort, die Bevölkerung sei „Herr des Territoriums der Gemeinde und Subjekt der Verwaltung des sozialistischen Eigentums" (Art. 9 Abs. 3). Die Formel wird in zwei langen Kompetenzkatalogen konkretisiert, die dem Gemeinderat zwar im Prinzip eine umfassende Zuständigkeit für sämtliche Fragen der sozialen, kulturellen, infrastrukturellen, wirtschaftlichen und sonstigen Versorgung der Bevölkerung zuweisen (Art. 11, 12), aber aufgrund ihrer globalen, unbestimmten Aussagen nur begrenzt praktikabel sind. Das gilt insbesondere für die diversen Koordinations- und Kontrollbefugnisse gegenüber den auf Gemeindegebiet tätigen Wirtschaftsbetrieben und gesellschaftlichen Institutionen.

Die Gemeinden verfügen über eigene Einkünfte, die sich aus Abgaben der Betriebe, aus Grundsteuern, Beiträgen, Gebühren, Bußgeldern und Nutzungen des Gemeindevermögens zusammensetzen, deren Tarife bzw. Sätze aber vom Ministerrat festgelegt werden (Art. 14 Abs. 2). Sie sind die Grundlage des Haushaltes, den die Gemeinden in Übereinstimmung mit den verbindlichen Richtlinien des Ministerrats im Rahmen der staatlichen Gesamtplanung aufstellen.

Die *unterste* Verwaltungsebene bilden die „Bürgermeistereien" (*kmetstva*). Sie sind nicht nur in Landgemeinden, sondern – mit Ausnahme von Sofia – inzwischen auch in Großstädten (Burgas, Varna, Plovdiv, Sliven, Pleven, Ruse, Pernik, Stara Zagora) anstelle von Rayons eingerichtet worden[69]. Rechtlich gesehen, sind die Bürgermeistereien keine Amts- bzw. Verwaltungsaußenstellen der Gemeinden, sondern selbständig gebildete Bürgervertretungen mit eigenem Haushalt[70]. Tatsächlich liegt ihre Funktion darin, gewisse Aufgaben der Ordnungsverwaltung bürgernah zu erfüllen, darauf hinzuwirken, daß öffentliche und individuelle Bautätigkeit im Rahmen der Dorf- und Stadtteilentwicklungsplanung geordnet erfolgt, sowie ergänzende Maßnahmen zur Versorgung der Bevölkerung mit sozialen, kulturellen und sonstigen Dienstleistungen, auch in privaten Formen, zu treffen.

Die Kompetenzregelung der örtlichen Volksräte ist eingebettet in den vom Prinzip des Demokratischen Zentralismus (vgl. I.3.) bestimmten Organisationsaufbau der territorialen Verwaltungseinheiten (vgl. unten 2.b). Gemäß Art. 123 Verf. „leiten und kontrollieren" die höherstufigen Volksräte (als Vertretungskörperschaften) die nachgeordneten Volksräte; sie sind außerdem befugt, deren gesetzeswidrige bzw. fehlerhafte Normativakte aufzuheben (Art. 124 Abs. 1). Entsprechende Befugnisse besitzen die Exekutivkomitees der Volksräte gegenüber den ihnen untergeordneten Exekutivkomitees (Art. 124 Abs. 2). Außerdem dürfen sie die gesetzeswidrigen (fehlerhaften) Normativakte der nachrangigen Volksräte aussetzen und eine verbindliche Entscheidung desjenigen Volksrates veranlassen, der zur Aufhebung des betreffenden Aktes befugt ist (Art. 124 Abs. 3). Im übrigen sind die territorialen Volksräte, wie bereits vermerkt, den obersten Staatsorganen, namentlich DS und Ministerrat, unterstellt (Art. 93 Nr. 20; Art. 103 Nr. 12, Nr. 15 Verf.).

---

[69]) Dekret vom 17.12.1987 (DV. (1987) 89); Art. 66 Abs. 3 Gesetz über die Volksräte i. d. F. vom 10.12.1987 (DV. (1987) 97).
[70]) Art. 68 Gesetz über die Volksräte i. d. F. vom 1.12.1978 i. V. m. Art. 7 des „Vorläufigen Reglements" vom 18.12.1987.

In der Praxis wichtiger als diese für die örtlichen Vertretungskörperschaften und ihre Exekutivkomitees geltenden Unterstellungsverhältnisse ist das Über-Unterordnungsverhältnis zwischen den Fachministerien und den Fachabteilungen in den örtlichen Verwaltungsbehörden (vgl. dazu 2.b).

Die jüngste Verwaltungsreform hat trotz ihrer Betonung des Selbstverwaltungsgedankens an der hierarchischen Organisationsstruktur nichts geändert; und eine solche Änderung ist – zumindest unter der gegenwärtigen Partei- und Staatsführung – vorläufig auch nicht zu erwarten.

b) Die Organisationsstruktur der territorialen Verwaltungseinheiten

Das formaljuristisch gesehen, höchste und demnach wichtigste Organ ist der „Volksrat" (*Naroden săvet*); er vereinigt in sich alle Kompetenzen und ist gemäß dem Prinzip der Gewalteneinheit (vgl. I.2.) nicht nur zur Normsetzung, sondern auch zum Normenvollzug ermächtigt (Art. 113 Verf.). Er wird nach demselben Wahlrecht wie die NSb (vgl. II.1.), allerdings – seit 1971 – für eine Legislaturperiode von nur 2 ½ Jahren gewählt (Art. 6 Abs. 2 Verf.). Aus den Wahlergebnissen zu den Volksräten vom 28.2.1988 geht hervor, daß den Gebietsräten durchschnittlich 150, den Gemeinderäten 95 und den Bürgermeistereien 6 Volksvertreter angehören[71]. Die Gebietsräte[72] müssen mindestens viermal im Jahr, die Gemeinderäte mindestens sechsmal im Jahr zusammentreten (Art. 116 Verf.)[73]; zu den Sitzungen können außer Staatsfunktionären auch Vertreter von Parteien und Massenorganisationen sowie einzelne Bürger hinzugezogen werden[74]. Ausführlich regelt die Geschäftsordnung der Volksräte darüber hinaus die Zusammenarbeit mit der OF, den Gewerkschaften, dem DKMS und den sonstigen gesellschaftlichen Organisationen (Punkt 53–60)[75].

Die Volksräte bilden Ausschüsse (Art. 118 Abs. 1 Verf.; Art. 29 ff. Gesetz über die Volksräte), deren Hauptaufgabe nicht so sehr darin besteht, die Plenarentscheidungen vorzubereiten und die Verwaltung zu kontrollieren, sondern im Gegenteil „Transmissionsinstrumente"[76] der Verwaltung zu sein, um die Durchsetzung ihrer Maßnahmen gegenüber der Bevölkerung zu erleichtern und sie zur Arbeit des Rates heranzuziehen (Art. 29 Abs. 1 Gesetz über die Volksräte).

Den Kern der örtlichen Verwaltung stellt das vom Volksrat eingesetzte „Exekutivkomitee" (*Izpălnitelen komitet*) dar, das je nach der Größe bzw. Bedeutung der Verwaltungseinheit bis zu 17 Personen (Sofia) umfassen kann (vgl. Art. 43 Gesetz über

---

[71]) RD. 1.3.1988 (eigene Berechnung).
[72]) Die Regelung galt für die Bezirksräte, muß aber sinnvollerweise auf die „Gebiete" übertragen werden.
[73]) Die Initiative zur Einberufung liegt im übrigen bei 1/5 der Ratsmitglieder, abgesehen vom Exekutivkomitee und dem übergeordneten Organ der Staatsmacht: vgl. Punkt 2 der Instruktion des Präsidiums der NSb vom 29.4.1965 über die Organisation und Arbeitsformen der Volksräte (DV. (1965) 37); Art. 24 ff. Gesetz über die Volksräte.
[74]) Punkt 17, 19 der Instruktion bzw. Geschäftsordnung von 1965.
[75]) Diesen Bestimmungen liegt die in der Zeit Chruščevs propagierte Konzeption einer Integration von Sowjets und gesellschaftlichen Organisationen im Sinne einer „Vergesellschaftung des Staates" zugrunde. Sie wurde unter Brežnev nicht weiter verfolgt.
[76]) Spasov/Želev (Anm. 2) II, S. 227.

die Volksräte). Die Position des Exekutivkomitees im hierarchischen Gefüge der Verwaltung wird durch das *Prinzip der doppelten Unterstellung,* das ein Aspekt des Demokratischen Zentralismus ist, bestimmt: Einerseits ist das Komitee, horizontal gesehen, dem Volksrat als seinem Kreationsorgan sowohl dienstlich als auch fachlich verantwortlich und rechenschaftspflichtig und kann von ihm jederzeit abberufen werden (Art. 118 Abs. 1 Verf.); andererseits ist es auch gegenüber den höheren Exekutivkomitees und gegenüber dem Ministerrat weisungsgebunden, wobei es sich hier allerdings nur um eine Fachaufsicht handelt.

Der Schwerpunkt der vom Exekutivkomitee zu leistenden Arbeit besteht in der Leitung der allgemeinen Verwaltung des Territoriums, in der Koordinierung der von den Fachabteilungen beim Vollzug der zentralen Staatspolitik getroffenen Entscheidungen. Hier liegt zugleich der kritische Punkt der örtlichen Verwaltungsorganisation überhaupt, da in der Arbeit der Fachabteilungen (-organe) der Volksräte regionale bzw. lokale und zentrale bzw. ministerielle Interessen aufeinander stoßen.

Die *Fachabteilungen* sind zwar Untergliederungen der Volksräte und werden, formell betrachtet, von diesen gebildet (Art. 118 Abs. 1 Verf.), doch ihre Kompetenzen werden als untere staatliche Fachverwaltungsbehörden vom Ministerrat definiert (Art. 65 Gesetz über die Volksräte), und so unterliegen sie der Weisung der Ministerien und sonstigen Zentralbehörden (Art. 107 Abs. 1 Verf.). Diese gehen denen der Exekutivkomitees unbedingt vor; über sie vor allem vollzieht sich die zentrale Lenkung der örtlichen Verhältnisse. Die Eigenständigkeit der örtlichen Verwaltung, der Räte und ihrer Exekutivkomitees, erfährt dadurch die stärksten Limitierungen.

Fachabteilungen bestehen für: Planung; Finanzen; Arbeit; Preisbildung; kommunale Dienstleistungen; örtliche Industrie; Handel; Bauwesen; Land- und Forstwirtschaft; Transportwesen; Nachrichtenwesen; Volksbildung und Jugendarbeit; Kunst und Natur; Gesundheitswesen; Sozialfürsorge und Rentenwesen; Verwaltungsdienstleistungen; öffentliche Ordnung und sozialistische Gesetzlichkeit; Umweltschutz.

3. Sonderverwaltungsbereiche

Sonderverwaltungsbereiche, d. h. staatliche Aufgabengebiete, die unter der Leitung eines Ministeriums auch auf den unteren Ebenen durch einen eigenen Behördenapparat außerhalb der Volksräte verwaltet werden, gibt es auch in Bulgarien, sind aber eher eine Ausnahmeerscheinung[77]). Zu nennen sind hier neben dem Verkehrswesen (Eisenbahnen) und dem Nachrichtenwesen (Post) vor allem der auswärtige Dienst, was in der Natur der Sache liegt (und auf welchen hier nicht weiter eingegangen wird), ferner – mit Abstrichen – die Landesverteidigung sowie, als Teil des Innenministeriums (seit 1969), der Staatssicherheitsdienst.

Die wesentlichen staatsleitenden Entscheidungsbefugnisse auf dem Gebiet der *Landesverteidigung* und des inneren Notstandes hat der DS inne (vgl. II.2.). Die

---

[77]) Vgl. dazu Kostadinov, G.; Dermendžiev, I.; Vodeničarov, A.: Administrativno pravo. Specialna čast (Verwaltungsrecht. Besonderer Teil). Sofia 1973, insbes. S. 337 ff. (zit. als: Administrativno pravo).

laufende allgemeine, militärisch-politische Lenkung dieses Sektors unter Einschluß der Zusammenarbeit mit den WP-Staaten liegt allerdings nicht bei ihm, sondern bei dem von ihm ernannten, seit 1971 bestehenden Staatskomitee für Verteidigung (Art. 93 Nr. 10 Verf.)[78]). Seine personelle Zusammensetzung wird zwar geheimgehalten, aber soviel ist bekannt, daß es sich um ein relativ kleines Organ handelt, dem der DS-Vorsitzende vorsteht und dem Persönlichkeiten der Parteiführung (Politbüro) und der Streitkräfte angehören.

Die (technische) Verwaltung der Streitkräfte (Organisation, Beschaffungswesen, Personalwesen, Wehrersatzwesen usw.) wird hingegen vom Ministerrat bzw. vom Verteidigungsministerium besorgt (vgl. auch das Kapitel „Landesverteidigung" von W. Nolte).

Die *mittlere* Verwaltungsebene bilden die Wehrkreise (*voennite okrăzija*). Soweit es sich nicht um Militär-, sondern um Zivilverwaltungsangelegenheiten der Streitkräfte handelt, besitzen sie zugleich den Status von Fachabteilungen der regionalen Volksräte und unterstehen sowohl dem Verteidigungsminister als auch dem betreffenden Volksrat. Dieser wirkt vor allem an der Verwaltung des Ersatzwesens und der Reserve sowie an der Versorgung der Streitkräfte mit. Die *unteren* Organe der Landesverteidigung sind die Truppeneinheiten.

Der *Staatssicherheitsdienst (služba po sigurnostta)* bildet im Innenministerium einen selbständigen Behördenzug, der im Unterschied zu den Polizeiorganen (Miliz) nicht in die örtlichen Volksräte (als Fachabteilungen) eingegliedert ist. Rechtsgrundlagen der Institution sind nicht veröffentlicht; die Staatsrechtsliteratur beschränkt sich auf ein Minimum an Informationen. Von zentraler Bedeutung ist die Unterordnung des Staatssicherheitsdienstes unter die Parteiführung, woraus sich die für diese Institution typische extrakonstitutionelle Stellung ergibt[79]): „Das Komitee für Staatssicherheit entfaltet seine Tätigkeit unter der unmittelbaren Fürsorge, Leitung und Kontrolle des ZK der BKP. Als Organ für den Kampf gegen den Klassenfeind richtet es die Tätigkeit auf eine zeitgemäße Aufdeckung und Unterbindung der Wühltätigkeit der feindlichen Dienste und Zentren gegenüber der Volksrepublik Bulgarien. Das Komitee ergreift Maßnahmen zur Bewahrung der Bürger vor ihrer Verstrickung in eine staatsfeindliche Tätigkeit und fördert die patriotische und internationalistische Erziehung der Werktätigen." Die konkreten Aufgaben des Staatssicherheitsdienstes sind der Schutz der politischen und ökonomischen Grundlagen der sozialistischen Ordnung, der Staatsgrenzen, ferner die Grenzkontrolle und die Sorge für eine erhöhte politische Wachsamkeit der Bürger.

4. Das Verwaltungsverfahren

Die bulgarische Verwaltungsrechtswissenschaft faßt heute die Gesamtheit der Rechtsvorschriften, welche die Hervorbringung von Verwaltungsmaßnahmen (Ent-

---

[78]) Dazu Bălgarskite institucii (Anm. 48), S. 89.
[79]) A.a.O., S. 102/103. Auf die Arbeit des bulgarischen Staatssicherheitsdienstes ist im Zusammenhang mit dem Attentat auf den Papst (1981) etwas Licht gefallen. Vgl. dazu: Die Zeit. 21.1.1983, S. 9.

scheidungen) regeln, unter einem (weiten) Begriff des „administrativen Prozesses" zusammen und bezieht dabei auch die Herausgabe von Verwaltungsvorschriften, die Behandlung von „Vorschlägen, Signalen, (formlosen) Beschwerden und Bitten"[80]) durch die Behörden und den gerichtlichen Rechtsschutz ein[81]). Das „Verwaltungsverfahren", d. h. die verfahrensmäßige Ordnung des allgemeinen Kontaktverhältnisses zwischen Verwaltung und Bürger, ist hiervon nur ein Ausschnitt. Nach der kommunistischen Machtergreifung stand es im Zeichen „revolutionärer" administrativer Willkür zunächst unter einem ungünstigen Stern. Nachdem andere sozialistische Staaten vorausgegangen waren, verabschiedete man 1970 ein Verwaltungsverfahrensgesetz und ließ 1979 eine verbesserte Neufassung folgen[82]). Es regelt die Herausgabe des Verwaltungsaktes (verwaltungsrechtliche Verträge fehlen), die förmliche Beschwerde, Vollstreckung, Verwaltungsstrafen und den gerichtlichen Verwaltungsrechtsschutz (zu ihm unter V. 5.).

Verwaltungsakte sind Individualakte (Art. 2 Abs. 2 VwVfG), „welche von den Leitern der Zentralbehörden, von den Exekutivkomitees der Volksräte und anderen vollziehend – verfügenden (d. h. hoheitlich handelnden – O. L.) Organen erlassen und durch welche Rechte und Pflichten begründet oder die Rechte und gesetzlichen Interessen einzelner Bürger oder Organisationen berührt werden." Der Erlaß eines Verwaltungsaktes kann auf Antrag des Bürgers oder auf Initiative der Verwaltung unter Mitteilung an den Bürger eingeleitet werden. Im Zweifel ist das unterste Verwaltungsorgan (Bürgermeisterei; Gemeinde) sachlich zuständig; es hat Anträge gegebenenfalls an die zuständige Stelle weiterzuleiten; die vorgesetzte Behörde darf den Vorgang nicht ohne gesetzliche Ermächtigung an sich ziehen. Der Sachverhalt wird von Amts wegen festgestellt, wobei der Bürger zur Mitwirkung verpflichtet ist; er besitzt rechtliches Gehör und darf einen Vertreter seiner Interessen hinzuziehen. Das Recht der Akteneinsicht besitzt er nicht. Befangene Amtspersonen sind ausgeschlossen. Die Behörde hat grundsätzlich binnen sieben Tagen zu entscheiden, bei klärungsbedürftigen Umständen binnen einem Monat. Fristüberschreitung gilt als Ablehnung. Die Entscheidung hat schriftlich zu ergehen und muß – im Rahmen des Gesetzes – die dem Bürger günstigste Möglichkeit vorsehen; bei Ablehnung ist sie zu begründen. Vor Ablauf der Beschwerdefrist darf der Verwaltungsakt nicht vollzogen werden, es sei denn, die sofortige Vollziehung wurde aus einem der gesetzlich bestimmten (Art. 16 VwVfG) wichtigen Gründe angeordnet. Der mit Verstreichen der Beschwerdefrist unanfechtbar gewordene Verwaltungsakt besitzt Bestandskraft. Zugunsten des Vertrauens des Bürgers darf er nur unter erschwerten Voraussetzungen aufgehoben werden[83]).

---

[80]) Vgl. das entsprechende Gesetz vom 25. 6. 1980 (DV. (1980) 52).
[81]) Dermendžiev, I.: Administrativen proces na NRB (Das Verwaltungsverfahren in der NRB). Sofia 1981 (zit. als: Dermendžiev, Proces); Cvetanov, C.: Administrativnyj process v NRB (Das Verwaltungsverfahren in der NRB), in: SGiP. (1986) 8, S. 100–109 (104–106) (zit. als: Cvetanov, Process).
[82]) Gesetz über das Verwaltungsverfahren vom 31. 10. 1979 (DV. (1979) 90).
[83]) Vgl. dazu Lazarov, K.: Pravni sredstva za ostranjavanie na nedejstvitelnostta na administrativnite aktove (Rechtsmittel zur Beseitigung der Unwirksamkeit von Verwaltungsakten), in: Socialističesko pravo (Sozialistisches Recht). (1985) 3, S. 28–41; Dermendžiev, I.: Administrativen akt (Der Verwaltungsakt). Sofia 1985, S. 30 ff.

Der Bürger kann innerhalb eines Monats bei der nächsthöheren Behörde Beschwerde einlegen (Devolutiveffekt); eine Wiedereinsetzung in den vorigen Stand bei Fristversäumung ist möglich. Dem Bürger steht es – seit 1979 – frei, gleich vor Gericht zu gehen. Die Beschwerde hat aufschiebende Wirkung (Suspensiveffekt). Sie erstreckt sich auf die Rechtmäßigkeit und die Zweckmäßigkeit des Verwaltungsaktes.

Von der Beschwerdemöglichkeit ausgenommen sind alle Akte des DS, des Ministerrates, der Zentralbehörden, der Gebietsexekutivkomitees sowie Planungs- und Organisationsakte (Art. 3; 20 VwVfG). Darunter fallen auch innerbehördliche Akte, d.h. nach der Rechtsprechung des Obersten Gerichts[84] technische Instruktionen, dienstliche Rundschreiben, Anstaltsordnungen und konkrete innerdienstliche Weisungen ohne rechtliche Außenwirkung.

Über die Beschwerde ist in der Regel binnen 14 Tagen, längstens in einem Monat zu entscheiden; andernfalls kann der Bürger Untätigkeitsklage erheben.

5. Die Verwaltungskontrolle

Die Kontrolle über die zentralen und örtlichen Behörden gehört zu den Kompetenzen von NSb (Ständige Ausschüsse; Abgeordnete), DS und Ministerrat. Sie wird von einer Vielzahl von Kontrollorganen teils unter ihrer Leitung, teils außerhalb derselben ausgeübt, wobei die im staatlichen Bereich tätigen Parteiorganisationen eine allgemeine politische Richtungs- und Wirkungskontrolle vornehmen (vgl. den Beitrag von W. Höpken, Politisches System), während die Staatsanwaltschaft ein Hauptinstrument der Gesetzlichkeitskontrolle ist (dazu unten IV.2.).

Die wichtigste Stütze der Partei- und Staatsführung zur laufenden Kontrolle der Verwaltung sind die „Organe der Staats- und Volkskontrolle". Sie stellen eine hierarchisch aufgebaute Sonderbehörde dar, die auf allen Verwaltungsebenen durch „Komitees" vertreten sind und vom „Komitee für Staats- und Volkskontrolle beim Ministerrat" (vgl. oben III.1.) gelenkt werden[85]. Außer diesem unterstehen sie unmittelbar dem ZK der BKP; die örtlichen Parteiorganisationen dürfen in entsprechender Weise den Komitees Kontrollaufträge erteilen.

Die Komitees, die sich vor Ort in Zusammenarbeit mit den Massenorganisationen auch auf ehrenamtliche Kommissionen und Kontrolleure stützen, haben die Aufgabe zu prüfen, ob und wie die Direktiven der Partei und die Beschlüsse der höchsten Staatsorgane auf dem Gebiet vor allem der Wirtschaftspolitik, in geringerem Maße der Sozial-, Kultur- und Rechtspolitik sowie zum Arbeitsstil der Verwaltung auch

---

[84] Vgl. Sădebna praktika na Vărchovnija săd na Bălgarija (Gerichtspraxis des Obersten Gerichts Bulgariens), Graždanska kolegija (Kollegium in Zivilsachen). 1980, S. 180; 1982, S. 152; 1985, S. 161; 1986, S. 221 – ständige Rechtsprechung. Vgl. auch Dermendžiev, I.: Problemi na administrativnoto pravorazdavanie (Probleme der Verwaltungsjustiz). Sofia 1976, S. 214ff. (zit. als: Problemi); Cvetanov, Process (Anm. 81), S. 102f.

[85] Bezeichnung und Unterstellungsverhältnisse haben im Laufe der Jahre geschwankt. Im Januar 1986 wurde das Komitee wieder dem Ministerrat zugeordnet (DV. (1986) 9). Rechtsgrundlagen sind das Gesetz vom 3.7.1974 (DV. (1974) 54) sowie die weiteren Novellierungen 1976 und 1982 und die Verordnung von ZK der BKP und Ministerrat vom 10.1.1977 (DV. (1977) 98).

tatsächlich durchgeführt werden. Ihrer Kontrolle entzogen sind die Parteien, die ideologische Arbeit der gesellschaftlichen Organisationen, die Justiz (Gerichte, Staatsanwaltschaft) und gewisse Bereiche des Verteidigungs-, Innen- und Außenministeriums. Ansonsten verfügen die Kontrollkomitees über weitreichende Funktionsbefugnisse: sie haben ein freies Zutrittsrecht zu den Behörden, Institutionen usw., dürfen Auskünfte und Erklärungen verlangen, Akten anfordern und prüfen, an den leitenden Verwaltungskonferenzen teilnehmen u. a. m.

Auf die Feststellung von Vollzugsdefiziten oder Rechtsverletzungen können sie mit einer Skala abgestufter Sanktionen reagieren: Beseitigung der Mängel in bestimmter Frist; Aussetzung von Verwaltungsmaßnahmen; Verwarnungen; öffentlicher Tadel; Übergabe leichterer Vergehen an die Kollegengerichte sowie – unter besonderen Voraussetzungen – die Verhängung von Disziplinarmaßnahmen bis hin zur Entlassung aus dem Dienst.

Die so konzipierte politische Erfolgs- und Vollzugskontrolle ist angesicht der Verschwommenheit der Kontrollmaßstäbe und der zweifelhaften Qualifikation der Kontrolleure sicherlich nicht geeignet, im Sinne Max Webers für ein Mehr an bürokratischer Rationalität und Effizienz zu sorgen, wohl aber ein scharfes Instrument vor allem des Parteiapparates, um seine Herrschaft über die Staatsverwaltung und die Masse der Staatsangestellten (zusätzlich) abzusichern.

IV. Die Rechtspflege

Die Rechtspflege ist ein weiter Funktionsbereich, dem viele Einrichtungen gewidmet sind; die Rechtsprechung ist nur ein, allerdings wesentlicher, Teil von ihr. Die wichtigsten Institutionen sind Gerichte und Staatsanwaltschaft. Dazu gesellen sich die Schiedsgerichtsbarkeit (in Wirtschaftssachen) und die gesellschaftliche Gerichtsbarkeit der Kollegengerichte. Eng verbunden mit diesen Institutionen ist die Arbeit der Rechtsanwaltschaft, der Notare und der Rechtswissenschaft sowie auf der Ebene des Ministerrats die des Ministeriums für Rechtspflege. An dieser Stelle kann nur die eigentliche Justiz, d. h. Gerichte und Staatsanwaltschaft als die für das Regierungssystem bedeutsamsten Einrichtungen, behandelt werden.

1. Die Gerichte[86])

Die Rechtsprechung ist verfassungsgemäß den Gerichten (*sădilište*) vorbehalten. Sie bilden ein einheitliches System, das allerdings die Schaffung von Fachgerichten für besondere Rechtsmaterien nicht ausschließt, sofern sie nur den allgemeinen Prin-

---

[86]) Rechtsgrundlagen sind: Art. 125–132 Verf.; Gerichtsverfassungsgesetz vom 9. 3. 1976 (DV. (1976) 23) mit den Änderungen von 1979, 1982 und 1986; Verordnung (Reglement) des Ministerrats vom 1. 1. 1978 über die Organisation der Arbeit der Rayon- und Kreisgerichte und Militärgerichte (DV. (1977) 89) mit den Änderungen von 1979, 1984 und 1985.

zipien der Rechtsprechung unterliegen; Sondergerichte im Sinne von Ausnahmegerichten sind jedenfalls verboten (Art. 126 Abs. 3 Verf.). Die einzige Gerichtsbarkeit solcher Art, die neben den ordentlichen Gerichten besteht, sind die Militärgerichte (Art. 33 ff. GVG). Keine „Gerichte" im Sinne der Verfassung sind die „Sonderjurisdiktionen" (*osobeni jurisdikcii*), worunter die Schiedsgerichtsbarkeit, die Schlichtungskommissionen in Arbeitssachen, die Kollegengerichte und gewisse streitentscheidende Sonderkommissionen innerhalb der Verwaltung fallen[87]).

Die *ordentliche* Gerichtsbarkeit entscheidet über Zivil-, Straf- und Verwaltungssachen. Sie ist dreistufig gegliedert, wobei die eingehenden Sachen grundsätzlich in zwei Instanzen behandelt werden: 1. die (109) *Rayongerichte*, deren Amtsbezirke durchschnittlich 2–3 Gemeinden umfassen; sie sind gewöhnlich die Eingangsgerichte[88]). Ihre Entscheidungen treffen sie in der Regel kollegial, durch 1 Berufsrichter und 2 Gerichtsbeisitzer, ausnahmsweise durch den Einzelrichter; 2. die (28) *Kreisgerichte*, deren Status durch die Gebietsgliederung (vgl. III.2.) vorläufig nicht berührt wurde. Sie werden überwiegend – in der Besetzung von drei Richtern – als Kassations-(Revisions-)instanz tätig, daneben – in einer Besetzung wie auf Rayonebene – erstinstanzlich für Zivilsachen höheren Streitwerts, für gewisse Ehe- und Familiensachen und für schwerwiegende Strafsachen. Dazu zählen alle gegen die Staatsordnung und gegen die Volkswirtschaft gerichteten Delikte.

Die *Militärgerichte* (Art. 33–40 GVG) sind nur zweistufig aufgebaut, d. h. ihre Eingangsinstanz ist entweder territorial (Rayon) oder funktional (Truppeneinheit) bestimmt; sie entscheiden über Straftaten, die von Soldaten oder Zivilbediensteten der Streitkräfte und zivilen Teilnehmern verübt wurden.

3. Die letzte Instanz ist das Oberste Gericht in Sofia: Es ist in ein Straf-, ein Zivil- und in ein Militärkollegium gegliedert und weist eine Mehrzahl von Funktionen auf: Erstens wird es als *Staatsgerichtshof* tätig, indem es erstinstanzlich über Amtsdelikte von Mitgliedern des DS und des Ministerrates entscheidet; vorbehalten ist ihm auch die Entscheidung über Amtsdelikte von Richtern, Staatsanwälten und Untersuchungsführern sowie schwerer Straftaten höherer Militärs. In allen diesen Fällen ist das Gericht mit drei Richtern und vier Gerichtsbeisitzern besetzt. Zweitens entscheidet das Oberste Gericht als Kassations- bzw. Revisionsinstanz in Gestalt von drei Richtern über die Urteile der Kreis- und der Militärgerichte; drittens entscheiden das Kollegium für Zivil- und das für Strafsachen (unter Einschluß der Militärrichter) jeweils über die Aufhebung *rechtskräftiger* Urteile der Vorinstanzen im (außerordentlichen) *Aufsichtsverfahren* – eine Relativierung des Prinzips der Rechtssicherheit, die für die sozialistischen Staaten typisch ist; viertens sichern die Kollegien die Einheitlichkeit ihrer Rechtsprechung, indem sie Auslegungsstreitigkeiten über Gesetzesvorschriften verbindlich entscheiden; fünftens kann das aus allen Richtern gebildete *Plenum* auf Vorschlag des Gerichtsvorsitzenden im Aufsichtsverfahren alle unten anhängigen Verfahren an das Oberste Gericht ziehen (Evokationsrecht), und sechstens ist das *Plenum* im Interesse einer einheitlichen Rechtsprechung aller Gerichte (einschl. Sonderjurisdiktionen) und der rechtspolitischen Steuerung ihrer Praxis be-

---

[87]) Vgl. Art. 43 Abs. 2 GerichtsverfassungsG.
[88]) Vgl. die Dislozierung vom 30.5.1979 (DV. (1979) 45).

fugt, verbindliche Auslegungs-(*tălkovatelni*) und Leitungsbeschlüsse (*răkovodni postanovlenija*) zu fassen.

Die (Berufs-)Richter und Gerichtsbeisitzer sind gleichberechtigt; sie werden auf fünf Jahre gewählt, und zwar auf Rayon- und Kreisebene von den wahlberechtigten Bürgern (in Ausnahmefällen auch vom Kreisrat), auf zentraler Ebene von der NSb (vgl. II.1.). Sie können vorzeitig abberufen werden. Besondere Qualifikationsanforderungen stellt das Gesetz an die Beisitzer nicht; die angehenden Richter müssen hingegen ein abgeschlossenes Jurastudium vorweisen, über praktische Erfahrung verfügen und „die notwendigen politischen, moralischen...Qualitäten" besitzen (Art. 65 Nr. 6 GVG). Im Amt befindlich, müssen sie, entsprechend dem ambivalenten Prinzip der sozialistischen Gesetzlichkeit (vgl. I.5.), nicht nur die Gesetze, sondern auch „die Regeln der sozialistischen Moral tadellos beachten" (Art. 73 Nr. 2 GVG) und sowohl ihre juristische als auch ihre politische Befähigung laufend erhöhen (Nr. 5). Die darin liegende Bindung an die Parteilichkeit und an die durch die demokratischen Formen der Gerichtsverfassung nur verschleierte Macht des Parteiapparates führen dazu, daß die von der Verfassung (Art. 129 Abs. 1) deklarierte „Unabhängigkeit" der Richter weder in persönlicher noch in sachlicher Hinsicht gewährleistet ist[89].

2. Die Staatsanwaltschaft

Die bulgarische Staatsanwaltschaft (Art. 133–135 Verf.) besitzt die dem Vorbild der UdSSR verpflichtete, für die sozialistischen Staaten insgesamt typische starke Kompetenzstellung im Sinne eines Hauptgaranten der „sozialistischen Gesetzlichkeit gegenüber allen staatlichen Institutionen, gesellschaftlichen Organisationen und jedem Staatsbürger"[90].

Sie bildet ein selbständiges einheitliches und geschlossenes Behördengerüst, das strikt hierarchisch aufgebaut ist und dem Prinzip der Einzelleitung folgt: An der Spitze steht der von der NSb auf fünf Jahre, also eine Legislaturperiode, gewählte und ihr bzw. dem DS untergeordnete *Generalstaatsanwalt*. Zusammen mit seinen Stellvertretern, Abteilungsleitern und in der Zentrale tätigen Staatsanwälten bildet er die Generalstaatsanwaltschaft (*glavna prokuratura*); sie fungiert zugleich als (beratendes) Kollegium (vgl. oben III.1.).

Auf den nachfolgenden Ebenen des Gerichtsaufbaus arbeiten (ebenfalls) nach dem Prinzip der Einzelleitung Staatsanwälte, die grundsätzlich denselben Eignungsvoraussetzungen unterliegen wie die Richter, aber nicht gewählt, sondern vom Generalstaatsanwalt nach dienstlichem Ermessen ernannt bzw. entlassen werden und an seine Weisungen gebunden sind (sofern das Gesetz nichts anderes vorsieht). Das strenge Einheitsprinzip rechtfertigt man damit, daß das Recht im ganzen Land völlig gleich angewendet werden müsse.

---

[89] In der Literatur wird dies indirekt damit eingeräumt, daß die Unabhängigkeit nur auf die staatlichen Organe und die „gesellschaftlichen Organisationen", also nicht auf die Partei bezogen wird. Spasov/Želev (Anm. 2) II, S. 261.

[90] Gesetz über die Staatsanwaltschaft vom 29.10.1980 (DV. (1980) 87).

Entsprechend den Gerichten gibt es eine *Militärstaatsanwaltschaft*. Ihr Leiter ist weisungsgebundener Stellvertreter des Generalstaatsanwalts und zugleich Vorgesetzter aller Militärstaatsanwälte bei den Wehrkreisen (Truppeneinheiten).

Die Generalkompetenz der Staatsanwaltschaft – umfassende präventive und repressive Sicherung der sozialistischen Gesetzlichkeit – untergliedert sich in zwei Hauptbereiche: die allgemeine Aufsicht und die lenkende Teilhabe an der Strafgewalt des Staates. Ein Nebenbereich ist die Wahrnehmung der Aufsicht im Zivilprozeß und darauf sich erstreckende Interventionen; er kann hier außer Betracht bleiben.

Die *allgemeine Aufsicht (obšt nadzor)* ermächtigt die Staatsanwaltschaft, zum einen sämtliche Rechtsakte der Zentralbehörden, örtlichen Volksräte, Wirtschaftsorganisationen, Betriebe, staatlichen Anstalten (z. B. Sozial- und Bildungseinrichtungen), Genossenschaften und (nichtökonomischen) gesellschaftlichen Organisationen daraufhin zu überprüfen, ob sie mit der Verfassung, den Gesetzen, Dekreten und Ministerratsverordnungen übereinstimmen, zum anderen die Gesetzestreue der Amtspersonen und Bürger zu kontrollieren. Sie erfüllt diese weitgespannte Aufgabe, indem sie jene Behörden in planmäßiger Abfolge von Amts wegen ordentlichen Revisionen unterzieht oder aber außerordentliche Untersuchungen vornimmt, wenn sie aufgrund bei ihr eingehender Informationen über Gesetzesverletzungen Veranlassung dazu sieht. Solche Informationen erhält sie durch verschiedene Kanäle. Besonders wichtig sind die Eingaben, Beschwerden und „Signale" aus der Bevölkerung[91]. Dazu treten Presseberichte, Materialien der anderen Kontrollorgane (vgl. III.5.), Prozeßakten, formelle und informelle Hinweise aus den Behörden, Einrichtungen und Organisationen selbst. Die allgemeine Aufsicht soll zwar ausdrücklich auch dem Schutz der Rechte des Bürgers dienen, doch liegt ihre eigentliche Funktion schon aus quantitativen Gründen nicht hier, sondern darin, gehäuft auftretende, „strukturelle" Rechtsverletzungen etwa aufgrund von Korruption zu unterbinden und vorbeugende Gegenmaßnahmen zu entwickeln, ferner ein gewisses Maß abstrakter Normenkontrolle zur Wahrung der Normenhierarchie zu gewährleisten (vgl. II.4.).

Die Schwächen der „allgemeinen Aufsicht" sind offenkundig, nämlich ihre „Uferlosigkeit", insbesondere durch die Einbeziehung der Wirtschaft, und die daraus resultierende personelle und sachliche Überforderung des Personals. Die praktische Wirkung der allgemeinen Aufsicht stand daher immer im umgekehrten Verhältnis zur Weite ihres Auftrages[92].

Die *Teilhabe an der Strafgewalt* des Staates, traditionelle Aufgabe einer Staatsanwaltschaft und auch in Bulgarien ihr Schwerpunkt, umfaßt ein Bündel von Aufsichts-, Untersuchungs- und Prozeßbefugnissen:

– Leitung und Aufsicht über das Ermittlungsverfahren, das ausnahmsweise von ihr selbst, im Regelfall von Polizei und Staatssicherheitsdienst durchgeführt wird;
– Erhebung der Anklage bei Gericht und Anklagevertretung im Hauptverfahren;
– Entscheidung über die Einlegung von gewöhnlichen Rechtsmitteln gegen Strafur-

---

[91]) Gesetz vom 25.6.1980 (DV. (1980) 52).
[92]) Muletarov, S.: Problemi na obštija nadzor za zakonnost, upražniavan ot prokuraturata (Probleme der allgemeinen Aufsicht über die Gesetzlichkeit, ausgeübt von der Staatsanwaltschaft), in: Socialističesko pravo (Sozialistisches Recht). (1983) 1, S. 15–20.

teile, eventuell über Anträge auf Überprüfung rechtskräftiger Urteile im Aufsichtsverfahren beim Obersten Gericht;
- Aufsicht über die Vollstreckung der Urteile, insbesondere über die Haft- und die Justizvollzugsanstalten, über den Strafvollzug.

Zur Erfüllung ihrer vielfältigen Aufgaben verfügt die Staatsanwaltschaft über ein breites Arsenal von juristischen Instrumenten: Zur Verhinderung drohender Rechtsverletzungen darf sie geeignete Vorbeugemaßnahmen ergreifen, insbesondere Amtspersonen und Bürger verwarnen oder Behörden Empfehlungen mit einer qualifizierten Bescheidungspflicht geben. Im Rahmen der allgemeinen Aufsicht kann sie von allen Behörden, Institutionen usw. umfassend Auskünfte insbesondere über von ihnen erlassene Rechtsakte verlangen, Akten einsehen und anfordern, Personen vernehmen, Überprüfungen an Ort und Stelle vornehmen, sich der Amtshilfe anderer Behörden bedienen. Die Staatsanwälte sind berechtigt, den Sitzungen der Exekutivkomitees der Volksräte (ihrer Verwaltungsebene) beizuwohnen.

Bei Aufdeckung behördlicher Rechtsverletzungen dürfen sie zwar nicht selbst unmittelbar durch entsprechende Verwaltungsmaßnahmen für Abhilfe sorgen, wohl aber „Protest" gegen rechtswidrige Normativ- und Verwaltungsakte mit aufschiebender Wirkung einlegen und so eine Entscheidung der betreffenden Behörde in kurzen Fristen herbeiführen. Sofern die gesetzlichen Voraussetzungen vorliegen, haben sie auch die Möglichkeit, den Verwaltungsakt vor Gericht anzufechten (vgl. V.4.). Noch stärker sind die Befugnisse im strafrechtlichen Ermittlungsverfahren, deren „Herr" die Staatsanwaltschaft ist; sie entscheidet über vorbeugende Sicherungsmaßnahmen (Haft usw.). Ähnlich stark sind ihre rechtschützenden Interventionsbefugnisse im Strafvollzug.

Der Generalstaatsanwalt hat darüber hinaus einige staats- und justizpolitisch bedeutsame Vorrechte: Er darf an den Sitzungen des Ministerrats teilnehmen, Entwürfe von Gesetzen bei der NSb und von Dekreten beim DS einbringen und die verbindliche Auslegung von Gesetzen beantragen. Was das letztere anbetrifft, kann er entsprechende Initiativen gegenüber dem Obersten Gericht (Plenum; Kollegien) ergreifen und auch auf dessen Plenarsitzungen zugegen sein.

Der Befolgung ihrer Maßnahmen und der Wirkung ihrer Aufsicht kann die Staatsanwaltschaft schließlich Nachdruck verleihen, indem sie gegebenenfalls die Einleitung von Disziplinarmaßnahmen gegen Amtspersonen beantragt. Sofern sie verbindliche Weisungen erteilen darf (Einhaltung von Fristen usw.), kann sie die Beachtung durch die Auferlegung von Geldbußen erzwingen.

V. Die Rechtsstellung des Einzelnen

Die Verfassung der NRB bekennt sich zwar ebenso wie die Ungarns (§ 54 Abs. 1) zu den „Menschenrechten" (Präambel; Art. 3), und sie hat unter anderem die UN-Menschenrechtspakte vom 19.12.1966 über bürgerliche und politische bzw. über wirtschaftliche, soziale und kulturelle Rechte ratifiziert (23.7.1970)[93], aber sie di-

---

[93] DV. (1970) 60; (1976) 43. – Zu Ungarn s. Brunner (Anm. 16).

stanziert sich von dem klassischen Konzept der freiheitlichen Menschenrechtsidee. Sie interpretiert jene Bestimmungen als Teil des „demokratischen" Völkerrechts, das einer marxistisch-leninistischen Interpretation zugänglich sei und daher ein Verständnis der Menschenrechte als „Klassenrechte" nicht ausschließe[94]). Darüber hinaus steht Bulgarien auf dem Standpunkt, daß die Bestimmungen der Menschenrechtspakte nicht unmittelbar geltender Teil des bulgarischen Staatsrechts seien, sondern zunächst einer der sozialistischen Gesellschaftsordnung entsprechenden gesetzlichen Transformation bedürften[95]). Die Grundrechte der bulgarischen Verfassung sind daher ihrer Substanz nach nicht Rechte, die jedem Bulgaren kraft seiner ihm innewohnenden unentziehbaren Menschenwürde zukommen und vom Staat nur anerkannt werden, sondern Rechte, die er erst aufgrund der sozialistischen Umgestaltung des Landes von Partei und Staat empfangen habe. Sie sind wesensmäßig Staatsbürgerrechte. Folgerichtig leitet die bulgarische Staatsbürgerschaft (*bălgarsko graždanstvo*) den Grundrechtsteil ein, treten allein die „Bürger" als Grundrechtsträger auf. Ausländer und Staatenlose haben daher Rechte nicht kraft der Verfassung, sondern erst aufgrund besonderer Regelungen[96]). Eine Ausnahme macht hier nur das Asylrecht (Art. 65), dessen Gewährung ein Privileg solcher Ausländer ist, die wegen „fortschrittlicher" politischer Aktivitäten verfolgt werden.

1. Die Staatsbürgerschaft[97])

Infolge dieser ideologischen Gesamtperspektive besitzt die Staatsbürgerschaft einen hohen Stellenwert. Sie gilt nicht lediglich als ein äußerliches Merkmal, sondern gemäß dem sozialistischen Prinzip der Kollektivität als exklusives persönliches Rechtsverhältnis zwischen Staat und Bürger, das durch die verfassungsmäßigen Rechte und Pflichten ausgestaltet wird und auch durch den Auslandsaufenthalt grundsätzlich keine Veränderungen erleidet. Die technische Ausgestaltung des Staatsangehörigkeitsrechts ist in vieler Hinsicht traditionell geprägt (z. B. Erwerb der Staatsbürgerschaft hauptsächlich nach dem Abstammungsprinzip; Möglichkeit der Einbürgerung nach fünfjährigem Aufenthalt), wobei ihm ein starker *etatistischer* Zug eigen ist, der insbesondere in der Betonung der staatsbürgerlichen Treuepflicht Ausdruck findet. Ihre Verletzung kann zur strafenden Ausbürgerung führen, wenn der Staatsbürger (Art. 20 StaatsbürgerschaftsG) 1. illegal das Land verläßt, 2. nicht fristgerecht aus dem Ausland zurückkehrt, 3. sich der Wehrdienstleistung durch Auslandsaufenthalt entzieht, 4. den Staat vom Ausland aus schädigt oder durch unwür-

---

[94]) Dazu Georgiev, D.: Meždunarodnata zaštita na pravata na čoveka i ideologičeskata borba (Der internationale Schutz der Menschenrechte und der ideologische Kampf), in: Godišnik. 74 (1981), S. 200–226 (202f.).
[95]) So der Vertreter Bulgariens, Jankov, am. 16.4.1979 vor dem UN-Menschenrechtsausschuß bei der Erläuterung des bulgarischen Menschenrechtsberichts. Vgl. Covenant on Civil and Political Rights (CCPR) C/SR (Nr. 17); Genovski, M.: Osnovi na meždunarodnoto pravo (Grundlagen des Völkerrechts). 3. Auflage. Sofia 1969, S. 152ff.
[96]) Art. 2, 18ff. Gesetz über den Aufenthalt der Ausländer in der NRB vom 23.11.1972 (DV. (1972) 93); Popov, L.: Die Rechtsstellung des Ausländers in Bulgarien. Baden-Baden 1981.
[97]) Staatsbürgerschaftsgesetz vom 7.10.1968 (DV. (1968) 79); Spasov/Želev (Anm. 2) I, S. 190ff.

diges Verhalten kompromittiert, 5. in fremden Staatsdienst eintritt oder 6. ohne Genehmigung eine fremde Staatsangehörigkeit erwirbt. Daneben finden sich national-bulgarische Akzente: So verliert nur der Bürger *nicht*bulgarischer Volkszugehörigkeit durch Auswanderung seine Staatsbürgerschaft (Art. 16 Abs. 2 StaatsbürgerschaftsG). Für die Türken ist heute die Anwendung dieser Vorschrift dadurch ungewiß geworden, daß seit 1984 die Existenz dieser Minderheit offiziell geleugnet wird und ihre Angehörigen nunmehr als Bürger „bulgarischer Volkszugehörigkeit" hingestellt werden.

2. Die Grundrechte

Das Grundrechtskapitel der Verfassung (Art. 34 ff.) folgt in den Hauptzügen der in den 60er Jahren erarbeiteten sowjetischen Grundrechtskonzeption (die später auch in die UdSSR-Verfassung vom 7.10.1977 einging), weist daneben aber einige Besonderheiten auf. Im Vordergrund stehen die *sozio-ökonomischen* Rechte (Art. 37–47), beginnend mit dem Schutz und der Unterstützung von Ehe, Familie, Frauen und Jugend, gefolgt von den Rechten auf Arbeit, Erholung, Gesundheit, Sicherung im Alter, bei Krankheit und Erwerbsunfähigkeit, auf Bildung, Wissenschaft und Nutzung kultureller Güter. Es schließen sich die *persönlichen Rechte* (Art. 48–51) an: die Unverletzlichkeit der Person, der Wohnung, des Privatlebens und der persönlichen Ehre, des Korrespondenz- und Fernmeldegeheimnisses sowie die an anderer Stelle normierten Justizgrundrechte (Recht auf Verteidigung usw. – Art. 136 ff.) und der Schutz des persönlichen Eigentums (Art. 21); ferner die in kollektiven, organisierten Formen ausgeübten *politischen* Rechte (Art. 52–55): Recht zur Vereinigung in Organisationen und Verbänden verschiedener Zweckrichtungen, Gewissens- und Religionsfreiheit, Meinungs-, Presse-, Versammlungs- und Demonstrationsfreiheit sowie das Beschwerde- und Petitionsrecht; hinzu tritt das außerhalb des Kapitels geregelte Wahlrecht (Art. 6). Den Abschluß bilden Vorschriften über die Staatshaftung (Art. 56) und die *Grundpflichten* (Art. 57–64).

Nicht erwähnt sind die Freizügigkeit und das Recht auf gerichtlichen Rechtsschutz.

Die „Rechte, Freiheiten und Pflichten" gelten zwar nach Maßgabe gesetzlicher Vorschriften, doch sollen sie, wenn letztere fehlen, auch unmittelbar wirksam sein (Art. 9 Verf.)[98]. Eine die Bürgerfreiheit begünstigende praktische Bedeutung kann dieser Deklaration aus zweierlei Gründen nicht zukommen: zum einen, weil die Grundrechte unter dem generellen Verbot stehen, sie „zum Nachteil der gesellschaftlichen Interessen auszuüben", also unter einem Verfassungsvorbehalt, der eine Schranke aller Grundrechte darstellt, ob seiner Schwammigkeit beliebig interpretierbar ist und mit Hilfe der Gummitatbestände des politischen Strafrechts nach Belieben durchgesetzt werden kann; zum anderen, weil in Bulgarien weder ein demokratischer Gesetzgeber existiert, der für eine freiheitsfreundliche Ausgestaltung der Bürgerrechte sorgen, noch eine Verfassungsgerichtsbarkeit, an welche sich das Individuum zum Schutze seiner verfassungsmäßigen Rechte wenden könnte.

Der tatsächliche Standard der gesetzlichen Ausgestaltung in den Grundrechtsbe-

---

[98]) Spasov/Želev (Anm. 2) I, S. 204 ff.

reichen ist insgesamt dürftig⁹⁹); er weist breite normative Lücken insbesondere hinsichtlich der Pressefreiheit, Versammlungsfreiheit, Vereinigungsfreiheit und Koalitionsfreiheit sowie der Rechtsstellung der Religionsgemeinschaften auf. Besonders schwer wiegt der Umstand, daß ein Schutz *nationaler Minderheiten* in der Verfassung fehlt. Seit vielen Jahren sind die Staatsbürger vor allem türkischer Nationalität Objekt einer Politik der mehr oder weniger zwangsweisen Assimilierung an das Bulgarentum, die 1984/1985 in der behördlich erzwungenen Übernahme (christlich-) bulgarischer Namen, in massiven Verletzungen der Religionsfreiheit und anderer Menschenrechte einen Höhepunkt fand (vgl. das Kapitel von S. Troebst, Nationale Minderheiten). Der Staat verstieß damit nicht nur gegen seine völkerrechtlichen Menschenrechtsverpflichtungen, sondern auch gegen das Verbot der eigenen Verfassung (Art. 35 Abs. 2; 4), Bürger wegen ihrer „Nationalität" oder „Religion" zu diskriminieren.

Positive Aspekte hinsichtlich der Rechtsstellung des Einzelnen sind hingegen der gerichtliche Verwaltungsrechtsschutz (vgl. 4.), die Verbesserungen im Wahlrecht (vgl. II.1.) und das am 1.1.1989 in Kraft getretene bürgerfreundliche Staatshaftungsrecht¹⁰⁰).

3. Die Grundpflichten

Die starke Berücksichtigung der Staatsbürgerpflichten neben den Grundrechten ist ein Kennzeichen sozialistischer Verfassungen, das auch im Falle Bulgariens zutrifft. Verankert sind neben den Pflichten zur Verfassungstreue und zum Gesetzesgehorsam die Arbeitspflicht, Schulpflicht, Pflicht der Eltern zur „kommunistischen" Kindererziehung (Art. 38 Abs. 2), Pflicht zur Wahrung des sozialistischen Eigentums, Wehrpflicht, Pflicht zur Erhaltung des Friedens und Steuerpflicht. Sie alle gelten nicht lediglich als moralische Pflichten, sondern als Rechtspflichten, die wegen ihrer überragenden Bedeutung Verfassungsrang besitzen. Das der sozialistischen Grundrechtstheorie traditionell eigene Prinzip der „Einheit von Rechten und Pflichten" wird auch von der bulgarischen Staatsrechtslehre vertreten, jedoch neuerdings nicht mehr im Sinne eines rechtlichen Abhängigkeitsverhältnisses zwischen staatlicher Rechtegewährung und individueller Pflichterfüllung gedeutet, sondern nur noch als moralischer Wirkungszusammenhang verstanden¹⁰¹).

4. Der Verwaltungsrechtsschutz

Da nicht nur ein gerichtlicher, sondern überhaupt ein Grundrechtsschutz fehlt, kommt der Möglichkeit eines gerichtlichen Schutzes der in einfachen Gesetzen ver-

---

⁹⁹) Vgl. dazu: Menschenrechte in den Staaten des Warschauer Paktes. Bericht der Unabhängigen Wissenschaftlerkommission. Deutscher Bundestag. Drucksache 11/1344 (12.11.1987), S. 39 ff.; 57 ff.; 137 ff.; 168 ff.; 230 f. Violations of the Helsinki Accords. Bulgaria. Hrsg. von International Helsinki Federation for Human Rights. Wien, November 1986.

¹⁰⁰) Staatshaftungsgesetz vom 29.7.1988 (DV. (1988) 60).

¹⁰¹) Dazu Vălkanov, V.: Osnovnite zădălženija na graždanite v Narodna Republika Bălgarija (Die Grundpflichten der Bürger in der NRB). Sofia 1987, S. 45 ff.

brieften subjektiven Rechte des Bürgers gegenüber der Verwaltung erhöhte Bedeutung zu. Das gilt auch deswegen, weil die Behörden das in den Grundzügen durchaus rechtsstaatliche Verwaltungsverfahren (vgl. III.4.) bisher in beträchtlichem Maße mißachtet haben. Nicht zuletzt aus diesem Grunde war 1979 der Gerichtsschutz verstärkt, insbesondere die Klageerhebung alternativ neben der Verwaltungsbeschwerde eröffnet worden[102]). Art 33 Abs. 1 VwVfG gibt den Rechtsweg in Verwaltungssachen aufgrund einer Generalklausel (*obšta klauza*) frei, die zum einen voraussetzt, daß sich der Streit um einen „Verwaltungsakt" dreht (vgl. III.4.), und die außerdem durch eine (seit 1979 verkürzte) Reihe von Ausnahmen beschränkt ist (Art. 34); ausgenommen sind Verwaltungsakte, die „unmittelbar mit der Verteidigung und Sicherheit des Landes verbunden sind", die in Devisenangelegenheiten, zur hoheitlichen Festsetzung irgendwelcher Abgabenverpflichtungen, auf dem Gebiete der Raumordnung und Infrastrukturentwicklung oder von den Organen der Staats- und Volkskontrolle erlassen werden, oder gegen die in einem besonderen gerichtlichen Verfahren oder vor besonderen „Jurisdiktionsorganen" (*pred osobena jurisdikcija*) geklagt werden kann. Letzterer Fall kann dem gerichtlichen Verfahren ziemlich nahe kommen, wenn die betreffenden Organe gerichtsähnlich besetzt sind und eine zweite Instanz gegeben ist (Pensionssachen, Städtebausachen u. a.).

Ein wichtiger Unterschied zum Verwaltungsrechtsschutz in Rumänien (der in der Praxis immer weiter ausgedünnt worden ist), besteht darin, daß in Bulgarien auch Verwaltungsakte auf dem Gebiet der öffentlichen Sicherheit und Ordnung gerichtlich überprüft werden können (z. B. im Meldewesen). Aus einer Statistik des Obersten Gerichts (auf der Basis von 405 Fällen) geht hervor[103]), daß 80 % der Verwaltungsakte Zuzugsgenehmigungen betrafen, 4,8 % Entschädigungen im Zusammenhang mit dem Militärdienst, 1,6 % Eheschließungen mit Ausländern; der Rest war verstreut über die Gebiete von Eigentum (Wohnungen, Grundstücke) und von Beruf bzw. Arbeit. Die Zahl der Klagen ist nach Einführung der Verwaltungsgerichtsbarkeit (1970) sehr rasch angestiegen (1971: 127; 1972: 344; 1973: 537). 80 % von ihnen sind Verpflichtungsklagen wegen Untätigkeit der Verwaltung.

Das Gericht prüft allein die Rechtmäßigkeit des Verwaltungsaktes und dabei zugleich die Gesetzlichkeit des zugrundeliegenden Normativaktes – der einzige zulässige Fall einer (indirekten) gerichtlichen Kontrolle untergesetzlicher Normen. Kommt es zur Erkenntnis der Rechtswidrigkeit, hebt das Gericht den Verwaltungsakt auf und verweist die Sache zur Neuentscheidung an die Behörde zurück. Da jene in der Vergangenheit den Urteilen nur ganz ungenügend nachkamen, sind seit 1979 die Gerichte ermächtigt, bei wiederholter Aufhebung und klarer Sachlage anstelle der Verwaltung selbst zu entscheiden. Hier offenbart sich eine bedenkliche Schwäche der Justiz, die freilich nur einen Grundzug des Regierungssystems widerspiegelt, – die Vorherrschaft der Exekutive.

---

[102]) Dermendžiev, Proces (Anm. 81), S. 170 ff.; Leonhardt, P.: Der Verwaltungsrechtsschutz in Rumänien mit vergleichenden Hinweisen auf Bulgarien, in: Jahrbuch für Ostrecht. 25 (1984), S. 81–102.
[103]) Dermendžiev, Problemi (Anm. 84), S. 251 f.

Politisches System

Wolfgang Höpken, München

I. Einleitung – II. Die politischen Parteien: 1. Die Bulgarische Kommunistische Partei (BKP): a) Ideologie und Programm – b) Organisationsstruktur – c) Mitgliederentwicklung und Mitgliederstruktur – d) Parteielite – 2. Die Bulgarische Nationale Agrarunion (BZNS): a) Politische Entwicklung – b) Politisches Selbstverständnis und Aufgaben – c) Organisation und Mitgliederstruktur – d) Beteiligung an politischen Institutionen – 3. „Informelle Gruppen" und neue politische Parteien – III. Die Massenorganisationen – IV. Die politischen Institutionen (Wahlen, Parlament, Regierung und lokale Vertretungsorgane) – V. Die politische Kultur

I. Einleitung

Das heutige politische System Bulgariens ist in allen Bereichen ein Ergebnis der politischen und sozialen Transformation, die in den Jahren 1944–1948 von der BKP[1]) eingeleitet und durchgesetzt wurde. Die von ihr maßgeblich gestaltete Ordnung nach dem Staatsstreich vom 9.9.1944 knüpfte dabei zunächst formal noch an bestehende Institutionen und die Bestimmungen der Tărnovo-Verfassung von 1879 an; einschneidende personelle Eingriffe in Justiz, Verwaltung und Armee veränderten deren Charakter aber bereits in den ersten Monaten nach dem 9.9.1944 nachhaltig. Hinzu kam, daß mit der OF und deren Komitees zugleich eine im alten politischen System unbekannte Institution geschaffen wurde, die als Instrument der politischen Umgestaltung des Landes diente. Gleichwohl hielt die BKP in diesen Jahren des Übergangs zunächst noch an einem Mehrparteiensystem fest, das freilich von Anfang an hegemoniale Züge trug und das mit der schrittweisen Ausschaltung der Opposition immer mehr seinen formal pluralistischen Charakter aufgab. Beendet wurde diese erste Übergangsphase der Entwicklung des politischen Systems mit dem seit Herbst 1947 eingeleiteten rigiden Sowjetisierungskurs. Das nunmehr mit der endgültigen Ausschaltung der noch bestehenden Opposition und der Gleichschaltung der Bündnisparteien geschaffene politische System der *Volksdemokratie* hat seine institutionelle Form, vor allem aber seinen funktionalen Charakter in seinen wesentlichen Elementen praktisch unverändert bis zum Spätherbst 1989 erhalten. Mit der uneingeschränkten *Vormachtstellung* der BKP, einer ihr politisch untergeordneten, wenngleich formell unabhängigen Bauernpartei (BZNS) und als Transmissionsriemen fungierenden Massenorganisationen, mit funktionslosen Wahlen und einem ebenfalls

---

[1]) Bis zu ihrem V. Kongreß 1948 nannte sich die BKP „Bulgarische Arbeiterpartei (Kommunisten)" (BRP (k)). Der Vereinfachung halber wird im folgenden jedoch auch für die Jahre 1944–1948 die Bezeichnung BKP verwendet.

weitgehend entfunktionalisierten Parlament hat es sich in der Ära Živkov zwar *graduell* verändert, nicht jedoch dem Wesen nach.

Das von der bulgarischen Geschichtswissenschaft als „historisch" eingestufte *Aprilplenum* des ZK der BKP vom 2.–6.4. 1956, auf dem Todor Živkov mit seinem Vorgänger Vălko Červenkov abrechnete, hat für das politische System (wie für die politische Entwicklung überhaupt) keineswegs den vielfach behaupteten Charakter einer säkularen Zäsur gehabt. Seine Konsequenzen für den institutionellen Aufbau des politischen Systems waren gering, wenngleich zweifelsohne systemimmanente Korrekturen an der stalinistischen Praxis der politischen Institutionen in der Červenkov-Ära angebracht wurden.

Einen ebenfalls wenig fundamentalen Einschnitt in der Entwicklung des politischen Systems stellt die Verabschiedung der zweiten, noch in Kraft befindlichen *Verfassung von 1971* dar, mit der die Etappe der sogenannten entwickelten sozialistischen Gesellschaft eingeleitet wurde. Sie brachte zwar einige institutionelle Neuerungen, bewirkte aber keinen spürbaren funktionalen Wandel im Charakter des Systems. Auf die von Gorbačev ausgehende *perestrojka* hatte die bulgarische Führung um Todor Živkov auf dem Juli-Plenum des ZK der BKP 1987 zwar mit dem Versprechen einer Demokratisierung des politischen Systems und eines „neuen Modells des Sozialismus" reagiert; substantielle Reformen folgten dieser Ankündigung allerdings nicht. Erst mit dem erzwungenen Rücktritt Todor Živkovs als Generalsekretär der Partei und als Vorsitzender des Staatsrates im November 1989 deutet sich unter seinem Nachfolger Petăr Mladenov nunmehr auch in Bulgarien eine qualitativ neue Etappe in der Entwicklung des politischen Systems an. Der von Mladenov für die nahe Zukunft in Aussicht gestellte Übergang zu Meinungsfreiheit, Pluralismus politischer Organisationen und Parteien und freien Wahlen würde, eine konsequente Umsetzung in die Praxis vorausgesetzt, ähnlich wie in anderen osteuropäischen Staaten zuvor auch in Bulgarien das Ende des volksdemokratischen Systems alter Prägung bedeuten.

II. Die politischen Parteien

1. Die Bulgarische Kommunistische Partei (BKP)

a) Ideologie und Programm

Im Krieg und nach dem Staatsstreich vom 9.9. 1944 gab sich die BKP ideologisch und programmatisch zunächst ausgesprochen moderat. Bemüht, einen möglichst breiten Kreis an nicht-kommunistischen und bürgerlichen Bündnispartnern zu gewinnen, und mit Rücksicht auf die noch intakte Anti-Hitler-Koalition enthielt sich das vom Auslandsbüro der BKP in Moskau erarbeitete erste Programm der OF vom 17.7.1942 aller Zielsetzungen, die auf eine sozialrevolutionäre Umgestaltung Bulgariens nach dem Kriege hätten hindeuten können, und beschränkte sich im wesentlichen auf die Beendigung der Kriegsteilnahme Bulgariens und die Restitution der bürgerlich-liberalen Tărnovo-Verfassung[2]). Auch nach dem 9.9.1944 verzichtete die

---

[2]) Abgedruckt in: Otečestven front. Dokumenti i materiali. T. 1: 1941–1944, čast părva 22. juni

BKP auf ein eigenes Programm und ordnete sich zunächst dem erneuerten und konkretisierten OF-Programm unter. Mit seiner Forderung nach staatlichen Eingriffsmöglichkeiten in die Wirtschaft, nach Konfiskationen und der Beseitigung der sogenannten „parasitären" Privat-Industrien sowie nach Säuberung des Staatsapparates und Umgestaltung von Polizei und Armee ließ dieses Programm zwar Spielraum für Deutungen, war jedoch immer noch kein Programm einer sozialistischen Umgestaltung[3]). Hinsichtlich des Wirtschaftssystems verband die BKP ihr Plädoyer für einen ausgeweiteten Staatssektor mit der ausdrücklichen Ermunterung an „alle patriotischen Industriellen und Kaufleute", am Wiederaufbau teilzunehmen und mit dem Staat zusammenzuarbeiten[4]). Hingegen vermied die BKP nachdrücklich alles, was nach einer sozialistischen Revolution klang. Bei Aufstandsbeginn wurde jedes Überschreiten der programmatischen Grenzen des OF-Programms als schädlich verurteilt, und „linke" Übertreibungen, wie sie in einzelnen Regionen auftraten, wurden in die Schranken verwiesen. Die nach dem 9.9.1944 errichtete „neue Demokratie" wurde zwar durchaus als etwas anderes als eine rein „bürgerliche Demokratie" begriffen, auf keinen Fall jedoch sollte sie als „Diktatur des Proletariats" mißverstanden werden[5]). Die praktische Politik der BKP (vgl. das Kapitel „Domestic Politics" von J. D. Bell) wies freilich schon seit 1946 über diese noch gemäßigt klingende Programmatik hinaus.

Als Konsequenz aus der forcierten Sowjetisierung, die den osteuropäischen Volksdemokratien im Gefolge der Kominform-Gründungskonferenz von Szklarska Poręba verordnet wurde, nahm auch die BKP von ihrer gemäßigten OF-Programmatik Abschied. Auf dem XIII. Plenum des ZK am 14.10.1947 wurde der beschleunigte Übergang zum Sozialismus proklamiert, verbunden mit einer härteren Gangart gegen die Opposition sowie einer forcierten Nationalisierung und Überführung der Landwirtschaft in Kooperativen. Ideologisch bedeutete dies zugleich eine Neubewertung des September-Staatsstreichs und der Übergangsperiode seit dem 9.9.1944. Die September-Ereignisse wurden nun zum Beginn einer sozialistischen Revolution erklärt und die Volksdemokratie als spezifische Form der Diktatur des Proletariats interpretiert[6]). Diese programmatische und ideologische Neudefinition war freilich innerhalb der Parteiführung nicht unumstritten. Insbesondere Georgi Dimitrov verteidigte gegen Červenkov den Weg des langsamen Übergangs zum Sozialismus, gestützt auf ein Weiterbestehen einer von der KP geführten hegemonialen Parteienkoa-

---

1941-april 1944 (Die Vaterländische Front. Dokumente und Materialien. Bd. 1: 1941–1944, Teil 1: 22.6.1941-April 1944). Sofia 1987, S. 82f.

[3]) Abgedruckt in: Bălgarskata dăržavnost v aktove i dokumenti (Die bulgarische Staatlichkeit in Akten und Dokumenten). Sofia 1981, S. 368–372.

[4]) Vgl. in diesem Sinne das ZK der BKP im März und September 1945: Bălgarskata komunističeska partija v rezoljucii i rešenija na kongresite, konferenciite, plenumite i politbjuro na CK. T. IV: 1944–1955 g. (Die BKP in Resolutionen und Beschlüssen der Kongresse, Konferenzen, Plena und des Politbüros des ZK. Bd. IV: 1945–1955). Sofia 1955, S. 8, 31f. (künftig: BKP v rez.).

[5]) Vgl. u. a. Trajčo Kostovs Rede auf dem VIII. Plenum des ZK der BKP Ende Februar 1945, in: Kostov, T.: Izbrani proizvedenija 1944–1948 (Ausgewählte Werke 1944–1948). Sofia 1978, S. 130f.

[6]) Isusov, M.: Komunističeskata partija i revoljucionnijat proces 1944–1948 (Die Kommunistische Partei und der revolutionäre Prozeß 1944–1948). Sofia 1983, S. 268–275 (künftig: Isusov: BKP 1944/48). Einzige zugängliche Quelle des Plenums ist das knappe, nichtssagende Kommuniqué in: BKP v rez. (Anm. 4). T. IV, S. 79ff.

lition und gemischter Eigentumsformen, die er gleichsam als Elemente eines spezifischen, nicht-sowjetischen Weges zum Sozialismus ansah. Mit dem jugoslawisch-sowjetischen Konflikt vom Frühjahr 1948 freilich waren die vorsichtigen Ansätze einer solchen eigenständigen Deutung des weiteren politischen Weges nicht mehr haltbar. Dimitrov selbst mußte auf dem Plenum des ZK vom 27.6.1948 seine früheren Positionen wiederrufen. Auch er kritisierte nun die „legalistischen Illusionen" des friedlichen Übergangs vom Kapitalismus zum Sozialismus, die „falsche These" von der Koexistenz gemischter Eigentumsformen, die Vernachlässigung des Klassenkampfes und das zu langsame Tempo beim Übergang zum Sozialismus[7]). Auf dem V. Parteitag der BKP vom 18.–25.12.1948 wurde die *Volksdemokratie* von Dimitrov selbst in der bekannten und künftig über Bulgarien hinaus verbindlichen Definition neu gefaßt. Die Volksdemokratie wurde danach begriffen

– als Staat der Werktätigen unter der Führung des Proletariats,
– als Staat der Übergangsperiode auf dem Wege zum Sozialismus und
– als Diktatur des Proletariats[8]).

Die BKP verzichtete allerdings darauf, diese ideologische Neuorientierung in ein eigenes Parteiprogramm umzusetzen. Auch das Aprilplenum des ZK vom 2.–6.4.1956, obwohl es stets als Neubeginn einer politischen Ära hingestellt wird, führte nicht zu einer programmatischen Festschreibung der Parteipolitik. Erst im April 1971 gab sich die BKP ihr erstes formelles Parteiprogramm seit ihrem Gründungskongreß von 1919. Grundgedanke des Programms war die seit den 60er Jahren auf Moskauer Initiative hin entwickelte These von der *entwickelten sozialistischen Gesellschaft*, in der sich die Ostblock-Staaten außerhalb der UdSSR befänden. Nachdem der VII. BKP-Parteitag vom 2.–7.6.1958 deklamatorisch erklärt hatte, daß nunmehr mit dem Abschluß der vollen kooperativen Umgestaltung der Landwirtschaft der Sozialismus in Bulgarien gesiegt habe und die materiell-technische Basis für den Übergang zum Kommunismus gelegt werde[9]), begann man seit der zweiten Hälfte der 60er Jahre davon zu sprechen, daß auch Bulgarien nunmehr die Etappe der „entwickelten sozialistischen Gesellschaft" erreicht habe, mit der die Phase des Sozialismus abgeschlossen und der Übergang zum Kommunismus vorbereitet werde. Sie ist gekennzeichnet durch

– die absolute Herrschaft der sozialistischen Produktionsweise,
– ein hohes materiell-technisches Niveau,
– die Annäherung der beiden bestehenden Eigentumsformen, des staatlichen und des kooperativen Eigentums,
– ein Weiterbestehen der Klassen der Arbeiter und Bauern sowie der Schicht der Intelligenz, die sich aber stetig zur sozialen Homogenität – der *ednorodnost* – annähern, sowie

---

[7]) Novo vreme. (1948) 6–7, S. 515–528.

[8]) Dimitrov, G.: Političeski otčet na CK na BRP(k) pred V-ja kongres na partijata (Politischer Rechenschaftsbericht des ZK der BRP(k) an den V. Kongreß der Partei), in: Novo vreme. (1949) 1, S. 58 ff.

[9]) Migev, V.: Izgraždane na razvitija socializăm v Bălgarija (Der Aufbau des entwickelten Sozialismus in Bulgarien), in: Istoričeski pregled. 37 (1981) 3–4, S. 3–21.

- die Wandlung des Staates von einer „Diktatur des Proletariats" zum „allgemeinen Volksstaat" und der Kommunistischen Partei von einer Partei der Arbeiterklasse zu einer Partei, die auch die „Partei des ganzen Volkes" ist[10]).

Die praktische Relevanz dieses ersten und bislang letzten Parteiprogramms der BKP nach dem Kriege muß allerdings wohl als relativ gering angesehen werden. Die Prognosen der materiell-technischen Entwicklung und der Veränderung der sozialen Schichtung sind durch die reale Entwicklung widerlegt. Das Programm ist daher zunehmend zu einem Legitimationsfundus für politische Festtagsreden verkommen. Ähnlich wie in der UdSSR seit Gorbačev hatte man denn auch in Bulgarien und schon vor dem Sturze Živkovs damit begonnen, sich von der Behauptung einer „entwickelten sozialistischen Gesellschaft" zu distanzieren. Dem von Živkov auf dem Juli-Plenum des ZK 1987 als quasi-programmatischer Alternative formulierten Ziel eines bulgarischen „Selbstverwaltungs-Sozialismus" im Rahmen der bestehenden politischen Strukturen dürfte dabei allerdings keine längerfristige Gültigkeit mehr zukommen. Mit Živkovs Sturz im November 1989 sind vielmehr Forderungen nach einem erneuerten Parteiprogramm laut geworden, mit dem die gesellschaftspolitischen Zielperspektiven der BKP grundlegend neu definiert werden sollen. Wie weit die BKP dabei tatsächlich bereit sein wird, sich von marxistisch-leninistischen Ideologie- und Ordnungsvorstellungen zu lösen, ist bei Abschluß dieser Arbeit noch nicht exakt zu bemessen. Die Vorstellungen der neuen Führung um Petăr Mladenov zielen aber offenkundig auf einen durch bürgerlich-liberale Werte und Freiheitsrechte ergänzten „sozialistischen Rechtsstaat", in dem bestimmende, wenngleich nicht ausschließliche sozialistische Produktionsformen mit liberaler Rechtsstaatlichkeit und einem auf mehreren, voneinander unabhängigen politischen Kräften (Parteien?) beruhenden Parlamentarismus verbunden werden sollen[11]).

b) Organisationsstruktur

Nach dem Staatsstreich 1944 mußte die BKP sich zunächst einmal den neuen Bedingungen als legale und politisch bestimmende Partei organisatorisch anpassen. Die Parteispitze, Politbüro und ZK, wurden neu gewählt bzw. kooptiert[12]). Zugleich entwarf man ein neues *Statut*, da die Partei seit 1919 über kein schriftlich fixiertes Statut, das die organisatorische Bolschewisierung der Partei in den 20er Jahren berücksichtigte, mehr verfügte. Das als vorläufig geltende Statut von 1945 wurde vom

---

[10]) X. kongres na BKP (20.–25. april 1971). Stenografski protokol (X. Parteitag der BKP (20.–25.4.1971). Stenographisches Protokoll). Sofia 1971, S. 723–734; Iribadžakov, N.: Razvitoto socialističesko obštestvo (Die entwickelte sozialistische Gesellschaft), in: Novo vreme. (1971) 5, S. 104–124.

[11]) Zu Živkovs Vorstellungen von einem bulgarischen „Selbstverwaltungs-Sozialismus" vgl. dessen Rede auf dem Juli-Plenum des ZK: RD. 29.7.1987. Die politischen Zielvorstellungen der neuen Führung vorerst in der Rede Petăr Mladenovs auf dem Plenum des ZK der BKP vom 11.12.1989: RD. 12.12.1989.

[12]) Avramov, P.: Organizacionno izgraždane na BKP sled izlizaneto ot nelegalnosti (9. sept. 1944 – fevr. 1945 g.) (Der organisatorische Aufbau der BKP nach dem Austritt aus der Illegalität (9. Sept. 1944 – Febr. 1945)), in: Istoričeski pregled. 21 (1965) 2, S. 3ff. Siehe auch ausführlicher den Beitrag von John D. Bell, Domestic Politics, in diesem Band.

V. Parteitag am 18.–25.12.1948 ersetzt; dieses – 1954 modifizierte – Statut wurde auf dem VIII. Parteitag am 5.–14.11.1962 durch ein weiteres abgelöst, das mit kosmetischen Änderungen bis heute Gültigkeit besitzt. Sowohl das 1948 verabschiedete Statut als auch sein Nachfolger von 1962 waren dabei weitgehend eine Kopie der jeweils gültigen Statuten der KPdSU von 1939 und 1962. Änderungen waren im ganzen wenig substantiell. Als wesentlichere Modifikationen fallen lediglich die nach 1948 schrittweise erleichterten Aufnahmebedingungen sowie gewisse statuarische Anpassungen an die Entstalinisierung ins Gewicht, so die Ersetzung der 1945 und 1948 noch vorgeschriebenen offenen Abstimmung bei der Wahl der Parteiorgane durch die geheime Abstimmung ab 1954[13]). Ferner wurde in Übernahme des Chruščev-Statuts der KPdSU vom XXII. Parteitag 1961 der Personenkult als Verletzung der Leninschen Normen des Parteiaufbaus gebrandmarkt und die Kollektivität der Leitung als „oberstes Prinzip der Parteileitung" auch im 1962 verabschiedeten BKP-Statut verankert[14]). Als Konsequenz aus den Deformationen der Stalin-Zeit wurden zudem die formellen Rechte der Parteimitglieder erweitert und die Rolle des ZK graduell aufgewertet, indem man ihm die „Auswahl und Verteilung der leitenden Kader" ausdrücklich übertrug[15]).

Das Grundprinzip des Parteiaufbaus, der *Demokratische Zentralismus*, ist von diesen Modifikationen freilich nicht berührt gewesen. Seine Definition findet sich in Anlehnung an die klassischen Elemente des sowjetischen Parteistatuts in allen Nachkriegsstatuten in gleicher verbaler Form[16]). In jüngster Zeit ist dabei, offenkundig als Reflex auf die neue sowjetische Politik, noch besonders auf den Grundsatz der „Transparenz und Öffentlichkeit" der Arbeit der Parteiorgane verwiesen worden[17]) – ein Prinzip, das freilich angesichts der außerordentlich spärlichen Informationen, die über die Arbeit des Politbüros und des ZK an die Öffentlichkeit drangen, bislang nur formaler Natur war. Die neue Führung um Petăr Mladenov hat sich jedoch für die Zukunft zu größerer *glasnost* auch im Hinblick auf die Arbeit der Parteiorgane verpflichtet.

Mitglied der Partei kann grundsätzlich jeder werden, der das 18. Lebensjahr vollendet hat und Programm und Statut der Partei in Wort und Tat anerkennt, in einer der Parteiorganisationen mitarbeitet, sich aktiv am Aufbau des Sozialismus beteiligt, die Parteibeschlüsse ausführt und seinen Mitgliedsbeitrag zahlt[18]). Verändert haben sich allerdings die Modalitäten der Aufnahme in die Partei. Die strengsten Maßstäbe hatte hier noch das Statut von 1948 angelegt. Es verlangte bei der Bewerbung um den Parteieintritt bei Arbeitern Empfehlungen von zwei Mitgliedern mit mindestens dreijähriger Parteizugehörigkeit; Angehörige anderer Sozialgruppen benötigten gar die

---

[13]) Vgl. Art. 13 bzw. Art. 21 der Statuten von 1948 und Art. 26 des Statuts von 1954; alle abgedruckt in: BKP v rez. (Anm. 4). T. IV, S. 20, 61 und 459.

[14]) BKP v rez. (Anm. 4). T.V: 1956–1962. Sofia 1965, S. 942 (Art. 29).

[15]) Ebenda, S. 944 (Art. 35); VIII. kongres na BKP (5.–14.11.1962). Stenografski protokol (VIII. Parteitag der BKP (5.–14.11.1962). Stenographisches Protokoll). Sofia 1963, S. 156f.

[16]) Vgl. das Kapitel von Otto Luchterhandt, Regierungssystem.

[17]) XIII. kongres na Bălgarskata komunističeska partija (2.–5.4.1986). Stenografski protokol. čast treta (XIII. Parteitag der BKP (2.–5.4.1986). Stenographisches Protokoll, Teil III). Sofia 1987, S. 486 (Art. 14, Abs. g).

[18]) Ebenda, S. 481 (Art. 1).

Empfehlung von drei Parteimitgliedern, wovon einer fünf und die beiden anderen mindestens drei Jahre Mitglied der Partei gewesen sein mußten. Wer vor seinem Eintritt in die BKP einer anderen Partei angehört hatte, mußte die Empfehlung eines Parteimitglieds vorweisen, das bereits vor dem 9.9.1944 in die Partei eingetreten war und von vier Genossen, die bereits mindestens fünf Jahre Mitgliedschaft nachweisen konnten. Hinzu kam eine Kandidatenzeit von einem Jahr bei Arbeitern und von 1 1/2 Jahren bei allen anderen Bewerbern. Diese noch recht rigiden und sozial selektierenden Kriterien wurden in den folgenden Jahren jedoch zusehends erleichtert: Das geänderte Statut des VI. Parteitags vom 28.2.-3.3.1954 verzichtete bereits wieder auf die privilegierte Beitrittsmöglichkeit für Arbeiter und verlangte von allen Bewerbern, sofern sie nicht zuvor einer anderen Partei angehört hatten, lediglich drei Empfehlungen von Parteimitgliedern[19]). Diese Regelung wurde auch in bis heute gültiger Form in das Statut von 1962 übernommen. Seit 1966 ist zudem die bis dato obligatorische einjährige Kandidatenzeit weggefallen[20]) – einer der wenigen Punkte, in denen das BKP-Statut nicht dem der KPdSU folgt. Allerdings können Jugendliche bis zum Alter von 24 Jahren nur dann in die Partei aufgenommen werden, wenn sie Mitglied des DKMS sind. Die Pflichten des Parteimitglieds lassen sich mit den drei Begriffen *săznatelnost* (Bewußtsein), *organiziranost* (Organisiertheit) und *aktivnost* (Aktivität) umreißen[21]). „Bewußtsein" verlangt vom Parteimitglied, sich den Marxismus-Leninismus anzueignen, gegen Religiosität anzukämpfen, seine persönliche und berufliche Qualifikation zu verbessern, im gesellschaftlichen und wirtschaftlichen Leben vorbildlich zu wirken etc.; „Organisiertheit" bedeutet die aktive Betätigung in den Parteiorganisationen und die Umsetzung der Parteipolitik; und „Aktivität" steht für ein allseitiges, über die Parteitätigkeit hinausgehendes gesellschaftliches Engagement.

Auch im *Organisationsaufbau* folgt das Parteistatut der BKP, abgesehen von den verwaltungsmäßigen Besonderheiten des Landes, dem in der KPdSU und in den meisten anderen kommunistischen Parteien des Ostblocks gängigen Schema. Höchstes Organ der Partei ist danach der alle fünf Jahre stattfindende Parteitag, der aus Delegierten der Kreis-Parteikonferenzen beschickt wird. Wichtigste Aufgabe des Parteitags ist, neben der Entgegennahme des Rechenschaftsberichts und der Debatte der künftigen Politik, vor allem die Wahl des ZK und der Zentralen Revisions- und Kontrollkommission. Das ZK, das gegenwärtig aus ca. 220 Mitgliedern und ca. 140 (nicht stimmberechtigten) Kandidaten besteht, soll mindestens einmal in vier Monaten tagen und leitet formell die gesamte Parteiarbeit zwischen den Parteitagen. Sowohl seine Größe als auch seine relativ seltenen Sitzungen lassen diesen Anspruch aber zwangsläufig unerfüllt. Wie in allen anderen KP's auch obliegt die faktische Leitung der Partei, und damit der Politik überhaupt, auch in Bulgarien dem zumeist aus 7–11 Mitgliedern und ca. 5–7 Kandidaten bestehenden Politbüro. Das Politbüro wird ebenso wie das für die technisch-organisatorische Arbeit des ZK verantwortli-

---

[19]) BKP v. rez. (Anm. 4). T.IV, S. 159–161 (Art. 5 und 12) sowie S. 455 (Art. 5).
[20]) Otečestven front. 16.11.1966, S. 5.
[21]) Angelov, I. B.: Kriterii na členstvo v BKP (Kriterien für die Mitgliedschaft in der BKP), in: Akademija za obštestveni nauki i socialno upravlenie pri CK na BKP: Naučni trudove (künftig: NTAONSU). Serija partijno stroitelstvo. (1984) 4, S. 51–82.

che Sekretariat und der Generalsekretär der Partei vom ZK gewählt. Weder über die formelle Geschäftsgrundlage und die Sitzungshäufigkeit noch über die Arbeitsweise des Politbüros ist bislang etwas bekannt. Häufig lassen die knappen Kommuniqués der Sitzungen nicht einmal eine exakte Rekonstruktion der dort verhandelten politischen Fragen zu.

Neben dem Parteitag kann das ZK zu bestimmten anstehenden Fragen sogenannte „Nationale Parteikonferenzen" einberufen. Derartige Konferenzen haben in den vergangenen Jahren zumeist zu politischen, ökonomischen und sozialen Grundsatzfragen stattgefunden, so 1972 über die Entwicklung des Lebensstandards, 1978 über die wissenschaftlich-technologische Politik und 1988 zur Politik des „Umbaus" (*preustrojstvo*) der Partei. Bereits 1954 wurde der Nationalen Parteikonferenz allerdings das Recht genommen, den Bestand des ZK zu ändern.

Der *territoriale Aufbau* der Partei ist nach der letzten Verwaltungsreform vom 18.8.1987, mit der die vormals 28 Kreise (*okrăzi*) durch neun Bezirke (*oblasti*) abgelöst wurden, dreigliedrig: Am unteren Ende der Pyramide stehen die Parteigrundorganisationen, die in Arbeitskollektiven der materiellen und außermateriellen Sphäre, in Wohnvierteln und Armee-Einheiten mit mindestens drei Parteimitgliedern gebildet werden. Oberstes Organ der Parteigrundorganisation ist die Parteiversammlung, die als exekutives Gremium das Büro mit einem Sekretär an der Spitze wählt. Ähnlich aufgebaut sind auch die Gemeinde-Parteiorganisationen (bzw. in gleichem Rang die Rayon-Organisationen in größeren Städten und die Stadt-Parteiorganisationen), deren höchstes Gremium die Gemeinde-Konferenz ist. Die Konferenz wählt das Komitee mit einem Büro als Leitungsorgan sowie die Delegierten für die nächsthöhere Parteiebene – die Bezirks-Parteikonferenz. Die Bezirks-Parteiorganisationen sind in gleicher Weise strukturiert. Ihre Konferenz wählt zudem die Delegierten der Parteikongresse[22]).

c) Mitgliederentwicklung und Mitgliederstruktur

Nach dem 9.9.1944 öffnete die Partei ihre Tore in dem Bemühen, ihre im Krieg und der Illegalität nur schwache Mitgliederbasis zu verbreitern, zunächst weit für beitrittswillige Personen, wobei sie auch über das soziale Profil der neuen Mitglieder hinwegzusehen bereit war[23]). Das Ergebnis dieser *masovizirane*, mit der letztlich dem Erstarken der übrigen Parteien ein Riegel vorgeschoben und die vielfachen neuen staatlichen, politischen und ökonomischen Verwaltungsaufgaben „kadermäßig" bewerkstelligt werden sollten, war ein sprunghafter Anstieg der Mitgliederzahlen der BKP in den ersten 1 1/2 Jahren nach dem September-Staatsstreich (vgl. *Tabelle 1*). Eine derartige Explosion von 14000 vor dem September 1944 auf eine halbe Million Ende 1946 war in einem Agrarland wie Bulgarien letztlich weder mit dem Ideal einer Arbeiterpartei noch dem Anspruch, politische Avantgarde zu sein, in Einklang zu bringen. Mit dem Herbst 1947 und parallel zur härteren innenpolitischen Gangart der Sowjetisierung und zum Ausbruch des Kominform-Konflikts zwischen Jugoslawien und den übrigen Volksdemokratien änderte sich diese, vor allem auf numeri-

---

[22]) Näheres in: Kniga za partijnija sekretar (Buch für den Parteisekretär). Sofia 1987.
[23]) Dimitrov (Anm. 8), S. 83 ff.

Tabelle 1: Entwicklung der Mitgliederzahlen der BKP (1944–1986)

(bis zum 9.9.) 1944: 13 700*	1958: 484 255
(Jan.) 1945: 254 140	1962: 528 674
(Dez.) 1945: 427 714	1966: 611 179
(Okt.) 1946: 421 559	1971: 669 476
1946: 490 092**	1976: 789 796
1948: 493 658	1981: 825 876
1952: 409 948	1986: 932 055
1954: 455 251***	

* Georgi Dimitrov sprach auf dem V. Parteitag von 25 000 Mitgliedern, über die die Partei am Vorabend des 9.9. 1944 verfügt habe: Dimitrov, S. 83. Der bulgarische Historiker Avramov hat demgegenüber auf der Grundlage der Berichte der regionalen Parteiorganisationen im Archiv der BKP die oben genannte Zahl von 13 700 errechnet, die sich auch näherungsweise mit der von Trajčo Kostov 1945 genannten Zahl von 15 000 deckt (Kostov, S. 141).
** Einschließlich der ca. 21 000 durch die Vereinigung der BKP mit der BRSDP in die BKP übergetretenen ehemaligen BRSDP-Mitglieder.
*** 1954–1966 einschließlich der Kandidaten.
Quelle: Dimitrov (Anm. 8), S. 83; Avramov (Anm. 12), S. 19; Cvetanski (Anm. 26), S. 235; Atanasov, A.: Socialno-političeskata aktivnost na rabotničeskata klasa v Bălgarija (9.IX. 1944–1958 g.) (Die sozial-politische Aktivität der Arbeiterklasse in Bulgarien vom 9.9. 1944–1958), in: Istoričeski pregled. 43 (1987) 4, S. 16–19; VIII. kongres (Anm. 15), S. 142; XI. kongres (Anm. 29), S. 80; XII. kongres na BKP (31.3.–4.4. 1981). Stenografski protokol (XII. Parteitag der BKP (31.3.–4.4. 1981) Stenographisches Protokoll). Čast părva. Sofia 1981, S. 92; XIII. kongres. Čast treta (Anm. 17), S. 344.

sches Wachstum ausgerichtete Mitgliederpolitik jedoch grundlegend. Bis zum Ende des Jahres 1948 herrschte praktisch ein Aufnahmestop und die Partei begann, sich von sogenannten „karrieristischen" und ideologisch unzuverlässigen Elementen zu trennen[24]). Der V. Parteitag verschärfte sodann die sozialen Selektionskriterien und Aufnahmebedingungen für Neumitglieder. Ergebnis dieser restriktiveren Aufnahmepolitik sowie der zeitgleichen Säuberung der Partei im Zusammenhang mit dem Kostov-Prozeß in den Jahren 1949 bis 1952 war ein Rückgang der Mitgliedszahlen um ca. 90 000. Allein 1951 wuden 51 000 Mitglieder, 11 % der Parteimitgliedschaft, ausgeschlossen[25]). Die Säuberungen wurden dabei zugleich dazu benutzt, das Sozialprofil der Partei zu verbessern, indem von ihnen vornehmlich bäuerliche Elemente betroffen waren: Während unter den Ausgeschlossenen dieser Jahre nur 15 % Arbeiter und Angestellte zu finden waren, waren 57,3 % Bauern[26]). Seit Mitte der 50er Jahre

---

[24]) Vgl. Vălko Červenkov auf der Gründungskonferenz des Kominform im September 1947: Informacionnoe soveščanie predstavitelej nekotorych kompartii (Informationstreffen der Vertreter einiger Kommunistischer Parteien). Moskau 1948, S. 222f; ferner: BKP v rez. (Anm. 4). T. IV, S. 88.
[25]) Migev, V.: Organizacionnoto razvitie na BKP (1951–1956 g.) (Die organisatorische Entwicklung der BKP (1951–1956)), in: Izvestija na Instituta po istorija na BKP (künftig: III BKP). 57 (1987), S. 56.
[26]) Cvetanski, S.: Dejnostta na BKP za regulirane na socialnija i săstav (1944–1958) (Die Tätigkeit der BKP für die Regulierung ihrer sozialen Zusammensetzung (1944–1958)), in: III BKP (Anm. 25). 45 (1981), S. 227.

nahm der Mitgliederbestand der Partei zunächst mäßig, später stark zu, wobei insbesondere zwischen 1962 und 1966, 1971 und 1976 und zuletzt zwischen 1981 und 1986 zweistellige Zuwachsraten von 13 bis 17% zu verzeichnen waren. Die Abschaffung der Kandidatenzeit 1966, aber wohl auch das gewandelte Selbstverständnis der BKP als einer „Partei der Arbeiterklasse und des ganzen Volkes" seit Beginn der 70er Jahre dürften diesem Anstieg förderlich gewesen sein. Bis 1988 hat dieser kontinuierliche Mitgliederanstieg dazu geführt, daß fast 1 Mio. Bürger, d. h. jeder siebte Bulgare im Alter über 18 Jahre, Mitglied der BKP waren. Mit dieser Quote lag die bulgarische KP 1988 im RGW-Vergleich etwa im Mittelfeld, übertroffen noch von den kommunistischen Parteien der DDR, der ČSSR und Rumäniens, mit einem größeren Mitgliederanteil aber als die der UdSSR, Ungarns oder Polens[27]. Auch die periodischen Aktionen zum „Umtausch" der Parteibücher haben auf diesen steten Anstieg der Mitglieder keinen Einfluß gehabt. 1956/1957 sollen dabei 10 000–11 000 Parteimitglieder aus der Partei ausgeschlossen worden sein; 5800 wegen „Unregelmäßigkeiten", 2400 wegen der Weigerung, sich den Kooperativen anzuschließen, und 1800–2000 als „fremde und karrieristische Elemente"[28]. Zwischen 1978 und 1981 gingen 38 452 Mitglieder ihrer Parteibücher verlustig. Weitaus geringer lag die Zahl der Ausgeschlossenen im Zeitraum zwischen den beiden letzten Parteitagen (1981–1986), als lediglich 8545 Personen ihre Mitgliedschaft verloren[29].

Wenig aussagekräftig sind die verfügbaren Angaben zum *Sozialprofil* der BKP-Mitgliedschaft. Die ohnehin spärlichen Daten kranken nicht nur daran, daß die unscharfe Einteilung der Mitgliedschaft in Arbeiter, Bauern bzw. landwirtschaftliche Arbeiter sowie Angestellte und Intelligenz die Binnendifferenzierung der einzelnen Sozialgruppen kaum angemessen erfaßt. Unklar ist zudem die Erfassungsgrundlage, die dieser Kategorisierung zugrundeliegt (der ausgeübte Beruf, der einmal erlernte Beruf oder gar die familiäre Herkunft?). Ähnlich wie für die absolute Mitgliederzahl variieren die in der Literatur zu findenden Zahlen zudem für die Frühzeit der Nachkriegsepoche z. T. erheblich. Die in *Tabelle 2* wiedergegebenen Daten erlauben daher nur einige grobe Trends, mit denen sich die Entwicklung der BKP allerdings in die aus anderen kommunistischen Parteien geläufigen Entwicklungslinien einpaßt.

Die Öffnung der Parteimitgliedschaft nach dem 9.9.1944 bewirkte zunächst einmal einen erheblichen Zustrom bäuerlicher Schichten. Die Partei mußte sich dabei nicht zuletzt an die bäuerliche Bevölkerung wenden, um sich nicht gegenüber dem Lande, das immer noch die Masse der Bevölkerung stellte, zu isolieren und dieses Terrain dem BZNS zu überlassen. Es war aber nicht nur die aufgrund des geringen Industrialisierungsgrades nur kleine *Arbeiterschicht*, die ihren Anteil in der Partei zunächst bescheiden ausfallen ließ. Darüber hinaus wirkte sich auch eine in einigen

---

[27] Vgl. die Vergleichsangaben (für 1985–1988) bei R. Staar (Hg.): Yearbook on International Communist Affairs 1988. Stanford 1988, S. 253, 265, 275, 285, 304, 312.

[28] Migev, V.: Aprilskijat plenum na CK na BKP i organizacionnoto razvitie na partijata (1956–1958 g). (Das Aprilplenum des ZK der BKP und die organisatorische Entwicklung der Partei (1956–1958)), in: Istoričeski Pregled. 42 (1986) 3, S. 16.

[29] XI. kongres na BKP (29.3.–2.4.1976). Stenografski protokol (XI. Parteitag der BKP (29.3.–2.4.1976). Stenographisches Protokoll). Sofia 1976, S. 92; XIII. kongres na BKP (Anm. 17), S. 344 ff.; Angelov, I.: Kačestvenijat sästav na partijata (Die qualitative Zusammensetzung der Partei). Sofia 1988, S. 80 f.

Tabelle 2: Sozialstruktur der BKP-Mitgliedschaft (1944–1986; in %)

Jahr	Arbeiter	Bauern	Angest./Intell.	Sonstige
1944	26,5	51,9	8,0	13,6
1945	27,1	48,1	13,8	11,0
1946	27,2	45,1	14,6	13,2
1948	26,5	44,7	16,3	12,5
1954	34,1	39,8	17,9	8,2
1958	36,1	34,2	21,3	8,4
1962	37,2	32,1	23,6	7,2
1966	38,4	29,2	26,1	6,2
1971	40,1	26,1	28,2	5,6
1976	41,4	23,0	30,2	5,4
1981	42,7	*	*	*
1986	44,4	16,3	39,3**	

* = keine Angaben; ** = einschließlich Sonstiger

Quelle: Petrov, Z.: Socialno-klasovi i socialen sǎstav na partijata, in: NTAONSU (Anm. 21). Serija: partijno stroitelstvo. 121 (1980), S. 62 ff; Atanasov (s. Tab. 1), S. 16–19; Avramov (Anm. 12), S. 19; Cvetanski (Anm. 26), S. 243; Isusov, BKP 1944/1948 (Anm. 6), S. 191; VIII. kongres (Anm. 15), S. 142; XI. kongres (Anm. 29), S. 80; XII. kongres (s. Tab. 1), čast pǎrva, S. 92; XIII. kongres (Anm. 17), čast treta, S. 344.

Parteiorganisationen verbreitete „sektiererische Einstellung" gegenüber einem zu breiten Zustrom aus der Industriearbeiterschaft aus, der aus den Umstellungsproblemen der Partei von der Illegalität zur Herrschaftspartei resultierte[30]). Im Ergebnis öffnete sich die Schere zwischen Bauern- und Arbeiteranteil bis 1948 sogar und selbst in den wenigen industriellen Zentren, so Plovdiv und Sofia, verfügte die Partei nur über 40–55 % Arbeiter, viele davon zudem eher Handwerker als klassische Industriearbeiter[31]). Mit dem rigideren Kurs in der Mitgliederpolitik wurde dann jedoch der Zugang für nichtproletarische Mitglieder deutlich schwerer gemacht, so daß der Arbeiteranteil 1954 die auf dem V. Parteitag 1948 anvisierte Marge von 35 % erreichte. In den folgenden Jahren ist dieser Anteil nominell stetig gestiegen. Die in der Statistik fehlende Differenzierung nach Bildungsgrad, beruflicher Qualifikation und Sozialprestige macht diese Angaben allerdings wenig aussagekräftig. Aber auch die vorhandenen Angaben können nicht darüber hinwegtäuschen, daß selbst die gegenwärtig 44 % Arbeiteranteil an der Parteimitgliedschaft noch eine Unterrepräsentation dieser Sozialgruppe, gemessen an ihrem Bevölkerungsanteil von offiziell 60,6 %, bedeuten. Hingegen sind *Angestellte* und Angehörige der *Intelligenz*, die gegenwärtig 39 % der Mitgliedschaft stellen, gegenüber ihrem Bevölkerungsanteil von 23,3 % stark überrepräsentiert[32]). Lediglich in den Jahren bis 1954, als bewußte Restriktio-

---

[30]) Cvetanski (Anm. 26), S. 215.
[31]) Atanasov (s. Tab. 1), S. 17 ff.
[32]) Die Daten zur Sozialstruktur nach: Dimitrov, K. (Red.): Socialno-klasovata struktura na sǎvremennoto bǎlgarsko obštestvo (Die soziale Klassenstruktur in der gegenwärtigen bulgarischen Gesellschaft). Sofia 1986, S. 65 (künftig: Socialno-klasovata struktura).

nen den Zustrom der Angestellten in die Partei bremsten[33]), war die Steigerungsrate des Arbeiter-Zuwachses größer als die der Angestellten. Seit dem Wegfall dieser Barrieren hingegen ist das Wachstum der white-collar-workers spürbar größer gewesen. Für die numerische Größenordnung der Angestellten/Intelligenz-Gruppe gelten allerdings ähnliche methodische Vorbehalte wie hinsichtlich der Arbeiterschaft. Die wenig differenzierte Angestellten-Kategorie etwa umfaßt hochspezialisierte Hochschulabsolventen ebenso wie Verwaltungsangestellte oder nicht-physisch arbeitende Beschäftigte mit niedriger Qualifikation. Soziologische Querschnittsanalysen, die mit einem verfeinerten kategoriellen Raster arbeiten und stärker Intra-Schichten-Differenzierungen berücksichtigen, lassen demgegenüber auf eine auch innerhalb der statistischen Großgruppen noch erheblich schichtenspezifisch verteilte Neigung zum Parteieintritt zugunsten besser Qualifizierter und höherer Bildungsgruppen schließen[34]).

Der seit Anfang der 50er Jahre rückläufige Anteil an *Bauern* bzw. „landwirtschaftlichen Arbeitern" in der Parteimitgliedschaft korreliert schließlich mit dem allgemeinen Trend zur Deagrarisierung und dem absoluten Rückgang der landwirtschaftlich Beschäftigen, ist aber wohl auch auf eine immer noch geringere Anziehungskraft der Partei unter den im Agrarsektor Beschäftigten zurückzuführen.

Der *Frauenanteil* an der Parteimitgliedschaft ist in den vergangenen 40 Jahren deutlich gestiegen. Er war 1948 mit 13% nur marginal und erreichte selbst in den Industriezentren Plovdiv und Sofia, wo Frauen unter der Arbeiterschaft der hauptsächlich leichtindustriellen Betriebe sogar stärker vertreten waren als Männer, nur 10–11%; in den sozio-kulturell traditionalen Regionen Nordost- und Südost-Bulgariens kam er nicht über 4–6% hinaus[35]). Der seither sprunghafte Anstieg spiegelt dabei den verstärkten Drang von Frauen in die Arbeitswelt und den damit einhergehenden allgemeinen Säkularisierungs- und Gleichberechtigungstrend wider. Mit ca. 1/3 bleiben Frauen aber noch weit unter ihrem Anteil an der Bevölkerung und den Beschäftigten. Während nur 6,7% der weiblichen Bevölkerung Parteimitglieder sind, gilt dies für 14,1% der männlichen Bevölkerung. Hinzu kommt – näheres siehe im Abschnitt „Parteielite" –, daß der Anteil der Frauen in den leitenden Parteiorganen noch wesentlich geringer ausfällt.

Vollständige Angaben über die *Altersstruktur* liegen nur für einzelne Jahre vor. Auffällig bei den in *Tabelle 3* zusammengestellten Daten ist dabei vor allem der rapide Rückgang des Anteils junger Mitglieder bis 30 Jahre in den späten 50er und frühen 60er Jahren, der offenkundig auf eine in dieser Zeit restriktive Aufnahmepolitik zurückzuführen ist. Der VIII. Parteitag vom 5.–14.11.1962 kritisierte jedenfalls, daß in den vergangenen Jahren in vielen Parteiorganisationen praktisch überhaupt keine Jugendlichen aufgenommen worden seien[36]). Der dadurch begünstigte Alterungsprozeß der Parteimitgliedschaft, deutlich abzulesen auch am Rückgang der mittleren Altersgruppe bis 40 Jahre, geht zum einen darauf zurück, daß die in den ersten

---

[33]) Migev, Aprilskijat plenum (Anm. 28), S. 16; VIII. kongres (Anm. 15), S. 142.
[34]) Vgl. Socialno-klasovata struktura (Anm. 32), S. 132, 156, 261 ff.; Dimitrov, K.: Social-Class Differentiation on Social Activity, in: Society and Social Change. Hrsg. Bulgarian Sociological Association. Sofia 1986, S. 74–77.
[35]) Avramov (Anm. 12), S. 20.
[36]) VIII. kongres (Anm. 15), S. 142.

Tabelle 3: Geschlechts- und Altersstruktur der BKP-Mitgliedschaft (1945–1986; in %)

Jahr	Frauenanteil	bis 30 J.	30–40 J.	40–50 J.	50–60 J.	über 60 J.
1945	8					
1948	13,0	26,0	39,0	25,0	8,0	2,0
1954	19,3					
1958	20,4	21,3	35,5	25,0	13,2	5,0
1962	21,3	15,6				
1966	22,8					
1971	25,2	16,1	27,8	28,5	15,5	12,1
1976	27,5	15,0	25,4	26,8	17,9	14,9
1981	29,7	11,4				
1986	32,7	11,9				

Quelle: Atanasov (s. Tab. 1), S. 19; Petrov (s. Tab. 2), S. 62 ff.; VIII. kongres (Anm. 15), S. 142; XI. kongres (Anm. 29), S. 8; XIII. kongres (Anm. 17), čast treta, S. 344.

Nachkriegsjahren massenhaft in die Partei eingetretene Generation nunmehr die Altersstruktur der Partei nach oben verzerrt. Diese Entwicklung spiegelt jedoch auch den allgemeinen Alterungstrend der bulgarischen Bevölkerung wider und dürfte daher auch in den 80er Jahren, für die keine vollständigen Angaben zur Verfügung stehen, Gültigkeit haben. Schließlich deuten jüngere Angaben aber auch auf eine insgesamt nachlassende Beitrittsbereitschaft vor allem unter Jugendlichen hin. Während z. B. in den 80er Jahren in der KPdSU 70–75 % der neuaufgenommenen Parteimitglieder Jugendliche waren, war dies bei der BKP nur in 56–58 % der Fall[36a]).

Keine aktuellen Angaben liegen vor über die Repräsentanz der *Minderheiten* Bulgariens in der BKP, deren größte, die Türken, seit Ende 1984 ja ohnehin in ihrer Existenz bestritten wird. Anfang der 60er Jahre lag der Anteil der Parteimitglieder unter den Türken bei 2,9 %, während er unter den Bulgaren damals bei 6,5 % lag; am Ende der 60er Jahre bot sich mit 4,9 % BKP-Mitglieder unter der türkischen Bevölkerung gegenüber 7,3 % unter Bulgaren ein ähnliches Bild[37]). Aussagen aus der zweiten Hälfte der 70er Jahre, wonach die staatlichen Maßnahmen zur Entwicklung des ökonomischen und kulturellen Lebensstandards der türkischen Bevölkerung zu einer kontinuierlichen Erhöhung der Zahl der Parteimitglieder türkischer Herkunft beigetragen hätten[38]), deuten ebenfalls auf eine auch zu diesem Zeitpunkt noch bestehende geringere Verankerung der BKP unter dieser Bevölkerungsgruppe hin.

[36a]) Kosev, N.: Mestnite partijni organi (Die örtlichen Parteiorgane). Sofia 1989, S. 131.

[37]) Mizov, N.: Isljamăt v Bălgarija (Der Islam in Bulgarien). Sofia 1965, S. 142; Memišev, J.: Zadružno za socialističeskoto stroitelstvo na rodinata. Priobštavane na bălgarskite turci kăm izgraždaneto na socializăm (Gemeinsam für den sozialistischen Aufbau der Heimat. Die Einbeziehung der bulgarischen Türken in den Aufbau des Sozialismus). Sofia 1984, S. 136.

[38]) Ivanov, K.: Razvitie na săstava na partijata v uslovijata na socializma (Die Entwicklung der Zusammensetzung der Partei unter den Bedingungen des Sozialismus), in: NTAONSU (Anm. 21). Serija: partijno stroitelstvo. (1977) 96, S. 37.

Tabelle 4: Sozialprofil des ZK der BKP (1958–1986; in % der Mitglieder)

Jahr	Mitgl.	Frauen-anteil	Berufsstruktur				Altersstruktur			
			Partei-funktionäre	Angest. aus Staat/Wirtschaft	Wissenschaft/Kultur	Armee/Polizei	bis 40 J.	41–50 J.	51–60 J.	über 60 J.
1958	89	9,0								
1962	101	6,9								
1966	137	8,8	30,0	39,3	9,3	7,0	4,9	42,4	35,7	17,0
1971	147	7,8	26,2	43,6	8,7	10,2	13,2	46,7	29,2	10,9
1976	154	6,1	31,8	29,2	8,0	7,4	4,4	29,1	50,2	16,4
1981	197	6,2	33,8*	27,9	13,0	8,8	5,9	35,7	41,1	17,3
1986	195						4,4	15,0	35,3	34,1

* einschließlich gesellschaftspolitischer Organisationen

Quellen: VIII. kongres (Anm. 15), S. 870ff.; X. kongres (Anm. 10), S. 633ff.; XI. kongres (Anm. 29), S. 542ff.; XII. kongres (s. Tab. 1), část treta, S. 242ff.; XIII. kongres (Anm. 17), část treta, S. 199ff.

d) Parteielite

Die Parteielite der BKP umfaßt neben dem Generalsekretär die üblicherweise 7–11 Mitglieder und die 5–7 Kandidaten des Politbüros sowie die Mitglieder des Sekretariats der Partei und – deutlich abgestuft – die Mitglieder des ZK.

Dem *ZK* kommt formell die Leitung der Partei zu. Aufgrund seiner Größe und der relativ seltenen Sitzungen ist es in der Praxis aber letztlich eher ein sanktionierendes Organ der Beschlüsse des Politbüros. Seine Struktur ist dabei durch ähnliche Prozesse und Tendenzen gekennzeichnet, wie sie alle anderen kommunistischen Parteien des Ostblocks in den vergangenen 40 Jahren auch durchlaufen haben. Hinsichtlich des Sozialprofils bedeutet dies zunächst einmal einen deutlichen Trend hin zu höher qualifizierten white-collar-Vertretern und einen Rückgang der „Ideologen" der „Revolutionsjahre". Wie in der gesamten Bevölkerung ist auch der Bildungsstand unter den Mitgliedern des ZK stark gestiegen. 80 % der Mitglieder und Kandidaten sind heute Absolventen einer höheren oder Hochschulbildung, wohingegen nurmehr 10 % – vornehmlich die älteren Mitglieder – lediglich über Grundschulbildung verfügen. Neben der allgemeinen Verbesserung des Bildungsstandes geht dies aber auch auf eine gezielte Hinzuziehung von Spezialisten zurück, wie sie seit der Chruščev-Zeit auch von der BKP-Führung betrieben worden ist. Von ihrem Berufsfeld her ist das ZK durch Partei- und Staatsfunktionäre dominiert. Erstere, deren Anteil zwischenzeitlich von den Funktionären aus Staat und Wirtschaft überholt worden war, stellen mittlerweile mit 1/3 die relative Mehrheit des ZK, nicht zuletzt durch die Einbeziehung der regionalen Parteisekretäre in das ZK. Gestiegen ist der Anteil der aus Wissenschaft und Kultur kommenden ZK-Mitglieder, wohingegen der Anteil der Armee und Sicherheitsorgane, von geringen Schwankungen abgesehen, relativ konstant geblieben ist während der letzten 15 Jahre (vgl. *Tabelle 4*). Diese Entwicklung hat zwar einerseits zu einer Professionalisierung des ZK's beigetragen, andererseits aber auch dieses Gremium zu einer Domäne von white-collar-workers gemacht, wohingegen das „proletarische Element" heute praktisch kaum mehr im formell obersten Parteigremium repräsentiert ist. Der Arbeiteranteil, der 1971 noch bei 1/4 lag, liegt jetzt bei ca. 11 %. Während somit im Hinblick auf die sozialen und Bildungsmerkmale erhebliche Veränderungen innerhalb der ZK-Mitgliedschaft zu verzeichnen sind, die als Wechsel von der Ideologie zum Spezialistentum umschrieben werden können, hat sich die Repräsentanz von Frauen kaum substantiell verändert. Ein Anstieg ist lediglich zu verzeichnen, wenn man ZK und Kandidaten zusammennimmt, da der Frauenanteil unter den Kandidaten in den vergangenen Jahren gestiegen ist. Unter den Vollmitgliedern selbst hingegen ist ihr Anteil nicht nur gegenüber dem Anteil an der Mitgliedschaft völlig unterrepräsentiert, sondern er ist sogar rückläufig (vgl. *Tabelle 4*). Repräsentanten der einzigen zahlenmäßig relevanten ethnischen Minderheit, der Türken, sind innerhalb des ZK stets nur symbolisch, nie jedoch entsprechend ihres Mitgliederanteils oder gar ihres Bevölkerungsanteils vertreten gewesen. Zeitweilig, so z. B. zur Zeit des VII. und VIII. Parteitags zwischen 1954 und 1962, waren sie überhaupt nur durch einen Kandidaten repräsentiert; in den übrigen Jahren waren sie mit einem Mitglied und zwei bis vier Kandidaten vertreten. Paradoxerweise ist der Anteil türkischstämmiger Mitglieder im ZK und unter den Kandidaten gestiegen, nachdem die Parteiführung mit ihrer Namensänderungskampagne seit

Tabelle 5: Personelle Erneuerung im ZK (1958–1986; in Klammern %)

Jahr	Mitgl.	wieder-gewählt	nicht wieder-gewählt	vormals Kandidat	ohne Kandidatur direkt gewählt
1958	89				
1962	101	57 (64)	32 (36)	44 (44)	24
1966	137	79 (78)	22 (22)	58 (42)	33
1971	147	106 (77)	31 (23)	41 (28)	19
1976	154	121 (79)	26 (17)	33 (21)	22
1981	197	134 (87)	20 (14)	63 (32)	32
1986	195	161 (82)	36 (18)	34 (17)	26

Quelle: Wie Tabelle 4.

Ende 1984 der offiziellen Existenz einer türkischen Minderheit ein Ende gesetzt hat. Gegenwärtig gibt es, unter nunmehr bulgarischen Namen, drei türkische Vertreter im ZK und vier unter den Kandidaten des ZK[39]).

Hinsichtlich der personellen Erneuerung des ZK waren die größten personellen Fluktuationen in den späten 50er und 60er Jahren zu verzeichnen – ein Reflex auf die noch ungesicherte Position Živkovs und die seinerzeitigen Fraktionsauseinandersetzungen. Nachdem seine Stellung jedoch gefestigt war und insbesondere von der Mitte der 70er Jahre an bis zu seinem Sturz im November 1989 läßt sich hingegen ein Trend zu wachsender personeller Stabilität im ZK feststellen, bei dem zumeist weit über 70%, zuletzt sogar über 80% der Mitglieder von Parteitag zu Parteitag wiedergewählt wurden. Personelle Auffrischung kam in diesen Jahren der Ära Živkov zumeist nur über eine Vergrößerung des ZK zustande. Ergebnis dieser relativ hohen personellen Konstanz innerhalb des ZK war ein sich verstärkender Alterungsprozeß. Auch hier sind insbesondere die 80er Jahre zwischen dem XII. Parteitag (31.3.–4.4.1981) und dem XIII. Parteitag (2.–5.4.1986) auffällig, in denen sich der Anteil der über 60-jährigen verdoppelt hat und jetzt bereits über 1/3 des ZK ausmacht. Der Sturz Živkovs im November 1989 hat nunmehr auch zu ersten einschneidenden Veränderungen im ZK geführt, dessen personelle Erneuerung sich vermutlich auf dem für 1990 angekündigten außerordentlichen Parteitag der BKP fortsetzen dürfte. Insgesamt 25 Mitglieder wurden aus dem ZK abgewählt bzw. ausgeschlossen, darunter neben Todor Živkov und dessen Sohn Vladimir auch das ehemalige Politbüro-Mitglied Milko Balev, Wirtschaftsminister Stojan Ovčarov sowie viele der erst in den vergangenen zwei Jahren von Živkov in dieses Amt gerufenen Funktionäre[40]).

Anders als die oberste Parteispitze in der Sowjetunion haben das *Politbüro* und das *Sekretariat* der BKP als die eigentlichen politischen Schaltzentralen der Partei und

---

[39]) Die ZK-Mitglieder sind Kamen Kalinov (vormals Fachredin Chalilov; Chefredakteur der früher partiell türkischsprachigen Zeitung Yeni ışık-Nova Svetlina), Svetlana Dilova (vormals Salicha Adilova) und – seit Dezember 1988 – Radi Semov (vormals Rafet Sejdaliev); die Kandidaten sind: Aleksandăr Kolev (vormals Ali Aliev), Nadja Asparuchova (vormals Najde Ferchadova), Blaga Tatarova (vormals Elmaz Tatarova) und Juri Danailov (vormals Yumer Dachilov): RFE-RL Situation Report Bulgaria/4. 22.4.1986, S. 25; RD. 15.12.1988, S. 1.

[40]) RD. 17.11.1989; 9.12.1989.

des Landes in den 70er Jahren keine vergleichbaren Tendenzen hin zu einer Gerontokratie durchgemacht. Živkov hatte es in seiner Amtszeit stets verstanden, jüngere Funktionäre an die Parteispitze heranzuführen und sie der Garde der alten Živkov-Gefährten, die ihn seit den 50er und 60er Jahren auf dem Weg der Macht begleitet hatten, wie Verteidigungsminister Dobri Džurov (über 70 Jahre), Griša Filipov, Milko Balev und Penčo Kubadinski (alle über 60 Jahre), an die Seite zu stellen. Diese personelle Verjüngung diente freilich vorrangig der Machtsicherung der alten Führungsgarnitur und nicht zuletzt Živkovs selbst. Viele der in den 70er und 80er Jahren in die Führungsspitze aufgestiegenen jüngeren Funktionäre wurden daher nach relativ kurzer Zeit wieder ausgetauscht, wohingegen der Kern der älteren Politbüro-Mitglieder im wesentlichen stabil blieb. Das Altersgefüge des Politbüros hat sich so gegen Ende der Ära Živkov zunehmend nach unten verschoben und lag zuletzt bei Mitte 60. Die personalpolitische Fundamentalerneuerung des Politbüros nach dem Sturze Živkovs, bei der vom alten Politbüro lediglich der neue Generalsekretär Petăr Mladenov, Ministerpräsident Georgi Atanasov und Verteidigungsminister Dobri Džurov übrigblieben, hat nunmehr auch in diesem obersten Führungsorgan der Partei einen substantiellen Generationswechsel eingeleitet. Nach dem Ausscheiden der alten Gefährten Živkovs (Balev, Kubadinski, Filipov, Jotov) dominiert im neuen Politbüro die Generation der 50jährigen (Lukanov, Mladenov, Atanasov, Lilov, Pačov, Belčev sind zwischen 50 und 60 Jahre, Minčo Jovčev ist Ende 40), wohingegen lediglich noch Verteidigungsminister Džurov als Repräsentant der alten Generation in der Parteispitze verblieben ist.

An der *Spitze der Partei* stand mit Todor Živkov 35 Jahre lang der zuletzt dienstälteste Parteichef des Ostblocks. Der bei seinem Sturz im November 1989 fast 78 Jahre alte Živkov, Drucker von Beruf, gehört zur „Partisanengeneration" und war im Kriege in der Čavdar-Brigade eingesetzt, aus deren Kreis der Parteichef auch nach dem Aufstieg zur Macht immer wieder Weggefährten berief (z. B. Verteidigungsminister und Politbüro-Mitglied Dobri Džurov oder den zeitweiligen Ideologie-Sekretär des ZK Jordan Jotov). Nach dem Staatsstreich vom 9.9.1944 war er für die Arbeit der Miliz in Sofia verantwortlich und übernahm später die Leitung des Vorsitzes des Sofioter Stadtparteikomitees. Bei seinem Amtsantritt als Parteichef 1954 eher als schwache Führungsperson eingestuft, gelang es ihm bis zum Ende der 50er Jahre, sich innerparteilich nicht nur gegen seinen Vorgänger Vălko Červenkov durchzusetzen, sondern auch andere potentielle Konkurrenten auszubooten (Jugov, Terpešev). Nachdem seine anfangs noch ungesicherte Position 1965 ein letztes Mal durch den berühmt-berüchtigten „Militär-Putschversuch" in Gefahr geraten war[41]), hat er bis zu seinem Sturz, praktisch ungefährdet und im großen und ganzen auch ohne in seiner Position herausgefordert worden zu sein, Staat und Partei geführt. Die Gründe für diese Machtstabilität liegen zum einen in einer geschickten Personalpolitik während der Machtsicherungsphase zwischen 1954 und 1958, mit der er neue Leute seines Lagers und Vertreter der alten Generation verband. Durch das Hinführen jüngerer Kräfte in die Parteielite sicherte er seine Position, ohne jedoch sich durch diese selbst bedrohen zu lassen. Das kometenhafte Aufsteigen jüngerer Kader, gefördert durch

---

[41]) Vgl. hierzu den Beitrag von John D. Bell, Domestic Politics, sowie Bell, J.D.: The Bulgarian Communist Party from Blagoev to Zhivkov. Stanford 1986, S. 125 ff.

Živkov selbst, und deren spätere Abstufung in das zweite oder dritte Glied gehörte zum periodisch sich wiederholenden Verfahren seiner Machtsicherung. Boris Velčev, Aleksandăr Lilov, Stanko Todorov, der lange Zeit als Nummer zwei hinter Živkov gegolten hatte, sowie in jüngster Zeit auch die Anfang der 80er Jahre aufgestiegenen Čudomir Aleksandrov, Ognjan Dojnov und Stojan Markov sind derartige Beispiele einer Kaderpolitik, die zwar innovationsfreudig war, aber letztlich in erster Linie der Sicherung der eigenen Position diente. Der bulgarische Parteichef blieb daher trotz mehr als dreißigjähriger Amtszeit ohne klar erkennbaren Erben und machte immer wieder Nachfolgespekulationen zunichte. Zur Machtstabilisierung trug aber zeitweilig wohl auch ein gewisses Maß an persönlicher Legitimität bei, das der ansonsten völlig uncharismatische Parteiführer zu erringen vermochte durch eine Politik, die insbesondere seit den 70er Jahren politische Subordination unter die Moskauer Linie mit bulgarischem Nationalismus verband. Eine gewisse Volkstümlichkeit stützte diese Legitimation. Schließlich war die stets gesuchte Unterstützung in Moskau ein wesentlicher Faktor der Herrschaftssicherung für Živkov, auf die er sich sowohl zur Zeit Chruščevs als auch vor allem in der langen Brežnev-Ära verlassen konnte.

Insbesondere mit dem Amtsantritt Gorbačevs und den politischen Veränderungen in anderen Staaten Osteuropas, aber auch angesichts einer seit Mitte der 80er Jahre sich verschlechternden wirtschaftlichen Situation geriet die Akzeptanz seiner Führung jedoch zunehmend ins Wanken. Die Spätphase der Ära Živkov macht daher den Eindruck der Agonie und war bestimmt vom Interesse des Parteichefs an einem eruptionslosen Ausklingen seiner Herrschaft, ohne den Willen und die Kraft zu einem echten politischen Neubeginn. Seine Strategie, der sowjetischen *perestrojka* mit verbalem Reformradikalismus zu begegnen, tatsächliche politische Reformen aber dilatorisch zu behandeln, bewirkte einen zunehmenden Vertrauensverlust. Auf die traditionelle und vorbehaltlose Unterstützung aus Moskau konnte Živkov sich immer weniger stützen, das Verhältnis zum ersten Mann im Kreml blieb vielmehr, im Unterschied zu dessen Vorgängern Chruščev und Brežnev, distanziert, und eine zuletzt unberechenbar werdende Personalpolitik mit immer neuen „Kaderrotationen" zerstörte auch den stets gewahrten Elitenkonsens innerhalb der Parteiführung.

Nicht zuletzt, um einer ähnlich eruptiven Gefährdung der kommunistischen Parteiherrschaft wie in der DDR zuvorzukommen, sahen sich daher eine Gruppe von Parteiführern um den Außenminister Petăr Mladenov, Verteidigungsminister Dobri Džurov, Ministerpräsident Georgi Atanasov sowie Politbüro-Kandidat Andrej Lukanov veranlaßt, mit wohlwollender Unterstützung der Sowjetunion auf der Sitzung des ZK vom 10.11.1989 Živkov zum Rücktritt als Generalsekretär der Partei und als Vorsitzender des DS zu zwingen.

Zum neuen Generalsekretär und Nachfolger Živkovs im Amte des DS-Vorsitzenden wurde der langjährige Außenminister Petăr Mladenov gewählt. Auf zwei folgenden Sitzungen des ZK am 17.11. und 8.12.1989 gelang es Mladenov, praktisch alle alten Gefährten Živkovs (Milko Balev, Penčo Kubadinski, Griša Filipov, Jordan Jotov, Georgi Jordanov) sowie viele der von Živkov in den vergangenen zwei Jahren im Rahmen seiner vielen Personalveränderungen in Partei und Staat in führende Ämter gehievten Funktionäre (Petko Dančev, Ivan Panev, Stojan Ovčarov, Dimităr Stojanov u.a.) aus ihren Positionen zu verdrängen und so einen radikalen personalpolitischen Bruch mit der Živkov-Ära einzuleiten. An ihre Stelle traten zum einen bislang relativ unbekannte regionale Funktionäre (so die bisherigen führenden Funktionäre der BKP-Gebietskomitees Chaskovo, Plovdiv und Varna Minčo Jovčev, Pantelej Pačov als Mitglieder des Politbüros, Ivan Ivanov und Petko Petkov als Kandidaten des Politbüros und Dimo Uzunov als Sekretär des ZK) sowie einige jener bereits früher in politischen Führungsämtern tätigen Funktionäre, die jedoch mit dem alten Parteichef in Konflikt geraten waren. Zu ihnen gehören beispielsweise der 1983 angeblich wegen Kritik am Personenkult Živkovs als Mitglied des Politbüros und Sekretär des ZK entlassene, 1986 auch aus dem ZK abgewählte Aleksandăr Lilov, der nunmehr seine früheren Funktionen wieder übernommen hat, der jetzige Finanzminister Belčo Belčev oder auch der erst im Juli 1988 von Živkov geschaßte ZK-Sekretär Stojan Michajlov, der nunmehr sein Mandat als Mitglied des ZK wiedererhielt und stellvertretender Ministerpräsident wurde. Die personelle Basis der gegenwärtigen politischen Führung scheint somit aus neuen Regional-Funktionären einerseits und Živkov-Kontrahenten der 80er Jahre andererseits zu bestehen.

Zugleich mit der politischen Entmachtung Živkovs begann eine fundamentale Abrechnung mit seiner Person und seiner Amtsführung, die sich vor allem gegen seinen autoritären Führungsstil und seine „voluntaristische Kaderpolitik" sowie gegen seinen aufwendigen Lebensstil und den um ihn betriebenen Personenkult richtete. Im Gefolge dieser Kampagne verloren Živkov sowie sein Sohn Vladimir und sein enger Vertrauter Milko Balev nicht nur alle ihnen nach dem 10. 11. 1989 noch verbliebenen politischen Ämter, sondern sie wurden auch aus der Partei ausgeschlossen. Neben dem personalpolitischen Bruch mit der Živkov-Ära und der Abrechnung mit dem Amtsvorgänger sollten Maßnahmen der neuen Führung wie die „Nationalisierung" der Residenzen Živkovs und die Kürzung der Bezüge für den Generalsekretär der Partei den aufgestauten sozialen Unmut in der Bevölkerung dämpfen. Reformversprechen wie die Aussicht auf freie Wahlen im Mai 1990, der Verzicht auf die Verfassungsgarantie der führenden Rolle der Partei sowie erste ad hoc-Maßnahmen wie die die Abschaffung des berüchtigten § 273 des Strafgesetzbuches über verbale politische Delikte und die Auflösung der Staatssicherheitseinheit gegen „ideologische Diversion", die Vorbereitung eines Versammlungs- und Organisationsgesetzes und schließlich die faktische Duldung der oppositionellen Gruppen sollten ehrlichen Reformwillen signalisieren und den Reformdruck „von unten" kanalisieren.

Ob dieser Versuch einer Erneuerung des Systems „auf sozialistischer Basis" gelingt, ohne – wie in der DDR und der ČSSR – sich zu einer Existenzgefährdung der Partei und ihrer politischen Machtstellung auszuwachsen, war Ende 1989 noch offen. Die Ungeduld einer sich zunehmend politisierenden Öffentlichkeit könnte sich sehr schnell auch gegen die neue Führung richten, wenn diese – ähnlich wie die alte Živkov-Führung – hinter ihren eigenen Reformversprechen und hinter den Veränderungen in den übrigen sozialistischen Ländern zurückbleiben sollte. Bulgarien befindet sich am Beginn eines Umbruchs, in dem auch für die jetzige Parteielite die Perspektiven noch gänzlich unvorhersehbar sind.

2. Die Bulgarische Nationale Agrarunion (BZNS)

Der BZNS ist heute die einzige politische Partei neben der BKP, die die Beseitigung der pluralistischen Parteienstruktur in den Jahren 1944 bis 1948 organisatorisch überstanden hat – freilich um den Preis einer fundamentalen Veränderung ihres ideologischen Profils, ihrer politischen Rolle und der sie tragenden Parteielite. Trotz des vom BZNS aufrechterhaltenen Anspruchs, in der Kontinuität der alten, 1899 gegründeten Agrarunion und vor allem ihrer von Aleksandăr Stambolijski geprägten Ideologie und Politik zu stehen, hat der BZNS seit 1948 kaum mehr gemein mit seinem agrarpopulistischen Vorläufer aus der Zeit des ancien régime als den Namen.

a) Politische Entwicklung

Durch die zügige Wiedervereinigung seiner seit der Vorkriegszeit gespaltenen Flügel – dem eher konservativen *Vrabča-1* und dem stärker agrarpopulistischen *Pladne*-Flügel – gelang dem BZNS nach dem 9.9.1944 relativ schnell die organisatorische Festigung. Mit bereits im Frühjahr 1945 300 000 Mitgliedern (vgl. *Tabelle 6*) und einem breit gestreuten Netz an Grundorganisationen wurde er innerhalb weniger Wochen zur einzigen Partei, die in puncto Parteiorganisation und Mitgliederstärke wenigstens annähernd mit der BKP mithalten konnte[42]). Die Mitgliederbasis der Partei setzte sich wie schon vor dem Kriege ganz überwiegend aus Klein- und Mittelbauern bis zu 5 ha Grundbesitz zusammen. Darüber hinaus begann der BZNS aber auch in die städtische Mittelschicht einzudringen, die in ihm die einzige organisatorische und politische Gegenkraft zur BKP erblickte[43]). Ideologisch knüpfte der BZNS an die agrarsyndikalistische und populistische Programmatik der Vorkriegsphase an, basierend auf einer sogenanten „biologisch-materialistischen Weltanschauung", dem Kooperativgedanken sowie einer noch immer lebendigen Skepsis gegenüber Industriekapitalismus und Urbanismus[44]). Politisch bekannte er sich zwar zum Programm der OF, indem er Berührungspunkte mit seiner gemäßigt antikapitalistischen Programmatik entdeckte, und beteiligte sich an der Regierung. Allerdings gab es im Hinblick auf die Haltung zur OF und zur Politik der BKP erhebliche Nuancierungen innerhalb des BZNS. Während der „rechte" Flügel um Georgi M. Dimitrov (Gemeto) von Anfang an der Kooperation mit der OF skeptisch gegenüberstand, hielt der Flügel um Nikola Petkov, der schon im Kriege der Front beigetreten war, an der Perspektive einer dauerhaften Zusammenarbeit mit den Kommunisten auf der Basis des Programms der OF fest. Auch er war jedoch nicht bereit, den Anspruch auf Selbständigkeit aufzugeben und widersetzte sich der zunehmenden Machterweiterung der BKP.

---

[42]) Zur Frühphase des BZNS nach dem 9.9.1944 vgl. Isusov, M.: Političeskite partii v Bălgarija 1944–1948 (Die politischen Parteien in Bulgarien 1944–1948). Sofia 1978, S. 74 ff. (zit. als: Isusov, Pol. partii).

[43]) Zarčev, J.: BZNS i izgraždaneto na socializma v Bălgarija 1944/62 (Der BZNS und der Aufbau des Sozialismus in Bulgarien 1944–1962). Sofia 1984, S. 25 ff. (zit. als: Zarčev, BZNS 1944/62).

[44]) Vgl. Zarčev, J.: Deloto na Aleksandăr Stambolijski i razvitieto na BZNS sled pobedata na socialističeskata revoljucija (Das Werk Aleksandăr Stambolijskis und die Entwicklung des BZNS nach dem Sieg der sozialistischen Revolution), in: Aleksandăr Stambolijski. Život, delo, zaveti (A. Stambolijski. Leben, Werk, Vermächtnis). Sofia 1980, S. 128 ff.; Aslanov, L.: Za roljata na Bălgarskija zemedelski naroden săjuz v stroitelstvoto na socializma (Die Rolle des BZNS beim Aufbau des Sozialismus), in: BAN, Institut za istorija (Hrsg.): Socialističeskata revoljucija v Bălgarija. Istoričeski studii (Die sozialistische Revolution in Bulgarien. Historische Studien). Sofia 1965, S. 353 f.

Tabelle 6: Mitgliederentwicklung des BZNS 1944–1986

Sept. 1944: 37 827	1959: 120 000
Nov. 1944: 133 012	1962: 112 358
Frühj. 1945: 300 000	1966: 144 072
Okt. 1948: 165 000	1971: 116 363
1952: 116 000	1976: 120 000
1954: 109 441	1981: 120 000
1957: 112 787	1986: 120 000
	1989: 120 000

Quelle: Zarčev, BZNS 1944/62 (Anm. 43), S. 29, 32, 237, 284, 318; ders., Delo (Anm. 44), S. 145; Aslanov (Anm. 44), S. 375; 33. kongres na BZNS (29.11.–1.12. 1976). Sofia 1977, S. 78; Zemedelsko zname. 19.1. 1981 und 21.5. 1986; RD. 23.5.1989.

Trotz einer relativ starken Mitgliederbasis und einer intakten Organisationsstruktur, mit der er sich von den übrigen nichtkommunistischen Parteien unterschied, vermochte der BZNS gegen den Machtvorsprung der mit der Roten Armee im Rücken agierenden BKP nichts auszurichten. Abgesehen von der numerisch paritätischen Beteiligung der Agrarier an der ersten Regierung der OF und im ersten Nachkriegsparlament war er ansonsten in allen politischen Institutionen dem Einfluß der Kommunisten unterlegen. Innerhalb der Komitees der OF verfügte er nur über etwa 1/3 der Mandate gegenüber 54% der BKP und auch in den lokalen Machtorganen lag er weit hinter seinem kommunistischen Gegenpart zurück. Unter den 85 städtischen Bürgermeistern etwa stellte er 1945 lediglich zwei gegenüber 63 der BKP; auf dem Lande, der eigentlichen Domäne des BZNS, bestimmte er nur in 137 von 1165 Gemeinden (gegenüber 879 BKP-Bürgermeistern) das Geschehen[45].

Dieser geringere institutionalisierte Einfluß sowie vor allem die rigiden Repressionen durch die BKP und die von ihr beherrschten Organe in Staat und Polizei führten zwischen 1945 und Sommer 1947 zur schrittweisen Ausschaltung des BZNS als eigenständigem politischen Faktor. Der erzwungene Rücktritt Georgi M. Dimitrovs vom Parteivorsitz im Januar 1945, die ebenfalls erzwungene Abspaltung des Petkov-Flügels von der Partei im Mai 1945, der die Verhaftung und der Schauprozeß gegen Nikola Petkov im Laufe des Jahres 1947 folgten, sowie schließlich auch die Ausbootung des Petkov-Nachfolgers im Amte des Parteivorsitzenden, Aleksandăr Obbov, im Sommer 1947 sind die Stationen auf dem Wege der Umwandlung des BZNS in einen macht- und einflußlosen Juniorpartner der BKP[46]. Erst mit dem neuen Mann an der Spitze des BZNS, Georgi Trajkov, wurden ab Sommer 1947 die sogenannten „gesunden Kräfte" des „linken Flügels", die 1944 noch eine völlig untergeordnete Rolle innerhalb des BZNS gespielt hatten und auch nicht in der Parteileitung vertreten gewesen waren, bestimmend. Der Weg zu einer völligen ideologischen und programmatischen Neubestimmung von Rolle und Funktion des BZNS war damit geeb-

---

[45]) Ostoič, P.: BKP i izgraždaneto na narodnodemokratičnata dăržava. 9. septemvri 1944 – dekemvri 1947 (Die BKP und der Aufbau des volksdemokratischen Staates. 9.9.1944 – Dez. 1947). Sofia 1967, S. 76f.

[46]) Vgl. hierzu ausführlicher den Beitrag von John D. Bell, Domestic Politics.

net. Auf dem XXVII. Kongreß am 28./29.12.1947 sowie endgültig auf dem Plenum des „Obersten Unions-Rates" am 30.10.1948 ordnete sich die Partei ideologisch und politisch der BKP unter. Ähnlich wie diese bekannte sich nun auch der BZNS zum Sozialismus als seiner politischen Zielperspektive[47]). Zwar hatte er sich auch vorher schon des öfteren verbal für einen vage definierten Sozialismus ausgesprochen, der aber bis dahin verstanden worden war als Koexistenz sozialistischer Wirtschaftsformen vor allem in der Großindustrie und einer in Kooperativen organisierten, auf Klein- und Mittelbesitz beruhenden Landwirtschaft. Nunmehr hingegen akzeptierte er ein Sozialismus-Verständnis, das im Sinne der Diktatur des Proletariats und der schrittweisen Beseitigung aller privaten Verfügbarkeit über Produktionsmittel definiert war. Die Partei brach damit praktisch mit all jenen Elementen, die früher ihr ideologisches Selbstverständnis ausgemacht hatten. Die frühere Programmatik und Ideologie eines Aleksandăr Stambolijski wurde nunmehr zwar als eine in manchen Bereichen progressive, aber letztlich eklektizistische Ideologie abgetan, deren antiproletarische und antiindustrielle Ausrichtung nicht mehr zeitgemäß sei und der Anpassung an die neuen Bedingungen bedürfe. Drei Prinzipien, so Georgi Trajkov auf dem Oktober-Plenum 1948, sollten künftig für den politischen Kurs der Partei bestimmend sein:

1. Das Selbstverständnis des BZNS als „Klassenorganisation" der kleinen und mittleren Bauern, in der kein Platz für sogenannte „kapitalistische und Kulaken-Kräfte" sei, womit die Partei ihr noch 1944 erneuertes Selbstverständnis als einheitliche Organisation aller Bauern aufgab;
2. die Anerkennung des Sozialismus (im marxistisch-leninistischen Verständnis der BKP) als programmatisches Ziel auch des BZNS, was eine Absage an die agrarpopulistische und syndikalistische Programatik des alten BZNS bedeutete; sowie
3. die uneingeschränkte Anerkennung der führenden Rolle des Proletariats und seiner Partei, der BKP, womit der BZNS auf den von ihm nach dem 9.9.1944 verfolgten Anspruch verzichtete, das Bauerntum als gleichberechtigte „zweite Säule" auch eines volksdemokratischen Bulgariens zu betrachten[48]).

Mit dieser ideologischen und programmatischen Unterordnung unter die BKP einher ging eine weitere „Säuberung" der Partei in der Führung und unter den rank-and-file-Mitgliedern. Die Gesamtdimension dieser „Säuberungen" ist nicht exakt zu beziffern. Die Verringerung der *Mitgliederzahl* zwischen Oktober 1948 und den frühen 50er Jahren läßt jedoch erkennen, daß etwa 55 000 Parteimitglieder, etwa 1/3 der Gesamtmitgliedschaft, ausschieden (vgl. *Tabelle 6*). Ca. 60% der Führungsorgane der Bezirks- und Distrikt-Organisationen wurden ausgewechselt[49]). Die personelle Gleichschaltung verlief jedoch nicht reibungslos. Noch bis in die frühen 50er Jahre wurde immer wieder von Ausschlüssen „rechter Abweichler", selbst aus den Leitungsgremien der Partei, und von Maßnahmen gegen einzelne Grundorganisationen

---

[47]) Vankov, V.: Idejno-političeskata evoljucija na BZNS prez 1947–1948 g. (Die ideologisch-politische Evolution im BZNS 1947/48), in: Istoričeski pregled. 16 (1960) 5, S. 51–60; Isusov, Političeskite partii (Anm. 42), S. 433ff.

[48]) Vgl. die Rede Trajkovs auf dem Oktober-Plenum 1948: Trajkov, G.: Statii, reči, dokladi 1922–1968 (Aufsätze, Reden und Vorträge 1922–1968). Sofia 1969, S. 41–45.

[49]) Zarčev, BZNS 1944/62 (Anm. 43), S. 237.

berichtet. Die Neuorientierung der Partei bedeutete zugleich auch eine schrittweise Veränderung im Wandel der *Mitgliederstruktur* des BZNS. Nachdem seit 1948 bereits all jene ausgeschlossen worden waren, die unter den willkürlich und breit gefaßten Begriff des „Kulaken" fielen, wurden mit dem Beginn der Umwandlung der bulgarischen Landwirtschaft in Kooperativwirtschaften zudem Mitglieder der Kooperativen vorrangig in die Partei aufgenommen. Umgekehrt wurden BZNS-Mitglieder zu einem Eintritt in die Kooperativen genötigt. Schneller als die Struktur der Landwirtschaft im ganzen veränderte sich daher im Laufe der 50er Jahre der BZNS zu einer Partei von Kollektivbauern, die bereits 1951 zu über 60% aus Mitgliedern der Kooperativen bestand[50]).

1954 wurde der Transformationsprozeß des BZNS von einer ideologisch unpräzisen, agrarpopulistischen „All-Schichten-Partei" zu einer sozialistischen „Klassenorganisation" für abgeschlossen erklärt[51]). Ideologie und Rollenverständnis haben bis zum Sturz Živkovs keine substantiellen Änderungen mehr erfahren. Allenfalls graduelle Akzentverlagerungen waren spürbar. So war der BZNS in den Jahren des bulgarischen Stalinismus unter Červenkov 1950 bis 1954 ein vollends den Befehlen der BKP untergeordnetes Instrument der BKP bei der Kollektivierung der Landwirtschaft, dessen ohnehin geringes politisches Gewicht noch weiter abnahm. Die Mitgliedschaft ging weiter zurück, und viele Grundorganisationen bestanden nurmehr noch formal. Selbst unter der BZNS-Führung soll es Vorstellungen über eine Auflösung der Partei gegeben haben[52]). Die Haltung der BKP entsprach dabei der auch in anderen Volksdemokratien damals praktizierten Politik der weiteren Zurückdrängung von Bedeutung und Mitgliederzahl der noch bestehenden Bauernparteien. Nach dem Aprilplenum des ZK der BKP 1956 und vor allem im Zuge der „zweiten Entstalinisierung" 1961 wurde die Rolle des BZNS zumindest graduell aufgewertet, freilich ohne den 1948 gesetzten Rahmen seines Funktionsverständnisses zu sprengen. Immerhin aber wurde nunmehr das „sektiererische Verständnis" über die Beziehungen von BKP und BZNS und die „Unterbewertung seiner Rolle" in der Červenkov-Ära kritisiert und eine stärkere Beteiligung des BZNS an der Umsetzung der Politik zugestanden[53]). Der seit 1948 kontinuierlich rückläufige Mitgliederbestand der Partei durfte wieder aufgestockt werden; selbst eine Reihe alter Funktionäre, die im Zuge der Fraktionsauseinandersetzungen der ersten Nachkriegsjahre aus der Partei entfernt worden waren, durften nach vorheriger Selbstkritik wieder dem BZNS beitreten. Die gemäßigtere Haltung gegenüber dem BZNS war dabei nicht zuletzt auch durch die gewandelte Agrarpolitik der BKP motiviert, die, nach den Jahren der Umwandlung der Einzelwirtschaften in Kooperativen und einer fiskalischen und preislichen Abschöpfung der bäuerlichen Einkommen, sich um einen stärkeren

---

[50]) Ebenda, S. 227, 264.
[51]) Rešenie na razšireneto zasedanie na Upravitelnija sävet na BZNS, 8.–10.3.1954 (Beschluß der erweiterten Sitzung des Verwaltungsrates des BZNS, 8.–10.3.1954), in: Zemedelsko zname. 14.3.1954.
[52]) Aslanov (Anm. 44), S. 365f.; Zarčev, J.: BZNS i socializmät (1944–1971) (Der BZNS und der Sozialismus (1944–1971)), in: Istoričeski pregled. 35 (1979) 4–5, S. 68f. sowie der Rechenschaftsbericht an den 29. Parteitag, in: Zemedelsko zname. 6.4.1957.
[53]) Zemedelsko zname. 9.12.1961; BKP v rez. (Anm. 4). T. V, S. 75; Živkov, T.: Izbrani säčinenija. T. 2, S. 501f.

Rückhalt in der Bauernschaft bemühte. Ein aufgewerteter BZNS konnte dabei hilfreich sein. Angeblich sollen im Gefolge der innerparteilichen Auseinandersetzungen um die politische Linie der Partei nach dem XX. Parteitag der KPdSU 1956 auch Überlegungen vorgebracht worden sein, die über eine solche rein rollenimmanente Aufwertung des BZNS hinauswiesen. So soll der später aus seinen Positionen verdrängte Dobri Terpešev sich nach dem Aprilplenum für eine Umwandlung des BZNS in eine „Oppositionspartei" eingesetzt haben[54]). Inwieweit derartige, ex post erhobene Vorwürfe der Realität entsprechen, ist nicht festzumachen. Offenbar aber scheint es in der BKP und innerhalb der BZNS-Führung Bestrebungen gegeben zu haben, die Chance der Entstalinisierung zu einer substantielleren Ausweitung ihres Handlungsspielraums nutzen zu wollen. Im Mai 1956 wurden zumindest Maßnahmen gegen einzelne führende Funktionäre des BZNS ergriffen, die „ungesunde Ambitionen" gezeigt hätten[55]).

b) Politisches Selbstverständnis und Aufgaben

Ideologisch und in ihrem programmatischen Selbstverständnis war die Partei somit seit ihrem XXVII. Kongreß am 27.12.1947 und dem Oktoberplenum vom 31.10.–1.11.1948 festgelegt. Das Bekenntnis zum Sozialismus und zum Programm der BKP wurde auch für das gegenwärtig noch gültige Parteiprogramm der BKP von 1971 folgerichtig erneuert[56]). Entsprechend verfügte der BZNS denn auch über kein eigenes politisches Programm. Lediglich vier quasiprogrammatische Grundsätze hatte er in Anlehnung an das BKP-Programm auf seinem XXXII. Kongreß 1971 in seinem Statut verankert: 1. den Aufbau der entwickelten sozialistischen Gesellschaft als Aufgabe und Ziel des BZNS; 2. das Bündnis mit der BKP; 3. die Stärkung der bulgarisch-sowjetischen Freundschaft sowie 4. die Stärkung des Antiimperialismus, der Kampf für Frieden und Sicherheit und eine Politik der friedlichen Koexistenz[57]).

Aufgrund der fehlenden eigenen Programmatik waren denn auch die Aussagen der BZNS-Parteikongresse letztlich nicht mehr als ein Abklatsch der zuvor von der BKP festgelegten konkreten Politik, ohne die geringsten individuellen Akzentuierungen und allenfalls durch eine stärkere Berücksichtigung agrarpolitischer Fragestellungen geprägt.

Die konkreten politischen Aufgaben des BZNS ergaben sich somit lediglich aus einer arbeitsteiligen Umsetzung der von der BKP festgelegten politischen Zielsetzungen. In diesem Sinne betätigt sich der BZNS vor allem in zwei Sektoren: 1. bei der Umsetzung der Agrarpolitik sowie 2. auf dem Gebiet der Außenpolitik.

In der Agrarpolitik hatte der BZNS nach seiner Gleichschaltung zunächst die Funktion, die Umwandlung der Landwirtschaft in Kooperativen (TKZS) organisatorisch und mobilisierend zu unterstützen[58]). Nach Abschluß dieser faktischen Kol-

---

[54]) Zarčev, BZNS 1944/62 (Anm. 43), S. 283.
[55]) Zemedelsko zname. 13.5.1956; Zarčev, BZNS 1944/62 (Anm. 43), S. 287.
[56]) RD. 15.5.1971.
[57]) Zemedelsko zname. 21.10.1971.
[58]) Jotov, V.: Prinosăt na BZNS za pobedata na kooperativnija stroj na selo (Der Beitrag des BZNS zum Sieg des kooperativen Aufbaus des Dorfes). Sofia 1968.

lektivierung am Ende der 50er Jahre stützten die agrarpolitischen Aktivitäten des BZNS später die Zusammenlegung der einzelnen Kooperativen zu großen, industrieller Technik zugänglichen Kollektivwirtschaften und seit 1970 die Umwandlung der Kooperativen in APK ab[59]). Neben dieser organisatorisch unterstützenden Tätigkeit für die Realisierung der Agrarpolitik der Partei nimmt der BZNS über seine Mitglieder aber auch an der Verwaltung der APK teil[60]). Derartige Funktionen geben ihm somit zumindest die Möglichkeit, mit seiner fachlich-konsultativen Kompetenz auf die Agrarpolitik einzuwirken. Neben der Agrarpolitik findet der BZNS noch auf dem Felde der kulturellen und sozialen Entwicklung des Dorfes sowie in der Weiterbildung landwirtschaftlich Beschäftigter sein Wirkungsfeld.

Von anderen noch bestehenden Agrarparteien in den sozialistischen Ländern unterscheidet sich der BZNS durch eine größere internationale Aktivität, die auf der Zusammenarbeit mit den Schwesterparteien der sozialistischen Länder, den Genossenschaftsorganisationen vor allem in der Dritten Welt, aber auch auf nicht-kommunistische Parteien des Westens, von liberalen Parteien bis hin zu „grünen" Gruppierungen, beruht[61]). Allerdings beschränkt sich der BZNS auch hier ausschließlich auf eine Popularisierung der von der BKP festgelegten außenpolitischen Richtlinien.

Dieses fast 40 Jahre festgefügte ideologische und politische Profil des BZNS ist erst nach dem Sturze Živkovs im November 1989 in Bewegung geraten. Ähnlich wie die BKP, trennte sich auch der BZNS nach dem Rücktritt Živkovs von seinem langjährigen Vorsitzenden Petăr Tančev, der auch von seinem Amt als stellvertretender DS-Vorsitzender zurücktrat. In beiden Ämtern folgte ihm der bisherige Sekretär des Verwaltungsrates des BZNS, Angel Dimitrov. Mit ihm kündigte der BZNS nunmehr erstmals seit seiner Gleichschaltung die Ausarbeitung eines eigenen Programms sowie eigener Stellungnahmen und Lösungsvorschläge zu anstehenden politischen Fragen, vor allem im Agrarbereich, an. Gleichzeitig will sich der BZNS einer kritischen Revision seiner eigenen Geschichte stellen. Hierzu – und dies dürfte in der Tat von einiger Brisanz sein – wurde bereits eine Kommission zur Überprüfung des Urteils und der Hinrichtung Nikola Petkovs 1947 sowie der historischen Rolle aller bislang als „Konterrevolutionäre" und „Verräter" denunzierten Agrarier, die sich der Gleichschaltung widersetzt hatten, eingerichtet. Gegenüber der BKP hält die Partei zumindest gegenwärtig noch an dem Prinzip eines Bündnisses fest, will in ihm aber künftig die Rolle eines „wahren Partners" spielen, „mit eigenem Gesicht, eigenem Programm und eigenen Positionen". Eine weitere Bestimmung des politischen und ideologischen Standortes der Partei soll der ebenfalls für das Frühjahr 1990 einberufene Sonderkongreß des BZNS bringen[61a]).

---

[59]) Christov, Ch.: BZNS i razvitieto na socialističeskoto selsko stopanstvo (Der BZNS und die Entwicklung der sozialistischen Landwirtschaft), in: NTAONSU (Anm. 21), (1983) 2, S. 61–112.

[60]) 1976 stellte sie z.B. zwei der damals 146 Vorsitzenden von APK und 57 stellvertretende Vorsitzende: Černejko, G. A.: BZNS – vernyi sojuznik bolgarskich kommunistov (Der BZNS – ein wahrer Bundesgenosse der bulgarischen Kommunisten). Moskau 1979, S. 144.

[61]) Vgl. Zarčev, J.: Meždunarodnata dejnost na Bălgarskija zemedelski naroden săjuz (1956–1967) (Die internationale Tätigkeit des BZNS 1956–1967), in: III BKP (Anm. 25). 24 (1970), S. 69–107; Tančev, P.: Meždunarodnata dejnost na BZNS v služba na mira (Die internationale Tätigkeit des BZNS im Dienste des Friedens), in: Meždunarodni otnošenija. 11 (1982) 5; Černejko (Anm. 60), S. 149–169.

[61a]) Zemedelsko zname. 24.11.1989; 25.11.1989; 2.12.1989; 3.12.1989.

c) Organisation und Mitgliederstruktur

Anders als beispielsweise die DBD in der DDR, die sich in ihrem Statut ausdrücklich zum Organisationsprinzip des Demokratischen Zentralismus bekennt[62]), hat der BZNS auf eine formelle Übernahme dieser Organisationsform seines kommunistischen Bündnispartners verzichtet. Seine Organisationsstruktur spiegelt jedoch das Bemühen wider, die traditionellen innerparteilichen Institutionen des BZNS mit einer an der Praxis der BKP orientierten Binnenorganisation zu verbinden[63]). Aufgebaut ist der BZNS – anders als die BKP – ausschließlich auf dem Territorialprinzip. Grundorganisation ist die sogenannte *družba* – die „Kameradschaft", die aus mindestens fünf Parteimitgliedern bestehen muß. Auf die örtliche *družba* aufbauend werden gemäß der territorialen Verwaltungsstruktur des Landes Gemeinde-*družbi* und Bezirks-*družbi* gebildet.

Höchstes Organ des BZNS ist der Parteikongreß, der aus Delegierten, die auf den Wahlversammlungen der Bezirks-Organisationen gewählt werden, gebildet wird. Parteikongresse finden – ähnlich wie bei der BKP und in der Regel kurz nach deren Parteitagen – alle fünf Jahre statt. Der Kongreß wählt den sogenannten „Leitenden Rat" (*Upravitelen săvet*), der die Arbeit der Partei zwischen den Kongressen leitet, sowie die Revisions- und Kontrollkommission. Die Zahl der Mitglieder des „Leitenden Rates" wird vom Parteitag bestimmt; ihre Zahl ist in den vergangenen 40 Jahren nahezu ständig erhöht worden und betrug zuletzt 154 Vollmitglieder und 111 Kandidaten. Der „Leitende Rat" wählt seinerseits als engeres Führungsorgan der Partei einen „Ständigen Ausschuß" (*Postojanno prisăstvie*), bestehend aus dem „Sekretär des BZNS" als dem Parteivorsitzenden, gegenwärtig fünf Sekretären für die operative Tätigkeit des „Ständigen Ausschusses" sowie sieben Mitgliedern. Falls die Verabschiedung zentraler Beschlüsse zwischen den Parteitagen notwendig ist, kann der sogenannte „Oberste Unions-Rat" (*Vărchoven săjuzen săvet*) einberufen werden, der sich aus Delegierten der Bezirks-Organisationen, den Mitgliedern und Kandidaten des „Leitenden Rates" sowie denen der Revisions- und Kontrollkommission zusammensetzt[64]). Derartige Konferenzen des „Obersten Unionsrates" finden zumeist im Anschluß an entsprechende „Nationale Parteikonferenzen" der BKP und unter gleicher Themenstellung statt.

Mitglied des BZNS kann jeder werden, sofern er das 18. Lebensjahr vollendet hat. Vorrangig werden allerdings Personen aufgenommen, die im landwirtschaftlichen Milieu, in APK, Betrieben der verarbeitenden Nahrungsmittelindustrie oder in landwirtschaftlichen wissenschaftlichen und Verwaltungsinstitutionen tätig sind. Hingegen ist die Aufnahme städtischer Personenkreise limitiert[65]). Die Pflichten des BZNS-Mitglieds sind eng an jene im BKP-Statut angelehnt. Das Statut des BZNS

---

[62]) Vgl. Zimmermann, H. (Hrsg.): DDR-Handbuch. Bd. 1. Bonn 1985, S. 247.

[63]) Auch bulgarische Autoren betonen trotz der noch bestehenden Unterschiede die tendenzielle Annäherung in der innerparteilichen Arbeitsweise beider Organisationen: Tančev, E.: Săvmestnata rabota meždu BKP i BZNS i usăvăršenstvuvaneto na socialističeskata demokracija (Die gemeinsame Arbeit zwischen BKP und BZNS und die Vervollkommnung der sozialistischen Demokratie), in: Novo vreme. (1979) 12, S. 51; Aslanov (Anm. 44), S. 378.

[64]) Eine Zusammenfassung der Organisationsstruktur bei Černejko (Anm. 60), S. 11 ff.

[65]) Aslanov (Anm. 44), S. 369 f.

verlangt zwar kein Bekenntnis zum Marxismus-Leninismus, verpflichtet die Mitglieder aber auf die aktive Beteiligung am Aufbau des Sozialismus. Anders als die BKP kennt die Bauernpartei allerdings keine Bürgschaft bei der Mitgliedsbewerbung.

Die *Mitgliederentwicklung* spiegelt letztlich den Weg des BZNS von einer unabhängigen Gegenkraft zur BKP mit breiter Basis hin zu einer politisch zweitrangigen Bündnisorganisation der BKP wider. Der große Mitgliederbestand von über 300 000 im Frühjahr 1945 wurde dabei nach der Ausschaltung des Petkov-Flügels auf nicht viel mehr als 100 000 reduziert. Erst nach dem Aprilplenum von 1956 konnte der BZNS seinen während der Červenkov-Ära reduzierten Mitgliederbestand wenigstens etwas wieder aufforsten. Die Kongreßprotokolle des BZNS geben dabei den Mitgliederbestand seit 1957 konstant mit 120 000 an. Die wissenschaftliche Literatur hat demgegenüber mit Verweis auf das Parteiarchiv davon abweichende Mitgliederzahlen genannt, die der nachstehenden Tabelle zugrunde liegen. Auch diese Zahlen legen jedoch seit Ende der 50er Jahre eine nur geringe Fluktuation offen. Nach dem Sturz Živkovs wurde eingestanden, daß die BKP einen ungeregelten Mitgliederzuwachs über die Größe von 120 000 hinaus nicht zu akzeptieren bereit war.

Ähnlich spärlich wie die Angaben über den absoluten Mitgliederfluß sind auch die zugänglichen Informationen über das *soziale Profil* der BZNS-Mitglieder. Zumindest über den Anteil der Frauen an der Mitgliedschaft liegen dabei Angaben vor. Sie zeigen, daß der ursprünglich marginale Frauenanteil, der noch in den 60er Jahren bei nur knapp 5 % lag in den 70er und 80er Jahren substantiell gesteigert werden konnte. Die dabei mittlerweile erreichten 17 % sind freilich von einer auch nur annähernd proportionalen Vertretung der Frauen, gemessen an ihrem Anteil an der Gesamtzahl der landwirtschaftlich Beschäftigten, noch weit entfernt. Wenig läßt sich hingegen über die Sozialstruktur des BZNS aussagen. Entsprechend ihrer Aufnahmekriterien ist die Partei dabei nach wie vor eine fast ausschließlich auf dem Dorfe präsente Organisation. Trotz des permanenten Rückgangs des Anteils der Agrarbevölkerung sind nach wie vor 70 % der Parteimitglieder in der Landwirtschaft beschäftigt. Die soziale Zusammensetzung der Mitgliedschaft hat sich dabei parallel zur Umstrukturierung des Agrarsektors nach dem II. Weltkrieg verändert. Der Übergang zur Kollektivierung schloß dabei bereits am Ende der 40er Jahre jene, die unter dem weit gefaßten Begriff des „Kulaken" subsummiert wurden, von einer Mitgliedschaft aus. Zugleich wurden Kooperativbauern bei der Aufnahme bevorzugt. Im Ergebnis veränderte sich die Mitgliederstruktur bereits Anfang der 50er Jahre hin zu der einer Partei, in der neben Kooperativbauern, die 1951 allein 63 % der Mitglieder ausmachten, praktisch nur Kleinbauern vertreten waren[66]. Mit der Vollendung der Kollektivierung am Ende der 50er Jahre homogenisierte sich die Mitgliederstruktur des BZNS noch weiter. Für die 60er Jahre vorliegende Angaben zeigen dabei einen leichten Anstieg der Arbeiter und Angestellten zu Lasten der in der landwirtschaftlichen Produktion beschäftigten Mitglieder (vgl. *Tabelle 7*). Auch die Arbeiter und Angestellten sind jedoch innerhalb des weiteren Bereichs der Landwirtschaft beschäftigt, entweder in verarbeitenden Betrieben oder als Angestellte der APK, landwirtschaftlicher Behörden und wissenschaftlicher Einrichtungen.

---

[66] 80 % der 1951 noch existierenden Privatbauern unter den BZNS-Mitgliedern verfügten lediglich über bis zu 5 ha: Zarčev, BZNS 1944/62 (Anm. 43), S. 237.

Tabelle 7: Sozialprofil der BZNS-Mitglieder (in % der Mitglieder)

	Mitglieder	in der Landw. Beschäftigte	davon in TKZS	davon in DZS	Arbeiter	Angestellte
1962	112358	76,3	70,8	5,5	9,1	14,5
1966	144072	71,7	61,7	10,0	10,9	17,4
1971	116363	64,8	51,6	13,2	15,4	19,8

Quelle: Zarčev, Delo (Anm. 44), S. 145.

Für die späten 70er und 80er Jahre liegen keine nach Sozialgruppen getrennten Angaben mehr vor. Insgesamt dürfte aber entsprechend der allgemeinen Deagrarisierung und der Industrialisierung der landwirtschaftlichen Arbeit der Anteil der Angestellten angestiegen sein. Darauf deuten auch die wenigen Angaben über die berufliche Struktur der Beschäftigten hin, die einen stetigen Anstieg des Qualifikationsniveaus der Mitglieder, d. h. eine Zunahme der an Maschinen Beschäftigten und Spezialisten, suggerieren. Unverändert groß aber dürfte immer noch der Anteil an weniger und unqualifizierten Arbeitskräften unter den Mitgliedern sein.

d) Beteiligung an politischen Institutionen

Ähnlich wie in den beiden anderen sozialistischen Staaten DDR und Polen, in denen noch Bauernparteien existieren, ist auch der BZNS an den bestehenden politischen Institutionen in einer ebenso gesicherten wie unveränderbaren Weise beteiligt. Seine Repräsentanz in den Vertretungsorganen ist dabei nicht Ergebnis des Wahlausgangs, sondern des im Vorwege zwischen BKP und BZNS festgelegten Proporzes. Der numerische Anteil der Bauernpartei an den Parlamenten suggeriert dabei ein politisches Gewicht, das sie aufgrund ihrer programmatischen und politischen Abhängigkeit von der BKP de facto nicht besitzt. In der NSb ist die Partei dabei seit den 50er Jahren praktisch konstant mit etwa 1/4 der Abgeordneten vertreten (vgl. *Tabelle 10*). Innerhalb der obersten Organe des Staates ist sie in den 70er Jahren durch 4–5 Mitglieder des DS sowie durch 3–4 Mitglieder der Regierung repräsentiert. Mit Georgi Trajkov als stellvertretendem Ministerratsvorsitzenden sowie durch seine Nachfolger Petăr Tančev und den jetzigen Parteichef Angel Dimitrov als stellvertretende DS-Vorsitzende ist der BZNS stets auch mit einem formell ranghohen Staatsamt bedacht worden.

Auf kommunaler Ebene liegt der Repräsentanzanteil des BZNS bei etwa 20%, weist jedoch in den letzten Jahren sogar einen leicht rückläufigen Anteil auf (vgl. *Tabelle 11*). Gleiches gilt für die Übernahme exekutiver Funktionen, bei denen der BZNS wesentlich geringer bedacht wird, als dies sein Parlamentsanteil verlangen würde. Insbesondere Leitungsfunktionen wie die Position eines Vorsitzenden regionaler Exekutivorgane der Volksräte (*narodni săveti*) oder Bürgermeister werden zum ganz überwiegenden Teil mit BKP-Funktionären besetzt.

Bis zum Sturz Živkovs konnte der BZNS kaum als Partei sensu stricto begriffen werden. Der Verzicht auf eigenständige ideologische und programmatische Akzentuierungen, die nicht frei fluktuierender Bewegung überlassene Mitgliederzahl sowie die im Vorwege durch Absprache festgelegte Repräsentanz in politischen Institutionen machten ihn eher zu einer korporativen Institution, der im Gefüge des politischen Systems die Funktion arbeitsteiliger Umsetzung der Politik der BKP zukam. Zugleich übernahm er Sozialisationsfunktionen für agrarische Sozialgruppen, die immer noch für die BKP weniger leicht zu erreichen sind. Politischer Einfluß beschränkte sich dabei vornehmlich auf fachlich-konsultative Kompetenz und spiegelte sich nicht in einer autonomen Interessenrepräsentanz agrarischer Bevölkerungsgruppen wider. Die politischen Veränderungen nach dem Sturz Živkovs haben für den BZNS nunmehr zweifelsohne einen größeren Handlungsspielraum eröffnet. Trotz der immer noch lebendigen Traditionen des Agrarpopulismus dürfte es ihm aber nicht leicht fallen, das in den Jahren der totalen Subordination unter die BKP verspielte Vertrauen zurückzugewinnen.

3. „Informelle Gruppen" und neue politische Parteien

Anders als in Polen oder der ČSSR fehlte es im Bulgarien der Nachkriegszeit an vergleichbaren dissidentischen Traditionen und entsprechend ausgebildeten Gruppen und Organisationen. Gleichwohl kam es auch hier schon vor dem Sturze Živkovs am 10.11.1989 als Reflex auf die Entwicklung in der Sowjetunion und in anderen osteuropäischen Ländern zur Gründung „informeller Gruppen". Obwohl Živkov selbst im Rahmen seines verbalen Bekenntnisses zur *perestrojka* und zu politischen Reformen die Legitimität nicht von der Partei kontrollierter Gruppen und Vereinigungen mehrfach anerkannt und auf der Nationalen Parteikonferenz im Januar 1988 sogar prophezeit hatte, daß diese künftig „aus dem Boden schießen werden wie die Pilze nach dem Regen", zeigte die Parteiführung in der Praxis diesen Gruppen gegenüber keinerlei Dialogbereitschaft und reagierte ausschließlich repressiv auf deren Aktivitäten. Der Sturz Živkovs war denn auch nicht, wie in der DDR oder der ČSSR, Ergebnis eines von den informellen Gruppen getragenen Massenprotestes, gleichwohl aber haben auch sie durch ihre Existenz und ihre insbesondere im Laufe des Jahres 1989 gestiegenen Aktivitäten zweifelsohne mit dazu beigetragen, daß sich der Außenminister Petăr Mladenov zusammen mit anderen Spitzenfunktionären am 10.11.1989 zum Schlag gegen Živkov entschloß. Nachdem mit dem Rücktritt Živkovs der Weg für eine mehr oder weniger unbehinderte Aktivität der „informellen Gruppen" freigeworden ist, ist deren politisches Gewicht weiter gewachsen, wie mehrere von ihnen organisierte Massenkundgebungen im November und Dezember 1989 gezeigt haben. Größe und organisatorische Struktur der Gruppen sind allerdings gegenwärtig noch instabil, ihr programmatisches Profil noch unscharf, und sie selbst befinden sich noch im Prozeß der Definition ihres künftigen Charakters und ihrer Stellung im politischen System. Von ähnlichen Organisationen in Ungarn, der ČSSR oder der DDR unterscheiden sich die „informellen Gruppen" Bulgariens aber nicht nur durch ihre vorerst noch geringere Größe und organisatorische Struktur sowie ihre weniger präzise ausgerichtete programmatische Festlegung, sondern nicht zuletzt auch durch die bei ihnen noch wesentlich geringere Distanzierung von der regierenden Kommunistischen Partei. Unter der Führung mancher der bestehenden Gruppen finden sich nicht wenige Parteimitglieder, die ihre Organisation nicht oder noch nicht als organisatorische und ideologische Konkurrenz zur BKP verstehen.

Von besonderer Bedeutung im Spektrum der seit 1988 entstandenen „informellen Gruppen" sind dabei vor allem der „Klub für die Unterstützung von *glasnost'* und *perestrojka*" (mittlerweile umbenannt in „Klub für *glasnost'* und Demokratie"/*Klub za podkrepa na glasnostta i preustrojstvoto* bzw. *Klub za glasnostta i demokracija*), die Umweltschutzorganisation *Eko-glasnost* sowie die „Unabhängige Gewerkschaft *Podkrepa*". Daneben bestehen noch eine Reihe weiterer, zumeist kleinerer Vereinigungen zum Schutze von Menschenrechten, religiösen Freiheiten und Umwelt.

Der „Klub für die Unterstützung von *glasnost'* und *perestrojka*" wurde zu Beginn des Jahres 1988 von namhaften Intellektuellen und Akademikern (darunter die Schriftsteller Blaga Dimitrova, Radoj Ralin, Georgi Mišev) gegründet; viele seiner führenden Vertreter gehörten bzw. gehören gleichzeitig der BKP an. Der „Klub" verstand sich zunächst nicht als politische Organisation, sondern als intellektuelles Diskussionsforum, das mit seinen Aktivitäten, Arbeitsgruppen, Vorträgen und Diskussionen eine Art intellektuelle Gegenöffentlichkeit schaffen wollte, um die politische Führung zur Einlösung ihrer *perestrojka*- und Reform-Versprechen zu veranlassen. Zumindest für einen Teil seiner Aktivisten war der „Klub" somit zunächst weniger dissidentische System-Opposition als durchaus system-loyale „pressure group" für mehr Reformbereitschaft der Parteispitze. Gleichwohl reagierte die Parteiführung auf den „Klub" rein repressiv. Ein öffentliches Auftreten wurde ihm untersagt, mehrere seiner Mitglieder wurden aus der Partei ausgeschlossen und polizeilichen Verhören unterzogen. Vor weitergehender strafrechtlicher und gerichtlicher Verfolgung dürfte sie wohl nur der Bekanntheitsgrad der „Klub"-Aktivisten sowie die Gefahr internationalen Protestes bewahrt haben. Nach dem Sturze Živkovs ist der „Klub" zu einem gewichtigen Faktor der Demokratiebewegung geworden. Entsprechend der Heterogenität seiner Mitglieder ist das ideologische Profil des „Klubs" gegenwärtig allerdings noch recht diffus. Hinter Forderungen nach Pluralismus, Mehrparteiensystem und Rechtsstaatlichkeit verbergen sich noch unterschiedliche ideologische Konzepte, die von einem demokratisch erneuerten Sozialismus in Anlehnung an die reformerischen Kräfte in der Partei bis hin zu einem völligen Bruch mit sozialistischen Politik- und Wirtschaftskonzepten reichen. Umstritten ist gegenwärtig auch noch die Frage des künftigen organisatorischen Charakters des „Klubs", d. h. ob er intellektuelles Diskussionsforum bleiben oder sich in Richtung auf eine Partei wandeln soll.

Nicht als Partei, sondern als auf Umweltschutz und Demokratie ausgerichtete Bürgerinitiative versteht sich auch die Organisation *Eko-glasnost*. Sie setzt die Arbeit des 1987 gebildeten „Komitees für Ruse" fort, das sich als erste größere Umweltschutzorganisation Bulgariens gegen die katastrophale ökologische Situation in der Donau-Stadt gewandt hatte. Namhafte Repräsentanten der Öffentlichkeit wie der Maler und ZK-Mitglied Svetlin Rusev, die Frau des Parlamentspräsidenten Stanko Todorov, Sonja Bakiš, sowie die Trainerin der bulgarischen Gymnastik-Nationalmannschaft, Neška Robeva, hatten sich damals dem Ruse-Komitee angeschlossen und waren dafür mit administrativen Gegenmaßnahmen bestraft worden. *Eko-glasnost* erregte mit seinen Aktivitäten vor allem im Frühjahr 1989 Aufmerksamkeit, als es die Anwesenheit des in Sofia tagenden KSZE-Forums für Umweltschutz für zunächst geduldete, dann von der Polizei brutal verhinderte Demonstrationen nutzte. Die mittlerweile auch rechtlich legalisierte Organisation, die nach eigenen Angaben ca. 800 Mitglieder hat, will freilich eine überparteiliche Bürgeriniative bleiben und versteht sich nicht als Konkurrenz zu den bestehenden Parteien.

Gleiches gilt für die „Unabhängige Gewerkschaft *Podkrepa*", deren Mitglieder in den letzten 1 1/2 Jahren der Ära Živkov strafrechtlicher Verfolgung und Repression ausgesetzt waren. Mehrere ihrer führenden Vertreter wurden im Frühjahr 1989 exiliert oder ins Gefängnis geschickt. Die Organisation, die sich am Vorbild der polnischen „Solidarität" orientiert, verfügt nach eigenen Angaben bereits über 15 000 Mitglieder (Stand: Dezember 1989).

Im Dezember 1989 haben sich die „informellen Gruppen" zu einer „Union der demokratischen Kräfte" zusammengeschlossen und damit einen ersten Schritt zu einer organisatorischen Vereinheitlichung getan. Programmatische Ziele der „Union", die sich als lockere Föderation von Einzelinitiativen begreift, sind: die Schaffung einer „bürgerlichen Gesellschaft", politischer Pluralismus, ein Mehrparteiensystem, Gewerkschaftsfreiheit, Rechtsstaatlichkeit, Entideologisierung und Entpolitisierung von Armee, Miliz, Wissenschaft, Forschung, Schulen und Hochschulen, Trennung von Partei und Staat sowie eine auf Gleichberechtigung aller Eigentumsformen basierende Wirtschaftsordnung. Ob es die „Union" freilich schaffen wird, bis zu den für Mai 1990 angekündigten „freien Wahlen" im ganzen Land ein echtes Gegengewicht zur BKP zu werden, bleibt abzuwarten.

Unabhängig von den „informellen Gruppen", die sich fast durchweg nicht als politische Parteien verstehen, haben sich in jüngster Zeit auch einige der 1948 von der BKP aufgelösten bzw. gleichgeschalteten Parteien neu gegründet, so z. B. die BRSDP, die von zwei ehemaligen Abgeordneten der BRSDP in der NSb neu ins Leben gerufen wurde, die ebenfalls 1948 aufgelöste „Radikal-Demokratische Partei" oder eine neue „Bauernpartei-Nikola Petkov". Inwieweit es sich hierbei allerdings bislang nur um Parteigründungen auf dem Papier handelt, ist gegenwärtig noch nicht zu erkennen.

III. Die Massenorganisationen

Zu den Massenorganisationen zählen im engeren Sinne die OF, die BPS sowie der DKMS, im weiteren Sinne noch der BNŽS (Frauenverband) sowie die „Dimitrov'sche Pionier-Organisation *Septemvrijče*" und die *Čavdar*-Kinderorganisation.

Die zahlenmäßig größte dieser Massenorganisationen ist die OF (vgl. *Tabelle 8*).

Seit Ende 1941 hatte das Auslandsbüro der BKP sich bemüht, die zum Bündnis Bulgariens mit Deutschland und zur Regierung in Opposition stehenden politischen Kräfte unter dem organisatorischen Dach einer Volksfront zu vereinen. Die Bestrebungen der BKP trafen zwar bei Teilen der BRSDP und des *Zveno* sowie bei dem von Nikola Petkov vertretenen *Pladne*-Flügel des BZNS auf Resonanz, nicht jedoch bei den damals wichtigsten bürgerlichen Oppositionskräften, der DP Mušanovs, der NP Burovs, der RP sowie des *Vrabča*-Flügels des BZNS[67]). Auch die formelle Institutio-

---

[67]) Vgl. hierzu Bell, Bulgarian Communist Party (Anm. 41), S. 66–73.

Tabelle 8: Mitgliederentwicklung der Massenorganisationen (in Klammern Organisationsgrad der entsprechenden Zielgruppe)

Jahr	OF	BPS	DKMS
1945	34 652	200 313	50 000
1947		576 000 (77 %)*	437 000
1948	950 000	722 968 (94 %)	568 000
1950	2 113 000	890 000 (92 %)	
1958	3 321 770 (58 %)	1 149 248	
1961	3 372 320 (64 %)	1 583 565 (94 %)	1 100 000 (70 %)
1981	4 388 000	2 984 567 (95 %)	1 500 000 (90 %)
1986		3 100 000 (95 %)	1 500 000 (90 %)

Quelle: Atanasov (s. Tab. 1), S. 17; Atanasov, A.: Rabotničeskata klasa v Bǎlgarija 1948–1958 (Die Arbeiterklasse in Bulgarien 1948–1958). Sofia 1987, S. 114; Otečestven front. 12.2. 1957; Istorija na mladežkite dvizenija v Bǎlgarija (Geschichte der Jugendbewegung in Bulgarien). Sofia 1972, S. 451 f.; Otečestven front. 15.6. 77, S. 6; Boev, Aprilskata linija (Anm. 75), S. 25 ff.

nalisierung eines Leistungsorgans in Gestalt eines durch Repräsentanten der BKP, BRSDP, des *Zveno* und der *Pladne*-Agrarier besetzten „Nationalrats der OF" im August 1943 vermochte der Front zunächst kein wirkliches politisches Gewicht zu verleihen[68]). Erst in den Wochen vor dem Staatsstreich am 9. 9. 1944 gewann sie unter den bürgerlichen Oppositionskräften stärkeres Gehör, obwohl sich auch dann kein namhafter Politiker aus ihren Reihen der OF offen anschließen mochte. Erst jetzt begann sich auch die organisatorische Basis der Front zu verbreitern. In den letzten August-Tagen wurden vermehrt OF-Komitees gegründet, die während des 9. 9. 1944 die Leitung des Staatsstreiches übernehmen sollten[69]). Nach dem Machtwechsel wurden dann innerhalb kürzester Zeit überall derartige Komitees gebildet, die – obwohl sie den Bündnischarakter der OF widerspiegeln sollten – von der BKP dominiert wurden und praktisch überall die lokale Verwaltungsgewalt übernahmen. Im Frühjahr 1945 stellte die BKP 54 % der Komitee-Mitglieder, der BZNS 33 %, und der Rest verteilte sich auf die BRSDP, *Zveno* und Parteilose[70]). Aus Rücksichtnahme auf die Alliierten und um die Bündnispartner im Inneren nicht durch Revolutionsfurcht zu verschrecken, bremste die BKP allerdings bereits im Oktober 1944 regionale „ultralinke" Tendenzen, die Komitees der OF zu rein kommunistischen Revolutionsorganen zu machen. Sie ordnete die abgestuft paritätische Besetzung der Komitees mit allen OF-Parteien an, eine Regelung, die freilich nicht „dogmatisch" verstanden werden und bestehende Komitees nicht um jeden Preis grundlegend neu politisch

---

[68]) Diese gestehen auch bulgarische Historiker ein: Šarlanov, D.: Otečestvenijat front i naj-novata istorija na Bǎlgarija (Die OF und die neueste Geschichte Bulgariens), in: Istoričeski pregled. 23 (1967) 2, S. 9 f. Vgl. ferner zur OF 1944–1948: Kopylov, A. A.: Otečestvennyj front i narodno-demokratičeskaja revoljucija v Bol'garii (Die OF und die volksdemokratische Revolution in Bulgarien). L'vov 1985.

[69]) Okrǎžno No. 4 na CK na BKP (26.8.1944) (Rundschreiben Nr. 4 des ZK der BKP (26.8.1944)), in: Bǎlgarskata dǎržavnost (Anm. 3), S. 355.

[70]) Aslanov, (Anm. 44), S. 357.

umbilden sollte. Zugleich setzte sie die alten lokalen Verwaltungsorgane wieder in ihre Funktionen ein und untersagte den OF-Komitees, die lokale Verwaltungsgewalt auszuüben. Die OF sollte sich stattdessen auf eine Kontrolle der lokalen Organe beschränken[71]). Gleichwohl blieben sie auch so die letztlich entscheidenden lokalen Machtorgane. Sie entschieden über die Besetzung der lokalen Amts- und Mandatsträger, und sie leiteten und überwachten die ersten Säuberungsaktionen in Staat, Justiz und Polizei.

Die BKP gab der OF von Anbeginn an einen Doppelcharakter. Obwohl sie ein formelles Bündnis mehrerer Parteien war, sollte die Front doch keine Koalition im klassischen Sinne sein, sondern zugleich auch eine einheitliche Bewegung, die die politische und soziale Neuordnung Bulgariens vollenden sollte. Ungeachtet ihres formellen Koalitionscharakters war die OF somit doch vor allem gedacht als Instrument der sozialen und politischen Revolutionierung des Landes.

Bis ins Jahr 1948 hinein blieb der Charakter der OF als Koalition mehrerer formell unabhängiger Parteien jedoch noch bestehen, auch wenn die Opposition bereits weitgehend ausgeschaltet und die Bündnispartner innerhalb der OF auf eine Statistenrolle degradiert waren. Die politische Zäsur für die OF kam, ähnlich wie für das gesamte politische System, mit dem von der Kominform-Gründungstagung ausgehenden Kurs forcierter Sowjetisierung. Nunmehr, so wurde als Folge dieser Radikalisierung der BKP-Politik beschlossen, müsse sich die OF wandeln von einer auf formeller Parität beruhenden Koalition hin zu einer „einheitlichen gesellschaftspolitischen Organisation" mit einer „verbindlichen Disziplin", einer Leitung und einem Programm, basierend auf dem Organisationsprinzip des Demokratischen Zentralismus[72]). Dabei war allerdings zunächst offenkundig noch nicht an eine Auflösung der nichtkommunistischen Parteien gedacht. Daß nurmehr ein gutes Jahr nach dem II. OF-Kongreß im Februar 1948, auf dem das neue Konzept einer einheitlichen politischen Massenorganisation durchgesetzt worden war, bis auf den BZNS dann trotzdem alle anderen Parteien in der OF aufgegangen waren, lag sicherlich zum einen an der weiteren ideologischen Verhärtung des BKP-Kurses im Gefolge des jugoslawisch-sowjetischen Konflikts, zum anderen aber auch daran, daß diese Parteien, die ihr politisches Gewicht ohnehin schon lange eingebüßt hatten, nach der Umwandlung der Front praktisch zum funktionslosen Anachronismus geworden waren.

In den folgenden Jahren des Červenkov-Stalinismus degenerierte die OF zunehmend zu einem reinen Transmissions- und Mobilisierungsorgan, dem selbst innerhalb einer solchen Funktionsbestimmung praktisch kaum Raum für ein Eigenleben gestattet wurde. Die OF-Komitees wurden letztlich auf die Rolle von technischen Hilfsorganen der lokalen Volksräte reduziert[73]). Ihre organisatorische Tätigkeit verflachte, ihre Mitgliederzahl stagnierte, und Červenkov postulierte auf dem III. OF-Kongreß im Mai 1952 offen die schrittweise Verschmelzung der OF mit den lokalen Volksräten[74]).

---

[71]) Kostov (Anm. 5), S. 28f; Bălgarskata dăržavnost (Anm. 3), S. 377ff.
[72]) Dimitrov, G.: Otečestven front, negovoto razvitie i predstojaštite mu zadači (Die OF, ihre Entwicklung und die vor ihr stehenden Aufgaben), in: Novo vreme. (1948) 1, S. 31.
[73]) Dokov, D.: Charakter i rolja na narodnite săveti u nas (Charakter und Rolle der Volksräte bei uns), in: Novo vreme. (1953) 5, S. 50.
[74]) Todorov, G.: Istoričeskoto značenie na Aprilskija plenum na CK na BKP za povišavane

Wie für das gesamte politische System, so bedeutete auch für die OF das Aprilplenum des ZK der BKP 1956 zwar keinen substantiellen Rollenwandel, wohl aber einen graduellen Abbau der hyperzentralistischen Gängelung. Die Partei hielt dabei prinzipiell an dem seit dem II. OF-Kongreß 1948 bestimmenden Verständnis von der OF als Transmissions- und Mobilisierungsorgan für die Parteipolitik fest, befreite die Komitees der Front allerdings von dem rein exekutiven Unterordnungsverhältnis gegenüber den lokalen Volksräten[75]). Der Rahmen operativ selbständig zu bearbeitender Aufgaben wurde erweitert, und auch die in der Červenkov-Zeit stagnierende Mitgliederzahl der Front wurde nach 1956 sprunghaft gesteigert. Allein zwischen 1957 und 1963 erhöhte die OF ihren Mitgliederbestand um 50%[76]). Mit ihren heute über 4,3 Mio. Kollektiv- und Individualmitgliedern[77]) sind mittlerweile ca. 2/3 aller Wahlberechtigten in der OF erfaßt. Auch nach dem Ende der Červenkov-Ära haben alle Beschlüsse der Partei über Rolle und Funktion der OF sich bis 1989 im Rahmen eines Funktionsverständnisses bewegt, das ihr die Rolle eines die Partei bei der Realisierung ihrer Aufgaben mobilisatorisch unterstützenden Organs zuweist[78]).

Die wesentlichen politischen Aufgaben der Front sind dabei neben der Vorbereitung, Organisation und Durchführung der Nominierungs- und Wahlprozedur bei den Wahlen zu den Vertretungsorganen vornehmlich erzieherischer, mobilisierender und kontrollierender Natur. Auf dem Gebiet einer parteikonformen Sozialisation hat sich die OF vor allem bei Alphabetisierungskursen (in den 50er und frühen 60er Jahren) engagiert, bei Atheismus- und Anti-Alkoholismus-Kampagnen sowie im Rahmen der vielfältigen Bemühungen von Partei und Staat, die sogenannte „sozialistische Lebensweise" in der Bevölkerung zu verankern. Neben den lokalen Volksräten und Gewerkschaften und gemeinsam mit ihnen beteiligt sich die OF zudem an der informativen Vermittlung der Parteipolitik „nach unten" und an der Organisation von Mobilisierungsaktionen zur Erfüllung dieser Politik, so vor allem in der Organisation von freiwilligen Arbeitseinsätzen u. ä. Durch die Beteiligung an Kommissionen der lokalen Volksräte sowie durch eigene Organe übernimmt sie zudem eine Reihe von Kontrollfunktionen, vor allem im Bereich der infrastrukturellen Versorgung und Leistungen[79]). Ihre wohl bedeutendste formelle Kompetenz liegt in dem ihr zusammen mit den Gewerkschaften in Art. 80 der Verfassung von 1971 verliehenen Recht auf Gesetzesinitiative. Welche Rolle die OF in einem reformierten politischen System spielen soll, ist gegenwärtig noch nicht auszumachen. Ihre künftige Rolle

---

räkovodnata rolja na partijata (Die historische Bedeutung des Aprilplenums des ZK der BKP für die erhöhte Führungsrolle der Partei). Sofia 1964, S. 165f.

[75]) Otečestven front. 20.1.1957. Allgemein zur OF nach dem Aprilplenum Boev, B.: Aprilskata linija na BKP i razvitie na Otečestvenija front (Die April-Linie der BKP und die Entwicklung der OF), in: III BKP (Anm. 25). 34 (1976), S. 159–200.

[76]) Otečestven front. 15.3.1963.

[77]) Gewerkschaften, Jugendverband und andere gesellschaftliche Organisationen sind Kollektivmitglieder der OF, wohingegen Mitglieder der beiden Parteien nur eine individuelle Mitgliedschaft erwerben können: Statut der OF, Art. 3 und 4, in: Otečestven front. 17.3.1963.

[78]) Vgl. die entsprechenden Grundsatzdokumente der Partei in: Otečestven front. 25.7.1968 und 6.2.1976, sowie Art. 1 des Statuts der OF.

[79]) Vgl. Stojnov, I.: Otečestvenijat front i razvitieto na socialističeskata demokracija (Die OF und die Entwicklung der sozialistischen Demokratie), in: NTAONSU (Anm. 21). Serija partijno stroitelstvo. (1977) 96, S. 46–106; Šarlanov (Anm. 68), S. 25 ff.

dürfte ganz wesentlich davon abhängen, in welcher Weise das Recht auf die Bildung politischer Vereinigungen oder Parteien und deren Zulassung zu Wahlen künftig ausgestaltet werden wird. Eine politisch homogenisierende Rolle wie bisher dürfte mit dem angekündigten Ziel einer pluralistischen Umgestaltung der bulgarischen Gesellschaft allerdings wohl kaum mehr in Einklang zu bringen sein.

Organisatorisch ist die OF entsprechend dem auch für sie geltenden Prinzip des Demokratischen Zentralismus aufgebaut; d. h. auf die in den einzelnen Siedlungseinheiten bestehenden Grundorganisationen bauen die Territorialkomitees auf Gemeinde- und Bezirksebene auf. Höchstes Organ der OF ist der Kongreß, der den Nationalrat (*Nacionalen săvet*) als leitendes Gremium für die Zeit zwischen den Kongressen wählt. Der ca. 400 Personen umfassende Nationalrat schafft sich ein Präsidium für die Leitung der Organisation zwischen den Nationalratstagungen, das seinerseits das Büro, bestehend aus dem Vorsitzenden, stellvertretenden Vorsitzenden, Sekretären und sonstigen Mitgliedern, wählt. Entsprechend dem Anspruch, eine die gesamte Gesellschaft repräsentierende Massenorganisation zu sein, sind im Nationalrat die Repräsentanten der wichtigsten gesellschaftlichen Organisationen und berufsspezifischen Interessengruppen vertreten. Während freilich die Grundorganisationen der OF noch ein recht ausgewogenes Verhältnis zwischen Vertretern der BKP, des BZNS und der Parteilosen aufweisen, findet sich auf höherer Ebene bei der Zusammensetzung der Leitungsorgane die auch für die Parlamente typische 2/3-Mehrheit der BKP. Unter den exekutiven Spitzengremien ist die kommunistische Dominanz sogar noch weitaus größer[80]).

Ein im wesentlichen durch Transmissions- und Mobilisierungsfunktionen bestimmtes Funktionsverständnis lag bislag auch den *BPS* zugrunde. Auch sie waren vor allem in den Jahren des Stalinismus fast ausschließlich durch exekutive Aufgaben für die Realisierung der Wirtschaftspolitik der Partei bestimmt. Die Organisation von „Stachanov"-Aktionen und die Kontrolle über die Arbeitsdisziplin und Planerfüllung gehörten zu den wesentlichen innerbetrieblichen Aufgaben[81]). Echte Interessenvertretungsfunktionen vermochten die Gewerkschaften zumeist selbst dort nicht zu übernehmen, wo ihnen diese normativ zustanden, so etwa bei Verletzungen der Arbeitsgesetze.

Nach 1957 änderte sich dies insofern, als die innerbetrieblichen Kompetenzen der Gewerkschaften, vor allem im Bereich des Arbeitsschutzes und der Planungstätigkeit, erweitert wurden[82]). Der paradigmatische Funktionsrahmen, der letztlich für alle Gewerkschaften des Ostblocks (mit Einschränkungen für Ungarn und Polen) bestimmend ist, blieb dabei aber auch für die BPS intakt. Danach lassen sich die

---

[80]) Boev (Anm. 75), S. 173f., 183 (mit Zahlen von 1958 für die höheren Organe und von 1975 für die Grundorganisationen); RD. 23.12.1989 (von 358 Mitgliedern des Nationalrats 229 BKP, 62 BZNS, von 18 Mitgliedern des Exekutivbüros 14 BKP).

[81]) Rešenie na Politbjuro na CK na BKP (2.3.1950) (Beschluß des Politbüros des ZK der BKP (2.3.1950), in: BKP v rez. (Anm. 4). T. IV, S. 25ff; Prachov, T.: Profesionalni săjuzi – škola na komunizma (Die Gewerkschaften – Schule des Kommunismus), in: Novo vreme. (1953) 10, S. 45–62; Todorov (Anm. 74), S. 178ff.

[82]) BKP v rez. (Anm. 4). T. V, S. 106ff.

Aufgaben der bulgarischen Gewerkschaften, die heute mit über 3 Mio. Mitgliedern über 95 % der Beschäftigten organisieren, sechs Aufgabenbereichen zuordnen[83]):

1. Die Transmissionsfunktion für die Politik der Partei, wobei sich weder in programmatischen Grundsatzfragen noch in tagespolitischer Hinsicht substantielle Differenzen zwischen gewerkschaftlichen und Parteipositionen ausmachen lassen. Offen vorgetragene Problemlösungsvorschläge, die auch nur in Nuancen von den Vorstellungen der Partei abwichen, ließen sich in der Politik der bulgarischen Gewerkschaften bis 1989 nicht erkennen.

2. Die Mobilisierung der Beschäftigten für die Erfüllung der Produktionsziele steht auch nach der Abkehr von den Formen der Zwangsmobilisierung der Červenkov-Zeit im Zentrum der gewerkschaftlichen Tätigkeit. Im Unterschied zu früher haben die Gewerkschaften hierbei zwar nunmehr stärkere Beteiligungsrechte, z. B. bei der Erstellung der Gegenpläne, erhalten. Ihre Kompetenzen erstrecken sich aber nach wie vor zu einem guten Teil in erster Linie auf die Operationalisierung der von der Partei vorformulierten Ziele und auf die Organisation pseudopartizipativer Mitwirkungsformen, wie vor allem den Produktionsberatungen, die eher dekorative Kampagnen zur Erteilung von Produktionsaufträgen sind als echte Teilhabe-Gremien.

3. Die Interessenvertretungs- und Schutzfunktion für die Beschäftigten, die freilich nicht gedacht ist als offen ausgetragener Konflikt mit der Betriebsleitung, sondern als Konsens suchender Dialog. Gerade auf dem Gebiet der innerbetrieblichen Gestaltung der Arbeitsbedingungen bieten sich aber den Gewerkschaften eine Reihe normativer Mitgestaltungsmöglichkeiten, die ihre Rolle im Betrieb deutlich von der in den 50er Jahren abheben.

4. Partizipative und konsultative Aufgaben im Bereich der staatlichen Politik, die sich vor allem in der Hinzuziehung der Gewerkschaften bei der Gestaltung der Arbeits- und Sozialpolitik ausdrücken, für die die Gewerkschaften auch Gesetzgebungsinitiative besitzen.

5. Verwaltungsaufgaben in eigentlich gewerkschaftsfremden Aufgabenbereichen, so vor allem bei der Wohnungsvergabe und der Organisation von Urlaub.

6. Schließlich eine allgemeine Erziehungs- und Sozialisationsfunktion im Sinne der Zielsetzungen der Partei.

In jüngster Zeit ist dieses immer noch in erster Linie auf dem Transmissions- und Mobilisierungselement aufbauende Funktionsverständnis der BPS allerdings nachdrücklich in die Kritik geraten. Auf dem X. Gewerkschaftskongreß im April 1987 wurde in Anlehnung an ähnliche *perestrojka*-Diskussionen in den sowjetischen Gewerkschaften ein neues Rollenverständnis gefordert, das stärker als bisher die Funktion der Interessenvertretung in das Zentrum gewerkschaftlicher Tätigkeit rücke und der Gewerkschaft mehr Eigeninitiative in wirtschafts- und sozialpolitischen Fragen zugestehe. Das vom Kongreß verabschiedete Statut der BPS hielt jedoch wie alle seine

---

[83]) Vgl. die Bestimmungen im Kodeks na truda (Kodex der Arbeit), in: DV. (1986) 26, Art. 5, 34, 35, 36, 37, 39, 42, 399. Kritisch zur bisherigen Rolle der Gewerkschaften jetzt auch Petkov, K.: Profsäjuzite i samoupravlenieto (Gewerkschaften und Selbstverwaltung), in: Novo vreme. (1987) 11, S. 27–41.

Vorläufer an der führenden Rolle der Partei und an der Verpflichtung zur Erziehung der Werktätigen im Geiste der „Ergebenheit zur Partei" fest[84]). Für die Praxis hatten aber selbst derartige vorsichtige und systemimmanente Reformansätze keine spürbare Bedeutung. Die faktische *perestrojka*-Verweigerung der alten Živkov-Führung ließ derartiges nicht zu; bereits erarbeitete Reformvorschläge der Gewerkschaftsführung wurden, wie nach dem Sturze Živkovs im November 1989 verlautete, von der Parteiführung nicht akzeptiert, und den Gewerkschaften sei nicht einmal die Wahrnehmung der ihnen rechtlich zustehenden Mitwirkungsmöglichkeiten gestattet worden. Künftig jedoch, so kündigte die BPS-Führung nach dem 10.11.1989 an, werden die BPS sich als konsequent von Staat und Partei autonome Interessenvertretungsorganisation der Beschäftigten profilieren[85]). Als erster symbolischer Schritt der Trennung der Gewerkschaften von der Partei gab der Vorsitzende des BPS-Zentralrates, Petăr Djulgerov, nach dem Sturz Živkovs sein Mandat als Kandidat des Politbüros der BKP freiwillig auf. Inwieweit sich die bulgarischen Gewerkschaften künftig zu tatsächlich autonomen Organisationen werden wandeln können, dürfte aber wohl nicht nur vom Gang des angekündigten politischen Reformprozesses abhängen, sondern nicht zuletzt auch vom Schicksal der von der alten wie von der neuen Führung in Aussicht gestellten Wirtschaftsreform. Die Funktionslogik einer an Marktprinzipien orientierten Wirtschaft würde, ähnlich wie beispielsweise in Ungarn, auch in Bulgarien zwangsläufig die bisherigen Mobilisierungs- und Transmissionsaufgaben der Gewerkschaften überflüssig machen und ihre sozialpolitischen und Vertretungs-Aufgaben stärker fordern.

Aus der vom RMS im November 1947 durchgesetzten Zwangsvereinigung mit den Jugendorganisationen der Bauernpartei, der Sozialdemokraten und des *Zveno*[86]) entstand der *DKMS*. Wie in allen sozialistischen Staaten Osteuropas dient er der Funktion der politischen Sozialisation der Jugend, der Organisation von Freizeitaktivitäten und der Mobilisierung zu „freiwilligen" Arbeitseinsätzen. Darüber hinaus erfüllt die Mitgliedschaft und Aktivität im DKMS, der 1989 mit 1,5 Mio. Mitgliedern etwa 90 % der Jugendlichen erfaßte, nicht zuletzt auch die Funktion eines gegebenenfalls karrierefördernden Loyalitätsbekenntnisses. Ob er die ihm aufgetragene Sozialisationsfunktion jedoch wirklich erfüllt, daran sind seit längerem und mehrfach Zweifel geäußert worden. 1967 und 1978 bereits kritisierte die Parteiführung selbst „Bürokratismus", „Formalismus" und „Imitation der Partei" an der Arbeit des DKMS[87]). Im Zusammenhang mit der aktuellen *preustrojstvo*-Diskussion ist diese selbstkritische Bestandsaufnahme noch sehr viel schärfer ausgefallen. Kritisiert wurde vor allem die bürokratische Verfilzung des DKMS mit den Partei- und Staatsinstitutionen, die es ihm unmöglich gemacht hätte, sich als Interessenorgan der Jugend zu profilieren, der Mangel an innerorganisatorischem Leben sowie die an den Interessen der

---

[84]) RD. 8.4.1987; Trud. 16.4.1987.
[85]) Trud. 20.11.1989; 27.11.1989.
[86]) Itschenskaja, D.: Der Weg zur einheitlichen sozialistischen Jugendorganisation in Bulgarien 1944–1947, in: Jahrbuch für die Geschichte der sozialistischen Länder Europas. 23 (1979) 1, S. 103–127.
[87]) Narodna mladež. 1.12.1967; Otečestven front. 20.7.1978; Mitev, P.-E.: Mladežta i socialnata promjana (Die Jugend und der soziale Wandel). Sofia 1988.

Jugendlichen vorbeigehenden Aktivitäten der Organisation. Die ritualisierte und phrasenhafte ideologische Sozialisierung erweise sich als zunehmend wirkungslos. Skepsis und Distanziertheit der Jugendlichen gegenüber dem DKMS seien die Folge. Alternative Kommunikations- und Freizeitformen, vor allem im Zusammenhang mit musikalischen Subkulturen, die auch in Bulgarien in Konkurrenz zur parteioffiziellen Jugendorganisation stehen, scheinen sich in den 80er Jahren in zunehmendem Maße als attraktiver erwiesen zu haben für die Jugendlichen als die Aktivitätsofferten der offiziellen Jugendorganisation der Partei.

Ähnlich wie im Falle der Gewerkschaften blieb diese selbstkritische Lagebestimmung des DKMS in der Spätphase der Ära Živkov aber ohne spürbare praktische Konsequenzen und führte lediglich zu oberflächlichen innerorganisatorischen Reorganisationsversuchen, die das Prinzip, „der erste Gehilfe und die Reserve der Partei zu sein und unter deren Leitung zu arbeiten"[88]), nicht in Frage stellte. Nach dem Sturz Živkovs bemühte sich der DKMS zwar ebenfalls rasch darum, sich vom Image eines parteibestimmten Jugendverbandes zu befreien. Es scheint allerdings fraglich, ob er die in den vergangenen Jahren entstandenen Legitimationsdefizite kurzfristig wird wettmachen können. Die faktische Duldung unabhängiger Gruppen nach dem 10.11.1989 hat denn auch vor allem unter der studentischen Jugend sehr schnell zur Gründung eines unabhängigen Studentenverbandes geführt, der das bisherige Organisationsmonopol des DKMS in Frage stellt. Ähnlich wie in anderen Ländern Osteuropas auch, dürfte der in Gang gekommene Prozeß der Pluralisierung des politischen Lebens sich letztlich auch dann gegen den DKMS wenden, wenn sich dieser zu ihm bekennt.

IV. Die politischen Institutionen (Wahlen, Parlament, Regierung und lokale Vertretungsorgane)

Die einzigen *Wahlen* in Bulgarien, deren Ergebnis nicht im Vorwege feststand und bei denen es einer Opposition gestattet war, zu kandidieren oder doch zumindest indirekt das Wahlgeschehen zu beeinflussen, waren die zur XXVI. NSb am 18.11.1945 sowie die zur ersten VNSb der Republik am 27.10.1946. Vergleichbares gilt auch für das Referendum über die Abschaffung der Monarchie am 8.9.1946. Alle späteren Wahlgänge, seien es die zur NSb oder zu den regionalen Vertretungsorganen, fallen in die Kategorie gelenkter Abstimmungen ohne die Möglichkeit, für oppositionelle Kandidaten zu votieren oder wenigstens zwischen mehreren Kandidaten auszuwählen.

Aber auch die ersten beiden Nachkriegswahlen entsprachen in ihrem formalen Procedere und vor allem wegen der sie begleitenden Behinderungen der Opposition kaum den Maßstäben parlamentarischer Demokratie. Für die ersten Wahlen nach dem September-Staatstreich im November 1945 hatte die Regierung der OF zwar durch die Herabsenkung des Alters für das aktive Wahlrecht von 21 auf 18 und für das passive von 30 auf 23 Jahre den Kreis der Wahlberechtigten gegenüber der formal

---

[88]) Vgl. Narodna mladež. 14.5.1987, 16.5.1987, 30.9.1987, 6.10.1987.

noch in Kraft befindlichen alten Tărnovo-Verfassung erheblich erweitert[89]). Dieser formalen Demokratisierung des Wahlsystems stand jedoch das von der OF auf Betreiben der BKP vereinbarte proporzdemokratische Wahlverfahren entgegen, mit dem die zur OF gehörenden vier Parteien im Vorwege die Mandate unter sich aufteilten. Lediglich die der Front angehörenden politischen Parteien sollten auf einer Einheitsliste zur Wahl zugelassen werden, und die zu vergebenen 276 Mandate sollten nach einem Schlüssel von je 94 Mandate für BKP und BZNS, 48 für den *Zveno*, 32 für die BRSDP und 8 Mandate für Parteilose verteilt werden[90]). Das Bemühen der BKP, die Wahlen auf diesem Wege zu einem reinen Plebiszit für die OF zu machen, scheiterte jedoch am Protest des oppositionellen BZNS-Flügels um Nikola Petkov (BZNS-NP) und des von der BRSDP abgespaltenen Oppositionsflügels um Lulčev. Auf Druck der Westalliierten, die sich an die Seite Petkovs gestellt hatten, mußte die BKP die ursprünglich für den August 1945 vorgesehenen Wahlen auf den November verschieben, die Parteien Petkovs und Lulčevs legalisieren und auch der DP Mušanovs und einem von der RP abgespaltenen oppositionellen Flügel (RP (*obedinenie*)) eine legale Existenz gewähren. Die realen Betätigungsmöglichkeiten dieser Parteien blieben aber eingeengt, so daß sie letztlich im November von sich aus auf die Teilnahme an den Wahlen verzichteten[91]). Die 88,2 % der bei einer Wahlbeteiligung von 85,6 % für die OF abgegebenen Stimmen brachten der BKP die nötige formelle Legitimation; sie waren allerdings alles andere als ein überzeugendes Ergebnis. Allein fast 650 000 Bürger waren der Wahl ferngeblieben und weitere 450 000 hatten ungültig oder offen gegen die OF votiert. Mithin 24,5 % aller wahlberechtigten Bürger Bulgariens hatten der BKP und der von ihr geführten Parteienkoalition die Zustimmung direkt oder indirekt versagt. In einzelnen Regionen fiel der offene oder verdeckte Dissens noch deutlicher aus[92]).

Nach dem weniger kontrovers verlaufenen Referendum um die Abschaffung der Monarchie im September 1946, das auch in Kreisen der Opposition keinen Widerstand hervorrief (zum Ergebnis vgl. *Tabelle 9*), bedeuteten die ein knappes Jahr später angesetzten Wahlen zur ersten VNSb nach Ausrufung der Republik die zweite und zugleich letzte Wahl im Nachkriegs-Bulgarien, deren Ausgang trotz des erheblichen Machtvorsprungs der BKP noch nicht völlig antizipierbar war. Angesichts des Drucks der Westalliierten und des noch nicht unterzeichneten Friedensvertrages verzichtete die BKP diesmal auf eine Einheitsliste und einen schon im Vorwege festgelegten Mandatsproporz. Alle Parteien, auch die Koalitionsparteien der OF, konnten

---

[89]) DV. (1945) 136.
[90]) Kostov (Anm. 5), S. 133 f.; BKP v rez. (Anm. 4). T. IV, S. 9. Vgl. auch Isusov, BKP 1944/48 (Anm. 6), S. 124; Dragoljubov, P.: Izbornite borbi i rabotata na BKP v Narodnoto săbranie (1945–1949) (Die Wahlkämpfe und die Arbeit der BKP in der NSb (1945–1949)), in: III BKP (Anm. 25). 13 (1965), S. 214 f.
[91]) Ausführlicher bei Bell, Bulgarian Communist Party (Anm. 41), S. 89 ff.; Minčev, M.: Organizacionno i političesko razvitie na otečestveno-frontovskite pravitelstva v Bălgarija (Sept. 1944–noemvri 1946) (Die organisatorische und politische Entwicklung der OF-Regierungen in Bulgarien), in: III BKP (Anm. 25). 60 (1988), S. 5–42.
[92]) In Ruse gaben 37 % der Wähler nicht der OF ihre Stimme oder blieben der Wahl fern, in Pleven waren es 30 %, in Sofia 25 %: Isusov, BKP 1944/48 (Anm. 6), S. 162; ders., Pol. partii (Anm. 42), S. 230 f.

Tabelle 9: Wahlergebnisse 1945 und 1946

Stimmenergebnis		Mandatsverteilung:	
a) Wahlen vom 18.11. 1945 (in Klammern %)			
wahlberechtigt:	4 501 035	Mandate:	276
abgegebene Stimmen:	3 853 097 (85,6)	BKP	94 (34,1)
für die Liste der OF:	3 397 672 (88,2)	BZNS	94 (34,1)
		BRSDP	31 (11,2)
ungültig, gegen die OF:	455 425 (11,8)	Zveno	45 (16,3)
		RP	11 (4,0)
		parteilos	1 (0,4)
b) Referendum über die Abschaffung der Monarchie vom 8.9. 1946			
stimmberechtigt:	4 509 354		
abgegebene Stimmen:	4 132 017 (91,6)		
gültige Stimmen:	4 008 417 (97,0)		
für die Republik:	3 833 183 (95,6)		
für die Monarchie:	175 234 (4,4)		
c) Wahlen vom 27.10. 1946			
wahlberechtigt:	4 506 669	Mandate:	465
abgegebene Stimmen:	4 252 570 (94,4)		
für die OF	2 981 189 (70,1)	für die OF	366 (78,7)
– BKP	2 260 407 (53,1)	– BKP	275 (59,1)
– BZNS	562 114 (13,2)	– BZNS	69 (14,8)
– BRSDP	79 511 (1,8)	– BRSDP	9 (1,9)
– Zveno	70 358 (1,6)	– Zveno	8 (1,7)
– RP	8 789 (0,2)	– RP	4 (0,9)
		– parteilos	1 (0,2)
für die vereinigte Opposition	1 205 530 (28,3)	für die vereinigte Opposition	99 (21,3)
für die DP	22 894 (0,5)	– BZNS-NP	90 (18,9)
für sonstige	298 (0,0)	– BRSDP-O	8 (1,7)
		– parteilos	1 (0,2)

Quelle: Isusov, Pol. partii (Anm. 42), S. 230f.; ders., Izborite (Anm. 93), S. 7f., 19.

diesmal unter eigenem Namen antreten; die Parteien der OF einigten sich auf Initiative der BKP allerdings auf eine gemeinsame Plattform[93]). Zudem hatte die BKP das Nominierungsverfahren kontrolliert und sichergestellt, daß auch von den anderen OF-Parteien nur „konsequente Anhänger der OF" aufgestellt wurden[94]).

[93]) Vgl. zur Wahl von 1946 Genčev, N.: Izborite za Veliko narodno săbranie prez oktomvri 1946 g. (Die Wahlen zur VNSb im Oktober 1946), in: Istoričeski pregled. 20 (1964) 2–3, S. 213–229; Isusov, M.: Izborite za konstitucionno săbranie i razpoloženieto na političeskite sili v Bălgarija prez 1946 g. (Die Wahlen zur konstituierenden Versammlung und die Lage der politischen Kräfte in Bulgarien 1946), in: Istoričeski pregled. 32 (1976) 4, S. 3–30.
[94]) Stankov, B.: Bălgarskata komunističeska partija i izborite za formiraneto na predstavitelnite dăržavni organi (Die BKP und die Wahlen der staatlichen Vertretungsorgane), in: NTAONSU (Anm. 21). Serija partijno stroitelstvo. (1977) 96, S. 139–172.

Tabelle 10: Wahlen zur NSb und Mandatsverteilung 1949–1986

	1949	1953	1957	1962	1966	1971	1976	1981	1986
Wahlberechtigt		4987587	5218602	5482607	5774251	6168931	6379348	6526782	6650739
Wahlbeteiligung (in %)		99,53	99,77	99,71	99,63	99,85	99,93	99,96	99,92
für die Kandidaten der OF (in %)		99,81	99,95	99,90	99,85	99,90	99,92	99,93	99,90
Mandatsverteilung (in Klammern %)									
– insgesamt	239	249	254	keine Angaben	416	400	400	400	400
– BKP	161 (67,4)	145 (58,2)	162 (63,8)		280 (67,3)	266 (66,5)	272 (68,0)	271 (67,7)	276 (69,0)
– BZNS	48 (20,0)	65 (26,1)	65 (25,6)		99 (23,8)	100 (25,0)	100 (25,0)	99 (24,8)	99 (24,8)
– parteilos	30 (12,6)*	39 (15,7)*	27 (10,6)*		37 (8,9)	34 (8,5)	28 (7,0)	30 (7,5)	25 (6,3)

* einschließlich der Vertreter des Jugendverbandes DKMS

Quellen: Atanasov (s. Tab. 1), S. 14f., 23f.; Otečestven front. 22.12.1953, S. 1; 25.12.1957, S. 1; 28.2.1962, S. 1; 1.3.1966, S. 1; 30.6.1971, S. 1; 2.6.1976, S. 1; 9.6.1981, S. 1; 11.6.1986, S. 1.

Die Opposition – bestehend aus dem Petkov-Flügel des BZNS, dem Oppositionsflügel der BRSDP und einzelnen unabhängigen Vertretern – hatte sich unter dem Namen der „Föderation für die Bauern- und Stadt-Arbeit" vereinigt. Ihr Programm knüpfte vor allem an der alten Tărnovo-Verfassung an, deren liberale Grundsätze sie dem volksdemokratischen Verfassungsentwurf der OF-Regierung entgegensetzte. Es war durchaus kein Programm *gegen* die Volksfront, wohl aber gegen eine von den Kommunisten dominierte und zum Instrument nicht-demokratischer Transformation des politischen Systems umgewandelte OF. In Opposition zur OF, aber nicht auf der Liste der vereinigten Opposition kandidierte auch noch die DP (zusammen mit der kleinen Gruppierung der RP (*obed.*)).

Ähnlich wie 1945 brachte auch die Wahl zur konstituierenden NSb der BKP ein Ergebnis, das numerisch als formelle Legitimation ihres Herrschaftsanspruchs dienen konnte. 70,1 % der Stimmen entfielen auf die OF, 53,1 % auf die BKP. Die anderen Parteien der OF mußten sich mit einer erheblich verringerten Stimmenzahl zufriedengeben (vgl. Tabelle 9). 28,3 % Stimmenanteil für die Opposition, der zudem wieder in einzelnen Regionen noch erheblich höher lag, spiegelten jedoch die trotz aller Schikanen nach wie vor erhebliche Stärke der Opposition gegen die Politik der BKP wider. Zusammen machten die für die Oppositionsparteien abgegebenen Stimmen, die ungültigen Stimmzettel sowie die der Wahl Ferngebliebenen 34 % der Bevölkerung aus, die der OF die Zustimmung versagt hatten. Die Oppositionsflügel des BZNS und der BRSDP hatten zudem ihre „Mutterparteien" innerhalb der OF bei weitem überflügelt. Die politischen Kräfte des Landes hatten sich nach den Wahlen von 1946 damit polarisiert zwischen der BKP, deren Koalitionspartner nunmehr endgültig politisch degradiert waren, und der Opposition außerhalb der OF. Die Mandatsverteilung, die der BKP 60 % der Sitze sicherte, sowie die Neubildung der Regierung, in der die BKP mehr als die Hälfte der Minister stellte und alle zentralen Ministerien besetzte, boten nunmehr die parlamentarische Legitimation für die weitere Radikalisierung des Volksdemokratisierungsprozesses, dem die Opposition weder innerhalb des Parlaments noch außerhalb viel entgegenzusetzen vermochte.

Alle Wahlen seit dem Oktober 1946 haben ihren funktionalen Charakter letztlich weitgehend verloren. Sie sind zu ritualisierten Mobilisierungsaktionen verkommen, deren realer partizipativer Effekt und Legitimationswert gegen Null tendiert. Die Wahlbeteiligung lag stets bei über 99,5 % und das Abstimmungsergebnis bei mindestens 99,8 % Stimmen für die Einheitsliste der OF (vgl. *Tabelle 10*).

Bulgarien hat sich bis zu den Kommunalwahlen von 1988 auch nicht den Luxus anderer sozialistischer Staaten, wie z. B. Ungarn, Polen oder selbst Rumänien, erlaubt, wenigstens eine kontrollierte Mehrkandidaten-Wahl zuzulassen, obwohl die Nominierung mehrerer Kandidaten, die im Wahlgesetz von 1949 noch nicht vorgesehen war und die bei der Wahlrechtsnovellierung von 1953 nicht mehr ausdrücklich ausgeschlossen wurde, seit 1973 dem Buchstaben des Gesetzes nach gestattet war[95]. Erst mit den *preustrojstvo*-Bemühungen der letzten Jahre ist das bisher praktizierte

---

[95] Vgl. Art. 39 des Wahlgesetzes von 1949: DV. (1949) 175; Art. 48 des Wahlgesetzes von 1953: DV. (1953) 14 und Art. 43 des Wahlgesetzes von 1973: DV. (1973) 54.

Einkandidaten-Wahlverfahren auch in Bulgarien in die Kritik geraten[96]). Mit der Wahlrechtsnovellierung vom Dezember 1987 soll das Nominierungs- und Wahlverfahren demokratisiert werden. Wesentliche Neuerungen sind dabei: Die Aufstellung mehrerer Kandidaten, die freilich theoretisch auch schon bei früheren Wahlen möglich gewesen wäre, wird erleichtert und ausdrücklich ermutigt. Neben den nominierungsberechtigten gesellschaftspolitischen Organisationen haben auch Bürger das Recht, die Vorschlagsliste der OF durch weitere Nominierungen zu ergänzen. Darüber hinaus ist der Kreis der zur Nominierung Berechtigten auf die Arbeitskollektive ausgedehnt worden, und die für eine Nominierung durch die Bürger notwendige Zahl an unterstützenden Voten wurde herabgesetzt[97]). Schließlich wurde das formale Abstimmungsverfahren insofern liberalisiert, als der Wähler nunmehr für jeden nominierten Kandidaten einen eigenen Stimmzettel erhält. Damit entfällt die ausdrückliche Streichung eines Kandidaten, mit dem man nicht einverstanden war. Der Umstand, daß man die Wahlzettel schon vor dem Abstimmungstag erhalten kann und die Wahl somit auch in den eigenen vier Wänden möglich ist, mildert den sozialen Druck, an der Wahl teilzunehmen, zumindest etwas. Ungeachtet dieser eher moderaten Demokratisierung sind freilich die Steuerungsinstrumente der Partei erhalten geblieben, die die Wahlen auch künftig in ihrem Ergebnis antizipierbar machen werden. So blieb es nach dem Gesetz von 1987 bei einer Einheitsliste der OF, der die Bürger allenfalls ergänzende Kandidaten hinzufügen können. Zudem sind alle Kandidaten verpflichtet, sich zur politischen Wahlplattform der OF zu bekennen, die letztlich nichts anderes darstellt als ein Surrogat der Parteiprogrammatik und -politik. Hinzu kommen die nach wie vor unangetasteten informellen Einflußkanäle der BKP auf die Nominierung der Kandidaten. In der Praxis ist das neue Wahlverfahren bislang lediglich bei den Kommunalwahlen vom Februar 1988 zum Tragen gekommen. Die Ergebnisse waren freilich wenig beeindruckend. Lediglich in 20% der Wahlkreise wurden überhaupt mehr als ein Kandidat aufgestellt. Mit durchschnittlich 1,2 Bewerbern pro Mandat nahm sich die effektive Wahlmöglichkeit der Bürger dabei nur wenig besser aus als bei früheren Wahlen. Auch die Tatsache, daß diesmal die Zahl der Gegenstimmen höher lag als bei vergleichbaren früheren Anlässen (bei der Wahl der Bezirks-Volksräte 0,8%, bei den Gemeindewahlen 0,93% und bei der Wahl der Bürgermeister 1,4%) ist angesichts der nach wie vor mikroskopischen Größenordnung wenig bedeutsam[98]). Ein substantieller Funktionswandel der Wahlen dürfte sich erst einstellen, wenn die nach dem Sturz Živkovs von der neuen Führung um Petăr Mladenov für das Frühjahr 1990 angekündigten „freien Wahlen" Wirklichkeit werden sollten. In welcher Form diese konkret vonstatten gehen werden, d. h. ob als echte Konkurrenz mehrerer Parteien und politischer Gruppierungen oder lediglich als Möglichkeit der Nominierung einzelner unabhängiger Kandidaten, ist zum gegenwärtigen Zeitpunkt allerdings noch nicht auszumachen.

---

[96]) Vgl. u. a. Prodanov, V.: Demokracija i izbornost (Demokratie und Wählbarkeit), in: Novo vreme. (1987) 11, S. 16ff.
[97]) DV. (1987) 98. Siehe hierzu auch den Beitrag von O. Luchterhandt, Regierungssystem.
[98]) Vgl. hierzu Höpken, W.: Demokratie in kleinen Schritten: Die Kommunalwahlen in Bulgarien, in: Südosteuropa. 37 (1988), S. 208–218.

Tabelle 11: Mandatsverteilung in den lokalen Vertretungsorganen (1949–1986, in %)

Jahr	Mandate	BKP	BZNS	parteilos
1949	35876	55,2	28,0	16,8
1952	59644	55,4	18,3	26,3
1956	58870	59,0	20,6	20,4
1971	53665	58,6	19,8	21,6
1976	55391	53,0	18,3	28,7
1981	53712	57,9	17,0	25,1
1983	54475	54,9	14,6	30,5
1986	54496	55,9	14,3	29,8
1988	61374	60,8	13,4	25,8

Quelle: Atanasov (s. Tab. 1), S. 21; Atanasov, Klasa (s. Tab. 8), S. 122, 125; Otečestven front. 30.6. 1971, S. 1, 2.6. 1976, S. 5, 9.6. 1981, S. 1; RD. 6.12. 1983, S. 1; SG. 1987, S. 14f.; RD. 1.3. 1988, S. 1.

Das Ergebnis der bisherigen Wahlen war ein seit 1949 mehr oder weniger konstant gehaltener Proporz von BKP, BZNS und parteilosen Abgeordneten in den verschiedenen Vertretungsorganen, deren zahlenmäßiges Verhältnis durch die im Vorwege festgelegte Einheitsliste der OF abgesichert war. Er verteilte im Falle der NSb die Abgeordnetensitze dabei zu ca. 2/3 auf BKP-Abgeordnete, zu 1/4 auf den BZNS und reservierte den Rest für Parteilose und Repräsentanten gesellschaftlicher Organisationen (vgl. *Tabelle 10*). Seit 1971 ist dabei ein konstant leichter Trend zugunsten der BKP-Mitglieder festzustellen, deren Anteil zuletzt bei fast 70 % lag. Die politische Bedeutung des numerisch immer noch relativ großen Anteils an Nicht-BKP-Abgeordneten wird freilich ohnehin durch das einigende programmatische Band der OF und den Grundsatz der Willenseinheit von BKP, BZNS und Parteilosen minimalisiert.

Auf lokaler Ebene liegt der festgeschriebene BKP-Anteil bei 56–60 %; die Repräsentanz Parteiloser ist hier mit ca. 1/4 deutlich größer. Auffallend ist der rückläufige Anteil an BZNS-Abgeordneten, der in früheren Jahren konstant bei ca. 1/5 der Abgeordneten lag, mittlerweile aber auf ca. 14–15 % abgesunken ist. Ursächlich hierfür dürfte wohl das nur begrenzte Mitgliederreservoir der Bauernpartei sein, das einer Wahrnehmung des ansonsten zugestandenen Beteiligungsspielraums Grenzen setzt. Die auf der Ebene der lokalen Vertretungsorgane zahlenmäßig geringere Präsenz der BKP gilt freilich nicht für die exekutiven Organe. Hier sichert die Partei auch personell ihren Führungsanspruch in weitaus stärkerem Maße ab, so beispielsweise unter den Bürgermeistern, die sie zu etwa 90 % stellt.

Von der sozialen Struktur her, und das hat das bulgarische Parlament mit denen westlicher Gesellschaften gemein, ist die NSb ausgesprochen unausgewogen zusammengesetzt. Der von Anfang an dominierende Angestelltenanteil unter den Abgeordneten ist seit dem Ende der 40er Jahre kontinuierlich gestiegen, so daß mittlerweile 3/4 aller Abgeordneten Angestellte sind. Der Arbeiteranteil ist hingegen, gemessen an den 60 % Bevölkerungsanteil, mit 12 % nur marginal. Bei weitem unterrepräsentiert sind im Parlament ähnlich wie in der Partei auch die Frauen. Über den Anteil der türkischen Minderheit lassen sich selbst für die Zeit vor dem nationalitätenpolitischen Einschnitt von 1984 keine genauen Angaben machen. Den Namen der Abge-

Tabelle 12: Sozialprofil der Vertretungsorgane (1949–1986)

Jahr	NSb					Lokale Vertretungsorgane				
	Frauen-anteil	Jugendliche (bis 30 J.)	Sozialstruktur			Frauen-anteil	Jugendliche (bis 30 J.)	Sozialstruktur		
			Arbeiter	landwirt. Beschäft.	Angest.	sonstige			Arbeiter	landwirt. Beschäft.	Angest.	sonstige
1949	4,7	4,3	7,6	18,1	67,7	6,5	15,9		10,4	56,2	33,1	0,4
1953*									9,9	49,2	40,9**	
1957	16,1	6,0										
1962	20,3	12,5					22,9					
1966							19,6					
1971							24,7					
1976	19,5	8,3					37,4	24,6	33,0	28,9	38,1**	
1981	21,7	8,3	13,5	7,3	79,2**		33,8	21,0	28,8	25,6	45,6**	
1983							37,0	21,8	31,9	25,2	42,9**	
1986	21,0	9,0	12,8	7,5	75,2	4,5	35,0	21,6	33,2	20,6	41,4	4,8
1988							29,1	12,1	24,1			

* lokale Vertretungsorgane 1952 ** Angestellte und sonstige.

Quelle: Atanasov (s. Tab. 8), S. 118; Dragoljubov (Anm. 90), S. 233 f.; Novo vreme. 29 (1953) 5, S. 42, Otečestven front. 28.2. 1962; 1.6. 1966; 30.6. 1971; 9.6. 1981; SG. 1987, S. 14 f.; RD. 6.12. 1983; 1.3.1988; Todorov (Anm. 74), S. 88.

ordneten nach dürfte er aber zwischen 1949 und 1981 bei minimal 2,5 % und maximal 4,3 % gelegen haben, in jedem Fall also deutlich unter dem Bevölkerungsanteil.

Die soziale Struktur der lokalen Vertretungsorgane ist ausgeglichener. Insbesondere die landwirtschaftlich tätige Bevölkerung ist hier stärker berücksichtigt (vgl. *Tabelle 12*). Der zuletzt bei 1/5 liegende Anteil dieser Bevölkerungsgruppe an den Abgeordneten verdeckt allerdings, daß landwirtschaftlich Beschäftigte vor allem auf der untersten Ebene der örtlichen Volksräte mit fast 30 % vertreten waren, während ihr Anteil auf den höheren Ebenen der Gemeinde- und Kreis-Räte bereits deutlich niedriger liegt. Eine gegenläufige Tendenz weisen auch hier vor allem die Angestellten auf.

Nicht nur von seiner Genesis gelenkter Wahlen her ist die politische Legitimation und Bedeutung des bulgarischen *Parlaments* begrenzt. Auch seine Aktivitäten und seine reale Bedeutung für die politischen Entscheidungsprozesse sind eher bescheiden zu bemessen und bleiben weiter hinter der ihm zugewiesenen Funktion als oberstes politisches und legislatives Entscheidungs- und Kontrollgremium und Leitungsorgan der Innen- und Außenpolitik des Landes zurück[99]). Wenn seit Anfang der 60er Jahre die in der Zeit Červenkovs völlig inaktive, untergeordnete und formalisierte Rolle der NSb kritisiert wird, deren Sitzungen verfassungswidrig häufig nicht stattfanden und deren legislative Tätigkeit durch Dekrete der exekutiven staatlichen Organe ersetzt wurden[100]), so wird man für die Živkov-Ära wohl zwar von einer regelmäßigeren, häufigeren und von den beteiligten Personen und Gremien her ausgeweiteten Parlamentstätigkeit sprechen können, kaum jedoch von einem grundlegenden Funktionswandel des Parlaments. Seine ihm zugewiesene legislative und kontrollierende Tätigkeit ist auch heute noch im Umfang bescheiden und in der Art ihrer Wahrnehmung formalisiert. An einer wirklichen Ausfüllung ihrer normativen Kompetenzen wird die NSb bereits durch ihre geringe Sitzungshäufigkeit von verfassungsgemäß dreimaligen, in der Praxis der vergangenen Jahre zumeist viermaligen „Sessionen" mit 1–2 Tagen Dauer gehindert. Gesetzesvorlagen, die in wichtigen Fragen ohnehin lediglich die Normierung der vom Politbüro und ZK im Vorwege festgelegten Maßnahmen sind, werden dabei akklamativ verabschiedet oder, was häufig geschieht, lediglich nach vorheriger Inkraftsetzung durch den DS ex post bestätigt. Die Debatten des Parlaments beschränken sich dabei auf propagandistische Bekräftigungen der Regierungspolitik, allenfalls auf technisch-sachliche Anfragen. Das Ritual der Einstimmigkeit bei der Verabschiedung wird nur in dissidentischen Einzelfällen durchbrochen, so dem Vernehmen westlicher Quellen nach bei der Verabschiedung der Territorial- und Verwaltungsreform im Sommer 1987, als eine Abgeordnete gegen die Schaffung neuer Kreise mit neuen Hauptstädten votiert haben soll[101]). Die verfassungsmäßig festgelegte Kontrollfunktion des Parlaments gegenüber dem Ministerrat und dem DS beschränkt sich auf die nicht weniger ritualisierte Entgegennahme und Absegnung des Rechenschaftsberichts dieser Institutionen. Inwieweit die für verschie-

---

[99]) Vgl. die Art. 66–89 der Verfassung von 1971; näheres siehe im Beitrag von O. Luchterhandt, Regierungssystem.

[100]) Todorov (Anm. 74), S. 85; Migev, V.: Development of Socialist Democracy in Bulgaria during the Period of Transition, in: Problems of Transition from Capitalism to Socialism. Ed. BAN Institute of History. Sofia 1975, S. 146.

[101]) Frankfurter Allgemeine Zeitung. 9.9.1987.

ne Ressorts gebildeten parlamentarischen Kommissionen Orte verstärkter inhaltlicher Debatten und echter Formulierung politischer Beschlüsse sind, ist schwer auszumachen. Derartige Kommissionen, die bisweilen über 80 Mitglieder haben, sind quasi professionelle Fachgremien, die an der technischen Ausarbeitung legislativer Akte beteiligt sind[102]). Dies macht auch sie eher zu Gremien, die vorgegebene politische Beschlüsse technisch und fachlich umsetzen und nicht politische Entscheidungen autonom gestalten.

Eine gewichtigere politische Rolle spielt zweifelsohne der 1971 wie in anderen osteuropäischen Staaten an Stelle des Präsidiums der NSb eingeführte, 23 Personen umfassende *DS*. Dem von der NSb gewählten und ihm Rechenschaft schuldigen DS obliegen nicht nur schon normativ erhebliche Rechte[103]), sondern er hat auch in der Praxis gegenüber der Tätigkeit des Parlaments eine dominierende Rolle. Wenngleich über seine interne Arbeitsweise so gut wie nichts bekannt ist, so läßt schon der von ihm produzierte Gesetzesoutput erkennen, daß er die legislative Tätigkeit der NSb zu einem guten Teil übernommen hat. Seine Zusammensetzung hat dabei eine Art korporativen Charakter, indem neben der BKP, die mit dem Parteivorsitzenden Živkov die autoritative Führung des DS stellt, der BZNS sowie die Massenorganisationen und wichtige gesellschaftliche Organisationen mit ihren Spitzenvertretern in ihm vertreten sind. Die BKP, die stets etwa die Hälfte ihres Politbüros und ZK-Sekretariats in den DS entsendet, nimmt dabei über diesen den entscheidenden Politik formulierenden Einfluß wahr.

Die *lokalen Volksräte* (*Narodni sǎveti*) und ihre Exekutivkomitees in den nunmehr neun Bezirken, den Gemeinden und örtlichen Vertretungsorganen sollen zugleich Organe der zentralen Staatsgewalt und der lokalen Selbstverwaltung sein. Ersterer Aspekt hat jedoch, auch wenn die Kompetenzen der örtlichen Organe in den vergangenen 30 Jahren ausgeweitet wurden, immer noch den Vorrang. Bis in die frühen 60er Jahre und insbesondere in der Červenkov-Ära unterlagen die örtlichen Volksräte dabei einem rigide gehandhabten demokratischen Zentralismus und wurden als Transmissionsriemen verstanden, die die politische Linie der Partei, ihre „anleitenden Weisungen für die organisatorische Durchführung dieser politischen Linie" und die Mobilisierung der Massen zu verwirklichen hatten[104]). Nach dem Aprilplenum, vor allem aber in den 60er Jahren, wurde die Rolle der Volksräte dann zumindest vom Umfang ihrer Kompetenzen her in mehreren Schritten aufgewertet. Die Tätigkeit ihrer Organe wurde regelmäßiger gestaltet, und der Kreis der von ihnen zu behandelnden Fragen wurde erweitert. Gegenüber den lokalen Wirtschaftsbetrieben, vor allem im infrastrukturellen Versorgungsbereich erhielten die Volksräte Kontrollkompetenzen, und auch die finanzielle Verfügungsmasse der lokalen Vertretungsorgane wurde ausgeweitet[105]). Seit Anfang der 70er Jahre erhielten die lokalen Vertretungsorgane zudem Beteiligungsrechte bei der Erstellung und Konkretisierung des Wirt-

---

[102]) Spasov, B.: Narodno sǎbranie (Die NSb). Sofia 1980, S. 38f.
[103]) Vgl. hierzu den Beitrag von O. Luchterhandt, Regierungssystem.
[104]) Dokov (Anm. 73), S. 48; Atanasov, A.: Rabotničeskata klasa v Bǎlgarija 1948–1958g. (Die Arbeiterklasse in Bulgarien 1948–58). Sofia 1987, S. 114.
[105]) Todorov (Anm. 74), S. 90f.; Petkanov, G.: Bjudžetna kompetentnost na narodnite sǎveti v NR Bǎlgarija (Die Budget-Kompetenz der Volksräte in der NRB). Sofia 1988, S. 79ff.

schaftsplans[106]). Der Rahmen zentral gelenkter Politikrichtlinien und Eingriffsmöglichkeiten der zentralen staatlichen Organe wurde dabei freilich nicht überschritten. Die Aufwertung der lokalen Räte blieb vielmehr im Rahmen operativer Dezentralisierung und Arbeitsteilung, und die koordinierende Tätigkeit der Partei verhinderte zusätzlich eine ungewünschte Autonomisierung des lokalen Politikraums. Mit der Territorialreform vom 29. 8. 1987 wurde ein neuerlicher Schritt unternommen, die operative Selbständigkeit der Gemeinden auszuweiten. Die autonome Investitionskompetenz der Kommunen für infrastrukturelle Vorhaben und ihre budgetäre Selbständigkeit sollen dabei gestärkt werden. Die zentral vorgegebenen Entwicklungspläne sollen stärker strukturbestimmenden Charakter haben und den Gemeinde-Volksräten eine größere Entscheidungskompetenz im Hinblick auf die infrastrukturelle Entwicklung der Gemeinde zukommen. Ähnlich wie in der Wirtschaft sollen damit auch hinsichtlich der Territorialgliederung die Entscheidungskompetenzen dezentralisiert werden[106a]). Für eine Bewertung der praktischen Ergebnisse der Reform ist es allerdings noch zu früh.

Plebiszitäre Willensbildungsformen haben in Bulgarien nur eine sehr untergeordnete Rolle gespielt und allenfalls akklamativen Charakter. Art. 78, Abs. 3, Art. 93, Abs. 2 und Art. 117 der Verfassung geben zwar der NSb, dem DS und den lokalen Volksräten die Möglichkeit der Durchführung von „Volksbefragungen" und „Volksentscheiden". Auf gesamtbulgarischer Ebene hat dieses Recht bislang allerdings nur im Zusammenhang mit der Verabschiedung der Verfassung von 1971 Anwendung gefunden. Auf lokaler Ebene sind hingegen in einzelnen Kreisen auch zu anderen Themen derartige „Volksbefragungen" durchgeführt worden[107]). In Anlehnung an ähnliche, von Chruščev eingeführte Organe wurden seit Mitte der 60er Jahre auch in Bulgarien verschiedenartige konsultative Beteiligungsformen auf lokaler Ebene in Gestalt von diversen Kommissionen, Bürgerbeteiligung an Arbeitsgruppen der lokalen Volksräte und Kontrollorgane eingeführt[108]). Inwieweit derartige unmittelbare Beteiligungsformen dabei dem Bürger echte Entscheidungsbefugnisse über alternative Sachalternativen geboten haben, ist freilich nicht zu klären.

Bereits die alte Živkov-Führung hatte seit 1987 mit ihrem verbalen Bekenntnis zur Notwendigkeit einer Reform des politischen Systems auch die Entfunktionalisierung der alten Vertretungsinstitutionen eingestehen müssen, ohne jedoch selbst durchgreifende Schritte zu deren Funktionswandel eingeleitet zu haben[109]). Die Vitalisierung

---

[106]) Otečestven front. 25.7.1968; DV. (1969) 60, S. 1–8.

[106a]) Geneški, M.: Teritorialnite obštnosti v NR Bălgarija (Die Territorialgemeinschaften in der NRB). Sofia 1989, S. 105–114.

[107]) Galcin, P.: Politikata i dejnostta na BKP za povišavane roljata na predstavitelnite organi na dăržavnata vlast (1966–1976) (Die Politik und Tätigkeit der BKP für die erhöhte Rolle der Vertretungsorgane der Staatsmacht (1966–1976)), in: NTAONSU (Anm. 21). Serija: istorija. (1977) 95, S. 233 ff.

[108]) Petkov, V.: Dejnostta na BKP za vnedrjavane i razvitie na obštestvenoto načalo v rabotata na narodnite săveti (1958–1971 g.) (Die Tätigkeit der BKP für die Einführung und Entwicklung des gesellschaftlichen Grundsatzes der Arbeit der Volksräte (1958–1971)), in: III BKP (Anm. 25). 43 (1980), S. 219–242.

[109]) Vgl. Höpken, W.: Perestrojka auf bulgarisch: Sofia und die Reformpolitik Gorbačevs, in: Südosteuropa. 36 (1987), S. 619–645.

der NSb und der örtlichen Parlamente war denn auch eines der vorrangigen Ziele, zu dem sich die neue Führung um Mladenov bekannte. Insbesondere die NSb soll künftig zu einem Ort politischer Sachdebatten und echter parlamentarischer Entscheidungskompetenz umgestaltet und der präjudizierende Einfluß der Parteiorgane auf deren Beschlüsse beseitigt werden. Legislative und kontrollierende Tätigkeit der NSb sowie deren Beziehungen zum Ministerrat sollen durch die für 1990 avisierte grundlegende Verfassungsreform neu bestimmt werden, mit der vermutlich auch der bislang für die Gesetzgebung so dominierende DS reformiert oder gar abgeschafft und durch ein Staatspräsidium oder einen Präsidenten ersetzt werden wird. Letztlich aber dürfte die Rolle des Parlaments in der Zukunft wohl ganz entscheidend davon abhängen, in welcher Art und Weise die ebenfalls für 1990 zugesagten „freien Wahlen" in die Praxis umgesetzt werden.

V. Die politische Kultur

Die normative politische Kultur des Landes ergibt sich aus den ideologischen Postulaten und Ansprüchen der „entwickelten sozialistischen Gesellschaft". In Adaption entsprechender sowjetischer Ideologie-Vorbilder wird danach angenommen, daß mit der „entwickelten sozialistischen Gesellschaft" sich zugleich auch ein entsprechendes Wertesystem, eine „sozialistische Lebensweise" (*socialističeskijat način na život*), entwickelt[110]). Elemente dieser „sozialistischen Lebensweise" sind danach[111]):

– „sozialer Optimismus", d.h. Vertrauen in die Zukunft,
– eine sozialistische Einstellung zur Arbeit und Interesse am sozialistischen Aufbau,
– „Kollektivismus",
– ein hohes Maß an politischer Aktivität,
– die Verfestigung grundlegender politischer Werte wie sozialistische Überzeugung, Patriotismus, Internationalismus,
– das Streben nach allseitiger Vervollkommnung der Persönlichkeit.

Insbesondere seit Mitte der 70er Jahre ist durch Kampagnen zur Überwindung traditioneller Verhaltensweisen, religiöser Relikte und gegen das Aufleben nichtsozialistischer Elemente der Alltagskultur versucht worden, diese politischen Werte in der Bevölkerung zu verankern. Die Partei hat sich dabei nicht ungeschickt darum bemüht, traditionale und nationale bulgarische Elemente in ihren Sozialisationskatalog aufzunehmen, um über diese sozialistische Werte und Normen in der Bevölkerung zu verankern. So wurde beispielsweise in Anknüpfung an traditionelle volkskulturelle Elemente ein differenziertes System „sozialistischer Rituale und Feste" entworfen[111a]). Es mangelt allerdings in der bulgarischen Soziologie und Politikwis-

---

[110]) Socialističeskijat način na život. Teorija i praktika (Die sozialistische Lebensweise. Theorie und Praxis). Sofia 1985, S. 216 ff; Živkov, T.: Izbrani săčinenija. T. 24. Sofia 1978, S. 231.
[111]) Vgl. statt vieler zusammenfassend Hadžinikolov, V.: Die sozialistische Lebensweise, in: Jahrbuch für Volkskunde und Kulturgeschichte. N.F. 22 (1979) 7, S. 27–48.
[111a]) Vgl. Osnovni nasoki za razvitie i usăvăršenstvuvane na prazničko-obrednata sistema v NRB (Die grundlegenden Richtungen der Entwicklung und Vervollkommnung des Fest- und Ritualsy-

senschaft bislang noch völlig an einer expliziten Auseinandersetzung mit Begriff und Inhalt von „politischer Kultur". Dementsprechend dürftig ist auch die Informationsgrundlage, auf der sich Aussagen zu realen Verankerung derartiger Werte gründen ließen. Immerhin deuten eine Reihe bulgarischer Analysen an, daß nicht nur das behauptete Ausmaß an „sozialistischer Lebensweise" überschätzt wird, sondern daß es nach wie vor massive, wenn nicht gar dominante Wertemuster und Verhaltensweisen gibt, die diesem ideologischen Anspruch entgegenstehen. Die wenigen industriesoziologischen Untersuchungen deuten an, daß auch Bulgarien noch weit entfernt zu sein scheint von einer „sozialistischen Einstellung zur Arbeit" und Bummelei, Fernbleiben von der Arbeit u. ä. erheblich verbreitet sind. Formelle politische Aktivität ist deutlich weniger ausgeprägt, als es die „sozialistische Lebensweise" verlangt, und zudem schichtenspezifisch verteilt; Rückzug ins Private und Priorität privater Werte und Ziele vor gesellschaftlichen sind immer noch bestimmend[112]. Passivität, politische Apathie und eine diffuse Verarbeitung der offiziellen Werte werden von soziologischen Untersuchungen besonders im Hinblick auf die Jugendlichen angedeutet. Traditionale Verhaltensweisen und Normen, wie z. B. die nach wie vor starken großfamiliären Bindungen, der Vorrang informeller Gruppenbeziehungen vor formalisierten und organisierten Assoziationen u. ä., haben trotz „Revolution" und massivem sozialem Wandel ihren Einfluß nicht verloren und stellen sich der Internalisierung „moderner" sozialistischer Kulturmuster retardierend entgegen[113]. *Vrăzkite* und *chododajstvo* – Beziehungen und Protektion – sind für Bulgarien traditionelle Formen der politischen Kultur, die unter veränderten sozialen Bedingungen neue Formen und Intensität angenommen haben. In welchem Maße die von einer „sozialistischen Lebensweise" abweichenden Werte und Verhaltensweisen dabei heute noch real ihren Platz behaupten, ist im einzelnen nur schwer auszumachen. *Religiosität*, über deren Verankerung allerdings keine langen Zeitreihen vorliegen, dürfte dabei im Ergebnis von Atheismus-Propaganda und Modernisierung erheblich zurückgegangen sein. Bei den bislang umfassendsten Umfragen über Religiosität 1962 und 1968 hatten sich 35,5 % bzw. knapp 20 % der bulgarischen Bevölkerung (unter der türkischstämmigen Bevölkerung waren die Werte jeweils deutlich höher) als religiös bezeichnet[114]. Neuere Angaben, deren Repräsentativität allerdings offen bleiben muß, deuten eine noch niedrigere Rate an religiösem Bekenntnis von 10–15 %, bei Jugendlichen noch darunter, an[115]. Allgemein war Religiosität bei Frauen stärker

---

stems in der NRB), in: DV. (1978) 42, S. 505 ff.; Mizov, N.: Praznici, obredi, rituali (Feiern, Sitten, Rituale). Sofia 1980.

[112] Socialističeskijat način na život (Anm. 110), S. 219 f, 226.

[113] Vgl. Roth, K.: Großstädtische Kultur und dörfliche Lebensweise: Bulgarische Großstädte im 19. und 20. Jahrhundert, in: Großstädte. Aspekte empirischer Kulturforschung. Berlin 1985, S. 363–376 (Schriften des Museums für Deutsche Volkskunde 13).

[114] Ošavkov, Z. (Red.): Sociologičeskata struktura na săvremennoto bălgarsko obštestvo (Die soziologische Struktur der gegenwärtigen bulgarischen Gesellschaft). Sofia 1976, S. 383–410.

[115] So wird für das Ende der 70er Jahre von ca. 11 % überzeugten, aber nicht sehr aktiv Glaubenden und von 6 % aktiv Glaubenden gesprochen: Tachirov, Š.: Socialističeskata obrednost i duchovno edinstvo (Sozialistischer Ritus und geistige Einheit). Sofia 1984, S. 75. Mit ähnlichen Zahlen für einzelne Städte auch jüngst: Krăstev, K.: Religioznostta i ateističnoto văzpitanie u nas (Religiosität und atheistische Erziehung bei uns), in: Političeska prosveta. (1987) 4.

verbreitet als bei Männern (1968: 57,4% Atheisten unter Frauen, 76,3% unter Männern), ausgeprägter bei älteren Jahrgängen (1968 waren 11,2% der 18–23-jährigen und 16,1% der 24–28-jährigen religiös, aber ca. 60% der 59–68-jährigen und fast 75% der über 68-jährigen) und tiefer verwurzelt in bäuerlichen Berufsgruppen als bei Arbeitern und Angestellten (1968 waren Angestellte zu 13,2% religiös, Arbeiter zu 24,4% und Kooperativbauern zu 46,7%). Das fehlende religiöse Bekenntnis bedeutet aber, wie bisweilen kritisiert wird, nicht immer zugleich auch eine bewußte atheistische Lebenseinstellung, sondern läßt durchaus noch Raum für diffuse Beziehungen zur Religiosität[116].

Die Internalisierung sozialistischer Werte und Normen wird aber nicht nur durch die Resistenz traditionaler politischer Kultur behindert, sondern es tauchen auch neue, freilich nicht weniger dem angestrebten sozialistischen Normensystem zuwiderlaufende Normen und Verhaltensmuster auf. „Konsumerismus" ist eine in diesem Zusammenhang viel kritisierte Erscheinung, mehr aber noch die Auswirkungen des sogenannten „Informations-Booms", d.h. die Verbreitung von Video, Telespielen u.ä., die, wie bulgarische Analysen beklagen, sich als kaum zu kontrollierendes Sozialisationsmedium erweisen[117].

Nicht zuletzt die mit dem Živkov-Sturz zunehmende Politisierung der Öffentlichkeit hat dabei in jüngster Zeit nachdrücklich die Erodierung der offiziellen marxistisch-leninistischen Ideologie erkennen lassen. Liberal-demokratische Werte, wie sie sich in der Forderung nach echtem Pluralismus, nach Rechtsstaatlichkeit und Entideologisierung des Lebens ausdrücken, gewinnen statt dessen auch in Bulgarien an Boden. In der radikalen Kritik an Živkov und dem mit ihm identifizierten System der Privilegien und des Nepotismus scheinen aber auch traditionelle und egalitäre Gesellschaftsvorstellungen neu belebt zu werden. Wie das politische System, so befindet sich auch die politische Kultur des Landes in einem Prozeß des Umbruchs und der Differenzierung, nachdem das parteioffizielle Gerüst an Normen und Wertorientierungen seine Verbindlichkeit zunehmend verliert.

---

[116] Naučen ateizǎm (Wissenschaftlicher Atheismus). Sofia 1987, S. 188f.
[117] Ateistična tribuna. (1987) 4, S. 65–69.

Rechtssystem

Christa Jessel-Holst, Hamburg

I. Zivilrecht: 1. Einführung – 2. Personenrecht – 3. Eigentumsrecht – 4. Schuldrecht – 5. Erbrecht – 6. Internationales Privatrecht – 7. Reformbestrebungen – II. Zivilprozeßrecht: 1. Einführung – 2. System und Zuständigkeit der Zivilgerichte – 3. Das Verfahren – 4. Besondere Verfahrensarten – 5. Zwangsvollstreckung – 6. Notarielles Verfahren – 7. Register für juristische Personen – 8. Internationales Zivilprozeßrecht – III. Familienrecht: 1. Einführung – 2. Eherecht – 3. Kindschaftsrecht – 4. Unterhalt – 5. Internationales Familienrecht – 6. Das Verfahren in Ehesachen – IV. Recht der Wirtschaft: 1. Einführung – 2. Abschluß und Erfüllung der Wirtschaftsverträge; Haftung – 3. Einzelne Wirtschaftsverträge – 4. Streitlösung – V. Arbeitsrecht: 1. Einführung – 2. Grundfragen des Arbeitsrechts – 3. Internationales Arbeitsrecht – 4. Arbeitsgerichtsbarkeit – VI. Strafrecht: 1. Einführung – 2. Ausgewählte strafrechtliche Sonderprobleme – 3. Verwaltungsstrafrecht – 4. Statistik und Kriminologie – VII. Strafprozeßrecht: 1. Einführung – 2. System und Zuständigkeit der Strafgerichte – 3. Das Strafverfahren – 4. Strafvollzug

I. Zivilrecht

1. Einführung

Das bulgarische Privatrecht war auch vor dem II. Weltkrieg nicht kodifiziert. Es gab zahlreiche Einzelgesetze, die jedoch nur wenige eigenständige Lösungen enthielten und in der Hauptsache den Gesetzbüchern anderer Staaten nachgebildet waren. Und zwar beruhte das bürgerliche Recht im wesentlichen auf den Prinzipien des romanischen Rechtskreises, vor allem auf dem italienischen Codice civile, das Handelsrecht dagegen hatte das ungarische Handelsgesetzbuch und damit mittelbar auch das Allgemeine Deutsche Handelsgesetzbuch zum Vorbild[1].

Heute sind in Bulgarien, im Gegensatz zu anderen sozialistischen Staaten wie etwa Rumänien oder Polen[2], keine Gesetze aus der Zeit bis zum II. Weltkrieg mehr in Kraft. Durch Gesetz vom 9.11.1951 wurden nämlich sämtliche damals noch bestehende Normativakte aus der Zeit vor dem 9.9.1944 pauschal aufgehoben[3].

---

[1] Dazu Iwanow, G.: Bulgarien, in: Rechtsvergleichendes Handwörterbuch für das Zivil- und Handelsrecht des In- und Auslandes. Hrsg. v. Schlegelberger, F. Berlin 1929, Bd. 1: Länderberichte, S. 16–19; Schöndorf, F.: Einführung in das geltende slavische Recht (Privat- und Prozeßrecht) in rechtsvergleichender Darstellung. Bd. 1: Bulgarien. Leipzig und Berlin 1922, S. V ff.

[2] Rechtsvergleichend z. B. Korkisch, F.: Das Privatrecht Ost-Mitteleuropas in rechtsvergleichender Sicht, in: Rabels Zeitschrift für ausländisches und internationales Privatrecht. 23 (1958), S. 201–230.

[3] Gesetz über die Aufhebung aller bis zum 9. September 1944 erlassenen Gesetze (*Zakon za otmenjavane na vsički zakoni, izdadeni do 9 septemvri 1944 g.*), Izv. (1951) 93.

Die wichtigsten geltenden Rechtsvorschriften im Bereich des Zivilrechts sind:

a) Personenrecht

Gesetz über die Personen und die Familie (*Zakon za licata i semejstvoto*, im folgenden: ZLS) (DV. (1949) 182 Fassung (1989) 46);

Zivilstandsordnung (*Naredba za graždanskoto săstojanie*) (DV. (1975) 75 Fassung (1988) 33).

b) Eigentumsrecht

Eigentumsgesetz (*Zakon za sobstvenostta*, im folgenden: ZS) (Izvestija na Prezidiuma na Narodnoto săbranie, im folgenden: Izv. (1951) 92 Fassung DV. (1989) 38);

Gesetz über das Eigentum der Bürger (*Zakon za sobstvenostta na graždanite*, im folgenden: ZSG) (DV. (1973) 26 Fassung (1989) 31);

Reglement für die Anwendung des Gesetzes über das Eigentum der Bürger (*Pravilnik za priloženie na Zakona za sobstvenostta na graždanite*) (DV. (1973) 45 Fassung (1984) 57);

Ordnung für Staatsvermögen (*Naredba za dăržavnite imoti*) (DV. (1975) 79 Fassung (1985) 37);

Ordnung für die Verwaltung der Vermögen von Ausländern im Inland (*Naredba za upravlenie na imuštestvata na čuždestranni lica v stranata*) (DV. (1969) 30);

Anordnung Nr. 322 des Ministerrats für die Verwaltung der Vermögen von einheimischen Personen im Ausland und für die Führung von zivilrechtlichen Vermögensstreitigkeiten zwischen einheimischen und ausländischen Personen (*Razporeždane za upravlenie na imuštestvata na mestni lica v čužbina i za vodene na graždanski imuštestveni dela meždu mestni i čuždestranni lica*) (DV. (1967) 90 Fassung (1983) 77).

c) Schuldrecht

Gesetz über Schuldverhältnisse und Verträge (*Zakon za zadălženijata i dogovorite*, im folgenden: ZZD) (DV. (1950) 275 Fassung (1982) 28);

Gesetz über Mietverhältnisse (*Zakon za naemnite otnošenija*) (DV. (1969) 53 Fassung (1986) 88);

Reglement für die Anwendung des Gesetzes über die Mietverhältnisse (*Pravilnik za prilagane na Zakona za naemnite otnošenija*) (DV. (1970) 40 Fassung (1979) 73).

d) Erbrecht

Gesetz über die Beerbung (*Zakon za nasledstvoto*, im folgenden: ZN) (DV. (1949) 22 Fassung (1985) 41).

Das bulgarische Recht gehört zum sozialistischen Rechtskreis, und die Rechtserneuerung nach 1944 stand unter dem „beherrschenden Einfluß des Sowjetrechts"[4]. Ein Paradebeispiel hierfür ist das Eigentumsrecht. Eine totale Rezeption hat jedoch

---

[4]) Vgl. Zweigert, K.; Kötz, H.: Einführung in die Rechtsvergleichung auf dem Gebiete des Privatrechts, Bd. 1: Grundlagen. 2. Aufl. Tübingen 1984, S. 333, 358.

nicht stattgefunden. Manche nationale Eigenheiten wurden bewahrt, und auch die Verbindung zu anderen Rechtskreisen ist nie völlig abgerissen. So ist es auch kein Zufall, daß im Jahre 1974 in Sofia eine vorzügliche Übersetzung des deutschen Bürgerlichen Gesetzbuchs von 1896 erschienen ist[5]).

Im Zuge der *preustrojstvo* ist abermals eine umfassende Rechtserneuerung geplant, deren Umfang und Richtung sich in Bulgarien jedoch erst vage abzuzeichnen beginnen[6]). Bisher sind Auswirkungen der „Umwandlung" auf das Zivilrecht, wie auch auf die meisten anderen Rechtsgebiete kaum spürbar, abgesehen von einer wesentlich größeren Meinungsvielfalt in den Medien. So kann neuerdings sogar der Begriff des „sozialistischen Rechtsstaats" (*pravova socialističeska dăržava*) zur Diskussion gestellt werden[7]). Gewisse Ausnahmen bilden vor allem das Wirtschafts- und das Arbeitsrecht, wo zahlreiche legislative Neuerungen zu verzeichnen sind. Positiv hervorzuheben ist auch das Staatshaftungsgesetz[8]), das rechtswidriges Verhalten von Amtsträgern in Verwaltung und Justiz, unabhängig vom persönlichen Verschulden, mit einer Schadenersatzpflicht belegt, einschließlich des Ersatzes des immateriellen Schadens. Eine völlige Neuordnung wird wohl frühestens nach der Verabschiedung der angekündigten Verfassungsänderung[9]) möglich sein. Im Ergebnis besteht jedenfalls Einigkeit, daß die *preustrojstvo* maßgeblich auch mit Mitteln des Rechts verwirklicht werden soll.

2. Personenrecht

Das Gesetz über die Personen und die Familie regelt in Teil I das Recht der natürlichen Personen (Art. 1–19) und in Teil III die juristischen Personen (Art. 131–154).

a) Natürliche Personen

Danach beginnt die Rechtsfähigkeit des Menschen mit dem Augenblick der Geburt (Art. 1). Personen unter 14 Jahren sind minderjährig (*maloletni*), Art. 3. Als „nichtvolljährig" (*nepălnoletni*) werden Personen im Alter von 14 bis zur Vollendung des 18. Lebensjahres bezeichnet. Die Volljährigkeit tritt mit der Vollendung des 18. Lebensjahres ein (Art. 2).

Bulgarische Personennamen bestehen aus dem Vor-, dem Vaters- und dem Familiennamen, wobei unter dem Vatersnamen der Vorname des Vaters mit Suffix zu verstehen ist. Auch bezüglich des Nachnamens des Kindes wird einseitig auf die

---

[5]) Germanski graždanski zakonnik (Deutsches Bürgerliches Gesetzbuch), übersetzt von A. Kožucharov. Sofia 1974.

[6]) Grundlegend dazu Mräčkov, V.: Nacionalnata partijna konferencija i socialističeskata zakonnost (Die nationale Parteikonferenz und die sozialistische Gesetzlichkeit), in: Dăržava i Pravo. (1988) 2/3, S. 5ff.

[7]) Nenovski, N.: Văznikvane i razvitie na teorijata za pravovata dăržava v buržoaznite strani (Entstehung und Entwicklung der Theorie vom Rechtsstaat in den bürgerlichen Staaten), in: Dăržava i Pravo. (1988) 6, S. 12–23.

[8]) Gesetz über die Verantwortlichkeit des Staates für Bürgern zugefügte Schäden (*Zakon za otgovornostta na dăržavata za vredi, pričineni na graždani*), DV. (1988) 60.

[9]) Vgl. den entsprechenden Parlamentsbeschluß DV. (1987) 65.

Person des Vaters (bzw. des Großvaters) abgestellt (Art. 6 I und II ZLS). Nur bei nichtehelichen Kindern ohne festgestellte Vaterschaft sind die Namen der Mutter maßgebend (Art. 6 III ZLS). Weitere Einzelheiten regelt die Zivilstandsordnung (Art. 7–18).

Der Wohnsitz (Art. 7 ZLS) wird begründet mit der Eintragung in das Einwohnerregister des Ortes, an dem der Betreffende sich mit der Absicht niedergelassen hat, dort ständig oder überwiegend zu bleiben (im einzelnen Art. 19–22 Zivilstandsordnung). Für bestimmte Ortschaften wie insbesondere die Hauptstadt Sofia sind gesetzliche Zuzugsverbote ergangen[10]).

b) Juristische Personen

Das Gesetz über die Personen und die Familie enthält, entsprechend der Geringschätzung der Rechtsfigur der juristischen Person zur Zeit seiner Entstehung[11]), lediglich drei kurze allgemeine Bestimmungen, denen zufolge juristische Personen Träger von Rechten und Pflichten sein können, sie diese Rechte und Pflichten über ihre Organe erwerben (Art. 131) und ihren Sitz am Ort ihrer Verwaltung haben (Art. 132). Für juristische Personen mit wirtschaftlicher Zielsetzung wird im übrigen auf Spezialgesetze verwiesen (Art. 133); dazu unten. Zum Register für die juristischen Personen bei den Bezirksgerichten siehe unten (II 7).

Juristische Personen mit nichtwirtschaftlicher, also ideeller Zielsetzung sind die Gesellschaften (*sdruženie*) (Art. 134–148) und die Stiftung (*fondacija*) (Art. 149–154). Juristische Personen mit wirtschaftlicher Zielsetzung sind vor allem die Firmen (*firma*) (vgl. Art. 2 I des DS-Erlasses Nr. 56 über die wirtschaftliche Tätigkeit[12]) sowie die Genossenschaften (*kooperacija*)[13]). Nach der Aufhebung des überkommenen Gesellschaftsrechts (HGB und GmbH-Gesetz) durch Erlaß des Präsidiums der NSb von 1951[14]) verlief die Entwicklung in diesem Bereich zunächst sehr zögerlich[15]). Eine umfassende Regelung enthielt erstmals wieder das „Reglement für den ökonomischen Mechanismus"[16]) in dem Kapitel „Bildung von Assoziationen der Wirtschaftsorganisationen" (*sdružavane na stopanskite organizacii*)

---

[10]) Vgl. die Ordnung für die zeitweise Beschränkung der Aufnahme neuer Einwohner in die Städte (*Naredba za vremenno ograničavane priemaneto na novi žiteli v gradovete*), DV. (1974) 94 Fassung (1986) 86 sowie die Durchführungsvorschrift DV. (1975) 4 Fassung (1980) 70. S. auch Kostov, D.: Mestožitelstvo i schodni ponjatija (Wohnsitz und ähnliche Begriffe), in: Dăržava i Pravo. (1989) 2, S. 39–46.

[11]) Nachweise bei Sárközy, T.: Die „juristische Person" in den sozialistischen Ländern, in: Rabels Zeitschrift für ausländisches und internationales Privatrecht. 47 (1983) S. 1–21; Slapnicka, H.: Die sozialistische Kollektivperson. Funktion und Struktur der juristischen Person in den europäischen Volksdemokratien. Wien, Köln, Graz 1969.

[12]) *Ukaz za stopanskata dejnost*, DV. (1989) 4 nebst Durchführungsvorschrift, DV. (1989) 15.

[13]) Genossenschaftsgesetz (*Zakon za kooperativnite organizacii*), DV. (1983) 102 Fassung (1989) 46.

[14]) Izv. (1951) 78.

[15]) Vgl. allgemein auch Brunner, G.: Handelsgesellschaften im Sozialismus?, in: Sozialistisches Wirtschaftsrecht zwischen Wandel und Beharrung. Hrsg. v. K. Westen, G. Brunner und F.-C. Schroeder. Berlin 1988, S. 89–147. Einzelheiten bei Tadžer, V.: Kooperativno i družestveno pravo na NRB (Genossenschafts- und Gesellschaftsrecht der NRB). Sofia 1985, S. 173–176.

[16]) *Pravilnik za ikonomičeskija mechanizăm*, DV. (1982) 9.

(Art. 130–149). Die Ordnung für die wirtschaftlichen Assoziationen von 1987[17]) wurde schon 1988 durch eine gleichnamige Vorschrift ersetzt[18]).

Daneben gibt es auch sonstige juristische Personen wie z. B. den Staat, die Volksräte (*narodni săveti*) (Art. 16 I des Gesetzes über die Volksräte[19]) u. a. staatliche Leitungsorgane[20]). Der Grundsatz der speziellen Rechtsfähigkeit (*specialna pravoposobnost*) der juristischen Person[21]), also beschränkt auf ihren Aufgabenbereich, war zunächst in allen sozialistischen Staaten vorherrschend, hat jedoch in den letzten Jahren teilweise erhebliche Auflockerungen erfahren[22]). In Bulgarien erklärt Art. 26 III ZZD Verträge der sozialistischen Organisationen für nichtig, die ihren Tätigkeitsgegenstand überschreiten. Zumindest für die Wirtschaftsorganisationen ist die Anwendbarkeit dieser Bestimmung aber zweifelhaft geworden[23]).

3. Eigentumsrecht

Das überkommene Sachenrecht[24]) wurde 1951 mit der Verabschiedung des Eigentumsgesetzes aufgehoben. In den Jahren zuvor waren zahlreiche Nationalisierungsmaßnahmen[25]) zum Zwecke der Vergesellschaftung der Produktionsmittel im Wege der Verstaatlichung von Privateigentum und der Kollektivierung von Landwirtschaft und Handwerk durchgeführt worden. 1973 erging zusätzlich das Gesetz über das Eigentum der Bürger, das insbesondere regelt, was der einzelne alles nicht haben darf. Und zwar können bulgarische Bürger im persönlichen Eigentum nur unbewegliche und bewegliche Vermögensgegenstände zur Befriedigung ihrer eigenen und der Bedürfnisse ihrer Familie haben, darüber hinaus auch Produktionsmittel (der Zusatz „geringfügige" Produktionsmittel wurde 1989 gestrichen) zur Ausführung von Hilfstätigkeiten und die daraus erzeugten Produkte (Art. 1 ZSG). Die individuelle Arbeitstätigkeit[26]) unterliegt in Bulgarien, anders als etwa in Ungarn, noch immer sehr

---

[17]) *Naredba za stopanskite sdruženija*, DV. (1987) 18.
[18]) DV. (1988) 28.
[19]) *Zakon za narodnite săveti*, Izv. (1951) 95 Fassung DV. (1978) 97.
[20]) Vgl. z. B. Petev, V.: Sozialistisches Zivilrecht. Berlin, New York 1975, S. 43–73.
[21]) Dazu Petev (ebenda) S. 54–56.
[22]) Vgl. z. B. § 28 II des ungarischen Zivilgesetzbuchs Fassung 1959 versus Fassung von 1977.
[23]) Weiteres bei Tadžer, V.: Izmenenija v specialnata pravoposobnost na stopanskite organizacii (Änderungen in der speziellen Rechtsfähigkeit der Wirtschaftsorganisationen), in: Socialističesko Pravo. (1982) 3, S. 3–11.
[24]) Insbesondere das Gesetz über die Vermögen, das Eigentum und die Servituten (*Zakon za imuštestvata, za sobstvenostta i servitutite*), DV. (1904) 29.
[25]) Im einzelnen aufgeführt bei Velinov, I.: Razvitie na veštnoto pravo (Entwicklung des Sachenrechts), in: Razvitie na socialističeskoto pravo v Bălgarija (Entwicklung des sozialistischen Rechts in Bulgarien). Hrsg. v. Radev, J. Sofia 1984, S. 161–193 (171–181).
[26]) Dazu Reglement für die kollektive und individuelle Arbeitstätigkeit der Bürger zwecks zusätzlicher Produktion von Waren und Dienstleistungen (*Pravilnik za kolektivnata i ličnata trudova dejnost na graždanite za dopălnitelno proizvodstvo na stoki i uslugi*, DV. (1987) 48) mit diversen Durchführungsvorschriften für das private Beherbergungswesen, Bewirtschaftung von Kleinobjekten wie Gaststätten usw., Handwerk, Produktion, Handel und Dienstleistungen, Privattaxis sowie Tätigkeiten in der Rechentechnik. Siehe auch Nončev, I.; Kirov, D.: Dobrovolnijat dopălnitelen trud (Freiwillige Zusatzarbeit). Sofia 1987.

weitgehenden Einschränkungen (Beschränkung auf ganz bestimmte Lebensbereiche, Verbot der Beschäftigung von Hilfskräften, Ausgestaltung als reine Nebentätigkeit, fehlende materielle u. a. Voraussetzungen), so daß auch auf diesem Wege legaler privater Wohlstand normalerweise nicht zu erreichen ist.

In der Verfassung ist das Eigentum relativ ausführlich geregelt (Art. 14–21, 28). Unterschieden wird zwischen staatlichem (*däržavna*) und genossenschaftlichem Eigentum (*kooperativna sobstvenost*), dem Eigentum von gesellschaftlichen Organisationen (*sobstvenost na obštestvenite organizacii*) sowie dem persönlichen Eigentum (*lična sobstvenost*) (Art. 14 Verf.)[27]. Das persönliche Eigentum der Bürger unterliegt zahlreichen Beschränkungen. Z. B. darf jeder Bürger im Inland nur höchstens ein Wohngebäude und ein Wochenendhaus haben. Im Grundsatz bildet dies zugleich auch die Obergrenze für eine Familie (Ehepaar mit seinen unverheirateten nichtvolljährigen Kindern), wobei ein Kind aber z. B. eine eigene Wohnung erben kann (im einzelnen Art. 2 ZSG). Allgemein können die Mitglieder einer Familie zwei selbständige Wohnungen besitzen, sofern sie wenigstens eine davon geerbt haben; Ehegatten, die vor der Eheschließung jeder eine eigene Wohnung hatten, dürfen jetzt beide behalten, jedoch bilden zwei Wohnungen die Obergrenze (Art. 4 ZSG Fassung 1986). Wer mehr Wohngebäude (Wohnungen) oder Wochenendhäuser besitzt als zulässig, muß den Rest innerhalb von 2 Jahren nach dem Erwerb veräußern (Art. 7); andernfalls erfolgt ein Zwangsverkauf durch den Volksrat (Art. 8). Tatsächlich ist die Wohnsituation in Bulgarien, besonders in den größeren Städten (Sofia!) sehr beengt, und manche Familie ist froh, nach langem Warten überhaupt nur *eine*, kleine Mietwohnung zu finden. Ausländer mit ständigem Wohnsitz in Bulgarien haben dieselben Rechte und Pflichten wie inländische Bürger (Art. 14 I ZSG). Rechte an unbeweglichem Vermögen können in der Regel nicht frei, sondern nur über den zuständigen Volksrat übertragen bzw. begründet werden, wobei die Preise vom Staat diktiert werden[28]. Durch Arbeit erworbenes Eigentum wird besonders geschützt (Art. 2 II ZS). Dagegen werden „ohne Arbeit erzielte" (*netrudovi*) Einkünfte, wie z. B. Vermögensvorteile aus unerlaubten Preisaufschlägen, zugunsten des Staates konfisziert (Art. 31 ff. ZSG).

Vermögenswerte von Ausländern in Bulgarien sowie von Inländern im Ausland unterliegen einer gesteigerten Kontrolle. So ist eine Genehmigung des Ministeriums für Wirtschaft und Planung erforderlich für Rechtsgeschäfte und Handlungen, durch die (a) Ausländer im Inland belegenes Vermögen anderen Ausländern oder Inländern zu deren Eigentum übertragen; (b) Inländer im Ausland belegenes Vermögen in das Eigentum ausländischer oder anderer inländischer Personen übertragen; (c) Inländer einem Ausländer Eigentum an ihrem Inlandsvermögen übertragen. Dasselbe gilt für die Begründung oder Übertragung sonstiger dinglicher Rechte [Art. 23 des Gesetzes über die Geschäfte mit Valutawerten und die Valutakontrolle (*Zakon za sdelkite s valutni cennosti i za valutnija kontrol*, im folgenden: ZSVCVK)][29].

---

[27] Das Eigentumsgesetz 1951 nennt zusätzlich auch die Form des privaten Eigentums (*častna sobstvenost*), Art. 2 I, 28 II.
[28] Ordnung für die Preise von unbeweglichem Vermögen (*Naredba za cenite na nedvižimite imoti*), DV. (1979) 99.
[29] DV. (1966) 51 Fassung (1989) 53.

4. Schuldrecht

Ursprung des bulgarischen Schuldrechts war das Gesetz über Schuldverhältnisse und Verträge von 1892[30]). Zu nennen ist ferner auch das Handelsgesetzbuch von 1897[31]). Mit dem Übergang zum Sozialismus wurde das Handelsrecht abgeschafft. Das Gesetz über Schuldverhältnisse und Verträge von 1950 regelt die schuldrechtlichen Beziehungen der Bürger untereinander und mit sozialistischen Organisationen. Daneben enthält es auch zahlreiche Bestimmungen nur für die Verhältnisse der sozialistischen Organisationen, die aber zu einem erheblichen Teil von später ergangenen Sonderregelungen überlagert werden (vgl. auch unten IV: Recht der Wirtschaft). Eine weitere Sondervorschrift war der Erlaß des DS Nr. 535 über die wirtschaftliche Zusammenarbeit zwischen bulgarischen juristischen Personen und ausländischen juristischen und natürlichen Personen von 1980[32]), an dessen Stelle die Art. 99–126 des DS-Erlasses Nr. 56 (s. Anm. 12) betr. die wirtschaftliche Tätigkeit ausländischer und gemischter Firmen im Inland getreten sind.

Von besonderem Interesse aus der Sicht des Auslands ist das Recht der unerlaubten Schadenszufügung, schon deshalb, weil es als lex loci delicti z. B. auch für Straßenverkehrsunfälle mit ausländischer Beteiligung maßgebend ist. Da Bulgarien einerseits ein beliebtes Urlaubsziel für deutsche Touristen, daneben auch Transitstation für in der Bundesrepublik lebende Gastarbeiter (hauptsächlich für Türken, aber auch für Griechen) für Besuche in der Heimat ist, findet es bei Unfällen innerhalb dieser Personengruppen u. U. auch vor deutschen Gerichten Anwendung. Einschlägig sind die Art. 45–54 ZZD[33]). Wer einem anderen schuldhaft einen Schaden zufügt, ist ihm zum Ersatz verpflichtet, wobei das Verschulden bis zum Beweis des Gegenteils vermutet wird (Art. 45 ZZD). Art. 50 begründet eine Gefährdungshaftung des Eigentümers und des Beaufsichtigenden für Schäden, die durch irgendwelche Sachen (wie z. B. Kraftfahrzeuge) entstanden sind. Der Schadensersatz umfaßt, neben allen direkten und unmittelbaren Folgen der Schadenszufügung, auch Nichtvermögensschäden, die das Gericht nach Billigkeit bemißt. Die Verjährungsfrist für deliktische Schadensersatzansprüche beträgt 5 Jahre ab der Entdeckung des Täters (Art. 110, 114 ZZD). Im Falle einer Haftpflichtversicherung durch das Staatliche Versicherungsinstitut (*Dăržaven zastrachovatelen institut*, DZI) kann der Geschädigte einen Direktanspruch gegen den Versicherer geltend machen (Art. 349 II ZZD)[34]).

---

[30]) *Zakon za zadălženijata i dogovorite*, DV. (1892) 268. Dazu ausführlich Schöndorf (s. Anm. 1) sowie auch Popov, L.: Razvitie na obligacionnoto pravo (Entwicklung des Schuldrechts), in: Razvitie (s. Anm. 25), S. 194–222 (194 ff.).

[31]) *Tărgovski zakon*, DV. (1897) 114.

[32]) *Ukaz za ikonomičesko sătrudničestvo meždu bălgarski juridičeski lica i čuždestranni juridičeski i fizičeski lica*, DV. (1980) 25 Fassung (1988) 26. Dazu z. B.: Bulgarisches Wirtschaftskooperationsrecht, Aspekte des Erlasses Nr. 535 vom 25. März 1980 aus bulgarischer Sicht, in: Rabels Zeitschrift für ausländisches und internationales Privatrecht. 49 (1985), S. 678–733 (deutsche Übers. S. 734–740).

[33]) Deutsche Übersetzung in: Jessel, Ch.: Kraftfahrzeug-Haftpflichtversicherung in Bulgarien, in: Versicherungsrecht. (1979), S. 701–704 (702, Anm. 10). Dazu auch Apostolov, I.: Jurisprudence de la cour suprême – A. Responsabilité civile délictuelle, in: Droit Bulgare. (1968), S. 40–77.

[34]) Ein gesetzlicher Forderungsübergang auf den Sozialversicherungsträger wird in Bulgarien nicht anerkannt, jedoch kann der Geschädigte seinen Anspruch gegen das DZI dem ausländischen

5. Erbrecht

Das Erbgesetz von 1949[35]) zählt zu den beständigsten bulgarischen Gesetzen der Nachkriegszeit; während seiner bisher fast 40-jährigen Geltungsdauer wurde es nur zweimal geringfügig geändert. Seit längerem wird aber eine Neuregelung vorbereitet, und zwar soll das künftige Zivilgesetzbuch auch einen erbrechtlichen Abschnitt enthalten. Einige veraltete Regelungen des Erbgesetzes dürften dann entfallen; statt dessen könnten erbrechtliche Einzelbestimmungen, wie sie jetzt verstreut in anderen Gesetzen zu finden sind[36]), mit der Grundregelung vereinigt werden.

Die bulgarische Verfassung garantiert das Erbrecht in Art. 27. Gesetzliche Erben sind in der ersten Ordnung die Kinder des Erblassers bzw. deren Abkömmlinge. In zweiter Linie erben die Eltern, danach, in der dritten Ordnung, die Geschwister bzw. deren Abkömmlinge gemeinsam mit Verwandten in aufsteigender Linie zweiten oder eines höheren Grades (Art. 5–8 ZN)[37]). Der überlebende Ehegatte hat ebenfalls ein gesetzliches Erbrecht, das recht originell ausgestaltet ist. Alleinerbe wird er nur dann, wenn überhaupt keine anderen gesetzlichen Erben vorhanden sind. Neben Erben der ersten Ordnung erbt er ein Kindsteil. Sofern der Erblasser vom überlebenden Ehegatten zusammen mit seinen Kindern beerbt wurde, konnte früher der Ehegatte gemäß Art. 14 VII SK (*Semeen kodeks*/Familienkodex) 1968[38]) nur am individuellen Vermögen des Erblassers beteiligt werden, partizipierte also nicht am Anteil, den der verstorbene Ehegatte am Gemeinschaftsgut besaß. Diese Bestimmung, die den Ehegatten in vielen Fällen kraß benachteiligte, ist mit dem Inkrafttreten des neuen Familienkodex weggefallen. Nach wie vor muß jedoch der Ehegatte den Nachlaß auch mit sehr entfernten Verwandten teilen (gegebenenfalls auch mit der Urgroßmutter oder etwa mit den Großneffen des Erblassers)[39]). Die Erbquote des Ehegatten hängt bei Zusammentreffen mit Erben der zweiten und dritten Ordnung von der Ehedauer ab. Und zwar erhält er, falls er zusammen mit Aszendenten oder mit Geschwistern (bzw. deren Kindern) erbt, die Hälfte, und wenn der Erbfall nach Ablauf von zehn Ehejahren erfolgt, zwei Drittel des Nachlasses. Erbt der Ehegatte dagegen gemeinsam mit Aszendenten und mit Geschwistern (bzw. deren Kindern), so erhält er vor Ablauf der Zehnjahresfrist ein Drittel, danach die Hälfte (Art. 9 ZN). Ein erbenloser Nachlaß

Sozialversicherungsträger durch Vertrag abtreten (Urteil Nr. 882 des bulgarischen Obersten Gerichts v. 12.6.1984, in: Socialističesko Pravo. (1984) 9, S. 80). Vgl. jedoch neuerdings auch das Urteil Nr. 450 des Obersten Gerichts vom 10.7.1986, demzufolge Ausländer in solchen Fällen keinen weitergehenden Rechtsschutz beanspruchen können als Bulgaren (Anspruch aus Forderungsabtretung verneint), nach: Jessel-Holst, Ch.: Rechtsprechung des Obersten Gerichts der Volksrepublik Bulgarien in den Jahren 1985–1986, in: WGO – Monatshefte für Osteuropäisches Recht. (1989), S. 95–107.

[35]) Deutsche Übers. in: Ferid, M.; Firsching, K.: Internationales Erbrecht. München. Loseblattsammlung. Länderteil Bulgarien.

[36]) Im einzelnen Nenova, L.: Graždanskijat kodeks i nasledstvenoto pravo (Zivilkodex und Erbrecht), in: Problemi na kodifikacijata na graždanskoto pravo v Narodna republika Bălgarija (Probleme der Kodifikation des Zivilrechts in der NRB). Hrsg. von der BAN. Sofia 1975, S. 227–255 (228).

[37]) Nach Tasev, Ch.: Bălgarsko nasledstveno pravo (Bulgarisches Erbrecht). 4. Aufl. Sofia 1987, S. 31 ff.

[38]) Vgl. Anm. 77.

[39]) Kritisch z. B. Nenova (Anm. 36), S. 240.

fällt dem Staat zu (Art. 11 ZN). Erben, die mit dem Erblasser in häuslicher Gemeinschaft gelebt und für ihn gesorgt haben, erhalten den üblichen Hausrat als gesetzlichen Voraus (Art. 12 ZN).

Durch Testament (*zaveštanie*) (Art. 13 ff. ZN) kann der Erblasser Erbeinsetzungen vornehmen und Vermächtnisse aussetzen. Voraussetzung ist, daß er volljährig ist. Über sein ganzes Vermögen kann der Testator nur zugunsten seiner gesetzlichen Erben, des Staates oder öffentlicher Organisationen verfügen, zugunsten anderer Personen dagegen nur über höchstens die Hälfte. Auch gibt es einen Pflichtteilsanspruch zugunsten der Abkömmlinge, Eltern und des Ehegatten (*zapazena čast*). Seine Regelung ist kompliziert (Art. 29 ZN) und sieht sehr unterschiedliche Quoten vor, wobei als frei verfügbarer Teil (*razpolagaema čast*) je nach Sachlage zwischen zwei Dritteln und einem Achtel des Nachlasses übrigbleibt. Gemeinschaftstestamente sind verboten (Art. 15 ZN). Die Form des Testaments kann notariell oder eigenhändig sein, wobei das eigenhändige Testament zur Gänze handschriftlich verfaßt sein, das Datum der Errichtung angeben und unterschrieben sein muß. Das Testament ist frei widerruflich. Der Erblasser ist berechtigt, einen oder mehrere Testamentsvollstrecker einzusetzen.

Voraussetzung für den Erwerb der Erbschaft ist ihre Annahme durch den Erben (Art. 48 ZN), die auf den Zeitpunkt der Eröffnung der Erbschaft, d. h. des Todes des Erblassers, zurückwirkt. Die Annahme kann durch schriftliche Erklärung an den Rayonrichter erfolgen, in dessen Sprengel die Erbschaft eröffnet wurde (d. h. am letzten Wohnsitz des Erblassers). Sie kann aber auch konkludent durch Handlungen zum Ausdruck gebracht werden, die unzweifelhaft die Annahmeabsicht erkennen lassen. Das Recht zur Annahme erlischt mit Ablauf von 5 Jahren nach der Eröffnung der Erbschaft.

Eine Ausschlagung der Erbschaft durch Inländer, die Vermögen im Ausland geerbt haben, erfordert die vorherige Zustimmung des Ministeriums für Wirtschaft und Planung (Art. 24 ZSVCVK, oben N. 29). Dasselbe gilt offenbar auch für die Ausschlagung einer Erbschaft durch einen Ausländer, wenn sich der Nachlaß im Inland befindet[40]. Genehmigungsfrei ist dagegen die letztwillige Verfügung zugunsten von ausländischen und inländischen Personen, mag auch der Nachlaß im Ausland belegen sein (vgl. Art. 23 III ZSVCVK). Für ausländische Staatsangehörige mit Wohnsitz im Ausland ist vorgesehen, daß sie in Bulgarien belegenes unbewegliches Vermögen überhaupt nur im Wege der Erbfolge erwerben können (Art. 14 II ZSG).

Besonders geregelt ist die Erbfolge in Urheberrechte (Art. 18 Urhebergesetz)[41]. Und zwar sind gesetzliche Erben in diesem Fall nur die Abkömmlinge, der Ehegatte und die Eltern gemäß den Bestimmungen des Erbgesetzes. Testamentarische Verfügungen sind unter den allgemeinen Voraussetzungen zulässig. Wichtig ist, daß Urheberrechte nur ein einziges Mal vererbt werden können. Stirbt also der gesetzliche oder der testamentarische Erbe vor Ablauf der 50-jährigen Schutzfrist, so geht das Urheberrecht in jedem Fall auf den Staat über[42]. Außerdem erhalten die Erben noch nicht

---

[40] Tasev (s. Anm. 37), S. 111 f.
[41] *Zakon za avtorskoto pravo*, Izv. (1951) 92 Fassung DV. (1972) 35.
[42] Tasev (Anm. 37), S. 107.

einmal das volle Urheberhonorar, sondern lediglich die Hälfte, falls es sich um Eltern, den überlebenden Ehegatten und Abkömmlinge bis zur Volljährigkeit bzw. Abschluß der Ausbildung (maximal bis zur Vollendung des 25. Lebensjahres) handelt. Sonstige Erben bzw. erwachsene Kinder bekommen gar nur 20 % der für den Urheber selbst vorgesehenen Vergütung[43]).

Die Erbschaftssteuer ergibt sich aus dem Gesetz über örtliche Steuern und Gebühren (Art. 22–32)[44]). Sie richtet sich nach der Nähe des Erben zum Erblasser sowie nach dem Umfang des Nachlasses, mit gewissen, jedoch nicht sehr bedeutenden Freibeträgen, und beträgt z. B. für Ehegatten und Verwandte in auf- und absteigender Linie zwischen 2 % (bei einem Wert von 800 Leva) und, bei einem Wert von mehr als 12 000 Leva, 1668 Leva zuzüglich 50 % von dem Teil, der 12 000 Leva übersteigt, kann also im Einzelfall ziemlich hoch sein.

6. Internationales Privatrecht

Das bulgarische Kollisionsrecht ist nur in Teilbereichen gesetzlich normiert. An erster Stelle ist hier das internationale Familienrecht zu nennen (unten III 5), daneben auch das internationale Arbeitsrecht (unten V 3), ferner auch das Recht der Seehandelsschiffahrt[45]). Im Verhältnis zu den anderen sozialistischen Staaten sind die bilateralen Rechtshilfeverträge zu beachten, die dem autonomen Recht vorgehen (dazu das Kapitel der Autorin, „Verträge" VIII 3). Das neueste Lehrbuch des bulgarischen Internationalen Privatrechts datiert von 1976[46]). Die Praxis der bulgarischen Gerichte in Sachen mit Auslandsberührung ist nicht leicht zugänglich, soweit es überhaupt eine gibt[47]), denn in 99 % der Fälle mit internationalem Element wenden die bulgarischen Gerichte ohnehin die lex fori (Recht des Gerichtsstands) an[48]). Das seit langem geplante Zivilgesetzbuch soll auch einen Abschnitt über das Internationale Privatrecht enthalten.

7. Reformbestrebungen

Das bulgarische Zivilrecht wird zu Recht insgesamt als reformbedürftig angesehen. Seit Jahren laufen die Arbeiten an einer Kodifikation, die auch schon zu entspre-

---

[43]) Art. 3 der Anordnung Nr. 257 des Ministerratsbüros über die Anwendung des Urheberrechtsgesetzes (*Razporeždane za prilagane na Zakona za avtorskoto pravo*), DV. (1972) 55.
[44]) *Zakon za mestnite danăci i taksi*, Izv. (1951) 104 Fassung DV. (1984) 55.
[45]) Dazu Damjanov, C.: Die Kollisionsnormen nach dem bulgarischen Kodex für die Seehandelsschiffahrt, in: WGO-Monatshefte für Osteuropäisches Recht. (1978), S. 153–167 (mit deutscher Übers. S. 168–175).
[46]) Kutikov, V.: Meždunarodno častno pravo na NR Bălgarija (Internationales Privatrecht der NRB). 3. Aufl. Sofia 1976.
[47]) Nachweise vor allem bei Čačev, L.: Sădebna praktika po graždanski sporove s meždunaroden element (Gerichtspraxis bei Zivilsachen mit internationalem Element). Sofia 1981.
[48]) Siehe Todorov, T.: Zakonăt na săda v bălgarskoto meždunarodno častno pravo (Lex fori im bulgarischen Internationalen Privatrecht). Sofia 1988.

chenden Entwürfen geführt haben[49]). Erschwert wird das Vorhaben vor allem durch den Umstand, daß der Regelungsbereich des geplanten Gesetzes wohl noch immer nicht völlig ausdiskutiert ist. Debatten gab es, neben der Frage nach dem richtigen Standort des Internationalen Privatrechts, vor allem um die Einbeziehung des Wirtschaftsrechts, die jetzt wohl zugunsten einer eigenständigen wirtschaftsrechtlichen Kodifikation entschieden worden sind.

II. Zivilprozeßrecht

1. Einführung

Die Ursprünge des ersten bulgarischen Zivilprozeßgesetzes (von 1892) liegen im russischen Recht, mit späteren Anleihen im österreichischen und deutschen Recht[50]). Nach dem 9.9.1944 galt zunächst zwar das alte Gesetz (in der Neufassung von 1930)[51]) fort[52]), jedoch wurde durch Änderungsgesetze[53]) ein schrittweiser Übergang zu einer Zivilgerichtsbarkeit nach sowjetischem Muster herbeigeführt[54]). Im Jahre 1952 wurde ein Zivilprozeßkodex (*Graždanski procesualen kodeks*, im folgenden: GPK) verabschiedet, der noch immer fortgilt, wenngleich mit zahlreichen zwischenzeitlichen Änderungen[55]).

2. System und Zuständigkeit der Zivilgerichte

a) Die Gerichte

Die Zivilgerichtsbarkeit ist dreistufig und wird von den Rayon- [bis 1973 „Volksgerichte" (*naroden săd*) genannt][56]) und Bezirksgerichten sowie dem Obersten Gericht ausgeübt[57]). [Das Bezirksgericht der Hauptstadt trägt den Namen „Stadtgericht" (*gradski săd*); Art. 32 Gerichtsverfassungsgesetz (*Zakon za ustrojstvoto na sădilištata*,

---

[49]) Vgl. auch den Sammelband Problemi (Anm. 36).
[50]) *Zakon za graždanskoto sădoproizvodstvo* (DV. (1892) 31). Dazu Iwanov (Anm. 1), S. 19.
[51]) Vgl. Siljanovski, D.: Graždansko sădoproizvodstvo (Zivilprozeß). Sofia 1938, S. 43.
[52]) DV. (1930) 256.
[53]) DV. (1948) 9 und 228.
[54]) Vgl. auch das Gesetz über die Schließung der Appellationsgerichte (*Zakon za zakrivane na apelativnite sădilišta*, DV. (1947) 289), Gesetz über den Aufbau der Volksgerichte (*Zakon za ustrojstvoto na narodnite sădilišta*, DV. (1948) 70) u.a.m. Dazu Janovski, B.: Razvitie na socialističeskija graždanski proces (Entwicklung des sozialistischen Zivilprozesses), in: Razvitie (Anm. 25), S. 330–361 (330 ff.).
[55]) Izv. (1952) 12 Fassung DV. (1989) 31. Die wichtigsten Novellen sind Izv. (1961) 50 und DV. (1983) 28.
[56]) Umbenennung DV. (1973) 88.
[57]) Vgl. auch das Reglement für die Organisation der Arbeit der Rayon-, Bezirks- und Militärgerichte (*Pravilnik za organizacijata na rabotata na rajonnite, okrăžnite i voennite sădilišta*, DV. (1977) 89 Fassung (1989) 42).

im folgenden: ZUS)⁵⁸)]. Das Rayongericht (*rajonnen säd*) verhandelt als Gericht der untersten Stufe im Regelfall in der Besetzung mit einem Berufsrichter und zwei Laien-Beisitzern bzw. in gesetzlich bestimmten Sonderfällen durch den Einzelrichter (Art. 21 ZUS). Auch das Bezirksgericht (*okrăžen säd*) bzw. das Stadtgericht Sofia – also die mittlere Ebene – ist im allgemeinen mit einem Berufsrichter und zwei Schöffen, als Berufungsinstanz jedoch mit drei Berufsrichtern besetzt (Art. 26 ZUS). Das Oberste Gericht (*Vărchoven săd*) verhandelt Berufungssachen mit drei Berufsrichtern (Art. 44 Nr. 2 ZUS).

b) Zuständigkeit

Die Rayongerichte sind zuständig für alle Zivilsachen, die nicht den Bezirksgerichten zugewiesen sind (Art. 79 GPK). Im Jahre 1983 wurde der Kompetenzbereich der Rayongerichte erheblich ausgeweitet und umfaßt jetzt z. B. auch alle Ehesachen. Damit verhandeln die Rayongerichte nach der Reform rund 90 % aller Zivilsachen⁵⁹). Vor die Bezirksgerichte (bzw. das Stadtgericht Sofia) gehören die folgenden Sachen (Art. 80 GPK): (a) Klagen auf Feststellung oder Anfechtung der Abstammung, Beendigung einer Adoption, Entmündigung bzw. deren Aufhebung; (b) Klagen mit einem Streitwert über 10 000 Leva; (c) sonstige Klagen kraft gesetzlicher Zuweisung. Das Oberste Gericht hat keine eigene erstinstanzliche Zuständigkeit in Zivilsachen, jedoch steht den höheren Gerichten ein Evokationsrecht gegenüber den Gerichten ihres Sprengels zu, so daß sie Fälle an sich ziehen und selbst entscheiden können (Art. 80 II GPK).

Der allgemeine Gerichtsstand bestimmt sich nach dem Wohnsitz des Beklagten; Unterhaltsklagen können auch am Wohnsitz des Klägers erhoben werden (Art. 81 GPK). Für Klagen gegen juristische Personen richtet sich der Gerichtsstand grundsätzlich nach dem Ort ihrer Verwaltung (vgl. Art. 89 GPK). Besondere Gerichtsstände sind insbesondere der Belegenheitsort von unbeweglichen Sachen (Art. 83), der Gerichtsstand der Erbschaft als Ort der Erbschaftseröffnung (Art. 84), der Gerichtsstand der unerlaubten Handlung, entweder als Begehungsort oder entsprechend dem Wohnsitz des Beklagten (Art. 85) u. a.

Gegen die Entscheidungen der Rayongerichte ist eine Berufung (*obžalvane*) bei den Bezirksgerichten möglich. Erstinstanzliche Entscheidungen der Bezirksgerichte können vor dem Obersten Gericht angefochten werden (Art. 196 GPK).

3. Das Verfahren

a) Die erste Instanz

Meist beginnt der Zivilprozeß mit einer Klage der interessierten Person; jedoch kann auch der Staatsanwalt den Antrag stellen (Art. 2 II GPK). Die Ladung muß jetzt mindestens 7 Tage im voraus erfolgen (Art. 41 V GPK Fassung 1983). Ziel des

---

⁵⁸) DV. (1976) 23 Fassung (1988) 91.
⁵⁹) Janovski (Anm. 54) S. 338.

Verfahrens ist die objektive Wahrheitsfindung unter aktiver Mitwirkung des Gerichts (Art. 137). Die Verhandlung ist grundsätzlich öffentlich (mit Ausnahmemöglichkeit im öffentlichen Interesse oder mit Rücksicht auf die Intimsphäre der Parteien (Art. 105 II GPK). Jede Partei muß diejenigen Umstände beweisen, auf die sie ihre Anträge oder Einwände stützt. Das Geständnis einer Partei ist nicht automatisch bindend, sondern wird vom Gericht mit Rücksicht auf alle Umstände des Falles gewürdigt (Art. 127). Auch ist das Gericht nicht auf die Beweisanträge der Parteien beschränkt, sondern kann selber von Amts wegen Beweise erheben und erhobene Beweise nachprüfen (Art. 129 GPK). Beweismittel sind: Zeugen, schriftliche Beweise, Sachverständige, Augenschein. Der Zeugenbeweis ist in bestimmten Fällen ausgeschlossen; insbesondere gilt dies für die Feststellung von Verträgen mit einem Wert über 500 Leva, außer Verträgen zwischen Ehegatten und nahen Angehörigen (Art. 133 GPK). Die Novelle 1983 sieht verschiedene Maßnahmen zur Verfahrensbeschleunigung vor, einschließlich einer Zusatzgebühr für Prozeßverschleppung. Das Urteil wird in geheimer Beratung mit Stimmenmehrheit der Richter gefällt (Art. 187 GPK), wobei das Gericht die Vollstreckung mit Rücksicht auf die Vermögenslage einer Partei oder auf andere Umstände einmal (nicht öfter) hinausschieben kann (Art. 191 GPK).

b) Die zweite Instanz

Die Berufung ist binnen 7 Tagen bei dem Gericht einzulegen, dessen Entscheidung angefochten wird (Art. 197 II GPK). In diesem Verfahren sind im Grundsatz als Beweismittel nur schriftliche Beweise sowie Geständnisse zugelassen; jedoch kann das Berufungsgericht, wenn es den Rechtsstreit in der Sache verhandelt, neue Beweise erheben und erforderlichenfalls auch die Zeugen und Sachverständigen erneut vernehmen (Art. 205 GPK).

Auch in der zweiten Instanz beschränkt sich das Gericht nicht auf die Erörterung der von den Parteien bezeichneten Berufungsgründe, sondern ist verpflichtet, von Amts wegen die Richtigkeit der Entscheidung im ganzen zu überprüfen (Kontrollfunktion). Dementsprechend kann es auch nicht angegriffene Bestandteile aufheben oder aber für Personen aufheben, die nicht selbst Berufungskläger sind (Art. 206 GPK). Die kassatorische Funktion der Berufungsinstanz wurde 1983 erheblich eingeschränkt (vgl. Art. 208 GPK), so daß es nur noch in wenigen Ausnahmefällen zu einer Zurückverweisung an die Vorinstanz kommt. Damit vollzieht sich in Bulgarien ein Wandel ähnlich wie in der DDR, Ungarn und der Tschechoslowakei[60]). Gründe für eine Urteilsaufhebung sind (Art. 207 GPK): Widerspruch zum Gesetz; wesentliche Verfahrensmängel; unvollständige Beweiserhebung; Unbegründetheit.

c) Überprüfung rechtskräftiger Entscheidungen und Wiederaufnahme

Rechtskräftige Entscheidungen der Gerichte bzw. der besonderen Rechtspflegeorgane (ausgenommen Ehescheidungen) können auf Betreiben des Generalstaatsan-

---

[60]) Dazu Stalev, Ž.: Reformata na GPK ot 8 april 1983 g. (Reform des GPK vom 8.4.1983), in: Pravna Misäl. (1983) 4, S. 68–77 (74).

walts sowie des Vorsitzenden des Obersten Gerichts im Aufsichtsweg durch das Oberste Gericht überprüft werden (Art. 225–230 GPK). Die Gründe sind dieselben wie für die Berufung (Art. 207, jedoch ohne den Fall der unvollständigen Beweiserhebung). Nachdem 1961 erstmals eine zeitliche Befristung eingeführt worden war, wurde diese 1983 verkürzt und vereinfacht und beträgt seitdem ein Jahr ab der Rechtskraft, mit einer Privilegierung für den Staat als Partei (im einzelnen Art. 226 GPK). Das Verfahren ist neuerdings in allen Fällen öffentlich. Auch wird im Regelfall nicht mehr kassiert und zurückverwiesen, sondern das Oberste Gericht trifft eigene Sachentscheidungen (Art. 229 GPK). Die Wiederaufnahme ergibt sich aus Art. 231 ff. GPK.

d) Gebühren und Kosten

Die Gerichtsgebühren sind vergleichsweise niedrig[61]), wurden jedoch für Ehesachen im Jahre 1985 spürbar angehoben. Im Falle des Obsiegens besteht ein Anspruch auf Kostenerstattung (Art. 64 GPK).

e) Befugnisse des Staatsanwalts im Zivilprozeß

Der Staatsanwalt kann ein Verfahren im Interesse eines Dritten in Gang setzen[62]) oder einem bereits anhängigen Verfahren als Partei beitreten in den gesetzlich bestimmten Fällen oder wenn er selbst dies im öffentlichen Interesse für geboten hält. Unter denselben Voraussetzungen kann er auch Stellungnahmen zu Zivilsachen abgeben (Art. 27 GPK). Außerdem ist er berechtigt, selbständig Berufung gegen gerichtliche Entscheidungen einzulegen, sogar wenn er an dem betreffenden Verfahren nicht teilgenommen hatte (Art. 30 GPK).

4. Besondere Verfahrensarten

Der dritte Teil des Zivilprozeßkodex regelt einige besondere Verfahrensarten wie insbesondere das Verfahren in Ehesachen (dazu unten III), in Zivilstandssachen, bei Entmündigung, gerichtlicher Teilung usw.

5. Zwangsvollstreckung

Die Zwangsvollstreckung ergibt sich aus Teil fünf, Art. 323–423 GPK. Lohnpfändungen werden, soweit es um Forderungen des Staates oder einer sozialistischen

---

[61]) Art. 53 ff. GPK sowie Behördentarif Nr. 1 für das Justizministerium (DV. (1970) 1 Fassung (1985) 52).
[62]) Außer bei Klagen, die eine streng persönliche Bewertung erfordern wie: Ehescheidung, Widerruf einer Schenkung usw. [Art. 3 II der Instruktion Nr. 3 für die Arbeit der Bezirks- und Rayon-Staatsanwaltschaften bei der zivilgerichtlichen Gesetzlichkeitsaufsicht (*Instrukcija za rabotata na okrăžnite i rajonnite prokuraturi po graždansko-sădebnija nadzor za zakonnost*, DV. (1983) 32)].

Organisation geht, in das Arbeitsbuch des Schuldners, bei Unterhaltsforderungen überdies auch in seinen Personalausweis eingetragen (Art. 395 IV GPK)[63]). Besondere Regeln gelten für die Vollstreckung in das Vermögen von sozialistischen Organisationen, darunter auch der staatlichen Unternehmen (Art. 399–413 GPK). Bestimmte Vermögensmassen sind dem Zugriff von Gläubigern entzogen, vgl. insbesondere Art. 402 GPK (Boden, Gebäude, Anlagen, Werkzeug usw.).

6. Notarielles Verfahren

Notarielle Aufgaben werden von den Notaren bei den Rayongerichten, bzw. in Ermangelung solcher vom Rayonrichter, dem Gerichtsvollzieher oder auch durch den zuständigen Volksrat oder die Bürgermeisterei (*kmetstvo*) wahrgenommen (siehe im einzelnen Art. 95–97 ZUS, Art. 465–488 GPK). Im Ausland versehen die bulgarischen diplomatischen und konsularischen Vertreter bestimmte notarielle Dienste (Art. 473a GPK).

7. Register für juristische Personen

Seit 1987 gibt es erstmals ein Register für die juristischen Personen und seit 1989 auch für die Firmen von Bürgern, das zunächst bei den Rayongerichten geführt wurde und neuerdings den Bezirksgerichten untersteht (Art. 489–501 GPK)[64]). Die Registereintragungen sind jedermann zugänglich und genießen öffentlichen Glauben (Art. 492f. GPK).

8. Internationales Zivilprozeßrecht

Die bulgarischen Gerichte sind zuständig für Klagen gegen Personen im Inland sowie für Klagen von Bulgaren gegen Personen mit ausländischem Wohnsitz (Art. 7 GPK), wobei die Bestimmungen über die örtliche Zuständigkeit (oben II 2) zugleich auch als solche über die internationale Zuständigkeit aufgefaßt werden[65]). Für Ehesachen genügt es, wenn ein Ehegatte bulgarischer Bürger ist (Art. 7 III n. F. GPK). Bei rein ausländischen Ehen muß entweder der Beklagte den Wohnsitz in Bulgarien haben, oder aber ein Gatte lebt in Bulgarien und die Gesetze des Staates, dem die Ehegatten angehören, schließen die bulgarische Zuständigkeit nicht aus (Art. 7 IV n. F.).

---

[63]) Vgl. auch die Instruktion Nr. 7 über die Eintragung der Pfändungsvermerke in das Arbeitsbuch und in den Paß (*Instrukcija za upisvane na zapornite săobštenija v trudovata knižka i pasporta*, DV. (1987) 93).

[64]) Siehe die Ordnung des Justizministers Nr. 9 über die Führung und Verwahrung der Register für Eintragungen (*Naredba za vodene i săchranjavane na registrite za opisvanijata*), DV. (1989) 42. Zu den Gebühren vgl. DV. (1989) 27.

[65]) Stalev, Ž.: Bălgarsko graždansko procesualno pravo (Bulgarisches Zivilprozeßrecht). 3. Aufl. Sofia 1979, S. 779.

Im Verfahren sind Ausländer den bulgarischen Bürgern gleichgestellt und brauchen daher z. B. auch keine Sicherheit für Prozeßkosten zu leisten[66]). Ein etwa für den Fall maßgebendes ausländisches Recht muß von der Partei bewiesen werden, die daraus für sich günstige Folgen ableiten will, sofern es dem Gericht nicht bekannt ist bzw. von diesem nicht ermittelt werden kann (Art. 132 GPK). Für den Rechtshilfeverkehr zwischen bulgarischen und ausländischen Gerichten gelten die Art. 88–110 des Reglements für die Organisation der Arbeit der Rayon-, Bezirks- und Militärgerichte[67]).

Für die Anerkennung und Vollstreckung ausländischer Gerichtsentscheidungen wurde früher die vertraglich verbürgte Gegenseitigkeit verlangt[68]). Seit 1983 genügt die faktische Gegenseitigkeit (Art. 303 I GPK), über deren Bestehen aus bulgarischer Sicht der Justizminister [seit 1966 (!) Frau Svetla Daskalova] entscheidet (Art. 303 II GPK)[69]). Im Verhältnis der Bundesrepublik Deutschland mit Bulgarien ist die Gegenseitigkeit im Schrifttum mehrfach befürwortet worden[70]). Bei Ehescheidungssachen genügt es, ganz unabhängig von der Gegenseitigkeit, die hier nicht verlangt wird, wenn der Beklagte bei Klageerhebung seinen Wohnsitz in dem Land hatte, in dem die Entscheidung ergangen ist (Art. 303 IV n. F.)[71]).

Die internationale Handelsschiedsgerichtsbarkeit ist 1988 erstmals durch ein Gesetz geregelt worden[72]). Die Zuständigkeit des Schiedsgerichts beruht auf einer entsprechenden Vereinbarung. Während bisher als Schiedsrichter nur bulgarische Bürger zugelassen waren, heißt es jetzt (Art. 11 II): „Schiedsrichter kann auch eine Person sein, die nicht Bürger der Volksrepublik Bulgarien ist." Die Entscheidung des Schiedsgerichts ist endgültig, kann aber unter besonderen Voraussetzungen (Art. 47 f.) vom Stadtgericht Sofia aufgehoben werden[73]).

---

[66]) Popov, L.: Die Rechtsstellung des Ausländers in Bulgarien. Baden-Baden 1981, S. 226. Ebenso Bundesgerichtshof 11.11.1981, Wertpapier-Mitteilungen 1982, S. 194 = Recht der internationalen Wirtschaft 1982, S. 213.
[67]) Anm. 57. Deutsche Übers. in: WGO-Monatshefte für Osteuropäisches Recht. (1982), S. 264–267.
[68]) Rechtshilfeverträge siehe unten „Verträge" VIII 3.
[69]) D. h. das Gericht muß im konkreten Fall beim Ministerium nachfragen, ob Gegenseitigkeit besteht. Dazu Damjanov, C.: Vzaimnost s ogled izpălnenie na čuždestranni sădebni i arbitražni rešenija (Gegenseitigkeit bei der Vollstreckung ausländischer Gerichts- und Schiedsgerichtsentscheidungen), in: Pravna Misăl. (1986) 5, S. 71 f.
[70]) Velinov, L.: Sădebnoto proizvodstvo po priznavane i dopuskane izpălnenieto na čuždestranni sădebni rešenija (Gerichtliches Verfahren zur Anerkennung und Vollstreckung ausländischer Gerichtsentscheidungen), in: Socialističesko Pravo. (1983) 8, S. 26–33 (27); Martiny, D.: Anerkennung ausländischer Entscheidungen nach autonomem Recht, in: Handbuch des internationalen Zivilverfahrensrechts. Hrsg. v. Max-Planck-Institut für ausländisches und internationales Privatrecht. Bd. III/1. Tübingen 1984, Rz. 1343; Jessel-Holst, Ch.: Anerkennung und Vollstreckung ausländischer Entscheidungen sowie Rechtshilfe in Zivilsachen nach dem bulgarischen Recht, in: WGO-Monatshefte für Osteuropäisches Recht. (1982), S. 255–267 (256).
[71]) Vgl. im übrigen die Art. 303–307 GPK; deutsche Übers. von Jessel-Holst, Ch. bei Bergmann, A.; Ferid, M.: Internationales Ehe- und Kindschaftsrecht, Länderteil Bulgarien. Frankfurt/M. Loseblattsammlung.
[72]) Gesetz über die internationale Handelsschiedsgerichtsbarkeit (*Zakon za meždunarodnija tărgovski arbitraž*, DV. (1988) 60).
[73]) Vgl. im übrigen das Kapitel der Autorin, Verträge, VIII 1.

III. Familienrecht

1. Einführung

Das bulgarische Familienrecht gehörte früher in die Zuständigkeit der Kirche, die auch eigene geistliche Gerichte unterhielt. Es galt das byzantinische kanonische, d. h. griechisch-orthodoxes Kirchenrecht[74]). Die erste sozialistische Kodifikation bildete die Gesetzesverordnung über die Ehe von 1945[75]), die abgelöst wurde vom Gesetz über die Personen und die Familie von 1949[76]). Dieses wiederum wurde weitgehend aufgehoben durch den Familienkodex von 1968[77]), der im Jahre 1985 außer Kraft getreten ist. Zu den Vorzügen des sozialistischen, und damit auch des bulgarischen Familienrechts nach 1944, gehört vor allem die Einführung der Gleichberechtigung der Geschlechter und die Gleichstellung der nichtehelichen mit den in der Ehe geborenen Kindern, die beide in Westeuropa zum Teil erst Jahre später erreicht werden konnten. Nichteheliche Lebensgemeinschaften als solche werden dagegen vom bulgarischen Familienrecht ignoriert, was die vergleichsweise konservative Einstellung der bulgarischen Gesellschaft verdeutlicht. (In Jugoslawien dagegen finden sich zahlreiche Rechtsvorschriften zur Regelung der Rechtsstellung des faktischen Lebensgefährten, bis hin zur Unterhalts- und erbrechtlichen Ansprüchen.)

Der geltende Familienkodex (*Semeen kodeks*, im folgenden: SK)[78]) betont besonders die sittlichen Grundlagen des Familienlebens (vgl. z. B. die neue ausführliche Präambel). Das Eherecht wurde etwas strenger gefaßt als bisher, unter Ausweitung des Verschuldensprinzips[79]). Im Falle einer Verschuldensscheidung kann das Gericht sogar die Entscheidung dem Arbeitskollektiv des schuldigen Teils oder aber der für ihn zuständigen gesellschaftlichen Organisation mitteilen (Art. 108 SK). Auch sind Scheidungen teurer geworden (vgl. oben II 3 d). Tatsächlich ist daraufhin die Zahl der Ehescheidungen jedenfalls im ersten Jahr zurückgegangen (von 14 361 im Jahre 1985 auf nur noch 10 042 im Jahre 1986), um 1987 wieder auf 11 687 anzusteigen[80]).

2. Eherecht

In Bulgarien ist die Zivilehe obligatorisch (Art. 6 SK). Neuerdings muß der Eheschließung in der Regel ein dreißigtägiges Aufgebot vorangehen (Art. 10 SK). Das Mindestalter beträgt 18 Jahre und kann vom Gericht ausnahmsweise auf 16 Jahre

---

[74]) Schöndorf (Anm. 1), S. 14; Iwanow (Anm. 1), S. 16.
[75]) *Naredba-zakon za braka*, DV. (1945) 108.
[76]) Dazu Mevorach, N.: Semejno pravo (Familienrecht). 2. Aufl. Sofia 1956. (Vgl. auch oben I 1 a).
[77]) DV. (1968) 23.
[78]) DV. (1985) 41. Dazu ausführlich Jessel-Holst, Ch., in: Bergmann; Ferid (Anm. 71).
[79]) Auch in Ungarn wurde das Eherecht kürzlich in Teilbereichen deliberalisiert; vgl. das Gesetz IV/1952 über die Ehe, die Familie und die Vormundschaft Fassung 1986 (Magyar Közlöny. 1986 Nr. 48), deutsche Übers. in: Jahrbuch für Ostrecht. 28 (1987) 1, S. 221–258.
[80]) Nach: SG. 1988, S. 78.

herabgesetzt werden (Art. 12 SK). In der Ehe sind die Gatten gleichberechtigt[81]). Sie können ihren Beruf frei wählen, sollen aber zusammenwohnen (Art. 16f. SK). Nach der Heirat kann jeder Gatte seinen Familiennamen beibehalten, oder einer von ihnen nimmt den Namen des anderen an bzw. fügt ihn dem eigenen hinzu (Art. 11 SK).

Das Ehegüterrecht sah bis 1968 die Gütertrennung vor. Der Familienkodex 1968 führte die Errungenschaftsgemeinschaft ein, jedoch beschränkt auf Sachen und Rechte an Sachen (Art. 13 a. F. SK). Seit 1985 gehören auch Geld-Guthaben zum Gesamtgut (Art. 19 n. F. SK). Voraussetzung für die Entstehung von Gesamtgut ist ein gemeinsamer Beitrag der Ehegatten zum Erwerb, der aber nicht nur in Geld und Arbeit, sondern auch in der Obsorge für die Kinder oder in Hausarbeit bestehen kann. Art. 19 III SK stellt zugunsten des Vorhandenseins eines gemeinsamen Beitrags eine gesetzliche Vermutung auf. In das persönliche Sondervermögen jedes Ehegatten fallen dagegen alle sonstigen während der Ehe erworbenen Gegenstände, sein vor der Eheschließung erworbenes Vermögen, die während der Ehe anfallenden Erbschaften und Schenkungen sowie bewegliche Sachen, die der gewöhnlichen persönlichen Nutzung oder der Berufsausübung dienen (Art. 20 SK). Eheverträge sind nicht zugelassen[82]). Die Ehegatten schulden einander Unterhalt (Art. 18, 80 SK).

Die Ehescheidung kann einvernehmlich erfolgen (Art. 100f. SK), also ohne gerichtliche Nachprüfung der Gründe, sofern sich die Parteien über sämtliche Folgen geeinigt haben und die Ehe mindestens drei Jahre bestanden hat. Die Entscheidung des Gerichts wird sofort rechtskräftig (zum Verfahren Art. 259a–c GPK). Für kontradiktorische Scheidungen gilt das Zerrüttungsprinzip, wobei jedoch nicht geschieden wird, wenn der Kläger schuldhaft die alleinige Ursache für die Zerrüttung gesetzt hat und der andere Teil die Ehe fortsetzen will, es sei denn, wichtige Umstände sprechen für die Scheidung. Das Scheidungsurteil trifft normalerweise auch einen Schuldausspruch (Art. 99 SK), der Auswirkungen auf den nachehelichen Unterhalt (Art. 83 I SK; siehe unten 5), die Sorgerechtsentscheidung (Art. 106 II SK), die Zuteilung der Familienwohnung (Art. 107 SK), die Prozeßkosten (Art. 270 GPK) u. a. haben kann.

3. Kindschaftsrecht

Ehelich und nichtehelich geborene Kinder sind in Bulgarien schon seit 1945 rechtlich vollkommen gleichgestellt (Art. 26 III Gesetzesverordnung über die Ehe). Die Abstammung von der Mutter ergibt sich aus der Geburt, auch im Falle der Empfängnis mit fremdem genetischem Material (Art. 31 SK). Als Vater gilt bis zum Beweis des Gegenteils der Ehemann der Mutter (Art. 32 SK), der diese Vermutung binnen einem Jahr seit Kenntnisnahme von der Geburt anfechten kann. Die Anfechtungsfrist für die Mutter beträgt ein Jahr ab der Geburt. Das Kind kann dagegen nicht selbst anfechten. Die Vaterschaft ist unanfechtbar, wenn die Mutter mit schriftlicher Zu-

---

[81]) Eingeführt durch die Gesetzesverordnung über die Gleichberechtigung der Personen beiderlei Geschlechts (*Naredba-zakon za izravnjavane pravata na licata ot dvata pola*, DV. (1944) 227).

[82]) Anders neuerdings Ungarn, vgl. Art. 27 II und III n. F. Ehe-, Familien- und Vormundschaftsgesetz (Anm. 79).

stimmung des Mannes künstlich befruchtet wurde oder mit fremdem genetischen Material empfangen hat (Art. 33 SK). Die Elternschaft kann auch anerkannt werden (Art. 35–39 SK). Auf gerichtliche Feststellung der väterlichen Abstammung können das Kind und die Mutter klagen (Art. 40 ff. SK). Im Falle der Anfechtung der Anerkennung seiner Vaterschaft kann auch der Anerkennende die Feststellungsklage erheben (Art. 37 II SK).

Die elterlichen Rechte und Pflichten werden von beiden Eltern „gemeinsam und getrennt" ausgeübt; im Streitfall entscheidet das Rayongericht (Art. 72 SK). Rechtshandlungen für und von Minderjährigen werden von den Eltern bzw. Vormündern (*nastojnik*) vorgenommen (Art. 3 ZLS); Nichtvolljährige im Alter von 14 bis 18 Jahren bedürfen hierfür zwar der Zustimmung ihrer Eltern bzw. Pfleger (*popečitel*), können aber kleine Verträge des Alltags zur Befriedigung ihrer laufenden Bedürfnisse selbständig abschließen und auch selbst über ihre persönlichen Arbeitseinkünfte verfügen (Art. 4 ZLS). Jeder Elternteil ist selbständig zur Vertretung des Kindes bzw. zur Genehmigung von dessen Rechtsgeschäften berechtigt, jedoch sind bestimmte Verfügungshandlungen genehmigungspflichtig bzw. nichtig (Art. 73 SK). Mit der Eheschließung werden Nichtvolljährige geschäftsfähig (Art. 12 III SK). Im Interesse des Kindes kann das Elternrecht beschränkt oder sogar gänzlich aberkannt werden (Art. 74 ff. SK).

Für die Adoption (Art. 49–67 SK) gibt es seit 1968 zwei Formen: Die Volladoption (*pălno osinovjavane*) (Art. 61 SK), die das Mündel vollkommen in die neue Familie integriert und die Rechtsbeziehungen zu den Blutsverwandten beendet, oder aber die einfache Adoption (*nepălno osinovjavane*) (Art. 62 SK), die das Rechtsverhältnis zur Herkunftsfamilie bestehen läßt und neue verwandtschaftliche Beziehungen lediglich zwischen dem Angenommenen und seinen Nachkommen und dem Annehmenden schafft, unter Wegfall der Erbberechtigung der leiblichen Eltern gegenüber dem Angenommenen und Übergang der Elternrechte und -pflichten auf den Annehmenden. Zur Volladoption kommt es bei Kindern unbekannter Eltern oder bei zur Adoption in einer Anstalt abgegebenen Kindern sowie auch bei einer ausdrücklich hierauf gerichteten Einwilligung aller Beteiligten, ansonsten bleibt es bei der unvollständigen Adoption. Die Adoption von Volljährigen ist unzulässig (Art. 49 SK), dasselbe gilt für die Annahme von Verwandten in gerader Linie sowie zwischen Geschwistern (Art. 52 I SK). Eine Ausnahme macht neuerdings Art. 52 II zugunsten von Großeltern, die ihr nichtehelich geborenes oder verwaistes Enkelkind annehmen dürfen. Zuständig ist das Rayongericht, das im Dekretsystem entscheidet (Art. 58 f. SK). Art. 145 II Strafkodex (Fassung 1982) stellt den Bruch des Adoptionsgeheimnisses unter Strafe. Das Annahmeverhältnis kann vom Gericht aufgrund beiderseitigen Einverständnisses von Annehmendem und Angenommenen, oder aber auf Antrag wegen schwerwiegender Verfahrensmängel oder Verfehlungen bzw. tiefgreifender Zerrüttung wieder beendet werden (Art. 64 SK). Davon abgesehen endet die einfache Adoption mit dem Tode des bzw. der Annehmenden. Eine Volladoption *kann* in solchem Fall im Interesse des Angenommenen auf Antrag gerichtlich beendet werden (Art. 65 I SK).

4. Unterhalt

Unterhalt bekommt nur, wer arbeitsunfähig und ohne ausreichendes eigenes Vermögen ist (Art. 79 SK). Jedoch haben nichtvolljährige Kinder einen unbedingten Unterhaltsanspruch gegen ihre Eltern (Art. 82). Ehegattenunterhalt erhält nur der an der Scheidung nicht schuldige Teil, und zwar höchstens drei Jahre lang, sofern nicht die Parteien eine längere Frist vereinbart haben, oder aber das Gericht kann die Frist verlängern, wenn sich der Berechtigte in einer Notlage befindet und der Verpflichtete ohne weiteres leistungsfähig ist. Der Anspruch endet mit der Wiederheirat des Berechtigten (Art. 83 SK). Die Unterhaltshöhe folgt den Bedürfnissen des Berechtigten sowie den Möglichkeiten des Verpflichteten, wobei für den Kindesunterhalt vom Ministerrat eine untere und eine obere Grenze (derzeit zwischen 30 und 100 Leva monatlich) festgesetzt wurden, die nur aus besonderen Gründen unter- bzw. überschritten werden dürfen (Art. 85 SK)[83]).

5. Internationales Familienrecht

Die familienrechtlichen Kollisionsnormen sind in Art. 129–143 SK enthalten[84]). Sie folgen dem Staatsangehörigkeitsprinzip und ergänzend auch dem Aufenthaltsrecht. Besonders betont wird der Schutz der bulgarischen Bürger, für die in aller Regel das bulgarische Sachrecht maßgebend ist. Für die Kindesannahme bulgarischer Bürger und für Unterhaltsansprüche gegen Bulgaren beansprucht Bulgarien jetzt gar die ausschließliche internationale Zuständigkeit (Art. 136 I 2, 139 SK). Die Art. 129ff. SK betreffen vor allem die bulgarischen Beziehungen zum Westen, da im Verhältnis zu den anderen sozialistischen Staaten Sonderregelungen in Rechtshilfeverträgen den Vorrang genießen (Art. 143; s. das Kapitel der Autorin, Verträge, VIII 3).

6. Das Verfahren in Ehesachen

Eheklagen sind in Art. 256–270 GPK geregelt. Für Ehescheidungen ist ein vorgeschalteter Sühnetermin mit anschließender Bedenkzeit vorgesehen.

---

[83]) Ministerratsverordnung Nr. 38 über die Festlegung der Unterhaltsgrenzen für nichtvolljährige Kinder gemäß Art. 85 I SK und über die Änderung der Behördentarife Nr. 1 und 3 (*Postanovlenie za ustanovjavane granicite na izdrăžkata na nenavăršilite pălnoletie deca po čl. 85 al. 1 ot Semejnija kodeks i za izmenenie na vedomstvenite tarifi no 1 i no 3*, DV. (1985) 52).

[84]) Dazu Jessel-Holst, Ch.: Die Neuregelung des bulgarischen Internationalen Familienrechts im Familienkodex von 1985, in: Rabels Zeitschrift für ausländisches und internationales Privatrecht. 51 (1987), S. 35–59, mit deutscher Übers. S. 228–234.

IV. Recht der Wirtschaft

1. Einführung

1984 wurde beschlossen, ein Wirtschaftsgesetzbuch zu schaffen, das jedoch noch aussteht[85]). Als erster Vorläufer kann das Reglement für den ökonomischen Mechanismus von 1982 gelten[86]), das am 1.1.1987 von dem Reglement für die Wirtschaftstätigkeit abgelöst wurde[87]). Dieses hatte jedoch nur ein knappes Jahr Bestand: ein neues, gleichnamiges Reglement wurde am 18.12.1987 verabschiedet (*Pravilnik za stopanskata dejnost*, im folgenden: PSD)[88]) und sollte eigentlich bis einschließlich 1990 gelten. Jedoch folgte bereits 1989 der DS-Erlaß Nr. 56 über die wirtschaftliche Tätigkeit (s. Anm. 12). Dieser Beitrag beschränkt sich in der Hauptsache auf das Wirtschaftsvertragsrecht sowie auf die staatliche Binnenarbitrage (zum Wirtschaftssystem vgl. das Kapitel von W. Gumpel, Wirtschaftssystem).

Eine Schlüsselrolle im System des NIM und der selbstverwaltenden Wirtschaftsorganisationen nehmen die Wirtschaftsverträge ein. Deshalb hat sich auch der bulgarische Gesetzgeber in den letzten Jahren gleich mehrfach mit ihnen befaßt[89]). Allgemeine Grundsätze enthielten die Art. 90f. des damaligen Reglements für die Wirtschaftstätigkeit. Ferner gilt das Gesetz über die Verträge zwischen den sozialistischen Organisationen (*Zakon za dogovorite meždu socialističeskite organizacii*, im folgenden: ZDSO)[90]) fort. Die umfassendste, aktuelle Regelung enthält die Ordnung für die Wirtschaftsverträge (*Naredba za stopanskite dogovori*, im folgenden: NSD) vom 30.1.1987[91]), die 1988/89 neu gefaßt worden ist[92]). Inhaltlich bietet sie in stattlichen 139 Artikeln eine vorweggenommene Kodifikation des Rechts der Wirtschaftsverträge.

Die Ordnung für die Wirtschaftsverträge gilt für juristische Personen, ausgenommen solche mit ausländischer Beteiligung sowie Firmen von Bürgern, die dem allgemeinen Zivilrecht (ZZD, oben I 1 c) unterliegen (vgl. Art. 1 n. F. NSD). Ihre Erstfassung unterschied zwischen vertikalen und horizontalen Vertragsbeziehungen und regelte, vertikal, in Art. 7–10 erstmals relativ ausführlich die sogenannten staatlichwirtschaftlichen Verträge, d.h. die wechselseitigen Beziehungen zwischen den für die Erteilung staatlicher Aufträge zuständigen Staatsorganen und den Wirtschaftsorga-

---

[85]) Dazu Jessel-Holst, Ch.: Reformen des Wirtschaftsrechts in Bulgarien, in: Sozialistisches Wirtschaftsrecht (Anm. 15), S. 253–279 (257f.).

[86]) *Pravilnik za ikonomičeskija mechanizăm*, DV. (1982) 9.

[87]) DV. (1987) 3.

[88]) DV. (1987) 100.

[89]) Vgl. die Ordnung für die Verträge zwischen den sozialistischen Organisationen (*Naredba za dogovorite meždu socialističeskite organizacii*, DV. (1973) 4) sowie die gleichnamigen Vorschriften (DV. (1976) 1 und (1980) 44). Allgemeine Grundsätze für die Rechtsbeziehungen der sozialistischen Organisationen untereinander enthält das Gesetz über die Schuldverhältnisse und Verträge (oben I 1).

[90]) DV. (1963) 85 Fassung (1977) 16.

[91]) DV. (1987) 19. Dazu Goleminov, C.: Novata pravna uredba na stopanskite dogovori (Neue rechtliche Regelung der Wirtschaftsverträge), in: Socialističesko Pravo. (1987) 5, S. 3–11.

[92]) DV. (1988) 5 sowie (1989) 41.

nisationen, denen die Aufträge erteilt werden. Diese Bestimmungen wurden im Jahre 1988 wieder aufgehoben (vgl. N. 92), jedoch wurden 1989 die staatlich-wirtschaftlichen Verträge in Art. 7–10 n. F. mit anderem Inhalt erneut hervorgeholt. Die horizontalen Vertragsbeziehungen der Wirtschaftsorganisation erfolgen in Gestalt der herkömmlichen Wirtschaftsverträge (Art. 11 ff. NSD).

2. Abschluß und Erfüllung der Wirtschaftsverträge; Haftung

Wirtschaftsverträge werden entweder aufgrund eines Kontrahierungszwanges oder aber frei eingegangen. Die Fälle einer Vertragsabschlußpflicht ergeben sich aus Art. 11 NSD. Abs. 1 begründet einen neuen Typ von Kontrahierungszwang, der sich aus dem „registrierten Gegenstand der Tätigkeit des Produzenten (Lieferers, Erbringers einer Leistung) im Rahmen von dessen Produktionskapazität" ergibt[93]. Weitere Vertragsabschlußpflichten enthalten die Abs. 2 und 3, und zwar werden vorrangig Verträge geschlossen, durch welche die Erfüllung von staatlichen Aufträgen hierfür gewährleistet wird. Zwei weitere Fälle, nämlich gemäß den festgesetzten Limits sowie zur Befriedigung von Verbrauchern bei dauerhaft begründeten Vertragsbeziehungen[94] wurden 1989 aufgehoben. Ein Vertragsabschlußzwang kann schließlich auch in anderen Fällen, durch Gesetz, Erlaß oder Akt des Ministerrats festgelegt werden.

Im Falle der Nicht- oder Schlechterfüllung des Vertrages ist die vertragstreue Partei verpflichtet, Realerfüllung zu verlangen und die Gegenseite haftbar zu machen. Die Zahlung einer Vertragsstrafe und von Schadenersatz befreit aber grundsätzlich nicht von der Pflicht zur Vertragserfüllung (Art. 21 NSD). 1988 wurde die Pflicht zur Geltendmachung von Vertragsstrafen und Schadenersatz für Ansprüche bis zur Höhe von 1 000 Leva aufgehoben (Art. 21 III NSD). Neuerdings wurde die Grenze auf 2000 Leva heraufgesetzt (Art. 21 II n. F.). Normalerweise wird die Vertragsstrafe auf den Schadenersatz angerechnet. In Rechtsvorschriften kann aber auch vorgesehen werden, daß in bestimmten Fällen die Vertragsstrafe kumulativ neben dem vollen Schadenersatz zu leisten ist (Art. 22 I).

3. Einzelne Wirtschaftsverträge

Das zweite Kapitel der Ordnung für die Wirtschaftsverträge regelt die folgenden Typen von Wirtschaftsverträgen: Kooperationslieferung, Lieferung von Waren für die Bevölkerung, Export, Import, Ankauf von landwirtschaftlichen Produkten, For-

---

[93] Vgl. auch Art. 6 des geltenden Reglements für die Wirtschaftstätigkeit (Anm. 88): „Außer den in den Normativakten festgesetzten Verboten ist das Unternehmen nicht berechtigt: 1. den Abschluß von Verträgen zur Befriedigung der Bedürfnisse der Verbraucher mit Waren und Dienstleistungen in Sortiment und Qualität gemäß dem für es festgelegten Tätigkeitsgegenstand und im Rahmen seiner Produktionskapazität zu verweigern."
[94] Vgl. auch den Beschluß Nr. 4 der Obersten Staatsarbitrage über dauerhaft begründete Vertragsbeziehungen als Quelle einer Kontrahierungspflicht (*Postanovlenie otnosno trajno ustanovenite dogovorni otnošenija kato iztočnik na zadălženie za dogovarjane*) in: Socialističesko Pravo. (1986) 7, S. 100–103.

schungs- und technologische Tätigkeit, Investitionstätigkeit, Organisation des Warentransports.

4. Streitlösung

Streitigkeiten der sozialistischen Organisationen untereinander sind der Zuständigkeit der ordentlichen Gerichte entzogen. Statt dessen gelangen sie vor die Staatsarbitrage (*dăržaven arbitraž*). Damit hat Bulgarien die traditionelle sozialistische Konzeption beibehalten[95]. Dagegen haben Jugoslawien (1954), Ungarn (1972) und zuletzt auch Rumänien (1985)[96] ihre Staatsarbitragen aufgelöst und die entsprechenden Kompetenzen auf die Gerichte übertragen.

Das System der Staatsarbitrage besteht aus der Obersten Staatsarbitrage (*Vărchoven dăržaven arbitraž*), den Bezirks- (Stadt-)Staatsarbitragen [*okrăžen (gradski) dăržaven arbitraž*] sowie den staatlichen Ressortarbitragen (*dăržaven vedomstven arbitraž*), die der Leitung durch den Hauptarbiter (*glaven arbităr*) der Obersten Staatsarbitrage unterstehen. Dabei ist die Oberste Staatsarbitrage dem Ministerrat und sind die Bezirks- (Stadt-)Staatsarbitragen der Obersten Staatsarbitrage zugeordnet. Staatliche Ressortarbitragen werden auf Beschluß des Ministerrats bei einzelnen Ministerien und anderen Behörden zur Lösung interner Streitigkeiten gebildet [Art. 3 des Gesetzes über die Staatsarbitrage (*Zakon za dăržavnija arbitraž*, im folgenden: ZDA)[97]]. Der Hauptarbiter der Obersten Staatsarbitrage und seine Stellvertreter werden vom Vorsitzenden des Ministerrats ernannt; die übrigen Arbiter der Obersten und der Bezirks- (Stadt-)Staatsarbitragen schließen Arbeitsverträge (!) mit dem Hauptarbiter der Obersten Staatsarbitrage, und die Arbiter der Staatlichen Ressortarbitragen mit den Leitern der jeweiligen Behörden nach Abstimmung mit dem Hauptarbiter der Obersten Staatsarbitrage (Art. 4 ZDA).

Die Zuständigkeit der Staatsarbitrage ist umfassend. Sie entscheidet vorvertragliche und zivilrechtliche Vermögensstreitigkeiten der sozialistischen Organisationen untereinander, ist zur Mitwirkung bei der Herstellung von vertraglichen Beziehungen in der Volkswirtschaft und zur Kontrolle des rechtzeitigen Vertragsschlusses der sozialistischen Organisationen untereinander aufgerufen und signalisiert von ihr festgestellte Mißstände den zuständigen Organen (Art. 1 ZDA). Neuerdings entscheidet die Staatsarbitrage auch Streitigkeiten zwischen Organisationen, die ein und derselben Vereinigung oder Assoziation angehören (§ 1 Schlußbestimmungen NSD). Für die vorvertraglichen Streitigkeiten von Unternehmen, die einer Vereinigung oder einem Volksrat zugeordnet sind, ist jetzt ein Dialog-Verfahren der beteiligten Leiter vorgeschaltet worden (Art. 14 n. F. NSD).

---

[95] Im einzelnen Jessel, Ch.: Die sowjetische Wirtschaftsarbitrage (Mit einer Übersicht über die Arbitragesysteme und arbitrageähnlichen Einrichtungen der osteuropäischen Volksdemokratien). Hamburg 1974.
[96] Dazu Tontsch, G.: Die Auflösung der staatlichen Arbitrage in Rumänien im osteuropäischen Vergleich, in: WGO-Monatshefte für Osteuropäisches Recht. (1986), S. 15–21.
[97] DV. (1950) 127 Fassung (1987) 24; Reglement für die Anwendung des Gesetzes über die Staatsarbitrage (*Pravilnik za prilagane na Zakona za dăržavnija arbitraž*, DV. (1977) 74).

Ersatz für Schäden, die den selbstverwalteten Organisationen durch Entscheidungen staatlicher Organe zugefügt wurden oder die aus der Nichterfüllung von deren Pflichten herrühren, kann gegen diese Organe vor der Staatsarbitrage eingeklagt werden (vgl. Art. 32 PSD Dez. 1987).

Funktional ist die Oberste Staatsarbitrage zuständig, wenn ein Ministerium oder eine andere Behörde Partei ist oder der Streit vertraulichen Charakter hat bzw., kraft Evokation, bei Streitigkeiten mit großem öffentlichen Interesse. Die staatlichen Ressortarbitragen werden bei Streitigkeiten innerhalb desselben Ministeriums bzw. einer sonstigen Behörde tätig. Innerhalb eines Unternehmens anfallende interne Streitigkeiten werden dagegen durch dessen Leiter oder ein von ihm bezeichnetes Organ gelöst (Art. 1 ZDA).

Am Beginn des Arbitrageverfahrens kann eine Klage der interessierten Partei stehen. Die Initiative kann aber auch vom Ministerrat oder einem Exekutivkomitee oder aber von der zuständigen Staatsarbitrage selbst ausgehen, sofern eine Vertragsverletzung durch schriftliche Beweismittel festgestellt ist (Art. 13 ZDA). Verhandelt und entschieden werden die Streitigkeiten durch den Arbiter und je einen Vertreter der Streitparteien, wobei das Ziel eine einvernehmliche Lösung ist. Im anderen Fall entscheidet der Arbiter allein. Bei wichtigen und komplizierten Sachen können auch zwei oder drei Arbiter mitwirken (Art. 17 ZDA). Entscheidungen der unteren Arbitrageorgane unterliegen der Überprüfung im Aufsichtswege durch die Oberste Staatsarbitrage, ausgenommen Vermögenssachen mit einem Beschwerdewert bis zu 1 000 Leva (Art. 23–23 b ZDA). Im übrigen ist der Ministerrat berechtigt, die Vollziehung von Entscheidungen der Obersten Staatsarbitrage sowie der Bezirks- (Stadt-) Staatsarbitrage auszusetzen oder davon Befreiung zu erteilen; entsprechendes gilt für die Leiter von Behörden mit eigener Ressortarbitrage im Hinblick auf deren Entscheidungen (Art. 25 ZDA). Der DS-Erlaß Nr. 56 (vgl. Anm. 12) hat in Art. 98 daneben auch die Möglichkeit eröffnet, Vermögensstreitigkeiten in Zusammenhang mit der wirtschaftlichen Tätigkeit durch schriftliche Vereinbarung einem freiwilligen Schiedsgericht (*dobrovolen arbitraž*) zu übertragen, dessen Entscheidungen nicht rechtsmittelfähig sind und zwangsvollstreckt werden können (im einzelnen s. Art. 144–151 der Durchführungsvorschrift).

V. Arbeitsrecht

1. Einführung

Das Arbeitsrecht wurde erstmals im Jahre 1951 kodifiziert[98]). Von diesem Kodex, der ganz von sowjetischen Vorstellungen geprägt war, gelten die Art. 145–170, 177 betreffend die staatliche Sozialversicherung bis zur Verabschiedung des geplanten Sozialversicherungsgesetzes vorläufig fort[98a]). Im übrigen gilt seit dem 1.1.1987 der

---

[98]) Izv. (1951) 91 Fassung DV. (1989) 46.
[98a]) Dazu Kirtschewa, E.: Stand und Entwicklung des Sozialversicherungsrechts in Bulgarien, in: Südosteuropa-Mitteilungen. (1989) 1, S. 24–44.

Arbeitskodex 1986 (*Kodeks na truda*, im folgenden: KT)[99]), der als eine der wichtigsten gesetzlichen Vorschriften zur Verwirklichung der *preustrojstvo* betrachtet wird. Sein Ziel ist die Selbstverwaltung der Arbeitskollektive. Mit diesem Kodex hat Bulgarien gesetzgeberisches Neuland betreten und in weitem Umfang auch eigene Lösungen entwickelt. Die Aufgaben und Tätigkeit der Gewerkschaften wurden ebenfalls neu definiert; auf dem X. Kongreß der BPS im April 1987 wurde eine neue Satzung und die Anpassung der Organisationsstruktur der Gewerkschaften an die Prinzipien der Selbstverwaltung der Arbeitskollektive beschlossen[100]).

2. Grundfragen des Arbeitsrechts

Art. 40 der Verfassung sichert jedem Bürger das Recht auf Arbeit und auf freie Berufswahl zu. Auf der anderen Seite trifft jeden arbeitsfähigen Bürger die Pflicht, eine gesellschaftlich nützliche Arbeit zu verrichten (Art. 59 Verf.)[101]). Der neue Arbeitskodex unterscheidet zwischen den primären und den Stamm-Arbeitskollektiven (*părvični i osnovni trudovi kolektivi*), Art. 12 KT. Dem ersteren gehören alle „Arbeiter" (*rabotnik*)[102]) einer Brigade oder dergleichen an (im einzelnen Art. 12 II). Das letztere umfaßt alle Arbeiter des Unternehmens und alle primären Arbeitskollektive (Art. 12 III). Die allgemeine Versammlung (*obšto săbranie*) des primären Arbeitskollektivs hat weitreichende Befugnisse erhalten, z. B. zur Wahl des Brigadiers, Annahme des kollektiven Arbeitsvertrages, Aufteilung der Gelder für Lohn und materiellen Anreiz entsprechend dem Beitrag des einzelnen usw. (Art. 20 KT). Auch kann der Unternehmensleiter einen Arbeiter, der unmittelbar in der materiellen Produktion arbeiten soll, nur mit Zustimmung der allgemeinen Versammlung der Brigade einstellen, in der er arbeiten soll (Art. 64 KT). Die allgemeine Versammlung des Stamm-Arbeitskollektivs wählt z. B. den Unternehmensleiter und den Wirtschaftsrat (*stopanski săvet*) und entscheidet andere grundlegende Fragen (Art. 27 KT). Die kollektiven Arbeitsverträge (sowohl des primären als auch des Stamm-Arbeitskollektivs mit dem Unternehmen) werden unter aktiver Mitwirkung der Gewerkschaften geschlossen (Art. 50 ff. KT). Das individuelle Arbeitsverhältnis beruht auf einem Arbeitsvertrag zwischen Arbeiter und Unternehmen, kann aber auch durch Wahl oder aufgrund einer Ausschreibung, aufgrund Einweisung sozial Schwacher durch das Büro für Arbeit und Soziales sowie durch Gerichtsentscheidung entstehen. Besondere Arbeitsplätze sind für „junge Spezialisten" (*mladi specialisti*) nach Abschluß der Ausbildung reserviert (Art. 77 ff. KT).

---

[99]) DV. (1986) 26 und 27 Fassung (1988) 6. Dazu Kirčeva, E.: Das bulgarische Arbeitsgesetzbuch von 1986, in: WGO-Monatshefte für Osteuropäisches Recht. (1988) 1, S. 59–84.

[100]) Siehe Höpken, W.: Die bulgarischen Gewerkschaften im Zeichen von „Perestrojka", in: WSI-Mitteilungen 1988, S. 244–249.

[101]) Bei unverschuldeter Arbeitslosigkeit besteht unter bestimmten Voraussetzungen ein befristeter Anspruch auf ein (geringfügiges) Überbrückungsgeld.

[102]) D. h. jede in einem Arbeitsverhältnis, sei es als Arbeiter, Angestellter oder als Mitglied einer Produktionsgenossenschaft, stehende Person. Vgl. § 1 Nr. 2 der Ergänzenden Bestimmungen zum KT.

3. Internationales Arbeitsrecht

Der Arbeitskodex enthält jetzt auch zwei allgemeine Bestimmungen zu Verhältnissen mit ausländischem Element. Und zwar beruft Art. 10 KT das bulgarische Sachrecht für alle arbeitsrechtlichen Verhältnisse mit bulgarischen und gemischten Unternehmen im Inland sowie auch für arbeitsrechtliche Verhältnisse von bulgarischen Bürgern mit ausländischen Unternehmen im Inland oder mit bulgarischen Unternehmen im Ausland, vorbehaltlich einer abweichenden Regelung durch Gesetz, Erlaß oder einen Staatsvertrag. Entsprechendes gilt für die arbeitsrechtlichen Verhältnisse von Bulgaren, die zur Arbeit ins Ausland in ausländische oder gemischte Unternehmen entsandt wurden, sowie von Ausländern, die zur Arbeit im Lande in bulgarischen oder gemischten Unternehmen aufgenommen wurden, und zwar auf der Grundlage internationaler Verträge. Gemäß Art. 11 KT werden im Ausland erworbene Rechte aus Arbeit in Bulgarien anerkannt auf der Grundlage eines Gesetzes, Erlasses, Aktes des Ministerrats oder Staatsvertrages.

Außerdem wurde auch die internationale Zuständigkeit normiert. Art. 370 KT sieht für Arbeitsstreitigkeiten zwischen ausländischen Arbeitern und gemischten Unternehmen mit Sitz in Bulgarien, wenn die Arbeit im Inland erbracht wird, eine ausschließliche Zuständigkeit der Gerichte vor. Und zwar verhandelt, je nach Streitwert, das Rayon- bzw. das Bezirksgericht am Sitz des Unternehmens. Dagegen bestimmt sich die Zuständigkeit für Arbeitsstreitigkeiten zwischen bulgarischen Arbeitern und bulgarischen Unternehmen im Ausland, wie auch die Zuständigkeit für Arbeitsstreitigkeiten von Bulgaren, die von bulgarischen Unternehmen zur Arbeit ins Ausland entsandt wurden, nach den allgemeinen Regeln (Art. 371; siehe unten 4. Vgl. im übrigen auch Art. 394 KT).

4. Arbeitsgerichtsbarkeit

Für Arbeitsstreitigkeiten sind, je nachdem, die Kommissionen für Arbeitsstreitigkeiten (*komisija za trudovi sporove*) (Art. 365 KT), die in allen Unternehmen mit mehr als 20 Arbeitern gebildet werden, die Gerichte (Art. 366 KT) oder aber die übergeordneten Verwaltungsorgane (Art. 369 KT) zuständig. Für die Arbeiter ist das Verfahren in allen Instanzen kostenlos (Art. 362 KT). Der neue Arbeitskodex hat die Rechtsstellung der Arbeiter verbessert. So kann der Arbeiter gegen eine rechtswidrige Entlassung nach eigener Wahl Klage vor dem Rayongericht oder vor der Kommission für Arbeitsstreitigkeiten erheben (Art. 366 II KT). Die Zuständigkeit der Administrativorgane wurde eingeschränkt. Hervorzuheben ist auch Art. 361 KT, der den Arbeitern die Möglichkeit gibt, sich in Arbeitsstreitigkeiten anwaltlich vertreten zu lassen.

Gegen die Entscheidungen der Kommissionen für Arbeitsstreitigkeiten steht, von geringfügigen Ausnahmen abgesehen, der Rechtsweg zu den Rayongerichten offen (Art. 392 KT). Die Entscheidungen der übergeordneten Verwaltungsorgane sind teils nicht beschwerdefähig; im übrigen kann Beschwerde beim nächsthöheren Verwaltungsorgan eingelegt werden. Weitere Rechtsmittel bestehen nicht (Art. 395 KT). Gegen die Entscheidungen der Rayongerichte kann Berufung bei den Bezirksgerichten eingelegt werden (Art. 196 GPK).

VI. Strafrecht

1. Einführung

Die erste bulgarische Strafrechtskodifikation datiert von 1896 und wurde vor allem vom ungarischen und vom niederländischen Strafgesetzbuch sowie vom russischen Strafgesetz-Entwurf inspiriert. (Zuvor hatte türkisches Recht gegolten, das seinerseits dem französischen Code pénal entnommen war[103]).) Von den nach 1944 hierzu ergangenen Änderungen ist insbesondere die stufenweise Aufhebung des Analogieverbotes zum Nachteil des Täters zu nennen[104]), die jedoch im Jahre 1956 wieder rückgängig gemacht wurde[105]). Entsprechendes geschah in den anderen sozialistischen Staaten; seit Anfang der 60er Jahre gilt in ihnen allen der Grundsatz des *nullum crimen sine lege*[106]). 1949 erging ein besonderes Militärstrafgesetz (aufgehoben 1956)[107]). Das Strafgesetzbuch (*Nakazatelen zakon*) von 1951[108]) entstand unter unmittelbarem sowjetischen Einfluß. Nach seiner Vervollständigung 1956[109]) wurde es in Strafkodex (*Nakazatelen kodeks*) umbenannt. [Durch Kodices (*kodeks*) werden in Bulgarien ganze Rechtszweige oder in sich abgeschlossene wichtige Teile davon geregelt. Sie bilden eine (besonders bedeutende) Unterart der Gesetze (*zakon*) im formellen Sinne; vgl. Art. 4 des Gesetzes über die Normativakte[110]).] 1958 wurde das Gesetz über die Bekämpfung der Kinderkriminalität verabschiedet[111]) [seit 1961: Gesetz über die Bekämpfung von gesellschaftswidrigen Erscheinungen von Minderjährigen und Nichtvolljährigen (*Zakon za borba srestu protivoobštestvenite projavi na maloletnite i nepălnoletnite*, im folgenden: ZBPPMN), vgl. unten 3 b, N. 122[112])].

Der geltende Strafkodex (*Nakazatelen kodeks*, im folgenden: NK) datiert von 1968[113]). Von den zahlreichen zwischenzeitlich ergangenen Änderungsgesetzen sind namentlich die von 1975, 1982, 1985, 1986 und 1989 hervorzuheben[114]). Während

---

[103]) Vgl. Dolaptschieff, N.: Die Entwicklung des Strafrechts in Bulgarien, in: Zeitschrift für die gesamte Strafrechtswissenschaft. 59 (1939), S. 76–82 (76f.). Strafgesetzbuch (*Nakazatelen zakon*, DV. (1896) 40). Zur historischen Entwicklung siehe Ljutov, K.; Michajlov, D.: Razvitie na nakazatelno pravo (Entwicklung des Strafrechts) in: Razvitie (Anm. 25), S. 393–412.

[104]) § 52 II der Gesetzesverordnung über die Versorgung und Preise (*Naredba-zakon za snabdjavane i cenite*, DV. (1945) 213, (1946) 232); Art. 1 des Strafgesetzbuchs 1896, Fassung DV. (1948) 80.

[105]) Izv. (1956) 12.

[106]) Vgl. Filar, M.; Weigend, E.: Die Entwicklung des Strafrechts in den sozialistischen Staaten Europas, in: Zeitschrift für die gesamte Strafrechtswissenschaft. (1986), S. 235–259 (241).

[107]) *Voenno-nakazatelen zakon*, DV. (1949) 21; Izv. (1956) 12.

[108]) Izv. (1951) 13, Berichtigung 16. Deutsche Übers. v. Lyon, Th.: Das Bulgarische Strafgesetzbuch vom 2.2.1951. Berlin 1957.

[109]) Izv. (1956) 12.

[110]) *Zakon za normativnite aktove*, DV. (1973) 27.

[111]) *Zakon za borba protiv detskata prestăpnost*, Izv. (1958) 13; (1961) 11.

[112]) Siehe auch das Reglement für die Organisation und Arbeit der Heime für die zeitweise Einweisung der Minderjährigen und Nichtvolljährigen (*Pravilnik za organizacijata i rabotata na domovete za vremenno nastanjavane na maloletni i nepălnoletni*, DV. (1976) 83).

[113]) DV. (1968) 26 Fassung (1986) 89 und 90. Deutsche Übers. v. Lyon, Th.; Lipowschek, A.: Das bulgarische Strafgesetzbuch vom 16. März 1968 (*Nakazatelen kodeks*) mit ergänzenden Vorschriften. Berlin 1973.

[114]) DV. (1975) 95 (dazu Jessel-Holst, Ch.: Neue Strafbestimmungen gegen Terrorismus und Flug-

die Novelle 1975 vorwiegend den Besonderen Teil des Strafkodex betraf (Schutz des bulgarischen Luftverkehrs, Betäubungsmittelmißbrauch usw.), reformierte die sehr umfangreiche Novelle 1982 sowohl den Allgemeinen als auch den Besonderen Teil[115]). Hervorzuheben ist namentlich die Dekriminalisierung bestimmter geringfügiger Verstöße (gegen das sozialistische Eigentum, Art. 218b, das Valuta-Regime, Art. 250 IV, und gegen die Militärdisziplin, Art. 406 III NK). Auch wird die Wiedergutmachung des Schadens in einigen Fällen kraft Gesetzes privilegiert (Art. 78a, 206 VI, 212a I NK). Hingegen wurden die Strafen für schwere Vermögensdelikte wie Aneignung gesellschaftlichen Eigentums (Art. 206), Großbetrug (Art. 212) und schwere Mißwirtschaft (Art. 219ff.) drastisch angehoben. Außerdem wurden neue qualifizierte Tatbestände für Wiederholungs- und gefährliche Rückfalltäter u. a. geschaffen. Das Änderungsgesetz 1985 befaßt sich mit terroristischen Akten sowie erneut mit dem Betäubungsmittelmißbrauch. Auch die umfassende Novelle 1986 betrifft hauptsächlich den Besonderen Teil, wobei jetzt insbesondere die Wirtschaftskriminalität sehr viel härter geahndet wird (z. B. Art. 196a, Diebstahl von sozialistischem Vermögen; Art. 203, Amtsunterschlagung; Art. 302a, Bestechung: Höchststrafe jetzt 30 Jahre und Vermögenseinziehung; Art. 220 II, absichtlicher Abschluß eines nachteiligen Geschäfts durch eine Amtsperson: Höchststrafe 10 Jahre; Art. 226, unerlaubte privatwirtschaftliche Tätigkeit: maximal 20 Jahre; Art. 250, Valutadelikt: maximal 15 Jahre). Weitere Strafverschärfungen betreffen Sittlichkeitsdelikte (Art. 149ff.), Raub (Art. 199 II) sowie die Schaffung neuer qualifizierter Unter-Tatbestände. Außerdem wurde die Obergrenze für Freiheitsstrafen generell angehoben (vgl. unten 3c); schließlich wurden in zahlreichen besonderen Tatbeständen höhere Geldstrafen angedroht. Auf der anderen Seite wurde aber auch das Täterprivileg für Wiedergutmachung des angerichteten Schadens erweitert (Art. 197, 205). Die jüngste Änderung von 1989 sieht die Aufhebung der Art. 280 und 281 NK (Republikflucht) vor und steht in engem Zusammenhang mit der Liberalisierung der Paß-Gesetzgebung (in DV. (1989) 38).

Der Strafkodex 1968 hat insgesamt das Verhältnis der Strafen mit zu denen ohne Freiheitsentziehung zugunsten der letzteren verschoben[116]). Der Anteil der Nicht-Freiheitsstrafen an den gerichtlichen Verurteilungen soll (einschließlich der bedingten Verurteilung) ca. 60 bis 65% betragen[117]). Gewachsen ist der Anteil der Besserungsarbeit (dazu unten 2c), die mehr als die Hälfte aller Strafen ohne Freiheitsentziehung ausmacht[118]). Darüber hinaus verzichten alle sozialistischen Staaten, und also auch Bulgarien, bei Ersttätern von geringfügigen Straftaten mit günstiger persönlicher Prognose zunehmend ganz auf strafrechtliche Sanktionen, sondern wählen

---

zeugentführung in Bulgarien, in: WGO-Monatshefte für Osteuropäisches Recht. (1984/85), S. 321–237); DV. (1982) 28; DV. (1985) 41 (dazu Jessel-Holst, aaO., sowie Lammich, S.: Zur jüngsten Strafrechtsentwicklung in Bulgarien, in: Juristenzeitung. (1985), S. 883–885); DV. (1986) 89, Berichtigung 90; DV. (1989) 37.

[115]) Siehe auch Teichler, G.: Zum Strafrecht und Strafverfahrensrecht der Volksrepublik Bulgarien, in: Neue Justiz. (1984), S. 492–494.

[116]) Ljutov; Michajlov (Anm. 103), S. 414.

[117]) Nach Teichler, G.; Willamowski, H.: Zur Entwicklung der Strafen ohne Freiheitsentziehung in sozialistischen Staaten, in: Neue Justiz. (1982), S. 349–353 (353 Anm. 5).

[118]) Vgl. die voranstehende Anm. (S. 351).

statt dessen andere, mildere Formen der Einwirkung (unten 2f)[119]. Wenn man diese Entwicklung in Beziehung setzt zu den im Gegenteil immer härter werdenden Sanktionen bei schwerwiegenden Delikten, so kann, für Bulgarien wie für ganz Osteuropa, von einer „sich öffnenden Schere der staatlichen Reaktion auf das Verbrechen" gesprochen werden[120].

2. Ausgewählte strafrechtliche Sonderprobleme

a) Die Straftat

Das bulgarische Recht kennt nur die einheitliche Bezeichnung *prestăplenie* (Straftat), unterscheidet also nicht, wie etwa die DDR, zwischen Verbrechen und Vergehen (zum Übertretungsrecht siehe unten 3)[121]. Eine Handlung ist nur dann strafbar, wenn sie „gesellschaftsgefährlich" (*obštestvenoopasno*) ist, d. h. wenn sie von der sozialistischen Rechtsordnung geschützte Interessen schädigt oder bedroht. Keine Straftaten sind deshalb Handlungen, die zwar formal einen gesetzlichen Straftatbestand verwirklichen, wegen ihrer Geringfügigkeit aber nicht oder nur in offensichtlich unbedeutendem Maße gesellschaftsgefährlich sind. Es gilt der Grundsatz des *nullum crimen sine lege* (Art. 9f. NK). Die Handlung wird nur dann bestraft, wenn sie schuldhaft, d. h. vorsätzlich (*umišleno*) oder fahrlässig (*nepredpazlivo*), begangen wurde (Art. 11 NK). Im Jahre 1982 wurde neben den traditionellen Rechtfertigungsgründen der Notwehr und des Notstandes mit dem „gerechtfertigten wirtschaftlichen Risiko" (*opravdan stopanski risk*) ein neuer eingeführt (Art. 13a NK). Er betrifft Handlungen, die begangen wurden zur Verwirklichung eines wichtigen, gesellschaftlich nützlichen Ergebnisses oder zur Abwendung von erheblichen Schäden. Voraussetzung ist, daß die Handlung den derzeitigen wissenschaftlich-technischen Errungenschaften und Erfahrungen entspricht, daß sie keinem ausdrücklichen gesetzlichen Verbot zuwiderläuft, nicht das Leben und die Gesundheit eines anderen gefährdet und der Täter alles in seiner Macht Stehende zur Vermeidung der eingetretenen schädlichen Folgen getan hat. Für die Frage, ob das Risiko „gerechtfertigt" war, kommt es auch auf das Verhältnis zwischen dem erwarteten positiven Ergebnis und den möglichen negativen Folgen sowie auf die Wahrscheinlichkeit ihres Eintritts an.

b) Strafrechtliche Verantwortlichkeit

Von der Vollendung des 18. Lebensjahres an wird die strafrechtliche Verantwortlichkeit vorausgesetzt. Nichtvolljährige (ab 14 Jahre) sind nur dann strafmündig, wenn sie ihre eigene Handlung begreifen und ihr Verhalten steuern konnten. Minder-

---

[119] Dazu Reuter, L.: Depönalisierung im Strafrecht der europäischen sozialistischen Länder, in: Neue Justiz. (1984), S. 405–408.

[120] Vgl. Filar; Weigend (Anm. 106), S. 254.

[121] Rechtsvergleichend hierzu Buchholz, E.; Griebe, W.: Neue Tendenzen im Strafrecht und Ordnungswidrigkeitenrecht der europäischen sozialistischen Länder, in: Neue Justiz. (1987), S. 63–66.

jährige unter 14 Jahren unterliegen allenfalls erzieherischen Maßnahmen (Art. 31 f. NK)[122]). Die Verantwortlichkeit entfällt bei fehlender Zurechnungsfähigkeit (Art. 33 f.).

c) Die Strafe

Der erklärte Strafzweck besteht in der Besserung des Verurteilten und seiner Erziehung zur Einhaltung der Gesetze und der Regeln des sozialistischen Zusammenlebens, in der vorbeugenden Einwirkung auf ihn sowie in der Generalprävention, nicht aber in der Zufügung von physischen Leiden oder der Erniedrigung der Menschenwürde (Art. 36 NK). Das Strafensystem des Art. 37 NK differenziert nicht nach Haupt- und Nebenstrafen oder Maßregeln. Es umfaßt: 1. Freiheitsentziehung; 2. Besserungsarbeit ohne Freiheitsentziehung; 3. Einziehung des vorhandenen Vermögens; 4. Geldstrafe; 5. Zwangsaufenthalt ohne Freiheitsentziehung; 6. Aberkennung des Rechts, ein bestimmtes staatliches oder gesellschaftliches Amt zu bekleiden; 7. Aberkennung des Rechts, einen bestimmten Beruf oder eine bestimmte Tätigkeit auszuüben; 8. Aberkennung des Rechts auf Wohnsitz an einem bestimmten Ort; 9. Aberkennung des Rechts, Orden, Ehrenbezeichnungen und Auszeichnungen zu erhalten; 10. Aberkennung eines militärischen Ranges; 11. gesellschaftlicher Tadel sowie 12. die Todesstrafe.

Die Mindest-Freiheitsstrafe betrug im Strafgesetzbuch 1951 einen Tag, im Strafkodex 1968 (Urfassung) einen Monat, und nach der Novelle 1982 beträgt sie jetzt drei Monate. Auf der anderen Seite wurde die zulässige Höchststrafe von zunächst 20 Jahren im Strafgesetzbuch 1951, nach einer vorübergehenden Ermäßigung auf 15 Jahre (Regelfall) im Jahre 1968, bei der letzten Reform vom Jahre 1986 wieder generell auf 20 Jahre heraufgesetzt[123]). Ebenfalls seit 1986 kann in Ausnahmefällen (umgewandelte Todesstrafe, Mehrfach- und Rückfalltäter, besonders bezeichnete Tatbestände) eine 30-jährige Freiheitsstrafe verhängt werden (Art. 39 II n. F. NK).

Die Besserungsarbeit (*popravitelen trud*) ist historisch zwar aus der ehemaligen Zwangsarbeit hervorgegangen[124]), dient aber heute als besondere Form der Bewährungsstrafe. Sie kann von drei Monaten bis zu einem Jahr betragen und wird am Arbeitsplatz des Verurteilten (und in Ermangelung eines solchen auf einer anderen geeigneten Arbeit) an seinem Wohnort verbüßt, wobei von seinem Arbeitslohn nach Maßgabe des Urteilsspruchs 10 bis 25 % zugunsten des Staates einbehalten werden. Auch wird die Dauer der Besserungsarbeit nicht auf die Dienstjahre angerechnet, und es gibt keinen bezahlten Urlaub. Die Tatsache der Verurteilung wird dem Arbeitskollektiv und der zuständigen gesellschaftlichen Organisation bekanntgegeben. Bei einem Verstoß gegen die Arbeitspflichten kann die Besserungsarbeit in eine Freiheitsstrafe umgewandelt werden [Art. 43 NK, Art. 133–141 Strafvollzugsgesetz (*Zakon za*

---

[122]) Vgl. auch das Gesetz über die Bekämpfung von gesellschaftswidrigen Erscheinungen von Minderjährigen und Nichtvolljährigen (Anm. 111) Fassung DV. (1988) 75.
[123]) Die lebenslange Freiheitsstrafe kennen lediglich Ungarn und die DDR; vgl. Filar; Weigend (oben Anm. 106) S. 252.
[124]) Filar; Weigend (Anm. 106), S. 250 f.

izpălnenie na nakazanijata, im folgenden: ZIN)[125]]. Bei Arbeitsunfähigkeit tritt an die Stelle der Besserungsarbeit eine Geldstrafe oder öffentlicher Tadel.

Die Strafe der Vermögenseinziehung spielte bisher z. B. in Republikfluchtfällen eine wichtige praktische Rolle und findet namentlich auch bei Wirtschaftsdelikten Anwendung.

Die Geldstrafe (Art. 47 NK) hatte zunächst eine vergleichsweise geringe Bedeutung, soll aber künftig häufiger eingesetzt werden[126]. In diesem Zusammenhang wurde die Mindesthöhe von 10 Leva (1968) auf 50 Leva (1982) angehoben. Der Höchstsatz ergibt sich aus dem jeweiligen besonderen Straftatbestand und wurde ebenfalls in zahlreichen Fällen angehoben. Bulgarien hat damit Anschluß an die Entwicklung in anderen sozialistischen Staaten gefunden, die mehrheitlich schon früher die Anwendung der Geldstrafe ausgeweitet haben[127] (zur Geldstrafe als Verwaltungsstrafe, Art. 78a NK, siehe unten f).

Das Institut der Todesstrafe wird als „zeitweilige", d. h. nur für eine Übergangsperiode bis zum endgültigen Sieg des Sozialismus vorgesehene[128]), und „außerordentliche" Maßnahme bezeichnet (Art. 37 II NK). Sie erfolgt durch Erschießen (vgl. Art. 128–132 ZIN). Das Strafgesetzbuch 1951 sah die Todesstrafe für 50 Fälle vor, nach dem Strafkodex 1968 waren es nur noch 29 Straftatbestände. Damit ist die bulgarische Regelung zwar im Vergleich mit den anderen sozialistischen Staaten streng[129]), wird aber in dieser Hinsicht von der Sowjetunion noch deutlich übertroffen[130]). Der Trend geht jedoch auch in Bulgarien weiter gegen die Todesstrafe. Neuerdings wird in Juristenkreisen sogar die völlige Abschaffung diskutiert[131]). Bereits im Jahre 1982 wurden die Art. 397 II und 400 NK (Militärdienst-Delikte in Kriegszeiten), die allein noch die Todesstrafe als einzige Sanktion vorgesehen hatten, durch die alternative Androhung einer Freiheitsstrafe ergänzt. Hat ein fremder Staat eine Person unter der Bedingung ausgeliefert, daß die Todesstrafe keine Anwendung finden soll, so tritt an ihre Stelle eine zwanzigjährige Freiheitsstrafe (Art. 38 III NK Fassung 1982). Auf Schwangere und grundsätzlich auch auf Personen unter 20 Jahren findet die Todesstrafe keine Anwendung (vgl. im übrigen auch unten e).

d) Strafaussetzung zur Bewährung

Das Gericht kann eine von ihm verhängte Freiheitsstrafe von bis zu 3 Jahren, Zwangsaufenthalt oder Entzug des Wohnsitzrechts auf einen Bewährungszeitraum

---

[125]) Vgl. unten Anm. 160.

[126]) Dazu Teichler (Anm. 115), S. 493.

[127]) Teichler; Willamowski (Anm. 117), S. 352.

[128]) Vgl. Nenov, I.: Nakazatelno pravo na Narodna republika Bălgarija. Obšta čast (Strafrecht der NRB. Allgemeiner Teil). Sofia 1972, S. 475f.

[129]) Als bisher einziges sozialistisches Land hat die DDR die Todesstrafe ganz abgeschafft (4. Strafrechtsänderungsgesetz, GBl. DDR (1987) I Nr. 31, S. 301).

[130]) Dazu Schultze-Willebrand, B.: Das Strafrecht der europäischen sozialistischen Staaten. Tübingen 1980, S. 350–352.

[131]) Milev, V.: Za ili protiv smărtnoto nakazanie (Für oder gegen die Todesstrafe), in: Obštestvo i Pravo. (1988) 3, S. 14–16; Spasov, M.: Edna alterniva na smărtnoto nakazanie (Eine Alternative zur Todesstrafe), in: Obštestvo i Pravo. (1988) 8, S. 12.

von 3 bis 5 Jahren bedingt aussetzen, wobei der Verurteilte nach der Novelle 1982 verpflichtet ist, während dieser Zeit zu arbeiten oder zu lernen (Art. 66–69a NK). Gleichzeitig ist das Gericht befugt, die zuständige gesellschaftliche Organisation bzw. das Arbeitskollektiv oder aber eine bestimmte Person mit der erzieherischen Einwirkung auf den Verurteilten zu betrauen. Davon abgesehen kann bei guter Führung während der Strafhaft die bedingt vorzeitige Entlassung des einsitzenden Täters angeordnet werden (Art. 70–73 NK).

e) Begnadigung und Amnestie

Der DS hat ein umfassendes Gnadenrecht inne und kann verhängte Strafen ganz oder teilweise erlassen (im Falle der Todesstrafe auch: sie umwandeln), Art. 74 NK, Art. 93 Nr. 21 Verf. Dagegen ist für Amnestien die NSb zuständig (Art. 78 Nr. 9 Verf.), die von ihrem Recht des öfteren Gebrauch gemacht hat (zuletzt 1989 in Verbindung mit der Aufhebung der Art. 280f. NK betr. Republikflucht)[132].

f) Absehen von der strafrechtlichen Verantwortlichkeit

Im Verlauf der letzten Jahrzehnte wurden mehrere Möglichkeiten neu geschaffen, im Einzelfall von der strafrechtlichen Verurteilung abzusehen und sie durch andere, schonende Formen der Einwirkung zu ersetzen[133]. Von 1968 datiert die Regelung der bedingten Strafbefreiung unter Übergabe zur gesellschaftlichen Bürgschaft (Art. 75f. NK), deren Voraussetzungen im Jahre 1982 noch erweitert wurden, und zwar kann die Strafbefreiung neuerdings bereits vom Staatsanwalt nach Abschluß der Voruntersuchung verfügt werden. In solchen Fällen wird die zuständige gesellschaftliche Organisation bzw. das Arbeitskollektiv mit der Umerziehung des Täters beauftragt.

Bei bestimmten geringfügigen Straftaten wie Beleidigung, leichter Körperverletzung oder Bagatelldiebstahl kann der Täter von der strafrechtlichen Verantwortlichkeit befreit und statt dessen den Kameradschaftsgerichten übergeben werden (Art. 77 NK). Das Gesetz über die Kameradschaftsgerichte (*Zakon za drugarskite sădilišta*, im folgenden: ZDS)[134] wurde im Jahre 1961 nach sowjetischem Vorbild erlassen; ähnliche Einrichtungen gibt es ferner auch in der DDR und in Rumänien[135]. Kameradschaftsgerichte gibt es in Städten und Dörfern, außerdem in den TKZS, Unternehmen, Einrichtungen, Organisationen, Hoch- und Fachhochschulen und Genossenschaften (Art. 3 ZDS). Die Mitglieder dieser Kameradschaftsgerichte werden von

---

[132]) Für die Nachkriegszeit vgl. die Amnestien in: DV. (1944) 196 und 204 (Beilage); (1946) 157; (1947) 146; (1950) 266; Izv. (1956) 29; (1958) 86; DV. (1964) 71; (1974) 87; (1981) 54 (dazu WGO-Monatshefte für Osteuropäisches Recht. (1981), S. 120) und (1984) 43 (vgl. WGO-Monatshefte für Osteuropäisches Recht. (1983), S. 305). Siehe auch Guneva, M.: Amnistija v Narodna republika Bălgarija (Amnestie in der NRB), in: Pravna Misăl. (1984) 5, S. 65–71. Zuletzt DV. (1989) 37.
[133]) Dazu Reuter (Anm. 119).
[134]) Izv. (1961) 50 Fassung DV. (1986) 27.
[135]) Siehe Knüsli, W.: Die gesellschaftliche Gerichtsbarkeit in Osteuropa. Bern, Frankfurt/M., Las Vegas 1978, S. 83f.

der allgemeinen Versammlung des betreffenden Kollektivs in offener Abstimmung auf eine Frist von 3 Jahren gewählt (Art. 4 I ZDS); sie können vorzeitig wieder abgewählt werden (Art. 6 ZDS). Die Kameradschaftsgerichte verhandeln auch über Fälle der Verletzung der Arbeitsdisziplin und -sicherheit, geringfügige zivilrechtliche Streitigkeiten u. ä. (Art. 7ff. ZDS). Sie können „Maßnahmen der gesellschaftlichen Einwirkung" verhängen sowie in begrenztem Umfang auch Schadenersatz zusprechen oder aber es bei der öffentlichen Verhandlung der Sache bewenden lassen (Art. 11 f. ZDS). Die Verhandlung ist im Regelfall öffentlich (Art. 17 ZDS); die Entscheidung wird öffentlich verkündet und am Arbeits- und Wohnsitz des Betroffenen bekanntgegeben. Rechtsmittel gibt es keine, jedoch können z. B. die Gewerkschaften u. a. Gremien das Kameradschaftsgericht verpflichten, einen Fall ein zweites Mal zu verhandeln, wenn ihnen die erste Entscheidung fehlerhaft erscheint (Art. 25 ZDS). Die Entscheidungen unterliegen der Zwangsvollstreckung (Art. 26 ZDS). Rechtsanwälte dürfen nicht hinzugezogen werden (Art. 28 ZDS).

Schließlich kann das Gericht, oder der Staatsanwalt nach Abschluß der Voruntersuchung, in leichten Fällen seit 1982 auch eine Befreiung von der strafrechtlichen Verantwortlichkeit aussprechen, an deren Stelle eine administrative Strafe (*administrativno nakazanie*), d. h. eine Ordnungsstrafe in einer Höhe zwischen 100 und 1 000 Leva festgesetzt wird. Wurde durch die Straftat ein Vermögensschaden verursacht, so muß dieser vorher ersetzt worden oder sein Ersatz gewährleistet sein (Art. 78 a NK). Auch insoweit hat die Sowjetunion Pate gestanden[136]). Vom Inkrafttreten der NK-Novelle 1982 am 1.7.1982 bis Ende 1983 haben die bulgarischen Gerichte in 1 850 Fällen derartige Strafen verhängt, davon in 1 600 Fällen auf Antrag der Staatsanwaltschaft[137]). Für das Verfahren gelten die Art. 454–460 Strafprozeßkodex. Die Verhängung der administrativen Strafe erfolgt durch das Rayongericht, dessen Entscheidung endgültig ist und allenfalls im Aufsichtswege überprüft werden kann.

Wenn die Voraussetzungen für mehr als eine Art der Befreiung von der strafrechtlichen Verantwortlichkeit gleichzeitig erfüllt sind, kann das Gericht bzw. der Staatsanwalt unter ihnen wählen (Art. 78 b NK), wobei in der Praxis die Entscheidung meist zugunsten der administrativen Strafe des Art. 78 a NK ausfällt[138]). Aufgrund vergleichbarer Angaben aus anderen sozialistischen Ländern wird vermutet, daß der Anteil der Straftaten, bei denen bei Erwachsenen von der strafrechtlichen Verantwortlichkeit abgesehen wird, bei etwa 20 bis 25 % liegen dürfte[139]).

g) Verjährung

Das Recht zur Strafverfolgung verjährt innerhalb von mindestens 2 und höchstens 20 Jahren, je nach gesetzlicher Strafandrohung (Art. 80 NK). Unverjährbar sind Straftaten gegen den Frieden und die Menschlichkeit (Art. 79 II NK).

---

[136]) Erlaß des Präsidiums des Obersten Sowjets der UdSSR v. 8.2.1977, Vedomosti Verchovnogo Soveta Sojuza Sovetskich Socialističeskich Respublik 1977 Nr. 7, Pos. 117.
[137]) Teichler (Anm. 115), S. 493.
[138]) Ebenda.
[139]) Nach Reuter (Anm. 119), S. 407.

h) Medizinische Zwangsmaßnahmen

Art. 89–92 NK sehen Maßnahmen zur medizinischen Behandlung im Falle der Unzurechnungsfähigkeit des Täters vor. Einzelheiten regelt auch die Instruktion Nr. 1 für die Tätigkeit der Gesundheitsorgane bei der Zwangseinweisung von Personen in psychiatrische Kliniken[140]).

3. Verwaltungsstrafrecht

Das Übertretungsrecht wird in Bulgarien, ähnlich wie in der Sowjetunion und den meisten anderen sozialistischen Staaten, dem Verwaltungsrecht und nicht etwa dem Strafrecht zugeordnet[141]). Das Gesetz über die administrativen Übertretungen und Verwaltungsstrafen (*Zakon za administrativnite narušenija i nakazanija*, im folgenden: ZANN)[142]) sieht für schuldhaft begangene Handlungen, welche die festgesetzte Ordnung der sozialistischen Staatsverwaltung verletzen und durch eine Rechtsvorschrift mit einer Verwaltungsstrafe bedroht sind (Art. 6), die folgenden Sanktionen vor: (a) gesellschaftlicher Tadel; (b) Geldbuße bis zu 300, im Wiederholungsfall 500 Leva; (c) zeitweilige Aberkennung des Rechts auf Ausübung eines bestimmten Berufes oder einer bestimmten Tätigkeit (Art. 13, 15 ZANN). Art. 20 ZANN sieht die Einziehung von Sachen, die zur Begehung der Übertretung gedient haben oder als Ergebnis der Übertretung erlangt worden sind, zugunsten des Staates vor. Zur Vorbeugung und Verhinderung drohender Übertretungen bzw. zur Beseitigung bereits eingetretener Schadensfolgen können ferner auch administrative Zwangsmaßnahmen verhängt werden (Art. 22f. ZANN). Geringfügige Sachen können an die Kameradschaftsgerichte abgegeben werden (Art. 28 Lit. „b" ZANN). Die Verhängung der Verwaltungsstrafe erfolgt durch das zuständige Verwaltungsorgan (im einzelnen Art. 47 ZANN), gegen dessen Strafbescheid (Art. 57 ZANN), ausgenommen Bagatellsachen, vor dem Rayongericht Beschwerde eingelegt werden kann (Art. 59 ZANN). Es entscheidet der Einzelrichter, und zwar endgültig (Art. 63 ZANN). Jedoch kann vor dem Bezirksgericht eine Überprüfung im Aufsichtswege bzw. die Wiederaufnahme stattfinden (Art. 65ff, 70ff. ZANN)[143]). Ferner kann nach dem Erlaß über die Bekämpfung des geringfügigen Chuliganismus (Rowdytums) von 1963[144]) eine Person, die das 16. Lebensjahr vollendet hat, vom Rayonrichter als Einzelrichter zu einer Verwaltungsstrafe von bis zu 15 Tagen Arrest in den Einrichtungen des Innenministeriums oder zu einer Geldbuße zwischen 5 und 50 Leva verur-

---

[140]) *Instrukcija za dejnostta na zdravnite organi pri nastanjavane na lica v psichiatrični stacionari po prinuditelen red*, DV. (1981) 58.
[141]) Rechtsvergleichend Lammich, S.: Grundzüge des Übertretungsrechts in den sozialistischen Staaten, in: Recht in Ost und West. (1980), S. 93–103 (93), sowie Bilinsky, A.: Das sowjetische Verwaltungsstrafrecht mit einem Überblick über das Recht anderer Ostblockstaaten, in: Jahrbuch für Ostrecht. 19 (1978), S. 9–64.
[142]) DV. (1969) 92 Fassung (1987) 24. Deutsche auszugsweise Übers. in: Lyon; Lipowschek (Anm. 113), S. 193–198.
[143]) Anm. 141.
[144]) *Ukaz za borba s drebnoto chuliganstvo*, DV. (1963) 102 Fassung (1979) 36.

teilt werden. Das Verfahren ist öffentlich; anwaltlicher Schutz wird nicht gestattet. (Zur Möglichkeit der Befreiung von der strafrechtlichen Verantwortlichkeit unter Verhängung einer Verwaltungsstrafe gemäß Art. 78 a NK siehe oben 2 f).

4. Statistik und Kriminologie

Von den sozialistischen Staaten Europas publizieren bisher nur Jugoslawien, Polen und Ungarn regelmäßig umfassende und allgemein zugängliche statistische Angaben zur Kriminalität. Dagegen herrscht in der UdSSR[144a]), Rumänien und Albanien nach wie vor strengste Geheimhaltung. Zwischen diesen beiden Polen nimmt Bulgarien einen Mittelplatz ein, insofern zwar auch heute noch keine absoluten Zahlen erhältlich sind, aber doch wenigstens seit den späten 60er Jahren die Nennung einzelner statistischer Informationen durch Fachleute in wissenschaftlichen Veröffentlichungen zugelassen wird[145]). Sie berichten von einer beträchtlichen Senkung der Kriminalität. So hätten z. B. die strafrechtlichen Verurteilungen im Zeitraum des 8. Fünfjahresplans (1981–1985) um 18% unter denen des 7. Fünfjahresplans (1976–1980) gelegen. Von den während des 8. Fünfjahresplans verurteilten Tätern hätten 25% eine Strafe ohne Freiheitsentziehung bekommen. Die verhängten Freiheitsstrafen hätten nur in 2,3% der Fälle auf zwischen 5 und 10 Jahren, in 1% auf über 10 Jahre gelautet. Unter den Straftaten seien die Wirtschaftsdelikte mit 28,3% aller Verurteilungen am häufigsten gewesen[146]). Insgesamt sollen zwischen 1965 und 1985 in Bulgarien über 500 000 Menschen wegen einer Straftat verurteilt worden sein. Dem standen gut 20 000 Freisprüche gegenüber, was einer Quote von ca. 4% entspricht[147]).

Das Interesse an kriminologischen Forschungen ist in Bulgarien seit den 60er Jahren deutlich gewachsen. 1967 wurde der Rat für kriminologische Forschungen bei der Generalstaatsanwaltschaft gegründet. Auf eine Initiative dieses Rates geht auch das Erscheinen der ersten systematischen Arbeit zur Kriminologie in Bulgarien im Jahre 1983 zurück, nämlich des Werkes *Osnovi na kriminologija v NRB* (Grundlagen der Kriminologie in der NRB), das 1987 auch in russischer Übersetzung erschienen ist[148]).

[144a]) In der UdSSR sind jedoch neuerdings Auflockerungstendenzen zu beobachten, vgl. Zur Entwicklung der Kriminalität in der Sowjetunion, in: Osteuropa. (1989), A 245–251.

[145]) Vgl. auch Kubiak, J.: Das Problem der Publizität von Informationen über die Kriminalität in den sozialistischen Staaten Europas, in: Osteuropa-Recht. (1986), S. 45–57.

[146]) Nach Ljutov, K.: Ukrepvane na zakonnostta. Intervju (Festigung der Gesetzlichkeit. Interview), in: Obštestvo i Pravo. (1986) 10, S. 5–7.

[147]) Popov, D.: Sădăt opravdava (Das Gericht spricht frei), in: Obštestvo i Pravo. (1988) 5, S. 12–14.

[148]) Eingehend Georgiev, G.: Centăr na kriminologičeski izsledvanijata (Po povod 20 godini ot săzdavaneto na Săveta za kriminologičeski izsledvanijata) [Zentrum für kriminologische Forschungen (Anläßlich des 20-jährigen Bestehens des Rates für kriminologische Forschungen)], in: Socialističesko Pravo. (1987) 7, S. 70–76.

VII. Strafprozeßrecht

1. Einführung

Bis 1951 galt das vor allem russischen Vorbildern entlehnte[149]) Strafprozeßgesetz von 1897 fort[150]), allerdings mit weitreichenden Änderungen besonders im Anschluß an die Verabschiedung der Dimitrov-Verfassung von 1947. Kurz darauf, im Jahre 1952, kam es zur Verabschiedung eines neuen Strafprozeßkodex[151]) nach sowjetischem Muster. Er wurde im Jahre 1974 durch den geltenden Strafprozeßkodex (*Nakazatelno-procesualen kodeks*, im folgenden: NPK)[152]) ersetzt. Die Novelle von 1982 hat, wie bei der Zivilgerichtsbarkeit, zu einer Kompetenzverlagerung nach unten, von den Bezirksgerichten auf die Rayongerichte geführt[153]).

2. System und Zuständigkeit der Strafgerichte

Für Strafsachen sind die Rayon- und Bezirksgerichte sowie das Oberste Gericht zuständig; außerdem gibt es eine spezielle Militärgerichtsbarkeit (Art. 33–40 ZUS)[154]). Die erste Instanz entscheidet mit einem Berufsrichter und zwei Laienbeisitzern (das Oberste Gericht mit drei Berufsrichtern und vier Schöffen). In der zweiten Instanz sind die Gerichte mit drei Berufsrichtern besetzt (Art. 23 f. NPK). Richter (und auch Staatsanwälte) sind bei der Ausübung ihres Amtes unabhängig und unterstehen nur dem Gesetz (Art. 129, 135 Verf., Art. 9 NPK). Jedoch wird dieses Prinzip eingeschränkt durch die Wahl der Richter auf eine Amtszeit von nur jeweils fünf Jahren (Art. 61 ZUS) mit der Möglichkeit der vorzeitigen Abberufung. Seit 1982 werden sämtliche Richter von der NSb bzw. vom DS, nicht mehr unmittelbar von der Bevölkerung gewählt; entsprechendes gilt auch für die Abberufung (Art. 80 III ZUS). Die *preustrojstvo* soll die Stellung und das Ansehen der Richterschaft aufwerten. Nachdem bereits eine spürbare Gehaltsverbesserung für höhere Justizkader erfolgt ist, wird gegenwärtig diskutiert, Richter nach 5-jähriger Bewährung auf Lebenszeit zu wählen. Außerdem soll die ungewöhnlich hohe Arbeitsbelastung der bulgarischen Richter reduziert werden, damit sie mehr Zeit für die einzelnen Fälle bekommen.

Auch in Strafsachen sind die Rayongerichte für alle die Sachen zuständig, die nicht einem höheren Gericht zugewiesen wurden (Art. 28 I NPK). Die Bezirksgerichte verhandeln bestimmte, in Art. 28 II NPK aufgelistete Tatbestände des Strafkodex. Unmittelbar vor das Oberste Gericht gelangen Straftaten von Mitgliedern von DS und Regierung sowie von Angehörigen des Justizapparats im Zusammenhang mit der Erfüllung ihrer Dienstpflichten (Art. 28 IV NPK). Übergeordnete Gerichte haben

---

[149]) Näheres siehe Lamouche, L.: Bulgarie, in: Annuaire de législation étrangère. 27 (1897), S. 788–831 (809).
[150]) *Zakon za uglavnoto sădoproizvodstvo* (DV. (1897) 77).
[151]) *Nakazatelno-procesualen kodeks* (Izv. (1952) 11).
[152]) DV. (1974) 80 Fassung (1986) 89.
[153]) DV. (1982) 28.
[154]) Vgl. Anm. 58.

für ihren Gerichtsbezirk ein Evokationsrecht inne (Art. 36 I NPK). Verhandelt wird vor dem Gericht, in dessen Sprengel die Tat verübt wurde (Art. 33 NPK). Auslandstaten von Ausländern werden von den Sofioter Gerichten verfolgt, für bulgarische Täter kommt es in solchem Fall auf den Ort der Voruntersuchung an (Art. 34 I NPK). Berufungsinstanz gegen Urteile des Rayongerichts ist das Bezirksgericht. Gegen dessen Entscheidungen erster Instanz kann Berufung beim Obersten Gericht eingelegt werden (Art. 38 NPK).

3. Das Strafverfahren

Die Verhandlung ist grundsätzlich öffentlich und mündlich (Art. 13, 18 NPK); es gilt das Prinzip der Unmittelbarkeit (Art. 17 NPK). Nach dem Gesetz gilt der Beschuldigte bis zu seiner rechtskräftigen Verurteilung als unschuldig und hat das Recht auf Verteidigung (Art. 14 NPK). Im Zeichen der *preustrojstvo* hat jedoch eine lebhafte Diskussion über die tatsächliche Praxis eingesetzt. Art. 138 II der Verfassung bestimmt: „Der Beschuldigte hat ein Recht auf Verteidigung", jedoch kann laut Art. 73 I NPK ein Strafverteidiger erst vom faktischen Abschluß der Voruntersuchung durch die Untersuchungsführer und Ermittlungsorgane (Art. 48 NPK) an hinzugezogen werden. Ausnahmen hiervon gelten lediglich für Minderjährige sowie mit Erlaubnis des Staatsanwalts, die aber in Wirklichkeit kaum jemals erteilt wird[155]. Die Zeitschrift *Obštestvo i Pravo* (Gesellschaft und Recht) hat im Jahre 1988 eine Roundtable-Konferenz mit Sofioter Strafverteidigern, darunter auch dem Vorsitzenden des Rates des Sofioter Anwaltskollegiums durchgeführt[156]. Das Echo darauf war so lebhaft, daß sich nach dem ersten Bericht noch zwei weitere Hefte mit dem Thema beschäftigten[157]. Im Ergebnis kamen alle beteiligten Juristen übereinstimmend zu dem Schluß, daß das Recht auf Verteidigung wirksamer ausgestaltet werden muß. Tatsächlich ist nach Auskunft der Anwälte das Vorverfahren dasjenige Verfahrensstadium, in dem sich der Ausgang des Prozesses entscheidet. Das Gericht bilde seine Überzeugung nicht so sehr aufgrund der mündlichen Verhandlung, sondern halte sich im Zweifel an die Ergebnisse der Voruntersuchung. Dort gemachte Aussagen können sogar gemäß Art. 277 und 279 NPK vor Gericht verlesen werden. Laut Art. 91 NPK darf eine Verurteilung nicht allein auf das Geständnis des Angeklagten gegründet werden. Doch wird das Geständnis in der Gerichtspraxis als „ungekrönte Königin der Beweismittel" bezeichnet. Die Rolle des Gerichts bestehe im Falle eines Geständnisses nicht in der objektiven Wahrheitsfindung, sondern in der Bestätigung des in der Voruntersuchung gemachten Geständnisses. Tatsächlich soll während der Voruntersuchung nicht selten auf Verdächtige erheblicher Druck ausgeübt werden,

---

[155] Dazu Obštestvo i Pravo. (1988) 2, S. 24f.; (1988) 6, S. 12 (Anm. 156f.).

[156] Krăgla masa na tema: Pravoto na zaštita v nakazatelnija proces. Zaštita na obvinjaemija – no otkoga? (Roundtable zum Thema: Recht auf Verteidigung des Beschuldigten – aber ab wann?), in: Obštestvo i Pravo. (1988) 2, S. 24–29.

[157] Chadzoljan, M.: Văprosi, koito otdavna čukat na vratata (Fragen, die seit langem an die Tür klopfen), in: Obštestvo i Pravo. (1988) 6, S. 12f.; Stojčev, N.: Săstezatelnost i pri predvaritelnoto razsledvane (Wettstreit auch in der Voruntersuchung), in: Obštestvo i Pravo. (1988) 7, S. 14f.

damit sie die Tat gestehen. In diesem Zusammenhang wird auch die Praxis der Untersuchungshaft kritisiert, die manchmal der Erzwingung von Geständnissen diene. Beklagt werden die lange Zeitdauer und die Isolierung während der U-Haft sowie die schlechten Haftbedingungen dort, die eine Verlegung in das Gefängnis als Erlösung erscheinen lassen könnten. Sobald der Beschuldigte in Untersuchungshaft genommen worden sei, verkehre sich die gesetzliche Unschuldsvermutung in ihr faktisches Gegenteil[158]). In dieselbe Kerbe schlägt der Beitrag von D. Popov in Heft 5 der Zeitschrift[159]). Danach soll in Bulgarien die Meinung verbreitet sein, Freisprüche seien so schwer zu finden wie einzelne Tropfen im Meer, und der Richter fungiere als eine Art Bestätigungsinstanz für die Anklagen der Staatsanwaltschaft. Um einen Angeklagten freizusprechen, müsse der Richter besonders mutig sein.

Die zweite Instanz überprüft die tatsächlichen und rechtlichen Grundlagen des Urteils; jedoch sind vor ihr nur schriftliche und gegenständliche Beweise zugelassen (Art. 312, 315 NPK). Das Urteil wird aufgehoben bzw. geändert bei einer Gesetzesverletzung, einem wesentlichen Verfahrensverstoß, unvollständigen Beweisen, Unbegründetheit des Urteils und im Falle einer offensichtlich ungerechten Strafe (Art. 328 NPK). Auch im Strafverfahren gibt es die Möglichkeit einer Überprüfung rechtskräftiger Entscheidungen im Aufsichtswege durch das Oberste Gericht, auf Vorschlag des Generalstaatsanwalts und des Vorsitzenden des Obersten Gerichts (Art. 349ff. NPK) sowie der Wiederaufnahme (Art. 359ff. NPK).

4. Strafvollzug

Freiheitsstrafen werden in Gefängnissen (*zatvor*) sowie in Besserungshäusern für Nichtvolljährige vollstreckt. Das Strafvollzugsgesetz[160]) regelt ausführlich die Rechte und Pflichten der Strafgefangenen. Die Novelle 1982 hat zu einer Einteilung der Gefängnisse in geschlossene, halboffene und offene Einrichtungen geführt (Art. 8, 12f., 44, 74 ZIN). Ein Staatsvertrag der sozialistischen Staaten von 1978 (vgl. unten das Kapitel der Autorin, Verträge, VIII 2) ermöglicht den Austausch von Strafgefangenen zwecks Strafverbüßung im Heimatland (dazu auch Art. 442–449 NPK).

---

[158]) Obštestvo i Pravo. (1988) 2, S. 26ff. Schon bei Pavlov, S.: Nakazatelen proces na Narodna republika Bălgarija (Strafprozeß der NRB). Sofia 1979, S. 286, findet sich der Hinweis, Art. 73 I NPK entspreche nicht in vollem Umfang der bulgarischen Verfassung und sei reformbedürftig.
[159]) Popov, D.: Sădăt opravdava (Anm. 147).
[160]) DV. (1969) 30 Fassung (1988) 26. Reglement für die Anwendung DV. (1982) 66.

Landesverteidigung

Wilhelm Nolte, Hamburg

I. Militärstrategische und wehrgeographische Lage – II. Militärpolitische Grundlagen – III. Militärische Kräfte zur Landesverteidigung: 1. Entstehung der BNA – 2. Struktur und Stärke der BNA und paramilitärische Kräfte – 3. Zur inneren Verfassung der BNA unter Führung der BKP – IV. Schlußbetrachtung

I. Militärstrategische und wehrgeographische Lage

Die Landesverteidigung Bulgariens, des südlichsten Partners der Großmacht UdSSR im WP, erscheint dem westlichen Betrachter zwiespältig. Die Frage der militärischen Sicherung des mit der DDR kleinsten und daneben bevölkerungsärmsten Mitglieds des WP wird er in landeseigener Literatur kaum problematisiert finden[1]). Die geostrategisch bedeutsame südeuropäische Landbrücke in den Nahen Osten heißt zwar nach einem der Hochgebirge Bulgariens Balkan-Halbinsel, doch ist der Balkan hier nicht einmal das höchste Gebirge. Auch ist Bulgarien nicht die unruhigste Region in dem einstigen „Pulverfaß Europas". Selbst, wer Bulgarien „im Herzen" des Balkan liegen sieht und hier „Prozesse, Erscheinungen und negative äußere Einflüsse" beobachtet, die „Besorgnis wecken", erwartet dennoch nicht, daß hier der nächste Weltkrieg entbrennen werde[2]).

Frieden und Sicherheit erscheinen vielmehr gefestigt. Die Militär-Weltmacht UdSSR ließe sonst nicht gleich zwei der sozialistischen Bruderstaaten (Bulgarien und Rumänien) militärisch ungedeckt. Auch pflegen die Außenminister aller Balkanstaaten, die der NATO wie des WP, miteinander politischen Verkehr. Erst jüngst tauschten sie „in einer konstruktiven Atmosphäre" ihre „Ideen...zur Entwicklung der multilateralen Zusammenarbeit" aus. Dabei ist ihnen die Vorstellung, „die Balkanhalbinsel in eine kern- und chemiewaffenfreie Zone zu verwandeln", gemeinsame „Aufmerksamkeit" und „weitere Erörterung" wert[3]). West und Ost machen hier bündnisübergreifende Sicherheitspolitik.

Das in der „internationalen Arena"[4]) von KSZE, KVAE, MBFR u. a. Konferenzen aktive Land (vgl. das Kapitel von K.-D. Grothusen, Außenpolitik) scheint von

---

[1]) Bebler, A.: Das Militärwesen in den Gesellschaftswissenschaften sozialistischer Länder, in: Österreichische Militärzeitschrift. 23 (1985) 2, S. 133–144.
[2]) Semerdshiew, A.: Die Verteidigungspolitik der Volksrepublik Bulgarien, in: Österreichische Militärzeitschrift. 26 (1988) 1, S. 11.
[3]) Gemeinsames Kommuniqué über das Treffen der Außenminister der Balkan-Länder vom 24. bis zum 26. Februar 1988 in Belgrad, in: Europa-Archiv. 43 (1988) 9, S. D237f.
[4]) Semerdshiew (Anm. 2), S. 11.

der Moskauer Zentrale am langen Arm geführt. Dabei liegt es geographisch in größerer Distanz zur politischen Metropole als alle anderen sozialistischen Bruderländer. Nur: es ist der fernen UdSSR ungleich fester verbunden als deren unmittelbare Anrainer. Sowjetischer Truppen im Lande bedarf es offenbar nicht. Umringt von in der NATO verbündeten Gegnern (Türkei und Griechenland) im Süden, von aus dem Pakt ausgeschiedenen Blockfreien (Albanien und Jugoslawien) im Westen sowie einem eigenwilligen Bündnispartner Rumänien im Norden steht Bulgarien unbeirrbar als südliche, sichere Bastion der Verteidigungsgemeinschaft. An Loyalität und Verläßlichkeit besteht kaum Zweifel[5]).

Die Funktion, einer Großmacht als Bastion dienen zu müssen, ist ein Paradigma der jüngeren Geschichte Bulgariens (vgl. das Kapitel von R. Crampton, Historical Foundations). Die bald fünf Jahrhunderte türkischer Fremdherrschaft hatte Bulgarien in einer nicht nur kulturell schwer erträglichen Unterordnung gehalten. Gleicherweise war es geopolitisch in eine Orientierung gedrängt, die den geographischen Hauptlinien der Region entgegenstehen. Die Befreiung durch Rußland im Russisch-Türkischen Krieg löste 1878 diese Fesseln. Und die Einbindung in die tiefe Südflanke des WP in der Mitte unseres Jahrhunderts führte Bulgarien in eine Rolle, die den geographischen Hauptlinien des Landes strategisch adäquat scheint. So betrachtet macht die erneute Unterordnung unter eine Großmacht geostrategisch Sinn; historisch erklärt sie sich aus der zweimaligen Befreiung durch „Rußland", zuletzt im II. Weltkrieg aus deutscher Vorherrschaft.

Die geographischen Hauptlinien Bulgariens sind in dem mitteleuropäischen Donaustrom, im langgestreckten Balkangebirge und im Flußlauf der Marica gezogen. Sie legen sich Nord-Süd-Bewegungen in den Weg. Im Südwesten ragen die Gebirgsstöcke Rila, Pirin und Rhodopen in Höhen bis über 2900 m wie Türme zum „reich gegliederte(n) Massiv der Thrakischen Masse" auf. Sie weisen Bewegungen aus dem Mittelmeerraum ab. Allerdings führen Donau und Marica in mäßigem Gefälle durch „weitgespannte Becken"[6]) an die Küsten des Schwarzen Meeres bzw. in die zur Türkei gehörige Thrakische Ebene. Sie öffnen hier Einlässe. Und sie zeichnen die strategischen Bewegungslinien vom Donaudurchbruch am Eisernen Tor durch die Nordbulgarische Platte bis zum (rumänischen) Donaudelta, bzw. von der Hauptstadt Bulgariens, Sofia, zwischen Balkan und Rhodopen auf den Bosporus zu. Wo die bulgarischen Flüsse in die Ägäis münden, da läuft Europa gegen Asien hin aus. Aber Asien fängt hier noch lange nicht an.

Weiträumige Bewegungen sind kaum irgendwo möglich. Von Norden nach Süden müßten sie die steilen Donauufer queren und den vielfach über 2000 m hohen West-Ost-Riegel des – im Kleinen Balkan zum Schwarzen Meer hin ausfächernden – Balkankammes überwinden. Raumgreifende Bewegungen von Süden – aus dem ägäischen Raum nach Norden – müßten die hoch aufragenden Gebirgsblöcke der Thrakischen Masse übersteigen oder sich im „tiefen Grabenbruch der Strumafurche"

---

[5]) Nelson, D.N.: Alliance Behaviour in the Warsaw Pact. Boulder Col. 1986, S. 111; Volgyes, I.: The Political Reliability of the Warsaw Pact Armies – The Southern Tier. Durham N.C. 1982, S. 24–40.
[6]) Heß, G.: Bulgarien – Landeskundlicher Überblick. Leipzig 1985 (alle landschaftsbezogenen Zitate aus dieser Quelle).

hindurch flußaufwärts zwängen. Diese bietet, zusammen mit den westlich liegenden Grenzgebirgen zu Jugoslawien hin, die nordwestlich von Sofia am Nordbalkan anschließen, einen natürlichen Schutz in oft cañonartigen Tälern. Ähnliche natürliche Barrieren sind auch für die aus dem Balkan zur Donau hin entwässernden Flüsse kennzeichnend. Sie unterbrechen die im Zuge der Donau ausgemachte Hauptlinie wiederholt. So ist im großen und ganzen „für viele Landesteile... der schroffe Wechsel zwischen gehobenen Gebirgsstöcken und zu tief eingesenkten Becken abgesunkenen Schollen" charakteristisch.

Die Landesnatur begünstigt Verteidigung, besonders gegenüber mobilen Kräften. Sie bietet vielfältige Gelegenheiten, sich an Graten und Schluchten, Pässen und Steilufern anzuklammern und festzuhalten.

Erst zur Türkei hin, wo das Ostbulgarische Hügelland mit nur „sanft ansteigenden und nur mittlere Höhen erreichenden" Bergen und Plateaus vom Maricabecken zur – allerdings häufig schroff abbrechenden – Schwarzmeerküste hinüberleitet, werden weiträumige Bewegungen gepanzerter Kräfte begünstigt. Auch liegt die Hauptstadt Sofia im Nordwesten des Landes in offener Hochebene und nahe der jugoslawischen Grenze vergleichsweise ungeschützt. Beide Regionen verbindet der unablässige, europäisch-asiatische Personen- und Gütertransit. Dieser aber liegt abseits der militärstrategischen Kernräume Europas[7]).

Gleichwohl kommt Bulgarien eine Schlüsselfunktion in Südosteuropa zu. Sie erklärt sich aus westlicher wie östlicher[8]) Sicht. Ungeachtet eines originären Eigeninteresses Bulgariens an seiner Verteidigung[9]) verbinden sich mit dessen geostrategischer Lage für Moskau eine Reihe vorteilhafter Optionen: So kann Bulgarien als Aufmarschgebiet gegenüber den NATO-Staaten Griechenland und Türkei dienen; von hier aus ist – über kurze Distanzen – der Zugriff auf Bosporus, Marmara-Meer und Ägäis möglich[10]). Von hier aus können gleichzeitig oder nachfolgend geführte See-Operationen der sowjetischen Schwarzmeerflotte zum Durchbrechen des Bosporus und der Dardanellen entlastet und landseitig gesichert werden.

Andererseits kann Bulgarien aus den NATO-Staaten von Süden her geführte Angriffe dank seiner günstigen Landschaftsstruktur und eigener Verteidigungskräfte zunächst abfangen[11]). Dabei bildet es einen Puffer gegenüber nach Norden geführten Offensiven und vermittelt hierin den nicht sofort verfügbaren sowjetischen Verstärkungskräften Zeitreserven für deren Aufwuchs und ihre Heranführung – aus dem Militärbezirk Odessa etwa[12]). Im übrigen kommt Bulgarien schon derzeit eine besondere strategische Rolle darin zu, daß es als bündnispolitische Klammer fungiert, die das autonomiebegierige Rumänien im WP räumlich einbindet.

---

[7]) Volgyes, I.: Regional differences within the Warsaw Pact, in: Orbis. 26 (1982) 3, S. 670; Peterson, Ph. A.; Hines, J. G.: Die sowjetische Friedens- und Kriegsstrategie in Europa, in: Wettig, G.: Sicherheit über alles!. Köln 1986, S. 77 ff.
[8]) Semerdshiew (Anm. 2), S. 14.
[9]) Volgyes (Anm. 5), S. 40.
[10]) Scherz, R.: Land- und Luftstreitkräfte in Europa – Ein militärischer Kräftevergleich, in: Stiftung Wissenschaft und Politik, SWP-Bericht-S-318. Ebenhausen 1985, S. 141 ff.
[11]) Scherz (Anm. 10), S. 154.
[12]) Scherz (Anm. 10), S. 155 f.

In westlicher Sicht grenzt Bulgarien an eine der „sensiblen Zonen"[13]) der NATO. An ihrer Südflanke ist sie durch den historisch überkommenen und in aktuellen Problemstellungen fortlebenden griechisch-türkischen Konflikt nicht weniger geschwächt[14]) als der WP möglicherweise durch Rumänien. Die aus diesem Grunde im makedonisch-thrakischen Raum zum Teil gegeneinander gerichteten Truppen der Türken und Griechen bilden zwar ein starkes militärisches Gegengewicht gegen die bulgarischen Truppen. Sie sind jedoch angesichts der geringen Raumtiefe zwischen Grenze und Küste auf das Gelingen ihrer hier geplanten Vorneverteidigung angewiesen. Denn auch die NATO bräuchte für die Nachführung von Verstärkungen Zeit – und die Gewißheit, daß die knappen Reserven nicht zugleich an der NATO-Nordflanke benötigt werden[15]).

Mit der NATO teilt Bulgarien die längste Grenze, davon mit der Türkei 259 km und mit Griechenland 493 km. Hiernach bildet Rumänien mit 609 km die nächstlange Grenze. An den Querseiten des an ein Rechteck erinnernden Territoriums liegen Jugoslawien im Westen mit 506 km gemeinsamer Grenze und im Osten die sich auf 378 km Länge hinziehende Küste des Schwarzen Meeres. Diese bietet in den Hochseehäfen Burgas und Varna wichtige Fährverbindungen in die Sowjetunion. Hier hat die Eisenbahnfähre nach Odessa strategischen Wert, weil auf ihr – an dem ungewissen Partner Rumänien vorbei – schwere, gepanzerte Verbände aus dem nächstgelegenen sowjetischen Militärbezirk herangebracht werden können.

In das Territorium des einzigen Nachbarn im WP, nach Rumänien, führen nur wenige strategisch-operativ nutzbare Wege. Denn die Donau ist auf den gemeinsamen 470 km Grenze nirgends leicht zu überbrücken. Die erste und einzige Eisenbahnbrücke wurde 1954 nahe dem Donauhafen Ruse über den Strom geschlagen, in zweiter Ebene trägt sie auch Radlastverkehr. Die nächste Straßenbrücke liegt 120 km stromabwärts bei Silistra. – Nach Jugoslawien hingegen bieten eine Vielzahl von Pässen Durchlaß durch die Grenzgebirge.

So umschließen Donau, Schwarzmeerküste, Gebirge und Flüsse ein Territorium von 110 994 km², auf dem je km² rund 81 Bürger zu verteidigen sind (vgl. das Kapitel von I. Matley, Geographical Foundations).

II. Militärpolitische Grundlagen

Die militärische Sicherung Bulgariens läßt sich nicht ohne weiteres als Gegenstand eigenständiger[16]) Militärpolitik erfassen. Einerseits bestimmt Bulgarien immer wieder den eigenen militärpolitischen Ort in seiner festen Einbindung in die Warschauer

---

[13]) Cremasco, M.: Der NATO-Abschnitt Südeuropa, in: Österreichische Militärzeitschrift. 24 (1986) 3, S. 226ff.
[14]) Vgl. Dabag, M.; Şen, F.; Yiallourides, Ch.: Der Griechisch-Türkisch-Zypriotische Konflikt als internationaler Modellkonflikt. Athen/Bochum/Bonn 1986.
[15]) Scherz (Anm. 10), S. 157.
[16]) Vgl. Höpken, W.: Die bulgarisch-sowjetischen Beziehungen seit Gorbatschow, in: Südosteuropa. 37 (1988), S. 611f.

Vertragsorganisation und in unverbrüchlicher Verbundenheit mit dem russischen Volk. Andererseits rückt es bei jeder Gelegenheit all jene militärpolitischen Fragestellungen in den Vordergrund, die sich in eine stringent durchgehaltene Linie von Kritik einfügen: Kritik von Gewaltbereitschaft anderer Gesellschaftssysteme, Kritik von Machtpolitik der Gegenmächte und ihrer Bereitschaft zu militärischen Eingriffen in die Geschicke von Drittstaaten, nicht zuletzt Kritik der Massenvernichtungswaffen der „nuklearen Pest"[17]).

Im Zusammenhang mit letzteren entfaltet Bulgarien seit Jahren eine Vielzahl eigener, im Einklang mit unmittelbaren Nachbarn (Rumänien, Jugoslawien, Griechenland) vorgetragener Initiativen für eine nuklearwaffenfreie und chemiewaffenfreie Zone Balkan. Doch sind diese Initiativen für die „internationalen Foren"[18]) gedacht und damit der Außenpolitik zuzuordnen.

Soviel Öffentlichkeit Bulgarien dieser Problematik verschafft, sowenig öffentlich führt es die Debatte einer auch in Innenpolitik, Finanzpolitik oder Gesellschaftspolitik anzusiedelnden Landesverteidigung. So konnte der bulgarische Finanzminister Belčev bei der Einbringung des Staatshaushalts für das Jahr 1987 die Begründung der Finanzmittel für Verteidigung auf den einen Satz beschränken: „Im Entwurf des Staatshaushaltsplanes sind die erforderlichen Mittel für die Verteidigung und Sicherheit des Landes vorgesehen"[19]). Tatsächlich verausgabt Bulgarien mit rund 30 % des Gesamtbudgets mehr als alle übrigen WP-Partner der UdSSR[20]).

Auch die BKP faßt sich gern kurz, so auf dem XIII. Parteitag 1986. Zwar gelte: „Die Verteidigung des sozialistischen Vaterlandes, die Festigung der Verteidigungskraft des Landes und die Garantierung seiner Sicherheit müssen erstrangige Sorge und Pflicht aller Partei- und Staatsorgane, eines jeden Kommunisten und aller bulgarischen Bürger sein". Doch widmet der umfangreiche Rechenschaftsbericht des ZK an den Parteitag der „erstrangigen Sorge" gerade diesen einen Satz sowie einen weiteren Absatz. Dieser mahnt die Notwendigkeit der „Festigung der Verteidigungsfähigkeit" und der „Erhöhung der Gefechtsbereitschaft" angesichts der „komplizierten internationalen Situation und wachsender militärischer Bedrohung von seiten des Imperialismus" an. Er betont die Ergebenheit der Parteikader in der BNA, behauptet ihre moderne Ausrüstung und unterstellt sie gedanklich sogleich wieder dem „Bündnis mit der Sowjetarmee und den Armeen der anderen sozialistischen Teilnehmerländer des Warschauer Vertrages", mit denen zusammen sie ein „zuverlässiger Verteidiger des Friedens und der sozialistischen Errungenschaften des Volkes" sei[21]).

Mit Sentenzen wie diesen wird öffentlich kaum mehr debattiert, als in der Verfassung Bulgariens zur Landesverteidigung nachzulesen steht. Hiernach ist „die Vertei-

---

[17]) Shiwkow, Th.: Ich glaube an die Zukunft der Menschheit, in: RD. 6.12.1986, nach: ZK der BKP (Hrsg.): Informationsbulletin. Sofia 30 (1987) 2, S. 86.

[18]) Rechenschaftsbericht des ZK der BKP an den XIII. Parteitag der BKP, in: XIII. Parteitag der Bulgarischen Kommunistischen Partei, 2. bis 5. April 1986 – Materialien. Berlin 1986, S. 77, 61; vgl. Höpken, W.: Der XIII. Parteitag der Bulgarischen Kommunistischen Partei, in: Südosteuropa. 35 (1986), S. 173.

[19]) Beltschew, B.: Die Hauptrichtungen der einheitlichen Finanzpolitik – Bericht zum Entwurf des Staatshaushaltsplanes 1987, in: RD. 25.12.1986, nach: Bulletin (Anm. 17), S. 66.

[20]) Nelson (Anm. 5), S. 20ff.

[21]) Rechenschaftsbericht (Anm. 18), S. 152.

digung des Vaterlandes... die oberste Pflicht und Ehrensache jedes Bürgers" (Art. 61 Abs. 1). Da „entscheidet (die NSb) über Kriegserklärung und Friedensschluß" (Art. 78 Abs. 10). Und der DS „erklärt den Kriegszustand im Falle eines militärischen Angriffs auf die Volksrepublik Bulgarien oder... zur Erfüllung von internationalen Verpflichtungen zur gemeinsamen Verteidigung..." (Art. 94 Abs. 10).

Hiermit sind die wenigen, in offiziellen Quellen nachvollziehbaren militärpolitischen Grundlagen angesprochen. Sie sind – wenn auch unter unmittelbarer Inkorporation des Bündnisfalles – vornehmlich nach innen gerichtet. Sie beschreiben vor allem die den Organen des Staates zugeordneten Kompetenzen (auch Ernennungen u. a.). Und sie erteilen hierüber hinausgehende Ermächtigungen. So soll der DS, wenn „unter den Kriegsverhältnissen keine Möglichkeit mehr zur Einberufung der Volksversammlung" besteht, per Erlaß „die Gesetze aufheben oder ändern" oder „auch die in der Gesetzgebung nicht geregelten Fragen regeln" können (Art. 95)[22].

Eine nach außen gewandte, eigenständige militärpolitische Betrachtung könnte Bulgarien etwa die Region, in die es eingebettet liegt, in den Blick nehmen lassen. Hier wäre z. B. nach regional notwendigen Ausrichtungen der eigenen Verteidigungspotentiale zu fragen. Es fände dann gewiß zu Akzentuierungen, die von eher plakativen, auf der außenpolitischen Oberfläche angesiedelten Forderungen nach einem nuklear- und chemiewaffenfreien Balkan hinleiten könnten zu Initiativen, die, auf einer unteren Ebene konkretisiert, zur Minderung von Spannungen in der Region beitrügen.

Eine solche Betrachtungsweise kann etwa die vorherrschende Vorstellung relativieren, daß die größere regionale Bedrohung von der Türkei ausgehe. So beklagt der Generalstabschef der BNA, die Türkei unterhalte die „stärkste Armee des Balkans wie auch des ganzen Mittelmeerraumes"[23]. Dabei stützt er seine Argumentation auf die Daten des renommierten Londoner Instituts für Strategische Studien. Diesen liest er jedoch nicht ab, was sie *auch* verdeutlichen: daß die Verhältnisse Soldaten je Einwohner bzw. Soldaten je km² nicht nur den Nachbarn Griechenland (2,0 % bzw. 1,6) über die Türkei (1,2 % bzw. 0,8) hinausheben; vielmehr überragt Bulgarien seinerseits (1,7 % bzw. 1,4) die Türkei in diesen Kenngrößen für das in der Region aufgebotene Wehrpotential.

Tabelle 1: Wehrpotential Bulgariens und der umliegenden Staaten im Verhältnis zur Einwohnerzahl und zur Landesgröße[24])

Land	Einwohner (E)	km²	Soldaten (S)	S = % E	S/km²
Rumänien	23 670 000	237 500	179 500	0,8 %	0,75
Jugoslawien	23 397 000	255 804	213 500	0,9 %	0,83
Bulgarien	8 976 255	110 994	152 800	1,7 %	1,37
Griechenland	10 434 000	131 944	209 000	2,0 %	1,58
Türkei	52 512 000	805 689	654 400	1,2 %	0,81

---

[22]) Brunner, G.; Meissner, B. (Hrsg.): Verfassungen der kommunistischen Staaten. Paderborn 1980, S. 45 ff.
[23]) Semerdshiew (Anm. 2), S. 14.

Vor einer näheren Betrachtung der militärischen Potentiale Bulgariens ist auf die vom Generalsekretär der KPdSU, Michail Gorbačev, ausgehenden Impulse zur Erneuerung von Demokratie und Gesellschaft zu verweisen, die auch in Bulgarien ihren Niederschlag finden. So wird inzwischen die im Westen entwickelte Begriffswelt „Strukturelle Nichtangriffsfähigkeit" aufgenommen und weitergedacht. Sie verbindet sich hier mit dem Selbstverständnis eines im Wesen auf Frieden ausgerichteten Sozialismus ebenso wie mit dem Bild vom „Gemeinsamen Haus Europa". So wurde auf einer internationalen Tagung in Varna im Oktober 1987 von bulgarischer Seite betont, es müsse „ein vernünftiges Maß" in der Stärke der Verteidigungskräfte gefunden werden. Und man sollte „Zahlenspiele" vermeiden, indem in Betracht gezogene Reduktionszonen zunächst eindeutig fixiert werden. Auch sollten Streitkräfte in Reduktionszonen bei Manövern vermindert werden[25]).

Solche Einlassungen, die von bulgarischer Seite zumeist im Einklang mit dem sowjetischen Konferenzteilnehmer vorgebracht wurden, mögen – wie andere balkanpolitische Aktivitäten – als „koordinierte regionalpolitische Umsetzung genereller sowjetischer Strategien"[26]) interpretiert werden. Doch läßt aufmerken, daß von bulgarischer Seite in der regionalen Nachbarschaft zum eigenwilligen Rumänien betont wurde, jeder Staat müsse „das Recht haben, einen selbstgewählten Weg der Sicherheit zu gehen"[27]).

---

[24]) International Institute for Strategic Studies (Hrsg.): The Military Balance 1987–1988. London 1987, S. 47f. (Zit. als: IISS/Balance). Hinweis: Die Daten zu den Streitkräften werden hier und im folgenden, wenn nicht ausdrücklich anders vermerkt, auf dem Stand der IISS/Balance 1987 belassen, auch wenn mit dem Jahrgangsband 1988/1989 neuere Daten vorliegen. Diese weisen in der Gesamtstärke – hier zugunsten nur der Landstreitkräfte – und in wenigen anderen Kategorien auch anderer Teilstreitkräfte moderat zu nennende Steigerungen aus. Ende Januar 1989 hat allerdings der WP selbst – mit Blick auf die Konferenz für Konventionelle Rüstungskontrolle ab März 1989 – einen ersten, ausführlicheren Kräftevergleich vorgelegt: Militärverlag des Verteidigungsministeriums der UdSSR (Hrsg.): Warschauer Vertrag und NATO – Kräfteverhältnis in Europa. Moskau 1989. Hier scheinen z. T. erhebliche Divergenzen gegenüber der IISS/Balance auf. Beispielsweise werden schon die Gesamtstreitkräfte Bulgariens auf nur 117500 Soldaten berechnet (S. 10 und 12). Diese und die weiteren Unterschiede werden – so ist zu hoffen – im Zuge der Konferenz aufgehellt werden. Hier können sie nicht aufgelöst werden. Von einer bloßen Gegenüberstellung wird im Interesse einer Gesamtschau abgesehen, die vor dem Zeitpunkt endet, von dem an offizielle Daten des WP vorliegen. Auch die vom WP angekündigten, einseitigen Truppenreduzierungen müssen im weiteren unberücksichtigt bleiben, da sie sich noch nicht in den gegebenen Strukturen niederschlagen. Die Rede ist von einer Reduzierung um 10000 Mann, 200 Panzern, 200 Artilleriesystemen, 20 Kampfflugzeugen, 5 Kampfschiffen und von einer Senkung des Verteidigungsetats um 15% (Schmidt, H. J.: Der Warschauer Pakt wird defensiv, in: Frankfurter Rundschau. 24.02.1989, S. 11).

[25]) Henning, C.: (Kurzbericht über) Tagung (der World Federation of Scientific Workers in) Varna, 18.–20. Oktober 1987 – „European Security and Non-Offensive Defence (NOD)", unveröffentlichtes Manuskript 26.10.1987, S. 2ff; vgl. Lapins, W.: Die Russen kommen – Kommen die Russen?, in: Truppenpraxis. 32 (1988) 3, S. 246–251, hier: S. 249.

[26]) Höpken (Anm. 16), S. 616.

[27]) Henning (Anm. 25), S. 2.

III. Militärische Kräfte zur Landesverteidigung

1. Entstehung der BNA

Der Entstehung der BNA wird in der militärbezogenen Literatur des Landes ungleich größere Aufmerksamkeit gewidmet als der Militärpolitik. Im Entstehungsprozeß nämlich wird – quasi stellvertretend für Militärpolitik – ein „Schlüsselmoment der Militärpolitik"[28]) gesehen. Auch die „bulgarische... militärwissenschaftliche Arbeit ist vor allem durch Werke militärischer und ziviler Historiker gekennzeichnet"[29]). Dabei setzt die „Geschichte der Bulgarischen Volksarmee" in der anliegenden Zeittafel beim Soldatenaufstand von Vladaja am 24.9.1918 ein – im Schatten der Großen Sozialistischen Oktoberrevolution in Rußland. Sie erinnert mit den Unruhen des Jahres 1923 und dem „Beginn des antifaschistischen Volksaufstandes" am 23. September den Anlaß des alljährlichen Tages der BNA. Von hier springt sie flugs in die Kriegsjahre 1941 ff. und zum „Tag der Befreiung Bulgariens", dem Tag des „bewaffneten antifaschistischen Volksaufstandes" am 9.9.1944.

Einen Tag zuvor, am 8.9.1944, hatten sowjetische Truppen die rumänisch-bulgarische Grenze überschritten. 10 Tage hiernach wurde die Armee Bulgariens „dem Oberbefehlshaber der 3. Ukrainischen Front, Marschall der Sowjetunion F.I. Tolbuchin, operativ unterstellt". Aus dieser Unterstellung unter sowjetische Führung hat sich die bulgarische Armee bis heute nicht wieder gelöst. In dieser Unterstellung haben die bulgarischen Truppen in zwei Perioden des „Vaterländischen Krieges Bulgariens" an der „Befreiung Ostjugoslawiens" (Oktober bis November 1944) und an der „Befreiung Südungarns und Nordwestjugoslawiens" (Dezember 1944 bis März 1945) mitgewirkt[30]). Dabei sahen sich die bulgarischen Truppen wegen ihrer „bürgerlichen Auffassungen über die Vorbereitung und Durchführung des Krieges, der Operation und des Gefechts... in vielerlei Hinsicht hinter dem Niveau der Kriegskunst" insbesondere der sowjetischen Streitkräfte „zurückgeblieben". In der zweiten Periode konnte immerhin eine „solide Basis für die weitere Entwicklung... für den weiteren fruchtbringenden Einfluß der sowjetischen Kriegskunst geschaffen (werden), ohne die die moderne Bulgarische Volksarmee nicht vorstellbar ist"[31]).

Gerade weil hier besondere militärische Leistungen nicht zu vermerken sind[32]), ist schlüssig, wenn die BNA sich „aus der sozialistischen Revolution vom 9.9.1944 hervorgegangen" sieht[33]). Sie „wurde 1944 durch die revolutionäre Umgestaltung der alten Armee formiert", dabei war das „Wichtigste..., daß sie mit revolutionärem Geist erfüllt"[34]) wurde. Semerdžiev meint heute, der in den Nachkriegsjahren gelei-

---

[28]) Semerdshiew (Anm. 2), S. 12.
[29]) Bebler (Anm. 1), S. 136.
[30]) Semerdshiew, A.; Christow, F.; Penkow, S.: Geschichte der Bulgarischen Volksarmee. Berlin 1977, Zeittafel S. 291 ff.; s. auch das Kapitel „Außenpolitik" von K.-D. Grothusen.
[31]) Geschichte der BVA (Anm. 30), S. 138, 143.
[32]) Vgl. Autorenkollektiv unter Leitung von Panow, B.W.: Geschichte der Kriegskunst. Moskau 1984, Berlin 1987; die in der „Geschichte der BVA" (Anm. 30) herausgehoben betrachteten Kämpfe an der Südwestflanke der Roten Armee finden in diesem Werk keine Erwähnung.
[33]) Geschichte der BVA (Anm. 30), S. 5.
[34]) Kriegskunst (Anm. 32), S. 537.

stete Aufbau der „Armee der jungen Volksmacht" sei „originell", weil die „Truppen der monarchofaschistischen Macht nicht aufgelöst, nicht liquidiert wurden"[35]. In der von ihm mitverfaßten „Geschichte der BVA" wird freilich eine gründliche „Säuberung der Armee" belegt, indem Georgi Dimitrov zitiert wird: „Unter der Führung unserer Partei wurde eine Reihe reaktionärer Verschwörungen aufgedeckt und mit starker Hand liquidiert", und: „Die Armee wurde konsequent von reaktionären Offizieren gereinigt"[36].

Besondere militärische Traditionen scheinen weniger an herausragende Kampfesleistungen in den Weltkriegen geknüpft. Sie greifen weiter in die Geschichte zurück und erinnern an die Zurückschlagung der türkischen Armee durch bulgarische Landwehr zusammen mit russischen Truppen am Šipka-Paß im hohen Balkan (1877), die Abwehr serbischer Truppen bei Slivnica (1885) und die Niederringung türkischer Truppen während des 1. Balkankrieges bei Lozengrad (1912)[37]. Einen näheren Bezug zur Gegenwart vermitteln Benennungen von Schulen, Kasernen oder Soldatenklubs, indem sie an Persönlichkeiten aus den revolutionären Anfängen der Volksrepublik gemahnen. Etwa ehrt jede Einheit den ersten kommunistischen Ministerpräsidenten mit einem nach ihm „Dimitrov-Zimmer" benannten Kulturraum[38]. Namen stehen damit für den bewußt tradierten parteilichen Ansatz der Entwicklung der BNA in ihrer ersten Etappe.

Eine zweite Entwicklungsetappe setzt „gegen Mitte der 50er Jahre" in der Zeit der Gründung des WP ein. In der ersten Etappe hatte „auf der Grundlage... der sowjetischen Militärwissenschaften" die Ausformung einer „modernen Armee sozialistischen Typs" im Vordergrund gestanden. Dabei war in ihrer „Organisationsstruktur... ein abgestimmtes System von Politorganen" eingefügt worden. In der zweiten Etappe hingegen rücken mehr militärische Gesichtspunkte in den Blick: mit der Einführung „neuer, moderner Bewaffnung" aus den Händen der „uneigennützigen... Sowjetunion und... (der) anderen sozialistischen Staaten", mit Voranschreiten der Mechanisierung und Motorisierung, mit einer „scharfen" Erhöhung der Feuer- und Stoßkraft der Mot-Schützenverbände hält „eine militärtechnische Revolution" in der BNA Einzug. Sie wird nun auf die „Führung von aktiven und hochbeweglichen Kampfhandlungen" vorbereitet und damit befähigt, „zu jeder Zeit... dem Aggressor einen vernichtenden Schlag zu versetzen"[39].

2. Struktur und Stärke der BNA und paramilitärische Kräfte

Ungeachtet dieser selbst zugedachten Befähigung sind nach Meinung des Generalstabschefs Semerdžiev „die Streitkräfte der VR Bulgarien... recht begrenzt". Und

---

[35]) Semerdshiew (Anm. 2), S. 13.
[36]) Geschichte der BVA (Anm. 30), S. 75, 83, 159, 259.
[37]) Semerdshiew (Anm. 2), S. 13.
[38]) Anonym: Streitkräfte (Bulgariens). Unveröffentlichtes Manuskript, dem Autor auf Anforderung übersandt von der Botschaft der Volksrepublik Bulgarien, Bonn, 24.07.1987; Geschichte der BVA (Anm. 30), S. 268.
[39]) Botschaft (Anm. 38), S. 11f.

Landesverteidigung

„sie übersteigen...nicht den Bedarf ihrer Verteidigung"[40]). Eine nähere Betrachtung[41]) ergibt das folgende Bild.

Die BNA hält insgesamt 152 800 Mann unter Waffen, davon dienen 94 000 Soldaten als Wehrpflichtige. Daneben stehen 216 500 Soldaten im Reservestatus verfügbar. Die drei Teilstreitkräfte teilen sich hierein, wie die Tabelle 2 ausweist.

Tabelle 2: Soldaten in der BNA und in den Teilstreitkräften

Aufteilung	Aktive Soldaten 152 800 = %	davon Wehrpflichtige 94 000 = %	zusätzliche Reserven 216 500 = %
Landstreitkräfte	110 000 = 72,0	70 000 = 74,5	182 500 = 84,4
Luftstreitkräfte	34 000 = 22,2	18 000 = 19,1	20 000 = 9,2
Seestreitkräfte	8 800 = 5,8	6 000 = 6,4	14 000 = 6,4

Paramilitärische Kräfte werden in 16 Regimentern der Grenztruppen mit insgesamt 15 000 Mann gesehen. Auch sind 150 000 Mann Territorialmiliz zu nennen sowie 7500 Mann der Sicherheitspolizei. Eine andere Quelle macht hier andere Angaben[42]). So ist ein eindeutiges Bild nicht zu gewinnen. Hinweise der bulgarischen Botschaft in Bonn: „In den Bestand der bulgarischen Volksarmee treten auch die Grenztruppen, die Bautruppen und die Truppen des Ministeriums für das Transportwesen (Eisenbahntruppen) ein"[43]), helfen da kaum weiter.

Die *Landstreitkräfte* (LandSK) sind mehr als doppelt so groß wie die beiden anderen Teilstreitkräfte zusammen. Bemerkenswert, daß einerseits ihr Personalanteil an Wehrpflichtigen in etwa diesem Verhältnis entspricht. Demzufolge sind sie – mehr als Luftwaffe und Marine – im Kriegsfall auf Personalaufwuchs aus den Reserven angewiesen. Dieser dominiert dem Umfang nach die aktiven Kräfte. Daß weitere 500 000 Mann in einer Art zweiter Reserve geführt werden, ist hierbei noch unberücksichtigt.

Anderen Informationen zufolge belaufen sich die Reserven insgesamt auf 200 000 bis 250 000. Dabei wird angemerkt, daß ihre Fortbildung kaum der westlicher Armeen gleichkomme[44]).

Die LandSK sind in drei Armeen gegliedert, die jede zugleich einen Wehrbereich führt. Die Wehrbereiche erstrecken sich über die ganze Tiefe des Landes von der Nordgrenze gegenüber Rumänien bis zur Südgrenze gegenüber Griechenland und der Türkei. Nur ein Wehrbereich hat eine gemeinsame Grenze mit einem anderen Staat, die es hiergegen zu verteidigen gelten könnte: Wehrbereich I zu Jugoslawien. Und nur ein Wehrbereich (III) grenzt an das Schwarze Meer, gegenüber dem amphibische Anlandungen abzuwehren wären.

---

[40]) Semerdshiew (Anm. 2), S. 15.
[41]) IISS/Balance (Anm. 24), ebenda.
[42]) Keegan, J.: World Armies – Second Edition, London 1983, S. 82 f.
[43]) Botschaft (Anm. 38), S. 16.
[44]) Keegan (Anm. 42), S. 82.

Tabelle 3: Gliederung der bulgarischen Landstreitkräfte[45]

Wehrbereich I	Wehrbereich II	Wehrbereich III
1. Armee, Sofia	2. Armee, Plovdiv	3. Armee, Sliven
1. GardeMotSchtz Div(A) Sofia	2. MotSchtzDiv(A) Stara Zagora	3. MotSchtzDiv Burgas
28. MotSchtzDiv Blagoevgrad	17. MotSchtzDiv Chaskovo	18. MotSchtzDiv(A) Šumen
	19. MotSchtzDiv(A) Pazardžik	7. MotSchtzDiv Jambol
	5. PzBrig Kazanläk	13. PzBrig Sliven
	11. PzBrig Karlovo	24. PzBrig Ajtos
		9. PzBrig Knjaževo
(1) SCUD-WerferBrig Samokov	(1) SCUD-WerferBrig Karlovo	(1) SCUD-WerferBrig Jambol
		(1) LuftlandeRgt Burgas

Aus der Kräftegruppierung und ihrer Dislozierung ist abzulesen, daß sich die bulgarischen LandSK mit dem Rücken an den rumänischen Bündnispartner anlehnen. Denn die große Masse der Verbände ist auf der Südseite des Balkan, also zum Gegner hin stationiert. Bewegungsvorhaben nach Norden würden immer erst den langgestreckten Gebirgszug überqueren müssen. Nur eine der acht MotSchützen-Divisionen liegt auf der Nordostflanke des Kleinen Balkan, aber keine der Panzerbrigaden.

Damit ist die BNA auf eine Verteidigung eingerichtet, die nahe an der Grenze zu den NATO-Gegnern aufgenommen werden soll. Nicht auszuschließen ist, daß hierbei die Panzerbrigaden für Gegenangriffe eine grenzüberschreitende Rolle zugewiesen erhalten. Denn sie liegen mit drei von fünf Brigaden im südostbulgarischen Hügelland versammelt. Überdies können die beiden anderen aus geschützter Flankenlage in jene Region hineinstoßen, die vor allen anderen Landesteilen als panzergünstig zu charakterisieren gewesen war.

Die vorstehenden Überlegungen sind an *konventionelle* Waffen eines eher rückständigen Standards geknüpft. Denn Bulgarien gehört trotz seiner besonderen Treue zur Sowjetunion nicht zu den bevorzugt mit neuen Waffen belieferten Ländern im WP[46]. Im *nuklearen* Zusammenhang muß erwähnt werden, daß in Bulgarien 27 mobile Abschußgestelle für SCUD-Raketen und 39 mobile Abschußrampen für FROG-Raketen disloziert sind. Diese – auch durchwegs veralteten – Waffenträger können

---

[45] Zusammengestellt nach: Keegan (Anm. 42), S. 83; (anonym): Die Streitkräfte der Warschauer-Pakt-Staaten Rumänien und Bulgarien, in: Österreichische Militärzeitschrift. 24 (1986) 6, S. 562; IAP-Dienst Sicherheitspolitik – Warschauer Pakt Streitkräftepotential. 2. Aufl., 1987, S. 23f.

[46] Keegan (Anm. 42), S. 82; nach IISS/Balance (Anm. 24), S. 234, stehen nur noch in Bulgarien und Rumänien Panzer des Baujahres 1940 (T 34). Nach IAP-Dienst, S. 24, sind erst rund 10 % der insgesamt 2150 Panzer vom neueren (!) Typ T 72.

ebenso mit konventionellem wie mit chemischem oder nuklearem Sprengkopf (mit niederem KT-Wert) bestückt werden, doch sollen nukleare Sprengköpfe in Bulgarien nicht gelagert sein[47]).

Die *Luftstreitkräfte* (LuftSK) sind in zwei Luftwaffendivisionen mit zusammen sieben Luftkampfregimentern gegliedert. Zwei Regimenter sind zur Kampfunterstützung der LandSK vorgesehen. Vier Regimenter fliegen in Abriegelungsrollen. Ein Regiment hat eine Aufklärungsrolle. Es ist hierfür u. a. mit dem sonst nur in der Sowjetunion geflogenen Fernaufklärer FOXBAT (MIG-25) ausgestattet. Offensichtlich wird der Fernaufklärung besonderes Gewicht beigemessen. Hingegen fällt bei der übrigen Ausstattung der bulgarischen Luftwaffe mit insgesamt rund 270 Kampfflugzeugen die Vielzahl der Flugmuster auf: MIG-17, MIG-21PFM, MIG-23BM, MIG-23B/G, MIG-25, Su-22 und Su-25. Dies erschwert sowohl die Wartung als auch die Einsatzführung. Je ein Transportregiment, ein Helikopterregiment (mit 1 Kampfhubschrauberschwadron), ein Ausbildungsregiment sowie ein Fallschirmjägerregiment und eine Luftabwehrdivision runden das Bild einer weitgehend ausgewogenen Luftwaffe ab. Ihre größeren Standorte sind Balčik, Burgas, Ignatievo, Karlovo, Plovdiv, Sofia, Tolbuchin und Jambol[48]).

Die bulgarischen *Seestreitkräfte* (SeeSK) sind, gemessen an ihrer seestrategisch günstigen Nähe zu den Meerengen, die Europa von Kleinasien trennen, unverhältnismäßig klein und schwach gerüstet. Offensichtlich ist ihnen im Verbund mit Seeoperationen des WP keine größere Rolle als die der Küstenverteidigung und der Grenzsicherung (Donau) zugedacht. Auch hat diese Teilstreitkraft in den letzten Jahren große Einbußen im Personalumfang verkraften müssen, obwohl der Umfang der Gesamtstreitkräfte nahezu konstant geblieben ist. Hingegen verzeichnet die Luftwaffe – zunächst sehr zu Lasten der LandSK – im gleichen Zeitraum einen enormen Zugewinn an Personal.

Tabelle 4: Entwicklung der bulgarischen Seestreitkräfte[49]) im Vergleich zu den anderen Teilstreitkräften

	1987	1984	1981	1978	87 : 78
Seestreitkräfte	8 800	8 500	10 000	10 000	− 12 %
Luftstreitkräfte	34 000	33 800	34 000	25 000	+ 36 %
Landstreitkräfte	110 000	105 000	105 000	115 000	− 4 %

Auch in der Ausrüstung der SeeSK zahlt sich die enge Verbundenheit Bulgariens mit den Partnern des WP nicht aus: Sie sind keineswegs modern ausgerüstet. An größeren Einheiten sind 3 Fregatten der Riga-Klasse (aus 1957/58) und 4 Untersee-

---

[47]) Arkin, W. M.; Fieldhouse, R. W.: Nuclear Battlefields – Global Links in the Arms Race. Cambridge M. A., 1985, S. 264.
[48]) Keegan (Anm. 42), ebenda; IISS/Balance (Anm. 24), ebenda; IAP (Anm. 45), ebenda.
[49]) Nach IISS/Balance (Anm. 24), (die betreffenden Jahrgangsbände).

boote der Romeo-Klasse (1971/72 und 1985/86 erworben) zu nennen. Diese alten Schiffstypen sind, wie die meisten übrigen (und kleineren) Einheiten, von der UdSSR übernommen. Sie bedürfen z. T. umfangreicher Renovierung, um sie einsatzfähig zu machen. Die SeeSK sind gegliedert in die Schwarzmeerflotte, Marineflieger (Hubschrauber), Küstenverteidigung (u. a. Artillerie), Marinebasen, die Donauflottille, Rückwärtige Dienste und Ausbildungseinrichtungen. Das Marinehauptquartier befindet sich in Burgas, weitere Marineanlagen sind in Varna, Sozopol, Vidin, Atija und Balčik[50]).

Allerdings macht der Marinesektor mit seinem Renovierungsbedarf und in beschränktem Umfang auch Eigenbau von kleineren Schiffseinheiten einen bemerkenswerten Anteil einer eigenen *Rüstungsindustrie* Bulgariens aus[51]). Sie scheint in offiziellen Wirtschaftsberichten freilich ebensowenig auf wie die landeseigene Produktion von Handfeuerwaffen und Munition[52]).

3. Zur inneren Verfassung der BNA unter Führung der BKP

Mit rund 62 % Wehrpflichtigen in den Streitkräften und unter Hinzurechnung der zuvor beschriebenen, die Gesamtstreitkräfte in ihrem Umfang um ein Mehrfaches übersteigenden Reserven ist die BNA für ihr Personalaufkommen auf Wehrpflicht angewiesen. Die Verfassung fordert jeden Bürger auf, „zur Sicherung und Festigung des Friedens beizutragen" (Art. 63 Abs. 1) und stellt „Kriegsanstiftung und Kriegspropaganda" als „die schwersten Straftaten gegen den Frieden und die Menschheit" unter Strafandrohung (Art. 63 Abs. 2). Der politisch gefaßte Appell wird in Art. 61 Abs. 1 dahingehend konkretisiert, daß „die Verteidigung des Vaterlandes... die oberste Pflicht und Ehrensache jedes Bürgers ist". Art. 62 endlich „verpflichtet alle Bürger entsprechend den Gesetzen" zum „Wehrdienst"[53]).

Der Wehrdienst dauert in LandSK und LuftSK zwei Jahre, in den SeeSK drei Jahre. Die Wehrpflichtigen treten ihren Militärdienst in der Regel nach einer vormilitärischen Ausbildung an, die „Tausende Offiziere, Unteroffiziere und Soldaten" der BNA unterstützen. So haben sie bei der „Ablegung des Fahneneides in Städten und Ortschaften" und „in einem feierlichen Zeremoniell" eine Vorstellung von dem, was sie beschwören: „... ein ehrlicher, tapferer, disziplinierter und wachsamer Soldat zu sein, militärische und staatliche Geheimnisse streng zu wahren und widerspruchslos alle militärischen Vorschriften und Befehle... zu erfüllen...". Sie beeiden auch, „... bis zum letzten Atemzug... der Volksregierung treu ergeben zu sein". Und sie versprechen, „... die Heimat mutig, geschickt, in Ehre und Würde zu schützen,... für die Erringung des vollständigen Sieges über die Feinde..."[54]).

---

[50]) Nach IISS/Balance (Anm. 24), ebenda; Keegan (Anm. 42), ebenda; sowie Vego, M.: East European Navies, in: Naval Forces. 8 (1987) 2, S. 114–118; Breyer, S.: Im Schatten des „Großen Bruders" – Die Marinen Bulgariens und Rumäniens heute, in: Marine-Rundschau. 84 (1987) 4, S. 229–233.
[51]) Vego (Anm. 50), S. 118.
[52]) Keegan (Anm. 42), ebenda.
[53]) Brunner/Meissner (Anm. 22), S. 59.
[54]) Geschichte der BVA (Anm. 30), S. 268, 286f.

Der Wehrpflichtige wie der Berufssoldat leisten als Bürger der Volksrepublik einen Eid auf eine Armee, die von der herrschenden Partei zusammen mit dem militärisch-politischen „Befreier" UdSSR noch vor der Republik begründet wurde. Die Bindung der Armee an die BKP ist damit von besonderer Qualität, hat sie ihre Existenz doch der Partei mehr als dem Staat zu verdanken. Sie vergilt es ihr durch Verbundenheit: „88 % aller Offiziere sind Mitglieder der BKP. Sie sind jene mächtige Kraft, die die Parteilinie durchsetzt... und sie zu vorbildlicher Erfüllung der militärischen Pflicht inspiriert"[55]).

Unter der unangefochtenen Führung der Armee durch die Partei ist „die Armee... eine Schule" der Gesellschaft. „Sie erzieht die Soldaten zu kollektivem Denken und Handeln in höchster Form... und sie macht sie zu würdigen Bürgern der sozialistischen Gesellschaft"[56]). Die Führungsfähigkeit der Partei ist vielfach abgesichert: z. B. durch ein dicht organisiertes Netz von Politorganen in allen Truppenteilen, durch Politoffiziere in den Kommandoebenen und durch Vortragsrecht des Chefs der Politischen Hauptverwaltung der Volksarmee sowohl beim Minister der Volksverteidigung wie beim Chef des Sekretariats des ZK. Dekrete des Ministers der Volksverteidigung zu Grundfragen parteipolitischer Arbeit bedürfen der Mitzeichnung des Leiters der politischen Hauptverwaltung. Die Politorgane in den Streitkräften erlassen für alle unterstellten Kommandeure wie für die Partei-, Gewerkschafts- und DKMS-Organisationen in den Streitkräften verbindliche Anweisungen. Dabei dient parteipolitische Arbeit in der Armee, neben gesellschaftspolitischen Vorhaben, auch „der Erhöhung der Gefechtsbereitschaft der Truppen" und der „ständigen Festigung der Ordnung und der Disziplin der Soldatenkollektive"[57]) (vgl. das Kapitel „Regierungssystem" von O. Luchterhandt).

Die Grundlagen der Führungsbefähigung im militärischen wie im politischen Sinne werden in sorgfältiger Ausbildung der Offiziere und Unteroffiziere an einer Vielzahl von militärischen Lehranstalten gelegt. Dabei haben die Lehranstalten für Offiziere den Rang von Hochschulen oder Militärakademien, die für Unteroffiziere den von Mittelschulen. Zu nennen sind hier:

– Militärakademie Georgi Stojkov Rakovski in Sofia
– Offiziershochschule (der Landstreitkräfte) Vasil Levski in Veliko Tărnovo
– Fliegervolkshochschule Georgi Benkovski in Dolna Mitropolija
– Marinevolkshochschule Nikola Jonkov Vapcarov in Varna.

Die Ausbildung dauert zwischen 4 und 5 Jahre und schließt mit einem Diplom ab, dabei überwiegt die ingenieurwissenschaftliche Ausbildung. Bis zu 70 % der Offiziere verfügen über einen Hochschulabschluß[58]). Das hiermit gewonnene gesellschaftliche Ansehen wird darüber hinaus bevorzugt finanziell vergütet. So verdient ein Offizier unter Einrechnung verschiedener Vergünstigungen zwischen 50 und 70 % mehr als Beschäftigte in vergleichbarer ziviler Stellung[59]).

---

[55]) Geschichte der BVA (Anm. 30), S. 259.
[56]) Semerdshiew (Anm. 2), S. 13; Geschichte der BVA (Anm. 30), S. 268.
[57]) Volgyes (Anm. 5), S. 32; Botschaft (Anm. 38), S. 23 f.
[58]) Botschaft (Anm. 38), S. 22–24.
[59]) Botschaft (Anm. 38), S. 19–21; Volgyes (Anm. 5), S. 36.

IV. Schlußbetrachtung

„Der gesamte Aufbau der bulgarischen Volksarmee wird vom Zentralkomitee der Bulgarischen Kommunistischen Partei und vom Ministerrat geleitet. Ihre unmittelbare Führung erfüllt das Ministerium für Volksverteidigung."[60]) Der Minister, Dobri Džurov, ist Armeegeneral und Mitglied des Politbüros des ZK der BKP. Sein Stellvertreter, Generaloberst Christo Dobrev, Mitglied des ZK der BKP, ist Stellvertreter auch des Oberkommandierenden des WP für Bulgarien[61]). Im Sinne eines operativen Kommandos führt keiner von beiden die eigenen Truppen. Denn diese unterstehen – im Frieden wie im Krieg – dem sowjetischen Oberbefehlshaber der Truppen im Strategischen Operationsgebiet Südwest, Armeegeneral Gerasimov[62]).

Sowjetischen Kommando folgt die BNA seit jeher: sichtbar in Manövern im eigenen Lande, in Ländern anderer Partner und zur See[63]). Bulgarien nutzt diese und jede andere Gelegenheit zum Erweis seiner Festigkeit im Bündnis. Es muß ein Interesse hieran haben, denn Eigenständigkeit wird Bulgarien im militärischen Sektor nicht erlangen können. Auf die Unterstützung der Sowjetunion bleibt es – bei Notwendigkeit der Verteidigung des Landes – angewiesen. Aber solange auf dem Balkan Frieden bleibt, kann Bulgarien – ohne fremde Truppen im Lande – auf sich gestellt sein. Dies bleibt es umso sicherer, je selbstverständlicher es dem Pakt dient.

---

[60]) Volgyes (Anm. 5), ebenda.
[61]) Botschaft (Anm. 38), S. 15.
[62]) Nach: Nor-Mesek, N.; Rieper, W.: Das Oberkommando der Sowjetischen Streitkräfte. Hrsg. v. Institut für Sowjet-Studien. Frankfurt a. Main 1985, Tafeln 6 und 16; Schulz-Torge, J.: Die Führung der UdSSR in Partei, Staat, KGB und Militär. Hamburg 1988, S. 955; Hines, J. G.; Petersen, Ph. A.: Sowjetische Führungskonzepte im Wandel – Schwerpunkt Operationsgebiet, in: Internationale Wehrrevue. 1986, 3, S. 287 ff.
[63]) Flor, R.: Manöver in Europa 1975–1983 – Grundlagenmaterial – Teil 3: Manövererfassungsblätter WP und N/N. Hrsg. v. Institut für Strategische Grundlagenforschung an der Landesverteidigungsakademie Wien. Wien 1984.

Wirtschaftssystem

Werner Gumpel, München

I. Die Transformation der Wirtschaftsordnung – II. Die Einführung der Planwirtschaft – III. Maßnahmen zur Steigerung der Effizienz des Wirtschaftssystems: 1. Grundprobleme – 2. Die Wirtschaftsreformen der 60er und 70er Jahre – 3. Das Konzept der *preustrojstvo* vom Dezember 1986: a) Die Einführung der Selbstverwaltung in der Wirtschaft – b) Änderungen in der Planung – c) Veränderungen im Bereich der Preisbildung – d) Die Einführung der „Firma" – e) Die Reform des Bankensystems – IV. Zukunftsaussichten

I. Die Transformation der Wirtschaftsordnung

Das Wirtschaftssystem der NRB ist in deren Verfassung vom 18. 5. 1971 festgeschrieben[1]). Es sind insbesondere die Art. 13–33, in denen es dargestellt und der Rahmen, in dem sich die wirtschaftlichen Aktivitäten im Lande vollziehen können, abgesteckt wird. Wie die Wirtschaftssysteme der anderen sozialistischen Staaten Ost- und Südosteuropas basiert es auf dem Stalin-Modell der Sowjetunion, das im Zeitablauf verschiedentlich variiert wurde, wobei die umfangreichsten und tiefgreifendsten Veränderungen in den Jahren 1987 und 1988 eingebracht wurden.

Art. 13, Abs. 1 der Verfassung sagt eindeutig: „Das Wirtschaftssystem der Volksrepublik Bulgarien ist sozialistisch. Es gründet sich auf das gesellschaftliche Eigentum an den Produktionsmitteln, schließt die Ausbeutung des Menschen durch den Menschen aus und entwickelt sich planmäßig zu einer kommunistischen Wirtschaft." Damit ist das wichtigste Grundcharakteristikum sozialistischer Wirtschaftssysteme verfassungsrechtlich verankert.

Das *gesellschaftliche Eigentum* an den Produktionsmitteln ist gleichzusetzen mit dem *sozialistischen Eigentum*, das in den Art. 14–20 definiert wird. Dieser Begriff erfaßt das *Staatseigentum*, das auch als „allgemeines Volkseigentum" bezeichnet wird, und als die „höchste Form des sozialistischen Eigentums" gilt, das *genossenschaftliche Eigentum* und das *Eigentum der gesellschaftlichen Organisationen*. Eine neue Eigentumsform ist insbesondere im Bereich der Landwirtschaft entstanden, wo es *staatlich-genossenschaftliche Unternehmen* gibt, das sind Genossenschaften mit staatlicher Kapitalbeteiligung. Ebenso wie den Staatsunternehmen weist der Staat diesen Vermögen zur Bewirtschaftung und Verwaltung zu. Er kann ihnen auch das

---

[1]) In deutscher Sprache abgedruckt in: Brunner, G.; Meissner, B. (Hrsg.): Verfassungen der kommunistischen Staaten. Paderborn 1980, S. 50 ff.

Nutzungsrecht an bestimmten staatlichen Vermögen abtreten. Im Zusammenhang mit den Reformen der Jahre 1987/88 wird eine Neudefinition des Begriffs „sozialistisches Eigentum" diskutiert.

Die *gesellschaftlichen Organisationen*, wie BPS, DKMS, Sportorganisationen usw. sollen mit Hilfe ihres Eigentums die ihnen vom Staat zugewiesenen Aufgaben erfüllen. Dabei können sie auch in speziellen, vom Gesetz vorgesehenen Fällen eine ihren Zielen entsprechende wirtschaftliche Tätigkeit ausüben.

Privates Eigentum an den Produktionsmitteln gibt es nur im kleingewerblichen Bereich und, als Ausnahmefall, in der Landwirtschaft sowie für die Ausführung „häuslicher Produktion seitens der Werktätigen". Diese Produktionsmittel dürfen beim Einsatz persönlicher Arbeit der Bürger und ihrer Familien eingesetzt werden. Ein spezielles Gesetz bestimmt, welche Produktionsmittel erworben und in welchem Ausmaß sie eingesetzt werden können.

In Bulgarien verlief die *Sozialisierung der Industrie* sehr schnell. Die am 9.9.1944 an die Macht gekommene OF-Regierung stellte alle größeren Betriebe entweder unter die Kontrolle der Staatsorgane oder der Gewerkschaften. Eine Sozialisierungsabsicht wurde noch im Oktober 1945 bestritten; vielmehr wurde versichert, daß das Privateigentum unangetastet bleiben solle. In Wirklichkeit waren damals jedoch die Sozialisierungsvorbereitungen bereits in vollem Gange[2]. Mit der Verfassung vom 4.12.1947 erhielt der Staat das Recht zur Sozialisierung von Wirtschaftsunternehmen (Art. 10, Kap. II). Bereits drei Wochen nach Annahme dieser Verfassung, am 26.12.1947, wurde ein Gesetz verabschiedet, das die Verstaatlichung der gesamten bulgarischen Industrie mit Ausnahme der kleineren Betriebe mit handwerklichem Charakter vorsah.

Die erste große Enteignungswelle setzte mit dem Gesetz vom 26.12.1946 ein[3]. Ihm war eine Reihe anderer Gesetze vorausgegangen, die die Errichtung eines beachtlichen Staatssektors ermöglichten. Nach demselben Muster war in der Sowjetunion und später in den anderen sozialistischen Staaten Ost- und Südosteuropas verfahren worden. Zunächst wurde ein Staatssektor bei teilweiser Beibehaltung eines privaten Wirtschaftssektors geschaffen. Durch die gezielte Förderung des Staatssektors bei gleichzeitiger Diskriminierung der privaten Unternehmer wurde der Privatsektor laufend verkleinert. Schließlich wurde er völlig beseitigt.

Entsprechende Regelungen wurden in Bulgarien schon bald nach dem Staatsstreich von 1944 getroffen. Hierzu gehörten ein Gesetz über die Aburteilung von Kriegsverbrechern, deren Eigentum konfisziert wurde, ein Gesetz über die Konfiskation von illegal oder durch Kriegsgewinne erworbenen Eigentums sowie zwei Gesetze zur Schaffung eines Staatsmonopols für Tabak und Alkohol. Durch diese Gesetzgebungsakte wuchs der Anteil der sozialistischen Staatsunternehmen von 6 auf 16,6% der Industrieunternehmen des Landes. Wird der genossenschaftliche Sektor mit einem Anteil von 8% hinzugezählt (ihm wurde unter den neuen Bedingungen des

---

[2] Vgl. Rochlin, R. P.: Die Wirtschaft Bulgariens seit 1945 (DIW-Sonderhefte, NF Nr. 38, Reihe A). Berlin 1957, S. 64.
[3] Ebenda.

volksdemokratischen Systems sofort ein sozialistischer Charakter zugesprochen), so gehörten bereits Ende 1946 fast 25 % der Wirtschaft dem sozialistischen Sektor an[4]).

Das Gesetz vom 26.12.1947 brachte dann die schnelle und konsequente Verwirklichung der Sozialisierungspläne der Kommunisten. Der Enteignung unterlagen die Unternehmen der Privatindustrie und der Montanindustrie sowie die Banken. Von den insgesamt ca. 7000 nationalisierten Unternehmen, unter ihnen 1150 Kleinbetriebe, wurden etwa 4000 den zuständigen Industrieministerien (sektoral gegliederten Verwaltungsbehörden für die Industrie) unterstellt, ca. 3000 wurden den Kommunen übergeben. Die letzteren waren relativ kleine Unternehmen von im allgemeinen nur lokaler Bedeutung, die auf der Basis von lokal verfügbaren Rohstoffen arbeiteten. Die etwa 4000 größeren Unternehmen unterlagen einem *Konzentrationsprozeß*. Ihre Zahl war bis 1948 auf Grund von Fusionen auf 1739 gesunken[5]). Mit der Bildung von Großbetrieben sollten die Voraussetzungen für die Einführung der Planwirtschaft geschaffen werden. Je geringer die Zahl der Betriebe in der Volkswirtschaft, desto einfacher ist nämlich die Erstellung und die Vollzugskontrolle des Volkswirtschaftsplanes. Auch ausländische Unternehmen und Beteiligungen wurden verstaatlicht. Das in Bulgarien vorhandene deutsche und italienische Kapital wurde von der Sowjetunion beschlagnahmt. Aus ihm wurden die gemischten bulgarisch-sowjetischen Gesellschaften gebildet, die unter sowjetischer Leitung standen. Gegen eine von Bulgarien zu zahlende Entschädigung in unbekannter Höhe wurden die gemischten Gesellschaften in den Jahren 1954 und 1955 der bulgarischen Regierung übergeben. Hierzu gehörten neben der Luftfahrtgesellschaft Tabso die Schiffahrtsgesellschaft des Landes, einige Betriebe der Montanindustrie (Blei-, Zink-, Silber- und Erdölförderung) sowie der Bau- und Baumaterialienwirtschaft. 1948 befanden sich 93 % der industriellen Produktionskapazitäten des Landes in Staatshand. Weitere 2 % gehörten zum genossenschaftlichen Sektor. 1953 hatte sich der Anteil des privaten Sektors auf 1,4 % vermindert. Damit konnte die Sozialisierung als abgeschlossen betrachtet werden.

Mit der Transformation der Eigentumsordnung in der Industrie waren die Grundlagen für die Einführung der sozialistischen Planwirtschaft sowjetischer Prägung geschaffen.

Auch die *Landwirtschaft*[6]) erfuhr eine sozialistische Umgestaltung. Dies geschah aus politischen, wirtschaftlichen und sozialen Gründen, sollte sie doch nicht nur den politischen Zielen der kommunistischen Regierung untergeordnet, sondern auch in die angestrebte planwirtschaftliche Ordnung eingefügt werden. Die Transformation der Eigentumsordnung in der Landwirtschaft konnte auf dem bestehenden Genossenschaftswesen aufbauen. Bulgarien verfügte bereits Ende des letzten Jahrhunderts über ein relativ gut ausgebautes Genossenschaftswesen der traditionellen Art[7]).

Das erste Gesetz über die Kollektivwirtschaften und die Maschinen- und Traktoren-Stationen nach sowjetischem Vorbild wurde 1945 verabschiedet. Eine Zwangs-

---

[4]) Roussinov, S.: Economic Development of Bulgaria after the Second World War. Sofia o.J., S. 18.
[5]) Ebenda, S. 19.
[6]) Zur Organisation der Landwirtschaft siehe den Beitrag von I. Grosser in diesem Band.
[7]) Roussinov (Anm. 4), S. 21; Die Umgestaltung. (1988) 1, S. 1–5.

kollektivierung größeren Ausmaßes setzte erst in der zweiten Hälfte des Jahres 1948 ein und wurde in den Jahren 1949 und 1950 verstärkt fortgesetzt. 1956 waren 77 % der landwirtschaftlichen Nutzfläche und 75 % aller Bauernhöfe kollektiviert, 1959/60 gab es praktisch keine privaten Bauern mehr. Ihr Anteil an der landwirtschaftlichen Nutzfläche machte zu diesem Zeitpunkt nur noch 0,8 % aus[8]).

Neben die TKZS traten Staatsgüter, die jedoch in Relation zu den TKZS von nur untergeordneter Bedeutung blieben.

Während in den anderen sozialistischen Staaten Ost- und Südosteuropas verschiedene Typen von landwirtschaftlichen Produktionsgenossenschaften gegründet wurden, die sich im jeweiligen Sozialisierungsgrad unterschieden, wurde in Bulgarien nur ein Typ nach sowjetischem Vorbild geschaffen.

II. Die Einführung der Planwirtschaft

Der I. Fünfjahresplan wurde für die Jahre 1949–1953 erarbeitet und verkündet. Er wurde in nur vier Jahren erfüllt. Mit ihm setzte die eigentliche Industrialisierung Bulgariens ein. Nach sowjetischem Vorbild wurde die Schwerindustrie (Produktionsabteilung A) bei den staatlichen Investitionen gegenüber der Konsumgüterindustrie (Produktionsabteilung B) bevorzugt. Für die Schwerindustrie wurden 86 % der für die Industrie zur Verfügung stehenden Investitionsmittel aufgewendet, für die Konsumgüterindustrie nur 14 %[9]). Damit wurden die Wurzeln für die später auftretenden strukturellen Ungleichgewichte in der bulgarischen Volkswirtschaft gelegt. Sie gehören zu den wichtigsten Ursachen der fast 50 Jahre währenden Unterversorgung der bulgarischen Bevölkerung mit Lebensmitteln und industriellen Konsumgütern.

Die Industriepolitik des I. Fünfjahresplans war auf eine gleichmäßigere industrielle Erschließung des Landes und damit nicht nur auf sektorale, sondern vor allem auch auf regionale Effekte abgestellt. Die Industrie des Landes war in den Agglomerationsräumen um Sofia und Plovdiv konzentriert, wenn von einigen minder wichtigen Ballungsgebieten abgesehen wird. Nun wurden neue industrielle Standorte auch in Südbulgarien, wie in Dimitrovgrad, Kărdžali und Rudozem, geschaffen. Das Land verzeichnete in allen Jahren dieses Plans hohe wirtschaftliche Wachstumsraten, was jedoch in der Versorgung der Bevölkerung keinen sichtbaren Ausdruck fand. Allerdings sind die damals veröffentlichten Statistiken sehr widersprüchlich.

1953 trat der II. Fünfjahresplan in Kraft. Damit war die Planung fest institutionalisiert. Während der Laufzeit dieses Plans konnte die Wachstumsdynamik der vorhergehenden Jahre allerdings nicht mehr aufrecht erhalten werden. Dafür wurde der III. Fünfjahresplan bereits nach drei Jahren, im Jahre 1960, erfüllt.

Mit der Übernahme des sowjetischen Planungstyps wurden auch die entsprechen-

---

[8]) Vgl. hierzu Dobrin, B.: Bulgarian Economic Development Since World War II. New York 1973, S. 44 ff., und Dellin, L. A. D. (Ed.): Bulgaria. New York 1957, S. 287 ff., sowie Lampe, J. R.: The Bulgarian Economy in the Twentieth Century. London 1986, S. 124 ff.

[9]) Vgl. Planovo Stopanstvo. (1954) 6, S. 1.

den Planungsinstitutionen adaptiert. Dies fand in einem hierarchisch aufgebauten Planungssystem seinen Ausdruck, an dessen Spitze eine Staatliche Plankommission (*Dăržavna planova komisija*) stand. Diese war ein Organ des Ministerrats und erarbeitete die Volkswirtschaftspläne in enger Interaktion mit diesem, dem ZK der BKP und den Industrieministerien sowie einigen weiteren zentralen Behörden, wie dem Staatlichen Preiskomitee (*Komitet po cenite*) und dem Komitee für Wissenschaft und technischen Fortschritt (*Komitet za nauka i techničeski progres*). Dieser Plan wurde im alten, bis Mitte der 60er Jahre geltenden System über die Industrieministerien und die Wirtschaftsvereinigungen an die Betriebe weitergeleitet, wobei diese ein Einspruchsrecht hatten. Ein Einspruch konnte, mußte aber nicht zu einer Planänderung führen. Die Planung war imperativ.

Die Durchsetzung der Planauflagen erfolgte mit Hilfe eines komplizierten und umfangreichen Systems von Kennziffern, deren Erfüllung von den übergeordneten Behörden kontrolliert wurde. Sie waren das wichtigste Instrument der Planerstellung, des Planvollzugs und der Plankontrolle. In einem einstufigen Bankensystem waren die Betriebe an eine Bank (Tochter oder Filiale der BNB) gebunden, der sie, ebenso wie andere Betriebe der gleichen und anderer Branchen, zugewiesen waren. Diese vollzog die Plankontrolle durch die „Kontrolle über den Lev": Da sämtliche Zahlungsvorgänge einschließlich der Aufnahme von Krediten und deren Bedienung nur über sie möglich waren, erhielt sie einen genauen Einblick in die Wirtschaftstätigkeit des Betriebes und konnte damit eventuelle Abweichungen vom Plan erkennen. Wurden solche festgestellt, konnten unverzüglich die übergeordneten Instanzen verständigt und damit staatliche Interventionen veranlaßt werden. Zudem gab es die Institution der gesellschaftlichen (Volks-) Kontrolle, einer Institution, die sich aus Vertretern der Partei und verschiedener gesellschaftlicher Organisationen zusammensetzte. Dieser war der Betriebsdirektor zur Auskunft verpflichtet. Auch sie hatte das Recht und die Pflicht, die übergeordneten Behörden bei Unregelmäßigkeiten in der Wirtschaftstätigkeit und bei der Planerfüllung zu informieren. Damit war der Betrieb in ein perfektes Kontrollsystem eingebettet, das es ihm unmöglich machte, aus dem Plansystem auszubrechen[10]. Dieses System der Planung hat im Rahmen der seit Mitte der 60er Jahre durchgeführten Reformen zwar Änderungen erfahren, war im Prinzip jedoch bis 1987 gültig.

Wichtigstes Planungsorgan war die *Staatliche Plankommission*, die gemeinsam mit den territorialen Planungsorganen die langfristige, mittelfristige und Perspektivplanung für die gesamtwirtschaftliche, die sektorale und die territoriale Entwicklung durchführte. Hierzu stellte sie den Bedarf der Volkswirtschaft an materiellen Ressourcen fest und erarbeitete Bilanzen und Pläne zur Verteilung der wichtigsten Roh- und Brennstoffe, der Elektrizitätserzeugung, der Materialien und Ausrüstungen sowie einer Reihe anderer Güter der industriellen und landwirtschaftlichen Produktion. Das Ergebnis ihrer Recherchen legte sie der Regierung vor. Gleichzeitig erstellte sie gemeinsam mit der Kommission für Wissenschaft und Technik Pläne für die Einführung neuer Technologien und die Modernisierung der Produktionskapazitäten.

---

[10] Vgl. Gumpel, W.: Sozialistische Wirtschaftssysteme. Die sozialistischen Staaten. Bd. 1. München 1983, S. 89 ff.

Unter Beteiligung der Industrieministerien und auf der Grundlage von Vorschlägen des Ministeriums für Außenhandel erarbeitete sie die Export- und Importpläne des Landes, die Teil des Volkswirtschaftsplans waren. Im Rahmen der Zusammenarbeit der sozialistischen Staaten innerhalb des RGW hatte sie für die Koordinierung der nationalen Entwicklungsplanung mit der der anderen RGW-Staaten Sorge zu tragen. Darüber hinaus mußte sie eine effiziente Kontrolle der rechtzeitigen Planerfüllung gewährleisten. Zur Erfüllung all dieser Aufgaben bedurfte es einer laufenden Kommunikation mit dem staatlichen Preiskomitee, das zentral die Bewertung der wichtigsten Güter durchführte bzw. Kalkulationsvorschriften für die dezentrale Preisbildung erließ und selbst oder durch seine territorialen Organe die dezentral gebildeten Preise bestätigte und fixierte.

Wichtige staatliche Planungsorgane waren auch einige der funktionalen Ministerien (z. B. das Finanzministerium) sowie die BNB bzw. das Bankensystem. Dabei war die Rolle des Finanzministeriums besonders so lange bedeutsam, als die Investitionen in der Volkswirtschaft zentral, d. h. aus dem Staatshaushalt finanziert wurden.

Bis zur Reform des Bankensystems im Jahre 1987 liefen sämtliche Zahlungen des Staates und der Wirtschaft, auch die Kredite, über die BNB und deren Organe. So hatte sie nicht nur den Geldumlauf gemäß den Geldeinnahme- und Geldausgabenbilanzen der zentralen Instanzen zu planen und zu verwirklichen, sie hatte auch die Kreditpläne für die Wirtschaft zu erstellen. Gemeinsam mit der *Außenhandelsbank* war sie Trägerin des staatlichen Valutamonopols, eines wichtigen Bestandteils des staatlichen Außenhandelsmonopols. Zu ihrem Aufgabenbereich gehörte auch die Finanzkontrolle der Ministerien und Behörden.

Die *Industrieministerien* waren die administrativen Führungsorgane der wichtigsten Branchen. Ihre Hauptaufgaben waren die Produktionsplanung für die ihnen unterstellten Vereinigungen und Betriebe sowie die Kontrolle des Planvollzugs. Entscheidend für die Effizienz ihrer Tätigkeit war eine wirkungsvolle Interaktion und eine gute Koordination der Tätigkeit der verschiedenen Ministerien in den komplementären Bereichen. Dadurch sollte ein ungestörter Ablauf des Wirtschaftsprozesses ermöglicht werden. Gleichzeitig sollte dadurch eine optimale Ressourcenallokation gewährleistet werden. In der Praxis wurde jedoch immer wieder über eine mangelhafte Koordination der Tätigkeit der einzelnen Ministerien geklagt.

Die *Wirtschaftsvereinigungen* (*obedinenie*), im Jahre 1964 geschaffen, können am besten als „sozialistische Konzerne" charakterisiert werden. Sie waren Führungsorgan einer Anzahl von Unternehmen der gleichen Branche und galten als „ökonomische Grundeinheit" der Volkswirtschaft. Bis zu ihrer Gründung waren sog. Vereinigte Unternehmen (*obedineni predprijatija*) die Führungsorgane der Staatsbetriebe, wobei die ihnen angeschlossenen Unternehmen keine rechtliche Selbständigkeit besaßen. Sie hatten den Status von Filialen. Die Wirtschaftsvereinigungen stellten in der Planungshierarchie das Zwischenglied zwischen Unternehmen und Ministerien dar. Die angeschlossenen Unternehmen blieben auch nach 1964 Filialen der Vereinigung, nunmehr jedoch mit „relativer Selbständigkeit"[11]).

---

[11]) Vgl. Planovoe chozjajstvo. (1971) 11, S. 26 f.

Die Wirtschaftsvereinigungen verfügten über besondere „innere Abteilungsfilialen", die aus Vereinigten Betrieben, Fabriken, Kombinaten oder Basen bestehen konnten. Die Abteilungsfilialen hatten eigene Niederlassungen, eigene Benennungen, verfügten über ein eigenes Verrechnungskonto bei der Bank und erstellten eigene Bilanzen. Die Abteilungsfilialen waren keine juristischen Personen, und ihre wirtschaftliche Selbständigkeit war eng limitiert. Im Falle ihrer Zahlungsunfähigkeit trat die Vereinigung für sie ein. Den Wirtschaftsvereinigungen konnten Außenhandelsunternehmen angegliedert werden, die eigene Rechtspersonen waren.

Der hohe Konzentrationsgrad der Wirtschaft und das schwer durchschaubare Geflecht von wirtschaftlicher Unselbständigkeit und Selbständigkeit der Unternehmen sowie der hohe Bürokratisierungsgrad, der sich aus der Planbürokratie und ihrem hierarchischen Aufbau ergab, bedeuteten eine enge Limitierung der betrieblichen Autonomie und des betrieblichen Aktionsradius. Die Anpassungsfähigkeit an neue wirtschaftliche Situationen und Entwicklungen war außerordentlich gering, falls sie überhaupt vorhanden war.

Die staatlichen *Unternehmen* bzw. *Betriebe* (*predprijatie*) (beide Termini werden synonym gebraucht) stellen die unterste Leitungsebene dar. Zunächst waren sie jedoch reine Befehlsempfänger mit nur sehr geringen Dispositionskompetenzen. In der Arbeitsorganisation spielen die Arbeitsbrigaden, die nach sowjetischem Vorbild geschaffen wurden, eine entscheidende Rolle. Die sog. *Wirtschaftsleiter* (*răkovoditeli*), gemeint ist das Management vom Brigadeleiter (Brigadier) bis zum Betriebsdirektor bzw. Direktor einer Wirtschaftsorganisation, sind bei ihrer Tätigkeit für die Berücksichtigung der staatlichen Interessen bei allen zu treffenden Entscheidungen verantwortlich.

Die Unternehmen sind bis zu den Reformen der sog. „Umgestaltung" (*preustrojstvo*) verpflichtet gewesen, „Gegenpläne" zu den staatlichen Plänen zu erstellen. Durch diese sollten Produktionsreserven aufgedeckt werden, denn Aufgabe des Gegenplans war es, die staatlichen Planaufgaben zu überbieten. Da die Unternehmen bei der Erstellung ihrer Plankennziffern um die Verpflichtung zur Gegenplanung wußten, verschwiegen sie in der Regel den übergeordneten Behörden vorhandene Kapazitäten, um Spielraum für den Gegenplan zu haben. Aus diesem Grunde wurde die Gegenplanung in der DDR als wenig sinnvoll erkannt und 1980 abgeschafft. In Bulgarien hat Todor Živkov noch im Jahre 1984 den Gegenplan als „das Hauptinstrument der sozialistischen Wirtschaftsleitung" bezeichnet. Er forderte sogar, „die Rolle des Gegenplans aufzuwerten"[12]).

Durch ihre Einbindung in die Planungs- und Verwaltungshierarchie waren die Unternehmen ebenso wie die Wirtschaftsvereinigungen der Willkür der Bürokratie unterworfen. Sie hatten eine Vielzahl von Detailregelungen und staatlichen Anweisungen zu beachten, die sie kaum durchschauen konnten, über deren Erfüllung sie jedoch Rechenschaft ablegen mußten. Auch Živkov hatte dieses erkannt, als er ausführte: „Die Wirtschaftsleitungen und die Arbeitskollektive können sich im Wirr-

---

[12]) Shivkov, T.: Probleme und Methoden bei der Gestaltung des entwickelten Sozialismus in der Volksrepublik Bulgarien. Sofia 1984, S. 87.

warr von Artikeln, Paragraphen und Punkten der verschiedenen Vorschriften und Instruktionen nur schwer zurechtfinden"[13]).

Unter den gegebenen Umständen konnten die Unternehmen nur sehr begrenzt eine eigene *Investitionspolitik* verfolgen. Wollten sie selbst aktiv werden, so konnte dies nur im Rahmen des Plans geschehen, d.h., sie mußten ihre Investitionswünsche bei den übergeordneten Behörden anmelden, diese gaben sie über die einzelnen Hierarchie-Stufen an die Zentrale weiter, wo die Entscheidung getroffen wurde. Bei erfolgter Genehmigung wurde das Investitionsvorhaben in den Plan aufgenommen und, je nach Verfügbarkeit der gewünschten Investitionsgüter, in der nächsten oder einer weiter in der Zukunft liegenden Planperiode verwirklicht. Einen Handel mit Investitionsgütern gab es nicht, diese wurden vielmehr zugeteilt. Die Unternehmen bemühten sich, Maschinen möglichst über den Bedarf hinaus zu erhalten, um beim Ausfall von Produktionskapazitäten über Reserven zu verfügen und damit die Planaufgaben erfüllen zu können. Das galt umso mehr, als die Ersatzteilversorgung unzureichend war. Bei allgemeiner Kapitalknappheit führte dies zu einer ungeheuren Verschleuderung von Produktivkapital, durch die der Volkswirtschaft schwerer Schaden zugefügt wurde. Erst in der Mitte der 60er Jahre wurde versucht, durch eine aus dem Gewinn zu zahlende Produktionsfondsabgabe und die Aufwertung der Rentabilität als Plankennziffer, diesem Zustand ein Ende zu setzen.

Da die Investitionen zentral finanziert wurden und ein materielles Interesse an ihrer Tätigkeit aufgrund des starren Lohn- und Prämiensystems nicht bestand, war den „Leitern" auf den verschiedenen Planungsebenen ihre Realisierung ziemlich gleichgültig. Auch kümmerten sie der zu ihrer Durchführung benötigte Zeitraum und ihre Wirtschaftlichkeit wenig. 20 Jahre nach den ersten Reformen des Wirtschaftssystems stellte Todor Živkov im Jahre 1984 fest: „Heute noch passieren beispielsweise folgende Dinge: Der Bau neuer Objekte oder die Rekonstruktion und Modernisierung werden in Angriff genommen, ohne daß die Notwendigkeit, ja sogar die Effektivität der Investitionen bewiesen sind. Oftmals haben die Projekte ein niedriges Niveau und sind bei ihrer Genehmigung moralisch überholt, oder aber man beginnt mit dem Bau von Objekten ohne Entwurfs- und Kostenunterlagen, oder bei vielen Objekten wachsen die Voranschlagskosten unaufhörlich und beträchtlich, oder aber die Inbetriebnahme der Bauvorhaben wird weit über den Abgabetermin hinaus verzögert, die projektierten Kapazitäten werden schleppend verwirklicht usw. – Warum ist das so?... Weil eine moderne Organisation des Investitionsprozesses fehlt, die nicht auf guten Vorsätzen, sondern auf der unmittelbaren ökonomischen Interessiertheit, auf dem ökonomischen Vorgehen beruht"[14]).

Diese Mißwirtschaft wurde begünstigt durch die Abkapselung der bulgarischen Binnenwirtschaft von der Außenwirtschaft. Das *staatliche Außenhandelsmonopol* gab den Unternehmen in dem System, das bis 1987 galt, keinerlei Recht zu eigenen außenwirtschaftlichen Aktivitäten, sie hatten nicht einmal das Recht zur Kontaktaufnahme mit ihren ausländischen Abnehmern oder Lieferanten.

---

[13]) Ebenda, S. 91.
[14]) Ebenda, S. 92f.

Die bulgarischen Unternehmen wurden dementsprechend nicht mit der Konkurrenz der westlichen Industriestaaten konfrontiert und sahen daher keinen Grund zur Hebung ihrer wirtschaftlichen Effizienz, mit dem Ergebnis, daß die bulgarische Wirtschaft in ihrer technischen Entwicklung immer weiter hinter den westlichen Industriestaaten zurückblieb. Das Außenhandelsmonopol, das eigentlich dem Schutz der heimischen Industrie dienen und eine schnelle extensive Industrialisierung sichern sollte, wurde so zum Hemmschuh der Wirtschaftsentwicklung[15]).

III. Maßnahmen zur Steigerung der Effizienz des Wirtschaftssystems

1. Grundprobleme

Das streng zentralistische Wirtschaftssystem mit seiner starren Planung und administrativen Preisbildung wurde mit fortschreitender Industrialisierung Bulgariens immer mehr zu einer Fessel der Produktivkräfte. Die gewachsene Wirtschaft mit ihrer diversifizierten Struktur ließ sich immer schwieriger und nur mit steigendem Aufwand von einem einzigen Zentrum aus steuern. Das zeigte sich in allen Bereichen der Industrialisierungspolitik. Es entstanden ernsthafte Disproportionen und Fehlallokationen[16]). Dies war auch ein Ergebnis der sog. Prioritätenplanung, also einer bewußt schwerpunktmäßigen Entwicklung der Wirtschaft.

Die einseitige Entwicklung der Industrie und hier die Bevorzugung der Schwerindustrie, hatte ein Zurückbleiben der Konsumgüterindustrie und der Landwirtschaft zur Folge, mit dem Ergebnis einer unzureichenden Versorgung der Bevölkerung mit industriellen und landwirtschaftlichen Konsumgütern. Der Dienstleistungssektor wurde ebenfalls vernachlässigt und blieb unterentwickelt. Die Priorität der gesamtwirtschaftlichen vor den einzelwirtschaftlichen Zielen führte zu Verlusten auf der Mikroebene und beeinträchtigte den ohnehin geringen Aktionsradius der Unternehmen.

Die von Bulgarien ausgewiesenen Wachstumsraten waren zwar über Jahrzehnte hinweg hoch (was zweifellos auch an der niedrigen Ausgangsbasis der Daten lag), doch entstanden als Folge der geschilderten Industrialisierungspolitik weitreichende Fehlentwicklungen, die besonders nach Erreichung eines höheren Entwicklungsstandes wachstumshemmend wirkten und zu Friktionen führten. Die Politik der extensiven Industrialisierung führte zwar zum Entstehen neuer Industrien, jedoch um den Preis einer Überalterung der Produktionskapazitäten als Folge unterlassener oder nicht ausreichender Ersatz- und Modernisierungsinvestitionen. Langlebigkeit der

---

[15]) Zur Bedeutung des Außenhandelsmonopols im Rahmen der sozialistischen Entwicklungsstrategie vgl. Gumpel, W.: Das Außenhandelssystem der sozialistischen Balkanstaaten in seinen Konsequenzen für deren internationale Wirtschaftsbeziehungen, in: Südosteuropa im Entwicklungsprozeß der Welt. Festschrift für Hermann Gross. Hrsg. von W. Althammer, W. Gumpel. München-Wien 1979, S. 40 ff.
[16]) Vgl. Feiwel, G. R.: Industrialisation in Postwar Bulgaria, in: Osteuropa Wirtschaft. 23 (1978) 1, S. 5.

Produktionsgüter galt als Tugend. Die Industrialisierung erfolgte unter Vernachlässigung der Arbeitsproduktivität. Sie vollzog sich damit unter Bevorzugung der quantitativen, bei Vernachlässigung der qualitativen Aspekte der Produktion. Hierzu gehörte u. a. auch die Vernachlässigung der Entwicklung ganzer Wirtschaftszweige, wie des Verkehrssektors oder der Wohnungswirtschaft, in denen aus der Substanz gelebt wurde. Bei schnellem Wirtschaftswachstum hatte besonders die immer unzureichender werdende Verkehrsinfrastruktur negative Auswirkungen.

Die detaillierte zentrale Planung führte, verbunden mit unzureichenden materiellen Anreizen, zur Interesselosigkeit von Management und Arbeitern. Die wirtschaftlichen Entscheidungen wurden auf den oberen Ebenen der Planungshierarchie konzentriert, Marktbeziehungen kamen nicht einmal in Ansätzen zustande. Die Wirtschaft lebte von und mit dem Dekret, war also eine Befehlswirtschaft. Damit war den Unternehmen die Fähigkeit genommen, auf Änderungen der volks- und weltwirtschaftlichen Datenkonstellation elastisch zu reagieren. Zudem führte der umfangreiche und schwerfällige Planungsapparat zu einer hohen Kostenbelastung der Betriebe und der Volkswirtschaft, wobei Fehlplanungen wegen des hohen Zentralisierungsgrades an der Tagesordnung waren und zusätzliche Friktionen und Kosten verursachten. All dies hat zu einer Zementierung des Entwicklungsrückstandes gegenüber den westlichen Industriestaaten geführt. Sollte er überwunden werden, so bedurfte es einer tiefgreifenden Umgestaltung des bulgarischen Wirtschaftssystems. Dies wurde zwar von den bulgarischen Politikern erkannt, jedoch wurden die Konsequenzen viel zu spät und nur unzureichend gezogen. Es blieb bei einem Kurieren an Symptomen, wobei auch dieses nur halbherzig vorgenommen wurde.

2. Die Wirtschaftsreformen der 60er und 70er Jahre

Nachdem in der Sowjetunion insbesondere durch den bahnbrechenden Aufsatz von Prof. J. Liberman in der „Pravda" vom 9.9.1962 der Weg für eine Reformdiskussion mit anschließenden Reformen freigegeben worden war, wurden auch in Bulgarien Reformen des Leitungssystems erörtert. Auf dem VIII. Parteitag der BKP im November 1962 wurden erstmalig Reformen der Lenkungsmethoden in der Volkswirtschaft angekündigt. Zur Verkündung der Grundzüge des angestrebten Reformsystems kam es allerdings erst im Jahre 1964. Die Reformen begannen als „ökonomisches Experiment" am 1.4.1964 in 30 Industrieunternehmen[17]). Ab 1965 sollte das Experiment auf eine größere Zahl von Wirtschaftszweigen ausgedehnt werden, u. a. auf die Konsumgüter- und die Lebensmittelindustrie sowie auf die TKZS, die DZS und den Handel, aber auch die chemische und pharmazeutische Industrie.

Ziel der Maßnahmen war, ähnlich wie bei der im Jahre 1963 in der DDR durchgeführten Wirtschaftsreform, die Abkehr von den rein administrativen Methoden der Leitung der Volkswirtschaft und der Übergang zu ökonomischen Leitungskriterien. Die Gängelung und Bevormundung der Unternehmen sollte vermindert werden.

---

[17]) Vgl. Feiwel, G. R.: Growth and Reforms in Centrally Planned Economies. The Lessons of the Bulgarian Experience. New York 1977, S. 96.

Nachdem die Experimente zufriedenstellend verlaufen waren, wurden im Dezember 1965 die „Thesen zur Neugestaltung der Planung und Lenkung der Volkswirtschaft" veröffentlicht[18]). Ihr Inhalt wurde für eine öffentliche Diskussion freigegeben. Im April 1966 wurde das Reformprogramm unter Berücksichtigung der Diskussionsergebnisse vom ZK der BKP angenommen und beschlossen[19]).

Hauptanliegen der Wirtschaftsreform war, der mittleren und unteren Leitungsebene der Volkswirtschaft mehr Dispositionskompetenzen zu gewähren. Die hierfür vorgesehenen Maßnahmen waren zunächst recht weitgehend. Wichtigster Schritt war der Ausbau der *Wirtschaftsvereinigungen* bzw. Trusts, die die mittlere Leitungsebene der bulgarischen Wirtschaft darstellen sollten. Die Betriebe sollten im Rahmen des „Neuen Systems der Leitung der Volkswirtschaft" (*Nova sistema na răkovodstvo na narodnoto stopanstvo*) ein größeres Maß an Autonomie erhalten. Hierzu wurde das ausufernde Kennziffernsystem reduziert. Künftig sollten nur noch vier Hauptkennziffern für die Unternehmen verbindlich sein. Die Unternehmen erhielten die Berechtigung, in allerdings sehr begrenztem Maße selbständig zwischenbetriebliche Lieferverträge abzuschließen, wobei diese genehmigungspflichtig blieben.

Eine Änderung erfuhr auch die *Investitionsfinanzierung*. Der Staat rückte von der zentralen Finanzierung der Wirtschaft aus dem Staatshaushalt ab, die bis dahin dominierend war. Fortan sollten die Investitionen der Unternehmen aus dem Gewinn und aus Bankkrediten erfolgen, lediglich für große Erweiterungsinvestitionen und Unternehmungsneugründungen sowie Infrastrukturinvestitionen sollten weiterhin Mittel aus dem Staatshaushalt zur Verfügung stehen. Diese Regelung sollte zu einem effizienteren Mitteleinsatz führen. Zu diesem Zweck sollten die Unternehmen verstärkt mit „wirtschaftlicher Rechnungsführung" arbeiten, das bedeutete Eigenbilanzierung mit Gewinn- und Verlustrechnung. Für die Schwerindustrie behielten allerdings die Zuweisungen aus dem Staatshaushalt nach wie vor entscheidende Bedeutung. Auch blieben die Investitionsentscheidungen weiterhin zentralisiert.

Um die Verzerrungen der Preisstruktur im Lande zu beseitigen und zu einer rationaleren *Preisbildung* zu gelangen, war vorgesehen, die Inlandpreise den Weltmarktpreisen anzunähern. Neben die Gruppe der staatlich fixierten Festpreise sollte eine Gruppe von Preisen treten, die sich innerhalb einer Ober- und einer Untergrenze frei bewegen. Für eine beschränkte Anzahl von Gütern lokaler Bedeutung sollten sich die Preise frei bilden können.

Ähnlich den Reformkonzepten anderer sozialistischer Staaten sollten die Arbeitnehmer durch eine Stimulierung ihrer *materiellen Interessiertheit* zu höherer Arbeitsleistung angeregt werden. Dies sollte durch eine Veränderung des Lohnsystems erreicht werden. So war vorgesehen, einen Teil der Löhne und Gehälter von der Höhe der erwirtschafteten Gewinne abhängig zu machen.

Der aus der zentralen Planung resultierende hohe Konzentrationsgrad der Wirtschaft hatte im Zeitablauf in weiten Bereichen der Industrie zu Monopolsituationen geführt. Die Reformmaßnahmen sollten zu deren Abbau und zur Verhinderung des Entstehens neuer Monopolunternehmen führen.

---

[18]) Vgl. Feiwel (Anm. 17), S. 91 ff.
[19]) Vgl. RD. 4.12.1965 und 29.4.1966, sowie Planovoe chozjajstvo. (1971) 11, S. 26 ff.

Nicht betroffen von der Reform war das Außenhandelssystem. Damit blieb die weitgehende Abschottung des Binnenmarktes von den Auslandsmärkten erhalten.

Die wichtigste Neuerung war, daß die Planung im Rahmen vorgegebener Kennziffern nunmehr in den Betrieben erfolgen sollte, wobei allerdings den übergeordneten Organen ein Einspruchsrecht verblieb. Damit sollte der Volkswirtschaftsplan wirklichkeitsnäher und vollziehbarer werden. In der bulgarischen Literatur wurde dies „Planung von unten" genannt.

In der Realität änderte sich jedoch wenig oder nichts. Den Unternehmen wurden auch weiterhin nicht die vorgesehenen vier, sondern erheblich mehr Kennziffern auferlegt, die zentrale Planung wurde sogar noch verstärkt[20]). Anläßlich des IX. Parteitags (1966) kritisierte Živkov, daß „niemals neue Planungsmethoden ausgearbeitet worden" seien[21]). Die Unternehmen blieben auch weiterhin zentralen Weisungen unterworfen, insbesondere hatten sie sich den Anordnungen der Wirtschaftsvereinigungen unterzuordnen.

Im November 1968 wurde mit einem „Dekret über die stufenweise Anwendung und Weiterentwicklung des Neuen Systems der Wirtschaftsleitung" das System erneut modifiziert. Die „Planung von unten" wurde unter dem Vorwand, daß die „wissenschaftlich-technische Revolution" eine Rezentralisierung erforderlich mache, abgeschafft. Die zentral gesetzten bindenden Kennziffern, Limits und Normative wurden fühlbar vermehrt, die Kompetenzen der Wirtschaftsvereinigungen reduziert. Gleichzeitig wurden neue zentrale Institutionen, wie ein „Komitee für wirtschaftliche Koordination" und ein „Ministerium für Versorgung und staatliche Reservehaltung", geschaffen. Letzteres hatte dafür Sorge zu tragen, daß alle zwischenbetrieblichen Verträge wieder zentralen Vorgaben untergeordnet wurden. Auch die Preise wurden wieder zentral gesetzt oder fixiert[22]).

Die im Zuge der Reformen gebildeten „Wirtschaftskomitees", mit denen den Arbeitern ein begrenztes Mitwirkungsrecht an den Unternehmensentscheidungen gegeben worden war, wurden umbenannt und umgebildet. Vorsitzender dieses Komitees wurde jeweils der Unternehmensdirektor, die Rechte der Gewerkschaften in den Komitees wurden erweitert.

In der *Landwirtschaft* liefen die Reformen auf einen umfangreichen Konzentrationsprozeß hinaus, der seinen Ausdruck in der Schaffung der APK fand.

Auch in den folgenden Jahren wurden verschiedene Änderungen in den bulgarischen Wirtschaftsmechanismus hineingetragen. Zu ihnen gehörte insbesondere die Auflösung des Landwirtschaftsministeriums und seine Ersetzung durch den NAPS im März 1979. Er bedeutete eine weitere Verstärkung des Konzentrationsprozesses in der Landwirtschaft durch die Zusammenfassung aller staatlichen und genossenschaftlichen agrarischen Wirtschaftsorganisationen einschließlich der wissenschaftlichen Dienste, des Baus und der Instandhaltung sowie der Aufkauf-, Absatz-, Versorgungs- und Handelsbetriebe unter einem Dachverband. In ihn gingen auch die APK

---

[20]) Vgl. Dellin, L. A. D.: Bulgarien, in: Osteuropa Wirtschaftsreformen. Hrsg. H. Gross. Bonn 1970, S. 78 f.

[21]) Vgl. RD. 15.11.1966.

[22]) Vgl. Feiwel (Anm. 17), S. 100 ff.

ein. Er sollte eine straffere zentrale Führung der Landwirtschaft ermöglichen, die auch die TKZS noch stärker erfaßte[23]). Anläßlich des X. Parteitages der BKP (1971) wurde noch einmal auf die besondere Bedeutung der zentralen Planung und Leitung der Volkswirtschaft hingewiesen.

Am 29.12.1981 bestätigte der Ministerrat erneut einen „Neuen Wirtschaftsmechanismus" (NIM), der am 1.1.1982 in Kraft trat[24]). Er war bereits im Jahre 1977 von T. Živkov angekündigt und in den Jahren 1978 und 1979 eingeleitet worden. Die Neuerungen des Jahres 1982 wurden als Fortsetzung und Verbesserung der Reformen von 1979 bezeichnet. Erneut standen „wirtschaftliche Rechnungsführung" (*stopanska smetka*) und die „ökonomischen Hebel des materiellen Interesses" im Mittelpunkt der Regierungsmaßnahmen. Die Eigenerwirtschaftung der für den Wirtschaftsprozeß erforderlichen Mittel stellte das Kernstück der „neuen" Regelungen dar. Es waren vor allem vier Elemente, die den NIM bestimmten[25]):

1. Die zentrale Wirtschaftsplanung sollte erhalten bleiben. Die Wirtschaftseinheiten sollten auch weiterhin mit verbindlichen Planzielen konfrontiert werden.
2. Alle Wirtschaftsorganisationen sollten sich selbst wirtschaftlich erhalten und unabhängig von staatlichen Subventionen sein. Alle Verträge für den Erwerb von Vorprodukten, für den Absatz der Güter sowie für die Inanspruchnahme von Dienstleistungen sollten von den Unternehmen selbständig abgeschlossen werden.
3. Die Rolle monetärer Stimuli sollte verstärkt werden. Die Höhe der Löhne wurde vom wirtschaftlichen Erfolg des Unternehmens abhängig gemacht. Die Einkommensgarantie für das Management entfiel.
4. Nach Planerfüllung sollten die Unternehmen auf eigene Rechnung zusätzliche Produktionen und Dienstleistungen erbringen können.

Auch in diesem neuen NIM blieb die Macht der *Industrieministerien* ungebrochen. Das Bankensystem war in der Kreditvergabe von ihren Weisungen abhängig. In der *Preispolitik* wurde erneut die Angleichung der Inlands- an die Weltmarktpreise gefordert, so wie bereits 17 Jahre zuvor. Für die Mehrzahl der Güter sollten die Preise nach staatlichen Kalkulationsvorschriften errechnet und danach von den Behörden fixiert werden, wobei Änderungen möglich waren. Bei einer Reihe anderer Güter sollten die Preise frei aushandelbar sein, wobei allerdings ein staatlich gesetzter Höchstpreis nicht überschritten werden durfte.

Die Wirtschaftsreform des Jahres 1982 brachte eher eine Stärkung der zentralen Behörden als eine Dezentralisierung. Bei strenger zentraler Kontrolle wurden gewisse Dispositionskompetenzen auf die mittlere Leitungsebene (Wirtschaftsvereinigungen) verlagert, ohne daß dies mit mehr Rechten (dafür jedoch mit mehr Pflichten) für die Wirtschaftsvereinigungen und die Unternehmen verbunden gewesen wäre.

Die sich über mehr als 20 Jahre erstreckenden Reformbemühungen der Regierung waren dank ihrer Halbherzigkeit und Inkonsequenz ohne den gewünschten Erfolg

---

[23]) Vgl. hierzu Gumpel, W.: Agrarische Organisationsreform in Bulgarien, in: Wissenschaftlicher Dienst Südosteuropa. 29 (1980) 1/2, S. 23 ff.; Wirtschaftsnachrichten aus Bulgarien. (1979) 5, S. 1; Ekonomičeskaja gazeta. (1979) 47, S. 20; vgl. a. den Beitrag „Landwirtschaft" von I. Grosser.
[24]) RD. 30.12.1981; 15.1.1982.
[25]) Vgl. RD. 6.6.1981 sowie RFE-RAD Background Report 12 (Bulgaria) 2.7.1982.

geblieben. Im Gegenteil, die Leistung der Wirtschaft wurde vor allem in den 80er Jahren immer unbefriedigender. Während nämlich das produzierte Nationalprodukt bis etwa Mitte der 70er Jahre vergleichsweise hohe Wachstumsraten von ca. 8 % jährlich aufwies, trat in den folgenden Jahren eine deutliche (ungeplante) Abnahme der Wachstumsraten ein[26]). Im Jahre 1983 belief sich die Wachstumsrate auf 3 %, 1986 auf 5,5 %. Trotz „wirtschaftlicher Rechnungsführung" und Eigenwirtschaftlichkeits-Postulat waren immer mehr Unternehmen in die roten Zahlen gelangt und zu einer Bürde für Staatshaushalt und Volkswirtschaft geworden[27]). Dies war u. a. die Folge einer Planung, die den Wirtschaftsprozeß bis ins Detail zu erfassen versuchte. Zudem wurde der Plan entgegen allen Reformpapieren als staatliche Direktive an die Unternehmen gegeben.

Auch die Preispolitik war bis 1986 nicht den Reformkonzepten gefolgt. Eine Annäherung an die Weltmarktpreise hatte nicht stattgefunden. Steuersystem und Gewinnabführungssystem für die Unternehmen waren veraltet. Das einstufige Bankensystem machte eine Ökonomisierung des Kreditwesens, soweit dies unter den gegebenen Planungsbedingungen überhaupt denkbar war, unmöglich. Das Lohnsystem war den Arbeitern kein Anreiz zu quantitativ und qualitativ zufriedenstellender Leistung.

Auch die Investitionsfinanzierung war praktisch unverändert geblieben und wurde von der zentralen Finanzierung aus dem Staatshaushalt dominiert. Die Produzentenmonopole bestanden noch immer. Sie nutzten ihre Macht nicht nur, indem sie qualitativ schlechte Produkte erzeugten, um den Plan leichter erfüllen zu können, sondern sie nahmen auch auf die zentrale Preisbildung Einfluß und konnten auf diese Weise zusätzliche Gewinne realisieren.

Besonders hemmend wirkte sich die mangelnde Interessiertheit der Wirtschaftssubjekte aus. Sie war auch durch die verschiedenen Reformen nicht verbessert worden. Dies führte zu Passivität, Unwirtschaftlichkeit ganzer Wirtschaftszweige, Ausschußproduktion und zur Bilanzfälschung, wodurch wiederum falsche Informationen an die zentralen Wirtschaftsorgane gelangten. Die Entfremdung der Menschen von ihrer Tätigkeit nahm immer mehr zu. Die Arbeiter konnten sich für das von ihnen erarbeitete Geld wegen der herrschenden Mangelwirtschaft nicht die gewünschten Güter und Dienstleistungen kaufen. Gleiches galt für die Unternehmen. „Geld zu haben, heißt häufig nicht, irgendeinen wirklichen Wert zu besitzen.... Das Unternehmen kann Geld in seinen Fonds zur Verfügung haben, aber das hat keine reale Bedeutung, wenn es einige Jahre darauf warten muß, bis es Maschinen und Ersatzteile erhält und die Aufträge erfüllt werden, wenn es Jahre warten muß, bis es eine Bau- und Montageorganisation findet für die Erweiterung seiner Produktionsmöglichkeiten oder für technologische Erneuerungen, für den Bau eines Wohnblocks oder eines Erholungsheims. Nachdem der Bau begonnen hat, dauert es drei bis fünf weitere Jahre."[28])

---

[26]) Vgl. Grosser, I.: Bulgarien: Zwischenbilanz des „Neuen Wirtschaftsmechanismus" (Berichte des Bundesinstituts für ostwissenschaftliche und internationale Studien Nr. 34). Köln 1984, S. 5.
[27]) Vgl. hierzu Angelov, I.: Novijat ikonomičeski mechanizăm trjabva da zaraboti (Der neue ökonomische Mechanismus muß zu wirken anfangen), in: Novo Vreme. 63 (1987) 3, S. 44ff.; in deutscher Übersetzung in: Südosteuropa. 36 (1987), S. 345ff.
[28]) Ebenda, S. 352.

3. Das Konzept der preustrojstvo vom Dezember 1986

Der Ausweg aus dieser Wirtschaftssituation soll eine „Umgestaltung" des Wirtschaftssystems sein, die, beginnend auf den unteren Ebenen der Wirtschaftsleitung, die Arbeitenden zu effektiverer Tätigkeit zwingt und damit die vorhandenen Leistungsreserven mobilisiert. Sie zu verdecken, war bisher Anliegen der Wirtschaftssubjekte gewesen. Zu diesem Zweck soll ein System wirtschaftlicher Interessiertheit und Verantwortlichkeit geschaffen werden, das die Arbeitenden zu einer tatsächlichen Leistungserbringung anhält. Bilanzverfälschungen und Normerfüllung nur auf den Abrechnungsbögen sollen unmöglich werden.

Der Beginn der *preustrojstvo* liegt zeitlich vor Verkündung der sowjetischen *perestrojka*. Das „Regelwerk über die wirtschaftliche Tätigkeit" wurde am 23.12.1986 vom Plenum des ZK der BKP bestätigt und am 29.12.1986 vom Ministerrat verabschiedet[29]). Es trat am 1.1.1987 in Kraft. Es wird ergänzt durch ein am 18.12.1987 angenommenes und am 1.1.1988 in Kraft getretenes weiteres Regelwerk sowie durch eine Anzahl weiterer Gesetze komplementären Charakters. Mit Erlaß Nr. 56 vom 9.1.1989 über die Wirtschaftstätigkeit folgte die Verkündung weiterer Umgestaltungsmaßnahmen. T. Živkov betonte vor den Delegierten der BKP-Landeskonferenz am 28.1.1988, daß die laufende *preustrojstvo* „undenkbar wäre ohne die Entwicklungen in der Sowjetunion seit dem XXVII. Parteitag der KPdSU"[30]).

Wie auch bei den vorhergehenden Reformansätzen, die offiziell stets als „Vervollkommnung des Wirtschaftsmechanismus", nicht aber als Reform bezeichnet wurden, sind auch dieses Mal wieder die Reformansätze in der Konzeption unvollständig und teilweise widersprüchlich und verwirrend.

a) Die Einführung der Selbstverwaltung in der Wirtschaft

Kernstück der bulgarischen „Umgestaltung" ist die Einführung der *Selbstverwaltung* in allen Bereichen der Wirtschaft, aber auch in den territorialen Einheiten des Landes. Von der „Herrschaft im Namen des Volkes" solle zur „Herrschaft durch das Volk" übergegangen werden, formulierte Živkov[31]). „Die Selbstverwaltung ist die Bahn, auf der der gesamte Prozeß der Umgestaltung verläuft."[32]) Dabei ist jedoch nicht an die Übernahme des auch in Bulgarien als diskreditiert betrachteten jugoslawischen Modells gedacht, sondern an eine wirtschaftliche Eigenständigkeit der Unternehmen, unter Beibehaltung zentraler Leitungselemente und zentraler Kontrolle.

---

[29]) Vgl. DV. (1987) 3; (1987) 100 sowie (1988) 3. Zum Inhalt der Reformen vgl. Angelov (Anm. 27), sowie ders.; Intenzifikacija, predpriemčivost i ikonomičesko sărevnovanie (Intensivierung, Unternehmungsgeist und wirtschaftlicher Wettbewerb), in: Novo Vreme. 62 (1986) 7, S. 36–50; Arojo, Z.: Samoupravlenie i ikonomičesko regulirane (Selbstverwaltung und wirtschaftliche Regulierung), in: Novo Vreme. 63 (1987) 2, S. 27 ff.; Höpken, W.: „Perestrojka" auf bulgarisch: Sofia und die Reformpolitik Gorbatschows, in: Südosteuropa. 36 (1987), S. 618–45; Dimitrov, V.: Die neue Organisationsstruktur der Wirtschaft, in: Bulgarischer Außenhandel. 36 (1987) 3, S. 30 f.
[30]) FAZ. 29.1.1988.
[31]) Vgl. Novo Vreme. 63 (1987) 10, S. 7.
[32]) Vgl. RD. 29.7.1987.

Der Grundgedanke der Reform besteht darin, daß der „Staat als Besitzer des sozialistischen Eigentums (Produktivkapital, Umlaufvermögen der gesamten Volkswirtschaft) die Aufgabe hat, die langfristigen Ziele der wirtschaftlichen Entwicklung und die Strategie, durch die sie erreicht werden können, festzulegen, ohne sich in die Tätigkeit der Arbeitskollektive einzumischen, die wiederum als Verwalter des ihnen anvertrauten Eigentums mit umfassenden Befugnissen ausgestattet und selbständig wirtschaftlich tätig sind"[33]).

Die Einführung der Selbstverwaltung setzte eine Umgestaltung der *Leitungshierarchie* voraus. Die Pyramidstruktur der staatlichen Leitungsorgane, die über Jahrzehnte für die sozialistischen Volkswirtschaften Ost- und Südosteuropas charakteristisch war, wurde formal abgeschafft. Hierzu wurde in der ersten Etappe der Umgestaltung die branchenmäßig gegliederte Leitung aufgehoben. Das bedeutete die Beseitigung der Industrieministerien, die nach Wirtschaftszweigen gegliedert waren. Das geschah bereits zu Beginn des Jahres 1986. Zum 1.1.1988 wurde auch das Ministerium für Handel aufgelöst, so daß seit diesem Zeitpunkt nur noch ein einziges Fachministerium besteht, das Ministerium für Verkehrswesen. Gleichzeitig wurden als Hilfsorgane der Regierung ein Wirtschaftsrat, ein Rat für Land und Forstwirtschaft und ein Sozialrat ins Leben gerufen, die aber bereits im August 1987 wieder aufgelöst wurden. Seit dem 1.1.1988 gibt es auch keine Staatliche Plankommission mehr, bisher wichtigstes Organ der Wirtschaftsleitung und Spitze der Planpyramide. Neben dem Ministerium für Handel wurde auch das Finanzministerium aufgelöst und mit ihm das Staatskomitee für Forschung und Technologie, das Komitee für Arbeit und Sozialwesen und das Staatliche Preiskomitee. An ihre Stelle traten als neue Ministerien das Ministerium für Land- und Forstwirtschaft, das Ministerium für Außenwirtschaft und das Ministerium für Wirtschaft und Planung (*Ministerstvo na ikonomikata i planiraneto*) als neues Superministerium, das die Aufgaben der Staatlichen Plankommission, des Finanzministeriums, des Staatlichen Komitees für Forschung und Technologie, des Komitees für Arbeit und Sozialwesen und des Staatlichen Preiskomitees übernimmt. Sie alle stellen jetzt Abteilungen des neuen Ministeriums dar, so daß Änderungen nur formal eingetreten sind. Die bulgarische Regierung erhofft sich von dieser Umorganisierung eine bessere Koordinierung der Tätigkeit dieser Organe.

Das Ministerium für Wirtschaft und Planung soll im Rahmen der Selbstverwaltung künftig keine detaillierten und verpflichtenden Pläne mehr erarbeiten, sondern lediglich die gesamtstaatliche wirtschaftliche Entwicklungspolitik und -strategie sowie Normative für die Wirtschaftstätigkeit der Unternehmen.

Das Ministerium für Außenwirtschaft (*Ministerstvo na vănšnoikonomičeskite vrăzki*) nimmt keine branchengebundenen operativen Funktionen mehr wahr, da das Außenhandelsrecht auf die Selbstverwaltungsorganisationen und die von ihnen gegründeten Außenhandelsunternehmen übergegangen ist. Das Ministerium soll nur noch „die Staatspolitik auf dem Gebiet des Außenhandels verwirklichen und die Interessen des Staates vertreten"[34]).

---

[33]) Vgl. Die Umgestaltung. (1987) 1, S. 1.
[34]) Vgl. ebenda., S. 6.

Auch die mittlere Leitungsebene wurde vollkommen umgestaltet. Sie bestand bisher aus den sog. Wirtschaftsvereinigungen. An ihre Stelle traten „Wirtschaftsvereinigungen neuen Typs" und „Assoziationen".

Bei den Wirtschaftsvereinigungen neuen Typs[35]) (*asociaciite ot nov tip*) handelt es sich um Gruppen von Produktions- und Handelsunternehmen, Forschungsinstituten und anderer Einrichtungen, die ein gemeinsames wirtschaftliches Interesse verbindet. Zu ihnen gehören auch die APK und die Kombinate, die als im allgemeinen vertikal gegliederte Konzerne bezeichnet werden können. Die Wirtschaftsvereinigung verfolgt eine gemeinsame Investitions- und Marktpolitik sowie eine gemeinsame Politik im wissenschaftlich-technischen Bereich. Sie koordiniert die Tätigkeit der beteiligten Unternehmen, übernimmt die Personalschulung, die Versorgung mit Informationen usw. Eine unmittelbare wirtschaftliche Tätigkeit übt sie nur in Ausnahmefällen aus, z. B., wenn sie von einem ihrer Unternehmen damit beauftragt wird. In der Regel übt sie auch gegenüber den in ihr zusammengeschlossenen Unternehmen keine Leitungstätigkeit aus, wobei die Energiewirtschaft, das Nachrichtenwesen sowie der Eisenbahn- und der Flugverkehr Ausnahmen darstellen. Sie wird durch Abführungen der ihr angeschlossenen Unternehmen finanziert. Auch sie wird von einem Wirtschaftsrat und einem Direktor geleitet, in geheimer Wahl gewählt wird jedoch nur der Direktor. Der Wirtschaftsrat dagegen setzt sich aus den Direktoren der zusammengeschlossenen Unternehmen sowie je einem Vertreter der Arbeitskollektive sowie der zuständigen Bank zusammen.

Bei der Assoziation (*asociacija*) handelt es sich um eine neue Form der Leitung großer branchenüberschreitender Produktionskomplexe aus Wirtschaftsvereinigungen und anderen Wirtschaftsorganisationen. Auch ihre Mitglieder behalten ihre wirtschaftliche und rechtliche Selbständigkeit. Ähnlich den Wirtschaftsvereinigungen organisieren die Assoziationen die Tätigkeiten von gemeinsamem Interesse und verfolgen eine einheitliche Technologie-, Investitions- und Marktpolitik. Sie können gemeinsame Handels- und Dienstleistungsunternehmen gründen. Die Regierung kann die Ausübung staatlicher Funktionen an sie delegieren. In einem solchen Fall sind ihre Beschlüsse für alle Betriebe und Organisationen verbindlich, unabhängig ob diese der betreffenden Assoziation angehören oder nicht. In ihnen ist daher nach wie vor ein zentralistisch-imperatives Element erhalten geblieben.

Die Leitungsorgane der Assoziation (Verwaltungsrat, Kontrollrat und Vorsitzender) werden gewählt. Jede Selbstverwaltungsorganisation ist berechtigt, einer Assoziation als ordentliches Mitglied und einer unbegrenzten Zahl von Assoziationen als außerordentliches Mitglied anzugehören. Die Assoziationen bestreiten ihre Ausgaben durch Beiträge ihrer Mitglieder. Sie sollen jedoch in keinem Fall Verwaltungs- oder Leitungsinstitutionen sein und auch nicht die aufgelösten Ministerien ersetzen. Jedoch sind die von den kollektiven Organen gefaßten Beschlüsse für alle Mitglieder verbindlich, wobei aber eine unmittelbare Einmischung in die Tätigkeit der Mitglieder unterbleiben soll.

---

[35]) Hierzu und zu den Assoziationen vgl. Dimitrov, V.: Die neue Organisationsstruktur der Wirtschaft, in: Bulgarischer Außenhandel. 36 (1987) 3, S. 30f.

Obwohl Unternehmen, Wirtschaftsvereinigungen und Assoziationen keine hierarchische Pyramide darstellen sollen und alle Selbstverwaltungsrechte ihrer Mitglieder erhalten bleiben, handelt es sich bei ihnen doch um Leitungsorgane, die den Einfluß des Staates in den Unternehmen zur Geltung bringen und dessen Ziele durchsetzen können. Die bulgarische Regierung ist der Meinung, daß die neue Organisationsstruktur der Wirtschaft Beschlußfassungen erleichtert und auch zusätzliche Möglichkeiten einer Zusammenarbeit mit ausländischen Firmen eröffnet. An dieser Sicht der Dinge sind jedoch erhebliche Zweifel berechtigt. Durch die „freiwillige" Verlagerung von unternehmerischen Entscheidungen und die faktische Abtretung von Dispositionskompetenzen sowie durch die Übernahme von staatlichen Aufgaben durch die Assoziationen und die damit verbundene Kommandogewalt wird vielmehr den Unternehmen ein Teil der Selbstverwaltungsrechte wieder genommen. Das bedeutet auch eine Einschränkung ihrer Entscheidungsfreiheit. Daß die Assoziationen eine Art Ersatz für die aufgelösten Ministerien darstellen, geht nicht nur aus dem enthüllenden Satz hervor: „Als große Wirtschaftseinheiten verbinden die Assoziationen objektiv die Interessen der zu ihnen gehörenden Betriebe mit den Interessen des Staates"[36]. Es wird auch deutlich an den bisher registrierten Assoziationen, die weitgehend der Gliederung der bisherigen Industrieministerien entsprechen. So gibt es jeweils eine Assoziation für Energiewirtschaft, für Elektronik, für Investmaschinenbau, für Konsumgüterindustrie, für pharmazeutische Industrie und medizinischen Gerätebau, für Metallurgie und mineralische Rohstoffe, für Versorgungsfragen, für Bauwesen usw. Auch der NAPS hat die Gestalt einer Assoziation angenommen. Die Assoziationen werden vom Staat kontrolliert.

Die Genossenschaften (*kooperacii*) sollen im Rahmen der Umgestaltung der Wirtschaft wieder an Bedeutung gewinnen und jene Organisationsform darstellen, in deren Rahmen sich auch individuelle Aktivitäten vollziehen können. In den vergangenen Jahrzehnten waren sie in ihrer Tätigkeit zunehmend eingeengt und staatlich reglementiert worden. In der Landwirtschaft wurden sie faktisch beseitigt. Ein großer Teil der Produktionsgenossenschaften des Handwerks wurde verstaatlicht. Auch das 1983 verabschiedete Gesetz über die Genossenschaftsorganisation[37], das nur noch drei Arten von Genossenschaften zuließ (Konsumgenossenschaften, Produktionsgenossenschaften des Handwerks und Produktionsgenossenschaften der Behinderten) war auf eine Einschränkung des Tätigkeitsbereichs der Genossenschaften abgestellt. So sind heute nur noch 394 Genossenschaften im Zentralen Genossenschaftsverband (*Centralen kooperativen săjuz – CKS*) zusammengefaßt, die in Handel und Gastronomie, im gewerblichen Bereich (Herstellung von Lebensmitteln und industriellen Konsumgütern), im Dienstleistungsbereich, im Tourismus sowie im Aufkauf von landwirtschaftlichen Erzeugnissen tätig sind[38].

Die restriktive Genossenschaftspolitik der vergangenen Jahre wird heute als unbegründet, die These, daß die Genossenschaft eine provisorische Wirtschaftsform sei, die zu einer Verschmelzung von staatlichen und genossenschaftlichen Betrieben sowie

---

[36] Vgl. Die Umgestaltung. (1987) 1, S. 11.
[37] Zakon za kooperativnite organizacii, in DV. (1983) 102, S. 1257–1262.
[38] Vgl. Die Umgestaltung. (1988) 1, S. 2f.

zur Verstaatlichung der Genossenschaften zu führen habe, als „unwissenschaftlich" und „unbrauchbar" bezeichnet[39]). In den vom Politbüro des ZK der BKP 1987 verabschiedeten „Vorstellungen zur Weiterentwicklung der Genossenschaftsbewegung entsprechend dem Kurs auf ein qualitativ neues Wachstum"[40]), in denen die Rolle der Genossenschaften im Umgestaltungsprozeß definiert werden, werden die Genossenschaften als „eine effektive Form zur Förderung der individuellen und kollektiven Arbeit" bezeichnet. Sie sollen nunmehr zu einer Einrichtung von Dauer werden. In ihnen sollen, wenn das wirtschaftlich gerechtfertigt ist, auch staatliche Betriebe und Organisationen vertreten sein können (kollektive Mitglieder). Eine obligatorische Mitgliedschaft in Genossenschaftsverbänden ist nicht mehr vorgesehen. Der CKS wird in eine Assoziation der Genossenschaftsorganisationen umgewandelt.

b) Änderungen in der Planung

Auch im reformierten System wird es eine zentrale staatliche Planung geben. Sie wird jedoch in ihrem Inhalt grundsätzlich verändert und soll sich auf die „strategischen Entwicklungsprobleme der Volkswirtschaft" beschränken, während die Produktions- und die ihnen komplementären Pläne selbständig von den Unternehmen erstellt werden. Die staatliche Planung soll dagegen „die Priorität der gesellschaftlichen vor den Gruppeninteressen" sicherstellen[41]).

Bis zur Einführung des Reformsystems wurde der Plan, wie an anderer Stelle dargelegt, nach Branchen und Betrieben aufgeschlüsselt. Er war für die verschiedenen Wirtschaftseinheiten verbindlich. Im System der *preustrojstvo* dagegen erstellt die Zentrale einen „Plan für die sozialökonomische Entwicklung" Bulgariens für einen Fünfjahreszeitraum oder eine längere Periode. Dieser soll keine Plandirektive, sondern ein Planentwurf und den unteren Wirtschaftseinheiten Information, nicht dagegen Anweisung sein. Allerdings wird auf die Unternehmen, wie gezeigt, auch weiterhin Einfluß genommen, um eine Durchsetzung der staatlichen Ziele zu garantieren. So müssen diese ihren Planentwurf auf der Grundlage des Staatsplanentwurfs erarbeiten sowie auf der Grundlage der „staatlichen Normative zur Lenkung der Wirtschaftstätigkeit". Im übrigen benutzen sie als Planungsgrundlage die Ergebnisse eigener Marktforschung und Erhebungen. Wichtigste Grundlage des Planes sind die mit den Lieferanten und Abnehmern geschlossenen Verträge sowie die mit den Banken getroffenen Vereinbarungen.

Die Planbilanzen der Unternehmen werden zu einem Teil des nationalen Bilanzsystems, deren Kernstück eine „technologische Verflechtungsbilanz" sein soll, d. h. eine Art Input-Output-Tabelle für die Volkswirtschaft. Sie sollen miteinander abgestimmt werden, wozu es eines dauernden Dialogs bedarf. Ein solcher „Dialog" soll aber auch

---

[39]) Vgl. Shivkov, T.: Grundlagen der Konzeption für die weitere Gestaltung des Sozialismus in Bulgarien. Sofia 1987, S. 10 sowie: Die Umgestaltung. (1988) 1, S. 2.
[40]) Vgl. RD. 3.4.1987, S. 1–3.
[41]) Vgl. Die Umgestaltung. (1987) 1, S. 13, sowie: Rechenschaftsbericht des Zentralkomitees der BKP an den XIII. Parteitag. Sofia 1986, S. 124, und Trud. 5.9.1987, S. 2, sowie: Die Umgestaltung. (1989) 3, S. 3.

zwischen den Betrieben und den staatlichen Planungsorganen stattfinden. Er wird als „Hauptinstrument zur Konkretisierung der nationalen Ziele und Staatsaufgaben sowie zur Sicherung der Ressourcen" bezeichnet[42]). Differenzen zwischen dem Entwurf des Staatsplanes und den Planentwürfen der Firmen sollen durch ihn überwunden werden. Dieser „gleichberechtigte Dialog" wird so lange geführt, bis der Plan endgültig bestätigt ist. führt der Dialog zu keiner Einigung, so werden die strittigen Fragen dem Ministerrat vorgelegt.

Auch im NIM bedient sich der Staat neben der direkten Intervention eines „Systems ökonomischer Hebel" (einer Art wirtschaftspolitischen Instrumentariums), mit dem er auf die Wirtschaftssubjekte einwirkt. Bei ihnen handelt es sich vorwiegend um Steuern, Preise, Kredit und Zins sowie staatlich gesetzte Wechselkurse[43]). Mit diesem Instrumentarium, das, wie auch schon in der Vergangenheit, durch ein System materieller Anreize ergänzt wird, will der Staat vor allem Einfluß auf die Investitionstätigkeit der Betriebe und damit auf die Gestaltung der Wirtschaftsstruktur nehmen.

Der *Investitionsprozeß* wurde vereinfacht. Die zentrale Finanzierung aus dem Staatshaushalt soll wieder einmal eingestellt werden. Wie schon in früheren Reform-Modellen soll die Investitionsfinanzierung nunmehr aus Eigenmitteln (Abschreibungen und Gewinne) sowie mittels Bankkrediten erfolgen. Bürokratische Einschränkungen in Form von Genehmigungsverfahren und Abstimmungen mit einer Reihe von Behörden und Organisationen wurden abgeschafft. Allerdings bestehen eine Reihe von mehr oder weniger limitierenden Vorschriften, die von den Firmen einzuhalten sind. Dazu gehört die Verpflichtung zur vollen Auslastung der Produktionsanlagen und zur Durchführung nur eines und keiner weiteren Vorhaben mit eventuell überfälligen Bauterminen. Die investierenden Betriebe müssen vor Tätigung der Investition sichergestellt haben, daß die für die zusätzliche Produktion erforderlichen Rohstoffe und Vorprodukte verfügbar und der Absatz der für die erweiterte Produktion vorgesehenen Güter garantiert ist. Mindestens 35% der Investition müssen mit Eigenmitteln finanziert werden. Die verbindliche Festlegung von Baufristen soll der in sozialistischen Ländern weit verbreiteten Verzögerung der Fertigstellung von Investitionsvorhaben entgegenwirken. Bei Terminverzug müssen die ausführenden Firmen 2% des mittleren jährlichen Wertes der nicht beendeten Arbeiten an den Staatshaushalt abführen[44]). Alle Investitionsobjekte unterliegen im Entwurf einer verbindlichen technisch-wirtschaftlichen Begutachtung, damit Fehlinvestitionen vermieden werden.

Zur Finanzierung größerer Vorhaben steht ein *staatlicher Kreditfonds* zur Verfügung. Seine Mittel werden von der neu gegründeten Wirtschaftsbank (*Stopanska banka*) verwaltet. Sie stehen nur für fest umrissene Wirtschaftszweige und Vorhaben zur Verfügung und dienen der Kreditierung des Baus von Betrieben der Energiewirtschaft, des Bergbaus, des Verkehrswesens, des Schiffbaus, des „schweren Investi-

---

[42]) Vgl. Thesen des Dreizehnten Parteitages der Bulgarischen Kommunistischen Partei. Sofia 1986, S. 94.
[43]) Vgl. Novosti. (1987) 35 vom 2.9.1987.
[44]) Vgl. Dimitrov, V.: Neuregelung der Investitionen, in: Bulgarischer Außenhandel. 36 (1987) 6, S. 2.

tionsmaschinenbaus", der Hüttenindustrie und von Meliorationsvorhaben. Die Tilgungsfrist für die Mittel aus diesem Fonds beläuft sich auf zehn bis zwanzig Jahre, der gewährte Vorzugszins liegt bei 2,5%[45]). Sinn dieser Regelung ist die Bevorzugung sog. strukturbestimmender Investitionen und damit die Kapitalallokation in jenen Bereichen, die den zentralen Zielsetzungen entsprechen.

Sowohl in der Planung als auch im Bereich der Investitionen als einem wesentlichen Teil der betrieblichen Aktivitäten bleibt daher trotz aller gegenteiligen Äußerungen in den NIM-Papieren ein bestimmender staatlicher Einfluß erhalten, so daß von einer wirklichen Dezentralisierung oder von der Einführung eines Marktmechanismus kaum gesprochen werden kann.

c) Veränderungen im Bereich der Preisbildung

„Der Mechanismus der Preisbildung ist entscheidend zu verbessern", heißt es in den „Thesen des XIII. Parteitags der BKP"[46]). Dabei sei dem Einfluß der Weltmarktpreise Rechnung zu tragen. Im Rechenschaftsbericht des ZK der BKP auf demselben Parteitag wird gefordert, daß die Preisbildung „von jeglichen Erscheinungen der Bürokratie und des Subjektivismus befreit werden" solle[47]).

Die Schwierigkeit, vor der alle sozialistischen Staaten stehen, ist das Problem, bei fehlenden Knappheitspreisen zu einer effizienten (optimalen) Ressourcenallokation zu gelangen und ein Gleichgewicht zwischen den Einkommen der Bevölkerung und dem zur Verfügung stehenden wertmäßigen Güter- und Dienstleistungsangebot herzustellen. Da die Preise entweder willkürlich gesetzt werden oder aber auf der Grundlage zentral vorgeschriebener Kalkulationsvorschriften zustande kommen und der Genehmigung durch die Preisbehörde bedürfen, besteht die oben dargelegte Problematik auch im NIM weiter fort. Die Halbherzigkeit und Inkonsequenz der bulgarischen Reformvorhaben zeigt sich besonders im Bereich der Preisbildung. Zweifellos stellt die Preisreform aber den schwierigsten Teil der Wirtschaftsreform dar.

Anläßlich des ZK-Plenums vom 13.11.1987 stellte Živkov jedenfalls fest, daß die Großhandelspreise des Landes den Weltmarktpreisen nur allmählich angenähert werden könnten, auch wenn dadurch die Reformen auf anderen Gebieten verzögert würden. Er regte an, die Preisreform in zwei Schritten durchzuführen: Zunächst sollen die Großhandelspreise festgesetzt werden, die bis zum Ende des laufenden IX. Fünfjahresplans in Kraft bleiben sollen. Als zweiter Schritt soll dann mit Beginn des X. Fünfjahresplans im Jahre 1991 eine grundlegende Preisreform durchgeführt werden[48]). Wie diese aussehen soll, bleibt bisher offen. Vorläufig soll so verfahren werden, daß der Staat einen Höchstpreis festlegt, die konkreten Preise werden unter Beachtung der staatlichen Kalkulationsvorschriften von den in kommerzielle Beziehungen tretenden Betrieben vereinbart. „Ungerechtfertigte Gewinne" sollen ausge-

---

[45]) Ebenda.
[46]) Thesen des XIII. Parteitags (Anm. 42), S. 96.
[47]) Rechenschaftsbericht des ZK der BKP (Anm. 41), S. 57.
[48]) Vgl. RD. 2.12.1987; 10.12.1987, sowie: Dimitrova, N.: Cenite i cenoobrazuvaneto – dejstven regulator na intenzivnoto ikonomičesko razvitie (Die Preise und die Preisbildung – wirksamer Regulator der intensiven wirtschaftlichen Entwicklung), in: Ikonomika. (1987) 12, S. 30 ff.

schlossen werden. Fallen sie dennoch an, sind sie an den Staatshaushalt abzuführen[49]). Der Erlaß vom 9.1.1989 sieht drei Arten von Preisen vor:

1. Preise für Waren und Dienstleistungen, die „entsprechend den Weltmarktpreisen sowie der Nachfrage und dem Angebot auf dem Binnenmarkt festgesetzt" werden. „Die konkreten Preise werden zwischen den Firmen vereinbart".
2. Fest- oder Höchstpreise im Einzelhandel, die vom Staat für „bestimmte Waren und Dienstleistungen von besonders großer Bedeutung für den Lebensstandard der Bevölkerung" festgesetzt werden.
3. Industrieabgabe-Höchstpreise für Roh- und Werkstoffe und Transportleistungen, die entsprechend einer vom Ministerrat beschlossenen Liste festgesetzt werden.

Ein wirtschaftlicher Wettbewerb zwischen den Betrieben derselben Branche soll zur Anhebung der Arbeitsproduktivität und damit zu sinkenden Stückkosten sowie zur Erzeugung besserer Qualität führen, die dann in niedrigeren Preisen Ausdruck finden. Bei der gegebenen Betriebsgrößenstruktur der bulgarischen Wirtschaft würde dies allerdings zunächst die Zerschlagung der in vielen Branchen bestehenden monopolistischen „Markt"-Struktur durch Teilung der Großbetriebe und die Neugründung von kleinen und mittleren Betrieben voraussetzen[50]). Unter den gegebenen Bedingungen von einer „freien Vereinbarung" der Preise zu sprechen, heißt Entwicklungen als vollzogen zu betrachten, für die noch Jahre erforderlich sind, wenn sie jemals erfolgen werden.

d) Die Einführung der „Firma"

Die bis Ende 1988 durchgeführten Reformen haben sich in weiten Bereichen als nicht erfolgreich erwiesen. Besonders die Assoziationen scheinen sich nicht bewährt zu haben[51]). Aus diesem Grunde wurde die Wirtschaft mit Erlaß vom 9.1.1989 erneut umorganisiert[52]). Offiziell wurden die Assoziationen zwar noch nicht abgeschafft, da sie jedoch mit dem Inhalt des Erlasses weitgehend unvereinbar sind, werden sie wohl in absehbarer Zeit verschwinden oder aber neue Formen annehmen. Neue Grundeinheit der Wirtschaft sind die sog. Firmen, die im Rahmen der verschiedenen zugelassenen Eigentumsformen gebildet werden können und wirtschaftlich selbständig agieren sollen. Neben dem Staatseigentum an den Produktionsmitteln gibt es, wie bisher, das genossenschaftliche Eigentum, das Eigentum der gesellschaftlichen Organisationen und, in dieser Form neu, das Eigentum von Privatpersonen an Produktionsmitteln. Dieses unterliegt allerdings, wie noch zu zeigen ist, gewissen Beschränkungen. Auch ausländische Bürger dürfen Eigentum an Produktionsmitteln im Rahmen der dafür geltenden Gesetze erwerben. Daneben gibt es die Form des „gemischten Eigentums" (*smešena sobstvenost*).

---

[49]) RD. 14.11.1987.
[50]) Ebenda.
[51]) Vgl. Izvestija. 22.2.1989, S. 5.
[52]) DV. (1989) 4.

Die „Firma" (*firma*)[53]) entsteht durch Registrierung beim Bezirksgericht und kann in verschiedenen Formen gegründet werden. Einzelne Personen und Personengruppen können, auch ohne eine Firma registrieren zu lassen, wirtschaftlich aktiv werden. Mit Ausnahme der Einmann- und Kollektivfirmen ist die Firma eine juristische Person. Für alle vier möglichen Firmenformen werden gleiche Bedingungen für ihre Tätigkeit garantiert. Sowohl die Gründung als auch die Liquidation und die Reorganisation einer Firma kann durch ein staatliches Organ, eine gesellschaftliche Organisation (z. B. die BPS), eine Bank, eine bereits bestehende Firma oder durch eine Einzelperson erfolgen.

Für die Firma gilt das Prinzip der Selbstverwaltung und der Eigenwirtschaftlichkeit. Das bedeutet, daß sie selbständig über ihre Organisations- und Produktionsstruktur und über die Art der Firmenleitung entscheidet. Firmen, die juristische Person sind, können ohne besondere Genehmigung Außenhandelstransaktionen tätigen, wobei der Staat allerdings hierfür besondere Bedingungen sowie Quoten festlegen und den Im- und Export bestimmter Güter und Dienstleistungen untersagen kann.

Die Firma hat das Recht, ihr Vermögen zu verpachten. Der Staat übernimmt keine Verantwortung für die Verpflichtungen der Firma, sie kann also nicht ohne weiteres mit staatlichen Subventionen rechnen. Sie hat das Recht zur Ausgabe von Belegschaftsaktien (*trudovi akcii*), bei denen es sich um Namensaktien mit einem Nennwert von je 50 Leva handelt, von denen das Belegschaftsmitglied nicht mehr als 200 Stück besitzen darf. Sie sind vererbbar, müssen jedoch nach dem Eintritt des Erbfalls an die Firma veräußert werden, wenn der Erbe nicht in einem arbeitsrechtlichen Verhältnis zu ihr steht. Rentner dürfen ihre Belegschaftsaktien behalten, wenn sie mindestens zehn Jahre in der Firma gearbeitet haben. Aus dem Besitz von Belegschaftsaktien leitet sich nur ein Recht auf Dividende, nicht jedoch ein Eigentumsrecht ab.

Leitungsorgane der Firma sind die Vollversammlung der Belegschaft (*obšto săbranie na trudovija kolektiv*), der Verwaltungsrat (*upravitelen săvet*), der Aufsichtsrat (*kontrolen săvet*) und der Geschäftsführer (*răkovoditel*). Während der Belegschaftsversammlung nur das Recht der Planerörterung sowie der Einflußnahme auf soziale Fragen zukommt, liegen die eigentlichen Entscheidungskompetenzen beim Verwaltungsrat und beim Geschäftsführer, wobei die Mitglieder des Verwaltungsrates zur Hälfte plus ein Mitglied von den das Kapital gebenden Organen und Organisationen benannt werden, der Rest wird von der Vollversammlung gewählt. Die Wahl erfolgt für fünf Jahre.

Der Geschäftsführer, der dem Verwaltungsrat qua Amt angehört, arbeitet nach dem Prinzip der Einzelleitung, der Verwaltungsrat darf sich daher nicht in dessen Tätigkeit einmischen, kann ihn jedoch unter bestimmten Bedingungen abberufen.

Der Aufsichtsrat ist ein reines Kontrollorgan. Über seine Zusammensetzung macht der Erlaß Nr. 56 keine Aussagen.

Die Unternehmensformen, in denen sich die Firmen organisieren können, sind die Aktienfirma (*akcionerna firma*), die Firma mit beschränkter Haftung (*firma s ograni-*

---

[53]) Vgl. hierzu und zum folgenden den Erlaß Nr. 56 über die Wirtschaftstätigkeit (Anm. 52).

čena otgovornost), die Firma mit unbeschränkter Haftung (*firma s neograničena odgovornost*) und die Firmen natürlicher Personen (*firmi na graždane*).

Eine Aktienfirma kann nur von juristischen Personen gegründet werden. Sie emittiert Namens- und Inhaberaktien (*na prinositel*), wobei bulgarische Bürger nur Namensaktien erwerben dürfen, eine Veräußerung der Aktien ist damit zunächst ausgeschlossen. Organe sind die Hauptversammlung (*obšto săbranie*) der Aktionäre, der Verwaltungsrat, der Aufsichtsrat und der Geschäftsführer, wobei die Hauptversammlung sowohl den Verwaltungsrat als auch den Aufsichtsrat wählt oder ihrer Funktionen enthebt.

Während die Firmen mit beschränkter und unbeschränkter Haftung mit der Ausnahme, daß die letzteren auch Aktien begeben können, keine besonders zu erwähnenden Eigenheiten haben, erwecken die Firmen der natürlichen Personen in Hinblick auf das sozialistische Wirtschaftssystem besonderes Interesse. Sie können Einpersonen-, Kollektiv- und Gemeinschaftsfirmen (*edinolični, kolektivni, družestveni*) sein. Ihr wirtschaftlicher Aktionsradius ist durch spezielle Gesetze und Erlasse beschränkt. Auch in Hinblick auf eine außenwirtschaftliche Betätigung sind sie mit den anderen Firmentypen nicht gleichberechtigt[54]). Das Grundkapital muß mindestens 10 000 Leva betragen. Die natürlichen Personen sind verpflichtet, in den von ihnen registrierten Firmen persönlich mitzuarbeiten. Das Gesetz gestattet die Beschäftigung von bis zu zehn Arbeitskräften, bei saisonbedingten Tätigkeiten entfällt in diesem Bereich jegliche Beschränkung.

Die Teilhaber dieses Firmentyps haften gemeinschaftlich für die Verbindlichkeiten bis in Höhe ihrer eingebrachten oder einzubringenden Einlagen; reichen diese nicht aus, auch mit ihrem persönlichen Vermögen. Jeder Bürger darf sich an einer Firma natürlicher Personen auch dann beteiligen, wenn er ein arbeitsrechtliches Verhältnis mit einer anderen Firma unterhält.

Die Gemeinschaftsfirma natürlicher Personen ist juristische Person, nicht dagegen die sogen. Einmannfirma. Beide müssen, um aktiv werden zu können, beim Bezirksgericht registriert werden.

In dem Erlaß Nr. 56 wird zum ersten Mal in der bulgarischen sozialistischen Rechtsgeschichte der Versuch unternommen, die durch Zahlungsunfähigkeit erforderliche Firmenliquidation relativ ausführlich zu regeln. Die Folgen der Zahlungsunfähigkeit einer Firma müssen von dieser selbst und den Gläubigern getragen werden, was zu mehr Vorsicht bei der Wahl der Partner führen und den Staatshaushalt entlasten soll. Zahlungsunfähige oder für insolvent erklärte Firmen können jedoch staatliche Hilfe oder, nach Einigung mit den Gläubigern, deren Unterstützung in Anspruch nehmen. Erst wenn dies ohne die erwünschte Wirkung bleibt, wird die Liquidation der Firma eingeleitet. Damit dürfte es bei der bisherigen Praxis einer Subventionierung unrentabler Unternehmen bleiben.

Die Firmen sind zwar offiziell in der Gestaltung ihrer Unternehmenspolitik autonom, sie müssen jedoch mit den „zuständigen Staatsorganen" Absprachen über ihre Beteiligung an der Erfüllung des Staatsplanes „auf der Basis von gegenseitigen Vereinbarungen und Staatsaufträgen" treffen. Staatsaufträge „dürfen nur zur Erfüllung

---

[54]) Vgl. Die Umgestaltung. (1989) 3, S. 2.

internationaler Verpflichtungen und der Aufgaben der Sozialpolitik, zur Erreichung strategischer, technologischer und Marktziele, wie auch zur Gewährleistung der nationalen Sicherheit sowie wichtiger nationaler Bilanzen vergeben werden". Sie sollen nicht mehr als zwei Drittel der Firmenkapazität binden. In der Praxis bedeutet dies, daß sie in allen Bereichen der Wirtschaft als Lenkungsinstrument eingesetzt werden können und der allmächtige Einfluß des Staates auf die Firmen erhalten bleibt. „Die Wirtschaftstätigkeit der Firmen muß der ökonomischen Strategie des Staates entsprechen."[55])

Der Erlaß Nr. 56 dürfte im Hinblick auf die Neugestaltung des Wirtschaftssystems noch nicht das letzte Wort darstellen. Seine Verwirklichung, so die sowjetische Tageszeitung *Izvestija* dürfte große Schwierigkeiten bereiten. „Die Idee", so die sowjetische Zeitung sarkastisch, „fällt nicht immer mit der Realität zusammen. Doch wir zollen unseren Respekt, daß Bulgarien diesen Schritt gewagt hat."[56])

e) Die Reform des Bankensystems

Im Jahre 1987 wurde in Bulgarien ein neues Bankensystem eingeführt[57]), das als eine wesentliche Voraussetzung für die Verwirklichung des NIM betrachtet wird. Während bisher sämtliche Bankoperationen im Zusammenhang mit der Finanzierung von Investitionen und der Kreditierung von Wirtschaftsaktivitäten von der BNB durchgeführt wurden, gehen diese Tätigkeiten im Rahmen des NIM auf acht neu gegründete Handelsbanken über, die die Rechtsform einer Aktiengesellschaft haben, deren wichtigster Aktionär allerdings die BNB ist. Andere Aktionäre können Wirtschaftsorganisationen der verschiedenen, an anderer Stelle geschilderten Arten, sein.

Die neuen Handelsbanken, die ihre Tätigkeit offiziell am 1.9.1987 aufnahmen, arbeiten auf kommerzieller Grundlage. Dementsprechend gelten auch für sie die Grundsätze der Eigenwirtschaftlichkeit und der wirtschaftlichen Rechnungsführung. Wie bisher sind die Firmen entsprechend ihrer Branchenzugehörigkeit einer bestimmten Bank zugeordnet. Unabhängig davon haben sie aber die Möglichkeit, bei einer anderen Bank einen Kredit aufzunehmen, wenn diese günstigere Konditionen bieten kann als die Hausbank. Dies soll ein Element des Wettbewerbs in das Bankgeschäft bringen. Im nach wie vor starren System kann sich die Gewährung besserer Konditionen allerdings allein auf den Bankservice beziehen.

Das *Bankensystem* Bulgariens hat gegenwärtig (1989) folgende Struktur[58]):

Die *BNB* fungiert als Noten- und Staatsbank. Sie leitet, koordiniert und kontrolliert die Tätigkeit aller anderen Banken, bestimmt den Geldumlauf und den Hauptzinssatz und übt andere Notenbankfunktionen aus. Sie ist die „Bank der Banken" und als „Organ mit funktioneller Rechtsstellung" direkt dem Ministerrat unterstellt

---

[55]) Ebenda, S. 3.
[56]) Izvestija. 22.2.1989.
[57]) DV. (1987) 46.
[58]) Vgl. Postanovlenie Nr. 33 ot 3 juni 1987 i. za preustrojstvoto na bankovata sistema, in: DV. (1987) 46, S. 2, sowie: Pravilnik za bankite, ebd., S. 2ff.; Die Umgestaltung. (1987) 4, S. 1–3.

und somit weisungsgebunden. Sie verfügt über Bezirksfilialen und Zweigstellen. Die Bezirksfilialen („Bezirksbanken") arbeiten nach dem Prinzip der innerbetrieblichen Rechnungsführung und erstellen ihre eigene Bilanz.

Die BNB wird von der Regierung am Entscheidungsprozeß der staatlichen Kredit- und Zinspolitik beteiligt und hat diese durchzusetzen; sie ist zusammen mit den Handelsbanken an der Aufstellung des Staatsplans sowie des Kredit- und Geldumlaufplans beteiligt. Die BNB führt die laufenden Konten der Wirtschaftsorganisationen und gibt den Handelsbanken Informationen über die finanzielle Situation ihrer Kunden. Banken, Versicherungsorgane und Staat deponieren ihre „frei verfügbaren Mittel" bei der BNB, die auch den Zahlungsverkehr zwischen den Banken abwickelt. In gleicher Weise werden die Regionalbanken der BNB tätig.

Die sogenannten spezialisierten Handelsbanken (*specializirani tărgovski banki*) sind wirtschaftlich selbständig und von der BNB unabhängig. Ihre kommerzielle Tätigkeit erstreckt sich vorerst (Stand 1989) nur auf den Finanz- und Kreditbereich, sie sind daher keine Universalbanken und können nur von Unternehmen, nicht aber von Privatpersonen in Anspruch genommen werden. Für diese ist die Staatliche Sparkasse (*Dăržavna spestovna kasa*) zuständig, die auch die Kontenführung für Selbstverwaltungsorganisationen von lokaler Bedeutung übernehmen kann. Die Handelsbanken sind teilweise sektoral gegliedert. Es handelt sich dabei um die Wirtschaftsbank (Sofia), die Bank für Wirtschaftsinitiative (*Banka za stopanski iniciativi*) (Sofia), die Biochim-Bank (Sofia), die Bank Elektronika (Sofia), die Agrar- und Genossenschaftsbank (Plovdiv), die Bank Avtotechnika (Sofia), die Transportbank (Varna) und die Bauwirtschaftsbank (Sofia). Zur finanziellen Abwicklung der Außenwirtschaftstätigkeit der bulgarischen Wirtschaft wurde außerdem die Bulgarische Außenhandelsbank mit Sitz in Sofia gegründet.

Die neuen Banken werden u. a. auch bankfremde Tätigkeiten wahrnehmen. So werden sie sich an der Erstellung der Pläne der selbstverwalteten Wirtschaftseinheiten beteiligen und sollen auch beim Planvollzug mitwirken. Im internationalen Bereich sollen sie sich an Investitionen zur Gründung gemeinsamer Unternehmen bzw. zur Durchführung gemeinsamer Produktionen im RGW-Bereich beteiligen sowie Mitglied von Bankenkonsortien für gemeinsame Investitionsvorhaben im In- und Ausland werden. Auch die Gründung gemeinsamer Banken mit ausländischen Partnern soll möglich werden. Ein Beispiel für die hier gegebenen Möglichkeiten ist die Gründung der Bayerisch-Bulgarischen Handelsbank GmbH im Oktober 1986 durch die Bulgarische Außenhandelsbank und die Bayerische Vereinsbank. Hier werden 51 % des Kapitals von 20 Mio. DM von der Bayerischen Vereinsbank und 49 % von der Bulgarischen Außenhandelsbank gehalten.

Seit Mai 1989 können Zweigstellen der BNB in den größeren Wirtschaftszentren in Aktienbanken umgewandelt werden. Die neuen Handelsbanken erhielten das Recht, einzelne BNB-Zweigstellen als Filialen zu erwerben[59]). Ende August 1989 wurde vom Verwaltungsrat der BNB die Gründung von 32 Banken in der Form von Aktiengesellschaften interessierter Firmen zugelassen. Sie dürfen keine Zweigstellen besitzen. Die bestehenden Handelsbanken übernehmen 27 BNB-Zweigstellen gegen Be-

---

[59]) Vgl. Erlaß Nr. 19 vom 19. 5. 1989, in: DV. (1989) 42.

zahlung. Gleichzeitig wurde der Tätigkeitsbereich der Handelsbanken erweitert. Sie erhielten das Recht, nicht nur Investitionen, sondern auch das Umlaufvermögen der Firmen zu kreditieren. In Verbindung damit erhielt die BNB das Recht auf Einführung von Mindestreserven zugesprochen[60]). Damit ist allerdings die bulgarische Bankenreform noch nicht abgeschlossen. Weitere Veränderungen werden folgen.

Unter den gegebenen Umständen, besonders wegen der Beschränkung des Tätigkeitsfeldes der Handelsbanken, kann das neue bulgarische Bankensystem kaum als zweistufiges Bankensystem im westlichen Sinne bezeichnet werden, zumal die Führung der Geschäftskonten der Unternehmen auch weiterhin Monopol der Staatsbank bleibt. Bulgariens Bankenreform bleibt damit vorerst z. B. hinter dem in Ungarn verwirklichten Modell zurück.

IV. Zukunftsaussichten

Partei und Regierungs Bulgariens haben klar erkannt, daß die Anforderungen der modernen Zeit mit dem nach sowjetischem Vorbild geschaffenen und seither nur wenig veränderten Wirtschaftssystem nicht bewältigt werden können. Die in den Jahren 1986, 1987, 1988 und 1989 durchgeführte „Umgestaltung" erweitert die Grenzen der seit mehr als 20 Jahren angestrebten „Vervollkommnungen" des Systems. Ob eine wirkliche Selbstverwaltung der Staatsunternehmen möglich ist und diesen ein Maß an Autonomie gewährt wird, das ein eigenständiges unternehmerisches Handeln möglich macht, erscheint bei der gewählten Konstruktion des Wirtschaftsmechanismus zweifelhaft. Der Einfluß der Zentrale auf die Unternehmen bleibt auch unter den Bedingungen der *preustrojstvo* erhalten. Der Monopolisierungsgrad der Wirtschaft, der bei dem gegebenen Kapitalmangel nur langfristig beseitigt werden kann, verhindert die Einführung tatsächlicher Marktbeziehungen. Daran würde auch die Einführung freier Preise nichts ändern. Eine sofortige Freigabe der Preise würde freilich bei der gegebenen Mangelsituation zu starken Preissprüngen führen. Aufgrund des hohen Monopolisierungsgrades der Wirtschaft würde sie kein oder nur ein sehr beschränktes Angebotswachstum bewirken. Das geltende Preis- und Lohnsystem und das unzureichende Güterangebot bewirken eine unzureichende Stimulierung zu quantitativ und qualitativ besserer Produktion, die Mangelwirtschaft bleibt damit bestehen.

So befindet sich die bulgarische Wirtschaft in einem verhängnisvollen circulus vitiosus, den zu durchbrechen nur eine wirklich „radikale Umgestaltung" des Wirtschaftssystems imstande wäre. Da die bulgarische Staatsführung diesen Schritt aus politischen und ideologischen Gründen scheut (er könnte zur Transformation nicht nur des wirtschaftlichen, sondern auch des politischen und gesellschaftlichen Systems führen), ist kein grundlegender Wandel der wirtschaftlichen Situation im Lande zu erwarten. Auch in Zukunft wird vielmehr eine „Politik der halben Schritte" in Form von in unregelmäßigen Zeitabständen durchgeführten „Umgestaltungen" und „Vervollkommnungen" die Entwicklung des bulgarischen Wirtschaftssystems bestimmen.

---

[60]) Die Umgestaltung. (1989) 20, S. 1–3.

Industry and Handicrafts

Marvin R. Jackson, Tempe/Arizona

I. Introduction – II. Industry and Handicrafts before 1944 – III. The Overall Place of Industry and Handicrafts in the Economy of Socialist Bulgaria: 1. Shares of Labor, Capital and Output in Industry and Handicrafts – 2. From „Under-" to „Over-industrialization" – 3. Alternative Measures of Over-industrialization – IV. The Growth of Industrial Output: 1. Secular Decline and Fluctuations – 2. Bulgarian Growth Compared to Other Socialist Countries – V. Regional Patterns of Industrialization – VI. The Structure of Bulgarian Industry: 1. Relative Output Growth and Labor Absorption – 2. International Comparisons of Bulgarian Industrial Structure – 3. Comparative Evolution of Bulgarian Industrial Structure since 1965 – VII. Industrialization and the Role of Foreign Markets: 1. The Role of Exports in Bulgarian Industrialization – 2. Industrial Policy and the CMEA – 3. The Failure of Bulgarian Industry in Western Markets – VIII. Increasing Productivity and Prospects for Economic Maturity: 1. Analysis of Production Functions in Bulgarian Industry – 2. Partial Productivity Ratios – IX. Summary of Bulgarian Industrialization 1950 to 1989

I. Introduction

Industrialization has played no lesser a role in the overall economic development strategies of Bulgaria's communist party leaders than elsewhere in socialist Eastern Europe[1]). As the following analysis demonstrates, Bulgarian industrialization deviated in some important aspects from the common socialist pattern. But the economy has not avoided the need for „restructuring" industry and „intensifying" growth processes in industry. Furthermore, Bulgarian industry has so far failed to penetrate competitive international markets. In this respect it faces the very same bottlenecks facing all socialist economies. In Bulgaria, as elsewhere, it is unsatisfactory performance of industry, more than any other sector, that stimulates leaders to seek economic reforms[2]).

---

[1]) For useful surveys, especially of the earlier years, see Popov, N. et al.: Ikonomika na Bŭlgariiâ. Vol. II. Ikonomika na Bŭlgariiâ prez prekhodniiâ period ot kapitalizma do sotsializma (The Economy of Bulgaria during the Transition Period from Capitalism to Socialism). Part 3. Sotsialisticheska industrializatsiiâ – osnova za izgrazhdane na materialno-tekhnicheskata baza na sotsializma (Socialist industrialization – a foundation for building the material-technical base of socialism). Sofia 1972, p. 153–232; Spirkov, P.; Shapkarev, P.: Socialist Industrialization – the Basis of Building the Material and Technical Foundations of Socialism, in: Institute of Economics, Bulgarian Academy of Sciences: Social and Economic Development of Bulgaria 1944–1964. Sofia 1964, p. 44–80; Zlatev, Z.: Socialist Industrialization in Bulgaria, in: Institute of History, Bulgarian Academy of Sciences: Problems of the Transition from Capitalism to Socialism in Bulgaria. Sofia 1975, p. 173–200.

[2]) Jackson, M.: Bulgaria's Attempt at „Radical Reform". Berichte des Bundesinstituts für ostwissenschaftliche und internationale Studien. No. 2. Köln 1988. See also the contribution by W. Gumpel in this volume.

It follows that, if one aims to describe and understand the development of industry and handicrafts in Bulgaria during the forty years of rule by the BKP one must do more than enumerate the specific characteristics of the country's growth and structure. Bulgarian industry makes sense only if one sees it in a proper comparative perspective. Thus, what follows incorporates ample reference to the experiences of other countries as well as identifiing and explaining the relevant analytical studies of industrialization in Europe that include the Bulgarian case.

Before turning to these details, a warning about statistics is important, more so because of the comparative analysis to follow. The more specific defects in the published record of Bulgarian industrial statistics are: (1) no separate categories for industry and handicrafts (as is the case, for example, with Yugoslav data); (2) large unidentified residuals in the distribution to branch statistics, and since 1970 no publication of data for nonferrous metals; (3) no publication of the values of branch output in current prices (although this information is circulated in Bulgaria in *Razshireno Sotsialistichesko Vŭzproizvodstvo v NRB* (Extended Socialist Reproduction in NRB) which has not been released to foreigners or to the United Nations); (4) no publication of data by standard industrial classifications of branches and sub-branches (as is the case in Hungary, Poland and Yugoslavia), so little is known about complex branches like the machine-building; and (5) no good connections between industrial production data and foreign trade in industrial products, especially at the sub-branch level. In addition, the generally available comparative compilations of Bulgarian and other socialist country data usually follow different rules of classification. For example, data published about Bulgaria in the CMEA Yearbook often differs in detail from official Bulgarian data. Mixed sources often lead to false impressions.

II. Industry and Handicrafts before 1944

The earliest enumeration of Bulgaria's national accounts by Kiril Popov indicated that in 1911 industry and handicrafts together contributed only about 13 percent of the gross output of all sectors in the economy. But in spite of a small relative size the two sectors had grown by nearly 15 percent a year since 1904[3]).

Details of subsequent industrial development are reported in the chapter „Historical Foundations" by Richard Crampton. Still, it is important here to show that rapid industrial growth in the country did not begin just with the advent of socialism. For example, by 1922 gross output of industry and handicrafts exceeded the 1911 level by 60 percent and by 1930 by more than 4 times in real terms. Although output declined in the early 1930's later growth (industry alone) was enough to average a respectable 7 percent a year for the whole decade[4]). Thus, industrial growth rates were about as fast before socialism as after.

---

[3]) Lampe, J.; Jackson, M.: Balkan Economic History 1550 to 1950. Bloomington IN 1982, p. 162, 334.

[4]) Jackson, M.; Lampe, J.: The Evidence of Industrial Growth in Southeastern Europe Before the Second World War, in: East European Quarterly. XVI (1983) 4, p. 392–398.

Bulgarian industry continued to grow in the first two years of the Second World War and fell below the 1939 peak only in 1944 by a small 3 percent. Then the 1939 level was exceeded by 12 percent in 1945 and by nearly 60 percent in 1948 and 112 percent by 1950. This was a momentum not found in the other socialist countries.

III. The Overall Place of Industry and Handicrafts in the Economy of Socialist Bulgaria

Even though Bulgaria gained a step on other East European countries because of the relatively better conditions in the country during the Second World War, the place of industry in the economy remained quite low. From the various East European sources of data in Table 1 industrial output per capita was only 40 percent of that in the Soviet Union.

Table 1: Estimates of Per Capita Industrial Output in the Socialist Countries as a Percent of the USSR

Country	as cited in[1])				
	Wilczynski			Montias	
	1950	1965	1970	1955	1957
Bulgaria	40	70	80	37	40
Czechoslovakia	150	119	104	na	na
GDR	na	150	138	142	129
Hungary	80	80	68	91	62
Poland	70	80	73	74	76
Romania	30	50	58	49	50
Yugoslavia	na	na	na	38	na
USSR	100	100	100	100	100

[1]) Data are from different East European sources. They are not consistent one with another.

Source: Wilczynski, J.: Technology in Comecon. New York 1974, p. 275; Montias, J.: Economic Development in Communist Romania. Cambridge MA 1967, p. 8.

1. Shares of Labor, Capital and Output in Industry and Handicrafts

The shift of labor into industry in Bulgaria was remarkable in any of the periods shown in Table 2. The shift was relatively greater between 1950 and 1960 when Bulgaria shot past Romania. This phenomenal transition even exceeded that of Romania from 1970 to 1980.

By 1970 Bulgaria's share of labor force in industry exceeded that of Poland and by 1980 that of Hungary. Now it approaches the level of Czechoslovakia and must be nearing a maximum expected share. In fact, as suggested by table 3, Bulgaria could well do with a reduction of the share of labor in industry and an increase in the share of services.

Table 2: The Shares of Industry in the Economies of the Socialist Countries

	1950	1960	1970	1970#	1980#	1985#	1986#
A. Employment							
Bulgaria	7.9	21.9	30.4	38.8	43.2	45.8	46.0
Czechoslovakia	27.9	36.1	37.6	47.3	47.6	47.1	46.9
GDR	39.7	41.4	41.7	49.6	50.9	50.4	50.0
Hungary	19.7	29.8	38.0	43.2	41.4	38.7	38.5
Poland	20.8	25.5	29.2	37.6	39.0	37.1	37.0
Romania	12.0	15.1	23.0	30.5	43.8	44.2	–
USSR				37.9	38.5	38.4	38.4
B. Fixed Capital¹)							
Bulgaria	11.8*	20.4	33.1	33.7	36.3	38.3	38.6
Czechoslovakia	29.0	32.2	34.7	33.7	34.8	35.9	30.9
GDR	27.4*	29.6	36.4	42.2	44.4	45.2	45.6
Hungary	–	25.3	25.0	22.1	25.0	25.6	25.6
Poland	–	17.6	23.6	22.5	23.2	25.8	25.5
Romania	19.5	27.7	36.6	36.9	43.5	45.2	–
USSR				29.7	31.8	32.8	32.9
C. National Product¹)							
Bulgaria	36.8	45.6	49.1	51.1	51.0	61.2	63.6
Czechoslovakia	62.5	63.4	62.1	61.1	65.0	61.2	61.2
GDR	47.0	56.4	60.9	57.6	68.5	63.3	63.3
Hungary	48.6	60.1	43.6	42.6	44.2	47.2	47.2
Poland	37.1	47.0	57.5	54.6	54.9	48.7	47.3
Romania	43.4	42.1	60.1	59.1	59.3	62.7	–
USSR	57.5	52.3	51.2	51.1	51.5	45.5	43.9

* – 1952.   # – Data since 1970 have been revised; employment shares published by the CMEA secretariat are „industry and construction". ¹) The price basis for fixed capital and national product shares is highly variable across countries and not always clearly defined in the CMEA yearbook; cross-country and time-series comparisons should be made with caution.

Sources: Alton, T.: Economic Growth and Resource Allocation in Eastern Europe, in: Reorientation and Commercial Relations of the Economies of Eastern Europe. Papers submitted to the Joint Economic Committee, Congress of the United States. Washington 1974, p. 263, 267. Statisticheski ezhegodnik stran-chlenov soveta ekonomicheskoĭ vzaimopomoshchi 1971. Moscow 1971, p. 46. Statisticheski ezhegodnik stran-chlenov soveta ekonomicheskoĭ vzaimopomoshchi 1987. Moscow 1987, p. 42.

2. From „Under-" to „Over-industrialization"

In a broader and more accurate international comparison, Bulgaria and the other socialist countries in Eastern Europe have gone from „under-industrialized" to „over-industrialized" countries. Before discussing the extent of this change in Bulgaria's own case, the meaning of these terms need to be explained.

„Under-" and „Over-industrialization" refer to measurements presented in Tables 3 and 4. Behind these calculations is the generally known phenomenon that the shares of labor force found in the major sectors of an economy vary across all countries as a function of the level of GNP per capita. In fact, the expected change in the share of labor force found in industry as GNP per capita rises has been measured many times, as it was by the author in the case of Table 3. In this case it is estimated using data for more than thirty capitalist countries, most of them in Europe, for two years, 1970 and 1980. From the parameters of the regression equations one can estimate what would be expected to be the labor shares of the socialist countries if they behaved like capitalist ones. All that such a prediction involves is to enter in the regression equation the actual per capita GNP for each socialist country and then solve for its predicted labor share in industry. The numbers in Table 3 are then the result of dividing the actual labor shares by the predicted labor shares.

Table 3: Ratios of Actual to Calculated Normative Shares of Labor Force in Industry[1])

Country	Ofer				Jackson	
	1940	1950	1960	1967	1975	1980
Bulgaria	.40	.51	.84	1.01	1.45	1.54
Romania	.45	.53	.62	.73	1.57	1.67
Yugoslavia	.51	.74	.83	.78	1.16	1.30
Greece	NC	.89	.72	.68	.90	.94
Spain	1.24	1.06	1.10	1.01	1.22	1.27
Portugal	1.08	.98	1.12	1.01	1.44	1.38
Turkey	NC	NC	NC	NC	.62	.60
Czechoslovakia	1.14	1.02	1.17	1.20	1.60	1.58
GDR	1.45	1.47	1.25	1.25	1.55	1.55
USSR	.91	.95	.99	1.00	1.45	1.54
Hungary	.78	.85	1.07	1.10	1.52	1.42
Poland	.62	.91	1.03	1.03	1.42	1.43

[1]) „Normal" shares are calculated from an equation fitting the share of industrial labor force to the level of GNP per capita for 35 capitalist countries, using each country's actual GNP per capita. NC = not calculated.

Source: Jackson, M.: Economic Development in the Balkans Since 1945 Compared to Southern and East-Central Europe, in: Eastern European Politics and Societies. I (1987) 3, p. 429.

Consider, for example, the numbers in Table 3 for Bulgaria, Spain, Portugal, and the USSR for the year 1967. All of these numbers are about 1.00 which tells us that in 1967 the actual share of labor force in industry for these four countries was almost identical to what would be predicted for them, given their levels of GNP per capita. In 1975 and 1980, according to the author's calculations, the socialist countries all had much larger shares of labor force in industry than would be expected on the basis of their GNP's per capita. Hence, they are considered „over-industrialized".

Bulgaria went from a situation of having only half or less than a „normal" industrial labor share in 1940 and 1950 to having an actual share close to 50 percent more than normal for a country with its level of GNP per capita. It was not quite as „over-industrialized" as neighbor Romania, but it came no where close to its other neighbor, Yugoslavia, which looked almost „capitalist" in this sense.

3. Alternative Measures of Over-industrialization

Estimates similar to those presented in Table 3 have been published. The results usually differ in detail as a consequence of differences in samples by year and country, techniques for estimating per capita GNP in common units, or specifications of the normal equation. But conclusions are similar, even when the indicator of share of output is used in place of share of labor[5]).

Table 4 explores two better indicators of the extent of Bulgaria's over-industrialized labor force. Both are calculated from the indicator of relative industrial labor in Table 3 and similar calculations (not shown here) for the shares of urbanized population and labor force in services.

The numbers in Part A of the table compare shares of industrial labor force to shares of urban population. For example, if in one year Bulgaria's ratio of actual to predicted shares of industrial labor force was the same as the ratio of its actual to predicted shares of urban population, then the number 100 would be entered in Table 4 for that year.

Table 4: Indicators of Relative Over-industrialization in Bulgaria Compared to Other Socialist Countries

Country	Ofer				Jackson	
	1940	1950	1960	1967	1975	1980
A. Ratio of Industrial Labor Share to Urban Population Share						
Bulgaria	67	74	110	126	144	144
Czechoslovakia	118	108	127	125	167	161
GDR	112	106	106	109	133	135
USSR	118	117	117	112	149	160
Hungary	102	116	147	155	183	167
Poland	89	121	116	126	158	155
Romania	79	100	88	113	196	192
Yugoslavia	133	160	145	141	165	180
B. Ratio of Services Labor Share to Industrial Labor Share						
Bulgaria	79	58	64	78	72	67
Czechoslovakia	71	71	82	79	89	89
GDR	68	63	68	70	72	72
USSR	97	82	79	87	91	91
Hungary	117	114	92	104	93	93
Poland	100	71	63	72	77	79
Romania	83	70	59	77	72	73
Yugoslavia	102	76	80	95	111	114

Source: Calculated from Tables 3 and data given in the source for Table 3.

---

[5]) Because of different factor proportions and shares of profits and indirect taxes, output shares are usually different from labor shares. The estimation of output shares in comparable terms presents significant problems, but can be found in Gregory, P.: Cross Section Comparisons of the Structure of

As shown in the table, in 1940 and 1950 Bulgaria's relative urbanization, while quite low, was not as low as its relative industrialization. By 1960 and to an increasing extent thereafter, the country's relative industrialization surpassed its relative urbanization (which, by the way, only reached „normal" levels in the last decade). While all the socialist countries show this tendency for urbanization to be dominated by industrialization, Bulgaria's relative distortion is smaller than all other socialist countries shown except the GDR.

Part B of Table 4 compares the relative commitment of labor to industry compared to services. In this case, Bulgaria is recently more distorted than the other socialist countries shown in the table. In this case, 100 (as in Poland's case in 1950) indicates that a country has the same relative commitments, given its level of GNP per capita, to both services and industry. Bulgaria's low ratio indicates that its relative overcommitment of labor to industry is matched with a relative under-commitment of labor to services. Bulgaria's policy makers have been especially faithful to Marx's idea of the productivity of the material sectors of production.

IV. The Growth of Industrial Output

1. Secular Decline and Fluctuations

There has been so much growth of industrial output from 1950 to 1987 in Bulgaria that it is hardly useful to show this in terms of a simple index number. Rather in Figure 1 are graphed the annual growth rates recorded in official Bulgarian statistics for gross industrial output and net material product generated in industry, a value added measure. Both figures tell a similar story:

- there is an obvious downward trend, although one showing less clearly in the case of contribution to net material product because slower input growth partly offsets slower output growth;
- there has been significant instability in industrial growth, especially before about 1963 and expecially in industry's contribution to net material product, something which may be connected to the pricing of imported materials.
- since 1965 the growth rate of industry's contribution to net material product has a distinctive cyclical quality in that growth is low as the beginning of a five-year period and rises and then falls again at the end of the period.

GNP by Sector of Origin: Socialist and Western Countries, in: Kyklos. 24 (1971) 3, p. 444–454; Askana, B.: Wirtschaftsstrukturen in Osteuropa: ein Vergleich mit Westeuropa, in: Forschungsberichte 6, Wiener Institut für internationale Wirtschaftsvergleiche. Wien, September 1972; Ofer, G.: Industrial Structure, Urbanization, and Socialist Growth Strategy – An Historical Analysis, 1940–1967, in: Research Report No. 54, Department of Economics, The Hebrew University of Jerusalem. Jerusalem, March 1974, p. 33/34; and Winiecki, J.: The Overgrown Industrial Sector in Soviet-Type Economies: Explanations, Evidence, Consequences, in: Comparative Economic Studies. XXVIII (1987) 4, p. 24.

Figure 1: Bulgarian industrial output growth.

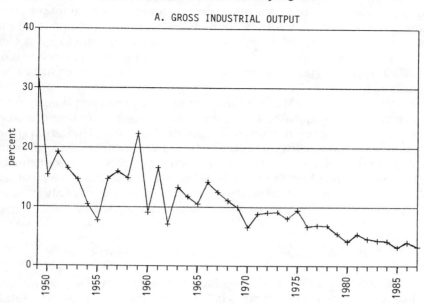

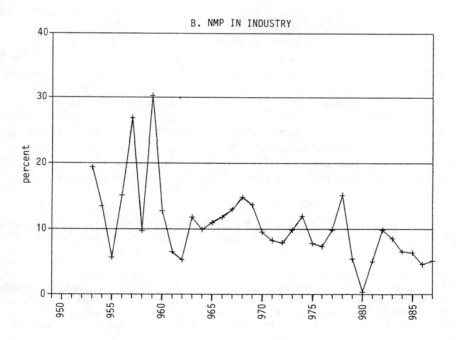

The retardation of Bulgarian industrial growth is exceptional by available international comparisons with either the other socialist countries or a sample of capitalist countries. Such a conclusion is born out by Pryor's estimates covering both official and western recalculations of the growth rates of industrial output for the socialist countries for the period from 1950 to 1979. Bulgaria's growth rate retardation by either measure was the greatest in Pryor's sample of eight socialist and sixteen capitalist countries[6].

Bulgaria's industrial output also turns out to have been exceptionally unstable when compared internationally. This is the common result from several studies. In one, Pryor calculates standard errors of western recalculations of industrial growth in constant prices of the socialist countries and compares them to a sample of data from capitalist countries. While he finds no significant differences across systems for the sample period covering 1950 to 1979, he does show that Bulgaria's industrial growth had the largest standard error of all the socialist countries and was only exceeded by three capitalist economies in the sample (Finland, Spain, and Sweden)[7].

2. Bulgarian Growth Compared to Other Socialist Countries

Bulgaria's official measures of gross industrial output by five-year periods are compared with other socialist countries in Part A of Table 5. In such terms Bulgaria's best relative performance was in 1956–1960 when its growth rate surpassed all others. During the 1960's Bulgaria's growth was second only to Romania, while during the 1970's it shared second place with Poland. In both extreme periods, 1951–1955 and 1986/87, Bulgaria occupied the middle of the group.

The real question is knowing how much growth ought to be expected from Bulgaria, given allocations of resources to this end and other factors that are commonly expected to influence growth. Comparative productivity will be examined below. Aside from productivity, it turns out that growth rates of national product and industrial output tend to vary across countries according to the level of national product per capita. As development levels rise, growth rates tend to fall. Therefore, one basis of what to expect from Bulgaria is its level of national product per capita. Because that indicator has been relatively low for Bulgaria as well as for Romania and Yugoslavia, one would have expected them to have high growth rates.

---

[6] Pryor's estimates are of a coefficient, r, in a regression, $gr = b + 2c(t)$, where gr = the percentage of growth in any year, and $2c$ = the „retardation coefficient". See Pryor, F.: Growth and Fluctuations of Production in O.E.C.D. and East European Countries, in: World Politics. XXXVII (1985) 2, p. 224.

[7] Pryor, F. L.: A Guidebook to the Comparative Study of Economic Systems. Englewood Cliffs NJ 1985, p. 116/117. Using another measure for the period 1958 to 1975 and data for individual branches of industry (comparing only Romania, Poland, Bulgaria, Czechoslovakia, and Hungary), Anderson concludes that „regardless of measure used, Bulgaria has the highest instability in every industrial branch". Anderson, E. E.: Central Planning and Production Instabilities in Eastern Europe, in: Slavic Review. 42 (1983) 2, p. 226.

It should be noted that controversy exists over the most appropriate way to compare instability internationally and that the measures used in the cited works are open to criticism.

Fortunately, one can again turn to the work of Pryor for empirical measurement of the connection between growth rates of industrial output and level of GNP per capita. He bases his test on western recalculations of industrial growth for the socialist countries and official growth for the capitalist countries. For the sample covering 1950 to 1979, he finds that growth rates across countries are significantly correlated with development levels, but do not differ across economic systems. Since Pryor does not consider individual country performance, this author took his results and performed a simple test to see if Bulgaria's industrial growth has been as fast as expected according to Pryor's regression estimates. This is done by dividing its actual growth rate by a predicted growth rate using Pryor's results. The result leads to a conclusion

Table 5: Comparison of Bulgarian Growth Rates of Industrial Production with Other Socialist Countries (average per year)

Country	Five Year Time Period							
	51–55	56–60	61–65	66–70	71–75	76–80	81–85	86/87
A. Official Gross Industrial Production Indices								
Bulgaria	13.7	15.9	11.7	10.9	9.1	6.0	4.6	3.6
Czechoslovakia	10.9	10.5	5.2	6.7	6.7	4.6	2.7	2.7
GDR	13.7	8.7	5.8	6.6	6.5	4.9	4.2	3.7
Hungary	13.2	7.6	7.5	6.1	6.4	3.4	1.9	2.8
Poland	16.2	9.9	8.5	8.4	10.4	4.7	0.3	4.0
Romania	15.1	10.9	13.8	11.9	12.9	9.6	3.8	6.1
USSR	13.2	10.4	8.6	8.5	7.4	4.4	3.7	4.3
B. Western Recalculations								
Bulgaria	10.8	14.2	8.4	8.7	5.5	3.4	1.8	1.3
Czechoslovakia	4.1	9.3	2.9	4.1	3.9	2.7	1.6	1.6
GDR	11.5	6.8	3.6	4.1	3.3	2.9	1.9	2.7
Hungary	8.7	5.4	6.4	3.4	2.6	2.5	1.4	1.8
Poland	9.7	7.7	6.5	6.3	7.6	0.7	0.0	1.4
Romania	7.7	9.2	10.0	11.2	9.4	4.4	2.2	4.2
C. Ratio of Growth Implied in Western Recalculations to Official Gross Output[1])								
Bulgaria	.974	.985	.970	.980	.967	.975	.973	.978
Czechoslovakia	.938	.989	.978	.975	.973	.981	.989	.989
GDR	.980	.982	.979	.976	.970	.980	.977	.990
Hungary	.960	.979	.989	.974	.964	.991	.995	.979
Poland	.944	.980	.981	.981	.974	.961	.997	.975
Romania	.935	.984	.966	.993	.969	.952	.984	.982

[1]) calculated as (1 + growth rate)/(1 + growth rate).

Sources: Western recalculations are from various reports and papers of the Research Project on National Income in East-Central Europe, the latest of which is: Alton, T. et al.: Economic Growth in Eastern Europe 1970 and 1975–1986. Occasional paper no. 95, Research Project on National Income in East Central Europe. New York 1987. A complete listing of the Project's research papers are listed in this volume.

that Bulgaria's industrial growth is not only faster than predicted for the period, 1950 to 1979, but also more so than was the case for either Romania or Yugoslavia[8]).

Information is also provided in Table 5 on comparisons in terms of the data used by Pryor. These western recalculations tend to reduce the growth of all socialist countries by roughly the same proportions. This is shown in the bottom part of the table where it can be seen that Bulgaria's case shows no major deviations[9]).

V. Regional Patterns of Industrialization

Sofia has by far the greatest concentration of absolute industrial activity with about 13 percent of gross industrial output and 30 percent more than Burgas, Bulgaria's second largest center. Plovdiv and Stara Zagora follow in that order[10]). But Sofia turns out not to be the most intensely industrialized area measured in terms of Table 6. There the intensity of regional industrialization is measured as the percentage of a region's net material product generated by industry. Since this measure counts only the Marxist notion of „productive" activities, it may well exaggerate the relative rank of Sofia, with its great concentration of government services. Instead, the most intensely industrialized region is Gabrovo, with its administrative center of the same name, Bulgaria's oldest industrial center.

Table 6: Regional Ranking of Industrialization in 1980 according to Share of NMP in Industry (national percent = 51)

Rank	Region	Percent	Rank	Region	Percent
1.	Gabrovo	76	15.	Pleven	45
2.	Sofia City	63	16.	Khaskovo	44
3.	Stara Zagora	62	17.	Vidin	43
4.	Lovech	60	18.	Varna	43
5.	Pernik	60	19.	Shumen	42
6.	Sofia Region	59	20.	Îambol	42
7.	Burgas	55	21.	Veliko Tŭrnovo	41
8.	Plovdiv	55	22.	Mikhailovgrad	39
9.	Sliven	53	23.	Tŭrgovishte	37
10.	Vratsa	52	24.	Silistra	36
11.	Pazardzhik	51	25.	Razgrad	35
12.	Ruse	50	26.	Tolbukhin	31
13.	Kiustendil	46	27.	Blagoevgrad	30
14.	Smolîan	46	28.	Kŭrdzhali	12

Calculated from official Bulgarian statistics.

---

[8]) Pryor (n. 7), p. 76–78. The ratios, actual: predicted, were: Bulgaria 9.48 : 7.81; Romania 9.45 : 8.26; and Yugoslavia 8.93 : 8.66.

[9]) The comparison in the table divides (1 + growth rate) by (1 + growth rate) rather than (growth rate)/(growth rate). The latter is meaningless when growth is zero or negative, and tends to exaggerate differences as growth rates approach zero.

[10]) SG. 1984, p. 542.

Industry and Handicrafts 315

The first column in Table 7 shows yet another indicator of relative regional industrialization in how much per capita NMP in industry varied across the regions in 1980. So Burgas, which was three times the national per capita level, generated twelve times the per capita NMP in industry as did the weakly developed regions of Îambol and Kŭrdzhali.

Table 7 provides a contrast between the relative levels achieved in 1980 and the recorded growth of industrial output in the regions by selected periods back to 1952 (unfortunately the measure of level is based on net output while the measure of growth is based on gross output). Thus, one can see if there has been any tendency

Table 7: Bulgarian Regions By Relative Amounts of NMP Generated in Industry per Capita in 1980 and Relative Growth of Gross Industrial Output by Major Sub-periods from 1952 to 1983 (nation level or growth = 100)

Region	1980	52–56	57–60	61–65	66–70	71–75	76–80	81–86
		(ratio of regional to national growth)						
Burgas	319	105	97	124	118	112	93	88
Pleven	178	115	103	87	105	93	110	91
Gabrovo	156	101	87	84	91	97	90	100
Stara Zagora	146	94	102	143	101	99	116	114
Plovdiv	128	100	98	101	90	102	101	102
Sofia City	119	99	102	95	94	93	94	98
Sofia Region	115	82	124	101	99	90	102	109
Lovech	112	92	125	99	111	103	97	110
Pernik	105	121	80	80	80	80	92	96
Ruse	101	102	101	114	108	98	102	108
Veliko Tŭrnovo	100	92	90	114	101	105	98	103
Nation	100	100	100	100	100	100	100	100
Sliven	87	103	90	90	83	102	117	104
Vidin	85	83	138	121	174	115	87	86
Shumen	78	92	121	120	120	104	101	107
Tŭrgovishte	70	67	136	128	108	105	99	94
Blagoevgrad	68	83	94	98	92	134	110	106
Pazardzhik	66	91	90	98	90	96	102	109
Mikhailovgrad	59	94	115	99	104	95	110	93
Smolîan*	56	78	474	85	66	86	93	106
Kîustendil	55	87	95	81	91	119	94	98
Razgrad	49	87	160	139	160	127	116	116
Tolbukhin	45	146	114	116	113	113	109	89
Varna	39	125	111	90	110	98	108	94
Vratsa	39	104	103	110	118	105	103	103
Khaskovo	36	97	92	93	89	89	88	98
Silistra	28	82	139	111	145	126	86	119
Îambol	25	95	103	96	108	89	93	94
Kŭrdzhali	23	107	51	67	80	108	97	108

Note: After 1957 some changes in the regional attribution of activity took place, from Kŭrdzhali to Smolîan, Khaskovo and Îambol regions.

Source: SG. 1972, p. 460; 1984, p. 544; 1987, p. 538.

toward regional equality of industrial output per capita over the period of observations.

Before considering the table, note should be taken of the author's calculation of the regional distribution of per capita NMP in industry for both 1971 and 1980 (not shown in the table). The calculation reveals clearly that regional industrialization grew more unequal during this period. Table 7 reinforces this point by the obvious lack of any clear tendency for the regions below the national average to experience growth faster than the average (that is, to have numbers over 100 in the various time periods in the table).

Looking below the national average reveals a relatively clear separation. There are two slowly growing regions that have above average industrialization – Gabrovo and Pernik. Among the regions with less than average industrialization, those growing slowly are all in the southeastern part of the country – Iambol, Sliven, Khaskovo, Kŭrdzhali, Smolĩan, and Pazardzhik, where the Turkish minority is concentrated (cf. the chapter „Nationale Minderheiten" by S. Troebst). Below average regions that tend to grow more rapidly – Vidin, Shumen, Tŭrgovishte, Razgrad, Tolbukhin, Silistra, and Vratsa – are in the north. Probably most of Bulgaria's regional distribution of industry can be accounted for either by the location of natural resources or the lower cost of location in already developed areas[11]).

VI. The Structure of Bulgarian Industry

1. *Relative Output Growth and Labor Absorption*

Early socialist industrialization in Bulgaria was aimed, as elsewhere in Eastern Europe, at building a base of heavy industry. This shows clearly in Table 8 in the relative growth of industrial branches compared to the growth of total gross output. The very high elasticity of ferrous metals in 1951–1955 reflects both the virtual absence of output at the beginning of the period as well as the commissioning in 1953 of Bulgaria's first major facility, the Lenin complex at Pernik. Then came another period of high relative growth in 1961–1965 as a consequence of bringing on line the Kremikovtsi Works outside of Sofia in 1963. Heavy industrial emphasis is also reflected in the figures for electric power and building materials.

By the 1960's, however, Bulgarian policy makers turned to the machine building and metalworking industries. No other branch has claimed as much attention over the whole period, although data for the 1970's highlights the concentration on electrical engineering and electronics, the focus of high technology hopes in the country today[12]). Chemicals also acquire a greater role in the 1960's with a continuing em-

---

[11]) For example, much of the development in the southeast is due to the expansion of nonferrous metals mining and processing based on ores found in the Rhodope Mountains.

[12]) See, for example, Kovacheva, Z.: Bŭlgarskoto mashinostroene – rozhba na aprilskata ikonomicheska politika na partiĩata (The Bulgarian Machine-building Industry – an Offspring of the April Economic Policy of the Party), in: Ikonomicheska misŭl (Economic thought). XXXI (1986), p. 73–84.

Table 8: Relative Growth of Branches by Periods

Period	51–55	56–60	61–65	66–70	71–75	76–80	81–85	86–88
Growth of Gross Industrial Output	1.90	2.04	1.75	1.67	1.54	1.34	1.25	1.14
Elasticity of Branch Output*								
1. Energy	1.49	1.13	1.14	1.11	.84	1.10	1.00	.98
2. Fuels	1.08	.73	1.34	1.23	.98	.97	–	–
3. Coal	–	–	–	–	.61	.86	.83	.98
4. Ferrous metals	5.36	1.52	1.90	1.40	1.09	.98	.91	.94
5. Nonferrous metals	1.45	1.27	.97	.76	– (not available) –			
6. Machinery, metalworking	–	–	–	–	1.15	1.07	1.09	.96
7. Electrical, electronics	–	–	–	–	1.71	1.41	1.49	1.30
8. Items 6 and 7	1.27	1.45	1.33	1.23	1.29	1.18	1.24	1.10
9. Chemicals, rubber	1.40	1.47	1.25	1.58	1.12	1.20	1.12	1.03
10. Building materials	1.71	1.07	1.24	.96	1.01	1.07	.87	.91
11. Wood processing	.83	.73	.76	.76	.86	.87	.93	.93
12. Paper and pulp	.87	.82	.98	1.24	1.15	.91	.95	.96
13. Glass and ceramics	1.17	1.58	1.37	1.11	.98	1.03	.88	.98
14. Textiles	–	–	.75	.90	.92	.96	.94	.96
15. Clothing	–	–	.81	1.11	.92	.86	.98	.97
16. Items 14 and 15	1.07	.96	.78	.96	–	–	–	–
17. Leather	.65	.88	.81	1.02	.89	.83	1.08	1.04
18. Printing	.76	.75	.72	1.05	.79	1.22	.87	.92
19. Foods	.76	.90	.96	.79	.86	.87	.91	.94

* Elasticity is branch growth in the period divided by the growth of gross industrial output.

phasis in recent years on biotechnology, a part of the chemical branch not reflected in the statistical data[13]).

The gamut of light industry, including food products, never realized higher than average growth even though this was the case for clothing/textiles in 1951–1955. Slower relative growth of these sectors, particularly marked in the case of foods, meant, as shown in Table 9, significantly shrinking shares of a much larger industrial pie.

As will be discussed below, output results from applying capital and labor, plus generating improvements in productivity. This means that Tables 8 and 9 reveal little about the allocation of labor that was also a very important part of Bulgarian industrialization.

In order to follow the relative emphasis in labor allocation, in Table 10 have been calculated the increases in industrial labor, both various measures of industry as a whole and the separate branches. It shows the remarkable step up of labor absorption in industry after 1956. In terms of labor, this appears to have been a giant step, if not a great leap forward.

---

[13]) See, Gurov, R.: Aprilski kurs za uskoreno razvitie na khimicheskata promishlenost (The April strategy for accelerated development of the chemical industry), in: Ikonomicheska misŭl (Economic thought). XXXI (1986) 4, p. 106–112.

Table 9: The Branch Structure of Bulgarian Industry (percentages of gross output in constant prices, variable years**)

Branch	1939	1952	1960	1970	1980	1985	1987	1988
Energy	1.8	2.1	2.0	2.5	4.0	3.8	4.1	3.7
Fuels	4.6	3.2	2.8	4.6	–	–	–	–
Coalmining	–	–	–	–	1.5	1.4	1.5	1.3
Ferrous metals	0.2	0.2	1.1	3.2	4.2	3.6	3.4	3.1
Non-ferrous metals	0.3	3.5	4.4	3.2	–	–	–	–
Machinery/metalworking	2.4	10.0	12.4	16.5	20.2	27.1	29.3	29.4
– machinery/metalworking	–	–	–	–	15.6	15.3	15.7	15.0
– electrical/electronics	–	–	–	–	8.2	11.8	13.6	14.4
Chemicals	1.9	3.1	3.7	7.5	8.8	9.3	9.3	8.8
Building materials	1.8	2.2	3.1	3.7	3.6	2.9	2.9	3.6
Wood processing	10.3	7.6	6.3	3.7	3.4	3.0	2.9	2.8
Paper	1.5	1.1	0.9	1.0	1.6	1.4	1.3	1.3
Glass/ceramics	0.3	0.6	0.6	0.9	1.1	0.9	0.8	0.8
Textiles	19.8*	14.7	13.5	9.1	5.4	5.6	5.5	5.1
Clothing		4.1	5.5	4.9	1.8	2.2	2.2	2.2
Leather	2.1	3.7	2.3	1.9	1.3	1.3	1.3	1.3
Printing	1.7	0.9	0.6	0.5	0.6	0.4	0.4	0.4
Foods	51.2	39.2	33.5	25.4	22.1	23.9	22.5	23.3
Total Output	100.0	100.0	100.0	100.0	100.0	100.0	100.0	100.0

* textiles and clothing.   ** Bulgarian data are not generally published in current prices: 1939, 1952 in 1956 prices; 1960, 1970 in 1962 prices; 1980 in 1971 prices; 1985, 1987 in 1982 prices.
Sources: SG. 1972, p. 110; Statisticheski spravochnik 1989 (Statistical handbook 1989), p. 124.

The machinery/metalworking branch led the way and clearly all heavy industrial branches greatly enlarged their labor forces. But the food branch absorbed nearly as much labor as machinery/metalworking, possibly many of the wives of its workers, while the textile/clothing/leather group also took in well over 50 thousand new workers, considering their importance in the unallocated cooperative industry total given at the bottom of the table. It would appear that much larger portions of increased output in light industry were accounted for by labor than in the case of heavy industries.

2. International Comparisons of Bulgarian Industrial Structure

The general pattern of changes in the branch structure of Bulgarian industry conforms more-or-less with that found historically in the more developed capitalist countries[14]). The question is whether any deviations can be observed from the expected quantitative dependence of branch structure on the level of national product per

---

[14]) Paretti, V.; Block, G.: Industrial production in Western Europe and the United States 1901 to 1939, in: Banca Nazionale del Lavoro Quarterly Review. 39 (1956), S. 56–87.

Table 10: Allocation of Marginal Labor in Industry and Handicrafts (thousand additional workers and employees)

	1952	1956	1960	1965	1970	1975	1980	1985	1986	1987
Total Occupied Persons	118	111	313	170	224	179	97	–	8	32
Total Employees	140	89	293	182	210	178	71	–	–	–
Total in Branches	128	84	299	174	211	137	66	45	17	7
In State Enterprises	113	72	258	176	186	152	87	–	–	–
Energy	3	3	2	3	2	3	6	5	2	–
Fuels	4	13	6	9	4	–	–	–	–	–
Coal mining	–	–	–	–	–	–7	3	3	0	0
Ferrous metals	0	4	4	12	8	2	3	0	2	1
Non-ferrous metals	7	8	12	11	–3	(data not published)				–
Machinery/metalworking	25	10	55	60	69	75	39	35	6	2
Machinery/metalworking	–	–	–	–	–	42	21	13	3	1
Electrical/electronics	–	–	–	–	–	33	19	22	4	1
Chemicals	9	4	6	14	23	–	–	–	–	–
(new definition)	–	–	–	–	–	17	9	10	3	–2
Building materials	2	6	15	14	2	11	3	2	0	3
Wood processing	1	5	23	3	0	–	–	–	–	–
(new definition)	–	–	–	–	–	2	–8	0	–2	–2
Paper	0	2	1	2	2	4	0	1	0	1
Glass	2	2	4	5	4	4	3	0	0	–1
Textiles	15	4	32	–2	22	18	–1	–6	0	0
Clothing	0	3	13	11	9	6	2	15	2	0
Leather	4	0	5	5	7	2	1	5	0	0
Printing	2	0	2	0	2	0	2	0	0	–1
Food	27	0	53	21	25	–	–	–	–	–
(new definition)	–	–	–	–	–	3	–7	0	2	1
Other	13	10	23	5	12	(not available)			–	–
In Cooperatives	15	12	40	–2	25	–15	–22	–	–	–

Sources: SG. 1972, p. 133; 1983, p. 167; Statisticheski izvestiiâ (Statistical bulletin). (1987) 4, p. 22.

capita[15]). Such deviations have been expected as a consequence of socialist development strategies that emphasized both high initial investment rates and relative autarky, the latter arising not only from barriers to trade with capitalist countries, but also systemic failures.

The first published effort to identify the effects of system on industrial structure with a structural model is the work of Gregory based on data from 1955 to 1963[16]).

---

[15]) Chenery, H.: Patterns of Industrial Growth, in: American Economic Review. 50 (1960) September, p. 624–654.

[16]) Romania, in contrast to Bulgaria, is found by Gregory to be the only East European country with slightly less than „normal" shares of industry (and normal total manufacturing) and it had at the time of Gregory's sample the largest positive percentage deviations in the case of heavy industry. Its metal products branch was, so to speak, too large while its food branch was too small. Like all the other East European economies in the sample, it also had a heavy-intermediate products branch that was above average. Gregory, P.: Socialist and Nonsocialist Industrialization Patterns. New York 1970.

He concludes that „heavy" industry had significantly larger shares under socialism. For example, the six East European countries averaged 3 percent smaller shares of food and light (mostly clothing, textiles, footwear) industries, a probably insignificant 1 percent larger metal products industry, and a 7 percent larger heavy intermediate-products industry than would be expected from capitalist countries at the same development level.

In terms of its branch structure Bulgaria is found by Gregory to be nearly a normal „socialist" country, but with only a moderately below capitalist-normal share in the food branch in place of the large shortfalls in the food branch's share shown by other socialist countries.

The Economic Commission for Europe provides a complementary view of differences in socialist structure, but unlike Gregory using no regression techniques to test for differences[17]). Table 11 shows some of its results in terms of a simple comparison of the branch structures of the Soviet Union and the six East European countries with two groups, West I, the more developed capitalist countries in Western Europe, and West II, the four Southern European countries (data for Yugoslavia are provided by the author). As might be expected, the branch shares of „the East" usually fall in between those of the more and the less developed countries of Europe.

Table 11: East West Differences in Industrial Structure, 1964–1966 (percent)

	Western Europe		Eastern Europe			
	I	II	All	Bul.	Rom.	Yug.**
Food, tobacco	11.9	16.8	12.1	18.4	9.8	9.9
Textiles	7.3	12.2	10.8	11.2	11.1	15.5*
Clothing, footwear	8.9	11.8	7.0	5.2	5.3	(*)
Leather	0.8	1.6	1.5	0.8	4.1	3.3
Wood products	7.1	9.5	7.2	5.3	16.5	10.0
Paper	3.8	1.7	1.3	1.0	1.5	1.9
Printing	4.6	3.3	1.2	0.9	1.4	3.2
Chemicals	6.3	5.6	5.7	4.2	5.9	6.0
Petroleum, coal	0.6	0.5	1.2	0.5	2.9	7.1
Non-metalic minerals	4.8	5.9	6.7	6.2	7.3	8.8
Metals, engineering	40.2	27.6	38.0	25.8	33.6	33.5
Miscellaneous	3.7	3.5	7.7	20.5	0.6	0.8
Total	100.0	100.0	100.0	100.0	100.0	100.0

I = developed countries; II = less developed countries; All = average for Soviet Union and CMEA Six; Bul. = Bulgaria; Rom. = Romania; Yug. = Yugoslavia; ** classification might not be consistent; clothing and footwear included with textiles.

Sources: UN-ECE: Structure and Change in European Industry. New York 1977, p. 229; Statistički godišnjak Jugoslavije (Statistical Yearbook of Yugoslavia). Belgrade 1971, p. 86.

---

[17]) UN-ECE: Structure and Change in European Industry. New York 1977, p. 84–88.

Industry and Handicrafts

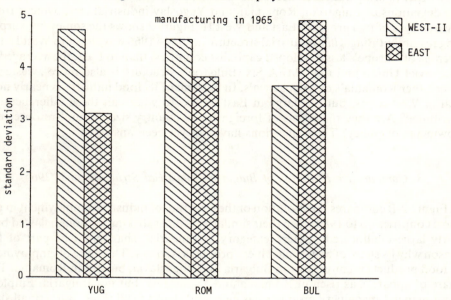

Figure 2: Deviations from employment shares.

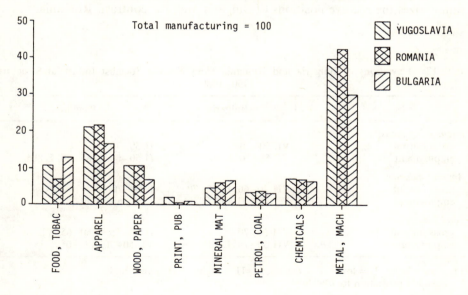

In order to bring out differences in the Bulgarian pattern, the author has calculated the deviations of Bulgarian, Romanian and Yugoslav industrial employment from the averages of two groups – East and West II. Figure 2 shows the somewhat surprising result that Bulgaria's industrial structure in 1964–1966 was closer to West II, the average of Europe's less developed capitalist countries, than to East, the average for the Soviet Union and the CMEA Six. Bulgaria's structure is also more „western" than either Romania's or Yugoslavia's. In particular, its food industry is nearly normal in West-terms, but too large in East-terms. To what can these differences be attributed? Are they the effects of foreign trade, country size, natural resource endowments or policy? These questions have not yet been answered.

3. Comparative Evolution of Bulgarian Industrial Structure since 1965

Figure 2-B compares the evolution of the structure of industrial employment in the three countries up to 1980 when their similarity is most striking, although flawed by a fairly large unallocated „other" category in Bulgaria. That might be part of the reason why its share of metal-machinery products is so low. The share of employment in food products is converging in Bulgaria and Yugoslavia, but not in Romania. The share of apparel has risen in Romania and Yugoslavia, but not Bulgaria. Employment in metal-machinery products has increased shares in all three. But a small shift of Bulgaria labor from food to apparel and a small shift of Romania labor from metal-machinery to food would make the three nearly identical.

In a second effort to trace Bulgaria's branch structure more recently, the author updated a study of the ECE that compares only seven socialist countries. Table 12 summarizes the relative positions of Bulgaria and, for contrast, Romania.

Table 12: Deviations of Bulgaria and Romania from Normal Socialist Industrial Structures, 1950–1980

	Bulgaria	Romania
Engineering industry		
gross output	VL 50–70	H 50–70
employment	VL 50–70, L 80*	H 50–60, L 65–70, E 80*
Apparel industry		
gross output	VH 50–60, H 65–70	L 50–70
employment	Variable H and L	L 50–65, H 70
Food industry		
gross output	VH 50–70	H 50–55, L 60–65, VL 70
employment	VH 50–70, E 80*	VL 50–70, VL 80*

VL = very low; L = low; E = expected; H = high; VH = very high.
* – author's projection to 1980.

Source: From data in: UN-ECE: Structure and Change in European Industry. New York 1977, p. 169–189; and country yearbooks.

By comparison to the other socialist countries, Bulgaria's food industry took unusually large shares of employment and provided large shares of output. Its engineering industry took, by contrast, unusually small shares of employment and provided small shares of output[18]). Both branches exhibited these deviations in all five observation periods, from 1950 to 1970, showing no tendency to decline as Bulgarian per capita GNP rose. The author's estimates for 1980 show engineering employment with little relative change, but the share of employment in the food industry declined to the level expected for a socialist country[19]).

VII. Industrialization and the Role of Foreign Markets

Although many more details on foreign trade are to be found in the contribution by R. Schönfeld to this volume, there has been such a great influence of foreign trade on Bulgaria's industrialization that the connection must be discussed here.

1. The Role of Exports in Bulgarian Industrialization

A country's foreign trade dependence normally is greater as the country is smaller, and smaller as the country's level of development is lower. This means that Bulgaria has been subject to contradictory influences quite apart from any policy and systemic influences acting upon it. According to measures of foreign trade dependence, in the mid-1950's it shared a common tendency of socialist countries to have unusually low levels of foreign trade compared to GNP, and while it did have higher levels of dependence than neighboring Romania, it was still below all other European countries in the CMEA[20]).

A special Bulgarian feature began to emerge in the 1960's when it had become the most trade-dependent of all European CMEA members, and by 1975 had nearly

---

[18]) This conclusion has been reinforced by the author's calculations of socialist country branch deviations for an unweighted average of all countries in the group. Bulgaria has the largest deviations from the average in terms of output and employment shares for both 1965 and 1979. But, at the same time, its overall deviation was much reduced by 1979 compared to 1965. These calculations are available from the author and were based on data published by Tuitz, G.: Structural Changes and Productivity: Development in Manufacturing Industries of the European Centrally Planned Economies, in: Forschungsberichte 85, Wiener Institut für internationale Wirtschaftsvergleiche. Wien, April 1985.

[19]) That Bulgaria's machinery and metalworking branch is still rather small for a socialist country, but almost the share expected by regressions on capitalist country data is the finding of Winiecki for 1979. Winiecki, E.; Winiecki, J.: Manufacturing structures in centrally planned economies; patterns of change and institutional factors, in: Jahrbuch der Wirtschaft Osteuropas. 12 (1987), p. 225.

[20]) For a more complete explanation and presentation of the statistical methods behind the estimations of foreign trade dependence, see Jackson, M.: Economic Development in the Balkans Since 1945 Compared to Southern and East-Central Europe, in: Eastern European Politics and Society. I (1987) 3, p. 437–441.

reached trade-dependence levels that would have been typical for a capitalist country of similar size and development level. Unfortunately, this position was being sustained by both borrowing from the West and implicit subsidization from the Soviet Union in the form of low import prices for oil. By 1980 when both stimuluses were removed, Bulgaria's trade dependence fell to about 80 percent of a level expected for a country of its size and GNP per capita, but heavier borrowing from the West pushed it back up again to „normal" levels by 1988.

Another measure of trade dependence, the ratio of exports to production of industrial products, had reached an estimated 16 percent in 1970, second in CMEA to Hungary's 17 percent. By about 1980, Bulgaria's export share moved up to 24 percent, still only lagging behind Hungary, but by a wider margin (Hungary's share reached 31–32 percent)[21]). As shown in Table 13, the share of industrial output exported has fallen in the last two years.

The numbers in Part A of the table show the growth in industrial output and export of various categories that took place in each five-year period since 1950. The tendency for industrial growth to slow down is shown plainly in the first column. It is equally

Table 13: Industrial Output and Exports

Date	Total Industrial Output	Total Exports	Total Industrial Goods	From Industrial Materials	From Nonindustrial Materials
A. Increase in the period (end year compared to beginning year = 100)					
1951–55	183.5				
1956–60	199.2	279.2	286.4	268.3	294.7
1961–65	174.1	205.5	212.2	318.9	167.3
1966–70	168.0	180.7	189.5	223.0	162.6
1971–75	154.7	160.8	170.0	219.2	115.3
1976–80	133.8	182.9	184.1	211.7	126.2
1981–85	124.7	141.6	143.7	155.1	109.6
1986–88	113.9	100.1	100.6	103.2	89.4
B. Increase compared to increase in industrial output					
1951–55	100.0				
1956–60	100.0	140.2	143.8	134.7	148.0
1961–65	100.0	118.0	121.9	183.2	96.1
1966–70	100.0	107.6	112.8	132.7	96.8
1971–75	100.0	103.9	109.9	141.7	74.5
1976–80	100.0	136.7	137.6	158.2	94.3
1981–85	100.0	113.6	115.2	124.4	87.9
1986–88	100.0	87.9	88.3	90.6	78.5

Source: SG., various issues. Statisticheski spravochnik 1989 (Statistical handbook), p. 121, 200.

---

[21]) Montias, J.: Industrial policy and Foreign Trade in Bulgaria. Eastern European Politics and Society. 2 (1988) 3, S. 523, citing Bogomolov, O.: Strany sotsializma v mezhdunarodnom razdelenii truda (The Countries of Socialism in International Division of Labor). Moscow 1986, p. 301.

clear that all categories of exports except those industrial products from nonindustrial (mostly agricultural) materials. In this case, the relative growth is more easily compared in Part B of the table. There is a significantly decreasing stimulus to industrial growth coming from the export sector.

2. Industrial Policy and the CMEA

Although initially in conflict with CMEA foreign trade pricing arrangements, Bulgaria soon found ways to press for its advantage in that organization's development of specialized production[22]. In 1964 the only country with a smaller share of total CMEA exports covered by „specialization" was Czechoslovakia (4.5 percent compared to Bulgaria's 6.0 percent). By 1981 Bulgaria's share was 38.1 percent, then the highest in CMEA. Since then it appears that other countries have caught up, but Bulgaria still accounts for about 16 percent of all CMEA trade covered by specialization, a figure that marginally exceeds even the GDR[23].

The most intense Bulgarian interaction with CMEA under specialization agreements has been in machine building. But it began slowly. At the Berlin CMEA meetings in 1956, Bulgaria and Romania were each recommended for specialization in only 7 percent of the 600 most important types of mass-produced machinery and equipment. Both countries probably paid little attention to this. In Bulgaria's case it started up production of refrigerators in 1956 and in 1957 television sets, bulldozers, equipment for the automobile industry. Typewriters and electronic calculators were initiated around 1962, equipment for the chemical and cellulose industries in 1968 and for the metallurgical industry in 1969[24].

By 1965, hauling and lifting equipment made up nearly two-thirds of Bulgaria's so-called „specialized" exports in CMEA. Tractors and agricultural machinery and means of transportation took up the other third. But all „specialized" exports were only 10 percent of total Bulgarian exports of machinery and equipment. Such arrangements still could not be considered a real force generating economies of scale in production since most exports were scattered in small volume items.

The share of total exports of machinery and equipment falling in the „specialized" categories did reach half by 1975. By then the share of hauling and lifting equipment in what was „specialized" fell to a third, while another third was found in the new growth industry, electronics and computing, and 10 percent in transportation equipment.

---

[22]) Kaser, M.: COMECON. Oxford 1965, p. 141/142.
[23]) See Simai, M.: Exports and Export Performance, in: Vajda, I.; Simai, M.: Foreign Trade in a Planned Economy. Cambridge 1971, p. 117, and for recent years the usual statistical „commentaries" published in CMEA's journal, Ekonomicheskoe sotrudnichestvo stran-chlenov (Economical Cooperation of the Member Countries).
[24]) Montias (n. 21), p. 529–533.

Table 14: Evidence of Successful Industrial Policy in Branches of Bulgarian Machine-Building[a]

Branch	1960 to 1965	1965 to 1970	1970 to 1975
Hauling and lifting Equipment	yes	yes	no
Metalworking Machinery	yes	no	no
Power and Electrotechnical Equipment	no	no	no
Tractors and Agricultural Machinery	yes	no	no
Equipment for Light Industry	(export data not identified)		
Equipment for Food Industry	yes	yes	no
Ships and Other Vessels	no	yes	no
Radio-electronics	—[b]	yes	yes
Instruments and Automation Equipment	—[b]	—[b]	yes

(a) Based on both production and exports growing faster than total machinery and equipment production and exports.
(b) Export and production shares insignificant.
Source: Montias (n. 21), p. 528.

Montias observes that Bulgaria's transformation from its mostly domestically consumed metal-working industry to the electrotechnical and electronics branches was the most rapid in CMEA. And while Bulgaria shows extensive evidence of having passed what he calls „the litmus test of industrial policy" in the 1960's, he concludes that „only a few sub-branches of the machine-building and electronics industry and still fewer sub-branches of the chemical industry can properly qualify as building blocks of an industrial policy"[25]. And by the 1980's Bulgaria found itself heavily dependent upon export sectors like the lifting and hauling machinery branch that made inefficient use of imported materials and energy whose costs were rising rapidly in terms of their export values.

3. The Failure of Bulgarian Industry in Western Markets

Bulgaria has proven to be an exceptionally loyal member of the CMEA. Its share of foreign trade with the socialist countries has been since 1950 very high, yet it probably has had the choice of selling more of its food products in western markets. If Bulgarian policy makers had used this opportunity, as those in Romania did, then they would have been required to gradually shift its trade back to CMEA as industrial origin exports grew as a percentage of the total.

---

[25] Ibid., p. 15, 21.

Just how loyal Bulgaria was in 1970 was measured by Hewett through the estimation of a gravity model of foreign trade. He found that CMEA had a more powerful tendency to pull trade away from nonmembers than the EEC. Consequently, Bulgaria's trade with the Soviet Union and the GDR were, respectively, five and four times the levels if these countries had been western partners not bound by a tariff union. Its trade with the West, like Hungary's, was only 30 percent of what it would have been under those more normal conditions[26]).

Table 15: Bulgarian Exports of Some Industrial Commodities

Commodity group	1986			1987		
	Total	to CMEA	%	Total	to CMEA	%
	(mil. valuta leva)			(mil. valuta leva)		
Machinery, equipment	7719.8	6833.7	88.5	8358.7	7317.8	87.5
Minerals, fuels	1071.3	405.3	37.8	977.1	370.6	37.9
Chemicals	443.8	243.2	54.8	420.3	241.0	57.3
Construction material	271.0	258.0	95.2	258.3	243.3	94.2
Processed foods	1759.7	1573.8	89.4	1671.4	1456.2	87.1
Other consumer goods	1434.7	1252.5	87.3	1458.6	1265.8	86.8

Source: Statisticheski izvestiĩa (Statistical bulletin). (1987) 4, p. 55; (1988) 4, p. 56.

There have been intervals, such as 1961–1965, when the growth rate of Bulgarian exports to the West led the CMEA[27]). Bulgaria has also mounted a comparatively strong organizational effort in western markets[28]). Yet both the pull of socialist ties and the poor quality of Bulgaria's export products is reflected in Table 15 showing the tiny shares of its industrial exports going outside the CMEA. Its geographical „diversification" is strictly limited to easily marketed fuels and chemicals that present no technological challenges and are made from crude oil imported from the Soviet Union. Recently, PlanEcon estimated that over 40 percent of total Bulgarian exports to the developed West is made up of fuels. One has to go far down the PlanEcon list of Bulgarian exports to OECD countries to the 13th rank to find the first complex export, industrial lift trucks, an item that is only 1.29 percent of Bulgaria's exports and 0.54 percent of the OECD import market[29]). A more comprehensive view of

---

[26]) Hewett, E.: A Gravity Model of CMEA Trade, in: Brada, J.: Quantitative and Analytical Studies in East-West Economic Relations. Bloomington IN 1976, p. 1–16.
[27]) See the data in Simai (n. 23), p. 118.
[28]) For example, as of November, 1977, there were 35 Bulgarian companies counted in the West (including banks and other financial institutions), more than enumerated for Romania, the GDR or Czechoslovakia. See McMillan, C.: Direct Soviet and East European Investment in the Industrialized Western Economies, in: Institute of Soviet and East European Studies, Carleton University Working Paper No. 7. Ottawa, January 1978, p. 12.
[29]) PlanEcon Report. IV (June 3, 1988) 22–23, p. 1, 21.

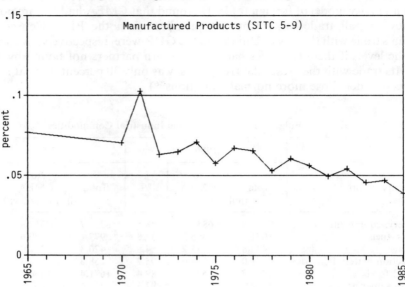

Figure 3: Bulgaria's Share of OECD Imports.

Bulgaria's discouraging failure to maintain market shares in OECD's imports of manufactured goods is clearly shown in Figure 3[30]).

VIII. Increasing Productivity and Prospects for Economic Maturity

Bulgaria's failure to penetrate western markets with industrial exports is probably the most telling evidence that unproductive uses have been made of the now significant shares of resources committed to industrialization. But it does not explain the evolution of outputs and inputs to industry in a way that hints of changes in the ratio of outputs to inputs over time or compared with other socialist or similarly situated capitalist countries.

1. Analysis of Production Functions in Bulgarian Industry

There is now an extensive literature attempting to explain the economic downturn in Eastern Europe in terms of empirically estimated production functions, or the

---

[30]) Also, for a reflection of doubt concerning Bulgaria's chances for electronics exports in the West, see Business International: Bulgaria: High Goals for Electronic Growth, in: Business Eastern Europe. May 26, 1986, p. 1.

measurement of changes in outputs and inputs of fixed capital and labor[31]). Most of the work has focused on the Soviet Union and has resulted in a major disagreement among the specialists on the best explanation of that country's industrial growth retardation. One point of view is that neutral technological progress or aggregate input productivity has been falling. Another plausible explanation is that technology has not permitted adequate substitution of fixed capital for labor. Consequently, the attempt to maintain growth by high rates of investment in the face of constrained labor supplies does not work.

Besides the estimates of the parameters of neutral technological change and the substitution of capital for labor, the statistical techniques also permit an evaluation of the extent to which economies of scale have been realized. This would be very important evidence in the evaluation of Bulgaria's export-oriented industry.

It is unfortunate that the few efforts by western scholars to estimate Bulgarian industrial production functions seem to have floundered on the poor quality of published statistics, especially those for fixed capital stocks. For example, the research of Kyn and Kyn in the cases of both Bulgaria and Romania resulted either in statistically insignificant coefficients or implausible estimates when compared with research on other countries[32]).

A possible problem with the Kyns' research might also have been the sample period, 1948 to 1968, when data problems were especially grave. A hint of that is the choice of years from 1960 to 1982 by a Bulgarian specialist, who unlike the usual practice of his colleagues, actually published the estimated coefficients of the regressions (although, unfortunately, not as much other information as would be normal for a western scholar). The most interesting result is the lack of realized economies of scale in both estimates. The other results raise as many questions as answers for those especially interested in Bulgaria growth processes[33]).

2. Partial Productivity Ratios

Lacking the more powerful techniques for comparative measures of productivity change in Bulgarian industry, consideration can be given to so-called partial produc-

---

[31]) For an excellent, clearly written explanation of the statistical techniques and results of research on the Soviet Union and Eastern Europe, see Brada, J.: The Slowdown in Soviet and East European Economic Growth, in: Osteuropa-Wirtschaft. 30 (1985) 2, p. 116–128.

[32]) Kyn, O.; Kyn, L.: Factor Productivities in East European Countries, in: Altmann, F.; Kyn, O.; Wagener, H.: On the Measurement of Factor Productivities. Göttingen 1976; Kyn, O.; Kyn, L.: Trends in East European Factor Productivity, in: Jahrbuch der Wirtschaft Osteuropas. 7 (1977), p. 71–90.

[33]) For example, the branches with the greatest technological progress are foods and wood processing. In terms of capital: labor substitution, Bulgarian branches fall into two sharply divided groups. One (including energy, fuels, ferrous metallurgy, machine-building and metalworking, chemicals, and paper) displays unity of capital: labor factor substitution. The other (including food, textiles, clothing, leather, wood products, and construction materials) suggests nearly fixed proportions or near zero elasticity of substitution. Antonov, V.: Proizvodstveni funktsii s obshteni faktori (Production functions with general factors of production). Ikonomicheska misŭl. (1985) 7, p. 106–118.

tivity measures which are available comparatively, but which are based on accounting rather than economic techniques. In these terms, one focus of Bulgarian planners has been effort to direct larger portions of investments in industry to technological upgrading of plant and equipment rather than the construction of wholly new facilities.

The plan for 1981–1985 called for 70 percent of investments in the material sector to be used for modernization, reconstruction and expansions of existing facilities[34]). But in industry which takes the bulk of investments, achievements, as shown in Table 16, have fallen short of this goal and have clearly not shown an upward trend.

Table 16: Share of „Intensively" Used Capital Investments in Bulgarian Industry (percent)

	1978	1980	1983	1985	1986	1987
Modernization, reconstruction and expansion of existing facilities	66.6	64.0	61.3	65.3	62.0	–
Modernization and reconstruction of existing facilities	40.2	42.3	40.1	30.7	30.4	38.0

Source: SG. 1984, p. 174; 1987, p. 172; Statisticheski spravochnik. 1988, p. 36.

Since the Bulgarian management system has failed to realize greater shares in re-equipping, it comes as no surprise that industrial output per unit of fixed capital is falling. The figures in Table 17 suggest that Bulgaria has recently ranked among the worst of the socialist countries, although an appraisal of Romania in terms of honest output statistics would no doubt make its performance even worse.

Bulgaria has also tended to consume the highest levels of energy and other raw materials in the CMEA. Consequently, it has had much room for improvement, a fact which no doubt helps explain its rather good comparative ranking in Part B of Table 17.

The datum most often used by socialist countries to measure the „intensity" of economic development is the simple ratio of output growth to growth of the labor force, something, of course, that does not itself identify why the ratio increases. As suggested above, the usual source of increase has been increasing the amount of fixed capital per laborer, a simple formula which seems to have encountered little success in recent years in all socialist countries.

Bulgaria's record in such terms is spotty. Not only has it failed to register continuous gains. It has also the smallest share of output growth attributed to „increased labor productivity"[35]). This poor performance can not be attributed to a failure to

---

[34]) RD. December 11, 1981.
[35]) Again, such a comparison demands qualification because of Romania's politically inflated statistics.

Industry and Handicrafts

Table 17: Capital and Material Productivity in Bulgaria and Other Socialist Countries (percent per year).

	1981–85	1986
A. Industrial Output per Unit of Fixed Capital Investments		
Bulgaria	− 3.1	− 1.9
Czechoslovakia	− 2.5	− 2.1
GDR	− 0.8	− 1.0
Hungary	− 2.5	na
Poland	− 2.6	2.3
Romania	− 4.6	− 0.9
Soviet Union	− 2.7	− 0.7
B. Material Intensity of Industrial Production[1])		
Bulgaria	− 2.5	− 1.6
Czechoslovakia	− 0.1	− 0.5
GDR	− 0.9	− 1.3
Hungary	− 0.9	3.1
Poland	1.5	0.1
Romania	− 1.8	− 0.4
Soviet Union	− 0.2	0.7

[1]) ratio of gross output index to net output index.

Source: UN-ECE: Economic Survey of Europe in 1987–1988. New York 1988, p. 162/163.

Table 18: Growth of Output per Unit of Labor as a Percent of Industrial Output Growth

	1981–85	1986	1987
Bulgaria	64	68	58
Czechoslovakia	81	84	100
GDR	93	107	108
Hungary	185	126	162
Poland	325	95	115
Romania	63	96	102
Soviet Union	81	96	108

Source: UN-ECE: Economic Survey of Europe in 1987–1988. New York 1988, p. 161.

provide increased supplies of fixed capital. Rather the problem, as now admitted by the country's leadership, is that Bulgaria's management system has clearly failed to meet its latest challenges.

IX. Summary of Bulgarian Industrialization 1950 to 1989

The main points covered in this chapter can now be enumerated:
(1) Bulgaria began the period with an industrial sector that was second only to Albania in its smallness, producing on a per capita basis 40 percent or less of per

capita industrial output in the Soviet Union. Today the country probably equals or exceeds per capita industrial output in Poland, Hungary or even the Soviet Union.

(2) From having smaller shares of its labor force in industry than would have been expected, given its per capita GNP in 1950, Bulgaria arrived at a position in 1980 of having about 50 percent greater shares in industry than would be normal development. This state of „over-industrialization" is shared by other socialist countries where, by comparison, Bulgaria's over-industrialization is the greatest considering the small share of the labor force found in services.

(3) International comparisons show that Bulgaria's industrial output has grown at rather higher rates than might be accounted for by its level of GNP per capita. But by the same international comparisons, it has experienced especially great fluctuations and one of the most pronounced recent retardations of growth.

(4) Regional inequality of industrialization in Bulgaria increased from 1971 to 1980, measured by the leva value of net material product in industry in the regions. The most industrialized regions have more than twice the share of labor force in industry as do the least developed regions, the latter being generally found in the southeastern part of the country.

(5) By 1965 Bulgaria acquired an industrial structure that was unusual for a socialist country in that the food sector was not smaller than would be normally expected, while the heavy industrial sectors were not so exaggerated. Since then, the country has tended to converge with other socialist countries in this regard.

(6) Bulgaria also acquired an unusually high foreign trade dependence for a socialist country, based on unusually strong commitments of its trade with the Soviet Union and the GDR. While at first this position was based on agricultural development, later it grew from Bulgaria's use of CMEA specialization in order to expand both production and exports in selected sub-branches of the machine-building and electrical-electronics industries.

(7) Bulgaria's successful industrial policies have depended on its ability to trade in the CMEA and have had no evident success in developed market economies where Bulgarian market shares continue to fall.

In the 1980's Bulgaria's continued industrialization is caught in a squeeze. Rising raw material costs have reinforced Soviet demands for better quality Bulgarian goods so that what were advantages of commitments to CMEA have turned into disadvantages. Seemingly endless Soviet markets seem to have made Bulgarian enterprises noncompetitive. The question for the future is, how can Bulgaria upgrade its industrial output in terms of the quality needed for western markets when so much of it is tightly meshed in long-term cooperation with enterprises in other socialist countries?

Land- und Forstwirtschaft

Ilse Grosser, Wien

I. Volkswirtschaftliche Bedeutung der Land- und Forstwirtschaft – II. Produktionsfaktoren: 1. Boden – 2. Arbeitskräfte und Einkommen – 3. Anlagekapital und Investitionen – III. Produktionsergebnisse: 1. Wachstum und Struktur – 2. Pflanzenproduktion – 3. Tierproduktion – IV. Privatwirtschaften – V. Nahrungsmittelverbrauch – VI. Agraraußenhandel – VII. Forstwirtschaft – VIII. Eigentums- und Organisationsstruktur: 1. Bodenreform, Kollektivierung und Betriebskonzentration – 2. Vertikale Integrationsansätze: Agrar-Industrie-Komplexe und Industrie-Agrar-Komplexe – 3. Organisationsexperimente seit 1979 – IX. Ziele und Instrumente der Agrarpolitik 1986–1990

I. Volkswirtschaftliche Bedeutung der Land- und Forstwirtschaft

Bulgarien war vor und nach dem II. Weltkrieg eines der wirtschaftlich am wenigsten entwickelten Länder Europas; die überwiegend kleinbetrieblich strukturierte und kaum technisierte Landwirtschaft bildete noch 1948–1950 den Lebensunterhalt für 86 % der Erwerbstätigen in der materiellen Sphäre, trug zu 58 % zum produzier-

Tabelle 1: Volkswirtschaftliche Bedeutung der Land- und Forstwirtschaft (LW und FW) 1948–1987 (% von insgesamt)

Jahr	Produziertes Nationaleinkommen[1]		Erwerbstätige (mat. Sphäre)		Anlagevermögen (mat. Sphäre)[2]	Exporte[3]	Importe[3]
	LW	FW	LW	FW	LW		
1948	58,0	1,0	85,6	0,2	28,0[4]	88,0[5]	13,9[5]
1957	34,0	0,0	75,5[7]	0,4[4]	24,0	60,7[6]	13,7[6]
1960	26,6	0,7	60,2	0,9	24,9	56,4	16,7
1970	16,5	0,7	40,5	0,6	20,5	43,4	15,9
1980	10,8	0,4	28,7	0,5	16,2	24,4	9,7
1985	12,9	0,4	24,8	0,5	12,5	18,5	9,5
1986	14,9	0,4	24,3	0,6	12,4	17,0	8,5
1987	12,2	0,4	23,4	0,7	12,0	16,2	8,5

[1] Vergleichbare Preise; ab 1970 inkl. Dienstleistungen in der Pflanzenproduktion. –
[2] Anschaffungswerte: 1948–1960 inkl. Forstwirtschaft: ab 1981 ohne Arbeits- und Nutztiere. –
[3] RGW-Nomenklatur Gruppen 5–8 vergl. Text Abschnitt IV. – [4] 1952. – [5] 1950. – [6] 1955. –
[7] 1956.

Quelle: SG., versch. Jahrgänge; Statističeskij ežegodnik stran-členov Soveta Ekonomičeskoj Vzaimopomošči (Statistisches Jahrbuch der Mitgliedsländer des Rates für Gegenseitige Wirtschaftshilfe). Moskau. Versch. Jahrgänge.

ten Nationaleinkommen und zu 88 % zum Export bei. Im Zuge des rapiden Strukturwandels und besonders der Industrialisierung des Landes nach der kommunistischen Machtübernahme gingen diese Anteile – bei wachsender Agrarproduktion – langfristig stark zurück. In den 80er Jahren (bis 1987) entfielen auf die Landwirtschaft ein Sechstel, gemeinsam mit der Nahrungs- und Genußmittelindustrie etwa ein Viertel des produzierten Nationalproduktes und ein Viertel der Erwerbstätigen in der materiellen Sphäre (Tabelle 1). Bulgarien gehört, neben Ungarn und Rumänien, zu den europäischen RGW-Nettoexporteuren bei Produkten landwirtschaftlichen Ursprungs, die in den 80er Jahren rund ein Fünftel des Gesamtexports ausmachten und auch dringend benötigte Hartwährungseinnahmen brachten – sie gingen zu rund einem Fünftel in die Nicht-RGW-Länder.

Kennzeichnend für die bulgarische Agrarpolitik sind der frühe Abschluß der Kollektivierung, eine relativ rasche Mechanisierung der Produktion und die Dominanz des sozialistischen Sektors (87 % der landwirtschaftlichen Nutzfläche (LN)) mit einer extrem großbetrieblichen Struktur, die erst heute wieder ernsthaft in Frage gestellt wird. In den 80er Jahren traten in der Landwirtschaft Krisenerscheinungen zutage, die durch ungewöhnliche Dürreperioden verschärft wurden.

Um für die langfristige Analyse die oft starken jährlichen Schwankungen der Agrarproduktion auszuschalten, beruhen aus Gründen der Vergleichbarkeit sämtlicher in der Folge angeführten jahresdurchschnittlichen Veränderungen auf dem Vergleich zwischen jeweils zwei Fünfjahresperioden (nicht von zwei Eckjahren einer Fünfjahresperiode)[1]).

II. Produktionsfaktoren

1. Boden

Bulgarien (110 912 km^2) besteht zu mehr als zwei Dritteln aus Flach- und Hügelland mit einer Seehöhe von unter 600 m^2). Die *LN* macht 56 % bzw. fast 0,7 ha je Einwohner aus – die höchste Relation unter den sechs europäischen RGW-Partnern der UdSSR, an die nur Rumänien und Ungarn mit mehr als 0,6 ha herankommen. So gesehen sind die Voraussetzungen für die Befriedigung des Ernährungsbedarfs der Bevölkerung und für potentielle Netto-Agrarexporte relativ günstig.

Mit 5,77 Mio. ha hatte die LN erst 1964 das Vorkriegsniveau (1939) wieder überschritten. Seit dem Höhepunkt des Jahres 1978 (6,21 Mio. ha) ist die LN kontinuierlich zurückgegangen (Tabelle 2). Dies ist eine bei zunehmenden Flächenansprüchen für Industrie und Infrastruktur typische Entwicklung, steht aber im Widerspruch zu dem immer noch geltenden agrarpolitischen Ziel, im Sinne einer Produktionssteigerung alle irgendwie nutzbaren brachliegenden Flächen, vor allem solche im Gebirgs-

---

[1]) Alle angeführten Zahlenangaben beruhen, wenn nicht anders festgehalten, auf offizieller bulgarischer Statistik.
[2]) Information Bulgaria: a short encyclopedia of the People's Republic of Bulgaria (Countries of the world information series). Ed. by The Bulgarian Academy of Science (zit. als: Information Bulgaria). Oxford u. a. 1985, S. 13 ff.

Land- und Forstwirtschaft

und Vorgebirgsland sowie Streu- und Splitterflächen, einer agrarischen Nutzung zuzuführen. Angesichts des mangelnden Interesses der dazu auch wenig geeigneten Großbetriebe (mit ein Grund für das Brachfallen von Böden) bieten sich dafür vor allem die Privatwirtschaften an, die seit der zweiten Hälfte der 70er Jahre stärker gefördert werden (vgl. IV). In jüngster Zeit wurden radikale Maßnahmen gegen die illegale Verbauung (vor allem mit privaten Wochenendhäusern) von zur landwirtschaftlichen Nutzung vorgesehenen Flächen angekündigt[3]).

Tabelle 2: Bodennutzung 1960–1987

	Landwirtschaftl. Nutzfläche[1]) 1000 ha	davon: Dauergrünland (%)	Dauerkulturen (%)	Ackerland (%)	Anbaufläche[2] 1000 ha	davon: Getreide (%)	Industriepflanzen (%)	Gemüse (%)	Feldfutterpflanzen[3]) (%)
1960	5672,0	18,5	6,1	75,4	3991,1	63,6	13,1	3,6	19,7
1970	6010,1	24,7	6,4	68,9	3631,8	62,5	14,6	4,2	18,7
1980	6184,8	32,5	5,7	61,9	3700,0	60,0	12,1	4,3	23,6
1985	6169,3	33,1	5,2	61,8	3731,5	53,6	12,6	4,6	29,2
1986	6166,9	33,0	5,0	61,9	3747,5	59,6	12,1	4,6	23,7
1987	6165,3	33,1	4,9	62,0	3762,3	55,6	12,0	4,5	27,8

[1]) Bis 1974 Stand 1.1., ab 1975 Stand 1.7. – [2]) Posevna plošt: frühjahrsproduktive Fläche ohne Zwischen- und Zweitkulturen, vernichtete Winter- und Frühjahrssaaten; ab 1973 inkl. Blumen, Umgruppierung von Soja aus Industriepflanzen in Getreide. – [3]) Ohne Getreide.

Quelle: SG., versch. Jahrgänge.

Aufgrund des insgesamt sehr begrenzten Potentials einer Ausweitung der LN liegen die bodenbezogenen Möglichkeiten einer Erhöhung bzw. Stabilisierung der Produktion vor allem in Meliorationsmaßnahmen. Im trockenheitsanfälligen Bulgarien hatten die bewässerten Flächen (i. allg. für Getreide, Futterkulturen, Zuckerrüben, Obst, Gemüse) bereits 1965 ein Fünftel von Ackerland und Dauerkulturen ausgemacht, 1981 waren es zwar 28 %, die bewässerten Flächen aber um 15 300 ha geringer als 1979. Zudem sind viele Anlagen überaltet, in typischen Jahren werden nur 80 % von ihnen überhaupt mit Wasser, oft in zu geringen Mengen, versorgt[4]). Ausbau und

---

[3]) Vgl. DV. (1988) 19, S. 1 ff.; RD. 6.7.1988.
[4]) Cook, E.: Prospects for Bulgarian Agriculture in the 1980's, in: East European Economies: Slow Growth in the 1980's. Vol. 3: Country Studies on Eastern Europe and Yugoslavia. Selected papers submitted to the Joint Economic Committee Congress of the United States (zit. als: Cook). Washington 1986, S. 73.

Modernisierung der Bewässerungsanlagen sollen ab 1990 zu jährlichen Zunahmen der neu bewässerten Flächen um 50 000 ha führen – das mehr als Dreifache der Periode 1981–1985[5]).

Langfristig wurde die *Bodennutzung* deutlich von Ackerland auf Dauergrünland verlagert. Entfielen 1939 noch drei Viertel der LN auf Ackerland, waren es 1987 nur mehr 62%. Die parallele Zunahme bei Dauergrünland, die besonders in den 60er und 70er Jahren stattfand[6]), ließ den Anteil an der LN von einem Fünftel auf ein Drittel ansteigen. Auch die Dauerkulturflächen nahmen langfristig zu, hatten aber 1967 flächen- und anteilsmäßig einen Höhepunkt erreicht, seit 1977 ist ihr Rückgang kontinuierlich (Tabelle 2). Im osteuropäischen Vergleich ist in Bulgarien der Anteil von Dauergrünland (in der Balkanregion spielen extensiv genutzte Gebirgsweiden eine erhebliche Rolle) und Dauerkulturen relativ hoch, jener von Ackerland relativ niedrig.

Innerhalb der Anbauflächen (Tabelle 2) ging langfristig der Anteil von Getreide, besonders von Brotgetreide, erheblich zurück, während besonders Feldfutterpflanzen (ohne Getreide), aber auch Industriepflanzen und Gemüse an Gewicht gewannen. Die mit Abstand bedeutendste Kategorie war 1981–1987 Getreide mit 59% der Anbaufläche, gefolgt von Futterkulturen (vor allem Grün- und Silomais und Rauhfutter auf Ackerland) mit 25%, Industriepflanzen mit 12% und Gemüse (inkl. Kartoffel und Melonen) mit 4,5%. Die beiden letztgenannten Kulturgruppen haben in Bulgarien einen im osteuropäischen Vergleich relativ hohen Anteil.

Eine wesentliche Ursache der aktuellen Probleme in der Pflanzenproduktion, besonders der erhöhten Dürreanfälligkeit, ist die langfristige Verschlechterung des *Bodenzustandes*. Abgesehen von unzureichender hat häufig falsche Bewässerung zu einer Ausschwemmung des Humus und Übersalzung des Bodens geführt, die Umstrukturierung der Tierbestände zugunsten der Schweinehaltung zu einem Mangel an wertvollem Stallmist von Rindern und geringerer Humusbildung. Dies hat auch die Erosionsprobleme verschärft: Etwa 80% des Ackerlandes soll von Wasser-, etwa ein Drittel von Winderosion betroffen sein[7]).

2. Arbeitskräfte und Einkommen

Anzahl und Gewicht der in der Landwirtschaft *Erwerbstätigen* gingen im Zuge der Industrialisierung und Urbanisierung des Landes sowie der Umstrukturierung und Mechanisierung der Landwirtschaft langfristig stark zurück. Der Rückgang der Erwerbstätigen hält, in gebremsten Maße (1981–1987: um jährlich 1,4–3,5%), immer noch an; mit knapp einem Viertel liegt der Anteil der Landwirtschaft an den Erwerbstätigen in der materiellen Sphäre (ein Fünftel von insgesamt) in Bulgarien immer noch relativ hoch. Trotz der ebenfalls relativ hohen Arbeitsintensität (nicht ganz 4 ha

---

[5]) DV. (1987) 99, S. 5.
[6]) Die sprunghafte Zunahme 1975/76 war vermutlich Folge einer Bodenrevision des Jahres 1974, wodurch die Agrarbetriebe gezwungen waren, bisher brachliegendes Land als Dauergrünland in ihr Bodeninventar aufzunehmen.
[7]) Zemědělské noviny. XLIV (1988) 148, S. 7.

Ackerland je Beschäftigten) herrscht saisonal und spartenweise (Rinder, Obst, Gemüse) im sozialistischen Sektor Arbeitskräftemangel[8]).

Die Steigerung der *Arbeitsproduktivität* erlaubte langfristig beträchtliche Produktionszuwächse. Ausschlaggebend dafür waren Konzentration und Spezialisation sowie Mechanisierung der Produktion und steigender Auslastungsgrad der Arbeitskraft[9]). 1981–85 nahm die Arbeitsproduktivität auf Basis der Bruttoproduktion zwar noch um 3,4% p. a. zu, ging aber auf Basis des in der Landwirtschaft produzierten Netto-Materialprodukts, das sich tendenziell weit schwächer entwickelt als die Bruttoproduktion (vgl. III.1.), bereits um 1,3% p.a. zurück. Mit nur 60% des Durchschnitts der materiellen Sphäre hat sich der Niveaurückstand der Landwirtschaft seit 1970 vergrößert[10]). Die Indikatoren der Arbeitsproduktivität beziehen sich sämtlich auf die Zahl der im sozialistischen Sektor voll Erwerbstätigen, nicht auf den tatsächlichen Arbeitseinsatz – unter Berücksichtigung des Auslastungsgrades der Arbeitskraft und der in den Privatwirtschaften und Hilfsbrigaden erbrachten Arbeitsleistung lägen Niveau bzw. Wachstumsraten um einiges niedriger. Überalterung und mangelnde Qualifikation der Arbeitskräfte bilden zunehmend ein Problem.

Während ursprünglich Genossenschaftsbauern die überwiegende Mehrheit der landwirtschaftlichen Arbeitskräfte gebildet hatten, sind es seit den frühen 70er Jahren zunehmend Arbeiter und Angestellte der sozialistischen Agrarbetriebe. Der Rückstand des *Lohnniveaus* (ohne Berücksichtigung des Arbeitseinkommens von Genossenschaftsbauern) in der Landwirtschaft auf den gesamtwirtschaftlichen Durchschnitt hatte sich in der zweiten Hälfte der 70er Jahre auf unter 5% verringert (1971–1975: 12%), erhöhte sich jedoch in den 80er Jahren wieder auf mehr als 8%. Das Haushaltseinkommen pro Kopf lag jedoch bei landwirtschaftlichen Erwerbstätigen 1982–1987 um 2–11% über dem landesweiten Durchschnitt. Ausschlaggebend dafür sind die relativ große Bedeutung – fast ein Drittel – ihres Naturaleinkommens bzw. Einkommens aus den privaten Nebenwirtschaften und die unterdurchschnittliche Haushaltsgröße[11]).

3. Anlagekapital und Investitionen

Ausgehend von dem extrem niedrigen Entwicklungsniveau erforderte die Modernisierung der Landwirtschaft, die sich besonders anfangs auf Agrartechnik-Importe aus der UdSSR stützte, einen erheblichen Kapitalaufwand. Nach einem auch im Rahmen des „großen Sprunges" spektakulären Investitionsstoß 1958/59[12]) verlang-

---

[8]) Vgl. Cook, S. 74, und Economic Survey of Europe in 1987–1988, prepared by the secretariat of the Economic Commission for Europe (Geneva) (zit. als: ECE). New York 1988, S. 209.

[9]) Die versteckte Arbeitslosigkeit vor dem II. Weltkrieg wird auf 1 Mio. geschätzt; vgl.: 35 godini socialističeska Bălgarija (35 Jahre sozialistisches Bulgarien). Hrsg. unter der Leitung von D. Mičev, G. Atanasova, N. Gečev (Zit. als: 35 godini). Sofia 1979, S. 118.

[10]) ECE, S. 209.

[11]) Offizielle Einkommensschätzungen aufgrund von Haushaltserhebungen (SG.). Bis 1980 wurden entsprechende Daten nur für Genossenschaftsbauern veröffentlicht, deren Pro-Kopf-Haushaltseinkommen zuletzt um 17% unter Durchschnitt lag.

[12]) Die Brutto-Anlageinvestitionen in die Landwirtschaft (zu laufenden Preisen) stiegen allein 1959 auf mehr als das Doppelte an.

samte sich das Wachstum der *Agrarinvestitionen* stärker als jenes der gesamten Investitionen in die materielle Sphäre. Ausgehend von einer Kapitalintensität von nur etwa 50 % des Durchschnitts der materiellen Sphäre (1970)[13] schwächte sich das Wachstum der Brutto-Anlageinvestitionen in die Landwirtschaft von rund 6 % p. a. (1971–1975) auf unter 2 % p. a. 1981–1985 (laufende Preise) ab. Während der Agrarsektor 1961–1965 mehr als ein Viertel der Investitionen in die materielle Sphäre erhalten hatte, war es 1981–1987 nur mehr rund ein Zehntel. Sein Anteil am Anlagevermögen des produzierenden Bereichs ging bis 1987 auf 12 % zurück (1965: 24 %)[14]. Die *Kapitalproduktivität* weist langfristig einen rückläufigen Trend auf. Gemessen an der Bruttoproduktion ging sie in den 70er Jahren um 4–5 % p. a. zurück, 1981–1985 um 0,5 p. a., aber gemessen an Nettomaterialprodukt um etwa 5 % p. a. Die Landwirtschaft gehört zu den Sektoren mit niedrigster Kapazitätsauslastung[15].

Trotz des langfristig hohen Wachstums der *Ausstattung* mit Energieressourcen[16] liegt der Stromverbrauch je Beschäftigtem als Indikator für die Ausstattung mit verschiedenen Anlagen im unteren Bereich Osteuropas, die Ausstattung mit Traktor-PS je ha Ackerland, wie in Rumänien und Ungarn, um die Hälfte unter dem Niveau der ČSSR und DDR[17]. Angesichts dessen ist der kontinuierliche Rückgang der physischen Zahl der Traktoren (1987 gegenüber 1977 um fast 20 %) als problematisch zu sehen, obgleich er eine Erneuerung des Maschinenparks in Richtung auf leistungsstärkere und schwerere Traktoren nicht ausschließt; diese beeinträchtigen allerdings durch Bodenverdichtung den Bodenzustand. Die Ausstattung mit Mähdreschern bezogen auf die Getreide-Anbaufläche ist, trotz eines Rückgangs der absoluten Zahl (1987 gegenüber 1977 um 40 %) im RGW-Vergleich besser als bei Traktoren[18].

---

[13] ECE, S. 209.

[14] Seit 1984 nur mehr Angaben zu laufenden Preisen, seit 1981 statistische Umgruppierung von Arbeits- und Nutztieren aus Anlagemitteln (Investitionen und Kapital) in Umlaufmittel, über die keine Daten veröffentlicht werden. Unter der Annahme, daß 1981–1985, einer Periode schwacher Tierbestandsentwicklung, der Anteil der Investitionen in die „Grundherden" (1976–1980: 30 %) zurückging, liegt die Zunahme der Investitionen inkl. Tiere unter der errechneten Zunahme exkl. Tiere (2 % p. a. zu laufenden Preisen). Durch die Umgruppierung sind die angeführten Anteile für 1981–1985 nach unten verzerrt.

[15] Vgl. RD. 19.6.1985; Ikonomičeski život. XX (1985) 31, S. 1 ff.

[16] 1981–1985 nahm der Stromverbrauch der Landwirtschaft gegenüber dem Vorjahrfünft um nur 2 % p. a. zu, die akute Energiekrise 1985 bedeutete für die Landwirtschaft eine weit überdurchschnittliche Abnahme des Stromverbrauchs um 8,4 %.

[17] ECE, S. 209.

[18] Ebenda.

III. Produktionsergebnisse

1. Wachstum und Struktur

Die Landwirtschaftsproduktion nahm nach dem II. Weltkrieg zunächst mit beträchtlichen Wachstumsraten zu. Die offiziellen bulgarischen Angaben über die Bruttoproduktion (einschließlich Vorleistungen bzw. Produktionskosten und Doppelzählungen von Futter, Saatgut u. a.) zu vergleichbaren Preisen zeigen nach einer letzten Wachstumsbeschleunigung 1966–1970 für die 70er Jahre eine deutliche Abschwächung auf rd. 2 % p. a., 1981–1985 betrug die Zunahme der Agrarproduktion nur mehr 1,2 % p. a. Somit hat sich die Korrelation mit den Fünfjahresplänen, die Wachstumsraten zwischen 3,2 und 3,7 % p. a. vorgesehen hatten, drastisch verschlechtert. Die Produktionsausfälle der Jahre 1983 und 1985 wurden zwar in den jeweils folgenden Jahren fast kompensiert, durch die Rückgänge von 1987 und 1988 lag das Produktionsniveau 1988 um mehr 8 % unter dem bislang besten des Jahres 1982 (Tabelle 3)[19]. Somit ist auch das Produktionsziel des laufenden Fünfjahresplans außer Reichweite gerückt. Das in der Landwirtschaft produzierte Nettomaterialprodukt wuchs i. d. R. langsamer bzw. ging stärker zurück als die Bruttoproduktion[20]; dies weist tendenziell auf einen steigenden Anteil von Vorleistungen (und Abschreibungen) hin. Das Wachstum der materiellen Inputs war in Bulgarien seit 1970 rascher als in jedem anderen osteuropäischen Land[21]. Wenn auch Ausdruck eines Nachholbedarfs, ist dies gleichzeitig ein Indikator für die zu hohe Materialintensität, schlechte Futterverwertung und andere Ineffizienzerscheinungen, die die Rentabilität der Landwirtschaftsproduktion zusätzlich zu der Entwicklung der relativen Preise von Inputs und Output beeinträchtigen.

Ausschlaggebend für das langfristige Entwicklungsmuster der Agrarproduktion sind zunehmende Probleme in der Pflanzenproduktion, denen zunächst noch relativ hohe Zuwächse der Tierproduktion gegenüberstanden. Das Wachstum der Pflanzenproduktion ging in den 70er Jahren jahrfünftweise spürbar zurück und näherte sich 1981–1985 mit 0,2 % p. a. der Stagnation (Tabelle 3). Wiederholte und teils schwere Mißernten schlugen sich in erheblichen jährlichen Schwankungen der Agrarproduktion nieder und bildeten in den letzten Jahren einen gesamtwirtschaftlich zunehmend destabilisierenden Faktor.

Langfristig nahm die *Tierproduktion* wesentlich rascher und weniger ungleichmäßig zu als die Pflanzenproduktion, eine deutliche Wachstumsverlangsamung trat erst 1981–1985 (2,4 % p. a.) ein, als sich die verschlechterte Futterbasis verstärkt bemerkbar machte. Der Beitrag der Tierproduktion zur Bruttoproduktion stieg von etwas mehr als einem Drittel in der ersten Hälfte der 50er Jahre auf mehr als die Hälfte, wäre

---

[19]) Möglicherweise stehen die Landwirtschaftsprobleme der letzten Jahre auch mit dem Minderheitenproblem der Türken in Zusammenhang (vgl. dazu auch die Kapitel von Troebst, S.: Nationale Minderheiten und Whitaker, R.: Social Structure), was sich aber kaum nachweisen läßt.
[20]) In schlechten Landwirtschaftsperioden steigen typischerweise die Vorleistungen, vor allem die teureren Kraftfutterkäufe (Rauhfutterkäufe kommen kaum in Frage) aus den zentralen Fonds, ungewöhnlich stark, um drohende Ausfälle in der Tierproduktion in Grenzen zu halten.
[21]) Vgl. ECE, S. 209.

Tabelle 3: Wachstum und Struktur der Agrarproduktion[1]). 1966–1988 (jahresdurchschnittliche Veränderung in %)

	Netto-material-produkt	Bruttoproduktion			Struktur der Bruttoproduktion	
		insgesamt	Pflanzen-prod.	Tier-prod.	Pflanzen-prod.	Tier-prod.
1966–1970[2])		4,8	4,8	4,8	65,5	34,5
1971–1975[2])		2,2	1,3	3,8	58,7	41,3
1976–1980[2])		2,1	0,7	4,0	54,7	45,3
1981–1985[2])	− 3,4	1,2	0,2	2,4	46,9	53,1
1985	− 20,6	− 12,3	− 22,5	− 2,9	42,2	57,8
1986	22,4	11,7	22,7	3,7	46,3	53,7
1987	− 14,6	− 5,1	− 8,8	− 1,9	44,5	55,5
1988		− 0,7	− 1,7	0,1	44,1[3])	55,9[3])

[1]) Vergleichbare Preise: 1966–1970 Preisbasis 1962, 1971–1980 Preisbasis 1971, 1981–1987 Preisbasis 1982. − [2]) Veränderung gegenüber Vorjahrfünft bzw. Anteil als Periodendurchschnitt. − [3]) Errechnet

Quelle: SG., versch. Jahrgänge; RD. 23.2.1989.

aber ohne die wiederholten Rückschläge in der Pflanzenproduktion in dieser Periode auf einem geringeren Niveau (Tabelle 3)[22]). Generell beruht der im internationalen Vergleich relativ hohe Anteil der Pflanzenproduktion auf der vergleichsweise großen Bedeutung intensiver Bodennutzungsformen (Obst, Gemüse, Industriepflanzen) und, wie in den übrigen RGW-Ländern, vermutlich auf einer Verzerrung durch die Doppelzählung von Futter[23]).

Die *Produktionsstruktur in regionaler Sicht* läßt sich, ausgehend von den natürlichen Anbaubedingungen in folgende grobe Zonen gliedern: Im Norden (Varna, Razgrad, ein Teil von Loveč, Michajlovgrad) liegen in West-Ost-Richtung Ebene und Hügelland entlang der Donau mit dem Balkangebirge als südlicher Begrenzung. In gemäßigt kontinentalem Klima überwiegen hier Schwarzerdeböden mit Getreideanbau (Weizen, Mais), Sonnenblumen, Rüben, Gemüse und Wein sowie Tierhaltung (Schweine, Geflügel). Südlich des Balkanmassivs (Weidewirtschaft) schließt die Berg- und Becken-Übergangszone an, gefolgt vom Osogovo-Rhodopen-Massiv. In diesen beiden Zonen herrscht gemäßigt kontinentales, übergangskontinentales sowie übergangsmediterranes Klima. Im vorwiegend gebirgigen Westen (Region Sofia) sind von besonderer Bedeutung Tierhaltung (Milchwirtschaft, Schafzucht), Kartoffelbau, Gemüse- und Obstproduktion, sowie teils Tabakanbau. Im mittleren Teil (Plovdiv, Chaskovo) dominieren Tabak-, Gemüse- und Weinbau, angebaut werden auch Reis,

---

[22]) Langfristig dürfte das Gewicht der Tierproduktion durch inadäquate Preisbereinigung (überdurchschnittliche Zunahme der Preise für die Tierproduktion) statistisch nach oben verzerrt sein.

[23]) Vgl. dazu Wädekin, K.-E.: Sozialistische Agrarpolitik in Osteuropa. II: Entwicklung und Probleme 1960–1976 (Giessener Abhandlungen zur Agrar- und Wirtschaftsforschung des europäischen Ostens (im folgenden: Giessener Abhandlungen 67) (zit. als: Wädekin II). Berlin 1978, S. 95f.

Baumwolle und ätherische Pflanzen, während die Viehzucht (Milchrinder, Schafe) vorwiegend auf das Bergland beschränkt ist. Im Osten (Burgas, einschließlich Schwarzmeerküste) spielen neben Wein Getreide und Tierzucht (Schafe, Schweine, Geflügel) eine größere Rolle[24]).

2. Pflanzenproduktion

Neben Konzentration und Spezialisierung, zeitweisen Zunahmen der Anbauflächen, Bewässerung und moderneren Produktionstechnologien wurde die langfristige Steigerung der Pflanzenproduktion von der Anwendung ertragreicheren Sortensaatguts und steigender Mengen an Pflanzenschutzmitteln und Mineraldünger gestützt. Die Lieferungen von Mineraldünger liegen mit 195 kg/ha Ackerland (1987) insgesamt auf einem soliden Niveau, hinter dem bereichsweise umweltschädigende Überdüngung steht; die Versorgung mit – vor allem aus dem Westen importierten – Pflanzenschutzmitteln ist schmäler.

In den 80er Jahren erhöhten sich die jährlichen Schwankungen der Pflanzenproduktion: War 1982 das bislang erfolgreichste Jahr, kamen die Mißernten in Häufung (1980, 1983, 1985, 1987, 1988) und Ausmaß (besonders 1985) jenen der 50er Jahre nahe. 1988 lag das Produktionsniveau um ein Zehntel unter jenem von 1982. Das generell zur Trockenheit neigende Klima war durch extreme Dürreperioden und teils durch Fröste gekennzeichnet. Jedoch liegen die Gründe dafür, daß die Auswirkungen ungünstiger klimatischer Gegebenheiten nicht zu einem größeren Teil aufgefangen werden konnten, in der erhöhten Dürreanfälligkeit des Bodens (s. o.), in einem niedrigen Anteil des relativ trockenresistenten Mais am Ackerland (1981–1985: 15% gegenüber etwa einem Drittel bzw. einem Viertel in Rumänien und Ungarn) sowie in der mangelnden Flexibilität des überzentralisierten Planungs- und Leitungssystems.

Die *Getreideproduktion* ist mit einem (wertmäßigen) Anteil von fast einem Drittel (Durchschnitt 1981–1987: 31%) und als agrarpolitische Priorität immer noch der wichtigste Sektor der Pflanzenproduktion. Langfristig beruhen die Produktionszunahmen, bei rückläufiger Anbaufläche, auf stark steigenden Hektarerträgen[25]). Diese erreichten 1981–1985 bei Mais mit 4,8 t westlichen Standard, lagen aber bei Weizen (3,8 t) und Gerste (3,6 t) darunter[26]). 1981–1985 nahm die Getreideproduktion um nur 0,6% p. a. zu – der Rekordernte im Jahr 1982 (10,2 Mio. t) stand ein Mißernte-Rekord im Jahr 1985 (5,5 Mio. t) gegenüber. 1986–1988 lag die Getreideernte mit im Schnitt 8 Mio. t nicht nur um ein Fünftel unter dem Planziel für 1986–1990, sondern auch um 4% unter dem Niveau von 1981–1985. Im Gegensatz zu den 70er Jahren

---

[24]) Vgl. Pospelowa, G.; Fließ, H.: Schlachttier- und Fleischproduktion in Osteuropa: Bulgarien (Giessener Abhandlungen 112). Berlin 1981, S. 15 ff.; Wirtschaftsnachrichten aus Bulgarien. 27 (1987) 11, S. 1, 3. Die zur Orientierung in Klammern angeführten Städte sind die Hauptstädte der im August 1987 geschaffenen neun Regionen (oblasti) ohne Sofia-Stadt. Vgl. dazu auch das Kapitel O. Luchterhandt: Regierungssystem.
[25]) Eine Ausnahme war die Periode 1976–1980, als die Getreideanbauflächen ausgedehnt wurden, aber die Erträge besonders von Mais und Gerste nur schwach zunahmen (1,5% und 2,3%).
[26]) ECE, S. 209.

nahmen bis 1987 Anbaufläche und Produktion von Weizen bei relativ schwacher Entwicklung der Hektarerträge überdurchschnittlich zu; auf ihn entfiel nun wieder mehr als die Hälfte der Getreideproduktion. Gleichzeitig gingen nun die Anbauflächen von Mais und Gerste zurück, was bei Mais im Zusammenhang mit dem anhaltenden Mangel an hochwertigem Saatgut, speziellen Pflanzenschutzmitteln und spezieller Agrartechnik steht. Bei Mais war der Flächenrückgang 1981–1985 noch durch erhebliche Steigerungen der Hektarerträge ausgeglichen worden (die Produktion stagnierte), 1986 und 1987 gingen auch diese zurück; die durchschnittliche Produktion lag 1986–1988 um ein Füftel unter dem Zeitraum 1981–1985. Die Produktion von Gerste war trotz steigender Hektarerträge bereits in der ersten Hälfte der 80er Jahre stark rückläufig, blieb aber 1986–1988 im Schnitt fast unverändert (Tabelle 4).

Auf *Industriepflanzen* entfiel 1981–1987 wertmäßig fast ein Viertel der Pflanzenproduktion. Die Produktion von Zuckerrüben steckt schon seit den frühen 70er Jahren in einer Krise, die, ähnlich wie bei Mais, auch auf einem Mangel an speziellem Saatgut (Monogerm) und spezieller Agrartechnik beruht. Die Hektarerträge, die sehr sensibel auf eine Verschlechterung der Bodenqualität reagieren, sind seit der ersten Hälfte der 70er Jahre rückläufig und gingen in den 80er Jahren, ebenso wie die Produktion, besonders stark zurück. Auf der Tabakanbaufläche wird zu 84% (1981–1987) Orienttabak kultiviert; hier setzten sich die langfristigen Rückgänge von Produktion und Anbaufläche bis 1987 fort. Bei Sonnenblumen wurden 1981–1985 Anbau und Produktion, nach Rückgängen in den 70er Jahren, wieder stärker betrieben; es folgten jedoch 1987 und besonders 1988 erhebliche Produktionsausfälle (Tabelle 4).

Auf den traditionsreichen Anbau von Gemüse und Obst entfiel 1981–1987 jeweils etwa ein Sechstel der Pflanzenproduktion. Die Wachstumsraten der *Gemüseproduk-*

Tabelle 4: Pflanzenproduktion 1971–1988

	1971–1975[1])		1976–1980[1])		1981–1985[1])		1985		1986		1987		1988
	P[2])	E[3])	P[2])	E[3])	P[2])	E[3])	P[2])	E[3])	P[2])	E[3])	P[2])	E[3])	P[2])
Getreide	7494,8	3,3	8088,4	3,5	8357,2	3,8	5491,7	2,7	8629,3	3,9	7395,0	3,5	7965,
davon: Weizen	3192,9	3,4	3512,5	3,7	4173,4	3,9	3067,5	2,9	4326,6	3,8	4148,6	3,8	4712,
Mais	2505,3	4,0	2651,8	4,0	2655,5	4,8	1350,4	3,1	2848,1	5,0	1857,6	3,7	1625,
Zuckerrüben	1711,1	29,3	1827,3	29,0	1084,5	22,5	823,9	16,8	869,5	20,3	736,5	18,8	676,
Sonnenblumen	439,6	1,7	391,9	1,7	449,7	1,7	364,7	1,4	488,7	1,9	410,3	1,5	367,
Orienttabak	126,0	1,2	118,8	1,2	109,0	1,2	101,5	1,2	106,7	1,2	108,5	1,4	91,
Gemüse[4])	1681,6		1740,6		1624,9		1505,7		1488,5		1599,6		
davon: Tomaten[5])	782,6	28,1	830,9	25,9	821,5	26,7	781,0	24,6	760,3	23,7	827,5	26,5	808,
Obst	2125,7		1963,3		2100,7		1821,5		2001,7		1775,4		
davon: Trauben	1053,3	5,5	1027,4	5,8	1079,6	6,6	905,4		923,6		942,6		928,
Grün- und Silomais	4071,8	13,2	4865,8	16,0	5746,1	15,1	5544,3	10,3	6227,3	19,9	6079,4	14,3	
Luzerne[6])	1570,6	5,6	1880,6	6,3	1837,5	5,7	1548,5	4,7	2122,9	6,1	1952,6	5,4	

[1]) Durchschnitt. – [2]) Produktion in 1000 Tonnen. – [3]) Ertrag in Tonnen je Hektar. – [4]) Inkl. Glashausproduktion [5]) Ertrag nur von Feldtomaten. – [6]) Umgerechnet in Heueinheiten, Ertrag nur von Altkulturen.

Quelle: SG. versch. Jahrgänge; RD. 23.2.1989.

tion (ohne Kartoffeln, Melonen) schwächten sich von Jahrfünft zu Jahrfünft deutlich ab, 1981–1985 ging die Produktion um 1,4 % p. a. zurück (Tabelle 4). Die nun nicht mehr zunehmende Anbaufläche läßt auf eine gleichfalls schwache Entwicklung der Produktivität schließen, die sich 1986/87 noch verschlechtert haben muß – auch eine Erweiterung der Anbaufläche konnte einen spürbaren Produktionsrückgang nicht verhindern. Von besonderer Bedeutung in Produktion und Export sind Tomaten und grüne Paprika, wo allerdings Produktionssteigerungen seit der zweiten Hälfte der 60er bzw. 70er Jahre nur durch vergrößerte Anbauflächen erreicht werden konnten. In den 80er Jahren nahm die Produktion bei beiden ab, bei Paprika vor allem wegen des weiter ständig sinkenden Hektarertrags, bei Tomaten zunächst wegen der Reduktion der Anbaufläche, später ebenfalls wegen Ertragsproblemen.

Bei *Obst* (inkl. Trauben) war das hohe Produktionswachstum der 60er Jahre stark von einer Flächenzunahme mitgetragen worden; in den 70er Jahren ging die Produktion stärker zurück als die Fläche, was auf sinkende Produktivität hinweist. Nach einer mäßigen Erholung 1981–1985 (+ 1,4 % p. a.) fiel die Obstproduktion 1986/87 im Schnitt um 10 % hinter 1981–1985 zurück. Bei stets abnehmender Anbaufläche muß die Produktivität in der ersten Hälfte der 80er Jahre kräftig zugenommen haben, danach aber gesunken sein (Tabelle 4). Von den bepflanzten Dauerkulturflächen entfiel 1981–1987 (Durchschnitt 291 000 ha) mehr als die Hälfte (56,5 %) auf Weingärten, 42 % auf Obstgärten und 1,3 % auf Beerenkulturen. Im Weinbau sind die fruchttragenden Weingartenflächen, vor allem bei den arbeitsintensiveren, daher oft privat kultivierten Tafeltrauben, seit der ersten Hälfte der 70er Jahre rückläufig. Die seit der zweiten Hälfte der 70er Jahre wieder steigenden Hektarerträge schlugen sich erst 1981–1985 in einer Produktionszunahme nieder, der jedoch schon 1986–1988 hohe Ausfälle folgten. In der Obstproduktion i. e. S. haben traditionell Äpfel und Pflaumen (1981–1987: 24 % bzw. 16 % der Obstgartenfläche) das größte Gewicht, langfristig überdurchschnittlich zugenommen haben Nüsse (14 %) und Kirschen (9 %). Der zunehmende Anteil der fruchttragenden an den gesamten Obstbauflächen illustriert die Umstrukturierung von Hochstämmen mit stark wachsenden Unterlagen zugunsten von (niedrigeren) Stämmen mit mittel- und schwachwachsenden Unterlagen, deren Jugendphase nur zwei bis vier Jahre dauert. Dies entspricht dem weltweiten Trend in Richtung auf intensivere Kulturen, und gilt in Bulgarien besonders für Äpfel, aber auch für Pflaumen, Pfirsiche und Aprikosen.

Bei den *Feldfutterpflanzen* ohne Getreide (1981–1987: 8 % der Pflanzenproduktion) nahmen Produktion und Flächen langfristig kräftig zu. Die Erweiterung der Anbauflächen bei den Hauptkulturen Luzerne und Grün- und Silomais, wo sie in witterungsbedingtem Zusammenhang mit der Abnahme bei Körnermais steht, hielt in den 80er Jahren an. Dies führte 1981–1985, bei erstmals leicht sinkenden Hektarerträgen, nur bei Grün- und Silomais zu Produktionssteigerungen (Tabelle 4). Nach den bei beiden Kulturen guten Produktionsergebnissen der Jahre 1986/87 dürfte die Rauhfutterproduktion 1988 einen schweren Einbruch erlitten haben.

3. Tierproduktion

In der Tierwirtschaft war der Übergang zu industrieller Haltung (die teils mit der fleischverarbeitenden Industrie integriert ist) besonders spürbar, die Produktionssteigerungen waren wesentlich bedingt durch die Vergrößerung der Futterbasis, die Verbesserung der Tierzüchtung und der veterinärmedizinischen Versorgung. Während der relativ hohe Anteil von Dauergrünland in Bulgarien eine günstige Voraussetzung für die Rinder- und Schafhaltung und die Milchwirtschaft ist, lieferte die relativ rasche Entwicklung der Getreideproduktion in den 70er Jahren die Basis für eine Ausweitung der Geflügel- und Schweinehaltung. Wie bereits angeführt, litt die Tierproduktion in den 80er Jahren merklich unter den Problemen in der Pflanzenproduktion; sie erlitt in zwei Jahren (1985 und 1987) Rückgänge und lag 1988 auf dem Niveau von 1983.

1986 wurden 773 100 t *Fleisch* ohne sog. Subprodukte (Innereien und Nebenprodukte der industriellen Fleischverarbeitung) erzeugt – dies bedeutet gegenüber 1970 eine Zunahme um 86 %, gegenüber 1980 um 13 %. In der Struktur der Fleischproduktion hatte die Schweinezucht immer schon das höchste Gewicht. Durch weit überdurchschnittliche Zunahmen bei Geflügel in der zweiten Hälfte der 60er Jahre, der Periode des Aufbaus moderner Großbetriebe für dessen Haltung, erhöhte sich sein Anteil an der Fleischproduktion bis 1970 auf 22 %, jener bei Schwein ging auf 35,5 % (1960: 14 % bzw. 52 %) zurück. Während seither der Anteil von Geflügel mit etwas mehr als einem Fünftel (1987: 22 %) stabil blieb, hat er sich beim Schwein (auf Kosten von Rind, Schaf und Ziege) wieder auf fast die Hälfte (1987: 48 %) erhöht. Das Gewicht von Schwein und Geflügel an der Fleischproduktion liegt mit etwa zwei Drittel (ebenso wie in Rumänien) niedriger als im übrigen Osteuropa[27]. Hatten besonders Rind, aber auch Schaf und Ziege in den 60er Jahren noch an Anteil an der Fleischproduktion gewonnen und 1970 jeweils rund ein Fünftel ausgemacht, ist ihr Gewicht seither deutlich zurückgegangen (1987: 17 % bzw. 13 %, Tabelle 5).

Tabelle 5: Tierproduktion 1971–1987

Jahr	Fleisch[1])	darunter (in 1000 Tonnen):				Milch Mio. l	Hühnereier Mio. Stück	Wolle Tonnen
		Rind	Schwein	Schafe u. Ziegen	Geflügel			
1971–1975[2])	502	95	201	86	117	1 676	1 721	32 091
1976–1980[2])	653	116	299	83	149	1 973	2 128	34 469
1981–1985[2])	722	132	331	99	157	2 401	2 577	35 138
1985	737	136	334	106	158	2 462	2 742	33 751
1986	775	133	372	102	167	2 523	2 820	33 163
1987	773	133	372	98	169	2 513	2 829	31 550

[1]) Ohne Subprodukte. – [2]) Durchschnitt.
Quelle: SG., versch. Jahrgänge.

---

[27]) Vgl. ebenda, S. 208.

Die Strukturverschiebungen in der Fleischproduktion beruhen vor allem auf unterschiedlichem Wachstumstempo der *Tierbestände*. Diese hatten sich nach einer zögernden Entwicklung in den 60er Jahren (mit Ausnahme von Geflügel) in den 70er Jahren rasch erhöht – am raschesten beim Schwein, gefolgt von Geflügel und Rind, wo die Rückgänge der 60er Jahre wieder mehr als wettgemacht wurden. Die Bestände an Schafen nahmen vergleichsweise langsam zu, jene an Ziegen holten 1976–1980 wieder auf. In den 80er Jahren entwickelten sich die Tierbestände schwach (Tabelle 6). Die geplante Umstrukturierung zugunsten von Rindern und Schafen, um Bedarf und Import von Futterkonzentraten für Schweine und Geflügel zu senken[28]), wurde verfehlt. Die Bestandszahlen von Rindern (ohne Büffel) sind seit einschließlich 1982 von Jahr zu Jahr rückläufig und lagen Ende 1988 um ein Zehntel unter dem Stand von 1980; der entsprechende Rückstand bei Kühen, deren Anzahl sich 1988 immerhin stabilisierte, betrug 8%, bei Schafen (Abnahmen seit 1984) sogar 18%. Diese Entwicklung ist entscheidend durch die schlechte Rauhfutterversorgung bestimmt. Spürbar über dem Niveau von 1980 lagen 1988 (nach Rückgängen 1982–1984) nur die Bestände an Schweinen (fast 9%), etwa auf gleichem Niveau jene an Geflügel.

Tabelle 6: Tierbestände[1]) 1971–1988 1000 Stück

	Rinder[2])	davon Kühe[2])	Schweine	Schafe	Ziegen	Geflügel
1971–1975[3])	1497	631	3030	9924	305	35796
1976–1980[3])	1761	704	3653	10188	382	40703
1981–1985[3])	1765	692	3814	10538	486	41600
1985	1706	670	3912	9724	460	39227
1986	1678	653	4050	9563	441	39735
1987	1649	646	4034	8886	428	41424
1988	1615	648	4134	8593		41810

[1]) Zum Jahresende. – [2]) Ohne Büffel. – [3]) Durchschnitt.
Quelle: SG., versch. Jahrgänge; RD. 23.2.1989.

1981–1985 betrugen die jahresdurchschnittlichen Produktionszunahmen gegenüber 1976–1980 bei Fleisch 2,1%, bei *Milch und Eiern* 4%. Wesentlich schwächer war die Entwicklung in den Jahren 1987 und 1988. Das – abgeschwächte – Produktionswachstum beruhte vor allem auf Zuwächsen in der Tierleistung. Bulgarien liegt hinsichtlich der Milchleistung je Kuh (1987: 3449 l), einem guten Indikator für das Entwicklungsniveau der Landwirtschaft, seit den frühen 70er Jahren unverändert im RGW-Mittelfeld. Bis 1987 gewährleistete die relativ hohe Leistungssteigerung trotz rückläufiger Bestände steigende Produktionsmengen von Kuhmilch (Anteil an der gesamten Milchproduktion 1987: 84%); die Abnahme der Milchleistung im Jahre 1988 ist für die schlechte Rauhfutterversorgung symptomatisch.

---

[28]) Cook, S. 78.

Die schleppende Entwicklung der Tierbestände, die zudem durch zusätzliche Futterimporte (vgl. VI) gestützt werden mußte, steht im Widerspruch zu den Zielen der bulgarischen Agrarpolitik. Strukturelle Gründe sind das ungelöste *Futterproblem*, eine offenbar relativ hohe Mortalität bei Jungtieren und verhältnismäßig geringe Reproduktionsraten[29]). Der Kern des Futterproblems ist die schlechte Futterverwertung, die sich seit 1970 nur bescheiden verbessert haben dürfte[30]). Sie steht wesentlich mit dem zu geringen Eiweißgehalt des Futters (aber auch teils mit schlechten Haltungsbedingungen und Tierzüchtung) in Zusammenhang[31]). Diese Mangelerscheinungen und die inadäquate Mischfutterindustrie machen Importe von Futtereiweiß aus den westlichen Industrieländern erforderlich, die die Hartwährungsposition belasten.

IV. Privatwirtschaften

Private Haupterwerbsbauern mit privatem Grundeigentum spielen in Bulgarien seit Anfang der 60er Jahre so gut wie keine Rolle mehr – der „private" Sektor besteht überwiegend aus kleinen und kleinsten *Nebenerwerbswirtschaften* vor allem landwirtschaftlicher Erwerbstätiger und Rentner. Sie werden auf Familienbasis (die Anstellung bezahlter Arbeitskraft wurde generell verboten) und auf Grundlage eines permanenten Nutzungsrechtes an Parzellen (i. d. R. bis zu 0,5 ha) geführt, die aber im sozialistischen Eigentum bleiben. Die ideologisch problematische Existenz eines solchen Sektors wurde unter den gegebenen Bedingungen als ökonomische Notwendigkeit betrachtet: Die Privatwirtschaften haben für den sozialistischen Sektor eine wichtige Entlastungsfunktion, ihre Spezialisierung liegt, bei einem ausnehmend geringen Mechanisierungsgrad, in den Bereichen Tierwirtschaft und arbeitsintensive Pflanzenkulturen. Als Ergebnis einer 1977/78 einsetzenden Lockerung gegenüber der privaten Landwirtschaft stieg ihr *Beitrag zur gesamten Agrarproduktion* von etwa 25% Anfang der 80er Jahre auf etwa 30% Mitte der 80er Jahre[32]).

Auf den privaten Sektor entfallen 10% der LN des Landes – die auf den ersten Blick beeindruckende Bodenproduktivität beruht wesentlich auf Futterlieferungen von den Agrarbetrieben, die in der privaten Tierproduktion veredelt werden, und dem relativ hohen Anteil teurerer Pflanzenprodukte (Obst, Trauben, Gemüse, Tabak). Von den Tierbeständen werden bei der Ziege 99%, beim Schaf und bei Geflügel etwa ein Drittel, bei Rindern etwas mehr, bei Schweinen etwas weniger als ein Fünftel privat gehalten. 1987 erzeugten die Privatproduzenten von den gesamten *Produktionsmengen* bei Fleisch 41%, bei Eiern 50%, bei Milch 25% sowie bei Obst und

---

[29]) Vgl. ebenda, S. 78.
[30]) Vgl. ECE, S. 209; der spezifische Futterverbrauch kann für die Produktion von 1 kg Fleisch auf 6–8 Getreideeinheiten geschätzt werden, vgl. Lukas, Z.: Animal Production in Socialist Countries 1970–1985, Wiener Institut für Internationale Wirtschaftsvergleiche, Forschungsbericht Nr. 137 (zit. als: Lukas). Wien 1988, S. 4.
[31]) Vgl. Wädekin II, S. 88 und 95f. und Lukas, S. 4.
[32]) Vgl. Grosser, I.: Private Landwirtschaft in Bulgarien (Giessener Abhandlungen 154) (zit. als: Grosser). Berlin 1988, S. 62.

Gemüse 44 % bzw. 31 %. Bereits etwa 40 % der privaten Produktion werden an den sozialistischen Sektor oder auf den Genossenschaftsmärkten verkauft.

Vom Staat besonders gefördert werden Privatwirtschaften, die sich vertraglich an einen sozialistischen Agrarbetrieb binden, und Grenzformen, wo von einzelnen Familien oder Personen im Auftrag des Betriebes nur mehr einzelne Produktionsphasen ausgeführt werden, z. B. Viehmast oder Viehaufzucht oder nicht-mechanisierte Arbeiten im Obst-, Gemüse- oder Tabakbau (sog. Individual-Akkord oder Familien-Akkord)[33]). Für die Zukunft ist eine spürbare Liberalisierung des privaten Sektors zu erwarten (vgl. IX).

V. Nahrungsmittelverbrauch

Der tägliche Pro-Kopf-Kalorienverbrauch ist mit 3 634 cal. (1983–86) gewährleistet, hat damit aber gegenüber 1979–1981 stagniert. Auch in Bulgarien hat in der Ernährungsstruktur (Kohlehydrate vs. Eiweiß) eine Substitution von Mehl und -produkten durch eiweißhaltige Produkte (Fleisch, Milch, Eier) stattgefunden. Jedoch wird der Eiweißverbrauch in Bulgarien immer noch zu einem weit geringeren Teil (46 %) aus tierischen Produkten gedeckt als im europäischen Schnitt (58 %). Die strukturelle Deckung des Eiweißverbrauchs tierischen Ursprungs hat sich 1970–1987, mit Ausnahme von Eiern, deren Pro-Kopf-Verbrauch sich mehr als verdoppelte (1987: 263 Stück), nicht wesentlich verändert. Bei Fleisch liegt Bulgarien im RGW-Mittelfeld, 1987 war mit 78 kg allerdings ein Rückgang um 1 % zu verzeichnen, der Verbrauch an Milch und Milchprodukten (1987: 278 kg pro Kopf umgerechnet auf Frischmilch) ist als zufriedenstellend zu betrachten. Der Pro-Kopf-Verbrauch ist bei Obst (1987: 114 kg), wo er trotz einer Erholung in den 80er Jahren seit 1970 um ein Viertel zurückgegangen ist, und bei Gemüse (1987: 147 kg) im RGW-Rahmen relativ hoch[34]). Hinter diesen auf offizieller Statistik beruhenden Angaben steht allerdings eine Verschlechterung der Versorgung auch mit einigen Grundnahrungsmitteln in den letzten Jahren – ausdrücklich genannt wurden u. a. verschiedene Arten von Fleisch und Fleischprodukten, Milchprodukte, Bohnen, Kartoffel, Obst, Gemüse, Knoblauch und Pflanzenfette und -öle[35]).

VI. Agraraußenhandel

Infolge der enttäuschenden Ergebnisse der Landwirtschaftsproduktion hat der positive Beitrag des Agrarsektors zur *Handelsbilanz* in den letzten Jahren abgenommen[36]). Zu laufenden Preisen verschlechterte sich die Export-Import-Relation im

---

[33]) Ebenda, S. 47–50.
[34]) Die angeführten Angaben beruhen bei Kalorien auf FAO Production Yearbook 1987 (vol. 41). Rom 1988, S. 246, 248; bei Pro-Kopf-Verbrauch (mit Ausnahme von Obst: SG) auf Statističeskij ežegodnik stran-členov soveta ekonomičeskoj vzaimopomošči. Moskau 1988, S. 84f.
[35]) Vgl. RD. 30.1.1987; 27.1.1988; 23.7.1988.
[36]) Vgl. dazu auch das Kapitel von Schönfeld, R.: Außenwirtschaft.

Tabelle 7: Außenhandel mit Waren agrarischen Ursprungs[1]) 1970–1987 Mio. Valuta-Leva

	1970	1980	1981	1982	1983	1984	1985	1986	1987
Exporte	1 018	2 172	2 253	2 491	2 582	2 902	2 557	2 277	2 235
Importe	342	808	1 016	905	1 041	1 084	1 361	1 227	1 207
Saldo	+ 676	+1 364	+1 237	+1 586	+1 541	+1 818	+1 196	+1 050	+1 028

[1]) Warengruppen 5 bis 8: Rohstoffe und Zwischenprodukte aus Land- und Forstwirtschaft für Nicht-Nahrungsmittel; Lebendvieh; Rohstoffe für Nahrungs- und Genußmittel; Lebensmittel.

Quelle: SG., versch. Jahrgänge.

Agrarhandel von 270% (1980) auf 185% (1987) (1970: 300%), der Rekordüberschuß im Agrarhandel des Jahres 1984 verringerte sich bis 1987 um fast die Hälfte, um sich 1987 zu stabilisieren (Tabelle 7). Seit 1985 mußte Bulgarien wieder Nettoimporte an Getreide (vorwiegend Futtergetreide) tätigen, die 1985 und 1986 eine nie dagewesene Größenordnung von 1 Mio. t erreichten, die Importe von Ölkuchen und Futtermehl stiegen allein 1985–1987 auf insg. 1,4 Mio. t[37]). Beide Warengruppen müssen aus dem Hartwährungsbereich bezogen werden.

In den bulgarischen Agrarexporten dominiert mit einem Anteil von rund drei Vierteln die *Warengruppe* Lebens- und Genußmittel, die den mit Abstand höchsten und als einzige der vier Untergruppen bis heute bestehenden Überschuß bringt (Konserven, Wein, Fleisch, Fisch, Milchprodukte, frisches Obst und Gemüse, Tabakerzeugnisse u.a.). An zweiter Stelle folgen Exporte von Rohstoffen für die Produktion von Nahrungs- und Genußmitteln (inkl. Tabak), denen seit 1985 höhere Importe (inkl. Getreide) gegenüberstehen. Bei anderen Rohstoffen und Zwischenprodukten aus Land- und Forstwirtschaft für die Produktion von Nicht-Nahrungsmitteln (inkl. Futterkonzentrate und -zusätze im Import, ätherische Öle im Export) fällt traditionell ein Handelsbilanzdefizit an. Von quantitativ untergeordneter Bedeutung ist der Handel mit Lebendvieh.

Regional gesehen nahm der RGW-Raum als Nettoimporteur von Agrarprodukten 80% der entsprechenden Exporte Bulgariens auf, lieferte aber nur 48% der Importe (Durchschnitt 1982–1987)[38]). Die binnenwirtschaftliche Pufferfunktion hatte besonders 1985 und 1986 der Handel mit den Nicht-RGW-Ländern übernommen, wo die bulgarischen Exporte überdurchschnittlich zurückgingen (1986 spielte auch Černobyl' eine Rolle), die Importe überdurchschnittlich zunahmen. Der entsprechende Handelsbilanzüberschuß wandelte sich 1985 in ein Defizit, das sich 1986 auf umgerechnet 300 Mio. US-$ erhöhte. 1987 wurde der Stabilisierung der Agrarhandelsbilanz mit den Nicht-RGW-Ländern Priorität eingeräumt.

---

[37]) FAO Trade Yearbook. Rom, versch. Jahrgänge.

[38]) Beide Anteile sind wegen der Überbewertung des Transferrubels gegenüber dem US-$ nach oben verzerrt und durch unterschiedliche Preisstrukturen auf dem RGW-Markt und dem Weltmarkt beeinflußt.

VII. Forstwirtschaft

Der Beitrag der Forstwirtschaft zum produzierten Nationaleinkommen ging von 1 % in den 60er Jahren im Laufe der 70er Jahre auf 0,4 % (1979) zurück und hat sich seither auf dieser Größenordnung stabilisiert. Hatten 1960 noch 0,9 % der Erwerbstätigen der materiellen Sphäre in der Forstwirtschaft gearbeitet, sind es seit 1970 0,5–0,7 %. Vom gesamten Territorium entfällt, ohne Bergkiefern, rund ein Drittel auf Waldland (1987: 3,87 Mio. ha). Mit Bäumen bestanden waren 3,32 Mio. ha, davon 36 % mit Nadelwald und 64 % mit Laubwald, davon wiederum 58 % mit hochstämmigen, 42 % mit niederstämmigen Bäumen. Der gesamte Holzschlag (liegend) ging von 6,2 Mio. Festmetern 1970 auf 4,2 Mio. 1987 zurück, auf Bauholz entfiel davon stets etwa die Hälfte. In jüngster Zeit wurden Maßnahmen gegen das offenbar weit verbreitete illegale Abholzen und gegen die Verbauung und andere zweckfremde Nutzung der staatlichen Forste gefordert[39]).

VIII. Eigentums- und Organisationsstruktur

1. Bodenreform, Kollektivierung und Betriebskonzentration

In ihrer ersten Etappe der Nachkriegszeit war die bulgarische Agrarpolitik von *Bodenreform und Kollektivierung* gekennzeichnet. Die Sozialisierung der Landwirtschaft setzte bereits unmittelbar nach Beginn der kommunistischen Machtübernahme ein. Zwar entstanden 1944/45 auch schon die ersten Staatsgüter (*dăržavno zemedelsko stopanstvo*, DZS) und Maschinen-Traktoren-Stationen (*mašinno-traktorna stancija*, MTS), der Schwerpunkt lag jedoch in Bulgarien auf der Schaffung der TKZS. Ausschlaggebend dafür waren die kleinbetriebliche Struktur der Landwirtschaft[40]) und genossenschaftliche Traditionen aus der Vorkriegszeit. Der wellenartig vor sich gehende Kollektivierungsprozeß wurde in Bulgarien schon 1959 praktisch zum Abschluß gebracht: Von der Agrarfläche entfielen 1959 83 % auf die landwirtschaftlichen Genossenschaften, 4 % auf Staatsgüter, 9 % auf Hofwirtschaften der Genossenschaftsbauern und nur mehr 1,4 % (1957: 14 %) auf private Einzelbauernwirtschaften.

Gegen Ende der 50er Jahre begann man mit energischen *Betriebsvergrößerungen*: Die Zahl der TKZS verringerte sich durch Zusammenlegung von 3 290 (1958) auf 932 (1960). Mit einer Durchschnittsfläche von über 4 000 ha und 1 120 ständigen Genossenschaftsbauern waren die bulgarischen Kollektivgüter, wie auch die DZS, die mit Abstand größten außerhalb der Sowjetunion[41]).

---

[39]) Vgl. RD. 22.5.1988, S. 2.

[40]) Die Privatbauern besaßen zu zwei Dritteln (1946) bis zu 5 ha Land, und selten mehr als 1–3 Kühe (1944); vgl. Information Bulgaria, S. 430, und: 35 godini, S. 119.

[41]) Modern Bulgaria – History, Policy, Economy, Culture. Editor in chief G. Bokov. Sofia 1981, S. 289; Wädekin, K.-E.: Sozialistische Agrarpolitik in Osteuropa. I: Von Marx bis zur Vollkollektivierung (Giessener Abhandlungen 63). Berlin 1974, S. 198; Wädekin II, S. 48.

2. Vertikale Integrationsansätze: Agrar-Industrie-Komplexe und Industrie-Agrar-Komplexe

Im April 1970 leitete ein Plenum des ZK der BKP[42]) die nächste Etappe der Agrarpolitik ein, die unter dem Zeichen der Intensivierung und Industrialisierung der Landwirtschaft stand. Diesen Zielen sollten die weitere Konzentration und Spezialisierung der Produktion und Ansätze vertikaler (agro-industrieller) Integration mit vor- und nachgelagerten Bereichen, besonders mit der Nahrungsmittelindustrie, dienen. Zunächst wurden 1970/71 als überwiegend horizontale Integrationsform 170 riesige APK geschaffen, in die sich 662 TKZS, 158 DZS und 99 spezialisierte Betriebe „freiwillig" mit Genehmigung des Ministerrates und der Bezirksvolksräte zusammenschlossen. Auf einen APK entfielen 1970 im Durchschnitt 24 291 ha Agrarfläche und 6479 Beschäftigte. An den APK konnten sich auch Betriebe und Organisationen in vor- und nachgelagerten Bereichen der Agrarproduktion beteiligen. Innerhalb der APK verloren die konstituierenden TKZS und DZS seit 1975 ihre Selbständigkeit und wurden zu „Abteilungen" ohne Rechtspersönlichkeit und auf interner wirtschaftlicher Rechnungsführung umfunktioniert. Formal wurde das Prinzip gewählter Leitungsorgane bis hinauf zum Vorsitzenden des APK, das von Anfang an aus der genossenschaftlichen Ordnung übernommen worden war, beibehalten.

Ab etwa 1973 experimentierte man zunehmend mit vertikalen Integrationsformen der Landwirtschaftsproduktion und der verarbeitenden Industrie – dazu gehören die Industrie-Agrar-Komplexe (*promišleno-agrarni kompleksi*, PAK) und die Wissenschafts-Produktions-Komplexe (*naučno-proizvodstveni kompleksi*, NPK), von denen es 1979 zehn bzw. acht gab. Die dominierende Form der Landwirtschaftsproduktion ist jedoch bis heute der APK geblieben. Die Leitung des neuen makroökonomischen APK war 1976 dem 1968 durch Zusammenlegung entstandenen Ministerium für Landwirtschaft und Nahrungsmittelindustrie (*Ministerstvo na zemedelieto i chranitelnata promišlenost*) übertragen worden.

1973 schuf man neue Regionaleinheiten, die sog. Siedlungssysteme (*selištni sistemi*)[43]), die zwischen Bezirken und Gemeinden einzuordnen sind und die Bevölkerung mit Grundnahrungsmitteln aus eigener Produktion versorgen sollten, was auch der landwirtschaftlichen Nebentätigkeit von Privatpersonen und Institutionen neue Impulse verlieh. Die nun als überdimensioniert betrachteten APK wurden aufgespalten und in ihrem Umfang in etwa den neuen Siedlungssystemen angeglichen: 1979 gab es 252 Siedlungssysteme und 268 APK mit einer immer noch riesigen Durchschnittsfläche von 13 570 ha.

3. Organisationsexperimente seit 1979

Unter dem Druck der unbefriedigenden Entwicklung der Landwirtschaftsproduktion wurde 1979 mit organisatorischen Umstrukturierungen und unter dem Namen

---

[42]) Vgl. Wiedemann, P.: The Origins and Development of Agro-Industrial Development in Bulgaria, in: Agricultural Policies in the USSR and Eastern Europe. Ed. R. A. Francisco; B. A. Laird. Boulder, Colorado 1980, S. 98.

[43]) Vgl. dazu auch das Kapitel von Luchterhandt, O.: Regierungssystem.

„Neuer Wirtschaftsmechanismus" (NIM) mit Reformexperimenten in der Landwirtschaft begonnen, die später auf die gesamte Wirtschaft ausgeweitet wurden[44]). Sie sahen eine Einschränkung der detaillierten zentralen Direktivplanung und eine erhöhte wirtschaftliche und finanzielle Autonomie und Verantwortlichkeit (Selbstfinanzierung) der APK und ihrer Untereinheiten, der Brigaden, vor. Diese blieben mit im Schnitt etwa 1 300 ha, in der Getreideproduktion bis zu 5 000 ha Ackerland immer noch sehr groß dimensioniert und in Untereinheiten gegliedert[45]). 1979 wurde das Ministerium für Landwirtschaft und Nahrungsmittelindustrie durch den NAPS ersetzt, der auf dem „freiwilligen wirtschaftlichen Bündnis" von staatlichen und genossenschaftlichen Agrarproduzenten (APK, PAK, Vereinigungen), von Organisationen in den Bereichen Wissenschaft, Forschung und Entwicklung, Aufkauf, Versorgung, Absatz und Handel, und von Betrieben (Nahrungsmittelindustrie, Agrartechnik, Bau) beruht, die alle wirtschaftlich und organisatorisch selbständig bleiben. Er basiert auf dem Prinzip von unten gewählter Leitungsorgane, denen andererseits staatliche Funktionen übertragen werden – so erhielt auf zentraler Ebene der NAPS den Status eines Ministeriums. Auf Bezirksebene sind ihm entsprechende Bezirks-Agrar-Industrie-Verbände (*okrǎžni agrarno-promišleni sǎjuzi*, OAPS) nachgeordnet. In der Praxis scheinen die ohnehin bescheidenen und überwiegend administrativen Dezentralisierungsabsichten auf der regionalen Ebene (OAPS) steckengeblieben zu sein, so daß sich die Entscheidungsspielräume für die APK, besonders aber für Brigaden und ihre Glieder, kaum erweiterten[46]).

IX. Ziele und Instrumente der Agrarpolitik 1986–1990

Angesichts der besorgniserregenden Entwicklung befaßte sich 1985 (neben dem zweiten regulären Kongreß des NAPS) ein ZK-Plenum[47]) speziell mit der künftigen Entwicklung der Landwirtschaft und der Nahrungs- und Genußmittelindustrie, die im 9. Fünfjahresplan für 1986–1990 strukturpolitisch wieder in den Vordergrund gerückt sind. Die angestrebte Effizienz- und Produktivitätssteigerung soll vor allem durch Forschung und Entwicklung, neue Technologien, „Biologisierung" und eine Reform des Planungs- und Leitungssystems herbeigeführt werden.

Für 1986–1990 ist eine vergleichsweise bescheidene Zunahme der *Agrarproduktion* gegenüber 1981–1985 um 1,5–1,9 % p.a. geplant (gegenüber dem schlechten Jahr 1985 um geschätzte 5,5–6,2 % p.a.). Der Akzent liegt auf der Stabilisierung der Produktion, sektoral auf der Pflanzenproduktion. Die Getreideproduktion soll um 3,6 % p.a (auf 10 Mio. t jährlich) steigen, das Futter-Eiweißproblem durch Produk-

---

[44]) Vgl. dazu auch das Kapitel von Gumpel, W.: Wirtschaftssystem.
[45]) ECE, S. 209; Grosser, S. 11.
[46]) Vgl. Wyzan, M.: The Bulgarian Experience with Centrally-Planned Agriculture: Lessons for Soviet Reformers? Paper presented at the conference on „Soviet Agriculture and Food Systems in Comparative Perspective", held at the Kennan Institute for Advanced Russian Studies in Washington, DC, on April 4, 1986, S. 21.
[47]) RD. 26.3.1985.

tionssteigerungen bei Sonnenblumen, Hülsenfrüchten, Soja, Futtererbsen, Luzerne u. a entschärft werden. Gegenüber dem Durchschnitt 1981–1985 soll bis 1990 die Gemüseproduktion (besonders Glashausprodukte) um 6,2–8,1 % p. a. steigen, die Obstproduktion (besonders Edelobst und Desserttrauben) um 3,5–4,4 % p.a. Die für 1990 geplanten Produktionsmengen implizieren bei Fleisch (830000–840000 t Schlachtgewicht) vermutlich eine Stagnation, bei Milch eine Zunahme um 5,2–5,9 % p. a. und bei Eiern um 3,1–4,4 % p. a. gegenüber 1981–1985[48]).

Die angestrebte Wende im *technologischen Bereich* beinhaltet die Modernisierung des Maschinenparks[49]), bessere Ersatzteilversorgung, Bodenmelioration, moderne Ertragssteuerungsmethoden in Pflanzen- und Tierproduktion, Entwicklung und Anwendung neuer Sorten, Hybride, Tierrassen und Biotechnologien (in Pflanzenschutz, Düngung, Futtermitteln und -zusätzen; Gentechnik und Genetik, Embryotransplantationen); letztere stehen allerdings teils erst im Anfangsstadium der Entwicklung.

Nach einigermaßen überstürzten Reorganisationen der Landwirtschaftsleitung auf zentraler Ebene, deren letztes Ergebnis die Wiedereinrichtung eines Ministeriums für Land- und Forstwirtschaft im August 1987 ist[50]), wurde Ende 1987 ein Paket von Reformen und wirtschaftspolitischen Maßnahmen, teils speziell für die Landwirtschaft, verabschiedet. Schon im September 1988 kritisierte T. Živkov anläßlich einer Politbüro-Sitzung die unzureichenden Ergebnisse der Umgestaltung in der Landwirtschaft und skizzierte weitere *Reformen*. Deren Verabschiedung verzögerte sich bis Mai 1989, nachdem schon zu Jahresanfang vorzeitig eine neue Runde genereller Wirtschaftsreformen verabschiedet worden war, die grundsätzlich auch die Landwirtschaft betrifft[51]). Obgleich es sich nicht um eine echte marktwirtschaftliche Reform handelt, ist im einzelnen fraglich, inwieweit die Landwirtschaft – ein auch in den meisten westlichen Marktwirtschaften in hohem Maße staatlich regulierter und gestützter Bereich – einbezogen werden wird. Konkretisierungen und Sonderregelungen in Form von Durchführungsbestimmungen stehen noch aus.

Die genannten Reformdokumente zeigen eine sich im Laufe der Zeit akzentuierende Tendenz in Richtung Dezentralisierung, Entbürokratisierung und Diversifizierung der Eigentums- und Wirtschaftsformen. Zunächst sollte die wirtschaftliche und finanzielle Autonomie der Brigaden (vergleichbar den Betrieben in der Industrie) auf Basis einer bulgarischen Version von Selbstverwaltung drastisch erhöht werden, nun sollen sie durch andere, unter gleichwertige ökonomische Bedingungen zu stellende, Wirtschaftsformen ersetzt werden. Grundsätzlich soll auch in der Landwirtschaft die sog. Firmenorganisation errichtet werden, wobei es sich um mit größerer Selbständigkeit ausgestattete und gewinnorientierte Unternehmen verschiedener Rechtsform

---

[48]) RD. 26.12.1986.
[49]) Im Landwirtschaftsmaschinenbau ist eine Produktionssteigerung um rund 10% p.a. geplant.
[50]) Im März 1986 wurde wieder ein Ministerium für Land- und Forstwirtschaft gegründet und damit der NAPS praktisch entmachtet. Dieses Ministerium wurde bereits Ende 1986 durch einen – kurzlebigen – „Rat für Land- und Forstwirtschaft" beim Ministerrat ersetzt; die Funktionsteilung zwischen dem neuen Ministerium und dem NAPS ist nicht geklärt.
[51]) Die folgenden Ausführungen beziehen sich auf: DV. (1987) 99, S. 2–8; (1988) 3, S. 1–20; 4, S. 1–15; 11, S. 2–5; 81, S. 1ff.; (1989) 39, S. 1–39; RD. 28.9.1988; 11.1.1989, Beilage; 17.2.1989, Beilage. Zu den Reformen vgl. das Kapitel von W. Gumpel, Wirtschaftssystem.

handelt. Ihre Bildung, Reorganisation und Auflösung soll überwiegend durch Registrierung bei den Bezirksgerichten, also nicht mehr durch staatliche Administrativakte, erfolgen. Die Reorganisationen, deren konkrete Gestalt bislang unklar ist, dürften die Aufspaltung überdimensionierter Wirtschaftseinheiten mit sich bringen. Während die APK zunächst nur in ihren Funktionen eingeschränkt werden sollten, scheinen sie nun aufgelöst zu werden. Als grundlegende Organisationsform der Landwirtschaftsproduktion sollen genossenschaftliche Strukturen wieder hergestellt werden, darunter auch kleine Kooperativen. Weitere Schwerpunkte sind die Zulassung privater Vollerwerbswirtschaften (die Möglichkeiten zum Betrieb von Nebenwirtschaften bleiben aufrecht) und die Anwendung des Pachtsystems. Privatwirtschaften können von nun an bis zu zehn ständig Beschäftigte und eine unbegrenzte Zahl von Saisonarbeitern einstellen und werden i. d. R. auf Basis von Verträgen betrieben, die entgeltlich oder unentgeltlich das Recht auf (und die Pflicht zur) Bodennutzung für 10–50 Jahre fixieren. Bestimmungen hinsichtlich der Größe von Privatwirtschaften sind – noch ausständigen – administrativen Beschlüssen überlassen. Privatpersonen, Familien und Kollektive, aber auch Genossenschaften und Firmen können Land, Dauerkulturen, und andere Produktionsmittel vertraglich für 5–50 Jahre pachten. Verpächter können Staatsorgane, Gemeinden und Bürgermeisterämter und Unternehmen sein, nicht jedoch Private. Die Pächter, mit Ausnahme jener in Gebirgs- und Vorgebirgsregionen, können zur Produktion und Lieferung bestimmter Produktmengen verpflichtet werden.

Auch für die Landwirtschaft wurden zentrale Plandirektiven formal abgeschafft, ihre Funktionen jedoch teils von den sog. Staatsaufträgen (gedacht als Übergangslösung) übernommen; diese dürfen nun maximal zwei Drittel der Kapazitäten beanspruchen. Die zentrale Inputzuteilung soll allmählich durch ein Großhandelssystem ersetzt werden, eine Liberalisierung der Absatzmöglichkeiten u. a. die Einrichtung regionaler Warenbörsen bringen.

Die Liberalisierungen im Außenwirtschaftsbereich bedeuten auch für die Agrarproduzenten ein eigenes Außenhandelsrecht. Angestrebt werden vor allem Technologieimporte zur Modernisierung der Landwirtschaft (und der verarbeitenden Industrie); neben Technologieimport gegen Agrarexport im Rahmen der betrieblichen Selbstfinanzierung sollen zunehmend neuere Formen wie Konsortien, Kapitalbeteiligungen und Zollfreizonen genutzt werden.

Auf der konzeptuellen Seite birgt das Preissystem ein besonderes Spannungsfeld. Derzeit hält die bulgarische Führung noch an stabilen, staatlich fixierten und hoch subventionierten Einzelhandelspreisen für Grundnahrungsmittel fest, die teils ebenfalls staatlich fixierten Großhandelspreise (und das System der Produzentensubventionen) sind im APK im wesentlichen unangetastet geblieben. Sie würden somit selbst im Falle dezentraler Entscheidungen keine Signalwirkung in Richtung effizientere Ressourcenallokation ausüben.

Die *wirtschaftspolitischen Maßnahmen* der Jahre 1988 und 1989 umfassen Zuschläge auf die Aufkaufpreise (Subventionserhöhungen ab 1988), Steuerbegünstigungen im Rahmen der Steuerreform, Umschuldung der Landwirtschaftsorganisationen, Maßnahmen zur Hebung des Qualifikationsniveaus und gegen die Abwanderung vom Lande und aus der Landwirtschaft vor allem jüngerer Arbeitskräfte (finanzielle Anreize, Versorgungsprioritäten, Verbesserung der ländlichen Infrastruktur) und zusätzliche Begünstigungen für Gebirgs- und Vorgebirgsregionen und „entvölkerte" Gebiete, darunter solche im Grenzland (z. B. Befreiung von Staatsaufträgen).

Der Plan 1986–1990 hat auf eine drastische Verbesserung von Produktivität und Wirtschaftlichkeit in der Landwirtschaftsproduktion gesetzt. Die bisherigen agrarpolitischen Maßnahmen sind insofern gescheitert, als die Ziele des laufenden Fünfjahresplanes in weite Ferne gerückt sind. Gleichzeitig wird zunehmend eingestanden, daß die Erholung der Agrarproduktion von außerordentlicher Bedeutung nicht nur für die Nahrungsmittelversorgung, sondern auch für die Wirksamkeit einkommenspolitischer Anreize (Reformen) in der gesamten Wirtschaft ist. Dazu kommt ihre außenwirtschaftliche Bedeutung, vor allem für die notwendige Konsolidierung im Hartwährungsbereich. Dementsprechend zeichnet sich eine Neuformulierung der Wirtschaftspolitik ab, die die Landwirtschaft, bereits im Plan für 1989, in den Kreis der Prioritätszweige aufrücken läßt. Ein neues Entwicklungsprogramm für die Landwirtschaft (mit vorrangiger Behandlung des Eiweißproblems, von Wein- und Obstbau, Zuckerrübenanbau, Schafhaltung und Bewässerung) dürfte auch einen neuerlichen Versuch bringen, die vorgelagerten Bereiche (Maschinenbau, Chemie, Bau, Transport u. a.) auf die Bedarfsdeckung der Landwirtschaft und der Nahrungs- und Genußmittelindustrie umzuorientieren. Der erforderliche Modernisierungsschub im Agrarbereich müßte auch Änderungen in der Investitionspolitik bedingen. Die rasante Abfolge reformpolitischer Erklärungen und Maßnahmen, die zu einem beträchtlichen Teil nicht in die Praxis umgesetzt wurden, hat in den letzten Jahren auch für die Landwirtschaft zu vielfach unklaren Regelungen und beträchtlicher Verunsicherung geführt. Für die nach 1990 in Aussicht gestellten weiteren Reformen, einschließlich einer fundamentalen Reform des Preissystems, zeichnen sich noch keine klaren Konturen ab. Zu der Vielzahl von Unsicherheitsfaktoren und dem ohnehin erheblichen Handlungsbedarf kam im Frühjahr 1989 der Massenexodus bulgarischer Türken. Bis August hatten über 310 000 Personen das Land in Richtung Türkei verlassen. Der Abfluß von Arbeitskraft aus dem Nordosten und Südosten des Landes trifft in erster Linie die Landwirtschaft – kurzfristige Notmaßnahmen zur Begrenzung der Produktionsverluste beinhalten zusätzliche Pflichtarbeit der Bevölkerung[52]). Durch diese jüngsten Ereignisse sind beabsichtigte Reformen und die Entwicklung nicht nur in der Landwirtschaft in verstärktem Maß gefährdet.

---

[52]) Vgl. z. B. RD. 23. 6. 1989; 21. 6. 1989; International Herald Tribune. 13. 7. 1989.

Bergbau und Energiewirtschaft

Jochen Bethkenhagen, Berlin

I. Die Stellung des Bergbaus in der Volkswirtschaft – II. Verfügbarkeit und Aufkommen von nichtenergetischen Rohstoffen: 1. Buntmetallurgie – 2. Eisenmetallurgie – III. Die Energiewirtschaft: 1. Die Verfügbarkeit von Energierohstoffen – 2. Produktion von Primärenergie – 3. Elektrizitätswirtschaft – 4. Energieverbrauch – 5. Außenhandel

I. Die Stellung des Bergbaus in der Volkswirtschaft

Gut 5 % der Beschäftigten in der bulgarischen Industrie arbeiten im Bergbau, dessen Anteil an der industriellen Bruttoproduktion knapp 5 % beträgt. Dieses Ergebnis ist – wie für die extraktiven Produktionszweige weltweit üblich – nur mit einem hohen Kapitalaufwand zu erreichen. Fast ein Sechstel aller Investitionen für die Industrie flossen 1986 in diesen Bereich (vgl. Tabelle 1).

Tabelle 1: Anteil des Bergbausektors[1]) an der Gesamtindustrie (1987; in %)

Produktionsanteil (Brutto)	5,4
Beschäftigtenanteil	6,1
Grundmittelanteil[2])	12,2
Investitionsanteil	13,0

[1]) Kohlenbergbau und Eisenmetallurgie. – [2]) 1985; Anschaffungswerte.
Quelle: SG. 1988, S. 114 ff.; Statističeski ežegodnik stran-členov Soveta Ekonomičeskoj vzaimopomošči. 1988.

Im Gegensatz zu anderen südosteuropäischen Staaten – insbesondere zu Ungarn – begann eine forcierte Industrialisierungspolitik in Bulgarien erst nach dem II. Weltkrieg. Die Rohstoffbasis hierfür war anfangs sehr gering. Relativ schnell wurde jedoch mit dem Aufbau der Buntmetallurgie begonnen, die zunächst sogar in ihrer Bedeutung die Eisenmetallurgie übertraf. Die Gewinnung größerer Mengen an Buntmetallen bildete die Grundlage für die Aufnahme der Produktion von Produkten mit einem hohen NE-Metallgehalt, wie Elektromotoren, Akkumulatoren, Elektrokarren, Hebefahrzeuge und Elektrokabel.

II. Verfügbarkeit und Aufkommen von nichtenergetischen Rohstoffen

1. Buntmetallurgie

Von größerer Bedeutung sind die Vorräte an Kupfer sowie an Blei-Zink-Erzen. Als Nebenprodukte beim Schmelzen fallen darüber hinaus einige seltene Metalle wie Molybdän, Cadmium oder Silber an. Die sicheren und wahrscheinlichen Vorräte an Kupfer werden auf rd. 2,5 Mio. t (Metallinhalt) geschätzt[1]). Unter Beteiligung der ČSSR wurde die östlich von Sofia gelegene Kupferhütte von Zlatica-Pirdop errichtet, in der vor allem die Erze aus den Tagebauen von Medet und Elšica aufbereitet werden. Ihr Metallgehalt beträgt etwa 0,4 %. 1985 erreichte der Kupferkomplex von Elacite, in der Nähe von Sofia, seine vorläufige Endkapazität. Bei einer Jahreskapazität von 6 Mio. t Erzen mit einem Kupferinhalt von 0,4 % können hier jährlich 24 000 t Kupfer gewonnen werden[2]).

Tabelle 2: Produktion und Verbrauch von NE-Metallen (in 1 000 t)

	1970	1975	1980	1985	1986	1987
Blei						
Bergwerksproduktion	98,5	108	100	97	97	95
Raffinadeproduktion	–	110	118	116	114	112
Raffinadeverbrauch[1])	–	95	110	113	108	106
Kupfer						
Bergwerksproduktion[1])	40,3	55	62	78	80	80
Raffinadeproduktion	38,3	52	63	73	74	76
Raffinadeverbrauch	34,5	48	55	65	69	71
Zink						
Bergwerksproduktion	76,4	83	70	68	70	68
Verbrauch	28	40	75	75	71	72
Cadmium[2])						
Raffinadeproduktion	–	–	200	175	170	160
Verbrauch	–	–	80	80	80	60
Silber[2])						
Bergwerksproduktion	25	26	24	26	26	26
Mangan	33	35	49	38	37	38

[1]) Für 1975 Schätzung (Metallstatistik). – [2]) In t.

Quellen: Metallgesellschaft (Hrsg.): Metallstatistik, Frankfurt, verschiedene Jahrgänge; SG., verschiedene Jahrgänge.

---

[1]) Vgl. den Beitrag von Matley, I. M.: Geographical Foundations (einschl. der dort enthaltenen Landkarten), sowie Bundesanstalt für Geowissenschaften und Rohstoffe: COMECON. Rohstoffwirtschaftlicher Überblick. Hannover 1979 (Rohstoffwirtschaftliche Länderberichte. Bd. XXII), S. 151.

[2]) Vgl. Bureau of Mines (Hrsg.): Minerals Yearbook 1985. Vol. III. Washington 1987, S. 170. In einer anderen Quelle wird die Jahresförderkapazität mit 15 Mio. t Erzen bei einem Kupfergehalt von 0,3 % (45 000 t Cu p. a.) angegeben. Vgl. Mining Annual Review. (1987), S. 476.

Blei-Zink-Erze lagern vor allem im östlichen Teil des Rhodopenmassivs bei Gorubso. Ihre Verwertung erfolgt in erster Linie im Hüttenkombinat von Kărdžali, das unter sowjetischer Beteiligung errichtet wurde. Weitere Standorte der Blei- und Zinkgewinnung sind Plovdiv, Rudozem und Pazardžik[3]). Die Förderung von Blei und Zink weist einen leicht rückläufigen Trend auf. Als Bleiprodukt der Förderung (Untertagebau) werden jährlich etwa 25 t Silber und um 180 t Cadmium gewonnen (vgl. Tabelle 2).

2. Eisenmetallurgie

Der Aufbau einer eigenen Eisen- und Stahlindustrie erfolgte in Bulgarien – anders als in den meisten anderen Mitgliedstaaten des RGW – erst relativ spät. Bis 1965 war das Hüttenwerk in Pernik bei Sofia mit seiner geringen Jahreskapazität von 0,2 Mio. t Roheisen die wichtigste Produktionsstätte. Inzwischen ist die Roheisenproduktion im Lande auf 1,7 Mio. t gestiegen, die Stahlproduktion erreichte 1987 rd. 3 Mio. t (vgl. Tabelle 3).

Tabelle 3: Entwicklung der Eisen- und Stahlproduktion (in 1000 t; 1960–1987)

Jahr	Eisenerz			Roheisen[1])		Stahl	Walzgut	Hüttenkoks[2])	
	Produktion		Import	Produktion	Import	Produktion	Produktion	Produktion	Import
	roh	Eisengehalt							
1960	415	188	–	192	117	253	193	20	344
1965	1804	585	1004	695	165	588	431	733	264
1970	2409	792	1133	1251	295	1800	1420	837	465
1975	2337	775	1918	1560	330	2265	2495	1364	357
1980	1886	590	2235	1583	413	2565	3213	1348	446
1981	1754	537	2280	1571	435	2484	3351	1381	407
1982	1552	474	2360	1617	399	2584	3253	1274	483
1983	1803	554	2313	1674	407	2831	3235	1270	502
1984	2063	622	2286	1621	665	2878	3354	1186	544
1985	1985	607	2215	1754	404	2944	3326	1087	664
1986	2179	661	2248	1651	425	2965	3347	1156	471
1987	1850	559	2308	1706	483	3045	3225	1134	309

[1]) Einschließlich Eisenlegierungen. – [2]) Feuchtigkeitsgehalt 6 %.
Quelle: SG., verschiedene Jahrgänge.

Drei Großbetriebe bilden die eisenmetallurgische Basis des Landes: Die Leninwerke in Pernik, das Hüttenwerk von Kremikovci, das 1965 in Betrieb genommen wurde, sowie das Feinstahlwalzwerk von Debelt bei Burgas, das im Verlauf des

---

[3]) Vgl. Harke, H., Rosenkranz, E. und Mücke, E.: Geographie ausgewählter RGW-Länder. Gotha 1983, S. 121.

9. Fünfjahresplans (1986–1990) fertiggestellt werden soll. Unter den Stahlveredlern nimmt die Produktion von Mangan in Bulgarien einen wichtigen Platz ein. Die Produktion liegt jährlich bei 40 000 t, sie reicht aber für den Eigenbedarf nicht aus. Vielmehr müssen jährlich noch rd. 90 000 t, vor allem aus der UdSSR, importiert werden.

III. Die Energiewirtschaft

1. Die Verfügbarkeit von Energierohstoffen

Die Energiewirtschaft in Bulgarien muß ihren Bedarf an fossilen Brennstoffen, das sind vor allem Kohle, Erdöl und Erdgas, überwiegend durch Importe decken. Die Vorräte an Erdöl, Erdgas und Steinkohle sind sehr gering; lediglich die Braunkohlevorkommen haben eine größere wirtschaftliche Bedeutung. Allerdings handelt es sich überwiegend um Lignite, also um eine holzartige Braunkohle mit einem niedrigen Heizwert.

Die gesamten Bilanzvorräte Bulgariens an Kohle wurden zuletzt mit 4,4 Mrd. t angegeben (vgl. Tabelle 4). Etwa vier Fünftel der Vorräte wurden nach 1956 erkundet. Darüber hinaus sind 2 Mrd. t noch nicht bilanziert und es werden weitere 2,6 Mrd. t

Tabelle 4: Gewinnbare Kohlevorräte (1979; in Mio. t)

Lignit		4 067
davon:		
Becken von:		
Marica-Ost	2 777	
Marica-West	154	
Vorkommen von:		
Kjustendil	26	
Belobrežk	44	
Stanjanci	28	
Čukurovo	9	
Sofia	549	
Elchovo	200	
Braunkohle		330
davon:		
Becken von:		
Bobov Dol	182	
Černo More	66	
Pernik	56	
Pirin	19	
Steinkohle		26
davon:		
Balkanbecken	24	
Anthrazit		7
davon:		
Becken von Svoge	6	
Insgesamt		4 430

Quelle: Elman, J.: Uhelný průmysl v BLR (Die Kohlenindustrie in der NRB), in: Uhli. (1985) 1, S. 35.

an Reserven vermutet. Die Vorräte sind auf 34 Lagerstätten verteilt. Die meisten sind relativ klein und weisen für den Abbau sehr ungünstige geologische Strukturen auf[4]).

In Bulgarien wird die Braunkohle in zwei Gruppen eingeteilt: Die höherwertige Braunkohle im engeren Sinn ist durch Heizwerte im Bereich von 2000 bis etwa 4000 kcal/kg, die Lignitkohle durch Heizwerte von 1000 bis 2000 kcal/kg charakterisiert.

Gut 90 % der gewinnbaren Kohlevorräte sind minderwertige Lignite, die in anderen Ländern erst gar nicht abgebaut werden. Der hohe Gehalt an Asche (bis über 43 % im wasserfreien Zustand) und Wasser (bis über 60 %) macht die Nutzung der Kohle sehr aufwendig. Günstig sind indes die Abbaubedingungen, denn etwa 90 % der Lignitvorkommen eignen sich für den Tagebau.

Im Gegensatz zu seinem nördlichen Nachbarn Rumänien[5]) verfügt Bulgarien über keine nennenswerten Vorräte an Erdöl und Erdgas. Die wichtigsten Erdöllagerstätten befinden sich bei Tjulenovo an der Schwarzmeerküste und bei Dolni Dăbnik in der Nähe von Pleven. Erkundungsarbeiten nach Erdöl und Erdgas werden in Zusammenarbeit mit der Sowjetunion im Schwarzmeerschelf durchgeführt; über etwaige Erfolge ist bisher aber nichts bekannt geworden.

Tabelle 5: Wasserkraftwerke: Leistung und Stromproduktion

Jahr	Leistung in MW	Stromproduktion in Mio. kWh	Auslastung[1]) in %
1970	816	2152	30,1
1975	1793	2452	15,6
1980	1868	3713	22,7
1985	1975	2236	12,9
1986	1975	2326	13,4
1987	1975	2538	14,7

[1]) Tatsächliche Stromerzeugung in % der maximal möglichen Stromproduktion (8760 h).
Quelle: SG. (verschiedene Jahrgänge), S. 212, 214 und S. 229f.

Nicht unbedeutend ist hingegen das hydroenergetische Potential des Landes[6]). Insgesamt gibt es in Bulgarien rund 90 Wasserkraftwerke; allerdings sind 90 % der Leistung auf 25 Werke konzentriert. Bei ihnen handelt es sich zumeist um hydroenergetische Systeme (Kaskaden, Stauanlagen), die auch wasserwirtschaftliche Funktio-

---

[4]) Zu Einheiten vgl. den Beitrag Matley, I. M.: Geographical Foundations (einschl. der dort enthaltenen Landkarten), sowie Elman, J.: Uhelný průmysl v BLR (Die Kohlenindustrie in der NRB), in: Uhli. 33 (1985) 1, S. 35 ff; Tilmann, W.: Der Braunkohlenbergbau in Bulgarien, in: Braunkohle. 36 (1984), 6/7; Bundesanstalt für Geowissenschaften und Rohstoffe (Anm. 1), S. 146 ff.
[5]) Vgl. Matley, I. M.: The Geographical Basis of Romania, und Schönfeld, R.: Industrie und gewerbliche Wirtschaft, beide in: Grothusen, K.-D. (Hrsg.): Südosteuropa-Handbuch. Band II: Rumänien. Göttingen 1977, S. 245 f. und S. 303 ff.
[6]) Vgl. Gumpel, W.: Die Entwicklung der bulgarischen Elektrizitätswirtschaft, in: Energiewirtschaftliche Tagesfragen. 32 (1982) 1, S. 38.

nen (Wasserregulierung, Wasserversorgung, Bewässerung) haben. Die Möglichkeiten zur Stromproduktion werden häufig durch die Auswirkungen der wahrzunehmenden wasserwirtschaftlichen Aufgaben beeinträchtigt. Die größten Wasserkraftwerke Bulgariens befinden sich an der Matonica (775 MW, mehrere Kraftwerke), Stara Reka (228 MW), Arda (274 MW) und am Iskăr (80 MW)[7]. Darüber hinaus gibt es zahlreiche kleine Laufwasserwerke.

Größtes Neubauprojekt ist das Pumpspeicherwerk von Čaira im Rila-Gebirge. Die vorgesehenen vier Turbinen sollen eine Gesamtleistung von 864 MW erbringen. Pumpspeicherwerke werden zur Deckung der Nachfragespitzen eingesetzt. In der nachfrageschwachen Zeit wird Wasser in die Höhe – in Čaira 700 m – gepumpt und bei Bedarf zum Antrieb der Turbinen wieder in die Tiefe gestürzt.

2. *Produktion von Primärenergie*

Angesichts der Ressourcenarmut des Landes ist der Handlungsspielraum für die Steuerung der Energieproduktion in Bulgarien relativ gering. Dennoch lassen sich drei Phasen der Produktionsentwicklung unterscheiden (vgl. Tabelle 6):

– Rückgang (1971 bis 1974)
– Stagnation (1975 bis 1978)
– leichte Expansion (1979 bis 1987).

In der ersten Phase verminderte sich die Inlandsproduktion von Primärenergie – das ist die Förderung von Brennstoffen sowie die Stromerzeugung aus Wasserkraft, nicht aber die Kernenergieproduktion, da die die Energie „enthaltenden" Brennstäbe importiert werden müssen – um rd. 20 %. Zu jener Zeit war vor allem das Erdöl zu relativ günstigen Bedingungen von der UdSSR und auf dem Weltmarkt verfügbar, so daß der Druck zum Ausbau der eigenen Ressourcen gering war. Dies änderte sich mit der ersten Ölpreisexplosion (1973). Auch in Bulgarien erfolgte eine stärkere Rückbesinnung auf die eigenen Ressourcen, so daß zunächst einmal der Rückgang der Energieproduktion gestoppt wurde. Mit dem zweiten Ölpreisschock (1979) setzte sich

Tabelle 6: Produktion von Primärenergie (in PJ[1]))

	1970	1975	1980	1985	1986	1987[2])
Insgesamt	291	261	285	267	299	313
Braunkohle	228	218	219	225	257	268

[1]) Peta-Joule = 10^{15} Joule. 1 Peta-Joule entspricht 0,03412 Mio. t Steinkohleneinheiten (SKE). –
[2]) Vorläufig.

Quellen: SG., verschiedene Jahrgänge; Datenbank RGW-Energie des DIW.

---

[7]) Harke, H., Rosenkranz, E. und Mücke, E. (Anm. 3), S. 120.

weltweit die Überzeugung durch, daß die Energiepreise am Weltmarkt auf absehbare Zeit noch bleiben werden. Der 8. Fünfjahresplan (1981–1985) sah daher im Energiebereich eine Verminderung der Einfuhrabhängigkeit und eine Erweiterung der Energieproduktion vor.

Verglichen mit diesem Ziel waren die Erfolge allerdings sehr bescheiden. Die Braunkohleförderung konnte am Anfang der 80er Jahre zwar etwas gesteigert werden. 1985 war sie aber kaum höher als 1980. Deutlich zurück ging zudem die Stromerzeugung aus Wasserkraftwerken, der zweitwichtigsten inländischen Energiequelle Bulgariens (vgl. Tabellen 5 und 7). Angesichts dieser Mißerfolge haben die Planer in den 9. Fünfjahresplan (1986–1990) ein moderateres Ziel eingesetzt: Nunmehr soll bis 1990 die Kohleförderung auf 39 Mio. t gesteigert werden – ein durchaus realisierbares Ziel, wenn man bedenkt, daß 1987 bereits 37 Mio. t gefördert wurden (1985: 31 Mio. t). Auf das schlechte Produktionsergebnis im Jahre 1985 hatte die bulgarische Regierung mit kräftigen Lohnerhöhungen (15 bis 20 %) für Bergleute und für andere Beschäftigte im Energiesektor reagiert. Außerdem wurden die Investitionen in den Braunkohletagebauen erhöht[8]).

Fast drei Viertel der bulgarischen Braunkohleförderung stammen aus dem Kombinat Marica-Ost, zu dem neben den beiden Großtagebauen (Trojanovo Nord und Süd) drei Kraftwerke mit einer installierten Leistung von 2 360 MW – das entspricht 36 % der gesamten Wärmekraftwerksleistung – und eine Brikettfabrik gehören. Angesichts der großen Vorräte und der relativ günstigen Erschließungsbedingungen konzentrieren sich die bulgarischen Ausbaupläne für Kohle sehr stark auf diese Lignit-Lagerstätte bei Dimitrovgrad. Im 9. Fünfjahresplan (1986–1990) soll die Produktionskapazität u. a. durch die verstärkte Ablösung des Zugbetriebes durch moderne Förderbandanlagen erweitert werden. Anfang der 80er Jahre sahen die Planungen für Marica-Ost noch eine Kapazitätserweiterung bis 1990 auf 45 Mio. t pro Jahr vor. Diese Pläne sind bei der Ausarbeitung des endgültigen 9. Fünfjahresplans (1986–1990) offenbar deutlich nach unten korrigiert worden (geplante Gesamtförderung in Bulgarien 1990: 39 Mio. t). Zusätzlicher Bedarf an Kohle entsteht durch den Bau neuer Kraftwerksblöcke im Kraftwerk 2 von Marica-Ost. Die Planungen sehen vor, die Leistung der in unmittelbarer Tagebaunähe befindlichen Wärmekraftwerke auf 3 360 MW zu erhöhen.

Die in Marica-Ost auch anzutreffenden höherwertigen Lignitkohlen werden in einer nahegelegenen Brikettfabrik verarbeitet. Allerdings ist die Brikettproduktion in Bulgarien relativ gering; sie beträgt pro Jahr 1,2 bis 1,5 Mio. t (zum Vergleich DDR: 50 Mio. t). Die Briketts werden fast ausschließlich im Haushaltssektor verwendet. Für die Produktion von einer Tonne Briketts müssen rd. 3 t Rohbraunkohle eingesetzt werden. Der Bau der Brikettfabriken erfolgte in enger Zusammenarbeit mit der DDR, die den größten Teil der Ausrüstungen lieferte.

Insgesamt haben sich im Kohlenbergbau Bulgariens in den zurückliegenden 20 Jahren beträchtliche Strukturveränderungen vollzogen. Der Anteil der heizwertarmen Lignitkohle an der gesamten Braunkohlenförderung stieg von 61 % im Jahre

---

[8]) Vgl. DV. 1.11.1985, S. 10 und The Times. 26.11.1985.

Tabelle 7: Die Förderung von Kohle (in 1 000 t; 1960–1987)

Jahr	Insgesamt		davon[1]) Braun- kohle	davon Lignit	Stein- kohle[2])
	brutto	netto			
1960	17 147	15 986	10 060	5 356	570
1965	26 254	25 042	24 489	14 926	552
1970	31 411	29 251	28 854	21 971	397
1975	28 949	27 845	27 515	21 060	330
1980	31 571	30 213	29 945	24 153	267
1981	30 585	29 241	28 996	23 338	246
1982	33 550	32 215	31 974	26 437	241
1983	33 829	32 390	32 147	26 805	243
1984	33 913	32 359	32 136	26 617	223
1985	32 480	30 657	30 880	25 272	223
1986	36 792	35 222	35 015	29 896	207
1987	38 492	36 819	36 621	31 403	198

[1]) Nettoförderung. – [2]) Einschließlich Anthrazit.

Quelle: SG., verschiedene Jahrgänge.

1965 über 77 % im Jahre 1975 auf 82 % im Jahre 1985[9]). Zugenommen hat auch die Bedeutung der Tagebauförderung: Wurden 1965 rd. zwei Drittel der Kohle im Tagebaubetrieb gewonnen, so waren es 1987 rd. vier Fünftel.

Die Produktion der übrigen Brennstoffe ist von ganz geringer Bedeutung. Die geförderte Steinkohlenmenge war mit 0,2 Mio. t 1986 halb so hoch wie 1970 und die Erdgasförderung ist von 0,5 Mrd. cbm (1970) auf einen Erinnerungsposten von 0,02 Mrd. cbm zusammengeschrumpft. Die Lagerstätte in der Region Loveč ist offenbar nahezu ausgebeutet. Nachdem die Erdölförderung in den 70er Jahren von 0,3 Mio. t (1970) auf 0,1 Mio. t (1978) zurückgegangen war, bemüht man sich wieder stärker um die Nutzung der geringen Vorräte. Die Fördermenge hat sich in den 80er Jahren bei 0,3 Mio. t stabilisiert. Wegen seines hohen Harzanteils wird das Öl fast ausschließlich zu Heizöl verarbeitet.

3. Elektrizitätswirtschaft

Im Zeitraum 1970 bis 1984 wurde die inländische Stromerzeugung deutlich erhöht, im Jahresdurchschnitt um 6,1 %. Allerdings reichte die Inlandserzeugung nicht aus, um den noch stärker steigenden Bedarf zu decken. Während 1970 noch der Stromexport etwas geringer als der entsprechende Import war, mußten in den darauf folgen-

---

[9]) Diese Entwicklung ist bei der Umrechnung der gesamten Braunkohlenfördermenge in Heizwerteinheiten berücksichtigt worden. Von 1970 bis 1979 wurde ein durchschnittlicher Heizwert von 1 890 kcal/kg und von 1980 an ein Wert von 1 750 kcal/kg (SKE-Faktoren von 0,27 bzw. 0,25) angenommen.

Bergbau und Energiewirtschaft

Tabelle 8: Stromproduktion nach Kraftwerksarten

	1970	1975	1980	1983	1984	1985	1986	1987
				in Mrd. kWh				
Wärmekraftwerke	17,4	20,2	25,0	27,0	28,7	26,3	27,4	28,5
Wasserkraftwerke	2,2	2,5	3,7	3,4	3,3	2,2	2,3	2,5
Kernkraftwerke	0,0	2,6	6,2	12,3	12,7	13,1	12,1	12,4
Insgesamt	19,5	25,2	34,8	42,6	44,7	41,6	41,8	43,5
				in %				
Wärmekraftwerke	89,0	80,2	71,6	63,3	64,2	63,1	65,6	65,6
Wasserkraftwerke	11,0	9,7	10,7	7,9	7,3	5,4	5,6	5,8
Kernkraftwerke	0,0	10,1	17,7	28,9	28,5	31,5	28,9	28,6
Insgesamt	100,0	100,0	100,0	100,0	100,0	100,0	100,0	100,0

Quelle: SG., verschiedene Jahrgänge.

den Jahren zeitweise über 10 % des inländischen Strombedarfs aus ausländischen Quellen gedeckt werden (vgl. Tabelle 9). Bulgarien importiert Strom zu über 90 % aus der Sowjetunion, die restlichen Einfuhren stammen aus den übrigen RGW-Staaten und Jugoslawien.

Als in den Jahren 1985 und 1986 die Stromproduktion zurückging (− 7 %) bzw. stagnierte, konnte allerdings nur ein Teil des Produktionsausfalls durch zusätzliche Importe ausgeglichen werden. Diese reichten aber nicht aus, um einen Rückgang im Stromangebot und damit eine deutliche Verlangsamung im Wirtschaftswachstum zu verhindern[10]). Die Energiekrise in den Jahren 1985 und 1986 machte die Anfälligkeit der bulgarischen Stromversorgung deutlich. Statt einer als optimal angesehenen Reservekapazität von 22 % betragen die tatsächlichen Reserven nach Angaben des ehemaligen Ministers für Energiewirtschaft und jetzigen Vorsitzenden der Assoziierung Energiewirtschaft (*Asociacija Energetika*), Nikola Todoriev, lediglich 3 bis 10 %[11]). Kommt es zu extremen Witterungsbedingungen – Dürre im Sommer, die die Flüsse austrocknet und die Stromproduktion aus Wasserkraft einschränkt oder starke Kälte im Winter, die die Braunkohlenförderung in den Tagebaubetrieben behindert und die Bekohlung der Kraftwerke beeinträchtigt – oder zu ungeplanten Ausfällen in den Elektrizitätswerken infolge mangelnder Wartung oder fehlender Ersatzteile, so führt dies zu einem Rückgang im Stromangebot. Alle diese ungünstigen Faktoren kamen neben organisatorischen Fehlleistungen während der Winter 1984/85 und 1985/86 zusammen und führten das Land in die seit 20 Jahren schwerste Energiekrise[12]). Strom für Industriebetriebe wurde rationiert, z.T. mußten großflächige Stromabschaltungen vorgenommen werden. Um die Verbraucher zu größerer Sparsamkeit zu

---

[10]) Vgl. Lodahl, M.: Die wirtschaftliche Entwicklung in Bulgarien in den achziger Jahren, in: Vierteljahreshefte zur Wirtschaftsforschung des DIW. (1987) 4, S. 341ff.

[11]) Todoriev, N.: Erwartet uns eine neue Energiekrise?, in: Bulgarien. (1987) 7/8, S. 6.

[12]) Vgl. Höpken, W.: Energiepolitik und Energieprobleme in Bulgarien, in: Südosteuropa. 37 (1988), S. 89.

motivieren, wurden die Preise für Elektroenergie drastisch erhöht: für private Abnehmer um 41 %, für Betriebe um 58 %[13]). Allerdings ist das Preisniveau für die privaten Haushalte noch immer gering, und die Betriebe können die erhöhten Energiekosten oft auf den Staat überwälzen. Daher blieben die freiwilligen Sparmaßnahmen unzureichend, und das Zwangssparen mußte für längere Zeit aufrechterhalten werden[14]). Aber auch Verbote können häufig nicht durchgesetzt werden. Zwar soll im Falle einer Überschreitung der vorgegebenen Verbrauchskontingente der fünffache Strompreis bezahlt werden; häufig fehlt es aber an Meßgeräten[15]). Auch das im Oktober 1984 ausgesprochene Verbot, in Industriebetrieben und kommunalen Einrichtungen elektrisch zu heizen, kann nicht überall durchgesetzt werden, weil viele Gebäude keine Schornsteine haben oder die empfohlenen Nachtspeicheröfen gar nicht angeboten werden[16]).

Tabelle 9: Stromaufkommen in Mrd. kWh

	1970	1975	1980	1983	1984	1985	1986	1987
Produktion	19,5	25,2	34,8	42,6	44,7	41,6	41,8	43,5
Import	0,2	4,1	4,9	5,3	5,9	7,5	5,4	5,3
Export	0,3	0,4	1,0	2,8	3,3	3,0	1,5	1,0
Nettoimport	− 0,1	3,7	3,9	2,5	2,6	4,5	3,9	4,3
Inlandsverbrauch	19,4	28,9	38,7	45,1	47,3	46,1	45,7	47,8

Quelle: SG., verschiedene Jahrgänge.

Zentrales Problem der bulgarischen Stromversorgung ist letztlich aber nicht das unzureichende Angebot, sondern der überhöhte Stromverbrauch. Wie Tabelle 10 zeigt, ist der Stromverbrauch je Einwohner in Bulgarien im internationalen Vergleich recht hoch. Fast alle europäischen Mittelmeerländer weisen einen deutlich geringeren Pro-Kopf-Verbrauch aus. Lediglich in Frankreich war der Stromverbrauch 1986 noch um 10 % höher. Für die überhöhte Nachfrage ist vor allem das Wirtschaftssystem verantwortlich zu machen, das Stromeinsparungen nicht ausreichend motiviert, sondern die Elektrizitätsverschwendung fördert.

Etwas entspannt wurde die Stromversorgungslage mit der Inbetriebnahme eines 1 000 MW-Reaktors im Kernkraftwerk von Kozloduj im Dezember 1987. Damit erhöhte sich die Kernkraftwerksleistung auf insgesamt 2 760 MW (vgl. Tabelle 11), das ist nach der ČSSR die höchste installierte Kernenergieleistung unter den kleineren Mitgliedstaaten des RGW. 1986 stammten knapp 30 % der bulgarischen Stromproduktion aus Kernkraftwerken. Dieser Anteil dürfte mit der Inbetriebnahme des

---

[13]) Vgl. RD. 16.9.1985; Grosser, I.: Bulgarien – Krise in Energie und Landwirtschaft bremst Wirtschaftswachstum, in: Bolz, K. (Hrsg.): Die wirtschaftliche Entwicklung in den sozialistischen Ländern Osteuropas zur Jahreswende 1985/86. Hamburg 1986, S. 20.
[14]) RD. 21.2.1985.
[15]) RD. 22.2.1985.
[16]) RD. 25.2.1985.

neuen Reaktorblocks auf über 35 % angestiegen sein und damit etwa dem entsprechenden Wert in der EG gleichkommen. Angesichts der geringen Brennstoffvorräte wird der Kernenergie in Bulgarien große Bedeutung zugemessen. 1974 nahm der erste 440 MW-Reaktor in Kozloduj an der Donau seinen Betrieb auf. Weitere drei 440 MW-Leichtwasserreaktoren folgten in den Jahren 1975, 1980 und 1982. Alle diese Reaktoren stammen aus der UdSSR; sie sind nicht mit dem im Westen üblichen Berstschutz ausgestattet. Erst der 1 000 MW-Reaktor, der ursprünglich bereits 1985 seinen Betrieb aufnehmen sollte, hat ein Containment. Bulgarien ist das erste der kleineren RGW-Staaten, in dem ein 1 000 MW-Reaktor fertiggestellt worden ist.

Tabelle 10: Stromverbrauch[1]) je Einwohner

	1980	1986	1980	1986
	kWh		Bulgarien = 100	
Bundesrepublik Deutschland	5 450	6 364	150	125
DDR	4 876	5 687	137	112
Frankreich	4 303	5 297	121	104
Bulgarien	3 564	5 090	100	100
Rumänien	2 654	–	74	–
Italien	2 900	3 572	81	70
Ungarn	2 483	2 983	70	59
Jugoslawien	2 275	2 805	64	55
Spanien	2 451	2 795	69	55
Griechenland	2 104	2 495	59	49
Türkei	472	667	13	13

[1]) Nettoverbrauch

Quelle: United Nations: Annual Bulletin of Electric Energy Statistics for Europe. New York 1987.

Die Planungen sahen für 1988 die Inbetriebnahme eines weiteren 1 000 MW-Reaktors in Kozloduj vor; mit 3 760 MW würde dieses Werk dann seine Endleistung erreichen. Dieses Ziel ist erneut nicht erreicht worden. Mit dem Bau eines zweiten Kernkraftwerk wurde bereits begonnen. Es entsteht ebenfalls an der Donau, in Belene. Hier sollen vier 1 000 MW-Reaktoren in den 90er Jahren ihren Betrieb aufnehmen. Bis zum Jahr 2000 sollen rd. 60 % des Stromes in Kernkraftwerken produziert werden[17]).

Das Unglück von Černobyl' hat bisher nicht zu einer Kursänderung in der bulgarischen Kernenergiepolitik geführt. Allerdings dürfte es mitverantwortlich für die Verzögerungen beim Ausbau der Kernenergiekapazitäten sein[18]). So sind nach dem

---

[17]) RD. 15.8.1986.
[18]) Vgl. Bethkenhagen, J.: Kernkraft kommt im RGW erst langsam voran, in: Energiewirtschaftliche Tagesfragen. 87 (1987) 10, S. 798 ff; derselbe: Nuclear Power in the USSR and Eastern Europe, Post Chernobyl, in: The Economist Intelligence Unit (Hrsg.): Eastern Europe and the USSR. London 1988, S. 27 ff.

Unglück an den bereits 1980 entwickelten 1000 MW-Reaktoren die Sicherheitseinrichtungen überprüft und konstruktive Veränderungen vorgenommen worden[19]). Ob allerdings an den Plänen festgehalten wird, auch Kernheizwerke zu bauen, ist derzeit schwer zu beurteilen. Derartige Heizhäuser müßten wegen der hohen Verluste beim Fernwärmetransport in unmittelbarer Nähe der Verbrauchszentren gebaut werden und stellen daher ein erhöhtes Sicherheitsrisiko dar.

Störfälle traten bereits im Kernkraftwerk von Kozloduj auf. Nikola Todoriev räumte ein, daß 1982 ein Ventilschaden zum Austritt von Radioaktivität im Kraftwerksraum geführt habe; ein weiterer Zwischenfall ereignete sich 1986, als 7 km vom Kernkraftwerk entfernt ein Wärmekanal einstürzte. Todoriev erklärte, daß keine Gefahr für die Bevölkerung bestanden habe; er verwies ferner darauf, daß im Kernkraftwerk nach dem Erdbeben von 1977 keine Schäden beobachtet worden seien[20]).

Tabelle 11: Kraftwerksleistung nach Kraftwerksarten in MW

	1970	1975	1980	1983	1984	1985	1986	1987
Wärmekraftwerke	3301	4387	5449	5978	6063	6508	6508	6508
Wasserkraftwerke	816	1793	1868	1895	1975	1975	1975	1975
Kernkraftwerke	0	880	880	1760	1760	1760	1760	2760
Insgesamt	4117	7060	8197	9633	9798	10243	10243	10743

Quelle: SG., verschiedene Jahrgänge.

4. Energieverbrauch

Angaben über den Primärenergieverbrauch[21]) werden in Bulgarien systematisch nicht veröffentlicht. Bulgarien zählt zu den wenigen Ländern, die der Economic Commission for Europe (ECE), einer UN-Organisation, keine Daten über die Primärenergiebilanz des Landes zur Verfügung stellt[22]). Die Angaben in den Tabellen 12 und 13 beruhen daher auf Schätzungen auf der Grundlage der lückenhaften Produktions- und Außenhandelsstatistiken.

In der Entwicklung des Primärenergieverbrauchs lassen sich zwei Phasen deutlich unterscheiden:

1970 bis 1980: Starke Verbrauchssteigerung
1981 bis 1987: Gedämpftes Wachstum.

---

[19]) Vgl. Todoriev, N. (Anm. 11), S. 6.
[20]) Ebd.
[21]) Primärenergieverbrauch ist der Verbrauch an Energieträgern, die in einer Volkswirtschaft produziert, aber noch nicht umgewandelt worden sind (z. B. Kohle, Erdgas, Erdöl; auch Wasserkraft und Kernenergie werden als Primärenergie eingestuft) sowie der Außenhandelssaldo mit Energierohstoffen und umgewandelter Energie (z. B. Koks, Benzin).
[22]) Vgl. Economic Commission for Europe (Hrsg.): Annual Bulletin of Energy Statistics for Europe. New York 1987, S. 3.

Die hohen Preissteigerungen auf den Weltenergiemärkten haben sich in den 70er Jahren auf den Energieverbrauch in Bulgarien überhaupt nicht ausgewirkt. Mit einer Jahresdurchschnittsrate von fast 6 % expandierte der Primärenergieverbrauch nahezu ungebrochen. Hierfür sind vor allem systemimmanente Gründe verantwortlich. Die bulgarische Währung ist – wie die in den anderen RGW-Staaten – eine reine Binnenwährung. Die Inlandspreise werden weitgehend unabhängig von den Weltmarktpreisen festgelegt. Eine administrative Anpassung der Energiepreise im Inland an die neuen Preise am Weltmarkt wurde kaum vorgenommen; die Wirtschaft blieb von den weltwirtschaftlichen Veränderungen weitgehend abgeschirmt. Anpassungsprozesse, wie sie sich in den westlichen Industriestaaten vollzogen, blieben aus. Während z. B. in der Bundesrepublik Deutschland der Primärenergieverbrauch 1980 nur um 3 % höher war als 1973, stieg er im selben Zeitraum in Bulgarien um 40 %.

Erst nach dem zweiten Ölpreisschock setzte sich auch in Bulgarien das Bewußtsein durch, daß das Expansionstempo im Energieverbrauch gedrosselt werden müsse. So betrug die Verbrauchszunahme im Zeitraum 1981 bis 1986 nur noch knapp 1 % im Jahresdurchschnitt.

Tabelle 12: Verbrauch von Primärenergie

	1970	1975	1980	1985	1986	1987[2])
	in Mio. t[3])					
Braunkohle	28,9	27,5	29,9	30,7	35,0	36,6
Steinkohle	5,9	7,1	7,2	8,4	7,7	8,3
Mineralöl	8,6	12,4	15,2	13,0	13,1	13,4
Erdgas	0,5	1,3	4,2	5,5	5,8	6,1
Primärstrom[1])	2,1	8,7	13,8	19,9	18,4	19,4
dar.: Kernenergie	0,0	2,6	6,2	13,1	12,1	12,4
	in PJ[4])					
Braunkohle	228	218	219	225	257	268
Steinkohle	134	161	165	194	178	190
Mineralöl	362	521	635	544	548	561
Erdgas	17	45	146	191	202	212
Primärstrom[1])	24	102	162	233	215	227
dar.: Kernenergie	0	30	72	154	141	146
Insgesamt	765	1 047	1 327	1 387	1 399	1 458
	Anteile in %					
Braunkohle	29,8	20,8	17,3	16,2	18,3	18,4
Steinkohle	17,5	15,4	12,4	14,0	12,7	13,0
Mineralöl	47,3	49,7	49,6	39,2	39,2	38,5
Erdgas	2,2	4,3	8,5	13,8	14,4	14,6
Primärstrom[1])	3,2	9,8	12,1	16,8	15,4	15,6
dar.: Kernenergie	0,0	2,9	5,7	11,1	10,1	10,0
Insgesamt	100,0	100,0	100,0	100,0	100,0	100,0

[1]) Wasserkraft, Kernenergie, Außenhandelssaldo. – [2]) Vorläufig. – [3]) Erdgas in Mrd. cbm, Primärstrom und Kernenergie in Mrd. kWh. – [4]) PJ – Peta-Joule = 10^{15} Joule. 1 Peta-Joule entspricht 0,03412 Mio. t Steinkohleneinheiten (SKE).

Quellen: SG., verschiedene Jahrgänge; Datenbank RGW-Energie des DIW.

Erreicht wurden die Energieeinsparungen in erster Linie durch Zuweisung geringerer Verbrauchskontingente. Sparanreize über hohe Preise gibt es in Bulgarien lediglich bei Benzin. Mit 1,20 Leva für einen Liter zählt der Benzinpreis zu den höchsten in Europa. So muß ein Bulgare für 100 l Benzin gut 50 % eines Durchschnittseinkommens aufwenden (DDR: rd. 15 %; Bundesrepublik Deutschland: rd. 5 %).

Auch im 9. Fünfjahresplan (1986–1990) wird der Energieeinsparung eine wichtige Bedeutung zugemessen. Im Vergleich zu 1985 soll 1990 der spezifische Verbrauch je 100 Leva Nationaleinkommen bei wichtigen Brennstoffen um 17 % geringer sein. Trotz der bisher erreichten Einsparungen ist der Primärenergieverbrauch je Einwohner in Bulgarien noch immer unverhältnismäßig hoch. Mit 155 Tera-Joule war er 1985 nur um 15 % geringer als in der Bundesrepublik Deutschland.

Verändert hat sich im Beobachtungszeitraum die Struktur des Primärenergieverbrauchs (vgl. Tabelle 12). Stark zurückgegangen ist die relative Bedeutung der Braunkohle. Sie deckte 1970 noch 30 % des Verbrauchs, 1987 hingegen nur noch 18 %. Zurückgegangen ist auch der Mineralölanteil – von 50 % (1975) auf zuletzt rd. 40 %. Stark an Bedeutung gewonnen haben dagegen Erdgas und Kernenergie, die 1970 praktisch noch ohne jegliche Bedeutung waren und 1987 rd. 15 % bzw. 10 % des bulgarischen Energieverbrauchs deckten. Insgesamt weist der Energieverbrauch in Bulgarien eine relativ „saubere" Struktur auf, denn die bei der Verbrennung die Luft stark belastende Kohle hat nur einen Anteil von knapp einem Drittel.

5. Außenhandel

Ein wesentliches Kennzeichen für die Energiewirtschaft Bulgariens ist ihre hohe Importabhängigkeit. Den hohen Zuwachs im Primärenergieverbrauch in den 70er Jahren deckte Bulgarien ausschließlich durch die Ausweitung der Importe (vgl. Tabelle 13). Erhöht wurden in jener Zeit vor allem die Erdöl- und Erdgaseinfuhren. Der mit Abstand wichtigste Energielieferant ist die Sowjetunion; Bulgarien bezieht von dort nahezu alle Importe.

Für diese einseitige Ausrichtung sind vor allem politische Gründe maßgebend. Wie alle kleineren RGW-Staaten verfolgt auch Bulgarien das Ziel, eine im Blockmaßstab autarke Energieversorgung zu sichern[23]). Die enge Bindung an die UdSSR bietet zudem den Vorteil, daß die Energiebezüge im Rahmen der Koordinierung der Fünf-

Tabelle 13: Primärenergieaufkommen (Anteile in %)

	1970	1975	1980	1985	1986	1987[2])
Produktion	38,0	24,9	21,5	19,2	21,4	21,5
Import	63,9	75,5	79,8	84,4	80,3	79,2
Export	1,9	0,4	1,3	3,7	1,7	0,7
Verbrauch[1])	100,0	100,0	100,0	100,0	100,0	100,0

[1]) Ohne Bestandsveränderungen. – [2]) Vorläufig.

Quellen: SG., verschiedene Jahrgänge; Datenbank RGW-Energie des DIW.

jahrespläne im voraus mengenmäßig fixiert werden und somit eine Grundlage für die Ausarbeitung der mittelfristigen Volkswirtschaftspläne bilden.

Auch die Preise waren über einen längeren Zeitraum für Bulgarien günstig. Dies ist ein Ergebnis der im RGW-Intrablockhandel geltenden Preisbildungsregeln. Danach werden die ausgetauschten Waren mit Preisen bewertet, die aus dem Durchschnitt der Weltmarktpreise in den vorangegangenen fünf Jahren bestimmt werden. Preisausschläge am Weltmarkt werden durch dieses Verfahren gedämpft. So waren die sowjetischen Erdölpreise für Lieferungen in den RGW in den 70er Jahren z. T nur halb so hoch wie die Weltmarktpreise. Der drastische Rückgang der Energiepreise kehrte indes Vor- und Nachteile um. Nunmehr profitiert die UdSSR von diesem Prinzip. 1986 war der von ihr in Rechnung gestellte Ölpreis doppelt so hoch wie der Weltmarktpreis[24]. Allerdings werden durch die mittelfristige Festschreibung von Liefermengen und durch die Dämpfung der Preisveränderungen Anpassungsprozesse verzögert. Während z. B. in den westlichen Industriestaaten der Ölverbrauch nach den kräftigen Preissteigerungen in den Jahren 1973 und 1979 gesenkt wurde, nahm er in Bulgarien noch bis 1980 zu. Erst danach ging er zurück: von 1980 bis 1985 von 15 auf 13 Mio. t[25]. Hierfür dürfte in erster Linie die Kürzung der sowjetischen Exporte in die RGW-Länder um rd. 10 % im Jahre 1982 verantwortlich gewesen sein.

Die Erdgasimporte – sie stammen ausschließlich aus der Sowjetunion – konnte Bulgarien seit der Aufnahme der Bezüge im Jahre 1974 auf 6 Mrd. cbm (1987) steigern. Die Ausweitung ihrer Liefermengen macht die Sowjetunion seit Mitte der 70er Jahre von der Beteiligung der RGW-Länder an der Erschließung der Erdgaslagerstätten abhängig. Bulgarien hat sich z. B. am Bau von Erdgasleitungen beteiligt, die von den Vorkommen in Orenburg, Urengoj und Jamburg zur sowjetischen Westgrenze führen. Derartige Beteiligungen erfolgen durch die Gewährung von Devisen-Krediten für den Kauf, durch die Lieferungen von Ausrüstungen sowie durch die Entsendung von Arbeitskräften für den Bau der Leitungen und Nebeneinrichtungen. Die Leistungen Bulgariens werden von der UdSSR in Form von Erdgaslieferungen zurückgezahlt[26].

Eine sehr enge Bindung an die UdSSR besteht auch im Bereich der Kernenergie. Die in Kozloduj eingesetzten Druckwasserreaktoren sind in der Sowjetunion entwickelt und gebaut worden. Die eingesetzten Brennstäbe stammen ebenfalls aus der UdSSR. Insofern hat der Ausbau der Kernenergie die Importabhängigkeit der Ener-

---

[23] Vgl. auch Bethkenhagen, J.: Bergbau und Energiewirtschaft, in: Grothusen, K.-D. (Hrsg.): Südosteuropa-Handbuch. Band V: Ungarn. Göttingen 1987, S. 328f.

[24] Vgl. Bethkenhagen, J. (Bearb.): Auswirkungen des Ölpreisverfalls auf die UdSSR, in: Wochenbericht des DIW. 53 (1986) 17, S. 212ff.

[25] Auch hier handelt es sich um Schätzungen. Von 1977 an werden von der bulgarischen Statistik Angaben über die Ein- und Ausfuhren von Öl nicht mehr ausgewiesen. Unklarheit besteht daher auch, ob und ggf. in welchem Ausmaß Bulgarien Rohöl ohne oder nach Verarbeitung reexportiert hat. Bulgarien soll etwa 3 bis 5 Mio. t Rohöl pro Jahr aus Libyen, Iran, Irak und Algerien beziehen, die nach Verarbeitung zu Mineralölprodukten in westliche Länder exportiert werden. Vgl. Financial Times. 7.9.1984. Diese Vermutung läßt sich allerdings statistisch nicht verifizieren.

[26] Vgl. Arakeljan, G.: Gemeinsamer Bau von Gasindustrieobjekten, in: Außenhandel der UdSSR. (1987) 1, S. 14f.

gieversorgung Bulgariens nicht vermindert, sondern weiter erhöht[27]). Auch der Brennstoffkreislauf steht unter sowjetischer Kontrolle, denn die abgebrannten Brennstäbe werden nach einer Zwischenlagerung in Kozloduj in die Sowjetunion zur Wiederaufarbeitung bzw. End- oder Zwischenlagerung zurückgesandt. Bulgarien ist Unterzeichner des Atomwaffensperrvertrages. Damit prüfen auch Inspektoren der „Internationalen Atomenergieorganisation" (IAEO) in Wien, ob das Uran ausschließlich für friedliche Zwecke verwendet wird. 1986 unterzeichnete Bulgarien ein gemeinsames Programm zum Ausbau der Kernenergie in den RGW-Staaten. Danach sollen bis zum Jahr 2000 die Kernkraftwerksleistungen in den kleineren Mitgliedstaaten von derzeit 8 000 auf 50 000 MW erweitert werden.

Bulgarien ist Gründungsmitglied der 1962 gebildeten „Vereinigten Energieverbundsysteme der RGW-Länder" (VES). Ziel der Vereinigung mit ihrer Schaltzentrale in Prag („Zentrale Dispatcherverwaltung") ist die Gewährleistung von Stromlieferungen, vor allem im Falle von unvorhergesehenen Störfällen. Da in allen RGW-Ländern die Stromversorgung sehr angespannt ist, ist die Leistungsfähigkeit des RGW-Verbundsystems trotz der Gesamtkapazität von rd. 160 000 MW in Spitzenlastzeiten sehr gering.

---

[27]) Die Kernenergie wird in der Primärenergiebilanz deshalb auch als Import behandelt.

Handel, Versorgung und Verkehr

Franz-Lothar Altmann, München

I. Handel und Versorgung: 1. Die Etablierung des „sozialistischen" Binnenhandelssystems – 2. Organisation und Formen des Handels – 3. Versorgung, Einkommen und Preisentwicklung – 4. Exkurs: Geplante Veränderungen bei der Preisbildung – II. Transport und Verkehr: 1. Geographische und historische Grundlagen – 2. Leistungen des Transportwesens – 3. Eisenbahntransport – 4. Straßenverkehr – 5. Fluß- und Seeschiffahrt – 6. Luftverkehr – 7. Rohrleitungstransport

I. Handel und Versorgung

1. Die Etablierung des „sozialistischen" Binnenhandelssystems

Vor dem II. Weltkrieg beruhte das System des Binnenhandels in Bulgarien auf privatwirtschaftlicher Grundlage. Private Händler und Kooperativen bildeten die Träger eines Systems, in welchem die landwirtschaftlichen Produkte sowohl von Händlern als auch von den landwirtschaftlichen Produzenten direkt auf den Wochenmärkten in allen Städten und Dörfern verkauft wurden, während andererseits die Landbevölkerung mit den benötigten Industriegütern und anderen Waren über Geschäfte und regelmäßig stattfindende Verkaufsmessen versorgt wurde. Umherziehende Händler ergänzten dieses System. Nach der letzten offiziellen Vorkriegsangabe, die sich auf den Zensus vom 31.12.1934 stützt, existierten Mitte der 30er Jahre in Bulgarien knapp 41000 Handelsunternehmen mit insgesamt 60000 Beschäftigten (einschließlich Unternehmern), woraus erkennbar wird, daß diese Handelseinrichtungen von sehr kleiner Größe waren und zumeist nur den Eigentümer selbst und bestenfalls noch eine Familienhilfe ernährten[1]). Die Anzahl der unabhängigen Händler war bis zum Jahr 1944 noch deutlich angewachsen und hatte ihren Höchststand in jenem Jahr mit 92500 erreicht[2]).

Eine besondere Bedeutung kam in der Vorkriegszeit für Bulgariens Binnenhandel den Verbrauchergenossenschaften (*potrebitelna kooperacija*) zu. 1938 existierten 165 mit insgesamt 96283 Mitgliedern, wobei erwähnt werden sollte, daß diese Verbrauchergenossenschaften sich fast ausschließlich (93 % aller Mitglieder) in den Städten organisiert hatten[3]). Nach dem Kriege begann man 1947 zunächst, eine Reihe von

---

[1]) Statističeski godišnik na carstvo Bălgarija (Statistisches Jahrbuch des Königreichs Bulgarien). Sofia 1939, S. 310/11.
[2]) Čakalov, A.: Nacionalnijat dochod i razchod na Bălgarija (Nationaleinkommen und -ausgaben Bulgariens). Sofia 1946, S. 92/93.

staatlichen Handelsorganisationen zu errichten, wie z. B. *CHOREMAG* (*Choteli, restoranti, magazini* / Hotels, Restaurants, Kaufhäuser), *NARMAG* (*Naroden magazin* / Volkskaufhaus) und ähnliche mehr. Auf diese Weise stieg der staatliche Anteil am Einzelhandelsumsatz von 16% im Jahre 1947 auf 25% im Jahre 1948 und erreichte 1949 immerhin bereits 44%. Gleichzeitig sank der Anteil des privaten Sektors am Einzelhandelsumsatz von 56% im Jahre 1947 über 31% im Jahre 1948 auf 13% im Jahre 1949, drei Jahre später, d. h. 1952, war der Anteil des privaten Handels unter 1% gefallen[4]). In diesem Jahr erfolgte auch die Veröffentlichung des Regierungserlasses über den Binnenhandel (20. 2. 1952), der festlegte, daß derselbe in Übereinstimmung mit dem staatlichen Wirtschaftsplan und entsprechend den Weisungen des Ministeriums für Binnenhandel durchzuführen sei. Der Ministerrat erhielt den Auftrag, die Organisation des Binnenhandels zu übernehmen, wobei der Großhandel Staatsbetrieben und Kooperativen übertragen wurde. Für den Einzelhandel wurde in dem Erlaß zunächst festgeschrieben, daß er staatlichen Handelsbetrieben, Verbraucher- und allgemeinen Genossenschaften, landwirtschaftlichen und handwerklichen Genossenschaften (jedoch nur für den Vertrieb ihrer eigenen Produkte) und auch privaten Personen übertragen werden sollte. Letztere benötigten für ihren Geschäftsbetrieb eine spezielle Genehmigung, die nur für jeweils ein Jahr ausgestellt wurde. Wenig später erlassene Durchführungsverordnungen (18. 3. 1952) stellten ausdrücklich fest, daß Privatpersonen sich nicht im Großhandel betätigen dürften.

Die restriktive Handhabung der Bestimmungen des Jahres 1952 führte dazu, daß bereits 1953 nur mehr 0,4% des gesamten Einzelhandelsumsatzes in Bulgarien im privaten Sektor abgewickelt wurden. Man stellte jedoch sehr schnell fest, daß wichtige Funktionen des Privathandels vom staatlichen und kooperativen Handel nicht ausgefüllt werden konnten und erließ am 12. 2. 1954 eine Verordnung, die das private Handwerk, den privaten Einzelhandel und auch Fliegende Händler wieder begünstigen sollte. Eine Reihe von weiteren Bestimmungen legte beispielsweise fest, daß der Handel mit gebrauchten Gegenständen nur in Geschäften mit besonderer Genehmigung erfolgen dürfe, daß der Viehhandel im Staatsmonopol durch das Staatsunternehmen *ZEMSNAB* (*Zemedelsko snabdjavane* / Landwirtschaftliche Versorgung) abgewickelt werden sollte, daß der Handel mit Gold, Silber, Platin und Edelsteinen ebenfalls dem Staat vorbehalten bleiben sollte und daß Verkäufe, die zu höheren Preisen als den staatlich festgelegten erfolgten, unter Strafe stünden[5]).

Von Anfang an spielte im sozialistischen Bulgarien die Handelstätigkeit der Genossenschaften eine wichtige Rolle. Schon 1946 waren gut 30% des Einzelhandelsumsatzes von Kooperativen abgewickelt worden, zwei Jahre später, 1948, betrug ihr Anteil bereits 43,5%. Bis zum Jahre 1952, d. h. bis zu dem Jahr, in welchem der Umbau des Handelssystems als weitgehend abgeschlossen betrachtet werden kann, hatte dann der sozialistische Sektor insgesamt einen Anteil von 99,3% am gesamten

---

[3]) Eine ausführliche Darstellung der Situation im Binnenhandel Bulgariens in der Zeit vor und unmittelbar nach dem II. Weltkrieg findet man in: Bulgaria. Ed. L. A. D. Dellin. New York 1957, S. 333–340 (Kapitel „Trade", verfaßt von Ivanko Gabensky).

[4]) Todorov, N. u. a.: Stopanska istorija na Bălgarija 681–1981 (Wirtschaftsgeschichte Bulgariens). Sofia 1981, S. 479.

[5]) Vgl. Gabensky, I.: Trade, in: Dellin (Ed.) (Anm. 3), S. 336.

Einzelhandelsumsatz, darunter entfielen 47,8 % auf den genossenschaftlichen Bereich.

Oberstes Leitungsorgan für den Binnenhandel war zunächst 1947 das Ministerium für Handel und Lebensmittelversorgung (*Ministerstvo na tǎrgovijata i prodovolstvieto*), das 1948 geteilt wurde, und zwar in ein Ministerium für Binnenhandel (*Ministerstvo na vǎtrešnata tǎrgovija*) und eines für Außenhandel (*Ministerstvo na vǎnšnata tǎrgovija*). Bei dieser Teilung blieb es bis 1957, als die beiden Ministerien wieder zu einem Handelsministerium (*Ministerstvo na tǎrgovijata*) zusammengefaßt wurden. 1959 erfolgte wieder eine Zweiteilung, so daß bis 1971 ein Außenhandelsministerium und ein Binnenhandelsministerium existierten. Letzteres wurde 1971 in „Ministerium für Binnenhandel und Dienstleistungen" (*Ministerstvo na vǎtrešnata tǎrgovija i uslugite*) umbenannt und bestand als solches bis 1984, als es mit dem Ministerium für Leichtindustrie (*Ministerstvo na lekata promišlenost*) zu dem neuen Ministerium für Produktion und Handel mit Konsumgütern (*Ministerstvo na proizvodstvoto i tǎrgovijata s potrebitelski stoki*) vereinigt wurde. Dieses fusionierte 1986 mit dem Außenhandelsministerium und trug bis zum 31. 12. 1988 die Bezeichnung „Handelsministerium" (*Ministerstvo na tǎrgovijata*). Im Zuge der am 18. 8. 1987 von der NSb verabschiedeten strukturellen und personellen Veränderungen im Ministerrat wurde mit Wirkung vom 1. 1. 1988 auch das Handelsministerium aufgelöst. Dem neuen Ministerium für Wirtschaft und Planung (*Ministerstvo na ikonomikata i planiraneto*) wurde der Bereich Binnenhandel zugeschlagen; für den Außenhandel ist seither ein eigenes Ministerium für Außenwirtschaftsbeziehungen (*Ministerstvo na vǎnšnoikonomičeskite vrǎzki*) zuständig[6]).

2. Organisation und Formen des Handels

Wenn im Falle Bulgariens der Begriff „Handel" (*tǎrgovija*) im Sinne von Handelsorganisation im Binnenhandel (*vǎtrešna tǎrgovija*) gebraucht wird, so ist damit ausschließlich der Einzelhandel gemeint, was auch im SG seine Bestätigung findet. Dies ist darauf zurückzuführen, daß es einen zwischengeschalteten Großhandel im westlichen Sinne (noch) nicht gibt, der zwischen den Produzenten und den verschiedenen Verkaufsstellen eine Verteilungs- und Marktfunktion übernehmen könnte. Die verschiedenen Verkaufsorganisationen, auf die weiter unten noch eingegangen wird, erhalten die zu verkaufenden Produkte direkt vom Produzenten zu sogenannten Produzentenabgabepreisen, die in etwa den im Westen gebräuchlichen Großhandelspreisen entsprechen, ohne daß eine Großhandelsinstitution zwischen Produzent und Verkaufsorganisation zwischengeschaltet ist.

Auch die Zulieferungen an die Produktionsbetriebe mit Rohstoffen, Vor- und Zwischenprodukten, Ersatzteilen, Maschinen und Einrichtungen erfolgen nicht über einen Großhandel, sondern werden über ein staatliches Zu- und Verteilungssystem

---

[6]) Zu den organisatorischen Veränderungen vgl.: Bǎlgarskite dǎržavni institucii 1879–1986. Enciklopedičen spravočnik (Die bulgarischen Staatsinstitutionen. Enzyklopädisches Nachschlagewerk). Sofia 1987.

organisiert, das in seiner Grundstruktur eine nachgeordnete Behörde der Staatlichen Plankommission (*Dăržavna planova komisija*) ist und die Produktionsmittelzuteilungen entsprechend den aus den Planaufgaben sich ergebenden Ansprüchen durchführt.

Die derzeit in Bulgarien unternommenen Reformbestrebungen zielen darauf ab, sowohl das traditionelle Zuteilungssystem, das bisher die Zulieferungen zwischen den einzelnen Produzenten durchführte, durch ein Großhandelssystem zu ersetzen, als auch zwischen Produzent und Einzelhandel schrittweise ein Großhandelssystem einzubauen. Die Beziehungen zwischen den Unternehmen sowie zwischen ihnen und den anderen sozialistischen Organisationen und auch privaten Händlern sollen auf der Grundlage von Wirtschaftsverträgen organisiert werden[7]).

Tabelle 1: Einrichtungen des Einzelhandels nach Warenarten und Eigentumsformen (Anzahl)

Warenarten	1980			1987		
	Staats-betriebe	Genossen-schafts-betriebe	Privat-betriebe	Staats-betriebe	Genossen-schafts-betriebe	Privat-betriebe
Lebensmittelgeschäfte	6 188	7 162	2	7 401	7 636	–
Geschäfte für Nicht-lebensmittelwaren	7 464	5 717	63	8 662	5 789	26
Gemischtwarenläden	238	4 174	–	339	4 019	–
Buden und Kioske	4 178	1 728	460	4 709	1 992	766
Insgesamt	18 068	18 781	525	21 111	19 436	792

Quelle: SG. 1988, S. 318.

Wie aus Tabelle 1 ersichtlich, existierten Ende 1987 41 339 Einzelhandelseinrichtungen in Bulgarien. Die Anzahl der Staatsbetriebe und der Genossenschaftsbetriebe war annähernd gleich, in privatem Eigentum fand man nur 792 Geschäfte, wobei diese vorwiegend Kioske und Buden waren. Auch hier ist aber im Zuge der Reform geplant, daß private Handelstätigkeit in verstärktem Maße zugelassen wird, wobei auch vorgesehen ist, daß staatliche Handelsunternehmen in einer Art Leasingverfahren das Management von kleineren Einrichtungen an Privatpersonen abtreten. Insgesamt gab es 7717 Selbstbedienungsläden, darunter 4194 für Lebensmittel und 2398 für Nichtlebensmittelwaren.

Im RGW-Vergleich läßt sich im übrigen feststellen, daß unter den Ländern, die bereits Privatbetriebe im Einzelhandel zulassen, Bulgarien mit 1,7% Anteil an der Gesamtzahl der Einzelhandelseinrichtungen sich noch sehr bescheiden ausnimmt gegenüber Privatanteilen von 37,3% in Ungarn, 35,2% in der DDR, 17,4% in Polen

---

[7]) Vgl. Pravilnik za stopanskata dejnost, in: DV. (1987) 100. Eine deutsche Übersetzung des ‚Regulativs für die Wirtschaftstätigkeit' erschien in: Südosteuropa. (1988), S. 308–345.

und sogar 78,2% in Vietnam (alle Angaben 1986). Gleichzeitig muß aber festgehalten werden, daß in der Sowjetunion, in der Tschechoslowakei, Rumänien, der Mongolei und Kuba bisher überhaupt keine privaten Geschäfte existierten, in der Mongolei sogar Genossenschaftsbetriebe unbekannt sind. In der Tschechoslowakei und der Sowjetunion sollen nunmehr ebenfalls im Zuge der Reformen private Einzelhandelsläden zugelassen werden[8]).

Die kleine Durchschnittsgröße der privaten Einzelhandelseinrichtungen in Bulgarien bringt jedoch mit sich, daß der Gesamtumsatz derselben 1987 nur 3,6 Mio. Leva gegenüber 4901,7 Mio. Leva im genossenschaftlichen Einzelhandelsbereich und 11 839 Mio. Leva im staatlichen Einzelhandel ausmachte und somit ganze 0,02% erreichte.

Von den insgesamt 4 108 459 Beschäftigten in der NRB waren im Jahr 1987 308 355 Arbeiter und Angestellte für den Bereich des Handels ausgewiesen, allerdings schloß diese Zahl auch Personen ein, die im sogenannten Großhandel und vor allem im öffentlichen Restaurationswesen tätig waren. Eine genauere Unterteilung ist nur für Arbeiter im SG zu finden; hier sind von insgesamt 170 140 ein Anteil von knapp 47% dem Einzelhandel zuzurechnen, ein etwas größerer Anteil (48,1%) entfällt auf das öffentliche Restaurationswesen, der Rest verteilt sich auf Großhandel und Ankauf[9]).

In der bulgarischen Statistik wird unter Binnenhandel auch das öffentliche Restaurationswesen eingeordnet. Ende 1987 gab es 26 645 sogenannte Einrichtungen der öffentlichen Verpflegung, darunter 4496 Restaurants, Gaststätten und Imbißstuben, 3622 Wein- und Bierstuben, 4719 Eis-, Milch- und Kaffeestuben, 6553 Kantinen und 4469 Buden bzw. Kioske[10]). In der internationalen RGW-Statistik wurden für das Jahr 1986 für Bulgarien 28 927 Einheiten aufgezählt, wobei hier auch die Unterscheidung nach Eigentumsformen durchgeführt wird. Von der eben genannten Zahl entfielen auf staatliche Betriebe 17 182, 11 700 waren im Eigentum von Genossenschaften, und ganze 45 waren Ende 1986 in privater Hand. Dies sind knappe 0,2%, während zum Vergleich in Ungarn 27,2%, in der DDR 30% (1985) und in Polen 19% von Einrichtungen dieser Art in privatem Besitz waren. In den übrigen RGW-Ländern existierten 1986 private Gaststätten noch nicht, im Zuge der derzeitigen Reform sind jedoch mittlerweile in der UdSSR und der Tschechoslowakei ebenfalls die ersten entstanden[11]).

Das bislang noch vorherrschende System der internen Organisation des Binnenhandels (einschließlich des öffentlichen Restaurationswesens) ist mehrstufig insofern ausgelegt, als auf der untersten Stufe die Handelsgeschäfte zu finden sind, die dann in der mittleren Stufe entsprechend ihrer Eigentumsformen in staatlichen oder genossenschaftlichen Organisationen zusammengefaßt sind. Die wenigen Privatbetriebe sind in keinen Vereinigungen organisiert. Für ihre Mitglieder sind die Handelsorganisationen verantwortlich für den Ankauf der Waren. Sie sind entweder auf nationaler

---

[8]) Statističeskij ežegodnik stran-členov soveta ekonomičeskoj vzaimopomošči (Statistisches Jahrbuch der RGW-Mitgliedsländer). (1987). Moskau 1987, S. 271–275.
[9]) SG. 1988, S. 324.
[10]) SG. 1988, S. 321.
[11]) Statističeskij ežegodnik (Anm. 8), S. 277–279.

Ebene organisiert, wie z. B. *NARMAG, Naroden restorant* (Volksrestaurant) oder *Obleklo i obuvki* (Kleidung und Schuhe), oder stellen nur lokale Organisationen dar, wie *Gradeška tărgovija* (Städtischer Handel), *Narodna kooperacija* (*NARKOOP* / Genossenschaft des Volkes) oder *Selska kooperacija* (*SELKOOP* / Dorfgenossenschaft). Die obersten Aufsichts- und Planungsorgane stellen schließlich das Ministerium für Wirtschaft und Planung sowie – für die lokalen Handelsorganisationen noch zwischengeschaltet – die Handelsabteilungen der jeweiligen Volksräte dar.

Eine Vorstellung von der gesamtwirtschaftlichen Bedeutung des Bereichs Handel, materiell-technische Versorgung und Ankauf gibt sein Anteil am volkswirtschaftlichen Gesamtprodukt eines Jahres. Die beiden hierfür in Bulgarien verwendeten Gesamtgrößen, das gesellschaftliche Produkt und das Nationaleinkommen, zeigten für das Jahr 1987 nur Leistungsanteile dieses Sektors von 4,0 bzw. 7,5 %. Diese Anteilszahlen sind im übrigen in den 80er Jahren stark zurückgegangen, 1980 lag beispielsweise der Beitrag des weiteren Bereichs des Handels zum Nationaleinkommen noch bei 9,8 %[12]).

3. Versorgung, Einkommen und Preisentwicklung

Obwohl insgesamt die Anzahl der Einzelhandelseinrichtungen zwischen 1970 und 1987 um gut ein Drittel erweitert wurde und vor allem neue Supermärkte entstanden waren, muß doch festgestellt werden, daß das Einzelhandelssystem in Bulgarien immer noch eine ungünstige Größenstruktur (durchschnittliche Ladengröße – Selbstbedienungsläden eingeschlossen – 50 qm) sowie überaus hinderliche Organisationsformen aufweist. Der Konsument muß sich mehrfach anstellen, um die Ware erst zu bestimmen, dann bezahlen zu dürfen und schließlich die Ware ausgehändigt zu bekommen. Selbstbedienungsläden machten 1987 noch nicht einmal ein Viertel aller Einzelhandelseinrichtungen aus, und das Warenangebot ist trotz deutlicher Verbesserungen zu Beginn der 80er Jahre in Struktur und Qualität bei weitem noch nicht zufriedenstellend. Immerhin war Bulgarien zu Beginn der 80er Jahre im Vergleich mit anderen sozialistischen Ländern relativ gut versorgt, was vor allem die Grundbedürfnisse im Lebensmittelbereich anbetraf. Infolge mehrerer schlechter Erntejahre traten jedoch seit Mitte der 80er Jahre wieder häufiger Versorgungslücken bei Nahrungsmitteln auf, der Planerfüllungsbericht 1987 nennt hierbei einzelne Arten von Fleisch und Fleischprodukten, Obst, Gemüse, Kartoffeln, Knoblauch, rote gemahlene Paprika, Bohnen und pflanzliche Speisefette. Probleme traten neuerdings auch bei Backwaren, insbesondere bei Brot, auf. Engpässe werden zur Zeit auch bei Industrieprodukten (Schuhe, Unterbekleidung und Fernsehapparate) und einigen Dienstleistungen berichtet[13]).

Über die Entwicklung des Einzelhandelsumsatzes gibt Tabelle 2 Auskunft. Die in Klammern gesetzte parallele Entwicklung der Einzelhandelspreise ergibt in der Gegenüberstellung zu den nominalen Umsatzzahlen die reale Ausweitung des Waren-

---

[12]) SG. 1988, S. 143.
[13]) Grosser, I.: Bulgarien 1987/88, in: Die wirtschaftliche Entwicklung in den sozialistischen Ländern Osteuropas zur Jahreswende 1987/88. Hrsg. K. Bolz. Hamburg 1988, S. 16.

Tabelle 2: Entwicklung des nominalen Einzelhandelsumsatzes je Einwohner (einschließlich Gaststätten) (U) und der Einzelhandelspreise (P), 1970–1987

Jahr	Einzelhandelsumsatz insgesamt		davon Lebensmittel (einschließlich Gaststättenverzehr)		industrielle Konsumgüter	
	1970 = 100 U (P)	1980 = 100 U (P)	1970 = 100 U (P)	1980 = 100 U (P)	1970 = 100 U (P)	1980 = 100 U (P)
1980	175 (123)	100 (100)	157 (139)	100 (100)	189 (112)	100 (100)
1982	191 (124)	109 (101)	168 (140)	108 (101)	210 (113)	111 (101)
1984	203 (127)	116 (103)	176 (146)	113 (105)	226 (113)	119 (101)
1987	225 (133)	129 (108)	185 (156)	118 (112)	262 (118)	138 (105)

Quelle: SG. 1988, S. 328, 349.

umsatzes. Hierbei wird deutlich ersichtlich, daß eine schnellere Umsatzausweitung bei industriellen Konsumgütern als bei Lebensmitteln erfolgt ist. Tabelle 3 gibt einen Überblick über die Entwicklung des Einzelhandelsumsatzes im staatlichen, genossenschaftlichen und privaten Handel sowie im Gaststättenbereich seit 1980. Es wird dabei deutlich, daß sowohl in den Einzelhandelsläden als auch im Gaststättenbereich die stärkeren Umsatzzuwächse im staatlichen Sektor erfolgt sind.

Hinsichtlich der offiziellen Preisveränderungen für Konsumgüter kann man in Bulgarien unterschiedliche Entwicklungen feststellen. Von 1970 bis 1978 stieg der offizielle Konsumentenpreisindex lediglich insgesamt um 3,2 Punkte, was auch im Intra-RGW-Vergleich deutlich die geringste Preissteigerung in all diesen Ländern bedeutete. 1979 wurde dann erstmalig ein größerer Preissprung von 4,6 % verzeichnet, wobei die Begründung offiziell lautete, daß sowohl die Großhandelspreise als auch die Ankaufspreise für landwirtschaftliche Erzeugnisse angehoben wurden, um Anreize für die Produktion von Konsumgütern zu schaffen und Subventionen abzubauen. Ein Teil der Preissteigerungen wurde auch in das Jahr 1980 verlegt, wo der Einzelhandelspreisindex nochmals um 14 % zulegte. In diesem Zusammenhang wurde noch eine zweite Begründung angeführt, nämlich der sich stark entwickelnde Tourismus nach Bulgarien. Die Preise wurden angeblich erhöht, um Subventionen bei Produkten einzuschränken, die von Ausländern gekauft wurden, was zum Teil eine Bestätigung durch ein Dekret vom November 1981[14] erfuhr, das Ausländern verbot, eine lange Liste von (vermutlich stark subventionierten oder knappen) Nahrungsmitteln und dauerhaften Konsumgütern aus Bulgarien mitzunehmen und das beträchtliche Exportzölle (200 bis 300 %) für einige andere Produkte erließ. Diese Maßnahme zielte offensichtlich auf Touristen aus Polen und Rumänien sowie teilweise aus Griechenland und Jugoslawien ab, zu einer Zeit, als in diesen Ländern starke Versorgungsprobleme entstanden waren[15]. Zwischen 1981 und 1985 bewegten sich die jährlichen

---

[14] DV. (1981) 86.
[15] Vgl. Feiwel, G. R.; Feiwel, I.: Bulgarien, in: Die Wirtschaft Osteuropas und der VR China zu Beginn der 80er Jahre. Hrsg. H.-H. Höhmann. Stuttgart 1983, S. 241.

Tabelle 3: Entwicklung des nominalen Einzelhandelsumsatzes nach Eigentumsformen, in Mio. Leva

Jahr	Einzelhandelsumsatz insgesamt				davon: in Einzelhandelsläden				im Gaststättenbereich			
	insges.	staatlich	genossensch.	privat	insges.	staatlich	genossensch.	privat	insges.	staatlich	genossensch.	privat
1980	12084	8248	3832	3,1	9674	6753	2917	3,1	2410	1495	915	0
1982	13316	9187	4125	3,7	10659	7513	3142	3,6	2656	1674	982	0,1
1984	14311	9927	4379	4,1	11434	8096	3333	4,1	2877	1831	1046	0
1987	16744	11839	4902	3,6	13609	9809	3796	3,5	3135	2030	1105	0,1
1980 = 100	138,6	143,5	127,9	116,1	140,7	145,3	130,1	112,9	130,1	135,8	120,8	–

Quelle: SG. 1988, S. 331.

Preissteigerungen zwischen 0,3 und 1,7 % (1985), um erst 1986 mit 3,5 % wieder eine Beschleunigung zu erfahren, bevor man 1987 offiziell die Preise nur um etwas weniger als 1% steigen ließ. Diese offiziellen Preissteigerungsraten sind jedoch mit Vorsicht zu behandeln, da es wie in den übrigen sozialistischen Ländern durchaus auch eine beachtliche versteckte Inflation gibt. Die latente Übernachfrage nach Konsumgütern verleitet die Produzenten dazu, ihre Produkte ein wenig zu verändern, ohne die Qualität meßbar zu verbessern, um hierdurch eine Preisanhebung durch die Preisfestsetzungsbehörde zu erwirken. Gleichzeitig wird die Produktion des billigeren Produkts, für das immer noch Nachfrage besteht, eingeschränkt, wobei das „neue" Produkt nicht, das alte hingegen weiterhin in die Berechnung des Preisindexes eingeht. Die tatsächlichen Preissteigerungen müßten zudem auch die Preise berücksichtigen, die auf den verschiedenen nichtlegalen Märkten bezahlt werden.

Wenn weiter oben festgestellt wurde (vgl. Tabelle 2), daß der Index der staatlichen Einzelhandelspreise von 1970 bis 1987 um 33 % gestiegen war, so wird gleichzeitig für den Zuwachs des Realeinkommens je Einwohner eine Steigerung um 85,6 % ausgewiesen. Das durchschnittliche Jahreseinkommen von Arbeitern und Angestellten betrug 1987 2812 Leva, wobei sich durchaus Unterschiede in den Durchschnittseinkommen zeigen. Im Gegensatz zu anderen RGW-Ländern findet man das höchste Durchschnittseinkommen im Bereich Wissenschaft, die niedrigste Einkommensgruppe sind die Beschäftigten im Bereich Handel, materiell-technische Versorgung und Ankauf.

Im Ergebnis zeigt sich in der Versorgung mit langfristig genutzten Konsumgütern im Jahre 1987, daß von 100 Haushalten 97 einen Fernsehempfänger, 91 elektrische Waschmaschinen, 94 einen Haushaltskühlschrank, 39 einen Personenkraftwagen und 47 einen Telefonanschluß besitzen. Beim Verbrauch wichtiger Grundnahrungsmittel pro Kopf der Bevölkerung lassen sich für das Jahr 1987 folgende Angaben finden: 74,0 kg Fleisch, 8,5 kg Fisch, 195,4 l Milch, 270 Eier, 35 kg Zucker, 117,6 kg Gemüse und 114 kg Obst. Bulgarien steht hierbei im Vergleich mit anderen sozialistischen Ländern vor allem bei Gemüse und Obst sowie bei Weizen- und Roggenerzeugnissen relativ gut versorgt da, weil in diesen Bereichen die Pro-Kopf-Produktion des Landes deutlich über dem RGW-Durchschnitt liegt.

4. Exkurs: Geplante Veränderungen bei der Preisbildung

Im Zuge der derzeit laufenden Reformbestrebungen soll grundsätzlich der Prozeß der Preisfestsetzung auf der Unternehmensebene erfolgen. Bis einschließlich 1987 hatten die zentralen Staatsorgane praktisch alle Preise in Bulgarien bestimmt. Im neuen reformierten System sollen die Unternehmen die Großhandelspreise für Waren und Dienstleistungen auf der Grundlage der Preise bilden, zu denen diese Waren auf repräsentativen ausländischen Märkten verkauft werden. Hierbei sollen die erwarteten Änderungen der internationalen Preise, d.h. vor allem die erwartete Inflation, sowie das Verhältnis von Angebot und Nachfrage auf dem Binnenmarkt berücksichtigt werden. Die so festgesetzten Preise werden Maximalpreise darstellen und unterliegen der Registrierung. Die Unternehmen können nach eigenem Ermessen Produkte zu einem geringeren Preis als dem eben erwähnten Grenzpreis absetzen. Da nicht von vornherein davon ausgegangen werden kann, daß von Anfang an echte Marktverhältnisse in Bulgarien bestehen, wurde festgelegt, daß die Vorschläge für die Großhandels- und Einzelhandelspreise mit den Hauptverbrauchern abgestimmt werden. Für die Einzelhandelspreise werden hierbei die Empfehlungen der BPS und der Verbraucherräte bei der OF mitberücksichtigt. Eine Reihe von Zusatzbestimmungen regelt die Aufschläge für Luxuswaren, Delikatessen und Markenwaren, für Ersatzteile und für die Ankaufpreise landwirtschaftlicher Produkte. Insgesamt ergibt sich der Eindruck, daß auch das neue reformierte Preisbildungssystem noch keinesfalls nach den Regeln einer freien Marktpreisbildung funktionieren wird, sondern die staatlichen Organe weiterhin weitreichende Kontroll- und Einflußmöglichkeiten sich vorbehalten werden. Im übrigen wurde gleichzeitig mit den neuen Bestimmungen zur Preisbildung eine Liste von etwa 60 vom Ministerrat und ca. 80 von den Ressortministerien festgesetzten Preisen veröffentlicht, die für grundlegende Waren und Dienstleistungen sowie für einige Produktionsmittel zentral bestimmt werden[16]).

Der Umbau des Großhandelspreissystems nach den hier nur kurz wiedergegebenen neuen Bestimmungen, der im Ergebnis eine Annäherung der binnenwirtschaftlichen Preisrelationen an die der Weltmärkte bringen soll, soll bis Ende 1990 durchgeführt werden. Beginnend mit dem Jahr 1991 wird in einer zweiten Phase der Preisreform der Bereich der Konsumgüterpreise in Angriff genommen, wobei die ungarischen Erfahrungen kräftige Preissteigerungen im Einzelhandelsbereich erwarten lassen. Daß dies auch von offizieller Seite so erkannt wird, bestätigt die Ankündigung, daß die Löhne und Gehälter begleitend entsprechend der „geplanten und begrenzten Inflation" angehoben werden sollen.

II. Transport und Verkehr

1. Geographische und historische Grundlagen

Bei einer heutigen Gesamtfläche von 110 994 km² ist Bulgarien als kleineres südosteuropäisches Land traditionell klassisches Transitland, das allerdings wegen seiner verkehrsmäßig ungünstigen starken Zerklüftung – über die Hälfte des bulgarischen Territoriums hat hügeligen oder Bergcharakter – nicht leicht zu erschließen ist. Nach der Eroberung der Balkanhalbinsel wurden die alten Balkanwege an das osmanisch-türkische Wegesystem eingeschlossen und entwickelten sich zu lebendigen Verkehrsadern der allgemeinen Wirtschaft in Südosteuropa. Der belebteste Weg auf dem Festland war der alter Römerweg von Singidunum über Serdica (heute Sofia) nach Konstantinopel, der in der Türkenzeit die Hauptverkehrsader zwischen der Hauptstadt und den europäischen Gebieten des Imperiums war. Belebt waren auch die Handelswege von Plovdiv nach Dubrovnik durch Samokov, Skopje, Prizren und von der Donau ins Rhodopengebirge und nach Istanbul, durch Nordostbulgarien, durch

---

[16]) Vgl. Naredba za cenite (Anordnung über die Preise), in: DV. (1988) 3. Deutsche Übersetzung in: Südosteuropa. (1988), S. 330–345.

das Balkangebirge nach Karnobat und Ajtos. Wasserwege erleichterten teilweise den Handel. Die Donau diente als Verbindung zu der Walachei, zur Moldau, zu Polen und Ungarn, die Flüsse Marica und Struma, die in ihrem Unterlauf schiffbar sind, erleichterten den Wassertransport zum Ägäischen Meer. Hafenstädte am Schwarzen Meer ermöglichten Transportverbindungen sowohl in nördlicher Richtung nach Constanța und Odessa als auch nach Süden, nach Istanbul. Die Ausbreitung des Handels mit Österreich-Ungarn in der zweiten Hälfte des 18. Jh. beeinflußte auch den Transport auf der Donau in Richtung Nordwesten. Wichtiges Umschlagszentrum war damals die Stadt Svistov (heute Svištov).

Zur Zeit der Befreiung von der türkischen Oberherrschaft im Jahre 1878 hatte Bulgarien nur zwei Eisenbahnlinien, die Ruse-Varna-Linie und die privat errichtete Eisenbahnlinie des österreichischen Baron Hirsch von der türkischen Grenze (Svilengrad) über Plovdiv nach Belovo. Erst 10 Jahre später, im Jahr 1888, wurde Bulgarien zum ersten Mal in das europäische Eisenbahnnetz Wien-Belgrad-Sofia-Istanbul eingeschlossen[17]). Bereits im Jahre 1885 wurde durch das Eisenbahngesetz festgelegt, daß das Eisenbahnwesen in Bulgarien in der Hand des Staates liegt, eine grundsätzliche Bestimmung, die seither keine Änderung mehr erfahren hat.

Zum Ende des II. Weltkriegs muß für Bulgarien festgestellt werden, daß es in bezug auf verkehrsmäßige Erschließung gegenüber seinen Nachbarländern deutlich zurücklag. Bis zum Jahr 1947 wurden auch von der kommunistisch geführten Regierung keine konkreten Maßnahmen getroffen, um die Rückständigkeit des Transportwesens zu beseitigen. Erst die Nationalisierungsgesetze des Jahres 1947 verfügten die Beschlagnahme aller in Privatbesitz befindlichen Transportmittel, diese wurden fortan vom Staat bzw. von Kooperativen verwaltet. Der im selben Jahr aufgestellte Zweijahresplan ordnete 15 % aller Investitionsmittel dem Transport- und Nachrichtenwesen zu. Im darauffolgenden 1. Fünfjahresplan (1949–1953, 1952 vorzeitig erfüllt) wurden sogar 22 % der Gesamtinvestitionen diesem Sektor laut Plan zugeordnet, tatsächlich mündeten jedoch nur 17,2 % in diese Verwendung. Der 2. Fünfjahresplan (1953–1957) bedachte das Transport- und Nachrichtenwesen immerhin noch mit 12 % aller Investitionsausgaben.

Die außergewöhnliche strategische Bedeutung Bulgariens für die Sowjetunion (direkte Grenzen mit der Türkei, Griechenland und Jugoslawien, lediglich 25 bis 50 km vom Ägäischen Meer entfernt) brachte es mit sich, daß die Pläne für die Erneuerung, Modernisierung und vor allem Erweiterung des Transport- und Nachrichtenwesens in Bulgarien in der Nachkriegszeit direkt von Moskau entworfen wurden. Bis zum Jahre 1952 unterstand die allgemeine Eisenbahnverwaltung im bulgarischen Transportministerium noch direkt dem sowjetischen General Markov[18]). Viele der neuerbauten, erweiterten oder verbesserten Verkehrsverbindungen hatten vor allem strategische Bedeutung. Hinzu kamen die sehr stark intensivierten Wirtschaftsbeziehungen, die Bulgarien nach dem II. Weltkrieg mit der Sowjetunion einging und für die spezielle Transportsysteme errichtet werden mußten, wie beispielsweise die neue

---

[17]) Peneva-Vincze, L.: Über die Frage des Warentransports in Bulgarien, in: Traditionelle Transportmethoden in Ostmitteleuropa. Hrsg. A. Paládi-Kovacs. Budapest 1981, S. 73–77.
[18]) Rangeloff, G.: Transportation and Communications, in: Dellin (Ed.) (Anm. 3), S. 370.

Trans-Balkan-Eisenbahnlinie, die täglich 700 t Uranerz aus der Gegend nördlich von Sofia nach Burgas am Schwarzen Meer zur Verschiffung in die Sowjetunion brachte.

Die Verwaltung des Transportwesens unterliegt dem Ministerium für Transport (*Ministerstvo na transporta*), das seit 1947 „Ministerium für Eisenbahn-, Automobil- und Wasserverkehr" (*Ministerstvo na železopătnite, avtomobilnite i vodnite săobštenija*) hieß, 1949 in „Ministerium für Transport" umbenannt wurde und zwischen 1957 und 1966 mit dem Ministerium für Post, Telegrafen- und Telefonwesen (*Ministerstvo na poštite, telegrafite i telefonite*) fusioniert wurde zum Ministerium für Transport und Nachrichtenwesen (*Ministerstvo na transporta i săobštenijata*). Seit 1966 ist das Nachrichtenwesen wieder ausgegliedert, und das Transportministerium trägt seinen Namen bis heute.

2. Leistungen des Transportwesens

Mit 105 Mrd. Tonnenkilometern (tkm) wies Bulgarien 1987 eine Transportleistung aus, die fast an die der Tschechoslowakei (107 Mrd. tkm) herankam, d. h. an die Leistung eines Landes, das nicht nur in der wirtschaftlichen Entwicklung deutlich weiter ist, sondern auch bei insgesamt größerem Territorium länger gestreckt ist und 6 Mio. mehr Einwohner hat. Ungarn, das 20 % kleiner ist und gut 10 % mehr Einwohner hat, erreichte 1986 nicht einmal die Hälfte der tkm-Leistung Bulgariens[19]). Bei diesen Zahlen muß aber darauf hingewiesen werden, daß 65,2 % der tkm-Leistung des bulgarischen Warentransportes auf den Seeverkehr entfallen, wobei die Handels- und Tankerflotte vor allem Fremdfrachten transportiert, so daß der größte Teil der hierbei erzielten tkm im Grunde genommen die Gesamtleistung des bulgarischen Transportwesens verzerrt darstellt (vgl. Tabelle 4).

Tabelle 4: Leistungen des Waren- und Personenverkehrs, nach Verkehrsträgern gegliedert, 1987

Verkehrsträger	Gütertransport		Personentransport	
	Mio. t	Mrd. tkm	Mio. Personen	Mrd. Personenkm
Eisenbahn	82,5	17,8	109,7	8,1
Kraftfahrzeug	917,5	16,7	939,8	19,9
Flußschiffahrt	4,1	2,0	0,3	0,02
Seeschiffahrt	25,9	67,5	0,4	0,03
Pipeline	21,0	1,0	–	–
Luftverkehr	24 (Tsd. t)	42 (Mio. tkm)	2,8	3,6
Insgesamt	1 051,0	105,0	1 053,0	31,6

Quelle: SG. 1988, S. 295, 308.

---

[19]) Statističeskij ežegodnik (Anm. 8), S. 247.

3. Eisenbahntransport

Das gesamte Schienennetz der bulgarischen Eisenbahn beträgt 6497 km, darunter allerdings 2197 km Bahnhofgleise. Von den 4300 km freien Strecken waren 1987 58,3% elektrifiziert, was ein im internationalen Vergleich sehr hoher Wert ist: 1986 hatte Ungarn 25,7% elektrifiziert (allerdings von einer Gesamtlänge von 7875 km), die DDR wies gar nur 19,7% (Elektrifizierung von 14005 km) auf, und auch Polen konnte mit 38,8% (von 26848 km) diesen Anteil ebenso wenig erreichen wie die UdSSR mit 34,8% (von 145576 km) und die ČSSR mit 26,9% (von 13116 km). Die in Klammern gesetzten Gesamtstreckenlängen zeigen allerdings auch, daß die Streckendichte in Bulgarien mit 38,7 km Gleislänge je 1000 km^2 relativ gering ist. Andere RGW-Länder haben eine weit höhere Streckendichte, wie beispielsweise Ungarn mit 85 km/1000 km^2, die DDR mit 129 km/1000 km^2, Polen mit 85,9 km/1000 km^2, Rumänien mit 47,1 km/1000 km^2 und die Tschechoslowakei mit 103 km/1000 km^2. Immerhin konnten wegen des hohen Elektrifizierungsgrades 1987 bereits 80,3% der Gütertransportleistung (gemessen in tkm) im elektrischen Betrieb befördert werden.

Eine Besonderheit stellen 245 Restkilometer der früher vorherrschenden Schmalspur (760 mm Spurbreite) dar, sie stellen die Verbindung zwischen Septemvri und Pazardžik einerseits und den in Pirin-Gebirge gelegenen Orten Razlog, Bansko und Dobriniště andererseits her.

Insgesamt können neun Hauptverbindungslinien im bulgarischen Eisenbahnwesen aufgezeigt werden:

a) Kalotina-Dragoman-Sofia-Pazardžik-Plovdiv-Svilengrad. Diese ist ein Teil der internationalen Magistrale, die Europa mit dem Nahen und Mittleren Osten verbindet.

b) Sofia-Mezdra-Pleven-Gorna Orjachovica-Kaspičan-Varna. Diese Linie wird auch die nordbulgarische Magistrale genannt.

c) Die am Südrand des Balkans entlangführende Strecke von Sofia über Karlovo, Sliven, Karnobat nach Burgas und Varna.

d) Ruse-Gorna Orjachovica-Veliko Tărnovo-Dăbovo-Stara Zagora-Dimitrovgrad-Podkova. Diese stellt die Nord-Süd-Verbindung zwischen den südlichsten Landesteilen und der Donaugegend dar.

e) Sofia-Pernik-Stanke Dimitrov-Blagoevgrad-Kulata. Diese Linie stellt sowohl die Verbindung zwischen dem bulgarischen Industriezentrum Sofia als auch der aus dem nordöstlichen und östlichen Europa kommenden internationalen Linie mit Griechenland her.

f) Sofia-Pernik-Radomir-Kjustendil-Gjueševo, eine der beiden Hauptverbindungen nach Jugoslawien.

g) Mezdra-Vraca-Vidin. Diese Linie ist sowohl für die Erschließung des nordwestlichen Teils Bulgariens als auch als Anschluß an die Verkehrsbedingungen im RGW von Bedeutung.

h) Plovdiv-Čirpan-Stara Zagora-Jambol-Karnobat-Burgas.

i) Ruse-Samuil-Kaspičan. Diese Linie ist die älteste in Bulgarien bestehende Eisenbahnlinie und verbindet die Industriegebiete von Ruse und Varna[20].

---

[20] Geografija na Bălgarija. Ikonomičeska geografija (Geographie Bulgariens. Wirtschaftsgeographie). Sofia 1981, S. 364.

4. Straßenverkehr

Der größte Teil der Beförderungen von Lasten und Personen im Inland entfällt auf Kraftfahrzeuge, lediglich bei einem Vergleich der geleisteten tkm im Warenverkehr können die bulgarischen Eisenbahnen noch einen leichten Vorsprung gegenüber dem Kraftfahrzeuggewerbe aufweisen (vgl. Tabelle 4). 1987 wurden 87,3 % aller beförderten Güter (gemessen in t) mit Kraftfahrzeugen befördert, 89,2 % des Personentransports (gemessen an der Anzahl der beförderten Personen) erfolgte mittels Kraftfahrzeugen. Auch bei der Personenkilometerleistung sind die Beförderungen durch Kraftfahrzeuge mit 63 % an der gesamtstaatlichen Beförderungsleistung deutlich vorne. In diesen Angaben sind im übrigen die behördlichen und innerstädtischen Personenbeförderungen nicht enthalten.

Das Straßennetz Bulgariens hatte 1987 eine Gesamtlänge von 36 908 km, darunter 90,9 % mit festem Belag. Im Ausbau befindet sich derzeit ein Autobahnnetz, das in Form eines Dreiecks auf einer südlichen Route Sofia mit Plovdiv und Burgas (*Trakia*), auf einer nördlichen Linie Sofia mit Botevgrad und Varna (*Chemus*) und schließlich mit einer kürzeren Nord-Süd-Richtung entlang des Schwarzen Meeres die beiden großen Hafenstädte Varna und Burgas (*Černo More*) verbinden soll. Ende 1987 waren von den gut 1100 geplanten Autobahnkilometern erst 242 fertiggestellt. In beiden Fällen war der Autobahnbau von Sofia ausgehend begonnen worden, wobei die südliche Trasse schon deutlich weiter fortgeschritten ist.

Neben diesen 242 km Autobahn wies Ende 1987 Bulgarien 2938 km Straßen erster Ordnung, 3812 km Straßen zweiter Ordnung, 6277 km Straßen dritter Ordnung und 23 639 km Straßen vierter Ordnung aus. Insgesamt ergab dies 332,8 km Straßen je 1000 km^2.

Die wichtigsten Straßenverbindungen im Überlandverkehr sind:
a) Kalotina-Sofia-Plovdiv-Svilengrad. Sie stellt ein Teilstück der internationalen europäischen (RGW-) Magistrale Nord-Süd dar, die in Danzig beginnt und über Preßburg (Bratislava), Budapest und Sofia bis Istanbul läuft.
b) Kulata-Blagoevgrad-Sofia-Botevgrad-Pleven-Bjala-Ruse. Sie stellt die Verbindung zwischen den nördlichen Landesteilen und Rumänien mit Griechenland her.
c) Gjuešsevo-Kjustendil-Pernik-Sofia-Botevgrad-Loveč-Veliko Tărnovo-Šumen-Varna. Diese Straßenverbindung beginnt an der jugoslawischen Grenze und ist vor allem für den binnenwirtschaftlichen Transport von vorrangiger Bedeutung.
d) Sofia-Karlovo-Sliven-Burgas. Diese sehr gut asphaltierte Streckenführung stellt die schnellste Verbindung zwischen Sofia und dem Schwarzen Meer her.
e) Ruse-Polski Trămbeš-Veliko Tărnovo-Gabrovo-Šipkapaß-Kazanlăk-Stara Zagora-Chaskovo-Kărdžali. Diese Streckenführung ist die direkte Nord-Süd-Verbindung von dem Industriegebiet in Ruse nach dem Süden des Landes.

Bulgarien ist ins internationale Transportwesen durch *SOMAT* (*Stopansko obedinenie meždunaroden avtomobilen transport* / Wirtschaftsvereinigung Internationaler Autotransport), das größte Lastbeförderungsunternehmen Europas, überaus stark integriert. Neben den normalen Straßentransporten nach den europäischen Ländern und Asien unterhält SOMAT Roll-on-Roll-off-Verkehrslinien auf der Donau bis Deggendorf und von Burgas bis Thessaloniki, Limassol auf Zypern, Tartus in Syrien, Marseille in Frankreich und Barcelona in Spanien.

Für die Personenbeförderung standen 1987 im Überlandverkehr 5207 Omnibuslinien zur Verfügung, die auf insgesamt 196 754 km Streckenlänge 4895 Ortschaften bedienten. Innerstädtische Autobuslinien gab es in 158 Städten, hierbei sind vor allem die ungarischen Ikarusbusse im Einsatz. Für den städtischen Personenverkehr sind daneben noch Trolleybusse und Trambahnen eingesetzt. Bis zum Jahr 1965 gab es Trolleybusse nur in Sofia und Plovdiv, seit 1986 zusätzlich auch noch in den Städten Varna, Pleven, Sliven und Kazanlǎk sowie seit 1987 auch in Gabrovo, Pernik und Tolbuchin. Die Gesamtlänge der befahrenen Strecken betrug Ende 1987 in allen diesen Städten zusammen 300 km, zum Einsatz kamen 506 Trolleybusse. Trambahnen findet man nur in Sofia, wo 1987 auf einer Gesamtlänge von 175 km 390 Triebwagen zur Verfügung standen. Ebenfalls in Sofia wurde damit begonnen, ein Untergrundbahnnetz mit sowjetischer Unterstützung aufzubauen. Archäologische Funde im Zentrum der Stadt haben zunächst den Ausbau behindert und verteuert. Einige Teilstrecken am südlichen Stadtrand wurden jedoch bereits 1986 fertiggestellt, weitere Teile der Linie, die zu dem neuen Wohnviertel Ljulin führen soll, erwarten ihre Fertigstellung im Jahre 1990.

5. *Fluß- und Seeschiffahrt*

Die bulgarische Handelsflotte zusammen mit den Schiffen der Schwarzmeer- und Hochseefischerei und der Fahrgastflotte nimmt den 18. Platz in der Welt in Bezug auf die Gesamttonnage ein. Hierbei verfügt sie über Tanker (darunter auch der 100 000-Tonnen-Tanker „Chan Asparuch"), Trockengutfrachter, Mehrzweckfrachter, Containerschiffe und Fähren mit einer Gesamttonnage von knapp 1,9 Mio. Bruttoregistertonnen.

Bulgarien hat zwei wichtige Wasserwegverbindungen. Die erste ist das Schwarze Meer mit den Haupthäfen Burgas und Varna, von denen neun feste Linienverbindungen mit ausländischen Häfen bestehen, darunter die sogenannte Westeuropäische, die Mittelmeerlinie, die Fernöstliche Linie u. a. m. Regelmäßige Linienverbindungen bestehen auch zwischen den beiden Häfen Varna und Burgas einerseits und den sowjetischen Häfen Odessa, Il'ičevsk, Novorosijsk und Ždanov, woher Bulgarien vor allem seine Rohstoffe aus der UdSSR bezieht. Im Jahre 1978 wurde noch eine neue Fährverbindung Varna-Il'ičevsk eröffnet, auf der ständig vier Fährschiffe verkehren. Die gesamte jährliche Tonnenleistung soll auf 8 Mio. t ausgelegt sein und für die wirtschaftliche Integration der beiden Länder Bulgarien und UdSSR eine wichtige Rolle spielen[21]).

Die zweite Anbindung an den internationalen Schiffsverkehr ermöglicht die Donau, die auf eine Länge von 470 km Bulgariens Grenze nach Rumänien bildet. Sie stellt einen wichtigen Transportweg sowohl für Waren in die UdSSR als auch nach Rumänien, Jugoslawien, Ungarn, die Tschechoslowakei, Österreich und die Bundesrepublik Deutschland dar. Über die Häfen Lom und Ruse wird der größte Teil des über die Donau führenden Ex- und Imports abgewickelt. Einige Häfen sind für be-

---

[21]) Ebenda, S. 371.

stimmte Produkte spezialisiert, wie z. B. Lom für Erze und Koks oder Silistra für Holzmaterialien. Weitere wichtige Donauhäfen sind Vidin, Orjachovo, Svištov und Somovit.

Hauptsitz der bulgarischen Flußschiffahrt ist Ruse. Von hier sowie von Lom nimmt die Ostlinie ihren Beginn, die zu den sowjetischen Häfen Reni und Izmail führt und die die wichtigste und am höchsten belastete Linie darstellt. Die zweite, die sogenannte Westlinie, führt von Lom nach Bratislava. Mit der Sowjetunion hat Bulgarien außerdem ein gemeinsames Transportunternehmen *DUNAJTRANS* mit Sitz in Ruse gegründet, ferner ist Bulgarien neben Ungarn, der UdSSR und der ČSSR auch Mitglied in der internationalen Wirtschaftsvereinigung *INTERLEICHTER*. Dieses Unternehmen führt Fluß- und Seetransporte mit Hilfe moderner Leichtertechnologie durch und soll vor allem die Donauanliegerstaaten beim Übergang vom Fluß- zum Seeverkehr unterstützen.

6. *Luftverkehr*

Die bulgarische Zivilluftfahrt wurde 1947 gegründet, als die erste Linie zwischen Sofia und Burgas ihren Betrieb aufnahm. 1948 wurde dann eine bulgarisch-sowjetische Luftverkehrsgesellschaft mit dem Namen *TABSO* begründet, die 1954 in alleiniges bulgarisches Eigentum überging und den Namen *BALKAN* erhielt, unter dem die bulgarischen Flugzeuge auch heute noch national und international verkehren. Das nationale Luftverkehrsnetz erreichte 1987 eine Länge von 2670 km, hinzu kamen 133 545 km internationale Luftlinien, die von *BALKAN* bedient werden. Damit hat Bulgarien nach der UdSSR (1 156 000 km) und der DDR (142 000 km) das drittlängste Flugverkehrsnetz des RGW mit deutlichem Abstand vor Polen, Kuba und der Tschechoslowakei, die zwischen 84 000 und 88 000 km Netzlänge aufweisen können.

Im Güterverkehr nahm Bulgarien 1986 mit 25 000 t Beförderungslast nach der UdSSR und der DDR den dritten Platz unter den sozialistischen Ländern ein, in der tkm-Leistung reichte es mit 43 Mio. tkm jedoch nur zum vierten Platz, da hier die Tschechoslowakei mit 58,3 Mio. tkm eine höhere Jahresleistung aufweisen konnte.

Der Personenverkehr sieht hingegen die bulgarische Luftlinie nach der Sowjetunion (116 Mio. Passagiere) schon an zweiter Stelle mit 2,8 Mio. für 1987. In der Passagierleistung, d. h. gemessen in Mio. Passagierkilometern, nahm Bulgarien 1986 unter den RGW-Ländern jedoch nur den dritten Platz ein, da hier Polen mit 3159 Mio. Passagierkilometern Bulgarien mit 2961 Passagierkilometern knapp überholt hatte.

Insgesamt besitzt Bulgarien 13 Flughäfen: Sofia, Varna, Burgas, Ruse, Plovdiv, Tărgovište, Stara Zagora, Gorna Orjachovica, Silistra, Chaskovo, Pleven, Vidin und Jambol. Die wichtigsten inländischen Flugverbindungen sind hierbei die Anbindungen der Städte Varna, Burgas und Ruse an die Hauptstadt Sofia. Der Flugpark der bulgarischen Luftfahrtgesellschaft *BALKAN* setzt sich ausschließlich aus sowjetischen Flugzeugen der Typen Tupolev, Yak und Antonov zusammen.

7. Rohrleitungstransport

Der Rohrleitungstransport begann in Bulgarien mit der Errichtung einer Leitung für Rohöl von dem Hafen *Družba* bei Burgas zu dem Erdölverarbeitungskombinat bei Kameno im Jahre 1975 zum Weitertransport des aus der Sowjetunion per Schiff angelieferten Rohstoffes. Wegen der geringen eigenen Vorräte an Primärenergiequellen ist von großer Bedeutung auch noch die Gasleitung, die ebenfalls aus der Sowjetunion Erdgas zuführt[22]. Das Erdgasleitungssystem stellt die Form eines Rings dar, dessen Zuleitung von Norden durch Rumänien erfolgt. Der nördliche Teil des Rings versorgt die Industrieunternehmen in Devnja, Pleven, Gabrovo, Vraca, Kremikovci, Sofia und Pernik. Der südliche, später fertiggestellte Zweig transportiert Erdgas nach Plovdiv, Dimitrovgrad, Jambol, Sliven, Chaskovo u. a. m. Vorgesehen ist weiter die Verlegung eines Rohrleitungssystems für den Transport von Erdöl und Erdölderivaten, das scherenförmig von Burgas ausgehend den Süden und Norden Bulgariens versorgen soll[23].

---

[22] Vgl. hierzu auch Höpken, W.: Energiepolitik und Energieprobleme in Bulgarien, in: Südosteuropa. (1988), S. 73–94.
[23] Geografija (Anm. 20), S. 378.

Tourismus

Magarditsch A. Hatschikjan, St. Augustin

I. Natürliche Bedingungen und Schwerpunkte des Tourismus – II. Fremdenverkehrsregulierung und Fremdenverkehrspolitik – III. Reiseverkehrsentwicklung 1970–1986

I. Natürliche Bedingungen und Schwerpunkte des Tourismus

Trotz der relativ kleinen territorialen Ausdehnung besitzt Bulgarien aufgrund landschaftlicher Vielfalt und günstiger klimatischer Bedingungen gute natürliche Voraussetzungen für den Tourismus. Verschiedene Gebirgszüge – das Rila-Gebirge, das Pirin-Gebirge, der Balkan, die Rhodopen –, zahlreiche Gebirgsseen und selbstverständlich die Schwarzmeerküste gehören zu den wichtigsten Naturschätzen des Landes auch im Hinblick auf den Tourismus. Hinzu kommen klimatische Vorzüge, die das Land seiner Lage im Übergangsgebiet zwischen einem (nach Norden hin) milden Kontinental – und dem (nach Süden hin) mediterranen Klima verdankt[1].

Dennoch wurden erst in der zweiten Hälfte der 60er Jahre die strukturellen und organisatorischen Grundlagen für den internationalen Massentourismus *nach* Bulgarien geschaffen. Naturgemäß stand als Zielgebiet zunächst die Schwarzmeerküste im Vordergrund, die auch bis heute der Hauptanziehungspunkt für ausländische Urlauber und die Haupteinnahmequelle für Sofia im Bereich des Tourismus geblieben ist. In der zweiten Hälfte der 70er Jahre folgte ein spürbarer Ausbau der Kapazitäten für den Wintersport, der seither zum zweiten Standbein im bulgarischen Touristik-Angebot geworden ist. Relativ unterentwickelt blieben hingegen, soweit es den internationalen Reiseverkehr anbelangt, die Möglichkeiten zur Nutzung der Gebirgsseen, der Jagdreviere und der Städte für den Tourismus.

II. Fremdenverkehrsregulierung und Fremdenverkehrspolitik

Bis Mitte der 80er Jahre war das 1966 gegründete Tourismuskomitee beim Ministerrat (*Komitet po turizma pri Ministerskija săvet*), seit 1977 das Staatskomitee für Tourismus (*Dăržaven komitet po turizma*) die wichtigste Regulierungsinstanz der bul-

---

[1]) Eine gute Übersicht bieten Dinev, L.; Mišev, K.: Bălgarija. Kratka geografija (Bulgarien. Kurze Geographie). Sofia 1980. Siehe auch Petrov, P.: Bulgaria on the Geographical Map, in: Modern Bulgaria. History, Policy, Economy, Culture. Sofia 1981, S. 128–154. Vgl. das Kapitel von I. Matley, Geographical Foundations.

garischen Touristikwirtschaft, zuständig für die Erarbeitung der fremdenverkehrspolitischen Leitlinien, für die Planung und Durchführung der fremdenverkehrspolitischen Maßnahmen und für die Kontrolle eines Netzwerks staatlicher touristischer und wirtschaftlicher Unternehmen (darunter „Balkantourist"). Im Zuge der 1986 in Gang gesetzten Reorganisierungswelle in der bulgarischen Wirtschaftsstruktur[2]) wurde als Branchenassoziation die „Bulgarische Assoziation für Tourismus und Erholung" (*Bălgarska asociacija za turizăm i otdich* – BATO) de facto mit den Aufgaben des Staatskomitees für Tourismus betraut. Der Unterschied zur Situation vor 1986 besteht – zumindest auf dem Papier – darin, daß sowohl die Assoziation als auch die ihr zuzuordnenden Wirtschaftseinheiten (Unternehmen, Institute, Brigaden) auf der Grundlage von „Selbst-Verwaltung" und „Selbst-Finanzierung" tätig sein sollen. Das wichtigste und bekannteste der zur BATO gehörenden Unternehmen ist das nunmehr als „sich selbst verwaltende Organisation" titulierte „Balkantourist" mit mehr als 30 Filialen („Touristische Komplexe") im ganzen Land.

Nach der relativ raschen und starken Expansion des Touristik-Sektors in den 60er und 70er Jahren begannen sich schon in der zweiten Hälfte der 70er Jahre die negativen Auswirkungen der einseitigen fremdenverkehrspolitischen Orientierung auf den organisierten internationalen Badetourismus abzuzeichnen. Dies führte Ende der 70er Jahre zu ersten größeren Ansätzen einer Umorientierung, die sich auch in Umgewichtungen innerhalb der Kapitalinvestitionsstruktur niederschlug und vornehmlich zum Ziel hatte, die übermäßige saisonale Konzentration des Touristik-Angebots zu überwinden[3]). Trotz dieser Versuche blieben infolge finanzieller und organisatorischer Barrieren die strukturellen Schwachstellen – übermäßige regionale und zeitliche Konzentration des Reiseverkehrs, Monokultur des jeweiligen Angebots, schwache Qualität im gesamten Dienstleistungsbereich – weiterhin deutlich spürbar. Angesichts der in der ersten Hälfte der 80er Jahre unübersehbaren Stagnation und selbst Rückentwicklung im Reiseverkehr entbrannte – nicht zufällig nach dem Einbruch 1986 infolge des Černobyl'-Effekts – erneut die Debatte um den notwendigen Kurswechsel in der Fremdenverkehrspolitik[4]). Forderungen nach einer Diversifikation der anzubietenden Urlaubs- und Freizeitmöglichkeiten zielen – wie etwa in Zusammenhang mit den Heilbädern an der Schwarzmeerküste, mit den noch unzureichenden bzw. ineffektiv genutzten Kapazitäten im Gebirge oder mit dem sowohl quantitativ wie qualitativ äußerst beschränkten Angebot an Sportstätten – vor allem auf die

---

[2]) Vgl. hierzu vor allem Höpken, W.: Wirtschaftsreform in Bulgarien, in: Südosteuropa. 36 (1987), S. 45–57; Altmann, F.-L.: Wirtschaftsreformen in Südosteuropa und der ČSSR – Versuch einer vergleichenden Gegenüberstellung, in: Südosteuropa. 37 (1988), S. 280–294, hier insbesondere, S. 284–287; vgl. das Kapitel „Wirtschaftssystem" von W. Gumpel.

[3]) Die Ziele zu Beginn der 80er Jahre sind zusammengefaßt in Petrov, V.: A Country of Tourism, in: Modern Bulgaria (Anm. 1), S. 442–466, hier S. 450 ff.

[4]) Siehe hierfür insbesondere die Dokumentation einer von der Redaktion der Zeitschrift „Ikonomičeska misăl" organisierten Debatte: „Krăgla masa" po problemite na stopankija turizăm v NR Bălgarija („Runder Tisch" über die Probleme des Tourismus in der NRB), in: Ikonomičeska misăl. 32 (1987) 4, S. 24–52. Bemerkenswerterweise enthielten die vom XIII. Parteitag der BKP (der Anfang April 1986, also kurz vor der Černobyl'-Katastrophe, stattfand) verabschiedeten Thesen über Aufgaben und Ziele der ökonomischen, politischen, sozialen und kulturellen Entwicklungen bis zum Jahre 2000 nicht ein einziges Wort zum Thema Tourismus.

angestrebte ganzjährliche Nutzung der traditionellen Urlaubsgebiete und die Erschließung *qualitativ* neuer Quellen für den Tourismus nach Bulgarien vor allem unter dem Gesichtspunkt des Konkurrenzkampfs um westliche Touristen. Der Erfüllung dieser Forderungen stehen indes nicht nur Kapital- und Devisenmangel sowie die nun schon chronischen Defizite an Qualität und Vielfalt in den Einzelhandels- und Dienstleistungsangeboten entgegen, wie sie in Umfragen westlicher Reiseunternehmen regelmäßig bestätigt werden[5]). Auch die bereits angesprochenen jüngeren Reorganisierungsmaßnahmen im Wirtschaftsordnungssystem haben infolge ihrer Inkonsistenz eher Konfusion und neue Organisationsprobleme vor allem im Hinblick auf die territoriale Koordinierung der tourismusbezogenen Aktivitäten und die Gewährleistung einer reibungslosen Versorgung der Touristen hervorgerufen[6]).

III. Reiseverkehrsentwicklung 1970–1986

Nach dem ersten Boom in den 60er Jahren, in deren Verlauf sich die Anzahl ausländischer Gäste (von einem allerdings sehr niedrigen Ausgangsstand aus) mehr als verzwölffachte, verzeichnete Bulgarien auch im darauffolgenden Jahrzehnt einen kontinuierlich wachsenden Strom ausländischer Besucher, deren Zahl sich zwischen 1970 (mehr als 2,5 Mio.) und 1979 (rd. 5,12 Mio.) mehr als verdoppelte. Nach einem zwischenzeitlichen Rückgang der absoluten Besucherzahl in den Jahren 1982 und 1983 kletterte sie ab 1984 wieder in die Höhe und erreichte 1986 den bisherigen Rekordstand von mehr als 7,5 Mio.[7]). Allerdings geben diese Ziffern ein unzutreffendes, verzerrendes Bild wieder. Wie die statistischen Angaben über die Zahl der Übernachtungen und den Zweck der Besuche, differenziert nach Herkunftsländern, ausweisen, hat sich im Tourismus insgesamt eine Stagnation festgesetzt. Der enorm aussehende Anstieg der absoluten Besucherzahl ist fast ausschließlich auf die ab 1984 sprunghaft anwachsende Zahl von jugoslawischen „Handels-Touristen", auf die in den 80er Jahren kontinuierlich angestiegene Zahl von türkischen Transitreisenden

---

[5]) Dem Autor liegen Ergebnisse von Befragungen westdeutscher Touristen durch Reiseveranstalter über ihre Eindrücke von dem Urlaubsaufenthalt in Bulgarien vor, die ein einheitliches Bild vermitteln. Um ein typisches Resultat anzuführen: Auf die auf die Beurteilung des touristischen Leistungsangebots zielende Bitte, 14 angegebene Einzelpunkte anhand der allgemeinen Schulnoten (von „sehr gut" bis „mangelhaft") zu bewerten, kam es zu folgenden Ergebnissen: Nur in einem einzigen Fall – nämlich Bademöglichkeiten und Strandleben – fiel die durchschnittlich vergebene Note besser als „gut" aus (1,776). Schlechter als „befriedigend" wurden das Unterhaltungsangebot im Hotel (3,587), die Einkaufsmöglichkeiten (3,241), das Verpflegungsangebot (3,055) sowie die Kureinrichtungen (3,040) bewertet, und auch der Kontakt zu den Einheimischen (2,959) sowie Komfort und Service im Hotel (2,957) wurden als kaum besser als „befriedigend" eingestuft. Ergebnisse bulgarischer Untersuchungen sind zu finden und analysiert bei Tončev, C.: Turističeskoto obsluživane – săstojanie, problemi i zadači (Das touristische Dienstleistungsangebot – Zustand, Probleme und Aufgaben), in: Ikonomičeska misăl. 32 (1987) 6, S. 35–44.
[6]) Dieses Problem wird ausführlich diskutiert in Marinov, V.; Băčvarov, M.: Za integralen podchod kăm problemite na stopanskija turizăm (Für ein integrales Herangehen an die Probleme des Tourismus), in: Ikonomičeska misăl. 32 (1987) 12, S. 71–82, hier S. 79f.
[7]) SG. 1986, S. 441, und 1987, S. 449.

sowie auf den überproportional stark wachsenden Strom polnischer Besucher zurückzuführen. Demgegenüber ist – in umgekehrtem Verhältnis zur Entwicklung des Tourismus etwa nach Ungarn im selben Zeitraum – die Zahl westlicher Touristen und vor allem ihrer Übernachtungen in Bulgarien während der 80er Jahre stetig gesunken[8]). Unter dem Gesichtspunkt der Zahlungsbilanz muß folglich sogar von einer deutlichen Rückentwicklung ausgegangen werden.

In den 80er Jahren gewann der Individualtourismus im Verhältnis zum organisierten zahlenmäßig an Bedeutung, doch sind, wie bulgarische Untersuchungen und statistische Angaben belegen, die Bedingungen für Individualtouristen nach wie vor erheblich schlechter als diejenigen für die Gruppenreisenden[9]). Dies hängt mit der generellen Schwierigkeit für Sofia zusammen, für die seit Ende der 70er Jahre häufig

Tabelle 1: Entwicklung des Reiseverkehrs von und nach Bulgarien, 1960–1986

	1960	1965	1970	1975	1980	1981	1982	1983	1984	1985	1986	1987
Ausländische Besucher (Gesamtzahl in Mio.)	0,2	1,08	2,53	4,05	5,49	6,05	5,65	5,77	6,14	7,30	7,57	7,59
darunter aus der Bundesrepublik Deutschland				0,18	0,22	0,17	0,18	0,16	0,15	0,13	0,19	0,23	0,27
davon Touristen										0,12	0,10	0,10
Zahl der Übernachtungen von Ausländern (in Tausend)					15855	16066	17601	16666	16869	17241	18001	16723	19134
darunter aus der Bundesrepublik Deutschland					2186	2322	2403	1974	1615	1397	1766	1392	1775
Bulgarische Besucher im Ausland (Gesamtzahl in Mio.)				0,31	0,68	0,76	0,76	0,55	0,47	0,48	0,53	0,56	0,54
darunter in die Bundesrepublik Deutschland					3272	13077	16922	19103	18079	15097	17780	15476	11763	11448
davon Dienstreisen											11389	8270	8021

---

[8]) SG. 1987, S. 451. Von erheblicher Bedetung ist vor allem der starke Rückgang der von Touristen aus der Bundesrepublik Deutschland (dem seit langem mit Abstand zahlenmäßig größten Bestandteil der westlichen Touristen) realisierten Übernachtungen in Bulgarien, deren Zahl von 1980 bis 1986 um fast die Hälfte fiel (von 2,322 Mio. auf 1,392 Mio.).
[9]) Ausführlich diskutiert bei Marinov/Băčvarov (Anm. 6), S. 73 f. Siehe auch den Artikel: Svetlini i senki v sezona na počivkite (Licht und Schatten in der Urlaubssaison), in: RD. 13.8.1988.

als notwendig propagierte Intensivierung in der Touristik-Wirtschaft durch eine Diversifikation und qualitative Verbesserung des Angebots den dafür erforderlichen Strukturwandel in der Realität durchzusetzen. Immer noch werden Privatquartiere nur unzureichend, und wenn überhaupt, dann in auffallend disproportionalen Maßstäben, genutzt. Obwohl die Privatquartiere inzwischen hinsichtlich der Bettenanzahl den größten Posten innerhalb des bulgarischen Touristik-Angebots einnehmen (mit 27,6% der Betten vor den Erholungsheimen mit 21% und den Hotels mit 19,2%), macht die Zahl der dort übernachtenden Besucher lediglich weniger als ein Zehntel sowohl der Gesamtzahl der Touristen als auch der Gesamtzahl ausländischer Touristen aus, die Zahl der realisierten Übernachtungen (wiederum als Anteil sowohl aller Übernachtungen wie auch aller Übernachtungen ausländischer Besucher) rund ein Fünftel. Im übrigen ist ein überproportional hoher Prozentsatz der Privatquartiere in der Region an der Schwarzmeerküste konzentriert (68,3%), wohingegen er in den Gebirgsgegenden verschwindend gering (unter 1%) geblieben ist[10]).

Die Gesamtzahl bulgarischer Reisender ins Ausland erhöhte sich in den 70er Jahren stetig, erreichte 1981 den bisherigen Rekordstand von mehr als 750 000, fiel 1982 und 1983 drastisch, stieg aber ab 1984 wieder langsam an[11]). Allerdings gibt auch diese Ziffer kein realistisches Abbild der Entwicklung wieder, denn in ihr sind sowohl die „Privat"-(Tourismus, Familienbesuch, krankheitsbedingter Auslandsaufenthalt) als auch die Dienstreisen ins Ausland enthalten, wobei die Dienstreisen zwischen einem Drittel und zwei Fünftel der Gesamtzahl ausmachen. Bezogen auf die Gesamtbevölkerung, erreichte der Anteil der aus privaten Gründen ins Ausland reisenden Bulgaren Mitte der 80er Jahre lediglich rd. 4%, wobei die häufigsten Reiseziele die UdSSR, Rumänien, die DDR, Jugoslawien, Griechenland, Ungarn und die Tschechoslowakei sind. Rd. 13% aller aus privaten Gründen ins Ausland reisenden Bulgaren fuhren 1986 in ein westliches Land, wobei hier allerdings allein der Anteil Griechenlands rd. zwei Drittel ausmachte. Bezieht man diese Zahlen auf die Gesamtbevölkerung Bulgariens, so ergibt sich für 1986 das Ergebnis, daß kaum mehr als 0,5% aller Bulgaren (zieht man den griechischen Anteil ab, so verbleiben sogar nur rd. 0,2%) ins westliche Ausland reisten.

Relativ große Bedeutung für den Inlands-Tourismus kommt dem offiziell als „Sozial-Tourismus" apostrophierten Zweig zu, der vor allem unter sozialpolitischen und ideologischen Aspekten zu bewerten ist. Von verschiedenen Ministerien, den Ge-

Tabelle 2: Zweck der Reisen von ausländischen Besuchern nach Bulgarien (Angaben in Mio.)

	Gesamtzahl	Tourismus	Dienstreise	Transit	Auf Einladung	Sonstiges
1985	7,30	2,5	0,43	3,69	0,55	0,13
1986	7,57	2,11	0,46	4,04	0,71	0,25
1987	7,59	2,36	0,46	3,99	0,55	0,24

---

[10]) Zahlenangaben nach: Turizăm (Tourismus). Sofia 1987, S. 68–87. Siehe auch Marinov/Băčvarov (Anm. 6), S. 76ff.
[11]) SG. 1987, S. 452.

werkschaften, Jugendverbänden und anderen Institutionen organisiert, bietet er durch ein Netzwerk von Erholungsheimen und Schülerlagern für einen nicht unerheblichen Teil der Bevölkerung relativ preisgünstige Urlaubs- und Ferien-Möglichkeiten[12]).

Tabelle 3: Struktur des Touristik-Angebots

	Hotels	Camping	Privatquartiere	Erholungsheime
Bettenanzahl (in % der Gesamtbettenanzahl)	19,2	14,4	27,6	21,0
Anteil der Übernachtenden	52,8	5,8	9,2	11,3
Anteil an Übernachtungen von Ausländern	75,3	13,7	9,4	–

Quellen: SG. 1986, S. 441–444; 1987, S. 449–452, und 1988, S. 439–442; Turizăm. Sofia 1987, S. 68–87.

---

[12]) Grundlegende Aspekte des „Sozial-Tourismus" werden in verschiedenen Aufsätzen des Sammelbandes: Problemi na socialnata i ikonomičeska efektivnost na otdicha i kurortnoto lečenie (Probleme der sozialen und wirtschaftlichen Effektivität von Erholungswesen und Kurbehandlung). Sofia 1981, erörtert.

Außenwirtschaft

Roland Schönfeld, München

I. Einführung: 1. Ressourcenbedingte Außenhandelsabhängigkeit – 2. Einbindung in den „sozialistischen Weltmarkt" – II. Der institutionelle Rahmen der Außenwirtschaft: 1. Das sozialistische Außenwirtschaftsmonopol – 2. Reformexperimente mit der Außenwirtschaftsordnung – III. Die Entwicklung des Außenhandels und der Außenhandelspolitik: 1. Veränderungen der Warenstruktur – 2. Beständigkeit der regionalen Orientierung – der RGW-Markt – 3. Haupthandelspartner Sowjetunion – 4. Wirtschaftsbeziehungen zu den nichtsozialistischen Ländern – 5. Formen der Unternehmenskooperation

I. Einführung

1. Ressourcenbedingte Außenhandelsabhängigkeit

Bulgarien hängt mangels quantitativ und qualitativ ausreichender eigener Bodenschätze mit fortschreitender Industrialisierung in hohem und immer noch zunehmendem Maße von der Einfuhr ausländischer Rohstoffe und Energieträger ab. Zwar verfügt das Land über Kohlen-, Kupfer-, Blei- und Zink-, ja sogar über Erdöl-, Erdgas- und Uranlagerstätten, doch reicht keines dieser Vorkommen auch nur annähernd aus, um den Bedarf der Wirtschaft zu decken.

Dabei ist die Importabhängigkeit auf dem Energiesektor besonders kritisch. Selbst im Vergleich zu den sämtlich mehr oder weniger rohstoffarmen sozialistischen Ländern Ostmittel- und Südosteuropas weist Bulgarien mit 33 % den niedrigsten Grad der Selbstversorgung mit Energieträgern aus[1]. Es ist bestenfalls gelungen, den Einfuhranteil am gesamten Energieverbrauch, der zwischen 1970 und 1980 von 59,6 auf 71,0 % wuchs, in den 80er Jahren – durch verschärfte Bewirtschaftung, nicht durch sparsameren Umgang mit knapper Energie – zu stabilisieren (1985: 67,3 %)[2].

Darüber hinaus war Bulgarien im Verlauf der Modernisierung seiner Volkswirtschaft mangels eigener Ressourcen stets auf ausländische Kapital- und technische Hilfe angewiesen. Hierfür wie auch als Garant einer zureichenden Energie- und Rohstoffversorgung bot sich nach dem II. Weltkrieg die Sowjetunion an. Seine eindrucksvolle Entwicklung vom Agrar- zum industriellen Schwellenland hat das sozialistische

---

[1] Kohle, Öl und Gas zusammengenommen. Ungarn deckt 57, die ČSSR 68, die DDR 73, Rumänien 88 % seiner Energieversorgung aus eigenen Quellen. COMECON-Data 1985. Hrsg. Wiener Institut für Internationale Wirtschaftsvergleiche, S. 425. Vgl. die Kapitel von I. Matley, Geographical Foundations, und J. Bethkenhagen, Bergbau und Energie.

[2] Ebenda, S. 436. Dazu ausführlich Höpken, W.: Energiepolitik und Energieprobleme in Bulgarien, in: Südosteuropa. 37 (1988), S. 73–94.

Bulgarien vor allem sowjetischer Unterstützung zu danken. Zwar fehlte es nicht an eigenen Anstrengungen. Nachdem die BKP der Wirtschaft das in der siegreichen UdSSR offensichtlich mit Erfolg erprobte System der zentralistischen Planung und Leitung von Produktion und Verteilung aufgezwungen hatte, suchte sie unter schweren materiellen Opfern der Bevölkerung und durch Mobilisierung aller Arbeitskraftreserven die Armut und Rückständigkeit des Landes mit Brachialgewalt zu überwinden. Doch nur mit fortwährender finanzieller und technischer Hilfe der Sowjetunion konnte der Industrialisierungsprozeß in einem Tempo erzwungen werden, das noch in der Zwischenkriegszeit niemand für möglich gehalten hätte.

2. Einbindung in den „sozialistischen Weltmarkt"

Sowjetische Spezialisten ersetzten die entmachteten und von ihren Posten vertriebenen Führungskräfte der Kriegs- und Vorkriegsjahre in der Wirtschaftsverwaltung, in den Produktionsbetrieben, im Handel und in den Staatsgütern. Sie gewährleisteten sowjetische Kontrolle, dienten aber auch dazu, eine breite Schicht bulgarischer Technokraten heranzubilden, denen die Wirtschaftsplanung und die Leitung der neuen Industriebetriebe anvertraut werden konnte. Ein Instrument sowjetischen Einflusses bei der Neuorganisation der bulgarischen Wirtschaft waren gemeinsam betriebene Unternehmen, in welche die UdSSR die aufgrund des Pariser Friedensvertrages vom 10.2.1947 enteigneten deutschen Firmenanteile einbrachte[3]).

Im Rahmen von sogenannten Investitionsabkommen[4]) lieferte die UdSSR seit Ende der 40er Jahre Maschinen und Fabrikausrüstungen, schließlich Hunderte von kompletten Industrieanlagen in nahezu allen Branchen. Gleichzeitig wurde der mit dem Industrieaufbau rasch zunehmende Rohstoff- und Energiebedarf überwiegend aus sowjetischen Vorkommen gedeckt. Als Gegenleistung übernahm die Sowjetunion zunächst vor allem landwirtschaftliche und mineralische Rohstoffe sowie Nahrungsmittel, dann aber in wachsendem Umfange die aus den neuerrichteten Anlagen fließenden Industrieprodukte. Die gewaltige Kapazität des sowjetischen Marktes machte einen solchen bilateralen Warenaustausch, der keiner konvertierbaren Währung bedurfte, überhaupt erst funktionsfähig.

Es entsprach dem politischen Willen der sowjetischen und der bulgarischen Führung, daß der Außenhandel von den traditionellen Partnerländern in Mittel- und Westeuropa ab- und dem „sozialistischen Weltmarkt" zugekehrt wurde. Doch die mehr oder weniger sklavische Imitation des sowjetischen Wirtschaftssystems ließ dem Land schließlich auch keine andere Wahl. Der qualitative und technologische Standard der bulgarischen Industrieprodukte war und blieb systembedingt niedrig und reichte nicht aus, um einen angemessenen Absatz auf den hart umkämpften Märkten der „kapitalistischen" Länder zu gewährleisten. Hier zeigten sich die bulga-

---

[3]) Vgl. Spulber, N.: The Economics of Communist Eastern Europe. New York, London 1957, S. 193f.

[4]) Das erste Abkommen dieser Art wurde am 18.3.1948 für 20 Jahre geschlossen. Vgl. Sovetsko-bolgarskie otnošenija 1944–1948. Dokumenty i materialy. Moskau 1969, Nr. 150, S. 408–414.

rischen Exporteure weder ihren Konkurrenten aus den alten Industriestaaten noch jenen aus anpassungsfähigeren industriellen Schwellenländern gewachsen.

Erst durch die sozialistische Umgestaltung Bulgariens wurde die UdSSR, die in der Zwischenkriegszeit trotz geographischer Nähe und guter politischer Beziehungen zwischen beiden Ländern über unbedeutende Anteile an der bulgarischen Ein- und Ausfuhr nicht hinausgekommen war, zu einem übermächtigen Handelspartner. 1955, am Ende des ersten Jahrzehnts der kommunistischen Herrschaft, wickelte Bulgarien 48,9 % seines Außenhandelsumsatzes mit der Sowjetunion und weitere 37,7 % mit den übrigen sozialistischen Partnerstaaten im RGW – mit der DDR, der Tschechoslowakei, Polen, Ungarn und Rumänien – ab[5]). Somit beanspruchte der „sozialistische Weltmarkt" fast neun Zehntel des bulgarischen Warenverkehrs mit dem Ausland.

II. Der institutionelle Rahmen der Außenwirtschaft

1. Das sozialistische Außenwirtschaftsmonopol

Das staatliche Außenwirtschaftsmonopol, nach Lenin ein unabdingbares Erfordernis jeder „gesellschaftlichen Produktion nach vorherbestimmten Plan", bedeutet die ausschließliche Befugnis staatlicher Organe, den Handel und Kapitalverkehr betreffende Vereinbarungen mit dem Ausland zu treffen, d. h. Waren und Dienstleistungen ein- und auszuführen, Kredite in anderen Ländern aufzunehmen oder dorthin zu vergeben, Valuta-, Transport- und Versicherungsoperationen durchzuführen und wissenschaftlich-technische Erkenntnisse (Patente, Lizenzen, Know-how) auszutauschen. Das eigens für die Kontrolle des Warenverkehrs mit dem Ausland geschaffene Ministerium für Außenhandel (*Ministerstvo na vănšnata tărgovija*) kann das Recht, Auslandsgeschäfte zu tätigen, an spezielle staatliche Außenhandelsunternehmen, in Einzelfällen auch an staatliche Produktionsbetriebe übertragen. Das Valutamonopol als Teil des Außenwirtschaftsmonopols, der die internationalen Geldbeziehungen erfaßt, wird von der staatlichen Zentralbank und anderen staatlichen Organen wahrgenommen. Das Außenwirtschaftsmonopol sichert, daß nur solche Außenhandels- und Valutatransaktionen durchgeführt werden, die dem Willen der Parteiführung und den von ihr gesteckten wirtschaftspolitischen Zielen entsprechen. Es erlaubt die restlose Ein- und Unterordnung des Außenhandels im gesamten Volkswirtschaftsplan und die Abschirmung der Binnenwirtschaft gegenüber störenden Einflüssen des kapitalistischen Weltmarkts.

In Bulgarien wurde die völlige Monopolisierung der Außenwirtschaft nach dem sowjetischen Organisationsschema in wenigen Jahren nach Kriegsende schrittweise verwirklicht. Dieser Absicht der kommunistisch beherrschten Regierung kam die Tatsache entgegen, daß die außenwirtschaftlichen Transaktionen hier von jeher staat-

---

[5]) SG. 1960, S. 261 (errechnet).

licher Kontrolle unterlagen und es einen auch nur begrenzt freien Außenhandel seit der Weltwirtschaftskrise nicht mehr gegeben hatte[6]).

Das Valutamonopol der BNB, die seit ihrer Gründung 1879 eine staatliche Institution gewesen war und die Ziele der Regierung zu verwirklichen hatte, wurde lediglich fortgeführt und verschärft. Den Außenhandel mit der UdSSR und den übrigen sozialistischen Ländern wickelte die Regierung im Rahmen streng bilateraler Vereinbarungen ab, die Warenmengen, Preise und Zahlungsbedingungen rigoros festlegten[7]).

2. Reformexperimente mit der Außenwirtschaftsordnung

Die Nachteile dieser starren Monopolisierung der Außenwirtschaft waren wohl längst erkannt, ehe die sowjetische Führung mit dem aufsehenerregenden Liberman-Artikel in der *Pravda* im September 1962 das Startzeichen für ein offizielles Nachdenken über die Mängel des Planwirtschaftssystems auch in den Bruderländern gegeben hatte. So waren vorsichtige Modifizierungen des Außenwirtschaftssystems schon als Bestandteil der im November 1962 vom VIII. Parteitag der BKP beschlossenen Reformexperimente vorgesehen. Einigen Staatskonzernen räumte die Regierung versuchsweise erhebliche Freiheiten im Kontakt mit ausländischen Kunden und Lieferanten ein, die sie rasch wieder zurücknahm, als schwerwiegende Unregelmäßigkeiten aufgedeckt und führende Manager vor Gericht gestellt werden mußten. Immerhin erwog das Juliplenum 1968 des ZK der BKP, bestimmte Kooperationsformen mit kapitalistischen Unternehmen zu gestatten und setzte erstmals die Konvertierbarkeit des Lev im Rahmen eines sozialistischen Währungsverbunds als Ziel der bulgarischen Wirtschaftspolitik[8]).

Dem eklatanten Rückgang des Entwicklungstempos in den 70er Jahren, chronischen Leistungsbilanzdefiziten und einer rasch zunehmenden Verschuldung des Landes, sowohl gegenüber dem Haupthandelspartner Sowjetunion als auch in konvertierbaren Währungen, versuchte die bulgarische Führung durch eine Wiederbelebung der Reformdiskussion entgegenzuwirken. Dabei wurde den maßgebenden Kreisen offensichtlich klar, daß die für einen erneuten Wachstumsschub der Exporte notwendige Erweiterung der Produktionskapazitäten und Verbesserung der Produktqualität nur zu schaffen war, wenn man auch das verkrustete, überbürokratisierte Leitungssystem der Außenwirtschaft flexibler gestaltete, den Betrieben Anreize für die Ausfuhrproduktion bot, die Möglichkeiten für den Technologietransfer verbesserte und selbstverantwortliches, von ökonomischen Interessen bestimmtes Handeln der Menschen in diesem Bereich honorierte, nicht bestrafte.

---

[6]) Schönfeld, R.: Die Balkanländer in der Weltwirtschaftskrise, in: Vierteljahresschrift für Sozial- und Wirtschaftsgeschichte. 62 (1975), bes. S. 198 ff., 207 ff.
[7]) Spulber (Anm. 3), S. 101 f., 162 f., 425 f.
[8]) RD. 25.7.1968. Vgl. auch Vogel, H.: Rolle und Entwicklung der Wirtschaftsreform in Bulgarien seit 1965, in: Höhmann, H. H.; Kaser, M. C.; Thalheim, K. C. (Hrsg.): Die Wirtschaftsordnungen Osteuropas im Wandel. Ergebnisse und Probleme der Wirtschaftsreformen. Band I. Freiburg im Br. 1972, bes. S. 237 f.

So befaßte sich der 1979 verkündete, in vorsichtigen und tastenden Schritten angelegte „Neue Wirtschaftsmechanismus" (NIM) bald auch mit dem Außenwirtschaftssystem. Zweifellos setzte die Verschlechterung der Zahlungsbilanzsituation, insbesondere das Scheitern der Westexportstrategie, aber auch die Unzufriedenheit der sowjetischen Führung mit dem Zustand der bulgarischen Wirtschaft und dem Leistungsniveau der Exportindustrie die BKP in den 80er Jahren unter einen ständigen Handlungsdruck, immer neue Reformschritte einzuleiten. Einen wirkungsvollen Auftakt inszenierte die bulgarische Regierung mit dem Dekret Nr. 535 vom 25.3.1980, das die Gründung gemeinschaftlicher Produktions-, Handels- und Dienstleistungsunternehmen mit Partnerfirmen aus kapitalistischen Ländern gestattete[9]). Damit war Bulgarien nach Rumänien, Ungarn und Polen der vierte RGW-Mitgliedsstaat, der – immerhin sieben Jahre vor der Sowjetunion – westliche Direktinvestitionen in der eigenen Wirtschaft wünschte.

Als weitere Reformetappe wurde ab 1982 eine vorsichtige Dezentralisierung im Außenwirtschaftsbereich angestrebt[10]). So erhielten zunächst die übergeordneten Wirtschaftsorganisationen – Wirtschaftsvereinigungen, Kombinate, APK –, seit 1984 auch die Produktionsbetriebe selbst das prinzipielle Recht, Einfuhren und Ausfuhren direkt, also ohne die obligate Zwischenschaltung staatlicher Außenhandelsunternehmen, zu tätigen. Genehmigungen für jede dieser Transaktionen müssen jedoch nach wie vor beim Ministerium für Außenhandel und beim zuständigen Branchenministerium eingeholt werden, die sich somit eine lückenlose Kontrolle über das Auslandsgeschäft der Betriebe sichern und unerwünschte Abschlüsse verhindern können.

Die Ein- und Ausfuhrrechte der Wirtschaftsorganisationen wurden in der Ende 1986 verabschiedeten „Verordnung über die Wirtschaftstätigkeit" (*Pravilnik za stopanskata dejnost*) präzisiert[11]). Daß solche Aktivitäten streng überwacht werden, zeigt die Verpflichtung des Handelsministers, dem Ministerrat den Entzug der Ein- und Ausfuhrrechte vorzuschlagen, wenn Betriebe „die vorgeschriebenen Bedingungen und Anforderungen für ein selbständiges Auftreten auf dem Binnen- und Außenmarkt systematisch verletzen, qualitativ nicht ensprechende Produkte anbieten, ihre Vertragsverpflichtungen nicht erfüllen und durch dieses Fehlverhalten dem Lande nachteilige wirtschaftliche und handelspolitische Folgen entstehen..."[12]).

Seither haben Wirtschaftsorganisationen entsprechend ihrer Umwandlung in „sich selbst verwaltende Organisationen" auch für ihre „Selbstfinanzierung in konvertiblen Währungen" zu sorgen. Während ihnen bisher Auslandslieferungen und -bezüge über das zuständige Außenhandelsunternehmen in Binnenwährung – und zu Binnenpreisen – abgerechnet wurden, bilden sie nunmehr mit den aus direkten Auslandsgeschäften fließenden Devisen sogenannte Valutafonds, die nach Abzug der

---

[9]) DV. (1980) 25. Ausführlicher dazu siehe unten S. 417/18.
[10]) Vgl., auch zum folgenden Grosser, I.: Bulgarische Außenwirtschaftsreformen in den achtziger Jahren, in: Haendcke-Hoppe, M. (Hrsg.): Außenwirtschaftssysteme und Außenwirtschaftsreformen sozialistischer Länder. Ein intrasystemarer Vergleich. Berlin 1988, S. 143–159.
[11]) DV. (1987) 3.
[12]) Ebenda.

vorgeschriebenen Abführungen an den Staat ihrer Verfügung unterstehen. Der Valutafonds kann durch zusätzliche Devisenkäufe beim Staat oder bei der Außenhandelsbank (*Bălgarska vănšnotărgovska banka*) angereichert werden, nicht benötigte Devisen kaufen die Außenhandelsbank oder andere Handelsbanken auf[13]).

Um die Selbstfinanzierung der Betriebe zu erleichtern, wurde allen im Rahmen der Bankreform im Juni 1987 geschaffenen acht branchenorientierten „Handelsbanken" (*Tărgovski banki*) das Recht erteilt, Valutakredite zu vergeben, insbesondere um Modernisierungsinvestitionen, den Einkauf „effektiver" Rohstoffe oder eine bessere Versorgung des Binnenmarktes zu ermöglichen. Die Handelsbanken können Kredite im Ausland aufnehmen, sich an internationalen Bankenkonsortien beteiligen, am internationalen Devisenmarkt spekulieren und mit ausländischen Banken gemeinschaftliche Kreditinstitute, auch in Bulgarien, gründen. Eine besondere Verantwortung für sämtliche Valutaoperationen kommt nach dem Willen der Reformer der Außenhandelsbank zu, die nicht nur die Auslandsaktivitäten der anderen Handelsbanken überwacht, sondern auch die Valutakonten der Betriebe und deren „Selbstfinanzierung in konvertiblen Währungen" kontrolliert[14]).

Da die Handelsbanken offenbar nicht in der Lage sind, den Bedarf der im Außenhandel tätigen Betriebe an konvertierbaren Devisen auch nur annähernd zu befriedigen, greift neuerdings der Staat ein, um aus den Beständen der BNB harte Währungen an die Interessenten meistbietend zu versteigern. Auf einer ersten Auktion der eigens dafür vom Ministerium für Wirtschaft und Planung (*Ministerstvo na ikonomikata i planiraneto*) und von der BNB gegründeten Behörde[15]) am 22.6.1988 wurde 1 Mio. US-$ angeboten und zu Preisen zwischen 5,0 und 12,0 Leva pro Dollar zugeschlagen[16]). Daß somit das Mehrfache des offiziellen Ankaufskurses (0,8465 Leva zuzüglich Prämie, die den Kurs in etwa verdoppelt) erzielt und sogar der Schwarzmarktkurs (4,0–6,0 Leva) übertroffen wurde, zeigt den eklatanten Devisenmangel.

Durch derartige Maßnahmen wird das bulgarische Wechselkurssystem weiter verkompliziert und den Zielen der Reformpolitik entgegengewirkt. Tatsächlich besteht für sämtliche Valutageschäfte nach wie vor ein System multipler Wechselkurse. Dem offiziellen An- und Verkaufskurs für kommerzielle Deviseneinnahmen werden interne Valutakoeffizienten, sogenannte „Korrektive", hinzugeschlagen, die bislang je nach Währungsart und Warengruppen variierten. Ab 1.1.1988 wurde das Wechselkurssystem insofern vereinheitlicht, als die obligatorischen Abführungen der Betriebe an den Staat zu einem Basiskurs abgerechnet, zusätzliche Devisenverkäufe aber mit einer Prämie zu diesem Kurs belohnt werden, die angeblich nicht mehr nach Warengruppen differenziert ist. Unterschiedlich sind dem Vernehmen nach die Prämien, die den offiziellen Dollar- und Rubelkursen hinzugerechnet werden[17]). Unverkennbar ist das Bemühen, mit Hilfe der Wechselkurspolitik die Außenhandelstätig-

---

[13]) DV. (1987) 100.
[14]) DV. (1987) 46.
[15]) DV. (1988) 28.
[16]) Nikolaev, R.: Bulgaria Auctions off Hard Currency, in: Radio Free Europe Research, Vol. 13, No. 30, 29.7.1988, S. 19 ff.
[17]) Grosser (Anm. 10), S. 156, 157 f.; auch Jackson, M.R.: Bulgarian Economic Reforms and the GATT, in: Südosteuropa. 36 (1987), S. 551.

keit der Betriebe zu steuern, Exporte in die „richtige" Richtung zu lenken und unerwünschte Einfuhren zu verhindern.

Als erster Schritt zu der auch in Bulgarien als Fernziel betrachteten Konvertibilität der Währung müßte jedoch nach ungarischem Vorbild der Wechselkurs vereinheitlicht werden. Aber der überbewertete Lev wurde bisher nicht abgewertet, gegenüber den konvertiblen Währungen sogar ein neuer Wechselkurs eingeführt, der bei Ankäufen von seiten in- und ausländischer natürlicher Personen gilt und das Dreifache des Kurses für kommerzielle Transaktionen beträgt[18]. Folgerichtig setzt sich Bulgarien zunächst für eine Konvertibilität der RGW-Währungen ein. Ein bulgarisch-sowjetisches Abkommen, das erste dieser Art in der sozialistischen Wirtschaftsgemeinschaft, sieht vor, die Konvertierbarkeit der beiden Partnerwährungen in den bilateralen Wirtschaftsbeziehungen schrittweise herzustellen[19]. Wie weit und mühevoll der Weg zur freien Konvertierbarkeit des Lev ist, wird deutlich, wenn man bedenkt, daß die Devisenbewirtschaftung und damit die Manipulation des Wechselkurses erst dann aufgehoben werden kann, wenn die „Warenkonvertibilität" hergestellt ist, also Lev-Guthaben nicht nur in gewünschte Währungen umgetauscht, sondern auch jederzeit und uneingeschränkt zum Kauf beliebiger und international begehrter bulgarischer Produkte verwendet werden können.

So zeigt auch die neueste Reformetappe im Außenwirtschaftsbereich die für den NIM kennzeichnende Kombination von marktorientierter Liberalisierung mit allgegenwärtiger Lenkung und Kontrolle des Wirtschaftsgeschehens durch die Staatsorgane. Noch ist die Gängelung und Bevormundung der Betriebe durch übergeordnete Behörden unverkennbar. An die Stelle der abgeschafften Plandirektiven für den Außenhandel treten Staatsaufträge, die zukünftig nicht mehr zugewiesen, sondern an den Meistbietenden versteigert werden sollen. Doch die Betriebe sind verpflichtet, bei der Ausarbeitung ihrer Pläne die langfristigen Exportverpflichtungen des Landes – namentlich aufgrund der Vereinbarungen mit den RGW-Partnern – sicherzustellen. Andererseits dürfen zusätzliche Exporte nur dann durchgeführt werden, wenn dem Binnenmarkt keine notwendigen Ressourcen entzogen werden und die „Bedürfnisse der Bevölkerung erfüllt sind"[20]. Devisenakkumulationen der Betriebe sind unter diesen Bedingungen kaum möglich. Der Großteil ihrer Devisenerlöse muß nach wie vor an die Außenhandelsbank abgeliefert werden[21].

Die Eingriffsrechte des Staates in diesem empfindlichen, auch politisch bedeutsamen Wirtschaftsbereich sind offenbar auch unter dem neuesten Reformschub enorm. Die im Außenhandel tätigen Betriebe werden mit Mauern des Mißtrauens umgeben. Inwieweit die neueste „Verordnung" bisher überhaupt – gegen den Widerstand in der Verwaltung, aber auch in den Betrieben selbst – in die Praxis Eingang fand, ist aufgrund der zurückhaltenden bulgarischen Informationspolitik nicht feststellbar.

---

[18]) Grosser, I.: Bulgarien 1988/89. Wirtschaftswachstum und Reformen beschleunigt, Hartwährungsverschuldung kritisch, in: Bolz, K. (Hrsg.): Die wirtschaftliche Entwicklung in den sozialistischen Ländern Osteuropas zur Jahreswende 1988/89. Hamburg 1989, S. 24.

[19]) Sofioter Nachrichten. (1987) 28.

[20]) Grosser (Anm. 10), S. 151; Höpken, W.: Wirtschaftsreform in Bulgarien, in: Südosteuropa. 36 (1987), S. 50.

[21]) Nikolaev (Anm. 16), S. 21.

Zweifellos fehlt es den Wirtschaftsorganisationen mit Außenhandelsabteilungen an ausgebildetem Personal, an Marketing-Fachleuten und nicht zuletzt an geeigneten Betriebsleitern. Wie sollten auch über Nacht aus Befehlsempfängern der Ministerien verantwortungsbewußte, risikobereite und entscheidungsfreudige Manager werden? Von westlichen Unternehmen, die im Bulgarienhandel tätig sind, ist zu erfahren, daß der durch die Reformen hervorgerufene Kompetenzwirrwarr und Unsicherheiten der bulgarischen Partner über die Durchsetzbarkeit ihrer neuen Rechte die Geschäftsmöglichkeiten beeinträchtigen.

III. Die Entwicklung des Außenhandels und der Außenhandelspolitik

1. Veränderungen der Warenstruktur

Die rasche Industrialisierung Bulgariens war nicht nur von einer Vervielfachung der Außenhandelsumsätze begleitet, sondern ermöglichte auch einen imposanten Wandel der Exportwarenstruktur. Während Vorkriegsbulgarien fast ausschließlich Nahrungs- und Futtermittel, Lebendvieh und landwirtschaftliche Rohstoffe ins Ausland lieferte und mit einem Tabakanteil von zumeist über 40 % monokulturartige Züge aufwies[22], zeigte die Zusammensetzung der Ausfuhr in den vier Jahrzehnten sozialistischer Entwicklungspolitik immer stärker den Charakter eines industriellen Schwellenlandes, das die vom Ausland bezogenen Güter mit einem zunehmenden Anteil industrieller Fertigprodukte bezahlt.

Besonders eindrucksvoll ist der Wandel der Warenstruktur des bulgarischen Außenhandels seit den 60er Jahren, also mit Beginn des forcierten Industrialisierungsprogramms, das vom VII. Parteitag der BKP als „Großer Sprung nach vorn" im Juni 1958 beschlossen worden war[23]. Zwar hatten sich die Einfuhren von Maschinen und Industrieanlagen schon zwischen 1948 und 1958 vervierfacht. Doch von 1960 bis 1980 nahmen sie in etwa gleichem Tempo wie die gesamten Importe von 324,8 Mio. Verrechnungs-Leva (VL) auf 2932,3 Mio. VL, bis 1987 noch einmal auf 5582,5 Mio. VL zu. Dabei beanspruchte diese Warengruppe regelmäßig 40–50 % des Einfuhrwerts. Auch die Zunahme der importierten Energie- und industriellen Rohstoffe von 179,9 Mio. VL (1960) auf 5701,0 Mio. VL (1987) zeigt den enorm gewachsenen Rohstoffbedarf der bulgarischen Wirtschaft – wie auch die langfristigen Veränderungen des Einfuhrpreisniveaus. Für die Warengruppe Brennstoffe, mineralische Rohstoffe und Metalle wurden 1987 32,4 % der gesamten Einfuhrkosten aufgewandt. Dagegen kamen importierte industrielle Konsumgüter, die den Lebensstandard der Bevölkerung verbessern halfen, über ein Zehntel des Wertes der Auslandsbezüge nie hinaus[24].

---

[22]) South-Eastern Europe. A Political and Economic Survey. The Royal Institute of International Affairs (Ed.). London 1939, Tab. d, S. 168.
[23]) Trud. 3.6.1958. Vgl. Brown, J. F.: Bulgaria Under Communist Rule. New York 1970, S. 83ff.
[24]) SG. 1980, S. 381; 1988, S. 363.

Tabelle 1: Warenstruktur des bulgarischen Außenhandels (Anteile an den gesamten Ausfuhren bzw. Einfuhren in Prozent)

Export	1960		1970		1980		1987	
	Mio. VL	%	Mio. VL	%	Mio. VL	%	Mio. VL	%
Maschinen und Ausrüstungen	86,4	12,6	679,4	27,3	3948,7	50,7	8359,7	58,8
Brennstoffe, mineral. Rohstoffe, Metalle	61,7	8,2	190,4	6,9	1334,0	12,7	980,8	8,8
Chemische Produkte, Düngemittel	14,8	2,1	80,1	3,6	366,9	2,8	420,5	3,7
Landwirtschaftl. Rohstoffe	170,4	26,3	286,7	10,0	193,8	5,0	560,4	4,5
Nahrungsmittel	206,5	31,7	731,1	30,8	1592,0	15,6	1674,6	11,4
Industrielle Konsumgüter	119,8	17,7	344,4	20,1	786,9	9,4	1460,2	10,2
Sonstige Waren	9,0	1,4	32,4	1,3	298,0	3,8	345,8	2,6

Import	1960		1970		1980		1987	
	Mio. VL	%	Mio. VL	%	Mio. VL	%	Mio. VL	%
Maschinen und Ausrüstungen	324,8	44,7	869,3	40,3	2932,3	45,4	5582,5	43,5
Brennstoffe, mineral. Rohstoffe, Metalle	179,9	23,9	622,8	28,4	3552,3	28,3	5701,0	32,4
Chemische Produkte, Düngemittel	48,3	6,2	162,8	8,4	523,3	6,7	704,3	6,4
Landwirtschaftl. Rohstoffe	102,8	13,6	288,7	12,9	689,8	8,8	1081,6	9,5
Nahrungsmittel	20,3	2,8	52,7	2,3	112,3	1,8	125,0	1,1
Industrielle Konsumgüter	56,5	7,8	121,9	6,6	367,8	7,2	656,4	5,4
Sonstige Waren	7,5	1,0	24,1	1,1	105,1	1,8	216,5	1,7

Quelle: SG. 1980, S. 381; 1987, S. 373; 1988, S. 363.

Noch ausgeprägter spiegeln die Veränderungen der Exportwarenstruktur den imponierenden Industrialisierungsfortschritt des Landes wider. Bulgarien verkaufte im Jahre 1960 für 86,4 Mio. VL Maschinen und Ausrüstungen ins Ausland, was einem Anteil von 12,6 % der gesamten Ausfuhren entsprach. Bis 1980 waren die Lieferungen in dieser Warengruppe auf 3948,7 Mio. VL, bis 1987 auf 8359,7 Mio. VL oder 50,7 bzw. 58,8 % der Gesamtexporte gestiegen. Der Anteil der landwirtschaftlichen Rohstoffe war zwischen 1960 und 1987 von 26,3 auf 4,5 %, der Anteil der Nahrungsmittel von 31,7 auf 11,4 % gesunken. Der Export industrieller Konsumgüter, der 1960 immerhin 17,7 % der Auslandslieferungen ausmachte, ging bis 1987 anteilmäßig auf 10,2 % zurück[25]).

Dabei sollte nicht übersehen werden, daß diesem Strukturwandel ein erheblicher Schönheitsfehler anhaftet. Bulgarische Industrieprodukte, selbst moderne Erzeugnisse der seit den 70er Jahren stark ausgebauten Elektrotechnik und Elektronik sind auf den hart umkämpften Märkten der westlichen Industrieländer kaum abzusetzen. Maschinen und Ausrüstungen, aber auch industrielle Konsumgüter werden zum Großteil, manche Artikel fast ausschließlich in den RGW-Raum, insbesondere in die Sowjetunion, geliefert. Der Konkurrenz des Weltmarktes als Gradmesser für den international erreichten technologischen und qualitativen Standard sind die bulgarischen Drehbänke, Elektromotoren, Elektrokarren, elektronischen Rechengeräte, Schreibmaschinen, Telefonapparate, Traktoren und Mähdrescher offensichtlich nicht gewachsen. Im Vergleich mit der Exportwarenstruktur anderer RGW-Staaten schneidet Bulgarien, das bei der Gründung der sozialistischen Wirtschaftsgemeinschaft das am wenigsten entwickelte Schlußlicht bildete, sogar mit einer Spitzenposition ab. Maschinen und Ausrüstungen sowie Transportmittel stellten nach der RGW-Statistik im Jahre 1987 60,6 % der bulgarischen, 58,0 % der tschechoslowakischen, 62,9 % der polnischen, 48,0 % der ostdeutschen und 35,2 % der ungarischen Ausfuhr[26]). Es versteht sich, daß der niedrigere Investitionsgüteranteil anderer, fortgeschrittener Mitgliedsländer durch deren höhere Westexportquote bewirkt wird. Das soll den Modernisierungserfolg der bulgarischen Wirtschaft nicht schmälern, zeigt aber deutlich deren besondere Abhängigkeit vom RGW-Markt.

2. Beständigkeit der regionalen Orientierung – der RGW-Markt

Die regionale Orientierung des bulgarischen Außenhandels zeigt seit den 50er Jahren eine bemerkenswerte Konstanz. Ein Vergleich der Ländergruppenanteile 1960 mit jenen des Jahres 1987 demonstriert Beständigkeit im Festhalten an einer frühzeitig beschlossenen politischen Anlehnung, deren Folge eine demonstrative außenwirtschaftliche Schwerpunktbildung war. In beiden Jahren wurden etwas mehr als vier Fünftel des gesamten Außenhandels mit den Mitgliedsländern des RGW abgewickelt, mehr als die Hälfte der gesamten Warenumsätze mit der Sowjetunion[27]).

---

[25]) Ebenda. 1988: 60,8 %, 11,8 % bzw. 10,7 %. Sofioter Nachrichten. 5.4.1989.
[26]) Statističeskij ežegodnik stran-členov Soveta Ekonomičeskoj Vzaimopomošči (Statistisches Jahrbuch der Mitgliedsländer des Rates für gegenseitige Wirtschaftshilfe) 1988. Moskau 1988, S. 344 ff.
[27]) RGW 1960: 80,1 %, 1987: 80,2; UdSSR 1960: 53,2, 1987: 59,2. SG. 1961, S. 306; 1988, S. 367 f.

Tabelle 2: Exportwarenstruktur der RGW-Mitgliedsländer 1987 (Anteile am jeweiligen Gesamtexport, in Prozent)

	Bulgarien	Ungarn	DDR	Polen	Rumänien[1]	ČSSR	UdSSR
Maschinen, Ausstattung und Transportmittel	60,6	35,2	48,0	62,9	36,9	58,0	15,5
Brennstoffe, mineralische Rohstoffe, Metalle	7,1	11,2	16,7	14,4	22,0	12,3	56,1
Rohstoffe, auch bearbeitet, Rohstoffe zur Nahrungsmittelherstellung, Nahrungsmittel	16,2	23,7	6,8	5,1	13,3	5,9	7,1
Industrielle Konsumgüter	10,6	18,1	16,0	14,3	17,3	15,8	2,6
Chemische Produkte, Düngemittel, Kautschuk, Baumaterial u. a. Waren	5,5	11,8	12,5	3,3	10,5	8,0	18,7

[1] 1986

Quelle: Statističeskij ežegodnik stran-členov SEV (Statistisches Jahrbuch der Mitgliedsländer des RGW) 1988. Moskau 1988, S. 344 ff.

Von dieser Regel gab es im Zeitverlauf nur geringfügige Abweichungen. Die seit Ende der 60er Jahre verstärkten Einkäufe in den „kapitalistischen" Industriestaaten – damit folgte Bulgarien dem Beispiel der UdSSR und anderer sozialistischer Bruderländer – wurden mit dem Scheitern der Westexportstrategie seit Anfang der 80er Jahre wieder eingeschränkt. Gelungen schien bis 1985 eine auch relative Absatzsteigerung in einigen Ländern der Dritten Welt, die womöglich mit dem Verfall der

Tabelle 3: Wichtigste Handelspartner Bulgariens (Anteile am gesamten Export und Import in Prozent) 1987

Export	%	Import	%
1. Sowjetunion	61,1	1. Sowjetunion	57,3
2. DDR	5,5	2. DDR	5,7
3. Tschechoslowakei	4,9	3. Tschechoslowakei	5,0
4. Polen	4,3	4. Bundesrep. Deutschland	4,9
5. Libyen	3,4	5. Polen	4,8
6. Irak	2,9	6. Rumänien	2,2
7. Rumänien	2,1	7. Ungarn	2,0
8. Ungarn	1,8	8. Kuba	1,8
9. Kuba	1,4	9. Österreich	1,6
10. Bundesrep. Deutschland	1,2	10. Schweiz	1,4
11. Schweiz	1,0	11. Großbritannien	1,2
12. Griechenland	1,0	12. Italien	1,2
13. Jugoslawien	0,7	13. Libyen	1,0
14. Italien	0,6	14. Brasilien	0,9
15. Syrien	0,6	15. Jugoslawien	0,8
16. Großbritannien	0,6	16. Belgien	0,8

Quelle: SG. 1988, S. 367 f.

Tabelle 4: Länderstruktur des bulgarischen Außenhandels (Anteile am Gesamtexport und -import in Prozent)

	1960	1970	1975	1980	1981	1982	1983	1984	1985	1986	1987	1988[1]
Exporte												
in sozialistische Länder	82,9	79,3	80,0	70,8	69,1	71,4	76,4	75,5	77,0	83,2	82,6	84,5
in RGW-Länder	80,2	77,4	77,6	68,8	67,3	69,9	75,2	74,3	75,7	81,7	81,5	83,0
in die UdSSR	53,8	53,8	54,6	49,9	48,4	51,6	56,0	55,7	56,6	61,1	61,1	62,8
in nicht-sozialistische Länder	17,1	20,7	20,0	29,2	30,9	28,6	23,6	24,5	23,0	16,8	17,4	15,5
in entwickelte Industrieländer	9,8	14,2	9,3	15,8	13,4	11,4	10,5	9,1	8,5	6,9	6,8	6,4
in Entwicklungsländer	7,3	6,5	10,7	13,4	17,5	17,2	13,1	15,4	14,5	9,9	10,6	9,1
Importe												
aus sozialistischen Ländern	83,2	76,2	72,3	78,9	75,4	77,2	79,8	79,9	77,0	77,1	80,2	76,7
aus RGW-Ländern	80,1	74,8	70,8	77,1	73,9	76,0	78,4	78,5	75,5	75,8	78,9	75,3
aus der UdSSR	52,5	52,5	50,7	57,3	54,7	55,9	58,1	59,0	56,1	56,4	57,3	53,7
aus nichtsozialistischen Ländern	16,8	23,8	27,7	21,1	24,6	22,8	20,2	20,1	23,0	22,9	19,8	23,3
aus entwickelten Industrieländern	11,8	19,1	23,6	17,2	23,0	16,7	13,9	13,8	15,2	15,4	15,3	15,5
aus Entwicklungsländern	5,0	4,7	4,1	3,9	4,6	6,1	6,3	6,3	7,8	7,5	4,5	7,8

[1]) Vorläufig.

Quelle: SG., entspr. Jahrgänge; Iznos i vnos. (1988) 4.

Erdöl- und sonstigen Rohstoffpreise auf dem Weltmarkt ein vorläufiges Ende gefunden hat.

Während Rumänien, aber auch Ungarn und Polen frühzeitig bemüht waren, die ihnen in den Nachkriegsjahren aufoktroyierte Konzentration des Warenverkehrs auf den von der Sowjetunion geschaffenen Block sozialistischer Länder zu mildern und ihren Außenhandel auch regional zu diversifizieren, stellte sich Bulgarien den Zwängen und Widrigkeiten des kapitalistischen Weltmarktes nur begrenzt. Das Land ging keine vermeidbaren Risiken ein, scheute Experimente und setzte auf Bewahren. In kluger Einschätzung der Leistungsfähigkeit seiner Wirtschaft suchte es ökonomische Rückendeckung vor allem im RGW. Mit der Gründung des RGW am 25. Januar 1949 als Instrument zur internationalen Koordination der Entwicklungsplanung strebte die sowjetische Führung an, ihren ideologisch-politischen Einfluß auf die regierenden kommunistischen Parteien in den Mitgliedsländern zu stärken und ein dauerhaftes Mitspracherecht bei der Gestaltung der Produktionsstruktur dieser Volkswirtschaften im ökonomischen und strategischen Interesse der UdSSR zu gewinnen[28].

Zweck des RGW war laut Gründungprotokoll, den Wiederaufbau und die Industrialisierung zu fördern, die Rohstoffgewinnungskapazitäten zu erweitern, die Exportkonkurrenz der Mitgliedsländer untereinander zu beseitigen und „die Wirtschaften der Unterzeichnerstaaten auf der Grundlage eines vom Rat entwickelten ökonomischen Generalplanes zu koordinieren"[29].

Bulgarien wurde vom Gründungsdatum an in diese Organisation eingebunden und engagierte sich ab Mitte der 50er Jahre immer stärker in deren Spezialisierungs- und Kooperationsabkommen. Die bulgarische Führung lehnte es ostentativ ab, weltpolitisch günstige Konstellationen – wie Rumänien den chinesisch-sowjetischen Konflikt – zum Widerstand gegen sowjetische Integrationswünsche zu nutzen. Im Gegenteil, sie kam solchen Bestrebungen mit besonderer Willfährigkeit nach.

Zweifellos hat die am wenigsten entwickelte Volkswirtschaft im RGW vom Technologietransfer aus den fortgeschritteneren Partnerländern und den Kredithilfen der Gemeinschaftsbanken zur Modernisierung der Produktionsstruktur erheblich profitiert. Zwar blieb Bulgarien in dieser internationalen Arbeitsteilung zunächst vordringlich mit der Erzeugung und Verarbeitung von Obst und Gemüse, Genußmitteln und tierischen Produkten betraut. Auf der XII. RGW-Ratssitzung in Sofia im Dezember 1959 erhielt Bulgarien den Auftrag, seine Gemüse- und Obstlieferungen an die Partnerländer bis 1965 zu verdoppeln[30]. So förderte die staatliche Wirtschaftspolitik konsequent die in anderen, einseitig auf Industrialisierung eingeschworenen sozialistischen Ländern meist vernachlässigte Landwirtschaft, ein Umstand, der dem

---

[28] Schönfeld, R.: Der Rat für gegenseitige Wirtschaftshilfe als Instrument sozialistischer ökonomischer Integration und sowjetischer Hegemonie, in: Brunner, G.; Schweisfurth, Th.; Uschakow, A.; Westen, K. (Hrsg.): Sowjetsystem und Ostrecht (Festschrift für Boris Meissner). Berlin 1985, S. 687–700. Vgl. das Kapitel von K.-D. Grothusen, Außenpolitik.

[29] Kommuniqué und Protokoll über die Gründung des RGW, in: Uschakow, A.: Integration im RGW (COMECON), Dokumente. 2. Aufl. Baden-Baden 1983, S. 19f.

[30] RD. 17.12.1959. Vgl. Brown (Anm. 23), S. 86f. Vgl. das Kapitel von I. Grosser, Landwirtschaft.

bulgarischen Export zugute kam, als sich seit Mitte der 70er Jahre die außenwirtschaftlichen Rahmenbedingungen drastisch verschlechterten.

Aber Bulgariens Loyalität wurde andererseits mit besonderem Entgegenkommen und Verständnis der Sowjetunion belohnt, die sich bulgarischen Industrialisierungswünschen nie verweigerte. Bulgarien konnte sich im RGW gleichzeitig auf die Produktion von Transport- und Hebegeräten, bestimmten Werkzeug- und Landmaschinen sowie einer Reihe von chemischen Erzeugnissen spezialisieren. So wurden 1987 96 % der in Bulgarien hergestellten Elektrokarren, 92 % der Motorkarren, 100 % der Telefonapparate, Traktoren und Mähdrescher, 98 % der Schiffe und 82 % der kalzinierten Soda im RGW-Raum verkauft[31]). Seit den 70er Jahren setzte die Regierung vor allem auf den Ausbau der wachstumsfördernden Elektrotechnik und Elektronik, stellte elektronische Rechengeräte, computergesteuerte Maschinen und Industrieroboter in wachsendem Umfang auch für den RGW-Export her. Die Ausfuhrproduktion des Elektronenrechners „Elka" wurde von jeher zum Großteil in die Partnerstaaten geliefert.

Den Nutzen engstmöglicher wirtschaftlicher Zusammenarbeit mit den übrigen sozialistischen Ländern wußte die bulgarische Führung richtig einzuschätzen. Der Anteil der aufgrund bilateraler Spezialisierungs- und Kooperationsabkommen im RGW gewonnenen Industrieprodukte am Gesamtexport wuchs rasch, im Maschinenbausektor schon Anfang der 80er Jahre auf über 50 %. Besonders intensiv wurde die Arbeitsteilung mit der Sowjetunion. Mehr als drei Viertel der ausgeführten „spezialisierten Erzeugnisse" werden dorthin geliefert[32]). Die Spezialisierungs- und Kooperationsabkommen haben wesentlich dazu beigetragen, die bulgarischen RGW-Beziehungen zu stabilisieren und dem Land die Möglichkeit zu geben, seine Warenbezüge

Tabelle 5: Regionalstruktur des Außenhandels der RGW-Mitgliedsländer (in Prozent des Gesamthandels) 1987

	Sozialistische Länder	RGW-Länder	Entwickelte kapitalistische Länder	Entwicklungsländer
Bulgarien	81,4	80,2	11,1	7,5
Ungarn	53,7	49,5	38,4	7,9
DDR	68,8	66,6	27,2	4,0
Kuba	88,3	86,5	8,3	3,4
Mongolische VR	97,4	94,9	2,4	0,2
Polen	76,4	72,7	19,5	4,1
UdSSR	67,0	61,7	21,8	11,2
ČSSR	79,1	75,4	16,6	4,3

Quelle: Statističeskij ežegodnik stran-členov SEV (Statistisches Jahrbuch der Mitgliedsländer des RGW) 1988. Moskau 1988, S. 342.

---

[31]) SG. 1988, S. 369 ff.
[32]) Wass von Czege, A.: Spezialisierung und Kooperation im RGW. Interaktionsstruktur und Verhaltensmuster, in: Schönfeld, R. (Hrsg.): RGW-Integration und Südosteuropa. München 1984, Tab. 2 u. 3, S. 76.

aus diesem Raum mit eigenen Industrieprodukten abzugelten. In der Intensität des RGW-Handels, gemessen am gesamten Warenaustausch mit dem Ausland, wird Bulgarien mit einem Anteil von 81,5 % der Exporte und 78,9 % der Importe (1987) nur von der Mongolischen Volksrepublik und von Kuba übertroffen. Dabei fallen die Defizite mit fast allen RGW-Partnern von insgesamt 236 Mio. VL (1987) ins Auge, die 1988 durch Ausfuhrsteigerungen und Einfuhrbeschränkungen in Überschüsse verwandelt wurden[33]).

Auch das Drängen der UdSSR, die Mitgliedsländer des RGW sollten sich stärker an den Erschließungs-, Förder- und Transportkosten der an sie gelieferten sowjetischen Energieträger und Rohstoffe beteiligen, fand in Sofia meist offenere Ohren als anderswo[34]). Im „Komplexprogramm" des RGW von 1971 war empfohlen worden, „den steigenden Bedarf der Industrie an Erzeugnissen der Brennstoff-, Energie-, Metallurgie- und anderen Rohstoffzweige auf der Grundlage der Vereinigung der Anstrengungen der interessierten Länder zur Entwicklung dieser Zweige besser zu decken"[35]). Dies betraf in erster Linie die Rohstoffvorkommen der Sowjetunion. Um die Blockversorgung zu sichern, sah sie sich gezwungen, immer stärker auf abgelegene und nur mit steigendem Kapitaleinsatz zu erschließende Lagerstätten zurückzugreifen, deren Produktion über riesige Entfernungen und fast ausschließlich auf Landrouten in die Verbrauchszentren des RGW verfrachtet werden mußte. Die 1973 einsetzende internationale Ölpreishausse konnte die Verhandlungsposition der Sowjetunion nur verstärken. Bei rasch verbesserten terms of trade im sowjetischen Westhandel wurden Brennstoffe zu „harten", jederzeit und überall zu steigenden Preisen und gegen konvertible Währung verkäuflichen Waren. Im Intra-RGW-Handel lieferte die UdSSR Energieträger, vor allem Erdöl, nach wie vor in bilateraler Verrechnung, also im Tausch gegen zweit- und drittklassige Industrieprodukte, und aufgrund der modifizierten Preisformel von 1975[36]) jahrelang zu erheblich unter den Weltmarktnotierungen liegenden Preisen. Die Abhängigkeit der kleineren RGW-Länder von den sowjetischen Lieferungen nahm entsprechend zu, und es war im Interesse der eigenen Versorgungssicherung vernünftig, sich an den geforderten „Gemeinsamen Investitionen" im RGW zu beteiligen.

War Bulgarien in den Bau der Erdölleitung *Družba* in den 60er Jahren noch nicht eingeschaltet, so gehörte es schon zu den Unterzeichnerstaaten des Generalabkommens über das bedeutendste Investitionsvorhaben des RGW in den 70er Jahren. Im Rahmen dieses ehrgeizigen Projekts trugen die Partnerstaaten von 1974 an nicht nur

---

[33]) Statističeskij ežegodnik stran-členov SEV 1988, S. 342; SG. 1988, S. 367f. (errechnet); Grosser (Anm. 18), S. 22; Sofioter Nachrichten. 5.4.1989.

[34]) Schönfeld, R.: Gemeinsame Investitionen im RGW und die Beteiligung der südosteuropäischen Mitgliedsländer, in: ders. (Hrsg.) (Anm. 32), S. 101–126.

[35]) Komplexprogramm für die weitere Vertiefung und Vervollkommnung der Zusammenarbeit und Entwicklung der sozialistischen ökonomischen Integration der Mitgliedsländer des RGW, in: Uschakow (Anm. 29), S. 1085ff.

[36]) Mit der auf sowjetisches Drängen 1975 vereinbarten „Bukarester" Formel wurden die Intra-RGW-Preise aufgrund des Durchschnitts der Weltmarktpreise der vorangegangenen 5 Jahre jährlich neu berechnet. Bei den (bis 1983) steigenden Weltmarktnotierungen für Erdöl waren die Forderungen im RGW stets entsprechend niedriger. Ab 1985 stiegen die RGW-Preise, soweit keine Sonderkonditionen vereinbart waren, offenbar über das Weltmarktniveau.

zur Erschließung des Erdgasvorkommens von Orenburg in der UdSSR bei, sondern verlegten gemeinsam die 2676 km lange Gasleitung *Sojuz* von Orenburg bis zur sowjetischen Westgrenze. Bulgarien übernahm den fünften Bauabschnitt (km 2208–2766) mit drei Verdichterstationen in eigener Regie und stellte Arbeitskräfte für die Fertigstellung des ungarischen Bauabschnitts zur Verfügung. Für die gemeinsame Errichtung eines Zellstoffwerks in Ust'Ilimsk bei Irkutsk in Ostsibirien lieferten bulgarische Firmen Wand- und Dachplatten, Elektrokarren und Kabel. Außerdem waren bulgarische Jugendbrigaden am Bau beteiligt. Erhebliche Leistungen erbrachte das Land auch für den Bau eines Asbest-Kombinats in Kiembaev im südlichen Ural sowie für die metallurgischen Kombinate in der Kursker Magnetanomalie und in Krivoj Rog. Auch zu der 750 kV-Hochspannungsleitung von Vinnica (Ukrainische SSR) nach Albertirsa in Ungarn trug Bulgarien bei. Seit 1982 errichten die Sowjetunion, Bulgarien und Rumänien gemeinsam ein Kernkraftwerk in Konstantinovsk am Don, ebenfalls mit einer 750 kV-Hochspannungsleitung, die nach Măcin in der rumänischen Dobrudscha und von dort zur bulgarischen Grenze führt. Bei allen diesen Projekten wie auch in der sowjetischen Holzwirtschaft sind bulgarische Facharbeiter und Ingenieure beschäftigt, deren Zahl 1984 mit 27000 angegeben wurde. Da es sich wohl vorwiegend um Spezialisten handelt, fehlen sie zweifellos in der Binnenwirtschaft[37]).

Sämtliche erbrachten Leistungen der an den gemeinsamen Investitionen beteiligten Mitgliedsstaaten werden der UdSSR kreditiert und von dieser aus der anlaufenden Produktion des betreffenden Projekts mit Lieferungen abgegolten. Bulgarien sichert sich damit einen beträchtlichen Teil der notwendigen Versorgung mit Energieträgern, Strom, Metallerzen und anderen Rohstoffen bis weit in die 90er Jahre.

Auch wenn man in Betracht zieht, daß in Systemen willkürlich festgesetzter Planpreise und Wechselkurse der optimale Ressourceneinsatz bei internationalen Investitionen praktisch ausgeschlossen bleibt, weil realistische Kostenrechnungen nicht möglich sind, so kann man doch davon ausgehen, daß die Beteiligung an solchen gemeinsamen RGW-Vorhaben für ein rohstoffarmes Land wie Bulgarien durchweg vorteilhaft ist. Die Ersparnis an konvertierbaren Devisen, die auf dem Weltmarkt für Energieträger und Rohstoffe aufgewendet werden müßten, ist über einen längeren Zeitraum enorm.

3. Haupthandelspartner Sowjetunion

Der intensive Warenaustausch mit der Sowjetunion, der seit vier Jahrzehnten fast ständig mehr als die Hälfte des gesamten Außenhandels beansprucht, verschaffte Bulgarien kaum zu überschätzende materielle Vorteile. Eine hohe Einfuhrabhängigkeit von der Führungsmacht im sozialistischen Lager wurde bewußt und wohl nicht nur aus politischem Kalkül in Kauf genommen. Von den beiden „Ölpreisschocks" 1973/74 und 1979/80 und der Hausse auf den internationalen Rohstoffmärkten bis

---

[37]) Schönfeld (Anm. 34), S. 114ff. Zu den bulgarischen „Gastarbeitern" in der UdSSR vgl. Gumpel, W.: Die bulgarisch-sowjetischen Wirtschaftsbeziehungen – Partnerschaft oder Bindung?, in: Osteuropa. 36 (1986), S. 272ff.

Anfang der 80er Jahre blieb die bulgarische Wirtschaft weitgehend ausgespart. Sowjetisches Erdöl notierte mindestens bis 1985, jahrelang sogar erheblich, unter den Weltmarktpreisen. Einfuhren aus der UdSSR konnten ausschließlich und bis vor wenigen Jahren vermutlich meist problemlos mit bulgarischen Exportprodukten, vorwiegend solchen der heimischen Industrie, verrechnet werden, deren Qualität und technologischer Standard den Anforderungen westlicher Absatzmärkte nicht genügten. Als Bulgarien seit 1975 wegen der erheblichen Verschlechterung seiner internationalen Austauschrelationen (terms of trade)[38] wachsende Schwierigkeiten hatte, den vollen Wert der Rohstoffbezüge mit entsprechenden Gegenlieferungen auszugleichen, wurde diese Unterdeckung von der Sowjetunion mit großzügiger Kreditierung überbrückt. Von 1975 bis 1985 kumulierte Bulgarien im bilateralen Verrechnungsverkehr mit der UdSSR Jahr für Jahr Defizite in Höhe von insgesamt 3,6 Mrd. VL[39].

Tabelle 6: Außenhandel Bulgariens mit der UdSSR (Mio. VL)

	1960	1965	1970	1975	1980	1981	1982	1983	1984	1985	1986	1987
Importe	389	689	1118	2653	4743	5451	6134	6951	7580	7898	8098	8056
Exporte	360	718	1261	2481	4445	4768	5616	6619	7230	7776	8155	8437
Saldo	−29	+29	+143	−172	−298	−683	−518	−332	−350	−122	+57	+381

Quelle: SG. 1980, S. 385f.; 1987, S. 377f.; 1988, S. 367f.

Die bulgarische Regierung, seit 1980 erfolgreich um die Verminderung der Auslandsschuld in konvertierbaren Währungen bemüht, glich somit die entstehenden Kapitalversorgungslücken jahrelang wenigstens zum Teil mit sowjetischen Clearing-Krediten aus, um der Bevölkerung und der Wirtschaft eine allzu harte Austerity-Politik zu ersparen. Erst 1985 gelang es, das chronische Defizit Bulgariens in der bilateralen Handelsbilanz mit der UdSSR nennenswert zu reduzieren. 1986 wurde erstmals seit 1974 wieder ein Überschuß von 57 Mio. VL erzielt, der 1987 durch vermehrte Ausfuhr bei stagnierenden Importen auf 381 Mio. VL, 1988 sogar auf 1,6 Mrd. VL anwuchs[40]. Der dadurch bewirkte Ressourcenabfluß trug zweifellos dazu bei, die Versorgungskrise auf dem bulgarischen Binnenmarkt und den Kapitalmangel der Wirtschaft zu verschärfen. Weltmarktfähige Produkte wurden zur Befriedigung sowjetischer Bedürfnisse der Ausfuhr in den Hartwährungsraum entzogen. Sinkende Preise der aus der UdSSR importierten Energieträger bewirkten eine Verbesserung der bulgarischen terms of trade – 1987 um 6 % –[41], die den Defizitabbau erleichterten. Doch es ist zu vermuten, daß diese auf den Ausgleich der bilateralen Clearing-

---

[38]) PlanEcon Report, Vol. IV, Nos. 22–23. Washington D.C., 3.6.1988, S. 24. Die terms of trade werden durch das Verhältnis des Index der Ausfuhrpreise zum Index der Einfuhrpreise ausgedrückt und geben an, ob ein Land durch die internationalen Preisbewegungen im Zeitverlauf mehr oder weniger Exportgüter aufwenden muß, um dasselbe Importvolumen zu finanzieren.
[39]) SG. 1976, S. 356f.; 1980, S. 385f.; 1987, S. 377f. (errechnet).
[40]) SG. 1988, S. 367f.; Grosser (Anm. 18), S. 22.
[41]) PlanEcon Report (Anm. 38), S. 5.

konten und die Rückführung der Rubelschulden ausgerichtete bulgarische Handelspolitik der 80er Jahre auf massiven Druck der sowjetischen Führung zustandekam.

Eine Wende im Verhalten Moskaus wurde 1985 auch ausländischen Beobachtern deutlich, als Bulgarien wegen der unzureichenden Effizienz seiner Wirtschaft und der mangelhaften Qualität der im Tausch gegen weltmarktfähige Rohstoffe in die UdSSR gelieferten Exportprodukte erstmals öffentlich gescholten wurde[42]). Die bisher gepflegte Kameradschaft und herzliche Einmütigkeit mit der Sowjetunion schien seit Gorbačevs Amtsantritt getrübt. Den Auftakt gab der sowjetische Botschafter in Sofia, Leonid Grekov, der sich im Juli 1985 über Funktionsstörungen und Fehlinvestitionen in der bulgarischen Wirtschaft beklagte. Den Pressekommuniqués zufolge fehlte es bei diversen Treffen zwischen Gorbačev und Živkov nicht an Ermahnungen an die bulgarische Adresse, sich „nicht auf den Lorbeeren auszuruhen", sondern „die Effizienz der Zusammenarbeit zu erhöhen... und bestehende Probleme zu lösen"[43]).

Konsequenzen aus den sich offensichtlich häufenden Reklamationen wegen qualitativ unzureichender, technologisch rückständiger oder gänzlich ausbleibender bulgarischer Lieferungen zog die sowjetische Führung bereits bei der Formulierung des im Juni 1986 mit Bulgarien geschlossenen langfristigen Abkommens über die Entwicklung der wirtschaftlichen und wissenschaftlich-technischen Zusammenarbeit bis zum Jahre 2000[44]). Darin sagte sie zwar zu, dem Partner weiterhin Rohstoffe und Energieträger „auf der Grundlage der koordinierten Pläne und langfristigen Vereinbarungen" zur Verfügung zu stellen. Doch Bulgarien mußte seinerseits versprechen, „konsequent die Struktur der Produktion und des Exports (zu) entwickeln, um der Sowjetunion die notwendigen Produkte, insbesondere Nahrungsmittel und Konsumgüter, einige Arten von Konstruktionsmaterialien und Ausrüstungsgegenständen sowie Maschinen von hoher Qualität und technischem Weltniveau zu überlassen". In reichlich gouvernantenhaftem Ton wurde die bulgarische Regierung aufgefordert, „in Zusammenarbeit mit der Sowjetunion die notwendigen Maßnahmen im Bereich der Kapitalinvestitionen (zu) ergreifen, die auf weitere Vervollkommnung der Struktur der Volkswirtschaft, vor allem auf die Entwicklung von Produktionen mit niedrigen Energie- und Rohstoffkosten sowie auf eine effiziente Ausnutzung der Energie- und Rohstoffressourcen gerichtet sind"[45]).

Darüber hinaus mußte sich Bulgarien verpflichten, auch in Zukunft Kapital und Arbeitskräfte für gemeinsame Investitionen zur Erschließung sowjetischer Rohstoffvorkommen bereitzustellen. Als engste Form der bilateralen Kooperation sollen bulgarische Produzenten mit sowjetischen Partnerunternehmen gemeinsame „Wissenschafts- und Produktionsvereinigungen" gründen, von denen sich Bulgarien einen rascheren Technologietransfer aus der UdSSR, diese sich wohl auch eine direktere

---

[42]) Vgl. Höpken, W.: Die bulgarisch-sowjetischen Beziehungen seit Gorbačev, in: Südosteuropa. 35 (1986), S. 619ff.
[43]) Zitiert ebenda, S. 621.
[44]) Dălgoročna programa za razvitie na ikonomičeskoto i naučno techničeskoto sătrudničestvo meždu NR Bălgarija i SSSR za period do 2000 godina (Langfristiges Abkommen über die Entwicklung der wirtschaftlichen und der wissenschaftlich-technischen Zusammenarbeit zwischen der NRB und der UdSSR im Zeitraum bis zum Jahre 2000), in: Ikonomika. (1985) 8.
[45]) Ebenda, S. 6. Deutscher Text von Höpken (Anm. 42), S. 629.

Kontrolle über die bulgarische Industrieproduktion verspricht. Dabei sollte nicht übersehen werden, daß Bulgarien zu den Pionieren der wenigen Gründungen gemeinsamer Produktionsunternehmen im RGW-Rahmen gehört[46]). Die erhebliche Zahl sowjetischer Facharbeiter, Techniker, Ingenieure und sonstiger „Berater", die in allen wichtigen Sparten der bulgarischen Wirtschaft tätig ist, würde sich durch die noch stärker intensivierte Zusammenarbeit im Forschungs- und Produktionsbereich weiter erhöhen.

Tabelle 7: Anteile sowjetischer Lieferungen an verschiedenen Rohstoffimporten Bulgariens (in Prozent)

	1970	1975	1980	1981	1982	1983	1984	1985	1986	1987
Steinkohle (1 000 t)	2 149	2 515	4 900	5 090	5 480	5 367	5 338	5 528	5 322	5 600
aus UdSSR (%)	100,0	100,0	100,0	100,0	97,3	97,4	96,9	94,5	98,2	96,6
Koks (1 000 t)	465	357	446	407	483	502	544	664	471	309
aus UdSSR (%)	29,7	78,4	75,8	76,4	69,2	54,6	48,3	21,5	11,0	16,8
Eisenerz (1 000 t)	1 133	1 918	2 235	2 280	2 360	2 313	2 286	2 215	2 248	2 308
aus UdSSR (%)	91,2	87,5	100,0	100,0	96,0	95,4	95,4	95,4	100,0	95,3
Roheisen (1 000 t)	295	330	413	435	399	407	665	404	425	483
aus UdSSR (%)	71,9	97,6	97,6	94,3	100,0	92,2	60,9	89,7	88,9	88,4
Zellulose (1 000 t)	79	83	141	131	131	159	158	161	151	159
aus UdSSR (%)	75,9	83,1	84,4	79,8	90,1	91,8	90,2	88,0	74,3	70,5
Baumwolle (1 000 t)	60,6	51,4	63,8	56,2	59,0	88,7	66,9	87,3	79,8	68,6
aus UdSSR (%)	70,7	81,5	74,1	81,1	68,0	55,3	72,0	57,4	62,6	76,7

Quelle: SG. 1984, S. 402 ff.; 1987, S. 393 ff.; 1988, S. 383 ff.

Die Bedeutung der Wirtschaftsbeziehungen zur UdSSR ist kaum zu überschätzen. Bulgarien verdankt der sowjetischen Aufbauhilfe nicht nur seine rasche Industrialisierung, sondern auch die fortgesetzte Sicherung der Energie- und Rohstoffzufuhr. Zwei Drittel des gesamten Brennstoffbedarfs wird aus sowjetischen Quellen gedeckt. Mehr als neun Zehntel der Erdöleinfuhren stammen aus der UdSSR[47]). Die Abhängigkeit von sowjetischen Eisenerz-, Roheisen- oder Zelluloselieferungen ist nicht weniger augenfällig. Auch die im Industriesektor verwendeten Maschinen und Fabrikausrüstungen sind überwiegend sowjetischer Bauart. Nach bulgarischen Angaben stellen die mit Unterstützung der UdSSR errichteten Betriebe fast die Hälfte des industriellen Anlagevermögens des Landes[48]), trotz einer leistungsfähigen einheimi-

---

[46]) 1964 wurde „Intransmasch" (Produktion innerbetrieblicher Transportsysteme) aufgrund eines bulgarisch-ungarischen Abkommens in Sofia, mit einem Filialbetrieb in Budapest, gegründet, 1965 die ungarisch-bulgarische „Agromasch" (Herstellung landwirtschaftlicher Ernte- und Verarbeitungsmaschinen). Vgl. Schönfeld (Anm. 34), S. 107 f.

[47]) 1987 lieferte die UdSSR 12,9 Mio. t Erdöl und 6071 Mio. m³ Erdgas. Vnešnaja torgovlja SSSR v 1987 g. Moskau 1988, S. 62.

[48]) Bašikarov, P.: Ikonomičeskata integracija i sābližavaneto sās SSSR (Wirtschaftliche Integration und die Annäherung an die UdSSR), in: 40 godini socialističeska vānšna tārgovija na NR Bālgarija (40 Jahre sozialistischer Außenhandel der NRB). Bd. 1. Sofia 1985, S. 88. Vgl. Höpken (Anm. 42), S. 624.

schen Investitionsgüterindustrie. Die UdSSR lieferte seit Beginn der sozialistischen Industrialisierung Hunderte von kompletten Industrieanlagen in allen Branchen, als herausragende Beispiele die Stahlwerke Kremikovci bei Sofia und *Lenin* in Dimitrovo, das petrochemische Kombinat bei Burgas und das Kernkraftwerk Kozloduj. Ein „Vertrag über die weitere Entwicklung der Zusammenarbeit auf dem Gebiet der friedlichen Nutzung der Atomenergie" vom 27.4.1967 sicherte der bulgarischen Wirtschaft schon frühzeitig die technische und finanzielle Unterstützung der Sowjetunion beim Aufbau einer eigenen Atomstromerzeugung[49]).

Unter den als Gegenleistung in die UdSSR gelieferten bulgarischen Industrieprodukten expandiert die Sparte „Maschinen und Ausrüstungen" besonders kräftig. Dagegen ist es auch 1987 nicht gelungen, die Ausfuhr der von sowjetischer Seite vordringlich gewünschten hochwertigen Konsumgüter und Nahrungsmittel zu steigern[50]). Von wachsender Bedeutung im bulgarisch-sowjetischen Handel sind dagegen Computer und Computerteile, Elektronenrechner und Telekommunikationsgeräte. Diese in enger Kooperation mit japanischen Firmen erstellte bulgarische Produktion wird für die Raumfahrt-, aber auch für die Rüstungsindustrie der UdSSR immer unentbehrlicher[51]).

Doch selbst in diesem wachstumsintensiven Fertigungsbereich hat die willkürliche Anpassung eines Großteils der Produktionskapazitäten an den sowjetischen Einfuhrbedarf womöglich hohe volkswirtschaftliche Kosten verursacht. In Bulgarien hergestellte Anlagen zur elektronischen Datenverarbeitung sind – wie die meisten Industrieprodukte des Landes – auf dem Weltmarkt nicht absetzbar, weil sie dem raschen technologischen Fortschritt im Westen hinterherhinken, weil sie qualitative Mängel aufweisen und kein Service-Netz unterhalten wird. Der problemlose Absatz in der Sowjetunion hat es den bulgarischen Produzenten bisher erspart, sich auf Gedeih und Verderb der internationalen Konkurrenz zu stellen. Steigende Qualitätsansprüche der sowjetischen Abnehmer werden daran kaum Wesentliches ändern, eher noch die wenigen weltmarktfähigen bulgarischen Ausfuhrprodukte dem heilsamen Konkurrenzdruck entziehen. Die vom sowjetischen Markt ausgehenden Wachstumsimpulse sind zu gering, um der bulgarischen Wirtschaft zu dem Innovationsschub zu verhelfen, der notwendig ist, um eine durchgreifende Modernisierung nicht nur der Industrie, sondern aller Wirtschaftssektoren, auch der Landwirtschaft, einzuleiten. Der Nutzen weitgehender Versorgungssicherung wird durch die Kosten langfristigen Verharrens auf dem Niveau eines zweitklassigen Industriegüterproduzenten vermutlich mehr als aufgewogen.

4. Wirtschaftsbeziehungen zu den nichtsozialistischen Ländern

Diese Priorität der RGW-Orientierung mit einer besonders engen wirtschaftlichen Anlehnung an die Sowjetunion hat die sozialistische Außenhandelspolitik Bulgariens

---

[49]) Vgl. das Kapitel von J. Bethkenhagen, Bergbau und Energie.
[50]) PlanEcon Report (Anm. 38), S. 12.
[51]) Ivanova, A.; West, B.: Bulgaria's Growing Technological Importance to the USSR, in: RFE Research, Bulgarian SR/7 29.7.1988, S. 23 ff.

nie ernsthaft in Frage gestellt. So spielte der Warenaustausch mit den westlichen Industrieländern stets nur eine marginale Rolle. Selbst die Periode der Entspannung, die andere sozialistische Länder zu euphorischen Öffnungen gegenüber dem kapitalistischen Warenangebot verführt hatte, wurde von Bulgarien nur vorübergehend zu verstärkten Einkäufen auf dem Weltmarkt genutzt. Das Scheitern der Westexportstrategie, der Hoffnungen auf eine rasche Steigerung der Exportleistungsfähigkeit durch Kapitalgüter- und Technologieeinfuhren aus den entwickelten Marktwirtschaften, wurde rechtzeitiger erkannt als in anderen sozialistischen Ländern. Als 1979 die Nettoverschuldung des Landes in konvertierbaren Währungen auf 3,7 Mrd. US-$ angestiegen war, reagierte die bulgarische Führung prompt und eher als die Regierungen Polens, Rumäniens oder Ungarns mit energischen Einfuhrrestriktionen. Obwohl sich seit dem ersten Ölpreisschock von 1973/1974 die Preisstrukturen auf dem Weltmarkt erheblich zuungunsten Bulgariens verschoben und eine Verschlechterung der terms of trade um ungefähr 20% bewirkt hatten, gelang es 1979 und 1980, die Westexporte zu steigern und dank dieser kombinierten Ausfuhrförderungs- und Einfuhrdämpfungspolitik in beiden Jahren Handelsbilanzüberschüsse zu erzielen[52].

Die bulgarische Exportwirtschaft profitierte geschickt vom zweiten, 1979 einsetzenden Ölpreisboom, indem sie zunehmende Mengen des meist von der Sowjetunion im bilateralen Tauschhandel bezogenen Erdöls zu Derivaten verarbeitete und diese gegen harte Währungen auf den westlichen Märkten verkaufte. Wenn auch dieses Geschäft unter dem Zusammenbruch des internationalen Ölmarktes in der ersten Hälfte der 80er Jahre litt, besorgte es 1987, bei wieder anziehenden Preisen, mehr als 40% der Deviseneinnahmen aus dem Export in die westlichen Industrieländer[53]. Die Verschuldung in konvertierbaren Währungen ging unmittelbar zurück und konnte bis Ende 1984 bei netto 1,4 Mrd. US-$ eingegrenzt werden. Doch die zur Sicherung des außenwirtschaftlichen Gleichgewichts ergriffenen Maßnahmen, nicht zuletzt auch die verschlechterten außenwirtschaftlichen Rahmenbedingungen und der Ressourcenabfluß durch den Schuldenabbau beeinträchtigten die Wachstumsraten der Produktion. 1985 und 1986 massierten sich Maschinen- und Anlagenkäufe im Hartwährungsraum. Auch ließen eine katastrophale Mißernte und Störungen in der Energieversorgung die Einfuhren außerplanmäßig steigen. Das Defizit im Handel mit den westlichen Industrieländern nahm 1985 auf 925 Mio. US-$ dramatisch zu und war damit erstmals seit 1978 wieder höher als der im Warenaustausch mit der Dritten Welt erzielte Überschuß. Prompt machten sich Liquiditätsprobleme bemerkbar, die Bulgarien zwangen, nach fünfjähriger Abstinenz wieder in internationalen Finanzmärkte in Anspruch zu nehmen. Bis Ende 1986 hatte die Nettoverschuldung in konvertierbaren Währungen auf 3,3 Mrd. US-$ zugenommen. Nach westlichen Schätzungen führten Leistungsbilanzdefizite und der Abwertungseffekt des Dollar bis Ende 1988 zu einem weiteren Anstieg der Hartwährungsschulden auf netto 5,9 Mrd. US-$ (brutto 7,1 Mrd. US-$)[54].

---

[52]) Grosser (Anm. 10), S. 158f.
[53]) PlanEcon Report (Anm. 38), S. 3.
[54]) Nach Berechnungen des Wiener Instituts für internationale Wirtschaftsvergleiche. Grosser (Anm. 18), S. 25; Economic Bulletin for Europe. Vol. 40. United Nations, Genf 1988.

Obschon der seit Anfang der 80er Jahre anhaltende Abwärtstrend der Ausfuhren in die westlichen Industrieländer inzwischen abgefangen werden konnte, stieg das 1986 erreichte Rekorddefizit der Handelsbilanz mit dieser Region von 1,36 Mrd. US-$ 1988 auf 1,47 Mrd. US-$[55]). Bei der nach wie vor strikten staatlichen Überwachung des Außenhandels ist zu vermuten, daß dies das Ergebnis einer gezielten Politik ist und die bulgarische Wirtschaftsführung das Defizit und eine zunehmende Hartwährungsverschuldung in Kauf nimmt, um mit Hilfe verstärkter Westimporte das technologische und qualitative Niveau der einheimischen Produktion – insbesondere im Hinblick auf Lieferverpflichtungen gegenüber der UdSSR – anzuheben. Bemerkenswert sind die erfolgreichen Bemühungen, die Handelsbilanz mit den Entwicklungsländern zu verbessern. Trotz fortdauernder Einnahmeschwäche der Erdölförderländer infolge des niedrigen Dollarkurses gelang es Bulgarien, seine Exporte in die Dritte Welt 1987 um 21,8 % zu steigern. Dieser Nachfrageboom kam vor allem der bulgarischen Maschinen-, aber auch der Waffenindustrie zugute[56]). Durch flankierende Maßnahmen zur Beschränkung der Einfuhr konnte der Überschuß im Warenaustausch mit dieser Region 1987 gegenüber dem Vorjahr von 268 auf 992 Mio. US-$ fast vervierfacht werden. Von den rigorosen Importrestriktionen waren die Erdölkäufe in den arabischen Ländern besonders stark betroffen, deren Wert einbruchartig um mehr als 60 % zurückging. Insgesamt wurden die Einfuhren aus Libyen um 71, aus dem Iran um 60, aus Algerien sogar um 90 % verkürzt. Da die bulgarischen Importe 1988 wieder stark zunahmen, verringerte sich der Handelsbilanzüberschuß mit den Entwicklungsländern auf 267 Mio. US-$[57]).

Doch der Wert dieser Überschüsse bulgarischer Forderungen an Entwicklungsländer wird von westlichen Beobachtern skeptisch beurteilt[58]). Die Gesamtsumme bulgarischer Exportkredite an die Dritte Welt könnte sich nach deren Schätzungen auf 4,6 bis 5,3 Mrd. US-$ belaufen[59]). Ein wesentlicher Teil davon ist vermutlich zur Zeit oder auf Dauer nicht einbringlich – soweit diese Kredite nicht ohnehin auf sowjetischen Wunsch als Entwicklungshilfe vergeben und längst abgeschrieben wurden. So tragen die bulgarischen Überschüsse im Warenaustausch mit der Dritten Welt nur in Grenzen dazu bei, Leistungsbilanzdefizite mit den westlichen Industrieländern abzudecken oder die Verzinsung und Tilgung der Schulden in konvertierbaren Währungen zu finanzieren. Außerdem ist gerade dieser Handel mit seiner Konzentration auf wenige Länder – Libyen und Irak nahmen 1987 59,6 % der bulgarischen Ausfuhren in die Entwicklungsländer auf – höchst verletzlich gegenüber Preisschwankungen auf den Weltrohstoff- und -energiemärkten.

Im Westhandel hat Bulgarien in den 80er Jahren weiter an Boden verloren. Auf dem Gemeinsamen Markt vermochten sich die bulgarischen Exporteure mit ihrem

---

[55]) PlanEcon Report (Anm. 38), S. 1 ff.; Grosser (Anm. 18), S. 25.
[56]) Die bulgarischen Waffenexporte in die Entwicklungsländer werden von westlicher Seite für 1987 auf 470 Millionen US-$ (1986 auf 360 Millionen US-$) geschätzt. Ebenda, Tab. 4, S. 11.
[57]) Bundesstelle für Außenhandelsinformation: Nachrichten für den Außenhandel (BfAI: NfA). 18. 4. 1988; PlanEcon Report (Anm. 38), S. 3, 5; Grosser (Anm. 18), S. 22.
[58]) So von PlanEcon, Washington, D. C. Vgl. Report (Anm. 38), S. 6, 10.
[59]) Ebenda, S. 1 ff.

unangepaßten, qualitativ und technologisch unzureichenden Sortiment schlechter durchzusetzen als andere, marktwirtschaftlich orientierte industrielle Schwellenländer. Auch 1987 hat Bulgarien im Handel mit den Mitgliedsländern der EG mit einem gegenüber dem Vorjahr (745 Mio. VL) nur geringfügig verringerten Passivsaldo von 673 Mio. VL abgeschlossen[60]). Zu diesem Defizit trug der Warenaustausch mit der Bundesrepublik Deutschland beträchtlich bei. Während sich die bulgarischen Einfuhren aus der Bundesrepublik schon bis Mitte der 70er Jahre zügig, aber ungleichgewichtig entwickelt[61]) und in der ersten Hälfte der 80er Jahre noch einmal wertmäßig fast verdoppelt hatten, stagnierte der Warenabsatz auf dem bereits 1981 erreichten Niveau. Auch 1988 waren nur 20,6 % der Bezüge durch Lieferungen gedeckt und die bilaterale Handelsbilanz schloß mit einem Defizit von 1 243 Mio. DM (1 210 Mio. DM in 1987 = 535 Mio. VL)[62]).

Die Ursache der Unausgewogenheit des bulgarischen Außenhandels mit dem industrialisierten Westen zeigt der Warenaustausch mit der Bundesrepublik Deutschland allzu deutlich. Bestanden die deutschen Ausfuhren nach Bulgarien 1988 zu 96,7 % aus Erzeugnissen der gewerblichen Wirtschaft, davon knapp die Hälfte Maschinen und elektrotechnische Geräte, so setzten sich die bulgarischen Lieferungen in die Bundesrepublik überwiegend aus landwirtschaftlichen Produkten, Rohstoffen, Halbwaren und Konsumgütern zusammen. Maschinen und elektrotechnische Geräte stellten 6,1 % der bulgarischen Exporte[63]). Mit Gütern der Ernährungswirtschaft (19,6 %) sowie Textilerzeugnissen und Bekleidung (21,2 %) konkurriert Bulgarien auf besonders empfindlichen Märkten, wo die neuaufgenommenen Mitglieder der EG – Griechenland, Spanien und Portugal – mit einem ähnlichen Sortiment und zu Inlandsbedingungen operieren. Es ist der bulgarischen Führung bewußt, daß die Beseitigung des bedenklichen Ungleichgewichts im Westhandel wie auch die langfristige Stabilisierung des Warenaustauschs mit der Sowjetunion einer flexiblen Anpassung der Exportproduktion an die Bedarfsstruktur und das Anspruchsniveau auf dem Weltmarkt bedarf. Dazu werden seit einigen Jahren erhebliche Anstrengungen unternommen. Dem Ziel, die Reaktionsfähigkeit im Auslandsgeschäft zu beschleunigen, dienen die geplanten oder bereits realisierten Reformen des Außenwirtschaftssystems. Um den Zugang zum Welthandel zu erleichtern, stellte Bulgarien im September 1986 den Antrag auf Vollmitgliedschaft im GATT, der originellerweise damit begründet wurde, daß sich die bulgarische Außenwirtschaftspolitik bereits an marktwirtschaftlichen Prinzipien orientiere[64]).

---

[60]) BfAI (Anm. 57).

[61]) Schönfeld, R.: Bulgariens Außenhandelspolitik und die Rolle der deutschen Wirtschaft, in: Südosteuropa. 31 (1982), S. 398 ff.

[62]) Der Deutsche Osthandel 1987 (Studien-Reihe 59). Hrsg. vom Bundesministerium für Wirtschaft. Bonn, Juni 1988; SG. 1988, S. 367 f.; Grosser (Anm. 18), Tab. IV d, S. 42 f.

[63]) Grosser (Anm. 18), Tab. IV d, S. 42 f.

[64]) Dazu Jackson (Anm. 17), S. 544–559.

5. Formen der Unternehmenskooperation

Die bulgarische Regierung hat, dem Beispiel anderer RGW-Länder folgend, bestimmte Formen langfristiger Kooperation zwischen einheimischen Wirtschaftsorganisationen und Unternehmen im kapitalistischen Ausland, wie Lizenzgeschäfte, Produktionsteilung u. ä., schon in den 60er Jahren zugelassen. Im Rahmen des NIM wurden schließlich Gemischte Handels- und Produktionsgesellschaften in westlichen Volkswirtschaften und auf bulgarischem Territorium gestattet sowie die Errichtung von Zollfreizonen angekündigt.

Der rechtliche Rahmen für die Gründung und den Betrieb von Gemischten Gesellschaften wurde zunächst durch den Erlaß Nr. 535 über die „wirtschaftliche Zusammenarbeit zwischen bulgarischen juristischen Personen und ausländischen juristischen und natürlichen Personen" aus dem Jahre 1980 abgesteckt[65]). Im Jahre 1987 trug die bulgarische Wirtschaftsführung der inzwischen erfolgten Reform der Betriebsverfassung und den Wünschen ausländischer Interessenten mit der Verordnung Nr. 31 über die „Tätigkeit der selbstverwalteten Wirtschaftsorganisationen mit ausländischer Investititionsbeteiligung" und der Verordnung Nr. 49 über die „Durchführung der Kontrolle der wirtschaftlichen Tätigkeit selbstverwalteter Wirtschaftsorganisationen mit ausländischer Investitionsbeteiligung"[66]), im Januar 1989 schließlich mit dem Erlaß Nr. 56 „Über die Wirtschaftstätigkeit"[67]) Rechnung. Damit wurde die bulgarische Joint-Venture-Gesetzgebung dem Stand der entsprechenden Rechtsentwicklung in Ungarn weitgehend angepaßt und eine der liberalsten Regelungen dieser Art im RGW geschaffen. Am Gesellschaftskapital kann das westliche Unternehmen auch mit mehr als 49 % beteiligt sein. Die Gemischte Gesellschaft kann praktisch in jedem Produktions- und Dienstleistungszweig der bulgarischen Wirtschaft tätig werden und ist in das staatliche Planungs- und Leitungssystem nicht integriert. Die Vorsitzenden des Direktorenrates (Geschäftsführung) wie auch des Verwaltungsrates (Aufsichtsrat) müssen bulgarische Staatsbürger sein. Für Beschlüsse dieser Organe ist Einstimmigkeit vorgeschrieben, womit die Interessen der Teilhaber geschützt, Entscheidungsfindungen aber erschwert werden.

Die Verpflichtung der Gemischten Gesellschaft, für den Retransfer der Gewinne benötigte Devisen selbst zu erwirtschaften, beeinträchtigte bisher die Rechte des ausländischen Investors und schränkte die Produktionsziele des Unternehmens ein. Auch durch die zeitliche Befristung des Joint Venture-Vertrages (15 Jahre, Genehmigung des Verlängerungsantrags bleibt vorbehalten) und die trotz zwischenstaatlicher Investitionsschutzabkommen immer noch unzureichend geregelten Eigentumsrechte – der ausländische Teilhaber kann nicht Eigentum an bulgarischen Immobilien erwerben – wurden die Investitionsbedingungen gegenüber konkurrierenden Standorten in westlichen Industrie- oder Dritte Welt-Ländern verschlechtert. Diese und ande-

---

[65]) DV. (1980) 25. Vgl. Schönfeld, R.: Joint Ventures mit westlicher Kapitalbeteiligung in sozialistischen Ländern, in: Brunner, G. (Hrsg.): Wirtschaftsrecht, Internationaler Handel und Friedliche Koexistenz aus osteuropäischer Sicht. Berlin 1982, bes. S. 79f., 83f., 89f.
[66]) DV. (1987) 50 und 63.
[67]) DV. (1989) 4; Ikonomičeski život. (1989) 22 (Beilage); BfAI: NfA (R). 1.2.1989.

re Gründe[68]) haben bisher dazu beigetragen, daß bisher nur neun Joint Ventures mit westlicher Kapitalbeteiligung auf bulgarischem Territorium errichtet wurden, und zwar drei mit japanischen, zwei mit amerikanischen und je eine mit Schweizer, französischen, englischen und deutschen Gesellschaftern. Der Erlaß Nr. 56 gestattet dem ausländischen Investor nunmehr, seinen Gewinnanteil und gegebenenfalls auch seine Liquidationsquote bei der BNB in die Währung einzutauschen, „in der die Investition erfolgt ist" (Art. 120, Abs. 2 u. 3). Genehmigungspflichtig bleibt die Gründung einer GmbH, wenn die ausländische Beteiligung mehr als 49 %, einer AG, wenn diese mehr als 20 % beträgt (Art. 103 u. 104). Nach wie vor kann die Gesellschaft mit ausländischer Beteiligung aber nur ein befristetes Nutzungsrecht an bulgarischen Immobilien erwerben (Art. 123), der Eigentumserwerb an Grund und Boden bleibt ausdrücklich ausgeschlossen (Art. 126). Es bleibt abzuwarten, ob der Erlaß Nr. 56 die erhofften Anreizwirkungen entfaltet, die wesentlich vom gesamten Reformfortschritt abhängen.

Im Juli 1987 wurde die Errichtung zollfreier Wirtschaftszonen in See- und Binnenhäfen, internationalen Flughäfen, Transportzentren, Verkehrsknotenpunkten und bestimmten Industriebetrieben beschlossen. Dort können ausländische Firmen Zollfreilager unterhalten und entweder allein oder zusammen mit einem bulgarischen Partner Produktions- und Handelsbetriebe gründen, Vertretungs-, Versicherungs- oder Finanzierungsgeschäfte tätigen. Alle Zahlungen müssen in konvertibler Währung erfolgen, Gewinne sind steuerfrei, solange sie in der Zollfreizone verbleiben[69]). Der bulgarischen Führung ist in den 80er Jahren mehr denn je bewußt geworden, daß es zur flexiblen Anpassung der Industriestruktur an den raschen technologischen Wandel der Weltwirtschaft der verstärkten Inanspruchnahme finanzieller und technischer Unterstützung der westlichen Industrieländer, aber gleichzeitig auch einer tiefgreifenden, vor dem Überbordwerfen sozialistischer Prinzipien nicht zurückscheuenden Reform des Systems der Außenwirtschaftslenkung bedarf. Dazu wurden bereits entscheidende erste Schritte unternommen. Die politische Demokratisierung des Landes wird auch den Prozeß der Liberalisierung und der regionalen Umorientierung der bulgarischen Außenwirtschaft beschleunigen. Ein kräftiges Voranschreiten Bulgariens in dieser Richtung sollte von den westlichen Handelspartnern in jeder nur möglichen Weise ermutigt und gefördert werden.

---

[68]) Vgl. Untersuchung über die Voraussetzungen und gesetzlichen Rahmenbedingungen für eine langfristige Unternehmenskooperation zwischen deutschen und bulgarischen Unternehmen in Bulgarien, im Auftrag des Bundeswirtschaftsministeriums erstellt von Roland Berger & Partner GmbH, München, Dezember 1987, S. 71 f.
[69]) DV. (1987) 55 und 86.

Raumplanung und Umweltschutz

Wolf Oschlies, Köln

I. Raumplanung und historische Landesentwicklung – II. Aus der Geschichte des Umweltschutzes in Bulgarien – III. Ökologische Ängste der Gegenwart: 1. Bodenzerstörung – 2. Wasser: knapp und verschwendet – 3. Luftverseuchung – 4. Denkmalschutz als „patriotische Mission" – 5. Hände weg von der Kernkraft? – 6. Sorgenkind Sofia

I. Raumplanung und historische Landesentwicklung

Gerade unter dem weiter gefaßten Blickwinkel von Umweltbelangen sieht Bulgarien sich in wachsendem Maße mit Problemen konfrontiert, die aus drei Grundcharakteristika des Landes resultieren:

1. Als frühere Randprovinz des Osmanischen Reichs, die Bulgarien rund 500 Jahre lang war, hat es immer noch mit den Folgewirkungen seines historischen Schicksals zu tun;
2. als „agro-industrielles" (bzw. „industriell-agrarisches") Land muß Bulgarien ein hohes Maß demographischer und ökonomischer Auswirkungen in Kauf nehmen, die auf dem Weg von agrarischer Rückständigkeit zu industrieller Moderne unvermeidlich sind;
3. als „sozialistisches Land" mit einer (erst neuerdings gelockerten) zentralen Wirtschaftsplanung hat Bulgarien schließlich mit systemimmanenten Belastungen zu kämpfen, die alle auf den Primat der Planerfüllung *vor* der Ökologie zurückzuführen sind.

Diese drei Momente sind zumeist aufs engste ineinander verwoben, so daß bei gewissen Prozessen nicht mehr auszumachen ist, welche auslösenden Faktoren sie vorrangig stimulieren – die Binnenwanderung beispielsweise kann zu fast gleichen Teilen die Umkehrung historischer Fluchtbewegungen, die Sogwirkung neuer Industrien oder die Abwanderung aus ökologisch meistgefährdeten Gebieten sein. Oder auch umgekehrt: Förderungsprogramme, die Neuansiedlungen von Menschen und Industriekapazitäten in bestimmten Gebieten beabsichtigen, versanden in der zähen Kohäsion von Miniregionen, in die kein „Zugereister" so bald hineinkommt. Erleichtert wird Bulgariens Lage immerhin durch den Umstand, daß es seit seinem Wiedereintritt in die europäische Staatenfamilie (1878) relativ geringe Territorialveränderungen erlebte, damit auch geringere regionale Entwicklungsgefälle verkraften mußte. Wenn es in der bulgarischen Geschichte gelegentlich zu Territorialveränderungen kam – 1885 Wiedervereinigung von Nord- mit Südbulgarien, 1940 Anschluß der Süddobrudscha –, dann fußten diese so einsehbar auf dem Nationalitätenprinzip, daß sie fortan Bestand hatten (vgl. das Kapitel „Außenpolitik" von K.-D. Grothusen).

Das soll wiederum nicht heißen, daß Bulgarien nie Probleme mit der Raum- und Regionalplanung gehabt hätte. Vielmehr resultierte der Zwang, sich mit gewissen Regionen gesondert zu befassen, bereits aus verschiedenen grundlegenden Gegebenheiten:

1. Bulgarien weist eine klare geomorphologische Zonengliederung auf, wobei jede Zone die ganze Landesbreite von West nach Ost einschließt. In Nordsüd-Richtung schließen sich die folgenden Zonen aneinander an: „Mösische Platte – Donau-Plattformebene", „Gesamtbalkanisches Kettensystem", „Rila-Rhodopen-Region" (vgl. das Kapitel „Geographical Foundations" von I. Matley).

2. In Westost-Richtung weist Bulgarien eine weitere Zonengliederung auf, die vor allem dialektal und soziokulturell festzumachen ist: In Ostbulgarien dominiert die *Jakane*-Sprechweise, die auch die Normen der bulgarischen Standardsprache setzt (vgl. Kapitel „Massenmedien und Sprachkultur" des Autors). Im Westen gibt es die *Ekane*-Sprechweise, deren „unbulgarische" Intonation die Kulturausstrahlung der Hauptstadt mindert.

3. Nachdem sich die Osmanenherrschaft auf dem Balkan gefestigt hatte (frühes 15. Jh.), wurden die Slawen auf ihre Uranfänge – Stammesorganisation, Großfamilienwirtschaft – zurückgeworfen, und vor den Türken zogen sie sich in die sicheren Berge zurück. Diese politische und regionale Isolierung ließ ethnische Kleinstgemeinschaften von hohem Kohäsionsgrad und mit viel ursprünglichem Brauchtum entstehen, was faktisch einer immer noch spürbaren Mikrorayonierung des ganzen Landes gleichkam. (Wie eingangs erwähnt, ist die langsame Umkehrung dieser Absetzbewegung eine der Triebkräfte der bulgarischen Migration.)

4. Traditionelle Stiefkinder bulgarischer Raumplanung sind die peripheren Regionen Dobrudscha (NO), Pirin (SW) und Rhodopen (S). In früheren Jahrzehnten wurden sie vom Eisenbahnbau (der gerade zu „bourgeoisen" Zeiten sehr energisch vorangetrieben wurde und das Land weitblickend erschloß) vernachlässigt – in neuer Zeit bei der Dislozierung von Industrieanlagen und beim Straßenbau.

Seit der Wiederentstehung des bulgarischen Staates wurde versucht, Raumplanung über die administrative Aufgliederung zu lösen, was Bulgarien seit über 100 Jahren eine wechselnde „Buntscheckigkeit" verlieh, die indessen ohne spürbare Effizienz blieb: 1878 – 8 Gouvernements (*gubernija*), 1880 – 21 Kreise (*okrăg*), 1887 – 26 Kreise, 1901 – 12 Kreise, 1934 – 7 Gebiete (*oblast*), 1944 – 9 Gebiete (vermutlich vermehrt um die im Krieg eroberten makedonischen Regionen), 1947 – ca. 100 Bezirke (*okolija*), 1949 – 15 Kreise, 1959 – 30 Kreise, 1971 – 28 Kreise, 1987 – 9 Gebiete. Erst die jüngste Territorial-Verwaltungsreform vom August 1987 (international vielfach als politischer Versuch, die etablierten Bürokratien durcheinanderzuwirbeln, angesehen) kann beanspruchen, raumplanerisch geglückt zu sein – die neuen Gebiete sind annähernd gleich groß, industriell und infrastrukturell gleich versorgt, sie integrieren stärker als bisher Randregionen, ihre Zentren sind voneinander gleich weit entfernt und untereinander gut verbunden (vgl. den Beitrag „Regierungssystem" von O. Luchterhandt).

In „sozialistischer" Zeit diente Raumplanung auch als jenes „Verbindungsglied", das die zentrale Wirtschaftsplanung so nach Branchen/Regionen aufgliedern sollte, daß ein gesamtstaatliches-gesamtwirtschaftliches Entwicklungsgleichgewicht herauskam. Dieser Aufgabe widmete sich vor allem das 1960 geschaffene „Institut für

Raumplanung" (*Institut za rajonno planirane*), das spezielle Entwicklungsprogramme für einzelne Regionen – Touristengebiet an der Schwarzmeerküste, Kohlegebiet Pernik, Industrierevier Devnja u. a. – entwarf.

Darüber hinaus bedeutet „Raumplanung" seit langem, die Stadt-Land-Unterschiede einzuebnen und die „Selbstversorgung" überschaubarer Regionen zu sichern. Mit der Förderung „persönlicher Wirtschaften" in der „sozialistischen" Landwirtschaft wurde ab 1973 eine wichtige Voraussetzung dafür geschaffen. 1973 schritt man auch zur Bildung von „Siedlungssystemen" (*selištni sistemi*): Alle Siedlungen einer bestimmten Region werden wie Viertel einer fiktiven Großstadt angesehen, als solche verwaltet und versorgt.

Dieses Konzept hat sich relativ gut bewährt, allerdings im Landesinneren mehr als in den Grenz- und einigen Bergregionen. In ihnen ist gewissermaßen eine „Entwicklung" abgebrochen, die im übrigen Bulgarien zwar identisch begann, aber anders weiterging: Bis 1957 bestand in Bulgarien eine „normale" Migration, da die kollektivierte Landwirtschaft etwa soviele Menschen freisetzte, wie die extensiv fortschreitende Industrialisierung aufnehmen konnte. In den Jahren 1957–1963 überwog die Landflucht die industriellen Aufnahmemöglichkeiten um ein Vielfaches, was zu einem „Migrationsverlust" (*migracionna zaguba*) in Gestalt von Massenarbeitslosigkeit führte. In den 60er Jahren wandelte sich das Bild dergestalt, daß nunmehr ein „schreiender" Arbeitskräftemangel in der Industrie auftrat, der erst nach 1972 ausgeglichen werden konnte.

Allein manche Grenzregionen scheinen vielfach noch bei den Gegebenheiten von 1963 zu verharren. Bulgariens Randzone bildet einen nahezu geschlossenen Gürtel dünnstbesiedelter Gebiete (0–20 E./km), in denen der Trend zur „Entvölkerung" anhält. Dazu tragen besonders bei: eine niedrige Natalität (unter 5 bis max. 10‰), eine hohe Mortalität (20 – über 35‰), ein aus beiden resultierender niedriger natürlicher Zuwachs (0–7,5‰), eine ungünstige Altersstruktur, ein Trend zur dauernden oder saisonalen Abwanderung, eine „stark ausgeprägte versteckte Arbeitslosigkeit in der Landwirtschaft" (*silno izrazena skrita selskostopanska bezrabotica*), die Sogwirkung benachbarter Industriezentren u. a. m.[1]).

Die von diesen Erscheinungen meistbetroffenen Regionen liegen in der Nachbarschaft von Ländern, die entweder blockfrei (Jugoslawien) sind oder der NATO angehören (Türkei, Griechenland). Nun unterhält Bulgarien zwar zu Griechenland ein traditionell freundschaftliches Verhältnis (dessen Anfänge Mitte der 60er Jahre gelegt wurden und das in den späten 80er Jahren besonders gut entwickelt war), kann es als WP-Mitglied aus grundsätzlichen strategischen Erwägungen heraus aber nicht zulassen, nahezu entvölkerte Regionen an seinen Grenzen zu haben. Deswegen wurde im Mai 1982 ein Grenzland-Förderungsprogramm beschlossen[2]), das zunächst aus den

---

[1]) Minkov, M. (Hrsg.): Charakteristika na bălgarskoto naselenie (Charakteristik der bulgarischen Bevölkerung). Sofia 1984, S. 138 ff.

[2]) Vgl. Postanovlenie Nr. 22 ot 10 maj 1982 g. za uskoreno socialno-ikonomičesko razvitie na selištni sistemi ot četvărti i peti funkcionalen tip, ot graničnite rajoni i ot Strandžo-sakarskija kraj prez osmata petiletka i do 1990 g. (Verordnung Nr. 22 vom 10. Mai 1982 über eine beschleunigte sozioökonomische Entwicklung von Siedlungssystemen des 4. und 5. Funktionstyps, von Grenzregionen und des Gebiets Strandža-Sakar im 8. Fünfjahresplan und bis 1990), in: DV. (1982) 42.

genannten Gründen – traditionell verfestigte Siedlungsstrukturen – nicht recht vorankam, zudem die Gefahr in sich barg, wegen der ethnischen Zusammensetzung der Grenzlandbevölkerung (mit ihren starken Anteilen von Makedoniern, Griechen, Türken und Pomaken) inneren Unfrieden bei der Titularnation auszulösen. Um dieser Gefahr zuvorzukommen (wohl auch um ersten Anfängen eines islamischen Fundamentalismus unter den Muslimen zu wehren), startete Sofia Mitte der 80er Jahre eine „Bulgarisierungskampagne". Sie sollte die innere Kohäsion *aller* Bevölkerungsteile stärken, zudem raumplanerische Aktivitäten durch den nationalen Appell erleichtern. Tatsächlich war die Kampagne so übereilt und ungeschickt inszeniert, daß Bulgarien sich in kürzester Zeit vor der Weltöffentlichkeit praktisch des Genozids an seinen nationalen Minderheiten angeklagt sah[3]) (vgl. die Beiträge „Außenpolitik" von K.-D. Grothusen und „Domestic Politics" von J.D. Bell).

Zumindest *ein* Gutes haben die bulgarischen Grenzregionen – sie sind ökologisch in einer Weise intakt, die sich im übrigen Bulgarien kaum noch findet. Dafür ein Beispiel: Vor hundert Jahren hatte Sofia unter 20 000 Einwohner – derzeit über 1,3 Mio., d.h. 14% der Gesamtbevölkerung des Landes (wo 6% das demographische Optimum wären). In der Stadt sind 14% der bulgarischen Industrieproduktion konzentriert, ebenfalls eindeutig zu viel. Eine 1987 publizierte „Ökologische Karte" Sofias sprach eine deutliche Sprache: fünf- bis achtfach höhere Raten der Erkrankungen der Atmungsorgane, der Haut und des Kreislaufs allein in den Jahren 1981–1985, CO-Belastung zehn- bis neunzigfach *über* den zulässigen Normen etc.[4]). Einige Hundert Industriebetriebe belasten die Umwelt, am meisten die Stahlwerke Kremikovci und *Lenin* (NO und SO), veraltete und dringend sanierungsbedürftige Großanlagen auf unzureichenden Erzlagerstätten, die die Hauptstadt samt umliegendem „Sofioter Feld" tagtäglich mit ihren immensen Schadstoffemissionen überziehen.

Im SW von Sofia (und neuerlich zu seinem „Gebiet" gehörend) erstreckt sich das Piringebirge – eine so dünn besiedelte natürliche und unversehrte Region, daß 1967 hier der „Pirin-Nationalpark" eingerichtet wurde. Er ist zwar nicht der älteste bulgarische Nationalpark, mit 26 479 ha Ausdehnung aber mit Abstand der größte (zum Vergleich: Der älteste Park *Vitoša* wurde 1933 geschaffen und umfaßt als zweitgrößter Park 12 100 ha).

Gerade die Unterschiede Sofia – Pirin illustrieren die ganze Spannbreite der Raum- und Ökoproblematik Bulgariens. Sofia steht für die Schattenseiten von Industrialisierung, Intensivierung und Urbanisierung. Pirin – das ist sozusagen die „heile Welt" früherer Zeiten. Das wiederum heißt beileibe nicht, Bulgarien sei in der Vergangenheit eine ökologische Idylle gewesen!

---

[3]) Oschlies, W.: Mononationales Bulgarien – mit kleinen Schönheitsfehlern, in: Europäische Rundschau. 3 (1986), S. 125–128.
[4]) Conkova, S.: Orientir za dejstvie (Orientierungshilfe zur Handlung), in: Anteni. 11.3.1987.

II. Aus der Geschichte des Umweltschutzes in Bulgarien

Es wäre reizvoll, eine Geschichte Bulgariens unter ökologischem Aspekt zu schreiben. Sie müßte im Jahre 811 einsetzen, als der altbulgarische Chan Krum ein Waldschutzgesetz erließ. In späteren Jahrhunderten war Bulgarien als zentrales Balkanland die Beute vieler Herren und Schauplatz ungezählter Kriege und Aufstände, und dieses wechselvolle Schicksal hinterließ ökologische Wunden, die partiell schon in vorbulgarischer Zeit geschlagen wurden: Bereits die Anfänge des Bergbaus in römischer, mehr noch in türkischer Zeit sind bis heute in rücksichtslos ausgebeuteten Fundstätten und aufgetürmten Halden nachzuvollziehen. Mit den Türken kam im späten Mittelalter der fast totale Niedergang der bulgarischen Regionen, und als im Juni 1553 Hans Dernschwamm, Beauftragter des Handelshauses Fugger, nach Bulgarien kam, notierte er über dessen Hauptstadt: „Sophia scheint eine große statt sein gewesen vor zeiten, ist noch groß genug, ohne mauren und bevestigung, von schlechten niederen baursheusern von holz, nichts in die hoche gebaut, auswendig mit zeunen verfridet alle wie saustell, damit sie nur trucken sitzen"[4a]).

Gegen die Türken regte sich zu allen Zeiten bulgarischer Widerstand, der Natur und Menschen gleichermaßen in Mitleidenschaft zog: Türkische Rache ließ bulgarische Siedlungen in Flammen aufgehen oder ganze Wälder für freies Schußfeld fallen, Vertreibungen bedingten neue Rodungen usw. Als der österreichische Ethnograph F. Ph. Kanitz (1829–1904) in den 60er und 70er Jahren des vergangenen Jahrhunderts durch Bulgarien reiste, war es vor allem der schlechte Zustand der Wälder, der seine Besorgnis erregte[5]). Ähnlich sahen es die ersten bulgarischen Zeitungen – *Stupan* (Landwirt), *Dunav* (Donau) u.a. –, die bereits lange vor der Befreiung des Landes besorgte Artikel publizierten, ob den Wäldern auch genügend Schutz und Aufmerksamkeit zuteil würden. Jahrzehnte vor 1878 begannen auch Bemühungen, Zeugnisse bulgarischer Vergangenheit zu restaurieren bzw. in Museen der Nachwelt zu überliefern.

Als alte „Bauernnation" hatten (und haben) Bulgaren stets ein gewissermaßen „instinktives" Verhältnis zur Natur, mit und von der sie lebten; altbulgarische Sitten, Feiern und Sprichwörter künden davon (vgl. das Kapitel „Volkskultur" von K. Roth)[6]). Auf der anderen Seite bewirkte die allgemeine Rückständigkeit, die die Türkenherrschaft mit sich gebracht hatte, einen vielfach rücksichtslosen Umgang mit der Natur: Nach 1878 wurden z.B. die Wälder Gemeindeeigentum – und so erbarmungslos abgeholzt, daß der junge Staat mit einem eigenen Waldgesetz dazwischentreten mußte (1883). Ähnlich war es mit Jagd, Fischfang u.a.

Es waren gerade die größten bulgarischen Literaten, die Ökologie früh als patriotisch-aufklärerischen Auftrag verstanden. Ivan Vazov setzte sich bereits 1884 als Abgeordneter für Belange des Umweltschutzes ein, als späterer Volksbildungsmini-

---

[4a]) Vgl. Hans Dernschwam's orientalische Reise 1553–1555 – aus Handschriften im Auszuge mitgetheilt von Prof. H. Kiepert, in: Globus – Illustrierte Zeitschrift für Länder- und Völkerkunde. 52 (1887), S. 186–235, hier: S. 202.

[5]) Kanitz, F.: Donau-Bulgarien und der Balkan. Bd. I–III. 2. Aufl. Leipzig 1882, passim, speziell II, S. 115.

[6]) Vakarelski, Ch.: Bulgarische Volkskunde. Berlin 1969, passim.

ster (August 1897–Januar 1899) führte er Schulgärten als Beitrag zur lokalen Wiederaufforstung ein; Aleko Konstantinov („Der Glückliche") regte um 1890 „touristische" Vereinigungen an, also Wander- und Naturschutzbewegungen (und wie seit einigen Jahren ein Gedenkstein im Sofioter Zentrum bezeugt, gelang ihm das auch). Bereits Ende des vorigen Jahrhunderts entstanden in rascher Folge Gesellschaften für Naturschutz (z. B. 1896 *Bălgarsko Prirodoizpitatelno Družestvo* – Bulgarische Gesellschaft für Naturforschung), wurden Museen gegründet, wurde mit Ausgrabungen und Konservierungen begonnen u. a. m.

Nach dem I. Weltkrieg wurde der Umweltschutz systematisch in drei Richtungen vorangetrieben – organisatorisch (z. B. *Komitet za zaštita na bălgarskata priroda* – Komitee für den Schutz der bulgarischen Natur, 1919; *Săjuz za zaštita na prirodata* – Verband für Naturschutz, 1928), praktisch (Gründung des Nationalparks (*Naroden park*) Vitoša im Februar 1933 sowie der Reservate (*rezervat*) Silkozija (Burgas), Parangalica (Rila), Bajuvi dupki, Suchodol, Džindžirica (alle Pirin), Oborište, Šipka, Buzludža und Vola (alle Balkangebirge) bis 1935) und wissenschaftlich (z. B. durch die erstmalige Erstellung von agrogeologischen und Bodenkarten durch Nikola Puškarov (1874–1943). Daneben wurden urbanistische Maßnahmen vollendet wie die Generalsanierung Sofias, die unter Dimităr Petkov (1858–1907) bereits Ende des 19. Jh. eingesetzt hatte. Alle diese (und weitere) Bemühungen schlugen sich im Gesetz über den Naturschutz in Bulgarien (*Zakon za zaštita na prirodata v Bălgarija*) vom 15. 3. 1936 nieder, das interessanterweise dem Naturschützerverband das Recht einräumte, Gesetzesübertretungen zu ahnden. Nicht einmal der II. Weltkrieg konnte den praktischen Umweltschutz in Bulgarien stoppen, wie etwa das 1942 wiederhergestellte staatliche Waldmonopol bewies.

Später sah es für etwa fünf Nachkriegsjahre so aus, als könne die alte Tradition mit einigen „kosmetischen" Korrekturen bruchlos fortgeführt werden. So benannte sich der Verband am 17. 2. 1946 in „Bulgarischer Nationalverband für Naturschutz" (*Bălgarski naroden săjuz za zaštita na prirodata*) um und machte weiter wie bisher. Und tatsächlich schien die Chance real, bulgarische Tradition des Umweltschutzes und „sozialistische Industrialisierung" unter einen Hut zu bringen, fundiert gefördert von wissenschaftlich ausgewiesenen Naturschützern wie dem Pharmazeuten Aleksi Petrov (1889–1974), dem Zoologen Krăst'o Tuleškov (1901–1976) u. a. Der Naturschutz wurde zu einer wahren Massenbewegung, die erstaunliche Erfolge aufzuweisen hatte: Bis Anfang der 50er Jahre wurden u. a. 6 Nationalparks, 39 Reservate und 26 „Geschichtsplätze" (*istoričeski mestnosti*) geschaffen. Und dann brach alles zusammen. Die „sozialistische" Industrialisierung, die zentrale Wirtschaftsplanung durften nicht mehr als Verursacher von Umweltschäden genannt werden – folglich wurden 1951 alle Naturschutzorganisationen aufgelöst, alle Naturschutzgesetze ersatzlos gestrichen. Kurz: „In den 50er Jahren starb der Naturschutz für eine bestimmte Zeit ab"[7]).

Mit der Gründung der „Naturschutzkommission bei der BAN" (*Komisija po zaštita na prirodata pri BAN*), die auf sowjetisches (!) Drängen hin erfolgte, kam 1958

---

[7]) Rizov, K.: Razvitie na prirodozaštitnoto delo v Bălgarija (Entwicklung des Naturschutzwesens in Bulgarien). Sofia 1987.

wieder etwas Bewegung in diese vernachlässigte Sphäre. Am 13.9.1960 wurde die „Anweisung für Naturschutz" (*Ukaz za zaštita na prirodata*) erlassen, nachdem kurz zuvor bei der „Hauptleitung für Wälder" (*Glavno upravlenie na gorite*) bereits ein „Sektor für Naturschutz" (*Sektor po zaštita na prirodata*) geschaffen worden war. Langjähriger Leiter des „Sektors" war Marin Toškov, ein wissenschaftlich wie publizistisch gleich hochbegabter „Einzelkämpfer", der mit Hunderten Aufsätzen und zehn Büchern die bulgarische Gesellschaft ökologisch sensibilisierte. Erfolge blieben nicht aus: Die ganzen 60er Jahre über wurden einschlägige Gesetze und Verordnungen erlassen (z. B. 1963 Gesetz über den Schutz von Luft, Gewässern und Böden vor Verschmutzung (*Zakon za opazvane na văzducha, vodite i počvite ot zamărsjavane*), 1967 Gesetz zum Naturschutz (*Zakon za zaštita na prirodata*) u.a.), wurden bei Organisationen und Institutionen spezielle „Kommissionen" geschaffen (z.B. 1962 Kommission für Naturschutz (*Komisija za zaštita na prirodata*) beim Bulgarischen Touristikverband (*Bălgarski Turističeski Săjuz, BTS*)), fand die Öko-Thematik Eingang in bulgarische Medien. Es war aber auch allerhöchste Zeit. 1969 untersuchten drei Chemiker den Reinheitsgrad bulgarischer Flüsse (in die, ohne Donau und Schwarzes Meer, alle 24 Stunden 2,85 Mio. m³ Abwasser strömten) und kamen zu dem Schluß, „daß sich die Verschmutzung der Flüsse mit Schadstoffen mit jedem vergangenen Jahr erhöht hat, wodurch die Schäden, die der Volkswirtschaft zugefügt werden, ununterbrochen anwachsen"[8]).

In den 70er Jahren kam es zu Öko-Aktivitäten von geradezu verwirrender Vielfalt: Im Juli 1971 wurde das bisherige Waldministerium in „Ministerium für Wälder und Umweltschutz" (*Ministerstvo na gorite i opazvaneto na prirodnata sreda*) umbenannt, und so entstand (heißt es) das erste Umweltministerium der Welt. Im Juni 1976 wurde das Ministerium wieder auf seine ursprüngliche Aufgabe reduziert, allein die Forstwirtschaft zu leiten; an seiner Stelle entstand im Januar 1977 beim Ministerrat das „Komitee für den Schutz der natürlichen Umwelt" (*Komitet za opazvane na prirodnata sreda, KOPS*), das seither als eine Art „Superministerium" mit Weisungsbefugnis für alle anderen Ministerien wirkt. Zusätzlich entstanden Öko-Gremien bei Staats-, Partei- und Gesellschaftsorganen, die wiederum von Dachgremien überwölbt wurden – etwa vom „Gesamtnationalen Komitee für Naturschutz" (*Obštonaroden komitet za zaštita na prirodata*) von 1971, das fortan den Mai als „Monat des Naturschutzes" ausrichtete. Daneben stand die bulgarische Presse, die nahezu kollektiv „grün" wurde und mit jedem Jahr ernster, kompetenter und aggressiver gegen ökologische Sünden auftrat.

Aus zwei Gründen mußte sich die Aggressivität der Medien akkumulieren. Zum einen blieb die bulgarische Öffentlichkeit weithin wenig an Umweltproblemen interessiert – sie sprangen noch nicht allenthalben ins Auge, zudem bot der Alltag noch andere Sorgen in Fülle. Zum zweiten kümmerten sich die „sozialistischen" Großbetriebe von Industrie und Landwirtschaft geradezu demonstrativ *nicht* um ökologische Belange oder gar Auflagen. Ohnmächtig mußte – und muß noch – die Presse zuschauen, wie nicht wenige Unternehmen ungerührt die Umwelt verseuchten, dafür

---

[8]) Cačev, C. et al.: Zamărsjavane na rekite v Bălgarija săs suspendirani veštestva (Verschmutzung der Flüsse in Bulgarien mit Abfallstoffen). Sofia 1973.

pro Jahr etwa 80 000 Leva „Strafe" zahlten und im nächsten Jahr mit ihren Schadstoffemissionen fortfuhren.

III. Ökologische Ängste der Gegenwart

1. Bodenzerstörung

Gerade in den 70er Jahren wurde das ökologische Dilemma „realsozialistischer" Staaten in der bulgarischen Presse ausgesprochen oder wenigstens angedeutet: Planerfüllung und Umweltschutz werden von demselben Staatsapparat in Auftrag gegeben, wobei der Plan höchste Priorität genießt und Öko-Investitionen zumeist als „unproduktiv" angesehen werden. Im Konfliktfall verweist der Staat auf seine (guten) Umweltgesetze, die Betriebe aber verweisen auf ihre Planauflagen – letztlich geschieht nichts, und den Schaden hat die Umwelt.

Grundsätzlich besteht diese Lage bis zur Gegenwart, in manchen Bereichen, etwa bei der Luftverseuchung, hat sie sich noch erheblich verschärft. Geändert hat sich jedoch die Einstellung der Bevölkerung, die einfach sensibler gegenüber Umweltfragen geworden ist. (Mit-)Auslöser dessen waren Mitte der 70er Jahre die Anfänge des Sofioter Metrobaus. Zwei Trassen waren geplant, die sich im Zentrum Sofias kreuzen sollten – also genau dort, wo die heißen Quellen der Stadt entspringen, wo der Untergrund sandig-weich ist, wo schon in der Vergangenheit bei jeder kleinsten Grabung Altertümer ans Licht kamen, wo die Reste des antiken Serdica (slaw. *Sredec*) noch ihrer Ausgrabung harren. Als diese Pläne bekannt wurden, brach ein wahrer Sturm los, der laufend eskalierte, dabei von zwei Institutionen noch „geschürt" wurde – der Wochenzeitung „Anteni" (gegr. 1971) und dem „Klub Freunde der Sofioter Architektur" (*Klub Prijateli na sofijskata architektura*), der um 1979 entstand und sich seither zu einer informellen „Bürgerinitiative" entwickelt hat: unabhängig, kompetent, einflußreich[9]). Beider (und anderer) Bemühen hatte Erfolg: 1981 wurden die Metro-Streckenpläne revidiert, wobei das engste Zentrum nunmehr völlig ausgespart blieb.

Die 80er Jahre hatten in den Bulgaren bereits das Gefühl einer allseitigen ökologischen Bedrohung wach werden lassen, das durch die Atomkatastrophe im sowjetischen Černobyl' (April/Mai 1986) noch vertieft wurde. Aus der gesamten engagierten und ausführlichen Öko-Debatte schälten sich drei Haupt- und zwei Nebenprobleme heraus: Zur ersten Gruppe gehört die Verseuchung von Boden, Wasser und Luft, zur zweiten Fragen des Denkmalschutzes und der Stadtsanierung.

Die Bodenproblematik ist in Bulgarien doppelt schwierig. Zum einen besteht eine durchgehende Rechtsunsicherheit in Grundstücksfragen. So kommt es immer wieder vor, daß per Behördenanweisung private Wohnsiedlungen eingeebnet werden, weil man Raum für neue Stadtviertel benötigt – zum Schaden der Bürger, die dort vor 20 Jahren mit offizieller Genehmigung und auf eigene Kosten ihr Häuschen errichte-

---

[9]) Detailliert Prodev, S. (Interview): Freunde der Sofioter Architektur, in: Südosteuropa. 37 (1988), S. 420–425.

ten[10]). Zum zweiten ist Boden ein knappes Gut, mit dem jedoch bemerkenswert sorglos umgegangen wird. Nur 61 % des bulgarischen Territoriums werden dem „landwirtschaftlichen Fonds" zugerechnet, lediglich 42 % sind landwirtschaftlicher Kulturboden. Und der bröckelt immer mehr ab: In den Jahren 1960–1988 gingen 227 600 ha Boden verloren, etwa die Hälfte davon für Bauzwecke. Seit 1980 entfielen 67 % der jährlichen Bodenverluste auf bestes Ackerland, 1987 waren es 87 %. Hinzu kommen Erosionsverluste an noch bebautem Boden, die in erster Linie den Produktionsbedingungen der „sozialistischen" Landwirtschaft anzulasten sind (so der Sofioter Bodenkundler Nejčo Ončev 1984): Großgerät (das durch sein Gewicht die Ackerkrume bis zur Wasserundurchlässigkeit verdichtet) benötigt für seinen Einsatz freie Riesenflächen – zu denen dann die erodierende Kraft von Wind und Regen ungehinderten Zugang hat. Minimalschätzungen beziffern die Jahresverluste auf den Gegenwert von 2 Mio. t Getreide[11]).

Im Frühjahr 1988 kam es nach langen Jahren guter Versorgung wieder zu langen Schlangen vor Lebensmittelläden – Krise als Folge des blinden Raubbaus am Boden? Bulgarische Gerichte sind seit Jahren damit befaßt, unlösbare Fälle zu lösen: TKZS klagen gegen Industriegiganten (wie das Chemiewerk Devnja bei Varna, den Energiekomplex Marica-iztok im zentralen Südbulgarien), weil in deren Nachbarschaft die Erträge, die laut planwirtschaftlichen Auflagen zu erbringen sind, durch Bodenverseuchung praktisch auf Null zurückfielen. Dabei tun die beteiligten Kontrahenten nur, was ihre „sozialistische" Pflicht ist – ihre jeweiligen Pläne zu erfüllen.

2. Wasser: Knapp und verschwendet

Industrieller und städtebaulicher Bodenraub ist im Grunde noch das kleinere Problem – gemessen etwa an der industriellen Schadstoffbelastung des Wassers. Von allen Balkanstaaten hat Bulgarien die geringste Wassermenge zur Verfügung – 2180 m^3 pro Kopf und Jahr. Seit 1982 hat das Land zudem nur Dürrejahre erlebt, die z. B. 1986 zu einem Defizit von mindestens 2 Mrd. m^3 führten. Für die Zukunft rechnet man mit weit größeren Fehlbeträgen, die sich z. B. im Jahre 2020 auf 4,6 Mrd. m^3 belaufen werden[12]).

Im Juli 1987 prüfte das Komitee für Staats- und Volkskontrolle den gesamten Wasserhaushalt Bulgariens. Das Ergebnis fiel so aus, daß die Regierung am 24. 2. 1988 strenge Wasser-Sparmaßnahmen verfügte. Deren Erfüllung wurde im weiteren Verlauf des Jahres kontrolliert – mit unbefriedigendem Ergebnis. Zwar waren die Talsperren zu 60 % gefüllt, aber das Trinkwasserdefizit betrug dennoch 51 Mio. m^3. Ursache dessen war vor allem der „Durst" der Industrie. Seit 1983 ist die Entnahme von Trinkwasser für Industriezwecke gesetzlich verboten, doch zeigte dieses Verbot keinerlei Wirkung. Allein in Sofia gibt es 15 Industriebetriebe ohne eigene Was-

---

[10]) Avramov, K.: Ot pozicija na silata (Aus der Position der Stärke), in: RD. 15. 6. 1988.
[11]) Petrov, V. (Interview): Adresi na plodorodieto (Adressen der Fruchtbarkeit), in: Kooperativno selo. 9. 2. 1988; Manolov, A.: Prirodata ni e učitel (Die Natur ist unser Lehrer), in: Anteni. 4. 5. 1988.
[12]) Radoev, C.: Kădeto e teklo... (Wo es geflossen ist...), in: Narodna kultura. 48, 28. 11. 1986.

serquelle, die sich mit 2,2 Mio. m³ jährlich aus dem städtischen Vorrat bedienen. Und im übrigen Land gibt es Dutzende ähnlicher Fälle. Vorgesehen ist, daß die Betriebe ihre Abwässer selber klären und wiederverwenden; weil das allein in Sofia 17 Betriebe *nicht* tun, wird der hauptstädtische Wasserhaushalt um jährlich weitere 3,5 Mio. m³ geschädigt[13]).

Die bulgarische Wasserversorgung arbeitet so, als sei das Land eine kleine Insel in einem unerschöpflichen Süßwassermeer. Wasser wird zu symbolischen Preisen von 0,2 Stotinki pro m³ (für die Landwirtschaft) bis 3,5 Stotinki (für die Industrie) verkauft. Insgesamt werden rund 30 % des Trinkwassers für die Industrie abgezweigt – im Kohlerevier von Pernik (W) gar 45,9 %. Erschwerend kommt hinzu, daß weitere 30 % des Trinkwassers (ca. 470 Mio. m³/Jahr) in einem brüchigen Leitungsnetz spurlos versickern. Allein in Sofia beträgt dieser Verlust 70 Mio. m³ – und das ist *mehr* als der Gesamtverbrauch der Sofioter. Die Leitungen bestehen aus Asbest-Zementröhren mit Gummidichtungen, und bei ihnen gab es 1987 85000 „Havarien", allein 19000 in Sofia.

Die geringfügigen Umweltstrafen – 1987 wurden in Sofia 40 Betriebe mit einer Gesamtsumme von 1 Mio. Leva belegt – bewirken gar nichts, und „zu verzeichnen ist eine alarmierende Tendenz zur Verschlechterung der Kennziffern für Trinkwasser hinsichtlich der Nitrate, Nitrite, Phosphate (...) und anderer chemischer Verunreinigungen". In ganz Bulgarien sind zahlreiche Regionen ausgewiesen, wo diese Trinkwasserverunreinigungen die zulässigen Normen erheblich übersteigen. Die Gründe dafür sind bekannt. In Sofia z. B. mißt das Wasserleitungsnetz 3477 km, die Abwässerkanalisation aber nur 1710 km, d. h. das Gros der Abwässer wird direkt in die vorbeifließenden Flüsse geleitet. Fehlplanungen industrieller Standorte verschärfen die Lage noch: Im südbulgarischen Plovdiv wurde für 30 Mio. Leva eine Abwässerkläranlage gebaut – und *hinter* ihr die „Industriezone Nord", aus der die Abwässer von 30 Betrieben ungereinigt in den Fluß Marica strömen. Vereint machen industrielle Wasserverschmutzung und landwirtschaftliche Überdüngung (deren Folgen sich im Grundwasser wiederfinden) immer größere Trinkwasserkontingente fast unbrauchbar: 1985 zählte man über 300 Siedlungen mit zusammen ca. 400000 Einwohnern, die Wasser benutzen mußten, das als Trinkwasser ungeeignet war. Anfang der 60er Jahre wurden im Bezirk Stara Zagora Nitratmengen von 20 mgr/l gemessen – 1983 waren es 480 mgr/l (bei einer Zulässigkeit von 50 mgr/l). Und Stara Zagora war kein Einzelfall in Bulgarien[14]).

Besonders übel dran sind die bulgarischen Flüsse, von denen überhaupt nur die Donau ganzjährig Wasser führt. Seit Jahrzehnten sind in Bulgarien die Verursacher der Flußverschmutzung namentlich bekannt – alle die Betriebe, die seit 20 und mehr Jahren pro Sekunde 120 l Giftwasser ablassen, Textilwerke, deren Abwässer Flußufer kilometerweit blau oder rot einfärben, Elektrizitätswerke, die ihren Klärschlamm

---

[13]) Bobčev, St.: Uništožavat, no si plaštat (Man zerstört, aber man zahlt), in: Stăršel. 2207, 27.5.1988.

[14]) Iliev, G. et al.: Voda ili žažda? (Wasser oder Durst?), in: Trud. 10 (5.1988); Angova, T.: Vodata, kojato ja ima i... njama (Wasser, das es gibt und nicht gibt), in: Zemedelsko zname. 21.6.1988; Vačev, D.: I Marica mătna šava (Und trübe schwappt die Marica), in: Stăršel 2204, 6.5.1988; Sokolova, Z.: Bezvredna označava li chubava? (Bedeutet schadlos auch schön?), in: RD. 19.6.1988.

den Flüssen mitgeben, landwirtschaftliche Kollektivwirtschaften, die dasselbe mit ihrem Dünger tun.

1983 hatte der Bulgarische Journalistenverband (*Săjuz na bălgarskite žurnalisti, SBŽ*) die originelle Idee, jeder bulgarischen Zeitung einen Fluß zur fürsorgenden „Patenschaft" zu übergeben. 1986 wurde deprimierende Bilanz gezogen – die Flüsse bleiben verseucht wie zuvor, weil Betriebsdirektoren sich nicht um Abwässer kümmern und die Kommunen sich taub stellen. Die Folgen davon beschrieb im Juni 1987 ein Sofioter Nachrichtenmagazin:

„Die Verschmutzung der Oberflächengewässer mit schädlichen Chemikalien und Schwermetallen führt in einigen Regionen zur chemischen Verseuchung des fruchtbarsten Ackerbodens, der sich entlang der Flußtäler ausbreitet. Solche Böden gibt es an den Ufern von Ogosta, Timok, Iskăr, Jantra, Marica u. a. Jährlich werden für Abwässerreinigung gewaltige Mittel aufgewendet, aber dennoch hat sich die allgemeine Lage des Flußnetzes nicht wesentlich gebessert. Mit dem chaotischen Bau von Reinigungsstationen und -anlagen kommen wir in die Situation, ein Faß ohne Boden zu füllen, da wir die gereinigten Gewässer, die die Stationen verlassen, in verseuchte Flußläufe einleiten"[15]).

3. Luftverseuchung

Verseuchtem Wasser kann man notfalls noch ausweichen, verseuchter Luft nicht, besonders dann nicht, wenn sie unaufhaltsam überall eindringt. In dieser Lage befindet sich Bulgarien ausgangs der 80er Jahre, wozu drei Umstände beigetragen haben:

– Industrielle Standortwahl erfolgte in der Vergangenheit oft ohne Blick für geomorphologische Gegebenheiten, so daß in der Regel eine einzige falsch plazierte Fabrik ganze Täler und Niederungen mit gasförmigen Schadstoffemissionen durchsetzte. In Bulgarien reihen sich entsprechende Beispiele: Das Sofioter Feld wird durch die fehlgeplanten Stahlwerke Kremikovci und *Lenin* gefährdet, das nordbulgarische Kajlăš-Tal durch ein Zementwerk, das subbalkanische Rosental (von dem Bulgarien sein schönstes Epitethon „Rosenland" entlieh) durch ein Zellulosekombinat usw.
– Alle diese (und weitere) Fabriken leiden unter der technologischen Rückständigkeit „realsozialistischer" Industrie. Wenn z. B. überhaupt Filteranlagen vorhanden sind, beseitigen diese im besten Fall 95 % der reinen Staubemission. Die eigentliche Gefahr aber geht von der Schwefel- und Stickoxyd-Emissionen aus, für deren Eliminierung es gute Filter westlicher Provenienz gibt. Für Osteuropa aber sind sie zu teuer, und entsprechende Anlagen heimischer Produktion stehen zwischen Elbe und Vladivostok nicht bereit.
– Die Luftverseuchung ist das Hauptproblem der grenzüberschreitenden Umweltbelastung. Viel kommentiert wurde z. B. die Lage, die sich im Dreiländereck DDR – Polen – ČSSR ergeben hat; weniger bekannt sind die Zustände an der rumänisch-

---

[15]) Kunišev, P.: Težkijat danăk na industrializacijata (Die schwere Steuer der Industrialisierung), in: Otečestvo. 11, 9.6.1987, S. 10.

bulgarischen Grenze. In Giurgiu an der Donau hat Rumänien mehrere Chemiewerke installiert, deren Chlorabgase durch vorherrschende Nordwinde ins bulgarische Ruse geweht werden. Dort stiegen in der zweiten Hälfte der 80er Jahre Erkrankungen, Totgeburten etc. in einem Maße an, daß die exakten Daten der Luftbedrohung unter amtlichem Verschluß gehalten wurden. Diese Politik des Verschweigens verschärfte die Situation gleich mehrfach: Die allgemeine Furcht – erkennbar etwa an dem neuen Ausdruck „Ruse-Lunge" – stieg noch an, öffentliche Proteste gegen den „chemischen Krieg eigener Art" (wie er von Rumänien gegen Bulgarien geführt werde) wurden im Frühjahr 1988 laut, und Intellektuelle nahmen den Fall Ruse zum Anlaß, eine radikale Wende der bulgarischen Umwelt- und Informationspolitik einzufordern[16]). Mit Verboten und Versetzungen der Wortführer des Protestes schuf die Regierung gewaltsam Ruhe, erreichte aber dennoch Abmachungen mit Rumänien, die Besserung der Lage hoffen ließen.

Ruse ist kein Einzelfall – die Politik des Verschweigens ist noch allgemeine Norm. In Sofia gibt es beispielsweise 211 Betriebe, von denen bekannt ist, daß sie die Luft verschmutzen; unbekannt, weil streng gehütetes Geheimnis, ist, in welchem Maße sie es tun. Seit Jahren gibt es eine Regierungsanordnung, diese Betriebe aus der Hauptstadt zu verlegen – geschehen ist nichts. Hinzu kommt, daß von den rund 1 270 000 Autos in Bulgarien die meisten in Sofia zugelassen sind oder durch die Hauptstadt fahren. Man schätzt, daß 45–60 % der Sofioter Luftverschmutzung auf sie zurückgehen. Genau weiß es niemand, weil der exakte Grad der Luftverseuchung geheim gehalten wird – „ganz allgemein kann man nur sagen, daß er die zulässigen Normen nicht um Prozente übersteigt, sondern um ein zweistelliges Mehrfaches"[17]).

4. Denkmalschutz als „patriotische Mission"

„Wenn der Türke zu Geld kommt, nimmt er Frauen – der Bulgare baut ein Haus", besagt ein altbulgarisches Sprichwort. Weil es zutrifft, gibt es in Bulgarien heute relativ wenig Mietwohnungen nach deutscher Art, dafür aber rund 40 000 Baudenkmäler. Ganze Orte (Arbanasi, Etăra, Žeravna, Kotel, Koprivštica, Melnik, Široka Lăka u. a.) und Ortsteile (Kirchen von Nesebăr, Altstädte von Veliko Tărnovo und Plovdiv), über 100 Klöster im Land, Ruinen altbulgarischer Hauptstädte und Festungen und anderes mehr sind Baudenkmäler bulgarischer Größe. Sie zu schützen, ist eine bulgarische Leidenschaft, deren Anfänge bis in die Mitte des vorigen Jahrhunderts zurückreichen. Ab der Jahrhundertwende wurden die Restaurierungsbemühungen höchst energisch vorangetrieben, ab 1924 durch die wirksame Pressure group der Gesellschaft *Bălgarska Starina* (Bulgarisches Altertum) effizient propagiert und gemanagt.

Seit den frühen 50er Jahren obliegen Restaurierungs- und Konservierungsarbeiten dem Nationalinstitut für Kulturdenkmäler (*Nacionalen institut za pametnicite na kul-*

---

[16]) Wortlaut des Protests in: Orbita. 9, 27. 2. 1988.
[17]) Krumev, R.: Văzduchăt, kojto veče viždame (Die Luft, die wir schon sehen), in: Orbita. 29, 18. 7. 1987.

turata, NIPK), das gute Arbeit leistet und noch bessere leisten könnte – wenn es nicht wie bisher bei der Zuteilung von Mitteln, Materialien und Fachleuten benachteiligt würde. Im nordbulgarischen Svištov haben z. B. vor 200 Jahren berühmte Baumeister wie Kol'o Fičeto mit 200 Handwerkern pro Bau gearbeitet. So kam Svištov in den Besitz von 110 „Kulturdenkmälern", die heute von abgezählten *fünf* NIPK-Mitarbeitern erhalten werden sollen. Und ähnliche Beispiele gibt es in Bulgarien in Fülle. Diese Versäumnisse aber rühren an das patriotische Sentiment jedes Bulgaren – es verfallen Zeugnisse von Bulgariens Rolle als „das neben Hellas und Rom dritte klassische Land", die Wiege slawischen Schrifttums; Kirchen werden nicht restauriert, die über Jahrhunderte der Türkenherrschaft das Flämmchen bulgarischer Nationalkultur hüteten. Kurz: Denkmalschutz hat in Bulgarien eine „patriotische Mission", die sich nicht darin erschöpfen darf, daß der Regierungssitz des Zweiten Bulgarischen Reichs (12.–14. Jh.), der *Carevec*-Hügel in Veliko Tărnovo (N), als Modell im Maßstab 1 : 1 rekonstruiert wird. Denkmalschützerische Fürsorge verlangen auch andere Baulichkeiten – kleine Dorfkirchen, alte Speicher und Magazine, das Sofioter *Majčin dom* (Mutterhaus), die altehrwürdige Geburtsklinik, in der nahezu alle Sofioter, die heute um 50 Jahre alt sind, das Licht der Welt erblickten, und viele andere Gebäude mehr – verlangen die Bulgaren, die sich bereits in informellen Vereinigungen wie den „Freunden der Sofioter Architektur" zusammenfinden und dabei von einer ökologisch wachen Presse unterstützt werden.

5. Hände weg von der Kernkraft?

Bulgarien ist ein rohstoff- und kapitalarmes Land, für das lange Zeit ausgemachte Sache war, daß an der Kernkraft kein Weg vorbeiführe. Bereits 1969 wurde mit dem Bau des KKW Kozloduj (N) begonnen, dessen fünfter Block im Winter 1986/87 ans Netz ging. Mitte der 80er Jahre wurde auf der Donauinsel Belene mit dem Bau eines zweiten KKW begonnen. Aber nach Černobyl' ist alles anders – der Schock saß gerade bei Bulgaren tief!

Die Schockwirkung hat bislang drei eskalierende Phasen durchlaufen. Am Anfang stand die bulgarische Černobyl'-Berichterstattung, die dem aufmerksamen Leser mit allen journalistischen Möglichkeiten (und Tricks) verdeutlichte, welche Katastrophe bei den Sowjets eingetreten war und wie diese sie vertuschen wollten. Die zweite Phase war die Abwendung der Öffentlichkeit von der Kernkraft – sie kam in angstvolles Gerede, Fachschulen und das Studienfach Kernphysik wurden allgemein gemieden. Und die dritte, selbstkritische Phase markierte im Oktober 1987 Generalleutnant Coco Cocev, Stellvertretender Verteidigungsminister Bulgariens. Er gab einen Bericht, der als Offenbarungseid bulgarischer Kernenergiepolitik anzusehen ist: keine wissenschaftlich begründeten Normen für die radioaktive Höchstbelastung, ungenügend qualifizierte Kader, allein auf Kriegszwecke ausgerichtete Strahlenmeßinstrumente, keine Nahrungs- und Futtermittelvorräte für Kernunfälle, keinerlei Ernstfall-Vorbereitung der gesamten bulgarischen Bevölkerung[18]).

---

[18]) Cocov, C.: Pouki za vsekigo i za vsički (Lehren für jeden und für alle), in: RD. 28.12.1987.

6. Sorgenkind Sofia

Gibt es in Bulgarien eine „Urbanisierung des Landes" – oder eine „Rustifizierung der Städte"? Tatsache ist, daß eine Landflucht die Städte aufbläht, während auf dem Land freier Wohnraum nicht genutzt wird. Die größten Städte legen sich laufend Satellitensiedlungen zu, die die bestehende Wohnraumnot kaum mildern, dabei aber die ökologischen und infrastrukturellen Probleme der Städte potenzieren. Viertel wie Galata (Varna, 25000 Einwohner), Rodopska jaka (Plovdiv, 80000 E.), Krajmorie (Burgas, 70000 E.) u. a. wurden auf der grünen Wiese errichtet, verschlangen Naherholungsgebiete, ohne daß man geprüft hatte, ob nicht durch eine vernünftige Sanierung der bestehenden Stadtviertel der benötigte Wohnraum zu gewinnen wäre.

Das größte urbanistische Sorgenkind Bulgariens ist Sofia, dessen stolzes Motto *Raste no ne staree* (Wächst, aber altert nicht) durch ein hypertrophes Aufquellen der Stadt nahezu pervertiert wurde. Sofia heute: übervölkerte Satellitenviertel bei „abgetötetem" Stadtkern; Boulevards, zu deren Verbreiterung 1985 rund 3300 alte Bäume gefällt wurden (ohne daß das Verkehrschaos dadurch behoben wurde); planlose Industriebauten, die oft genug ohne amtliche Genehmigung errichtet wurden; Lärm und Staub; ein in den Jahren halbiertes Grünmassiv; Parks, die mit jedem Jahr kleiner werden. Eine rundum bedrohte (Haupt-)Stadt, deren düstere Perspektive Bulgariens prominentester Architekt Ljuben Tonev im Januar 1988 malte:

„Nehmen wir zum Beispiel Sofia. Bei der kürzlichen Begutachtung seiner ökologischen Lage wurde konstatiert, daß selbige alarmierend ist – wegen übermäßiger Verseuchung von Luft, Boden und Wasser und wegen der Lärmbelästigung. (...) Die bislang ergriffenen Maßnahmen erweisen sich als bei weitem unzureichend, den ökologischen Verfall aufzuhalten und zu überwinden"[19]).

Und was bringt die Zukunft – für Sofia, für Bulgarien? Es gibt ein Reformklima im Lande, das vor allem wirtschaftlich „greift". Aber werden reformierte, allein auf Gewinn und Konkurrenz orientierte Betriebe mit der Umwelt pfleglicher umgehen als ihre zentralverwalteten Vorgänger? Und es gibt ein *glasnost'*-Klima in der Öffentlichkeit, das zudem in einer ökologisch zuträglichen Weise national grundiert ist. Wird die angestrebte Kooperation mit dem Westen auch moderne Öko-Technologie ins Land holen? Werden die berechtigten Öko-Ängste der Bulgaren den – im Grunde gutwilligen, in seinen Möglichkeiten aber noch begrenzten – Staatsapparat zu konzeptionellen Umorientierungen bewegen? Können neue Verdienstmöglichkeiten in der Landwirtschaft den infrastrukturellen Druck auf die Städte mindern? Führen die Erfahrungen, die z. B. Polen und die Tschechoslowakei mit der ökologischen Devastierung ganzer Landstriche gemacht haben, in Bulgarien zu einem Einlenken fünf vor Zwölf?

Bulgarien steht an einem Scheidewege. Und das Eingeständnis dessen wird nicht mehr verschwiegen. Aber hat man auch Rezepte für die Zukunft?

---

[19]) Tonev, L.: Ekologijata – Važna zadača i pred mladežta (Die Ökologie – eine wichtige Aufgabe auch vor der Jugend), in: Mladež. (1988) 1, S. 59; ein drastischer Bericht über die ökologische Gesamtsituation Sofias wurde auch in deutscher Sprache veröffentlicht; vgl. Popiliewa, P.: Mit Gasmaske und Schutzumhang durch Sofia, in: Sofioter Nachrichten. 9.12.1987, S. 12.

Population Structure

Robert N. Taaffe, Bloomington/Indiana

I. General – II. Population Growth: 1. Overall – 2. Age-Sex Composition – 3. Fertility – 4. Mortality – 5. Natural Change – 6. International Comparisons – III. Population Effects of International Migration since 1946 – IV. Urbanization and Population Change: 1. Urban Population Growth – 2. Sources of Urban Population Growth: a) Migration – b) Natural Urban Population Increases – c) Legal Redefinition of Villages – 3. City-Size Distribution and Inter-Urban Migration – V. Rural Population Change – VI. Spatial Pattern of Population – VII. Implications and Prospects

I. General

One of the most significant changes which has occurred in Bulgaria during the Communist era has been the transformation of the country from an agrarian state with all the demographic features of a traditional society into an industrialized nation in an advanced stage of the demographic transition. Since 1946, Bulgarian population change has been characterized by significant declines in birth rates, death rates (until 1975), and natural increases as well as by the pronounced aging of the population. Bulgaria has entered a phase of stagnant population growth from which it will not escape in the remainder of this century. The Bulgarians are more likely to experience negative population growth in the future than a major expansion of their population.

II. Population Growth

1. Overall

The changes in the population of Bulgaria from 1920 to the end of 1987 can be seen in Table 1 which is based on census totals from 1920 to 1985 and official estimates since then[1]).

Bulgaria has experienced a substantial increase in the magnitude of its population in the 69 years since 1920. During this interval, the country has gained 4.1 million people for a relative increase of 85%. The population declined in only three years of

---

[1]) The end of the year population totals after 1956 are based on the official projections to December 31 of the December 1 censuses for 1965 and 1975 and the December 4 census of 1985. The summary of these data as well as most national statistics are published by the Tsentralno Statistichesko Upravlenie (Central Statistical Administration).

Table 1: Population Growth (1920–1988 in thousands) and Sex Composition

Year	Population (Dec. 31)	No. of Females/1,000 males
1920	4,847.0	1,002
1946	7,029.3	999
1956[a]	7,613.7	1,004
1965	8,230.8	1,000
1975	8,731.4	1,003
1985	8,949.9	1,018
1987	8,976.3	1,010
1988	8,985.8	N.A.

Sources: SG. 1988, p. 36; Sofia News. March 1, 1989, p. 4.

[a] The population data for 1956 are for December 1.

this period. The emigration of Turks was responsible for national population decreases in 1950/1951 and from 1977 to 1978[2]). The most recent decline of 21,600 from 1984 to 1985 apparently reflects the revision of population figures from the results of the 1985 census.

With some modest exceptions, the rate of population growth has undergone a secular decline (Table 2). Approximately 53% of the population growth since 1920 occurred in the 26 years prior to 1946 and the subsequent 42 years to 1988 have accounted for only 47% of the population gains. With the exception of the small increases in the 1957–1965 period, every stage of the Bulgarian demographic experience since 1920 has been characterized by a significant decline in absolute and relative growth.

Table 2: Average Annual Population Growth (1920–1988 in thousands and %)

Years	Average Growth thousands	Average annual % increase
1920–1946	83.9	1.4
1947–1956	64.9	0.8
1957–1965	68.6	0.8
1966–1975	50.1	0.6
1976–1985	21.9	0.2
1986–1988	12.0	0.1

Sources: SG. 1988, p. 37; Sofia News. March 1, 1989, p. 4.

From 1920 to 1946, the population expanded by an average of 84,000 a year for an impressive annual growth rate of 1.4%. However, the present average increase of 12,500 is only one-seventh of the pre-1946 level and the rate of increase is now only

[2]) See the section on international migration.

7% as high as in the earlier period. The only increases in population growth averages since 1946 occurred in the 1957–1965 period, despite a relaxation of abortion laws, because of the reduced growth levels in the preceding 1947–1956 period resulting from the exodus of 154,000 Turks in 1950 and 1951. Since 1975, the magnitude of population increments and relative growth have been declining at precipitous rates. The Bulgarian population reached seven million in 1946 and the eight-million level was attained in 1962 or one million people were added in a 16-year span. According to current projections, the population will reach nine million by early 1990 which means that the most recent one-million increment will have taken 28 years. In the highly improbable event that the recent gains of 12,000 are maintained, 85 years will be required to bring Bulgarian population to the level of ten million[3]). The severe reduction in population growth in Bulgaria is beneficial to the extent that population pressures have greatly lessened. However, this dramatic change has induced a wide range of demographic and socioeconomic problems which will be increasingly evident in the future.

2. Age-Sex Composition

As Figure 1 indicates, Bulgaria has an age-sex pyramid which is similar to the geometric form of industrial countries in an advanced stage of the demographic transition. Specifically, the lack of a broad base sloping upwards to the apex indicates an old population with a relatively low share of children and young people and a limited capacity for growth. The number of people in the 50–54 age group of 602,100 is virtually identical to the 602,200 children in the 0–4 age bracket. A relatively low 42% of the population is under 30 years of age whereas a high 31% is 50 or over[4]). As is the usual case in a demographically declining country, the age distribution of the Bulgarian population has changed rapidly since 1946 when the number of people under 30 constituted 46.5% of the total population and the over-50 group accounted for a 25% share.

The average age of the Bulgarian population is increasing at an accelerating rate. In the half-century from 1900 to 1950, the average age rose slowly from 26 years at the turn of the century, to 27.3 at mid-century. However, this average increased sharply to 33.5 by 1975 and continued to rise to 36.0 in 1985[5]). Bulgaria has aged to such an extent that it is just slightly below the age level of the GDR and Hungary, which are regarded as demographically old countries, and substantially above the average age

---

[3]) This conflicts sharply with the unrealistically optimistic estimate of Georgi Dimitrov in December, 1948 that Bulgaria would have ten million people by 1960 (cited in: Oschlies, W.: Bulgarriens Bevölkerung Mitte der 80er Jahre – Eine demographische und sozialpolitische Skizze (Berichte des Bundesinstituts für Ostwissenschaftliche und Internationale Studien – BOIS. 17) Köln 1986, p. 3).

[4]) Naselenie 1986 (Population 1986). Sofia 1988, p. 5.

[5]) Kharakteristika na bŭlgarskata naselenie (Characteristics of the Bulgarian Population). Ed. by M. Minkov. Sofia 1984, p. 108; Baldwin, G.: Population Estimates and Projections for Eastern Europe: 1950–2000, in: East European Economies: Slow Growth in the 1980's. Joint Economic Committee of Congress. Washington 1985, p. 273; Naselenie 1986, p. XI.

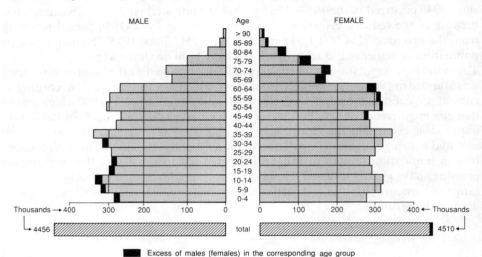

Figure 1: Age-sex pyramid of Bulgarian population (December 31, 1986).

of the other Balkan countries. Long-term projections indicate a stabilization or relatively slow increase in the average age of Bulgaria[6]).

The sex structure of the Bulgarian population shows a striking balance between the number of males and females (Table 1). Bulgaria has the most even sex distribution among the countries in Eastern Europe essentially because it did not experience major losses of its male population during the Second World War and the resulting deficits in males. With modest variations, the current level of 1,010 females per 1,000 males has remained relatively stable since 1920 when the country had 1,017 females/1,000 males. In percentage terms 50.5% of the population in 1987 was female. As Table 1 indicates, Bulgaria shares the standard age pattern of sex distribution. From the age of 45 on, females numerically exceed males because of greater female longevity whereas males are predominant in the population under 30 because of the excess of male births.

As in every East European country and the USSR, the labor participation of women in Bulgaria is extremely high. Over two million females (2,048,018) were in the Bulgarian work-force in 1987. Women constitute 49.8% of the workers and employees in the towns and villages of Bulgaria or, in effect, the labor force is equally divided between males and females as is the population in general[7]).

---

[6]) Baldwin (note 5), p. 273.
[7]) Statisticheski spravochnik. (1988), p. 46/47.

3. Fertility

Every country undergoing industrialization and urbanization has experienced a long-term decline in the rate of births. This decline in fertility in Bulgaria can be seen in Table 3.

Table 3: Births and Birth Rates (1920–1987 in thousands and ‰)

Year	Births in thousands	Birth Rates per 1 000 Population
1920	192.7	39.9
1946	179.2	25.6
1956	147.9	19.5
1965	125.8	15.3
1975	144.7	16.6
1985	119.0	13.3
1987	116.7	13.0

Sources: SG. 1988, p. 39.

At present, births in Bulgaria have descended to record lows in the post-1920 era in both absolute and relative terms. The number of births in 1987 was only 60 % as high as in 1920, despite the expansion of the population base by about four million in this period, and the birth rate is only one-third the 1920 level.

Crude birth rates do not consider the age structure or sex composition of the population. A more accurate measure is the net fertility rate, or the number of female births in relation to the number of females in the 15 to 49 age group, which is shown in Table 4.

Table 4: Net Fertility (1920–1987 in thousands and ‰)

Year	No. of Females 15–49	Female Births	Female Births/1 000 females 15–49
1920	1,204.0	93.1	77.3
1946	1,900.9	86.7	45.6
1956	1,981.0	71.7	36.2
1965	2,091.5	61.0	29.2
1975	2,188.3	70.3	32.1
1985	2,114.4	58.0	27.4
1987	2,130.5	56.9	26.7

Sources: Derived from data in: Demografiĭa na Bŭlgariĭa (Demography of Bulgaria). Sofia 1974, p. 57–61; SG. 1976; SG. 1988, p. 37–39.

The number of females in the child-bearing age group of 15–49 increased in every inter-censal period from 1920 to 1975. The only decline in this age-sex category occurred in the 1975–1985 period. Despite the growing number of women in the reproductive ages in most of the time-span since 1920, the net fertility rates and number of female births have pursued the same path of secular decline as crude birth rates.

To a considerable extent, the decline of Bulgarian fertility levels reflects the aging of the population, particularly the increasing share of women in the upper age brackets of the reproductive contingent, and a sharp decline in the birth levels of women over 30 years of age[8]. Related to this change is the shrinking size of the Bulgarian family. Only 5.3% of all births in 1985 involved a fourth child or more[9].

The aging of the population also affects birth rates by contributing to decreased marriage rates. From a 1946 level of 11.0 marriages per 1,000 population, the marriage rate has descended to a figure of 7.4 in 1985 (Figure 2). This primarily is a result of the persistent decline in the number of people in the marriage-prone 20–24 age group rather than a change in attitudes toward marriage in a country where only about one percent of the population never marries[10]. Accompanying the decline in marriages has been an increase in divorces. In 1985, there were 14,361 divorces, which is equal to 21.5% of the 66,682 marriages in that year[11]. The number of births outside marriage amounted to 13,954 in 1985 or 12% of the total number of births. Over one-half of the illegitimate births occurred among teen-agers[12].

Perhaps the most significant indicator of the future level of births and family size is the attitude of Bulgarians concerning the ideal number of children in their family (Table 5). In this 1977 survey the average number of children desired by wives was

Figure 2: Birth rates, death rates, natural increase, and marriage rates per 1,000 population 1920–1986.

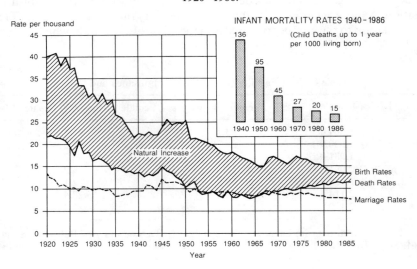

[8] Naselenie 1986, p. 41/42.
[9] Ibid.
[10] Demografiia na Bŭlgariia (Demography of Bulgaria). Sofia 1974, p. 144.
[11] Naselenie 1986, p. 6 and 228.
[12] Naselenie 1986, p. 42.

Table 5: Ideal Family Size among Bulgarian Married Couples under 40 (1977)

	Actual Number of Children						
	0	1	2	3	4	5	Total
Desired *Wives*	1.69	2.07	2.16	2.74	2.75	2.91	2.19
Number *Husbands*	1.65	2.10	2.25	2.77	2.77	3.20	2.25

Source: Kharakteristika na Bŭlgarskoto Naselenie (Characteristics of the Bulgarian Population). Ed. by M. Minkov. Sofia 1984, p. 130.

2.19. A 1985 census indicated that the desired number of children among young wives had descended to only 2.07[13]).

The prospects for a significant turnaround in the decline of birth rates in Bulgaria seem remote inasmuch as the young married couples, including those with more than three children, now regard the two-child family as the ideal. This is evident in the results of surveys and in recent demographic experience.

The Bulgarian population no longer is reproducing itself. The number of children which a Bulgarian woman will have in her reproductive life-time has gone below two, or below the level of zero population growth. More precise indicators of this trend are gross reproduction rates, or the number of female children a woman will have in her reproductive lifetime. In 1920, the gross reproduction coefficient was a very high 2.65. This figure declined sharply by 1946 to 1.43 and reached an estimated zero population growth level of 1.05 in 1968[14]). By 1982, only 0.93 females were estimated to be born in the reproductive lifetime of a Bulgarian woman and the country was headed toward ultimate negative growth[15]).

The government has actively pursued pro-natalist policies, including generous maternity leaves before and after births, monetary stipends to mothers, and the provision of extensive day-care facilities to allow mothers to retain their employment[16]). However, these measures seem to have had little effect in stimulating births. In contrast to policies stressing incentives for births, restrictions on abortions have had immediate, short-term effects on birth levels. In 1956, Bulgaria became the first East European country to adopt the liberalized policies toward abortion of the Soviet Union, which had removed most of the legal constraints on abortions a year earlier. Within a few years, the abortion levels had a six-fold increase and by 1966 the annual number of legal abortions had reached 101,000 and, when combined with 18,000 other abortions, almost equaled the number of births[17]). To stop the precipitous decline in births (from 148,000 in 1956 to 123,000 in 1966), the government passed a

---

[13]) Minkov, M.: Demografskoto razvitie – tendentsii i problemi (Demographic Development – Trends and Problems), in: Novo Vreme. (1987), p. 30.
[14]) Myers, P.: Demographic trends in Eastern Europe, in: Economic Developments in countries of Eastern Europe. Joint Economic Committee of Congress. Washington 1970, p. 89.
[15]) Baldwin (note 5), p. 274.
[16]) Minkov (note 13), p. 34–38; cf. chapter „Social Structure" by R. Whitaker.
[17]) Myers (note 14), p. 95.

decree in December, 1967 establishing a complex and rigid set of guidelines restricting the availability of legal abortions[18]). One year later, the number of births had increased to 141,000 for a 13% gain and a partial return to the birth levels of the pre-liberalization period. These gains were short-lived and by 1969 the number of births resumed its characteristic decline. This prompted the government in 1972 to reinforce and expand the constraints on abortion enacted in 1967[19]). As was the case after 1967, the number and rates of births increased sharply for the next two years, but since 1974 abortion controls have become a formality. In 1985, the 119,000 births were far less than the 130,000 legal abortions[20]).

The basic causes for the secular decline in fertility are associated with the usual demographic consequences of the transition to an industrialized urban society in general and are intensified by some specific Bulgarian features. According to Bulgarian surveys, the most important impediments to increased births are: 1) the increasing level of education; 2) the inability of the family to care for children inasmuch as both parents are employed full-time and the child-care functions of grandparents are often eliminated by the movement to cities; 3) the frequent conflicts between the professional careers of women and large families; 4) crowded urban housing; 5) the lack of domestic help; and, 6) the inadequacies of governmental stipends to mothers[21]).

4. Mortality

Death rates in Bulgaria have undergone two phases of change – a long-term decline from 1920 to 1965 and increasing mortality rates since then (Table 6). The death rates declined primarily as a result of improvements in health care and the relative youthfulness of the population. The more recent and unwelcome increases can be attributed essentially to the aging of the population. This aging has been sufficiently

Table 6: Deaths and Death Rates (1920–1987 in thousands and ‰)

Year	Deaths in thousands	Death Rates in ‰
1920	103.5	21.4
1946	95.8	13.7
1956	71,2	9.4
1965	67.0	8.1
1975	90.0	10.3
1985	107.5	12.0
1987	107.2	12.0

Sources: SG. 1988, p. 39/40.

---

[18]) Ibid.
[19]) Demografiía (note 10), p. 80.
[20]) Minkov (note 13), p. 37.
[21]) Kharakteristika (note 5), p. 133–137.

rapid to give Bulgaria a high death rate which is exceeded only by Hungary and the GDR in Eastern Europe and is higher than that of any of the demographically old, industrialized countries of Western Europe. The closest rival in this respect in 1985 was the Federal Republic of Germany which had a death rate of 11.5 (Table 9).

Approximately 60% of the deaths in Bulgaria in 1985 were caused by heart and circulatory diseases and this share has risen substantially from a level of 53.5% in 1977. By contrast, deaths from cancer were a distant second, accounting for 13.7% of the 1985 mortalities. This figure was slightly lower than the 14.1% cancer share in 1977. Substantial progress has been made in reducing deaths from respiratory diseases, which are the third most important cause. From 1977 to 1985, the share of respiratory diseases in mortalities declined from 11.0% to 7.7%[22]).

A major source of the significant reduction in death rates has been the sharp decline in the level of infant mortality in the Communist era (Figure 2). The 1986 level of 15.4 deaths in the 0–1 age bracket per 1,000 live births is only a little more than one-tenth of the 1940 level. Although the infant mortality rate in Bulgaria is still higher than in the industrialized countries of Western Europe, only the GDR and Czechoslovakia in Eastern Europe had lower rates in 1985 (Table 9). The basic reason for the Bulgarian success in reducing infant deaths is the concentration of 99.4% of all births in health institutions, particularly maternity clinics and hospitals[23]). Infant mortality rates in Bulgaria should reach West European levels in the near future. The only negative consequence of this is that reductions in infant mortality no longer will contribute significantly to reductions in overall death rates or to increased life expectancies.

Another demographic attainment of Bulgaria has been a substantial increase in the average life-span of its population in general and for both males and females since 1920 (Table 7). Until 1970, most of the dramatic gains in life expectancies were associated with major improvements in health care which resulted in a substantial reduction in age-specific death rates and, particularly, in infant mortality rates. As Table 7 indicates, the overall life-expectancy levels have not increased, in effect, since

Table 7: Life Expectancy (1921 to 1986 in years)

Years	Overall Average	Males	Females	Female – Male (Years)
1921–1925	44.64	44.35	44.98	0.65
1956–1957	65.89	64.17	67.65	3.48
1969–1971	71.11	68.58	73.86	5.28
1974–1976	71.31	68.68	73.91	5.23
1978–1980	71.14	68.35	73.55	5.20
1984–1986	71.19	68.17	74.39	6.22

Sources: Naselenie 1986 (Population 1986). Sofia 1988, p. 227; Statisticheski spravochnik. (1988), p. 187.

---

[22]) Smŭrtnost na naselenie v Bŭlgariĩa po prichini (Mortalities of the Population of Bulgaria by Reasons). Sofia 1977, insert; Naselenie 1986, p. 254.
[23]) Naselenie 1986, p. 56.

1969–1971. This stabilization of life expectancies over the past 15 years has resulted from a very slow but persistent decline in male expectancies, apparently derived from the increased rate of cardio-vascular deaths, and a counterbalancing, slow increase in average female life-spans. As in every developed country, female life expectancies exceed those of males. The current Bulgarian differential of 6.22 years is substantial but not uncommon.

5. Natural Change

The changes from 1920 to 1986 in the rates of births, deaths, marriages, and infant mortality are depicted graphically in Figure 2. Despite occasional increases, the long-term decline in all these demographic measures since 1920 is evident. The only indicator which has experienced a directional reversal is the average death rate since the late 1960's. By 1986, the downward-sloping birth-rate curve almost touched the rising mortality curve or, in other terms, the rate of natural population increase was close to zero. The absolute and relative changes in natural increase are shown in Table 8. In

Table 8: Natural Population Increases (1920–1987 in thousands and ‰)

Year	Total Natural increases	Natural increases ‰
1920	89.7	18.5
1946	83.6	11.9
1956	76.8	10.1
1965	58.8	7.2
1975	54.7	6.3
1985	11.5	1.3
1987	9.5	1.0

Sources: SG. 1988, p. 39/40.

addition to the secular declines since 1920, the absolute population increases and the relative growth rates have plummeted more rapidly since 1975 than any population projection anticipated. The present natural increase of only 9,500 people a year is only slightly more than one-tenth of the 1920 level but is also only one-sixth of the 1975 natural growth figure. Since 1975, the birth rate has declined from 16.6 to 12.9 and there has been an unexpected increase in death rates from 10.3 to 12.0. There are remarkable changes in a 12-year span. The annual rate of natural increase of 1.0 indicates that Bulgaria is precariously close to the negative growth experienced by the GDR and Hungary in Eastern Europe and some of the Germanic countries in Western Europe (Table 9).

6. International Comparisons

The Bulgarian demographic experience has been similar to that of other countries of Eastern Europe, with the exception of Albania, and also has much in common with Western Europe (Table 9).

Table 9: International Comparisons of Demographic Rates (1985)

Country	Birth Rates ‰	Death Rates ‰	Infant Mortality ‰	Natural Inc. ‰
Eastern Europe				
Bulgaria	13.3	12.0	15.4	1.3
Albania	26.2	5.8	28.0[a]	20.4
Czechoslovakia	14.5	11.8	14.0	2.7
GDR	13.7	13.5	9.6	0.2
Hungary	12.2	13.8	20.4	−1.6
Poland	18.2	10.2	18.4	8.0
Romania	15.8	10.9	25.6	4.9
Yugoslavia	15.9	9.1	28.8	6.8
USSR	19.4	10.6	26.6	8.8
Western Europe				
Greece	11.7	9.3	14.0	2.4
West Germany	9.6	11.5	9.6	−1.9
France	14.1	10.1	8.0	4.0
Italy	10.1	9.5	10.9	0.6
Austria	11.5	11.8	11.0	−0.3

Source: Naselenie 1986 (Population 1986). Sofia 1988, p. 438/439; Neues Albanien. (1989) 1, p. 36.
[a] 1987.

Bulgaria is in a more advanced stage of the demographic transition than most East European countries. Bulgarian birth rates are lower than in any of these countries, except Hungary, but are slightly higher than in the West European countries shown in Table 9 (with the exception of France). Apart from Hungary and the GDR, the death rates in Bulgaria exceed those of all the other East European countries (and are substantially higher than the West European examples above) despite the relatively low level of Bulgarian infant mortalities. Bulgaria, Hungary, the GDR, and Czechoslovakia are among those European countries, both East and West, with negligible or even negative rates of population growth.

III. Population Effects of International Migration since 1946

Historically, the magnitude of the population of Bulgaria has been profoundly affected by international migration. This international movement since 1946 has been dominated by the return of large numbers of the Turkish minority in Bulgaria to their ethnic homeland. Since 1946, the Communist regime in Bulgaria has instituted strict migrational controls designed to reduce emigration in general. The only major exceptions to these stringent migrational barriers have been occasional periods when large numbers of Bulgarian Turks have been expelled or allowed to be repatriated voluntarily. The only non-Turkic group emigrating en masse since 1946 consisted of the 34,000 Jews allowed to leave the country in the 1948–1951 period[24]). The Turkish emigration flow can be seen in Table 10.

Table 10: Turkish Emigration from Bulgaria (1946–85)

Years	Total number of Turks emigrating
1946–1949	2,694
1950/1951	154,393
1952–1968	105
1969–1973	33,751
1974–1976	4,278
1977/1978	72,743
1979–1985[a]	102

Sources: Türkiye Istatistik Yilliği (Statistical Yearbook of Turkey). Ankara 1959, p. 111; 1963, p. 97; 1973, p. 74; 1979, p. 75; 1985, p. 97; Naselenie 1986 (Population 1986). Sofia 1988, p. 407.
[a] Only 74 people emigrated from Bulgaria in 1985. They are assumed to be Turks.

The largest emigration of Turks resulted from the Bulgarian program, which started in August, 1950, to expel a substantial share of the Turkish minority. These expulsions ended in 1951 after 154,393 Turks were transported to the borders of Bulgaria and accepted by the Turkish government. The Turkish state has become strongly involved in the future of Bulgarian Turks and played a key role in negotiating emigration in the 1970's. In 1969–1973, 33,751 Bulgarian Turks went to the Mother country and the last major exodus from Bulgaria (before 1989) took place in 1977/1978 when 73,000 Turks left. By contrast, only 28 Turks emigrated from Bulgaria in the six-year span encompassing 1979 through 1984. Even if all the out-migrants from Bulgaria in 1985 were Turks, it is obvious that the severe restrictions on Turkish repatriation were maintained inasmuch as a grand total of 74 people emigrated from Bulgaria in 1985[25]). In mid-February, 1985, Turkey declared its willingness to receive 500,000 of the beleaguered Turks in Bulgaria but this offer was rejected by the Bulgarian government.

One of the reasons why Bulgaria has chosen to "Bulgarize" its Turkish minority rather than allow large-scale repatriation until 1989 is the significant effect that Turkish migration losses would have on the demographically declining and labor-scarce country. From 1946 to 1985, 268,066 Turks emigrated from Bulgaria but the effects

---

[24]) Demografiiā (note 10), p. 214/215; cf. chapters „Nationale Minderheiten" by S. Troebst, and „Außenpolitik" by K.-D. Grothusen.
[25]) Naselenie 1976, p. 407.

on population and the labor force have been much greater because the emigration data do not consider the lost natural increases of the Turkish emigrees, who have substantially higher birth rates than the Bulgarians. On May 29, 1989, Bulgaria removed the restrictions on Turkish emigration and a mass exodus of Turks began, which reached 310,000 until August, 1989[26]).

IV. Urbanization and Population Change

1. Urban Population Growth

One of the most important changes in Bulgaria has been the extremely rapid urbanization of the country since 1946 as a consequence of the drive to industrialize (Table 11). In 1946, only 1.74 million Bulgarians lived in cities or only about one-fourth of the national population. In the ensuing four decades, the urban population has swelled to 5.96 million which means that Bulgaria has become a country in which two-thirds of the population is urban.

Table 11: Urban Growth (1920–1987 in thousands and % of Population)

Year	Urban Population in thousands	Urban % of Population
1920	966.4	19.9
1946	1,735.2	24.7
1956	2,556.1	33.6
1965	3,828.4	46.5
1975	5,067.0	58.0
1985	5,807.5	64.9
1987	5,959.4	66.4

Sources: SG. 1988, p. 37.

2. Sources of Urban Population Growth

a) Migration

The growth of Bulgarian cities primarily is a result of a massive exodus from the villages to the towns, which persists to the present day[27]). The data in Table 12 point out that as the rural population became smaller, the ability of the villages to sustain a massive outpouring of migrants diminished from an annual average of 92,700 in 1965–1967 to a level of 66,900 in 1984/1985. The share of rural-to-urban migration in

---

[26]) The Times. February 19, 1985, p. 6, and March 27, 1985, p. 10.
[27]) Taaffe, R.: Urbanization in Bulgaria, in: Études Balkaniques. 10 (1974) 3, p. 50–63.

total migrational flows has declined from 54.6 to 40.6 % in this twenty-year interval. Despite the substantial losses of the young population in villages, the dominant age-group in migration, the intensity of rural migration to cities, as measured by the number of urban-bound villagers per 1,000 rural population, has actually increased from an annual average of 16.0 in 1960–1962 to a 21.7 average in 1984/1985. The shrinking of the rural population has affected the ability of villages to continue supplying the same magnitude of migrants for residence in cities but the increasing average age of the villagers has not been accompanied by a diminished propensity to migrate. A larger share of the villagers than ever before moves to cities[28]).

Table 12: Rural-Urban Migrational Streams (1960–1985 annual averages in thousands)

Years	Rural-to-Urban	Urban-to-Rural	Net Urban Migrational Increases
1960–1962	78.4	8.0	70.4
1965–1967	92.7	12.0	80.7
1971–1973	80.8	14.0	66.8
1981–1983	64.9	17.9	47.0
1984/1985	66.9	19.6	47.3

Sources: Naselenie (Population). Sofia 1981, p. 447; 1982, p. 415; 1983, p. 398; 1984, p. 398; 1988, p. 414; Demografska Statistika (Demographic Statistics). Sofia 1967, p. 274; 1968, p. 274; 1969, p. 234; Demografiià na Bŭlgariià (Demography of Bulgaria). Sofia 1974.

In addition to the reduced base of rural population, net urban migrational gains have been declining in recent years because of the surprising increases in the number of people leaving cities for temporary and long-term residence in villages. From 1960–1962 to 1984/1985, average yearly urban-to-rural migration more than doubled from 8,000 to 19,600 and in the latter period constituted almost 18 % of the total migrational movement in Bulgaria. In 1985, 39 % of these migrants left cities for rural employment, most frequently as agricultural specialists, farm machinery operators and mechanics, and, particularly, in rural service sectors[29]). Over 60 % of the urban out-migrants, however, left towns because of such factors as family motives, the completion of education, and retirement. These rural migrational gains are not nearly large enough to overcome the migrational losses of villages.

b) Natural Urban Population Increases

The natural population gains of Bulgarian cities were increasingly important as a source of urban growth until the mid-1970's. Since then, the natural increases in cities

---

[28]) A fuller discussion of urban-rural migration up to the mid-1970's can be found in Minkov, M.: Migratsiià na naselenieto (Migration of the Population). Sofia 1972, and Taaffe, R.: The Impact of Rural-Urban Migration on the Development of Communist Bulgaria, in: Population and Migration Trends in Eastern Europe. Ed. by H. Kostanick. Boulder, Colorado 1977, p. 157–179.

[29]) Naselenie 1986, p. 431; Demografiià (note 10), p. 227/228.

Population Structure

Table 13: Natural Urban Population Increases (1946–1987 in ‰ and thousands)

Year	Births ‰	Deaths ‰	Natural Increase ‰	Absolute Natural Increases
1946	24.6	13.1	11.5	19.8
1956	17.5	7.3	10.2	25.5
1965	14.7	6.2	8.5	31.8
1975	19.1	7.7	11.4	58.1
1985	13.8	8.7	5.1	30.2
1987	13.7	8.8	4.9	29.0

Sources: SG. 1988, p. 41.

have played a diminishing role as a contributor to the expansion of the urban population because of sharply reduced birth rates and slowly increasing death rates (Table 13).

The sudden increase in birth rates in the 1965–75 period reflects the substantial expansion of births after the strict controls on abortions were imposed in 1967 and reinforced in 1972. These urban birth increases were not matched by birth gains in the countryside where abortions are less common. The sharply reduced rates and absolute numbers of natural population change in cities since the mid-1970's indicate that the youthful urban population at the start of the Communist era has been replaced by a more mature urban population with a pronounced aversion to large families.

In 1984/85, natural urban increases accounted for only one-third of the total urban growth resulting from the combined effect of natural population increases and migration. This was equivalent to the natural-increase share in the early stages of Communist-era urbanization and substantially below the 1971–1973 level of 42%.

c) Legal Redesignation of Villages

If natural increases and net urban migration were the only sources of growth, the urban population of Bulgaria would be much smaller. A major source of Bulgarian urban growth has been the legal redefinition of villages into cities or the annexation of settlements into existing cities. From 1946 to 1971, several hundred villages or smaller settlements with a total population of 840,000 were urbanized and these administrative changes accounted for 35% of overall Bulgarian urban growth[30]. This process has continued after 1971 but at a slower rate. From 1972 to 1985, 56 villages, with a combined population of 213,300, were legally redesignated as cities and a large number of smaller settlements were annexed by cities[31]. The population of the reclassified villages amounted to 21% of total urban growth in this period.

---

[30] Demografiĭa (note 10), p. 575; cf. chapter „Geographical Foundations" by I. Matley.
[31] Naselenie 1986, p. 261–276.

3. City-Size Distribution and Inter-Urban Migration

The urban structure of Bulgaria is dominated by the 25 cities which had a population over 50,000 in 1985 and, particularly, by the primate city of Sofia (Figure 3 and Table 14).

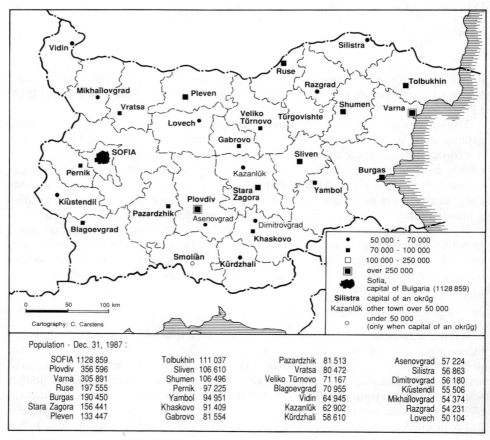

Figure 3: Cities with a population over 50,000 (December 31, 1987).

Population - Dec. 31, 1987:

SOFIA 1128 859	Tolbukhin 111 037	Pazardzhik 81 513	Asenovgrad 57 224
Plovdiv 356 596	Sliven 106 610	Vratsa 80 472	Silistra 56 863
Varna 305 891	Shumen 106 496	Veliko Tŭrnovo 71 167	Dimitrovgrad 56 180
Ruse 197 555	Pernik 97 225	Blagoevgrad 70 955	Kiustendil 55 506
Burgas 190 450	Yambol 94 951	Vidin 64 945	Mikhaĭlovgrad 54 374
Stara Zagora 156 441	Khaskovo 91 409	Kazanlŭk 62 902	Razgrad 54 231
Pleven 133 447	Gabrovo 81 554	Kŭrdzhali 58 610	Lovech 50 104

The population of Sofia now exceeds one million and comprises one-fifth of the national urban population. Sofia is so dominant that its population is almost equal to that of the combined total of the next five largest cities, including: Plovdiv (343 t); Varna (303 t); Ruse (185 t); Burgas (183 t) and Stara Zagora (151 t). Almost one-half the urban population lives in the ten cities with over 100,000 inhabitants and two-thirds of the urban residents are found in the 25 cities with over 50,000 people.

At the other end of the urban hierarchy, the 143 cities with fewer than 10,000 inhabitants in 1985 accounted for 60% of the 237 cities in Bulgaria but only one-

Table 14: City-Size Distribution (1985)

Size	Number	Population in thousands	% of Urban Population
over one Million	1	1,121.8	19.3
500–one Million	0	0	0
100–500	9	1,606.8	27.7
50–100	15	1,033.3	17.8
10–50	69	1,307.3	22.5
0.3–10	143	738.3	12.7

Source: Naselenie 1986 (Population 1986). Sofia 1988, p. 261–276.

eighth of the urban population. Most of these cities are redesignated villages and are slowly dying out. In 1985, 134 cities, or 57% of the total number had net migrational losses and nearly all of those cities were small[32]). Redesignating a village as a city, apparently, has not stopped out-migration[33]).

The volume of inter-urban migration has increased significantly and primarily has involved movement from small to large cities (Table 15).

Table 15: Inter-Urban Migration (1965–1985 in thousands and %)

Years	Average Annual Migration in thousands	% of All Migration
1965–1967	33.4	19.7
1971–1973	44.4	27.9
1981–1983	54.6	38.9
1984–1985	62.7	38.1

Sources: Naselenie (Population). Sofia 1981, p. 447; 1982, p. 415; 1983, p. 398; 1984, p. 398; 1988, p. 414; Demografska Statistika (Demographic Statistics). Sofia 1967, p. 274; 1968, p. 274; 1969, p. 234.

Bulgaria is rapidly approaching the last phase of the migration transition in which migration among cities exceeds the volume of rural-to-urban flows. In 1984/1985, the average inter-urban migrational flow of 62,700 was only a little below the rural-to-urban movement of 66,900.

---

[32]) Naselenie 1986, p. 409–413.
[33]) Devedzhiev, M.: Demografski i ikonomicheski problemi na malkite novi gradove (Demographic and Economic Problems of Small New Cities), in: Planovo Stopanstvo. (1981) 5, p. 44–55.

V. Rural Population Change

The decline of rural population in absolute and relative terms has been a persistent feature of Bulgarian development since 1946. The 1987 level of three million rural occupants is 2.3 million fewer than in 1946. The current total is only 57% of the figure at the start of Communist rule and represents just one-third of the Bulgarian population compared to three-fourths in 1946 (Table 16).

Table 16: Rural Population (1920–1987 in thousands and % of total)

Year	Rural Population in thousands	% of Total Population
1920	3,880.6	81.1
1946	5,294.1	75.6
1956	5,057.6	66.4
1965	4,402.4	53.5
1975	3,664.4	42.0
1985	3,142.4	35.1
1987	3,016.8	33.6

Sources: SG. 1988, p. 37.

One of the most significant features of the Bulgarian demographic experience has been the recent emergence of negative population changes in the countryside as a result of excesses of deaths over births in addition to the traditional large-scale rural population losses attributed to net migrational deficits. Since 1975, rural death rates have been higher than birth rates. This is the demographic cost of persistently high-levels of the out-migration from villages of people under 30, comprising 75% of the migrants in 1976–85, and the aging of the rural population[34]). The average age of the

Table 17: Natural Rural Population Change (1921–1987 in thousands and ‰)

Year	Birth Rates ‰	Death Rates ‰	Natural Increase ‰
1921	42.3	22.1	20.2
1946	25.9	13.9	12.0
1956	20.5	10.4	10.1
1965	15.9	9.8	6.1
1975	13.0	14.0	− 1.0
1985	12.3	18.3	− 6.0
1987	11.7	18.1	− 6.4

Sources: SG. 1988, p. 42.

---

[34]) Petkov, L.: Usloviiâ za vŭzproizvodstvo na rabotnata sila v selskoto stopanstvo (Conditions for the Reproduction of the Work-Force in Agriculture), in: Ikonomicheska Misŭl. (1987) 11, p. 48–58.

Bulgarian villagers is now over 40, as compared to an urban figure of 33 years, and this aging has been a major component of increased rural death rates and reduced rural birth rates which have led to negative natural change (Table 17)[35]).

The relative importance of natural change and migration in the decline of rural population is still heavily weighted toward migrational losses but the natural decreases are becoming more important (Table 18).

Table 18: Sources of Rural Population Change (1947–1985 annual averages in thousands)

Years	Rural Natural Increase	Rural Net Migration	Rural Change
1947–1950	66.4	− 33.1	33.3
1951–1955	53.3	− 73.6	− 20.3
1961–1965	36.1	− 75.6	− 39.5
1971–1973	3.9	− 66.8	− 62.9
1981–1985	− 13.3	− 47.2	− 60.5

Sources: SG. 1987, p. 37; Demografiià na Bŭlgariià (Demography of Bulgaria). Sofia 1974, p. 221–228; and Table 12.

Figure 4: Rural population decline 1965–1986.

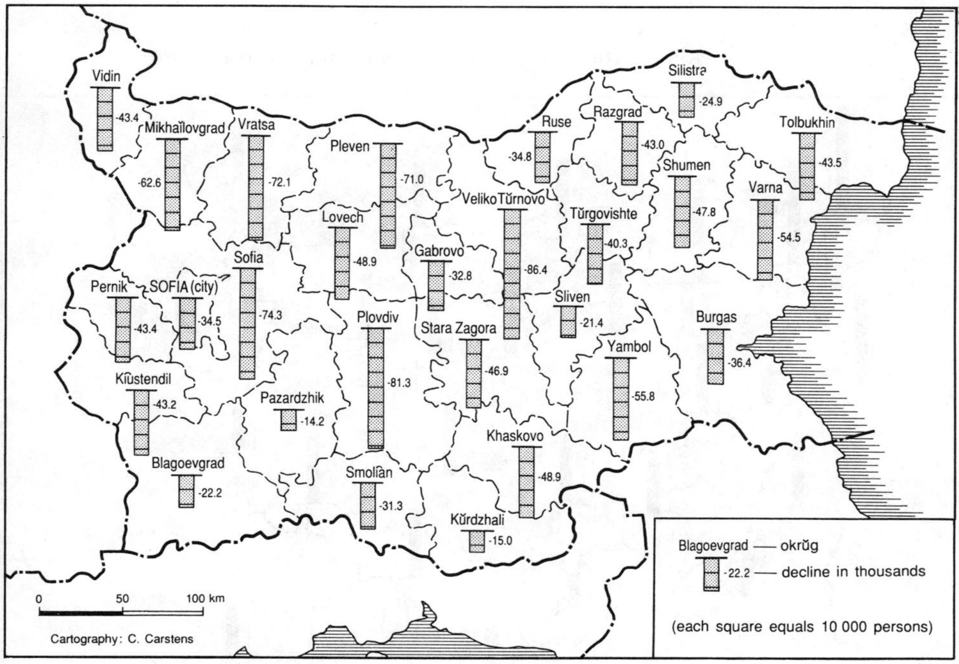

[35]) Derived from data in: Naselenie 1986, p. 5.

Since 1971, the losses of rural population have remained at a high level because the declining magnitude of net rural migration has been counterbalanced, to a considerable extent, by natural decreases.

The spatial pattern of rural population change can be seen in Figure 4. Every one of the 28 *okrŭgs* (abolished in 1987) experienced a net loss in the number of its rural inhabitants from 1965 to 1986. The heaviest losses have occurred in the western half of the densely settled Danubian Tableland, which is located between the Balkan Mountains and the Danube River. The greatest loss was experienced by Veliko Tŭrnovo, which had a decline of 86,400 villagers. Other substantial losses occurred in the fertile Maritsa Valley, particularly around Plovdiv, and in the Sofia Region. The smallest declines were in the borderlands of the Rhodope mountains because of the high birth rates of the Turkish minority.

Every *okrŭg* also had net rural migrational losses and the negative levels of natural population change in the countryside are now almost as pervasive (Figure 5). In 1986, only three of the *okrŭgs* had positive levels of natural change. The highest figures were in the Turkish-settled *okrŭgs* in the eastern Rhodope, particularly in Kŭrdzhali where a high birth rate of 18.1 and a low death rate of 7.2 resulted in a substantial natural increase of 11.0. The greatest natural declines were in the western half of the Danubian Tableland. For example, Vidin *okrŭg*, in the northwestern corner of Bulgaria,

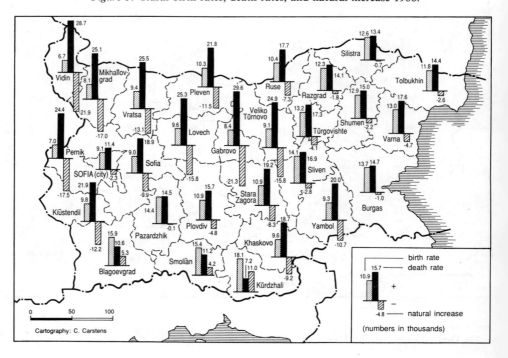

Figure 5: Rural birth rates, death rates, and natural increase 1986.

recorded only 513 births in its villages compared to 2,190 deaths for an extraordinary natural increase of − 21.9‰ in 1986[36]). Similar declines occurred in Gabrovo, Mikhaĭlovgrad, and Pernik *okrŭgs*.

Despite the persistent decline of rural population and the transformation of large numbers of villages into cities, the number of villages in Bulgaria has remained surprisingly stable. In 1966, there were 4,444 villages and 1,078 smaller settlements[37]). By 1986, the number of villages had only declined slightly to a total of 4,423 although the number of smaller settlements had dwindled to 656[38]). Apparently, many of the smaller places were annexed by cities and others were elevated to village status, which had the statistical effect of replacing villages transformed to cities. Many of the villages are in the process of becoming depopulated and, in 1980, approximately one-fourth of the villages had fewer than 200 people. In that year, however, 1,255 villages had more than 1,000 inhabitants, including 12 villages with over 5,000 people which are prime candidates for urban redesignation[39]).

VI. Spatial Pattern of Population

The spatial pattern of population change from 1965 to 1986 is depicted in Figure 6. The major gains in absolute and relative terms have been in *okrŭgs* centered on large cities with over 100,000 inhabitants in 1986. The city of Sofia had an increase of 315,700 from 1965 to 1986, which represents a 36% gain. The absolute growth of Sofia city was three times greater than in any other *okrŭg* despite legal restrictions on migration to the capital. Special permits are required to move to Sofia but through a variety of devices Bulgarians have been able to circumvent these barriers. A common method is to obtain permission to reside temporarily in Sofia and then obtain frequent extensions. In the early 1970's, for example, one-seventh of the population of Sofia consisted of temporary residents[40]). The second largest numerical increase in population from 1965 to 1985 occured in Plovdiv *okrŭg* and amounted to 113,800. The percentage increase of 18%, however, was only one-half the relative growth of Sofia. Next to Sofia city, the highest percentage growth increases were in Varna *okrŭg*, where the addition of 99,800 people represented a 27% gain. Other major increases were recorded for the okrŭgs of Burgas (70,400 and 19%) and Stara Zagora (61,800 and 18%).

At the other extreme, nine of the 28 *okrŭgs* experienced population losses essentially because rural and small-town losses exceeded the increases of the larger cities in the *okrŭgs*. Most of these *okrŭgs* are in the Danubian Tableland, where agricultural

---

[36]) SG. 1987, p. 470/471; cf. chapter „Regierungssystem" by O. Luchterhandt.
[37]) SG. 1966, p. 370.
[38]) SG. 1987, p. 458.
[39]) Kharakteristika (note 5), p. 107.
[40]) Minkov (note 28), p. 110–116.

Figure 6: Population change 1965–1986.

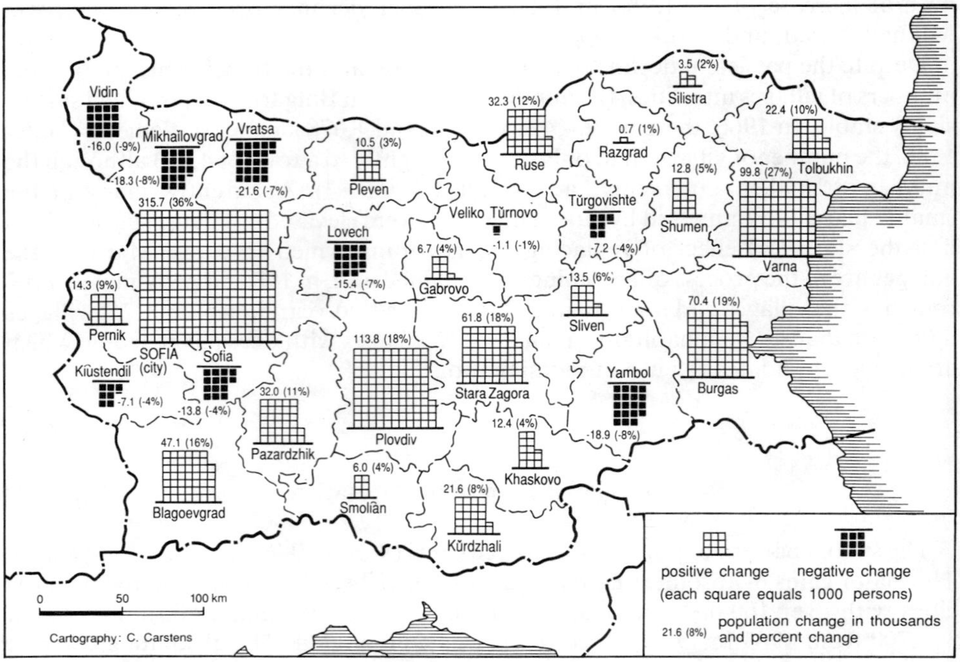

losses have been massive because of net migrational decreases and negative rates of natural change[41]).

The distribution of population in 1986 is shown in Figure 7. There is a strong positive correlation between urbanization and population size. Approximately 40% of the Bulgarian population resides in six heavily urbanized *okrŭgs*. Slightly over 13% of the national population resides in each of three groups of highly urbanized *okrŭgs*: 1) Sofia city; 2) Plovdiv and Varna; and, 3) Ruse, Burgas and Stara Zagora. The Bulgarian people are gravitating in large numbers to the most urban *okrŭgs*. Only four relatively small *okrŭgs* with large rural Turkish populations, Kŭrdzhali, Razgrad, Silistra, and Tŭrgovishte, still have more people living in villages than in cities. At the present rate of change, however, only Kŭrdzhali *okrŭg* will have a majority of rural inhabitants by 1990.

---

[41]) These changes represent a continuation of trends documented earlier by Devedzhiev, M.: Teritorialni aspekti na estestvenoto i mekhanichnoto dvizhenie na naselenieto v NR Bŭlgariiâ (Territorial Aspects of Natural and Migrational Movement of the Population of the NRB), in: Statistika. (1980) 1, p. 26–41.

Figure 7: Population – total, urban, and rural (December 31, 1986).

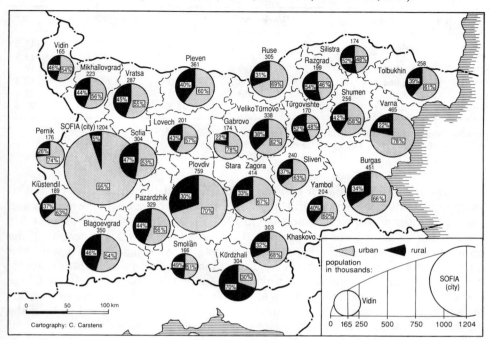

VII. Implications and Prospects

An important implication of the drastic decline of Bulgarian population growth and the aging of its population concerns the size of the labor-age group (Table 19). The relative share of the population in work-force ages remained remarkably stable around the level of 58% until 1975. By 1987, this share had dropped to 56% and the absolute number of people in this category declined by almost 54,000. The most significant changes, however, have been the persistent increases in the number and relative importance of the population over the work-force age and the corresponding decline of future entrants into the work-force since 1956. In 1987, there was near-equality in the share of the over-age population (21.6%) and that of the underage group (22.6%), which is an extraordinary transformation from the 11.7% over-age share in 1946, which was only two-fifths of the under-age percentage of 29.8%. The long-term decline in the under-age group and the large numbers of people in the older age-brackets of the labor force indicate that the negative trends in the age structure and size of the labor pool will persist in the foreseeable future even though the size of the actual labor force has increased recently from the level of 4,094,664 in 1985 to 4,108,459 in 1987, which is a gain of almost 14,000 workers and employees[42]).

---

[42]) SG. 1988, p. 110.

Table 19: Population in Relation to Work-Force Age (1946–1987 in thousands and %)

Year	Under Work-Force Age	%	Work-Force Age[a]	%	Over Work-Force Age	%
1946	2,092.5	29.8	4,117.0	58.5	819.8	11.7
1956	2,136.7	28.1	4,486.8	58.9	90.2	13.0
1965	2,112.4	25.7	4,789.0	58.2	1,326.5	16.1
1975	2,061.4	23.6	5,058.1	58.0	1,608.1	18.4
1985	2,046.7	22.9	5,013.2	56.0	1,888.8	21.1
1987	2,029.3	22.6	5,004.5	55.8	1,942.4	21.6

Source: Statisticheski spravochnik. (1988), p. 181; SG. 1988, p. 38.
[a] The work-force age is 16–54 for females and 16–59 for males.

As in the entire Communist era, the major trends at present involve continued sharp reductions in the agricultural labor force and rapid increases in the number and share of industrial workers. From 1980 to 1987, the agricultural sector lost 131,575 members of its labor force and comprised only one fifth, or 821,470 people, of the economically active Bulgarian population in 1987[43]). Although Bulgaria still has a higher level of labor intensity in its agriculture than West European countries, significant agricultural labor problems are evident, particularly those associated with age and education. Approximately, 14% of the agricultural labor force consists of farmers over the retirement age, compared to a 3% industrial share, and 40% of the agricultural workers are over 50 years of age in contrast to an industry level of 20.3%[44]). Another labor problem related to the massive exodus of young people is the relatively low educational level of the remaining villagers. In 1985, 90% of the agricultural workers had no more than a basic level of formal education[45]).

Bulgaria will find it increasingly difficult to sustain the recent pace of the expansion of its industrial labor force. In 1987, 1,437,507 people were employed in industry or 38.1% of the national work-force. By comparison to 1980, the number of people in the industrial labor-force increased by 68,587, which represents a 5% gain[46]). Demographic impediments should slow down this growth considerably. These include the sharply diminished possibilities for large-scale movement to cities from the demographically dying countryside and the rapid decline in urban birth rates.

To arrest the dramatic decline in natural population increases, Bulgarian demographic planners are stressing the urgency of encouraging three-children families in at least 30% to 40% of the young married households in order to bring birth rates up to the level of 16‰–17‰ and have an optimal annual population increase of 22,000 people[47]). The primary approach will be to improve the existing birth incentives

---

[43]) Ibid.
[44]) Petkov (note 34), p. 49; Cook, E.: Prospects for Bulgarian Agriculture in the 1980's, in: East European Economies: Slow Growth in the 1980's. Joint Economic Committee of Congress. Washington 1985, p. 74.
[45]) Petkov (note 34), p. 49/50.
[46]) SG. 1988, p. 110.
[47]) Minkov (note 13), p. 29–38.

involving housing, financial assistance, expanded day care facilities, and a wide range of additional programs. A newer approach calls for a mass-media campaign to idealize the three-child family and overcome the strong prejudices of urban residents toward larger families, which apparently are regarded by many as a throwback to the rural past of Bulgaria. The goal of these programs is not to return to the high birth rates at the start of the Communist era but rather to avert negative population growth in the future.

Long-term population projections offer little hope for the reversal of the demographic decline of Bulgaria. The US Census Bureau recently estimated that by the year 2000 Bulgaria will have a probable population of 9.26 million[48]. In the past, population projections for Bulgaria, including one by the US Census Bureau in 1981, consistently predicted population totals which were too high because of the frequent underestimation of birth rate declines, increases in mortality rates, and natural rural population decline. In 1974, Bulgarian demographers projected the lowest birth rate by 1985 would be 14.3 and the highest death rate to be 10.9. This would result in the lowest projected natural increase of 3.6 and a national population of 9,215,000[49]. The actual 1985 rates were 13.3 for births, 12.0 for deaths, a natural increase of 1.3, which has since descended to the level of 1.0 in 1987[50]. The 1985 population of 8,949,900 was more than one-quarter of a million below the lowest 1974 projection and even further below the prediction of Georgi Dimitrov in 1948 that Bulgaria would have 10 million people by 1960.

The Bulgarian population should continue its slow rate of growth or virtual stagnation perhaps until the turn of the century. Unless unforeseen demographic changes occur, however, Bulgaria ultimately could have negative growth as the mounting curve of death rates, characteristic of an aging society, crosses the persistently declining birth rate curve. The rural population has declined rapidly as a direct result of the abandonment en masse of villages by young, urban-bound migrants. This massive exodus from the countryside also has affected demographic change by contributing to the aging of the rural population, which has led to the pervasive natural negative growth in the villages. The once-crowded Bulgarian countryside, which was regarded by economic demographers as a classic example of rural overpopulation, has entered into a phase of chronic demographic decline. The movement of Bulgaria into the final phase of the demographic transition and the aging of a formerly youthful population will have significant economic effects which will intensify the need for technological change and increased labor productivity in every sector.

---

[48] Baldwin (note 5), p. 270/271. This is the medium projection. The high projection for the year 2000 is 9,464,000 and the low projection, which seems to be the most accurate is 9,062.
[49] Demografiía (note 10), p. 493–518.
[50] Naselenie 1986, p. 6/7, and SG. 1988, p. 39/40.

Social Structure

Roger Whitaker, Boston/Massachusetts

I. Planned Social Change: 1. The Role of the Communist Party – 2. Marxist Development Theory – II. The Bulgarian Peasant Legacy: 1. The Village and the Family – 2. The Party's Response to Inherited Circumstances – III. The Emergent Social Structure: 1. The Party's Strategy – 2. Socialized Agriculture – 3. New Occupational Opportunities – 4. The Role of Education – 5. Labor Shifts away from Agriculture – 6. Social Class Mobility – IV. The Family as a Changing Social Institution: 1. The „Ideal" Socialist Family – 2. Labor Force Participation and Women's Quest for Equality – 3. The Declining Tradition of Large Families – 4. Efforts to Increase the Birth rate – 5. Sex Roles within the Home – 6. The Division of Labor within the Household – 7. The Three Generation Household – V. Tradition and Modernization

I. Planned Social Change

1. The Role of the Communist Party

Out of the upheaval of World War II, the BKP assumed political power and charted a radical new course for the development of the Bulgarian society. The Party undertook the formidable task of transforming a peasant social system into an industrial socialist society. To administer this radical change, the Party drew heavily upon the Soviet model of development. Using the pervasive power of the State and a highly centralized planning apparatus, the Party mobilized resources (including human resources) to promote rapid industrialization and economic growth. In order to promote increasing social and economic equality in addition to rapid growth, the Party socialized ownership of the means of production by nationalizing non-agricultural sectors of the economy and by collectivizing agriculture. Further, the Party assumed control of the social institutions which structured community life in order to enhance the new socialist order (cf. chapter by W. Gumpel, Wirtschaftssystem).

„The formation, growth, and change of social structure is significantly an outcome of human purpose and will, and especially of the purpose and will of leaders and entrepreneurs who can mobilize others."[1]) In the case of Bulgaria, after 1944, the BKP became the propulsive force designing and managing the development of the Bulgarian social structure. The Party was explicit in its values and norms, conscious of its mission, certain of its destination. The Party established the goals and priorities

---

[1]) Warner, K.: Structural Matrix of Development, in: Sociological Perspectives of Domestic Development. Ed. by G. M. Beal, R. C. Powers, E. W. Coward. Iowa 1971, p. 97.

of the society and defined the values and purposes upon which the new social structure should be based[2]).

However, it is one thing for a revolutionary political party to assume the power of the State and quite another for it to use the State's power to bring about revolutionary change. No matter how resolute the BKP has been in articulating the Soviet interpretation of Marxist-Leninist development theory, the actual process of administering changes in Bulgaria's social structure has necessitated the adaptation of ideological principle to sociological reality – an arduous task in Bulgaria since the Party came to power in a society that did not resemble the type of society that Marx assumed would exist prior to the onset of a socialist social order.

2. Marxist Development Theory

According to Marx, socialist revolutions were expected to take place in the world's most economically advanced social systems where highly developed, large-scale capitalist enterprises in industry, commerce, and banking would be expropriated by masses of organized workers. Marx believed that under capitalism, in agriculture no less than in industry, large-scale production would be dominant at the time of the revolution. Furthermore, Marx presumed that the population would be highly differentiated into clearly defined classes with a small minority of rich industrialists and farmers and a growing majority of industrial and agricultural wage laborers. Marx's revolutionary prophecy was based upon the alliance of these industrial and agricultural working masses against the capitalists of town and country. Marx further presumed that after the victorious socialist revolution, the highly developed industries would provide the material resources to help agriculture further develop. Industry would be used to assist large-scale agriculture to transform itself along socialist cooperative lines[3]).

II. The Bulgarian Peasant Legacy

1. The Village and the Family

As is well known, the world chain of capitalism broke in its weakest links, in agrarian societies with very limited industrial resources, small industrial working classes and masses of peasants engaged in under-capitalized, small-scale agriculture. This was nowhere more evident than in Bulgaria which was simply not an industrial society with an attendant large working class at the end of World War II. Instead, Bulgaria was still part of Europe's granary, part of the agricultural half of Europe

---

[2]) Aspaturian, V.: Marxism and the Meaning of Modernization, in: The Politics of Modernization in Eastern Europe: Testing the Soviet Model. Ed. by C. Gati. New York 1974, p. 7.

[3]) Cliff, T.: Marxism and the Collectivization of Agriculture, in: International Socialism. 19 (1964) Winter, pp. 4/5.

supplying foodstuffs and raw materials to Europe's industrial states when the BKP assumed political power (cf. chapter by R. Crampton, Historical Foundations). By the end of World War II Bulgaria remained a part of the „peasant belt of Europe" which stretched from the Baltic Sea to the Aegean. Three-fourths of Bulgaria's population lived in villages and the overwhelming majority of these villagers were engaged in small-scale, primitive farming on land which was owned and operated by families who had inherited the land from their ancestors[4]).

Table 1: Population by Census, 1887–1946

Year	Total	in Cities	in Villages	% Urban
1887	3,154,375	593,547	2,560,828	18.8
1900	3,744,283	742,435	3,001,848	19.8
1920	4,846,971	966,375	3,880,596	19.9
1934	6,077,939	1,302,551	4,775,388	21.4
1946	7,029,349	1,735,188	5,294,161	24.7

Source: SG. 1988, p. 33.

As in all peasant societies, Bulgaria's social structure before World War II was built upon the twin pillars of tradition – the village and the family, and neither could be fully understood without reference to the other. The village established the limits of social contact for most people while the family was where the individual learned the knowledge and skills which were prescribed as norms for all villagers[5]).

Kinship was the principal organizing force within the village social structure. The extended family was the basic unit of residence and domestic function as well as the major source of social and economic organization for people in the community. The village labor force was allocated by families who worked privately owned farms and those who were unable to work (children, the elderly, the infirm) were cared for by their kin. The status of an individual was, by and large, determined by the status of his family within the community. A son inherited his father's occupation and status. There was little social or geographical mobility and little separation of the worlds of home and work. The family functioned as the major community institution socializing children and controlling the behavior of community residents. The family was, in short, at the very core of the community social structure, organizing the social, economic, and spiritual life of the peasantry.

---

[4]) See, as examples, Gerschenkron, A.: Economic Backwardness in Historical Perspective. Cambridge 1966; Kyurkchiev, M.: Bulgarian Agriculture Today and Life in the Villages. Sofia 1974; Sanders, I.: The Peasant Community and the National Society in Southeastern Europe: An Interpretive Essay, in: Balkanistica. III (1976), pp. 23–41; or Wolff, R.: The Balkans in Our Times. Cambridge, Massachusetts 1974.

[5]) The Family and Its Culture: An Investigation in Seven East and West European Countries. Ed. by M. Biskup, V. Filias, I. Vitanyi. Budapest 1984.

The internal structure of the peasant family before World War II was based upon the needs of the family as the major unit of production in the agrarian economy. The status and roles of individual family members were tailored to meet the needs of the family as a productive unit. The rights and obligations associated with different family members were typically defined by their age and sex. The entire matrix of family roles and relationships was intimately tied to the agrarian social structure where adult males controlled the family's major economic resource – land.

The authority of the family's eldest male over his wife and children was essentially unchallenged by tradition or by law. After all, he owned the land upon which the welfare of the entire family depended. The ideology of duty and submission to authority and fate were rarely challenged since values were oriented to the timeless traditions of peasant life supported by religious interpretations of the sacred relationship between a man and his land.

2. The Party's Response to Inherited Circumstances

Many of the characteristics of the prewar peasant social structure in Bulgaria were not necessarily obstacles to the centrally planned socialist developments after the coup of 1944. Some traditional aspects of Bulgarian peasant life have been tolerated or adapted by socialist policy makers while others have, ironically, been conducive to the development of a new social structure. Nevertheless, there is no question but that many of the dominant features of the peasant way of life were inimical to the development goals being articulated by the BKP. As examples, strong attachment to private land was incompatible with socializing the means of agricultural production. A narrow village social orientation was contrary to the Party's intention to progressively eliminate distinctions between villages and towns. Finally, the strong patriarchal familism of Bulgaria's prewar peasants obstructed the socialist goal of emancipating individuals, especially women, from presocialist family forms. Therefore, after 1944, the BKP faced the choice of introducing radical reforms in the countryside or enduring certain ideological anomalies. The Party chose to do both, with consequences which have been traumatic for some, dramatic for all.

III. The Emergent Social Structure

1. The Party's Strategy

Essential to the BKP's strategy of transforming Bulgaria into a socialist social system has been its resolve to progressively eliminate social class distinctions and to distribute goods and services on a more equitable basis than would, presumably, have resulted if Bulgaria had followed a capitalist development strategy. The Party's determination to rapidly develop and industrialize the Bulgarian economy has been complemented by other, more normative indicators of socialist development such as the expansion of the public sector of the economy, the enhancement or reduction of certain social classes or groups, and the promise of increasingly equal opportunities for all citizens to study or work (cf. chapter „Schulwesen" by P. Bachmaier).

2. Socialized Agriculture

The cornerstone of the Party's socialist foundation was laid with its resolve to eliminate private ownership of agricultural land which would inevitably trigger a complex set of political, economic and social reactions of great pace and scope. In fact, of all of the significant changes introduced in Bulgaria after the BKP assumed political power, none could rival the importance of reorganizing the basis of the peasant economy. More quickly than in any other East European country and with a speed rivalled only by the 1928–32 period in the Soviet Union, BKP leaders after World War II assaulted a tradition of private farming which was at the very core of the pre-socialist peasant social structure. By the end of 1952, over one-half of the arable land had been collectivized (cf. I. Grosser's chapter, „Landwirtschaft").

Table 2: Collectivization of Agriculture, 1945–1952 (Percentage of Arable Land)

Country	1945	1946	1947	1948	1949	1950	1951	1952
Bulgaria	3.0	3.5	3.7	6.2	11.3	43.0	47.5	51.0
Czechoslovakia					5.4	16.5	19.0	37.9
Hungary					0.5	2.6	8.1	18.2
Poland					0.3	2.2	3.5	4.8
Romania					0.1	2.7	3.1	7.2

Source: Stillman, E.: The Collectivization of Bulgarian Agriculture, in: Collectivization of Agriculture in Eastern Europe. Ed. I. T. Sanders. Lexington, Kentucky 1958, p. 70.

3. New Occupational Opportunities

Bulgaria's rapidly changing economy after World War II opened a plethora of new occupational opportunities for the country's working population. As is well known (cf. W. Gumpel's chapter „Wirtschaftssystem"), the BKP and its government apparatus committed the nation's resources to rapidly develop an industrial base for the national economy. The newly-created industrial enterprises needed a massive influx of both skilled and unskilled manual labor as well as executive and managerial talent. The Party's commitment to expanding and more equitably distributing social services to all localities (e. g. health clinics, schools), meant that many new, highly trained professionals were needed. Also, the burgeoning bureaucratic and administrative needs of the state required the recruitment of new employees. The labor needs for these expanding activities combined with the restricted need for manual labor on the newly consolidated and mechanized cooperative farms to create a new structure of employment opportunities for the population.

4. The Role of Education

Universal, compulsory education was enforced shortly after the BKP assumed political power and the schools became the institution which mediated the occupational aspirations of youth and the labor needs envisioned by centralized economic planners. The curricula of the general schools were designed to prepare youth for active participation in the restructured economy and large numbers of special vocational schools were created to train students to assume needed occupations. Education thus became both the major vehicle for the individual to achieve social mobility and the mechanism by which the Party helped ensure that the anticipated labor needs of the economy would be met. As Bulgarians, especially young Bulgarians, took advantage of the opportunities to prepare for new occupations through education, intergenerational and intragenerational shifts in occupation and social class were made possible, even inevitable.

5. Labor Shifts away from Agriculture

The restructured labor needs and opportunities which were fostered by Bulgaria's postwar development strategy clearly influenced the career options of people from all social classes, but it was especially the peasantry, the overwhelming majority of the population, which provided the obvious recruitment pool for new occupational roles. Rural youth were simultaneously „pulled" to the city and „pushed" from the countryside as Bulgaria's policies of industrial growth and agricultural collectivization were carried out.

A massive shift of rural labor from agriculture to industry was especially evident in the first two decades after the Party's development plans went into effect. Between 1948 and 1968, 1,750,000 active age men and women left work in agriculture, reducing the proportion of the national work force in agriculture from 81.9 percent to 39.1 percent[6]). For Europe's quintessential peasant society, this shift was nothing short of

Table 3: Employed Population by Economic Sector, 1980–1987 (percentages)

Sector	1980	1983	1987
Material Production	83.0	82.8	81.9
Industry	35.2	36.8	38.1
Agriculture	23.8	21.6	19.2
Construction	8.2	8.3	8.3
Trade	8.0	8.3	8.5
Transport	5.9	5.8	5.7
Other	1.9	2.0	2.1
Non-Material Production	17.0	17.2	18.1

Source: SG. 1988, p. 110.

---

[6]) Hoffman, G.: Regional Development Strategy in Southeast Europe. New York 1972, p. 53.

astonishing. The reduction in the agricultural work force has continued even in this decade so that latest figures indicate that only one in five active Bulgarians is engaged in the agricultural sector.

The obvious corollary of the depletion of the ranks of agricultural workers has been the dramatic increase in the number of Bulgarians working in industry, construction, and transportation – the major occupational indicators of Bulgaria's rapid economic development. Between 1948 and 1968, the number of workers in these categories increased from 743,000 to 2,409,000[7]). By the middle of the 1980s, while less than one-fifth of the work force remained in agriculture, nearly one-half was employed in industry and construction.

6. Social Class Mobility

The radical reorganization of employment opportunities in Bulgaria since World War II and the attendant shift of the work force to urban settings (65 percent of Bulgarians now live in areas classified as urban, including 18 percent in the capital city of Sofia), have obviously also meant significant intragenerational social as well as geographical mobility[8]).

The largest study conducted on the process of social mobility within Bulgaria during the initial decades of industrialization and agricultural collectivization was carried out in the late 1960s by the Institute of Sociology of the BAN[9]). That nationwide survey showed that nearly two-thirds of those individuals who were members of the working class not in agriculture, (defined as those performing manual labor in the State-owned sector of material production) were *new* members. Neither they nor their parents were workers at the end of World War II and the largest recruitment pools for these new working class members were, not surprisingly, poor and middle size farmers[10]).

A second major category of employment, according to Bulgarian researchers, is made up of office employees and intellectuals. They are considered to represent a stratum rather than a class because they are not involved in material production and include occupations such as artist, teacher, physician, director of an enterprise, nurse, secretary or policeman. The new members of this stratum in the first two and one-half decades after World War II were also shown in the Institute's study to have been drawn from the ranks of former farmers and to have grown in size by nearly four times during the period under review[11]). Only the class of cooperative farmers, de-

---

[7]) European Marketing Data and Statistics. London 1987, pp. 81, 83, 85.

[8]) SG. 1988, p. 33.

[9]) Sociology was not accepted as an academic discipline in the BAN until the late 1960s. The study of Town and Village in 1968 was the first important survey research conducted by the Institute and it helped to establish the academic credibility of Sociology within the BAN.

[10]) Mironov, I.: Incomes and Socio-Class Structure in Bulgaria, in: Bulgarian Journal of Sociology. I (1978), p. 92.

[11]) Minkov, M.: Development of the Social-Class Structure of the Socialist Society of Bulgaria, in: Contemporary Sociology in Bulgaria. Sofia 1978, p. 202.

fined as those engaged in material production in agriculture where the means of production were owned cooperatively rather than by the State, has been recruited from its own milieu. For example, nine out of every ten cooperative farmers in 1968 were formerly farmers at the time of the coup d'état or their parents were then farmers[12]. Unfortunately, the Sociology Institute's investigation did not examine possible differences in social mobility patterns experienced by Bulgaria's minority groups. Although no official data are available on the different opportunities afforded Bulgaria's Turkish or Gypsy populations, it is well known that the intergenerational and intragenerational mobility patterns experienced in these minority communities have been far less impressive than those of the general Bulgarian population. Despite this limitation and the fact that the Institute's three broad categories of worker, employee/intellectual, and cooperative farmer mask very significant sociological differences within each category, the Institute study did document the dramatic shifts in the social class structure in Bulgaria during the first 20 years of centrally planned socialist development. In the 20 years since that study, many Bulgarians may have reached a „mobility plateau" and doubts are now being raised about the opportunities available to some newly employed youth to exceed the occupational aspirations of their parents. Some observers have predicted that the social class structure will become increasingly „stable" and that class positions will become increasingly „hereditary" as the rate of economic growth and expansion become much more modest than during the initial years of Bulgaria's socialist development[13].

The socialization of agriculture in Bulgaria rendered obsolete the historical connections between class, status, and land ownership. The legacy of traditional class inequalities where class positions were defined as much by heritage, family name and estate as they were by productive forces, dies hard. The families of important landowners before World War II are still well known in most villages, but the process of separating the historical convergence of land ownership, status, and power is well under way. Socialized agriculture, rapid industrialization, and the resultant shift in employment opportunities for young people have dramatically altered the attachment to private land for which the grandparents of today's youth were so noted. Politically, economically, and sociologically, that represents one of the most significant achievements of the BKP in pursuit of its goal of transforming Bulgaria into an industrially-based, socialist social system.

---

[12] Dobrianov, V.: Changes in the Socio-Class Structure of Bulgaria, in: Bulgaria Past and Present. Ed. by T. Butler. Columbus, Ohio 1976, p. 157.

[13] Connor, W.: Social Change and Stability in Eastern Europe, in: Problems of Communism. XXVI (1977), p. 25.

IV. The Family as a Changing Social Institution

1. The „Ideal" Socialist Family

The family is arguably the most resilient of all institutions which make up a social system. Unlike other institutions in contemporary Bulgaria which organize public roles and relationships, the family is private and has no State-appointed representative to administer socialist policy. However, despite the tenacity of many of its time honored traditions, the structure and function of the Bulgarian family have undergone considerable change since World War II as the family tries to satisfy the enduring needs and interests of its members within a radically altered political, economic and cultural environment.

There is very little written about the precise form of the „ideal" family in a socialist society but Bulgaria's Family Code offers some general outlines of the government's view[14] (cf. chapter by Ch. Jessel-Holst, „Rechtssystem").

The new Family Code, adopted by the NSb in May 1985, specifies that spouses have equal rights and obligations within the marriage and „the relations between the spouses are built upon mutual respect, common care for the family, goodwill and faithfulness"[15]. As for relations between generations, the Code specifies that, „parents are obliged to care for their children and to prepare them for socially useful activity", while, „the children are obliged to respect their parents and to help them", and, „the adult children are obliged to care for their elderly, disabled and sick parents"[16]. Mapping these general principles onto traditional peasant patterns of family organization has not always been easy. An examination of changes in the roles and relations between ages and sexes shows striking examples of both continuity and change since World War II.

2. Labor Force Participation and Women's Quest for Equality

Each change in Bulgaria's family system has had obvious significance for the day-to-day lives of individuals and these changes, taken together, probably represent the broadest and most rapid rate of change in the history of the family as a social institution. However, no change has been as important, or as contested, as the changing role of women and especially important in this respect has been women's participation in paid labor.

One of the most important changes in sex role allocation throughout the modern world has been the entry of great numbers of women into the work force outside the home. In Bulgaria, this development has been directly and consistently encouraged by socialist development planners. The government has affirmed the rights of women to participate in the work force on an equal basis with men. The State has encouraged

---

[14] DV. (1985) 41. Note: The 1985 Code replaced the Family Code of 1968.
[15] Ibid., p. 8.
[16] Ibid., p. 20.

women to work outside the home because the economy needs their labor and because, according to Marxist theorists, true equality between the sexes is predicated upon equality and independence within the workplace, freeing women from traditional forms of material dependency. With such encouragement and because most families cannot reach or sustain a standard of living they desire without at least two family members' earnings, the overwhelming majority of Bulgarian women of working age are employed and in the 1980s, their ranks have approached nearly one-half of the total work force.

Table 4: Women Workers and Employees by Economic Sector, 1980–1987 (Percentage of total who are women)

Sector	1980	1983	1987
Total	47.1	49.2	49.8
Industry	47.6	48.9	49.2
Agriculture	45.3	48.5	47.7
Construction	17.8	19.7	20.1
Trade	62.7	64.4	65.4
Transport	17.3	19.8	21.1
Communications	59.1	59.8	62.3
Education	74.3	75.8	76.4

Source: SG. 1988, p. 113.

The distribution of new working women throughout various sectors of the economy has been reasonably even since World War II although one could argue that women are often subject to a „covert" form of sexual differentiation – a form of quasi-egalitarianism as many women have moved from traditional to neo-traditional roles. This may be supported by the fact that some young women continue to aspire to and dominate certain „nurturing" professions such as primary school teaching and nursing. Also, on an interpersonal level within the workplace, the tenacious spirit of male superiority continues to be expressed by some men who do not feel comfortable with female supervisors regardless of their abilities. Despite the dramatic improvement in the status of working women in post-war Bulgaria, it remains clear in the late 1980s that neither legal guarantees of sexual equality nor women's active labor force participation can quickly or completely eliminate some traditional aspects of male-female relations inside or outside the home.

3. The Declining Tradition of Large Families

One certain consequence of women leaving the traditional home to seek paid employment in the new, post-war industrial economy has been the drastic reduction in the Bulgarian birth rate. The birth rate declined from a post-war high of 25.6 (per 1000 population) in 1946 to a low of 15.3 in 1972. After a set of incentives for couples

Table 5: Birth Rates in Cities and Villages, 1930–1987 (per 1,000 population)

Year	Total	in Cities	in Villages
1930	31.4	23.8	33.4
1940	22.2	16.8	23.7
1950	25.2	24.9	25.3
1960	17.8	16.1	18.8
1970	16.3	18.0	14.6
1980	14.5	15.7	12.4
1986	13.4	14.3	11.7
1987	13.0	13.7	11.7

Source: SG. 1988, pp. 40–42.

to have children took effect, the birthrate increased slightly to 17.2 in 1974 but since then the rate has fallen again to an all-time low of 13.0 in 1987.

The Bulgarian tradition of the large family has clearly passed. Before World War II, a man's local prestige was based, in part, upon the number of children and especially sons that he had. Three or four children were the norm. Today, most couples expect to have only one or at most two children.

In the 1930s, children were perceived as „gifts of God". There were few thoughts and even fewer actions to prevent the birth of children. In the peasant agricultural economy before World War II, children were frequently seen as economic assets – either for their labor contribution to the family farm or their earnings from non-agricultural employment. Any physically and mentally healthy woman who did not marry was considered a failure and furthermore, any married woman who did not bear children was pitied[17]. Childbearing and child-rearing were the primary obligations of women to comply with the expectations of the community.

Many of the factors supporting the tradition of large families have been obliterated in Bulgaria today. First, with the secularization of public life, increased education and a more scientific outlook on life processes, women today know of the possibility and the advisability of smaller families. Second, without private farmland, the rural family does not have the need for extra farmhands to work the family's holdings. Instead, today, children may be seen as putting additional and unnecessary pressure on the family's finances or limited living space (especially in urban apartment buildings). Finally, children may also be seen as interrupting a wife's promising or enjoyable career, or at least causing some loss of household income when she is not at work.

This situation shows that the interests of the collective society, as represented by the State, and the interests of the single family may at times conflict. The singular family may believe that its private well-being depends upon a limited family size. The State, by contrast, may believe that an increased birth rate is necessary for the well-being of the general society with its anticipated labor needs.

---

[17] Sanders, I.T.: The Sociology of a Bulgarian Shopski Village. Ph. D. Dissertation, Cornell University, 1938.

4. Efforts to Increase the Birth rate

In order to reverse the precipitous decline in the Bulgarian birth rate, the government and public organizations have announced measures to ensure special protection and care for mothers and they have initiated many incentives and material benefits for working women to have more children.

Special protection involves both prenatal and postnatal care. To begin with, there is an impressive network of mother-care consultation centers that administer to the needs of pregnant women. This care is free of cost to the patient as are all hospital costs related to the delivery. The pregnant woman is also protected in her workplace. She cannot legally be refused a job for which she is qualified. The pregnant worker cannot be dismissed or moved to another job without her consent although she has the right to shift from hard or noxious work to a more appropriate position during her pregnancy.

An expectant mother may take leave from her workplace 45 days before her due date. She receives her full normal pay during this leave and if she is having her first child, she receives her full salary for a period of four months after the birth. For this first childbirth, she then receives the official minimum wage for a period of 20 additional months if she continues to be on leave. For a woman bearing her second child, she receives five months at full salary after the birth and the minimum wage for 19 more months while for a third child, the formula is full pay for 6 months and the minimum wage for an additional 18 months[18].

When a child is born, parents receive a lump sum cash payment from the State which increases in value for each additional child so that a third child results in a payment of 500 leva, five times greater than the sum paid for a first child. After the birth of a child, parents also begin to receive monthly support allowances valued at 15 leva for a first child, 25 to 30 leva for a second child and 45–50 leva for a third child. These payments are probably not very important in a couple's decision to have a child since the average annual household income in Bulgaria in 1987 was reported to be 7627 leva[19].

The Bulgarian government's protection and support for childbearing in the early years is laudable in principle, appreciated in practice. There is, nevertheless, a price to be paid by some women who take full advantage of the generous social benefits encouraging motherhood. A woman who takes leave to care for a series of infants loses sustained contact with the workplace which may, temporarily at least, preclude her advancement to positions of additional responsibility or authority, hence obviating the fulfillment of her potential work talents on an equal basis with men. Hilda Scott has summarized this dilemma by stating that East European socialist societies „... need women's productive power, and they need their reproductive power; but without much more effective measures than they have been able to take to date, one cannot be had without sacrificing some of the other"[20].

---

[18] Kyuranov, C.: The Bulgarian Family Today. Sofia 1984, pp. 8–11 (cit. as: Kyuranov).
[19] SG. 1988, p. 98.
[20] Scott, H.: Does Socialism Liberate Women? Boston 1974, p. 136.

5. Sex Roles within the Home

The impact of women's labor force participation upon roles and relations within the home has, in many respects, been dramatic. Marital decisions related to issues such as the allocation of household resources, vacation plans, recreational activities or child rearing decisions are increasingly carried out on a consulting basis of reciprocal respect. The one area of family life probably least changed by women's labor force participation or legal guarantees of sexual equality concerns the distribution of responsibility for the care of the household. Although it is true that working wives allocate much less time to the home than do stay-at-home wives, husbands of working wives do almost as little as husbands of stay-at-home wives. This has been shown to be true in recent studies conducted in the United States, the Soviet Union, Sweden, Finland, France and elsewhere[21]. Although it has been shown that the fathers of infants and better educated and younger husbands may do a bit more than others, the overwhelming fact is that men's domestic contribution doesn't change much whether or not they work, or whether or not their wives work[22].

6. The Division of Labor within the Household

The typical Bulgarian household in the late 1980s surely offers no exception to the general pattern of inequities in terms of the distribution of housecare responsibilities that is evident in most other countries. It is true that the burdens of housecare have been lightened somewhat in the 1980s by the general improvement in family living standards, including ownership of various home conveniences.

Table 6: Ownership of Consumer Products, 1980–1987 (Percentage of Households)

Product	1980	1983	1987
Washing Machine	71	81	91
(Automatic)	3	8	17
Refrigerator	76	88	94
Television	75	87	97
(color)	7	17	35
Telephone	24	34	47
Radio	88	92	94
Automobile	29	34	39

Source: SG. 1988, p. 102.

---

[21] Haavio-Mannila, E.: Convergence Between East and West: Tradition and Modernity in Sex Roles in Sweden, Finland and the Soviet Union, in: Women and Achievement: Social and Motivational Achievement. Ed. by Midnick et al. Washington 1975, pp. 71–84.

[22] Goode, W.: Why Men Resist, in: Rethinking the Family: Some Feminist Questions. Ed by B. Thorne, M. Yalom. New York 1981, p. 155.

Additionally, it is evident that some younger, better educated, urban husbands have assumed increased responsibility to share in handling some household chores. And recent survey data from Bulgaria show that men, in theory, recognize the importance of sharing household responsibilities[23]). By and large, however, the practical division of household labor continues to be based upon traditional sex roles with women assuming an inordinate share of the responsibility to care for the children and home. One typical response to the burdens of child and home care faced by Bulgaria's young working parents has been their reliance upon their retired parents and grandparents.

7. The Three Generation Household

Most newly married couples expect to eventually purchase or rent an apartment or home of their own. A 1979 study by the Institute on Youth in Bulgaria confirmed the intentions of most young people to live with their parents after marriage only temporarily[24]). The State is now trying to improve the opportunities for new couples to live alone. Since July 1985, the State has offered substantial loans to newly married couples to construct or purchase a home with generous repayment terms, especially for those who have several children. Even so, most couples live with parents, usually the husband's, for at least some time after marriage. Since many of these new couples will have a child within the first few years of their marriage, three (or even four) generation households are still common. Also, with impressive improvements in the average life expectancy in Bulgaria, three and even four generation households may be likely.

Table 7: Life Expectancy, 1921–1986 (in years)

	1921–25	1935–39	1956–57	1965–67	1974–76	1978–80	1984–86
Total	44.64	51.75	65.86	70.66	71.31	71.14	71.19
Men	44.35	50.98	64.17	68.81	68.68	68.35	68.17
Women	44.98	52.56	67.65	72.67	73.91	73.55	74.39

Source: SG. 1988, p. 106.

The financial burden of neolocal residence is not the only reason why three generation households persist in Bulgaria in the late 1980s. Many people prefer that married couples with children live together with their aging parents rather than separately. Practical considerations underlie the preferences of many people, both young and old, for living together. Retired parents may find it easier to live with their children in a shared household rather than try to maintain an independent home on a meager

---

[23]) Kyuranov (note 18), p. 15.
[24]) This study titled „Choosing a Marriage Partner" was conducted by the Institute on Youth in 1974 under the guidance of K. Vasilev. Portions of the data from the study are reported in Kyuranov (note 18), pp. 36/37.

pension provided by the State. Although the average annual amount of a pension has increased to 1 236 leva in 1987, no one can expect to support themself adequately on this alone since the average household income in 1987 was 7 627 leva[25]). In addition to this, many retired Bulgarians take great pleasure in caring for the children of their working sons and daughters because they remain vital in a full and busy house. From the point of view of young married couples, the three generation household means that the older, often retired, parents can help care for grandchildren and help to maintain the home, allowing both younger partners to work outside the home. Grandparents help to cook, wash, clean, shop, and care for the children as a daytime visit to any of Bulgaria's playgrounds or parks would make clear.

Retired parents or in-laws can, of course, compound rather than ease many of the household responsibilities of working mothers. Tensions may develop between generations or between the younger married partners whose relationship may be strained by living with the aging parents of one spouse. This may play a role in Bulgaria's rate of divorce which reached 16 divorces (per 10,000 population) in 1983 (20.4 in cities, 8.7 in villages), before new restrictions made it more difficult to divorce, lowering the rate to 11.2 in 1986 (14.3 in cities, 5.4 in villages) while in 1987, the divorce rate increased again to 13.0 (16.4 in cities, 6.4 in villages)[26]). Even in cases where three or four generations living together causes strife it may be routine for a retired grandparent to pick up a child from school, do occasional food shopping or provide babysitting for the younger couple. The role of retired Bulgarians in child and home care is not restricted to those who live in three generation households, but such a domestic arrangement clearly facilitates intergenerational dependencies. The ways in which the enduring needs and interests of the family are met are always adjusting to the context within which the family functions. The persistence of the three generation household in contemporary Bulgaria indicates that one such adjustment involves the adaptation of traditional solutions to new social, economic and political circumstances.

V. Tradition and Modernization

Peasant traditionalism and socialist modernity are not mutually exclusive. Some elements of Bulgaria's traditional social system and way of life have not necessarily been impediments to planned change nor have they simply given way to a new industrial and urban culture in the process of socialist development. There is no doubt that the transformation of much of Bulgaria's social system since World War II has been profound but the State's policy-making leaders have responded to specific pre-socialist traditions in at least four ways[27]).

---

[25]) SG. 1988, pp. 96, 98.
[26]) Ibid. p. 78.
[27]) For a fuller discussion of the Party's response to tradition, see Whitaker, R.: Experiencing Revolutionary Change: The Role of Tradition, in: Bulgaria Past and Present. Sofia 1982, pp. 109–116.

First, some of Bulgaria's pre-war traditional values and norms have been preserved or promoted by socialist policy-making leaders because they are conducive to, or even essential for, the planned development process. Examples include: establishing folklore groups and preserving historical sites which are used in patriotic campaigns to foster pride in Bulgaria's heroic past; portraying the traditional joint family with its shared resources as a natural base for the establishment of cooperative farms; preserving a tradition of children caring for their aging parents in part to reduce cost to the State; and encouraging a tradition of large families to ensure future labor resources.

Second, there are certain traditional values, norms and practices which are sufficiently innocuous or inconsequential for the goals of socialist development that policy-making leaders have tolerated their persistence. These leaders have decided that the financial, social, or political costs of opposing certain „undesirable" traditions are too great to warrant serious effort to change them or that over time they will diminish in importance. Examples in contemporary Bulgaria could include some traditional peasant-based health care practices concerning pregnancy and childbirth or the persistence of certain traditional religious practices such as ecclesiastical weddings, baptism and funerals.

Third, some specific traditions associated with Bulgaria's peasant legacy have now been adapted to contemporary needs. This, in fact, is the probable fate of most time-honored patterns in social life within the context of planned social change. There are numerous examples of this adaptive process but most noteworthy may be the State's secularization of certain traditionally religious ceremonies (e. g., name day and civil marriage ceremonies), and the allowance of auxiliary (private) farm plots for cooperative farm members.

Finally, there are some elements of Bulgaria's presocialist social system which if left unchallenged would clearly impede the process of planned socialist development. These traditions have, therefore, been opposed or prohibited by policy-making leaders. The principal examples of traditions which have been opposed by the Bulgarian political leadership are the private ownership of agricultural land upon which the peasant social structure was constructed including the consequent historical correlation between landownership, power and prestige in community life and the subordinate role of women within the home and village.

The commonly held beliefs that tradition and modernity are mutually exclusive social experiences and that Bulgaria's socialist development necessarily involves the end of all pre-socialist patterns of organization distort the complex process of planned social change. The transformations of the Bulgarian community and family since World War II have been profound. Yet, as some traditional peasant attributes have lost contemporary meaning in the face of change, others have been preserved, adapted or promoted. The dynamic interaction between pre-socialist social attributes and the goals of Bulgarian socialist development makes it clear that to understand the present, one must consider the inherited past as well as the anticipated future.

Nationale Minderheiten

Stefan Troebst, Berlin

I. Vorbemerkung – II. Grunddaten und internationaler Vergleich – III. Historischer Hintergrund – IV. Nationale Minderheiten und ethnisch-religiöse Gruppen: 1. Nationale Minderheiten: a) Türken – b) „Makedonier" – c) Roma – d) Armenier – e) Russen – f) Griechen – g) Tataren – h) Juden – i) Sonstige – 2. Ethnisch-religiöse Gruppen: a) Pomaken – b) Gagausen – V. Nationalitätenpolitik 1944–1989

I. Vorbemerkung

Etwa 1/6 der Einwohner Bulgariens gehört nicht dem Staatsvolk der südslawischen Bulgaren, sondern einer der zahlreichen nationalen Minderheiten und ethnisch-religiösen Gruppen[1]) des Landes an. In deutlichem Gegensatz zum numerischen, sozioökonomischen, politischen u. a. Stellenwert dieses Minderheitenanteils stehen Umfang und Dichte einschlägiger Informationen bulgarischer Herkunft, seien sie nun amtlicher, wissenschaftlicher oder anderer Art. Dieses Informationsdefizit ist auf eine 1956 beschlossene und ab 1958 durchgeführte Wende in der staatlichen Nationalitätenpolitik zurückzuführen (s. V.). Seitdem sind nicht nur Quantität und Qualität der offiziellen Minderheitenstatistiken, sondern zugleich Intensität und Bandbreite bulgarischer geistes- und sozialwissenschaftlicher Forschung in diesem Bereich stark zurückgegangen[2]). Aus diesem Grunde basiert ein Großteil der nachstehenden Angaben auf Daten und Veröffentlichungen der 50er und 60er Jahre.

II. Grunddaten und internationaler Vergleich

Mit einem Minderheitenanteil, der nach den letzten amtlichen Angaben von 1965 bei 12,11 % (Tab. 1) liegt, unter Einschluß der staatlicherseits nicht mitgezählten ethnisch-religiösen Gruppen (Tab. 2) hingegen über 15 % betragen dürfte, steht das

---

[1]) Die – nicht unproblematische – Differenzierung zwischen nationalen Minderheiten und ethnisch-religiösen Gruppen, letztere als deutlich unterscheidbare Zwischenstufe zwischen den erstgenannten und dem Staatsvolk, erfolgt hier in Anlehnung an Weber, M.: Wirtschaft und Gesellschaft. Grundriß der verstehenden Soziologie. Tübingen 1985, 5. Aufl., S. 238.

[2]) Daher sind auch die bisherigen Übersichtsdarstellungen wenig informativ. Vgl. zuletzt Georgeoff, P. J. (with the assistance of D. Crowe): National Minorities in Bulgaria, 1919–1980, in: Eastern European National Minorities, 1919–1980. A Handbook. Ed. by S. M. Horak. Littleton, CO, 1985, S. 274–308.

Land in dieser Hinsicht auf einer Stufe mit Rumänien (1977: 10,9% Minderheiten) und dem Nationalitätenstaat Jugoslawien (1981: 13,2% Nichtslawen). Bulgarien rangiert somit deutlich vor den anderen Balkanstaaten Griechenland (1951: 4,4% Minderheiten) und Albanien (1989: 2,0% Minderheiten). Obwohl seit 1965 keine bulgarische Nationalitätenstatistik mehr veröffentlicht worden ist, kann selbst bei Anrechnung der Erfolge staatlicher Assimilations- und Aussiedlungspolitik von einem weiter wachsenden Minderheitenanteil ausgegangen werden. Dies ist in erster Linie auf das generative Verhalten der Muslime, v. a. der mit ca. 10% bzw. 1 Mio. stärksten Minderheit der Türken, zurückzuführen. Geburtenrate und natürliches

Tabelle 1: Bulgaren und nationale Minderheiten in Bulgarien 1946–1965 nach amtlichen Angaben (absolut u. in %)

Nationalität	1946		1956		1965	
Bulgaren	6 073 124	86,40	6 506 541	85,46	7 231 243	87,89
Türken	675 500	9,61	656 025	8,62	780 928	9,49
„Makedonier"	*		187 789	2,47	9 632	0,12
Roma			197 865	2,60	148 874	1,81
Armenier			21 954	0,29	20 282	0,25
Russen			10 551	0,14	10 815	0,13
Griechen			7 437	0,10	8 241	0,10
Juden			6 027	0,08	5 108	0,06
Tataren			5 993	0,08	6 430	0,08
Rumänen			3 749	0,05	763	0,01
Deutsche			747	0,01	795	0,01
Serben	280 725	3,99	484	0,01	577	0,01
Tschechen			1 199	0,02	1 012	0,01
Sonstige Slawen			1 100	0,01	974	0,01
Albaner			1 105	0,01	503	0,01
Ungarn			671	0,01	583	0,01
Karakatschanen			2 085	0,03		
Aromunen			487	0,01	1 106	0,01
Sonst. Nichtslawen			1 900	0,02		
Gesamtbevölkerung	7 029 349	100,00	7 613 709	100,02	8 227 866	100,01

Quellen: *1946:* [Centralno statističesko upravlenie pri Ministerskija săvet,] Rezultati ot prebrojavaneto na naselenieto na 1 dekemvri 1965 godina (tri procentova reprezentativna razrabotka) (Ergebnisse der Volkszählung vom 1. Dezember 1965 [Dreiprozentige repräsentative Ausarbeitung]). Sofia 1966, S. 45; *1956:* [Centralno statističesko upravlenie pri Ministerskija săvet,] Prebrojavane na naselenieto v Narodna republika Bălgarija na 1. XII. 1956. Obšti rezultati (semejstva, kategori naselenie, nacionalnost i ravnište na obrazovanie) (Volkszählung in der NRB am 1. XII. 1956. Allgemeine Ergebnisse [Familien, Bevölkerungskategorien, Nationalität und Bildungsniveau]). Kniga II. Sofia 1960, S. 106–109; *1965:* [Centralno statističesko upravlenie pri Ministerskija săvet,] Rezultati ot prebrojavane na naselenieto na 1. XII. 1965 g. Tom I, Čast părva: Obšto za NR Bălgarija (Ergebnisse der Volkszählung vom 1. XII. 1965. Bd. I, erster Teil: NRB insgesamt). Sofia 1968, S. 12.

* Zwei von jugoslawischer Seite veröffentlichte Zahlenangaben widersprechen sich: 1971 hieß es, beim Zensus vom 25.12.1946 seien für *ganz* Bulgarien 169 544 „Makedonier" (= 2,41%) gezählt worden (o. A., Šta, zaista, govore činjenice, in: Borba. 19. 8. 1971, S. 3), wohingegen 1975 allein für den Bezirk Blagoevgrad für 1946 die Zahl 252 908 (= 3,60%) genannt wurde (Vuković, P.: U službi starog, in: Politika. 7. 12. 1975, S. 2).

Wachstum (Per-annum-Durchschnittswerte) lagen im Zeitraum 1975–1984 in kompakt türkisch besiedelten Regionen wie etwa dem Ostrhodopen-Bezirk Kărdžali[3]) bei 29,7 bzw. 14,8 % (Landesschnitt im selben Zeitraum 15,0 bzw. 4,2 %). Noch krasser fällt dieser Unterschied aus, vergleicht man die Verhältnisse in den ländlichen Teilen des Bezirkes Kărdžali mit denjenigen auf dem bulgarischen Dorf insgesamt (23,3 bzw. 16,3 %; Landesschnitt: 12,8 bzw. − 2,4 %)[4]). Angaben aus den 80er Jahren zufolge beträgt der Jugendsockel der unter 15jährigen in türkischen Ballungsgebieten derzeit 35,3 % (Landesschnitt: 21,3 %)[5]). Der Exodus von ca. 1/4 der türkischen Bevölkerung (ca. 3 % der Gesamtbevölkerung) im Sommer 1989 hat die Relationen allerdings verschoben (s. u., IV.1.a.).

Aussagen über die geographische Verteilung der Minderheiten sind problematisch, da auch hier die letzten amtlichen bulgarischen Daten aus dem Jahre 1965[6]) und die letzte (sowjetische) Nationalitätenkarte aus dem Jahr 1964[7]) stammen. Nationale Minderheiten und ethnisch-religiöse Gruppen siedeln im Südwesten (Pomaken), Südosten (Türken, Pomaken) und Nordosten (Türken) des Landes, wohingegen der Nordwesten einen geringen Minderheitenanteil aufweist. Die genannte stärkste Gruppe der bulgarischen Türken siedelt relativ geschlossen in den beiden Ballungsräume des Deli orman-Vierecks Ruse-Silistra-Varna-Šumen und in den östlichen Rhodopen.

Ein deutlicher Unterschied zwischen Bulgarien und seinen Nachbarstaaten ist in bezug auf die Rechtsstellung der Minderheiten auszumachen: Während die Verfassungen der anderen südosteuropäischen Staaten personalrechtliche, z. T. sogar territorialrechtliche Minderheitengarantien enthalten, kennt die bulgarische Verfassung vom 16. 5. 1971 keinen kollektiven Minderheitenbegriff. Im Gegensatz zur sog. Dimitrov-Verfassung vom 4. 12. 1947, in deren Art. 79 nationalen Minderheiten (*nacionali malcinstva*) das Recht auf Muttersprache (*majčin ezik*) und nationale Kultur (*nacionalna kultura*) garantiert wurde, ist in der neuen Verfassung nur noch von „Bürgern nichtbulgarischer Abstammung" (*graždane ot nebălgarski proizchod*) die Rede. Letztgenannten, so heißt es in Art. 45, Absatz 7, wird als einzige minderheitenrechtliche Konzession „das Recht, außer der obligatorischen Erlernung der bulgarischen Sprache auch ihre eigene Sprache (*svoi ezik*) zu lernen", zugestanden. Dem steht entgegen, daß es seit den 70er Jahren kein Minderheitenschulwesen mehr gibt. Gleichfalls im Gegensatz zu den übrigen Staaten Südosteuropas gibt es in Bulgarien auch keine verfassungsmäßige Verankerung der Rechte auf Gebrauch der Muttersprache im außerhäuslichen Bereich oder auf kulturelle Entfaltung, etwa in Form von Vereinen. Auch hinsichtlich der Verfassungs*wirklichkeit* unterscheidet sich Bul-

---

[3]) Vor 1959 Kreis des Bezirks, seit 1987 Teil des Gebiets Chaskovo.
[4]) Höpken, W.: Modernisierung und Nationalismus: Sozialgeschichtliche Aspekte der bulgarischen Minderheitenpolitik gegenüber den Türken, in: Nationalitätenprobleme in Südosteuropa. Hrsg. v. R. Schönfeld. München 1987, S. 255–280, hier S. 268.
[5]) Höpken (Anm. 4), S. 267.
[6]) Rezultati: Obšto 1965 (wie Tab. 1).
[7]) In: Narody zarubežnoj Evropy (Die Völker des europäischen Auslandes). Hrsg. v. S. A. Tokarev u. N. N. Čeboksarov. T. I. Moskau 1964, zwischen S. 302 u. 303. Vgl. auch die detailliertere Karte für das Jahr 1926 bei Kosack (wie Tab. 2), Beilage.

garien in der Behandlung nationaler Minderheiten negativ von seinen Nachbarn. Beobachtern der gegenwärtigen bulgarischen Minderheitenpolitik „stellt sich sogar die Frage, ob die 1985 kulminierende Kampagne zur Zwangsbulgarisierung der Türken, bei der es u. a. zu Mißhandlungen und Tötungen gekommen ist, nicht schon den Tatbestand des Völkermordes im Sinne von Art. II der Genozid-Konvention erfüllt hat"[8]).

Tabelle 2: Ethnisch-religiöse Gruppen in Bulgarien 1926–1973 (bulgarische und westliche Schätzungen absolut und in %)

Ethn.-rel. Gruppe	1926		1956		1970		1973	
Pomaken	102 351	1,87	130 000	1,71	ca. 170 000	ca. 2,02		
Gagausen	4 362	0,08					ca. 5 000	ca. 0,06
Gesamtbevölkerung	5 478 741		7 613 709		ca. 8 400 000		ca. 8 650 000	

Quellen: *1926:* Kosack, H.-P.: Ein Beitrag zur Methodik der Bevölkerungskarten. Nationalitätenkarte von Bulgarien, in: Zeitschrift der Gesellschaft für Erdkunde zu Berlin. (1937) 9–10, S. 348–372, hier S. 359; *1956*: Penkov, I.; Penkova, M.: Ikonomičeskata geografija na Narodna republika Bălgarija. Učebnik za učitelskite institucii (Wirtschaftsgeographie der NRB, Lehrbuch für Lehrerbildungsanstalten). Sofia 1956², S. 26; *1970*: [CK na BKP,] Bjuletin. Nr. 5, avgust 1970, S. 2 (nach Monov, C.: Prosvetnoto delo sred bălgarite s mohamedanska vjara v Rodopskija kraj prez godinite na narodnata vlast [1944-1968] [Das Bildungswesen bei den Bulgaren mit mohammedanischem Glauben im Rhodopengebiet in den Jahren der Volksmacht (1944–1968)], in: Rodopski sbornik. III [1972], S. 9–51, hier S. 11); *1973*: Guy Hérard, L'Europe des ethnies. Paris 1973², S. 184.

III. Historischer Hintergrund

So groß das Interesse des bulgarischen Staates an den bulgarischen Minderheiten in den Nachbarländern und in Übersee seit jeher ist, so gering ist dasjenige an den nationalen und ethnisch-religiösen Minderheiten im eigenen Land. Aus diesem Grund liegen kaum ältere, geschweige denn neuere historische, ethnographische oder soziologische Untersuchungen über einzelne Minderheiten vor, so daß diesbezüglich vorwiegend auf nichtbulgarische Darstellungen zurückgegriffen werden muß[9]).

Die Geschichte der nationalen Minderheiten und ethnisch-religiösen Gruppen im 1878 gegründeten, 1885 mit Ostrumelien vereinigten bulgarischen Staat ist die Geschichte eines Schrumpfungs-, Konzentrations- und Assimilationsprozesses. Stellten die Minderheiten 1880/81 noch 1/3 der Bevölkerung der beiden bulgarischen Teil-

---

[8]) Brunner, G.: Zusammenfassung, in: Menschenrechte in den Staaten des Warschauer Paktes. Bericht der unabhängigen Wissenschaftlerkommission. Bonn 1988 (= Bundestags-Drucksache 11/1344), S. 229.
[9]) V. a. auf Crampton, R. J.: Bulgaria, 1878–1918: A History. Boulder, CO, New York, NY, 1983 (s. bes. die Tabellen auf S. 176 u. 348).

staaten dar (Türken allein 1/4)[10], so war ihr Anteil 1965, wie erwähnt, auf 1/6 geschrumpft (Türken allein 1/10). Neben der Immigration von Bulgaren hat v. a. die Emigration von ca. 1,1 Mio. Türken, Pomaken und Roma ins Osmanische Reich bzw. in die Türkei im Zeitraum 1878–1989 die ethnischen Relationen verschoben[11]).

Nicht nur das Vorhandensein starker Minderheiten überwiegend islamischer Konfession, sondern auch die Einstellung von Staat und Staatsvolk diesen Minderheiten gegenüber müssen im Zusammenhang mit dem komplexen „osmanischen Erbe" des bulgarischen Nationalstaats gesehen werden. Bestandteil dieses „Erbes" ist auch die Existenz der hier als ethnisch-religiöse Gruppen bezeichneten Minderheiten von Pomaken und Gagausen. Dem liegt die in den autonomen konfessionellen Gemeinschaften (*millet*) der osmanischen Spätphase institutionalisierte gesellschaftliche Grenzziehung entlang konfessioneller Trennungslinien[12]), nicht ethnischer, sprachlicher o. a., zugrunde. Daher sind die Mehrzahl der Nationalitätenprobleme in Bulgarien nicht nur in einem Nationalismus vs. Kommunismus-Zusammenhang zu sehen; sie sind zugleich – wenn nicht vor allem – die Antwort islamisch-traditionaler Teilgesellschaften auf staatlich-profane Modernisierungsansprüche. Derartige Ansprüche werden von seiten des Staates seit 1878 kontinuierlich gestellt, wobei die Zäsurjahre 1934 (Errichtung eines autoritär-korporativen Regimes mit assimilatorischen Zielsetzungen), 1958 (Beginn der assimilatorischen Phase in der Nationalitätenpolitik der Nachkriegszeit) und 1984 (Einsetzen massiven Assimilationsdrucks v. a. auf die Türken) jeweils das Erreichen einer neuen qualitativen Stufe markieren.

IV. Nationale Minderheiten und ethnisch-religiöse Gruppen

1. Nationale Minderheiten

a) Türken

Einige Charakteristika dieser mit Abstand stärksten Minderheit wurden bereits in den Abschnitten II und III genannt; nachstehend daher noch einige Kennziffern: 86,24% der 1956 gezählten 656025 Türken (1965: 780928) lebten auf dem Lande, 69,95% allein in den drei (damaligen) Bezirken Chaskovo, Ruse und Kolarovgrad (Šumen)[13]). Die höchste regionale Konzentration wurde 1956 in den Ostrhodopen erreicht, wo der Kreis Kărdžali-Land im Bezirk Chaskovo mit 89,37% türkischer Bevölkerung an der Spitze lag. Das Bildungsniveau der Türken in Bulgarien war damals extrem niedrig: Einer Analphabetenrate von 36,24% stand eine Hochschul-

---

[10]) Ebenda, S. 176.

[11]) Jackson, M. R.: Changes in Ethnic Populations of Southeastern Europe: Holocaust, Migration and Assimilation – 1940 to 1970, in: Nationalitätenprobleme (Anm. 4), S. 73–104, bes. S. 78–80.

[12]) Vgl. zu den Spätfolgen des *millet*-Systems in Bulgarien Karpat, K. H.: *Millets* and Nationality, in: Christians and Jews in the Ottoman Empire. Ed. by B. Braude & B. Lewis. Vol. I. New York, London 1982, S. 141–169, bes. S. 165–167.

[13]) Diese, wie auch sämtliche nachfolgenden Daten für 1956 stammen aus Prebrojavane 1956 (wie Tab. 1), diejenigen für 1965 aus Rezultati: Obšto 1965 (ebenda).

absolventenrate von 0,04% gegenüber (Landesschnitt seinerzeit: 13,09% bzw. 1,73%; Bulgaren: 9,87% bzw. 1,93%). Und noch 1965, als die Analphabetenrate landesweit 9,47% betrug, gab es im (neuen) Bezirk Kărdžali, dessen Bevölkerung zu diesem Zeitpunkt zu 49,02% aus Türken bestand, 21,0% Analphabeten. Bis 1975 war es gelungen, die Bildungsstruktur partiell zu verbessern, doch gab es immer noch einen überproportional großen Anteil von Türken ohne Schulbildung sowie einen unterproportionalen Anteil bei Mittel-, höheren und Hochschulabschlüssen[14]).

Dies schlug sich auch in der Sozialstruktur nieder: 1975 etwa waren 29,0% aller Türken Genossenschaftsbauern – ein Beruf, den damals nur 6,7% aller Bürger des Landes ausübten; 4,9% türkischen Angestellten stand eine Angestelltenquote von 26,7% im Landesschnitt gegenüber; und nur der Anteil der türkischen Arbeiter (64,4%) deckte sich mit dem Landesschnitt (64,2%). Allerdings war die Mehrheit von ihnen in der Landwirtschaft (56,1%), nicht in der Industrie (20,9%) beschäftigt.

Die breite Palette türkischer Regionalzeitungen ist 1959 und erneut 1968 stark reduziert worden. 1981 gab es neben der Monatsschrift *Yeni hayat* (Neues Leben) nur noch die Wochenzeitung *Yeni ışık* (Neues Licht). Unter dem Titel *Nova svetlina* (Neues Licht) wird sie vom ZK der BKP dreimal wöchentlich herausgegeben, seit 1985 ausschließlich in bulgarischer Sprache[15]). Das mehrstufige türkische Schulwesen ist ab 1958 schrittweise abgebaut worden und in den 70er Jahren verschwunden[16]).

Die Türken Bulgariens besitzen keine eigenen Vereine bzw. Kultur- und Bildungsorganisationen. Zuständig für ihre kulturellen u.a. Belange waren bis Ende 1984 spezielle „Kommissionen für die türkische Minderheit" (*Türk azınlığı komisyonu*) in den Führungsgremien von BKP und OF.

Seitdem gelten die bulgarischen Türken in offizieller Sicht als „bulgarische Muslime", werden also wie die Pomaken dem bulgarischen Staatsvolk zugerechnet. Ihre islamisch-arabischen Vor-, Vaters- und Familiennamen wurden 1984/85 auf administrativem Wege durch christlich-slawische Namensformen ersetzt, das Türkische als Minderheitensprache landesweit abgeschafft und die Möglichkeit weiterer Auswanderung bzw. Familienzusammenführung, wie bis 1978 bzw. 1983 in Abkommen mit der Türkei vertraglich geregelt, ausdrücklich verneint. Die intensive, „wissenschaftlich" verbrämte Propagierung dieser neuen Sichtweise auch im Ausland hat die Beziehungen Bulgariens zur islamischen Welt getrübt und ein bis dahin wenig dringliches, internes Minderheitenproblem zu einem zentralen Konfliktpunkt in den Beziehungen vor allem zum NATO- und Nachbarstaat Türkei gemacht. Um die Jahreswende 1984/85 sowie erneut im Mai 1989 kam es zu schweren Zusammenstößen

---

[14]) Vgl. hierzu sowie zum folgenden Höpken (Anm. 4), S. 264–266, und Memišev, J.: Zadružno v socialističeskoto stroitelstvo na rodina (Priobštavane na bălgarskite turci kăm izgraždaneto na socializma) (Einig im sozialistischen Aufbau der Heimat (Die Einbindung der bulgarischen Türken in den Aufbau des Sozialismus)). Sofia 1984, hier S. 167–189.

[15]) Eine Übersicht der im Zeitraum 1944–1969 erscheinenden türkischsprachigen Blätter s. in: Bălgarski periodičen pečat 1944–1969. Bibliografski ukazatel (Bulgarische Periodika 1944–1969. Bibliographischer Wegweiser). T. II. Sofia 1975, S. 430–436.

[16]) Bachmaier, P.: Assimilation oder Kulturautonomie. Das Schulwesen der nationalen Minderheiten in Bulgarien nach dem 9. September 1944, in: Österreichische Osthefte. 26 (1984), S. 391–404.

zwischen Angehörigen der Minderheit, Miliz und Militär, und im Sommer 1989 wurden ungefähr 310 000 bulgarische Türken (Stand Mitte August) in die Türkei ausgewiesen.

b) „Makedonier"

Die „Makedonier" werden hier als einzige nationale Minderheit in Anführungszeichen gesetzt, da von den Ergebnissen der bulgarischen Volkszählungen der Jahre 1946, 1956 und bedingt auch 1965 abgesehen nur wenig auf ihre tatsächliche Existenz hindeutet. Den historischen Hintergrund dieses merkwürdigen Sachverhaltes bildet der Ende des 19. Jh. entstandene, als Makedonische Frage bezeichnete Konflikt zwischen Bulgarien, Serbien und Griechenland, der derzeit in Form zweier scharfer Kontroversen zwischen Bulgarien und Griechenland auf der einen sowie Jugoslawien bzw. der jugoslawischen Teilrepublik Makedonien auf der anderen Seite seine Fortsetzung findet[17]. Während Bulgarien ebenso wie Griechenland die Existenz eines makedonischen Ethnicums generell in Abrede stellt, postuliert Jugoslawien das Vorhandensein eines solchen nicht nur für die eigene (vardar)makedonische Republik, sondern zugleich für das zu Bulgarien gehörende Pirin-Makedonien (1946–1987 Bezirk Blagoevgrad, seitdem Teil des Gebietes Sofia), für das nordgriechische Ägäisch-Makedonien sowie für das ostalbanische Grenzgebiet um Bilishti. Die „Ethnogenese" der 1965 einem – nach jugoslawischer Lesart: – „statistischen Genozid" zum Opfer gefallenen „Makedonier" Bulgariens fällt in die nationalitätenpolitisch turbulente Phase 1944–1958. Die Makedonien-Strategie von Partei und Staat in Bulgarien beinhaltete damals die Anerkennung eines makedonischen Ethnicums sowohl im Innern, also in Pirin-Makedonien, als auch nach außen, in bezug auf Jugoslawien und Griechenland. Die offizielle bulgarische Ansicht von der Existenz einer nationalen Minderheit der „Makedonier" im Lande überdauerte den bulgarisch-jugoslawischen Bruch von 1948 und besaß bis 1953 volle Gültigkeit. Diese verlor sie zwar sukzessiv in der Entstalinisierungsphase, doch zögerte man mit der Verkündung einer neuen Sprachregelung. So erklärte etwa ein hoher Parteifunktionär noch im September 1958, in Bulgarien „hindert niemand einen Bürger, sich als Makedonier zu deklarieren, wenn er sich als solcher fühlt"[18]. Beim Zensus von 1965 gaben im Pirin-Bezirk Blagoevgrad nur noch 1437 Personen als Nationalität „Makedonier"[19] an, während es 1956 noch 178 862 gewesen waren (Tab. 1). Der Anteil der „Makedonier" an der Bezirksbevölkerung war also binnen zehn Jahren von 63,65 % auf 0,47 % gesunken. Die Zahl der „Makedonier" im übrigen Bulgarien veränderte sich jedoch nur wenig (1956: 8927, 1965: 8195). Unmittelbar nach dem Zensus vom 1.12.1965 sprach RD nicht mehr von „Makedoniern", sondern von „den Auswanderern aus Makedonien als untrennbarem Bestandteil der bulgarischen Nation". Diese Kurswende war be-

---

[17] Troebst, S.: Die bulgarisch-jugoslawische Kontroverse um Makedonien 1967–1983. München 1983; Kofos, E.: The Macedonian Question: The Politics of Mutation, in: Balkan Studies. 27 (1986), S. 157–172.
[18] Reč na dr. Dimităr Ganev (Rede des Genossen D. Ganev), in: RD. 22.9.1958, S. 1–2, hier S. 2.
[19] Rezultati: Obšto 1965 (wie Tab. 1), S. 500.

reits im März 1963 von einem geheimen ZK-Plenum zur Makedonischen Frage beschlossen worden[20]).

1956 entfielen 92,25% der Makedonier auf den Pirin-Bezirk Blagoevgrad, in dessen fünf Kreisen ihre Stärke unterschiedlich war: Blagoevgrad (Gorna Džumaja) 52,19%, Goce Delčev (Nevrokop) 45,78%, Petrič 82,62%, Razlog (Mechomija) 49,09% und Sandanski (Sveti Vrač) 89,49%. Während die „Makedonier" im Pirin-Gebiet überwiegend Landbewohner waren, siedelten sie im übrigen Bulgarien in den Städten, v. a. in Sofia, Varna, Burgas, Plovdiv und Chaskovo.

Ein Relikt des makedonienpolitischen Kurses der BKP der 50er Jahre ist der „Bund der makedonischen Kultur- und Bildungsvereine in Bulgarien" (*Săjuz na makedonskite kulturno-prosvetni družestva v Bălgarija*), dessen „Zentrale Leitung" ein *Bjuletin* publiziert[21]). Das makedonischsprachige Schulwesen im Bezirk Blagoevgrad ist in den frühen 50er Jahren in das bulgarische eingegliedert worden. Bezeichnenderweise spielte und spielt national motivierter Dissens von „Makedoniern" in Bulgarien keine Rolle. Dies mag nicht nur mit der Künstlichkeit des „Makedonier"-Konzeptes, sondern auch mit dem auf einen Beschluß von ZK und Ministerrat vom 4. 7. 1968 „Über die Verbesserung der Ökonomie des Bezirkes Blagoevgrad"[21a]) hin begonnenen, Mitte der 80er Jahre seinen Höhepunkt erreichenden ambitionierten Entwicklungsprojekt für das Pirin-Gebiet zusammenhängen.

c) Roma

Während den letzten greifbaren amtlichen Angaben zufolge die Zahl der Roma in Bulgarien (*cigani*, Selbstbezeichnung *rom*) im Zeitraum 1956–1965 um 1/4 auf 148 874 zurückgegangen sein soll (Tab. 1), wird sie im Ausland auf deutlich über 200 000 geschätzt[22]).

Nach religiösen und sprachlichen Kriterien werden die bulgarischen Roma in drei Gruppen eingeteilt: a) orthodoxe, bulgarischsprachige „bulgarische Roma" (*erlija* u. a.), b) muslimische, türkischsprachige „türkische Roma" (*chorachane*), und c) orthodoxe, rumänischsprachige „vlachische Roma" (*kopanari* u. a.). Darüber hinaus spricht eine im Abnehmen begriffene Zahl der Roma das lange schriftlose neuindische Romani. Den Volkszählungsangaben von 1965 zufolge sprachen 42,56% der Roma als Hauptsprache Bulgarisch, 22,81% Türkisch und 34,24% Romani. 1965 lebten 61,6% der Roma in ländlichen Siedlungen, 38,4% in städtischen. Siedlungsschwerpunkte waren die Bezirke Plovdiv, Tărgovište und Chaskovo. Neueren Infor-

---

[20]) O. A.: V služba na socializma, mira i razbiratelstvoto (Im Dienste des Sozialismus, des Friedens und der Verständigung), in: RD. 27.12.1965, S. 3. Zum Plenum von 1963 vgl. Troebst (Anm. 17), S. 98, sowie jetzt detailliert Grigorova, Ž.: Balkanskata politika na socialističeska Bălgarija 1944–1970 (Die Balkanpolitik des sozialistischen Bulgarien 1944–1970). Sofia 1985, S. 290–292.
[21]) Ebenda. Zum *Bjuletin* vgl. Bălgarskata istoričeska nauka. Bibliografija. T. 4: 1975–1979 (Die bulgarische Geschichtswissenschaft. Bibliographie). Sofia 1981, S. 330, 355 u. 877.
[21a]) Monov (Tab. 2), S. 48.
[22]) Vgl. hierzu sowie zum folgenden: Silverman, C.: Bulgarian Gypsies: Adaption in a Socialist Context, erscheint in: Nomadic Peoples. Nos. 21/22, Ms. 1987, 20 S. (mit weiterführender Literatur); Genov, D.; Marinov, V.; Tairov, T.: Ciganskoto naselenie v NRB po pătja na socializma (Die Zigeunerbevölkerung in der NRB auf dem Wege zum Sozialismus). Sofia 1964.

mationen zufolge soll die Stadt Sliven mit 30 000 Roma ein Zentrum der „bulgarischen Roma" geworden sein.

Obwohl den Roma das Nomadisieren in einer eigens erlassenen Anweisung des Ministerrates „Über die Regelung der Fragen der Zigeunerbevölkerung" vom 17.12.1958[22a]) untersagt wurde, ist ihre Berufsstruktur noch zu einem großen Teil traditional-mobil. Roma leben zwar offiziell seßhaft, sind aber häufig monatelang als Musiker, Bärenführer, Pferdehändler, Wanderhandwerker u.a. unterwegs. Diejenigen Roma, deren Lebensweise stationär ist, stehen fast ausschließlich in Arbeitsverhältnissen mit extrem niedrigem Sozialprestige (Stadtreinigung). 1965 waren nur 40,8 % der Roma als erwerbstätig gemeldet (Landesschnitt: 51,9 %). Einer neueren Untersuchung zufolge ist die Besetzung „ökonomischer Nischen" (C. Silverman) typisch für die beruflichen Aktivitäten der bulgarischen Roma.

Das Bildungsniveau der Roma war in der Vergangenheit äußerst niedrig: So waren 1956 trotz des damals noch existenten Roma-Schulsystems[23]) 55,89 % aller über 7 Jahre alten Angehörigen dieser Minderheit Analphabeten (Landesschnitt: 13,09 %; Bulgaren: 9,87 %). Über die gegenwärtige Schulsituation liegen nur spärliche Daten vor. 1975 soll es in Bulgarien 145 Internate gegeben haben, in denen 10 000 Roma-Kinder aus halbnomadischen Familien zwangsweise lebten[24]).

Die 1946 gegründete „Kultur- und Bildungsorganisation der Zigeunerminderheit in Bulgarien" (*Kulturno-prosvetna organizacija na ciganskoto malcinstvo v Bălgarija*) ist im Laufe der 50er Jahre aufgelöst bzw. in die OF eingegliedert worden. Anstelle der kurzlebigen, auf Romani erscheinenden Zeitschriften *Romano-esi* (Roma-Stimme) (1946–1949), *Nevo drom* (Neuer Weg) (1949–1950) und *Neve romă* (Neuer Rom) (1957) begann die OF 1959 mit der Herausgabe der überwiegend bulgarischsprachigen Monatsschrift *Nov păt / Nevo drom* (Neuer Weg), die seit 1968 als *Nov păt* nur noch auf Bulgarisch erscheint[25]).

d) Armenier

Im Zeitraum 1896–1922/24 gelangten mehrere Wellen armenischer Flüchtlinge aus dem Osmanischen Reich, der Türkei und der UdSSR nach Bulgarien, wo sie zusammen mit einer dort seit dem Mittelalter lebenden kleinen armenischen Minderheit 1926 mit 27 322 Personen 0,5 % der Bevölkerung stellten. Seit der Zwischenkriegszeit gibt es eine Emigrationsbewegung nach Westeuropa und nach Übersee. Ein armenisches „Repatriierungskomitee" (*Komitet po repatriacija*) strebte 1946–1950

[22a]) Georgieva, I.: Izsledvanija vărchu bita i kulturata na bălgarskite cigani v Sliven (Untersuchungen zu Lebensweise und Kultur der bulgarischen Zigeuner in Sliven), in: Izvestija na etnografskija institut i muzej. IX (1966), S. 25–50, hier S. 32, Anm. 12.

[23]) Bachmaier (Anm. 16), S. 399/400.

[24]) Puxon, G.: Rom: Europe's Gypsies. London 1975², S. 13 (= Minority Rights Group Report, No. 14). Diese Angabe wird durch einen bulgarischen Zeitungsbericht bestätigt, demzufolge „auf Beschluß des ZK der BKP" in den Jahren 1962 und 1963 insgesamt 7000 Roma-Kinder neu in Internatsschulen aufgenommen wurden (Otečestven front. 15.3.1963, S. 4).

[25]) BPP II (Anm. 15), S. 63, 68/69 u. 181/182. Vgl. auch Puxon (Anm. 24), S. 13.

die Auswanderung in die Armenische Sozialistische Sowjetrepublik an, doch kam es erst 1955/1956 zu einem kurzfristigen Emigrationsschub[26]).

Von den 1956 gezählten 21 954 Armeniern (1965: 20 282) wohnte 1/4 in Plovdiv und 1/5 in Sofia. Auch die übrigen waren überwiegend Städter; nur 3,43 % lebten auf dem Land.

Gleich den Juden in Bulgarien werden die Armenier von staatlicher Seite als „Vorzeigeminderheit" behandelt, was seinen Grund nicht zuletzt in der Existenz der erwähnten Sowjetrepublik hat. Dies bedeutet zum einen, daß eine Erwähnung der Armenier in Bulgarien als Ethnicum auch derzeit noch möglich ist, wenngleich unter dem obligaten Hinweis darauf, daß sie ein integraler Bestandteil des bulgarischen Volkes sind, und zum anderen, daß die am 22.10.1944 in Sofia gegründete „Kultur- und Bildungsorganisation ‚Erevan' der Armenier in Bulgarien" (*Kulturno-prosvetna organizacija ‚Erevan' na armencite v Bălgarija*) samt der ihr angegliederten „Armenischen progressiven Jugendorganisation" (*Armenska mladežka progresivna organizacija (ŽAF)*) in streng abgestecktem Rahmen weiter tätig sein kann. Die „Zentrale Leitung" von ‚Erevan' gibt die Wochenzeitung *Erevan* heraus, deren Text zu Teilen armenisch ist[27]).

Das private armenische Schulwesen wurde 1946 vom Staat übernommen und 1962 mit dem bulgarischen fusioniert[28]).

e) Russen

Die 1956 gezählten 10 551 Russen (1965: 10 815) lebten zu 1/3 in der Hauptstadt, während der Rest relativ gleichmäßig auf alle übrigen Bezirke verteilt war. 3/4 der Russen wohnten in Städten. Auffallend war 1956 der Altersaufbau der russischen Minderheit: Über die Hälfte war über 60 Jahre alt, darunter 3/4 Männer, und nur knapp 5 % waren Kinder bis zu 8 Jahren. Die große Mehrheit der Russen waren sog. weiße Emigranten, die ihre russische Heimat im Zuge des Bürgerkrieges 1918–1922 verlassen mußten und von denen insgesamt 29 000 zunächst in Bulgarien blieben[29]). Kleinere Gruppen sind Nachfahren von Don- und Zaporoger Kosaken, die im 18. Jh. eingewandert sind, oder von orthodoxen Altgläubigen, die zwischen 1830 und 1840 immigrierten und noch im Jahre 1961 die gesamte Bevölkerung der Dörfer Ajdemir (Bezirk Silistra) und Kazaško (Bezirk Varna) stellten[30]).

---

[26]) Art. Armenci (Armenier), in: Enciklopedija Bălgarija (Enzyklopädie Bulgarien). T. 1, Sofia 1978, S. 121; Pejkov, I. (Red.): Pătevoditel po fondovete na Centralnija Dăržaven Archiv na NRB (Führer durch die Bestände des Zentralen Staatsarchivs der NRB). Sofia 1975, S. 251. Vgl. auch Kasabjan, Ž. M.: Očerki istorii armjanskoj obščiny v Bolgarii (1896–1970 gg.) (Grundzüge der Geschichte der armenischen Gemeinschaft in Bulgarien 1896–1970). Erevan 1986.
[27]) Pejkov (Red.) (Anm. 26), S. 250; Bălgarski periodičen pečat. Vestnici, spisanija, bjuletini i periodični sbornici 1981. Godišen ukazatel (Bulgarische Periodik. Zeitungen, Zeitschriften, Bulletins und periodische Sammelbände 1981. Jahresverzeichnis). Sofia 1983, S. 15.
[28]) Bachmaier (Anm. 16), S. 398/399.
[29]) Vgl. Karte 41 bei Kosack (wie Tab. 2), S. 355.
[30]) Vgl. zu diesen *lipovani* genannten Russen: Geografija na Bălgarija (Geographie Bulgariens). Hrsg. v. A. S. Beškov & E. B. Valev. T. 2. Sofia 1961, S. 5.

f) Griechen

Die 1956 gezählten 7437 Griechen (1965: 8241) teilten sich in 2/3 Stadtbevölkerung, konzentriert in Sofia, Plovdiv, Varna und Pomorie, und 1/3 ländliche Bevölkerung in den Räumen Kazanlăk und Burgas. Die griechische Minderheit in Bulgarien besteht zum einen aus den Resten der beiden Gruppen der Schwarzmeer- und nordthrakischen Griechen (1900: 70887 bzw. 1,89 % der damaligen Gesamtbevölkerung), deren Hauptteil im Zeitraum 1900–1926, v. a. nach den Pogromen von 1906[31]) nach Griechenland ausgewandert ist[32]), zum anderen aus politischen Emigranten, die im Zuge des griechischen Bürgerkrieges 1946–1949 ins Land gekommen sind. Als „Organ der griechischen Politemigranten in Bulgarien" erscheint seit 1949 die griechischsprachige Wochenzeitung *Lefteria* (Freiheit)[33]).

g) Tataren

Im Gegensatz zu den von der osmanischen Zentralgewalt in der zweiten Hälfte des 19. Jh. ebenfalls in Nord- bzw. „Donaubulgarien" sowie in der Dobrudscha angesiedelten Tscherkessen verließen die aus der Krim stammenden Tataren die Region nach 1878 nicht vollständig. 86,37 % der 1956 gezählten 5993 muslimischen Tataren (1965: 6430) siedelten in Dörfern Nordost-Bulgariens.

h) Juden

Nachdem im Zeitraum 1946–1956 39206 der 1946 gezählten 44209, überwiegend sephardischen Juden (*evrei*) aus Bulgarien nach Palästina, ab 1948 nach Israel ausgewandert waren[34]), wurden 1956 nur noch 6027 Juden gezählt (1965: 5108). Diese lebten ausschließlich in Städten, über die Hälfte davon in Sofia, v. a. im Minderheitenviertel Jučbunar (heute Dimitrov-Stadtbezirk). Jüdische Gemeinden gab es weiter in Plovdiv, Stanke Dimitrov (Dupnica), Kjustendil, Ruse, Pleven, Burgas und Varna. Aufgrund hohen Bildungsniveaus üben Angehörige der jüdischen Minderheit überwiegend qualifizierte Berufe aus.

Trotz der antisemitischen Politik der bulgarischen Regierungen während des II. Weltkrieges gelang den beiden wichtigsten jüdischen Dachorganisationen 1944 eine rasche Neuformierung: Das konservative, für weltliche *und* religiöse Belange zuständige „Zentrale Konsistorium der Juden in Bulgarien" (*Centralna konsistorija*

---

[31]) Crampton (Anm. 9), S. 296–298.
[32]) Vgl. Karte 46 bei Kosack (wie Tab. 2), S. 364. – Aus bulg. Sicht sind die Griechen um Elchovo gräzisierte Bulgaren (*karioti*) (Art. Gărci (Griechen), in: EB (Anm. 26). T. 2. Sofia 1981, S. 206).
[33]) BPP GU 1981 (Anm. 27), S. 31.
[34]) Vasileva, B.: Săzdavaneto na Izrael i izselvaneto na evreite ot Bălgarija (1944–1949 g.) (Die Gründung Israels und die Aussiedlung der Juden aus Bulgarien 1944–1949), in: Izvestija na Bălgarskoto istoričesko družestvo (Mitteilungen der Bulgarischen Historischen Gesellschaft). 38 (1986), S. 303–331, bes.S. 312–314; Israel, S.: The Bulgarian Jews During the Years of People's Rule, in: Annual of the Social, Cultural and Educational association of the Jews in the People's Republic of Bulgaria. 6 (1971), S. 112. Vgl. auch Oschlies, W.: The Jews in Bulgaria since 1944, in: Soviet Jewish Affairs. 14 (1984), 2, S. 41–54.

na evreite v Bǎlgarija) wurde dabei von Partei und Staat unterstützt. Dies war bei der unabhängigen „Zionistischen Einheitsorganisation" (*Edinna cionistka organizacija*), deren Politik maßgeblich von ihrer sozialistischen Unterorganisation *Poale Zion* bestimmt wurde, nicht der Fall. Trotz der engen Kooperation mit dem „Zentralen Konsistorium" gründeten sowohl die BRP (k) als auch die OF eigene jüdische Kommissionen bzw. Komitees (*Centralna evrejska komisija pri CK na BRP (k)* und *Centralen evrejski komitet na OF*). Das letztgenannte Komitee gab die Zeitung *Evrejski vesti* (Jüdische Nachrichten) heraus, welche zwar politisch gegen das Organ der Zionistischen Einheitsorganisation, *Cionističeska tribuna* (Zionistische Tribüne), Front machte, in der Auswanderungsfrage hingegen mit dieser weitgehend konform ging.

Seit dem Ende der 40er Jahre gibt es anstelle der vier genannten jüdischen Organisationen nur noch zwei: Für religiöse Belange ist nun der „Israelitische geistliche Zentralrat" (*Centralen izrailtjanski duchoven sǎvet*) zuständig, und nicht-religiöse Interessen können theoretisch von der „Gesellschaftlichen Kultur- und Bildungsorganisation der Juden in der NRB" (*Obštestvena kulturno-prosvetna organizacija na evreite v NRB (OKPOE)*) wahrgenommen werden. Zionistische Organisationen gibt es in Bulgarien nicht mehr. Die Zentrale Leitung der OKPOE gibt weiterhin die „Jüdischen Nachrichten", allerdings nur 14-tägig, sowie ein wissenschaftliches „Jahrbuch" (*Godišnik*) mit einer englischen Parallelversion heraus[35]. In all diesen Publikationen wie auch in denjenigen das „Zentralrats" wird die bulgarische Sprache, nicht das umgangssprachliche Judenspanisch bzw. Ladino (*džudezmo*) oder das Hebräische, verwendet.

Das 1941 abgeschaffte und 1944 wiederhergestellte jüdische Schulwesen ist mit dem Exodus der späten 40er Jahre verschwunden. Auch andere jüdische Einrichtungen wie die Sofioter Bank „Galua" (*Banka „Galua"*), das Jüdische Krankenhaus und Klinik (*Evrejska bolnica i klinika*) oder das Jüdische Wissenschaftliche Institut an der BAN (*Evrejski naučen institut kǎm BAN*) wurden bulgarischen Institutionen angeschlossen[36].

i) Sonstige

Mit 3749 Mitgliedern war 1956 die *rumänische* Minderheit die stärkste unter den kleineren Minoritäten, doch schon 1965 zählte sie nur noch 763 Personen. 1956 waren die Rumänen zu mehr als 4/5 Dorfbewohner mit Siedlungsschwerpunkten um die Städte Vraca und Pavlikeni im Norden des Landes. Auch in den damaligen Bezirken Pleven, Ruse und Burgas wurden jeweils etliche hundert Rumänen gezählt. Sie alle bildeten die „Nachhut" einer noch 1926 33 634 Personen (0,61 %) starken Minderheit, die durch eine anhaltende Aussiedlungsbewegung nach Rumänien mit Höhepunkten um 1939/40 und nach 1944 verkleinert worden ist[37].

3/4 der 1956 gezählten 2085 orthodoxen *Karakatschanen* (*karakačani*, Selbstbezeichnung *vlachó*) (1965: keine Angabe) bewohnten damals als Winterquartiere Dörfer nahe den Städten Sozopol und Sliven. Bei ihnen handelt es sich um transhumante

---

[35]) BPP GU 1981 (Anm. 27), S. 14, 470 u. 514. Zum Annual s. Anm. 34.
[36]) Bachmaier (Anm. 16), S. 394–397; Vasileva (Anm. 34), S. 329/330.
[37]) Vgl. Karte 47 bei Kosack (wie Tab. 2), S. 365.

Hirtennomaden, die einen nordgriechischen Dialekt sprechen. Aufgrund eines Erlasses des Ministerrates vom Frühjahr 1954[38]) sind die Karakatschanen seßhaft gemacht worden und betreiben nur noch zum Teil Bergweidewirtschaft.

Knapp die Hälfte der 1956 gezählten 1105 *Albaner* (1965: 503) stellten die Einwohner des zu 4/5 von orthodoxen Albanern bewohnten Dorfes Mandrica im Südosten des Landes (nahe Ivajlovgrad)[39]). Weitere 95 Albaner wohnten in einem Dorf im Pirin-Gebirge, der Rest in Sofia und anderen Städten.

Die 1956 gezählten 484 *Serben* (1965: 577) lebten ganz überwiegend in Städten, darunter über 1/3 in Sofia. Bei dem Rest, der Dörfer um Vraca und Plovdiv bewohnte, handelte es sich um ältere serbische Siedlungen, während die Stadtbevölkerung z. T. aus politischen Flüchtlingen, die nach 1948 aus Jugoslawien gekommen waren, besteht. Von 1949 bis 1954 erschien für sie 14tägig die serbische Zeitschrift *Napred* (Vorwärts)[40]).

Die *Aromunen* Bulgariens tauchten in der offiziellen Statistik zuletzt 1956 unter der pejorativen Bezeichnung *kucovlasi* auf. Die damals gezählten 487 Angehörigen dieser orthodoxen, rumänischsprachigen Minderheit lebten fast ausschließlich in den beiden Städten Peštera und Velingrad (Lădžene) des Bezirks Plovdiv. Sie stellen den Rest einer vormals größeren Minderheit von Schafhirten dar, die 1928 und 1930 nach Rumänien ausgesiedelt worden war[41]).

Die Stärke der überwiegend hauptstädtischen, vornehmlich weiblichen Minderheiten der *Tschechen, Ungarn* und *Deutschen* (Tab. 1) ist im Zeitraum 1956–1965 annähernd konstant geblieben.

Bei den in der bulgarischen Statistik in „andere Slawen" und „andere Nichtslawen" unterschiedenen *übrigen nationalen Minderheiten* (Tab. 1) handelte es sich 1956 zum einen um 1100 Polen, Ukrainer, Kroaten u. a., (1965: 974), die in den Bezirken Pleven und Plovdiv sowie in der Hauptstadt konzentriert waren, zum anderen um 1900 Personen (1965: keine Angabe) nicht genannter nationaler Zugehörigkeit.

2. Ethnisch-religiöse Gruppen

a) Pomaken

Die Pomaken, amtlich als „mohammedanische Bulgaren" (*bălgari-mochamedani*) bezeichnet und nationalitätenstatistisch den Bulgaren zugeschlagen[42]), sind „Muslime bulgarischer Zunge" (F. Bajraktarević)[43]). Selbst in der modernen bulgarischen

---

[38]) Marinov, V.: Prinos kăm izučavaneto na proizchoda, bita i kulturata na karakačanite v Bălgarija (Beitrag zur Erforschung von Herkunft, Lebensweise und Kultur der Karakatschanen in Bulgarien). Sofia 1964 (dt. Res.).

[39]) Sokolova, B.: Die albanische Mundart von Mandrica. Wiesbaden 1983, S. 5–9.

[40]) BPP II (Anm. 15), S. 430.

[41]) Beškov/Valev (Anm. 30), S. 6. Vgl. auch Winnifrith, T. J.: The Vlachs: The History of a Balkan People. London 1987, S. 25–27.

[42]) Vgl. aus bulgarischer Sicht Monov (wie Tab. 2).

[43]) Bajraktarević, F.: Art. Pomaken, in: Enzyklopädie des Islam. Bd. 3. Leiden, Leipzig 1936, S. 1159–1162; Silverman, C.: Art. Pomaks, in: Muslim Peoples. A World Ethnographic Survey. Ed. by R. V. Weekes. Westport, CT, 1984. Vol. 2, S. 612–616.

anthropologischen Forschung wird aber darauf hingewiesen, daß die Pomaken „seit mehreren Jahrhunderten eine isolierte Bevölkerung darstellen, da sie sich nur untereinander verheiraten"[44]).

Die Pomaken, deren Zahl zuletzt 1970 von bulgarischer Seite mit 170000 beziffert wurde (Tab. 2), leben heute fast ausschließlich südlich der Marica in „topographischen Rückzugslagen" (H.-P. Kosack), wo sie in erster Linie Ackerbau unter Gebirgsbedingungen betreiben.

Die Pomaken besaßen weder vor noch nach 1944 ein Verbandswesen oder eigene Institutionen, sondern waren seit 1934 beständig das Objekt staatlichen wie privaten Assimilierungsdrucks. Zu Beginn der 70er Jahre wurden ihre islamisch-arabischen Namen durch christlich-slawische ersetzt.

b) Gagausen

Die Reste der in Bulgarien im Verschwinden begriffenen ethnisch-religiösen Gruppe der orthodoxen, einen osmanisch-türkischen Dialekt sprechenden Gagausen[45]) sind noch in Dörfern dreier Regionen des Landes zu finden: Um die Städte Varna und Vălčidol herum, nahe der Schwarzmeerstadt Kavarna sowie im Landesinneren, in der Umgebung der Stadt Topolovgrad. Im Gegensatz zu den Gagausen in der UdSSR, deren Vorfahren z. T. aus heute bulgarischen Gebieten eingewandert sind, sind diejenigen in Bulgarien schriftlos und besitzen keinen minderheitenrechtlichen Status. Von staatlicher Seite werden sie den Bulgaren zugerechnet[46]). Die Gagausen, über deren Zahl auch inoffiziell nichts verlautet (Tab. 2), betreiben Weinbau, Landwirtschaft und Fischerei.

V. Nationalitätenpolitik 1944–1989

In der Nationalitätenpolitik von Regierung und Partei Bulgariens lassen sich mehrere Perioden unterscheiden: Zwischen 1944 bis 1948 gab es eine aktive muttersprachliche Alphabetisierungspolitik gegenüber den Minderheiten. Parallel zum expandierenden, konfessionell geprägten Minderheitenschulwesen entstand ein Minderheitenverbandswesen. 1948 wurde dann vom V. Parteitag der BKP eine Politik der „Einbindung (*priobštavane*) in den Aufbau des Sozialismus" proklamiert. Durch die schrittweise Aufwertung des Bulgarischen von der ersten Fremdsprache zur Hauptunterrichtssprache sowie durch die Reduzierung des muttersprachlichen Minderheitenschulunterrichts auf die unteren Schultypen und -klassen sollten die Grundlagen dieser „Einbindungs"-Politik gelegt werden. In dieselbe Richtung zielten Bemühun-

---

[44]) Boev, P.: Die Rassentypen der Balkanhalbinsel und der Ostägäischen Inselwelt und deren Bedeutung für die Herkunft ihrer Bevölkerung. Sofia 1972, S. 208.

[45]) Zajączkowski, W.: Art. Gagauz, in: Encyclopaedia of Islam. Vol. II. Leiden, London 1965, S. 971–972; Hoppe, E. M.: Die türkischen Gagauzen-Christen, in: Oriens Christianus. 41 (1957), S. 25–137; Siedlungskarte in: Tokarev/Čeboksarov (Anm. 7).

[46]) Art. Gagauzi, EB (Anm. 26). T. 2, S. 17.

gen, Angehörige von Minderheiten für die Partei und andere gesellschaftliche Organisationen zu rekrutieren. Zugleich stieg nicht zuletzt im Zusammenhang mit der 1949 einsetzenden Kollektivierungswelle der politische Druck auf die meisten Minderheiten an. Die dritte Phase begann im Jahr 1958. Damals wurde eine bereits auf dem „historischen" Aprilplenum von 1956 beschlossene Kursänderung in die Tat umgesetzt[47]). Von nun an steuerten die mit der Nationalitätenpolitik befaßten Ministerien, Parteiinstanzen und die OF einen eindeutigen Assimilationskurs, welcher im Zuge der 1965 eingeleiteten Politik der „nationalen Rückbesinnung" weiter verschärft wurde. Im Zeitraum 1971–1974 wurde sodann das Konzept von der „einheitlichen sozialistischen bulgarischen Nation" (*edinna socialističeska bălgarska nacija*) ausgearbeitet, welches den theoretischen Rahmen für die praktische, auch Repressalien beinhaltende Politik der Beseitigung aller sog. „ethnodifferenzierenden Rezidive der Vergangenheit" abgab. 1984 schließlich kündigte sich mit der Einführung eines neuen Leitmotivs eine weitere Forcierung an: Nun war die Rede von der „im Aufbau befindlichen kommunistischen Nation in der NRB" (*izgraždašta se komunističeska nacija v NRB*)[48]).

Wie dieser neuerliche „Aufbau" konkret vor sich gehen würde, führten Regierung und Partei noch Ende 1984 mit der Zwangsbulgarisierung der Türken vor[49]). Erst im Verlaufe der dadurch ausgelösten innen- und außenpolitischen Krise wurde eine „wissenschaftliche" Rechtfertigung nachgeschoben: Wie anthropologische und ethnogenetische Untersuchungen gezeigt hätten, handle es sich bei den bislang irrtümlich als „Türken" bezeichneten Staatsbürgern um im 16. und 17. Jh. gewaltsam islamisierte und türkisierte Bulgaren, die aufgrund eben dieser Forschungsergebnisse ihre türkische Identität freiwillig zugunsten ihrer eigentlich bulgarischen aufgegeben hätten[50]).

Obwohl seit 1984/85 von einer *Nationalitäten*politik im Wortsinn in der NRB nicht mehr gesprochen werden kann, da aus staatlicher Sicht die nationalen Minderheiten

---

[47]) Die Richtlinien des Aprilplenums tauchten in einer Vorlage des Politbüros vom 21.6.1958 auf, die von einem ZK-Plenum vom 2.–4.10.1958 als „Thesen des ZK der BKP zur Arbeit unter der türkischen Bevölkerung" angenommen wurde (Memišev (Anm. 14), S. 128–136).

[48]) Erstmals tauchte diese Formel bei Memišev (Anm. 14), S. 197, dessen Buch im Mai 1984 erschien (ebenda, S. 199). Im selben Monat soll das Politbüro die im Dezember 1984 einsetzende Kampagne gegen die Türken beschlossen haben. Vgl. Memişoğlu, H. (i. e. J. Memišev!): Bulgarian Oppression in Historical Perspective. Ankara 1989, S. 26.

[49]) Vgl. drei Amnesty International-Publikationen: (1) Bulgaria: Imprisonment of Ethnic Turks. Human Rights Abuses during the Forced Assimilation of the Ethnic Turkish Minority. London (April) 1986; (2) Bulgaria: Continuing Human Rights Abuses against Ethnic Turks (EUR 15/01/87). London (Juli) 1987; und (3) Bulgaria. Imprisonment of Ethnic Turks and Human Rights Activist (EUR 15/01/89). London (February) 1989, sowie weiter: Laber, J.: Destroying Ethnic Identity: The Turks of Bulgaria. An Updata (A Helsinki Watch Report). New York, NY, Washington, DC, (September) 1987; [99th U. S. Congress, 2d Session,] Country Reports of Human Rights Practices for 1985. Washington, DC, (Februar) 1986, S. 926–936 („Bulgaria"); [One Hundredth U. S. Congress, First Session,] Hearing before the Commission on Security and Cooperation in Europe. Part I: National Minorities in Eastern Europe. The Turkish Minority in Bulgaria. February 3, 1987, Washington, DC, 1987.

[50]) Troebst, S.: Zum Verhältnis von Partei, Staat und türkischer Minderheit in Bulgarien 1956–1986, in: Nationalitätenprobleme (Anm. 4), S. 231–253, hier S. 250–252.

und ethnisch-religiösen Gruppen sämtlich im bulgarischen Staatsvolk aufgegangen sind und somit nicht mehr existieren – wobei die Frage nach der Sonderstellung von Armeniern und Juden noch einer amtlichen Antwort harrt –, gelten vier 1974 aufgestellte Leitsätze auch weiterhin. Sie besagen im einzelnen folgendes:

1. Bulgarien ist ein „mononationaler Staat" (*edinonacionalna dăržava*); 2. das bulgarische Volk setzt sich aus mehreren in der Vergangenheit in ethnischer Hinsicht verschiedenen, nunmehr aber voneinander „untrennbaren Bestandteilen" (*nerazdelni časti*) zusammen; 3. die „einheitliche sozialistische bulgarische Nation", bzw. mittlerweile die „im Aufbau befindliche kommunistische Nation in der NRB", ist zum einen das Ergebnis einer jahrhundertelangen historischen Schicksalsgemeinschaft, zum andern dasjenige der gemeinsamen Erfahrung des Aufbaus von Volksmacht, Sozialismus und Kommunismus seit 1944; und 4. zwischen ethnischer Zugehörigkeit und Religion – gemeint ist v. a. der Islam – gibt es keinen unmittelbaren Zusammenhang, d. h. aus dem verfassungsmäßig garantierten Recht auf Religionsfreiheit können keine nationalen Minderheitenrechte abgeleitet werden[51]).

Bereits 1970, also noch vor der Propagierung all dieser Leitsätze, Konzepte und Theorien hatte Staats- und Parteichef Todor Živkov das Endziel dieser Politik klar umrissen:

„‚Assimilation' – das ist ein bürgerlicher Begriff. Das ist nicht unser [Begriff], kein kommunistischer Begriff. Wir sind entschieden gegen Assimilation als Methode des Einpflanzens und des Formierens von Nationalbewußtsein. So sieht unser Weg nicht aus. Unser Weg ist derjenige gemeinsamer und gleichberechtigter Vorwärtsbewegung im Namen der Gesamtinteressen des ganzen Volkes. Hier handelt es sich nicht um Assimilation. Es handelt sich vielmehr um die schrittweise Annäherung aller Werktätigen, um die Umwandlung des ganzen Volkes in Erbauer von Sozialismus und Kommunismus. Wenn wir unter Assimilation das Verschwinden der Volksgruppen, ihre Umwandlung in eine andere Qualität, verstehen – gestatten Sie mir diesen Scherz –, dann können wir auch hinsichtlich der bulgarischen Nation von Assimilation sprechen: Sie verwandelt sich sukzessive in eine kommunistische Nation."[52])

Erst zwei Jahrzehnte später, im Mai 1989, hat die bulgarische Führung, an deren Spitze noch immer T. Živkov steht, indirekt eingeräumt, daß ihr Assimilationskonzept gescheitert ist. Das „Verschwinden der Volksgruppen", also die Homogenisierung des bulgarischen Nationalstaates, wird seitdem nicht mehr durch Assimilation allein, sondern auch durch Deportation bewerkstelligt.

---

[51]) Troebst (Anm. 50), S. 237–239. Vgl. auch die Dokumentationen in: Südosteuropa. 34 (1985), S. 359–367 u. 486–506.

[52]) Živkov, T.: Politikata na BKP kăm narodnostnite grupi v stranata e politika marksistkaleninska (Die Politik der BKP gegenüber den Volksgruppen im Lande ist eine marxistisch-leninistische) (Rede vom 3. 7. 1970), in: ders.: Izbrani proizvedenija (Ausgewählte Werke). T. 18. Sofia 1976, S. 95–110, hier S. 105.

Schulsystem

Peter Bachmaier, Wien-Klosterneuburg

I. Entwicklung des Bildungswesens: 1. Einleitung – 2. Die Übergangsphase (1944–1948) – 3. Das Bildungswesen in der Stalin-Ära (1948–1956) – 4. Partielle Entstalinisierung und Polytechnisierung (1956–1969) – 5. Die Reform von 1969: Mittlere Allgemeinbildung für alle – 6. Die Reform von 1979: Professionalisierung – II. Die Vorschulerziehung – III. Das allgemeinbildende Schulwesen – IV. Die Berufsschulen – V. Die Fachmittelschulen – VI. Die Lehrerbildung – VII. Pädagogische Wissenschaft und Bildungsforschung – VIII. Offene Fragen und Ausblick

I. Entwicklung des Bildungswesens

1. Einleitung

Das moderne weltliche Bildungswesen entstand in der ersten Hälfte des 19. Jh. als selbständige Einrichtung der bulgarischen Gemeinden und war Ausdruck des wachsenden Nationalbewußtseins, das sich gegen die politische Unterdrückung durch das Osmanische Reich und die kulturelle Abhängigkeit von der griechischen Geistlichkeit richtete. Der demokratische Geist des bulgarischen Bildungswesens setzte sich nach der Befreiung 1878 fort und blieb bis zu einem gewissen Grad bis in die 40er Jahre unseres Jahrhunderts erhalten.

Die Bulgaren orientierten sich beim Aufbau der neuen Kultur in der Zeit der nationalen Wiedergeburt vorwiegend nach Mittel- und Westeuropa, obwohl der Einfluß Rußlands aus politischen Gründen ebenfalls eine gewisse Rolle spielte. Das bulgarische Bildungswesen übernahm deshalb in der Struktur, im Unterrichtsinhalt und in der Verwaltung wesentliche Elemente aus der deutschen, österreichischen und französischen Bildungstradition[1]).

---

[1]) Tschauschov, S. P.: Die Entwicklung des bulgarischen Bildungswesens. Halle 1944 (Pädagogik in Geschichte, Theorie und Praxis IX); Istorija na obrazovanieto i pedagogičeskata misăl na Bălgarija (Geschichte des Bildungswesens und des pädagogischen Denkens Bulgariens). T. I–II. Sofia 1975; Russel, W. F.: Schools in Bulgaria. With Special Reference to the Influence of the Agrarian Party on Elementary and Secondary Education. New York 1924; Bachmaier, P.: Die Kulturpolitik Österreich-Ungarns gegenüber Bulgarien im Ersten Weltkrieg, in: Österreichische Osthefte. 23 (1981), S. 430–451; Paskaleva, V.: Sredna Evropa i zemite po dolnija Dunav prez XVIII–XIX vek. (Mitteleuropa und die Länder an der unteren Donau im 18. und 19. Jh.). Sofia 1986; Nurižan, Ž.: Prijateli na Bălgarija (Freunde Bulgariens). Sofia 1940; Čilingirov, S.: Protiv čuždite učilišta (Gegen die fremden Schulen). Sofia 1935; Buržoazni pedagogičeski văzgledi u nas do 1944 godina (Bürgerliche pädagogische Anschauungen bei uns vor 1944). Sofia 1964, S. 111–131.

2. Die Übergangsphase (1944–1948)

Der 9.9.1944 bedeutete nicht nur die Machtergreifung der OF, sondern auch den Beginn des sich etappenweise vollziehenden Übergangs zu einem Bildungswesen sowjetischer Prägung[2]).

Das Ministerium für Volksbildung (*Ministerstvo na narodnata prosveta*) wurde von 1944 bis 1946 von Nichtkommunisten geleitet, aber alle wesentlichen Entscheidungen wurden vom Nationalrat der OF beschlossen, in dem die BRP(k) die Macht hatte. Der Nationalrat und die bulgarische Regierung wiederum wurden in ihrer politischen Tätigkeit bis Februar 1947 von der ACC beaufsichtigt, in der die Sowjetunion den Vorsitz führte und auch den entscheidenden Einfluß hatte[3]).

Die OF bezeichnete ihre Politik im Bereich des Bildungswesens in der ersten Phase als „Demokratisierung", die in Wirklichkeit eine Mischung von genuin demokratischen Maßnahmen mit einer zunehmenden Bürokratisierung und Politisierung der Schule war. Das neue Regime eliminierte zunächst den Einfluß der nationalistischen Ideologie auf allen Ebenen des Schulwesens und entließ Lehrer, die sich unter dem alten Regime exponiert hatten. Gleichzeitig wurden jedoch auch viele Lehrer verfolgt, deren weltanschauliche Einstellung und berufliche Tätigkeit keinesfalls als „faschistisch" oder „chauvinistisch" bezeichnet werden konnte, sondern die nur bestrebt waren, den Schülern das nationale kulturelle Erbe zu vermitteln. Die dogmatische, ahistorische Linie der bulgarischen Kommunisten führte dazu, daß die Schule ihre Funktion, die kulturelle Kontinuität in der Gesellschaft zu gewährleisten, nicht mehr erfüllen konnte[4]).

„Demokratisierung" bedeutete auch freien und unentgeltlichen Zugang für alle (mit Ausnahme der Kinder der „Bourgeoisie" und politisch belasteter Personen) und die massenhafte Errichtung von neuen Schulen, vor allem auf dem Land. Die Anzahl der Gymnasien stieg von 135 im September 1944 auf 203 im Dezember 1944 und auf 275 im Mai 1945. Für diese überstürzte Expansion des Bildungswesens gab es jedoch weder genügend Schulgebäude noch Lehrer, und viele dieser Maßnahmen mußten bald wieder zurückgenommen werden. An den Gymnasien wurden „bürgerliche"

---

[2]) Von westlichen Darstellungen des Bildungswesens der NRB sind vor allem zu nennen: Apanasewicz, N.; Rosen, S.: Education in Bulgaria. Hrsg. U.S. Department of Health, Education and Welfare. Studies in Comparative Education. Washington 1965; Brown, J.F.: Bulgaria Under Communist Rule. London 1970. (Ch. 10: Education); Georgeoff, P.J.: The Education System of Bulgaria. Hrsg. U.S. Department of Health, Education and Welfare. Education Around the World. Washington 1977; Oschlies, W.: Bulgariens Kulturentwicklung 1944–1975. Teil I–II. Köln 1976 (Berichte des Bundesinstituts für ostwissenschaftliche und internationale Studien. (1976) 1–2).

Bulgarische Darstellungen: Atanasov, Ž.: Istorija na bălgarskoto obrazovanie – lekcionen kurs (Geschichte des bulgarischen Bildungswesens – Vorlesungen). Sofijski universitet „Kliment Ochridski", Filial Blagoevgrad. Sofia 1977 (Weiterhin: Atanasov, Istorija); Atanasov, Ž.: Borbata na BKP za korenno preustrojstvo na obrazovanieto (Der Kampf der BKP für die radikale Umgestaltung des Bildungswesens), in: Bălgarskata komunističeska partija i kulturata (Die BKP und die Kultur). T. 2. Sofia 1983, S. 336–388; Čakărov, N.: Sovremennaja škola i pedagogika v Narodnoj Respublike Bolgarii (Die gegenwärtige Schule und Pädagogik in der NRB). Moskau 1987.

[3]) Čičovska, V.: The Character of Cultural Policy in Bulgaria (1944–1948), in: Études historiques. 13 (1985), p. 225–259.

[4]) Čičovska, Character (Anm. 3), S. 231.

Fächer wie Religion, Latein und Griechisch abgeschafft und die Dauer der Schulzeit um ein Jahr verkürzt[5]).

Eine der wichtigsten Aufgaben, denen sich das neue Regime gegenübersah, war die Bekämpfung des Analphabetismus und des Bildungsrückstandes, die jedoch mit politischer Propaganda verbunden wurde. Es wurde ein umfangreiches System von Abendschulen eingeführt: einjährige Abendschulen für Analphabeten, zweijährige Abendschulen für Halbanalphabeten, ein zweijähriger Abendkurs für Erwachsene zum Erwerb der progymnasialen Bildung und ein vierjähriges Abendgymnasium für Berufstätige. Trotzdem gelang eine wirkliche Überwindung des Analphabetismus, der vor dem II. Weltkrieg 23 % der Bevölkerung umfaßt hatte, erst in den 50er Jahren[6]).

Die politische Linie der Negation der nationalen Kultur und der Förderung der „proletarischen" Schichten hatte positive Auswirkungen für die nationalen Minderheiten, denen eine kulturelle Autonomie zugebilligt wurde. Im Oktober 1946 wurden alle Schulen der türkischen, jüdischen und armenischen Minderheit, insgesamt etwa 1000 Schulen mit fast 2000 Lehrern und etwa 70 000 Schülern vom bulgarischen Staat übernommen, was von den Vertretern der Minderheiten einhellig begrüßt und als Beitrag zur Förderung ihrer eigenen Kultur verstanden wurde[7]).

Die BRP(k) machte auf ihrem 10. ZK-Plenum im Juli 1946 auch Zugeständnisse an Jugoslawien in der makedonischen Frage, indem sie Pirin-Makedonien eine Kulturautonomie gewährte. Im Hinblick auf eine spätere Vereinigung der Region mit der Republik Makedonien im Rahmen einer Balkan-Föderation wurde in den Schulen der Unterricht in makedonischer Sprache eingeführt. Im November 1947 wurde etwa 100 Lehrern aus der Republik Makedonien gestattet, die Kinder in den Schulen der Piriner Region in makedonischer Sprache zu unterrichten. „Makedonisch" wurde als eigenes Fach zwei Stunden wöchentlich unterrichtet. Die Tätigkeit der jugoslawischen Lehrer wurde im Juli 1948 nach dem Bruch zwischen Jugoslawien und der Sowjetunion eingestellt, doch bestand die Kulturautonomie der Piriner Region in eingeschränktem Umfang bis 1956 weiter[8]).

3. Das Bildungswesen in der Stalin-Ära (1948–1956)

Im Jahre 1948 wurde, vorbereitet vom neuen Minister für Volksbildung, Kiril Dramaliev, das erste „sozialistische" Bildungsgesetz Bulgariens beschlossen, das der entscheidende, aber noch nicht endgültige Schritt zur Übernahme des sowjetischen Schul- und Bildungssystems war. Nach dem neuen Gesetz war die Erziehung von

---

[5]) Čičovska, V.: Bulgaria's Cultural Development (1944–1958), in: Problems of the Transition from Capitalism to Socialism in Bulgaria. Sofia 1975, S. 201 ff.

[6]) Atanasov, Istorija (Anm. 2), S. 333.

[7]) Bachmaier, P.: Bulgariens Weg zur neuen Schule. Die Bildungs- und Wissenschaftspolitik der Vaterländischen Front, 1944–1948. Wien 1984, S. 29 ff.

[8]) Dimitrov, G. V.: Za taka narečenata „kulturna avtonomija" v Blagoevgradski okrăg (1946–1948) (Über die sogenannte „Kulturautonomie" im Kreis Blagoevgrad, 1946–1948), in: Isto-ričeski pregled. 35 (1979) 6, S. 77–82.

„Erbauern des Sozialismus" das Ziel der Schule; die Lehrpläne in Kindergärten, Grundschulen, Gymnasien, Fachmittelschulen und Hochschulen wurden vereinheitlicht, und der Marxismus-Leninismus war die einzige Weltanschauung, die von jetzt an in den Schulen und Hochschulen gelehrt werden durfte[9]).

Durch das neue Gesetz wurde das ausländische Schulwesen, das eine lange, zum Teil sogar bis in die erste Hälfte des 19. Jh. zurückreichende Tradition hatte, beseitigt. Während die deutschen Schulen ihre Tätigkeit bereits 1944 eingestellt hatten, wurden jetzt auch die französischen Lyzeen, das amerikanische protestantische College und die österreichische katholische Mädchenschule „Sancta Maria" als „Agenturen ausländischer Mächte" geschlossen. Der Vorwurf, der später wieder zurückgenommen wurde, war ungerecht, denn die meisten dieser Schulen waren Missionsschulen, die sich – mit Ausnahme der deutschen Schulen in den letzten Jahren ihres Bestehens – nie mit politischer Propaganda befaßt hatten. Bulgarien verlor dadurch ein wichtiges Bindeglied zur europäischen Kultur[10]).

1952 wurde, nicht ohne Widerstand des Ministers Dramaliev, der eine gewisse kulturelle Eigenständigkeit beibehalten wollte, eine weitere Umgestaltung des Bildungswesens durchgeführt, die die totale mechanische Übernahme des sowjetischen Bildungssystems bis zu den kleinsten Details bedeutete. Die nationalen Traditionen im Bildungswesen, die auf die Zeit der Wiedergeburt der bulgarischen Nation zurückgingen, wurden völlig mißachtet und beseitigt. Statt der alten Trimestereinteilung wurden Quartale eingeführt, die die Kontrolle der Schüler durch ständige Prüfungen verstärken sollten. Die alte, differenzierte Struktur des Schulwesens wurde abgeschafft und durch eine zentralisierte Einheitsschule ersetzt, in der die Lehrer den letzten Rest von Selbständigkeit verloren und der gesamte Unterricht streng reglementiert wurde[11]).

Das sowjetische System, das Vălko Červenkov jetzt endgültig durchsetzte, bedeutete vor allem eine bürokratisierte Schule, ein System endloser Vorschriften, Kennziffern und Kontrollen, dem Schüler, Lehrer und Direktoren in gleicher Weise unterworfen waren. Die Lehrer wurden zu Beamten, die selbst von bürokratischem Geist durchdrungen waren und den Sinn ihrer Arbeit nur mehr in der genauen Erfüllung der bis ins kleinste festgelegten Vorschriften sehen sollten. Hinter diesem bürokratischen System, das die Lehrer zu Rädchen in einer großen Maschine machte, stand die stalinistische Pädagogik, deren Ziel die absolute Unterwerfung des Menschen unter den Willen des Staates war. Es war eine Pädagogik der gezielten moralischen Deformation, der Vernichtung der menschlichen Würde, der Zerstörung der kulturellen Werte und ihrer Reduzierung auf unbedingten Gehorsam[12]).

Das bulgarische Bildungswesen übernahm jetzt die sowjetischen Lehrpläne, die sowjetischen Lehrbücher, die sowjetischen Methoden des Unterrichts, die methodischen Vereinigungen, Fachkommissionen und pädagogischen Beratungsstellen. Die pädagogische Theorie wurde mit sowjetischer Hilfe vom „Pädologismus" gesäubert,

---

[9]) Atanasov, Istorija (Anm. 2), S. 336.
[10]) Bachmaier, Bulgariens Weg zur neuen Schule (Anm. 7), S. 50.
[11]) Atanasov, Istorija (Anm. 2), S. 348 ff.; Dramaliev, K.: Săstojanie i zadači na narodnata prosveta (Lage und Aufgaben der Volksbildung), in: Narodna prosveta. (1951) 1, S. 13–32.
[12]) Siehe Stalinskaja pedagogika (Die Stalinsche Pädagogik), in: Učitel'skaja gazeta. (1988) 70.

es wurde die führende Rolle des Lehrers und der Schule in der Erziehung sowie die direkte Verbindung der Erziehung mit der Politik und die Bedeutung des Kollektivs für die Erziehung betont[13]).

Eine besondere Rolle wurde den Kinder- und Jugendorganisationen „Septemberkinder" (*septemvrijčeta*, nach 1956 *čavdarčeta*, d. h. Čavdarkinder, für die Schüler der Elementarschule), der Pionierorganisation (*pionerska organizacija*, für die Schüler der Progymnasialstufe, d. h. heute für die 10–14-jährigen) und dem DKMS (für die 15–35jährigen) zugedacht, die die Aufgabe erhielten, den Schülern durch Veranstaltungen in und außerhalb der Schule die marxistisch-leninistische Weltanschauung zu vermitteln und sie politisch im Sinne des Regimes zu erziehen.

Die „proletarische" und „internationalistische" Linie der BKP unter Červenkov hatte eine besondere Förderung des rückständigsten Teiles der Bevölkerung, der türkischen Minderheit, zur Folge. Durch die Verordnung des Ministerrates vom 18.1.1951 und den Beschluß des Politbüros vom 26.4.1951 wurde eine breite Kampagne zur Überwindung des Analphabetismus in Gang gesetzt, die den Anteil der Analphabeten unter der türkischen Bevölkerung von ca. 80 % (1944) auf 36,2 % im Jahr 1956 senkte. Türkische Jugendliche wurden an Gymnasien, Fachmittelschulen, Berufsschulen und Hochschulen bevorzugt aufgenommen, obwohl ihnen häufig entsprechende Bulgarischkenntnisse fehlten. Zur Organisation der türkischen Lehrerausbildung in Šumen, Kărdžali, Razgrad und an der Universität Sofia wurden Spezialisten aus der türkischsprachigen Sowjetrepublik Azerbajdžan eingesetzt, und türkische Jugendliche aus Bulgarien wurden zum Studium nach Baku geschickt[14]).

4. Partielle Entstalinisierung und Polytechnisierung (1956–1969)

Das Aprilplenum des ZK der BKP von 1956 bedeutete für das Bildungswesen eine partielle, aber nicht vollständige Überwindung des stalinistischen Systems. Jene Bestimmungen im Gesetz von 1952, die die nationalen Traditionen negierten, wurden durch eine Verordnung wieder aufgehoben. Die Quartalseinteilung mit ihrem strengen Prüfungssystem wurde abgeschafft und die Trimesterform, die es vorher gegeben hatte, wiedereingeführt.

Die absolute Zentralisierung des Schulwesens wurde etwas gemildert, der Frontalunterricht gelockert, die Reglementierung der Lehrer vermindert, die Übernahme sowjetischer Lehrbücher eingeschränkt und die Tür zum westlichen Ausland ein wenig geöffnet. Die Presse des Landes begann zum ersten Mal, Beiträge über die Probleme des Bildungswesens zu veröffentlichen. Das gesamte Ausmaß der Auswirkungen des Stalinismus auf das bulgarische Bildungswesen wurde jedoch nicht erkannt.

Mit der Verordnung vom 1.6.1957 begann die schrittweise Einführung des Arbeitsunterrichts in den allgemeinbildenden Mittelschulen und eine Annäherung an die tatsächlichen Anforderungen der Gesellschaft[15]).

---

[13]) Čakărov, (Anm. 2), S. 52 ff.
[14]) Memišev, Ju.: Zadružno v socialističeskoto stroitelstvo na rodinata. Priobštavane na bălgarskite turci kăm izgraždaneto na socializma (Gemeinsam im sozialistischen Aufbau der Heimat. Die Eingliederung der bulgarischen Türken in den Aufbau des Sozialismus). Sofia 1984, S. 103 ff.
[15]) Atanasov, Istorija (Anm. 2), S. 351; Čičovska, Development (Anm. 5), S. 227.

Die nächste größere Veränderung des Schulwesens erfolgte 1959 mit dem zweiten und bisher letzten Bildungsgesetz der NRB, mit dem die Schulpflicht von sieben auf acht Jahre (1 Jahr über die Grundschule hinaus) verlängert wurde. Die allgemeinbildenden Mittelschulen erhielten die Aufgabe, den Schülern auch polytechnische und Berufsbildung zu vermitteln und wurden mit Fabriken, TKZS, DZS und anderen Betrieben in Verbindung gebracht[16]).

Das System der Mittelschulen nach der siebenjährigen Grundschule hatte nach 1959 folgende dreigliedrige Struktur:

1) das vierjährige Gymnasium (*gimnazija*), das den Schülern Allgemeinbildung in Verbindung mit polytechnischer Erziehung vermittelte und sie in erster Linie zum Hochschulstudium vorbereiten sollte;
2) die mittlere Fachschule (*technikum*, vier Jahre), für mittlere Spezialisten;
3) die Berufsschule (*profesionalno-tehničesko učilište* – PTU, zwei- bis dreijährig) bildete Facharbeiter aus[17]).

Nach 1959 begann die eigentliche Expansion des bulgarischen Bildungswesens, die vor allem den Bereich der Berufsbildung erfaßte. 1962 wurden die ersten mittleren Berufsschulen (*sredni profesionalno-tehničeski učilišta*, SPTU) gegründet, die einen vollständigen Mittelschulabschluß vermittelten und die PTU in den 70er Jahren fast völlig ersetzten.

In dieser Zeit wurden auch die ersten Schritte zur Differenzierung des Bildungssystems unternommen: In Loveč wurde 1959 an Stelle des früheren amerikanischen College das erste Sprachgymnasium mit wahlweise Englisch, Französisch oder Deutsch als Unterrichtssprache gegründet. Es folgten weitere Sprachgymnasien für begabte Kinder, in denen der Unterricht fast ausschließlich in der jeweiligen westlichen Fremdsprache erteilt wurde, sowie Spezialschulen für Mathematik, Naturwissenschaften, Sport, klassische Sprachen und Kunst. Schulen mit russischer Unterrichtssprache ab der 1. Klasse der Grundschule hatten allerdings bereits seit der zweiten Hälfte der 40er Jahre existiert.

Das Aprilplenum, das den wissenschaftlich-technischen Fortschritt der Gesellschaft besonders betonte, bedeutete auch eine entscheidende Wende in der Minderheitenpolitik. Das ZK kritisierte am türkischen Schulwesen den „Selbstzweckcharakter" sowie Mängel in der materiellen Ausstattung und in der politischen Erziehung.

Im Schuljahr 1957/58 besuchten 104 291 Kinder der türkischen Minderheit die Grundschulen, etwa 6000 die Gymnasien, Fachmittelschulen und Berufsschulen, 1436 Türken studierten an Lehrerbildungsanstalten, 150 an Pädagogischen Hochschulen, 375 an bulgarischen Hochschulen und 30 an Hochschulen in der Sowjetunion.

Das ZK der BKP stellte fest, daß die forcierte Förderung der türkischen kulturellen Eigenständigkeit die Gefahr der „Selbstisolation" und „Entfremdung" der Türken

---

[16]) Zakon za po-tjasna vrazka na učilišteto s života i za po-natatăšnoto razvitie na narodnoto obrazovanie v NRB (Gesetz über die engere Verbindung der Schule mit dem Leben und die weitere Entwicklung der Volksbildung in der NRB), in: Narodna prosveta. (1959) 8, S. 10.
[17]) Atanasov, Istorija (Anm. 2), S. 354.

von der bulgarischen Bevölkerung mit sich brächte, und beschloß am 28.6.1958, das türkische Schulwesen aufzulösen und in das bulgarische Schulwesen zu integrieren, wobei Türkisch weiterhin nur mehr als eigenes Fach fakultativ gewählt werden konnte[18]).

5. Die Reform von 1969: Mittlere Allgemeinbildung für alle

Ein entscheidender Schritt zur Einführung der mittleren Allgemeinbildung für alle Jugendlichen wurde im Juli 1969 durch das Bildungsplenum des ZK eingeleitet, das eine stärkere Hinwendung zur Allgemeinbildung bedeutete, während die Polytechnisierung eingeschränkt und der Plan der Berufsausbildung in den Gymnasien zeitweise nicht mehr weiterverfolgt wurde[19]).

Die erste Hälfte der 70er Jahre brachte besonders nach der Verkündung der „einheitlichen sozialistischen Nation" in der Verfassung von 1971 eine Verstärkung der ideologischen und politischen Erziehungsarbeit, die sich auch auf das Schulwesen der bulgarischen Türken auswirkte. Das Plenum des ZK der BKP vom Februar 1974 beschloß die Integration der bulgarischen Türken mit der bulgarischen Bevölkerung. Danach wurde die kulturelle Eigenständigkeit der bulgarischen Türken, die die Führung der BKP als Hindernis für die Errichtung einer säkularisierten, wissenschaftlich-technischen, sozialistischen Zivilisation sah, beendet, und der Türkischunterricht in den Schulen wurde endgültig abgeschafft. Seit damals kann von einem türkischen Schulwesen in Bulgarien nicht mehr gesprochen werden.

Gleichzeitig muß festgestellt werden, daß die bulgarischen Türken in dieser Epoche bedeutende kulturelle Fortschritte machten, wie an folgenden Zahlen erkennbar ist:

Tabelle 1: Schüler und Studierende unter den bulgarischen Türken, 1957–1971

Schuljahr	Türk. Schüler u. Studierende insgesamt	Türk. Schüler an Gymn., Fachmittel- u. Berufsschulen	Türk. Hochschüler
1957/58	110 291	ca. 6 000	375
1962/63	152 203	7 221	–
1970/71	181 279	21 617	795

Quelle: Zahlen nach: Ju. Memišev: Zadružno v socialističeskoto stroitelstvo na rodinata (Vereint im sozialistischen Aufbau der Heimat). Sofia 1984, S. 103 ff., S. 188 ff.

Nach 1975 übte Ljudmila Živkova, die Vorsitzende des Komitees für Kultur (Komitet za kultura), einen deutlichen Einfluß auf das Bildungswesen aus, der sich in den Jahren 1980/1981 noch verstärkte.

---

[18]) Popov, G.N.; Jordanov, G.D.: BKP na čelo na masovoto dviženie za izučavane na ruski ezik v NRB (1944–1962) (Die BKP an der Spitze der Massenbewegung für das Studium der russischen Sprache in der NRB, 1944–1962), in: Izvestija na Visšata partijna škola pri CK na BKP. 24 (1965), S. 293–310; Memišev (Anm. 14), S. 103–127.

[19]) Schivkov, T.: Über Fragen der Bildung, in: Ausgewählte Reden. Wien 1973.

Auf Initiative von Ljudmila Živkova wurde die ästhetische Erziehung in den Schulen verstärkt und durch ein Nationalprogramm für Ästhetik in allen Bereichen der Gesellschaft ergänzt, so daß Bulgarien auf diesem Gebiet eine führende Rolle unter den RGW-Ländern erreichte; die besonders begabten Kinder wurden in der 1976 errichteten Grundschule in Gorna Banja durch die Anwendung der Suggestopädie und anderer moderner Lerntechniken besonders gefördert; der Entwicklung der kindlichen Kreativität diente die 1979 gegründete internationale Bewegung „Banner des Friedens"; die Errichtung eines klassischen Gymnasiums in Sofia im Oktober 1977 mit den Schwerpunkten Latein, Griechisch und Altbulgarisch sollte die Verbindung zu den Wurzeln der bulgarischen Kultur wieder herstellen[20]).

6. Die Reform von 1979: Professionalisierung

Im Juliplenum des ZK 1979 wurde neuerlich eine weitreichende Bildungsreform beschlossen, die das Ziel hatte, eine einheitliche polytechnische Mittelschule (*edinno sredno politechničesko učilište* – ESPU) für alle Schüler zu errichten, d. h. daß die achtjährige Grundschule und letztlich die drei bestehenden Typen von Mittelschulen, die allgemeinbildende Mittelschule (Gymnasium), die Fachmittelschule (Technikum) sowie die Berufsschule (SPTU) zu einer einzigen elfklassigen (später zwölfklassigen) Einheitsschule verschmelzen sollten, die allen Schülern sowohl Allgemeinbildung wie auch eine konkrete Berufsausbildung vermittelte[21]).

In der 11. Klasse, die das Kernstück der ganzen Reform war, wurden die Schüler ab 1981/82 in einem Berufsausbildungszentrum (*učebno-profesionalen kompleks* – UPK) für einen konkreten Beruf ausgebildet. Am Ende des Schuljahres legten sie zuerst die Matura in den allgemeinbildenden Fächern und dann eine Facharbeiterprüfung ab, so daß sie mit 17 Jahren das Recht hatten, sich entweder für die Aufnahme an der Hochschule zu bewerben oder aber einen Posten als Facharbeiter in einem Betrieb anzunehmen[22]).

1981 wurde ein Nationalprogramm für die Computerisierung des Bildungswesens beschlossen, das weitgehend erfüllt wurde. Im Schuljahr 1985/86 wurde das Fach Informatik als Pflichtfach in der 10. Klasse mit je zwei Stunden in der Woche eingeführt, inzwischen aber auf 1 Stunde reduziert, und an allen Mittelschulen wurden Computerkabinette für die Schüler errichtet[23]).

---

[20]) Memišev (Anm. 14), S. 178–195; Zhivkova, L.: Her Many Worlds – New Culture and Beauty – Concepts and Action. Second enlarged ed. Oxford 1986, pp. 125–135, 155–159, and 194–204; Oschlies, W.: Wiedereinführung der klassischen Bildung in Bulgarien, in: Gymnasium. (1978), S. 339–342.

[21]) Tezisi za razvitieto na obrazovatelnoto delo v Narodna republika Bălgarija (Thesen über die Entwicklung des Bildungswesens in der NRB). Sofia 1979.

[22]) Osnovni položenija na sădăržanieto i organizacijata na učebno-văzpitatelnata rabota v ESPU (Grundlegende Bestimmungen des Inhalts und der Organisation der Unterrichts- und Erziehungsarbeit in der einheitlichen polytechnischen Mittelschule). Hrsg. Ministerstvo na narodnata prosveta. Sofia 1982.

[23]) Sendov, B.: The Second Wave – Problems of Computer Education, in: Ennals, R.; Gwyn, R.; Zdravchev, L.: Information Technology and Education – The Changing School. Chichester 1986, pp. 14–22.

Die Jugendorganisationen, die ursprünglich nur für die politisch-ideologische Erziehung zuständig waren, erweiterten ihren Aufgabenkreis durch die Gründung von Jugendklubs für Robotertechnik, Mikroelektronik und Bionik, zu denen in den letzten Jahren die Klubs für Computertechnik kamen[24]).

Gegen den Plan der Integration von Allgemeinbildung und Berufsbildung gab es Widerstand von seiten der Volkswirtschaft, die ein vermindertes Niveau der Berufsausbildung bei Technikern und Facharbeitern feststellte, wie auch von seiten der Universitäten und Hochschulen, die sich über die mangelnde Allgemeinbildung der Studenten beklagten. Im Februar 1985 beschloß das ZK auf einem Plenum, das sich mit der Modernisierung der Gesellschaft und der wissenschaftlich-technischen Revolution beschäftigte, die Integration aufzuschieben: Die zwei traditionellen Zweige des bulgarischen Bildungswesens hätten, wie es im ZK-Beschluß heißt, ihre Möglichkeiten noch nicht völlig ausgeschöpft und sollten deshalb weiter bestehen bleiben[25]).

Im Oktober 1985 begann das Ministerium für Volksbildung mit einer Disziplinkampagne, die das Tragen von Schuluniformen, die Einführung einer Sperrstunde für alle Jugendlichen bis 19 Jahren ab 21 Uhr und eine Reihe von Sanktionen bei Verstößen gegen die Schulordnung vorsah. Diese Maßnahmen, die von den Eltern größtenteils mit Unverständnis aufgenommen wurden, mußten zwei Jahre später wieder zurückgenommen werden[26]).

Im Juli 1987 wurde eine gewisse Dezentralisierung des Bildungswesens durch Übertragung von Kompetenzen an die regionalen Schulräte und an die Schulen beschlossen.

Am 19. und 20.7.1988 wurden die Fragen des Bildungswesens erneut auf einem Sonderplenum des ZK der BKP über den geistig-kulturellen Bereich diskutiert, wo auch ein gewisser Einfluß sowjetischer Reformideen erkennbar war. Die Konferenz beschloß, die Einheitlichkeit und Professionalisierung des bulgarischen Bildungswesens abzuschwächen und statt dessen eine gewisse Differenzierung zu fördern. Es wurde geplant, in der Oberstufe der normalen ESPU Wahlfächer einzuführen, die den individuellen Neigungen der Schüler besser entgegenkommen, und versuchsweise eine „profilierte" ESPU einzuführen, die sich auf eine bestimmte Richtung spezialisiert[27]). Im wesentlichen blieb das Juliplenum 1988 jedoch im Rahmen des bestehenden Bildungssystems, es ging über die Thesen von 1979 nicht hinaus und vermied es, zu wichtigen aktuellen Fragen Beschlüsse zu fassen.

---

[24]) Cvetanova, M.: Prazni maratoni (Sinnlose Marathonläufe), in: Anteni. 18 (1988) 19; Janeva, K.: V delnika njama fanfari (Im Alltag gibt es keine Fanfaren), in: Anteni. 17 (1987) 34.

[25]) Živkov, T.: Za njakoi novi viždanija i podchodi v razrabotvaneto i proveždaneto na naučno-techničeskata politika na Narodna republika Bălgarija (Über einige neue Gesichtspunkte und Methoden in der Entwicklung und Durchführung der wissenschaftlich-technischen Politik der NRB), in: RD. 15.2.1985. Zu den Zielsetzungen der Bildungsreform siehe Mavrov, G.: Problemi na strategijata na obrazovanieto (Probleme der Strategie des Bildungswesens). Sofia 1986.

[26]) Učilištnata disciplina (Die Schuldisziplin), in: Učitelsko delo. (1987) 52.

[27]) Umgestaltung im Bildungswesen, in: BTA-Bulletin. (1988) 28; Rešenie na Plenuma na CK na BKP, săstojal se na 19 i 20 juli 1988 god. (Beschluß des Plenums des ZK der BKP vom 19. und 20. Juli 1988), in: Učitelsko delo. (1988) 30.

II. Die Vorschulerziehung

Die Vorschulerziehung konnte sich in Bulgarien bis zum II. Weltkrieg nur schwach entwickeln, da ein allgemeiner gesellschaftlicher Bedarf nicht vorhanden war. Dennoch wurde schon 1882 der erste öffentliche Kindergarten gegründet, und 1944 gab es bereits 243 staatliche Kindergärten mit 287 Erzieherinnen und 11 337 Kindern. Dazu kamen noch 25 Missionskindergärten mit 1203 Kindern[28]).

Nach dem 9.9.1944 begann die Regierung, ein einheitliches System von Kindergärten für drei- bis siebenjährige Kinder aufzubauen, das in den 50er Jahren besonders stark expandierte. Das Hauptaugenmerk galt in den letzten Jahrzehnten dem Ausbau des Netzes an Vorschuleinrichtungen und ihrer materiellen Ausstattung, weil man einen möglichst großen Anteil der Kinder frühzeitig beeinflussen wollte.

1970 gab es bereits 8037 Kindergärten mit 331 960 Kindern und 1986 4977 Kindergärten mit 349 131 Kindern. Der Rückgang in der Anzahl der Kindergärten ist auf den Bau größerer Einrichtungen in zentral gelegenen Orten zurückzuführen, während gleichzeitig ein Teil ländlicher, wenig frequentierter Einrichtungen geschlossen wurde. Die Anzahl der Kindergärtnerinnen hat sich zwischen 1956 und 1986 annähernd verdreifacht, so daß eine Kindergärtnerin heute im Durchschnitt 15 Kinder gegenüber 27 im Jahre 1956 betreut. 1986 waren mehr als 90 % aller Kinder im Kindergarten untergebracht[29]).

Tabelle 2: Kindergärten (Vorschuleinrichtungen)

	1944	1950	1960	1970	1980	1986	1987
Kindergärten	243 (25)	4432	6570	8037	6185	4977	4840
Erzieherinnen	287	7418	11 873	18 185	28 996	28 718	28 659
Kinder	11 337 (1 203)	221 924	284 356	331 960	420 804	349 131	344 396

(Die Zahlen in Klammern für 1944 bezeichnen die privaten Missionskindergärten.)
Quelle: SG. 1950–1988.

Es gibt acht verschiedene Arten von Kindergärten:
- ganztägige Kindergärten: für Kinder, deren Eltern berufstätig sind; sie sollen zum Haupttyp der Kindergärten ausgebaut werden;
- wöchentliche Kindergärten: für Kinder, deren Eltern auch nach 20 Uhr noch berufstätig sind;
- halbtägige Kindergärten: werden an Grund- und Mittelschulen sowie an ganztägigen Kindergärten und vereinigten Kindereinrichtungen errichtet;

---

[28]) 100 godini predučilištno vązpitanie v Bǎlgarija. Materiali na jubilejnata sesija v grad Svištov (100 Jahre Vorschulerziehung in Bulgarien. Materialien der Jubiläumstagung in der Stadt Svištov). Sǎstaviteli: Šejtanova, C. u.a. Sofia 1984.
[29]) Petrova, E.; Šejtanova, C.; Slavova, R.: Predučilištnoto vązpitanie v NRB (Die Vorschulerziehung in der NRB). Sofia 1979, S. 29 ff.

- zeitweilige Kindergärten: für Kinder, deren Eltern zeitweilig in einem Betrieb in einer anderen Region arbeiten;
- Sommerkindergärten: für Kinder, deren Eltern zur Erntezeit in landwirtschaftlichen Betrieben arbeiten;
- Sonderkindergärten: für Kinder mit körperlichen oder psychischen Behinderungen;
- Kindersanatorien: für Kinder, die häufig an schweren Krankheiten der oberen Atemwege oder an anderen Krankheiten leiden;
- Kinderspielplätze: werden während des Sommers bei Schulen mit halbtägigem Aufenthalt der Kinder errichtet[30]).

1979 wurde als Ziel formuliert, daß alle Fünfjährigen in den Kindergärten erfaßt werden sollten. 1981 wurde ein neues Programm für die Erziehung und Entwicklung der Kinder im Alter von drei bis sechs Jahren beschlossen, das substantielle Veränderungen in den pädagogischen Methoden vorsah. Die Kinder sollen sich gesellschaftlich nützliche Gewohnheiten aneignen, die ihnen den Übergang zur 1. Klasse der Grundschule erleichtern. Sie sollen durch eine geschickte Auswahl der zu erwerbenden Kenntnisse und Fähigkeiten und nicht auf dem Wege einer formalen Reduzierung des Lehrmaterials entlastet werden[31]).

Für jede Altersgruppe ist weiterhin ein genau festgelegtes Tagesregime vorgesehen, das aber der Kindergärtnerin auch die Möglichkeit geben soll, es selbständig zu gestalten. Diese neuen Unterrichtsformen sollen durch typische, dem Alter angepaßte Spiele verwirklicht werden. Für jede Altersgruppe gibt es auch entsprechende Lehrbücher.

Das neue Programm wurde mit der schrittweisen Herabsetzung des Schuleintrittsalters auf sechs Jahre in Übereinstimmung gebracht, die Mitte der 80er Jahre abgeschlossen wurde, so daß heute die Kinder die Kindergärten nur bis zum sechsten Lebensjahr besuchen. Gleichzeitig wurden auch die Ausbildung der Kindergärtnerinnen reformiert und Fortbildungskurse für sie organisiert, damit die neuen pädagogischen Methoden in die Praxis umgesetzt werden können[32]).

III. Das allgemeinbildende Schulwesen

Die 1979 beschlossene ESPU sollte bis 1985 schrittweise zum einzigen Schultyp werden. Sie ist einheitlich, weil sie theoretisch alle Jugendlichen von der 1. bis zur 11. Schulklasse umfaßt, nicht in selbständige, abgeschlossene Lehrgänge aufgeteilt ist und Allgemeinbildung mit Berufsbildung verbindet. Sie ist allgemeinbildend und

---

[30]) Petrova u. a. (Anm. 29), S. 30f.
[31]) Decata i mirăt. Sbornik s materiali ot meždunarodnija kolokvium na svetovnata organizacija za predučilištnoto văzpitanie (Die Kinder und die Welt. Sammelband mit Materialien des Internationalen Kolloquiums der Weltorganisation für Vorschulerziehung). Hrsg. Ministerstvo na narodnata prosveta. Sofia 1987, S. 43–55.
[32]) Nikolova, J.: Săstojanie i razvitie na detskite zavedenija (Lage und Entwicklung der Kindereinrichtungen), in: Decata i mirăt (Anm. 31), S. 199–202.

Schaubild: Aufbau des bulgarischen Bildungssystems ab 1979
(ohne Berücksichtigung prozentualer Anteile)

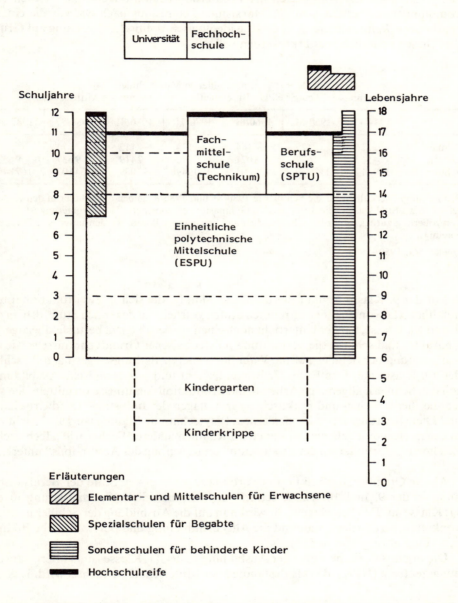

Die einheitliche polytechnische Mittelschule (*edinno sredno politechničesko učilište* – ESPU) hat folgende Stufen:
1.–3. Schuljahr: Elementarbildung (*načalen kurs*)
4.–8. Schuljahr: Progymnasialkurs (*progimnazialen kurs*)
1.–8. Schuljahr: Grundschule (*osnovno učilište*)
9.–11. Schuljahr: Gymnasialkurs (*gimnazialen kurs*)
11. Schuljahr: Berufsausbildungszentrum (*učebno-profesionalen kompleks* – UPK)

polytechnisch, weil sie den Unterricht mit der Arbeit verbindet und die Schüler mit den Grundlagen der Hauptarten der Produktion bekanntmacht. Sie ist auch eine kommunistische Schule, weil der Marxismus-Leninismus nach wie vor die einzige zugelassene Weltanschauung ist und die ideologisch-politische Erziehung auf Grund der Thesen neuerlich verstärkt werden soll[33]).

Tabelle 3: Allgemeinbildende Mittelschulen
(früher Gymnasien, heute ESPU, d. i. einheitliche polytechnische Mittelschulen)

	1944/45	1950/51	1960/61	1970/71	1980/81	1986/87	1987/88
Schulen	216	129	144	134	112	74	74
Lehrer	4563	4627	8021	6270	7419	9637	9637
Schüler	159517	113259	158004	100949	97089	164107	167845

Anmerkung: Die Zahlen für die Schuljahre 1980/81 und 1986/87 geben die Schüler in den Klassen IX–XI der ESPU wieder, die dem früheren Gymnasium entsprechen. Die Verringerung ist auf ihre Vergrößerung zurückzuführen. Schulen, die nahe beieinander liegen, werden unter eine Direktion vereinigt.
Quelle: SG. 1950–1988.

Mit der 9. Klasse beginnt die Berufsausbildung, die sich in zwei funktional und inhaltlich klar voneinander getrennten Stufen vollzieht: in der ersten Stufe, d. h. in der 9. und 10. Klasse, hat der Unterricht noch einen vorberuflichen, berufsfeldbezogenen Charakter und schließt die Vermittlung polytechnischer Grundkenntnisse sowie die Vorbereitung der Schüler auf die Wahl des weiteren Bildungsweges nach Abschluß der 10. Klasse ein. Das Fach „Arbeitsunterricht und polytechnische Ausbildung" soll den Schülern allgemeine Arbeits- und Produktionskenntnisse vermitteln. Sie sollen die theoretischen und praktischen Grundlagen der Industrie-, Landwirtschafts- und Dienstleistungsarbeit kennenlernen. Polytechnische Bildung wird aber nicht nur in einem eigenen Fach, sondern auch im Rahmen anderer Fächer wie „Technisches Zeichnen", „Grundlagen der Produktion" und „Aufbau des Automobils" unterrichtet[34]).

An die Orientierungsfunktion der profilbezogenen ersten Stufe der Berufsausbildung in der 9. und 10. Klasse schließt sich die berufliche Spezialisierung in der 11. Klasse an. Das Schwergewicht wird nun auf die Ausbildung der Schüler in einem konkreten Beruf gelegt, während die Allgemeinbildung und polytechnische Bildung fast völlig aufgegeben werden.

Die organisatorische Form der Ausbildung in der 11. Klasse ist das Berufsausbildungszentrum (UPK), das als Bestandteil der Mittelschule betrachtet wird. Das Be-

---

[33]) Tezisi za razvitieto na obrazovatelnoto delo v Narodna republika Bǎlgarija (Anm. 21).
[34]) Osnovni položenija za profesionalnata podgotovka (Grundbestimmungen über die Berufsausbildung). Sofia 1981.

Tabelle 4: Unterrichtsstunden an allgemeinbildenden Mittelschulen (ESPU), I.–X. Klasse

Fach	Unterrichtsstufen									
	I	II	III	IV	V	VI	VII	VIII	IX	X
	Anzahl der Unterrichtswochen									
	32	32	32	34	34	34	34	34	36	34
	Unterrichtsstunden pro Woche									
A. Allgemeinbildender Unterricht										
1. Bulg. Sprache und Literatur	8	8	7	7	6	5	5	5	4	3
2. Russisch	–	–	3	3	2	2	2	2	2	2
3. Westl. Sprache	–	–	–	–	3	3	3	2	2	–
4. Mathematik	4	4	4	5	5	4	4	4	4	4
5. Informatik	–	–	–	–	–	–	–	–	–	1
6. Physikal. und chem. Erscheinungen	–	–	–	–	–	2	–	–	–	–
7. Physik	–	–	–	–	–	–	2	2	3	3
8. Chemie	–	–	–	–	–	–	2	2	3	2
9. Naturkunde	–	–	1/0	1/2	2	–	–	–	–	–
10. Biologie	–	–	–	–	–	2	2	2	1	2
11. Heimatkunde	1	1	0/1	2/1	–	–	–	–	–	–
12. Geschichte	–	–	–	–	2	2	2	2	2	2
13. Geographie	–	–	–	–	2	2	2	2	2	–
14. Psychologie	–	–	–	–	–	–	–	–	–	1
15. Gesellschaftskunde	–	–	–	–	–	–	–	–	–	2
16. Bild. Kunst	1	1	1	1	1	1	1	1	–	–
17. Musik	1	1	1	1	1	1	1	1	–	–
18. Grundl. d. Ästhetik	–	–	–	–	–	–	–	–	1	1
19. Körpererziehung u. Sport	3	3	3	2	2	2	2	3	2	2
20. Arbeits- u. polytechn. Erziehung	2	2	2	2	2	2	2	3	4	5
21. Milit. Elementarunterricht	–	–	–	–	–	–	–	–	2	1
A insgesamt	20	20	22	24	28	28	30	31	32	31
B. Wahlfächer	–	–	–	2	2	2	2	2	2	2
C. Freifächer, außerunterrichtl. und außerschulische Tätigkeit	2	2	2	2	2	2	2	2	2	2

rufsausbildungszentrum, dessen Aufbau die schwierigste Aufgabe der Bildungsreform ist, wird als relativ selbständige Lehranstalt von einem eigenen Direktor geführt.

Der einjährige Lehrgang wurde zunächst als ausreichend angesehen, um den Jugendlichen eine praktische Berufsausbildung zu vermitteln.

Auf dem Februarplenum des ZK von 1985 und auf dem Januarplenum 1986 wurde beschlossen, die traditionelle Teilung in ein allgemeinbildendes und ein berufsbildendes Schulwesen beizubehalten und die Idee von der Integration der beiden Zweige nur mehr als „Perspektive" zu sehen. Statt dessen wird von der „Annäherung" der Allge-

Tabelle 5: Unterrichtsstunden an allgemeinbildenden Mittelschulen (ESPU), XI. Klasse

Fächer	1. Periode	2. Periode	3. Periode
	Zahl der Unterrichtswochen		
	17	9	10
A. Allgemeinbildende Fächer			
1. Bulg. Sprache u. Lit.	2	2	-
2. Körpererz. u. Sport	2	1	-
3. Gesellsch. u. Persönlichkeit	2	-	-
4. Informatik	2	2	-
A insgesamt	8	5	-
B. Allgemeintechn. und Spezialfächer			
1. Elektrotechnik u. Elektronik	3	-	-
2. Automatisierung d. Produktion	-	4	-
3. Ökonomie d. Produktion	2	-	-
4. Theorie d. Berufs u. d. Spezialisierung	8	10	-
B insgesamt	13	14	-
C. Produktionsunterricht			
1. Unterrichts- und Laborpraxis	10	12	-
2. Produktionspraxis	-	-	42
C insgesamt	10	12	42
A + B + C insgesamt	31	31	42
D. Wahlfächer	2	2	2
E. Freifächer	2	2	2

Quelle (Tab. 4 u. 5): Ukazanie (Anm. 46).

meinbildung und der Berufsbildung gesprochen, während das Ziel der Einheitsschule für alle praktisch aufgegeben ist[35]).

Unter dem Eindruck des Bildungsplenums des ZK der KPdSU vom Februar 1988 wurde eine Differenzierung des Unterrichts durch wahlweise-obligatorische Fächer und ein neues, objektiveres System in der Beurteilung der Schüler eingeführt[36]).

Auf den ZK-Sitzungen von 1985 und 1986 wurde eine Reform der Berufsausbildungszentren beschlossen, die das Ziel anstrebte, eine neue Liste der Berufe aufzustellen, die an den Zentren gelehrt werden, damit sie sich von den Fachschulen unter-

---

[35]) RD. 15.2.1985.
[36]) Učitelsko delo. (1988) 30.

scheiden und tatsächlich den Wünschen und Möglichkeiten der Schüler an den Mittelschulen entsprechen[37]).

Auf dem Sonderplenum des ZK über die Umgestaltung im geistig-kulturellen Bereich am 19. und 20. 7. 1988 wurde auch die erzieherische Funktion der Schule hervorgehoben, indem der weltanschaulichen, politischen, ethischen, rechtlichen und ästhetischen Entwicklung der Jugend Vorrang eingeräumt wird[38]).

Der Unterricht in Fremdsprachen spielt an den Mittelschulen traditionell eine große Rolle, wobei Russisch ab der 3. Klasse drei Stunden (ab der 5. Klasse zwei Stunden) wöchentlich obligatorisch ist. Der Unterricht in einer westlichen Fremdsprache ist ab der 5. Klasse drei Stunden (ab der 10. Klasse zwei Stunden) pro Woche Pflicht, kann aber schon vorher fakultativ besucht werden. Unter den westlichen Fremdsprachen steht im Gegensatz zu anderen osteuropäischen Ländern noch immer Französisch an erster Stelle, gefolgt vom Englischen, das aber erst Mitte der 80er Jahre die deutsche Sprache vom zweiten Platz verdrängen konnte[39]).

Tabelle 6: Zahl der Schüler an Gymnasien, die den Unterricht in westlichen Fremdsprachen besuchten

	1944/45	1950/51	1960/61	1970/71	1980/81	1986/87	1987/88
Französisch	84052	266053	163595	143724	172911	303195	296925
Englisch	1152	18150	15213	18557	51230	165122	183178
Deutsch	70727	77298	60497	56354	83300	160165	159910

Quelle: SG. 1950–1988.

Eine gewisse Differenzierung zeigt sich in den Spezialschulen (für die die Bezeichnung „Gymnasium" beibehalten wurde) für Schüler mit besonderen Begabungen und Interessen, die in den 60er Jahren in allen Großstädten Bulgariens gegründet wurden. Die Bewerber, die die 7. Klasse mit einem guten Zeugnis beendet haben, müssen eine strenge Aufnahmeprüfung ablegen, die den Schulen einen elitären Charakter gibt. Die Ausbildung dauert fünf Jahre, d. h. ein Jahr länger als der Gymnasialkurs der normalen ESPU.

An den 16 deutschsprachigen Gymnasien werden jährlich 125 Schüler neu aufgenommen, doch gibt es etwa fünfmal so viele Kandidaten. An den Schulen gibt es Lehrer aus der DDR, doch am jährlichen Fortbildungskurs für Germanisten im Sommer unterrichten auch zwei österreichische Lehrer. Österreich verfügt auch über ein ständiges Lektorat für deutsche Sprache und österreichische Literatur an der Universität Sofia. Es gibt auch 13 französische und 20 englische Gymnasien sowie 20 Schulen mit russischer Unterrichtssprache.

---

[37]) Teoretični osnovi na profesionalnata podgotovka (Theoretische Grundlagen der Berufsausbildung). Hrsg. Ministerstvo na narodnata prosveta. Sofia 1986.
[38]) Jotov, J.: Dălboko i plodotvorno preustrojstvo na duchovnija život (Tiefgreifende und fruchtbare Umgestaltung des geistigen Lebens), in: Učitelsko delo. (1988) 30.
[39]) Fremdsprachen in der Schule, in: Sofioter Nachrichten. 4.3.1983.

Darüber hinaus gibt es 20 Spezialschulen für Mathematik, eine für Naturwissenschaften (Physik, Chemie und Biologie), 16 für Sport, 21 künstlerische Mittelschulen und ein Gymnasium für klassische Sprachen[40]).

Bulgarien nimmt für sich in Anspruch, der Behindertenerziehung eine besondere Aufmerksamkeit zu widmen und kann auf eine bedeutende Förderung des Sonderschulwesens hinweisen. 1983 wurde an der Pädagogischen Hochschule Blagoevgrad und später auch an der Universität Sofia die Fachrichtung „Defektologie" eingerichtet, die von Pädagogen studiert werden kann. Bulgarien übernimmt auf diesem Gebiet vor allem die Erfahrungen der Humboldt-Universität in Ostberlin, mit der die Pädagogische Hochschule Blagoevgrad einen Vertrag über Professoren- und Studentenaustausch abgeschlossen hat[41]).

Tabelle 7: Behindertenschulen
(Schulen für geistig Behinderte, Schwererziehbare, Taubstumme, Blinde und Sprachbehinderte)

	1944/45	1950/51	1960/61	1970/71	1980/81	1986/87	1987/88
Schulen	4	11	20	116	129	128	128
Lehrer	43	115	987	2155	2373	2369	2364
Schüler	208	976	8090	16870	17420	17272	16764

Quelle: SG. 1950–1988.

IV. Die Berufsschulen

Die Berufsbildung für Facharbeiter und Handwerker wurde vor dem II. Weltkrieg in erster Linie durch eine Ausbildung am Arbeitsplatz in den industriellen und gewerblichen Betrieben durchgeführt. Die Industrialisierung des Landes und die Kollektivierung der Landwirtschaft erforderten jedoch ein Heer von qualifizierten Arbeitskräften, für die die traditionelle Form der Berufsbildung bei weitem nicht mehr ausreichte.

Die Regierung sah sich deshalb gezwungen, ein gänzlich neues Berufsschulwesen nach sowjetischem Vorbild aufzubauen, da es dafür keine entsprechenden eigenen Traditionen gab.

Das Gesetz über Volksbildung von 1948 sah eine wesentliche Verbesserung der Berufsbildung vor, die dem Ministerium für Volksbildung unterstellt wurde. Es wurden Schulen für die Ausbildung von Facharbeitern (*učilišta za podgotovkata na kvalificirani rabotničeski kadri*) eingerichtet, die sich zunächst nur langsam entwickelten (siehe Tab. 8).

---

[40]) Georgiewa, K.: Das deutschsprachige Gymnasium, in: Sofioter Nachrichten. 23.9.1987; Die Diskussion um die Schule geht weiter, in: Sofioter Nachrichten. 16.9.1987.
[41]) Mandatna programa, 1983–1987 godina (Mandatsprogramm für die Jahre 1983–1987). Hrsg. Visš pedagogičeski institut. Blagoevgrad 1983.

Es gab industrielle, Bau-, Transport-, Fernmelde- sowie land- und forstwirtschaftliche Schulen, die Facharbeiter in Kursen mit einer Dauer von ein bis drei Jahren ausbildeten[42]).

Die wirkliche Expansion begann nach der Bildungsreform von 1959 mit der Umwandlung dieser Schulen in beruflich-technische Schulen (*profesionalno-techničeski učilišta* – PTU) und nach 1969 in mittlere beruflich-technische Schulen (*sredni profesionalno-techničeski učilišta* – SPTU), die auch einen Mittelschulabschluß vermitteln. Das Berufsschulwesen erhielt eine breitere institutionelle Auffächerung und größere Flexibilität in seinem Bildungsangebot.

Die Thesen von 1979 sahen die Integration der Berufsbildung mit den Fachmittelschulen und den allgemeinbildenden Mittelschulen zu einem neuen, einheitlichen Schultyp (ESPU) vor. Der Lehrplan der Berufsschulen wurde an den der ESPU angeglichen, d.h. daß der Anteil der allgemeinbildenden Fächer erhöht und die Ausbildung generell auf drei Jahre festgelegt wurde[43]).

Da die allgemeinbildende Mittelschule (ESPU) heute ebenfalls eine Berufsausbildung in den Klassen 9 bis 11 anbietet, ist der Begriff der berufsbildenden Schule nicht mehr eindeutig, doch läßt sich erkennen, daß die Tendenz heute nicht zur Auflösung der SPTU, sondern zu ihrem weiteren Ausbau als Einrichtung mit eigenem Profil und einer hochwertigen Berufsausbildung geht.

PTU und SPTU haben nach ihrem Höhepunkt im Schuljahr 1980/81 mit insgesamt 151 200 Schülern infolge der Bildungsreform einen Rückgang auf 111 907 Schüler im Schuljahr 1986/87 erlitten, doch stellen Berufsschulen und Fachmittelschulen (*technikumi*) zusammen noch immer etwa 75% der bulgarischen Schüler[44]).

Die Anzahl der Schüler in den einzelnen Berufsschulen wird von der staatlichen Planungskommission im Einvernehmen mit dem Ministerium für Kultur, Wissenschaft und Bildungswesen (*Ministerstvo na kulturata, naukata i prosvetata*) gemäß dem Bedarf an qualifizierten Arbeitskräften in den einzelnen Zweigen der Volkswirtschaft im Fünfjahresplan und in den Jahresplänen festgelegt.

Der Lehrplan der einzelnen Berufsschulen wird vom Ministerium für Kultur, Wissenschaft und Bildungswesen gemeinsam mit den einzelnen Industrieministerien aufgestellt. Die Berufsschulen erteilen gleichzeitig mit dem theoretischen Unterricht auch praktischen Unterricht in eigenen Werkstätten und Versuchsbetrieben, und die Schüler müssen außerdem ein Produktionspraktikum in „Basisbetrieben" absolvieren, die einen Sondervertrag mit der Schule abgeschlossen haben[45]).

Die Stundentafel der SPTU sieht folgende Verteilung der Unterrichtsfächer vor:

Allgemeinbildende Fächer: 42%
Körpererziehung und Sport: 8,75%
Theoretische und allgemein-technische Fächer: 17,25%
Produktionsunterricht: 32%

---

[42]) Atanasov, Istorija (Anm. 2), S. 348.
[43]) Tezisi (Anm. 21).
[44]) SG. 1987.
[45]) Stoew, T.: Welche Fortbildungsmöglichkeiten gibt es außer der allgemeinbildenden Oberschule? Sofia 1988.

Die wöchentliche Belastung der Schüler durch Unterricht und praktische Übungen beträgt 36 Stunden[46]).

Tabelle 8: Berufsschulen

	1944/45	1950/51	1960/61	1970/71	1980/81	1986/87	1987/88
Schulen	323	187	236	328	300	264	264
Lehrer	1130	1564	2835	8454	9435	7704	7457
Schüler	28018	35724	42123	130292	151200	111907	107967

Quelle: SG. 1950–1988.

V. Die Fachmittelschulen

Die ersten Gewerbeschulen in Bulgarien entstanden um die Jahrhundertwende, und in den 30er Jahren gab es bereits 65 mittlere Berufsschulen mit etwa 20000 Schülern. Durch das erste „sozialistische" Bildungsgesetz von 1948 wurden diese Schulen dem Ministerium für Volksbildung unterstellt, das sich zunächst bemühte, ihre materielle Ausstattung zu verbessern. In den 50er Jahren bildeten sich die zwei Typen von berufsbildenden Schulen heraus: die zwei- bis dreijährige Berufsschule für die Ausbildung von Facharbeitern und die vierjährige mittlere Berufsschule oder Fachmittelschule (*sredno profesionalno učilište,* später nach sowjetischem Vorbild *technikum* genannt) für die Ausbildung von Technikern und mittleren Spezialisten[47]).

Auf dem VII. Parteitag der BKP im Juni 1958 wurden die Richtlinien für den 3. Fünfjahresplan (1958–1960) angenommen, der den Vorrang für die Schwerindustrie, insbesondere für Maschinenbau, Schwarz- und Buntmetallurgie, chemische Industrie, Elektrogewinnung, Kohleindustrie und Produktion von Baumaterialien festlegte. Daraus folgte, daß das Land einen sehr großen Bedarf an Spezialisten für die Produktion hatte, und ihrer Ausbildung daher besondere Aufmerksamkeit schenken mußte.

Durch die Bildungsreform von 1959 wurden Fachmittelschulen für Industrie, Landwirtschaft, Verkehrswesen, Handel und Gesundheitswesen geschaffen, die ihren Absolventen die Qualifikation eines mittleren Spezialisten in einem bestimmten Beruf vermittelten. Die Schulen erhielten Werkstätten, physikalische und chemische Kabinette, Laboratorien und Versuchsstationen und schlossen Verträge mit Betrieben und TKZS ab, die den Schülern die Möglichkeit gaben, ein Produktionspraktikum zu absolvieren[48]).

---

[46]) Ukazanie za organizirane na učebno-vǎzpitatelnata rabota prez učebnata 1988/89 godina (Weisung zur Organisation der Unterrichts- und Erziehungsarbeit im Schuljahr 1988/89). Hrsg. Ministerstvo za kulturata, naukata i narodnata prosveta. Sofia 1988, S. 5.

[47]) Atanasov, Istorija (Anm. 2), S. 311.

[48]) Aprilskata politika na BKP i razvitieto na profesionalnata podgotovka (Die Aprilpolitik der BKP und die Entwicklung der Berufsausbildung). Hrsg. Ministerstvo na narodnata prosveta. Sofia 1984.

Die Schulen erhielten auch das Recht, die Hochschulreife zu verleihen, so daß in den 60er Jahren bereits der größte Teil jener Jugendlichen, die an einer Hochschule studieren wollten, den Weg über das Technikum wählte. Die Absolventen des Technikums wurden jenen des Gymnasiums in jeder Beziehung gleichgestellt.

Es wurden auch Fachmittelschulen für Abend- und Fernstudenten errichtet, die Berufstätigen die Möglichkeit gaben, ohne Unterbrechung der Arbeit eine mittlere Fachausbildung zu erwerben. Die Nachfrage danach war jedoch gering, weil man höhere berufliche Positionen auch ohne den Abschluß einer Mittelschule erreichen konnte, und Mitte der 70er Jahre wurden die meisten Abendschulen wieder geschlossen[49]).

Die Unterschiede zwischen den beiden zur Hochschule führenden Bildungswegen, dem Gymnasium, das Allgemeinbildung ohne Berufsausbildung vermittelte, und der Fachmittelschule, die Spezialisten ausbildete, wurden seit den 60er Jahren zunehmend zu einem Problem.

Das Bildungsplenum des ZK im Juli 1969 beschloß, daß der größere Teil der Schüler nach dem Abschluß der achtjährigen Grundschule in berufsbildende Schulen oder direkt in die Produktion übergehen sollte. Es wurde auch der Versuch gemacht, daß Absolventen des Gymnasiums nach der Matura in zwei Jahren zusätzlich den Abschluß einer Fachmittelschule erwerben konnten, aber das konnte sich nicht durchsetzen[50]).

Durch die Bildungsreform von 1979 sollte auch die Fachmittelschule neu gestaltet werden: Sie sollte entweder durch Aufnahme allgemeinbildender Fächer zu einer normalen ESPU umgebaut oder aber zu einem Berufsausbildungszentrum (UPK) im Rahmen einer ESPU reduziert werden. Langfristig sollte die Fachmittelschule als eigener Schultyp aufhören zu bestehen und der Einheitsschule Platz machen. Die Veränderung der Struktur der Ausbildung sollte mit einer inhaltlichen Modernisierung eng verbunden werden, die folgendes umfaßte:

– enge Verbindung mit der Produktion;
– Erhöhung des Niveaus der wissenschaftlich-technischen Bildung;
– Verstärkung des theoretischen und praktisch-angewandten Niveaus der Unterrichtsfächer;
– Betonung solchen Wissens, das zum selbständigen, schöpferischen Denken anregt;
– neue Bestimmung des Inhalts der Berufsausbildung[51]).

Die Thesen von 1979 sahen vor, daß der Schülerstrom, der nach der 8. Klasse der Grundschule in die Fachmittelschule oder Berufsschule geht, systematisch abgebaut und in die ESPU umgeleitet werden sollte. Dieses Ziel konnte nicht erreicht werden, und im Februar 1985 wurde auf Grund der großen Schwierigkeiten bei der Verwirklichung an Stelle der Vereinheitlichung beschlossen, Fachmittelschulen und Berufsschulen bestehen zu lassen. Die Differenzierung unter den Schultypen wurde durch die Beschlüsse der letzten Jahre wieder verstärkt, und seit Mitte der 80er Jahre hat der Zustrom zu den Fachmittelschulen wieder zugenommen.

---

[49]) Aprilskata politika na BKP (Anm. 48).
[50]) Čakărov (Anm. 2), S. 82.
[51]) Tezisi (Anm. 21).

Die ältesten und populärsten Fachmittelschulen sind die Mechanik-Schulen, die in der Warm- und Kaltbearbeitung von Metallen ausbilden. Neuere Richtungen sind Schulen für Elektronik und Elektrotechnik, chemische und Gummiindustrie, Energetik und Kühltechnik. In Sofia gibt es spezialisierte Schulen für optoelektronische Rechentechnik und Industrieelektronik, Robotertechnik, Rundfunk- und Fernsehtechnik sowie Fernmeldetechnik. Diese Bereiche sind mit den progressiven Richtungen der Wirtschaftsentwicklung Bulgariens verbunden und erschließen den Absolventen berufliche Aufstiegsmöglichkeiten[52].

Im Schuljahr 1986/87 gab es in Bulgarien 237 Fachmittelschulen mit 104 953 Schülern, davon 77 543 ordentliche Schüler, 9263 Abendschüler und 18 147 Fernschüler. In diesen Schulen wurden Spezialisten in 151 Fachrichtungen und 24 Fachgruppen ausgebildet. Der Unterrichtsinhalt gliederte sich in einen allgemeinbildenden, allgemein-technischen, speziell-theoretischen und Produktionszyklus[53].

Tabelle 9: Fachmittelschulen*)
(*Technikumi*, vor 1969 auch mittlere Berufsschulen /*sredni profesionalni učilišta*/ genannt)

	1944/45	1950/51	1960/61	1970/71	1980/81	1986/87	1987/88
Schulen	62	175	231	246	234	237	248
Lehrer	792	2690	5307	9045	9415	10014	10619
Schüler	21212	61591	93944	152919	97575	104953	115036

*) einschließlich der künstlerischen Mittelschulen
Quelle: SG. 1950–1988.

VI. Die Lehrerbildung

Die Lehrer hatten einst neben den Popen das höchste Prestige in der bulgarischen Gesellschaft, da sie die Träger der Kultur, der Bildung und der national-revolutionären Ideen waren. Ihr gesellschaftlicher Einfluß begann schon vor dem II. Weltkrieg zu sinken, doch erst in den 40er und 50er Jahren verloren sie endgültig ihre frühere Position.

Unmittelbar nach dem 9.9.1944 wurden umfangreiche Säuberungen unter der Lehrerschaft durchgeführt, die zuerst nur die exponierten Vertreter des autoritären Regimes, aber nach 1947 auch Anhänger demokratischer Parteien und schließlich alle erfaßte, die „nationale" Ideen vertraten oder in irgendeiner Weise nicht die politische Linie des neuen, volksdemokratischen Regimes teilten. Viele Tausende wurden aus dem Schuldienst entlassen und durch junge, rasch ausgebildete Lehrer ersetzt, die die sowjetische Pädagogik durchsetzen sollten[54].

---

[52]) Spravočnik za profesiite s širok profil (Handbuch der Grundberufe). Hrsg. Ministerstvo na narodnata prosveta. Sofia 1986.
[53]) SG. 1987, S. 416.
[54]) Čičovska, Character (Anm. 3), S. 227.

Die Lehrer erhielten eine Funktion in der neuen Gesellschaft als Erzieher der Jugend zu „Erbauern des Sozialismus", doch verloren sie unter dem Červenkov-Regime ihre Selbständigkeit und hatten nur mehr Direktiven innerhalb eines bis in jede Einzelheit festgelegten Systems auszuführen. Sie erhielten die Aufgabe, den Schülern die Weltanschauung des Marxismus-Leninismus und die politische Linie der BKP zu vermitteln, wobei keinerlei Abweichungen mehr möglich waren. Sie wurden außerdem noch durch außerunterrichtliche und außerschulische Tätigkeiten überlastet, da sie auch Erziehungsaufgaben in den Jugendklubs, der Verkehrserziehung und in Erste-Hilfe-Kursen übernehmen mußten.

Im Mittelpunkt des „sozialistischen Aufbaus" stand die industrielle Produktion, während das Bildungswesen eine untergeordnete Rolle spielte. Die BKP konzentrierte sich darauf, führende Positionen im Partei- und Staatsapparat zu besetzen und überließ das Bildungswesen weitgehend den Parteilosen[55]).

In den 60er und 70er Jahren wurden alle Lehrerbildungsanstalten schrittweise in Lehranstalten mit Hochschulcharakter umgewandelt. Fachhochschulen für die Ausbildung von Kindergärtnerinnen und Grundschullehrern gibt es heute in Sofia, Ruse, Burgas, Stara Zagora, Vraca, Tolbuchin, Pazardžik und Pleven.

Die Lehrer für allgemeinbildende Fächer für die Sekundarstufen I und II (Progymnasialkurs und Gymnasium, d. h. 4. bis 11. Klasse der ESPU) werden an den Universitäten Sofia, Plovdiv und Veliko Tărnovo sowie an den Pädagogischen Hochschulen von Šumen und Blagoevgrad ausgebildet. Es gibt weiter eine Hochschule für Körperkultur in Sofia, je eine Hochschule für Musik in Sofia und Plovdiv und eine Hochschule für Kunsterziehung in Veliko Tărnovo. Die Ausbildung der Lehrer für technische und spezielle Fächer an Mittelschulen findet an fünf ingenieuragronomischen und ökonomischen Hochschulen statt. In Sliven ist eine neue Pädagogische Hochschule im Aufbau begriffen. In allen Fächern ist auch ein Fernstudium möglich, das aber ein Jahr länger dauert[56]).

Šumen ist eines der ältesten Bildungszentren Bulgariens, wo bereits im Jahre 1879 der erste Kurs für die Ausbildung von Grundschullehrern eröffnet wurde, aus dem 1919 eine Lehrerbildungsanstalt hervorging, die 1964 zu einer Filiale der Sofioter Universität „Kliment Ochridski" mit Hochschulcharakter ausgebaut wurde. Eine besondere Aufgabe der Filiale, an der die Fächer Türkische Philologie, Geschichte, Geographie und Mathematik gelehrt wurden, war die Ausbildung von türkischen Lehrern. 1971 wurde die Filiale zu einer Pädagogischen Hochschule mit einer Philologischen und einer Naturwissenschaftlichen Fakultät erhoben, die 1988 bereits 1400 ordentliche und 1200 Fernstudenten zählte[57]).

Blagoevgrad (Gorna Džumaja) im Piriner Gebiet hatte bereits 1923 eine Lehrerbildungsanstalt, die 1976 zu einer Filiale der Sofioter Universität „Kliment Ochridski" mit Hochschulcharakter und 1983 zu einer selbständigen Pädagogischen Hochschule erhoben wurde. Es gibt heute Fakultäten für Vorschulerziehung, Grundschulerziehung und polytechnische Bildung, zu denen in Zukunft eine Philologische und eine

---

[55]) Čičovska, Character (Anm. 3), S. 233.
[56]) Atanasov, Istorija (Anm. 2), S. 371.
[57]) Visš pedagogičeski institut Šumen, 1971–1981 god. (Die Pädagogische Hochschule Šumen, 1971–1981). Festschrift. Šumen 1981.

Naturwissenschaftliche Fakultät kommen sollen. Die Polytechnische Fakultät, die der Hochschule ihr besonderes Profil gibt und sich der besonderen Aufmerksamkeit der Regierung erfreut, bildet Lehrer für den polytechnischen Unterricht in ganz Bulgarien aus[58]).

Die Pädagogische Hochschule Blagoevgrad ist auch ein Zentrum für die Ausbildung von Lehrern für den Ökologieunterricht (seit 1976) und für Behindertenpädagogik (seit 1983), die sich vor allem an DDR-Erfahrungen orientiert. Die Hochschule beschäftigte 1988 insgesamt 370 Hochschullehrer, davon 76 habilitierte. Im selben Jahr hatte sie etwa 4700 Studenten, davon 1700 ordentliche und 3000 Fernstudenten[59]).

Bulgarien verfügt über ein entwickeltes System der Lehrerweiterbildung, das in den 50er Jahren geschaffen und zunächst dem Ministerium für Volksbildung und den Bezirksräten unterstellt war. Diese Weiterbildungskurse, die die Lehrer alle fünf Jahre absolvieren, dienen der fachlichen und politischen Weiterbildung und sind auch eine Voraussetzung für das Erreichen leitender Positionen. Seit 1981 bewertet ein Komitee aus drei Personen die Leistungen der Lehrer an jeder Schule nach einer vierstelligen Notenskala[60]).

Es gibt vier Institute für Lehrerweiterbildung, die nach 1979 in Fakultäten mit Hochschulcharakter verwandelt wurden: die Institute in Sofia, Varna (das der Pädagogischen Hochschule Šumen unterstellt wurde), Stara Zagora (das zur Universität Plovdiv kam) und Gabrovo (das an die Technische Hochschule Gabrovo angeschlossen wurde)[61]).

Das Zentralinstitut für die Weiterbildung der Lehrer und leitenden Spezialisten in Sofia wurde am 1.1.1953 gegründet und 1983 der Sofioter Universität „Kliment Ochridski" als eigene Fakultät angegliedert. Das Institut verfügt heute über 15 Lehrstühle, eine Schule für die Ausbildung von Pionierleitern und drei Abteilungen für Methodik. Es zählte 1988 insgesamt 160 Mitarbeiter, davon etwa 100 Hochschullehrer. Es besteht eine enge Zusammenarbeit mit Einrichtungen der Weiterbildung in der UdSSR[62]).

Der Lehrermangel ist eines der Hauptprobleme des bulgarischen Bildungswesens: Im Jahr 1987 haben mehr als die Hälfte der ausgebildeten Junglehrer den Dienst verlassen und sich eine andere Arbeit gesucht. Im Jahre 1988 fehlten allein in der Stadt Sofia 350 Lehrer. Die Gründe dafür sind die Arbeitsbelastung (durchschnittlich 12 bis 14 Stunden pro Tag), die durch die umfangreiche außerunterrichtliche und außerschulische Arbeit entsteht, die noch dazu unbezahlt ist, sowie das Fehlen mate-

---

[58]) Visš pedagogičeski institut Blagoevgrad – spravočnik (Pädagogische Hochschule Blagoevgrad – Handbuch). Blagoevgrad 1987.
[59]) Stoilov, D.: Čovek – obštestvo – priroda (Mensch – Gesellschaft – Natur). Blagoevgrad 1988.
[60]) Sistema za povišavane kvalifikacijata na učitelite i rǎkovodnite kadri na narodnata prosveta (System für die Erhöhung der Qualifikation der Lehrer und leitenden Spezialisten der Volksbildung). Sofia 1982.
[61]) Poslediplomnaja kvalifikacija pedagogičeskich kadrov – tendencii i perspektivi (Die postgraduale Weiterbildung der Lehrer – Tendenzen und Perspektiven). Sofia 1988.
[62]) 30 godini Centralen institut za usăvăršenstvuvane na učiteli i rǎkovodni kadri „Vela Blagoeva" (30 Jahre Zentralinstitut für die Weiterbildung der Lehrer und leitenden Pädagogen). Sofia 1983.

rieller Vorteile, die es für andere Berufsgruppen gibt wie Prämien, Urlaub in Erholungsheimen und Zuteilung von Sozialwohnungen[63]).

Wenn man alle Berufsgruppen Bulgariens in 16 Kategorien je nach ihren Löhnen und Gehältern einteilt, so sind die Lehrer in der 15., d. h. in der vorletzten Kategorie[64]).

Ergebnisse dieser Entwicklung sind die Feminisierung des Lehrerberufs und, durch die ständige Abwanderung der qualifizierten Kräfte, ein relatives Sinken des Qualifikations- und Bildungsniveaus der Lehrer, so daß 1987 nur 30% der Lehrer über Hochschulbildung verfügten[65]).

Der Lehrerberuf hat ein geringes Ansehen bei Männern, jungen Leuten und Personen mit Hochschulbildung, wie Soziologen anhand der Angaben einer Umfrage, die unter einer repräsentativen Gruppe von fast 3000 Lehrern durchgeführt wurde, feststellten[66]).

Der Verband der bulgarischen Lehrer (*Săjuz na bălgarskite učiteli*) ist heute eine gewerkschaftliche Organisation, die die Lehrer aller Arten und Stufen von Lehranstalten einschließlich der Hochschulen und der BAN vereinigt. In der Zeit von 1944 bis 1962 war der „Verband der Arbeiter im Bildungswesen" (*Săjuz na rabotnicite v prosvetata*) eine reine Berufsorganisation mit eng begrenzten Aufgaben. 1962 wurde der Verband reorganisiert: Er verlor die Hälfte der früheren Mitglieder wie z. B. Drucker, Schauspieler, Musiker und Museumsbeamte und wurde als Lehrerverband mit erweiterten Aufgaben wiedergegründet, der sich auch mit der Lehrerfortbildung beschäftigt[67]).

Der Lehrerverband verfügt über einen beträchtlichen politischen Einfluß, da 60 seiner Mitglieder auch dem Hohen Bildungsrat (*Visš učeben săvet*) angehören und keine Verordnung des Ministers für Volksbildung ohne die Unterschrift des Verbandes erlassen werden kann[68]).

Die Zeitung des Verbandes, *Učitelsko delo* (Lehrersache), die seit 1905 unter verschiedenen Titeln erscheint, veränderte 1981 ihre Konzeption: Sie wurde von einer eng begrenzten beruflichen Fachzeitschrift zu einer nationalen kulturpolitischen Wochenschrift, die sich an ein breites Publikum richtet und auch die Probleme der Jugend, Familie, Hochschule und Wissenschaft sowie der Kunst und Kultur miteinbezieht[69]).

Die Pädagogische Gesellschaft (*Pedagogičesko družestvo*), 1977 von Žečo Atanasov an der Universität Sofia als wissenschaftliche Vereinigung gegründet, informiert ihre Mitglieder vor allem über internationale Tagungen[70]).

---

[63]) Učitelsko delo. (1987) 46.
[64]) Učitelsko delo. (1987) 10.
[65]) Učitelsko delo. (1987) 15 und (1988) 16.
[66]) BTA-Informationsbulletin. (1988) 37.
[67]) Atanasov, Istorija (Anm. 2), S. 361.
[68]) Problemi na obrazovanieto (Probleme des Bildungswesens). Hrsg. Ministerstvo na narodnata prosveta. Sofia 1986.
[69]) Černaev, P.: Novijat vestnik – koncepcija na vestnika „Učitelsko delo" (Die neue Zeitschrift-Konzeption der Zeitschrift „Učitelsko delo"). Sofia 1984.
[70]) Information von Prof. Žečo Atanasov, Sofia, 4.6.1987.

VII. Pädagogische Wissenschaft und Bildungsforschung

Die Errichtung des kommunistischen Systems in Bulgarien erforderte nicht nur eine völlig neue Struktur des Bildungswesens, sondern auch eine neue Pädagogik zur wissenschaftlichen Absicherung und ideologischen Legitimation.

Die Pädagogik, die vor dem II. Weltkrieg an der Sofioter Universität gelehrt wurde – Herbartianismus, Sozialpädagogik und Reformpädagogik – war unvereinbar mit dem neuen Bildungssystem und wurde nach 1947 vollständig unterdrückt. Ihre Vertreter, die gute Beziehungen zur westeuropäischen Pädagogik hatten, wurden aus dem Dienst entlassen oder gezwungen, die marxistische Pädagogik zu akzeptieren.

Anfang der 50er Jahre wurde die sowjetische Pädagogik vollständig übernommen und zur allein zugelassenen pädagogischen Theorie erklärt.

Mit der Expansion des Bildungswesens entwickelte sich auch die pädagogische Wissenschaft. Heute gibt es eine Pädagogik an den Universitäten Sofia, Plovdiv und Veliko Tărnovo, an den Pädagogischen Hochschulen Blagoevgrad und Šumen sowie an den Lehrerfortbildungsinstituten in Sofia, Varna, Stara Zagora und Gabrovo. Die Pädagogik hat die Aufgabe, sowohl Grundlagenforschung als auch angewandte Forschung zur Unterstützung der Unterrichts- und Erziehungspraxis der Lehrer zu betreiben[71].

Das größte Zentrum der pädagogischen Forschung in Bulgarien ist das Institut für Bildungswesen (*Institut po obrazovanie*), früher Institut für Allgemeinbildung „Todor Samodumov", das 1950 als Forschungsinstitut der BAN gegründet wurde. 1964 wurde das Institut dem Ministerium für Volksbildung unterstellt und verlor dadurch seine direkte Beziehung zur Wissenschaft. Es beschränkte sich auf die Lösung praktischer Aufgaben der Schulentwicklung wie z. B. die Erstellung der Lehrpläne. Das Institut hat heute mehr als 200 Mitarbeiter in den Sektionen Allgemeinbildung, Berufsbildung und Hochschulbildung, die wiederum in zahlreiche Abteilungen unterteilt sind.

Das Institut für Bildungswesen kann die ihm gestellte Aufgabe, das Zentrum der pädagogischen Forschung des Landes zu sein, nur zum Teil erfüllen. Auf dem 1. Volksbildungskongreß am 12. und 13. 5. 1980 wurde „das schwerwiegende Zurückbleiben der einheitlichen wissenschaftlichen Absicherung des Bildungswesens" kritisiert und eine Hebung der Qualität der Bildungsforschung, die Überleitung der Forschungsergebnisse in die Praxis und die Auswertung der internationalen Erfahrungen im Bildungswesen gefordert[72].

Anfang der 80er Jahre wurde deshalb der wissenschaftliche Koordinationsrat (*Naučen koordinacionen săvet*) im Ministerium für Volksbildung gebildet, der die Aufgabe hat, die Forschungstätigkeit in den Instituten des Ministeriums, der BAN, der Hochschulen und in anderen Einrichtungen in ein einheitliches System zu brin-

---

[71]) Atanasov, Ž.: Pojava i razvitie na specialnostta pedagogika v Sofijskija universitet (Entstehung und Entwicklung des Faches Pädagogik an der Sofioter Universität), in: Narodna prosveta. (1987) 9, S. 77–91.

[72]) Institut de recherches sur l'éducation générale ‚Todor Samodumov'. Sofia 1984 (Informationsbroschüre des Instituts). Das Bildungswesen – Sache des ganzen Volkes. Materialien des Ersten Volksbildungskongresses, 12.–13. Mai 1980. Sofia 1980, S. 43.

gen. Es sollen insbesondere die Erfahrungen der fortgeschrittensten Industrieländer in Ost und West studiert werden. Dennoch kann man von keiner einheitlichen Planung der Bildungsforschung in Bulgarien sprechen.

Zu diesem Zweck wurden auch Forschungsgruppen außerhalb der etablierten pädagogischen Institute gegründet, die über eine gewisse Selbständigkeit verfügen und in der Lage sind, moderne pädagogische Methoden und Technologien aus anderen Ländern zu übernehmen.

Ein Beispiel dafür ist die „Problemgruppe für das Bildungswesen" (*Problemna grupa po obrazovanieto*) unter der Leitung von Blagovest Sendov und Bojan Penkov, die seit 1979 ein Experiment durchführt, bei dem die Methode des integrierten Unterrichts in der Grundschule angewendet wird. Die einzelnen Fächer, z. B. Bulgarisch und Mathematik, sind nicht scharf voneinander abgegrenzt, sondern durchdringen sich gegenseitig. Für den Unterricht werden eigene Lehrbücher verfaßt, die sich wesentlich von den üblichen Lehrmitteln unterscheiden. Besondere Aufmerksamkeit wird dem Unterricht in Informatik und Kunsterziehung gewidmet, um die schöpferische Entwicklung der Kinder anzuregen. Der Schulversuch, an dem sich 1988 etwa 60 Schulen im ganzen Land beteiligten, findet zunehmend das Interesse der Pädagogen anderer sozialistischer Länder[73]).

Eine andere Forschungsgruppe, das Laboratorium für pädagogische Diagnostik, das 1983 von Georgi Bižkov gegründet wurde, untersucht vor allem die Effizienz neuer Lehrinhalte und neuer Unterrichtsmethoden in Versuchsschulen, wofür geeignete Tests ausgearbeitet werden. Die Ergebnisse dieser unterrichtsbegleitenden Forschung werden direkt dem Koordinationsrat des Ministeriums vorgelegt[74]).

Eine originelle Theorie in der Pädagogik, die sich unabhängig von den offiziellen Tendenzen entwickelt hat, ist die in den 60er Jahren von Georgi Lozanov begründete Suggestopädie, die in den 70er Jahren zu einem bedeutenden Experiment im bulgarischen Bildungswesen wurde. Die Suggestopädie, die seit 1966 über ein eigenes Institut in Sofia verfügt, ist eine ganzheitliche pädagogische Methode, die mit den Mitteln der Tiefenentspannung und Suggestion die schöpferischen Kräfte des Menschen stimuliert und eine mühelose Aneignung von Lerninhalten ermöglicht. Die Methoden Lozanovs, die neue Erkenntnisse der Lernpsychologie und Gehirnforschung mit dem Wissen aus alten östlichen Traditionen verbinden, finden heute in den USA und Westeuropa unter der populären Bezeichnung Superlearning weite Verbreitung[75]).

---

[73]) Do korena na neštata – eksperimentăt na Problemna grupa po obrazovanieto pri BAN i MNP, 1979–1985 (Bis zur Wurzel der Sache – das Experiment der Problemgruppe für Bildungswesen bei der BAN und dem Ministerium für Volksbildung). Sofia 1986.

[74]) Bižkov, G.: Ocenačno-diagnostično izsledvane na rezultatite ot učebno-văzpitatelnata rabota v 5 klas na ESPU (Bewertungsdiagnostische Untersuchung der Ergebnisse der Unterrichts- und Erziehungsarbeit in der 5. Klasse der einheitlichen polytechnischen Mittelschule), in: Narodna prosveta. (1987) 4, S. 39–58; Bižkov, G.: Sravnitelna pedagogika (Vergleichende Pädagogik). Sofia 1986.

[75]) Lozanov, G. (ed.): Problems of Suggestology. Proceedings of the 1st International Symposium of the Problems of Suggestology in Varna, June 5–10, 1971. Sofia 1973; Lozanov, G.: Suggestology and Outlines of Suggestopedy. Translated by M. Hall-Pozharlieva and K. Pashmakova. London, 2nd printing 1980.

VIII. Offene Fragen und Ausblick

Das bulgarische Bildungwesen ist nach Zielsetzung, Struktur und Curriculum noch immer durch die Ende der 40er und Anfang der 50er Jahre geschaffenen Grundlagen geprägt, die bis heute nicht grundsätzlich in Frage gestellt werden. Das Bildungswesen weist ein hohes Maß an Kontinuität auf, und die Reformen von 1959, 1969 und 1979 haben die Grundlagen nicht beseitigt, sondern nur weitere Elemente hinzugefügt.

Die Bildungspolitik der NRB kann auf beträchtliche Erfolge verweisen: In den 50er Jahren wurde der Analphabetismus beseitigt, der besonders unter der ländlichen Bevölkerung und bei der türkischen Minderheit verbreitet war; in den 60er Jahren kam es zu einer Expansion des Berufsschulwesens und in den 70er Jahren zu einer faktischen Durchsetzung der allgemeinen mittleren Bildung, so daß vor allem die jüngere Generation der Bulgaren heute ein beträchtliches Bildungsniveau erreicht hat.

Die bulgarische Staats- und Parteiführung hat in immer neuen Anläufen versucht, dem Ziel einer Einheitsschule auch in der Struktur des Bildungswesens näherzukommen. Der letzte und zugleich radikalste Versuch, die 1979 beschlossene Integration von Allgemeinbildung und Berufsbildung wurde Mitte der 80er Jahre abgebrochen, aber nicht endgültig aufgegeben.

Die in der bulgarischen Öffentlichkeit geäußerte partielle Kritik an den Mängeln des Bildungswesens läßt erkennen, daß das Bewußtsein für notwendige Reformen in progressiven Kreisen der Lehrer, Erziehungswissenschaftler, Beamten der Bildungsverwaltung und politischen Funktionäre durchaus vorhanden ist, aber daß zu einer wirklichen *preustrojstvo* des Bildungswesens bisher der einheitliche politische Wille der Partei- und Staatsführung fehlt. Alle Konzepte, die auf Plenartagungen des ZK der BKP, Konferenzen des Lehrerverbandes und des Hohen Bildungsrates, Volksbildungskongressen etc. diskutiert und teilweise auch beschlossen wurden, konnten deshalb bis jetzt nicht verwirklicht werden.

Die Kritiker des gegenwärtigen Systems haben erkannt, daß die weitgehende Beseitigung der Traditionen der bulgarischen nationalen Wiedergeburt durch die „Maßnahmen" Ende der 40er und Anfang der 50er Jahre und die Übernahme eines fremden Bildungssystems in toto ein schwerer Fehler war und jede echte Erneuerung der bulgarischen Schule wieder an den nationalen Traditionen anknüpfen muß. Der Lehrerstand hat damals seine traditionelle soziale Rolle eingebüßt, und seine Schwäche ist heute der neuralgische Punkt des Bildungswesens.

In der Lehrerbildung gibt es deshalb Versuche zu einer Auflösung der starren Grenzen zwischen den Lehrerprofilen durch eine Integration zwischen den Ausbildungen von Kindergärtnerinnen und Grundschullehrern und durch eine Erhebung der Lehrerbildungsanstalten zu Pädagogischen Hochschulen. Aufmerksamkeit verdient auch die Eingliederung der Lehrerfortbildungsinstitute in die Universitäten und Hochschulen.

In der bulgarischen Gesellschaft werden heute – öffentlich oder auf internen Konferenzen – folgende grundlegende Probleme des Bildungswesens diskutiert, deren Überwindung gefordert wird:

Erstens ist die Struktur des Bildungswesens zu starr, und die Unifizierung zu weitgehend und begabungsfeindlich. Eine weitergehende Differenzierung der Schultypen und gleichzeitig ein differenzierter Unterricht innerhalb der einzelnen Schultypen sind notwendig. Die Schüler sollen in den oberen Klassen die Wahl zwischen einer naturwissenschaftlich-mathematischen und einer humanistischen Richtung haben, der einheitliche Lehrplan für alle Schüler von der 1. bis zur 11. Klasse sollte aufgegeben werden.

Zweitens sollten die traditionellen Unterrichtsformen wie Frontalunterricht und mechanisches Lernen durch moderne Diskussionsformen und moderne Technologien wie EDV-gestützten Unterricht und audiovisuelle Technologien ersetzt werden. Es soll die Notwendigkeit selbständigen Arbeitens bei Schülern wie bei Lehrern betont werden. Es wird eine Ausweitung von Unterrichtsinhalten gefordert, die die kreativen Fähigkeiten der Schüler entwickeln, wobei durch das Fach „Ästhetische Erziehung" ein guter Ansatz vorhanden ist.

Drittens sollte die zentralistische bürokratische Verwaltung und Schulaufsicht, die in einer kleinlichen Bevormundung der Direktoren und Lehrer durch unzählige Verordnungen, Regulative und Direktiven besteht, durch eine wirkliche Dezentralisierung ersetzt werden, die mehr ist als die Einführung der „Selbstfinanzierung" der Schulen.

Entscheidend ist, daß sich die Erkenntnis durchsetzt, daß eine bürokratische, von oben verordnete äußere Reform des Bildungswesens niemals zu einer neuen Schule und zur Lösung der wahren Probleme des Bildungswesens führt, wenn sie nicht durch eine innere Reform, eine neue Pädagogik, einen neuen Geist und eine Demokratisierung unter Mitwirkung der Lehrer ergänzt wird. Eine solche Reform des Bildungswesens, für die es durchaus Konzepte gibt, erscheint aber erst möglich, wenn sie durch eine Reform des politischen und sozialen Gesamtsystems abgestützt und begleitet wird.

Hochschulen und Wissenschaft

Milan Beneš, Berlin

I. Phasen und Tendenzen der Wissenschafts- und Hochschulpolitik: 1. Die Entwicklung bis 1944 – 2. Auseinandersetzung um eine marxistische Wissenschaft und Hochschule 1944–1948 – 3. Umbau nach sowjetischem Vorbild 1948–1956 – 4. Effektivierungsversuche im Zeichen des technischen Fortschritts 1956–1969 – 5. Integration von Hochschulen und Wissenschaft 1969–1979 – 6. Reformen der Gegenwart – II. Die Hochschulen: 1. Staatliche Verwaltung und Organisationsstruktur – 2. Institutionen – 3. Kategorien und Aufgaben des pädagogisch-wissenschaftlichen Personals – 4. Akademische Titel – 5. Das Studium: a) Zulassung – b) Organisation des Studiums – c) Didaktischer Aufbau – d) Die Erziehungsfunktion der Hochschule – e) Berufsbegleitendes Studium und Weiterbildung – 6. Soziale Absicherung – 7. Internationale Zusammenarbeit – III. Die Wissenschaft: 1. Allgemeines – 2. Leitung und Verwaltung – 3. Planung – 4. Das System der Forschungseinrichtungen: a) Die Akademien – b) Andere Einrichtungen – 5. Internationale Beziehungen

I. Phasen und Tendenzen der Wissenschafts- und Hochschulpolitik

1. Die Entwicklung bis 1944

Im bulgarischen Selbstverständnis reichen die Anfänge der bulgarischen Wissenschaft und wissenschaftlichen Bildung bis ins 9. Jh. zurück, in die Schaffenszeit der Apostel Kyrill und Method. Besondere Achtung genießt der Gründer der ersten bulgarischen Studienstätte, der Heilige Kliment Ochridski (840–916), nach dem später die älteste und bis in die Gegenwart bedeutendste Universität des Landes benannt wurde. Die mittelalterliche weltliche Forschung entwickelte sich insbesondere in der zweiten Hälfte des 14. Jh. Hier ist die Schule von Tărnovo hervorzuheben, die neben theologischen auch literarische, philosophische und naturwissenschaftliche Studien betrieb. Die moderne Wissenschaft verbreitete sich in Bulgarien erst in der Zeit der nationalen Wiedergeburt im 18. und 19. Jh., nachdem viele junge Bulgaren von ihren Studienaufenthalten im – meist westlichen – Ausland zurückgekehrt waren. Die mitgebrachten wissenschaftlichen Werke, Konzeptionen und Denkweisen dienten zugleich der Bildung und Aufklärung des Volkes. So kann es nicht verwundern, daß die bulgarische Wissenschaft sich besonders der Pflege enzyklopädischen Wissens zuwandte, zumal die Voraussetzungen für eine eigenständige Forschung im Osmanischen Reich nicht gegeben waren. Die bulgarischen Wissenschaftler studierten, arbeiteten und publizierten mehrheitlich im Ausland. Nach der nationalen Befreiung im Jahre 1878 entfalteten sich, nicht zuletzt als Folge der einsetzenden Industrialisierung, auch die Natur- und die technischen Wissenschaften, in denen Bulgarien am Anfang des 20. Jh. durchaus einige Erfolge vorweisen konnte. Die Philosophie und die Gesellschaftswissenschaften standen zu dieser Zeit vorwiegend unter dem Einfluß neukantianischer Ideen und der Werke von Berkeley, nach dem I. Weltkrieg auch von Bergson und Freud. Ende des 19. Jh. entstand auch eine bulgarische marxistische Forschung.

Die Geschichte der bulgarischen Wissenschaft ist untrennbar mit dem 30.9.1869 verbunden. Im rumänischen Brăila wurde die Bulgarische Literarische Gesellschaft (*Bălgarsko Knižovno Družestvo*) mit dem Ziel gegründet, „das bulgarische Volk allgemein aufzuklären und ihm den Weg zu seiner geistigen Bereicherung zu weisen"[1]). Die Gesellschaft, die 1878 nach Sofia übersiedelte, beschloß 1911, sich in Akademie der Wissenschaften (BAN) umzubenennen. Ein 1912 erlassenes Gesetz bestätigte sie in diesem Rang. Die BAN arbeitete damals in drei Klassen, der historisch-philosophischen, der naturwissenschaftlich-mathematischen und der gesellschaftswissenschaftlichen.

Etwas später als die Literarische Gesellschaft, im Jahre 1888, nahm in Sofia die erste Hochschule des Landes in Gestalt einer Höheren Pädagogischen Anstalt ihre Arbeit auf. Die ursprünglich historisch-philologische, mit der Lehrerbildung verbundene Ausrichtung wurde rasch überwunden, da 1889 eine physikalisch-mathematische und 1892 eine juristische Fakultät die Lehre aufnahmen. Einer Umgestaltung nach deutschem Vorbild im Jahre 1894 folgte zehn Jahre später ein Beschluß der NSb, durch den die Hochschule den Status einer Universität erhielt. Nach einem weiteren Ausbau bestand die Universität „Heiliger Kliment Ochridski" 1924 aus sieben Fakultäten. Vor dem II. Weltkrieg arbeitete in Sofia noch eine private „Freie Universität" mit drei Fakultäten, eine Kunst- und Musikakademie und in Varna und Svištov je eine Handelsakademie. Eine technische Ausbildung ermöglichte erst die 1942 in Sofia eröffnete Technische Hochschule. So arbeiteten im Studienjahr 1944/45 in Bulgarien 7 Hochschulen mit insgesamt nur 9 Fakultäten, an denen 803 Lehrkräfte[2]) unterrichteten, die mehrheitlich, ebenso wie die Mitarbeiter der BAN, nicht zu den Anhängern marxistischer Ideen gehörten.

2. Auseinandersetzung um eine marxistische Wissenschaft und Hochschule 1944–1948

Der Zeitraum zwischen dem Sieg der OF am 9.9.1944 und dem V. Parteitag der BKP (1948) kann als eine Übergangsperiode in der Entwicklung der bulgarischen Wissenschaft und des Hochschulwesens bezeichnet werden. Die OF kämpfte dafür, beide Bereiche nach sowjetischem Vorbild umzugestalten. Das Ziel war eine marxistisch ausgerichtete Wissenschaft, die dem „Volke dienen" und den wirtschaftlichen Aufbau unterstützen sollte. Damit verknüpft war das Bemühen, sozialistisch denkende Spezialisten auszubilden. 1945 wurde die erste Hochschulreform eingeleitet. Das Hochschulgesetz vom Juni 1947 beeinflußte die Studienpläne nachhaltig. Die marxistische Philosophie wurde ebenso Bestandteil des Studiums wie die Produktionspra-

---

[1]) Balewski, A.: Die bulgarische Akademie der Wissenschaften, in: Bulgarien heute – Geschichte, Politik, Wirtschaft, Kultur. Red. Georgi Bokov. Sofia 1982, S. 414.
[2]) SG. 1972, S. 367.

xis der Studenten. Administrative Eingriffe schränkten die Autonomie der Hochschule weitgehend ein, was jedoch auf heftigen Widerstand der Hochschullehrer, aber auch der Studentenschaft und einiger Politiker stieß. Personelle Konsequenz dieses Widerstandes war die Entlassung eines Teils der Lehrkräfte. Ein ähnliches Schicksal traf auch viele Wissenschaftler der BAN. Schon 1945 wählte eine Vollversammlung zum ersten Mal Vertreter der marxistischen Wissenschaft zu Mitgliedern der BAN, unter ihnen den bekannten Philosophen und späteren Akademiepräsidenten (1947) T. Pavlov. Am 1. 2. 1947 verabschiedete die NSb nach heftigen Auseinandersetzungen ein neues Gesetz, das die Akademie direkt unter die Kontrolle des Staates stellte und eine „ideologische Umgestaltung" sowie die Anbindung der Forschung an die staatliche Wirtschaftsplanung einleitete. Als positive Erscheinung dieser Zeitperiode kann das quantitative Wachstum des Hochschulsektors festgehalten werden: Die Studentenzahl stieg von 26 412 im Studienjahr 1944/45 auf 39 221 im Studienjahr 1948/49[3]). Priorität besaß dabei der Ausbau technischer und naturwissenschaftlicher Studiengänge. Auch das Haushaltsvolumen der Akademie betrug schon 1946 das Sechsfache des Jahres 1944.

3. Umbau nach sowjetischem Vorbild 1948–1956

Im Jahre 1948 begann ein neuer Abschnitt, der mit dem Aprilplenum des ZK der BKP 1956 endete. Das am 23. 12. 1947 gegründete „Komitee für Wissenschaft, Kunst und Kultur" (*Komitet za nauka, izkustvo i kultura*) sorgte, unter der Führung des späteren Ministerpräsidenten Červenkov, für eine distanzlose Übernahme der stalinistischen Hochschul- und Wissenschaftspolitik. Das neue Hochschulgesetz von August 1948 schuf die rechtliche Grundlage für die Umgestaltung des Hochschulwesens zu einer Ausbildungsstätte für sozialistische Kader. Die Aufgabe, eine sozialistische Intelligenz zu erziehen, übernahmen auch die nach sowjetischem Vorbild eingerichteten Arbeiter- und Bauernfakultäten. Marxistisch-leninistische Ideologie und Methodologie setzten sich uneingeschränkt als Leitlinie und Maßstab bei der Reorganisation der Wissenschaft durch, der auch solche zukunftsträchtigen Theorien wie die Kybernetik und die Relativitätstheorie zum Opfer fielen. Der V. Parteitag der BKP im Dezember 1948 besiegelte diese Entwicklung, die auch in der bulgarischen Selbstdarstellung oft heftig kritisiert wird.

4. Effektivierungsversuche im Zeichen des technischen Fortschritts 1956–1969

Die „politische Generallinie" des Aprilplenums des ZK der BKP im Jahre 1956 wird als eine Wende betrachtet, die den „dogmatisch-subjektivistischen" Entscheidungen im Bereich der bulgarischen Wissenschafts- und Hochschulpolitik der vorangegangenen Jahre ein Ende bereitete[4]). Die vorsichtige Liberalisierung der Gesell-

---

[3]) Ebenda.
[4]) Jachiel, N.: Nauka i politika v uslovijach naučno-techničeskoj revoljucii (Wissenschaft und Politik unter den Bedingungen der wissenschaftlich-technischen Revolution). Sofia 1987, S. 24f.

schaft änderte freilich nichts an dem Auftrag der BAN und des Hochschulwesens, die BKP und die Regierung beim Aufbau der sozialistischen Gesellschaft vorbehaltlos zu unterstützen. Dies bestätigt auch die neue Satzung der BAN von 1957 und das Hochschulgesetz vom 6.2.1958[5]). Die neue „schöpferische Atmosphäre"[6]) jedoch ermöglichte eine realistischere Diskussion der anstehenden Probleme und Aufgaben. Dazu zählte in erster Linie die Modernisierung der Wirtschaft, über deren Verlauf in Bulgarien damals äußerst optimistische Vorstellungen herrschten, die sich aus dem Gedankengut der Chruščev'schen Reformvorhaben nährten. Der technische Fortschritt, später mit dem umfassenderen Begriff „wissenschaftlich-technische Revolution" umschrieben, verlangte jedenfalls eine Neuorientierung in der Wissenschaftspolitik. Tatsächlich zeigten sich erste Ansätze einer fundierten Planung und Verwaltung der Wissenschaft, die Zahl der wissenschaftlichen Einrichtungen und Mitarbeiter stieg kräftig an, und die internationale Zusammenarbeit gewann an Bedeutung. Neue Forschungsrichtungen wie Kerntechnik oder Automatisierung konnten sich entwickeln. Auffallend war außerdem die Zunahme der zweckgebundenen Forschung außerhalb der Akademie und der Hochschulen. Unter gleichen Vorzeichen fand auch die Umgestaltung des Hochschulwesens statt. Die Kritik an den Hochschulen richtete sich vor allem gegen ihre „Losgelöstheit vom Leben", die dadurch überwunden werden sollte, daß man die „Praxis" zum Ausbildungsprinzip erhob. So sah z.B. ein gemeinsamer Beschluß des ZK der BKP und des Ministerrats von 1962 vor, den Anteil von Fernstudenten 1980 auf etwa 50% zu steigern[7]). Insgesamt scheint die Übernahme der Chruščev'schen Bildungsreform das Hochschulwesen weniger beeinflußt zu haben als das übrige Schulwesen.

5. Integration von Hochschulen und Wissenschaft 1969–1979

Der X. Parteitag der BKP (1971) verabschiedete die Konzeption einer entwickelten sozialistischen Gesellschaft, die den Anforderungen der wissenschaftlich-technischen Revolution gewachsen ist. Wissenschaftspolitisch schlug sich diese Konzeption in dem Bemühen nieder, die Wissenschaft in alle Bereiche des gesellschaftlichen Lebens zu integrieren und zur Grundlage jeder Tätigkeit werden zu lassen. Konkret verband sich damit insbesondere der Gedanke, die wissenschaftlichen Einrichtungen erstens mit der Produktion zu verbinden und gleichzeitig die anwendungs- und entwicklungsorientierte Forschung zu stärken. Zweitens sollten die wissenschaftlichen Einrichtungen mit dem Hochschulsektor zusammengelegt werden. Die schon 1969 eingeleitete, vom X. Parteitag bestätigte Hochschulreform folgte nach einer Änderung des Hochschulgesetzes (1972) dieser politischen Linie. 10 Fakultäten der Sofio-

---

[5]) Vgl. Izvestija na prezidiuma na narodnoto săbranie. 8 (1957) 45, S. 1–6, und Izvestija na prezidiuma na narodnoto săbranie. 9 (1958) 12, S. 3–5. Das Hochschulgesetz von 1958 bildet, trotz einiger Änderungen, bis in die Gegenwart die gesetzliche Grundlage des Hochschulwesens. 1988 wurde ein Entwurf vorgelegt, der die Grundlage eines neuen Hochschulgesetzes bilden soll.
[6]) Jachiel (Anm. 4), S. 27.
[7]) In: Izvestija na prezidiuma na narodnoto săbranie. 13 (1962) 83, S. 1–4. In Wirklichkeit lag dieser Anteil 1980 bei nur 23%.

ter Universität wurden mit 32 Instituten, 13 Zentrallaboratorien und zwei Wissenschaftsbereichen der BAN zu neun sog. „Einheitszentren für Wissenschaft und Kadervorbereitung" zusammengefaßt. Auch die gesamte medizinische sowie die landwirtschaftliche Forschung und Ausbildung erfolgte nunmehr in sog. „Komplexen für Wissenschaft und Lehre" (Akademien). Die Integration von Wissenschaft, Ausbildung und Praxis sollte offensichtlich durch Zusammenlegung der einzelnen Einrichtungen zu größeren Einheiten erreicht werden, etwa nach dem Vorbild der APK. Die übrigen Hochschulen blieben von dieser Entwicklung zunächst weitgehend unbeeinflußt, obgleich sie in ihrer Tendenz, wenn auch modifiziert, bis in die Gegenwart nachwirkt.

6. Reformen der Gegenwart

Dieses auf 15–20 Jahre angelegte Reformvorhaben wurde vom Juliplenum des ZK der BKP im Jahre 1979, das sich den Bildungsfragen widmete, nur zum Teil gewürdigt. Kritik galt vor allem der Verkürzung des Studiums zu Lasten der Grundlagenfächer und der praktischen Ausbildung. Das ZK beschloß eine grundlegende didaktische Reform sowie einige organisatorische Maßnahmen und verlangte, die Hochschulen in die Forschungs- und Entwicklungstätigkeit noch weitgehender einzubeziehen. Der Rechenschaftsbericht des ZK an den XIII. Parteitag der BKP (1986) wertete die nach dem Juliplenum erfolgten Veränderungen des Inhalts, der Formen und der Organisation der Hochschulbildung positiv, bemängelte jedoch, daß „zahlreiche Probleme" und eine „wesentliche Verzögerung" der Reform unübersehbar seien[8]). Die „Beschleunigung" der Reform, die manchmal auch als Reform der Reform bezeichnet wird, verfolgt folgende Ziele:

1. Die Hochschulen sollen flexibel die Nachfrage nach Spezialisten befriedigen, die die für die Epoche der wissenschaftlich-technischen Revolution notwendige Qualifikation, Adaptabilität und Mobilität aufweisen;
2. Die Hochschulen sollen ihre Forschungstätigkeit verstärken und sich an der Lösung praktischer Aufgaben beteiligen.

Diese Zielsetzung ist keinesfalls neu. Die Wege, auf denen sie realisiert werden soll, weichen allerdings von den bisherigen ab. Den Ausgangspunkt der neuen Konzeption bildet die auf dem XIII. Parteitag der BKP eingeleitete Integration von Wissenschaft, Kultur und Bildung sowie von Wissenschaft, Ausbildung und Praxis. Die beschlossenen Maßnahmen bewegen sich auf der schon seit 1971 festgelegten Linie, jedoch mit einem Unterschied: Die Hochschulen selbst sollen nämlich zu komplexen und multifunktionalen Zentren ausgebaut werden, in denen das Studium und die Lehre mit der Forschung, mit der Anwendung der Forschungsergebnisse in der Praxis und Produktion sowie mit der gesellschaftlichen und kulturellen Tätigkeit verbunden sind. Bei den Integrationsbemühungen steht somit nicht mehr die Zentralisierung oder der Aufbau immer größerer Einheiten im Vordergrund (ein Beispiel dafür ist die

---

[8]) Rechenschaftsbericht des Zentralkomitees der Bulgarischen Kommunistischen Partei an den XIII. Parteitag. Sofia, o. J., S. 113.

Ausgliederung von fünf Medizinischen Hochschulen aus der Medizinischen Akademie zum 1.1.1987); die Integration der genannten Bereiche soll an den Hochschulen selbst stattfinden. Die Technischen Hochschulen sollen z. B. nicht nur mit der Produktion zusammenarbeiten, sondern selbst eine Kleinserien- und Versuchsproduktion aufbauen. Gleichwohl wird eine noch engere Kooperation der Hochschulen mit anderen Forschungsinstitutionen, mit den Einrichtungen, in denen die Absolventen arbeiten, mit der Produktion sowie mit der gesellschaftlichen Sphäre angestrebt, die sowohl der wissenschaftlichen Arbeit als auch der Ausbildung Nutzen bringen soll. Dabei geht es nicht zuletzt darum, die zum Teil völlig unzulängliche Ausstattung der Hochschulen mit modernen technischen Mitteln zu verbessern, die für Lehre und Forschung notwendig sind. Aber auch hier besteht ein Unterschied zu den Vorstellungen der 70er Jahre, der sich aus der Selbstverwaltung ergibt, die zur gleichen Zeit zum Grundprinzip der gesellschaftlichen Leitung erhoben wurde: Die Selbstverwaltung birgt im Falle des Hochschulwesens nämlich mehr in sich als nur eine erweiterte Selbstbestimmung in Fragen der Lehre und Forschung. In ihrem Zeichen wird, anders als vorher, die Integration der Hochschule und der übrigen Bereiche als ein Dialog zwischen gleichgestellten selbständigen Einheiten und nicht als Zentralisierung verstanden.

Gleichzeitig steigen, nach einer längeren Stagnationsphase, wieder die Studentenzahlen. Für 1990 sind 118 000 Studenten eingeplant, so daß Bulgarien zu den auf diesem Gebiet führenden osteuropäischen Ländern aufschließt:

Tabelle 1: Studierende

	1944/45	1948/49	1960/61	1970/71	1980/81	1987/88
gesamt	26 412	39 221	54 965	89 331	85 330	116 407
Frauen			21 834	43 508	45 383	64 034
Fernstudenten			13 340	22 192	19 487	29 287

Quellen: SG. 1972, S. 367; SG. 1988, S. 411 f.

Tabelle 2: Studierende je 10000 der Bevölkerung

	1950/51	1960/61	1970/71	1980/81	1986/87
Bulgarien	46	70	108	98	124
DDR	16	58	84	78	79
Rumänien	33	39	75	87	69
UdSSR	69	111	188	196	181
Ungarn	35	45	78	95	93

Quelle: Statističeskij ežegodnik stran-členov SEV. Moskau 1987, S. 398.

Besonders in der zweiten Hälfte der 80er Jahre wurde nicht nur das Hochschulwesen, sondern auch die Wissenschaft vor völlig neue Aufgaben gestellt. Die Überlegungen zur Neuorganisation der Wissenschaft fanden in dem Projekt „Grundrichtungen und -aufgaben bei der Umgestaltung der Wissenschaftsfront" ihren Ausdruck, das vom Politbüro des ZK der BKP am 20.5.1988 vorgestellt wurde[9]). Angestrebt wird eine „totale Intellektualisierung", d. h. Verwissenschaftlichung jeder Tätigkeit im Bereich der Produktion, Leitung, Kultur und Bildung. Wenn Bulgarien nicht zu einer „technischen Provinz" verkümmern solle, so müsse jeder „Empirismus und Voluntarismus" bei der Durchsetzung der wissenschaftlich-technischen Revolution vermieden werden[10]). Dies setzt voraus, die administrativen Planungs- und Leitungsmethoden der Wissenschaft durch ökonomische Anreize und indirekte Leitungsmethoden zu ersetzen. Die staatlich ausgearbeiteten strategischen Wissenschaftspläne werden nunmehr als eine Plattform für Absprachen zwischen Forschungseinrichtungen, staatlichen Stellen oder wirtschaftlichen Organisationen aufgefaßt. Die Forschungseinrichtungen übernehmen dabei bestimmte Aufträge, die sie eigenverantwortlich erfüllen[11]). Dabei ist auch der Wettbewerb zwischen ihnen durchaus erwünscht. Die Finanzierung der Institutionen soll so durch die Finanzierung der Aufgaben ersetzt werden. Diese Prinzipien können natürlich für die Grundlagenforschung und für finanziell risikoreiche Aufgaben nur sehr bedingt gelten. Diese werden weiterhin aus verschiedenen Fonds und durch staatliche Zuwendungen finanziert. Als wichtigste Vorbedingung der neuen Politik gilt die Selbstverwaltung innerhalb der Forschergruppen, aber auch in ihren Beziehungen nach außen. Es geht darum, „die Rolle der unteren Ebene entscheidend" zu erhöhen[12]). Gerade in der „geistigen Sphäre" gäbe es keine Rädchen in einer Maschine, sondern schöpferisch tätige Menschen. Dazu gehöre, die Kompetenzen, aber gleichzeitig auch die Verantwortung der Leiter einzelner Einrichtungen zu erweitern.

Die angestrebte Selbstverwaltung setzt allerdings auch Selbstdisziplin und die Bereitschaft voraus, die staatlichen Aufträge zu erfüllen, um so mehr, als weiterhin feste staatliche Forschungs- und Ausbildungspläne vorliegen. Beabsichtigt ist nicht, die zentralisierte Leitung abzuschaffen, sondern sie zu effektivieren, oder, nach den Worten von T. Živkov, „mit einer weitreichenden Demokratie" zu „kombinieren"[13]). Das Problem, die administrativ kontrollierte Teilnahme durch selbstverantwortliches Handeln zu ersetzen, das gleichwohl mit den vorgegebenen Zielen nicht kollidiert, ist selbstverständlich durch die ökonomischen Anreize allein nicht zu bewältigen. Erforderlich ist auch ein entsprechender politisch-ideologischer Konsens über die gesellschaftlichen Ziele. Die vielfach geäußerte Kritik an einer nachlassenden ideologischen „Strenge"[14]) sowie an den Gesellschaftswissenschaften erscheint in diesem Zusammenhang nur folgerichtig. Den Gesellschaftswissenschaften wird vorgeworfen, ihre praktische Funktion verloren zu haben, also auch die Fähigkeit, die sozial-

---

[9]) Proekt: Osnovni nasoki i zadači za preustrojstvoto na naučnija front (Projekt: Grundrichtungen und -aufgaben bei der Umgestaltung der Wissenschaftsfront), in: RD. 20.5.1988, S. 1–3.

[10]) Dimitrov, I.: Nekotorye problemy perestrojki vysšego obrazovanija v Narodnoj Respublike Bolgarii (Einige Probleme der Umgestaltung der Hochschulbildung in der NRB), in: Sovremennaja Vysšaja Škola. 58 (1987) 2, S. 24.

[11]) Die ersten Versuche in dieser Richtung gab es schon in den 60er Jahren.

[12]) Shiwkow, T.: Die Wissenschaft – eine wirksame Produktivkraft. Sofia 1986, S. 286.

[13]) Shiwkow (Anm. 12), S. 287.

[14]) Shiwkow (Anm. 12), S. 228.

psychologischen Voraussetzungen der Reformen mitzugestalten. Auch die ideologische Erziehung der Studenten soll intensiviert und effektiviert werden.

II. Die Hochschulen

1. Staatliche Verwaltung und Organisationsstruktur

Mitte 1989 wurde die staatliche Verwaltung des Hochschulwesens reorganisiert[14a]. Das bis dahin für die Hochschulen zuständige Ministerium für Kultur, Wissenschaft und Bildung (*Ministerstvo na kulturata, naukata i prosvetata*) wurde zum Nationalen Rat für Bildung, Wissenschaft und Kultur (*Nacionalen săvet za obrazovanie, nauka i kultura*) umgebildet. Dessen Bestandteil ist das Komitee für Wissenschaft und Hochschulbildung (*Komitet za nauka i visše obrazovanie*), das offensichtlich die staatliche Leitung der Hochschulen übernehmen soll. Auch das Komitee für Kultur (*Komitet za kultura*), dem bisher die Institutionen der künstlerischen Hochschulbildung unterstanden, ging in den genannten Nationalen Rat ein. Es ist noch nicht ersichtlich, ob die landwirtschaftlichen und die medizinischen Hochschulen wie bisher den für diese Bereiche zuständigen Ministerien zugeordnet bleiben oder vom Komitee für Wissenschaft und Hochschulbildung mitverwaltet werden sollen. Ihre pädagogische Tätigkeit beaufsichtigte, ebenso wie in der künstlerischen Ausbildung, das bisherige Bildungsministerium ohnehin; größere Änderungen sind hier also nicht zu erwarten. Nicht anzunehmen ist, daß das Komitee Einfluß auf diejenigen Hochschulen gewonnen haben könnte, die der Kontrolle des bisherigen Bildungsministeriums entzogen waren: die Hochschulen der BKP, des Innenministeriums (*Ministerstvo na vătrešnite raboti*) und die Militärhochschulen. Einen Sonderstatus besitzt auch die theologische Akademie der BPC. 1980 wurde beim damaligen Ministerium für Volksbildung (*Ministerstvo na narodnata prosveta*) der Höchste Bildungsrat (*Visš učeben săvet*) gegründet. Er soll die Beschlüsse der Partei, der Regierung und des Kongresses für Volksbildung umsetzen und die bildungspolitische Tätigkeit koordinieren. Grundlegende Entscheidungen des Rates für Hochschulbildung sollen von einem Plenum gefällt werden, an dem Rektoren aller Hochschulen, Abgesandte von Ministerien und Komitees, Vertreter der BAN, der BKP, der Gewerkschaften, der Jugendorganisationen und der Hochschullehrer teilnehmen. Bei diesem Rat arbeitet ein Büro mit Abteilungen für methodische Fragen, wissenschaftliche Arbeit und Kaderfragen, Organisation und Ökonomie, Erhöhung der Qualifikation der Hochschulkader und für materielle Fragen der Studenten. Die staatliche Finanzierung der Hochschulen wird durch die Selbstfinanzierung aus der Auftragsforschung ergänzt. Zu einer weiteren Quelle sollen sich die Zuwendungen von Organisationen entwickeln, die an den Hochschulabsolventen interessiert sind.

Das 1987 beschlossene Selbstverwaltungsprinzip wirkt sich vor allem auf die Außenbeziehungen der Hochschulen aus. Eine gewisse Autonomie der inneren Verwal-

---

[14a]) Strukturni i personalni promeni v Ministerskija săvet (Strukturelle und personelle Änderungen im Ministerrat), in: RD. 5.7.1989, S. 1.

tung der Hochschule bestand auch früher. Die Wahl der Rektoren und Dekane von einer Vollversammlung der habilitierten Lehrkräfte in geheimer Abstimmung war schon in der ersten Fassung des Hochschulgesetzes vom 6.2.1958 verankert. Allerdings war der Rektor nicht nur dem Wahlgremium, sondern auch dem Volksbildungsminister verantwortlich. Zwei Verordnungen von 1958 und 1959 festigten darüber hinaus den Einfluß der BKP, des DKMS und der Gewerkschaftsorganisation. Die Änderungen des Hochschulgesetzes von 1972 und 1973 bekräftigten nochmals die Funktion der Vollversammlung. Sie gilt nunmehr als das höchste kollektive Leitungsorgan der Hochschule und der Fakultät. Neu ist die Mitbestimmung der nichthabilitierten Lehrkräfte, der Studenten und der in Bulgarien „Aspiranten" genannten Doktoranden sowie der wirtschaftlichen und wissenschaftlichen Organisationen, mit denen die Hochschule zusammenarbeitet. Der Anteil an nichthabilitierten Lehrkräften in der Vollversammlung kann bis zu 40% betragen. Die Vollversammlung wählt den Akademischen Rat, dem überdies die Dekane, die Hochschulsekretäre der BKP und des DKMS sowie der Gewerkschaftsvorsitzende angehören. Der von diesem Rat gewählte Rektor wird von dem zuständigen Minister ernannt. Analog dazu wird auch der Fakultätsrat gebildet, der den Dekan wählt. Die Wahl der Rektoren und Dekane, die habilitiert sein müssen, erfolgt alle vier Jahre. Sie werden in ihrer Arbeit durch mehrere Vertreter und Gremien, etwa für Bildung und Erziehung, für Forschung, für Weiterqualifizierung der Lehrkräfte usw., unterstützt. Die Verwaltung der Hochschule leitet ein Kanzler.

Das Politbüro-Projekt vom 20.5.1988 schlägt einige Veränderungen vor: Die Vollversammlung soll, in etwa gleicher Zusammensetzung wie bisher, das höchste Führungsorgan bleiben. Sie soll in allen grundsätzlichen Fragen der Organisation, Leitung und Tätigkeit der Hochschule entscheiden und in geheimer Direktwahl einmal in fünf Jahren den jeweiligen Leiter bestimmen. Zur Wahl sollen drei Kandidaten aufgestellt werden. Die Vorauswahl trifft allerdings eine Kommission, die kein Organ der Vollversammlung, sondern der übergeordneten administrativen Einheit ist. Der Minister beruft also die Kommission für die Wahl eines Rektors; der Rektor hat entsprechende Rechte bei der Wahl eines Dekans. Die Räte als kollektive Führungsorgane der jeweiligen Einheit sollen nur vom wissenschaftlichen Personal und von den Lehrkräften gewählt werden.

2. Institutionen

In Bulgarien wird zwischen Universitäten, die eine grundlegende wissenschaftliche Bildung vermitteln, und spezialisierten Hochschulen (Instituten) unterschieden. Durch einen Beschluß des Politbüros des ZK der BKP und des Ministerrates vom 18.5.1985 gilt die Kliment-Ochridski-Universität in Sofia als der führende Komplex für Lehre, Wissenschaft, Kultur und Ideologie im System der Hochschulbildung Bulgariens[15]). Eine ähnliche Rolle wird auch der geplanten Technischen Universität in Sofia zugewiesen. Die Entwicklung des Hochschulsystems zeigt die Tabelle 3.

---

[15]) In: DV. (1985) 42, S. 495/496.

Tabelle 3: Anzahl der Hochschulen und Fakultäten

	1944/45	1948/49	1960/61	1970/71	1980/81	1987/88
Hochschulen	7	12	20	26	28	30
Fakultäten	9	19	33	48	69	71

Quellen: SG. 1972, S. 367; SG. 1988, S. 411.

Eine Hochschulbildung kann in Bulgarien an folgenden Einrichtungen erworben werden:

Universitäten: Kliment-Ochridski-Universität Sofia (*1888 als Pädagogisches Institut, Universität seit 1904)[16]; Paisij-Chilendarski-Universität Plovdiv (*1961, 1972); Kiril i Metodij-Universität Veliko Tărnovo (*1971).

Pädagogische Hochschulen: Šumen (*1971); Blagoevgrad.

Sporthochschule „Georgi Dimitrov" (*1942, 1953). Zu der Hochschule gehört auch eine Militärfakultät.

Technische Hochschulen: Hochschule für Maschinenbau und Elektrotechnik „V.I. Lenin" Sofia (*1942, 1953); Hochschule für Maschinenbau und Elektrotechnik Varna (*1962); Technische Hochschule „Angel Kănčev" Ruse (*1954); Hochschule für Maschinenbau und Elektrotechnik Gabrovo (*1963); Hochschule für Architektur und Bauwesen Sofia (*1942); Chemisch-technologische Hochschule Sofia (*1945, 1953); Chemisch-technologische Hochschule „Prof. Dr. Asen Zlatarov" Burgas (*1962); Hochschule für Nahrungs- und Genußmittelindustrie Plovdiv (*1950, 1953); Hochschule für Bergbau und Geologie Sofia (*1953); Forstwirtschaftliche Hochschule Sofia (*1953).

Einigen Technischen Hochschulen sind *Technika* eingegliedert, die Studiengänge für Mittelschulabsolventen anbieten. Trotz der Beteiligung der Hochschullehrer und -einrichtungen an dieser Ausbildung sind die Abschlüsse mit dem Hochschuldiplom nicht gleichwertig.

Ökonomische Hochschulen: Hochschule für Wirtschaft „Karl Marx" Sofia (*1920 als Balkan-Nahost-Institut für Politische Wissenschaften, 1952); Hochschule für Volkswirtschaft „Dimităr Blagoev" Varna (*1920 als Handelsschule, 1953); Hochschule für Finanzwirtschaft „D.A. Cenov" Svištov (*1936 als Handelsschule, 1952/53).

Seit 1963 existiert das *Institut für Ausländische Studenten*.

Landwirtschaftliche Ausbildung: Landwirtschaftliche Akademie „Georgi Dimitrov" (*1921 als Fakultät an der Universität Sofia, 1972); Hochschule für Landwirtschaft „Vasil Kolarov" Plovdiv (*1945, 1950); Hochschule für Zootechnik und Veterinärmedizin Stara Zagora (*1974).

Medizinische Ausbildung: Medizinische Akademie (*1972); Medizinische Hoch-

---

[16]) Die erste Jahreszahl informiert über das Gründungsjahr. Allerdings sind die Vorläufer oft keine Hochschulen gewesen, sondern Privatschulen, Institute oder Fakultäten anderer Hochschulen. Die zweite Jahreszahl gibt darüber Auskunft, seit wann die gegenwärtige Form besteht.

schulen in Sofia (seit 1918 Fakultät, 1950), Plovdiv (*1945), Varna (*1961), Pleven und Stara Zagora.

Künstlerische Ausbildung: Bulgarisches Staatliches Konservatorium, Sofia (*1904, 1954); Hochschule für Dramatische Kunst „Krăst'o Sarafov" Sofia (*1948); Hochschule für Bildende Künste „N. Pavlovič" Sofia (*1896, 1954); Musikalisch-Pädagogische Hochschule Plovdiv (*1972).

Die *Akademie für Sozialwissenschaften und soziale Leitung* entstand 1969 auf der Grundlage der Parteihochschule (*1949). Sie untersteht dem ZK der BKP.

Die *Militärakademie* „Georgi Stojkov Rakovski" und fünf Offiziershochschulen sind dem Verteidigungsministerium (*Ministerstvo na narodnata otbrana*) zugeordnet.

Am 1.9.1987 wurde die Hochschule „Georgi Dimitrov" beim Innenministerium gegründet. Sie besteht aus drei Fakultäten (Staatssicherheit, Volksmiliz, Brandschutz).

Die *Theologische Akademie* „Sveti Kliment Ochridski" entstand 1950 durch Ausgliederung der Theologischen Fakultät (*1923) aus der Staatsuniversität Sofia.

3. Kategorien und Aufgaben des pädagogisch-wissenschaftlichen Personals

An Lehre und Forschung beteiligen sich ordentliche und korrespondierende Akademiemitglieder, Professoren, Ältere Wissenschaftliche Mitarbeiter I. und II. Grades, Dozenten, Lektoren (für Fremdsprachen, Zivilverteidigung, Sport), Assistenten und Wissenschaftliche Mitarbeiter. Eine ausdrückliche Lehrverpflichtung haben nur Professoren, Dozenten, Assistenten und Lektoren; auf Weisung des Rektors können auch die Wissenschaftlichen Mitarbeiter zur Lehre herangezogen werden. Die Professoren und die Älteren Wissenschaftlichen Mitarbeiter I. Grades müssen den Titel Doktor der Wissenschaften vorweisen oder eine Habilitationsarbeit vorlegen, die ähnlichen Anforderungen wie die Promotion zum Doktor der Wissenschaften entsprechen soll. Das Politbüro-Projekt vom 20.5.1988 hat angeregt, in Zukunft nur Inhaber des Doktortitels für diese beiden Kategorien zu berücksichtigen. Das Anfangs-Grundgehalt beträgt (1988) 550 Leva. Dozenten und Ältere Wissenschaftliche Mitarbeiter II. Grades müssen Kandidaten der Wissenschaften sein. Sie verdienen mindestens 450 Leva. Die freiwerdenden Stellen sind ausschreibungspflichtig, wobei über die Berufung die wissenschaftliche Qualifikation (nachzuweisen sind vor allem Veröffentlichungen), die berufliche Erfahrung sowie bei Lehrverpflichtung die pädagogische Eignung entscheiden. Die Assistenten und Wissenschaftlichen Mitarbeiter werden in einer Prüfung ausgewählt. Über die zahlenmäßige Entwicklung der Lehr-

Tabelle 4: Lehrkräfte an den Hochschulen

1944/45	1948/49	1960/61	1970/71	1980/81	1987/88
803	1666	3883	7125	12622	15941

Quellen: SG. 1972, S. 367; SG. 1988, S. 411.

kräfte informiert die Tabelle 4 (die Qualifikationsstruktur der bulgarischen Wissenschaftler ist in der Tabelle 5 wiedergegeben).

Zur Zeit wird der Status des Hochschullehrers, dessen Aufgabenfelder bislang stark mit der Lehre verbunden waren, neu durchdacht. Durch gesetzliche Regelungen sollen die bisher fehlenden Anreize geschaffen werden, selbständig zu forschen und die Studenten bei ihrer wissenschaftlichen und praktischen Arbeit anzuleiten. An der Sofioter Universität kann der Rektor schon jetzt durch eine Sonderregelung 30 % der Lehrkräfte für eine Forschungstätigkeit von der Lehre freistellen.

Auch die Kriterien für die Vergabe der akademischen Grade und Titel entsprechen nach einer vielfach geäußerten Kritik nicht mehr den gegenwärtigen Anforderungen. Neben der eigenständigen wissenschaftlichen Leistung soll auch die effektive Anwendung und Verbreitung der Wissenschaftsergebnisse stärker berücksichtigt werden.

4. Akademische Titel

Die wissenschaftlichen Titel, die in Bulgarien verliehen werden, sind „Kandidat der Wissenschaften" und „Doktor der Wissenschaften". Ersterer entspricht in etwa der deutschen Promotion, der andere ist mit einer Habilitation vergleichbar. Voraussetzung für beide Titel ist die Verteidigung einer Dissertationsarbeit, in der sich eine schöpferische wissenschaftliche oder anwendungsbezogene Leistung manifestiert. Der Erwerb des Doktortitels setzt eine Arbeit voraus, die eine „theoretische Verallgemeinerung und eine Lösung von Hauptproblemen der Wissenschaft oder der angewandten Wissenschaft sowie... einen bedeutsamen originellen Beitrag zur Wissenschaft" darstellt[17]). Diese Bestimmungen begünstigen im Grunde den kritisierten theoretischen Charakter der Dissertationen. Die Doktorarbeiten werden selbständig angefertigt. Der Weg zum Kandidatentitel führt dagegen hauptsächlich über einen besonderen Ausbildungsgang, die Aspirantur, die als Tages- oder Fernstudium absolviert wird. Das Politbüro-Projekt schlägt hier vor, die Aspirantur als Einheit von geregeltem Unterricht und der Einführung in die wissenschaftliche und pädagogische Arbeit zu gestalten. Der Kandidaten-Titel soll nicht mehr ausschließlich durch eine abgeschlossene wissenschaftliche Arbeit erworben werden, sondern ein Nachweis sein über das während der Aspirantur erworbene Wissen und über die herausgebildeten Fähigkeiten zur wissenschaftlichen Arbeit oder Lehre.

5. Das Studium

a) Zulassung

Bulgarien verfolgt, im Unterschied etwa zu Jugoslawien oder Polen, eine restriktive, bedarfsorientierte Zulassungspolitik. Die Auswahl von geeigneten Bewerbern gilt dabei als eine Grundbedingung für die Qualität der Hochschulbildung. Die Kriterien

---

[17]) Zakon za naučnite stepeni i naučnite zvanija (Gesetz über wissenschaftliche Grade und Titel), in: DV. (1972) 36, S. 1/2.

und der Ablauf des Zulassungsverfahrens sind äußerst detailliert geregelt; die jüngste Verordnung hat das damalige Ministerium für Kultur, Wissenschaft und Bildung am 22.1.1988 erlassen[18]). Der Kandidat muß grundsätzlich drei Voraussetzungen erfüllen: 1. Er muß ein Reifezeugnis (Diplom) der Sekundarstufe II besitzen, wobei nicht mehr wie früher eine Mindestnote vorgeschrieben ist. 2. Er muß eine Beurteilung des Schuldirektors oder der letzten Arbeitsstelle vorlegen. 3. Er darf nicht älter als 35 Jahre sein; für manche Studiengänge liegt das Zulassungsalter noch niedriger. Um das Fern- oder Abendstudium kann er sich bis zum 40. Lebensjahr bewerben.

Das Auswahlverfahren besteht aus anonymen schriftlichen Prüfungen in zwei studienbezogenen Fächern. Für einige Studienrichtungen sind auch Talentprüfungen, praktische Prüfungen (etwa im Sport) oder mündliche Prüfungen vorgeschrieben. Eine schriftliche Prüfung in Gesellschaftskunde ist obligatorisch. Die Prüfungsfächer und -inhalte bestimmte bisher das Bildungsministerium. Diese Aufgabe wird wohl dem neuen Komitee für Wissenschaft und Hochschulbildung zufallen. Neu ist, daß an acht technischen Hochschulen für die meisten Studienfächer keine Aufnahmeprüfungen notwendig sind. Der Grund dafür liegt im mangelnden Interesse an diesen Studienfächern. Die Hochschulen besitzen, was oft bemängelt wird, im Auswahlverfahren kein Mitspracherecht. Ausschlaggebend sind das Wissen der Bewerber, ihre Schulnoten und die Prüfungsergebnisse. Motive, Fähigkeiten und persönliche Eignung bleiben dagegen unberücksichtigt.

In diesem Verfahren gibt es aber eine Reihe von Ausnahmen. Einige davon sind didaktischer Natur. Vorteile haben Bewerber, die erfolgreich an den Jugendolympiaden oder der Bewegung „Für das wissenschaftlich-technische Schöpfertum der Jugend" teilgenommen haben. Besondere Regelungen gelten auch für die Angehörigen bestimmter Berufe oder Betriebe, meistens aus Landwirtschaft und Schwerindustrie, für die Absolventen der Vorbereitungskurse der Arbeiter- und Bauernjugend oder für Kandidaten aus den Grenzgebieten. Politisch motiviert sind die Ausnahmen für die „Helden der Arbeit" und „Helden der Volksrepublik Bulgarien".

Das Verhältnis der aufgenommenen Männer und Frauen soll 1 : 1 betragen, wobei Ausnahmen erlaubt sind. Tatsächlich ist Bulgarien aber das einzige sozialistische Land, das Männer bei der Hochschulzulassung durch festgelegte Quoten begünstigt. So waren z. B. Mitte der 80er Jahre 70 % der Studienplätze für Journalistik, Geologie und Veterinärmedizin für männliche Bewerber reserviert, an den technischen und medizinischen Hochschulen sowie bei universitären Studiengängen waren es 60 %.

b) Organisation des Studiums

Eine bulgarische Besonderheit ist das in drei Stufen gegliederte Studium. Diese Struktur wurde 1979 auf einem Plenum des ZK der BKP beschlossen und Anfang der 80er Jahre eingeführt. In der ersten Stufe sollen Grundlagenkenntnisse für eine ganze Berufsrichtung, z. B. Elektrotechnik, vermittelt werden. Sie dauert zwei Jahre. Eine vertiefte berufliche Orientierung, Prüfungen und Selektionsmaßnahmen bereiten den

---

[18]) In: DV. (1988) 14, S. 2–14. Diese Verordnung ist trotz ihres Umfangs im Verhältnis zu den früheren Bestimmungen stark vereinfacht worden.

Übergang auf die zweite Stufe vor. Hier soll, gleichfalls in zwei Jahren, breitprofiliertes Berufswissen, Erfahrung in schöpferischer Arbeit sowie Berufspraxis erworben werden. Die dritte Stufe, die ein Jahr dauert, dient vor allem der selbständigen Arbeit der Studenten in der Praxis oder in den Forschungseinrichtungen an oder außerhalb der Hochschule. Neben den Praktika wird noch Unterricht in spezialisierenden Fächern erteilt. In dieser Phase wird auch das Diplomprojekt vorbereitet. Das Studium endet mit einer Staatsprüfung, zu der sich der Student melden kann, wenn er alle vorgeschriebenen Prüfungen und Praktika absolviert hat. Geprüft wird im Marxismus-Leninismus und in den jeweiligen Spezialfächern. Außerdem muß der Student seine Diplomarbeit verteidigen. Die Studiendauer beträgt, mit Ausnahmen, 5 Jahre.

Seit Mitte der 80er Jahre steht eine Studienkonzeption zur Diskussion, die von verschiedenen Qualifikationsniveaus ausgeht. Angeregt wurde zunächst, neben einer verkürzten Massenausbildung, begabte Studenten für besondere Leitungsaufgaben und, als höchste Stufe, zur wissenschaftlichen Elite heranzubilden. Mit einer derartigen Aufteilung hat Bulgarien schon seit 1972 einige Erfahrungen sammeln können. Allerdings scheinen didaktische Probleme, besonders der Zeitpunkt und die Kriterien der Auswahl, eine andere Lösung bewirkt zu haben. Der Entwurf zum neuen Hochschulgesetz sieht jedenfalls nur eine Spezialisierung oder den Erwerb einer Zusatzqualifikation nach dem Abschluß des Erststudiums vor[19]).

Neben den ideologischen Fächern, dem Sport und der Zivilverteidigung ist sowie die praktische Ausbildung immer ein fester Bestandteil jedes Studiums gewesen. Eine neue Qualität erhielt sie unbestreitbar durch den Beschluß des Ministerrats „Über die berufliche Spezialisierung der Lernenden in der dritten Unterrichtsstufe" vom 17. 10. 1983 und die Verfügung des Bildungsministeriums vom 26. 6. 1987 „Über den berufspraktischen Unterricht der Hochschulstudenten"[20]). Der berufspraktische Unterricht hat zum Ziel, die theoretischen Kenntnisse zu bestätigen und zu vertiefen, sowie die praktische Berufsvorbereitung und die kommunistische Arbeitserziehung durch die Tätigkeit unter den realen Bedingungen der Praxis zu sichern. Unterschieden werden drei Typen von Praktika: 1. die unbezahlten Unterrichtspraktika (Laborarbeiten, Exkursionen etc.) in der I. und II. Studienstufe, die meistens in Einrichtungen der Hochschule stattfinden; 2. die Unterrichts- und Produktionspraktika, die überwiegend in den wirtschaftlichen Organisationen durchgeführt und auch bezahlt werden; 3. die berufliche Spezialisierung in der III. Ausbildungsstufe; hierbei soll der Student einen individuellen, bezahlten Auftrag in einer sozialistischen Organisation übernehmen. Eine andere Möglichkeit ist die selbständige Anfertigung einer wissenschaftlichen Arbeit oder die Teilnahme an der Forschungstätigkeit der Fakultät. Die übertragene Aufgabe kann auch mit dem Thema der Diplomarbeit übereinstimmen.

Das dreistufige Studium und die schrittweise Eingliederung in die Praxis dienen auch als Instrument der beruflichen Lenkung. Vor dem Beginn der beruflichen Spezialisierung, also am Ende der I. Stufe, schließen die Hochschulen mit den sozialistischen Organisationen Verträge ab, in denen der Bedarf an Absolventen mit bestimm-

---

[19]) NRB: Reforma vyššej školy (NRB: Hochschulreform), in: Učitel'skaja gazeta. (4. 2. 1988) 15, S. 3.
[20]) In: DV. (1983) 85, S. 1083–1085; DV. (1987) 81, S. 1–9.

ten Qualifikationsprofilen festgelegt wird. Die Hochschulen verpflichten sich, diese Spezialisten auszubilden, während die Organisationen verpflichtet sind, sie zu übernehmen und ihre Ausbildung zu unterstützen. Am Ende der II. Stufe können die Studenten einen individuellen Arbeitsvertrag unterzeichnen, der ihnen eine bestimmte Arbeitsstelle garantiert.

c) Didaktischer Aufbau

Die gegenwärtige didaktische Reform orientiert sich an den Thesen des Juliplenums des ZK der BKP von 1979. Hier wurde die Erziehung einer vielseitigen, perspektivisch allseitigen Persönlichkeit, die sich im Leben voll realisieren könne, beschlossen. Im Falle der Hochschulbildung ist darunter die Erziehung eines Spezialisten zu verstehen, die mehr als die Fachausbildung beinhaltet. Der Absolvent soll auch ideologisch gefestigt, dabei flexibel und selbständig sein, er soll die organisatorischen, sozialen und psychologischen Zusammenhänge seines Berufs kennen und das Bedürfnis nach ständiger Weiterbildung entwickelt haben. Es handelt sich also um die Erziehung eines Spezialisten für die Epoche der wissenschaftlich-technischen Revolution, ein Unterfangen, das seine Wurzel in den Reformen der Chruščev-Ära hat. Im Unterschied zu den früheren Reformen verfügt die bulgarische Pädagogik inzwischen über einen Bildungsbegriff, der den gewünschten Zielen mehr entspricht. Die Bildung, besonders an der Hochschule, wird als schöpferische Tätigkeit der Studenten verstanden, in der sie sich die geistige und materielle Kultur nicht nur aneignen, sondern sie auch verändern. Voraussetzung einer solchen Tätigkeit ist ein Kommunikationssystem, das die Studenten nicht zu Objekten des pädagogischen Prozesses degradiert[21]). Ob diese Definition der Realität gerecht wird, kann bezweifelt werden. Gleichwohl eröffnet sie Freiräume für eine notwendige pädagogische Reform.

Die konkreten Maßnahmen umfassen mehrere Bereiche: 1. Die Zahl der Studienrichtungen wird verringert: schon 1972 von 173 auf 145, die 1985 nochmals auf 134 reduziert wurden. Von 1979 an erfolgt das Studium in der I. Stufe in etwa dreißig übergreifenden Berufsrichtungen. Beabsichtigt ist, dadurch eine zu enge Spezialisierung zu vermeiden und die allgemeintheoretische Grundausbildung zu verbessern; 2. Modernisierung und Neustrukturierung der Unterrichtsinhalte. 3. Begabtenförderung und Individualisierung des Studiums, besonders bei überdurchschnittlichen Studenten der dritten Ausbildungsstufe; 4. das Lehrbuch wird weiterhin als Hauptstudienmittel betrachtet. Allerdings sind die Nachteile des reproduzierenden Erlernens eines standardisierten Wissens bekannt. Aktive Unterrichtsmethoden, Projekt, Rollenspiel, Diskussion sowie die Einbeziehung der Studenten in Forschung und Praxis sollen hier Abhilfe schaffen; 5. der Personalcomputer soll als Gegenstand und vor allem als Unterrichtsmittel in bedeutendem Umfang eingesetzt werden. Die Diskussion um den Programmierten Unterricht begann schon in den 60er Jahren; erst die Verbreitung des Personalcomputers schaffte die technische Grundlage für diese Lern-

---

[21]) Diese Konzeption wurde im wesentlichen von der sowjetischen Psychologie und Pädagogik übernommen.

form. Allerdings fehlen noch geeignete Programme, was jedoch kein spezifisch bulgarisches Problem ist.

Mit der Hochschuldidaktik und -pädagogik, denen ein zufriedenstellendes Niveau bescheinigt wird, beschäftigen sich neben dem Wissenschaftlichen Institut für Bildungsforschung beim Höchsten Bildungsrat auch Einrichtungen der Hochschulen, etwa das Laboratorium für Hochschulbildung an der Sofioter Universität oder das Forschungslaboratorium für technische Hochschulbildung an der Hochschule für Elektrotechnik und Maschinenbau in Sofia. Die pädagogische Vorbereitung der Lehrkräfte dagegen wird als verbesserungsbedürftig angesehen. Neben der geringen Bereitschaft zur pädagogischen, psychologischen und fachdidaktischen Qualifizierung wird die Schuld auch dem Fehlen eines verbindlichen Ausbildungssystems zugeschrieben. Die jungen Lehrkräfte, die sich zu etwa 50% aus den Absolventen der jeweiligen Hochschule rekrutieren, sind erst nach 3–5 Jahren in ihrem Beruf adaptiert.

d) Die Erziehungsfunktion der Hochschule

Die gewiß erheblichen Bemühungen um die weltanschauliche, ideologisch-politische und moralische Erziehung der Studenten haben bisher dieses „Kernstück des gesamten Bildungs- und Erziehungsprozesses" nicht auf das „Niveau der Forderungen der Partei" heben können[22]). Folgerichtig wird die Reform durch die Versuche begleitet, die ideologische Erziehung zu intensivieren und die Rolle der Parteiorganisation an der Hochschule zu stärken. Auch in diesem Bereich wächst die Einsicht, daß die ständigen Appelle der Verantwortlichen alleine nicht ausreichen. Deswegen wurde schon im Zuge der Hochschulreform vom 1969 versucht, dem Schematismus dieser Erziehung zu begegnen. Gegenwärtig werden besonders folgende Bedingungen einer erfolgreichen Erziehung zum kommunistischen Denken und Handeln genannt: Erstens soll die gesellschaftliche Aktivität der Studenten, ihre Teilnahme am Geschehen an und außerhalb der Hochschule, erhöht werden. Zweitens soll der dargebotene Stoff realitäts- und gegenwartsbezogen sein und mit Hilfe von aktivierenden, diskursiven Methoden vermittelt werden. Indes sind die Inhalte letztlich aus dem seit Stalin wenig veränderten Marxismus-Leninismus abgeleitet. Die propagierten schöpferischen Lernmethoden dürften daher schnell mit dem dogmatischen Weltbild kollidieren, das vermittelt werden soll. Die Erziehung ist nicht nur eine Aufgabe der Lehrkräfte für ideologische Fächer (Marxismus-Leninismus, Geschichte der BKP), sondern alle Mitarbeiter der Hochschule sollen sich daran beteiligen, indem sie die weltanschaulichen Grundlagen der jeweiligen Disziplin aufdecken und selbst als überzeugte Marxisten auftreten.

Eine gewichtige Rolle spielen auch die Hochschulorganisationen der BKP und der DKMS.

---

[22]) Shiwkow (Anm. 12), S. 155.

e) Berufsbegleitendes Studium und Weiterbildung

Abgesehen von den medizinischen Fakultäten bieten alle Hochschulen in fast jedem Studienfach die Möglichkeit des Fernstudiums an. Diese seit 1950 bestehende Studienform wurde besonders von der Bildungspolitik der 60er Jahre favorisiert. Gegenwärtig gewinnt sie erneut an Bedeutung, da der Bedarf an Hochschulabsolventen in den 90er Jahren nicht über das Tagesstudium zu decken ist. Im Abendstudium dagegen können nur insgesamt elf Fächer an einigen Hochschulen in Sofia studiert werden. Beide Studienformen umfassen das gleiche Pensum wie das Tagesstudium, und die Studiendauer verlängert sich meist um ein Jahr.

Verbessert wird gegenwärtig auch das schon bestehende Weiterbildungssystem der Hochschulen, das sich seit Anfang der 70er Jahre besonders schnell entwickelte, so daß fast alle Hochschulen über weiterbildende Einrichtungen verfügen. Gut ausgebaut sind die Ausbildungsgänge für Mediziner, Beschäftigte im Schulsektor und für Führungskräfte der Wirtschaft und Verwaltung. Ein periodisches Weiterqualifizierungssystem für die Angehörigen technischer Berufe befindet sich z. Zt. im Aufbau. Zu diesem Zweck wurde z. B. an der Technischen Hochschule in Ruse die erste eigene Fakultät eingerichtet.

6. Soziale Absicherung

Die ersten Unterstützungsfonds für Studenten sind schon 1947 eingerichtet worden. Im Studienjahr 1948/49 erhielten etwa 5% der Studenten ein Stipendium, 1987/88 waren es schon 55%. Die Vergabe der staatlichen Stipendien richtet sich nach zwei Kriterien: Leistung und materielle Lage. Je besser die Leistung ist, desto höher kann auch das anrechenbare Familieneinkommen sein. Stipendien können auch Ministerien, Behörden oder wirtschaftliche Organisationen vergeben, um ihren Bedarf an Spezialisten zu decken. Sonderstipendien erhalten hochbegabte Studenten, Mütter oder Leistungssportler, aber auch aktive Kämpfer gegen Kapitalismus und Faschismus, Helden der sozialistischen Arbeit und der NRB sowie leitende Funktionäre der Partei und Verwaltung. Die letztere Gruppe braucht keinen Leistungsnachweis zu erbringen. Die Höchstgrenze liegt bei 150 Leva, Aspiranten können 250 Leva erhalten[23]). Zur sozialen Unterstützung gehören darüber hinaus das subventionierte Mensaessen, verbilligte Fahrkarten sowie die Möglichkeit, in einem Wohnheim zu leben und studentische Freizeit- und Erholungseinrichtungen zu nutzen.

7. Internationale Zusammenarbeit

Die internationale Zusammenarbeit entfaltete sich von Anbeginn vor allem in den Beziehungen zu anderen sozialistischen Staaten. Insbesondere mit der UdSSR ver-

---

[23]) Vgl. Postanovlenie Nr. 40 „Za stipendiite na studentite ot visšite učebni zavedenija i aspirantite" (Beschluß Nr. 40 über Hochschul- und Aspirantenstipendien), in: DV. (1985) 64, S. 766–768 und die Änderung vom 21.4.1988, in: DV. (1988) 34, S. 1.

sucht Bulgarien, von einer Kooperation zu einer Integration des Hochschulbereichs überzugehen. Dazu gehören: 1. Abstimmung der Entwicklungspläne und Prognosen; 2. gemeinsame Lehrpläne und -bücher; 3. Koordination der Forschungspläne, die Spezialisierung einzelner Hochschulen und gemeinsame Forschung; 4. Zusammenarbeit in der kommunistischen Erziehung, z. B. durch Fortbildung der bulgarischen Lehrkräfte für ideologische Fächer in der UdSSR; 5. Austausch von Lehrkräften und Studenten. Die Richtlinien legt die Ständige Konferenz der Minister für Hochschulbildung sozialistischer Staaten fest, die alle zwei Jahre stattfindet. Zur Lösung der behandelten Fragen werden Experten- und Koordinationsgruppen gebildet. Die bulgarischen Wissenschaftler bearbeiteten z. B. von 1981 bis 1985 das Thema „Technische Unterrichtsmittel". Seit 1969 werden überdies regelmäßige Rektorenkonferenzen veranstaltet. Konferenzen, Seminare und Konsultationen, Kooperation zwischen einzelnen Hochschulen und bilaterale Absprachen sind weitere Formen der Zusammenarbeit. Vereinbarungen mit nichtsozialistischen Staaten ermöglichten Partnerschaftsverträge auch mit Hochschulen dieser Länder. In der Bundesrepublik Deutschland sind es die Universität des Saarlandes sowie die Universitäten Köln und Hamburg, die Vereinbarungen mit der Sofioter Universität abgeschlossen haben. Von den 4395 Bulgaren, die im Jahre 1987/88 im Ausland studierten, hielten sich 3470 in der UdSSR, 450 in der DDR auf. Für 1987/1988 erhielten 14 bulgarische Studenten und jüngere Hochschulabsoventen ein DAAD-Jahresstipendium für die Bundesrepublik Deutschland. 1988 wurde an der Universität Sofia erstmals ein DAAD-Lektor angestellt.
Die Mitarbeit im Rahmen der UNESCO sowie die Ausbildung von Spezialisten aus der Dritten Welt gehören zu den weiteren Schwerpunkten der internationalen Beziehungen.

III. Die Wissenschaft

1. Allgemeines

Zu den wissenschaftspolitischen Zielen der 80er Jahre gehört, die wissenschaftliche und die angewandte Forschung, die Entwicklung und Umsetzung in die Praxis zu einem Zyklus zusammenzuschließen. Alle Forschungseinrichtungen sollen so umgestaltet werden, daß sie diese komplexen Aufgaben erfüllen können. Gleichwohl sind drei Typen von wissenschaftlichen Organisationen zu unterscheiden. Die akademischen Einrichtungen konzentrieren sich auf die Grundlagenforschung und die wissenschaftlich-methodische Anleitung und Koordination anderer wissenschaftlicher Organisationen. Die Hochschulen sollen sich mit zukunftsorientierten, gesellschaftlich bedeutsamen Themen beschäftigen. Die in den Hochschulen betriebene angewandte Forschung soll sie nicht in Konkurrenz mit den Ingenieur-, Projekt- oder Entwicklungsbüros bringen. Denn erstens bliebe dadurch das hohe Qualifikationsniveau der Mitarbeiter ungenutzt, und zweitens dürfte die Hauptaufgabe der Hochschule, die Ausbildung, nicht durch kurzfristige ökonomische Effekte tangiert werden. Ein Kriterium für die Themenwahl ist somit, ob die Hochschulforschung die Lehre bereichert und den voraussichtlichen Qualifikationsbedarf berücksichtigt. Ein umfangreiches Netz von wissenschaftlichen Einrichtungen unterhalten auch Ministerien, Behörden, Staatliche Komitees und Betriebe. Diese erbringen vorwiegend wissenschaftliche Dienstleistungen auf den Gebieten der angewandten Forschung, der Entwicklung, Erprobung und Überführung in die Praxis.

2. Leitung und Verwaltung

Die unterschiedlichen Forschungsschwerpunkte spiegelten sich bis zum 1.1.1988 auch in der Struktur der staatlichen Verwaltungsstellen wider. Die wissenschaftliche Tätigkeit an der BAN, der medizinischen und landwirtschaftlichen Akademie, an den Hochschulen und anderen Forschungsinstituten wurde vom Komitee für Wissenschaft (*Komitet za nauka*) beim Ministerrat koordiniert. Das Komitee erstellte nationale Programme für die wissenschaftliche Grundlagenforschung sowie Prognosen für die Wissenschaft, Ökonomie, Demographie, Ökologie und die soziale und geistige Entwicklung des Landes. Unter seiner Beteiligung wurden auch Fünfjahrespläne für die wissenschaftliche Tätigkeit und ihre Finanzierung sowie für die Qualifizierung wissenschaftlicher Kader (Promotionen, Habilitationen, Spezialisierung im Ausland) ausgearbeitet. Für die einheitliche Politik zur Intensivierung der Volkswirtschaft durch Wissenschaft und Technik war das Staatskomitee für Forschung und Technologie (*Dăržaven komitet za izsledovanija i technologii*) verantwortlich. Beide Komitees, erst im April 1986 gegründet, wurden zum 1.1.1988 wieder aufgelöst. Ihre Aufgaben übernahmen die neugeschaffenen Ministerien für Wissenschaft, Kultur und Bildung (Grundlagenforschung) und für Volkswirtschaft und Planung (*Ministerstvo na ikonomikata i planiraneto*). Auch diese Reorganisation brachte wohl nicht die gewünschten Ergebnisse. Wie schon erwähnt[23a]), wurde Mitte 1989 die staatliche Leitung von Wissenschaft und Hochschulen zusammengefaßt und dem Komitee für Wissenschaft und Hochschulbildung unterstellt. Es ist anzunehmen, daß dieses Komitee nur für die Grundlagenforschung zuständig ist. Das Politbüro-Projekt vom 20.5.1988 betont die Richtlinienkompetenz der staatlichen Stellen für die Wissenschaftspolitik. Die staatliche Führung soll garantieren, daß die ökonomischen, technologischen, sozialen und ideologischen Vorstellungen der Partei und des Staatsapparates umgesetzt werden. Als gesellschaftliches Pendant zur staatlichen Führung ist ein Kongreß der selbstverwalteten wisssenschaftlichen Einrichtungen vorgesehen. Der Kongreß und die von ihm gewählten Gremien sollen selbstverantwortlich die staatliche Politik realisieren.

Die Tätigkeit auf dem Gebiet der angewandten Forschung, d.h. die Entwicklung neuer technischer Lösungen, die Überführung von wissenschaftlichen und technischen Erkenntnissen in die Praxis sowie die Ausnutzung von nationalen und internationalen Erfahrungen oder auch den An- und Verkauf von Lizenzen regelt eine Verordnung des Ministerrates von 1987[24]). Sie gilt für alle beteiligten Organisationen (staatliche Stellen, Wirtschafts- und Handelsorganisationen, Forschungsinstitute,

---

[23a]) Vgl. Promeni (Anm. 14a).
[24]) Vgl. DV. (1987) 17, S. 8–17.

Berufsverbände, Hochschulen, Akademien usw.). Der Grundgedanke dieser Verordnung ist, daß die interessierten Organisationen selbständig oder kooperativ selbstverwaltete Forschungszentren gründen und betreiben können. Die angewandte Forschung soll vor allem von sog. Programmkollektiven durchgeführt werden. In ihnen werden Spezialisten verschiedener Abteilungen und Einrichtungen zusammengezogen, die festumrissene Aufgaben und Aufträge übernehmen. Die Programmkollektive können, wenn der Auftrag ausgeführt ist, wieder aufgelöst werden. Bemerkenswert sind die vielfältigen Finanzierungsquellen. Neben staatlichen Fonds für wissenschaftliche und technologische Forschung, Forschungs- und Risikofonds der wirtschaftlichen Organisationen, Haushaltsmitteln der Akademien und Hochschulen können auch selbsterwirtschaftete Mittel, Bankkredite oder die von einem Auftraggeber zur Verfügung gestellten Mittel eingesetzt werden. Die Bezahlung der Mitarbeiter richtet sich nach der individuellen Leistung und dem Erfolg der Forschergruppe.

Ein Beispiel für diese Form der Forschungstätigkeit zeigt ein Experiment, das schon 1981 an vier technischen Hochschulen begann. Die Hochschulen erhielten die Erlaubnis, selbständig über die Erträge zu verfügen, die sie durch ihre Forschungs- und Entwicklungstätigkeit, durch Expertisen und durch den Verkauf von Unikaten, kleinseriell hergestellten Produkten sowie durch andere wissenschaftliche Dienstleistungen erwirtschafteten. Mit Hilfe von Devisenkrediten beschafften sie sich moderne technische Mittel und Einrichtungen und bauten Produktionsabteilungen auf, die auch für die Ausbildung der Studenten genutzt werden. So konnte die Technische Hochschule „V. I. Lenin" in Sofia schon 1985 52% ihres Haushalts aus selbsterwirtschafteten Mitteln decken. Die Löhne der an dem Experiment beteiligten Mitarbeiter lagen 40–50% über dem Tarif[25]. Allerdings wurde auch der Verwaltungsapparat um 15% aufgebläht und die Lehre zum Teil vernachlässigt; störend wirkte sich das Experiment auf die Beziehungen zu Kollegen aus, die nicht an der Einkommenserhöhung partizipieren konnten, etwa die Lehrkräfte für ideologische Fächer. Wohl aus diesem Grunde sieht das neue Politbüro-Projekt „neue Mechanismen der Bewertung und Stimulierung" der Lehrkräfte für Sprachen und Geisteswissenschaften vor[26].

3. Planung

Zu den Grundsätzen der staatlichen Forschungspolitik gehört der Versuch, die wissenschaftliche, gesellschaftliche und ökonomische Entwicklung miteinander abzustimmen. Der erste Forschungsplan wurde schon 1947 für die BAN ausgearbeitet. Trotz zahlreicher Parteibeschlüsse gelang es jedoch bis Ende der 70er Jahre nicht, die Forschungstätigkeit vollständig in die staatlichen Pläne der sozio-ökonomischen Entwicklung zu integrieren und den Eigeninteressen der wissenschaftlichen Einrichtungen wirksam entgegenzusteuern. Seit Ende der 70er Jahre wird versucht, nach dem sog. Ziel-Programm-Prinzip vorzugehen. Es besagt, daß Ziele (konkrete End-

---

[25] Vgl. Experimenty na vysokých školách v Bulharsku (Experimente an den bulgarischen Hochschulen), in: Vysoká škola. 35 (1986–1987) 5, S. 225–231.
[26] Proekt (Anm. 9), S. 2.

produkte), Organisationsformen, Ressourcen und die Dauer einzelner Forschungsvorhaben in den Plänen genau erfaßt werden sollen. Allerdings konstatierte T. Živkov noch 1985: „Über eine echte zielgerichtete programmäßige Organisation (der Wissenschaft – M. B.) und echte Zielprogramme verfügen wir gegenwärtig noch nicht"[27]).

Als Nachteil erwiesen sich auch die Defizite in der Wissenschaftsprognostik. Seit Ende der 70er Jahre können sich die Planer auf 20–30 Jahre vorausschauende Prognosen stützen, die, zum Teil in Abstimmung mit anderen RGW-Ländern entwickelt, in der „Nationalen Konzeption für die Entwicklung der Wissenschaft und des technischen Fortschritts bis 1990" zusammengefaßt sind[28]). Diese Prognosen dienten, gemeinsam mit den politischen und wirtschaftlichen Vorgaben, als Grundlage des strategischen „Nationalen komplexen Programms für die Entwicklung der Wissenschaft und des technischen Fortschritts in der Periode 1981–1990". Das Programm enthält Angaben zu folgenden vier Bereichen: 1. Entwicklung der für die gesamte Volkswirtschaft wichtigen Bereiche (Automatisierung, Elektronisierung, Atomenergie, neue Werkstoffe, Biotechnologie); 2. Veränderungen einzelner volkswirtschaftlicher Zweige bei Berücksichtigung technologischer und arbeitsorganisatorischer Fragen; 3. Entwicklung der Grundlagenforschung. Eines der 20 Unterprogramme ist das „Entwicklungsprogramm für Grundlagenforschung", das von der BAN koordiniert wird; 4. personelle, materielle und finanzielle Ausstattung und die angestrebte internationale Zusammenarbeit.

Dieses durch den Ministerrat gebilligte Programm[29]) ist eine der Vorlagen für die staatlichen Pläne. In die Fünfjahrespläne und die Jahrespläne gehen darüber hinaus aber auch die mittel- und kurzfristigen Forschungsvorhaben der einzelnen Ministerien, Wirtschaftszweige oder der ökonomischen und wissenschaftlichen Organisationen ein.

Um den Anschluß an die internationale Forschung zu gewährleisten, wendet Bulgarien eine selektive Forschungsstrategie an, die die Besonderheiten eines kleinen Landes berücksichtigt, das nicht auf allen Gebieten Spitzenforschung betreiben kann. Die Grundlage dafür bildet die arbeitsteilige Kooperation mit anderen sozialistischen Staaten sowie eine sorgfältige Auswertung internationaler Forschungsergebnisse[30]). Die Ausgaben für die Wissenschaft betrugen 1987 beachtliche 3,2 % des Nationaleinkommens; eine Spitzenposition im internationalen Vergleich nimmt Bulgarien damit jedoch nicht ein. Allerdings sind die Steigerungsraten hoch: 1960 lag der Anteil bei 0,5 %, 1980 bei 2,3 %, und 1990 sollen 3,6 % erreicht werden. Der Vorrang für die ökonomisch nutzbare Forschung läßt sich an einer Aufschlüsselung der Wis-

---

[27]) Shiwkow (Anm. 12), S. 281.

[28]) Gegenwärtig existieren mehr als 20 Prognosen bis zum Jahr 2000 und darüber. Vgl. Naučnotechničeskie programmy i upravlenie naučno-techničeskim progressom v socialističeskich stranach (Wissenschaftlich-technische Programme und die Leitung des wissenschaftlich-technischen Fortschritts in den sozialistischen Ländern). Moskau 1986, S. 311–329.

[29]) Die Nationalprogramme der einzelnen RGW-Staaten sind die Grundlage des 1985 beschlossenen „Komplexen Programms des wissenschaftlich-technischen Fortschritts der Mitgliedstaaten des RGW bis zum Jahr 2000". Vgl. Programmy (Anm. 28), S. 8.

[30]) Jachiel (Anm. 4), S. 71–74.

senschaftler nach Fachgebieten ablesen. 1987 waren 39,4% von ihnen im Bereich der technischen Forschung tätig, 1965 nur 25%. Dagegen nahm der Anteil der Naturwissenschaftler im gleichen Zeitraum von 19,5% auf 17,1% ab. Die Gesellschaftswissenschaften sind mit etwa 20%, gleich stark wie 1965, vertreten. Von 19% auf 15,4% ging die Rate im Bereich der Medizin zurück, und fast halbiert wurde der Anteil für die landwirtschaftliche Forschung (auf 8,5% im Jahre 1987)[31]. Die Anzahl der wissenschaftlichen Mitarbeiter und ihre Qualifikationsstruktur zeigt die Tabelle 5.

Tabelle 5: Anzahl der wissenschaftlichen Mitarbeiter

	1960	1970	1980	1987
gesamt	5848	12765	22601	30146
Akademiemitglieder	31	34	35	39
Korrespondierende Mitglieder	20	44	33	50
Professoren	383	718	986	1245
Dozenten	378	885	2008	2730
Ältere wiss. Mitarbeiter	516	1542	3468	4127
Wissenschaftliche Mitarbeiter	1663	5404	9172	13503
davon:				
Doktoren der Wissenschaft		103	645	1321
Kandidaten der Wissenschaft		2469	7945	9773

Quellen: SG. 1976, S. 132; SG. 1988, S. 150.

4. Das System der Forschungseinrichtungen

a) Die Akademien

Die BAN ist mit über 3000 wissenschaftlichen Mitarbeitern die größte und zugleich die führende wissenschaftliche Institution in Bulgarien. Sie arbeitet auf den Gebieten der geistes-, sozial-, naturwissenschaftlichen und der technischen Forschung. Die BAN ist aber zugleich eine Studien- und Weiterbildungsstätte, die ausdrücklich den Auftrag besitzt, eine wissenschaftliche Elite heranzuziehen. Ihr höchstes Führungsgremium ist die Generalversammlung, an der die ordentlichen und korrespondierenden Akademiemitglieder sowie Vertreter aus der Wissenschaft und aus anderen Institutionen teilnehmen. Der in einem Fünfjahresturnus gewählte Präsident und das Präsidium leiten die Tätigkeit der Akademie. Bei der BAN handelt es sich um eine staatlich finanzierte Haushaltsorganisation, die an den bulgarischen Gesamtausgaben für die Forschung mit fast 10% beteiligt ist. Eine weitere Finanzierungsquelle sind die Erträge der wissenschaftlichen Dienstleistungen und der Auftragsforschung, die inzwischen schon ein Viertel der Kosten decken können. Die Forschung erfolgt in den Wissenschaftlichen Vereinigungen, die aus Instituten, Zentren, Laboratorien

---

[31]) SG. 1976, S. 130; SG. 1988, S. 148.

und Abteilungen gebildet worden sind. Angeschlossen sind auch Betriebe für Kleinserien- und Versuchsproduktion und andere praxisorientierte Einrichtungen. Als Einheitszentren für Wissenschaft und Kadervorbereitung werden diejenigen Wissenschaftlichen Vereinigungen bezeichnet, die mit den Fakultäten der Sofioter Universität vereinigt sind. An der BAN bestehen Einheitszentren für: Mathematik und Mechanik, Chemie, Physik, Geowissenschaften, Biologie, Philosophie und Soziologie, Staats- und Rechtswissenschaften, Sprache und Literatur, Geschichte sowie die Wissenschaftlichen Vereinigungen für Kunstwissenschaft und für Grundprobleme der technischen Wissenschaften. Direkt dem Präsidium unterstehen die Institute für: Ökonomie, Internationale Beziehungen und sozialistische ökonomische Integration, Moderne soziale Theorie sowie die Zentren für: Bulgaristik, Wissenschaftswissenschaft, wissenschaftliche Information; die Zentralbibliothek und das wissenschaftliche Archiv, das Nationale Naturwissenschaftliche Museum, die Hauptverwaltung Hydrotechnik und Melioration, die Abteilung Bulgarische Enzyklopädie sowie ein Verlag mit angeschlossener Druckerei, in dem über 30 Zeitschriften und jährlich über 200 Bücher erscheinen.

Die Landwirtschaftliche Akademie ist Mitglied des NAPS. Sie ist eine Einrichtung für wissenschaftliche und angewandte Forschung sowie für Aus- und Weiterbildung von Spezialisten im Bereich der Land- und Forstwirtschaft, der Veterinärmedizin und der Lebensmitteltechnologie. Sie besteht aus 13 Forschungsinstituten und einem Institut für Weiterbildung landwirtschaftlicher Experten. Sie koordiniert die Arbeit einer Reihe anderer Institute. Ähnlich wie bei den Hochschulen ist ihr höchstes Leitungsorgan die Vollversammlung, die einen pädagogisch-wissenschaftlichen Rat wählt. Die Medizinische Akademie unter dem Ministerium für Volksgesundheit und soziale Fürsorge (*Ministerstvo na narodnoto zdrave i socialnite griži*) besteht aus 23 Forschungsinstituten und einem Wissenschaftszentrum. Angegliedert sind mehrere Produktionsbetriebe. Sie organisiert auch das postgraduelle Studium im medizinischen Bereich.

b) Andere Einrichtungen

An den Hochschulen sind Lehrstühle die Grundeinheiten der Lehre und Forschung. Eingerichtet wurden überdies Wissenschaftliche Forschungssektoren, Forschungslaboratorien, Klinika, Versuchsstationen, Außenstellen für Unterricht und Produktion sowie Kleinbetriebe, die sich auch an der angewandten Auftragsforschung beteiligen können.

Auch die Ministerien unterhalten eine Reihe von wissenschaftlichen Instituten und Zentren sowie Einrichtungen, die für eine schnelle Umsetzung der wissenschaftlichen Ergebnisse in die Praxis verantwortlich sind. Ausgesprochen spezialisiert und anwendungsbezogen ist die Tätigkeit der Forschungs- und Entwicklungsabteilungen der Wirtschaftsorganisationen und Betriebe. Schließlich beteiligen sich die Berufsverbände mit eigenen Einrichtungen oder in Kooperation mit anderen Organisationen an der Forschungs- und Entwicklungsarbeit. Zu ihnen gehören insbesondere der Verband der bulgarischen Wissenschaftler (*Săjuz na naučnite rabotnici*) und die Wissenschaftlich-technischen Verbände (*Naučno-techničeskite săjuzi*). Die Anzahl der Organisationen für angewandte Forschung ist der Tabelle 6 zu entnehmen.

Tabelle 6: Einrichtungen für angewandte Forschung

	1960	1970	1980	1987
gesamt	92	392	368	512
davon:				
Wissenschaftliche Institute	92	144	192	212
Wissenschaftliche Forschungssektoren an den Hochschulen		21	20	22

Quellen: SG. 1976, S. 130; SG. 1988, S. 148.

5. Internationale Beziehungen

Die internationale Zusammenarbeit erfolgt auf verschiedenen Ebenen: 1. die Mitgliedschaft bulgarischer Einrichtungen und Verbände in internationalen Organisationen. Hervorzuheben ist dabei die Mitarbeit an Programmen von UNO und UNESCO. Die meisten Beziehungen unterhält die BAN, die Mitglied in etwa 50 internationalen Organisationen ist. Die Landwirtschaftliche Akademie arbeitet z. B. im Ständigen Komitee für Landwirtschaft des RGW und in der FAO mit, die Medizinische Akademie in der WHO. Der Verband der bulgarischen Wissenschaftler ist seit 1948 Mitglied in der Weltföderation der Wissenschaftler, die Wissenschaftlich-technischen Verbände gehören der Weltorganisation der Ingenieurverbände (WFEO) an; 2. vertragliche und andere bilaterale Beziehungen zwischen einzelnen Einrichtungen (zuerst 1947 mit der UdSSR). Zu ihnen gehören der Austausch von Informationen und Mitarbeitern, gemeinsame Forschung, Konferenzen, Weiterbildung der Mitarbeiter. Die Beziehungen werden überwiegend mit sozialistischen Staaten gepflegt, die Bedeutung von Kontakten zu westlichen Einrichtungen nimmt aber zu. In der Bundesrepublik Deutschland ist es vor allem die DFG, die gemeinsame Vorhaben und den Wissenschaftleraustausch zwischen deutschen Einrichtungen und der BAN fördert. Forschungsstipendien vergibt die Alexander-von-Humboldt-Stiftung, und die Carl-Duisberg-Gesellschaft bietet Fortbildungsseminare an. Enge Beziehungen bestehen auch zur Südosteuropa-Gesellschaft; 3. im Rahmen des RGW werden weitergehende Formen der wissenschaftlichen Zusammenarbeit entwickelt. Dazu gehört die Abstimmung der Forschungspläne, mit der schon in der zweiten Hälfte der 60er Jahre begonnen wurde. Ein weiterer Schritt lag in der Arbeitsteilung und Spezialisierung sowie in gemeinsamen Forschungsvorhaben, die z. B. Mitte der 80er Jahre von 65 Koordinationszentren geleitet wurden. Zur gleichen Zeit bestanden zehn internationale Forschungsgruppen, zwei Laboratorien, fünf Forschungsinstitute und mehrere Vereinigungen für Wissenschaft und Produktion. Das älteste und mit 7000 Beschäftigten größte dieser Institute arbeitet seit 1956 in Dubno/UdSSR auf dem Gebiet der Kernforschung. Im Bereich der Grundlagenforschung dienen der Koordination auch die Treffen von Akademiepräsidenten der sozialistischen Länder, die alle zwei Jahre stattfinden. Die Arbeit an gemeinsamen Projekten wird von über 20 Problemkommissionen geleitet, in die jede Akademie ihre Vertreter entsendet. Des weiteren wurden von den Akademien einige internationale Zentren für die Weiterbildung wissenschaftlicher Kader gegründet. Die Forschungsschwerpunkte sind in dem 1985 beschlossenen „Komplexen Programm des wissenschaftlich-technischen Fortschritts der RGW-Mitgliedsländer bis zum Jahre 2000" festgelegt: Elektronik, Automatisierung, Biotechnologie, Atomenergie, neue Materialien und Technologien[32].

---

[32]) Vgl. Programmy (Anm. 28), S. 311–329.

Churches and Religious Communities

Marin Pundeff, Northridge/California*

I. Before 1944 – II. The Initial Changes, 1944–1947: 1. The Bulgarian Orthodox Church (BPTs) – 2. The Other Denominations – III. The Fundamental Changes, 1947–1953: 1. The General Provisions – 2. The BPTs – 3. The Other Denominations – IV. Developments since 1953: 1. General Provisions – 2. The BPTs – 3. The Other Denominations – V. Unrecognized Communities – VI. Inroads of Atheism

I. Before 1944

The oldest and most important of the churches and religious communities which the Bulgarian government recognizes today is the BPTs. A brief overview of its history before 1944 is necessary for understanding its status and condition since. The historical framework also provides perspective for the evolution of the other denominations in Bulgaria.

The first Bulgarian state in the Middle Ages (681–1014/18) became officially Christian in 864 by an act of its prince, Boris I, and under the auspices of the Patriarchate of Constantinople. The BPTs was organized as an archbishopric largely by Greek clergy using the Greek language and religious texts. Fearful of this subordination, Boris wanted an autocephalous patriarchate and turned to Rome, but Pope Nicholas I could not agree to it. The brief „union" ended in 870 when a council in Constantinople ruled that Bulgaria belonged in the East. A unique opportunity to stem the Greek influence presented itself in 886 when disciples of Cyril and Methodius, returning from the suppressed mission among the Moravian Slavs, found refuge in Bulgaria and began to spread Christianity and culture in the Slavic vernacular written in the new Glagolitic and Cyrillic scripts. Particularly notable was the work of Kliment, who became the first Slavic bishop at Ohrid. In 927, on arrangements with Constantinople, the BPTs was recognized as a separate patriarchate.

During the Byzantine reconquest (1014/18–1185) the patriarchate was abolished, but the see of Ohrid, elevated to an archbishopric, continued to function as a Slavic center. The second Bulgarian state (1185–1393/96) also entered into a brief union with Rome (1204–1235), which ended when, again on arrangements with Constantinople, the patriarchate was reestablished at Tŭrnovo. In the Turkish conquest it ceased to exist, and after 1453 its territory was taken over by the Patriarchate of

---

* The author is indebted to the East European Program of the Wilson Center, Washington, D.C., for support in the preparation of this chapter.

Constantinople. The archbishopric of Ohrid survived until 1767 when it, too, passed under the authority of Constantinople and its Greek (Phanariote) clergy.

During the nation's revival in the 19th century, removal of the Greek clergy and restoration of an autocephalous BPTs became the key goals. In 1870, the Ottoman government acceded to these demands and established an Exarchate for the Bulgarian areas of the empire but canonically subordinated to the Patriarchate. The latter responded by declaring the Exarchate schismatic and under anathema[1]).

Following the liberation of Bulgaria, the Treaty of Berlin in 1878 created a principality (after 1908, kingdom) and required it to guarantee the equality of all citizens regardless of religion and the freedom for all denominations (Orthodox Christians, Muslims, Catholics, Protestants, Armenians and Jews) in their internal organization and relations with religious superiors. The Tŭrnovo constitution of 1879[2]) thus stipulated freedom of religion, but introduced provisos that performance of rituals must not violate the laws, that no one could evade compliance with the laws because of religious convictions, and that all denominations, including the BPTs, while running their own religious affairs, were supervised by a cabinet minister. Since religious affairs were a treaty matter and involved religious authorities abroad, the supervision was vested in the ministry of foreign affairs.

The constitution further provided that Eastern Orthodox Christianity was the „dominant" religion, to which the monarch (except the first-elected princes) was required to belong. Bulgaria was „an inseparable part" of the Exarchate which included until the Balkan wars areas in Turkish Macedonia and Thrace and was headed by Exarch Ĭosif I residing in Constantinople. The BPTs's „supreme ecclesiastical authority" was its Holy Synod „wherever it might be located", and through it Bulgaria maintained „its unity with the Ecumenical Eastern Church in everything pertaining to the dogmas of the faith". Ĭosif's death in 1915 left the post vacant, and the BPTs in Bulgaria was governed by the Synod of metropolitan bishops (*mitropoliti*) heading the eleven eparchies in Bulgaria. Its administration and functions were regulated by the Exarchate's statute of 1871 as adapted to conditions in Bulgaria[3]). Its constitutional position entailed annual appropriations in the state budget under the ministry of foreign affairs, functions at state occasions, and control of the textbooks for religious instruction in the schools. The state also provided subsidies for the Muslim, Jewish, Armenian, and Catholic clergy[4]).

---

[1]) Sŭbev, T.: Uchredĭavane i diotsez na bŭlgarskata ekzarkhiĭa do 1878 g. (Establishment and territory of the Bulgarian exarchate until 1878). Sofia 1973, and Stanimirov, S.: Istoriĭa na Bŭlgarskata tsŭrkva (History of the Bulgarian church). Sofia 1925. For other sources on BPTs history, see Pundeff, M.: Hundert Jahre bulgarisches Exarchat, 1870–1970, in: Österreichische Osthefte. 12 (1970) 6, pp. 352–358.

[2]) For an English translation and discussion of the 1879 Constitution, see Black, C. E.: The Establishment of Constitutional Government in Bulgaria. Princeton 1943.

[3]) Vŭrgov, K.V.: Konstitutsiĭata na Bŭlgarskata pravoslavna tsŭrkva; istoriĭa i razvoĭ na ekzarkhiĭskiĭa ustav (The Constitution of the BPTs; history and evolution of the Statute of the Exarchate). Sofia 1920.

[4]) For extensive details, see the encyclopedic work of Tsankov, S.: Bŭlgarskata pravoslavna tsŭrkva ot osvobozhdenieto do nastoĭashte vreme (The BPTs from the liberation to the present time), in: Godishnik na Sofiĭskiĭa universitet; Bogoslovski fakultet (Annual of the Sofia University; Theolo-

II. The Initial Changes, 1944–1947

The entry of the Soviet army into Bulgaria in September, 1944, and the formation of the OF government (a coalition of Communists, Agrarians, Social Democrats, *Zveno*, and Independents) created the circumstances for fundamental changes. As a defeated country Bulgaria was placed under the authority of the ACC, chaired by its Soviet member, until the peace treaty took effect in 1947. Due to these constraints the initial changes were only a prelude to what was to come in 1947–1949 and after.

1. The Bulgarian Orthodox Church (BPTs)

There were basically two agendas for changes, those of the BPTs and of the Communists, and they converged on some points and sharply clashed on others. Church and lay leaders had long realized that the BPTs needed a process of renewal involving election of an exarch or patriarch, removal of the schism, improvement of the condition of the clergy, and invigoration of its work among the laity. They envisaged, of course, no diminished role for the BPTs as the state church. The chief proponent of this program was the Metropolitan of Sofia, Stefan (1878–1957), a strong-willed and well-educated hierarch, with a degree from the Kiev Theological Academy and a doctorate from the University of Fribourg (Switzerland), who aspired to become the BPTs's primate.

The Communists, on the other hand, were committed to the goal of eradicating all religion and replacing it by the „scientific" and atheistic Marxist outlook. However, being well attuned to the policies and wishes of the Soviet government, they were guided by Stalin's policy of allowing the Russian Orthodox Church (*Russkaîa Pravoslavnaîa Tserkov'*, RPTs) to elect a patriarch and assume a significant role in domestic and foreign affairs. The Russian patriarchate was intended to emerge after the war as the leader of Orthodoxy in the Balkans and elsewhere, and to be its effective supporter, the BPTs had to be strengthened by restoring its status (exarchate or patriarchate) and authority. The religious policy of the coalition itself was broadly stated in its program of September 17, 1944, favoring separation of the church from the state, introduction of civil marriage, and removal of the „intrusion of foreign factors" in the educational system[5]). The last point aimed at the foreign schools in the country, some of which had a religious orientation (see the chapter „Schulwesen" by P. Bachmaier).

The filling of the exarchal post[6]) and the lifting of the schism were speedily arran-

---

gical Faculty). XVI (1939), pp. 1–373, (Cit. as: Tsankov), which also covers the minority religions. The budget appropriation for the BPTs in 1938 was 71,980,000 leva, compared to 91,780,000 for the ministry of foreign affairs itself; DV. (1938) 1.

[5]) Ustanovîavane i ukrepvane na narodno-demokratichnata vlast, Septemvri 1944-mai 1945. Sbornik dokumenti. Ed. by V. Bozhinov et al. (Establishment and consolidation of the people's democratic power, September 1944-May 1945; collection of documents). Sofia 1969, pp. 113–136.

[6]) This was a tactical move to ease negotiations with the Ecumenical Patriarchate for the removal of the schism. Revival of the medieval patriarchate would have complicated and possibly even stymied them; on the restoration of the patriarchate, see below.

ged. On January 21, 1945, a *sŭbor* (council) of 96 delegates from the hierarchy and laity, elected Stefan exarch, and a month later, with the intercession of the Russian patriarch, the Ecumenical Patriarchate agreed to recognize him and thus lift the schism[7]). In his new role Stefan made it a point to stress the Russian assistance and began to build close ties with the RPTs, which was to him a model for relations with a Communist state and a potential protector. In June, 1945, he visited Patriarch Alekseĭ in Moscow amid a display of Slavic solidarity and in May, 1946, Alekseĭ spent ten days in Bulgaria for the commemoration of the millennium of the death of the national saint, Ivan of Rila. In July, 1948, Stefan journeyed again to Moscow for the 500th anniversary of the RPTs's autocephaly and the Pan-Orthodox meeting of church leaders. A major result of his visit was the establishment of a *podvorie* (church and residence) in Moscow as the BPTs „embassy" at the Russian Patriarchate and „living link" with the RPTs[8]).

The „classic" position of the Communists on the BPTs was formulated at the millennium ceremony by Georgi Dimitrov, who later in 1946 became prime minister. Speaking in the presence of the Russian patriarch, Dimitrov declared that the BPTs had great historic merits for preserving the Bulgarian's national consciousness during the centuries of Turkish rule. He was proud of it and proud of patriotic clergymen like Ivan Rilski, „a truly people's saint". However, the Church had also had in its ranks „traitors, scoundrels, and Judases from the point of views of the national interest of the Bulgarian people". The present Synod included some old men of „ossified brains and extremely conservative views". These old men needed to learn from the experience of the RPTs after the Revolution: at first it had failed to unterstand the spirit of the new times and had brought upon itself misfortunes, including persecution of clergymen for being tools of the counter-revolution. The BPTs could have a role to play if it became „a truly people's, republican, and progressive church"[9]). Church leaders did not respond directly, but in the preface of a book on the commemoration Stefan drew the philosophic battle line: „With all the external glitter and limitless claims of civilization in our democratic age, one still keenly feels the moral fissure, which is growing ever more fateful and fathomless. The causes of this tragic condition are hidden in the fact that no intoxication with technological progress and its material attainments can take the place of God in the soul of man or can satisfy the exalted human spirit created by God and dedicated to God. Yes, the more the idea of God and the immortality of the soul in the life of man are disparaged, the more dreadful becomes the spiritual indifference which inevitably ends in moral fall and spiritual death"[10]).

---

[7]) Lazov, D.: Ekzarkh Stefan I; zhivot, apostolstvo i tvorchestvo (Exarch Stefan I; life, mission, and works). Sofia 1947, pp. 257–259. The *tomos* of February 22, 1945, removing the schism and various related documents are in Tsŭrkoven Vestnik (Church gazette). May 19, 1945. Cf. Pundeff, M.: Church-State Relations in Bulgaria under Communism, in: Religion and Atheism in the USSR and Eastern Europe. Ed. by B. R. Bociurkiw and J. W. Strong. London 1975, pp. 328–330 and 346–347 (Cit. as: Pundeff).

[8]) Dukhovna Kultura (Spiritual culture). 59 (1979) 4, p. 20. An RPTs *podvorie* in Sofia was established in 1953.

[9]) Text in Dimitrov's Sŭchineniiâ (Works). Sofia 1954, vol. 12, pp. 186–190.

[10]) Sv. Ivan Rilski; sbornik po sluchaĭ 1000 godini ot smŭrtta mu (St. Ivan Rilski; collective volume on the occasion of the 1000th anniversary of his death). Sofia 1946, pp. 5–7.

The Communists pressed on with their plans. In September, 1946, the monarchy was replaced by a republic, eliminating the traditional church-state tie, and a month later the draft of what came to be called the Dimitrov constitution was published for discussion. The Synod issued a long and closely-reasoned statement which seemed to bear the imprint of Stefan's thinking and personality[11]. It raised strong objections to all sections „which radically change in a legal as well as moral sense the agelong relationship between the Bulgarian state and the Bulgarian Orthodox Church" and called for constitutional recognition of the fact, acknowledged by Dimitrov, that over the centuries the BPTs had played a central and vital role in the life of the nation.

To preserve this beneficial role the Synod asked for continued union of Church and State, especially since there was no history of antagonism between them or favoritism at the expense of the other religions in the country. The BPTs did not have „the ultraclerical spirit of the Roman Catholic Church" which might endanger, as in France or Mexico, the democratic republican government and the liberal national development. Nor did the Bulgarian nation have the background of religious heterogeneity and violent religious struggles, as did the Swiss Confederation, Holland, and the United States, which might compel the State to divorce itself from any leading church and take a neutral stand toward all. The negative views toward religion held by some persons and the idea that through separation the BPTs was to be crippled and destroyed could not be shared by any „true Bulgarian statesman". In any case, even in countries where there was hostility to religion and Christianity, „the Church has emerged invulnerable". If, however, the separation was to be enacted, provision should be made to preserve the loyal and benevolent relations between the State and the Church on the basis of recognition of the BPTs as a corporation of the same type as agencies of the State, as in Belgium, Holland, and France; recognition of the BPTs's rights of internal self-organization, self-government, ritual, teaching of the faith, and charity, as in Yugoslavia, the Soviet Union, and France; and assurance of state subsidies „as needed", as in Belgium. Holland, and Yugoslavia. The principle that religion was to be offered in the schools only as an elective subject was acceptable, but the stipulation concerning „secular education" contained a threat that an anti-clerical and anti-religious outlook would be fostered. For this reason the Synod requested a clause that the State would be „neutral in regard to the philosophical outlook".

The strongly-worded statement, with its allusions that Dimitrov was not a true Bulgarian statesman if he held the views of a true Communist and that even in the Soviet Union the Church had survived its ordeals, indicated that the BPTs was determined to fight for its rights and that the backbone of this determination was Stefan. He did not shrink from making his own views public. In the early part of 1947 he published with Georgiĭ Shavelsky, the last chaplain of the Russian imperial army and navy and a refugee in Bulgaria, a book on the issues of the time entitled *Sotsialniĭat vŭpros v svetlinata na Evangelieto* (The social question in the light of the Gospel), which openly and at length criticized the main tenets of the Communist outlook and equated Communism with Fascism and Nazism as varieties of materia-

---

[11] Text in Tsŭrkoven Vestnik. December 14, 1946.

lism seeking to destroy Christianity. Stefan and Dimitrov, representing Church and State, were thus set on a collision course, with the timing of the collision in Dimitrov's hands.

2. The Other Denominations

According to the last prewar census in 1934, in a total population of 6,077,939 there were 821,298 Muslims (Turks, Bulgarian-speaking Pomaks, Gypsies, and Tatars), 48,398 Jews, 45,704 Catholics (Roman Catholics and Uniats), 23,476 Armenians, and 8,371 Protestants (Congregationalists, Methodists, Baptists, Pentecostals, Adventists, and others).

The largest religious minority were the ethnic Turks (over 600,000) who were traditionally regarded as descendants of colonists settling in Bulgaria during and after the Ottoman conquest. Living in compact masses and isolated from the life of the Bulgarians, they maintained a strong sense of religious and ethnic identity. Their religious life was combined with that of the Muslim Bulgarians or Pomaks (about 120,000), that is Bulgarians who had converted to Islam under duress or by choice in the Ottoman period[12]); Muslim Gypsies (80,532); and Tatars (ca. 5,000). The postwar census in 1946 listed the Muslims at 934,418 (or 13.35 % of the total population of 7,029,349), of whom 675,500 were ethnic Turks. The community, regulated by a statute adopted in 1919[13]), was headed by a Chief Mufti residing in Sofia and regional muftis for the Turkish areas and the Pomaks in the Rhodope region. Before 1944, it had nine lower schools and one upper school (*medrese*) at Shumen (founded in 1922) to train Muslim clergy; a separate school for Pomak clergy was established in 1940 at Smolian[14]). The total subsidy from the state in 1939 was 1,701,320 leva[15]).

After 1944 the subsidy was discontinued until 1961 when it was resumed in undisclosed amounts. The Communists sought to win over the Turks by treating them in this period as a full-fledged ethnic minority, having its own schools and publications, but the atheist propaganda, which they also pressed, was counterproductive. In 1946, religious instruction in the schools of the recognized ethnic minorities (including Jews and Armenians) was declared optional, to be taught by lay teachers rather than by clergy[16]).

The Jews had a well-organized religious life until the calamities in World War II befell them. Most of them were Sephardics (Ladino-speaking) who arrived after their expulsion from Spain in 1492, but there were also some Ashkenasics (Yiddish-

---

[12]) For locations and estimated numbers of the Pomaks in Bulgaria, Greece, and Yugoslavia, see Tsankov (note 4), p. 286, and Shishkov, S.: Izbrani proizvedeniā (Selected works). Plovdiv 1965, pp. 169–274.
[13]) Text in DV. (1919) 65.
[14]) Tsŭrkvi i izpovedaniā v Narodna Republika Bŭlgariā (Churches and denominations in the NRB). Sofia 1975; issued by BPTs's Ecumenical Department also in Western languages, pp. 76–80 (Cit. as: Tsŭrkvi i izpovedaniā); Protsesŭt na preodoliāvane na religiāta v Bŭlgariā (The process of overcoming religion in Bulgaria). Ed. by Zhivko Oshavkov. Sofia 1968, p. 101.
[15]) Tsankov (note 4), p. 317.
[16]) DV. (1946) 234.

speaking) who came from countries north of the Danube[17]). The community was governed by a Central Consistory and a Chief Rabbi in Sofia, with consistories and rabbis in provincial centers. Because of language and rite differences, the Ashkenazics had separate synagogues in Sofia and Ruse. Integration into the country's life was substantial since there was no discrimination on religious grounds, and anti-Semitism was at most an isolated phenomenon[18]). In the inter-war period the community was dominated by the Zionists, who tended to a secular outlook. The state subsidy in 1939 was 65,520 leva.

Under Nazi Germany's influence and pressure, legislation against the Jews was enacted in January, 1941. As the so-called Law for the Defense of the Nation was being considered, the Synod of the BPTs addressed the prime minister and the president of the NSb, pointing out that „we are all sons of a heavenly Father, [that the law] could not be regarded as justified or beneficial in protecting the nation, [and that] if there are dangers to the nation, the measures against these dangers must deal with actions and not with ethnic and religious groups"[19]). With the Final Solution underway, the Bulgarian government delivered in secrecy the Jews from the Yugoslav and Greek territories occupied in 1941, but the arrangements for delivering the Jews from Bulgaria proper became known and aroused a wave of protests, demonstrations, and actions to save them from deportation. In the BPTs, particularly active was Metropolitan Stefan, who warned Tsar Boris of the consequences for him and the country and protected the Chief Rabbi from arrest in his residence. As a result no deportations to the death camps took place, and the government settled for expelling the Jews from Sofia to the countryside.

The changes in 1944 swept away these measures. Jewish religious life was revived around the Central Consistory, but the dominant role was assumed by the Jewish Central Committee of the OF, largely controlled by Communists. It began publishing a newspaper, *Evreĭski Vesti* (Jewish News, 1944-), for a period jointly with the consistory, as the conveyor of the new policies. In January, 1945, and April, 1946, it held national conferences at which the task was set to „wean away" the Jews from Zionism because it undermined their „spirit of patriotism" and led them to emigrate[20]). The census of 1946 listed 44,209 Jews, a drop of 4,189 from 1934 due to emigration.

The last of the recognized minorities, the Armenians were mostly refugees from persecution in Turkey and adherents of the nation's Gregorian Church. Before 1944, their religious life was organized as an eparchy headed by a bishop, with parishes in Plovdiv, Sofia and other Armenian centers. The state subsidy for the bishop's salary in 1939 was 18,000 leva. As in the case of the Jews, after 1944 the dominant role was played by a new *Erevan* progressive organization of the Armenians in Bulgaria, which

---

[17]) Mezan, S.: Les Juif espagnols en Bulgarie. Sofia 1925.
[18]) Chary, F. B.: The Bulgarian Jews and the Final Solution, 1940–1944. Pittsburgh 1972, pp. 27–36.
[19]) Quoted in Oliver, Kh. D.: Nie spasenite (We the saved). Sofia 1967, pp. 53/54.
[20]) Izrael, S.: Bŭlgarskite evrei v godinite na narodnata vlast (The Bulgarian Jews in the years of the people's power), in: Godishnik (Annual) of the Central Board of the Social, Cultural, and Education Association of the Jews in the People's Republic of Bulgaria. 6 (1971), pp. 113–137 (Cit. as: Izrael).

began publication of a newspaper, *Erevan* (1944–), to put across the new policies (see the chapter „Nationale Minderheiten" by S. Troebst).

The third of the Christian communities, the Bulgarian Catholics had a rather complex history going back to the 13th and 14th century, when Franciscan missionaries established communities in western Bulgarian regions. Among their converts were Orthodox heretics known as Paulicians (earlier Bogomils) along the Danube (Nikopol and Svishtov), in the Plovdiv area, and elsewhere. Under Ottoman rule their center was Sofia, which was raised to archbishopric in 1643. Clergy was educated in Rome, where a bishop of Nikopol, Filip Stanislavov, published the first Bulgarian book known as *Abagar* in 1651. Linked with Austria, many Catholics were forced to flee to the Banat region after the unsuccessful Chiprovtsi uprising in 1688. After the Crimean War a Uniat movement developed as a way of gaining independence from the Greek Patriarchate and support from the Catholic West, especially France[21]).

In the period after 1878 the Roman Catholics were organized in two bishoprics for Sofia-Plovdiv (see at Sofia) and Nikopol-Ruse (see at Ruse). The Uniats rose to a substantial number only after the wars of 1912–1918 when refugees from Macedonia and Thrace, where the Uniat movement arose, resettled in Bulgaria. To lead both, in 1925 the Vatican appointed an Apostolic Visitator (Angelo Roncalli, the future Pope John XXIII), who was elevated to Apostolic Delegate in 1931 with the rank of archbishop. Attempts to conclude a concordat were, however, resisted by the BPTs and the Bulgarian government, and diplomatic relations were never established. In 1926, the Vatican constituted the Uniats as an exarchate, in effect a bishopric, and appointed an exarch. The total number of Catholics before 1912 was over 32,000, which rose with the influx of Uniats to 40,347 in 1926 and 45,704 (including foreign residents) in 1934, by official census figures. Bulgarian Catholic statistics placed the number at 48,960 (42,400 Roman Catholics, of whom 26,500 were under the Sofia see and 15,900 under the Ruse see, and 6,560 Uniats). Their main publication was the weekly *Istina* (Truth) (1924–1949). Priests were trained in two seminaries (at Sofia run by Jesuits, and Svishtov run by Passionists), and at higher levels in Rome. For the laity, foreign Catholic clergy (mostly French) from various orders maintained a number of schools, as well as charities, which had *inter alia* missionary purposes. The most significant were the French colleges and boarding schools in Sofia and Plovdiv and the school of *Opera Italiana Pro Oriente* in Sofia[22]).

The developments in 1944–1947 did not significantly affect the Bulgarian Catholics. The war had already disrupted the work of the foreign clergy, especially the French, and after 1945 it was slow to regain the ground. The successor of Roncalli as Apostolic Delegate, Mgr. Giuseppe Mazzoli, died in that year and was replaced by Don Francesco Galloni, director of *Opera Italiana Pro Oriente* in Sofia.

---

[21]) Sofranov, I.: Histoire du mouvement bulgare vers l'Eglise Catholique au XIX siècle. I, 1855–1865. Rome 1960; Genchev, N.: Frantsiĭa v bŭlgarskoto dukhovno vŭzrazhdane (France in the Bulgarian spiritual revival). Sofia 1979.

[22]) Drenikoff, K.G.: L'Eglise Catholique en Bulgarie. Madrid 1968, pp. 17–28 (Cit. as: Drenikoff); Tsankov (note 4), pp. 290–298. Drenikoff provides a list of the orders (male and female) active in Bulgaria before 1944.

The last and smallest of the Christian communities, the Bulgarian Protestants had a recent, but culturally significant history. The first converts were made by American Methodist missionaries, who arrived in northern Bulgaria in 1857, and by missionaries of the American Board of Commissioners for Foreign Missions in Boston (mostly Congregationalists), who began their activities in 1858 in southern Bulgaria. Success in proselytizing was limited, but their publishing and educational activities filled acute needs before and after 1878. The most important among their religious publications was the first translation of the entire Bible into modern Bulgarian in 1871, which enjoyed wide use even among the BPTs clergy as well as laity, since BPTs did not issue such a Bible until 1925[23]). Also very influential was their weekly newspaper *Zornitsa* (Morning Star) (1876–1948), the first and longest-running weekly in Bulgarian, disseminating their theological and moral teachings. Their main schools were in Samokov (for boys and girls) and Lovech (for girls) in Bulgaria and the non-denominational Robert College in Constantinople, which educated a large number of Bulgarians holding leading positions after 1878. The establishment in Samokov was moved in 1926 to the village of Simeonovo, near Sofia, and named the American College, comparable in curriculum to the public secondary schools. The various sects united first in 1875 in the Bulgarian Evangelical Philanthropic Society and in 1909 in the Union of Evangelical Churches in Bulgaria headed by a common spokesman before the authorities and holding congresses every four years. Under its bylaws the union was a federation of internally autonomous denominations[24]).

The Bulgarian Protestants were thus closely linked with the parent churches in the United States (and to a lesser degree in Western Europe) and received financial and other support from them. The war disrupted their ties and led to the closing of the schools. After 1944, as Americans began to arrive in Bulgaria, efforts were made to reopen the schools, but the Communist government blocked them. Financial support to the Protestants was also effectively blocked by a law in 1946 on control of foreign currency transactions.

III. The Fundamental Changes, 1947–1953

1. The General Provisions

The Paris peace treaty (February 10, 1947) normalized Bulgaria's status and freed the Communists' hands to put in effect the drastic changes they had in mind. The treaty (Art. 2) did obligate Bulgaria to secure „the enjoyment of human rights and of the fundamental freedoms, including freedom of expression, of press and publica-

---

[23]) Pundeff, M.: Bulgaria's Cultural Reorientation after 1878, in: Papers for the V. Congress of Southeast European Studies, Belgrade, September, 1984. Ed. by K.K. Shangriladze and E.W. Townsend. Columbus 1984, pp. 300–320.

[24]) Tsankov (note 4), pp. 298–302.

tion, of religious worship, of political opinion and of public meeting"[25]), but when its enforcement mechanism was tested in 1950 (see below, p. 557), it proved ineffectual.

The first move was to enact the Dimitrov constitution (December 4, 1947). A number of its articles dealt explicitly or implicitly with religion, the BPTs, and the minority denominations. The main provisions were in Art. 78: „The citizens are guaranteed freedom of conscience and religious beliefs as well as freedom of performing the religious rituals. The church is separated from the state. A special law shall regulate the legal status, the questions of financial support, as well as the right of self-organization and self-government of the various religious communities. Misuse of church and religion for political purposes is prohibited, as is also the formation of political organizations on a religious basis." Art. 76 stipulated that only civil marriage was lawful, and Art. 79 proclaimed in regard to education that all schools were run by the state, that instruction was secular, and that „the national minorities have the right to schooling in their mother tongue and to develop their national culture, while the study of the Bulgarian language is obligatory".

The constitution thus explicitly ended the BPTs's official role and functions and took it, as well as the other denominations, out of the realm of education. By omission, it also ended all vestiges of the regime established by the treaty of Berlin. The way was now open to set up a new regime regarding religion in conformity with the Soviet model and to enact the special law envisaged by Art. 78.

The law was enacted on March 1, 1949. In introducing it, Dimitrov's deputy, Vasil Kolarov, spoke in tough and uncompromising terms on „what will not be tolerated": no church or clergyman would be allowed to preach against the new regime or conduct overt or covert activities to restore the old; no church or clergyman would be allowed to preach against the economic plans or be an agent of the imperialists and conspire with the remnants of capitalism against socialism. Kolarov singled out the Bulgarian Catholic and Protestant clergy as being agents of foreign centers and involved in traitorous activities that had to be stopped. The Vatican, in particular, he said, had shown interest in maintaining an outpost in Bulgaria, but since no concordat and diplomatic relations existed with it, the government had decided to terminate the activities and presence of Vatican representatives in the country[26]).

The law set forth a system of strict and thoroughgoing controls over the religious communities in line with the Soviet Law on Religious Associations of 1929. Since it is still in force, its provisions must be consulted for a full understanding of the position of the religious communities today[27]). Here only some clauses can be cited: The BPTs is singled out for special mention as „the traditional religion of the Bulgarian people, linked to its history, and as such, in form, substance, and spirit, could become a people's democratic church"; a denomination can exist and enjoy legal rights only if recognized by the State; recognition, taking the form of approval of a denomination's

---

[25]) Text of the treaty, with ratification dates, in: U.S. Department of State Publication 2973 (Washington, 1947).

[26]) RD. February 24, 1949.

[27]) Text in DV. (1949) 48; English translation in: The Church and State under Communism, issued by the U.S. Senate Committee on the Judiciary. Washington 1965; and German in: Kirche und Staat in Bulgarien und Jugoslawien: Gesetze und Verordnungen. Ed. by R. Stupperich. Witten 1971.

statute by the government official in charge of religious affairs – currently called *Predsedatel na Komiteta po vŭprosite na BPTs i religioznite kultove* (Chairman of the Committee for the Affairs of the BPTs and the Religious Cults; hereafter PK for short) and holding the rank of deputy foreign minister – can be withdrawn; clergy and other employees of denominations can be suspended or dismissed by the authorities; budgets must be submitted to PK and all financial activity is subject to PK control; denominations must submit all messages, circulars, and other papers and publications to PK; all officials must register with the authorities; minors are outside the range of activity of clergy; the denominations cannot operate hospitals, orphanages, etc., and can have contacts with denominations outside the country only with the prior permission of PK; anyone using churches and religion for propaganda against the government and its policies is punishable by imprisonment unless subject to another heavier penalty[28]).

2. The BPTs

The law was preceded and accompanied by police terror, sporadically used against churchmen since 1944. The number of those killed, tortured, and imprisoned is not known, but at one time the notorious Belene camp (on a Danube island) alone held 316 Orthodox priests[29]). What Stefan did to protect the clergy is also not known. Once the constitution was enacted, he took the position that it contained some „constructive provisions" and that the Church, being separated from the State and no longer constrained by a special status and considerations of state policy, was now able to begin a vigorous program of evangelical, educational, and charitable activities and deepen its roots among the people. The parish priests were accordingly instructed to increase Sunday-school activities and more effectively involve the lay *bratstva* (brotherhoods, 774 in 1939, which existed mostly around urban churches) in evangelical, educational, and charitable work. The priests were, furthermore, put on notice that separation from the State also signified that they should stay out of government-sponsored political organizations and out of politics in general[30]).

The showdown with Stefan began over the affairs of the BPTs eparchy in the United States. The eparchy, created in 1937 for the needs of the Bulgarian immigrants and placed under the supervision of the Metropolitan of Sofia, was headed by Bishop Andreĭ Velichki, who resided in New York. Apprehensive about the BPTs as a captive church in Bulgaria, Andreĭ convoked a *sŭbor* in 1947 in Buffalo, New York, which elected him bishop of an expanded eparchy of North and South America and Australia and moved to incorporate it under the laws of the State of New York in order to organize a self-contained religious life of the Orthodox Bulgarians overseas. Dimitrov stiffly demanded that Andreĭ be dismissed and refused to see Stefan until this was

---

[28]) Articles 26–28 dealing with offenses subject to imprisonment were superseded by the Criminal Code of February 13, 1951.
[29]) Tzanov, D.: Communist Struggle against Religion, in: Religion in Communist Dominated Areas. 19 (1980) 10-11-12, pp. 166–168.
[30]) Tsŭrkoven Vestnik. May 15, 1948.

done. Stefan and the Synod held that the dismissal might provoke a secession of Bulgarians emigrants but eventually yielded for the sake of workable relations with the government „and more particularly with the Prime Minister"[31]). Andreĭ, however, defiantly kept his eparchy.

Next, PK addressed a long communication to the Synod demanding that all church leaders stop criticizing the government, support its measures, acknowledge and preach that the State stood above the Church, counteract any propaganda against the party and the Soviet Union from the pulpit and in the religious press, display the portraits of the Communist leaders and preach love for them, prevent the polarization of opposition sentiments and activities around the churches, acknowledge and support the government organizations for children, youth, and women, and stop barring the lower clergy from joining political organizations and activities sponsored by the party. The communication was also sent to the eparchies and their subdivisions, the dean of the Faculty of Theology as well as the rector of the University of Sofia, the heads of the theological seminaries in Sofia and Plovdiv and the theological institute in Cherepish, the Union of Priests, the Orthodox Christian brotherhoods and church employees, and the periodicals *Tsŭrkoven Vestnik* (Church Gazette), *Naroden Pastir* (People's Shepherd, organ of the Priest' Union), *Tsŭrkoven Sluzhitel* (Church Employee), and *Pravoslaven Pastir* (Orthodox Shepherd) for the widest possible impact[32]).

The ensuing tug of war has remained shrouded in secrecy, but in July, 1948, the organ of the Synod explained that according to „assurance received from most authoritative persons", the PK's communication did not express the views of the government on relations between the Church and the State and on the mission of the BPTs; that it was to be regarded as „unsent, unreceived, and invalid"; and that the Synod's policy of asking the priests to stay out of politics and political organizations in order to devote themselves fully to their direct and proper concerns was in accordance not only with the tradition of the Church since the country's liberation in 1878, but with „*the view and practice of the Russian Orthodox Church*, which have been taken into account in organizing our own church life"[33]).

In his further efforts to protect the Church, Stefan had several discussions with Dimitrov's closest associates, Traĭcho Kostov and Vasil Kolarov, and realized that they wanted him out of the way as the price for a *modus vivendi*. On September 4–6 the Synod convened in a special meeting „for urgent consideration of certain important questions which needed immediate attention", according to an explanatory „Communication from the Holy Synod" which was published a month later and provided the only known details of the climax of the crisis[34]). At the meeting on September 6, described in the communication as „stormy", Stefan submitted his resignation, having already told an unnamed government official that he would do so. Published to allay „false and harmful rumors", the communication attributed his

---

[31]) Ibid.
[32]) Text in: Naroden Pastir. June 1, 1948.
[33]) Tsŭrkoven Vestnik. July 19, 1948; italics in the text.
[34]) Ibid., October 7, 1948.

resignation to his „imprudent" attitude toward his office „in a tense and strenuous time when the Holy Church is moving, not without pains, into new conditions of existence resulting from its separation from the State". It also castigated him for „autocratic" and „arbitrary" rule and mentioned his ambition to become patriarch. His functions as chairman of the Synod and Metropolitan of Sofia were temporarily assumed by the Synod's oldest number, Metropolitan Mikhail of Dorostol and Cherven, without any mention of the exarchal office, presumably because, in the light of subsequent developments, a decision had been reached to supersede it by restoring the patriarchate. Stefan himself was banished from Sofia and upon his death in 1957 was buried at the Bachkovo monastery.

With Stefan out, the Synod hastened on September 9 – the anniversary of the Communist seizure of power – to express to Dimitrov and Kolarov „most cordial and sincere" salutations and praised their „statesmanlike wisdom"[35]. On September 13, Mikhail, Metropolitan Paisiĭ of Vratsa, and Metropolitan Kliment of Stara Zagora paid a visit to the PK and announced „a complete understanding," while the PK assured the Priests' Union in a separate meeting that Dimitrov and Kolarov harbored „good will toward the Church and the priesthood" and stressed „heavily" that the State would continue to provide financial support. The Synod then issued a letter to all parish churches declaring that the priests were free to take an active part in Communist-sponsored organizations, that the Church would refrain from „any religious propaganda among the youth", that the constitution's provisions must be obeyed, that due respect was to be shown to the political leaders and the authorities, and that in the future only the religious and ethical truths of the Church were to be expounded from the pulpit[36].

The financial condition of the BPTs, despite the assurances of state support, became increasingly precarious. The nationalization of land cut severely into its holdings (valued, with buildings, at nearly 800 million leva in 1939), while inflation and currency reform practically wiped out its prewar liquid funds (370 million in 1939)[37]. If Dimitrov and Kolarov had committed themselves to provide support to the BPTs, Vŭlko Chervenkov, their successor in 1950–1956, had his own ideas of drastic Stalinism. The state support was discontinued and BPTs was put on a self-supporting basis, its main source of revenue now being the sale of candles. In the new hostile environment, however, the sale dropped from 150–180 tons per year before 1944 to 55 tons in 1953, and the state had to restore its subsidy, although apparently in amounts far below its pre-1944 equivalents[38]. The annual subsidy was not made public.

The vacant exarchal office was liquidated with the adoption of a new statute for the Church, approved by the government on December 31, 1950[39]. As expected, it made the BPTs a patriarchate in order to place it on equal footing with the Balkan Ortho-

---

[35] Ibid., September 21, 1948.
[36] Ibid., October 23, 1948.
[37] Full details of the BPT's finances before 1939 are provided in: Tsankov (note 4), pp. 303–363.
[38] Pundeff (note 7), p. 348.
[39] Text in: Supplement to Tsŭrkoven Vestnik for 1951.

dox patriarchates and provide the RPTs with an even stronger voice of support in international affairs. The selection of Metropolitan Kiril of Plovdiv three days later to be acting chairman of the Synod indicated that the agreements reached on the *modus vivendi* included his installation as patriarch.

Kiril's qualifications for the office were beyond dispute. Born in 1901 in Sofia, he studied theology at Belgrade and Chernovtsi, receiving a doctorate in 1927, as well as philosophy in Vienna and Berlin. His intellectual powers were evident early, as was his interest in public affairs, as he had served as secretary of the Synod (1935–1938) and president of the Sofia chapter of the nationalist Otets Paisiĭ All-Bulgarian Union founded by Stefan. Elevated to the Plovdiv see at the age of 37, he also had authority during World War II over areas annexed from Greece, and like Stefan in Sofia, he had much to do with saving the Jews in Plovdiv from deportation to the death camps. After the war he demonstrated adaptability in his account of the visit of the BPTs delegation to the Soviet Union in July, 1948[40]) and in becoming vice-president of the Bulgarian Committee for Defense of Peace and member of the World Peace Council. As Metropolitan of Plovdiv he also became biographer of some of his predecessors and later, as Patriarch, produced a large body of studies of other hierarchs and subjects of BPTs history. His sermons and speeches filled six volumes[41]).

Kiril's installation as Patriarch and Metropolitan of Sofia came on May 10, 1953. At the *sŭbor* of 107 delegates of clergy and laity, the PK declared that „the new relations" between Church and State had produced good results in the internal life of the Church: The BPTs was „freed from the heavy burden of functions not befitting it" and was able to „direct its resources exclusively into the field of religious questions where its real calling is". The Church, he said, was giving „uncoerced" support to the new order and was an active participant in the peace movement in the country and abroad. It was true to its traditions of „strict and unconditional" defense of national and religious independence and patriotism and was „in unison" with the people's aspirations. In his own detailed report on the state of the BPTs, including its poor financial condition, Kiril devoted only a page to „Relations with the State", pointing out that they were governed by the Lord's principle „Render to Caesar the things that are Caesar's and to God the things that are God's", that is, rendering to God faith and conscience and to the State „complete loyalty" and civil obligations. The Church had given evidence on many occasions since 1944 of this loyalty and its goodwill to cooperate, according to its abilities in terms of principles and actual resources, in the peace movement and other policies of the government and thus carry out its „patriotic duty"[42]). The two statements became the guidelines for the BPTs's role under Kiril.

The separation of the BPTs from the state also entailed separating the Faculty of Theology (established in 1923) from the University of Sofia in 1950 and constituting it as the BPTs's St. Kliment Okhridski Academy of Theology. The secondary theolo-

---

[40]) Plovdivski Kiril: Gosti na Ruskata tsŭrkva (Guests of the Russian Church). Plovdiv 1949.

[41]) On Kiril, see Koev, T.P.: Patriarch Kiril zum Gedächtnis, in: Kirche im Osten. 15 (1972), pp. 11–16; and Pundeff, M.: Patriarch Kiril of Bulgaria, 1901–1971, in: Slavic Review. 30 (1971) 2, pp. 471/472.

[42]) The full record of the *sŭbor* is in: Deĭaniĭa na tretiĭa tsŭrkovnonaroden sŭbor, Sofiĭa, 8–10 mai 1953 g. (Proceedings of the third church and lay council). Sofia 1953.

gical schools (seminaries) at Sofia and Plovdiv were merged also in that year and located at the Cherepish monastery, 75 km from Sofia.

3. The Other Denominations

The effect of the religious policies in this period was least painful on the Jews, simply because they received the option to emigrate as soon as Israel came into being. A mass exodus in 1948/49 left behind only about 6,000, most of them in Sofia and largely non-believers. The Jewish schools were declared closed for „lack of pupils", while religious life remained nominally possible at the synagogue in Sofia[43]).

The harshest treatment was reserved for the Protestants and the Catholics since they had ties with „hostile foreign centers" in the West. All foreign schools, with or without religious affiliation, were closed in 1948. As the Law on Religious Denominations was being passed, fifteen pastors from the Union of Evangelical Churches, secretly arrested earlier with other pastors, were put on trial and charged with espionage on behalf of the United States and England, high treason, foreign exchange speculation, and efforts to „restore the bourgeois capitalist regime"[44]). The leader, Vasil Ziapkov, was also charged with betraying secrets of the Bulgarian peace delegation in Paris to American and British delegates, although what apparently he did was to ask them to include in the peace treaty the clause for the protection of religious freedom. On March 5, 1949, Ziapkov and three other pastors were sentenced to life imprisonment and the rest to various prison terms. Other closed-door trials followed.

The question of what was happening to religious freedom in Bulgaria (as well as Hungary and Rumania) was taken by the United States and England to the United Nations General Assembly, which expressed deep concern and established and *ad hoc* Political Committee on Observance of Human Rights in these countries as bound by the peace treaties. The matter reached, however, a deadend when the International Court of Justice found, in two advisory opinions of March 30 and July 18, 1950, that the three countries could block the creation of joint commissions stipulated by the treaties to settle such disputes[45]). The severance of U.S. diplomatic relations with Bulgaria in 1950 removed American presence altogether until 1960. Isolated and leaderless, the Protestants slumped to a shadowy existence (see also the chapter „Außenpolitik" by K.-D. Grothusen).

The Catholics suffered a similar fate. Arrests of their leaders began in 1950, followed by one open trial and apparently several secret ones as well as executions without

---

[43]) Izrael (note 20), pp. 129/130; Oschlies, W.: The Jews in Bulgaria since 1944, in: Soviet Jewish Affairs. 14 (1984) 2, pp. 41–54.

[44]) The government version of the case is in: The Trial of Fifteen Protestant Pastors-Spies. Sofia 1949; for the travails of the Protestant clergy, see the account of two of the pastors, Popoff, H.: I Was a Communist Prisoner. Grand Rapids 1966, expanded in: Tortured for his faith. 1978, and Matheeff, M.: Document of Darkness; a document of 35 years of atheist-Communist terror against the Christians in the People's Republic of Bulgaria. St. Catharines, Ontario 1980; German ed.: Mit Jesus durch die Teufelszelle. Uhldingen-Mühlhofen 1973.

[45]) U.S. Department of State Bulletin. October 23, 1950, pp. 666–670.

trial. At the open trial Bishop Evgeniĭ Bosilkov, two editors of the suspended Catholic organ, *Istina*, and some thirty priests, nuns, and laymen were charged *inter alia* with spying for the Vatican, concealing weapons, and carrying on propaganda against Communism. The trial ended on October 3, 1952, with death sentences for Bosilkov and three others and various terms of prison for the rest[46]. On December 15 Pope Pius XII issued an encyclical protesting, without results, the „wave of terror". As in the case of the Protestants, the terror against the Catholics brought their life as a religious community to a virtual standstill until the 1970's.

The only Christian community that experienced no unsettling pressure in this period were the Armenians. Given the option to emigrate to the USSR, their number continued to drop. In religious affairs, jurisdiction over them was vested in the Armenian Gregorian bishop residing in Bucharest, Rumania.

Lastly, the Turkish minority was also the target of drastic measures. Islam gave the Bulgarian Turks a strong sense of religious and ethnic identity which stood in the way of the various cultural and economic changes, essentially aimed at amalgamation with the Bulgarian majority, that the Communists were bent on achieving. The method of dealing with the problem, which they adopted in August, 1950, was to thin out the Turkish areas and rid themselves of the most religious and recalcitrant Turks by planning to resettle within three months 250,000, or more than one-third of the minority, in Turkey. In the ensuing period until November, 1951, when Turkey closed the border to further deportations, nearly 155,000 Muslims, some of them Gypsies, were deported. Those who remained behind, as well as the Pomaks, were subjected to the constant pressure to communize and secularize their life[47]. Their religious life was regulated by a new statute approved in 1951 but not published.

IV. Developments since 1953

1. General Provisions

The 1947 constitution was superseded in 1971 by a new text which revalidated in its Articles 35, 38, 45, 52, and 53 the regime established earlier. There are, however, also significant innovations and changes of emphasis: parents must give their children a „Communist upbringing"; the upbringing of youth „in a Communist spirit is the duty of the entire society"; citizens of non-Bulgarian origin have the right to study their language „in addition to the compulsory study of Bulgarian", but the provision concerning the right to develop their national culture, which would involve religion, has been dropped. The rights of citizens include conducting „anti-religious propa-

---

[46] A „Bill of Indictment" was published in RD. September 21, 1952; for details see Drenikoff (note 22), and Broun, J. A.: Catholics in Bulgaria, in: Religion in Communist Lands. 11 (1983) 3, pp. 310–320.

[47] Kostanick, H. L.: Turkish Resettlement of Bulgarian Turks, 1950–1953. Berkeley 1957, pp. 65–82.

ganda". Lastly, religion cannot be invoked to refuse to fulfill obligations imposed by the constitution and the laws[48]).

The new constitution has not affected the 1949 Law on Religious Denominations. Its Articles 26–28 are now superseded by Articles 164–166 of the Criminal Code of 1968[49]).

2. The BPTs

In regard to the actual condition of the BPTs, as well as the other recognized communities, it should be noted at once that reliable and detailed information is very difficult to obtain. Bulgarian census statistics by religion have long been discontinued. The last official information of the size of the communities was released in 1975 (see Note 14). Data on the impact of atheist propaganda are even older. The Soviet phenomena of *samizdat* and *glasnost'*, furthermore, have not really reached Bulgaria yet (see the chapter „Domestic Politics" by J. D. Bell). The information, highly fragmentary, comes from incidental disclosures of Bulgarian officials and scholars, accounts of refugees, observations of foreign visitors, journalists, and scholars, and publications of such diverse organizations as the World Council of Churches in Geneva, Chevetogne Monastery in Belgium, Keston College in England, and others.

Under the leadership of Patriarch Kiril (1953–1971), the guiding theme of the BPTs in society was „patriotic service", which provided a common ground for Christians and Communists to work together. Promotion of patriotism and pride in the nation's history, heroes, and achievements became party policy since the early 1960's, under the leadership of Todor Zhivkov, and provided the BPTs with excellent opportunities to be seen in a favorable light, since many of these heroes and achievements were associated with it. In this atmosphere the BPTs elevated among its saints Paisiĭ, the author of the passionately patriotic *Istoriĭa Slavĭanobolgarskaĭa* of 1762 and Bishop Sofroniĭ of Vratsa, an ardent follower of Paisiĭ and author of the first book in modern Bulgarian. The party press began to publish pictures of monasteries as „citadels of the Bulgarian spirit" and historians returned to an almost traditional recognition of the BPTs's role in national history. Zhivkov himself publicly endorsed the theme, pointing out that „in contrast to the situation in other countries, our Church has always been patriotic" and that it had „a very meritorious record in the struggle against the foreign Turkish rule"[50]). Kiril on his part stressed that the Christian-Communist „dialogue is carried on every day through work and love of country" and that „in a family there can be both believing and non-believing members, but they love each other because they are bound together by blood. Our national family is like that. In it there are both non-believers and believers, but all work together for the wellbeing of our country"[51]).

---

[48]) Text in DV. (1971) 39; German translation of relevant articles in: Voss, E.: Die Religionsfreiheit in Osteuropa. Zollikon 1984, pp. 73/74.
[49]) Text in DV. (1968) 26.
[50]) Quoted in Tsŭrkoven Vestnik. September 21, 1968.
[51]) Slavĭani (Slavs). March 1969, pp. 18/19.

Another area of common ground which Kiril cultivated was the world peace movement sponsored by the Soviet Union, particularly the Christian Peace Conference. In 1961, the BPTs received recognition of its patriarchal status by the Patriarchate of Constantinople and became a member of the World Council of Churches, establishing a special department for ecumenical activities. Personally, Kiril involved himself increasingly in historical scholarship which earned him election as a member of the BAN, an atheist institution, in 1970.

Internally, under Kiril's stewardship, the BPTs continued to shrink. An index of this process was the drop of its salaried parish priests to 1,785 in 1966, compared to 2,825 in 1940[52]). The drop represented a considerable loss of ground, due undoubtedly to the pressures of atheist propaganda and the stranglehold the government has on the BPTs's finances, among other factors[53]). It should be noted that in the 1960's monks were allowed to return to Rila and other monasteries to lend them authenticity for Western tourists, whom the Communists, in need of hard currency, began to cultivate.

Kiril's successor, Metropolitan Maksim of Lovech, was installed on July 4, 1971, by a *sŭbor* or 101 delegates of clergy and laity[54]). Born in 1914 in a village near Lovech, he was educated at the Sofia seminary and the theological faculty of the University of Sofia, graduating in 1942. Unlike Kiril and Stefan, he has had no exposure to Western education and religious life. In this regard, obviously significant is the fact that he spent five years in Moscow (1950–1955) as head of BPTs's *podvorie* there. His stay gained him the good will and support of Patriarch Alekseĭ and other key figures in the RPTs. After his stint in Moscow, he served as general secretary of the Synod (1955–1960) and chairman of the editorial board of the BPTs periodicals, leading to his elevation to the Lovech see in 1960[55]).

At the *sŭbor*, following his election, Maksim declared that he would pursue the established policies. In contrast to Kiril, who provided at his election a detailed report on the state of the BPTs, however, he provided none. Information made public by the BPTs in 1975 indicates the number of parish priests as being „about 1,500", (down from 1,796 in 1963) and thus a further loss of staff and ground. The number of monks, whose ranks produce the higher clergy, was „about 200"[56]). The BPTs claims to have 3,200 churches and 500 chapels, but a great number of them are in disrepair and not used. Most of them were built between 1878 and 1944 (numbering 1,295 in 1880). The monasteries, including nunneries, are said to number about 120, but many of them, too, are not inhabited and are in disrepair; a lavishly illustrated volume published in

---

[52]) Pandurski, V. and others: NR Bŭlgariĭa i religioznite izpovedaniĭa v neĭa (The NRB and the religions denominations in it). Sofia 1966, p. 15; Statisticheski godishnik na Tsarstvo Bŭlgariĭa (Statistical Yearbook of the Kingdom of Bulgaria). 34 (1942), p. 787.

[53]) Additional data on the BPTs as of 1963, including churches abroad, in Klisarov, G. and others (eds.): Deset godini bŭlgarska patriarshiĭa, 10 mai 1953 – 10 mai 1963 (Ten years Bulgarian patriarchate). Sofia 1963, pp. 125–136.

[54]) The proceedings of the *sŭbor* are in: Tsŭrkovno-naroden patriarsheski izbiratelen sŭbor, 4 ĭuli 1971, Sofiĭa (Church-laity patriarchal election council). Comp. by T. Sŭbev and V. Veliĭanov. Sofia 1973.

[55]) Maksim's biography by Sŭbev is ibid., pp. 5–35.

[56]) Tsŭrkvi i izpovedaniĭa (note 14), pp. 31–37.

1974 presented only 76[57]). Parish life has been further curtailed by the dissolution of the *bratstva* ordered in 1982[58]).

The only evidence of growth is in the Bulgarian communities in the United States, Canada, and other countries. The problem with Bishop Andreĭ in New York was settled in 1963 when, after a visit by Metropolitan Pimen of Nevrokop, the Synod reinstated him as „canonical Metropolitan" of the eparchy[59]), and after his death installed in the see a vicar of Maksim for the Sofia eparchy. Growth of the communities, as well as considerations of building ties with them, have brought about the establishment of a second eparchy with the see at Akron, Ohio, and a deanery for Canada. The importance attached in Sofia to the BPTs in America was underscored by a prolonged visit to the communities in 1978 by Patriarch Maksim, then also acting head of the new eparchy[60]). These activities have provoked in many of them divisions between pro-Sofia and anti-Sofia factions.

The BPTs also has maintained parishes, with priests sent from Bulgaria, in Istanbul, Vienna, Budapest, and Bucharest, and other European cities which were consolidated in 1986 as an eparchy for Western Europe with the see at Budapest[61]). The BPTs still has a tenuous connection with Mount Athos, a great center of the Bulgarian national revival, where the number of Bulgarian monks has dwindled from 340 in 1912 to 11 residing at the Zograf monastery[62]). There are no BPTs parishes for the ethnic Bulgarians in the Soviet Union, 324,000 by Soviet count, living in Moldavia and the Ukraine.

For education of clergy and publishing on religious and religion-related subjects, the BPTs has at present the seminary and theological academy mentioned above, which have reportedly a combined enrollment of about 320 students[63]), and the *Sinodalno izdatelstvo* (the Synod's publishing office) established in 1938. The periodicals it publishes are *Tsŭrkoven Vestnik* for BPTs news and communications (since 1900; 32 issues per year, 4,000 copies, down from 6,200 in 1950), *Dukhovna Kultura* (Spiritual Culture), a monthly for „religion, philosophy, science, and art" (since 1920, 2,200 copies, down from 7,000 in 1950), and *Godishnik na Dukhovnata Akademiia „Sv. Kliment Okhridski"* (Yearbook of the St. Kliment Okhridski Theological Academy), (since 1950, 600 copies) for studies by professors in it and others. The

---

[57]) Chavrukov, G.: Bulgaria's Monasteries: Monuments of History, Culture, and Art. Sofia 1974; also available in German.

[58]) Broun, J.A.: Religious Repression in Bulgaria, in: Freedom at Issue. September–October 1987, pp. 27–31.

[59]) Tsŭrkoven Vestnik. July 6, 1963.

[60]) Veliânov, V.: Patriarshesko blagoslovenie na Akronska i Nĭuĭorkska eparkhiĭ (Patriarchal blessing of the Akron and New York eparchies). Sofia 1981.

[61]) For data on the BPTs churches in Western Europe, see V. Veliânov and others, eds.: Poklon pred trinadeset-vekovnata ni rodina (Bow before our 13-centuries-old fatherland). Sofia 1983, pp. 50–52 and 139–196. Tsŭrkoven Vestnik (May 21, 1986) mentions a Naredba (regulation) concerning the organization of the BPTs's eparchies abroad, but its text is not published.

[62]) Bolutov, D.: Bŭlgarski istoricheski pametnitsi na Aton (Bulgarian historical monuments on Mount Athos). Sofia 1961.

[63]) Tsŭrkvi i izpovedaniia, pp. 55–56, indicates „about 200" students at the seminary and 120 at the academy. For details, see Haertel, H.-J.: Zur Situation der Orthodoxen Priester in Bulgarien, in: Der Geistliche und seine Gemeinde in Osteuropa. Hrsg. von W. Kasack. Berlin 1986, pp. 148–159.

annual number of books published varies from a few to a dozen titles[64]). In 1982, the BPTs issued a new edition of the Bible, but it is not available at its bookstore in Sofia[65]). The BPTs also has an institute of Church History and Archives (*Tsŭrkovno-istoricheski i arkhiven institut*) established 1974 and publishing *Tsŭrkovno-Istoricheski Arkhiv* (Church History Archive) since 1981, and a Central Museum of Church History and Archaeology (*Tsentralen tsŭrkoven istoriko-arkheologicheski muzeĭ*), both in Sofia. They publish jointly occasional *Izvestiĭa* (Communications) (1978–).

The financial and economic affairs of the BPTs are handled by its *Vŭrkhoven tsŭrkoven sŭvet* (Supreme church council), which consists of lower clergy and laymen and has charge of the BPTs's budget, management of its assets, etc.[66]). The BPTs's income is primarily from the sale of candles (58%) and other religious objects and includes a 13% annual subsidy from the state, although Zhivkov has implied that the clergy depend much more heavily on the state for their salaries[67]).

3. The Other Denominations

The Bulgarian Turks have become the object of much international attention since 1984 when the Bulgarian government stepped up its campaign to erase their identity and, claiming that they were originally Bulgarians who in adaptation had turned Turks in religion, language, and customs, sought to restore them as Bulgarians. The campaign, in some cases backed by force and allegedly resulting in murders and arrests, focused on Bulgarianizing their names but also banned circumcision and other religious practices required by Islam[68]). Early signs of this policy were the pressure in 1971–1973 on the Pomaks, then estimated at about 170,000, to adopt Bulgarian names, and the ban on that term in favor of „Muslim Bulgarians". Such policies, while violations of human rights, are not without precedents in the Balkans. In Bulgaria, the BPTs undertook in 1913 to bulgarianize the Pomaks in the areas acquired from Turkey by making them Orthodox, and at times Muslim Gypsies were the object of similar efforts[69]) (see the chapter „Nationale Minderheiten" by S. Troebst).

The Muslim community (Turks, Pomaks, Gypsies, and Tatars) has experienced a drastic reduction of organized religious life. To begin with, the Turks were further thinned out by emigration of some 130,000 in 1968–1978 under an agreement with Turkey. The drop in the number of priests (imams or hodjas) has been precipitous

---

[64]) For full data, see the Bulgarian national bibliography: Bŭlgarski knigopis.

[65]) The print-run was only ca. 27,500; cf. the admirable work of the Metropolitan of Nevrokop, Pimen: Za Bibliĭata (Concerning the Bible). Sofia 1988, p. 226.

[66]) For details, see Vŭlkov, V.: Vŭrkhovniĭat tsŭrkoven sŭvet pri Sv. Sinod na Bŭlgarskata Pravoslavna Tsŭrkva (The supreme church council at the Holy Synod of the BPTs), in: Dukhovna kultura. 58 (1978) 6, pp. 25–32.

[67]) Todor Zhivkov – Statesman and Builder of New Bulgaria. Oxford 1982, p. 119 (Cit. as: Zhivkov).

[68]) For details, see Eminov, A.: The Status of Islam and Muslims in Bulgaria, in: Journal [of the] Institute of Muslim Minority Affairs. 8 (1987) 2, pp. 278–301.

[69]) Tsankov (note 4), pp. 286–288.

from a total of 2,715 in 1956 to 570 in 1982, according to Zhivkov who rounded out the numbers disclosed in 1965 (462 for the Turks, Gypsies and Tatars and 95 for the Pomaks) or „over 400", according to a 1987 source[70]). The official number of mosques in 1975 was 1,300 (120 in the Pomak areas), but they are rapidly disappearing from the Muslim villages, razed to make room for other buildings, and the imams are prohibited under the 1949 law to call the believers to prayer from the minarets. The *medrese* in Shumen is apparently closed and only occasional programs for minimal training of hodjas are permitted. The community is totally isolated from the Muslim world (except from some visits by high-ranking Soviet Muslims) and pilgrimages to Mecca are *de facto* impossible. As a result, a general ignorance of the tenets of Islam, even of its Five Pillars, has set in. The announced aim of the government is to produce a single amalgamated Bulgarian nation, and there are indications that for this purpose Bulgarian-speaking Pomak hodjas are assigned to Turkish areas[71]). The future of Islam and Muslim believers in Bulgaria is obviously bleak.

The Bulgarian Catholics like the Protestants, exist in harsh conditions. Until 1975 they were virtually isolated from Rome, except for attendance of the Second Vatican Council by one of the two Roman Catholic bishops and the Uniat bishop. Zhivkov's visit to the Vatican in that year to request access to its archives by Bulgarian historians preparing for the 1300th anniversary of the Bulgarian state, led to the appointment of two bishops in eparchies that had become vacant. Seminaries for the training of priests have remained closed but a few have been privately trained by older priests and after the visit of the Bulgarian foreign minister, Petŭr Mladenov, to the Vatican in 1978, two young priests were allowed to continue their studies in Rome[72]). Officially, in 1975 the Roman Catholics had „over 40 priests" and 30 churches and the Uniats had 17 churches and „over 20 priests", but the present numbers are much fewer. Publication of religious texts and literature is not possible. The two Catholic communities accept no subsidies from the state, in order to maintain their independence, and survive solely on their own resources. Their condition *in extremis* led a Bulgarian atheism expert to predict earlier that by 1975 they would die out.

The improvement of their condition, which began precisely in 1975, has been essentially due to the Communist government's need for good working relations with the Vatican because of the importance it attaches to national history in general and the historiographic controversies with Yugoslav Macedonia in particular. In addition to access to Vatican archives, it has sought to affirm Bulgaria's link with Cyril and Methodius by sending delegations on annual pilgrimages to the grave of Cyril in the San Clemente Basilica in Rome in conjunction with the national holiday (May 24) honoring the two brothers and their disciples. Evidence of the warming trend includes the permission in March, 1988, for the Bishop of Nikopol, Samuil Dzhundrin,

---

[70]) Mizov, N.: Isliâmŭt v Bŭlgariiâ; sŭshtnost, modernizatsiiâ i preodoliâvane (Islam in Bulgaria; essence, modernization, and defeat). Sofia 1965, pp. 194/195; Zhivkov (note 67), pp. 371–374; Slavova, M., ed.: Istinata za bŭlgarite-miûsiûlmani (The truth concerning the Muslim Bulgarians). Sofia 1987, p. 28.

[71]) Popovic, A.: L'Islam Balkanique: Les musulmans du sud-est européen dans la période post-ottomane. Berlin 1986, pp. 66–106.

[72]) Broun, J.A.: The Church in Bulgaria, in: Pro Mundi Vita: Dossiers. 3 (1986), pp. 15–17.

and some thirty Bulgarian pilgrims to visit the Vatican and the week-long trip by the Pope's special envoy for Eastern Europe, Archbishop Francesco Colasuonno, to Bulgaria where he conferred with the PK, Lîubomir Popov, and other officials and visited Catholic congregations in Sofia, Plovdiv, and Ruse[73]). On receiving the official Bulgarian delegation in Rome for the pilgrimage to Cyril's grave, as the Bulgarian news agency BTA reported on May 26, 1988, the Pope expressed his thanks for the hospitality accorded in Bulgaria to his envoy. A few weeks later the appointment of a new bishop, Georgi Iovchev, to the Sofia-Plovdiv bishopric, vacant since 1983, was announced in Rome.

The five Protestant denominations were officially indicated in 1975 as totaling „about 16,000" persons and having 101 houses of prayer and „about 265 pastors and preachers". The most numerous are the Pentecostals (about 6,000; 25 houses of prayer and 36 pastors), followed by about 5,000 Congregationalists (52 houses of prayer), about 3,000 Adventists (40 pastors), about 1,300 Methodists (15 houses of prayer and pastors), and about 650 Baptists (10 houses of prayer and 7 pastors)[74]). Unofficial figures reflecting a striking revival among the Pentecostals in the late 1970's place them at least at twice the official number, including the Tinchevists (followers of Pastor Stoîan Tinchev), a fundamentalist current in existence since 1928[7.5]). The revival was accompanied by various repressive measures and a trial of five leading Pentecostals in 1979.

Like the Catholics, the Protestants are unable to train their own clergy, publish religious literature, or receive it from abroad. A few pastors have been educated at the BPTs's Theological Academy, whether by tacit arrangement or chance. The Bible translated and published by the American missionaries in 1871 was reprinted in 1951 by the Oxford University Press for the British and Foreign Bible Society, but it reaches Bulgaria only if smuggled in. To preserve their independence the Protestants, too, do not accept subsidies from the state.

The last of the Christian communities, the Armenians are indicated as numbering 22,000 in 1975, with 10 priests for 12 parishes. They are under the jurisdiction of the Armenian Gregorian Church in Soviet Armenia through an archbishop residing in Bucharest. Under the Soviet aegis, relations between it and the BPTs have been close.

The Jewish community, estimated to number at present about 6,000 persons, has become largely secular. The religious consistories in 1957 gave way to the *Obshtestvena kulturno-prosvetna organizatsiîa na evreite v Narodna Republika Bŭlgariîa* (Social cultural-educational organization of the Jews in the NRB), which now represents the community. It continues to publish *Evreĭski Vesti* for news of the community, and since 1966 has published a *Godishnik/Annual* in which valuable studies on the history of the Jews in Bulgaria and the Balkans have appeared. For religious affairs there is a

---

[73]) Radio Free Europe Research, Weekly Record of Events in Eastern Europe, March 18 and April 1, 1988.

[74]) Tsŭrkvi i izpovedaniîa (note 14), pp. 67/68. For further details, see Mizov, N. and others: Protestantskite sekti v Bŭlgariîa (The Protestant sects in Bulgaria). Sofia 1972; and Mizov: Adventistite u nas (The Adventists in our country). Sofia 1972.

[75]) Davies, L.: Pentecostals in Bulgaria, in: Religion in Communist Lands. 8 (1980) 4, pp. 299–304.

Dukhoven izrailtĩanski sŭvet (Israelite Religious Council), but only the synagogues in Sofia, Samokov, and Vidin are occasionally open. There are no rabbis and only one cantor in Sofia[76]). Zionism and its religious roots are often attacked, as in *Pŭtishtata na Tsionizma* (The Ways of Zionism), a publication of the party in 1969 by Bogomil Raĭnov, a leading writer, publicist, and member of the BAN since 1974.

V. Unrecognized Communities

The largest of the prewar religious and quasireligious communities was the sect of Petŭr Dŭnov (1864–1944). The son of an Orthodox priest, Dŭnov studied medicine and theology in the United States (1888–1895) and founded in 1910 a religious community outside the BPTs and called the White Brotherhood. His teachings combined elements of Christianity, Buddhism, occultism, and belief in the reincarnation of the soul[77]). The sect claimed some 30,000 adherents in Bulgaria and followers in several other countries. At present its mode of existence and status are unclear. A government directive of 1962 concerning „registration of the Protestant sects and the White Brotherhood religious community (Dŭnovists)" has remained unpublished[78]), and Bulgarian sources indicate only that the number of Dŭnovists is insignificant. Other prewar organizations, which seem to have disappeared, included the Holy Orthodox Society (also known as The Good Samaritans), which sought to cultivate Christian piety at the grass-roots level, and the Free Masons. The latter had considerable influence since it attracted leading members of Bulgaria's elites. Efforts to restore its lodges after 1944 have reportedly been unsuccessful[79]), Western sources indicate the existence of Christian Brethren (5,000), Jehovah's Witnesses (1,000), Unitarians (500), and others[80]).

VI. Inroads of Atheism

In 1962, the BAN Institute of Philosophy conducted a comprehensive survey of 42,664 persons born before 1944 to assess the effects of the reductive containment of religion and the propaganda of atheism. The survey was carried out by some 3,000

---

[76]) Encyclopaedia Judaica. Yearbook for 1983–1985, pp. 232/233.

[77]) Mizov, N., ed.: Rechnik po ateizŭm (Dictionary of atheism). Sofia 1980, pp. 83/84, and: Entsiklopediĩa Bŭlgariĩa. Vol. 2 (1981), p. 475, citing one of Dŭnov's books; others are listed in Bŭlgarski knigopis for 1946 and 1947.

[78]) Ĭolova, G. and Kiskinova, L.: Spravochnik po zakonodatelstvoto na Narodna Republika Bŭlgariĩa (1944–1981 g.) (Guide to the legislation of the NRB, 1944–1981). Sofia 1982, p. 52. Also listed in the guide as not published are a resolution of the Council of Ministers of 1975 concerning the „improvement of the activity" of PK (p. 101) and the 1951 statute of the Muslim community (p. 52).

[79]) Georgiev, V.: Masonstvoto v Bŭlgariĩa (Masonry in Bulgaria). Sofia 1986, p. 434.

[80]) See, for example, Barrett, D. B., ed.: World Christian Encyclopedia. Oxford 1982, pp. 198–201.

investigators, mostly school teachers, among Bulgarians and the three ethnic *and* religious minorities in 108 towns and 822 villages across the country. The findings, published in 1968, were that only 32.76% of the Bulgarians were religious, while the percentage was 67.02 among the Turks, 38.58 among the Armenians, and 29.17 among the Jews[81]). As an attempt to arrive at a precise assessment, the survey is now described even in Bulgarian propaganda as „a flop"[82]). The efforts to inculcate the atheistic world view and way of life, however, go on unabated and involve publication of tracts showing science as victorious over religion, replacement of religious holidays and rites of baptism, marriage, and burial by socialist holidays and *rituali* for such occasions, and other programs[83]). Works by Bulgarian believers in atheism continue to claim decline in religiosity, but Western observers report indications of the opposite trend. With changes in favor of religion pending in the USSR, this trend is apt to become stronger.

---

[81]) Oshavkov (note 12 above) and Oshavkov, Zh., ed.: Sotsiologicheskata struktura na sŭvremennoto bŭlgarsko obshtestvo (The sociological structure of contemporary Bulgarian society). Sofia 1976, pp. 377–416.

[82]) Bulgaria. (April 1987), p. 8.

[83]) Oschlies, W.: Kirche und Religion in Bulgarien, in: Religionsfreiheit und Menschenrechte. Bilanz und Aussicht. Ed. by P. Lendvai. Köln 1983, pp. 180–202.

Massenmedien und Sprachkultur

Wolf Oschlies, Köln

I. Zur Geschichte der Massenmedien – II. Übergangszeit 1944–1948: 1. Die Parteien und ihre Organe – 2. Kommunistische Medienpolitik 1944/45 – 3. „Offenes Mehrparteiensystem" und Medienvielfalt – III. Medien als „Transmissionsriemen" (1948–1956) – IV. Jahre kultureller Selbstisolation (1956–1970) – V. Der lange Weg zur *glasnost'* (1971–1988) – VI. Sprachkultur: 1. Probleme der Orthographiereform – 2. Umgangs- und Mediensprache – 3. Gegen sprachliche Fremdeinflüsse – 4. Pro und contra Jugendsprache – 5. Dialekte als Sprachquelle

I. Zur Geschichte der Massenmedien

„Leseland" nennt sich stolz mancher osteuropäische Staat, mit großer Berechtigung auch Bulgarien. Lesend erwachten die Bulgaren aus einem jahrhundertelangen Geschichtsschlaf – durch die Lektüre der „Slavobulgarischen Geschichte", die der Athos-Mönch Paisij Chilendarski 1762 verfaßt hatte. Lesend betrieben und konturierten sie ihre nationalkulturelle „Wiedergeburt" (*văzraždane*), deren Profil mit jedem weiteren Jahrzehnt aus einer vielgestaltigen bulgarischen Presse hervorleuchtete, bis 1877/78 auch die nationale Befreiung und staatliche Rekonstituierung folgten. Diese Anhänglichkeit ans geschriebene Wort ist umso erstaunlicher, als nur relativ wenige Menschen überhaupt lesen und schreiben konnten: Noch 1893 betrug der Alphabetisierungsgrad der gesamten bulgarischen Gesellschaft nur 19,88 % (Männer 30,87 %, Frauen 8,37 %). Diese Diskrepanz – zwischen bestehendem Informationswillen und fehlender Kulturtechnik – wurde durch eine genuin bulgarische Bildungsinstitution überwunden, das im frühen 19. Jh. entstandene *čitalište* (Lesehalle), von dem aus gelesene und vorgelesene Erkenntnisse ihren Weg nahmen.

Wenn in den *čitališta* bald auch mehr und mehr bulgarische Periodika auslagen, dann geht das auf Anfänge lange vor der Befreiung Bulgariens zurück. „Gründungsvater" der bulgarischen Presse war der Lehrer Konstantin Fotinov (1790–1858), der 1844–1846 in Smyrna die Zeitschrift *Ljuboslovie* (Philologie) edierte. 1846 entstand auch die erste bulgarische Zeitung: Ivan Bogorov (ca. 1818–1892) gab in Leipzig ein

Tabelle 1: Bulgarische Presse bis 1877

	bis 1850	1851–1860	1861–1870	1871–1877
Zeitschr. im Osmanischen Reich	1	2	3	7
Zeitg. im Osmanischen Reich	1	2	9	12
Zeitschr. im Ausland	1	2	10	11
Zeitg. im Ausland	1	3	15	21

„bürgerliches, wirtschaftliches und literarisches Nachrichtenblatt" unter dem Titel *Bălgarski orel* (Bulgarischer Adler) heraus; 1847 verlegte er die Zeitung nach Istanbul und gab ihr 1848 (um türkischen Empfindlichkeiten vorzubeugen) den neuen Namen *Carigradski vestnik* (Konstantinopler Zeitung). Unter diesem Namen erschien sie bis 1861. Gute 15 Jahre später kam in Bukarest die erste bulgarische *Tages*zeitung heraus – Ivan Adženovs (ca. 1834–1903) *Vsekidneven novinar* (Täglicher Bote, 1877/78). Damit waren thematisch und formal die Grundkoordinaten gelegt, entlang derer sich das bulgarische Pressewesen rasch entwickelte (s. Tab. 1)[1].

Nach der Befreiung kam die bulgarische Presse auch nach Bulgarien selbst; vorher hatte es sie dort praktisch nicht gegeben, aber jetzt wurde die Zeitung *Marica*, die erstmalig am 25.7.1878 in Plovdiv erschien, der erste Bote einer bunten und laufend wachsenden Presselandschaft. In dem jungen Staat bildeten sich Parteien und weltanschauliche Gruppen, es gab außen-, innen- und wirtschaftspolitische Probleme, das soziale Leben diversifizierte sich, wissenschaftliche und künstlerische Interessen artikulierten sich – und all das (und weit mehr) schlug sich in der Schaffung immer neuer Druckmedien nieder, die durch das Pressegesetz von 1887 milde reglementiert und kaum gegängelt wurden[2].

Ins 20. Jh. trat Bulgarien als vollgültiges Zeitungsland ein, das fortan seine Genrevielfalt ausbaute, seine technische Basis pflegte und Verbindungen in alle Welt unter-

Tabelle 2: Die Presse 1940

Erscheinungsort:	Zeitungen	Zeitschriften
Sofia	278	335
Pleven	78	13
Šumen	53	20
Plovdiv	30	25
Vraca	29	2
Burgas	28	3
Stara Zagora	26	6
total	522	404
Erscheinungsweise		
täglich	23	1
wöchentlich 2–3mal	9	3
wöchentlich	141	9
monatlich 3mal	18	1
vierzehntägig	112	27
monatlich	73	260
zweimonatlich	2	20
vierteljährlich	–	15
zwanglose Folge	142	42
unbekannte Folge	2	26

---

[1]) Mišev, D. Văzraždane črez pečata (Wiedergeburt durch die Presse), in: Bălgarija 1000 godini. Sofia 1927, S. 601–663.

[2]) Topenčarov, V.: Bălgarskata žurnalistika 1885–1903 (Die bulgarische Journalistik). Sofia 1963.

hielt, vor allem über die 1898 gegründete „Bulgarische Telegraphenagentur" (*Bălgarska telegrafna agencija,* BTA).

Aus dem I. Weltkrieg ging Bulgarien als geschlagenes Land hervor, dem die Siegermächte harte Auflagen machten; das bewirkte einen wirtschaftlichen Druck, der zu Konzentrationserscheinungen auf dem Pressemarkt führte. In den frühen 30er Jahren war das überwunden, und mit 575 Periodika für rund 6 Mio. Einwohner erreichte Bulgarien einen Schnitt, der über dem Deutschlands und der USA lag. 1940 ergab sich eine weitere Steigerung (s. Tab. 2)[3].

Damals hatte Bulgarien seine Medienlandschaft durch die Einführung des Rundfunks erweitert. Erste Anfänge hatte 1928 eine Privatgesellschaft in Sofia gemacht; im Januar 1935 übernahm der Staat des Rundfunkmonopol, und Ende 1937 nahm der Großsender Vakarel (bei Sofia) den Sendebetrieb auf, wozu noch zwei Anstalten an der Küste und in Südbulgarien kamen. Daraufhin weitete sich das Hörernetz enorm aus. (s. Tab. 3)[4].

Tabelle 3: Rundfunk vor dem II. Weltkrieg

Jahr	Rundfunkempfänger
1936	20 531
1937	31 658
1938	46 600
1939	62 677
Okt. 1940	79 314

In den II. Weltkrieg kam Bulgarien ohne Parteien und von Zaren-Regierungen autoritär geleitet, zudem mit dem nationalsozialistischen Deutschland eng verbündet. Ganz nach deutschem Muster wurde die Presse „gleichgeschaltet", wofür die am 5.4.1941 ins Leben gerufene „Direktion für nationale Propaganda" zu sorgen hatte. Zwar machte Bulgarien nicht den deutschen Feldzug gegen die Sowjetunion mit, aber gegen seine vielfältigen Kriegsverstrickungen regte sich doch politischer Widerstand, dessen linker Flügel – Kommunisten, Sozialdemokraten, linke Agrarier u. a. – sich bereits 1942 zur OF zusammenschloß. Dieser stand mit der Rundfunkstation *Christo Botev*, die ab dem 23.7.1941 von sowjetischem Boden aus sendete, ein wirksames Medium zur Verfügung. In immer neuen, betont national gefärbten Appellen half sie mit, in Bulgarien jene fatalistische Haltung entstehen zu lassen, die das Land dazu brachte, sich in den ersten Septembertagen 1944 widerstandslos den einmarschierenden sowjetischen Truppen anheimzugeben[5].

---

[3]) Simonffy, A.v.: Hundert Jahre bulgarische Presse, in: Pester Lloyd. 17.7.1942.
[4]) Zahlen nach: Südost-Echo. (Wien) Nr. 5, 31.1.1941.
[5]) Nikolova, A.: Radiostancija „Christo Botev" za splotjavaneto na antifašistkite sili v Bălgarija (1941–9.IX.1944 g.) (Die Radiostation „Christo Botev" über den Zusammenschluß der antifaschistischen Kräfte in Bulgarien), in: Izvestija na Instituta po istorija na BKP. 50 (1983), S. 137–176.

II. Übergangszeit 1944–1948

1. Die Parteien und ihre Organe

Im Mai 1974 hat die Wochenzeitung *Pogled* (Blick), Organ des Bulgarischen Journalistenverbands (*Săjuz na bălgarskite žurnalisti*, SBŽ), eine Serie „Wie die Presse des neuen Bulgarien geboren wurde" veröffentlicht: Parteijournalisten der ersten Stunde erinnerten sich an die problemlose „Machtübernahme". Man konnte die nächstgelegene Redaktion übernehmen und dabei noch sicher sein, daß die Druckereien auch unter den neuen „Herren" bruchlos weiterarbeiten würden. Wenn es Probleme gab, dann waren sie interner Natur – weil niemand in der neu besetzten Redaktion wußte, wie es weitergehen sollte.

So war es – allerdings nur in den Anfangswochen. Bulgarien kehrte rasch zu einer fast pluralistischen Normalität zurück, die es gute drei Jahre lang nahezu ungeschmälert bewahrte. Mehrere Momente trugen dazu bei – Bulgarien trat an sowjetischer Seite in den Endkampf gegen Deutschland ein, in der regierenden OF mußte die BKP auf nichtkommunistische Partner Rücksicht nehmen, der sowjetische Einfluß war in Bulgarien nicht so total wie z. B. in Rumänien, wurde zudem durch die ACC begrenzt u. a. m.

Am 14.6.1934 waren alle bulgarischen Parteien aufgelöst worden – am 9.9.1944, dem Staatsstreich in Bulgarien, waren zumindest die wieder auf dem Plan, die für die nunmehr akzeptablen weltanschaulichen Strömungen standen und zudem in der OF zusammenarbeiteten: die BRP(k), der BZNS, die BRSDP und der *Zveno*.

Diese vier Parteien (zu denen im September 1945 noch Teile der RP stießen) stellten die Regierung der OF. Diese gab ab dem 9.9.1944 ihre gleichnamige Tageszeitung heraus, die bis Jahresende auf eine Auflage von 146 000 Exemplaren kam. Daneben besaßen die OF-Parteien eigene Zeitungen und Zeitschriften (s. Tab. 4)[6].

Tabelle 4: Entstehung der Parteipresse

Partei	Zeitung	Ersterscheinen	Auflage	Zeitschrift
BRP(k)	*Rabotničesko delo* (Arbeitersache)	18.9.1944	157 000	*Săvremennik* (Zeitgenosse, Jan. 1945)
BRSDP	*Narod* (Volk)	4.10.1944	–	*Socialističeska borba* (Sozialistischer Kampf, 1944)
BZNS	*Zemedelsko zname* (Landwirtschaftsbanner)	14.9.1944	28 000	*Zemedelska misăl* (Agrargedanke, 1944)
Zveno	*Izgrev* (Sonnenaufgang)	9.10.1944	–	*Brazda* (Furche, 15.1.1945)

---

[6]) Angaben nach Isusov, M.: Političeskite partii v Bălgarija 1944–1948 (Die politischen Parteien in Bulgarien). Sofia 1978, passim; soweit nicht anders ausgewiesen, beziehen sich alle Angaben, Zitate etc. zur bulgarischen Pressegeschichte der Nachkriegszeit auf dieses Werk.

Alle Parteien bildeten Jugend- und Kinderorganisationen, die ihrerseits eigene Blätter herausgaben. Die BRP(k) hatte den RMS und *Septemvrijče* (Septemberkind), für die ab September 1944 die Zeitung *Mladežka iskra* (Jugendfunke) erschien. Entsprechend dazu gab es beim BZNS die Organisationen *Zemedelski mladežki săjuz* (ZMS) (Agrarischer Jugendverband) und *Stambolijče* (Stambolijski-Kind), für die ab 1.10.1944 die Zeitung *Narodna mladež* (Volksjugend), ab 1945 auch *Mladežko zname* (Jugend-Banner) auf dem Zeitungsmarkt waren. Auch die relativ kleine, jedoch einflußreiche Partei *Zveno* (Kettenglied), in den 20er Jahren als überparteilicher „politischer Kreis" entstanden, besaß eine eigene Jugendorganisation, für die *Mladežko zveno* (Jugend-*Zveno*) ediert wurde.

Daneben gab es weitere Organisationen mit eigenen Blättern, etwa die Gewerkschaften und ihre Zeitung *Zname na truda* (Banner der Arbeit). Es gab die erstaunlich vielfältige Provinzpresse, die partiell in fortbestehenden privaten Verlagshäusern (*Chemus, Ch.G. Danov, Čipev* u.a.) gedruckt wurde; in ihr war die große Gruppe jener Journalisten tätig, die mit dem „Verband der Berufsjournalisten der Provinz" (*Săjuz na provincialnite profesionalni žurnalisti*) eine eigene Standesorganisation besaßen.

Bereits Ende 1944 waren in Bulgarien 322 Periodika mit einer Gesamtauflage von 778500 Exemplaren auf dem Markt[7]). Zu diesem Zeitpunkt sah es so aus, als könnten die Bulgaren ihre klassischen Vorlieben ungeachtet aller Veränderungen, die das Kriegsende mit sich geführt hatte, fortsetzen – möglichst viele politische Gruppierungen mit einer möglichst breiten Medienpalette zu haben.

2. Kommunistische Medienpolitik 1944/45

„Kollektiver Organisator, Agitator und Propagandist" ist, einem Diktum Lenins zufolge, die Presse für Kommunisten. Sie leiten bis heute daraus Konsequenzen für die Stellung der Medien und ihre Ausrichtung ab:

– Zeitungen und Zeitschriften können nur von parteilichen und gesellschaftlichen Organisationen bzw. staatlichen Ämtern herausgegeben werden und haben „gesellschaftlichen Zielen" zu dienen; da aber in diesen Gesellschaften die kommunistische Partei die „führende Rolle" spielt, ist sie auch presse- und informationspolitisch letzte Instanz.
– Die Presse ist „Waffe der kommunistischen Partei" beim „Aufbau des Sozialismus", für die „kommunistische Erziehung der Massen", sie ist weiterhin „kritische Tribüne gegen Schwächen", „Mittel zur Formung und Ausrichtung der öffentlichen Meinung", dient dem „Kampf gegen bourgeoise Ideologie und den Imperialismus, für die richtige Interpretation internationaler Ereignisse".

Es dauerte einige Jahre, bis auch die bulgarischen Kommunisten die Landespresse derart „im Griff" hatten, aber von Anfang an stand ihre Absicht dazu außer Zweifel. Am 9.9.1944 zählte die Partei 13700 Mitglieder, im Januar 1945 bereits 254140.

---

[7]) Newspapers and Magazines, in: Information Bulgaria. Oxford u.a. 1985, S. 851–859.

Dieser opportunistisch motivierte Zulauf und das Wohlwollen, das die Besatzungsmacht Sowjetunion den Kommunisten entgegenbrachte, hoben die Partei früh in eine dominierende Rolle im Nachkriegs-Bulgarien.

Aus dieser Position heraus arbeitete die Partei früh dafür, in Bulgarien die „führende Rolle" zu erlangen, und die Medienpolitik war dafür ein wichtiges Instrument. Es gab genügend Partei-Journalisten, da ja seit 1943 ein „Komitee der Journalisten bei der OF" (*Komitet na žurnalistite pri Otečestvenija front*) bestand. Zum Chef des „Ministeriums für Propaganda" (*Ministerstvo na propagandata*) wurde indessen ein Nichtkommunist bestellt: Dimo Kazasov (1886–1980), bulgarischer Spitzenpolitiker der Vorkriegszeit, „Regisseur" der Staatsstreiche von 1923 und 1934 und im Grunde Hauptgegner der Kommunisten, deren Aufstand von 1923 er in der wichtigen Position des Verkehrsministers raschest niederschlagen half. Exakt 20 Jahre später schloß er sich der OF an, und ab Herbst 1944 amtierte er als deren Propagandaminister. Hier hatte er eine doppelte Aufgabe – Säuberung der gesamten Presse von „monarchofaschistischen, großbulgarisch-chauvinistischen, reaktionären, volksfeindlichen" Ideen (was konkret auf Zeitungsverbote und Strafprozesse gegen Verlagsdirektoren und Chefredakteure hinauslief) und Ausrichtung der Informationspolitik auf die neuen Verhältnisse. Zu letzterem Zweck wurden im Ministerium vier Direktionen (*direkcija*) eingerichtet: „Nationalkultur", „Theater", „Funk" und „Presse". Auf dieser Ebene setzte die Partei an, um ihren Einfluß geltend zu machen. Pressechef wurde der Altkommunist Sava Ganovski (* 1897), Funkdirektor (also faktisch Chef von Radio Sofia) Orlin Vasilev (1904–1977), ebenfalls langjähriges Parteimitglied. Noch 1944 wurden beide ausgetauscht, wobei sich der kommunistische Einfluß in den Medien noch verstärkte: Funkchef wurde Karlo Lukanov (1897–1982), und an die Spitze der Presse trat Vladimir Topenčarov (* 1906), „Starjournalist" der bulgarischen Kommunisten und seit Kriegsende Chefredakteur von *Otečestven front*.

Das Ministerium initiierte in der unmittelbaren Folgezeit eine Reihe von Maßnahmen, die weitergehende Absichten gegenüber den Medien ahnen ließen: Die Wirksamkeit der noch bestehenden Privatverlage wurde über Papierzuteilungen eingedämmt. Das neue Pressegesetz ließ ab 1.12.1944 nur noch solche Zeitungen zu, die der Regierung genehm waren. Verlage und Bibliotheken wurden einer „Säuberung" (*čistka*) unterzogen, die von der Pressedirektion realisiert und anhand der von ihr aufgestellten schwarzen Buchlisten vorgenommen wurde. Und schließlich legte sich die Partei eine eigene Medienbasis zu: Aus mehreren früheren Privatverlagen, „die unter Parteikontrolle gestellt worden waren", bildete sie das neue Unternehmen „Parteiverlag" (*Partizdat*), dem noch der „Volksverlag" (*Narizdat*) angegliedert wurde; bereits Mitte 1945 war es das größte Unternehmen seiner Art in Bulgarien, das ein engmaschiges Netz parteieigener Buchhandlungen knüpfte[8]).

Zum 12.12.1944 verfügte das ZK die Bildung kommunistischer Gruppen bei allen Künstler- und verwandten Organisationen. Besondere Aufmerksamkeit kam dabei den Journalisten zu. Das Journalistenkomitee der OF übernahm die Führung in der „Gesellschaft der hauptstädtischen Journalisten" (*Družestvo na stoličnite žurnalisti*)

---

[8]) Janev, J.: Osnovni momenti v kulturnata politika na BRP(k) (1944–1945 g). (Grundmomente in der Kulturpolitik der BRP/k/), in: Izvestija na Instituta po istorija na BKP.55 (1986), S. 349–394.

und damit auch die Leitung der gut ausgebauten Pressevertriebsgesellschaft „Strela". An die Spitze der neuen Organisation trat Vladimir Topenčarov, der ihr binnen kürzester Zeit auch den Verband der Provinzjournalisten anschließen sollte. Mit Hilfe der nichtkommunistischen Regierungsparteien gelang das überraschend schnell, so daß bereits am 24. 12. der neue zentrale „Journalistenverband" (*Săjuz na žurnalistite*, SŽ) entstand. Mit dem SŽ milderte sich auch die bei den Journalisten laufende „Säuberung" – ursprünglich sollten 60 von ihnen vor Gericht gestellt werden, aber ein später revidiertes Verzeichnis führte nur noch 38 Namen an. Diese „Milderung" war symptomatisch für die halbdemokratische Übergangssituation im damaligen Bulgarien. Durch die frühe und organisatorisch glatte Zentralisierung des journalistischen Berufsstandes hatte sich die BKP keineswegs ein willfähriges Propagandainstrument geschaffen, wie die Folgen zeigten:

- Im Rundfunk stieg das professionelle Niveau an und sank die ideologische Verbindlichkeit: Es entstanden die ersten Fremdsprachenprogramme, und die Sofioter Zentrale war mit vielen Korrespondenten im ganzen Land verbunden. Noch am 31.10.1945 konstatierte RD halb befriedigt, halb bedauernd, die Radioprogramme besäßen „unbestreitbar einen Volks-, aber keinen Parteicharakter".
- Während vor allem die BRP(k) die „Säuberung" der anderen Verbände und ihre ideologische Ausrichtung betrieb, wurde sogar in der parteieigenen Presse offen darüber diskutiert, daß man für das eine wie für das andere keine klaren Kriterien besäße.
- Und als sich gar das Mehrparteiensystem in „Regierungsparteien" und „loyale Opposition" diversifizierte, demonstrierte der SŽ gewissermaßen Vielfalt in der Einheit: Selbst im Vorstand arbeiteten Partei- mit Oppositionsjournalisten zusammen.

3. „Offenes Mehrparteiensystem" und Medienvielfalt

Nach den relativ erträglichen Waffenstillstandsbedingungen vom Oktober 1944 zeigten sich bald tiefe Risse zwischen den Parteien der OF, aber auch zwischen den Flügeln dieser Parteien. Diese Entwicklung war angesichts der besonderen Situation Bulgariens unvermeidlich. Auf der einen Seite spielten die Kommunisten in der regierenden OF die dominierende Rolle und trachteten danach, ihren Einfluß maximal auszuweiten. Auf der anderen Seite gab es noch ausreichende Möglichkeiten, abweichende politische Meinungen zu formulieren und mit organisiertem Nachdruck zu vertreten. In einem RD-Artikel vom 20.9.1944 wurde beteuert, daß die bulgarische Regierung weder „kommunistisch" noch „sowjetisch" sei, weil sie unter besonderen Bedingungen entstanden sei und in ihrer Herrschaftstechnik auf die klassischen kommunistischen Instrumente verzichten könne[9].

Auch die Profilsuche der Regierungsparteien konnte nicht anders denn auf Kosten der Kommunisten ablaufen, beispielsweise bei der traditionell städtischen BRSDP, die nun die Landregionen entdeckte und dort mit den Kommunisten konkurrierte –

---

[9] Isusov (Anm. 6), S. 50.

besonders nachhaltig mit ihrer Landwirtschaftsbeilage *Narod-stožer* (etwa: Volk als Eichbaum), die jeden Sonnabend dem Parteiorgan *Narod* beigelegt wurde.

Durch eigenmächtige Aktionen und übereilte Kampagnen boten die Kommunisten genügend Reibungsflächen. Die Partei legte sich mit der Volksmiliz (*Narodna milicija*) eine Parteiarmee zu und betrieb eine „Säuberung" in der regulären Armee. Im Frühjahr 1945 forcierte sie den Aufbau eines monopolistischen Jugendverbandes, während die nichtkommunistischen Parteien noch damit beschäftigt waren, eigene Jugendorganisationen einzurichten. Schließlich sorgten die für August 1945 anberaumten Parlamentswahlen dafür, daß sich die Parteienlandschaft weiter differenzierte. Am 7.9.1945 wurden gleich vier neue Gruppierungen von den Gerichten offiziell bestätigt, zu denen in den folgenden Wochen noch zwei weitere kamen. Und jede dieser politischen Gruppen legte sich augenblicklich eine eigene Zeitung zu (s. Tab. 5).

Tabelle 5: Enstehung der Oppositionspresse 1944/45

Partei	Zeitung	Ersterscheinen
BZNS-Nikola Petkov	*Narodno Zemedelsko zname* (Nationales Landwirtschaftsbanner)	August 1945
BRSDP (*obedinena*)	*Svoboden narod* (Freies Volk)	14.9.1945
DP	*Zname* (Banner)	24.9.1945
RP (*obedinena*)	*Naroden glas* (Volksstimme)	11.11.1945
Anarchokomunističeska federacija v Bălgarija (Anarchokommunistische Föderation in Bulgarien)	*Rabotničeska misăl* (Arbeitergedanke)	Dezember 1944

Außer den Anarchokommunisten, die bereits Ende 1944 entstanden waren, wurden diese Parteien allgemein als „loyale Opposition" bezeichnet – zu Recht! Innenpolitisch stimmten sie generell dem Kurs der OF-Regierung zu, außenpolitisch galt für sie, was der oppositionelle BZNS-Führer Nikola Petkov im Februar 1946 so formulierte: „Immer mit Rußland und Jugoslawien, niemals gegen England und Amerika!"

Im Sommer 1945 war die „loyale Opposition" entstanden, wenige Monate später hatte sie partiell bereits spürbaren Einfluß erlangt, wie an den Mitgliederbewegungen abzulesen ist, speziell der der Partei Nikola Petkovs (s. Tab. 6)[10]).

Es verwundert nicht, den BZNS-NP als stärkste Oppositionsfraktion zu sehen, denn der OF-BZNS trieb ihm Unzufriedene förmlich zu. Das mußte selbst dessen oberster Repräsentant Aleksandăr Obbov (1887–1975) einsehen; 1945 war er Chef-

---

[10]) Isusov (Anm. 6), S. 266.

Tabelle 6: Mitgliedschaft der Parteien 1946

Partei	Mitglieder 1946	
	Jan.–März	April–Juni
BRP(k)	413 225	403 674
BZNS	152 788	152 861
BRSDP	29 039	30 574
Zveno	31 111	37 680
RP	5 595	3 995
BZNS-Nikola Petkov (NP)	53 531	53 642
BRSDP (o)	3 020	2 529
DP	1 607	1 287

redakteur des *Zemedelsko zname*, über dessen Charakter und Einfluß er urteilte: „Im Strauß der OF hat die Blume der Agrarunion keinen spezifischen Duft. Hier ist die Agrarunion nicht agrarisch, das ‚Landwirtschaftsbanner' nicht landwirtschaftlich. Wenn die Menschen so urteilen, werden sie sich fragen, warum sollen wir es kaufen, wenn wir in ihm dasselbe lesen, was auch in *Otečestven front* und *Rabotničesko delo* geschrieben steht"[11]).

Dieser Zwiespalt vertiefte sich noch, als die Kommunisten ab 1945/46 die Kollektivierung der Landwirtschaft betrieben und sich unter den Bauern Widerstand regte. Hinzu kam 1946 die Landreform, die von der oppositionellen Presse deutlich und einmütig als „gefährliches Experiment" gegen „alle ehrlichen und fleißigen bulgarischen Bauern" verurteilt wurde. Aber die Kommunisten waren nicht gewillt zurückzustecken, und am 25.4.1946 beschloß ihr Politbüro eine „Verstärkung der Enthüllungskampagne gegen die Opposition". Wichtigstes Mittel dafür war die Novellierung des Pressegesetzes, die zur selben Zeit vorgenommen wurde. Sie enthielt eine Fülle von „Gummiparagraphen": Pressemeldungen, die geeignet seien, „staatliche Interessen zu schädigen, die öffentliche Ordnung und Ruhe beeinträchtigende Stimmungen zu schaffen oder die Beziehungen Bulgariens zu anderen Ländern zu stören", sollten fortan strafrechtlich verfolgt werden. Damit war gegen die Presse faktisch jeglicher Willkür Raum gegeben, und das erste Exempel wurde sofort an dem Sozialdemokraten K. Pastuchov statuiert. Dieser hatte in einem Artikel dargelegt, daß die bulgarische Armee „aus einem Staatsorgan in ein Parteiorgan verwandelt" worden war, und wurde dafür zu fünf Jahren schweren Kerkers verurteilt. Ähnliche Fälle häuften sich, und bereits im Frühjahr schickte die BRSDP (o) eine Dokumentation an die Sozialistische Internationale, in der der „Massenterror gegen die Oppositionsparteien" geschildert und speziell das neugefaßte Pressegesetz als Terrorinstrument herausgestellt wurden. In Belgien und in der Schweiz wurde dieses Dokument veröffentlicht. Einen Effekt hatte das nicht, konnte es auch nicht haben, denn spätestens ab Ende 1946 war die bulgarische Opposition nur noch ein politischer Faktor auf Zeit. Wirtschaftspläne und Dimitrov-Verfassung von 1947 trugen die Hand-

---

[11]) Zit. n. Isusov (Anm. 6), S. 269.

schrift der Kommunisten. Diese gingen jetzt daran, mit ihren politischen Gegnern abzurechnen – beginnend bei deren Presse. Im Mai 1947 verschärfte die Partei ihre Kampagne gegen die Opposition, indem sie deren Zeitungen aus den Druckereien aussperrte, was ihrem Verbot gleichkam. Vergeblich waren Proteste der USA und Großbritanniens – die Opposition Bulgariens stand ohne eigene Presse da. Gleichzeitig begannen Gerichtsverfahren gegen die beiden Oppositionsführer, Petkov und Lulčev, die im Herbst für ersteren mit dem Todesurteil, für den sozialdemokratischen Führer aber mit langjähriger Freiheitsstrafe endeten. Am 26.8.1947 wurde der BZNS-NP (der sich nach Petkovs Verhaftung in „vereinigter" umbenannte) aufgelöst; sein nicht unbeträchtliches Vermögen, darunter über 6 Mio. Leva Guthaben der Parteizeitung *Narodno zemedelsko zname*, verfiel dem Staat. Als die BRP(k) im Dezember 1948 ihren V. Parteitag abhielt (und auf diesem den „Aufbau des Sozialismus" beschloß), war sie faktisch längst Alleinherrscherin in einem Land, in dem sich oppositionelle Parteien selbst aufgelöst hatten, andere mit den Kommunisten zwangsvereinigt wurden (BRSDP), wieder andere zu einem Schattendasein von kommunistischen Gnaden verurteilt waren (BZNS). Von der Parteien- und Medienvielfalt der unmittelbaren Nachkriegszeit blieb nichts übrig.

III. Medien als „Transmissionsriemen" (1948–1956)

Laut Lenin benötigt eine KP als „führende Kraft" gewisse „Transmissionsriemen" zu den sozialen Gruppen – für die Arbeiter Gewerkschaften, für die Jugend Jugendverbände usw. Entsprechend diesem Prinzip organisierten die bulgarischen Kommunisten die Medienlandschaft neu, wobei die Periodika inhaltlich auf die nunmehr herrschende Ideologie ausgerichtet, dabei aber bestimmten Themenbereichen und Lesergruppen zugeordnet wurden. So wurde etwa die Zeitung *Narodna mladež* (Volksjugend) 1948 Tageszeitung und Organ des im Dezember 1947 gegründeten zentralen „Verbands der Volksjugend" (*Săjuz na narodnata mladež, SNM*), der sich ab 1949 DKMS nannte. Und ähnlich erging es anderen Blättern.

Die Leitlinien der neuen Pressepolitik hatte der V. Parteitag der BRP(k) im Dezember 1948 abgesteckt. Auf diesem Kongreß gab sich die Partei ihren alten Namen BKP wieder und verfügte eine Dreiteilung der Medienlandschaft. Die Zeitungen wurden in „zentrale" (*centralen*), „Bezirks-" (*okrăžen*) und „Lokal-" (*mesten*) Blätter aufgeteilt. Die wichtigsten Zentralzeitungen waren die bekannten Partei-, Regierungs- und Verbandsorgane (*RD, Otečestven front, Zemedelsko zname, Narodna mladež* u.a.), zu denen 1951 noch die „Abendzeitung" (*Večerni novini*) kam. Bereits bei den Zentralblättern zeigte sich die zweite Aufteilung, nämlich die nach bestimmten Zielgruppen: 1944 entstand bereits die Tageszeitung „Volksarmee" (*Narodna armija*), die nunmehr als parteiliches Sprachrohr der Landesverteidigung diente. Ähnlich war es mit der Tageszeitung „Genossenschaftliches Dorf" (*Kooperativno selo*) von 1951, die die BKP-Standpunkte unter der Landbevölkerung verbreiten sollte.

Unterhalb der Zentral- standen die Bezirkszeitungen, von denen fünf Tageszeitungen waren; durchweg waren sie bereits 1944/45 entstanden, aber erst nach 1948 der BKP unterworfen worden: *Otečestven glas* (Vaterländische Stimme, Plovdiv), *Černo-*

morski front (Schwarzmeer-Front, Burgas), *Dunavska pravda* (Donau-Wahrheit, Ruse), *Pirinsko delo* (Pirin-Sache, Blagoevgrad) u. a.

Die bereits angesprochene zweite Teilung nach Zielgruppen war besonders bei den für die Jugend bestimmten Periodika deutlich. Es gab Tageszeitungen wie *Narodna mladež* (Volksjugend) und *Studentska tribuna* (Studententribüne, 1945), Zeitschriften (*Mladež*/Jugend, 1945; *Smjana*/Generation, 1945), dazu Blätter für jugendliche Interessen (z. B. *Nauka i technika za mladežta*/Wissenschaft und Technik für die Jugend, 1948), regionale Jugendblätter u. a. m.

Und schließlich gab es eine dritte Aufteilung nach eng gefaßten Sachgebieten, wobei sich die Presseorgane ausschließlich mit diesen zu befassen hatten. Einen besonderen Rang nahmen dabei Zeitschriften ein, die ein bestimmtes sensibles Gebiet im Sinne der Ideologie zu verbreiten hatten – etwa die Geschichte (*Istoričeski pregled*/Historische Rundschau), die Philosophie (*Filosofska misăl*/Philosophischer Gedanke), die Philologie (*Ezik i literatura*/Sprache und Literatur). Die relativ breite Palette der Kunst- und Literaturblätter nahm sich vielfach wie eine Reihe von Verordnungsblättern der Partei für bestimmte Berufsgruppen aus; inhaltlich waren sie unvergleichbar mit berühmten „bourgeoisen" Vorgängern wie etwa dem berühmten *Zlatorog* (Goldenes Horn), zumal in ihnen ein klassisches Element der bulgarischen Publizistik fast völlig fehlte: die Literatur- und Kunstkritik[12]).

Inhaltlich war die bulgarische Medienlandschaft sehr ausgedünnt worden, auch quantitativ verarmte sie. Eingangs der 50er Jahre erschienen 7 von 11 Tageszeitungen und 155 von 183 Zeitschriften in Sofia, so daß für die früher so rührige Provinzpresse kaum noch ein Betätigungsfeld blieb. Die Auflagenhöhe schwankte extrem, wobei der Löwenanteil für die kommunistische Zentralpresse reserviert war – beispielsweise hatten die 11 Tageszeitungen eine Gesamtauflage von 1 Mio. Exemplaren, von denen über 400 000 auf RD entfielen. Das war umso erheblicher, als die Zahl der Titel mit der endgültigen Machtübernahme der BKP deutlich zurückgegangen war (s. Tab. 7).

Tabelle 7: Auflagenzahlen in den 40er und 50er Jahren

	1944	1948	1950	1952	1953	1954	1955
Zeitungen (Tg., W.)							
Titel	302	92	63	65	67	70	79
Auflage (Mio./J.)	122	346	–	320	375	433	455
Zeitschriften							
Titel	121	246	164	79	92	96	99
Auflage (Mio./J.)	4,1	10,4	6,2	5,7	8,6	6,8	7,9

Dennoch war die bulgarische Presse der frühen 50er Jahre nicht nur eine langweilige Bleiwüste unter BKP-Regie. Nicht selten konnte man aus ihr auch entnehmen, wie es im Lande wirklich aussah. 1950/51 hatte es z. B. im Nordwesten Bulgariens und

---

[12]) Eckhard, T.: Bulgarische Publizistik, in: Blick nach Osten. 2 (1952) 4, S. 298–303.

anderswo heftige Bauernunruhen wegen der Zwangskollektivierung der Landwirtschaft gegeben, die ein solches Ausmaß erreichten, daß die Parteiführung den Kollektivierungsdruck deutlich mildern mußte; darüber wurde in der Presse ausführlich berichtet[13]). Und in der damaligen Presse fand sich laufend etwas, das man heute und seit langem vergeblich suchen würde: die Anerkennung einer eigenständigen makedonischen Nation. Zwar hatte sich Bulgarien Stalins Bannfluch über Tito anschließen müssen, und damit war es auch zu Ende mit den Plänen einer Wiedervereinigung von Pirin- und Vardar-Makedonien, aber bis in die frühen 60er Jahre hinein hielt Bulgarien an der Tatsache fest, daß im südwestlichen Pirin-Gebirge eben kaum „Bulgaren" leben, dafür aber knapp 200 000 „Makedonier". Über sie und ihre kulturell-sprachliche Eigenständigkeit wurde in der bulgarischen Presse damals laufend berichtet.

Generell aber waren die 50er Jahre eine Phase der Stagnation, in der jedoch technische Novitäten eingeführt wurden. Vor allem wurde das Radionetz zügig ausgebaut. Als 1947 die sowjetischen Besatzungstruppen Bulgarien wieder verließen, ließen sie große Mengen Funkgerät zurück, mit dem Drahtfunk in jene Dörfer gelegt wurde, die bislang noch nicht vom Rundfunk erfaßt worden waren. Bis Mitte der 60er Jahre wurden 2250 Dörfer mit Drahtfunk versehen, was die Zahl der Geräte von 183 000 (1944) auf 670 000 anwachsen ließ. Seit 1946 strahlte Radio Sofia ein zweites Programm aus, und 1951 wurde ein Kurzwellen-Sender für Fremdsprachenprogramme installiert. 1958 wurden die Programme erstmals rund um die Uhr ausgestrahlt, und 1962 kam ein drittes Programm hinzu.

Bereits 1951 experimentierte das Physikalische Institut der Sofioter Hochschule für Maschinenbau und Elektrotechnik (VMEI) mit dem Kabelfernsehen, was 1952 zu ersten Kabelsendungen führte. Ab dem 1. 5. 1954 wurde regelmäßig drahtlos gesendet, doch galt das noch als „Testphase". Den endgültigen Beschluß, in Bulgarien Fernsehen einzuführen, faßte das Politbüro im April 1958. Die erste Sendung erfolgte zum 7. 11. 1959, dem Jahrestag der russischen (!) Revolution. Als offizieller Geburtstag des Fernsehens gilt indessen der 26. 12. 1959. Anfänglich nutzten die bulgarischen TV-Macher technische Hilfe aus der DDR und besonders aus der Sowjetunion. Offenkundig eine Spätfolge davon ist, daß in Bulgarien bis heute Teile des sowjetischen zentralen TV-Programms ausgestrahlt werden – leichte Unterhaltungskost zum Wochenende, die zudem an Umfang immer weiter abnimmt.

IV. Jahre kultureller Selbstisolation (1956–1970)

Im April 1956 hatte das ZK der BKP eine Entstalinisierung („Beseitigung der Folgen des Personenkults") eingeleitet, und „April-Linie" wurde augenblicklich ein neues Schlagwort, das eine gewisse Verheißung enthielt. Bereits im Mai 1956 aber wurde ausgerechnet *Otečestven front* nachdrücklich darauf verwiesen, daß es für die

---

[13]) Migev, V.: Organizacionnoto razvitie na BKP (1951–1956 g.) (Die organisatorische Entwicklung der BKP), in: Izvestija na Instituta po istorija na BKP. 57 (1987), S. 52–96.

Presse nach wie vor enge Grenzen gäbe. Journalisten wie Vladimir Topenčarov hatten die verderblichen Einflüsse des Stalinismus offen beim Namen genannt, Satiriker wie Genčo Uzunov karikierten den politischen „Stil" im damaligen Bulgarien, Literaten wie Radoj Ralin und Blaga Dimitrova sprachen der Partei rundheraus das Recht ab, literarische und künstlerische Aktivitäten zu kontrollieren. Alle diese Versuche, mehr Meinungsfreiheit zu erlangen, versandeten gezwungenermaßen rasch.

Für gute 15 Jahre durchlebte Bulgarien eine Phase, in der Aufwand und Ertrag der Medienpolitik extrem auseinanderliefen. Die bulgarische Führung, die nach personellen und konzeptionellen Wandlungen ohne „Hausmacht" dastand, übertrieb ihre prosowjetische Loyalität in einem Maße, daß sie „katholischer als der Papst, türkischer als der Sultan" war (wie es ein vielzitiertes Sprichwort ausdrückte). Auf die bulgarische Bevölkerung prasselte eine intensive, langdauernde Propagandaoffensive herab – für „Wachsamkeit", für die „Erziehung des neuen Menschen", gegen „bourgeoise Ideologie", gegen Religion und hunderte Anlässe mehr. Die Propagandainstitutionen auf allen Stufen der Parteihierarchie wurden laufend verstärkt, Schulungen und „Seminare" lösten sich in endloser Folge ab, neue Zeitschriften entstanden – etwa 1966 *Političeska prosveta* (Politische Bildung) –, „Materialien" bulgarischer und sowjetischer Provenienz wurden in Millionenauflagen herausgebracht usw.[14]).

Diese Kampagnen hatten zumindest ein längerfristiges Gutes – in ihrem „Windschatten" hielt die empirische Sozialforschung wieder Einzug in Bulgarien. Man konnte z. B. schlecht atheistische Kampagnen starten, ohne zu wissen, wie die Menschen zur Religion standen; folglich begannen bereits um 1962 umfangreiche religionssoziologische Untersuchungen, die die Renaissance der Soziologie dort begründeten. Ganz allgemein aber verloren die Bulgaren in diesen Jahren fast gänzlich das Interesse an den heimischen Massenmedien, die sich ihnen in grauer Eintönigkeit präsentierten. Der einzige verbliebene Informationskanal waren ausländische Rundfunkstationen, und Zeitzeugen erinnern sich, daß zu keiner Zeit in Bulgarien mit solcher Leidenschaft fremde Sprachen wie die ganzen 60er Jahre über gelernt wurden...[15]).

Diese Situation fiel selbst treuesten Parteigängern des Regimes auf, die Abhilfe schaffen wollten. Zu diesen „Pionieren" zählte etwa Lozan Strelkov, ehedem als stellvertretender Chefredakteur des Schriftstellerorgans *Literaturen front* (Literaturfront, 1945) ein unerbittlicher Verfechter des Kunstdogmas vom „sozialistischen Realismus". Später wurde er Generaldirektor von BTA und bemühte sich in seiner neuen Funktion, Bulgariens kulturelle Isolation aufzubrechen. Plötzlich edierte BTA mehrere Zeitschriften – *Lik* (Bildnis), *Nauka i technika* (Wissenschaft und Technik), *Paraleli* (Parallelen) und andere –, die als interessante und unideologische Blätter höchst populär wurden, zumal sie eine gewisse Brücke von Bulgarien zum Westen schlugen.

---

[14]) Dimitrov, M.: Propagandistkata rabota na BKP za komunističeskoto văzpitanie na trudeštite se (1962–1966 g.) (Die propagandistische Arbeit der BKP für die kommunistische Erziehung der Werktätigen), in: Izvestija na Instituta po istorija na BKP. 26 (1971), S. 247–295.

[15]) Vgl. Markov, G.: Zadočni reportaži za Bălgarija (Auswärtige Reportagen über Bulgarien), Bd. I–II. Zürich 1980/81, passim.

Ähnliche Wandlungen machte ein anderer Hardliner vergangener Zeiten durch: Christo Radevski, führender Ideologe des bulgarischen Stalinismus. In den späten 50er Jahren wurde er auf den Posten des Chefredakteurs der Literaturzeitschrift *Septemvri* (September, 1948) abgeschoben. In seiner neuen Rolle verbündete er sich mit jungen Literaten und machte das Blatt zu ihrem Sprachrohr – *Septemvri* wurde ein populärer Geheimtip für bislang nie gelesene mutige Texte. Gegenstück zu *Septemvri* war die 1957 entstandene Zeitschrift *Plamăk* (Flamme), die von Andrej Guljaški in der herkömmlichen dogmatischen Weise redigiert wurde. Beide Blätter waren offizielle Organe des SBP, unterschieden sich aber extrem dank heterogener Auffassungen ihrer Schriftleiter. Dieser Konflikt wurde eine Zeitlang ausgetragen und dann durch die Absetzung Radevskis im Sinne der Dogmatiker beendet. Bulgariens Medienlandschaft blieb eintönig wie zuvor.

V. Der lange Weg zur *glasnost'* (1971–1988)

Die 70er Jahre fanden die bulgarischen Medien im Zeichen der großen, langen und folgenreichen Debatte um den *siv potok* (grauer Strom). Dieser Begriff war erstmals in einem Beschluß des Politbüros vom 15. 10. 1969 aufgetaucht und enthielt eigentlich eine Klage über „ideenloses und apolitisches" Schreiben, das wieder gegen eine revolutionär-parteilich-klassenmäßige Darstellungsweise ausgewechselt werden sollte. Aber die „Kreativen" drehten den Ideologen das Wort im Munde herum, und *siv potok* wurde fortan ein Synonym für jene politisch-ideologische Realitätsferne, die anderthalb Jahrzehnte für Bulgariens Literatur, mehr aber noch für Bulgariens Journalistik unumstößliches Dogma gewesen war. Diese Debatte war ein in Osteuropa einmaliger Fall, nach dem nichts mehr so war, wie es sich vorher präsentiert hatte; klassische Begriffe des ideologischen Repertoires – „Kompromißlosigkeit", „Kritik", „Aktivität" etc. – wurden nunmehr gegen die ideologischen Gralshüter gewendet, indem diese „diensthabenden Phrasen" (*dežurni frazi*) mit neuem Inhalt und neuer Wirksamkeit angefüllt wurden.

Zudem hatte die bulgarische Öffentlichkeit das erhellende Vergnügen, die Debatte anhand eines Grundsatzkonflikts der zwei führenden Literaturblätter zu verfolgen. Der orthodoxen Part spielte dabei *Literaturen front* (LF), im September 1944 entstanden und seit Jahrzehnten Organ des SBP; dieser fürchtete um seine organisatorische Unabhängigkeit samt ihren beträchtlichen materiellen Möglichkeiten und gab sich entsprechend parteikonform. Auf der Gegenposition stand *Narodna kultura* (NK), 1957 als Organ des Ministeriums für Bildung und Kultur (*Ministerstvo na prosvetata i kulturata*) (ab 1963: Komitee für Kultur und Kunst / *Komitet za kultura i izkustvo*) entstanden und mit einer wöchentlichen Auflage von 50 000 Exemplaren höchst populär; Anfang 1964 war NK mit *Literaturni novini* (Literarische Nachrichten) fusioniert worden, einem Literaturblatt, das mit einigen „gewagten" Artikeln den Zorn der LF und seiner Hintermänner erregt hatte.

Ab 1970 gerieten LF und NK in einen Streit miteinander, der fortlaufend eskalierte; er begann damit, daß NK ihrem Gegner das Recht bestritt, „die Tätigkeit unserer gesamten Presse mit Benotungen zu versehen", und er endete mit einer entlarvenden

Bestandsaufnahme des Verfalls bulgarischer Literatur und Publizistik. In diesem Streit machte ein russisches Wort „Karriere" – *kazionni*, was im Sinne von „staatseigen" oder „obrigkeitshörig" gebraucht wurde, und zwar so offen und abwertend, daß sich gerade Bulgariens beste Autoren fortan hüteten, *kazionni* zu sein, und dies durch einen demonstrativen Boykott von LF und ähnlichen Blättern bekundeten[16]).

In den 70er Jahren kam als neuer Grundzug ein nationalbewußter Pragmatismus in die bulgarische Politik, der mit jedem Jahr mehr der (unausgesprochenen) Prämisse folgte, daß „sozialistisch" sei, was Bulgarien zählbaren Nutzen bringe, und daß Neues gewagt und Nichtbewährtes aufgegeben werden müßten. Diese neue Sicht von Politik hatte medienpolitisch die besten Auswirkungen, speziell bei den Funkmedien. Bei der „Generaldirektion des Bulgarischen Radios und Fernsehen" (*Generalna direkcija na Bǎlgarskoto radio i televizija*) wurde 1970 ein soziologisches „Institut" für die Beobachtung der Einschaltquoten gegründet, und seine ersten Ergebnisse waren so ernüchternd, daß man augenblicklich zu gründlichen Programmreformen schritt. 1971 wurden drei Programme mit ausgeprägtem Profil erstmals ausgestrahlt: *Chorizont* (Pop-Musik, literarisch-publizistische Kurzbeiträge, Nachrichten, Kommentare), *Christo Botev* (klassische und Volksmusik, Literatur, Politik), *Orfej* (literarische und musikalische Sendungen auf gehobenem Niveau), „Sendungen für das Ausland" (in über einem Dutzend Fremdsprachen mit Schwerpunkten in Makedonisch und Türkisch); 1977 kam noch das Bildungsprogramm *Znanie* (Wissen) hinzu[17]). Ähnliches passierte im TV-Bereich, wo man aufgrund von Zuschauer-Polls die Programme änderte und „entpolitisierte"[18]). Zum 1.4.1977 emanzipierten sich Rundfunk und Fernsehen zu „eigenständigen Struktureinheiten", was bei beiden der Professionalität und Rezipientenrücksicht zugute kam.

Ganz allgemein bemühte sich Bulgarien seit Mitte der 80er Jahre verstärkt, keinen Bereich der Funkmedien auszulassen. Seit 1986 sind die zentralen Rundfunkprogramme landesweit auf UKW zu empfangen. Darüber hinaus senden regionale Studios aus Stara Zagora, Plovdiv, Šumen, Varna und Blagoevgrad. Die zwei zentralen TV-Kanäle werden (fast) gänzlich in Farbe ausgestrahlt; daneben bestehen noch TV-Studios mit eigenen Programmen in Plovdiv, Varna, Ruse und Blagoevgrad. Als „Medientor" zur Welt hat schließlich in den letzten Jahren die (1967 geschaffene) Agentur „Sofia-Press" an Profil gewonnen. Sie verbreitet den bulgarischen Standpunkt in der Welt, wozu sie u. a. ein eigenes Filmstudio, die Redaktion *Inter-Foto* und fremdsprachige Blätter in zehn Sprachen (darunter die *Sofioter Nachrichten*) unterhält.

Weniger auffällig, aber dennoch vorhanden waren positive Veränderungen in den Printmedien. Es entstanden neue Blätter, die sich inhaltlich von früheren Usancen absetzten und darauf ihren Erfolg bei den Lesern begründeten – 1973 etwa die Literaturzeitschrift *Sǎvremennik* (Zeitgenosse) oder 1975 das Nachrichtenmagazin *Otečestvo* (Vaterland), das mit seiner Themenvielfalt, Offenheit und mutigen Kritik der

---

[16]) Bulgariens Literatur im „grauen Strom", in: Wissenschaftlicher Dienst Südosteuropa. (1972) 4, S. 55–60.
[17]) Kostov, V.: Na radiotemi (Zu Rundfunk-Themen), in: Narodna kultura. (1971) 37.
[18]) Pisarev, P.: Programnite problemi na televizijata (Programmprobleme des Fernsehens), in: Narodna kultura. (1971) 11.

größte Zeitungserfolg der Nachkriegszeit wurde. Andere Blätter wandelten völlig ihr Profil, beispielsweise die Wochenzeitung *Anteni*. 1971 wurde sie zwecks Propagierung bulgarisch-sowjetischer Freundschaft geschaffen, aber ihre Trägergremien vergingen rasch. Fortan existierte *Anteni* als ein Blatt, „das niemandem gehört", das sich also noch eigenem Gusto Themen und Stil aussuchen konnte. Dabei stieß es als wohl erstes Organ auf die Öko-Problematik, die sich gerade in Sofia Mitte der 70er Jahre bei Konflikten um den Metrobau „hautnah" stellte. Mit intellektueller Aggressivität wandte sich *Anteni* den Problemen zu, wobei es früh jene national grundierte Darstellungsweise – nicht irgendeine Umwelt wird zerstört, sondern „unsere bulgarische" – pflegte, die mittlerweile für bulgarische Öko-Diskussionen charakteristisch ist (vgl. den Beitrag „Raumordnung und Umweltschutz" des Autors).

Ganz allgemein wurde die bulgarische Presse farbiger und mutiger, was ihr vermehrten Leserzuspruch einbrachte. Ihre Auflagenhöhe von 1974 stellt Tab. 8 dar. Nach der Territorialreform von 1987 ergaben sich in dieser Medienlandschaft partielle Veränderungen. Insgesamt wurden in Bulgarien rund 1 000 Periodika ediert, darunter 20 Tageszeitungen. Obwohl die früheren Bezirksblätter fortfielen, gab es mehr

Tabelle 8: Presse in den 70er Jahren

	Auflage	
	pro Ausgabe	Jahr
Tages-, Wochenzeitungen		
total: 573	6 660 000	930 000 000
zentrale: 56	5 312 000	858 200 000
Bezirks-: 32	562 000	105 500 000
lokale: 485	785 000	16 300 000
Tageszeitungen		
total: 13	2 211 000	729 600 000
zentrale: 8	–	–
Bezirks-: 5		
Rabotničesko delo	750 000	–
Kooperativno selo	270 000	–
Trud	250 000	–
Narodna mladež	233 000	–
Otečestven front	280 000	–
Wochenzeitungen		
Pogled (Blick, Organ des Journalistenverbandes	310 000	–
Stăršel (Hornisse, Satireblatt)	280 000	–
Zeitschriften		
total: 250	3 306 000	37 900 000
Ženata dnes (Frau heute)	374 000	–
Zdrave (Gesundheit)	160 000	–
Slavejče (Kleine Nachtigall)	127 000	–
Kosmos	100 000	–
Partien život (Parteileben, BKP)	47 000	–
Novo vreme (Neue Zeit, BKP)	33 000	–

Tageszeitungen (sog. „Gebiets-" bzw. „Gemeindezeitungen"). In den Auflagen waren gewisse Schwankungen zu verzeichnen: RD – 820 000 pro Ausgabe, OF – 300 000, *Kooperativno selo* – 193 000, *Večerni novini* – 117 000, *Zemedelsko zname* – 176 000, *Pogled* – 300 000 usw.[19]).

Nun sind Auflagenzahlen bei kommunistischen Periodika gewiß kein Maßstab, aber einiges sagen sie doch aus. Ein Blatt wie *Ženata dnes*, 1945 geschaffen, führte ein jahrzehntelanges Schattendasein und gewann erst Profil, als es sich auf die Wünsche der Leserinnen einstellte – Ratgeber zu Familienfragen, Schnittmusterbeilage, Rezepte etc. Das aber soll nicht heißen, daß es sich hier um ein flaches Hausfrauenblättchen handelte. *Ženata dnes* ist vielmehr eine mutige Zeitschrift, die vor keinem heißen Eisen zurückschreckt und beispielsweise 1973 die erste Dokumentation über Selbstmorde in Bulgarien publizierte.

Mit anderen Worten: *glasnost* ist nicht nur ein *bulgarisches* Wort – sie ist auch eine Eigenheit der bulgarischen Presse, die sich ab den frühen 70er Jahren immer mehr herausschälte. Jedes neue Problem – sozusagen von „Außenpolitik" und „AIDS" bis „Zentrale Planwirtschaft" – trug das Seine dazu bei, die Presse mutiger und informativer zu machen; und gravierende Ereignisse wie etwa die Černobyl'-Katastrophe vom April 1986 brachten die Presse (allen voran RD) beinahe in die Rolle eines öffentlichen Wächters und Anwalts. Als aus der Sowjetunion *glasnost'*-Anstöße kamen, wurden sie von bulgarischen Journalisten als willkommene Schützenhilfe aufgenommen, und in den nun folgenden Debatten wurden journalistische Binsenweisheiten „wiederentdeckt": daß die Presse nicht übermäßig kontrolliert und reglementiert werden darf, daß es keine „Tabu-Bereiche" geben soll, daß der Leserwunsch nach Information und Unterhaltung oberstes Gebot journalistischer Professionalität ist, daß sich die Menschen „anderswo" informieren, wenn sie es aus heimischen Medien nicht können.

Diese Debatten setzten 1986 ein, und bis Ende 1988 wurde praktisch kein Aspekt des Pressewesens ausgespart. Dies kann auch als Vorgriff auf eine bessere Zukunft aufgefaßt werden, wie sie am 6.8.1988 ein Politbüro-Beschluß „Über die qualitativ neue soziale Rolle der Presse in der NRB unter den Bedingungen der Reform" absteckte. Interessanteres hat das oberste BKP-Gremium selten beschlossen, und dem jetzigen Beschluß merkt man an, daß in ihn alle Fachdiskussionen der letzten Jahre eingemündet sind. Gleich zu Beginn wird z.B. als „wesentlicher Mangel" der Presse gerügt, daß sie und ihre Informanten schutzlos Staat und Partei gegenüberstehen. Ähnlich kritisch werden vermerkt: das „Bemühen", Vorgänge, Ereignisse und Fakten „als Geheimnis einzustufen" und somit die Menschen von ihnen zustehender Information auszuschließen; mangelnde Professionalität in der Presse; „Schablonen" und „Oberflächlichkeit" in Kommentaren; ein Übermaß an „Protokollen und offiziellen Materialien" u.a.m.

Alle diese Vorwürfe an die Presse sind berechtigt – aber wer hat eigentlich die Zeitungen so gemacht, wie sie sich bis in die späten 80er Jahre präsentierten? In

---

[19]) Viktorov, I.: Bălgarskijat periodičen pečat v cifri prez 1974 godina (Die bulgarische periodische Presse in Zahlen im Jahre 1974), in: Bălgarski žurnalist. (1974) 5, S. 30; neuere Zahlen bei Wetzel, F.: Das Medienspektrum Bulgariens, in: Neue Deutsche Presse (DDR). (1988), 7.

Zukunft soll alles anders und besser werden: „Die Hauptaufgabe der Presse ist heute, eine reichhaltige und glaubwürdige Information zur ganzen Komplexität des Reformprozesses und seiner Widersprüche bereitzustellen". Die Presse soll die „demokratische Kultur der Menschen" erhöhen, indem sie alle innovativen Prozesse kritisch begleitet und durch „Meinungsvielfalt" unterstützt.

Damit nicht genug: Fortan soll sich die Presse Bulgariens „selbstverwalten" und „selbsterhalten". Das wird beträchtliche Veränderungen in der bulgarischen Medienlandschaft nach sich ziehen: Ämter werden nicht mehr wie bisher als Herausgeber „ihrer" Blätter fungieren, gewisse Periodika gehen ein oder werden mit anderen zusammengelegt, Erscheinungsweisen ändern sich, Monopole fallen (etwa das der Firma „Bulgarreklama" auf Werbungsakquisition), Redaktionen werden „ausgedünnt" oder fusioniert, und vor allem werden die Bezugspreise steigen, und zwar kräftig: RD kostete z. B. 5 Stotinki, ab 1. Januar 1989 aber 11 Stotinki. Und die spottlustigen Sofioter malten sich schon Monate vorher das Chaos mit dem Wechselgeld aus, welches speziell die elfte Stotinka auslösen werde.... Vermutlich deswegen wurde der Preis bald wieder auf 10 Stotinki gesenkt.

VI. Sprachkultur

Wer immer in Bulgarien publizistisch tätig ist, sollte sich im eigenen Interesse bewußt sein, daß er für ein bis zum Purismus sprachsensibles Publikum arbeitet. Die ersten bulgarischen Periodika überhaupt waren philologischer Natur, die nachfolgende Medienvielfalt förderte die Sprachentwicklung und wirkte indirekt sprachelzieherisch – das bulgarische Medienpublikum registriert jeden und verzeiht kaum einen Sprachfehler. Bulgarien versteht sich als das – neben Hellas und Rom – „dritte klassische Land", aus dem Sprache und Schrifttum der Slawen kamen, und dieses Postulat nach einem intrakulturellen Primat entspricht dem wachen Bewußtsein der bulgarischen Öffentlichkeit für Reinheit und Schönheit der eigenen Sprache. Zu allen Zeiten wurde über sie ausführlich diskutiert, und seit einigen Jahren wird speziell die Sprache des Fernsehens kritisiert; in dieser haben sich gewisse Unachtsamkeiten verfestigt – sorgloser Umgang mit direkten Artikeln, Artikulationsfehler, Zusammenziehen von Wörtern und Wortgruppen, falsche Nominalbildungen, Verwendung von Dialektismen u. a. –, die sprachkritisch dokumentiert werden[20]).

Seit Ende des II. Weltkriegs hat es in bulgarischen Sprachdebatten immer wieder fünf Bereiche gegeben, die sich zu verschiedenen Zeiten in den Vordergrund schoben, ohne daß sie jemals gänzlich verschwunden wären. Sie sollen im folgenden kurz gewürdigt werden.

---

[20]) Brezinski, S.: Za ezika na televizionnite predavanija (Zur Sprache von TV-Sendungen), in: Văprosi na săvremennata žurnalistika. (1981) 2–3, S. 36–45.

1. Probleme der Orthographiereform

Als klassische Sprache des Slawentums hat das Bulgarische zu allen Zeiten viel archaisches Wort- und Schriftgut mit sich getragen, dessen „Gewicht" in der Neuzeit durch mehrere Orthographiereformen gemindert werden sollte. Die bislang letzte wurde am 27.2.1945 verkündet, und sie befreite die Sprache von Verzichtbarem. Daneben initiierte die Reform Entwicklungen, die je länger je mehr politischen Rückschlägen gleichkamen.

Die bulgarische Sprache weist eine Binnendifferenzierung in Dialekte auf, deren Hauptgruppen entlang der Nord-Süd-Linie Nikopol – Pirdop – Pazardžik – Goce Delčev geteilt sind. Östlich davon dominiert die *Jakane* – Sprechweise mit volltönenden Ja-Lauten, westlich das *Ekane*, in welchem „ja" als „e" gesprochen wird. Bis 1945 gab es mit dem Ѣ im bulgarischen Alphabet einen Buchstaben, der diese Sprachkonventionen schriftlich integrierte. Er wurde eliminiert, gleichzeitig erhob man das *Jakane* zur standardsprachlichen Norm[21]. Und seither schlägt man sich mit den negativen Folgewirkungen dieser Entscheidung herum: geminderte Kulturausstrahlung der Hauptstadt (weil Sofia Zentrum des *Ekane* ist), sprachdidaktische Probleme mit jeder neuen Schülergeneration, künstliche Barriere zwischen neuer und „alter" Literatur in Bulgarien, maximale Distanz zum (verwandten) Makedonischen u.v.m.

Bereits 1951 forderte eine „Nationalkonferenz" von Fachleuten eine erneute Rechtschreibungsreform, 1962 wurde dafür eine „Zentralkommission" eingesetzt. Konkret geschah nichts, und noch 1970 klagte der international angesehene Linguist Konstantin Popov: „Ein Vierteljahrhundert ist vergangen, seit die Orthographiereform in Kraft ist, aber immer noch hat sich die gewünschte Einheit in der sprachlichen Praxis (...) nicht eingestellt. Offen gesagt, es liegen Resultate vor, die mit der alten Rechtsschreibung nicht möglich gewesen wären"[22].

Momentan ist es nahezu ausgeschlossen, daß sich hier etwas ändern wird – auch wenn gerade seit den späten 70er Jahren Klagen und sprachpflegerische Bemühungen zunahmen. Grundsätzlich gibt es aber nur einen Ausweg, der sich zweifach unter politischem Aspekt verbietet: Wiederbelebung der „faschistischen" Orthographie vom August 1923 (die als reine Reform optimal war) und damit vergrößerte Distanz zur „zweiten Muttersprache Russisch" (dem das Bulgarische durch die Reform von 1945 „ähnlicher" geworden war).

2. Umgangs- und Mediensprache

Seit es regierende Kommunisten gibt, besteht auch ihre typische pathetische Verlautbarungs- und Befehlssprache[23]. Gerade in neuester Zeit wird in Bulgarien offen

---

[21] Kröter, W.: Die Reform der bulgarischen Rechtschreibung 1945, in: Zeitschrift für Phonetik und Allgemeine Sprachwissenschaft. (1953) 5–6, S. 409/410.
[22] Popov, K.: Po njakoi sporni i nerešeni vǎprosi na knižovnija pravogovor i pravopis (Zu einigen strittigen und ungeklärten Fragen der literarischen Aussprache und Rechtschreibung), in: Plamǎk. (1970) 1, S. 55–63.
[23] Vgl. Seliščev, A.M.: Jazyk revoljucionnoj epochi (Sprache der revolutionären Epoche). Moskau 1926.

ausgesprochen, daß Alltagskommunikation und „offizielle" Rede maximal auseinanderlaufen, daß das „offizielle" Bulgarisch – vulgär, euphemistisch, langweilig und stets auf Rückversicherung bedacht – die Sprache insgesamt trübt[24]).

Besonders heftig wurde eingangs der 70er Jahre gegen diese Sprachverhunzung polemisiert. Im Februar 1971 hatte der Wissenschaftler Emil Džakov einige „Gedanken zur Entwicklung der bulgarischen Sprache" geäußert und die Philologen um mehr Wachsamkeit gebeten. Ihm antwortete die bekannte Dichterin Blaga Dimitrova: Es sind die „Halbintellektuellen" mit ihren „risikolosen Standardphrasen", die die Sprache verderben und dies vor allem über die Medien tun. Blaga Dimitrova: „Wenn wir nur die Zeitungs- und ‚Vortrags'-Sprache der Quartalsversammlungen hernehmen, dann könnten wir zu wunderlichen Schlußfolgerungen gelangen: Unsere Landsleute haben kein Gedächtnis, da man ihnen unausgesetzt ein und dieselben Phrasen wiederholt, sie haben kein Gefühl für Humor, sie haben keine Leidenschaft zu suchen, zu entdecken, nachzudenken, sie sind überhaupt lethargisch und gefühllos. Es ist nur gut, daß wir hinterher wieder aus solchen Versammlungen herauskommen und die Zeitungen nach dem Durchblättern wegwerfen; dann tauchen wir wieder in die lebendigen Ströme der gesprochenen Sprache, die vor Scharfsinn, Schlagfertigkeit, unwiederholbarer Originalität blitzt, aus der gedankliche Energie funkelt."

Blaga Dimitrova erntete kaum Widerspruch, löste aber eine interessante Entwicklung aus. In nahezu allen Medien (vor allem in *Otečestven front* unter dem Titel *Ezik moj, drag moj*/Meine Sprache, meine Liebe) wurde fortan über Sprache in einer Weise diskutiert, die viel von späterer *glasnost'* vorwegnahm; zusätzlich gingen Literatur und Öffentlichkeit eine „heimliche Allianz" dergestalt ein, daß gewisse Autoren (Radoj Ralin, Nikolaj Chajtov u. a.) öffentlichen Widerwillen gegen bestimmte Sprachphänomene artikulierten und dabei politisch kritische Töne anklingen ließen[25]).

Bis Mitte der 80er Jahre hatte all das kaum Effekt, und so mußte noch 1984 auf einer Konferenz konstatiert werden: „Heutzutage wird die reinste bulgarische Sprache von den wenigstgebildeten (...) Leuten gesprochen, deren Bewußtsein die Aussagen von Journalisten, die für die Zeitung oder das Radio bestimmt sind, nicht aufnimmt"[26]). Und so startete im Dezember 1985 *Narodna kultura* eine neue Kampagne, in der die Leser eine „gemeinsame Front gegen Sprachenschund, gegen sprachliche Armut als Zeichen bürokratischen Denkens", kurz: gegen die „Antisprache" (*antiezik*), bilden sollten[27]).

---

[24]) Georgiev, Ž.: Ezikăt văv vsekidnevieto (Die Sprache im Alltag), in: Sociologičeski problemi. (1985) 1, S. 16–28; Jarămov, D.: Ezikăt, na kojto obštuvame (Die Sprache, in der wir verkehren), in: Rodna reč. (1988) 1.

[25]) Bulgarische Sprachprobleme, in: Wissenschaftlicher Dienst Südosteuropa. (1972) 5, S. 80–83.

[26]) Zit. n. Healing the Ailing Bulgarian Language, in: Radio Free Europe Research. (1984) 9, S. 9–12.

[27]) Vgl. Antiezikăt, ili ezikăt na bjurokrata (Die Antisprache oder die Sprache des Bürokraten), in: Narodna kultura. (1985) 51.

3. Gegen sprachliche Fremdeinflüsse

Seit Kriegsende kontinuierlich, periodisch verstärkt wehrt sich bulgarisches Sprachempfinden gegen ein Übermaß an fremder Lexik. Schon bald nach Kriegsende strömte ins Bulgarische ein Flut neuer Ausdrücke, zumeist russischer Provenienz, was von den Linguisten zunächst mit amüsiertem Fatalismus beobachtet wurde[28]). Jahre später empörte man sich über die Flut „unberechtigter und unnötiger Russizismen"[29]), von denen sich das Bulgarische dank bester Entsprechungen „leicht befreien könnte"[30]).

Kann es das wirklich? Eine eher pessimistische Antwort gab 1983 Kiril Kosev, Chef der „Politischen Hauptverwaltung" der BNA, mit seinen gescheiten „Gedanken über die heimische Sprache"[31]). Eine „Sprachverschmutzung" (*zamărsjavane na ezika*) konstatierte er – vor allem durch die sowjetische Mediensprache: sie schmuggelt laufend russische Wörter ins Bulgarische und infiziert dieses mit der typisch russischen Falschverwendung von Lehn- und Fremdwörtern („Rekonstruktion" statt Sanierung, „Regime" statt Ordnung, „Estrade" statt Unterhaltung etc.)

In neuerer Zeit kamen zu den Russizismen noch die Anglizismen (Amerikanismen), die in bulgarischer Schreibweise besonders auffallen, weil sie rein phonetisch adaptiert werden: *nou-chau* (know how), *dizajn* (design) usw. Je mehr Bulgarien sich der westlichen Welt öffnet, desto stärker wird ihre Zahl anwachsen[32]). Auch in Bulgarien stehen jene Einfallstore offen – Sport, Mode, Unterhaltung, Computerterminologie, Touristik usw. –, über die fremdes Wortgut eindringt[33]). Interessant ist dabei, daß diese vorwiegend westliche Lexik speziell die neuen Problemfelder besetzt, deren bloße Existenz offiziell erst sehr verspätet registriert wurde – derzeit in erster Linie die Ökologie.

Wie jeder moderne Staat muß auch Bulgarien mit solchen Entwicklungen leben – tut es aber mit größerem Widerwillen als andere. Die allgemein befürchtete Gefahr wurde von Nikolaj Chajtov so beschrieben: „Wird nicht in drei, vier Jahrzehnten die Zeit kommen, daß wir die ‚Balkanlegenden' mit dem Wörterbuch der im Bulgarischen ausgestorbenen Wörter lesen? Ganz zu schweigen von Vazov und Zachari Stojanov, die der heutigen jungen Generation bereits spürbare Schwierigkeiten verursachen. Was wird erst, wenn fremde und bulgarische Wörter je zur Hälfte da sind oder letztere gar in die Minderheit geraten"[34])?

---

[28]) Lekov, I.: Otraženie na obštestvenite promeni v leksikata na bălgarskija ezik (Widerspiegelung gesellschaftlicher Veränderungen in der Lexik der bulgarischen Sprache), in: Ezik i literatura. (1946) 1, S. 5–7.

[29]) Burin, I.: Nešto za rodnija ni ezik (Einiges zu unserer Muttersprache), in: Septemvri. (1978) 2, S. 221–228.

[30]) Popvasilev, S.: Bogat i zvučen – Besedi vărchu bălgarskija ezik (Reich und klangvoll – Unterhaltungen über die bulgarische Sprache). Sofia 1970, S. 41 ff.

[31]) Kosev, K.: Njakoi razmisli za rodnija ezik (Einige Überlegungen zur Muttersprache), in: Pogled. (1983) 21, S. 4.

[32]) Lazarov, A.: Običam te (Ich liebe dich), in: Trud. 19.10.1983.

[33]) Jordanova, L.: Novite dumi v săvremennija bălgarski ezik (Neue Wörter in der bulgarischen Gegenwartssprache). Sofia 1980 (Rodna reč omajna 16).

[34]) Chajtov, N.: Vălšebnoto ogledalo (Zauberspiegel), in: Septemvri. (1980) 8–9.

4. Pro und contra Jugendsprache

Ignorieren, ablehnen, tolerieren, feiern – in diesen Phasen haben sich die meisten osteuropäischen Länder mit dem fröhlichsten Sprachphänomen auseinandergesetzt, dem frech-respektlosen Jugendjargon. Wenn Bulgarien hierbei graduell eine gewisse Ausnahme machte, dann weil diese Sprachkonvention hier stets verständnisvolle wissenschaftliche Beobachter fand, die ihre metaphorische Vielfalt und poetische Expressivität zu schätzen wußten.

Sie alle stehen in der Nachfolge des bedeutenden Linguisten Stojko Stojkov (1912–1969), der 1946 seine Studie über den Sofioter Schülerjargon veröffentlichte (deren Material er während seiner Zeit als Lehrer selbst gesammelt hatte). Diese Arbeit bleibt nicht nur wegen ihrer Wortlisten interessant – zeitlos gültig ist auch, was Stojkov als Charakteristika für jeden Jugendjargon herausstellte: Semantisch veränderte, in metaphorischer Vielfalt gebrauchte Wörter stärken die Gruppenkohäsion und verschaffen dem jungen Individuum in der Gruppe Prestige[35].

Um 1970 tauchten in Bulgarien plötzlich zahlreiche Romane auf, in denen Probleme der Jugend in derem authentischen Jargon beschrieben wurden. Das löste bewegte Diskussionen aus, die das eigentliche Sprachphänomen positiv werteten: der freche Jargon ist ein willkommenes Gegengift gegen offizielle Sprachschludereien[36].

Diese Einstellung hat sich in den 80er Jahren generell noch verstärkt. Natürlich gibt es Gegenstimmen (die sich an den politischen Widerhaken dieser Sprachkonvention reiben), aber allgemein überwiegt Wohlwollen. Man sammelte und analysierte die lexikalischen Teile des Jargons – seine witzigen Verdrehungen, lakonischen Anspielungen, reaktionsschnellen Übernahmen, ironischen Sprüche, politischen Ketzereien usw. Das tat man in dem Bewußtsein, hier auf eine sprachliche Goldader gestoßen zu sein, aus der Anstöße für eine Belebung der Sprache generell zu entnehmen sind. Denn: „Im Jargon spiegelt sich die Lebensfähigkeit der Sprache. Nur in toten Sprachen gibt es keine Jargons"[37]. In diesem Bereich zeichnen sich sogar schon interessante „Rückkopplungen" ab: Sprachliche Belebung erzeugt ein neues Outfit der Medien. Beweis dafür ist seit Frühsommer 1988 die TV-Sendung *Dobro utro* (Guten Morgen), die ein Riesenerfolg unter jungen Bulgaren wurde, obwohl sie am frühen Morgen des Sonnabends ausgestrahlt wird; die Zuschauer honorieren eben, daß hier ganz bewußt gegen alte Denk- und Sprachschablonen vorgegangen wird – mit neuen Themen in jugendgemäßer Sprache und Offenheit.

---

[35] Stojkov, S.: Sofijskijat učeničeski govor (Der Sofioter Schülerjargon), in: Godišnik na Sofijskija Universitet-Istoriko-filologičeski fakultet. 42 (1945/1946).

[36] Vgl. Oschlies, W.: „Napred! Bezgrižni tarikati" – Soziolinguistische Bemerkungen zur Subkultur der bulgarischen Jugend, in: Festschrift für Wolfgang Gesemann. Bd. 3. Neuried 1986, S. 211–233.

[37] Vălkov, P.: Za žargona – nežargonno (Über den Jargon ohne Jargon), in: Narodna Kultura. (1988) 8; vgl. auch Karastojčeva, C.: Intelektualizacijata v săvremennija bălgarski mladežki sleng (Die Intellektualisierung im modernen bulgarischen Jugendslang), in: Ezik i literatura. 41 (1986) 1, S. 23–35; Dičev, I.: Igra na ezik (Sprachspiel), in: Mladež. (1987) 4; im Mai 1988 erschien schließlich noch eine soziolinguistische Studie über den bulgarischen Jugendjargon mit zahlreichen Beispielen zu diesem: Karastojčeva, C.: Bălgarskijat mladežki govor (Der bulgarische Jugendjargon). Sofia 1988.

5. Dialekte als Sprachquelle

Seit den späten 70er Jahren macht sich in Osteuropa ein Trend zum Regionalismus bemerkbar, der auch eine Renaissance regionaler Dialekte mit sich führt. Das ist wichtig, denn gerade Dialekte galten unter ideologischem Aspekt lange als „Sprache der Plebejer und Ausgebeuteten", die irgendwann einmal „absterben" würde.

Wenn diese Sichtweise in Bulgarien nicht so massiv wie anderswo galt, dann wegen des immer noch unverkennbaren Beitrags der Dialekte zur Genese der bulgarischen Hochsprache, wegen der Bedeutung der Mundartenforschung mit Blick auf bulgarische Ethnogenese und Siedlungsgeschichte und wegen der politisch postulierten Sprachenidentität Bulgarisch – Makedonisch.

Natürlich wünscht kein Bulgare, Radionachrichten oder wissenschaftliche Vorlesungen in einem Rhodopen-Dialekt zu hören, aber bedauernd konstatiert er, daß Dialekte einmal offiziell als „falsche und kulturlose Sprache" bezeichnet wurden. Denn Bulgarien ist ein Land, das auf relativ kleinem Territorium eine enorme Vielfalt der Mundarten bietet – bei der Arbeit am „Bulgarischen Dialektatlas" stellt man z. B. fest, daß selbst scheinbar kongruente Dialekte bei näherer Betrachtung weitgehende Differenzierungen aufweisen.

Seit langem dominiert eine durchweg positive Einstellung gegenüber Dialekten, die aus zwei Positionen herrührt. Die eine Position ist poetisch-sprachschöpferischer Natur und wird am nachhaltigsten von Nikolaj Chajtov vertreten. Er möchte die Dialekte stärker beachtet sehen – weil sie bulgarisch sind, weil ihre Lexik vielfach schöner als die standardsprachliche ist, weil mit ihrer Hilfe der Zustrom der Fremdwörter gebremst werden könnte, weil sie die Palette der Synonyme ungemein erweitern könnten[38]. Die andere Position ist sozialwissenschaftlich-utilitaristisch und nutzt Dialekte als Gradmesser für zahlreiche Entwicklungen: Die Untersuchung erhaltener altbulgarischer Phoneme (z. B. Nasale) gibt Aufschluß zur Sprachgeschichte, die Vielfalt der Dialekte zwingt zu schärferer Kategorienbestimmung im linguistischen Instrumentarium, Veränderungen der Dialekte bezeugen die Wirkung von Industrialisierung und sozialem Wandel, desgleichen sind sie Seismographen für Veränderungen der Stratifikation der Gesellschaft und ihrer regionalen Kulturen, Teile der Lexik und Syntax der Dialekte eignen sich für eine hochsprachliche Wiederbelebung, Dialekte sind (mögliche) Brücken zu den Sprachen von Nachbarvölkern, Diglossieformen zwischen Standardsprache und Dialekt lassen Rückschlüsse auf die Wirkung der gesamten Kultur- und Bildungspolitik zu.

Mit anderen Worten: „Das moderne bulgarische Dorf überwindet antagonistische und bestehende Unterschiede (...) Aber auf dem Weg seiner sozialistischen Entwicklung bewahrt es zahlreiche spezifische Besonderheiten, die es als spezifischen Siedlungstyp erhalten, welcher bestimmten sozialen Bedürfnissen in der gegenwärtigen Entwicklungsetappe entspricht. Warum soll unter diesen spezifischen Besonderheiten nicht auch der Dialekt sein, der immer noch wertvolle Sprachschätze in sich schließt"[39]?

---

[38]) Chajtov (Anm. 34).
[39]) Kožucharova, V.: Vzaimodejstvie meždu dialekt i knižoven ezik v săvremennoto bălgarsko selo (Wechselwirkung zwischen Dialekt und Literatursprache im modernen bulgarischen Dorf), in: Sociologičeski problemi. (1987) 1, S. 96–104.

Volkskultur

Klaus Roth, München

I. Voraussetzungen: Die Volkskultur im Übergang – II. Volkskultur nach 1944: 1. Volkskultur als Relikt – 2. Staatlich gelenkte und gepflegte Volkskultur – 3. Volkskultur in der Moderne

I. Voraussetzungen: Die Volkskultur im Übergang

Die traditionelle Volkskultur (VK) erlangte in Bulgarien aus historischen Gründen eine außerordentliche Bedeutung und ist für die sozio-ökonomische und kulturelle Entwicklung des Landes bis heute weitaus stärker bestimmend geblieben als etwa in Mitteleuropa. Dem Studium der VK und ihrer spezifischen historischen Voraussetzungen kommt daher für das Verständnis des heutigen Bulgarien eine entscheidende Rolle zu.

Unter VK wird im folgenden die Gesamtheit des kulturellen Systems, d. h. die gesamte materielle Kultur, die Verhaltensformen, Handlungen und Äußerungen sowie die Vorstellungen, Werte und Normen der großen Mehrheit der Bevölkerung verstanden. Die traditionelle VK des balkanischen Typs als ein kulturelles System, das auf der Patriarchalität gründet, bestand in Bulgarien in den ländlichen Regionen bis in die Zwischenkriegszeit. Diese *patriarchale Altkultur*[1]) ist durch eine Reihe von Merkmalen gekennzeichnet, die sowohl aus dem Wesen der patriarchalen Gesellschaftsform als auch aus dem Einfluß der osmanischen Herrschaft und Kultur herrühren. Die wesentlichsten seien angeführt:

1. Die überragende Bedeutung der *Sippe* und *Familie*. Die patriarchale Familie war nach Blutsverwandtschaft, Geschlecht und Alter strikt hierarchisch strukturiert. Die Mehrfamilie in der Form der *Zadruga* herrschte (in der westlichen Hälfte des Landes) bis zum ausgehenden 19. Jh. vor und verschwand erst um den II. Weltkrieg[2]). Die Bedeutung der Familie und der Verwandtschaft ist bis heute fast ungebrochen[3]).

Abkürzungen
BE   = Bălgarska etnografija (Bulgarische Ethnographie). Sofia 1976ff.
BF   = Bălgarski folklor. (Bulgarische Folklore). Sofia 1975ff.
BNT   = Bălgarsko narodno tvorčestvo (Bulgarisches Volksschaffen). 13 Bde. Sofia 1961–1965.
SbNU = Sbornik za narodni umotvorenija, nauka i knižnina (Sammlung für Volksschaffen, Wissenschaft und Literatur). Sofia 1889ff.

[1]) Vgl. Matl, J.: Die patriarchale Altkultur und der Weg zur Neukultur, in: Aspects of the Balkans. Continuity and Change. Ed. H. Birnbaum u. a. Paris 1972, S. 355–369.

[2]) s. Wilhelmy, H.: Hochbulgarien. 2 Bde. Kiel 1935/36. Bd. 1, S. 233–235; Vakarelski, Ch.: Bulgarische Volkskunde. Berlin 1969, S. 253–256.

[3]) Zu den positiven und negativen Auswirkungen des südslawischen Familismus vgl. Simić, A.:

2. Die weitreichende Bedeutung der *Sitte* und des *Gewohnheitsrechts*. Das System patriarchaler Rechtsnormen, Sitten und Brauchformen bestimmte über Jahrhunderte (neben dem orthodoxen und dem islamischen Recht) umfassend das sozialethische Verhalten der bulgarischen Bevölkerung. Es fand seinen Niederschlag in Institutionen wie der Kaufehe und dem Brautraub, der Wahlverwandtschaft (*pobratimjavane, kumstvo*) und dem Kodex der Ehre, der bäuerlichen Kooperation und dem Festhalten an rituellen und brauchtümlichen Formen[4]). Gerade das (historisch notwendige) Beharren bei traditionellen Normen und Werten förderte jedoch einen Konservatismus, der sich bei der Modernisierung dann hemmend auswirkte.

3. Die *Isolation* der Gemeinden und der *Stadt-Land-Gegensatz*. Bedingt durch die osmanische Verwaltungsstruktur blieb die weit überwiegend bäuerliche Bevölkerung in ihrem Denken und Handeln wie in ihrer Welterfahrung auf die Gemeinde begrenzt. Der Parochialismus wurde verstärkt durch den krassen Gegensatz zwischen osmanisch-islamischer Stadt und bulgarisch-christlichem Dorf[5]). Das daraus resultierende tiefe Mißtrauen gegenüber der Stadt als Herrschaftssitz hat lange Zeit nachgewirkt.

Die wichtigste Ursache dafür, daß die traditionelle VK eine so dominante Rolle spielte, war ohne Zweifel die lange Osmanenherrschaft. Durch die Beseitigung der autochthonen Eliten und ihrer Kultur, durch die Osmanisierung der Städte sowie durch die Einführung des auf der Religionszugehörigkeit basierenden osmanischen Verwaltungssystems (*millet*-System) wurde die Bevölkerung sozial nivelliert und in den Dorfgemeinden partikularisiert. Die VK erlangte dadurch im 15.–19. Jh. die Funktion und die Qualität einer alle Sozialschichten umgreifenden Kultur und konnte in vielen Bereichen Leistungen von großer Ausdruckskraft hervorbringen. Das Beharren bei der dörflichen VK gewährleistete damit über Jahrhunderte osmanischer Herrschaft hinweg die Bewahrung der kulturellen und ethnischen Identität[6]). Noch mehr in den Vordergrund trat diese Funktion der VK um die Mitte des 19. Jh., als, ausgelöst durch die romantische und national orientierte Rückwendung zur „Volkspoesie" und insbesondere das Vorbild Vuk Karadžićs, auch die bulgarische Volkspoesie in ihrem Wert für den nationalen Befreiungskampf entdeckt wurde. Bedeutende Sammler und Schriftsteller wie die Brüder Konstantin und Dimităr Miladinov, Marko Cepenkov, Stefan Verkovič, Petko Slavejkov, Georgi Rakovski, Kuzman Šapkarev u. a. machten seit etwa 1860 Aufzeichnungen der Volkspoesie in dem Bewußtsein, damit zur nationalen Wiedergeburt beizutragen. In dieser reichen *mündlichen Überlieferung* waren es neben den Volkserzählungen[7]) und lyrischen Liedern

---

Urbanization and Modernization in Yugoslavia, in: Urban Life in Mediterranean Europe. Ed. M. Kenny u. a. Urbana, Chicago 1983, S. 203–224, bes. 208–212.

[4]) Matl (Anm. 1), S. 356f.

[5]) Jelavich, Ch. and B.: The Establishment of the Balkan National States, 1804–1920. Seattle, London 1977, S. 4–9.

[6]) Zur Rolle der Kirche für die Wahrung des kulturellen Erbes vgl. das Kapitel „Churches and Religious Communities" von M. Pundeff.

[7]) Sammlungen von Märchen: Šapkarev, K. A.: Sbornik ot bălgarski narodni umotvorenija (Sammlung bulgarischen Volksschaffens). Sofia 1891–92; SbNU; BNT.

insbesondere die Heldenepen[8]), die ein hohes dichterisches Können offenbarten und die – in den Zyklen um die Kosovo-Schlacht, um Krali Marko und andere Helden – zusammen mit den Hajdukenliedern die Erinnerung an wichtige Ereignisse der balkanischen Geschichte wachhielten. Die Volkspoesie hat das Schaffen bulgarischer Dichter und Schriftsteller seither nachhaltig beeinflußt[9]).

Die *materielle VK* erreichte, bedingt durch die verbesserte wirtschaftliche Situation des bulgarischen Gebietes im Osmanischen Reich und die Entwicklung des Handwerks[10]), wohl aber auch unter dem Einfluß ausländischer Vorbilder in den letzten fünf Jahrzehnten osmanischer Herrschaft ihre höchste Blüte: Im Hausbau und in der Innenausstattung (Schnitzkunst), in der Möbel- und Keramikherstellung sowie in der Metallverarbeitung, vor allem aber in der Herstellung und Verzierung von Textilien (Teppiche, Trachten) und in der Malerei (Wandmalerei, Ikonenmalerei) zeigte sich hohe Differenzierung und beachtliches künstlerisches Niveau[11]).

Erst relativ spät ist versucht worden, die regionale Vielfalt und Differenzierung der VK systematisch zu erfassen und zu einer *kulturräumlichen Gliederung* zu gelangen. Unter Einbeziehung einer großen Menge von Elementen der materiellen, sozialen und geistigen VK kam Gavazzi 1956 zu einer kulturgeographischen Gliederung der Balkanhalbinsel, in der Bulgarien Anteil an sechs Kulturräumen hat[12]): (1) Die Donauebene gehört dem sich nördlich der Donau fortsetzenden „Ostdonaugebiet" an; (2) der größte Teil des Vorbalkans und des Balkangebirges bildet das „Balkan-Gebiet"; (3) das Strandžagebirge im Südosten ist dem bis ans Marmarameer reichenden „Thrakischen Gebiet" zuzurechnen; (4) das Gebirgsmassiv der Rhodopen gehört dem bis an die Ägäis reichenden „Rhodope-Gebiet" zu; (5) der Südwesten Bulgariens mit dem Pirin- und Rilagebirge ist Teil des „Makedonischen Gebiets", dessen Zentrum in Südjugoslawien und Nordgriechenland liegt; (6) eine Region sehr spezifischen Charakters bildet schließlich im Nordwesten um Sofia herum das „Šopen-Gebiet". Mit Ausnahme zweier Regionen (2 und 6) hat das heutige Bulgarien somit Anteil an volkskulturellen Regionen, die in heutige Nachbarländer hinüberreichen. Vakarelski, der sich auf das heutige bulgarische Staatsgebiet beschränkt, kommt zu einer recht ähnlichen Gliederung; Abweichungen ergeben sich dadurch, daß er stärker die „ethnographischen Gruppen" (Šopi, Dobrudžanci, Poljanci, Trakijci, Rupci, Balkanci, Makedonci) und ihre Dialekte betont[13]).

Die ersten Anzeichen des Zurückweichens der traditionellen VK zeigten sich um die Mitte des 19. Jh., als die reicheren Handwerker und insbesondere die Fernkaufleute der privilegierten Gebirgsstädtchen (Koprivštica, Gabrovo, Trjavna, Kotel

---

[8]) Sammlungen von Heldenepen: SbNU; BNT; Romanska, C. (Hrsg.): Bălgarski junaški epos (Das bulgarische Heldenepos). Sofia 1971 (=SbNU 53).

[9]) Vgl. das Kapitel „Literatur" von R. Lauer.

[10]) Paskaleva, V.: Die Entwicklung des Handwerks und die kulturelle Vermittlungsfunktion von Handwerkern bei der „Europäisierung" Bulgariens im 19. Jh., in: Handwerk in Mittel- und Südosteuropa. Hrsg. K. Roth. München 1987, S. 129–136; vgl. das Kapitel „Industry and Handicrafts" von M. Jackson.

[11]) s. Vakarelski (Anm. 2); Boschkov, A.: Die bulgarische Volkskunst. Recklinghausen 1972.

[12]) Gavazzi, M.: Die kulturgeographische Gliederung Südosteuropas, in: Südost-Forschungen. 15 (1956), S. 5–21, bes. 8–16.

[13]) Vakarelski (Anm. 2), Karte II.

u. a.) neben neuen Ideen und Vorstellungen auch Gegenstände westlicher Wohnkultur (wie Betten, hohe Tische und Stühle, Schränke, Eßgeschirr usw.) mitbrachten und damit den ersten Anstoß zum Wandel der materiellen Kultur gaben. Nach der Befreiung des Landes weitete sich die Übernahme westlicher Innovationen erheblich aus, konzentrierte sich aber zunächst auf Sofia und einige wenige größere Städte, die ein modernes Stadtbild mit neuem Straßen- und Verkehrsnetz, öffentlichen Gebäuden und bürgerlichen Wohnhäusern erhielten[14]. Der Wandel erfaßte alle Bereiche der Alltagskultur (materielle Kultur, soziale Formen und Verhaltensweisen, Vorstellungen und Normen), jedoch mit recht unterschiedlichem Tempo. Er wurde begünstigt durch die negative Bewertung der VK nach der Befreiung durch die junge bürgerliche Elite: Die VK galt nun nicht mehr als Ausdruck nationaler Identität, sondern als rückständig, primitiv und überfrachtet mit osmanischem Erbe, das der „Europäisierung"[15] im Wege stand. Die Modernisierung verlief in Südosteuropa nicht als Prozeß der imitativen Aneignung des Gesamtsystems der „*Neukultur*"[16], sondern vielmehr als partielle, selektive und adaptierende Übernahme westlicher Vorbilder[17]. Bezeichnend blieben daher cultural-lag-Phänomene, also Entwicklungsunterschiede zwischen verschiedenen Bereichen der Kultur, und Erscheinungen der oberflächlichen oder symbolischen Modernisierung[18].

Landflucht und Urbanisierung hatten nach der Befreiung zum starken Anwachsen einiger Städte und dort zur sozialen Differenzierung in eine kleine bürgerliche Elite und breite Schichten von Kleinbürgern und städtischem Proletariat geführt[19]. Durch eine aktive Bildungspolitik in wenigen Jahren alphabetisiert[20] und von der dörflichen VK entfernt, entwickelten letztere besonders in Sofia und Plovdiv eigene, zwischen VK und westlicher Kultur stehende Lebens- und Ausdrucksformen. Diese *städtische Popularkultur* äußerte sich in der alltäglichen Lebensweise (Wohnen, Kleidung, Nahrung), in den Formen der Unterhaltung und Freizeitgestaltung (Cafés, Tanzveranstaltungen usw.) sowie in neuen Sitten und Umgangsformen[21]; beach-

---

[14] s. Wilhelmy (Anm. 2), Bd. 2, S. 117–156.
[15] Zu „Europäisierung", „Entosmanisierung" und „osmanischem Erbe" s. Matl, J.: Die Europäisierung des Südostens, in: Völker und Kulturen Südosteuropas. München 1959, S. 218–236; ders.: Das orientalische Element in der Kultur der Balkanvölker, in: Beiträge zur Kenntnis Südosteuropas und des Nahen Orients. Bd. 2. München 1967, S. 71–82; Stavrianos, L. S.: The Influence of the West on the Balkans, in: The Balkans in Transition. Ed. Ch. and B. Jelavich. Berkeley, Los Angeles 1963, S. 184–226; Vucinich, W. S.: Some Aspects of the Ottoman Legacy, in: ebenda, S. 81–114; Lory, B.: Le Sort de l'Heritage Ottoman en Bulgarie. L'Exemple des Villes Bulgares 1878–1900. Istanbul 1985.
[16] Nach Matl (Anm. 1).
[17] Schmaus, A.: Die geistige Kultur der Südslawen, in: Südosteuropa-Jahrbuch. 3 (1959), S. 188f.; Roth, K.: Wie „europäisch" ist Südosteuropa?, in: Wandel der Volkskultur. Festschrift für G. Wiegelmann. Hrsg. N.-A. Bringéus u.a. Münster, Bd. 1, S. 225–28.
[18] Sundhaussen, H.: Neue Literatur zu Problemen der Industrialisierung und der nachholenden Entwicklung in den Ländern der europäischen Peripherie, in: Südost-Forschungen. 43 (1984), S. 287–303, bes. 290.
[19] Vgl. das Kapitel „Social Structure" von R. Whitaker.
[20] Vgl. das Kapitel „Schulsystem" von P. Bachmaier.
[21] Vgl. Georgiev, G.: Osvoboždenieto i etnokulturnoto razvitie na bǎlgarskija narod (Die Befreiung und die ethnokulturelle Entwicklung des bulgarischen Volkes 1877–1900). Sofia 1979; ders.: Sofija i Sofijanci (Sofia und die Sofioter 1873–1944). Sofia 1983.

tenswert ist darüber hinaus das Aufkommen neuer Ausdrucksformen wie der städtische Jahrmarktsgesang[22]), die vielen Stadtlieder[23]) sowie die sehr vielfältige Popularliteratur[24]). Diese städtische Popularkultur erreichte in der Zwischenkriegszeit mehr und mehr die ländlichen Regionen und nahm durch die Verbreitung der Massenmedien (Buchdruck, Radio, Schallplatte, Film) die Züge einer medialen Massenkultur an.

Das Leben der Bauern und Kleinhandwerker, die um 1930 noch über 80 % der Bevölkerung ausmachten, verlief bis in die Zwischenkriegszeit weiter in den Bahnen der traditionellen VK: Wenn auch einzelne Elemente dieser patriarchalen Kultur (wie etwa die Mehrfamilie, Brautraub und Kaufehe) langsam zurückwichen und das traditionelle Handwerk als Schöpfer der materiellen VK dem Ansturm ausländischer Industriewaren weichen mußte, so blieb sie doch als kulturelles *System* bestehen. Ihr Zusammenbruch vollzog sich dann jedoch in nur wenigen Jahren zwischen etwa 1925 und 1935, als – wohl infolge der Kriege und der durch sie bedingten Kulturkontakte und großen Bevölkerungsbewegungen – die Popularkultur und städtisch-bürgerliche Kultur auf die Dörfer vordrang[25]).

II. Volkskultur nach 1944

Obwohl die VK als ein das Leben der Menschen umfassend regulierendes System in der Zwischenkriegszeit durch neue Kulturformen verdrängt worden war, blieben dennoch auf dem Lande wesentliche Teilbereiche der Altkultur, insbesondere in der bäuerlichen Lebens- und Wirtschaftsweise und im Kleinhandwerk bis über den II. Weltkrieg hinaus erhalten. Einen zweiten tiefen Einschnitt brachte hier in den frühen 50er Jahren die breite forcierte Kollektivierung der Landwirtschaft und der massenhafte Einsatz der Handwerker in den neu errichteten Industriebetrieben. Innerhalb weniger Jahre wurde das *materielle* Erbe der für viele Jahrhunderte beherrschenden VK für die große Mehrheit der Bevölkerung obsolet. Doch auch nach diesen tiefgreifenden Prozessen der Urbanisierung, Modernisierung, Industrialisierung und Kollektivierung ist die VK keinesfalls verschwunden. Sie tritt uns heute vielmehr in drei verschiedenen Erscheinungsformen entgegen: 1. als Reliktkultur in marginalen Regionen, 2. als gelenkte und gepflegte VK und 3. als der modernen Zeit angepaßte VK.

---

[22]) Roth, K.: Der bulgarische Bänkelsang heute. Zum Wandel des Liedrepertoires eines Sängers, in: Festschrift für E. Klusen zum 75. Geburtstag. Hrsg. G. Noll u.a. Bonn 1984, S. 417–434.
[23]) Kaufman, N.: Bălgarski gradski pesni (Bulgarische Stadtlieder). Sofia 1968.
[24]) Roth, J. u. K.: Gattungen und Inhalte der bulgarischen Popularliteratur, in: Bulgarien. Internationale Beziehungen in Geschichte, Kultur und Kunst. Neuried 1984, S. 163–182.
[25]) Vgl. Wilhelmy (Anm. 2); Sanders, I.: Balkan Village. Lexington 1949, Westport ²1975; Georgiev (Anm. 21).

1. Volkskultur als Relikt

Die Vorgänge der Verdrängung der traditionellen VK verliefen in Bulgarien (wie auch anderswo) nicht gleichmäßig, sondern mit z. T. erheblichen regionalen und sozialen Unterschieden. In den stadtnahen und industrialisierten Regionen wurden die Stadt-Land-Unterschiede ausgeglichen und die durch Landflucht rapide wachsende Stadtbevölkerung[26] in den Modernisierungsprozeß einbezogen. Auf der anderen Seite standen periphere, meist gebirgige und wirtschaftlich unterentwickelte Regionen, in denen die zunehmend überalterte Dorfbevölkerung lange in traditionellen Lebensformen verharrte. In diesen marginalen Regionen, in denen Teile der VK als Rest und Relikt z. T. bis heute weiterbestehen, sind auch die meisten ethnischen und religiösen Minderheiten beheimatet.

a) Wenig erschlossene und kulturell *marginale Gebiete* sind zum einen die gebirgigen Regionen an der westlichen und südlichen Staatsgrenze wie etwa das Pirin-Gebiet, die südlichen Rhodopen und das Sakar- und Strandža-Gebiet, zum andern auch die Dobrudscha und Teile des östlichen Balkangebirges. Es ist die Reliktkultur solcher Regionen, die den Hauptteil der Untersuchungen der bulgarischen Ethnographie und Folklore bildet. Umfangreiche Forschungsexpeditionen wurden unternommen, die reiches Material an Epen und Liedern, Erzählungen und Bräuchen, Trachten und Geräten erbrachten und zu umfassenden Regionaldarstellungen und Sammelwerken führten[27]. Überall wird ein Zurückgehen und ein Funktionswandel der traditionellen Formen konstatiert und die Untersuchungen sind zumeist getragen von dem (romantischen) Gedanken, von der untergehenden VK soviel wie möglich zu sammeln und zu retten.

b) Die VK *religiöser Gruppen*[28] ist wenig erforscht. Wohl wegen ihrer marginalen Lage und gefördert durch die Religion blieben die *Pomaken*, islamisierte Bulgaren in den Rhodopen und im zentralen Vorbalkan, länger der traditionellen Kultur verhaftet[29]. Ihre kulturellen Ausdrucksformen ähneln weitgehend denen der benachbarten christlichen Bevölkerung, wie Kaufman am Beispiel der Liedüberlieferung aufgezeigt hat[30]; Unterschiede ergeben sich in den durch den Glauben bestimmten Bereichen (Riten, Bräuche, Vorstellungen). Das gleiche gilt auch für die um Plovdiv wohnenden *Katholiken* (Paulikianer).

c) Angesichts der Modernisierungspolitik des bulgarischen Staates und seines Strebens nach einer Gesellschaft, die durch „soziale und ideelle Einheit sowie die

---

[26] Anteil der Stadtbevölkerung: 1880 19,2%, 1934 21,4%, 1946 24,7%, 1965 46,5%, 1980 62,5% (Quelle: SG. 1987).

[27] Primovski, A.: Bit i kultura na rodopskite bălgari (Lebensweise und Kultur der Bulgaren in den Rhodopen). Sofia 1973 (SbNU 54); Dobrudža. Sofia 1976; Strandžanski folklor (Folklore aus Strandža). Sofia 1983 (SbNU 57); Kapanci. Sofia 1985; Plovdivski kraj (Region Plovdiv). Sofia 1986; vgl. als ältere Regionalstudien Kostov, S.; Peteva, E.: Selski bit i izkustvo v Sofijsko (Dorfleben und -kunst im Kreis Sofia). Sofia 1935, und Wilhelmy (Anm. 2).

[28] Vgl. das Kapitel „Churches and Religious Communities" von M. Pundeff.

[29] Vakarelski, Ch.: Altertümliche Elemente in Lebensweise und Kultur der bulgarischen Mohammedaner, in: Zeitschrift für Balkanologie. 4 (1966), S. 149–172; Primovski 1973 (wie Anm. 27).

[30] Kaufman, N.: Pesni na bălgarite mochamedani ot Rodopite (Die Lieder der islamischen Bulgaren in den Rhodopen), in: Rodopski sbornik. 2 (1969), S. 41–130.

ethnokulturelle und geistig-ideologische Vereinheitlichung der Nation"[31]) gekennzeichnet sein soll, wird für die *ethnischen Gruppen* die Wahrung der kulturellen Identität zunehmend schwieriger[32]). Folge des Bemühens um eine „einheitliche sozialistische Nation" ist, daß auch die Kultur der ethnischen Minderheiten nur geringe wissenschaftliche Beachtung findet. Eine Sonderstellung nehmen die als Bulgaren aufgefaßten *Makedonier* Südwestbulgariens ein, deren VK umfassend erforscht worden ist[33]).

Bei den ethnischen Gruppen in Bulgarien ist zu trennen zwischen den in den Städten lebenden Gruppen der Armenier, Juden, Griechen und Russen[34]), die – mit bestimmten eigenen Ausdrucksformen – der urbanen Kultur zugehören, und den Türken, Roma, Karakatschanen, Tataren, Aromunen und anderen Gruppen[35]), die in ländlichen, vor allem marginalen Regionen leben und ihre VK z. T. bis in die Gegenwart beibehalten.

Die *türkische* Bevölkerung Bulgariens, im wesentlichen in den drei ehemaligen Bezirken Šumen, Chaskovo und Ruse beheimatet und dominant in der Landwirtschaft tätig, hat sich, wie Tachirov in mehreren Tabellen indirekt nachweist[36]), in wichtigen Bereichen ihres religiösen und kulturellen Lebens dem Modernisierungs- und Assimilierungsdruck widersetzt; festzustellen ist sogar ein ausdrückliches Festhalten an den wichtigen islamischen Ritualen und Festtagen und eine geringere Akzeptanz neuer sozialistischer Rituale[37]). Auch in den Familienstrukturen, in der dörflich-agrarischen Lebensweise und im Alphabetisierungsgrad zeigen sich erhebliche Unterschiede zur bulgarischen Bevölkerung[38]). Der Assimilations- und Modernisierungsdruck auf die türkische Bevölkerung hat sich seit 1985 erheblich verstärkt.

Starkem Assimilationsdruck war schon in den 50er Jahren die kleine Gruppe der *Karakatschanen* ausgesetzt. Für die Hirtennomaden wurden „in den Städten und Dörfern kleinere oder größere Karakatschanenwohnviertel mit vollkommen modernen... Eigenheimen" eingerichtet, und sie wurden in neue Berufe und Lebensgewohnheiten eingewiesen[39]). Trotz der – z. T. forcierten – Anpassungsprozesse zeigt

---

[31]) Tachirov, Š.: Socialističeska obrednost i duchovno edinstvo (Sozialistisches Brauchtum und geistige Einheit). Sofia 1984, S. 5.

[32]) Vgl. das Kapitel „Nationale Minderheiten" von S. Troebst, sowie Höpken, W.: Modernisierung und Nationalismus: Sozialgeschichtliche Aspekte der bulgarischen Minderheitenpolitik gegenüber den Türken, in: Südosteuropa. 35 (1986), S. 437–457.

[33]) Vgl. Pirinski kraj (Die Region Pirin). Sofia 1980; Daskalova, D. u.a.: Narodna proza ot blagoevgradski okräg (Volksprosa aus dem Kreis Blagoevgrad). Sofia 1985 (SbNU 58).

[34]) 1965 lebten in Bulgarien 20282 Armenier, 10815 Russen, 8241 Griechen und 5105 Juden; s. das Kapitel „Nationale Minderheiten" von S. Troebst.

[35]) 1965 lebten in Bulgarien 780928 Türken, 148874 Roma, 6430 Tataren, 4178 Karakatschanen, 3749 Rumänen, 487 Aromunen und 484 Serben (wie Anm. 34).

[36]) Tachirov, Š.: Etnokulturni procesi sred bǎlgarskite turci (Ethnokulturelle Prozesse bei den bulgarischen Türken), in: BE. 5 (1980) 4, S. 3–16, hier S. 7–9.

[37]) Höpken (Anm. 32), S. 450–454.

[38]) Ebenda, S. 441 f.

[39]) Marinov, V.: Prinos kǎm izučavaneto na proizchoda, bita i kulturata na Karakačanite v Bǎlgarija (Beitrag zur Erforschung der Herkunft, Lebensweise und Kultur der Karakatschanen in Bulgarien). Sofia 1964, S. 137.

sich jedoch auch in dieser Gruppe ein Beharren bei traditionellen Formen etwa im Bereich der Familienbeziehungen und in der Berufsausübung als Hirten[40]).

Auch bei den *Roma* sind seit den 50er Jahren erhebliche Anstrengungen unternommen worden, sie seßhaft zu machen und sie in den Industrialisierungsprozeß einzugliedern. Die Folge war bei vielen Roma die – zumindest äußerliche – Assimilation unter Verlust der ethnischen Kultur. Ein beachtlicher Teil von ihnen ist jedoch halbnomadisch geblieben, bewahrt durch Endogamie die traditionelle Gruppenkultur und geht den seit langer Zeit typischen Wanderberufen (Musiker, Kesselflicker, Scherenschleifer, Altmaterialhändler usw.) nach; wie auch in anderen südosteuropäischen Ländern sind die Roma weithin zu professionellen Trägern der Volksmusiktradition geworden[41]). Ethnographische Arbeiten über die Roma liegen in sehr geringer Zahl vor[42]).

2. Staatlich gelenkte und gepflegte Volkskultur

Im Verhältnis des sozialistischen Bulgarien zur traditionellen VK lassen sich zwei Phasen unterscheiden: In den Jahren bis etwa 1965, der Phase forcierter Industrialisierung und Kollektivierung, standen zahlreiche Elemente der VK (wie etwa traditionelle Einstellungen und Verhaltensweisen) den sozio-ökonomischen Zielen entgegen. Die VK wurde eher negativ bewertet und hatte geringe kulturpolitische Bedeutung.

Wenn auch die negative Einstellung gegenüber den „fortschrittshemmenden" Elementen der VK blieb, so zeigte sich doch seit etwa 1965 eine differenzierte Bewertung, die zu einem tiefgreifenden Wandel der Kulturpolitik und zur massiven Pflege der VK führte. Die positivere Bewertung und Hinwendung zur VK hatte mehrere Ursachen: (a) Betont wurde nun, daß seit dem 19. Jh. in der VK als der Lebens- und Ausdrucksform der einfachen Bauern und Handwerker eine „demokratische" Tradition gewachsen und zudem eine „proletarische (!) künstlerische Kultur" entstanden sei, die im sozialistischen Staat Beachtung verdiene[43]). (b) Die VK war zudem schöpferische Leistung des eigenen Volkes und konnte – neben der Hochkultur – zur ästhetischen und nationalen Erziehung der Jugend beitragen. (c) Die VK wurde zu einem wesentlichen Element der zu schaffenden „einheitlichen sozialistischen Nation" insofern, als ihr bei der Formierung der „sozialistischen Lebensweise" eine wesentliche Rolle zugewiesen wurde. (d) Die VK konnte für die Außenrepräsentation des Landes eingesetzt werden; für den seit 1960 stetig wachsenden Tourismus[44]) wurde ein nationales Image entwickelt, das vor allem auf Relikte der VK („Folklore") rekurrierte. (e) Als Folge der überhasteten Industrialisierung und Urbanisierung kam – zuerst unter der

---

[40]) Vgl. Bonina, Z.: Săvremennoto karakačansko semejstvo (Die heutige Karakatschanenfamilie), in: BE. 6 (1981) 3/4, S. 39–49.

[41]) s. Silverman, C.: Bulgarian Gypsies: Adaptation in a Socialist Context, in: Nomadic Peoples. 21/22 (1986), S. 51–62, bes. S. 55f.

[42]) Vgl. Silverman (Anm. 41), S. 61f.

[43]) Parpulova, L.: Bălgarskata socialističeska kultura i folklorăt (Die bulgarische sozialistische Kultur und die Folklore), in: BF. 6 (1980) 4, S. 25–34, bes. S. 25f.

[44]) Vgl. das Kapitel „Handel, Versorgung und Verkehr" von F.-L. Altmann.

Stadtbevölkerung – das Gefühl des unwiederbringlichen Verlusts kultureller Identität auf, was zu einer nostalgischen Rückwendung zum Dorf und seiner Kultur führte.

Von besonderem Gewicht war der Einbezug der VK in die „sozialistische Kultur und Lebensweise", deren Durchsetzung in den Mittelpunkt der Kulturpolitik rückte. Die „sozialistische Lebensweise" umfaßt alle Seiten des sozialen und kulturellen Lebens des sozialistischen Menschen und damit „die Gesamtheit der typischen Lebensbedingungen, der Normen und Formen der Lebenstätigkeit, der gegenseitigen Beziehungen zwischen den Menschen"[45]). Der nationalen VK kam in diesem Konzept eine wichtige Rolle zu, denn es galt, „jene Einwirkungen zu erklären, die die nationalen Besonderheiten der Menschen in den sozialistischen Ländern auf deren Lebensweise ausüben..."[46]). Der Ethnograph hatte jene Merkmale aus der VK herauszuarbeiten, die die ethnische Spezifität begründen, um diese dann in die nationale sozialistische Kultur zu integrieren. Dabei war aber zu trennen zwischen „nützlichen" und „schädlichen" Elementen: Allein die für wertvoll und „fortschrittlich" erachteten Elemente durften zum Gegenstand staatlicher Volkskulturpflege werden (s. u.).

Ein zentraler Teil der „sozialistischen Lebensweise" ist das System der sozialistischen Festtage, Bräuche und Rituale[47]); es ist der bisher differenzierteste Versuch der Lenkung der heutigen VK in den sozialistischen Ländern. Aufgrund vorliegender Klassifizierungen[48]) können folgende Kategorien von Ritualen und Festen unterschieden werden: (a) Familiäre Lebenslauffeste: Namengebung (anstelle der Taufe), Eheschließung, Begräbnis und Totengedenken. Für jedes Ritual dieser und der nächsten Gruppe sind unter Mitwirkung von Ethnographen ausgefeilte Szenarien mit genauen Handlungsanweisungen für die Beteiligten erarbeitet worden; für die wichtigen Rituale gibt es mehrere Varianten. (b) Rituale der Einführung in soziale und politische Gruppen: feierliche Übergabe des Personalausweises, Verabschiedung der Rekruten, Schulabschlußfeier u. a. (c) Rituale, die mit dem Arbeitsleben verbunden sind: Einführung in das Arbeitskollektiv, Jubiläen[49]). (d) Feiertage im Jahreslauf: Neujahr, Tag der Geburtshilfe[50]), 1. März, Tag der Frau, Tag der ärztlichen Hilfe, Tag der Arbeit, Tag des bulgarischen Schrifttums (24. Mai), Tag des Viehzüchters, Tag der Befreiung u. a. Einige einst verbreitete Maskenbräuche (wie *lazaruvane, kuke-*

---

[45]) Markov, G. E.: Sovetskij obraz žisni i problemy etnografii (Sowjetische Lebensweise und Probleme der Ethnographie), in: Sovetskaja etnografija. (1976) 2, S. 3. Das in der Sowjetunion entwickelte Konzept wurde um 1970 in Bulgarien rezipiert und in zahllosen Publikationen behandelt: s. Todorov, D. (Hrsg.): Etnografija i sǎvremennost (Ethnographie und Gegenwart). Sofia 1976; Hadžinikolov, V.: Die sozialistische Lebensweise, in: Jahrbuch für Volkskunde und Kulturgeschichte. 22 (1979), S. 27–48; Parpulova (Anm. 43); Živkov, T. I.: Folklor i sǎvremennost (Folklore und Gegenwart). Sofia 1981 u. a.

[46]) Hadžinikolov (Anm. 45), S. 39.

[47]) Nikolov, J.: Ponjatijno-kategorialnijat aparat na socialističeskata praznično-obredna sistema (Begrifflich-kategorieller Apparat des sozialistischen Festtags- und Brauchsystems), in: BE. 5 (1980) 3, S. 3–16; Hadžinikolov (Anm. 45).

[48]) Lane, Ch.: The Rites of Rulers. Cambridge, London 1981; Nikolov, J.: Za tipologijata na socialističeskite rituali (Zur Typologie sozialistischer Rituale), in: BE. 10 (1985) 4, S. 37–46.

[49]) Nikolov (Anm. 48), S. 41 f.

[50]) Stamenova, Z.: Den na rodilnata pomošt i majčinstvoto (babinden) (Tag der Geburtshilfe und Mutterschaft [Hebammentag]), in: BE. 11 (1986) 3, S. 66–76.

ri, koleduvane[51])) sind in manchen Orten nach staatlichen Bemühungen in einer ästhetisierten und angepaßten Spielform wiederbelebt worden[52]. (e) Feiertage und Rituale des Staates, der Partei, der Organisationen[53]. Hinsichtlich der Akzeptanz und des Durchsetzungsgrades bestehen zwischen den einzelnen Feiertagen und Ritualen erhebliche Unterschiede; empirische Studien hierzu liegen kaum vor[54].

Die Erforschung, Pflege und Nutzung der VK für nationale, ideologische, edukative, kommerzielle und andere Ziele erfolgt in Bulgarien auf einer ganzen Reihe von Ebenen[55]:

a) Die *Dokumentation* und Erforschung der VK bildet die Basis für ihre Pflege und Nutzung. Der Volkskunde[56]) kommt daher eine Reihe wichtiger Funktionen zu. Sie soll

- die Relikte der traditionellen VK sammeln, dokumentieren und erforschen,
- die Ergebnisse in möglichst populärer Form publizieren,
- die erhobenen Materialien auf ihren Wert und ihre Nutzbarkeit für die Volkskulturpflege und die Eingliederung in die „sozialistische Lebensweise" überprüfen,
- konkrete Vorschläge für die Anwendung und Integration der Elemente der VK machen und
- die Übernahme der Vorschläge in Kommissionen oder Jurys überwachen oder sie empirisch untersuchen.

Die Erforschung der VK und die Publikation der Ergebnisse ist im Ansatz recht umfassend; die *Pflege* und folkloristische Nutzung betrifft hingegen nur jene Elemente, die expressiv-darstellender, ästhetischer und unterhaltender Art sind (s.u.).

b) In den Lehrplänen bulgarischer *Schulen* ist die „bulgarische Folklore" Teil des Literaturunterrichts, wo sie zur ästhetischen, ideologischen und nationalen Erziehung beitragen soll. Sie spielt daher in der Lehrerausbildung eine Rolle und wird an den Philosophischen Fakultäten der Universitäten Sofia, Tărnovo und Plovdiv sowie am Staatlichen Bulgarischen Konservatorium und an der Hochschule für Musik und Choreographie in Plovdiv gelehrt[57].

c) In den *Massenmedien* (Radio, Fernsehen, Film) sowie auf *folkloristischen Veranstaltungen* (in Fremdenverkehrsorten, in Konzerten, in Restaurants) werden an

---

[51]) Vgl. Vakarelski (Anm. 2), S. 312–328.

[52]) Kraev, G.: Chudožestvena samodejnost i promenite v maskaradnata obrednost (Laienkunst und der Wandel des Maskenbrauchtums), in: BF. 11 (1985) 1, S. 44–49.

[53]) Nikolov (Anm. 48), S. 40f.

[54]) Vgl. Mitkova, E.: Vlijanieto na socialnite procesi za utvărždavane na graždanskata pogrebalna obrednost văv Velikotărnovski okrăg (Der Einfluß sozialer Prozesse auf die Durchsetzung des bürgerlichen Begräbnisses im Kreis Tărnovo), in: BE. 3 (1977) 1, S. 57–66; Höpken (Anm. 32).

[55]) Vgl. Parpulova (Anm. 43).

[56]) Die Erforschung der Volkskultur geschieht in drei Instituten der BAN: Ethnographisches Institut (mit Museum), Institut für Folklore und Institut für Musikwissenschaft (alle in Sofia). Zur Wissenschaftsgeschichte vgl. Dinekov, P.: The Development of Bulgarian Folklore Studies, in: International Folklore Review. 1 (1981), S. 43–47; ders.: Bălgarski folklor (Bulgarische Folklore). Sofia 1972, S. 79–167; Etnografija na Bălgarija (Ethnographie Bulgariens). Hrsg. V. Hadžinikolov u.a. Bd. 1. Sofia 1980, S. 114–163.

[57]) Parpulova (Anm. 43), S. 30–32.

Gattungen fast nur Lieder, Musikstücke und Volkstänze dargeboten. Bei den als Solisten oder in staatlichen Ensembles auftretenden Sängern, Musikern und Tänzern, die in der Regel standardisierte, erneuerte *Tracht* tragen, handelt es sich überwiegend um professionelle Interpreten mit formaler Ausbildung am Staatlichen Bulgarischen Konservatorium, an einer Spezialschule für Volksmusikinstrumente (Kotel, Široka Lăka) oder im Fach Volkstanz an einer Ballettschule. Die Professionalisierung der Interpretation, der Bearbeitung, der Arrangements und der Choreographierung hat dazu geführt, daß die dargebotene Folklore in sehr hohem Maße ästhetisiert und zur rein artistischen Äußerung geworden ist, die allein der Unterhaltung dient. Die resultierende Standardisierung und Sterilität der geförderten und in großer Menge in den Medien gesendeten Volksmusik hat inzwischen im Lande öffentliche Kritik an der staatlichen Volksmusikpflege hervorgerufen, die für die geringe Attraktivität der Volksmusik verantwortlich gemacht wird[58].

d) Auf lokalen, regionalen und nationalen *Folklore-Festivals* werden von tausenden in langwierigen Auswahlverfahren ermittelten Laien oder (halb)professionellen Interpreten außer den dominierenden Liedern, Musikstücken und Tänzen auch Erzählungen und theatralische Inszenierungen von Bräuchen in Wettbewerbsform dargeboten. Bewertungsmaßstab der aus Ethnographen, Ethnomusikologen, Folkloristen u. a. bestehenden Jurys ist die „Authentizität" und die „Reinheit", d. h. der Verzicht auf nicht-bulgarische Elemente; die VK ethnischer Minderheiten ist nicht vertreten. Den vom *Centăr za chudožestvena samodejnost* (Zentrum für Laienkunst, Sofia) organisierten Festivals, an deren Spitze das alle fünf Jahre in Koprivštica stattfindende „Nationale Folklore-Festival" steht, wird, wie die umfassende Medienberichterstattung zeigt, große Bedeutung für die Erziehung der Bevölkerung beigemessen.

e) Die Einfügung und Benutzung von Elementen der VK betrifft in hohem Maße das System sozialistischer *Rituale* und *Festtage* (s. o.). Zu unterscheiden ist dabei zwischen zwei Arten der Nutzung: (1) Traditionelle Festtage und Rituale, vorwiegend solche religiöser Art, werden unter Wahrung eines Teils ihres Gehaltes und ihrer Form in sozialistische Rituale und Festtage umgewandelt. So ist der *Babinden* (Hebammentag, 8.1.) zum „Tag der Geburtshilfe und Mutterschaft"[59] und der *Gerg'ovden* (Hl. Georgstag, 23.4.) zum „Tag des Viehzüchters" umgewandelt worden. (2) Teile der VK werden in sozialistische Rituale, Feiern, Festtage eingebaut: Elemente der Volksarchitektur (restaurierte alte Gebäude) und der Inneneinrichtung (Wandbehänge, Teppiche) werden für Ritualsäle gewählt, Volkstrachten, Brauchrequisiten (wie Brot und Honig) und Brauchhandlungen, Inhalte der mündlichen Überlieferung (Lieder, Erzählstoffe, Sprichwörter) und Volksmusik werden vielfältig in neue Rituale einbezogen. In manchen Gemeinden kann ein „folkloristisches" Hochzeitsritual gewählt werden.

---

[58] Zur Volksmusik in den Medien vgl. Bojadžiev, G.: Narodnata muzika po radioto i săvremennijat slušatel (Volksmusik im Radio und der heutige Hörer), in: Problemi na bălgarski folklor (Probleme der bulgarischen Folklore). Sofia 1972, S. 257–260. Zur Kritik s. Roth, J.: Volksmusik und nationale Identität in Bulgarien, in: Südosteuropa. 35 (1986), S. 147–150; s. Kapitel „Musik" von B. Krader.

[59] Stamenova (Anm. 50).

f) Von nicht geringer Bedeutung für die Pflege der VK ist es, daß Elemente dieser Kultur in das Schaffen der Schriftsteller, Dichter, Komponisten, Maler, Bildhauer, Regisseure und anderer Künstler eingebunden werden. Diese „Kontakte mit der Folklore, direkt oder mittels der schon etablierten ästhetischen Norm," können Teil „konkreter künstlerischer Aufträge oder eines allgemeinen Schaffensstils" sein[60]).

g) Durch die Wirtschaftspolitik der Nachkriegszeit waren viele alte Handwerke untergegangen oder bedroht. Die auf Anregung des Ethnographen Christo Vakarelski um 1967 einsetzende staatliche *Handwerkspflege* hatte wesentlich die Aufgabe, diese Handwerke durch eine Vielzahl von Maßnahmen zu retten: In mehreren Orten des Landes wurden besondere Berufs- und Fachschulen (*technikum*) eingerichtet (z. B. für Keramik in Trojan); für verdiente Meister wurden Orden, Auszeichnungen und Titel (wie „Volks-Handwerksmeister"[61])) ausgesetzt; Handwerksbetrieben wird durch Gestellung von Werkstätten, Rohmaterial, Lagerräumen und durch Abnahme der Produktion direkte Unterstützung zuteil; in den Zentren restaurierter Altstädte (s. u. h) wurden Werkstätten mit Verkaufsläden eingerichtet. Eine wichtige Maßnahme war die im April 1967 auf Anordnung des Sekretariats des ZK der BKP vorgenommene Gründung der *Zadruga na majstorite na narodnite chudožestveni zanajati* (Genossenschaft der Meister der Volkskunst-Handwerke), die in den 70er Jahren einen großen Aufschwung nahm. Die über tausend Mitglieder haben ihre Werkstätten in allen Teilen des Landes, doch ist die Hälfte von ihnen in Sofia und Plovdiv tätig[62]). Die Prüfung der Handwerker und die Begutachtung ihrer Produktion erfolgt durch Kommissionen von Handwerksmeistern, Ethnographen, Künstlern, Architekten, Ökonomen und Juristen. Trotz der Bemühungen der Ethnographen, die Handwerker zur Herstellung „normaler", gebrauchsfähiger Gegenstände nach authentischen Vorlagen anzuhalten und so die alte materielle Kultur fortzuführen, weist die Produktion die Tendenz zum Kunst- und Hobby-Handwerk und zur individuellkünstlerischen Ausarbeitung auf[63]); viele Gegenstände sind nicht für den praktischen Gebrauch geeignet. Ein großer Teil der Produktion wird für die Ausgestaltung von Repräsentationsbauten, Ritualsälen und Restaurants oder für die Ausstattung der Tanz- und Musikensembles verwendet.

h) Für die Bewahrung und Pflege des Erbes der *Volksarchitektur* werden ganz erhebliche Mitte aufgewendet. Die Pflege städtischer Baudenkmäler geschieht durch die sorgfältige Restaurierung der Altstadt oder einzelner Straßenzüge in Plovdiv, Tărnovo, Koprivština, Loveč, Trjavna, Kotel u. a. Städten, wobei fast immer der Zustand der Wiedergeburtszeit, der Blüte des Handwerks und der VK, wiederhergestellt wird. Ländliche Baudenkmäler werden in der Regel ebenfalls in situ bewahrt, wobei einige gut erhaltene Dörfer (Boženci, Žeravna) zu Museumsdörfern erklärt und restauriert wurden. Freilichtmuseen mit translozierten Gebäuden sind noch selten; mehrere sind in Planung, doch ist bisher nur das Museum Etăra bei Gabrovo, das eine kleinstädtische Handwerkerstraße darstellt, in Betrieb. In den letzten Jahren

---

[60]) Parpulova (Anm. 43), S. 30.
[61]) Die Titel und Orden werden seit September 1987 nicht mehr verliehen.
[62]) Roth, K.: Die Pflege alter Handwerke im heutigen Bulgarien, in: Handwerk in Mittel- und Südosteuropa. Hrsg. ders. München 1987, S. 217–230, hier S. 221 f.
[63]) Ebenda, S. 228.

werden zunehmend Versuche unternommen, dekorative Elemente der traditionellen Bauweise in den modernen Wohnungsbau einzubringen.

3. Volkskultur in der Moderne

Die *tatsächliche* heutige VK, d. h. die Alltagskultur der großen Mehrheit der bulgarischen Bevölkerung in der Gegenwart, ist vielschichtig und widersprüchlich, da sie das Ergebnis verschiedener, einander z. T. entgegenwirkender Faktoren ist, wie: (a) hohe Geschwindigkeit des Übergangs von der Agrar- zur Industriegesellschaft. Der Einbruch der modernen Welt und des technischen Wandels in das Alltagsleben vollzog sich für die Mehrheit der Bevölkerung in den wenigen Jahren von 1950–1970; (b) rapide Urbanisierung und sozialer Wandel. Durch Industrialisierung und massenhafte Landflucht stieg der Anteil der Stadtbevölkerung von 24,7 % (1946) auf 62,5 % (1980), die Einwohnerzahl Sofias im gleichen Zeitraum von 366800 auf 1056900. Die Neubürger wurden weit überwiegend konzentriert in großen suburbanen „Wohnkomplexen" angesiedelt; (c) Einfluß des „real existierenden Sozialismus" auf die Kultur und Lebensweise des Volkes; ausschlaggebend waren dabei weniger die beabsichtigten Wirkungen der „sozialistischen Lebensweise" als vielmehr die konkreten alltäglichen Lebensbedingungen (wie Wohnsituation, Konsumangebot); (d) stetes Fortwirken des Erbes der patriarchalen VK sowie der osmanischen Kultur. Dieser Einfluß kann, wie die stabilisierende Rolle der engen Familienbeziehungen im Verstädterungsprozeß zeigt[64]), durchaus auch positiv sein; (e) weitgehendes Fehlen einer vorbildgebenden bürgerlichen Schicht. Die neuen Führungsschichten waren zum größten Teil dörflich-kleinstädtischer Herkunft und brachten eher traditionelle Verhaltensformen mit; (f) das Vorbild der westlichen Massenkultur. Konnte dieser Einfluß anfangs in Grenzen gehalten werden, so ist seit etwa zwanzig Jahren eine zunehmende Bedeutung vor allem der Medienkultur (Schallplatten, Toncassetten, Videobänder usw.) und der materiellen Kultur (technische Geräte, Kleidung) zu konstatieren, die von der Kulturpolitik mit Sorge betrachtet wird.

Bestimmend für die heutige VK sind damit gegenläufige Prozesse der Modernisierung bei gleichzeitiger Traditionalisierung: Die auch für andere Balkanländer nachgewiesene „Rustifizierung" der Städte[65]) etwa ist Folge u. a. der Ansiedlung Hunderttausender von Dörflern in den Wohnkomplexen der Großstädte: Sofia zog von 1946 bis 1980 über 700000 Landflüchtige an. Die Retraditionalisierung des städtischen Lebens findet ihren Ausdruck in starker Sozialkontrolle, im Beharren bei überkommenen Ernährungs- und Wohnweisen, in engen Bindungen ans Heimatdorf, im exzessiven Feiern von Familienfesten oder in traditionellen Formen der öffentlichen

---

[64]) Vgl. Simić (Anm. 3), S. 208–212.

[65]) Marcu, L.: Zeitgenössische soziologische Aspekte des Verstädterungsprozesses in Südosteuropa, in: Revue des études sud-est européennes. 9 (1971), S. 677–714 und 11 (1975), S. 513–552; Simić, A.: The Best of Two Worlds: Serbian Peasants in the City, in: Anthropologists in Cities. Ed. G. M. Foster. Boston 1974, S. 179–200, bes. 195f.; Roth, K.: Großstädtische Kultur und dörfliche Lebensweise. Bulgarische Großstädte im 19. und 20. Jh., in: Großstadt. Hrsg. H. Bausinger u. a. Berlin 1985, S. 363–376.

Unterhaltung[66]). Dieser Traditionalismus steht nicht nur im Kontrast zur Urbanisierung und zum Ausbau der Großstädte zu modernen Zentren, sondern auch zur raschen Übernahme von technischen Neuerungen, Kleidermoden und Trends der Medienunterhaltung. Das unmittelbare Nebeneinander von Tradition und Moderne, von modernen Verkehrsmitteln und traditionellen Formen des Umgangs mit ihnen, von technischen Geräten und abergläubischen Vorstellungen über sie, von neuesten Schlagern und alter Volksmusik, von modischer Kleidung und konservativem Nahrungsverhalten, von Videokultur und traditionellen Familienbeziehungen ist bezeichnend für die heutige VK Bulgariens.

Die Symbiose von Altem und Neuem betrifft auch die verbalen Ausdrucksformen. Festzustellen ist eine nahezu ungebrochene Kraft der *mündlichen Überlieferung* im Alltag, die auch durch die Medien kaum beeinträchtigt wird. Dabei sind es weniger die längeren und komplexen Gattungen der Volkserzählung wie etwa das Märchen, sondern vielmehr die kurzen Gattungen wie Sage und Memorabile, Schwank und Witz, Parodie und Redensart, die – gerade in den Großstädten – täglich erzählt werden und in ihren Formen und Inhalten, ihrem Realismus und im Einbezug der technisierten Lebenswelt ganz der Gegenwart angepaßt sind. Unzählbar sind die modernen *Sagen*, die meist grausige Ereignisse wie Unfälle und Verbrechen, ungewöhnliche Begegnungen und Erlebnisse im städtischen Milieu wiedergeben; die Fülle derartiger Erzählungen ist sicher z. T. auf die unzulängliche Information durch die Medien zurückzuführen. Noch größer ist freilich im alltäglichen Erzählen die Zahl der humoristischen Erzählungen, sowohl der traditionellen *Schwänke*[67]) als auch vor allem der *Witze*, die Afanasieva-Koleva zu Recht als die „lebendigste, aktivste und aktuellste Erscheinung der gegenwärtigen Folklore überhaupt" bezeichnet[68]), denn sie werden von jedermann überall und ständig erzählt; etwa zwei Drittel aller heute in Bulgarien erzählten Witze betreffen die Bereiche Politik und Sexualität[69]). Trotz ihrer großen Bedeutung im Alltagsleben sind Witze ebenso wenig erforscht wie die überall vordringenden Parodien und Sagen, die Sprache der Jugendlichen, Gruselgeschichten der Kinder u. a.[70]).

Unabhängig von staatlichem Einfluß entwickelt sich im privaten Bereich auch die *Liedtradition*, die zu kurzen und parodistischen Formen neigt und zunehmend durch Liederbücher beeinflußt ist[71]); die heutige *Musik* und *Tanztradition* bei privaten Anlässen[72]) ist gekennzeichnet durch die kreative Einbeziehung von Elementen der

---

[66]) s. Roth (Anm. 22).

[67])Ančev, A.: Nabljudenija värchu folklora v edno zveno na rabotničeska stroitelna brigada (Beobachtungen zur Folklore in einer Baubrigade), in: BF. 10 (1984) 1, S. 90–102.

[68]) Afanasieva-Koleva, A.: Vicăt folklor li e? (Ist der Witz Folklore?), in: Smechăt văv folklora (Das Lachen in der Folklore). Sofia 1987, S. 132–143, hier S. 132.

[69]) Ebenda, S. 135.

[70]) Erste Ansätze zur Erforschung dieser heute sehr wichtigen Gattungen enthalten einige Aufsätze im Band „Smechät väv folklora" (Anm. 68).

[71]) Stojkova, S.: Folklorät i kulturnite promeni (Die Folklore und die kulturellen Veränderungen), in: Folklor i obštestvo (Folklore und Gesellschaft). Sofia 1977, S. 31–36; Roth (Anm. 22).

[72]) Zu den „freien" Hochzeitsmusikern s. Georgiev, K.: Părva nacionalna srešta na svatbarskite orkestri (1. nationales Treffen der Hochzeitsorchester), in: BF. 12 (1986) 3, S. 90 f; s. auch N. Kaufman in: BF. 13 (1987) 1, S. 78 f.

durch Medien und Tonträger vermittelten jugoslawischen und griechischen Musik und der westlichen Unterhaltungsmusik.

Im *Jahreslaufbrauchtum* hat eine erhebliche Reduzierung stattgefunden, doch haben einige wenige Sitten wie das Überreichen von *survaknici* (geschmückte Neujahrsruten) und *martenici* (weiß-rote Anhänger zum 1. März) stark an Bedeutung gewonnen; die Requisiten werden in großer Vielfalt produziert und überall verkauft. Im *Lebenslaufbrauchtum* hingegen ist bei Abiturientenfeiern, Verabschiedungen der Rekruten und besonders bei Hochzeiten in den Städten wie auf dem Lande ein sehr traditionelles Verhalten festzustellen[73], das sich in der unvermindert sozial bindenden Wirkung der Wahlverwandtschaft mit Gevatter (*kum*) und Gevatterin (*kuma*), in den sehr hohen Gästezahlen und einem oft extrem hohen Aufwand äußert. Recht tief verwurzelt sind auch noch Teile des *Volksglaubens* und der Volksmedizin; weit verbreitet ist etwa der Glaube an den bösen Blick, an das Besprechen sowie an jenseitige Wesen.

Die aufgeführten Erscheinungen der VK in der Moderne sind Ausdruck einer Haltung, die geprägt ist durch selektiven und synkretistischen Umgang mit fremden und neuen Kulturelementen und zugleich durch ein Auseinanderklaffen im Tempo der Übernahme von neuen Objekten, Verhaltensformen und Einstellungen. Diese traditionelle Grundhaltung bestimmt auch die weitere Entwicklung der VK in Bulgarien.

---

[73] Vgl. Roth, J. u. K.: Hochzeit in einem ostbulgarischen Dorf, in: 1300 Jahre Bulgarien. Neuried 1981, S. 167–189.

Literatur

Reinhard Lauer, Göttingen

I. Traditionen der bulgarischen Literatur – II. Literatur der Übergangsphase (1944–1948) – III. Die Durchsetzung des Sozialistischen Realismus (1949–1956) – IV. Der Bulgarische Schriftstellerverband (SBP) – V. Die Neue Welle nach dem Aprilplenum: Die 60er Jahre – VI. Die Literatur der 70er Jahre: Junge Prosa und groteskes Drama – VII. Die Literatur der 80er Jahre: Humane Kybernetik – Ökologie – Weibliche Poetik – VIII. Zeittafel zur bulgarischen Nachkriegsliteratur

I. Traditionen der bulgarischen Literatur*

Die bulgarische Literatur unterscheidet sich von den meisten europäischen Literaturen durch einen eigenartigen Entwicklungsrhythmus. Hatte das mittelalterliche Schrifttum in Bulgarien auf der Basis der altbulgarischen (altkirchenslawischen) Sprache, mehr und mehr sich von byzantinischen Vorbildern lösend, bereits im 10. Jh. unter dem Zaren Simeon einen Höhepunkt erreicht, so kam in der langen Zeit der osmanischen Herrschaft das literarische Leben der Bulgaren fast zum Erliegen. Abgeschottet vom übrigen Europa, verloren die Bulgaren den Anschluß an die kulturellen Entwicklungen von Humanismus und Renaissance über Barock und Klassizismus bis zur Romantik, während sich unter den Bedingungen des osmanischen Herrschaftssystems und der bäuerlich-patriarchalischen Lebensformen zugleich eine reiche Volkskultur ausbilden konnte.

Die neue bulgarische Literatur setzt 1762 mit der zunächst nur handschriftlich verbreiteten *Istorija Slavjanobolgarskaja* (Slawisch-bulgarische Geschichte) des Paisij Chilendarski ein. Mit diesem Werk versuchte der Athos-Mönch, den Bulgaren das Gefühl für die eigene Sprache, Vergangenheit und nationale Würde neu zu wecken. Er leitete damit die Wiedergeburt (*văzraždane*) der bulgarischen Nationalkultur ein, die sich bis zur Befreiung Bulgariens im Russisch-Türkischen Krieg 1878 als ein äußerst dynamischer und vielschichtiger Vorgang darstellt. Im Verlaufe weniger Jahrzehnte wurde nicht nur das Neubulgarische als Literatursprache soweit formiert, daß in ihm die Elementarkenntnisse in allen wichtigen Wissensmaterien vermittelt werden konnten, sondern es wuchs inzwischen auch eine belletristische Literatur heran, die sich mehr und mehr imstande zeigte, die nationalen, intellektuellen und emotionalen Ansprüche der sich rasch entwickelnden bulgarischen Gesellschaft zu befriedigen. Die besonderen bulgarischen Bedingungen bewirkten zum einen, daß ein nationalpädagogischer, aufklärerischer Impuls über lange Zeit die Literatur bestimmte, zum anderen, daß im Zuge einer „beschleunigten Literaturentwicklung" (Georgi

---

* Die mit Sternchen* gekennzeichneten Titel liegen in deutscher Übersetzung vor.

Gačev)[1]) versäumte Phasen der europäischen Globalentwicklung in abreviierter Form „nachgeholt" wurden. So zeigt die Analyse der thematischen und stilistischen Phänomene der bulgarischen Literatur im 19. Jh. ebenso wie die Auswahl und der Modus der Rezeption fremder Literaturwerke, daß in sich verringerndem Abstand typische Ausdrucksformen des Barock, des Klassizismus, des Sentimentalismus und der Romantik gewonnen wurden.

Leitkulturen waren für die Bulgaren im 19. Jh. nacheinander die griechische, französische, russische und deutsche[2]). Dank der engen politischen und geistigen Beziehungen zu Rußland (hier erhielten viele junge Bulgaren, darunter die Dichter-Revolutionäre Christo Botev und Ljuben Karavelov, ihre Ausbildung) gewannen russische Vorbilder große Bedeutung für die bulgarische Literatur. Gesellschaftsbezogenheit und volksnahe Wirklichkeitsdarstellung, wie man sie im russischen Realismus vorgebildet fand, wurden zu bleibenden Orientierungsmarken in der bulgarischen Literatur nach der Befreiung. Wohl am deutlichsten folgte den russischen Wegweisern Ivan Vazov in seinem durch große Vielfalt der Themen und Gattungen ausgezeichneten Werk, das für die Bulgaren heute klassischen Rang besitzt. Bezeichnenderweise wurden über das Russische eine Zeitlang auch fremde Autoren, beispielsweise Heinrich Heine, nach Bulgarien vermittelt. Seit den 1890er Jahren zeichnete sich im Kreise um die Zeitschrift *Misăl* (Idee) eine Hinwendung zur deutschen Literatur und Philosophie ab. Durch den einflußreichen Literaturkritiker Krăst'o Krăstev und den Dichter Penčo Slavejkov wurde die neokantianische Ästhetik, namentlich die sog. „Gefühlsästhetik" Johannes Volkelts[3]), Grundlage einer neuen Literaturauffassung, die dem literarischen Kunstwerk einen Platz jenseits aller politischer Tendenz und Alltagswirklichkeit zuwies. Daß sich zu Anfang des 20. Jh. eine starke symbolistische Strömung mit deutlichem Affront gegen den Vazovschen Gesellschaftsrealismus abzeichnete, hängt mit der Etablierung der idealistischen Ästhetik aufs engste zusammen. Hervorragende lyrische Talente wie Pejo Javorov, Dimčo Debeljanov, Nikolaj Liliev und der mit der deutschen Kultur besonders eng verbundene Teodor Trajanov bezeichnen für die bulgarische Literatur nicht nur Gipfelpunkte des poetischen Ausdrucks, sondern zugleich auch den überzeugenden Anschluß an die europäischen Entwicklungen. Seither ist in der bulgarischen Literatur mit einer polaren Gegenströmung zum gesellschaftsrelevanten Realismus zu rechnen. Während aus diesem in der Zwischenkriegszeit ein starker ruraler Realismus mit kräftigen Erzählern wie Jordan Jovkov, Anton Strašimirov und Elin Pelin hervorgeht, folgen jener die Fortsetzer des Symbolismus um die Zeitschriften *Chiperion* (Hyperion, 1922–31), *Zlatorog* (Goldhorn, 1920–43) und *Bălgarska misăl* (Bulgarische Idee, 1925–44). Deutlich erkenn-

---

[1]) Gačev, G.: Uskorennoe razvitie literatury (na materiale bolgarskoj literatury XIX v.) (Beschleunigte Entwicklung der Literatur (am Material der bulgarischen Literatur des 19. Jh.)). Moskau 1964.

[2]) Lauer, R.: Zur Frage der Fremdorientierung in der bulgarischen Literatur, in: Kulturelle Traditionen in Bulgarien. Hrsg. von R. Lauer; P. Schreiner. Göttingen 1989 (Abhandlungen der Akademie der Wissenschaften in Göttingen. Phil.-Hist. Klasse. Dritte Folge. 177, S. 263–280.

[3]) Natev, A.: Cel i samocelnost na izkustvoto. Kritični nabljudenija vărchu neokantianskata estetika i nejnoto vlijanie v Bălgarija (Zweck und Selbstzweck der Kunst. Kritische Beobachtungen zur neokantianischen Ästhetik und ihren Einfluß in Bulgarien). Sofia 1960.

bar sind deutsche Impulse im kurzlebigen bulgarischen Expressionismus (Geo Milev) und im sog. „Diabolismus" (Svetoslav Minkov).

Für die spätere Literaturentwicklung sollte sich als überaus bedeutsam die Tatsache erweisen, daß bereits seit den 20er Jahren neben ruralen Realisten und Symbolisten eine beachtliche „linke", sozialistische Literatur bestand, die aufmerksam die kulturrevolutionären Entwicklungen in der Sowjetunion verfolgte. Die sozialrevolutionäre Avantgarde (Geo Milev), die sozialkritische Prosa (Georgi Karaslavov, Emil Koralov), das antifaschistische und antimonarchistische Engagement vieler junger Schriftsteller in den 30er Jahren (Kamen Kalčev, Andrej Guljaški, Pavel Vežinov, Nikolaj Chrelkov, Krum Penev, Krăst'o Belev u.a.) bildete eine beständige linke Opposition zur herrschenden Kultur. Die nach sowjetischen Vorbild geschaffenen Vereinigungen proletarischer Schriftsteller RLF (*Rabotničeski Literaturen Front/* Literarische Arbeiterfront, 1929–34) und der 1932 gegründete Bund der Schriftsteller des Arbeitskampfes (*Săjuz na trudovoborčeskite pisateli*) wurden zum Sammelbecken der linken antifaschistischen Autoren. Eine Tribüne fanden sie in den der BRP nahestehenden Zeitschriften *Zvezda* (Stern, 1932–34), *Štit* (Schild, 1933/34) oder *Nova literatura* (Neue Literatur, 1935/36). Hier wurde, wie im benachbarten Jugoslawien, eine offene Debatte um den „neuen Realismus" – so nannte man den in der Sowjetunion konzipierten Sozialistischen Realismus einstweilen – geführt. Die parteiliche Literaturkritik eines gestandenen, noch an Plechanov geschulten Marxisten wie Georgi Bakalov (1873–1939) versuchte, die sozialrevolutionäre Tradition der bulgarischen Literatur von Botev über Christo Smirnenski in die Gegenwart zu verlängern. Von nicht geringerer Bedeutung war das Wirken des marxistisch-leninistischen Theoretikers Todor Pavlov (1890–1977). Er hatte von 1932 bis 1936 als Professor für dialektischen Materialismus am Moskauer Institut für Philosophie- und Literaturgeschichte gewirkt und mit seiner *Teorija na otraženieto* (Widerspiegelungstheorie, 1936) einen maßgeblichen Beitrag zur theoretischen Fundierung des Sozialistischen Realismus geleistet. Mit Todor Pavlov stand ein entschiedener Gegner jeglicher idealistischer Ästhetik und militanter Kämpfer gegen formalistische und naturalistische Abweichungen bereit, die marxistisch-leninistische Kunsttheorie und den Sozialistischen Realismus durchzusetzen.

Der Ausbruch des II. Weltkrieges und die Option der bulgarischen Monarchie für die Achsenmächte verschärften die inneren Antagonismen noch weiter. Nicht wenige der antimonarchistisch und antifaschistisch, dabei prosowjetisch gestimmten Schriftsteller gingen in die Illegalität oder beteiligten sich an der bulgarischen Partisanenbewegung. Nikola Vapcarov (1909–1942), einer der begabtesten Lyriker aus dem linken Lager, dessen *Motorni pesni* (Motorenlieder*) 1940 unter dem Namen Nikola Jonkov erschienen waren, zählte zu den aktiven kommunistischen Widerstandskämpfern. Im März 1942 wurde er verhaftet und im Prozeß gegen das ZK der BRP zum Tode verurteilt. Vapcarovs von Optimismus und Tragik durchdrungene Poesie, nicht zuletzt die unmittelbar vor der Exekution geschriebenen Verse: „Der Kampf ist grausam und kennt keine Gnade. / Der Kampf, so sagt man, ist dem Epos gleich"[4]),

---

[4]) Zit. nach: Das Wort – meine Waffe. 1878–1978. Hundert Jahre bulgarische revolutionäre Lyrik. Ausgewählt von H.-J. Neschtschenko. Berlin 1978, S. 112.

sollten nach dem Zusammenbruch des alten Regimes zum Exempel einer antifaschistischen, progressiven Poesie werden.

II. Literatur der Übergangsphase (1944–1948)

Nach dem Sturz der Regierung und der Machtübernahme durch die OF am 9.9.1944 setzte eine politische und soziale Umgestaltung in Bulgarien ein, die alle Bereiche des Lebens, namentlich aber auch Kultur, Literatur und Kunst, erfaßte. Fortan war damit zu rechnen, daß die Literatur, ähnlich wie in den anderen sog. Volksdemokratien, in bislang unbekanntem Maße politisch instrumentalisiert und den politischen Zielen der Volksfront und der sie beherrschenden Kommunistischen Partei dienstbar gemacht wird. Von daher erklärt es sich, daß alle bisherigen Versuche, ein Periodisierungsmodell für die bulgarische Nachkriegsliteratur zu entwerfen, faktisch die Epochen der politischen Entwicklung, genauer: der Parteigeschichte, ihrer zeitlichen Gliederung unterlegen. So zeichnen sich die Jahre 1944–1948 als eine erste Phase ab, eine „Übergangsphase"[5]), in der die antifaschistischen, demokratischen Kräfte im Sinne der Volksfrontpolitik gesammelt und kulturpolitisch gebunden wurden. Der Beschluß der BKP auf dem V. Parteitag im Dezember 1948, den Aufbau des Sozialismus in Bulgarien in Angriff zu nehmen, leitete die zweite Phase der Kultur- und Literaturentwicklung ein, die von 1949 bis 1956, d.h. bis zum berühmten Aprilplenum der BKP, währte. Das politische „Tauwetter", das mit diesem Ereignis einsetzte, schuf die Voraussetzungen für die Ausbildung einer Literatur, die sich erst zögernd, später jedoch mit wachsendem Selbstvertrauen von politischen und dogmatischen Gängelungen befreite, ohne ihren „gesellschaftlichen Auftrag" jedoch jemals aus dem Blick zu verlieren. Bei der Betrachtung der literarhistorischen Prozesse schälen sich gegenwärtig für die 60er, 70er und 80er Jahre zwar bestimmte, durchaus zu unterscheidende thematische und künstlerische Tendenzen heraus, der geringe zeitliche Abstand und die erst in Ansätzen geleistete wissenschaftliche Sichtung der Materie lassen jedoch noch keine vorbehaltlose Periodisierung zu[6]). So scheint zur Zeit lediglich eine Darstellung nach dem Dekadenprinzip möglich und sinnvoll, bei der die genuinen innerliterarischen Gesichtspunkte und Gesetzmäßigkeiten zwar noch nicht voll hervortreten, während andererseits der Primat der politischen Entwicklung zurückgedrängt wird.

Die Volksfrontpolitik, die die Literatur in der „Übergangsphase" bestimmte, stand vor allem im Zeichen der Mobilisierung aller antifaschistischen Kräfte sowie der Reorganisation der Industrie und Landwirtschaft, wobei vorerst von durchgreifenden Sozialisierungsmaßnahmen Abstand genommen wurde. Die zunächst noch bestehenden bürgerlichen Oppositionsparteien und ihre publizistischen Organe wurden hingegen mit allen Mitteln bekämpft und bis zum Frühjahr 1947 praktisch ausgeschaltet. Schon Ende 1944 hatte Todor Pavlov, damals, bis zur Abschaffung der

---

[5]) Literatur Bulgariens 1944 bis 1980. Einzeldarstellungen. Hrsg. v. T. Shetschew; S. Stantschew u.a. Berlin 1981, S. 24.

Monarchie durch das Referendum im September 1946, einer der drei Regenten für den unmündigen Zaren Simeon II., das Programm einer „Vaterländischen Literaturfront" konzipiert, das das Bündnis von sozialistischen und bürgerlich-demokratischen Schriftstellern forderte. Wurde hier noch ästhetische und weltanschauliche Toleranz eingeräumt, so sollten doch die sozialistischen Autoren – gleichsam in edlem Wettstreit – bemüht sein, die Überlegenheit der Methode des Sozialistischen Realismus durch ihre Werke zu beweisen[7]). Die Aufgaben der bulgarischen Literatur formulierte dann Georgi Dimitrov in seinem vielbeschworenen Brief an den SBP vom 14.5.1945. Das bulgarische Volk, hieß es hier, brauche eine wahrhaft volkstümliche Kunstliteratur wie das Brot und die Luft zum Leben, eine Literatur, die durch ihre tiefe Wahrhaftigkeit und hohe Emotionalität das kulturelle und ideologische Niveau hebe, die die Vaterlandsliebe entwickele, die den Haß auf den Faschismus und jegliche Volksfeinde verstärke, die alles Faule und Zersetzende im Volksorganismus geißele, die die Luft von den Miasmen des großbulgarischen Chauvinismus und allem Obskurantismus reinige, die die Liebe zu echter Wissenschaft verbreite und zu heroischen Taten im Bereiche der Arbeit und der Kultur sowie im Kampf um die Verteidigung der Freiheiten und Rechte des Volkes anstachele, die das Gefühl der slawischen Einheit und der internationalen Solidarität und der ewigen Freundschaft mit dem Befreier Bulgariens, dem großen sowjetischen Volk, erziehe[8]). Dimitrov vertrat gleichfalls die von der Partei als zweckmäßig erkannte taktische Rücksichtnahme auf die demokratischen Schriftsteller; diese sollten erst allmählich und keinesfalls unter Zwang zur Annahme des Sozialistischen Realismus gebracht werden[9]).

In der Tat gelang es in Fortführung der virulenten antifaschistischen, linksbürgerlichen und sozialistischen Strömungen der 30er Jahre überraschend schnell, viele namhafte Dichter und Schriftsteller, gerade auch solche aus dem bürgerlichen Lager, auf der Plattform der OF zu vereinen. Natürlich wurde der SBP, der sich auf einer Vollversammlung am 30.11.1944 mit 70 Mitgliedern neu konstituierte, von kommunistischen Schriftstellern dominiert, doch schlossen sich schon bald angesehene bürgerliche Autoren der antifaschistischen Formation an, darunter nicht nur politisch neutrale Persönlichkeiten wie Elisaveta Bagrjana (geb. 1893), Dora Gabe (1888–1983), Atanas Dalčev (1904–1978), Stojan Zagorčinov (1889–1969) oder Konstantin Pet-

---

[6]) Die repräsentative Darstellung der bulgarischen Nachkriegsliteratur Kolevski, V.; Žečev, T.; Bojadžieva, V.: Očerci po istorija na bălgarskata literatura sled deveti septemvri 1944 godina (Skizzen zur Geschichte der bulgarischen Literatur nach dem 9.9.1944). Bd. I–II. Sofia 1979–80 (zit. als: Očerci), gliedert nach dem Gattungsprinzip: Theorie, Roman, Drama, Poesie, Kurzroman (*povest*) und Erzählung. Abgesehen von der „Übergangsperiode" 1944–1949 und dem Einschnitt des Aprilplenums 1956 lassen sich keine übergreifenden Periodisierungen erkennen. Vgl. auch Igov, S.: Problemi na periodizacijata na naj-novata bălgarska literatura (Probleme der Periodisierung der neuesten bulgarischen Literatur), in: Vtori meždunaroden kongres po bălgaristika (Zweiter Internationaler Bulgaristikkongreß) – Dokladi (Referate) 12: Bălgarskata literatura sled osvoboždenieto (1878) – Săvremenna bălgarska literatura (Die bulgarische Literatur nach der Befreiung (1878) – Zeitgenössische bulgarische Literatur). Sofia 1988, S. 485–492 (zit. als: Dokladi 12).

[7]) Literatur Bulgariens (Anm. 5), S. 24.

[8]) Dimitrov, G.: Săčinenija (Werke). Sofia 1951–1955, Bd. XI, S. 191 ff. (Übersetzung nach: Lauer, R.: Tendenzen der bulgarischen Gegenwartsliteratur, in: Südosteuropa-Mitteilungen. (1981) 3, S. 77.

[9]) Očerci (Anm. 6), Bd. I, S. 11.

kanov (1891–1952), sondern selbst Elin Pelin (1877–1949) und Angel Karalijčev (1902–1972), die in der Zeit der Monarchie zu den offiziell geachtetsten Vertretern der bulgarischen Literatur gezählt und sogar im nationalsozialistischen Deutschland Beachtung als „Blut und Boden"-Dichter gefunden hatten[10]). Ein angesehener Dichter wie Ljudmil Stojanov, der vom Symbolismus kam, aber schon in den 30er Jahren eine antifaschistische, prosowjetische Haltung eingenommen hatte, war in der Übergangsphase (1946–1949) Vorsitzender des SBP. So wird in der offiziellen Geschichtsschreibung mit unverhohlener Genugtuung vermerkt, daß in Bulgarien, im Unterschied zur Sowjetunion und einigen anderen sozialistischen Ländern, die bürgerlichen „wissenschaftlichen Kader", ebenso wie Schriftsteller und Dichter, nach dem 9.9.1944 fast ausnahmslos auf die Seite des Volkes übergegangen seien[11]), so daß es in Bulgarien eine „Krise" für die Intelligenz nicht gegeben habe.

Dennoch zeigt die sog. „Septemberliteratur", die unmittelbar nach dem Umbruch entstand, kein hohes künstlerisches Niveau. Ihre Themen fand sie im antifaschistischen Widerstandskampf und der Partisanenbewegung, sei es in der pathetisch-optimistischen Lyrik (Ogănja/Das Feuer 1946) eines Mladen Isaev (geb. 1907) oder den hochgelobten *Partizanski pesni* (Partisanenlieder, 1947) von Veselin Andreev (geb. 1918), sei es in Erzählungen und Kurzromanen wie *Pleneno jato* (Die gefangene Schar, 1948) von Emil Manov (1919–1982) oder *Po strămninite* (Auf steilen Pfaden, 1948) von Charalan Rusev (1914–1968). Im Zusammenhang mit dem Zweijahresplan (1947/1948) muß das Thema des industriellen Aufbaus gesehen werden. Aus der vom DKMS initiierten Brigadierbewegung gingen Sammelbände junger Autoren hervor (1948, 1951), in denen man die Anfänge einer neuen, optimistischen, in gewisser Weise sozialistisch-romantischen Lyrik erblickte. Aus dem „Brigadiermantel" (*Brigadirski šinel*) – so war ein Gedicht von Ivan Radoev (geb. 1930) überschrieben – sei damals die ganze junge bulgarische Poesie hervorgegangen[12]). Zum literarischen Idol der Bewegung wurde Pen'o Penev (1930–1959), in dessen Gedichten, im Ausdruck an Majakovskij und Vapcarov erinnernd, das Thema der kämpferischen Arbeit pathetisch aufklang: *Dobro utro, chora!* (Guten Morgen, Leute!, 1956), *Nie ot dvadesetija vek* (Wir vom 20. Jahrhundert, 1959). Enttäuscht durch die Aufdeckung des stalinistischen Personenkultes und im SBP wegen seines freien Lebenswandels angegriffen, suchte Penev im April 1959 den Freitod.

Auch einige ältere linksbürgerliche und sozialistische Autoren nahmen das Thema des antifaschistischen Kampfes auf. Von ihnen stammen die gelungensten Werke dieser Übergangszeit; so der Roman *Osădeni duši* (Verdammte Seelen*, 1945) über Franco-Spanien von Dimităr Dimov (1909–1966) (der Autor hatte sich 1943 zur medizinischen Spezialisierung in Madrid aufgehalten); dann die Erzählungen *V ticha večer* (An einem stillen Abend*, 1948) und *Kradecăt na praskovi* (Der Pfirsichdieb*, 1948) von Emilijan Stanev (1907–1979) sowie der Kurzroman *Tango* (1948) von Georgi Karaslavov.

---

[10]) Vgl. Krause, F.: Deutsch-bulgarische Kulturbeziehungen. Bibliographie. Berlin 1970, S. 148 ff., 172 ff.
[11]) Vgl. Kossev, D.; Christov, Ch.; Angelov, D.: Bulgarische Geschichte. Sofia 1963, S. 433.
[12]) Očerci (Anm. 6), Bd. II, S. 76.

III. Die Durchsetzung des Sozialistischen Realismus (1949–1956)

Die Beschlüsse des V. Parteitags der BKP im Dezember 1948, die auf den Aufbau des Sozialismus abzielten, setzten der Literatur engere Grenzen und machten der bisherigen Toleranz ein Ende. Die Durchsetzung des Sozialistischen Realismus als der verbindlichen künstlerischen Methode der neuen sozialistischen Literatur wurde nun rigoros betrieben; das Vorbild der Sowjetliteratur (Gor'kij, Šolochov, Furmanov, Polevoj, Majakovskij – letzterer in der einseitigen Deutung durch Todor Pavlov) gewann verbindlichen Charakter; die in der Sowjetunion aufgerollten Kampagnen gegen Formalismus, Dekadenz, Kosmopolitismus usw. wurden, wie im gesamten Ostblock, so auch in Bulgarien ungeprüft und unverändert abgespult mit all den verheerenden Folgen, die sich daraus für die künstlerische Eigenart und Qualität der Literatur ergaben. Zwangsläufig waren alsbald alle jene Deformationen zu verzeichnen, die für die sowjetische Literatur der ausgehenden Stalin-Zeit typisch sind: Schematismus und Schwarz-Weiß-Zeichnung der handelnden Personen, „Lackierung der Wirklichkeit", Konfliktlosigkeit, unbegründeter Optimismus u. ä. Selbst das Gefüge der Gattungen gestaltete sich nun nach dem Muster, das der Sozialistische Realismus vom sowjetischen Typus lieferte. Einer seiner Hauptpfeiler war der Produktions- oder Aufbauroman – etwa *MT-stanica* (MT-Station*, 1950) von Andrej Guljaški (geb. 1914) oder *Zavod 17* (Werk 17, 1953) von Nikola Marinov (1909–1982) – für die bulgarische Literatur vom Stoff her in der Tat eine gänzlich neue Gattung, die allerdings über den primitiven Schematismus ihrer sowjetischen Vorbilder nicht hinausgelangte. Ferner ist die Roman-Epopöe zu nennen, das große Epochenbild, in dessen Rahmen typische private Schicksale in Gestalt einer Familiengeschichte eingeflochten sind. Das monumentalste Beispiel dieser Gattung schuf in Bulgarien Georgi Karaslavov mit dem sechsteiligen Roman *Obiknoveni chora* (Gewöhnliche Menschen*, dt.: Stanka, 1952–1974). Den Strom der geschichtlichen Ereignisse vom Beginn des I. Weltkrieges bis zum Ende des II. Weltkrieges nutzte Karaslavov, um am Schicksal alltäglicher Menschen den politischen und Klassenkampf in der bulgarischen Gesellschaft nachzuzeichnen. Auch der historische Roman erlebte einen Aufschwung. Dimitär Talev (1898–1966) übertrug in seiner Tetralogie über den makedonischen Freiheitskampf im 19. Jh. (*Železnijat svetilnik*/Der eiserne Leuchter*, 1952; *Prespanskite kambani*/Die Glocken von Prespa*, 1954; *Ilinden*/Der Eliastag*, 1953; *Glasovete vi čuvam*/Ich höre eure Stimmen, 1966) die Gattungsstruktur der Roman-Epopöe auf einen historischen Stoff. Angesichts dieses Strebens zur großen epischen Form sprechen die Literaturhistoriker zu Recht von einer „epischen Welle" (*epičeska vălna*), die die bulgarische Literatur Anfang der 50er Jahre erfaßte.

Ein Teil der Schriftsteller aus dem bürgerlichen Lager, die man anfangs umworben und großenteils für die Sache der OF gewonnen hatte, wurde jetzt wieder zurückgestoßen und als reaktionär, idealistisch, formalistisch usw. gebrandmarkt. Selbst Dimitär Dimov, einer der besten Romanautoren der bulgarischen Literatur überhaupt, geriet mit seinem 1951 veröffentlichten Roman *Tjutjun* (Tabak*) in Schwierigkeiten. Er hatte in diesem Werk am Beispiel zweier Brüder, Boris und Pavel Morev, das Schicksal der bulgarischen Intelligenz zwischen Monarchie und sozialistischer Volksrepublik gezeigt. Während der eine Bruder zum erfolgreichen Manager in der von deutschen Konzernen beherrschten Tabakfabrik „Nikotiana" aufsteigt, kämpft der andere als kommunistischer Funktionär gegen Faschismus und Kapitalismus. In breiter Verästelung und unter Verzicht auf jegliche Schwarz-Weiß-Zeichnung seiner Figuren – nur die Vertreter des deutschen Kapitals erscheinen als unsympathische Karikaturen – hatte Dimov den Kampf des alten mit dem neuen Bulgarien geschildert und dabei stark auf die psychologisch-philosophische Dimension seines Themas abgehoben. Der Roman löste bei seinem Erscheinen äußerst widersprüchliche Reaktionen aus, die sich zur wohl erbittertsten literarischen Kontroverse im Nachkriegsbulgarien ausweiteten. Zwar blieb der von Pantelej Zarev erhobene Vorwurf des „Antirealismus" nicht unerwidert; Dimov fand Verteidiger, und der Streit wurde schließlich durch ein Machtwort der Partei zu seinen Gunsten entschieden. Dennoch sah er sich veranlaßt, den Roman nach Maßgabe „neuer ideologischer, erzählerischer und sprachlicher Möglichkeiten", wie er es selbst formulierte, umzuarbeiten[13]).

Die literarische Entwicklung in den 50er Jahren lief darauf hinaus, nicht nur den Sozialistischen Realismus in dogmatischer Enge durchzusetzen, sondern zugleich auch den Kanon der literarischen Tradition auf die realistisch-sozialengagierte Linie Botev-Vazov-Smirnenski-Vapcarov einzuengen und überhaupt die gesamte Weltliteratur in einseitiger Sicht zu präsentieren. In ideologischer Verblendung wurde die Abwertung und Verdrängung wesentlicher Traditionsstränge (*Misăl*-Kreis, Symbolismus, Avantgarde, Diabolismus) und einzelner bedeutender Gestalten der bulgarischen Literatur (Krăst'o Krăstev, Teodor Trajanov u. a.) vollzogen, was notwendig zu einer gefährlichen Verarmung der literarischen Perspektive führen mußte.

IV. Der Bulgarische Schriftstellerverband (SBP)

Eine entscheidende Rolle bei der ideologisch-politischen und ästhetischen Ausrichtung der Literatur in der Nachkriegszeit spielte und spielt nach wie vor der SBP. Aus alten Schriftstellervereinigungen hervorgegangen, die sich 1913 als einheitliche, über den Parteien stehende Organisation mit vorrangig berufsständischen Aufgaben konstituiert hatten, vertrat der SBP, über die materielle und soziale Absicherung seiner Mitglieder hinaus – auf diesem Felde wurden beachtliche Verbesserungen erzielt; heute erfreuen sich die bulgarischen Schriftsteller mancher Privilegien –, nach dem 9.9.1944 die politischen Ziele der OF, seit 1949 die der BKP. Im Verständnis der politischen Führung wurde der SBP zum Instrument der „kulturellen Revolution", durch die „der Überbau der neuen sozialistischen Wirtschaftsbasis", gegründet auf die „Prinzipien der proletarischen Ideologie", geschaffen werden sollte. Entsprechend dem leninistischen Grundsatz, sollte die zu schaffende Kultur ihrer Form nach national, ihrem Inhalt nach sozialistisch sein[14]).

Auf der Vollversammlung der Schriftsteller am 30.10.1944 kam es zur Neugründung des Verbandes. Im Frühjahr 1945 fand die I. Nationale Konferenz der bulgari-

---

[13]) Nach Očerci (Anm. 6), Bd. I, S. 171.
[14]) Nach Kossev (Anm. 11), S. 432. Vgl. Anweiler, O.; Ruffmann, K.-H. (Hrsg.): Kulturpolitik der Sowjetunion. Stuttgart 1973, S. 301.

schen Schriftsteller statt. Höchstes Organ des Verbandes war nunmehr die Vollversammlung (*obšto săbranie*), die alle zwei Jahre einberufen wurde und eine neue Leitung wählte. 1968 wurde durch Beschluß des Politbüros des ZK der BKP der im Vierjahresturnus abzuhaltende Kongreß des SBP als höchstes Organ eingesetzt[15]). Das vom I. Kongreß des Verbandes 1968 angenommene, 1972 und 1980 geänderte und ergänzte Statut des SBP läßt den politischen und organisatorischen Rahmen erkennen, in dem sich Literatur in Bulgarien in den Nachkriegsjahrzehnten bewegen mußte und konnte.

Nach seinem gültigen Statut sieht sich der SBP als Fortsetzer (*priemnik*) der Errungenschaften der fortschrittlichen Weltliteratur, vor allem der russischen klassischen und Sowjetliteratur[16]). Als „schöpferische Methode" wird der Sozialistische Realismus für die Mitglieder des Verbandes verbindlich vorgeschrieben. Dazu heißt es in der Präambel: „Diese Methode weist am wirksamsten den Weg zur Wiedergabe der Wirklichkeit in vielfältigen künstlerischen Formen und Stilen, zur Entdeckung neuer Prozesse und Tendenzen in ihr vom Standpunkt der marxistisch-leninistischen Weltanschauung aus. Die Methode des Sozialistischen Realismus eröffnet vor den bulgarischen Schriftstellern breiteste Möglichkeiten, die Werktätigen ideologisch und ästhetisch zu erziehen, ihre schöpferische Individualität zu äußern, ihre Begabung vollgültig zu entfalten, nach Inhalt und Form innovatorische Werke zu schaffen. Die

Schaubild: Organisatorische Gliederung des SBP

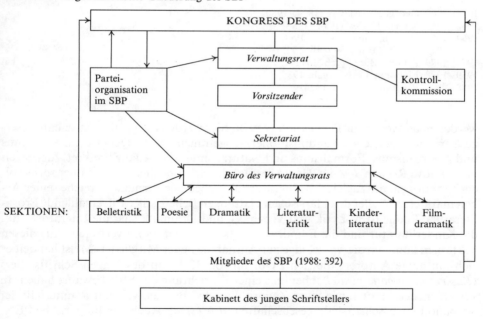

---

[15]) Rečnik na bălgarskata literatura (Wörterbuch der bulgarischen Literatur). Sofia 1976–82, Bd. III, S. 425.
[16]) Ustav na Săjuza na bălgarskite pisateli (Statut des SBP). Sofia 1984, S. 6.

Schöpfer der sozialistischen Literatur werden von den großen Aufbautaten des Volkes, von den Helden unserer Zeit inspiriert, ihre Inspiration ist der historische Optimismus unserer sozialistischen Welt"[17]). An diesem weittragenden Grundsatz halten die maßgeblichen Sprecher des Verbandes auch heute noch fest, obwohl die literarische Praxis sich vom ursprünglichen Konzept des Sozialistischen Realismus so weit entfernt hat, daß das Festhalten an dem Begriff für den Außenstehenden kaum noch nachzuvollziehen ist.

Die Organisationsform des SBP stellt sich in der Weise dar, daß vom Kongreß als seinem höchsten Leitungsorgan ein Verwaltungsrat (*Upravitelen săvet*) eingesetzt wird, der die Geschäfte in der Zeit zwischen den Kongressen führt. Der Verwaltungsrat wählt den Vorsitzenden des Verbandes (*predsedatel*), die Vizepräsidenten (*zamestnik-predsedatel*), die Sekretäre und das Büro des Verwaltungsrates (*Bjuro na Upravitelnija săvet*). Vom Büro des Verwaltungsrates wird die administrative Arbeit des Verbandes, die Leitung der Zeitschriften, Verlage und Gesellschaften, die Verwaltung des „schöpferischen Fonds" (*tvorčeski fond*) usw. durchgeführt. Die wichtigste Aufgabe des Büros besteht in der Koordination und Leitung der sechs „schöpferischen Sektionen" (*tvorčeski sekcii*) des Verbandes, die als die eigentlichen Umschlagplätze von literaturpolitischen Intentionen und schöpferischer Arbeit der Schriftsteller anzusehen sind. Hier vollzieht sich der Erfahrungsaustausch der Schriftsteller, hier

Tabelle 1: Vorsitzende des SBP 1958–1989

1958–1962 Georgi Karaslavov (1904–1980)
1962–1964 Kamen Kalčev (1914–1988)
1964–1966 Dimităr Dimov (1909–1966)
1966–1972 Georgi Džagarov (geb. 1925)
1972–1979 Pantelej Zarev (geb. 1911)
1979–1988 Ljubomir Levčev (geb. 1935)
1988–   Pavel Matev (geb. 1924)

werden neue Werke zur Diskussion gestellt, hier werden die großen Auseinandersetzungen um ästhetische Grundpositionen ausgetragen wie die Debatte um Realismus und Antirealismus, Formalismus und Naturalismus oder – ganz konkret – der Streit um Dimovs Roman *Tjutjun*. Heute verfügt der Schriftstellerverband über sechs solcher Sektionen, die zugleich die literaturpolitischen Schwerpunktbereiche seiner Arbeit markieren. Außer den klassischen Gattungen Belletristik (d. h. erzählende Prosaliteratur), Poesie (d. h. Lyrik und Versepik), und Dramatik sind die Literaturkritik, die Kinderliteratur und die Filmdramatik (*kinodramaturgija*) vertreten. Aus diesen Sektionen kommen die Vorschläge zur Aufnahme neuer Mitglieder. Meist handelt es sich um junge Autoren, die sich zuvor im sog. Kabinett des jungen Schriftstellers (*Kabinet na mladija pisatel*), ebenfalls einer Einrichtung des SBP, bewährt haben. In verschiedenen Städten wie Stara Zagora, Plovdiv, Burgas, Varna u. a. unterhält der Verband lokale Schriftstellergesellschaften (*družestva*). Auch das Bulgarische PEN-Zentrum, das, bereits 1926 mit Ivan Šišmanov als erstem Vorsitzenden gegründet,

---

[17]) Ustav (Anm. 16), S. 7.

1944 seine Tätigkeit im Zeichen der neuen politischen Prämissen fortsetzte, ist eine Abteilung des SBP und vertritt dessen ideologische und ästhetische Ziele.

In der Tat verfügt der SBP somit über sehr beachtliche Möglichkeiten zur Förderung, aber auch zur Gängelung seiner Mitglieder. Nicht nur unterstützt er sie wirkungsvoll bei so wichtigen Problemen wie der Wohnungsbeschaffung, der Sozialfürsorge, bei Informations-, Erholungs- und „schöpferischen" Reisen, sondern bietet ihnen, da er eine Reihe von literarischen Zeitschriften in Sofia und anderen Städten herausgibt und einen eigenen Verlag, *Bălgarski pisatel* (Bulgarischer Schriftsteller),

Tabelle 2: Titelproduktion des Verlags „Bălgarski pisatel"

Der am 20.12.1947 gegründete, dem SBP unterstehende Verlag legte von 1948 bis 1982 5406 literarische Titel vor. Die Jahresproduktion betrug:

1948: 37	1958: 104	1968: 253	1978: 216
1949: 50	1959: 136	1969: 197	1979: 177
1950: 57	1960: 161	1970: 205	1980: 180
1951: 30	1961: 163	1971: 202	1981: 207
1952: 71	1962: 170	1972: 194	1982: 207
1953: 69	1963: 186	1973: 177	1985: 215
1954: 64	1964: 149	1974: 182	1988: 157
1955: 88	1965: 188	1975: 178	
1956: 124	1966: 221	1976: 189	
1957: 124	1967: 248	1977: 181	

Angaben nach E. Furnadžieva; I. Furnadžiev: Izdatelstvo Bălgarski pisatel. Bibliografija (Der Verlag „Bulgarischer Schriftsteller". Bibliographie) 1948–1977. Sofia 1981; I. Furnadžiev: Izdatelstvo Bălgarski pisatel. Bibliografija 1978–1982. Sofia 1985.

betreibt, lukrative Publikationschancen. *Bălgarski pisatel* ist der bei weitem größte und einflußreichste Belletristikverlag in Bulgarien. 1947 als Hausverlag des SBP gegründet, legt er nicht nur die zeitgenössische, sondern auch die klassische bulgarische Literatur in großem Umfang vor, wobei die kommentierten Schulausgaben der *Biblioteka za učenika* (Bibliothek für den Schüler) einen nicht zu unterschätzenden Einfluß auf die Literaturverbreitung und literarische Bildung im Volk haben. Durchschnittlich erscheinen pro Jahr etwa 200 Titel mit einer Gesamtauflage von 3 000 000 Exemplaren[18]).

Tabelle 3: Wichtige Literaturzeitschriften und Almanache
Literaturen front (Literaturfront). Sofia 1944 ff.
Septemvri (September). Sofia 1948 ff.
Literaturna misăl (Literarische Idee). Sofia 1957 ff.
Narodna kultura (Volkskultur). Sofia 1957 ff.
Plamăk (Flamme). Sofia 1957 ff.
Prostori (Räume). Varna 1961 ff.
Trakija (Thrakien). Plovdiv 1968 ff.
Zornica (Morgenstern). Gabrovo 1972 ff.
Săvremennik (Zeitgenosse). Sofia 1973 ff.
Chorizont (Horizont). Stara Zagora 1974 ff.

---

[18]) Daten nach: Rečnik (Anm. 15), Bd. I, S. 166.

Die für das literarische Leben in Bulgarien nicht anders als monopolistisch zu nennende Stellung des SBP erhält ihre politische Operationalisierung durch die enge Anbindung des Verbandes an die BKP. Nicht nur zählt es zu den erklärten Aufgaben des SBP, das „Kriterium der klassengebundenen Parteilichkeit" (d. h. den Parteistandpunkt) zu bekräftigen und die Schriftsteller „um die Politik der BKP zusammenzuschließen"; vielmehr sichert auch die Organisationsstruktur des Verbandes der Parteiorganisation innerhalb des SBP wesentlichen Einfluß in Kongreß, Verwaltungsrat, Sekretariat und Büro des Verwaltungsrats.

Eine beträchtliche Steuerung und Stimulierung der literarischen Produktion geht von den zahlreichen Literaturpreisen aus, die von Staat und Gemeinden an Schriftsteller verliehen werden. Größtes Ansehen besitzt der 1949 von der NSb gestiftete Dimitrov-Preis (*Dimitrovska nagrada*), zu dem etwa 50 örtliche Preise treten. Auch den internationalen Literaturpreisen kommt eine richtungsweisende Funktion zu, so dem Christo-Botev-Preis (seit 1976; Laureaten: Aleksej Surkov, Miroslav Krleža, Rasul Gamzatov, Günther Wallraff u. a.) und dem Nikola-Vapcarov-Preis (seit 1979; Laureaten: William Meredith, Jarosław Iwaszkiewicz, Stefan Hermlin, Ernesto Cardenal u. a.).

V. Die Neue Welle nach dem Aprilplenum: Die 60er Jahre

Drei Jahre nach Stalins Tod und zwei Monate nach dem XX. Parteitag der KPdSU, der die Abrechnung mit dem Personenkult des Diktators und den Abweichungen von der sozialistischen Gesetzlichkeit einleitete, versuchte auch die BKP auf dem Aprilplenum, mit den stalinistischen Deformationen im eigenen Bereich aufzuräumen. Für die Literaturpolitik bedeutete dies, daß nunmehr dogmatische und schematische Auslegungen und Anwendungen der Doktrin des Sozialistischen Realismus angeprangert wurden, daß diese „schöpferische Methode" geöffnet, gleichwohl aber nicht grundsätzlich in Frage gestellt wurde. Überhaupt kann man nicht sagen, daß die Entdogmatisierung der Literatur in Bulgarien rasch um sich gegriffen hätte. Während in der UdSSR Schriftsteller wie Il'ja Erenburg, Aleksandr Tvardovskij oder Vera Panova noch im Jahre 1953 das literarische „Tauwetter" einleiteten und sich fortan, wenn auch mit gewissen Schwankungen, ein neues, freieres, kulturelles Klima verbreitete, verhielten sich die bulgarischen Schriftsteller zunächst einmal abwartend. Noch 1954 war Dimovs *Tjutjun* in überarbeiteter Form erschienen, diesmal mit einer jungen kommunistischen Tabakarbeiterin als Pendant zu der bürgerlichen Heldin Irina. Und 1958 veröffentlichte Emilijan Stanev die ersten Teile des Romans *Ivan Kondarev** (dt.: Heißer Sommer, 1958–1964), gleichsam das Gegenstück zu *Tjutjun*, in dem er die Lage um den Septemberaufstand 1923 beleuchtete. Dem Titelhelden, einem zum antifaschistischen Kämpfer heranreifenden Lehrer, wird in dem Roman als Vertreter der faschistischen Kräfte Aleksandăr Christakiev gegenübergestellt; der politische Kampf ist zugleich ein moralisches Ringen. Gattungsmäßig stellte der Roman, wie die Literaturkritik vermerkt, einen „Übergangstyp zwischen der Periode vor und nach dem Aprilplenum" dar[19]), indem er sich einerseits noch als monumen-

---

[19]) Očerci (Anm. 6), Bd. I, S. 211.

tale historische Roman-Epopöe, andererseits bereits als ein Werk zeigte, in dem die Menschen in der vollen Komplexität ihrer privaten und politischen Existenz dargestellt wurden.

Dem schematischen, einseitig politisch-gesellschaftlichen Menschenbild, das die Literatur, gelenkt und geleitet von einer wachsamen, sich normativ verstehenden Literaturkritik, bislang vermittelt hatte, erteilte nun auch die neue Parteispitze eine deutliche Absage. „Mehr unter dem Volk – näher dem Leben" (*Poveče meždu naroda – po-blizo do života*) lautete die Devise, unter die Todor Živkov die bulgarische Literatur in seiner großen Rede vor dem SBP am 8.4.1958 stellte. Zwar wurden hier den Schriftstellern die gleichen Aufgaben gestellt wie bisher (kommunistische Erziehung der Massen, Festigung des sozialistischen Bewußtseins, Formung der moralischen Eigenschaften und Charakterzüge des neuen Menschen) und die unveräußerliche Bedeutung des Sozialistischen Realismus festgeschrieben, doch wurden auch einst erwünschte Autoren wie Emil Manov und Todor Genov jetzt getadelt und der Literatur als Generalthema das Leben des Volkes nahegelegt: „Dieses Volk, sein reiches Leben, sein Kampf und seine heroische Arbeit für den Sieg des Sozialismus, seine Gedanken, Gefühle und Wünsche sind der Hauptgegenstand des gesamten künstlerischen Schaffens bei uns und müssen es sein"[20]. Mängel und Defizite der sozialistischen Gegenwart sollten zwar, ebenso wie die der überwundenen alten Welt, kritisch beleuchtet werden, doch so, daß die Errungenschaften der neuen Welt durch sie nicht verdunkelt würden. „Die Widersprüche, Konflikte und Gebrechen können und dürfen nicht isoliert von unseren großen Erfolgen, von den wahrhaft großen Taten der freien bewußten Arbeit des Volkes wiedergegeben werden. Weil für unser System nicht die Schwächen und Mängel charakteristisch sind, sondern das Neue, das Progressive, der Sozialismus. Weil die Schwächen und Mängel sich in heftigem Konflikt mit dem sozialistischen Ideal, mit unserer sozialistischen Praxis befinden. Weil die Lebenswahrheit so ist und in den Kunstwerken getreu widergespiegelt werden muß. Weil endlich die Aufgabe der Kritik nicht nur darin besteht, das Unrichtige, Ungesunde, Verfaulte zu treffen, sondern auch darin, das Neue, Richtige, Gesunde anzustacheln und zu befestigen"[21].

Verglichen mit den hier verkündeten Grundsätzen, nehmen sich die Ausführungen des Parteichefs in seiner zweiten großen Grundsatzrede zu Fragen der Literatur und Kunst *Komunističeskata idejnost – visš princip na našata literatura i izkustvo* (Die kommunistische Ideologie – höchstes Prinzip unserer Literatur und Kunst), gehalten am 15.4.1963 bei einem Treffen des Politbüros der BKP mit Funktionären der Kulturfront[22], wie der Versuch aus, die Literatur, die in den vorausgegangenen Jahren einige beachtliche Erfolge vorzuweisen hatte, wieder strenger am Zügel zu führen. Wieder wurde der Kampf gegen die „bürgerliche Ideologie", gegen Revisionismus und Dogmatismus beschworen, doch lag der entscheidende Akzent auf den Gefahren, die von der ersteren drohten, gefördert von finsteren Mächten in den USA und Westeuropa und aufgenommen von der bulgarischen Jugend in Form von Jazz, Mode, Erotik. Die detaillierten Einlassungen über pessimistische, dekadente und auf-

---

[20] Živkov, T.: Za literaturata (Über die Literatur). Sofia 1981, S. 20.
[21] Živkov (Anm. 20), S. 31 ff.
[22] Živkov (Anm. 20), S. 65 ff.

müpfige Töne in der Lyrik, die Auseinandersetzung mit den Dichterinnen Nevena Stefanova, Liljana Stefanova und Blaga Dimitrova, mit dem Erzähler Vasil Popov und dem Dichter Georgi Džagarov, die Polemik mit dem Literaturkritiker Boris Delčev – all das ließ erkennen, mit welchem Ernst die politische Spitze in Bulgarien die literarische Entwicklung verfolgte und im Griff zu behalten bemüht war. Dabei wurde zugleich versucht, die inzwischen als Dogmatiker geschmähten Autoren wie Georgi Karaslavov, Christo Radevski oder Ljudmil Stojanov dem Anathema zu entziehen.

Anfang der 60er Jahre war abzusehen, daß sich die neuen Tendenzen in der bulgarischen Literatur mit Macht durchsetzten. Die „neue Welle" (*nova vălna*) erfaßte alle Gattungen, zeigte sich aber zuerst in der Lyrik, wo das zeitweilig suspendierte „schöpferische Ich" wieder voll in seine Rechte eintrat. Lyriker, die in den Jahren zuvor geschwiegen hatten (Dora Gabe, Nikola Furnadžiev) oder deren Poesie in das Sperrfeuer der dogmatischen Kritik geraten war (Valeri Petrov), traten wieder an die Öffentlichkeit. Neue Talente wie Veselin Chančev, Georgi Džagarov und Ljubomir Levčev versuchten in ihren Versen, das gesellschaftspolitische Engagement mit neuem poetischem Ausdruck zu verbinden. Man hat von einer „Poesie der Offensive" (*poezija na nastăplenieto*) dieser „Aprilgeneration" gesprochen.

Selbst das Drama, sonst eher das Stiefkind der bulgarischen Literatur, nahm jetzt einen beachtlichen Aufschwung, und es waren zwei genuine Poeten, die dem Theater neue, attraktive Stücke lieferten: Valeri Petrov (geb. 1920) und Georgi Džagarov (geb. 1925). Valeri Petrov, noch aus der Vorkriegszeit bekannt als Verfasser stimmungsvoller, unpathetischer Dichtungen, später als begabter Shakespeare-Übersetzer, errang mit dem Drama *Kogato rozite tancuvat* (Wenn die Rosen tanzen*, dt.: Tanzende Rosen, 1961) einen ungewöhnlichen Erfolg. Das Stück mit dem Untertitel „Traumspiel mit Musik und Ballett" erinnert in der Kombination von scherzhaftem Spiel und Lyrismus an die frühen Komödien Shakespeares, in der Verwendung verfremdender Effekte an Brecht[23]). Herrschten in dieser lyrischen Komödie das Liebesthema und allgemeine philosophische Probleme vor, so griff Georgi Džagarov mit seinem Drama *Prokurorăt* (Der Staatsanwalt, 1965) mitten hinein in die sozialistische Wirklichkeit. Im Zusammenprall zwischen dem Staatsanwalt und dem Untersuchungsrichter um Recht und Gesetze wurden in dem Stück politische und psychologische Probleme der stalinistischen Epoche aufgearbeitet. Zählte Valeri Petrovs lyrisches Drama, wie auch die Dramen von Ivan Pejčev, Ivan Radoev, Božidar Božilov u. a., zu den charakteristischen Stücken der sog. „poetischen Welle" (*poetičeska vălna*), so bewegte sich Džagarov mit seinem *Prokurorăt* bereits auf den „analytisch-psychologischen" Dramentypus hin, der in den 70er Jahren Bedeutung gewinnen sollte[24]). Neben diesen neuen Ansätzen nahm sich das beliebte historische Drama eher konventionell aus, so die Stücke von Kamen Zidarov (geb. 1902) *Ivan Šišman* (1962) und *Kalojan* (1969), der damit an den Erfolg seines Dramas *Carska milost* (Zarengnade, 1955), das in der Zeit des Zaren Ferdinand spielt, anknüpfen konnte.

---

[23]) Očerci (Anm. 6), Bd. II, S. 316.
[24]) Veličkov, M.: Theater und Dramatik in Bulgarien. Einführung in ihre zeitgenössischen Entwicklungen, in: Südosteuropa-Mitteilungen. (1980) 1, S. 76.

Nach Lyrik und Drama sollte freilich bald die erzählende Prosa zum interessantesten Träger der neuen Tendenzen in der bulgarischen Literatur werden. Wiewohl das Gattungsspektrum nach wie vor den alten Produktionsroman (*proizvodstven roman*), den Partisanenroman – *Zvezdite nad nas* (Die Sterne über uns, 1962) von Pavel Vežinov – und insbesondere historische Romane wie die Romanchronik *Samuil* (Bd. I–III, 1958–1960) und der Paisij-Roman *Chilendarskijat monach* (Der Mönch von Chilendar, 1962) von Dimităr Talev oder *Vreme razdelno* (Trennende Zeit*, dt.: Schwur unter dem Halbmond, 1964) von Anton Dončev enthielt, zeigten sich als produktivste Erzählgattungen der Kurzroman (*povest*) und die Erzählung bzw. Novelle, Gattungen, die nicht mehr eine Totale, sondern nur einen begrenzten Ausschnitt der Wirklichkeit boten, oftmals betrachtet aus der individuellen Perspektive eines Helden. Es versteht sich, daß damit über die Problematisierung des politischen und sozialen Lebens hinaus Aspekte des Privaten und Intimen in den Vordergrund treten konnten und traten. Wichtiger war aber wohl in der damaligen politisch-geistigen Atmosphäre, daß die Autoren vorsichtig an bestimmte Tabuthemen rührten, deren Nennung oder Erörterung in der stalinistischen Epoche ausgeschlossen war. Das galt nicht nur für bestimmte „private" Tabus wie Ehebruch oder -scheidung und bestimmte psychische Probleme, sondern vor allem für die Erscheinungen, die sich unmittelbar aus den „Deformationen" der Stalin-Zeit ergeben hatten: Repression, Verfolgung, Deportation unschuldiger Menschen unter irgendeinem politischen Vorwand. Erzähler wie Kamen Kalčev (1914–1988) und Bogomil Rajnov (geb. 1919) fanden hier ihr neues Thema.

Eines der ersten Erzählwerke, das solche Fragen aufwarf und gestaltete, war Kamen Kalčevs Roman *Dvama v novija grad* (Zwei in der neuen Stadt, 1964). Der Held des Romans, der als Ich-Erzähler auftretende Jugendverbandsfunktionär Marin Maslarski, zählt zu den Opfern des Stalinismus: Er war aufgrund einer Denunziation gesetzwidrig „repressiert" und verhaftet und erst nach dem Aprilplenum rehabilitiert und freigelassen worden. Der Roman zeigt, wie Maslarski versucht, in einer neuen Stadt ein neues Leben mit seiner Frau, die ihn nach seiner Verhaftung verlassen hatte, zu beginnen. Das war, wenn auch – gemessen an den Werken der sowjetischen Tauwetter-Literatur – recht behutsam und relativ spät, ein Durchbruch; hier begann, wie es der Kritiker Tončo Žečev formuliert hat, „der Roman unserer reifen Gesellschaft", realisierten sich endlich die Anstrengungen, „das wahrhaft zeitgenössische Thema im Roman zu erfassen"[25]. Noch einmal gelang Kamen Kalčev ein bemerkenswerter literarischer Wurf – mit seinen *Sofijski razkazi* (Sofioter Erzählungen*, 1967), Prosastücken, mit einem Briefträger als vorgeschobenem Erzähler, der aus seiner beschränkt-verschmitzten Sicht die Kehrseite der Revolution beleuchtet. Das sich hier abzeichnende, vor allem aus der russischen Literatur bekannte *skaz*-Verfahren, d.h. die durch individuelle Sprachmerkmale bestimmte Erzählerrede, wurde in der Folgezeit von einigen begabten Erzählern zur virtuosen Vollendung gebracht, wobei auf das Element des Witzes und des Humors aus der nie versiegenden Quelle der bulgarischen Volkserzählung zurückgegriffen werden konnte. Der unbestrittene Meister dieser Erzählform ist Jordan Radičkov (geb. 1929). In vielen seiner Erzählungen – zwi-

---

[25]) Očerci (Anm. 6), Bd. I, S. 227.

schen 1959 und 1969 legte er nicht weniger als dreizehn Erzählbände vor, darunter *Nie vrabčeta* (Wir Spatzen*, 1968) und *Baruten bukvar* (Pulverfibel*, 1969) – steigern sich Humor und Ironie, etwa wenn er die Menschen und Vorkommnisse des fiktiven Dorfes Čerkazki schildert, bis zur Groteske, die an E. T. A. Hoffmann, Gogol', Bulgakov und den „magischen Realismus" von Borges gemahnt[26]).

Neben Radičkov konnten sich in den 60er Jahren Pavel Vežinov (geb. 1914) und Nikolaj Chajtov (geb. 1919) als eigengeprägte Erzähler profilieren. Vežinov hatte noch vor dem Krieg mit Erzählungen debütiert, die der Kritiker Bojan Ničev als Beispiel für einen bulgarischen „Neorealismus" deutet[27]); dann hatte er in der Nachkriegszeit eine Reihe von Romanen und Erzählungen vorgelegt. Sein ureigenstes Thema, die psychologischen und moralischen Probleme des zeitgenössischen Menschen in der sozialistischen Gesellschaft, fand er erst in den Novellenbänden *Momčeto s cigulkata* (Der Junge mit der Geige, 1963) und *Dăch na bademi* (Ein Hauch von Mandeln (1966). Vežinov arbeitete mit Kontrasten und Montagetechniken, in einige Erzählungen brachte er Phantastik und Groteske ein. Sein novellistisch komponierter Roman *Zvezdite nad nas* (Die Sterne über uns, 1966) mit dem Motiv der versehentlichen Hinrichtung stieß auf breites Interesse in der bulgarischen Leserschaft. Nikolaj Chajtov, aus den Rhodopen stammend, kam erst relativ spät zur Literatur. Seine Reisebeschreibungen (*Razbulena Rodopa*/Entschleierte Rhodopen, 1960), historischen Skizzen (*Chajduti*/Haiduken, 1960) und Erzählungen (*Iskrici ot ognište*/Funken vom Herdfeuer, 1959) kündigten ein starkes erzählerisches Talent an, das sich in dem Band *Divi razkazi* (Wilde Geschichten*, 1967) voll entfaltete. Seine besorgte Sicht der modernen urbanen Zivilisation, deren Vordringen nicht nur die Natur, sondern auch die Lebensform der bäuerlichen Welt zerstört, erinnert an die Vertreter der russischen Dorfprosa (Valentin Rasputin, Vladimir Solouchin). Wie Radičkov, so versuchte sich auch Chajtov immer wieder im *skaz*. Die sprachliche und stoffliche Authentizität seiner Skizzen und Erzählungen ebenso wie die menschliche Wärme, die aus ihnen strahlt, machten Chajtov zu einem der beliebtesten Autoren im heutigen Bulgarien.

Das mächtige Aufkommen der Dorferzählung – hier sind ferner Autoren wie Georgi Mičev, Vasil Popov und Dimităr Vălev zu nennen –, das von einigen Kritikern im Zusammenhang mit der naiven Kunst (*primitiv*) gesehen und als regionalistisch, ja, als „Talkessel-Literatur" (*kotlovinna literatura*) eingeschätzt wurde[28]), bedeutete nicht, daß nicht auch der Roman mit einigen beachtlichen Werken vertreten wäre. Aus der großen Zahl neuer Romane – allein im Jahre 1962 erschienen elf Romane, von denen sechs zeitgenössischen und fünf geschichtlichen Themen gewidmet waren[29]) – seien erwähnt: *Mărtvo vălnenie* (Toter Wellengang*, dt.: Und wenn ich dich zwingen muß, 1961) und die Kurzromane *Predi da se rodja. I sled tova** (Bevor ich zur Welt kam. Und danach, 1968, 1971) von dem begabten Erzähler Ivajlo Petrov (geb. 1923), der mit den Mitteln der Ironie und der Parodie das Leben der Bauern in der

---

[26]) Vgl. Tretner, A.: Jordan Raditschkow – Tscherkaski und die Welt, Nachwort zu: Raditschkow, J.: Dem Herrgott vom Wagen gefallen. Kurzgeschichten. Leipzig 1987, S. 336.

[27]) Literatur Bulgariens (Anm. 5), S. 286.

[28]) Očerci (Anm. 6), Bd. II, S. 291.

[29]) Žečev, T.: Săvremenni obrazi i idei (Zeitgenössische Gestalten und Ideen). Sofia 1964, S. 10ff.

Dobrudscha beschrieb. Mit den Romanen *Pătuvane kăm sebe si* (Reise zu sich selbst, 1965), *Otklonenie* (Abweichung*, dt.: Liebe auf Abwegen, 1967) und *Lavina* (Lawine, 1971) unternahm Blaga Dimitrova (geb. 1922), die zuvor insbesondere durch ihre Lyrik bekannt geworden war, erzählerische Experimente, indem sie an autobiographischem Material die Ort-Zeit-Relationen auflöste, komplizierte Montagetechniken einsetzte und narrative mit essayistischen Strukturen vermischte.

Ganz anders der historische Roman *Slučajat Džem* (Der Fall Cem*, 1966) von Vera Mutafčieva (geb. 1929). Vom Fach her Historikerin und Expertin für osmanische Geschichte, griff die Autorin hier den gleichen Stoff auf, der im Zentrum des Romans *Der verfluchte Hof* (1954) des jugoslawischen Nobelpreisträgers Ivo Andrić steht: das tragische Schicksal des osmanischen Prinzen Cem, der im 15. Jh. zum „Spielball zwischen Kirche und Thron" (so der Titel der deutschen Übersetzung) wurde. Für die Darbietung des Geschehens im politischen und kulturellen Kräftefeld zwischen Orient und Okzident wählte Vera Mutafčieva, im Unterschied zu Andrić, die Form der kriminalistischen Untersuchung. Die einzelnen Kapitel stellen fiktive „Aussagen" (*pokazanija*) der beteiligten Akteure aus den Jahren 1481 bis 1499 dar, aus denen sich mosaikartig das Bild der Epoche und des osmanischen Thronprätendenten ergibt.

VI. Die Literatur der 70er Jahre: Junge Prosa und groteskes Drama

In vielem bot die bulgarische Literatur in den 70er Jahren die Fortsetzung der Tendenzen, die sich nach dem Aprilplenum abgezeichnet hatten: fortschreitende Enttabuisierung im Thematischen, Überwindung des künstlerischen Schematismus, Komplizierung der psychologischen und ethischen Fragestellungen, Aufbrechen des Totalitätsanspruchs in der Literatur durch Subjektivierung und offene Strukturen in den Erzählgattungen. Namentlich der in den kurzen Prosaformen erreichte künstlerische Standard setzte sich bei Erzählern wie Nikolaj Chajtov, Pavel Vežinov und Ivajlo Petrov fort. Gleich am Beginn der 70er Dekade steht eines der gelungensten Werke der bulgarischen Literatur, Emilijan Stanevs historischer Roman *Antichrist* (Der Antichrist*, 1970). Schon wenige Jahre zuvor hatte sich Stanev der frühen Geschichte seines Volkes in dem Kurzroman *Legenda za Sibin, Preslavskija knjaz* (Legende von Sibin, dem Fürsten von Preslav, 1968) zugewandt; nun schrieb er über die Welt der mittelalterlichen Bogomilen, jener vom Manichäismus geprägten Häretiker, die einen eigentümlichen sozialen und geistigen Unruheherd auf der Balkanhalbinsel darstellten, der bis nach Italien und Frankreich hineinwirkte. Stanev legte also mit diesem Roman eine Wurzel der bulgarischen Geistestradition frei, zum anderen konnte er im historischen Gewande philosophische Fragen anschneiden, die die Stellung des Menschen in einer aufgewühlten Zeit des Umbruchs betrafen. Da der Roman aus der Ich-Perspektive des Helden erzählt wird, des Mönchs En'o, der sich zunächst den hesychastischen Mystikern anschließt, dann zu den ketzerischen Bogomilen stößt, um schließlich gegen die Türken für sein Volk zu kämpfen, konnte Stanev seinen Stoff wie eine altbulgarisch stilisierte Beichte – gleichsam in einem historisierenden *skaz* – darbieten, während die geschichtliche Welt nicht mit auktorialer

Omnipotenz, sondern allein durch das individuelle Prisma des Ich-Erzählers evoziert wurde. Mit anderen Worten, Stanev gelang hier eine Synthese von offenen narrativen Strukturen mit dem historischen Thema, die den *Antichrist* zu einem unverkennbaren Meisterwerk machte. Die bulgarische historische Prosa gewann hier Qualitäten, die sich mit den besten Werken dieses Genres in der jugoslawischen (Meša Selimović) oder russischen Literatur (Bulat Okudžava) durchaus messen können. (In den westlichen Literaturen gab es, soweit zu sehen, dazu lange kein Pendant.)

Auch weitere Erzählwerke der 70er Jahre zeigten Neuerungen in Inhalt und Form. Als das inhaltlich Neue erkannte der Kritiker Ivan Spasov „die delikate menschliche Welt" in den Romanen und Erzählungen dieses Jahrzehnts[30]), darunter von Pavel Vežinov *Noštem s belite kone* (Nachts mit weißen Pferden*, 1975), *Barierata* (Die Barriere, 1977), *Belijat guster* (Die weiße Eidechse, 1977) und *Ezernoto momče* (Der Seejunge, 1978); von Ivajlo Petrov *Ljubov po pladne* (Liebe am Mittag, 1976); von Diko Fučedžiev (geb. 1928), *Rekata* (Der Fluß*, dt.: Schatten über dem Fluß, 1974), *Zelenata pustinja* (Die grüne Wüste*. dt.: Das grüne Gras der Wüste, 1978) u. a. Es ging in dieser Literatur in zunehmendem Maße um allgemeinmenschliche Lebensprobleme wie Liebe, Krankheit und Tod, während das Produktionsmotiv zurücktrat. In der neu aufkommenden Science-Fiction-Literatur oder „wissenschaftlichen Phantastik" (*naučna fantastika*), wie man sie in Bulgarien nennt, wurde in futuristischen Projektionen bei Autoren wie Atanas Nakovski (*Bez senki*/Ohne Schatten, 1970), Pavel Vežinov (*Nad vsičko*/Über alles, 1973) oder Emil Manov (*Galaktičeska bufonada*/Galaktische Buffonade, 1978) der technische Fortschritt zur Diskussion gestellt.

Um die Dekadenwende trat zu den schon etablierten Schriftstellern eine Gruppe junger, um 1940 geborener Erzähler auf den Plan, die, wie der ungarische Bulgarist György Szondi zeigt, die typischen Ausdrucksmerkmale dieser Generation deutlich erkennen lassen[31]). Ihr gehörten u. a. an: Stanislav Stratiev (geb. 1941), Ljuben Petkov (geb. 1939), Dimităr Korudžiev (geb. 1941), Georgi Markovski (geb. 1941), Vladimir Zarev (geb. 1947). Fast alle diese Autoren pflegten die kleine, offene Prosaform, mit der sie, ideologisch weit unbefangener als ihre Väter, die brennenden Fragen und komplexen Probleme der modernen urbanen Gesellschaft, insbesondere natürlich die der eigenen Generation, artikulierten. Ihr Erzählton war „kritischer und selbstkritischer" als bei den Älteren und von Lyrisierung und Selbstironie befrachtet (G. Szondi). In vieler Hinsicht erinnerten die Werke dieser Autoren an die „junge Prosa" (*molodaja proza*) oder Jeans-Prosa, die sich nach dem Vorbild von J. D. Salingers *The Catcher in the Rye* (1951) in Ost und West, vor allem auch in der UdSSR und Jugoslawien, in den 60er Jahren ausbreitete. Das hat der Zagreber Literaturwissenschaftler Aleksandar Flaker am Beispiel von Stanislav Stratievs Kurzroman *Diva patica meždu dărvetata* (Die Wildente zwischen den Bäumen, 1972) herausgestellt. Der typische junge Erzähler, der hier auftrat, setzte sich gegen die gesellschaftlichen Verkrustungen und toten Traditionen zur Wehr und fand seinen obligatorischen Eva-

---

[30]) Spasov, I.: Čerti ot săvremennata bălgarska literatura (Grundzüge der zeitgenössischen bulgarischen Literatur). Sofia 1980, S. 66.

[31]) Sondi (Szondi), D. (G.): Edno pokolenie v bălgarskata literatura (Eine Generation in der bulgarischen Literatur), in: Dokladi 12 (Anm. 6), S. 493–498.

sionsraum in einer alten Burg³²). Die provokanten Züge der „jungen Prosa" freilich, die vor allem in Jugoslawien im Gebrauch eines vulgären Großstadtjargons und in unverblümten Sexualmotiven sich ausdrückte, waren in der bulgarischen Literatur nicht anzutreffen.

Stanislav Stratiev wurde in den folgenden Jahren auch durch eine Reihe effektvoller Komödien bekannt, mit denen er der Hausautor (und seit 1976 der Dramaturg) des Sofioter Satirischen Theaters wurde, einer der besten bulgarischen Bühnen. In *Rimska banja* (Das römische Bad*, 1974), *Sako ot velur* (Sakko aus Velour*, dt.: Das Schaf, 1976) und *Rejs* (Der Bus, 1979) brachte er groteske Situationen aus dem Leben des sozialistischen Alltags, insbesondere Auswüchse der Bürokratie, auf die Bühne, was durchaus in einem typologischen Zusammenhang mit dem westlichen absurden Theater gesehen werden kann³³). Überhaupt kennzeichnet eine Tendenz zu Groteskem und Absurdem die „belletristische Welle" (*beletrističnata vălna*) im bulgarischen Drama der 70er Jahre – so genannt nach den „Belletristen" (Prosaerzählern), die jetzt, nach den Poeten, als Dramatiker hervortraten; darunter Dragomir Asenov (geb. 1926) mit seinen differenzierenden Dramen wie dem im Milieu der technischen Intelligenz spielenden *Zlatnoto pokritie* (Die Golddeckung, 1974) und dem Militärstück *Krajat na denja* (Das Ende des Tages, 1975); Nikolaj Chajtov mit mehreren dramatischen Miniaturen und, allen voran, Jordan Radičkov. Dieser Autor, der in seinen Erzählungen den Volkswitz virtuos mit der Groteske zu verbinden wußte, hatte bereits mit seinem ersten Stück, *Sumatocha* (Tumult, 1965) bewiesen, daß sich seine Erzählmanier auf das Drama übertragen ließ. (In diesem Stück erzählen dreizehn Figuren je auf ihre Art die Geschichte von einem Fuchs, der, indem er sich totstellt, einem Bauern die Fische raubt.) Radičkov verfolgte diese Linie der ins Absurde treibenden Volksposse weiter und erreichte mit dem parabolisch zu deutenden Stück *Opit za letene* (Flugversuch, 1979), in dem ein irreales Flugerlebnis zweier bulgarischer Bauerngruppen vorgeführt wird, den unbestrittenen Höhepunkt seiner dramatischen Kunst. Die sog. „analytisch-psychologische" Dramatik, die sich, häufig in der Form des Kammerstückes, der Alltagsprobleme, namentlich der schwierigen sozialen Situation der Frauen, annahm – etwa in *Bjagstvoto* (Die Flucht, 1974) von Michail Veličkov oder *D-r Faustina* (Dr. Faustine, 1972) und *Nečakana srešta* (Unerwartete Begegnung, 1974) von Blaga Dimitrova – wirkte dagegen eher blaß, obwohl aus ihr der beste Dramatiker der Folgezeit, Konstantin Iliev (geb. 1937) hervorging, der, bekannt überdies als Übersetzer Büchners und Brechts, bereits mit *Prozorecăt* (Das Fenster, 1977) und *Bosilek za Draginko* (Basilikum für Draginko, 1978) Beachtung fand.

In die 70er Jahre fiel die weitgehende Rehabilitierung und Reintegrierung der vordem ausgeschalteten idealistischen und formalistischen, also nicht-mimetischen, Traditionen der bulgarischen Literatur, die seit 1949 Un-Literatur gewesen waren. Der ganze Javorov, der ganze Debeljanov, mit Ausnahme ihrer Sozialismus-Kritik auch Penčo Slavejkov und Krăst'o Krăstev, mit einigem Zögern selbst Teodor Trajanov wurden nun wieder in das literarische Erbe der Bulgaren eingereiht, das sich ohne sie

---

³²) Flaker, A.: Modelle der Jeans-Prosa. Kronberg/Ts. 1975, S. 198 ff., 226.
³³) Literatur Bulgariens (Anm. 5), S. 507.

freilich auch seltsam genug ausgenommen hatte. Möglicherweise gewann die aktuelle Lyrik aus diesem Prozeß einige Impulse. Stärker freilich war der Einfluß sowjetischer Vorbilder, etwa Evgenij Evtušenkos oder Andrej Voznessenskijs, zu erkennen, vor allem bei Ljubomir Levčev (geb. 1935), in dessen Gedichtbänden *Dnevnik za izgarjane* (Tagebuch zum Verbrennen, 1973) und *Svoboda* (Freiheit, 1975) das Öffentliche und das Politische mit Reflexion und Emotionalität zu einer neuen Form lyrischer Publizistik amalgamierte. Auch sein Altersgenosse Damjan P. Damjanov (geb. 1935) gelangte, vor allem in dem aus Vers- und Prosapassagen montierten Text *Tetradka po vsičko* (Heft für alles, 1978–80) zu einem neuen Konzept des lyrischen Ausdrucks. Frisch traten in den 70er Jahren einige Poeten auf – Boris Christov (geb. 1945), Marin Georgiev (geb. 1946), Tan'o Lisurov (geb. 1944), Mirjana Baševa (geb. 1947) u. a. –, für die der Zwiespalt zwischen Stadt und Dorf als unterschiedlichen Lebens- und Erfahrungsräumen zum beherrschenden lyrischen Thema wurde. Geborgenheit in der dörflichen Welt, Einsamkeit und Entfremdung in der Stadt, aber auch die gegenseitige Durchdringung beider Sphären, eine Problematik, die ja auch der erzählenden und dramatischen Literatur nicht fremd war, wurden in den recht konventionellen lyrischen Texten dieser Autoren artikuliert.

VII. Die Literatur der 80er Jahre: Humane Kybernetik – Ökologie – Weibliche Poetik

Die Literatur der letzten Jahre zeigt eine zunehmende Sensibilisierung der Autoren für die Fragen des menschlichen Zusammenlebens in Familie und Berufsleben, für die „humane Kybernetik", wie es Konstantin Iliev nennt. Dieser Autor bewegt sich auf dieser Linie, auch wenn er, wie in dem Zweipersonenstück *Nirvana* (1982) in die Vergangenheit zurückgreift und die Ehetragödie zwischen Pejo Javorov und Lora Karavelova als einen strindbergischen Kampf zwischen dem Mann und der Frau auf die Bühne bringt. In solchen Stücken gewinnt über die psychologische Analyse hinaus auch das Mythische und Archetypische wieder Raum, so daß sich hier eine Synthese der vorausgegangenen Strömungen im bulgarischen Drama abzeichnet. Auch in der Erzählliteratur begegnen jetzt reifere, kompliziertere Formen, begleitet von einer differenzierteren Sicht gerade auch der heiklen Probleme der bulgarischen Gegenwart. So kann in dem vielbeachteten Prosatext *Gradinata s kosovete* (Der Garten mit den Amseln*, 1984) von Dimităr Korudžiev selbst das Modell der „jungen Prosa" vertieft und zu neuer Aussage gebracht werden, indem die autobiographische Rechenschaft durch Elemente des Essays bereichert und der Weg der Selbstfindung über Militärzeit, Krankheit und Studium nachgezeichnet wird[34]).

Wenn nicht alles täuscht, kommt auch der große Gesellschaftsroman wieder zu Ehren, freilich als eine Gattung, die die frühere ideologische Befangenheit aufgege-

---

[34]) Očerci (Anm. 6), Bd. II, S. 178 ff.; vgl. Marčalis, N.: Beležki vărchu bălgarskata poezija ot 70-te godini (Anmerkungen zur bulgarischen Poesie seit den 70er Jahren), in: Dokladi 12 (Anm. 6), S. 509–516.

ben hat und in Komposition und Perspektive zu vielschichtigen Strukturen drängt. Das ist der Fall in Pavel Vežinovs *Vezni* (Die Waage, 1982) oder in Andrej Guljaškis *Skitnik brodi po sveta* (Ein Landstreicher zieht durch die Welt, 1982). Slav Ch. Karaslavov (geb. 1932) gar nähert sich mit dem auf mehrere Bände geplanten Romanwerk *Detronirane na veličijata* (Entthronung der Majestäten, 1985 ff.) der Roman-Epopöe der 50er Jahre, die aber nun, da sie ihren ideologischen Totalitätsanspruch aufgibt, eine neue ästhetische Qualität erreicht. Der meist diskutierte Roman der letzten Jahre war Ivajlo Petrovs *Chajka za vălci* (Wolfsjagd*, 1987) nicht nur, weil der Autor mit der Zwangskollektivierung der Landwirtschaft in der Dobrudscha ein lange Zeit gemiedenes „heißes Eisen" ansprach, sondern auch wegen seines unbestrittenen künstlerischen Ranges. Der Literaturkritiker Simeon Chadžikosev sieht als die wesentlichsten Transformationsprozesse in der bulgarischen Prosa unserer Tage das Vordringen der Phantastik und des Dokumentalismus, was er als Auswirkung des lateinamerikanischen „magischen Realismus", des sowjetischen Dokumentarromans und des amerikanischen „neuen Journalismus" sieht[35]).

Zu den brisanten Themen, an denen die Literatur der postmodernen Welt nirgends mehr vorbeisehen kann, zählen Ökologie und Umweltzerstörung. Es wird nun – etwa bei Nikolaj Chajtov, Vasil Popov, Jordan Radičkov u.a. – vorsichtig die Rechnung für die überstürzte und rücksichtslose Industrialisierung aufgemacht: literarische Rücknahme des einstigen stolzen Produktionsromans. Es ist auffallend, daß seit den 70er Jahren in zunehmender Zahl Dichterinnen (*poetesi*) und Schriftstellerinnen auf dem literarischen Plan erscheinen. Nach dem letzten Mitgliederverzeichnis (1987) zählt der SBP 35 weibliche Mitglieder von insgesamt 378. Mit Elisaveta Bagrjana, Dora Gabe und Blaga Dimitrova war das weibliche Element in der Nachkriegsliteratur niemals zu übersehen gewesen. In der Lyrik der 80er Jahre aber hat die Salzburger Slavistin Ute Bieber eine charakteristische „weibliche Poetik" (*ženska poetika*) in Gedichten von Blaga Dimitrova, Rada Aleksandrova (geb. 1943), Ekaterina Tomova (geb. 1946) und Rada Pančovska (geb. 1949) geortet, die sich aus der spezifischen Sichtweise und dem Erfahrungsbereich der Dichterinnen ergibt und in „weiblichen" Motiven und Metaphern realisiert wird[36]).

Betrachtet man die bulgarische Nachkriegsliteratur, die nun fast schon ein halbes Jahrhundert umfaßt – mehr als die literarhistorische Periode nach der Befreiung (1878–1918) und fast doppelt soviel wie die Periode zwischen den beiden Weltkriegen (1918–1944) –, so fällt auf, daß sich die Neuformierung nach dem Staatsstreich vom 9.9.1944 unter den Bedingungen des antifaschistisch-sozialistischen Staates relativ rasch und einheitlich vollzog, wobei insbesondere die Gewinnung der „bürgerlichen" Autoren zunächst im Zeichen der OF, später des Sozialismus, hervorzuheben ist. Im Gegensatz zu anderen Literaturen des Ostblockes, einschließlich Jugoslawiens, hat es bei den Bulgaren keine nennenswerte literarische Emigration gegeben – abgesehen von wenigen Ausnahmen wie dem in München lebenden Lyriker Christo Ognjanov

---

[35]) Chadžikosev, S.: Transformacionni procesi v săvremennata bălgarska proza (Transformationsprozesse in der zeitgenössischen bulgarischen Prosa), in: Dokladi 12 (Anm. 6), S. 440 ff.

[36]) Biber, U.: Săvremenni bălgarski poetesi (Zeitgenössische bulgarische Dichterinnen), in: Dokladi 12 (Anm. 6), S. 499–507.

(geb. 1911), der im Exil zwei Bände mit religiöser Lyrik vorgelegt hat (*Pătešestvie*/Reise, 1954; *Prevăplăštenija*/Verwandlungen, 1978). Ebensowenig hat sich nach dem Tauwetter eine literarische Opposition, sei es als Dissidentenbewegung, sei es als literarischer Untergrund, gebildet wie in der Sowjetunion oder in der Tschechoslowakei. Vielmehr ist die literarische Entwicklung durch ein beharrliches Festhalten an der Doktrin des Sozialistischen Realismus gekennzeichnet, und das heißt: am Realismusdogma, am Prinzip der Parteilichkeit und an der sozialpädagogischen Funktion der Literatur, die länger als anderswo restriktiv verstanden und normativ angewandt wurden. Hand in Hand mit dieser literaturpolitischen Linie ging die Kanonisierung eines ganz bestimmten Traditionsstranges der bulgarischen Literatur, des realistisch-sozialengagierten, bei gleichzeitiger Ausblendung der nicht-mimetischen Traditionen (Symbolismus, Avantgarde, Diabolismus usw.). Die Folge war, daß die Literatur sich, im Einklang mit den politischen Zielen der Partei- und Staatsführung, der jeweils erwünschten öffentlichen Themen annahm, während bis tief in die 60er Jahre die Sphäre des Privaten und Intim-Menschlichen im Hintergrund blieb. Modernismus und Neoavantgarde, wie sie in den westlichen Literaturen, jedoch auch in Jugoslawien, Polen und der UdSSR ausgebildet waren, fielen in Bulgarien aus. Es gab hier – von den wenig bekannten Lautgedichten des Sofioter Linguisten Mosko Moskov abgesehen – keine konkrete (visuelle) und nur wenig Ansätze zu einer experimentellen Poesie. Bezeichnenderweise wurden auch aus der sowjetischen Literatur, zu der doch ungemein enge, vielgestaltige Beziehungen bestehen, vornehmlich „offizielle" Tendenzen und Anregungen aufgenommen, nicht aber solche der informellen oder gar der Dissidentenliteratur.

Erst in allerletzter Zeit haben sich unter dem Eindruck der sowjetischen Öffnungspolitik auch in Bulgarien inoffizielle Diskussionsforen gebildet, die sich in Eingaben und Appellen für die Einhaltung der Menschenrechte, gegen Publikationsbeschränkungen und Verfolgungen von Schriftstellern einsetzen. Vor allem der im November 1988 gegründete *Klub za podkrepa na glasnostta i preustrojstvoto v Bălgarija* (Klub zur Stärkung der Transparenz und Umgestaltung in Bulgarien) drang mit Forderungen nach unvoreingenommener Erörterung brennender politischer und geistiger Fragen an die Öffentlichkeit. Zu den engagierten Vordenkern der inneren Erneuerung des Landes zählen bekannte Wissenschaftler und Schriftsteller, darunter Damjan Damjanov, Blaga Dimitrova, Dimităr Korudžiev und Valerie Petrov. Im Gefolge solcher Bestrebungen erschienen 1989 auch die ersten, von jüngeren Literaten herausgegebenen Samizdat-Publikationen, so die Zeitschrift *Glas* (Stimme, herausgegeben von Vladimir Levčev) und der Almanach für experimentelle Literatur *Most* (Brücke, herausgegeben von Edvin Sugarev).

In den 50er und 60er Jahren zeichnete sich bei den Autoren der mittleren Generation ein gewisser Verlust an jener Weltläufigkeit ab, die die ältere Generation – Elisaveta Bagrjana, Atanas Dalčev, Dimităr Dimov, Bogomil Rajnov – noch wie selbstverständlich besessen hatte. Erst seit den 70er Jahren machten sich Weltoffenheit und Interesse auch am ästhetischen Diskurs und den literarischen Strömungen des Westens bei den jüngeren Autoren wieder bemerkbar. Freilich hat es die List der literarischen Evolution so eingerichtet, daß die bulgarische Literatur am ehesten da wieder zu universaler Bedeutung gelangte, wo sie sich ganz auf das Regionale zurückgezogen hatte: in den dörflichen Grotesken von Nikolaj Chajtov und Jordan Radičkov. Steht auch vor jeder nationalen Literatur der Imperativ, das Ureigenste an Spielarten des Menschlichen und des Sozialen zu ihrem Gegenstand zu machen, so darf sie doch auch den Konnex zur weltweiten Modernität nicht verlieren, die nicht immer nur das Ephemer-Modische, sondern eben oft auch das Kreativ-Neue in der Kunst verkörpert. Keine Literatur, die am globalen Kommunikationsprozeß teilhaben will, kann darauf verzichten. 500 Jahre kultureller Abschottung in der Vergangenheit sind den Bulgaren eine bittere Lehre. Auf dem VI. Kongreß des SBP im März 1989 übten zahlreiche Schriftsteller scharfe Kritik am Apparat sowie der Machtkonzentration des Verbandes. Die Überwindung der noch immer wirksamen ideologischen Vorurteile und der „verbalen Wirklichkeit" (Blaga Dimitrova) der letzten vierzig Jahre wurde ebenso angemahnt wie die Forderung, den Sozialistischen Realismus durch einen „sozialistischen Pluralismus" (Stefan Prodev) zu ersetzen. Wieweit *preustrojstvo*, das bulgarische Pendant zu Gorbačevs *perestrojka*, die Literatur öffnen wird, bleibt abzuwarten.

VIII. Zeittafel zur bulgarischen Nachkriegsliteratur

1944 30. Oktober: Vollversammlung des SBP.

1945 Februar: Einführung der neuen Rechtschreibung. Frühjahr: I. nationale Konferenz der bulgarischen Schriftsteller. 14. Mai: Brief Georgi Dimitrovs an den SBP. 23.–27. September: Nationale Konferenz des SBP; Verkündung des Programms der Nationalliteratur.
Romane: Dimităr Dimov: *Osădeni duši* (Verdammte Seelen); Kamen Kalčev: *V kraja na ljatoto* (Am Ende des Sommers); Ljudmil Stojanov: *Zazorjavane* (Morgengrauen).
Drama: Kamen Kalčev: *Partizani* (Partisanen).

1946 *Erzählung:* Jordan Vălčev: *Boeve* (Kämpfe).

1947 20. Dezember: Gründung des Verlages „Bălgarski pisatel" (Bulgarischer Schriftsteller)
Lyrik, Versepik: Veselin Andreev: *Partizanski pesni* (Partisanenlieder); Mladen Isaev: *Poema za vintovkata* (Poem vom Gewehr); Krum Penev: *Epocha* (Eine Epoche).
Drama: Kamen Zidarov: *Carska milost* (Zarengnade).

1948 Dezember: V. Parteitag der BKP. Resolution zur Entwicklung der Literatur auf dem Wege des Sozialistischen Realismus. Beginn der Formalismusdebatte.
Sammelbände: Sbornik za brigadirskoto dviženie (Sammelband über die Brigadierbewegung); *Mladi avtori I* (Junge Autoren I).
Romane, Erzählungen: Georgi Karaslavov: *Tango**; Emil Manov: *Pleneno jato* (Die gefangene Schar); Nikola Marinov: *Interbrigadisti* (Interbrigadisten); Emilijan Stanev: *V ticha večer* (An einem stillen Abend*), *Kradecăt na praskovi* (Der Pfirsichdieb*); Dimităr Talev: *Văstanie v Čiprovec* (Aufstand in Čiprovec).
Drama: Orlin Vasilev: *Trevoga* (Alarm).

1949 Stiftung des Dimitrov-Preises durch die NSb.
Roman: Kamen Kalčev: *Sin na rabotničeskata klasa* (Ein Sohn der Arbeiterklasse).

1950 *Romane, Erzählungen:* Krăst'o Belev: *Tăkačkata Sava Michajlova* (Die Weberin Sava Michajlova); Andrej Guljaški: *MT-stancija* (Maschinen- und Traktorenstation); Emilijan Stanev: *Kogato skrežăt se topi* (Wenn das Eis schmilzt).
Drama: Andrej Guljaški: *Obeštanie* (Das Versprechen).
Dimitrov-Preise: Elisaveta Bagrjana, Krăst'o Belev, Nikolaj Chrelkov, Andrej Guljaški, Kamen Kalčev, Georgi Karaslavov, Krum Penev, Georgi Stamatov, Ljudmil Stojanov, Orlin Vasilev, Pavel Vežinov, Stojan Zagorčinov, Pantelej Zarev, Kamen Zidarov.

1951 *Sammelband: Mladi avtori II* (Junge Autoren II).
Romane: Dimităr Dimov: *Tjutjun* (Tabak*); Dimităr Metodiev: *Dimitrovsko pleme* (Das Dimitrov-Geschlecht).
Dimitrov-Preise: Božidar Božilov, Nikola Furnadžiev, Andrej Guljaški, Mladen Isaev, Christo Radevski, Stefan Savov, Pavel Vežinov.

1952 Die Kontroverse um Dimovs Roman *Tjutjun* wird durch ZK-Beschluß beendet.
Romane: Krăst'o Belev: *Devojkite ot zavoda* (Die Mädchen aus dem Werk); Georgi Karaslavov: *Obiknoveni chora* (Gewöhnliche Menschen*, dt.: Stanka), Dimităr Talev: *Železnijat svetilnik* (Der eiserne Leuchter*).
Dimitrov-Preise: Dimităr Dimov, Emil Koralov, Dimităr Metodiev, Bogomil Rajnov, Stefan Savov.

1953 Lyrikdebatte.
Lyrik: Elisaveta Bagrjana: *Pet zvezdi* (Fünf Sterne), *Samolet za Moskva* (Ein Flugzeug nach Moskau); Ivan Radoev: *Proletno razsămvane* (Frühlingserwachen); Ljudmil Stojanov: *Otvăd železnata zavesa* (Jenseits des Eisernen Vorhangs).
Romane: Nikola Marinov: *Zavod 17* (Werk 17); Dimităr Talev: *Ilinden* (Der Eliastag*).
Dimitrov-Preis: Orlin Vasilev (koll.).

1954 Diskussion „Bücher für die Menschen der Arbeit". Zweite Auflage von Dimovs Roman *Tjutjun*.
Lyrik: Veselin Chančev: *Stichove v palaskite* (Verse in den Patronentaschen); Georgi Džagarov: *Moite pesni* (Meine Lieder).
Roman: Dimităr Talev: *Prespanskite kambani* (Die Glocken von Prespa*).
Drama: Orlin Vasilev: *Štastie* (Glück).

1955 *Roman:* Krăst'o Belev: *Probudeni planini* (Erweckte Gebirge).

1956 *Lyrik, Versepik:* Georgi Džagarov: *Lirika* (Lyrik); Dimităr Metodiev: *Pesen za proverkata* (Das Lied von der Kontrolle).

1957 *Drama:* Kamen Zidarov: *Za čestta na pagona* (Um die Ehre der Schulterklappe).

1958 8. April: Rede Todor Živkovs *Poveče meždu naroda – po-blizo do života* (Mehr unter dem Volk – näher dem Leben) vor dem SBP.
Lyrik: Georgi Džagarov: *V minuta na mălčanie* (In Minuten des Schweigens); Aleksandăr Gerov: *Naj-chubavoto* (Das Schönste); Pen'o Penev: *Dni na proverka* (Tage der Prüfung); Liljana Stefanova: *Svetăt, kojto običam* (Die Welt, die ich liebe).
Romane: Emilijan Stanev: *Ivan Kondarev** (dt.: Heißer Sommer); Dimităr Talev: *Samuil*, Bd. I: *Štitove kamenni* (Samuil, Bd. I: Steinerne Schilde).
Drama: Ivan Pejčev: *Vsjaka esenna večer* (An jedem Herbstabend).

1959 *Roman:* Dimităr Talev: *Samuil*, Bd. II: *Pepeljaška i carskijat sin* (Aschenbrödel und der Zarensohn).
Komödie: Dimităr Dimov: *Ženi s minalo* (Frauen mit Vergangenheit).
Dimitrov-Preise: Veselin Chančev, Nikola Furnadžiev, Andrej Guljaški, Georgi Karaslavov, Dimităr Talev.

1960 17. Juni: Treffen Todor Živkovs mit einem Schriftstelleraktiv.
Lyrik, Versepik: Elisaveta Bagrjana: *Orljakăt izlita* (Der Schwarm fliegt aus); Valeri Petrov: *V mekata esen* (Im milden Herbst).
Drama: Milčo Radev: *Po trotoara* (Auf dem Bürgersteig).

1961 *Romane:* Dragomir Asenov: *Kafjavite chorizonti* (Die braunen Horizonte); Dimităr Dimov: *Vinovnijat* (Der Schuldige); Ivajlo Petrov: *Mărtvo vălnenie* (Tote Brandung,* dt.: Und wenn ich dich zwingen muß); Dimităr Talev: *Samuil*, Bd. III: *Pogibel* (Untergang).
Dramen: Georgi Džagarov: *Vratitete se zatvarjat* (Die Türen schließen sich); Valeri Petrov: *Kogato rozite tancuvat* (Wenn die Rosen tanzen*, dt.: Tanzende Rosen).

1962 *Romane:* Atanas Nakovski: *Marija protiv Piralkov* (Maria gegen Piralkov); Jordan Radičkov: *Obărnato nebe* (Umgekehrter Himmel); Ljudmil Stojanov: *Detstvo* (Kindheit); Dimităr Talev:

Bratjata ot Struga (Die Brüder aus Struga), *Chilendarskijat monach* (Der Mönch von Chilendar); Stojan Zagorčinov: *Ivajlo*.
Drama: Valeri Petrov/Radoj Ralin: *Improvizacija* (Improvisation); Kamen Zidarov: *Ivan Šišman*.

1963 *Lyrik:* Elisaveta Bagrjana: *Ot brjag do brjag* (Von Ufer zu Ufer).
Romane, Erzählungen: Diko Fučedžiev: *Nebeto na Veleka* (Der Himmel der Veleka); Miron Ivanov: *Pači jajca* (Enteneier); Pavel Vežinov: *Momčeto s cigulkata* (Der Junge mit der Geige).
Drama: Božidar Božilov: *Probnijat brak na Ani* (Annis Ehe auf Probe).

1964 Mai: Treffen der Schriftsteller der Balkanländer.
Lyrik: Blaga Dimitrova: *Ekspedicija kăm idnija den* (Expedition zum kommenden Tag).
Romane, Erzählungen: Anton Dončev: *Vreme razdelno* (Trennende Zeiten*); Andrej Guljaški: *Sedemte dni na našija život* (Die sieben Tage unseres Lebens); Kamen Kalčev: *Dvama v novija grad* (Zwei in der neuen Stadt); Liljana Stefanova: *Edna esen v Amerika* (Ein Herbst in Amerika).
Dimitrov-Preise: Dimităr Metodiev, Emilijan Stanev.

1965 *Lyrik:* Pavel Matev: *Čajkite počivat na vălnite* (dt.: Wie die Möwen ausruhen auf den Wellen*).
Romane, Erzählungen: Nikolaj Chajtov: *Divi razkazi* (Wilde Erzählungen); Blaga Dimitrova: *Pătuvane kăm sebe si* (Reise zu sich selbst*); Diko Fučedžiev: *Gnevno pătuvane* (Zornige Reise); Genčo Stoev: *Cenata na zlatoto* (Der Preis des Goldes).
Drama: Georgi Džagarov: *Prokurorăt* (Der Staatsanwalt).

1966 *Lyrik:* Blaga Dimitrova: *Obratno vreme* (Umgekehrte Zeit).
Romane, Erzählungen: Vera Mutafčieva: *Slučajat Džem* (Der Fall Cem*; dt.: Spielball von Kirche und Thron); Bogomil Rajnov: *Pătišta za nikăde* (Wege ins Nirgendwo); Pavel Vežinov: *Dăch na bademi* (Ein Hauch von Mandeln), *Zvezdite nad nas* (Die Sterne über uns*).
Drama: Miron Ivanov: *Mačovo bărdo* (Mačovs Hügel).
Dimitrov-Preise: Anton Dončev, Georgi Džagarov, Angel Karalijčev, Pavel Matev, Ilija Volen.

1967 *Lyrik, Versepik:* Blaga Dimitrova: *Otklonenie* (Abweichung), *Osădeni na ljubov* (Zur Liebe verurteilt); Dora Gabe: *Počakaj, slănce* (Warte noch, Sonne); Aleksandăr Gerov: *Svoboden stich* (Freier Vers); Dimităr Metodiev: *Pesen za Rusija* (Lied über Rußland); Valeri Petrov: *Dăžd vali-slănce gree* (Regen fällt – die Sonne scheint).
Romane, Erzählungen: Atanas Dalčev: *Fragmenti* (Fragmente*); Kamen Kalčev: *Sofijski razkazi* (Sofioter Erzählungen*); Georgi Mišev: *Matriarchat* (Matriarchat); Vasil Popov: *Korenite* (Die Wurzeln); Bogomil Rajnov: *Gospodin Nikoj* (Herr Niemand).
Drama: Jordan Radičkov: *Sumatocha* (Tumult).

1968 Mai: I. Kongreß des SBP; Annahme des Statutes.
Romane, Erzählungen: Ivajlo Petrov: *Predi da se rodja. I sled tova* (Bevor ich zur Welt kam... und danach*); Jordan Radičkov: *Neosvetenite dvorove* (Die unbeleuchteten Höfe); Emilijan Stanev: *Legenda za Sibin* (Legende von Sibin, dem Fürsten von Preslav*).
Lyrik: Blaga Dimitrova: *Migove* (Augenblicke); Ljubomir Levčev: *Recital* (Dichterlesung).

1969 Rede Todor Živkovs vor dem Aktiv der Sofioter Jugend.
Romane, Erzählungen: Vera Mutafčieva: *Poslednite Šišmanovci* (Die letzten Šišmans); Jordan Radičkov: *Baruten bukvar* (Pulverfibel*).
Dimitrov-Preise: Nikolaj Chajtov, Venko Markovski, Bogomil Rajnov, Pantelej Zarev.

1970 *Romane, Erzählungen:* Kol'o Georgiev: *Văzmožni i nevăzmožni priznanija* (Mögliche und unmögliche Bekenntnisse); Emilijan Stanev: *Antichrist* (Der Antichrist*).

1971 *Lyrik:* Ljubomir Levčev: *Strelbište* (Schießstand).
Roman: Blaga Dimitrova: *Lavina* (Lawine).
Drama: Kol'o Georgiev: *Izključitelen šans* (Eine exklusive Chance).
Dimitrov-Preise: Kostadin Kjuljumov (koll.), Jordan Radičkov, Liljana Stefanova, Pavel Vežinov (koll).

1972 II. Kongreß des SBP; Änderung und Ergänzung des Statutes.
Lyrik: Elisaveta Bagrjana: *Kontrapunkti* (Kontrapunkte).
Romane, Erzählungen: Gerčo Atanasov: *Dokato očakvame* (Solange wir warten); Nikolaj Chajtov: *Rodopskite komiti* (Die rhodopischen Freischärler); Dončo Dončev: *Počti ljubovna istorija* (Fast eine Liebesgeschichte); Andrej Guljaški: *Zavrăštaneto na inžener Nadin* (Die Rückkehr des Ingenieurs Nadin); Ilija Nikolčin: *Devet meseca i edna nošt* (Neun Monate und eine Nacht); Vărban Stamatov: *Flagman* (Flaggmann); Stanislav Stratiev: *Diva patica meždu dărvetata* (Die Wildente zwischen den Bäumen).
Dimitrov-Preise: Efrem Karanfilov, Ljubomir Levčev, Ivajlo Petrov.

1973 *Lyrik:* Ljubomir Levčev: *Zvezdopăt* (Sternenweg).
Romane, Erzählungen: Andrej Guljaški: *Zlatnijat vek* (Das Goldene Zeitalter); Genčo Stoev: *Ciklopăt* (Der Zyklop); Ljudmil Stojanov: *Vojna* (Krieg); Pavel Vežinov: *Nad vsičko* (Über alles); Blaga Dimitrova: *Otklonenie* (dt.: Liebe auf Umwegen*).
Drama: Jordan Radičkov: *Januari* (Januar).

1974 Diskussion über den Sozialistischen Realismus in der Zeitschrift „Plamăk".
Lyrik: Blaga Dimitrova: *Kak* (Wie).
Erzählung: Diko Fučedžiev: *Rekata* (Der Fluß*).
Dramen: Dragomir Asenov: *Zlatnoto pokritie* (Die Golddeckung); Nadežda Dragova/Părvan Stefanov: *Ženski godini* (Frauenjahre*); Georgi Džagarov: *Tazi malka zemja* (Dieses kleine Land).
Dimitrov-Preise: Dragomir Asenov, Stefan Karakostov, Ivan Pejčev.

1975 *Lyrik:* Stefan Canev: *Az pitam* (Ich frage); Dora Gabe: *Sgăstena tišina* (Verdichtete Stille); Marin Georgiev: *Selo* (Dorf).
Erzählungen: Nikolaj Chajtov: *Bodlivata roza* (Die Stachelrose); Jordan Radičkov: *Praška* (Schleuder); Pavel Vežinov: *Noštem s belite kone* (Nachts mit weißen Pferden*); Vladimir Zarev: *Denjat na netărpenie* (Der Tag der Ungeduld).
Drama: Dragomir Asenov: *Krajat na denja* (Das Ende des Tages).

1976 Stiftung des Internationalen Botev-Preises.
Lyrik: Božidar Božilov: *Amerikanska tetradka* (Amerikanisches Heft); Dora Gabe: *Glăbini* (Tiefen).
Erzählung: Pavel Vežinov: *Barierata* (Die Barriere).
Drama: Stanislav Stratiev: *Sako ot velur* (Sakko aus Velour*, dt.: Das Schaf).
Dimitrov-Preis: Pavel Vežinov.

1977 Juni: Internationales Schriftstellertreffen in Sofia.
Lyrik: Boris Christov: *Večeren trompet* (Abendtrompete).
Romane, Erzählungen: Vasil Popov: *Nizinata* (Die Niederung); Bogomil Rajnov; *Černite lebedi* (Die schwarzen Schwäne); Georgi Veličkov: *Štărkel v snega* (Storch im Schnee); Pavel Vežinov: *Belijat gušter* (Die weiße Eidechse), *Ezernoto momče* (Der Seejunge).
Drama: Konstantin Iliev: *Prozorecăt* (Das Fenster).

1978 *Epos:* Venko Markovski: *Predanija zavetni* (Heilige Überlieferungen).
Romane: Erzählungen: Diko Fučedžiev: *Zelenata treva na pustinjata* (Das grüne Gras der Wüste); Emil Manov: *Galaktičeska bufonada* (Galaktische Buffonade); Georgi Markovski: *Chităr Petăr* (Der schlaue Peter); Vera Mutafčieva: *Kniga za Sofroni* (Ein Buch über Sofroni); Ivajlo Petrov: *Esenni razkazi* (Herbsterzählungen); Vladimir Zarev: *Bitieto* (Das Dasein).
Dramen: Jordan Radičkov: *Lazarica*; Michail Veličkov: *Bjagstvoto* (Die Flucht*); Rusi Božinov: *Štastliveca ide* (Der Glückspilz kommt).
Lyrik: Ljubomir Levčev: *Pozdrav kăm ogănja* (Gruß zum Feuer).
Dimitrov-Preise: Nikolaj Christozov (koll.), Dora Gabe.

1979 Stiftung des Internationalen Vapcarov-Preises.
Erzählungen: Dimităr Korudžiev: *Stajata* (Das Zimmer); Pavel Vežinov: *Izmerenija* (Ausdehnungen).
Dramen: Konstantin Iliev: *Bosilek za Draginko* (Basilikum für Draginko); Jordan Radičkov: *Opit za letene* (Flugversuch); Stanislav Stratiev: *Rejs* (Der Bus).

1980 18. Dezember: Vollversammlung des SBP; Änderung des Statutes.
Lyrik: Blaga Dimitrova: *Prostranstva* (Räume).
Erzählungen: Dončo Končev: *Koliba v lozeto* (Die Hütte im Weinberg); Ivajlo Petrov: *Najdobrijat graždanin na Republikata* (Der beste Bürger der Republik).
Drama: Dragomir Asenov: *Cenata* (Der Preis).
Dimitrov-Preise: Aleksandăr Gerov, Diko Fučedžiev, Penčo Dančev, Tončo Zečev.

1981 *Romane:* Kamen Kalčev: *Probuždane* (Erwachen); Vera Mutafčieva: *Chan Asparuch*. Verbot des bereits ausgedruckten Romans *Lice* (Gesicht) von Blaga Dimitrova.

1982 *Romane, Erzählungen:* Andrej Guljaški: *Skitnik brodi po sveta* (Ein Landstreicher zieht durch die Welt); Atanas Nakovski: *Katastrofata* (Die Katastrophe); Pavel Vežinov: *Vezni* (Die Waage); Ivajlo Petrov: *Chajka za vălci* (Wolfsjagd, Erster Teil).
Dramen: Konstantin Iliev: *Nirvana*; Jordan Radičkov: *Košnici* (Körbe).
Dimitrov-Preis: Georgi Canev, Vera Mutafčieva (koll.), Genčo Stoev.

1983 *Erzählung:* Jordan Radičkov: *Nežnata spirala* (Die zarte Spirale).

1984 *Erzählungen, Prosa*: Dimităr Koruždiev: *Gradinata s kosovete* (Der Garten mit den Amseln*); Damjan P. Damjanov: *Tetradka po vsičko* (Heft für alles).
Dramen: Konstantin Iliev: *Odisej pătuva za Itaka* (Odysseus reist nach Ithaka); Stanislav Stratiev: *Maksimalistăt* (Der Maximalist).
Dimitrov-Preis: Evtim Evtimov, Efrem Karanfilov, Ljuben Stanev.

1985 *Roman:* Slav Ch. Karaslavov: *Detroniraneto na veličijata* (Entthronung der Majestäten).

1986 *Roman:* Ivajlo Petrov: *Chajka za vălci* (Wolfsjagd*, vollständige Ausgabe).
Dimitrov-Preis: Veselin Josifov, Slav Ch. Karaslavov, Leda Mileva, Stanislav Stratiev, Ljubomir Tenev.

1987 *Lyrik:* Blaga Dimitrova: *Labirint* (Labyrinth).

1988 3. November: Gründung des unabhängigen Diskussionsforums *Klub za podkrepa na glasnostta i preustrojstvoto v Bălgarija* (Klub zur Stärkung der Transparenz und der Umgestaltung in Bulgarien).
Prosa: Bogomil Rajnov: *Krajat na pătja* (Das Ende des Weges).

1989 9. März: VI. Kongreß des SBP.
April–Mai: Veröffentlichung kritischer Stellungnahmen verschiedener Schriftsteller in *Literaturen front*.
Erste bulgarische Samizdat-Ausgaben: *Most* (Brücke), I–II, und *Glas* (Stimme).

Theater

Gunnar Hille, Bonn

I. Voraussetzungen: Theater bis 1944 – II. Kulturpolitik und Bühnenschaffen: 1. 1944–1949 – 2. 1949–1956 – 3. 1956–1989 – III. Institutionen und Organisationen: 1. Ausbildungsstätten – 2. Staatliche Theateradministration – 3. Publikationsorgane – 4. Internationale Zusammenarbeit – IV. Statistischer Anhang

I. Voraussetzungen: Theater bis 1944

Historische Umstände sind dafür verantwortlich zu machen, daß die Theaterkunst in Bulgarien relativ jung ist. Sieht man von Frühformen des Theaterspiels wie Volksbräuchen und -belustigung, kultischen Handlungen usw. ab, so kann von einem bulgarischen Sprechtheater im heutigen Sinne erst seit Mitte des 19. Jh. die Rede sein, als sog. Dialoge, einfache Texte patriotischen oder unterhaltsamen Charakters, zu kleinen Bühnenstücken weiterentwickelt und von Laienspielern aufgeführt wurden.

1856 kam es in Lom und Šumen zu den ersten echten Theateraufführungen in Bulgarien. Hier und in den Folgejahren auch andernorts wurden zunächst v. a. ausländische Werke, oft Rührstücke, in stark bearbeiteter Form gespielt.

Dobri Vojnikov (1833–1878) und Vasil Drumev (1840?–1901) sorgten nach 1870 für erste gelungene Dramen.

Nach der Befreiung von der osmanischen Herrschaft (1878) wurden Theatergebäude mit festen Ensembles geschaffen: 1881 in Plovdiv das Theater *Luksemburg*[1]) und 1888 für die erste Sofioter Truppe *Osnova* (Grundlage) ein Holzbau mit über 300 Plätzen. 1891 wurde das Theater *Slavjanska beseda* (Slavisches Forum) eingeweiht, wo am 2.1.1891 auch die erste Opernvorstellung in Bulgarien stattfand[2]). Ab 1892 spielte in *Slavjanska beseda* ein neues Ensemble, *Sălza i smjach* (Träne und Lachen), das sich aus den besten Theaterkräften rekrutierte und ab 1904 den Namen *Bălgarski naroden teatăr* (Bulgarisches Nationaltheater)[3]) führte. 1907 konnte das Ensemble sein eigenes, monumentales Gebäude beziehen, das noch heute, mehrfach umgebaut, das Zentrum Sofias schmückt.

Um die Jahrhundertwende hatten sich in den größeren Städten des Landes in lockerer Besetzung weitere Ensembles gebildet, die meist von „Theatergesellschaf-

---

[1]) Vgl. Penev, P.: Istorija na bălgarskija dramatičen teatăr (Geschichte des bulgarischen dramatischen Theaters). Sofia 1975, S. 214–216.

[2]) s. Penev (Anm. 1), S. 252.

[3]) Die wörtliche Übersetzung „Volkstheater" ist im Deutschen irreführend und wird daher vermieden.

ten" oder Mäzenen unterstützt und von Männern, die im Ausland Theatererfahrung gesammelt hatten, geleitet wurden. Erst nach 1918, als auch das Theater einen allgemeinen Aufschwung nahm, konnten einige dieser Truppen in festen Stadttheatern aufgehen (Pleven 1918, Varna 1919, Burgas 1921, wenig später wurden auch in Lom, Šumen, Vidin und Pazardžik von den Kommunen unterstützte Theater geschaffen).

Das Bühnenschaffen zwischen den Weltkriegen ist v. a. mit dem Namen des Russen Nikolaj O. Masalitinov (1880–1961) verbunden, eines ehemaligen Mitarbeiters K. S. Stanislavskijs am Moskauer Künstlertheater, der 1925 an das *Naroden teatăr* berufen wurde. In den folgenden drei Jahrzehnten schuf Masalitinov hier mehr als 130 Inszenierungen und prägte die bulgarische Theaterkunst stark im Sinne seines psychologischen Realismus.

Modernistische Tendenzen wie G. Milevs verdienstvolle Versuche, als Regisseur und Theoretiker unter dem Einfluß von M. Reinhardt und V. Meyerhold (Mejerchol'd) das bulgarische Theater von einer abbildenden zu einer in das Wesen der Dinge eindringenden, stilisierenden Kunst fortzuentwickeln[4]), konnten sich gegen den vorherrschenden Realismus nicht durchsetzen.

Auch in Bulgarien gab es Versuche, „Arbeitertheater" unter Anlehnung an Piscator, Vachtangov u. a. zu machen (am interessantesten: Bojan Danovski), die die Behörden jedoch, v. a. ab 1939, zu verhindern suchten.

Das Repertoire der Bühnen von den Anfängen bis 1944 bestand – neben vielen Rührstücken – v. a. aus Klassikern wie Shakespeare, Schiller, Čechov, nach der Jahrhundertwende kamen jedoch immer mehr bulgarische Dramen dazu. Nach 1878 waren die wichtigsten Regisseure: V. Nalburov, R. Kaneli, Ch. Cankov, N. O. Masalitinov, N. Fol, B. Danovski; die bekanntesten Schauspieler: K. Sarafov, R. Popova, V. Kirkov, S. Ognjanov, A. Budevska u. a.

II. Kulturpolitik und Bühnenschaffen

1. 1944–1949

Nach dem Staatsstreich vom 9.9.1944 entwickelte sich die bulgarische Kulturpolitik in Übereinstimmung mit der gesamtpolitischen Linie der Regierung der OF; bis zur Ausrufung der Volksrepublik (15.9.1946) ging man sehr behutsam, bis zur Annahme der „Dimitrov-Verfassung" (4.12.1947) und v. a. danach immer selbstbewußter auf die utilitäre Benutzung der Kultur für die sozialistischen Ziele zu, um auf dem V. Parteitag der BKP im Dezember 1948 die Erhebung des „Sozialistischen Realismus" zur alleingültigen künstlerischen Methode in allen Bereichen der Kultur zu beschließen[5]).

---

[4]) Vgl. Milevs grundlegenden Aufsatz „Teatralno izkustvo" (Theaterkunst) von 1918, in: Milev, G.: Săčinenija (Werke). Bd. 2. Sofia 1976, S. 75–98.

[5]) Der in der UdSSR 1934 dekretierte Sozialistische Realismus war in Bulgarien Mitte der 30er Jahre zwar von einigen Literaturkritikern um G. Bakalov lebhaft begrüßt worden, fand aber vor 1944

Chronologisch: Bereits am 30.10.1944 wählte der SBP 70 neue Mitglieder in seine Reihen und schloß eine Anzahl nichtgenehmer Autoren aus. Zum Ehrenpräsidenten des SBP wurde jener Mann gewählt, dessen Name stellvertretend für die Kulturpolitik der Dogmatismus-Ära bis 1956 steht: Todor Pavlov war soeben aus dem sowjetischen Exil zurückgekehrt und übte in zahlreichen Parteiämtern und Funktionen seinen Einfluß als „Kulturpapst" aus. Er gab die Devise aus, die nicht völlig in Ungnade gefallenen nichtsozialistischen Schriftsteller[6]) nicht auszugrenzen, sondern sie vermehrt in die Aktionen der OF einzubeziehen, „um ihnen zu helfen, sich von ihrer Romantik, ihrem Symbolismus, Naturalismus usw. zu befreien"[7]).

Die von Pavlov zunächst vorgegebene, scheinbar tolerante kulturpolitische Linie, die den Sozialistischen Realismus als eine Methode unter mehreren darstellte, wurde von ihm selbst bereits im September 1945 durch Formulierung seines Endziels (die alleinige Anwendung des Sozialistischen Realismus) in einem sog. „Maximalprogramm" als Taktik entlarvt. Es dauerte jedoch noch drei Jahre, bis die BKP ihre Macht hinreichend konsolidiert hatte, um die Kultur ungehindert für Parteizwecke mißbrauchen zu können.

Zu diesem Zweck mußte man auch die Literaturkritik, die in Bulgarien auf eine mehr als hundertjährige, reiche Tradition zurückblicken konnte, zum Druckmittel, obersten Gericht und Indoktrinationsinstrument degradieren. Hierzu G. Dimitrov in einem Brief aus seinem Moskauer Exil an den SBP vom 14.5.1945: „Daneben ist es die Pflicht des Schriftstellerverbandes, mit Hilfe einer gesunden Literaturkritik sorgfältig die Wiese der bulgarischen Literatur von schädlichem Unkraut zu reinigen."[8])

Zwischen 1944 und 1949 entwickelten sich Bühnenschaffen und Theaterleben parallel zu den politischen Ereignissen. Zunächst herrschte Verwirrung um das Ausmaß der Einschränkungen. Mancher Regisseur, Schauspieler oder Autor widersetzte sich dem zunehmenden Druck der sozialistischen Kräfte, die immer mehr die Schlüsselpositionen besetzten. Andere paßten sich an, teils aus Überzeugung, teils aus Opportunismus, um sich den Verlust an künstlerischer Freiheit durch eine gesicherte Position (bei entsprechender Willfährigkeit) versüßen zu lassen.

2. 1949–1956

Die beiden bedeutendsten Regisseure der Vorkriegszeit, N.O. Masalitinov und B. Danovski, stellten ihre Kunst auf die Erfordernisse der Zeit ein. Beide hatte ja Erfahrungen mit dem Stanislavskij-System bzw. mit Agitationstheater, Richtungen, denen fortan wichtige Bedeutung zukam. Der Begriff „Stanislavskij-System" wurde nach

---

keine Anwendung. Der Sozialistische Realismus verpflichtet u.a. zur Parteilichkeit für die Idee des Sozialismus und zur Darstellung eines optimistischen, problemlosen Alltags mit einem fehlerlosen „positiven Helden" im Mittelpunkt (s. Kasack, W.: Lexikon der russischen Literatur ab 1917. Stuttgart 1976, s.v. „Sozialistischer Realismus").

[6]) Einige Literaten wurden von den neuen Machthabern liquidiert, so J. Badev, einer der führenden Literaturkritiker der Vorkriegszeit, und D. Šišmanov, Dramatiker und Politiker, Sohn Prof. I. Šišmanovs.

[7]) Zitat aus Pavlovs programmatischer Rede vor Künstlern und Funktionären vom Dez. 1944, abgedruckt in Pavlov, T.: Izbrani săčinenija (Ausgewählte Werke). Bd. 6. Sofia 1963, S. 130.

[8]) Dimitrov, G.: Za literatura i izkustvo (Über Literatur und Kunst). Sofia 1982, S. 148.

1944 auch in Bulgarien zum Synonym für Dogmatismus in der Theaterkunst. Das System, Anleitungen zur Schauspielkunst des bedeutenden russischen Regisseurs K. S. Stanislavskij (1863–1938), hat die vollständige Identifikation des Schauspielers mit seiner Rolle durch Verschmelzung seiner Physis mit dem inneren geistigen (russ. *duchovnyj*) Leben der Figur, u. a. mittels sog. „physischer Handlungen", zum Ziel. Der vom Sozialistischen Realismus geforderte positive Held wurde durch diese „physischen Handlungen", die sich bald auf typische Gesten und Intonation reduzierten, auch in der szenischen Realisierung stark schematisiert. „Das System wurde mit der Methode des Sozialistischen Realismus identifiziert... Aber konnte man denn die von Stanislavskij geforderte künstlerische Harmonie in einer Aufführung von schematischen Stücken, wie sie damals geschrieben und zumeist im Theater gespielt wurden, erreichen?... Die innovatorische Lehre Stanislavskijs wurde paradoxerweise zu einer retardierenden Kraft. Diejenigen, die den echten Stanislavskij verstanden, zogen es vor, nicht gegen die Entartungen zu opponieren. Die anderen, die ihn nicht verstanden, wurden eine leichte Beute der Entartungen."[9]

So hatte man bis 1949 zwar die Theater auf den Sozialistischen Realismus eingeschworen und Schlüsselpositionen entsprechend besetzt, mußte jedoch den Mangel an geeigneten bulgarischen Stücken beklagen (bis 1944 waren nur drei Dramen mit „revolutionärer Thematik" gespielt oder veröffentlicht worden). Hinzu kam, daß nun auch noch eine Klausel eingeführt wurde, die vorschrieb, daß 50 % des Repertoires aus bulgarischen Stücken zu bestehen hätten. Diese Vorgabe wurde „pedantisch eingehalten, ohne den künstlerischen Gehalt zu berücksichtigen"[10], wobei die Verbannung der großen Vorkriegsautoren wie I. Vazov, P. Javorov, P. J. Todorov u. a. als „bürgerliche" bzw. „dekadente" Schriftsteller den größten Verlust darstellte.

Folglich mußten als Vorbilder für schnell zu schaffende bulgarische Stücke sowjetische Vorlagen dienen, die sich mit der Warenproduktion (*proizvodstveni piesi*) oder dem revolutionären Kampf befaßten. Infolge der These, daß die Widersprüche in der sozialistischen Gesellschaft nichtantagonistischen Charakters seien, nahm seit 1950 die Tendenz zur Konfliktlosigkeit und Schönfärberei zu, was der Dramenkunst fast den Todesstoß versetzte. Die natürliche Folge waren Resignation und Erstickungserscheinungen bei Theaterleuten und Autoren.

Erst nach Stalins Tod begannen Künstler und Theaterpraktiker neue Hoffnung zu schöpfen. So wurden 1953 und 1955 nichtöffentliche Diskussionen mit den führenden Vertretern von Theater, Kritik und Kulturpolitik abgehalten.

Die Diskussion von 1953 setzte mit noch sehr verhaltener Kritik zunächst bei der Schauspielkunst an (B. Danovski forderte die Anwendung eines breiteren Spektrums des Stanislavskij-Systems)[11]. Daneben wurde sogar die Frage diskutiert, ob man sich einer einzigen Inszenierungsmethode zu unterwerfen habe, ohne sich aber zu einer negativen Antwort zu bekennen. Dennoch hatte diese Diskussion zur Folge,

---

[9] Bojadžiev, A.: Teatralnijat proces. Preživjano i razmisăl (Der theatralische Prozeß. Erlebnisse und Reflexionen). Sofia 1985, S. 15.
[10] Bojadžiev (Anm. 9), S. 53.
[11] Wir skizzieren hier die ausführliche Darstellung der Diskussionen bei Dobrev, Č.: Dramaturgični idei i teatralna metodologija (Dramaturgische Ideen und theatralische Methodologie). Sofia 1984, S. 5–88.

daß sich bis 1955 in einem eher geräuschlosen Prozeß zwei gegnerische Lager bildeten, die in der zweiten Diskussion 1955 heftig aufeinanderstießen.

Diese Veranstaltung war denn auch die „erste wirkliche und scharfe Attacke gegen die dogmatische und normative Ästhetik der Personenkults-Periode"[12]). Die Attacke wurde von jüngeren Theaterleuten wie L. Daniel, J. Ognjanova u. a. geritten, die den Mangel an guten Stücken, die klischeehaften Aufführungen und auch den „Angstkomplex" der Regisseure, gegen die Dogmen zu verstoßen, bemängelten. Dagegen sprach sich das gegnerische, meist aus Theaterkritikern bestehende Lager für die Beibehaltung der bestehenden „Theaterästhetik" aus und tat jede Form von Experimentieren als Formalismus, Ästhetizismus oder Naturalismus ab.

Michail Veličkov, später führender Vertreter der Richtung des Kammertheaters, warf bei der Diskussion der Theaterkritik „Schematismus und Simplifizierung" vor, was „zum Verfall ästhetischer Kriterien sowie zur Stimulierung des Primitivismus in der Kunst" beitrage[13]). Veličkov resümierte: „In der Theaterkritik haben sich viele schädliche Parasiten ein Nest geflochten und sich dort gemütlich eingerichtet: grober Soziologismus, Primitivismus, Unverständnis und Nichtbeachtung unserer nationalen Traditionen."[14]) Erst durch Rückbesinnung auf die eigenen Bühnenklassiker, so die Folgerung Veličkovs, könne in kurzer Zeit wieder gutes Theater auf bulgarischen Bühnen gezeigt werden.

In diesem Zusammenhang waren die Aufführung von V. Drumevs *Ivanko* von 1872 in Pleven (1955) und die darauf folgende kontroverse Diskussion ein weiterer Meilenstein zur Überwindung des Dogmatismus, nachdem sich die Nichtdogmatiker, die sich zu den Klassikern bekannten, durchgesetzt hatten.

Dennoch war der Weg zu einer Liberalisierung im Kulturleben noch längst nicht frei. Zu zahlreich waren die Verfechter der harten, dogmatischen Linie; und diese waren weniger unter den Theaterpraktikern als vielmehr in der Theater- und Literaturkritik zu suchen. Zur Klärung erwartete man nun von der Partei eine richtungsweisende Aussage über die Grenzen des künstlerischen Freiraums.

3. 1956–1989

Die offizielle Abkehr von der Stalin-Ära wurde in Bulgarien auf dem Plenum des ZK der BKP im April 1956 vollzogen, wo Todor Živkov als Erster Sekretär des ZK eine Bewertung des XX. Parteitages der KPdSU vornahm und seine Partei auf die neue sowjetische Linie festlegte.

Für das Theater bedeutete dies keineswegs eine abrupte Wende. Die seit 1953 ansatzweise festzustellenden Liberalisierungstendenzen setzten sich weiterhin nur recht mühsam fort. Die alten Dogmatiker, voran T. Pavlov, wollten sich nicht geschlagen geben und setzten ihre Polemiken gegen Neuerungen, die sie nun als ideologische Abweichungen, Verbeugung vor dem Westen usw. brandmarkten, fort.

---

[12]) Dobrev (Anm. 11), S. 6.
[13]) Zit. n. Dobrev (Anm. 11), S. 86.
[14]) Ebenda.

Dennoch trat seit 1956 eine allmähliche Wandlung zunächst des Bühnenrepertoires ein. Dieser Prozeß ist in Bulgarien nicht mit einem Autor oder gar Drama verbunden (erst 1963 konnte Emil Manov als erster Dramatiker in *Greškata na Avel* (Abels Fehler) mit den Verfehlungen der Partei während der Stalin-Ära abrechnen, Georgi Džagarovs *Prokurorăt* (Der Staatsanwalt) folgte 1965), sondern er erfaßte allmählich immer mehr Dramatiker, Regisseure und Kritiker, auch solche, die opportunistisch den Dogmatismus mitgetragen hatten.

Nun, Ende der 50er Jahre, kehrten auch die Vorkriegsdramen auf die Bühnen zurück: S. L. Kostovs Komödien, die Bühnenwerke Jovkovs, Todorovs, Vazovs u. a. Als Höhepunkt dieser Wiederkehr wurde dem Sofioter „Nationaltheater" der Name Vazovs als des Begründers eines nationalen bulgarischen Theaters beigegeben. Parallel hierzu fanden nun auch wieder westeuropäische und amerikanische Dramen auf die Spielpläne zurück.

Ein wichtiger Schritt zur Erneuerung und Diversifizierung im Theater war – nach entsprechendem Parteibeschluß – die Gründung des *Dăržaven satiričen teatăr* (Staatliches Satirisches Theater) im Herbst 1956. Die ursprüngliche Idee der Initiatoren Valeri Petrov und Radoj Ralin war es, humoristisches, kritisches und karikaturistisches Theater zu machen. Unter B. Danovskis Leitung (1958–65) wandte sich das Haus echten Komödien und Satiren zu und inspirierte Autoren wie Ivan Radoev und Jordan Radičkov. Der vielseitige Griša Ostrovski inszenierte hier in den 60er Jahren Shakespeare, Dürrenmatt, Frisch, O'Casey und Fo; Metodi Andonov, 1969–70 Direktor des Theaters, wagte sich als erster Regisseur an Radičkovs Dramendebut *Sumatocha* (Wirrwarr), das damals (1966) bei der Kritik noch auf Unverständnis und Ablehnung stieß. (Auch die weiteren Bühnenwerke dieses bedeutendsten bulgarischen Nachkriegsdramatikers wurden am „Satirischen Theater" uraufgeführt.)

1974 gelangte am „Satirischen Theater" mit *Rimska Banja* (Römisches Bad) erstmals ein Drama von Stanislav Stratiev zur Aufführung, weitere folgten bald. So nahmen zwei der wichtigsten Tendenzen der bulgarischen Nachkriegsdramatik, Radičkovs mythologisch-philosophische Dramen und Stratievs Satiren, an diesem Haus ihren Anfang. Später war es Mladen Kiselov, der als künstlerischer Leiter des Theaters (1979–83) durch große Inszenierungen von Dramen beider Autoren, daneben auch von Werken Radoevs, Veličkovs u. a. richtungsweisend wirkte.

Neben dem Aufstieg des „Satirischen Theaters" vollzogen sich nach 1956 weitere nennenswerte Prozesse im bulgarischen Theater, die hier nur anzudeuten sind, wie die – aus der UdSSR kommende – Bewegung der *edinomišlenici* (Gleichgesinnten), Ensembles von Theaterbesessenen, die sich Ende der 50er Jahre in mehreren Städten formierten. Theaterhistorisch am bedeutendsten waren die „Gleichgesinnten" am Theater in Burgas mit den Regisseuren Vili Cankov, Leon Daniel, Julija Ognjanova und Metodi Andonov. Sie suchten neue Wege der Zusammenarbeit im Ensemble, bemühten sich um junge Autoren und, stets von der konservativen Kritik beargwöhnt, auch um Brechts Bühnenkunst[15]).

---

[15]) Brecht, der – soweit ersichtlich – vor dem Krieg nur einmal inszeniert worden war („Dreigroschenoper", Regie N. Fol), wurde nun zu einer Zuflucht für die Neuerer. Doch wurde er, ähnlich wie zuvor Stanislavskij, als dessen Gegenstück er gesehen wurde, auf wenige theoretische Aussagen verengt, mit übergroßer Hochachtung inszeniert und vom Publikum nach Jahren schmaler Theater-

Auch wenn die Burgas-„Gleichgesinnten" Brecht zu wörtlich nahmen und dabei dessen Intentionen übersehen haben mögen, gaben sie doch wichtige Anstöße, die v. a. von den Anfang der 60er Jahre künstlerisch erfolgreichen Kleinstadtbühnen (Pazardžik, Dimitrovgrad, Sliven u. a.) aufgenommen wurden.

Im Frühjahr 1958 dekretierte das damalige Ministerium für Bildung und Kultur die Durchführung einer „Leistungsschau (*pregled*) des bulgarischen Dramas" alle fünf Jahre. Durch die Wettbewerbssituation dieser Veranstaltung (ein Vorläufer hierzu hatte bereits 1951 mit Stücken der dogmatischen Linie stattgefunden) wollte man die Qualität von Regie, Darstellung und Bühnenbild steigern, die Schaffung neuer Bühnenwerke anregen und den Blick auf bulgarische Dramen lenken[16]). In der Tat hat sich diese Form des Stimulierens und Bilanzierens weitgehend bewährt, die *pregledi* zeigen schonungslos Stand und auch Perspektiven der nationalen Bühnenkunst auf. Theaterhistorisch lassen sich an ihnen auch die wichtigsten Stationen der jüngeren bulgarischen Theatergeschichte nachvollziehen (so das Nebeneinander von „poetischer Welle" und „dogmatischen" Stücken 1959, Neuerungen durch „stilisiertes Theater" und kritische Dramen 1964).

1965 kam es im Organ des SBP *Septemvri* zu einer offenen Diskussion über die Rolle der Literaturkritik, die als Druckmittel abgelehnt und stattdessen als Gewissen und wohlmeinender Förderer des literarischen Prozesses reklamiert wurde. Zwar konnte dadurch kein Umbruch bei der parteigebundenen Kritik herbeigeführt werden[17]), doch führte die bessere, derartige Diskussionen ermöglichende Atmosphäre jener Zeit zu den eigentlichen Höhepunkten im bulgarischen Nachkriegstheater in den späten 60er und in den 70er Jahren: den Dramen Radičkovs, zu Satire und Kammertheater.

Die „kleine Form" des Kammerspiels[18]) wurde nach der Gründung der ersten kleinen Bühnen 1965 zu einem belebenden Element. Inzwischen hält sich, meist auf Initiative von Regisseuren und Schauspielern, fast jedes Theater im Lande eine Kleinbühne; daneben entstanden Theatercafés, Keller- und Studiotheater etc. Die Spezifik des Kammertheaters (Zuschauernähe, Verzicht auf äußere Effekte sowie Dekor und Schminke), v. a. jedoch die thematische Hinwendung zu familiären, intimen Problemen und die Konzentration auf das Wort und den Schauspieler (Abkehr vom sonst vorherrschenden Regietheater) haben dem Spielbetrieb neue Wege eröffnet. In Westeuropa werden v. a. M. Veličkovs Kammerdramen gespielt, weitere wichtige Autoren dieser Form sind Ivan Radoev, Stefan Canev, Konstantin Iliev u. a.

---

kost nicht verstanden. Daneben witterte die Kritik in Brecht – trotz seiner Biographie – den Vertreter eines experimentellen und somit abzulehnenden Theaters. Erst seit den 70er Jahren wird er häufiger gespielt.

[16]) Vgl. Bodjadžiev (Anm. 9), S. 55–57.

[17]) Noch 1986 beklagte E. Karanfilov die *grupovština* (dt. etwa „Cliquenwirtschaft"), das Bevorzugen bestimmter genehmer Gruppen seitens der Kritik ohne Rücksicht auf künstlerische Qualität, vgl. Diskussion in: Septemvri. 39 (1986) 1, S. 7–41.

[18]) Zu Enstehung und Tendenzen des bulgarischen Kammertheaters s. Verf.: Das bulgarische Kammertheater, in: Festschrift für Wolfgang Gesemann. Hrsg. v. H.-B. Harder, G. Hummel und H. Schaller. Bd. 1: Beiträge zur Bulgaristik. Neuried 1986, S. 103–110.

In den 80er Jahren ist es dem bulgarischen Theater nicht gelungen, an die Erfolge der 60er und 70er Jahre anzuknüpfen. Vielmehr läuft das Theater Gefahr, zur Boulevardkultur abzusinken, um der ihm erwachsenen Konkurrenz durch Fernsehen etc. zu trotzen. Theaterleute beklagen in den Medien die vermehrte Aufnahme von ästhetisch eher wertlosen Kassenschlagern in das Repertoire der Bühnen[19], die (offenbar erfolglos) den Zuschauer anlocken sollen, das Theater jedoch zur anspruchslosen Billigware machen.

Sinnvoller wäre es, die Angst der Behörden vor unbequemen Dramen wie Radičkovs *Obraz i podobie* (Abbild und Ebenbild)[20] zu überwinden und mit ihrer Aufführung für die Erschließung neuer Bereiche zu sorgen. Die erstmalige Aufnahme von Becketts „Warten auf Godot" in die Spielpläne zweier Häuser in der Saison 1987/88 war sicherlich ein Schritt in die richtige Richtung.

Hoffnungsvoll stimmten auch die Ankündigungen im Beschluß des Politbüros der BKP zur „Beschleunigung der Umgestaltung im geistigen Bereich" vom 27.3.1988[21]. Das ZK-Plenum vom Juli 1988 bestätigte zwar diesen Kurs, doch sind konkrete Ziele der Theater wie Selbstverwaltung, Repertoire-Autonomie etc. noch nicht erreicht worden. Erst mit Hilfe dieser Verbesserungen könnte es jedoch gelingen, den „intellektuellen Ansatz" im Theater durchzusetzen, „für den B. Danovski und M. Andonov kämpften"[22]. Das Interesse der Zuschauer im Lande sowie der Freunde des – an Talenten reichen – bulgarischen Theaters im Ausland würde dadurch mit Sicherheit gestärkt werden.

Insgesamt kann der Ausblick auf die Zukunft des bulgarischen Theaters – nach seiner Verarmung zwischen 1944 und 1956, einem gewissen Aufblühen in den 60er und 70er Jahren sowie einer Stagnation in den 80er Jahren – durchaus optimistisch sein, vorausgesetzt, es kommt endlich zu der lange angekündigten Umgestaltung im Theaterleben, die sich auch 1989 noch immer im Diskussionsstadium befindet[23]; denn erst, wenn den Theaterhäusern und ihren Künstlern die lebensnotwendige Autonomie zugestanden wird, kann sich die bulgarische Theaterkunst, ungehindert von politischer Einflußnahme und staatlicher Reglementierung, zu neuer Größe entwickeln und wieder Anschluß an das Welttheater vermitteln.

---

[19] Vgl. u.a. die Aussagen zur Dramatik von 1987 bei der traditionellen „Aprildiskussion" des SBP, abgedruckt in: Literaturen Front. 44 (1988) 17, S. 6f.

[20] Veröffentlicht in: Sävremennik. 14 (1986) 2, S. 283–329.

[21] Veröffentlicht u.a. in: RD. 27.4.88.

[22] Tenev, L.: Teatărăt i publikata (Das Theater und das Publikum), in: Narodna Kultura. 32 (1988) 13, S. 4.

[23] Vgl. Theater-Leitartikel in RD. 6.2.1989, betitelt: Neobchodimi promeni ili neopravdani riskove? (Notwendige Veränderungen oder ungerechtfertigte Risiken?), über die Diskussion um mögliche Strukturveränderungen im *Vazov*-Nationaltheater, denen Modellcharakter zukäme.

III. Institutionen und Organisationen

1. Ausbildungsstätten

Nachdem bis zum I. Weltkrieg eine gute, professionelle Ausbildung für bulgarische Schauspieler und Regisseure nur im Ausland zu erlangen war (man wandte sich v. a. nach Rußland und Deutschland), wurde zwischen beiden Weltkriegen eine Reihe von privaten Schauspiel- bzw. Theaterschulen gegründet. Auch einige Theater boten mehr oder weniger umfangreiche Ausbildungsgänge für junge Theaterpraktiker an.

1942 wurde die „Staatliche Theaterschule" mit zweijährigem Studiengang geschaffen, die dem Nationaltheater in Sofia angegliedert wurde. Nach dem Staatsstreich 1944 waren die dort Lehrenden gehalten, „die Erziehung der Studenten in Richtung des sozialistischen Geistes (zu) lenken"[24]. Ende 1948 wurde die Einrichtung zur „Staatlichen Theaterhochschule" erhoben, 1951 ihr der Name des Schauspielers K. Sarafov beigegeben, und seit 1954 heißt sie *Visš institut za teatralno izkustvo Krăstju Sarafov* (Hochschule für Theaterkunst), kurz VITIZ genannt. Hier werden in zehn verschiedenen, vier- und fünfjährigen Studiengängen Schauspieler, Regisseure, Puppenspieler, Theater- und Filmwissenschaftler, Kameraleute u. a. ausgebildet. VITIZ ist die einzige Ausbildungsstätte für Theaternachwuchs in Bulgarien.

2. Staatliche Theateradministration

Staatliche Stellen nehmen durch das Komitee für Kultur und die ihm seit 1987 unterstellte „Hauptdirektion Theater" in zwei wesentlichen Bereichen Einfluß auf die Schauspielhäuser. Die „Direktion" versorgt alle Theater im Lande mit den Texten ausländischer und bulgarischer Dramen. Vor allem für kleinere Häuser, die nicht über eigene Repertoire-Abteilungen verfügen, vermittelt die „Direktion" zwischen Autor und Theater und schließt entsprechende Verträge. Im Juni jeden Jahres werden mit allen Bühnen Gespräche über das Repertoire der nächsten Saison geführt, wobei die „Hauptdirektion" großen Einfluß auf die letztendliche Auswahl hat. Daneben gibt es auch andere „Filter" wie Verlage usf., die formal Sorge zu tragen haben, daß nur Dramen mit Niveau Verbreitung finden; eine gewisse Zensor-Funktion ist ihnen jedoch nicht abzusprechen. (Darüber hinaus muß jede Inszenierung von einem *chudožestven săvet* (künstlerischer Rat) vor der Uraufführung abgenommen werden.)

Daneben hat die „Hauptdirektion" die staatlichen Vorgaben hinsichtlich der Organisationsformen der Theater durchzusetzen. Sie entscheidet mit über Personalfragen, aber auch über die szenische Realisierung der Bühnenwerke. Im Zuge der *preustrojstvo* dürften jedoch diese Aufgaben den Theatern unmittelbar übertragen und der „künstlerische Rat" überflüssig werden.

---

[24]) Penev (Anm. 1), S. 985.

3. Publikationsorgane

Seit 1946 erscheint monatlich die Zeitschrift *Teatăr* (Theater), die sich mit dem bulgarischen und internationalen Theaterleben befaßt und in jeder Ausgabe ein vollständiges Drama abdruckt. Ebenfalls monatlich veröffentlicht die *Teatralna biblioteka* (Theaterbibliothek) zwei oder mehrere Dramen mit Kurzerläuterungen. Daneben bieten die Literaturzeitschriften *Plamăk* (Flamme) und *Săvremennik* (Zeitgenosse) vereinzelt ganze Dramen an. Als Buchveröffentlichungen stehen Dramentexte jedoch – wie auch andernorts – in Zahl und Auflage hinter Prosa und Poesie zurück. Mit dem Theaterleben in Form von Kritiken, Interviews etc. beschäftigen sich die Wochenzeitungen *Literaturen Front* (Literarische Front, Organ des SBP) und *Narodna Kultura* (Volkskultur, Organ des Komitees für Kultur), vereinzelt auch die Tagespresse sowie die elektronischen Medien.

4. Internationale Zusammenarbeit

Bulgarien ist Mitglied im Internationalen Theater-Institut (ITI). Am „Theater der Nationen", dem Festival dieser UNESCO-Unterorganisation, nehmen bulgarische Ensembles regelmäßig teil. 1982 war Bulgarien Ausrichter dieser Veranstaltung.

1987 fand in Sofia erstmals das Festival „Theater im Koffer" (mit großem Erfolg) statt, das hier fortan im Zweijahres-Turnus die kleine Theaterform durch Ensembles aus aller Welt einem breiten Publikum nahebringen soll.

Zwischen der Bundesrepublik Deutschland und Bulgarien ist es bisher nur vereinzelt zu Theatergastspielen gekommen. Nach dem Austausch von Kulturinstituten dürfte jedoch beiden Ländern der Zugang zur Theaterkunst des anderen mittels verstärkten Angebots von Literatur, Vorträgen, Gastinszenierungen und Besuchen von ganzen Ensembles erleichtert werden. Außerdem wäre ein größeres Angebot an Übersetzungen von Dramen beider Länder wünschenswert, um zunächst einmal die Textvorlagen einem breiteren Leserkreis vorstellen zu können.

IV. Statistischer Anhang[25]

Der Vergleich zu Ungarn, wo 26 der 55 Theater des Landes in Budapest stehen (1984 wurden dort insges. 681 Stücke in 12 570 Vorstellungen vor 5 812 000 Zuschauern gespielt[26]), zeigt, daß trotz der zahlenmäßigen und qualitativen Dominanz der Hauptstadttheater die Provinzbühnen in Bulgarien eine vergleichsweise größere Rolle spielen.

---

[25] Angaben aus: Centralno statističesko upravlenie, „Kultura" (Statistische Zentralverwaltung, „Kultur"). Sofia 1988.
[26] Vgl. Fazekas, T.; Mavius, G.: Theater, in: Grothusen, K.-D. (Hrsg.): Südosteuropa-Handbuch. Bd. 5: Ungarn. Göttingen 1987, S. 596/97.

Tabelle 1: Anzahl der Theater (Sprech-, Musik- und Puppentheater)

Jahr	Sprechtheater	Opern	Operetten	Puppentheater
1960	36	5	1	4
1965	24	5	1	6
1970	34	5	1	6
1975	36	7	1	11
1980	37	8	1	12
1985	37	8	1	19
1987	37(8)	8(1)	1(1)	20(1)

(in Klammern die Angaben für Sofia-Stadt)

Tabelle 2: Entwicklung des Sprechtheaters

	1960	1965	1970	1975	1980	1985	1987
Plätze (insgesamt)	17 668	13 475	17 519	18 955	19 265	18 328	18 012
Vorstellungen (insgesamt)	11 057	8 439	9 701	9 906	12 024	10 423	9 993
Besucher (in Tsd.)	4 765	3 696	4 165	4 340	4 553	3 816	3 660
Vorstellungen (pro Theater)	307	352	285	275	325	282	270
Besucher pro Theater	132 361	154 000	122 500	120 545	123 049	103 138	98 920
Besucher pro Vorstellung	431	438	429	438	379	366	366

1987 unterstanden 34 Theater finanziell dem Komitee für Kultur, drei dem Staatshaushalt. Die 34 Theater hatten 1987 bei 9 094 Vorstellungen 3 254 Mio. Zuschauer und Einnahmen aus dem Kartenverkauf in Höhe von 4 735 Mio. Leva. Die drei staatlichen Theater hatten 1987 in 899 Vorstellungen 406 000 Zuschauer und 797 000 Leva Einnahmen aus dem Kartenverkauf. Die Höhe der Subventionen seitens des Komitees für Kultur bzw. des Staatshaushaltes ist nicht bekannt.

Bei den 9 993 Vorstellungen der dramatischen Theater 1987 wurden 5 439 mal Dramen von bulgarischen, 1 653 mal Werke von sowjetischen und 2 901 mal Stücke von anderen ausländischen Autoren gezeigt.

An den 37 Schauspielhäusern waren 1987 4 345 Personen beschäftigt, darunter 206 „künstlerische Leiter" (Intendanten, Regisseure etc.), 1 517 „künstlerisch Ausführende" (Schauspieler), 1 562 „künstlerisch-technische" Mitarbeiter (Bühnen- und Maskenbildner etc.), 781 „hilfstechnische" Mitarbeiter (Bühnenarbeiter u. a.) sowie 279 Verwaltungsbedienstete.

Zum Vergleich: In der Bundesrepublik Deutschland und Berlin (West) haben in der Spielzeit 1986/87 die 433 im Deutschen Bühnen-Jahrbuch verzeichneten Theater insgesamt 179074 Plätze angeboten. An diesen Häusern waren ein Jahr zuvor 323 Bühnenleiter (Intendanten, Direktoren), 324 Dramaturgen, 564 Kostüm- und Bühnenbildner und 416 Regisseure (incl. Oper u. Operette), daneben 4861 Schauspieler (davon 1765 weibl.) beschäftigt[27].

---

[27] Deutsches Bühnen-Jahrbuch 1986/87 (95. Jg.). Hamburg 1988.

Film

Klaus Eder, München

I. Einführung – II. Die Organisation des Films – III. Der Film bis 1944 – IV. Der Neubeginn: 1. Alte Muster (1944–1948) – 2. Neue Muster (1948–1956) – V. Film und Poesie (1956–1968): 1. Die verlorene Jugend – 2. Abrechnung mit der Vergangenheit – 3. Neue Probleme, neue Helden – VI. Konsolidierung: Thematische und stilistische Vielfalt (1968–1989): 1. Die Entwicklung der Genres – 2. Das Bild des Arbeiters – 3. Landflucht – 4. Der Rückgriff auf kulturelle Traditionen – 5. Neuer Blick auf alte Themen – 6. 1 300 Jahre Bulgarien – 7. Tendenzen

I. Einführung

Der bulgarische Film ist im Westen weitgehend unbekannt geblieben. Einzelne Filme wie *Ikonostasăt* (Die Altarwand) oder *Kozijat rog* (Das Ziegenhorn) fanden außerhalb Bulgariens bei einem interessierten Publikum Anerkennung oder wurden bei internationalen Festivals ausgezeichnet wie *Zvezdi* (Sterne) 1959 in Cannes, *Obič* (Liebe) 1973 in Moskau oder *Avantaž* (Vorteil) 1978 in Berlin. Dennoch erreichten polnische oder sowjetische Filme unter Kennern größere Bekanntheit und Beliebtheit. Daß bulgarische Filme nicht die internationale Aufmerksamkeit fanden, die sie verdienen, liegt unter anderem am Fehlen eines herausragenden, international berühmten Regisseurs, der – wie Andrzej Wajda in Polen oder Andrej Tarkovskij in der Sowjetunion – das Interesse auf die gesamte Kinematographie des Landes hätte lenken können. Zum anderen ist der bulgarische Film jung. Auch wenn der erste Spielfilm 1915 entstand und seitdem einigermaßen regelmäßig Filme gedreht werden konnten, kann man von einer kontinuierlichen Filmarbeit doch erst seit den 50er Jahren sprechen, als mit Studios und Laboratorien die technischen Grundlagen der Filmproduktion bereitgestellt wurden. „The Bulgarian cinema came into being as a contemporary of the socialist revolution."[1]) Diese unter bulgarischen Filmhistorikern verbreitete Ansicht weist auf die kulturpolitische Aufmerksamkeit hin, die das sozialistische Bulgarien dem Film als „wichtigste der Künste" (Lenin) entgegenbrachte (nicht anders als in der Sowjetunion nach 1917 und in den anderen sozialistischen Ländern nach 1944/45). Seitdem bildete sich eine Kinematographie von thematischer und stilistischer Vielfalt und von hohem Niveau heraus, die nicht weniger interessant ist als andere sozialistische Kinematographien und die sich gleichzeitig in ihrer nationalen Prägung von ihnen unterscheidet. Die Geschichte, die Literatur, im weiteren Sinn die Kultur des Landes bildeten die Grundlage dieser Kinematographie, die nicht in erster Linie einem Unterhaltungsinteresse dient, sondern zusammen mit

---

[1]) The Bulgarian Art Feature Film. A Collection of Articles. Ed. by M. Nikolova. Sofia o. J., S. 8.

den anderen Künsten einen moralischen und ideologischen Anspruch wahrnimmt und darüber hinaus einen nationalen Charakter des Landes und seiner Menschen zu recherchieren, zu diskutieren und zu formen sucht. „Le cinéma bulgare s'est intégré à la vie du pays et reflète fidèlement et honnêtement ses problèmes, son passé et son présent."[2]) Diese kulturpolitische Absicht konnte keineswegs immer, aber doch in den besten Perioden der bulgarischen Filmgeschichte realisiert werden.

II. Die Organisation des Films

In den ersten vier Jahrzehnten des Jahrhunderts wurden jährlich nicht mehr als drei, vier Filme gedreht, manchmal war es auch nur einer. Insgesamt wurden von 1915 bis 1944 lediglich 47 abendfüllende Spielfilme hergestellt[3]). Bulgarien war – wie die umliegenden Balkanländer – kein Filmland. Den vereinzelten Bemühungen um eine nationale Kinematographie stand der Import ausländischer, vorwiegend amerikanischer Filme gegenüber. Es fehlten somit alle Voraussetzungen, eine funktionierende Film-Industrie aufzubauen. Dazu kam es erst nach 1944, dann allerdings systematisch. Zurückgreifen konnte man auf wenig: „Außer Begeisterung, außer dem Gefühl, auf der Höhe der Zeit zu sein, hatte man nichts als einige schrottreife Kameras."[4]) Der Film wurde 1948 nationalisiert und in einer eigenen Organisationsform (mit einem Generaldirektor im Rang eines Vizeministers an der Spitze) dem Kultusministerium unterstellt. Studios für Spielfilme, für Trickfilme, für Dokumentarfilme, für populärwissenschaftliche Filme wurden eingerichtet. Ein filmisches Zentrum wurde gebaut, das 1963 seine Arbeit aufnahm: *Kinocentăr Bojana* vor den Toren Sofias, das heute rund 25 abendfüllende Spielfilme pro Jahr herstellt. Diese „Filmstadt" am Fuße des Vitoša-Gebirges beherbergt verschiedene Produktionseinheiten sowie den technischen Park der bulgarischen Kinematographie. Diese Produktionseinheiten (fünf) wurden 1987 eingerichtet. Sie stehen unter der Leitung jeweils eines Regisseurs, haben einen jährlichen Etat von je rund 2,5 Mio. Leva und sind in ihren künstlerischen Entscheidungen autonom (1987 wurde die Zensur von Drehbüchern aufgehoben). Eine dieser Einheiten (*Debut*, geleitet von Zako Cheskija) widmet sich dem Nachwuchs. 1988 wurden in Bojana 24 Kinofilme, 22 Fernsehfilme, etwa 15 Dokumentarfilme und 60 Kurzfilme hergestellt. Der Kinobestand wurde auf einen Stand von etwa 3 450 Kinos ausgebaut. Das entspricht etwa der Zahl der Kinos in der weitaus größeren Bundesrepublik Deutschland. Allerdings entspricht die technische Ausrüstung der Kinos nicht dem internationalen Standard, beispielsweise ist in nur vier Kinos das Ton-System Dolby installiert. Auch der Kinobesuch ist in Bulgarien höher: Der statistische Kinobesuch pro Einwohner und Jahr lag in den 60er und 70er

---

[2]) Der damalige Generaldirektor der bulgarischen Kinematographie, Pavel Pisarev, 1975, in: Cervoni, A.: Les écrans de Sofia. Paris 1976, S. 97.

[3]) Eine verläßliche Filmographie 1915–1985 findet sich in: Holloway, R.: The Bulgarian Cinema. Cranbury, London, Toronto 1986, S. 141–209.

[4]) Der Regisseur Zachari Žandov, in: Ratschewa, M.; Eder, K.: Der bulgarische Film. Frankfurt 1977, S. 18.

Jahren bei dreizehn und ist in den 80er Jahren auf zehn gesunken. Zum Vergleich: In der Bundesrepublik sind es knapp zwei Kinobesuche pro Einwohner und Jahr. Der Eintrittspreis beträgt 0,50 Lev. Der staatliche Verleih bringt pro Jahr 160 bis 170 ausländische Filme in die Kinos. Wer heute in künstlerischen Bereichen des Films arbeitet, hat eine Ausbildung an einer Filmhochschule abgeschlossen, früher im Ausland, seit 1973 an der Sofioter Hochschule VITIZ. Der „Verband der Filmschaffenden" (gegründet 1918 als eine Vereinigung der Bühnen- und Filmschauspieler und 1944 als *Săjuz na kinodejcite* reorganisiert) übernahm die Vertretung sozialer und professioneller Belange aller kreativen Kräfte im Film – ohne allerdings in den letzten Jahren die politische Funktion und Macht zu gewinnen, wie sie dem sowjetischen Filmverband durch die Politik der *perestrojka* zuwuchsen. Zwei monatliche Zeitschriften informieren über das internationale Filmgeschehen: *Kino izkustvo* (Filmkunst, theoretisch orientiert), und *Filmovi novini* (Film-Nachrichten, populär). Außerdem gibt *Filmbulgaria*, die für den Import und den Export von Filmen zuständige Abteilung der staatlichen Kinematographie, ein regelmäßiges, in vier Sprachen übersetztes Bulletin über das bulgarische Kino heraus. Ein nationales Spielfilm-Festival findet alle zwei Jahre in Varna statt, für ausländische Kritiker und Festivaldirektoren eine willkommene Gelegenheit, sich über die neueste Produktion zu informieren. Weitere Festivals sind die in Plovdiv (Kurzfilme, jährlich), Tolbuchin (Trickfilme) und Smoljan (eine Schau des „jungen Films"). Das bulgarische Filmarchiv unterhält im Zentrum Sofias ein Kino, das filmhistorische Vorführungen anbietet.

III. Der Film bis 1944

Die Geschichte des bulgarischen Films bis 1944 ist in wirtschaftlicher und kultureller Hinsicht unbedeutend. Was an nennenswerten Filmen entstand, war das Werk enthusiastischer Einzelgänger. Zwar gab es die ersten Filmvorführungen (in Ruse) bereits im Frühjahr 1897, wenige Monate nach den ersten Filmvorführungen in Paris; zwar wurden erste Dokumentar-Aufnahmen bereits 1903 gemacht, kam die erste Wochenschau 1913 heraus (*Kino*). Doch der erste Spielfilm entstand erst 1915: *Bălgaran e galant* (Der Bulgare ist galant), die Imitation einer Hollywood-Komödie. Der Regisseur war Vasil Gendov (1891–1970), einer der Pioniere des bulgarischen Kinos. Von 1915 bis 1937 drehte er elf Spielfilme (die fast alle als verloren gelten). 1922 verfilmte er die populären Geschichten Aleko Konstantinovs um *Baj Ganju*.

Bis zum II. Weltkrieg basierte das bulgarische Kino auf der Adaption nationaler Literatur. Petăr Stojčev verfilmte Elin Pelins Roman *Zemja* (Erde, 1930) über den Abstieg einer Familie auf dem Land. Boris Grežov drehte *Bezkrăstni grobove* (Gräber ohne Kreuz, 1932), den ersten bulgarischen Tonfilm, nach Bončo Nestorovs Elegie auf die Opfer des Aufstands von 1923. Aleksandăr Vazov adaptierte Ivan Vazovs populäres Poem *Gramada* (Der Steinhaufen, 1936) über das Leid Bulgariens unter türkischem Joch. Diese Filme zeichneten ein realistisches Bild des Lebens in Dörfern und Kleinstädten. Die Hauptrollen wurden von bekannten Theaterschauspielern dargestellt.

IV. Der Neubeginn

1. Alte Muster (1944–1948)

Bis 1948 konnten noch private Firmen arbeiten (*Balkan-Film, Slav-Film, Rila-Film*). Ihre Filme versuchten, die Veränderungen im Land darzustellen, bedienten sich jedoch alter, melodramatischer Muster des Vorkriegsfilms: *Šte dojdat novi dni* (Neue Tage werden kommen, 1945), Regie Anton Marinovič, über Bauern, die gegen Landbesitzer revoltieren; *Bojka* (1947), Regie Dimităr Minkov, ein folkloristisches Hajduken-Drama. 1948/49 kam diese Produktion dann zum Erliegen. Im April 1948 wurde die nationale Film-Industrie verstaatlicht.

2. Neue Muster (1948–1956)

Kalin orelăt (Kalin, der Adler) von Boris Borozanov, 1950 noch unter privater Initiative begonnen, war der erste von der staatlichen Kinematographie fertiggestellte Film. Er erzählte von einem Helden aus dem Befreiungskrieg 1878, der nach fünfzehn Jahren der Verbannung in seine Heimat zurückkehrt und ein anderes Land vorfindet als das, für das er kämpfte. Der erste, von der neuen nationalen Kinematographie initiierte und hergestellte Film wurde *Trevoga* (Alarm, 1951) von Zachari Žandov (geb. 1911) über zwei Brüder, die in den letzten Tagen des II. Weltkriegs auf verschiedenen Seiten stehen. In der vereinfachenden Aufteilung von Positionen zeigte sich der Schematismus stalinistischer Kulturpolitik, der die ästhetische Entwicklung des bulgarischen Films in dieser ersten Periode behinderte.

Die meisten der bis 1955/56 hergestellten Filme wandten sich historischen Themen zu. „The upsurge and actual chronology of the Bulgarian cinema began with an interest in the historical life of the people, recreated in the full volume and in the most crucial moments of its development."[5]) Auf drei Perioden konzentrierte sich das Interesse: auf die Befreiung von rund 500 Jahren türkischer Herrschaft 1878; auf den Aufstand von 1923; und auf den Staatsstreich vom 9. 9. 1944, der zur Errichtung des sozialistischen Staates führte. Dem Film kam die Aufgabe zu, dem neuen Staat ein neues, kollektives Bild der eigenen Geschichte zu entwerfen. Dako Dakovski gestaltete in *Pod igoto* (Unter dem Joch, 1952, nach dem gleichnamigen Roman von Ivan Vazov) das Leben in einem bulgarischen Dorf 1876. Vom Aufstand 1923 handelte Zachari Žandov in *Septemvrijci* (Die Septemberkämpfer, 1954). Ebenfalls 1954 enstand eine filmische Erinnerung an den Dichter und Widerstandskämpfer Nikola Vapcarov, der 1942 ermordet worden war, *Pesen za čoveka* (Das Lied vom Menschen), Drehbuch Christo Ganev, Regie Borislav Šaraliev.

Die ersten Versuche, Gegenwarts-Filme zu machen, blieben unbeholfen und waren den ideologischen Schemata des Stalinismus verhaftet: *Tova se sluči na ulicata* (Es geschah auf der Straße, 1956) von Janko Jankov, die Liebesgeschichte zwischen einem Chauffeur und einer Laborantin; *Dve pobedi* (Zwei Siege, 1956) von Borislav

---

[5]) Milev, N.: Reaching Maturity, in: The Bulgarian Art Feature Film (Anm. 1), S. 27.

Šaraliev, eine Komödie, in der bekannte Schauspieler des Sofioter Nationaltheaters auftraten.

Dem Dorf als Schauplatz wandte sich Dako Dakovski (1919–1962) zu. In *Nespokoen păt* (Der unruhige Weg, 1955) beschrieb er das Leben von Bauern, die unter den neuen Bedingungen des Lebens viele der überlieferten Gewohnheiten aufgeben müssen. Weitere Filme Dakovskis über das Dorfleben waren *Tajnata večerja na Sedmacite* (Das geheime Abendmahl der Sedmaks, 1957) und *Stublenskite lipi* (Die Linden von Stublen, 1960).

V. Film und Poesie (1956–1968)

1. Die verlorene Jugend

Das Aprilplenum bestätigte 1956 die Beschlüsse des XX. Parteitags der KPdSU. Die kulturpolitischen Veränderungen machten sich zunächst in einer Reihe von Filmen über den antifaschistischen Widerstand bemerkbar. Der erste dieser Filme war 1958 *Na malkija ostrov* (Auf der kleinen Insel) von Rangel Vălčanov (geb 1928). Das Drehbuch schrieb Valeri Petrov (geb. 1920), der viel zum poetischen Stil des bulgarischen Films der späten 50er und der frühen 60er Jahre beitrug, zusammen mit dem Kameramann Dimo Kolarov und dem Komponisten Simeon Pironkov. *Na malkija ostrov* bedeutete für das bulgarische Kino einen Aufbruch. Vier Häftlinge, Teilnehmer des Septemberaufstands von 1923, die ihren Ausbruchsversuch von einer Gefängnisinsel im Schwarzen Meer mit dem Leben bezahlen, wurden von Petrov/Vălčanov nicht als Helden porträtiert; an ihrem Schicksal wurde der Sinn von Heldentum diskutiert und in Frage gestellt. „This is, in essence, a tragedy, better still an epic poem, a convention that did not fit easily into the prior precepts of Socialist Realism, but is wholly acceptable and appropriate within the country's rich literary tradition."[6] Der zur gleichen Zeit entstandene Film *Partizani/Života si teče ticho* (Die Partisanen/Das Leben fließt langsam dahin, 1958) von Binka Željazkova (Regie) und Christo Ganev (Drehbuch), ein kritischer Blick auf die Jahre des Stalinismus, wurde verboten.

Der Film nach 1956 war eine Antwort auf den Film vor 1956, eine Auseinandersetzung mit den ästhetischen Normen und Dogmen der Stalin-Zeit. Aus den starren Darstellungen und den schematisierten Menschenbildern im Film der 50er Jahre entwickelte sich nach 1956 ein differenziertes psychologisches Drama: der poetische Film. Diese bedeutende Stilrichtung im bulgarischen Film hatte ihr Pendant im filmischen Aufbruch Polens (Andrzej Munk, Andrzej Wajda), Ungarns (Zoltán Fábri) und der Sowjetunion (Michail Kalatozov). Die Autoren dieser poetischen Filme hatten am Widerstand teilgenommen. Im Widerstand hatten sie ihre Jugend verloren. „Ambitions appeared in the Bulgarian cinema to create author's films, supporting their generalizations and truths with personal experience and feelings."[7] Persönliche

---

[6] Holloway (Anm. 3), S. 85.
[7] Stefanov, I., in: The Bulgarian Art Feature Film (Anm. 1), S. 46.

Dimensionen erhielt die Tragik des Kriegs in *Zvezdi* (Sterne, 1959), einer Koproduktion Bulgariens mit der DDR. Der bulgarische Szenarist Anžel Vagenštajn (geb. 1922) schrieb das Drehbuch, Konrad Wolf führte Regie. In einem für das bulgarische Kino neuen Ton, der an Kalatozovs *Letjat žuravli* (Wenn die Kraniche ziehen, UdSSR 1957) erinnerte, wurde die tragische Begegnung zwischen einem deutschen Unteroffizier und einem jüdischen Mädchen geschildert. Die Filme dieser Periode erfaßten individuelle Charaktere und sahen sie vor dem Hintergrund der Kriegszeit. *Părvi urok* (Erste Lehre, 1960) wurde der zweite Film des Teams Petrov/Vălčanov: ein lyrisches Poem, eine heiter beginnende und tragisch endende Liebesgeschichte vor dem Hintergrund von Razzien der faschistischen Polizei 1942. *Bednata ulica* (Die arme Straße, 1960) von Christo Piskov variierte dieses Thema am Beispiel einer Liebe zwischen einer Schülerin und einem jungen Partisanen. Der Rückgriff auf eigene Erlebnisse und Erfahrungen kam in besonderem Maß in *A bjachme mladi* (Wir waren jung, 1961) zum Ausdruck, einem von Christo Ganev geschriebenen Film, den Binka Željazkova (geb. 1923) inszenierte, über eine Gruppe junger Partisanen, die Sabotageakte gegen Deutsche planen und ausführen. Nicht nur die Trauer über eine verlorene Jugend bestimmte diesen Film, eines der Schlüsselwerke der bulgarischen Kinematographie der 60er Jahre. Ganev/Željazkova teilten der neuen jungen Generation auch die Ideale ihrer eigenen Jugend mit.

Ende der 60er Jahre, unter dem Generaldirektor Christo Santov (1969–1971), verschlechterten sich die kulturpolitischen Bedingungen. Zahlreiche Filmemacher zogen es vor, im Ausland zu arbeiten. Nachfolger Santovs wurde 1971 Pavel Pisarev, unter dessen Leitung die bulgarische Kinematographie eine ihrer fruchtbarsten Perioden hatte.

2. Abrechnung mit der Vergangenheit

Die thematischen und stilistischen Neuerungen des bulgarischen Films Mitte der 60er Jahre fanden ihren besten Ausdruck in dem Film *Otklonenie* (Umweg, 1967), mit dem die Schriftstellerin Blaga Dimitrova als Szenaristin debutierte, Griša Ostrovski und Todor Stojanov als Regisseure. *Otklonenie* verband damals aktuelle Themen mit fortgeschrittenen stilistischen Ansätzen. Die Autoren legten die Analyse und Bilanz einer Generation vor, die ihre Jugend Ende der 40er Jahre hatte, in den ersten Jahren des sozialistischen Bulgariens. Erzählt wurde von den beiden Versuchen der Protagonisten Bojan (Ivan Andonov) und Neda (Nevena Kokanova, eine der bekanntesten Schauspielerinnen des Landes, fand hier eine ihrer besten Rollen), ihre Liebe zu verwirklichen. In den 40er Jahren waren die beiden an den Umständen gescheitert, in der Gegenwart scheitern sie an der eigenen Mutlosigkeit und Resignation. Die Autoren sympathisierten mit ihren Figuren. Ständig wechselten die Zeitebenen. Die Bilder ordneten sich nach einem „Bewußtseinsstrom". Ein verspäteter Einfluß der französischen *Nouvelle Vague* war hier zu spüren.

Otklonenie war ein folgenreicher Film: Er lieferte modellhaft die filmische Bilanz einer mittleren Generation. Ein Jahr nach *Otklonenie* legte Metodi Andonov (1932–1974) seinen Film *Bjalata staja* (Das weiße Zimmer, 1968) vor, eine Abrechnung mit dem Stalinismus. Ein Roman Bogomil Rajnovs lag dem Film zugrunde

(*Pătišta za nikăde*, Wege ins Nichts). Die Geschichte eines Intellektuellen wurde erzählt, des Wissenschaftlers Aleksandrov (Apostol Karamitev spielte diese Rolle, einer der beliebtesten bulgarischen Schauspieler; er starb 1973), der in der Zeit des Stalinismus versucht hatte, seine wissenschaftlichen, antidogmatischen Konzeptionen zu verteidigen und darüber depressiv wurde, erkrankte und starb. *Bjalata staja* war der erste Film, der offen die Opfer des stalinistischen Terrors benannte. In der Folge von Metodi Andonovs Film erschien eine Reihe von Filmen, die Probleme der Gesellschaft offen kritisierten. *Obič* (Liebe, 1972) von Ljudmil Stajkov (geb. 1937) schilderte eine junge Frau, die sich gegen den Konformismus ihrer Umwelt auflehnt. *Švedskite krale* (Die schwedischen Könige, 1968) von Ljudmil Kirkov erzählte vom enttäuschenden Ausflug eines hoch bezahlten Stahlarbeiters in ein internationales Bad am Schwarzen Meer.

3. Neue Probleme, neue Helden

In der ersten Hälfte der 60er Jahre versuchte man, den Kreis der Themen zu vergrößern. „Für die Filmemacher wurde es außerordentlich wichtig, die Gegenwart zu beschreiben und zu reflektieren und die neuen Probleme zu diskutieren, die die rasche sozialistische Entwicklung des Landes mit sich brachte."[8]) Valeri Petrov und Rangel Vălčanov interessierten sich in *Slănceto i sjankata* (Sonne und Schatten, 1962) dafür, das Thema von Krieg und Frieden auf eine allgemeinere, von der konkreten Vergangenheit losgelöste Weise zu diskutieren. *Slănceto i sjankata*, ein thematisch wie stilistisch von Alain Resnais' *Hiroshima mon amour* (Frankreich 1959) beeinflußter Film, wurde ein modernes Liebesgedicht, in dessen Hintergrund die Angst vor einem Atomkrieg stand.

Eine Verbreiterung der thematischen Grenzen wurde durch die Zusammenarbeit von Film und Literatur erreicht. Nikola Korabov (geb. 1928) verfilmte 1962 Dimităr Dimovs Roman *Tjutjun* (Tabak), den epischen Querschnitt durch eine Epoche, die Zeit vor und während des II. Weltkriegs. Dem Film *Kradecăt na praskovi* (Der Pfirsichdieb, 1964) von Vălo Radev (geb. 1923) lag eine Novelle von Emilijan Stanev über eine Episode aus dem I. Weltkrieg zugrunde; erzählt wurde auf eine psychologisierende Weise von der Liebe zwischen der Frau des Ortskommandanten von Tărnovo und einem serbischen Gefangenen. 1976 legte Radev eine weitere Literaturverfilmung vor, *Osădeni duši* (Verdammte Seelen), nach Dimităr Dimovs Roman aus dem Spanischen Bürgerkrieg. An die Linie historisch-politischer Filme knüpften der Szenarist Ljuben Stanev und der Regisseur Christo Christov (geb. 1926) mit dem Georgi-Dimitrov-Film *Nakovalnja ili čuk* (Hammer oder Amboß, 1972) an.

Andere Filme beschäftigten sich mit der Jugend. *Dvama pod nebeto* (Zwei unterm Himmelszelt, 1962) von Borislav Šaraliev, *Vălčicata* (Die Wölfin, 1965) von Rangel Vălčanov, *Măže* (Männer, 1966) von Vasil Mirčev, *Karambol* (Karambolage, 1966) von Ljubomir Šarlandžiev handelten von den Problemen der jungen Generation, zwischen der Bevormundung durch Eltern, Schule und Staat eine eigene Individuali-

---

[8]) Stefanov, I., in: M. Ratschewa; K. Eder (Anm. 4), S. 49.

tät zu entwickeln. Den gleichzeitigen Jugendrevolten im Westen gegenüber wurde hier von den Problemen freilich nur in abgemilderter Form gehandelt. Valeri Petrov (Drehbuch) und Borislav Šaraliev drehten 1966 den Film *Ricar bez bronja* (Ritter ohne Rüstung) über kompromißbereite Erwachsene, gesehen aus der Perspektive eines neugierigen Jungen.

VI. Konsolidierung: Thematische und stilistische Vielfalt (1968–1989)

1. Die Entwicklung der Genres

Die Versuche, einen bulgarischen Kriminalfilm zu schaffen, blieben bescheiden. Einen Detektiv und seinen Alltag beschrieb Rangel Vălčanov in *Inspektorăt i nošta* (Der Inspektor und die Nacht, 1963). Eine Reihe von Filmen entstand nach Romanen von Bogomil Rajnov, der die Figur eines intelligenten und mutigen Agenten der bulgarischen Spionage-Abwehr schuf.

Erfolgreicher waren die Versuche zu einer bulgarischen Komödie. Georgi Mišev schrieb eine Reihe von Drehbüchern, in denen er ein realistisches, teilweise auch satirisches Bild der bulgarischen Mittelklasse entwarf. Ljudmil Kirkov (geb. 1933) zeichnete in *Momčeto se otiva* (Ein Junge wird zum Mann, 1972, Drehbuch Mišev) einen 18jährigen Jungen, der in generationsbedingte Konflikte mit seiner Umwelt gerät und von kompromißbereiten Erwachsenen enttäuscht wird. Eduard Zachariev (geb. 1938) nahm die Vorlagen Miševs zum Anlaß von sozialer Satire und erfindungsreicher Beschreibungen kleinbürgerlicher Mentalität: *Ako ne ide vlak* (Wenn der Zug nicht kommt, 1967), *Prebrojavane na divite sajci* (Das Zählen der wilden Kaninchen, 1973), *Vilna zona* (Die Villengegend, 1975).

Großer Wert wurde von Anfang an auf Kinderfilme gelegt. Der bulgarische Kinderfilm erreichte hohes internationales Ansehen (Dimităr Petrov, Ivanka Gräbčeva, Mariana Evstatieva) und wird gerne zu internationalen Kinderfilm-Festivals (wie dem in Frankfurt) eingeladen. Auf den Dokumentarfilm spezialisierten sich Vasil Mirčev, Veselina Gerinska, Christo Kovačev, Nevena Toševa. Berühmt wurde der bulgarische Trickfilm (Todor Dinov, Don'o Donev), der bei den Festivals in Oberhausen oder Krakau immer wieder ausgezeichnet wurde.

2. Das Bild des Arbeiters

In den 50er Jahren hatte der bulgarische Film ein idealisiertes Bild des Arbeiters entworfen. In den 70er Jahren veränderte sich dieses Bild: Es wurde realistisch und psychologisch differenziert. An Kirkovs Film *Švedskite krale* knüpfte Ivan Terziev (geb. 1934) mit zwei Filmen an, *Măže bez rabota* (Männer ohne Arbeit, 1973) und *Silna voda* (Starke Wasser, 1975), deren Aufmerksamkeit nicht dem Bereich der Produktion galt, sondern den moralischen Problemen und Positionen der Menschen. *Nedelni mačove* (Fußball am Sonntag, 1975) von Todor Andrejkov schilderte auf eine beobachtende, fast dokumentarische Weise die Arbeitsbedingungen in einer kleinen

Bergarbeiterstadt. Stilistisch läßt sich hier von einem „inneren Dokumentarismus" sprechen, der einen oberflächlichen äußeren Realismus ablöste.

3. Landflucht

Ins Zentrum des filmischen Interesses rückte Mitte der 70er Jahre das soziale Thema der Landflucht. Fast alle 1974 beim nationalen Festival in Varna gezeigten Filme handelten davon. Diese Landflucht war das Ergebnis einer raschen industriellen Entwicklung des tradierten Agrarlandes. Sie warf andere als nur wirtschaftliche Probleme auf: soziale, psychologische, moralische. In Christo Christovs Film *Posledno ljato* (Der letzte Sommer, 1974, Drehbuch Jordan Radičkov) stand ein dickschädliger Bauer (Grigor Vačkov) im Mittelpunkt, der sich weigert, sein Stück Land zu verlassen, das bald von den Wassern eines Stausees überflutet werden wird. In *Dărvo bez koren* (Baum ohne Wurzeln, 1974, nach Nikolaj Chajtov) ließ Christo Christov einen Bauern in die Stadt ziehen, doch die Lebensumstände dort nicht ertragen. *Večni vremena* (Unvergängliche Zeiten, 1975) von Asen Šopov erzählte von einem Förster, der sich verzweifelt bemüht, die Menschen im Dorf zu halten. In *Seljaninăt s koleloto* (Der Bauer auf dem Fahrrad, 1974, Drehbuch Georgi Mišev) von Ljudmil Kirkov ist der Bauer zum Städter geworden und sehnt sich nach dem Dorf zurück, während eine Städterin, die im Dorf arbeitet, sich nach der Stadt sehnt. In diesen Filmen wurden die geistigen Dimensionen der Landflucht reflektiert.

4. Der Rückgriff auf kulturelle Traditionen

Eines der ambitionierten Unternehmen der bulgarischen Kinematographie wurde die Verfilmung von Dimităr Talevs Erzählung *Železnijat svetilnik* (Der eiserne Leuchter), die in die Jahre der bulgarischen Wiedergeburt im 19. Jh. zurückführt. Christo Christov und Todor Dinov, die beiden Regisseure, konzentrierten sich in ihrem Film *Ikonostasăt* (Die Altarwand, 1969) auf das Schicksal eines Holzschnitzers und Ikonenmalers und erzählten die Geschichte eines Künstlers, der seinem Gewissen folgt und damit gegen Recht und Ordnung verstößt. Diese Geschichte betteten sie in ein Tableau bulgarischer Volkskunst ein. Gedreht wurde *Ikonostasăt* – ein Film, der oft mit Andrej Tarkovskijs *Andrej Rublev* (UdSSR 1966/71) verglichen wurde – im Bačkovo-Kloster im Süden von Plovdiv, einem Zentrum der thrakischen Kunst.

1972 drehte Metodi Andonov nach einer Erzählung von Nikolaj Chajtov über die Zeit der Türkenherrschaft den Film *Kozijat rog* (Das Ziegenhorn), einen der erfolgreichsten Filme des Landes, der von rund 4,2 Mio. Bulgaren gesehen wurde. Chajtov, der Dichter der Rhodopen, war dem bulgarischen Kino als Drehbuchautor von Georgi Djulgerov gewonnen worden, der 1969 als Diplomarbeit an der Moskauer Filmhochschule eine Chajtov-Geschichte verfilmte, die er in Bulgarien 1971 noch einmal drehte: *Izpit* (Die Prüfung), über ein altes rhodopisches Ritual. Geschichten von Chajtov haben das bulgarische Kino in hohem Maß inspiriert. Andonovs *Kozijat rog* erzählte von einem Mann, einem Bauern, der in den Bergen lebt, und der seine Tochter (Katja Paskaleva) benützt, um sich an den Türken für den Mord an seiner Frau zu rächen. Metodi Andonov erzählte chronologisch, mit einer ökonomischen Dramaturgie. Die Kamera Dimo Kolarovs verharrte in langen Einstellungen auf die Menschen und ihre Umgebung; die weite, strenge, schöne Landschaft der Rhodopen spielte mit. Der poetische Realismus des Films ergab sich aus der Verbindung der Menschen mit ihrer sozialen und geographischen Umgebung. *Kozijat rog* war eine strenge, fast klassische Tragödie über einen Mann, den persönliches Leiden in einer schlimmen Zeit so sehr verblendet, daß er alle Maßstäbe verliert. Mit diesem Film errang das bulgarische Kino Weltniveau.

5. Neuer Blick auf alte Themen

Die persönlichen, emotionalen Filme der 60er Jahre, in denen ehemalige Partisanen von ihrer biographischen Erfahrung erzählten, hatten das Thema erschöpft. Der Film, den Christo Piskov 1973 zusammen mit Irina Aktaševa machte, *Kato pesen* (Wie ein Lied), wiederholte die Ideen und die Atmosphäre aus den frühen antifaschistischen Filmen noch einmal. Andere Regisseure derselben Generation versuchten, das Thema durch eine Erweiterung filmischer Ausdrucksmittel zu gestalten. Välo Radev führte in *Černite angeli* (Schwarze Engel, 1970, über eine Gruppe junger Partisanen, die einen bulgarischen Faschisten töten sollen), und Zako Cheskija führte in *Osmijat* (Der Achte, 1969) Elemente des Abenteuerfilms in das Genre des antifaschistischen Films ein, eine Antwort an die Polit-Thriller aus dem Westen. Eine Erneuerung gelang erst dem jungen Regisseur Georgi Djulgerov mit seinem Film *I dojde denjat* (Und der Tag kam, 1973). Djulgerov (geb. 1943) warf einen rationalen, analytischen Blick auf eine Vergangenheit, die er selbst nicht mehr erlebt hatte und nur aus den Erzählungen und den Filmen der älteren Generation kannte. Positiv wirkte sich die Zusammenarbeit mit dem Drehbuchautor Vasil Ak'ov aus, der im Widerstand war. Djulgerov stellte verschiedene revolutionäre Haltungen dialogisch gegeneinander, anhand der Geschichte einer in den Bergen versteckten Partisanengruppe in den Monaten vor dem 9.9.1944. Erst die Summe verschiedener Figuren ergab das Bild, das sich Djulgerov vom Revolutionär machte. Eine neue Sicht auf den Widerstand schlug auch Binka Željazkova in ihrem Film *Poslednata duma* (Das letzte Wort, 1973) vor. Sie versuchte, das Schicksal antifaschistischer, zum Tode verurteilter Mädchen und Frauen auf eine philosophische und moralische Ebene zu heben.

6. 1300 Jahre Bulgarien

Große Anstrengungen galten 1981 dem 1300. Jahrestag der Gründung des bulgarischen Staates. Die Kinematographie legte eine Reihe aufwendiger historischer Filme vor: *Chan Asparuch* von Ljudmil Stajkov, das Drehbuch schrieb die Schriftstellerin Vera Mutafčieva, über den Staatsgründer; *Boris* von Borislav Šaraliev, Drehbuch Anžel Vagenštajn, über den bulgarischen Fürsten[9]); *Konstantin filosof* (Konstantin,

---

[9]) *Chan Asparuch* wurde von 10,8 Mio. Zuschauern gesehen, *Boris* von 10,4 Mio.: mit Abstand die größten Publikumserfolge des bulgarischen Films.

der Philosoph) von Georgi Stojanov, über Kyrill und Method (1983 veröffentlicht); *Bojanskijat Majstor* (Der Meister von Bojana) von Zachari Žandov, über den unbekannten Maler der Fresken in der Bojana-Kirche bei Sofia; und *Mera spored mera* (Maß für Maß) von Georgi Djulgerov, über den Ilinden-Aufstand gegen die Türken in Makedonien im Jahr 1903. Daß eine der Qualitäten des bulgarischen Films im historischen Genre liegt, bewies schließlich Ljudmil Stajkov 1988 mit seinem Film *Vreme razdelno* (Zeit der Gewalt), einem Epos über die Unterdrückung der Bulgaren durch die Türken im 17. Jh., dem bulgarischen Beitrag zum Festival in Cannes 1988.

7. Tendenzen

Die wichtigsten Filme der 80er Jahre wurden von den Regisseuren der 60er und 70er Jahre gemacht (nicht anders als in vielen anderen, auch westlichen Ländern). Rangel Vălčanov porträtierte in *Lačenite obuvki na neznajnija vojn* (Die Lackschuhe des unbekannten Soldaten, 1979) auf grotesk-poetische Weise eine Kindheit in einem Dorf zwischen den Kriegen. 1988 drehte er eine parabelhafte und phantasievolle Komödie über eine Gruppe von Schauspielschülern in einer Examenssituation, *A sega nakăde?* (Und nun wohin?), ein Film, der die erzählerische Eleganz des Regisseurs bewies und seinen Ruf als bedeutendster bulgarischer Regisseur unterstrich. Christo Christov erzählte 1979 in *Barierata* (Die Barriere) von einem Komponisten an der Schwelle zu einem Nervenzusammenbruch. Unter jüngeren Regisseuren konnte sich Nikolaj Volev (geb. 1946) profilieren. In *Da običaš na inat* (Alles aus Liebe, 1986) erwies er sich als kritischer Betrachter der Gegenwart. Er griff einen Fall von Korruption auf (ein Lastwagenfahrer bereichert sich auf illegale Weise) und knüpfte daran zahlreiche moralische Fragen. Daß man in Bulgarien derart offen mit diesem Thema umgehen konnte, wurde vom Publikum durch regen Zulauf honoriert. Ein anderer, 1988 entstandener Film Nikolaj Volevs, *Margarit i Margarita* (Margarit und Margarita), wurde nicht freigegeben. Andere Regisseure einer jüngeren Generation (Krasimir Krumov, Ljudmil Todorov, Ivan Čerkelov, Nikolaj Bosilov, Adela Peeva) konzentrieren sich in ihren ersten Filmen auf Probleme heranwachsender Jugendlicher.

Ende der 80er Jahre zeichnete sich ein freierer Umgang mit dem Thema Stalinismus ab. Ivan Ničev stellte in *Ivan i Aleksandra* (Ivan und Alexandra, der bulgarische Beitrag in Berlin 1989) zwei junge Menschen in den Mittelpunkt, deren sentimentale und moralische Erziehung vom repressiven Klima der 50er Jahre geprägt wird. Für die Berlinale 1989 wurden zum ersten Mal auch einige in den 60er Jahren verbotene Filme freigegeben, darunter *Privărzanijat balon* (Der gefesselte Ballon, 1967) von Binka Željaskova, der das bulgarisch-rumänische Verhältnis berührt, und zwei Filme über die 50er Jahre, *Prokurorăt* (Der Staatsanwalt, 1968) von Ljubomir Šarlandžiev und *Ponedelnik sutrin* (Montag morgens, 1965) von Irina Aktaševa und Christo Piskov.

Ljudmil Stajkov leitet seit 1987 als Generaldirektor und Vizeminister für Kultur die Kinematographie – der seltene Fall, daß ein Regisseur den Posten eines Funktionärs bekleidet. Diese Entscheidung orientierte sich ohne Zweifel an der Moskauer

Entwicklung und an der Wahl des Regisseurs Elem Klimov zum Vorsitzenden des sowjetischen Filmverbands, auch wenn in Bulgarien im Gegensatz zur Moskauer Situation die wesentlichen filmpolitischen Entscheidungen bei der Generaldirektion der staatlichen Kinematographie verblieben und ein weitergehender Einfluß der sowjetischen Entwicklungen vorerst nicht auszumachen ist.

Bildende Kunst

Friedbert Ficker, München

I. Einführung: 1. Grundlagen und Voraussetzungen der neueren Kunst – 2. Die Kunst nach 1944 – 3. Wandlungen und gegenwärtige Situation – II. Kunstgattungen: 1. Zeichnung und Graphik – 2. Malerei – 3. Plastik – 4. Angewandte Kunst – 5. Architektur

I. Einführung

1. Grundlagen und Voraussetzungen der neueren Kunst

Unter den südosteuropäischen Ländern weist die Kunst Bulgariens bis zur Gegenwart eine bemerkenswerte Bindung an die Tradition und Geschichte des Landes sowie an das Volksleben auf. Historische Themen werden ebenso immer wieder behandelt, wie die Trachten, das Brauchtum oder die Volksarchitektur beliebte bildnerische Vorwürfe abgeben. Wir dürfen darin heute das Fortleben einer Entwicklung sehen, die auf die Zeit der nationalen Wiedergeburt und den damit verbundenen Kampf um die Befreiung von der osmanischen Fremdherrschaft zurückgeht.

Der bereits im 18. Jh. einsetzende Zerfall der überholten osmanischen Feudalordnung und der damit verbundene wirtschaftliche Niedergang des Osmanischen Reiches führte zur Entfaltung eigenständiger lokaler Wirtschaftszweige in den besetzten Ländern und zur Herausbildung privaten Wohlstandes. Damit war zugleich die Stärkung und Festigung des eigenen individuellen sowie des nationalen Selbstbewußtseins in den unterdrückten Völkern verbunden. Als Folge dieser Entwicklung blühten in Bulgarien verschiedene örtliche Handwerkszweige auf, wie die Keramik in Businci, die Teppichweberei in Čiprovci, ferner die Kupferschmiedekunst in Ustovo oder die Holzschnitzerei in Trjavna und in Samokov[1]). Dort entstand auch neben der für die künstlerische Weiterentwicklung in Bulgarien wichtigen Malerschule vor allem ein Zentrum für die graphischen Techniken des Holzschnittes und des Kupferstiches zur Herstellung der *Stampas*, der religiösen Einblattdrucke[2]).

Die jahrhundertelange Fremdherrschaft hatte auch in Bulgarien einen tiefen Bruch in der wirtschaftlichen und kulturellen Gesamtentwicklung zur Folge. So herrschte

---

[1]) Boschkov, A.: Bulgarische Volkskunst. Recklinghausen 1972; Wolfgramm, E.: Zur Rolle der Kunst in den zentralen Balkanländern während der Periode der „nationalen Wiedergeburt", in: Wissenschaftliche Zeitschrift der Hochschule für Architektur und Bauwesen Weimar. 15 (1968) 5, S. 535–540.

[2]) Sachariew, W.: Graphische Arbeiten der Schule von Samokow. Dresden 1968; Tomov, E.: Bulgarische Ikonen. Holzschnitte und Metallstiche. Ramerding 1982.

im späten 18. und im 19. Jh. unter den veränderten Bedingungen der zerbröckelnden Machtverhältnisse ein beachtlicher Nachholbedarf. Eine wichtige Rolle zu dessen Deckung spielten die zu Besitztum und Ansehen gelangten Handwerker- und Händlerfamilien. Über ihre geschäftlichen Verbindungen zu Westeuropa flossen auch Motive und Formelemente von dort in die heimische Kunst ein. So sind z. B. im *Chindlianov-Haus* in Plovdiv, das auch als *Haus des Armeniers* bekannt ist, unter den Wandmalereien in den Salons Darstellungen aus westeuropäischen Städten – darunter der Schiefe Turm zu Pisa, die Rialtobrücke in Venedig u. a. Motive – zu finden[3]).

Auf diesem Weg vollzog sich bald auch der geistige Austausch, der neue, die Wiedergeburtsbewegung befruchtende Gedanken wie auch das Formengut der westeuropäischen Kunst ins Land brachte und den aufstrebenden jungen Künstlern den Weg zu ihrer Ausbildung im Ausland wies. Von der zweiten Hälfte des 19. Jh. an studierten deshalb zahlreiche Bulgaren an den Akademien in Wien, München oder auch in Petersburg. Zu den Lehrmeistern in Bulgarien selbst wurden die beiden tschechischen Künstler J. V. Mrkvička (1856–1938) und J. Vešin (1860–1915), die im Gefolge der panslavistischen Bewegung ins Land kamen und als Lehrer an der 1886 gegründeten Akademie in Sofia tätig waren.

Besonders die Münchner Historienmalerei, deren Nachwirkungen in der bulgarischen Kunst bis zur Gegenwart zu spüren sind, bot sich im späten 19. und frühen 20. Jh. mit ihrer idealisierenden Verklärung und als typischer Ausdruck für romantisch-patriotische Ideen als ideales Vorbild zur repräsentativen Darstellung der eigenen Geschichte und der politischen Gegenwart an[4]). Die Münchner Akademie übte deshalb auf die bulgarischen Künstler bis in die Zeit kurz vor dem II. Weltkrieg eine große Anziehungskraft aus. Von dort gingen auch wichtige Anregungen zu einer Reform der bildenden Kunst in Bulgarien nach westeuropäischem Vorbild aus. Von N. Michajlov (1876–1960) über den Piloty-Schüler I. Angelov (1864–1924) oder den an Lenbach erinnernden Ch. Stančev (1870–1950) lassen sich bis zu D. Uzunov (1899–1986) zahlreiche an der Münchner Akademie ausgebildete Künstler anführen.

Mit der Orientierung nach Westeuropa war ein bedeutender Auftrieb im Kunstleben Bulgariens verbunden, das sich den verschiedensten Richtungen und Strömungen öffnete. Es kam zur Gründung von künstlerischen Vereinigungen wie der 1903 entstandenen Gruppe *Săvremenno izkustvo* (Gegenwartskunst), die sich zunächst am Jugendstil orientierte und die Europäisierung der bulgarischen Kunst unter Beibehaltung ihrer nationalen Eigenheiten anstrebte[5]). Als Gegengewicht gegen die mit dieser Entwicklung verbundenen kosmopolitischen Tendenzen entstand 1919 mit der Grün-

---

[3]) Mateev, M.: Stara architektura v Plovdiv (Die alte Architektur in Plovdiv). Sofia 1976; Old Plovdiv. Sofia 1977.

[4]) Ficker, F.: Die Münchner Akademie und die Kunst der Balkanvölker, in: Bulgarien. Internationale Beziehungen in Geschichte, Kultur und Kunst. Neuried o. J., S. 67–72; ders.: Das Geschichtsbild Ludwigs I., die Münchner Historienmalerei und ihre Bedeutung für die Kunst Bulgariens. Vortrag auf dem III. Internat. Symposium „Hochschulforschungen und -lehre der bulgarischen Geschichte..." in Smoljan/Pamporovo 1987 (im Druck).

[5]) Družestvo săvremenno izkustvo 1903–1933 (Die Gesellschaft für Gegenwartskunst 1903–1933). Katalog. Sofia o. J.; Ficker, F.: Penčo Kojčev, „Săvremenno izkustvo" und Anna Hähn-Josifova. Funkmanuskript. Köln 1988.

dung des Vereins *Rodno Izkustvo* (Heimatliche Kunst) die traditionsbewußte Heimatkunstbewegung, die in der bäuerlichen Welt ihre Vorbilder sah. Mit den ins Dekorative gehenden Verherrlichungen der bulgarischen Frau durch V. Dimitrov-Majstora (1882–1960) hat diese Richtung ihren Höhepunkt erreicht. Während *Rodno Izkustvo* sich von den aktuellen Zeitproblemen fernhielt, setzte sich die 1931 gegründete fortschrittliche Gruppe der *Neuen Künstler* kritisch mit Zeit und Umwelt auseinander und bezog den arbeitenden Menschen als vollwertiges Thema in die bulgarische Kunst ein. Bis 1944 findet sich so ein breites Spektrum an künstlerischen Darstellungsmöglichkeiten von der dekorativen Auffassung über Ansätze zur impressionistischen Gestaltung bis zur Neuen Sachlichkeit und zu expressionistischen Anklängen – ohne daß der Impressionismus und der Expressionismus voll zur Entfaltung kamen wie in Westeuropa.

2. Die Kunst nach 1944

Der grundlegende gesellschaftliche, politische und wirtschaftliche Umbruch nach dem Staatsstreich vom 9.9.1944 bedeutete auch für die bildende Kunst in Bulgarien eine Neuorientierung und zweifellos zugleich eine Neubewertung, wie sie Georgi Dimitrov formulierte: „Es besteht sowohl bei mir wie auch bei unserer Regierung ein besonderes Verhältnis zur Kunst im allgemeinen und den Künstlern im besonderen. Dieses Verhältnis unterscheidet sich grundlegend von jenem der Regierung vor dem 9. September 1944. Wir sind der Ansicht, daß unter den Faktoren, die unser Land wirtschaftlich, kulturell und politisch bestimmen, die Kunst mit allen ihren Gattungen einen sehr wichtigen Platz einnimmt."[6])

Bereits am 13.9.1944 erklärte der Sekretär der *Neuen Künstler* N. Šmirgela (geb. 1911) im Rundfunk: „Heute sind unsere Hände frei – übervoll von Begeisterung! Und glaubt, zusammen werden wir unsere neue Welt aufbauen, die schön und frei sein wird!"[7]) Eine Woche später gaben die neuen Vertreter der bulgarischen Künstler die Unterstützung der Volksmacht offiziell bekannt. Neben den antifaschistischen Kunstschaffenden, die nun die Führung übernommen hatten, stellten sich auch Maler, Graphiker und Plastiker dem Neuaufbau zur Verfügung, die am Widerstandskampf nicht unmittelbar teilgenommen hatten, wie z. B. D. Uzunov, der sich nach der Ernennung zum Rektor der Kunstakademie in Sofia im Jahre 1954 große Verdienste um die Entwicklung der bulgarischen Kunst erwarb.

Bereits die ersten Kunstausstellungen nach dem Kriege lassen die Anzeichen eines grundlegenden inhaltlichen und formalen Wandels unter dem Einfluß der BKP erkennen. Diese neuen Tendenzen wurden von Georgi Dimitrov klar herausgestellt: „Wir betrachten die Kunst – obwohl dieser Gesichtspunkt von uns als notwendig erachtet und nicht unterschätzt wird – nicht nur als Quelle höchster ästhetischer Genüsse für den Menschen. Vor allem aber betrachten wir die Kunst als Mittel zur

---

[6]) Katalog Ausstellung der heutigen bulgarischen Graphik. Berlin 1951, unpaginiert.
[7]) Sǎvremenno bǎlgarsko izobrazitelno izkustvo (Bulgarische Bildende Kunst der Gegenwart). Sofia 1982, S. 65.

Mobilisierung der moralischen, geistigen und physischen Kräfte unseres Volkes und unserer Jugend... Wir legen der künstlerischen Gestaltung des neuen Typus der Jugend, die den Aufbaubrigaden angehört, dem neuen Typus der Arbeiteraktivisten, überhaupt der Gestaltung des Aufschwungs der Arbeit, der das ganze Land ergriffen hat, große Bedeutung bei. Wir sehen auch die große Bedeutung der künstlerischen Formung der Heldentaten der Partisanen und der Kämpfer des Vaterländischen Krieges...."[8])

Diese Auffassung bestimmte die Linie in der Kunst nach dem V. Parteitag der BKP im Jahre 1948, auf dem der Kurs zum Aufbau des Sozialismus verkündet wurde. Zwar beteuerte man, daß Stilleben und Landschaften sowie andere vom Ästhetischen her bestimmte künstlerische Gestaltungen ihre Berechtigung hätten, doch erfuhr die vordergründige naturalistische Behandlung von Themen politischen Inhalts oder aus der Arbeitswelt eine einseitige Förderung, während z. B. ins Abstrakte gehende Werke als formalistisch abgelehnt wurden. Unter sowjetischem Einfluß entstand so eine Richtung, die analog der frühen Historienmalerei unter den Anregungen der Münchner Schule übertriebenes Pathos oder idealisierende Verklärung aufweist. Trotz beachtlicher Leistungen wie der 1949 erfolgten Eröffnung der Nationalgalerie in Sofia oder dem Beschluß der BKP von 1950 „Über den Zustand und die Aufgaben der Staatlichen Kunstakademie" wurde die künstlerische Entwicklung durch die dogmatische Anwendung der Stalin-Ždanovschen Definition des Sozialistischen Realismus[9]) empfindlich gehemmt[10]).

3. Wandlungen und gegenwärtige Situation

Nicht wenige Künstler widersetzten sich diesem Eingriff in ihre schöpferische Freiheit und beharrten auf ihrer persönlichen Ausdrucksweise, wie der Maler V. Barakov (geb. 1902). Inzwischen haben seine expressiv gestalteten Arbeiten ihre Anerkennung gefunden, wie seine seit 1963 erfolgten wiederholten Auszeichnungen zeigen.

Die Wende vollzog sich nach dem Aprilplenum des ZK der BKP von 1956 mit dem Aufruf an die Kunst- und Kulturschaffenden „Näher an das Leben, mehr unter das Volk"[11]). Damit war eine inhaltliche und formale Öffnung verbunden, die den Künstlern bis dahin nicht gekannte schöpferische Freiheiten zubilligte. Der damit verbundene Auftrieb führte zu einer beachtlichen Bereicherung des bildnerischen Schaffens. Ein weiterer Schritt in der künstlerisch-kulturellen Entwicklung wurde 1967 mit dem I. Kongreß der bulgarischen Kultur als der Grundlage zur Schaffung des Komitees für Kunst und Kultur und der damit verbundenen Leitung des künstlerisch-kulturellen Bereiches nach dem gesellschaftlich-staatlichen Prinzip vollzogen[12]).

---

[8]) Wie Anm. 6.
[9]) Vgl. dazu: Studienmaterial zur Kunstdiskussion für die künstlerischen Lehranstalten der DDR Nr. 1, 2, 5, 7, 8, 9. Berlin o. J. (als Manuskript gedruckt).
[10]) Die bulgarische Kunst, in: Allgemeine Geschichte der Kunst, Bd. VIII. Leipzig o. J., S. 441.
[11]) Živkova, L.: Die sozialistische Kultur und die gesellschaftlichen Prozesse der Gegenwart. Sofia 1977, S. 14/15.
[12]) Ebenda.

Die inhaltlich-formalen und organisatorischen Reformen zogen ein steigendes öffentliches Interesse an der Kunst nach sich, das zu einer vermehrten Ausstellungstätigkeit führte. Besondere Beachtung kommt hier der Berührung mit der Kunst anderer Länder zu. Die Künstler stellen sich seitdem nicht nur im eigenen Land dem Publikum, sondern bekommen nun auch Gelegenheit, sich im Ausland zu präsentieren. Umgekehrt erhalten sie durch internationale Ausstellungen in Bulgarien die Möglichkeit zum Vergleich und zur Leistungssteigerung. Die wachsende Bedeutung der Kunst drückt sich nicht minder in den zahlreichen Neugründungen von Galerien, Museen und Sammlungen bis in mittlere und kleinere Provinzstädte aus[13]). Endlich wurden als Erfolge der Neuorientierung ältere Künstler der Vorkriegszeit durch Gedächtnisausstellungen der Öffentlichkeit wieder bekannt gemacht[14]).

Mit der Öffnung nach innen und außen war eine völlig neue Definition des Begriffes „Sozialistischer Realismus" verbunden, der nicht mehr als vordergründige naturalistische Wiedergabe einer mehr statisch gesehenen Oberfläche verstanden wird, sondern als dynamischer Prozeß Vorgänge sichtbar zu machen versucht, die den Dingen innewohnen und damit deren eigentliches Wesen ausmachen oder in ähnlich bestimmender Weise dahinterstehen. Es ist deshalb längst keine Frage mehr, welche Sujets die Künstler wählen und ob diese gegenständlich oder abstrakt dargestellt werden. Dagegen scheint es nach der jüngsten Entwicklung, daß sich die oft geforderte Auseinandersetzung mit den Problemen von Zeit und Umwelt in der Kunst mehr auf die Interpretierung der von der Partei bestimmten Linie beziehen soll, nicht aber als ernsthafte Kritik zu verstehen ist.

II. Kunstgattungen

1. Zeichnung und Graphik

Die neuere bulgarische Graphik ist nicht ohne V. Zachariev (1895–1971) zu denken, der als Lehrer namhafter Zeichner und Graphiker wie P. Vălkov (1908–1956), V. Stajkov (1906–1970) oder D. Draganov (geb. 1908) vor allem den Holzschnitt zur Meisterschaft geführt hat und damit Maßstäbe für das folgende Schaffen setzen konnte. Während Zachariev die ältere volkstümliche Graphik zum Vorbild nahm und einen technisch vollendeten, mehr dekorativen Stil schuf, wandten sich seine Schüler der realistischen Darstellung zu. Im Bereich zwischen ornamental-dekorativer und realistischer Gestaltung hat sich die bulgarische Graphik bis zur Gegenwart bewegt, während heute in Westeuropa übliche Formen bis hin zur Gegenstandslosigkeit erst in jüngster Zeit Verbreitung finden.

Unter dem Eindruck der politischen Neuorientierung standen in den ersten Nachkriegsjahren Themen des revolutionären Befreiungskampfes im Vordergrund, so in den Zeichnungen von I. Beškov (1901–1958), B. Angelušev (1902–1966), A. Žendov

---

[13]) Popov, K.: Die demokratische Entwicklung der bulgarischen Kultur von heute. Sofia 1977.
[14]) s. dazu: Ausstellungskatalog Vaska Popova-Balareva 1902–1979. Sofia (1984).

(1901–1953) und I. Petrov (1903–1975) oder in den Holzschnitten von P. Kăršovski (geb. 1905) und D. Draganov. P. Vălkov behandelte dagegen Themen des Neuaufbaus, während sich G. Gerasimov (1905–1977) mit dem Leben des Volkes auseinandersetzte. Auch V. Stajkov wandte sich dem arbeitenden Menschen sowie der Landschaft zu. Er legte als Akademielehrer ebenso wie Beškov wesentliche Grundlagen für die Graphik in den letzten Jahrzehnten, die sich zu einer inhaltlichen und technisch-formalen Vielfalt entwickelte.

Einen breiten Raum nehmen Themen aus dem Volksleben und der Geschichte ein[15]), so in den Holz- und Linolschnitten von Z. Dăbova (geb. 1927), Z. Jončev (geb. 1924), Z. Zachariev (geb. 1937) und P. Kulekov (geb. 1924). L. Stoev (geb. 1939) gestaltet dagegen den schaffenden Menschen in großformatigen Holzschnitten. In ähnlicher Weise zielen die Graphiken T. Panajotovs (1927–1989) auf geradezu monumentale Wirkung hin. Dazu kommen neben der markanten Ausdrucksweise J. Minčevs (geb. 1923) die hintergründig aufgefaßten Motive Ž. Kosturkovas (geb. 1927) oder die locker gezeichneten und malerisch empfundenen Lithographien von A. Nejkov (geb. 1924) und Ch. Nejkov (geb. 1929).

Auffallend ist die vielfach hohe Meisterschaft in der sicheren Beherrschung der handwerklich-technischen Mittel, wie z. B. in der Radierung bei S. Stoilov (geb. 1944) oder bei dem jungen P. Marinov (geb. 1950). Ähnliches gilt in der Lithographie für L. Jordanov (geb. 1934) oder B. Stoev (geb. 1927). Meist ist damit eine Auffassung verbunden, die den Begriff „Realismus" über die herkömmliche statische Sicht hinaus erweitert durch dynamisch-kinematographisch aufgefaßte, nicht selten mehrschichtige Wiedergaben. Diese inhaltliche und formale Bereicherung ist Ausdruck des bereits genannten Wandels. So finden sich z. B. neben den topographisch bezogenen stimmungsvollen Radierungen von K. Gjulemetov (geb. 1938) oder den dekorativen Arbeiten von A. Angelov (geb. 1923) die neuesten abstrakten Kompositionen von I. Ninov (geb. 1946).

Eine bemerkenswerte Vielfalt und Qualität ist auch in den angewandten Bereichen der Graphik zu verzeichnen. Das zeigt sich beispielsweise in der Karikatur, die von ihrem Wegbereiter A. Božinov (1878–1968) über I. Beškov und A. Žendov bis zu dem heutigen Altmeister S. Venev (1904–1989) oder bis zu C. Cekov (Pseud. Karandaš) (geb. 1924) ein gleich hohes Niveau aufweist wie die Illustration. Dort hat I. Beškov die Voraussetzungen geschaffen, während B. Angelušev über die Buchgestaltung und über die Schrift Einfluß genommen hat. Zusammen mit A. Denkov (1925–1972) gehören Ch. Nejkov oder L. Zidarov (geb. 1923) zu den typischen gegenwärtigen Illustratoren. Einen beachtlichen Aufschwung hat die Kleinkunstform des Ex libris zu verzeichnen[16]). Neben P. Kăršovski sind hier P. Kulekov und G. Penčev (geb. 1924) besonders zu nennen. Den Grundstein für die Plakatkunst legte B. Angelušev. Dort führt der Weg über A. Poplilov (geb. 1916) zu dessen Schüler S. Kamenov (geb. 1936) als Beispiel für moderne visuelle Gestaltung. Endlich hat als Schöpfer eingetragener Warenzeichen S. Kănčev (geb. 1915) internationale Anerkennung gefunden.

---

[15]) Marazov, I.: Nacionalno-osvoboditelnoto dviženie v izobrazitelnoto izkustvo (Die nationale Befreiungsbewegung in der bildenden Kunst). Sofia 1979.
[16]) Tomov, E.: Ekslibris (Ex libris). Sofia 1977; Veličkov, P.: Sto bălgarski ekslibrisa (Hundert bulgarische Ex libris). Sofia 1985.

2. Malerei

Nach dem Staatsstreich vom 9.9.1944 hatte nicht nur die BKP ein verständliches Interesse an der Darstellung und Verherrlichung von Kampf und Sieg in der Malerei, sondern ebenso auch die daran beteiligten antifaschistischen Künstler. So schuf I. Petrov 1946 ein großes Wandgemälde *Der 9. September* zugleich im Gedanken an seinen im Widerstand umgekommenen Kollegen D. Grančarov, nachdem bereits ein Jahr früher N. Balkanski (1907–1977) eine ermordete *Partisanenhelferin* gemalt hatte. Doch stellten sich auch zahlreiche Maler aus der Heimatkunstbewegung wie V. Dimitrov-Majstora oder Z. Bojadžiev (1903–1976) in den Dienst der neuen Sache. Die Malerei der ersten Jahre nach dem Umsturz weist überhaupt eine breite Vielfalt malerischer Richtungen und Ausdrucksformen auf, die von den impressionistisch aufgefaßten Landschaften A. Michovs (1879–1974) bis zu den streng gebauten, expressiv wirkenden Gemälden von V. Barakov reicht.

In der folgenden Periode, die die *Allgemeine Kunstausstellung* von 1947 kennzeichnet, stand die Forderung nach der Parteilichkeit des künstlerischen Schaffens im Vordergrund. Zweifellos entstanden auch in dieser Zeit bedeutende Kunstwerke wie D. Uzunovs *Abschied* oder das Gemälde *Schwarze Kopftücher* von K. Conev (1896–1961), doch machte sich neben der inhaltlichen und formalen Einengung bald eine theatralische Pathetik bemerkbar, die teilweise zur plakativen Vergröberung von Farbe und Form führte. Andererseits kam es nicht selten zu einer Idealisierung wie in P. Panajotovs (geb. 1909) *Dreschen in der Kooperative*, die einen Rückgriff auf die Malerei des späten 19. und frühen 20. Jh. bedeutete.

Erst nach der vom Aprilplenum 1956 eingeleiteten Wende kam es wieder zu einer breiteren Entfaltung der unterschiedlichsten schöpferischen Kräfte[17]). So stehen neben den französischen Anregungen bei I. Nenov (geb. 1902) die an Dimitrov-Majstora erinnernde Pinselführung bei G. Genkov (geb. 1923) und A. Jaranov (geb. 1940) sowie das Vorbild Z. Bojadžievs bei R. Nedelčev (geb. 1938). Oder neben der in großen Formen gesehenen vitalen Malerei D. Kirovs (geb. 1935), der lapidaren Ausdrucksweise V. Petrovs (geb. 1939) und der eigenwilligen Formensprache von S. Kacarov (geb. 1937) stehen die heiteren Farbklänge V. Nedkovas (geb. 1908) sowie die experimentellen Kompositionen von G. Božilov (geb. 1935) und P. Dočev (geb. 1934). In der inhaltlichen und formalen Fülle spannt sich damit ein Bogen von den kritisch realistischen Arbeiten S. Janevs (geb. 1952), den ausdrucksstarken Kompositionen S. Rusevs (geb. 1933) oder den von der Neuen Sachlichkeit bestimmten Bildern von V. Kenarev (geb. 1951) über die Gestaltung menschlicher Schicksale bei L. Ruseva (geb. 1932), die landschaftlichen Strukturen von N. Conev (geb. 1928) und die Gefühls- und Empfindungswerte ansprechenden Farbkompositionen G. Baevs (geb. 1924) bis zu den von assoziativen Prozessen bestimmten Arbeiten des Nachwuchskünstlers D. Rusev (geb. 1957).

---

[17]) Ficker, F.: Bulgarische Kunst heute, in: Weltkunst. 57 (1987) 21, S. 3172; Aspekte bulgarischer Kunst heute, Ausstellungskatalog Ludwig, Aachen. Wien o. J.

3. Plastik

Die Plastik weist die gleiche Kontinuität und nahtlose Weiterentwicklung auf wie die Graphik und die Malerei, die durch die ältere Generation der Bildhauer aus der Zeit vor 1944 gewährleistet wurde. Sie haben nicht nur mit ihren eigenen plastischen Werken den Anschluß und Übergang hergestellt, sondern ihre bedeutendsten Vertreter wie M. Markov (1889–1966), I. Lazarov (1889–1952), L. Dalčev (geb. 1902) oder I. Funev (geb. 1900) haben darüber hinaus als Akademielehrer mit der Ausbildung des Nachwuchses für die Fortsetzung der guten bildhauerischen Tradition gesorgt.

Entsprechend ihrer Ausbildung an westeuropäischen Akademien haben diese Künstler die verschiedensten Anregungen für die bulgarische Plastik nutzbar gemacht, wie z. B. die impressionistisch aufgelockerte Oberfläche des Porträts *Asen Georgiev* von I. Funev oder die Akte von V. Emanuilova (geb. 1905) zeigen, die an Maillol denken lassen. Mit seinen erdhaft schweren, an Barlach erinnernden Darstellungen arbeitender Menschen hat dazu I. Lazarov wesentliche Vorarbeit für die Behandlung dieses nach 1944 bevorzugten Themas geleistet.

Beispiele dafür finden sich bei S. Rajnova (geb. 1919), N. Terziev (geb. 1927), B. Gondov (geb. 1935) oder I. Iliev (geb. 1922). Letzterer kommt zu einer geradezu übersteigerten Gestaltungsweise, deren monumentaler Anspruch bereits bei M. Markov vorgebildet ist und vor allem in Werken zum Widerstandskampf seine charakteristische Ausdrucksform gefunden hat. Von Arbeiten L. Dalčevs oder von S. Krumov (geb. 1922) führt hier der Weg über G. Apostolov (geb. 1923) bis zu I. Nešev (geb. 1927). Vollends kommen monumentale Form und pathetischer Ausdruck bei den Denkmälern zur Entfaltung, die einen wesentlichen Bestandteil der modernen Plastik darstellen[18] wie das *Monument der Sowjetarmee* oder das *Ehrenmal der gefallenen Antifaschisten* in Sofia, die *Gedenkstätte für den Aprilaufstand* in Panagjurište, das Denkmal *Borimečkata* bei Klisura oder das *Ehrenmal für die Gefallenen der Sowjetarmee* in Plovdiv.

Dazu kann die Porträtplastik auf bedeutende Leistungen verweisen, die von M. Kac (1889–1964), M. Markov und I. Funev über N. Šmirgela, I. Mandov (geb. 1914) und V. Ginovski (geb. 1927) bis zu V. Minekov (geb. 1928) reicht. Die mit dem Aprilplenum verbundenen Änderungen haben auch in der Plastik über das Konkret-Gegenständliche hinaus neue Möglichkeiten eröffnet, wie sie von V. Starčev (geb. 1935), A. Stanev (geb. 1947) oder G. Malakčiev (geb. 1931) vertreten werden.

4. Angewandte Kunst

Die angewandte Kunst kann auf eine lange Tradition in der Volkskunst zurückblicken. Die Holzschnitzerei, Keramik, Textilkunst und Teppichherstellung oder die Metallverarbeitung in Kupfer und Edelmetall weisen in der Vergangenheit einen hohen Leistungsstand mit einer reichen Fülle an Form und Dekor auf. Nach 1944

---

[18] Avramov, D.: Zur bulgarischen Kunst heute, in: Aspekte bulgarischer Kunst heute (Anm. 17), S. 16.

wurden diese schöpferischen Bereiche durch das neu gegründete Institut für bildende Künste der BAN systematisch erforscht und dem Kunstschaffen der neuen Gesellschaftsordnung praktisch erschlossen[19]). Über die jährlich stattfindenden Allgemeinen Kunstausstellungen setzte seit den Jahren 1954 und 1955 unter den jungen Künstlern ein wachsendes Interesse an den kunsthandwerklichen Techniken ein. Diese werden mit ihrem Formenschatz jedoch nicht einfach übernommen bzw. kopiert, sondern sie dienen als Grundlage und Anregung zur lebendigen schöpferischen Weiterentwicklung sowohl künstlerisch-formal als auch technisch und materialmäßig, um damit zu einer den veränderten technologischen, wirtschaftlichen und gesellschaftlichen Verhältnissen entsprechenden Gestaltung zu gelangen.

Eine reiche gestalterische Vielfalt weist z. B. die Textil- und Wandteppichkunst auf, zu deren bedeutendsten Vertretern M. Josifova (geb. 1905) mit ihren oft volkskunsthaften Motiven zählt. Aus dem reichen Schatz der volkskünstlerischen Tradition schöpft auch S. Askova (geb. 1918) mit ihren Stoffmustern – ähnlich wie G. Bakardžiev (1899–1972) in der Keramik.

5. Architektur

Neuen Aufgaben sah sich die Architektur nach dem 9.9.1944 gegenüber[20]). In der ersten Phase bis zum Aprilplenum 1956 standen vor allem öffentliche und gesellschaftliche Bauten im Vordergrund. In dem Bemühen um eine dem Inhalt nach sozialistische und der Form nach nationale Baukunst kam es allerdings nicht selten zu einer starren und formalistischen Anlehnung an Vorbilder der nationalen Tradition oder an als progressiv gewertete historische Perioden wie die Renaissance. Ein Beispiel dafür sind im Zentrum von Sofia das *Haus der Partei* (Architekt P. Zlatev), die Gebäude des *Staatsrates* und des *Ministerrates* sowie das *Hotel „Balkan"* und das *Zentrale Kaufhaus*. Ohne die unterschiedliche Funktion der einzelnen Gebäude genügend zu berücksichtigen, entstanden dort äußerlich formal zusammenstimmende eklektizistische Repräsentationsbauten[21]). Als geglückte Lösung ist allerdings der unterirdische Durchgang mit der Einbeziehung von Teilen des alten Serdica anzusehen. Historistischen Vorstellungen entsprechen die *Nationalbibliothek „Kyrill und Method"* (Architekten I. Vasil'ov, D. Colov) oder das *Aleksandăr-Stambolijski-Haus* (Architekt L. Paraškevanov), während das *Georgi-Dimitrov-Mausoleum* in seinen klaren strengen Formen ein Musterbeispiel für die funktionalistische Bauweise ist (Architekten G. Ovčarov, R. Ribarov).

Die zweite, von 1956 bis zur Gegenwart reichende Phase ist neben der allgemeinen künstlerisch-kulturellen Neuorientierung von der wirtschaftlichen und technologischen Entwicklung im Bauwesen bestimmt. Die Einführung von Typenprojektierung und serieller Bauweise machte es zwar möglich, mit der Errichtung großer Wohnkomplexe den Bedarf der Bevölkerung an Wohnraum rascher zu decken, doch war

---

[19]) Boschkov (Anm. 1), S. 25/26.
[20]) Berbenliev, P.: Kunstdenkmäler in Bulgarien. München, Berlin 1983, S. LVIII ff.
[21]) Die bulgarische Kunst (Anm. 10), S. 446.

damit eine Monotonie der Bauformen verbunden, die auf die historisch gewachsenen Stadtbilder keine Rücksicht nahm und mit der Zusammenballung der Menschen in den Hochhäusern die anonyme Massengesellschaft förderte. In der Folgezeit ist man deshalb wieder zum Bau kleinerer Einheiten mit differenzierterer Gliederung übergegangen, die den Strukturen der Städte besser gerecht werden und die historischen und kulturellen Objekte in die Gesamtplanung mit einbeziehen. Wirtschaftlichen Erwägungen entsprachen auch die mit der Entwicklung des Tourismus entstandenen Ferienkomplexe am Schwarzen Meer oder in den Rhodopen, wo man sich um die Einbindung der Landschaft in die architektonische Gestaltung bemühte.

Eine veränderte Einstellung zum Verhältnis von Funktion und Form ist auch bei den neueren öffentlichen Bauten festzustellen. Dort versucht man nunmehr, neueste bautechnische Möglichkeiten mit einer der Zeit angepaßten ästhetischen Gestaltung in Einklang zu bringen. Beispiele dafür sind die *Sporthalle „Universiada"* (Architekten A. Barov, I. Ivančev, I. Tatarov) und der *Kulturpalast* (Architekten A. Barov, A. Agura), beide in Sofia. Besonders letzterer ist mit der Parkanlage und dem axial aufgestellten Denkmal zu einer Gesamtkomposition zusammengefügt, bei der selbst die Kulisse des Vitoša-Gebirges im Hintergrund wirkungsvoll dazu beiträgt, den wuchtigen, aber dennoch in sich gegliederten Baukörper im Gesamteindruck wie in der Beziehung zu seiner Umgebung zu unterstützen.

Music

Barbara Krader, West Berlin, assisted by Gerald F. Messner, Geelong/Victoria

I. Introduction – II. Folk Music: 1. General Background – 2. Characteristics: a) Meters and Rhythms – b) Singing in Parts – c) Folk Musical Instruments – 3. Folk Music Regions – 4. Professional Folk Ensembles – 5. Folk Festivals – 6. New Developments – III. Medieval Church Music – IV. Secular Music – V. Music Training – VI. Music Research – VII. Music Journals, Professional Societies and Publishers

I. Introduction

The music of Bulgaria is discussed here under the three headings of folk, religious, and modern secular, the third category developing after 1878.

The music of the villages serves as a kind of national treasure, a feature of Bulgarian culture which is revered for its antiquity. K. Roth's chapter „Volkskultur" provides a necessary background for this folk music discussion.

A brief account is given of research and concert activity in medieval religious music.

The section on secular music focuses on compositions written after 1944.

II. Folk Music

1. General Background

The scholarly study of Bulgarian folk music began with Dobri Khristov (1875–1941), who published in 1913 a study[1] in which the basic principles of the asymmetric rhythms and meters had already been worked out. It forms the basis of all further work on the subject.

Between the world wars, Vasil Stoin (1880–1938) and a few collaborators notated in villages, by ear, about 24,000 folk songs and dance melodies and texts[2]. Of this some 13,600 tunes and song texts have been published with classification of meters, rhythms and scales, documenting a very archaic tradition.

---

[1] Khristov, D.: Ritmichnite osnovi na narodnata ni muzika (The Rhythmic Bases of our Folk Music), in: SbNU. 27 (1913), pp. 3–51.

[2] See Krader, B.: Vasil Stoin, Bulgarian Folk Music Collector, in: Yearbook of the International Folk Music Council. 21 (1980), pp. 27–42.

The Theory of Bulgarian Folk Music, by Stoîan Dzhudzhev, is the finest detailed analysis[3]). Two foreign scholars, the Austrian G. F. Messner and the American Timothy F. Rice did field research in the early 1970s on Bulgarian diaphony, and have made the results available[4]).

2. Characteristics

a) Meters and Rhythms

One must emphasize at the start that three-fifths of Bulgarian folk songs are dance songs in a strict tempo giusto rhythm, and that most of the chain dances are in 2/4 meter in a moderate to quick tempo[5]). Nevertheless the asymmetric meters, which were described as Bulgarian by Bartók, are of greatest interest[6]). Although such meters occur in other Balkan and also Asian folk music, in Bulgaria there is the greatest variety of them, with frequent occurrence.

It is characteristic that most of these songs and dance tunes are in very fast tempo. Therefore the time signatures are generally in sixteenths for tempi between 240 and 520 M. For slower tempi, between 180 to 240 M, the time signatures are marked in eighths[7]).

The key to the asymmetric meters is their combination of beats of different length, not (as is usual in western music) with a ratio of multiples of two, but in a ratio of 1 : 1 ½ or 2 : 3. It is thus a combination of duple and triple meters. The common Bulgarian meter 5/8 occurs as 2/8 + 3/8, or 3/8 + 2/8, ♪♫ or ♫♪. In a dance tune with drum accompaniment, usually the big drum (or the big stick, if only one drum) beats the basic rhythm, one beat for each duple or triple group, while the small drum (or the thin stick, when there is a single drum) beats – if the tempo is slow enough – all or most of the individual eighths or sixteenths.

The most frequent Bulgarian meters are: 5/16 (5/8), as 2 + 3 or 3 + 2 (two beats); 7/16 (7/8) 2 + 2 + 3 or 3 + 2 + 2 (three beats); 8/16 (8/8) 3 + 2 + 3 or 2 + 3 + 3 (three beats); 9/16 (9/8) 2 + 2 + 2 + 3 or 2 + 3 + 2 + 2 (four beats); 10/16 (10/8) 3 + 2 + 2 + 3 or 2 + 2 + 3 + 3 (four beats); 11/16 (11/8) 2 + 2 + 3 + 2 + 2 or 2 + 2 + 2 + 2 + 3 (five beats); 12/16 (12/8) 3 + 2 + 2 + 2 + 3 or 3 + 2 + 2 + 3 + 2 or 2 + 3 + 2 + 2 + 3 (five beats); 13/16 (13/8) 2 + 2 + 2 + 2 + 2 + 3 (six beats).

---

[3]) Dzhudzhev, S.: Teoriîa na bŭlgarskata narodna muzika (Theory of Bulgarian Folk Music). 4 vols. Sofia 1954–1961. 2nd ed. Bŭlgarska narodna muzika (Bulgarian Folk Music). 2 vols. Sofia 1970, 1975; see also his still valuable book: Djoudjeff, S.: Rhythme et mesure dans la musique populaire bulgare. Paris 1931.

[4]) Messner, G. F.: Die Schwebungsdiaphonie. Tutzing 1980; Rice, T. F.: Polyphony in Bulgarian Folk Music. Ph. D. dissertation, University of Washington 1977. Ann Arbor, University Microfilms International.

[5]) Katsarova, R.: Folk Music: Bulgarian, in: Grove's Dictionary of Music, 5th ed. London 1954, p. 206. Triple meters as dance rhythms were long thought not to exist in the Bulgarian tradition. But recently they were found to be common in southwestern Bulgaria (ibid.)

[6]) Bartók, B.: Der sogenannte bulgarische Rhythmus, in: Bartók, B.: Musiksprachen. Aufsätze und Vorträge. Leipzig 1972, pp. 94–105. Hungarian original published 1938. English translation in Bartók, B.: Essays. Ed. by B. Suchoff. New York 1976, pp. 40–49. Serious errors in translation.

[7]) Katsarova (n. 5), p. 207.

There are also many slow instrumental tunes, as well as the epic songs and others, which are unmeasured, in tempo rubato.

b) Singing in Parts

Although in most regions of Bulgaria, traditional singing is either performed solo, or in unison or in octaves, there is another totally different style of singing in seconds, an archaic tradition preserved in Bulgaria only in the western and southwestern regions. It is basically in two parts, with the intervals between the parts mostly major or minor seconds. The songs are nearly always sung by women, always in small groups, antiphonally, a cappella, with, in each group, one singer for the first part, and two or more singing the second part, which is a type of drone. This singing is rarely performed by men, then only in the Razlog district and in Ograzhden mountain villages[8]).

It requires much practice to perform these songs properly and achieve the right blending. The frequent second intervals, harsh to the western ear, are regarded by the singers and their listeners in their culture as beautiful and consonant.

The area of this singing is divided by Kaufman and others into subregions, including Central Western Bulgaria, Pazardzhik and Ikhtiman districts, and the Pirin district, each with clearly marked features[9]). In the first of these regions, the Shope area, the two-part ambitus is within a fourth, the tunes have a simple mode, as $a^1\ b^1\ c^2$. Many second intervals occur between the voices, and here the voices almost never cross[10]). Kaufman believes the diaphonic style here to be the most archaic in Bulgaria[11]).

c) Folk Musical Instruments

The best known folk musical instruments are the following, divided into stringed instruments, wind instruments and percussion.

The *gŭdulka* is a bowed stringed instrument with a pear-shaped body and a short neck. It may have three or four strings, and is played to accompany singing and dancing. The *tambura* is a long-necked fretted lute, plucked with a plectrum. It is most popular in southwest Bulgaria, and among Moslems in the Rhodopes. The *tambura* is often accompanied by a *daĭre*, a tambourine.

The most widespread wind instrument is the *kaval*, a rim-blown flute with a cylindrical base. It is associated with Thrace, but is played throughout the country. The *duduk* is a fipple flute with six fingerholes in front and sometimes one in back. The *dvoĭanka* is a double fipple flute, in which the melody pipe is like the *duduk*, while the second pipe has a single opening on the side, which sounds the second tone (not the lowest) of the melody pipe. All three flutes were shepherds' instruments. The *zurna* is

---

[8]) Kaufman, N.: Bŭlgarskata mnogoglasna narodna pesen (The Bulgarian Polyphonic Folk Song). Sofia 1968, p. 71.
[9]) Ibid., p. 20.
[10]) Ibid., pp. 27/28, 32.
[11]) Ibid., p. 22.

a shawm, an oboe type with double reed, with a loud rough quality. It is found in other Near Eastern countries as well. In Bulgaria it is commonly played by gypsies. Two *zurnas* and a *tŭpan* (drum) form a typical ensemble for dancing, one most found in southwest Bulgaria. The *gaĭda* is a bagpipe, possessing a melody pipe and one, sometimes more drone pipes, and the air bag of kidskin, to which another short pipe is attached, through which the player blows to fill it with air. There is a higher pitched bagpipe, called *dzhura gaĭda*, and a deeper one, called *kaba gaĭda*, the latter typical for the Rhodope mountains.

The *tŭpan* is a large double-headed cylindrical drum. It was once played mostly in southwest Bulgaria, with two *zurnas*. More recently it has spread more widely. The *daĭre* is a tambourine, used for rhythmic accompaniment of the *tambura*. The *tarabuka* is a goblet-shaped drum, with a single head, and is found among the Turks in Bulgaria[12]). These instruments are mentioned below in the section on folk music regions.

3. Folk Music Regions

Five regions are characterized here: Pirin, Rhodopes, Thrace, Dobrudja and North Bulgaria, and fifth, the so-called Central Western Bulgaria or Shope region. This account is very condensed. Our source, E. Stoin, treats the subject in far more detail[13]).

In the Pirin region, in southwest Bulgaria, two-part singing with the drone is found with features characteristic of this region, such as crossing of the parts. Binary rhythm predominates here, but asymmetric rhythms occur frequently, especially 7/8, as $3 + 2 + 2$. The *makedonsko khoro* has this meter. Triple meter, rare in Bulgaria, occurs here quite often in *khorovod* (dance) tunes. Many songs are unmeasured, without a regular beat, in tempo rubato. Harvest, working party, wedding and banquet songs include each forms. The chief musical instrument is the *tambura*, and the small high-pitched *gaĭda* is found here.

The center of the Rhodope regional style is located along the upper Arda river and the middle part of the Mesta river. Here mainly lyric songs remain, performed at work parties (*sedenki*), dances and at the feast table. Customary songs have nearly disappeared. The *khoro* is slower and quieter here than the uproarious Thracian and Shope dances. Binary meter predominates in moderate tempo. The asymmetric tunes are fewer than 10 % of the entire corpus. The lyric songs are often slow, often in 2/4, 3/4, 5/4 meter, or unmeasured. A pentatonic whole-tone scale is very characteristic of the area. The *gaĭda*, *kaval* and *tambura* are the most common instruments. Here the *gaĭda* is large, with a low register.

---

[12]) Based on Atanasov, V.: Bulgarian Folk Musical Instruments, in: The Folk Arts of Bulgaria. Pittsburgh (ca. 1976), pp. 188–212, illus.; see also EBMK, Narodni muzikalni instrumenti (Folk Musical Instruments) [by I. Kachulev], pp. 44–48, illus., bibliog. Atanasov wrote articles on all instruments mentioned above for the New Grove Dictionary of Musical Instruments. 3 vols. London 1984.

[13]) EBMK, section on folk music regions by E. Stoin, pp. 51–55; see her authoritative book: Muzikalno-folklorni dialekti v Bŭlgariia (Folk music dialects in Bulgaria). Sofia 1981, 378 pp.

Thrace extends south of the central and eastern Stara Planina mountain range to the Black Sea and the southern Bulgarian border. This is a rich area for carols and the customs attached to them, also for spring customs. Melodies here are usually in minor modes (aeolian and phrygian), rarely in major. The *kaval* is the classic instrument of Thrace, but the bagpipe is also played in all areas.

The folk music of Dobrudja in the northeast, and in northern Bulgaria generally, is affected by the migration of peoples from all areas of Bulgaria. The songs are mostly in 2/4 meter, but 5/16 and 9/16 are also found. The slow Dobrudjan song is unmeasured, and very ornamented. The *kaval* is wide-spread in the east, the *gŭdulka* along the Danube, and the *gaĭda* is found everywhere in the area.

In the Shope area, between the Stara Planina mountains and the Pirin region, and west to the Yugoslav border, two-part singing and epic recitatif are distinctive to the region. The epic singing may be accompanied by a *gŭdulka* or by a second voice acting as a drone, or it can be sung solo[14]. Distinctive in epic song is the melodic introduction on one vowel, in the form of a descending sequence with many tiny ornaments. Gradual melodic descent is also characteristic for the epic recitatif proper. These songs are usually in unmeasured rhythm. They tend to be sung at banquets. Binary meter is prevalent, especially in *khorovodni* (dance) melodies and *sedenkarski* songs. Dances in 3/4 meter occur here. Not many asymmetric rhythms are found, but they do include 5/16 and 7/16, and especially 9/16, for the Samokovsko and Radomirsko *khora*.

Unmeasured songs here are as frequent as those in a regular meter. Most of the harvest and ritual wedding songs are unmeasured, in tempo rubato with characteristic cries, most often an upward leap of a seventh. A narrow range predominates in this region's songs, usually a fourth or fifth.

4. Professional Folk Ensembles

The first was the State Ensemble of Folk Song and Dance (*Dŭrzhaven ansambŭl za narodni pesni i tantsi*), founded by Filip Kutev in 1951. Kutev remained its artistic director until his death in 1982. In 1980 it was composed of a women's chorus of 94, a mixed dance group of 35, an orchestra of 17 players, the orchestra directed by Stefan Dragostinov[15]. The repertory is based on folk music from the entire country in arrangements for orchestra and women's chorus. The dances are based on folk dances, but choreographed for the stage.

The second most important group was founded in 1954 in Blagoevgrad, originally called the State Ensemble for Macedonian Songs and Dances, later renamed the Pirin State Ensemble for Folk Songs and Dances (*Pirin Dŭrzhaven ansambŭl za narodni pesni i tantsi*). Its chief artistic director and conductor since 1956 has been Kiril Stefanov. The basic goal of the ensemble is „the stage transformation and populari-

---

[14] See Stoin, E.: Bŭlgarski epicheski pesni (Bulgarian Epic Songs). Sofia 1980. Focusses on the music.
[15] EB, vol. 2, 1981, article Dŭrzhaven ansambŭl..., pp. 482/483.

zing of arranged folklore from the Pirin region"[16]). It includes a chorus, an orchestra and a dance group. The repertory covers the entire Macedonian area[17]).

The other leading professional folk ensembles are also regional: Thrace (*Trakiĩa*), in Plovdiv, under Kiril Dzhenev, the Northern Ensemble (*Severnĩashki ansambŭl*) of Pleven, and Dobrudja, in Tolbukhin.

5. Folk Festivals

There is one all-Bulgarian festival, held in Koprivshtitsa, to which thousands of folk singers, dancers, instrumentalists, also story tellers and others come from all parts of Bulgaria to perform. The first was held in 1966, the second in 1971. Thereafter it has convened every five years. This festival strives to be authentic. Folklore and folk music specialists are deeply involved with preparations, ensuring that costumes, musical instruments, style of singing, texts, are acceptable (see chapter Volkskultur by K. Roth II, 2)[18]). There are many other regional festivals, some held every year.

6. New Developments

Another form of traditional music suddenly came to light in Bulgaria in 1985, when fifteen „wedding orchestras" met and played for two days in the Khaskovo district[19]). The folk music experts knew they existed, but had not taken them seriously. Now they listened, and realised that this was evolved from traditional music and very popular among those aged 18 to 30, the age group not present at the Koprivshtitsa Festival.

These wedding orchestras (*svatbarskite orkestri*) are instrumental groups, i.e., bands, of four to six local musicians who play for pay at weddings, christenings and other private family occasions in villages or towns. The instruments may include violin, clarinet, saxophone, trumpet, accordion, guitar and electric organ, and some folk instruments. The musicians have little or no formal training, but are highly skilled players, some virtuosi. Their improvization is especially admired by their fans, of whom ten thousand came to the 1986 session[20]).

This music is full of local traditional elements[21]), is developing spontaneously

---

[16]) EB, vol. 5, 1986, article Pirin, Dŭrzhaven ansambŭl..., p. 233.

[17]) Kaufman, N.: Bŭlgarski narodni khorove i ansambli (Bulgarian folk choruses and ensembles), in: BMz. 10 (1986) 2, pp. 71–78, here: p. 73.

[18]) Kaufman, D.: Razmisli na „Koprivshtitsa '86" (Thoughts on ‚Koprivshtitsa 1986'), in: BMz. 11 (1987) 1, pp. 77–83.

[19]) Georgiev, K.: Pŭrva natsionalna sreshta na svatbarskite orkestri (The first national meeting of wedding orchestras), in: BF. 12 (1986) 3, pp. 90/91.

[20]) Kaufman, N.: Vtora natsionalna sreshta na instrumentalnite grupi na bŭlgarska narodna muzika (The second national meeting of the instrumental groups of Bulgarian folk music), in: BF. 13 (1987) 1, pp. 78/79. Note author's renaming of the groups.

[21]) Kaufman, D.: Natsionalni i regionalni problemi v muzikata na svatbarskite orkestri (National and regional questions in the music of the wedding orchestras) in: Muzikalni khorizonti. (1989) 2, pp. 7–13. Brilliant analysis of regional folk instrumental styles in these bands.

through improvization and has a mass audience. It is now being discussed avidly by the musicologists.

III. Medieval Church Music

Research in medieval Bulgarian music has flourished since the late 1960s. Petŭr Dinev (1889–1980) laid the foundation for the Bulgarian scholarship, while Elena Toncheva is the outstanding figure from the 1950s, with the younger Kuĭumdzhieva.

Recent studies concentrate on newly found examples of the so-called *Bolgarskiĭ rozpev* (the Russian term for Bulgarian chant) found among Eastern Slavs in an Orthodox monastery in the Ukraine, and on Bulgarian music manuscripts from the Rila singing school of the early 19th century at the Rila monastery in southwestern Bulgaria.

In current musical life, composers in the 1980s have begun to use Bulgarian Orthodox church chants as themes. The choir of the Sv. Aleksandŭr Nevski Cathedral in Sofia has gained prestige as singers of Bulgarian and Russian liturgical choral music. The Bulgarian chamber music ensemble *Ĭoan Kukuzel*, directed by Taniâ Khristova, also specializes in such music.

On one matter, Bulgarian and western musicologists disagree. All Bulgarians assert that the important Byzantine composer and innovator of the 14th century, Joannes Koukouzeles (Bulgarian Ĭoan Kukuzel) was a Bulgarian, although foreign specialists, including E. V. Williams and M. Velimirović, consider this to be unproven[22]).

IV. Secular Music

From the years before 1944 we will mention only three men. Dobri Khristov (1875–1941) was a choral composer, teacher, theorist of Bulgarian folk music. His choral works are classics[23]). Pancho Vladigerov (1899–1978) was a child prodigy pianist, who studied and worked in Berlin until his return to Bulgaria in 1932. He is the best known Bulgarian composer internationally, admired for his brilliant orchestral works using folk themes. Petko Staĭnov (1896–1977), blind from childhood, composed, above all, choral and orchestral works. His orchestral tone poem *Trakiâ* (Thrace) and other pieces are much loved. He was also active in musical life, like Khristov[24]).

---

[22]) See Bibliography under New Grove Dictionary of Music. Williams is the leading authority on Koukouzeles. See also Braschowanowa–Stantschewa, L.: Die mittelalterliche bulgarische Musik und Joan Kukuzel. Graz u.a. 1984 (= Wiener musikwissenschaftliche Beiträge 12) for the Bulgarian view, and for existing documents of his work.

[23]) See biographies: Kamburov, I.: Dobri Khristov. Sofia n.d. [1942]; Krŭstev, V.: Dobri Khristov. Sofia 1954. Also EBMK, pp. 442–446.

[24]) Krŭstev, V.: Petko Staĭnov, zhivot i tvorchestvo (P.S. Life and Work). Sofia 1964, p. 34; see also EBMK, article on Staĭnov, pp. 397–401.

The new regime after 1944 imposed a more tightly organized and controlled musical life. Some earlier institutions continued, such as Sofia's most important orchestra, in 1949 renamed the Sofia State Philharmonic (*Sofiĭska dŭrzhavna filkharmoniĭa*), and the National Opera (*Narodna opera*). Among the new state professional musical undertakings were four state opera houses outside Sofia, opened between 1946 and 1953 in Stara Zagora, Varna, Ruse and Plovdiv.

In the first fifteen years, and especially after the often cited April Plenum in 1956, composers were urged to write works dedicated to the motherland and the Party, compositions reflecting events in the heroic past of the Bulgarian people, on Bulgarian-Soviet friendship, on socialist construction, music reflecting the mentality of contemporary man[25]. Along with other works, nearly all composers wrote mass songs and marches, modelled largely on Soviet revolutionary and mass songs.

There were new operas, mainly on medieval patriotic themes. An exception was *Antigone 43*, by L. Pipkov (1904–1974), using the Antigone theme placed in 1943. The music is dissonant, polytonal, sometimes atonal, with much dramatic recitatif[26]. L. Pipkov stands out as one of the most active composers and leaders in Bulgarian musical life, especially after 1944[27].

A new generation of composers arose in the 1940s, in particular Aleksandŭr Raĭchev (1922–), Lazar Nikolov (1922–) and Konstantin Iliev (1924–1988). Iliev and Nikolov, the former a student of A. Hába in Prague in the late 1940s, the latter a student of Vladigerov and of D. Nenov, experimented already in the 1940s and 1950s. Iliev in general used twelve-tone and aleatory techniques, occasionally combined with Bulgarian folk music elements in his rhythmic and intervallic structures[28]. Nikolov's second symphony (1960–1962) has been described as pointillist, the third (1976–1979) as more traditional, but with some use of twelve-tone and aleatoric structures[29].

A. Raĭchev, politically active and a talented and prolific composer, wrote heroic works at first, but lately uses more modern expressive means in traditional smaller forms[30].

A change of style came in the 1960s and 1970s, with fewer monumental works, more introversion, more works for smaller ensembles. In the 1970s there was opening to new western compositional practices.

The composers who stood out in this period include: Pencho Stoĭanov (1931–), Lilcho Borisov (1925–), Dimitŭr Khristov (1933–), Vasil Kazandzhiev (1934–), Krasimir Kĭurkchiĭski (1936–), Bozhidar Abrashev (1936–), Georgi Minchev (1939–).

---

[25] EB, vol. 4, 1984, survey article Muzika, p. 372.
[26] Krŭstev, V.: Ochertsi po istoriĭa na bŭlgarskata muzika (Essays on the History of Bulgarian Music). 2nd ed. Sofia 1977, pp. 640–646.
[27] Krŭstev, V.: Profili. Studii-eseta za 11 bŭlgarski kompozitori (Profiles: Studies of 11 Bulgarian Composers). Vol. 1. Sofia 1976. On L. Pipkov, pp. 217–265; see also Iliev, K.: Lĭubomir Pipkov. Monografiĭa. Sofia 1958.
[28] Brashovanova, L.: Iliev, Konstantin, in: New Grove Dictionary of Music and Musicians, 6th ed. London 1980.
[29] Brashovanova, L.: Nikolov, Lazar, in: ibid.
[30] EB, vol. 5, 1986, article Raĭchev, A., p. 692; see also Krŭstev, V.: Profili. Vol. 3. Sofia 1982; on A. Raĭchev, pp. 97–145.

Of these Kazandzhiev, especially, uses pointillistic timbres as well as aleatoric and sonoristic techniques[31]).

The next younger generation of composers includes: Emil Tabakov (1947–), Stefan Dragostinov (1948–), Rumen Bal'ozov (1949–), Bozhidar Spasov (1949–), I͡ulii͡a Tsenova (1948–), Rusi Tamarkov (1949–) and Aleksandŭr Kandov (1949–)[32].

In the 1980s there is a return to simplicity in composition. Polystylistics are used. There is less minimalism. Composers combine traditional and contemporary elements. After 1944 until the 1960s it was almost obligatory to use folk music characteristics, asymmetric rhythms, modal patterns, folk melodies as themes in Bulgarian art music. Not surprisingly, in the 1980s folk melodies or rhythms are less prominent, more apt to serve as structural models, if used at all.

V. Music Training

The Bulgarian State Conservatory (*Bŭlgarska dŭrzhavna konservatorii͡a*) in Sofia, thus named from 1954, is the advanced musical institution in Bulgaria for the professional training of instrumentalists, singers, conductors, composers, musicologists and music teachers.

Starting in 1904 as a private music school, in 1912 it became the State Secondary Music School, and in 1921 was reorganized into the State Music Academy (*Dŭrzhavna muzikalna akademii͡a*), the name it bore from 1921 to 1954.

In 1976/77 the Conservatory had 963 students and 160 instructors. From 1960 it has published the *Godishnik na Bŭlgarskata dŭrzhavna konservatorii͡a* (The Annual of the BDK), mainly on pedagogical and methodological problems[33]).

VI. Music Research

The BAN's Institute for Music, renamed Institute for Musicology (*Institut za muzikoznanie*) in the early 1970s, has been the leading scholarly research center for music in Bulgaria. Its first director was Petko Staĭnov, from 1948 to 1977. The second was Venelin Krŭstev, from 1977–1988. Under Staĭnov, music education and folk music collection were emphasized. From the 1960s more research was undertaken on medieval music. By the 1970s the history of Bulgarian music was emphasized, and a

---

[31]) EB, vol. 3, 1982, article Kazandzhiev, see also rather overblown article, Bozhikova, M.: Klastŭri i folklor: po treta simfonii͡a na Vasil Kazandzhiev (Clusters and Folk Music: on the Third Symphony of V.K.), in: BM. 39 (1988) 9, pp. 3–5.

[32]) For analysis of new works by Tabakov, Tamarkov, Kandov, B. Spasov, Dragostinov, see Spasov, B.: Traditionen in neuem Sinnzusammenhang: Über einige Besonderheiten des kompositorischen Schaffens in der modernen bulgarischen Musik, in: MusikTexte. Heft 19. April (1987), pp. 34–36; see also Krŭstev, V.: Nova Bŭlgarska Muzika '86 (Survey of the review of concerts of new Bulgarian music 1986), in: BMz. 10 (1986) 3, pp. 20–34.

[33]) EB, vol. 1, 1978, article Bŭlgarska dŭrzhavna konservatorii͡a, pp. 499/500.

multivolume history is now completed, according to Krŭstev[34]). From the 1970s research continued in medieval music, on Bulgarian opera, ballet, choruses, orchestral music and other subjects[35]).

The Institute for Musicology was dissolved in late 1988, and replaced in part by the Institute of Scientific Problems in Art (*Institut po problemi na izkustvoznanieto*). Within it is a Musicology Sector with three divisions: history, under E. Toncheva; theory, under Dimitŭr Khristov; ethnomusicology under Todor Todorov. Some folk music specialists left, to join a folk music section directed by N. Kaufman, in the Institute of Folklore.

VII. Music Journals, Professional Societies, and Publishers

The major current Bulgarian music journal is *Bŭlgarska muzika* (Bulgarian Music), from 1948. In the years 1948–1952 it was called *Muzika*. The journal is the organ of the Union of Bulgarian Composers and of the Committee for Culture (*Komitet za kultura*). Articles concern official policy, concert life, new works by composers, leading performers, Bulgarian music abroad, book and record reviews.

Other periodicals are *Muzikalen zhivot* (Musical Life), from 1981, and *Muzikalni khorizonti* (Musical Horizons), from 1973. The latter is the information bulletin of the Union of Bulgarian Musicians, and is distributed to the members. *Narodna kultura* (National Culture) is a weekly newspaper, begun in 1957, dealing with literature, music and other cultural fields. It includes music criticism and articles on music. *Khudozhestvena samodeĭnost* (Amateur Artistic Activity), published from 1954, is a popular magazine, concerning folk music groups and their performances and festivals. It is informative, for example, on the Koprivshtitsa Festival[36]).

The Union of Bulgarian Composers (*Sŭñuz na bŭlgarskite kompozitori*) was founded in Sofia in 1947. At first there were three sections, of composers, musicologists and concert artists. After 1954 the concert artists separated out, and in 1965 formed the Union of Musicians in Bulgaria (*Sŭñuz na muzikalnite deĭtsi v Bŭlgariĭa*). Members of the Union of Musicians include creative artists, technical artists, and administrators and government officials in music[37]).

The Union of Composers, among many other activities, arranges an annual series of concerts of new Bulgarian music, publishes at its expense works of Bulgarian composers, and sends the scores free to amateur and professional ensembles[38]).

In 1949 the new state publishing house *Nauka i Izkustvo* (Science and Art) founded a special music section for the publication of books on music and scores[39]). In 1975 a

---

[34]) Krŭstev, V.: Chetiri desetiletiĭa Institut za muzikoznanie (Four decades of the Institute of Musicology), in: BMz. 12 (1988) 4, pp. 3–6.
[35]) Ibid.
[36]) EB, vol. 4, 1984, article Muzikalen periodichen pechat (Musical Periodical Press), p. 374.
[37]) EB, ibid., article Muzikalni profesionalni sŭñuzi (Professional music unions), p. 376.
[38]) EBMK, article Sŭñuz na bŭlgarskite kompozitori, pp. 417/418.
[39]) EBMK, pp. 125/126.

new publisher, *Muzika*, was founded, which took the place of the former section, and is now the major publisher in this field[40]). In addition, important books on music are published by the BAN.

Abbreviations

BF   = Bŭlgarski folklor (Bulgarian Folklore). Sofia 1965–.
BM   = Bŭlgarska muzika (Bulgarian Music). Sofia 1948–.
BMz   = Bŭlgarsko muzikoznanie (Bulgarian Musicology). Quarterly journal from 1981.
EB   = Entsiklopediía Bŭlgariía (Encyclopedia Bulgaria). Vol. 1-. Sofia 1978–.
EBMK = Entsiklopediía na bŭlgarskata muzikalna kultura (Encyclopedia of Bulgarian Music). Sofia 1967.
IIM   = Izvestiía na Instituta za Muzika (Bulletin of the Institute of Music). Vols. 1–15; …za Muzikoznanie (…of Musicology), Vols. 16–18. Sofia 1952–1974.
SbNU = Sbornik za narodni umotvoreniía, nauka i knizhnina (Collection of Folklore, Science and Literature). Vol. 1-. Sofia 1889–.

---

[40]) EB, vol. 4, 1984, article Muzika. Dŭrzh. spetsializirano izdatelstvo za muz. literatura (Muzika. The State Specialized Publisher for Musical Literature), p. 374.

Sport und Körperkultur

Hans-Joachim Hoppe, Köln

I. Sport – Körperkultur – Tourismus – II. Geschichtliche Entwicklung – III. Sportorganisation und Sportverbände – IV. Breitensport und Schulsport – V. Spitzen- und Hochleistungssport – VI. Bulgarien und die Olympischen Spiele: 1. Geschichtlicher Überblick – 2. Die Olympischen Sommerspiele in Seoul 1988 – 3. Wintersport und Olympische Winterspiele

I. Sport – Körperkultur – Tourismus

In Bulgarien wird, wie im osteuropäischen Sprachgebrauch üblich, terminologisch zwischen „Sport", „Körperkultur" und „Tourismus" (auch: „Touristik") unterschieden. „Sport" (*sport*) bezeichnet den Leistungs- und Spitzensport, „Körperkultur" (*fizičeska kultura*) umfaßt als übergeordneter Begriff alle unter Anleitung systematisch vorgenommenen körperlichen Übungen und Betätigungen. Unter „Tourismus" (*turizăm*) wird nur zum kleineren Teil „Fremdenverkehr" verstanden, darüber hinaus Freizeitaktivitäten wie Wandern, Naturerkundung, Bergsteigen, Aufenthalt in Skihütten und in Jugendlagern in freier Wildbahn[1]).

II. Geschichtliche Entwicklung

Der moderne bulgarische Sport, die Körperkultur und Touristikbewegung haben ihre Anfänge in der Zeit des Unabhängigkeitskampfes in der Mitte des 19. Jh. Den ersten Turnverein (*gimnastičeska družina*) gründete 1867 im Dorf Eniköy (Tulčansko) der Revolutionär und Nationalheld Vasil Levski. Nach 1878 wurden Turnen und Gymnastik in der Schule als Unterrichtsfach und in der Armee als Pflichtdisziplin eingeführt. Es entstanden außerdem eine Vielzahl von Turn- und Sportvereinen. Der wichtigste war der 1888 gegründete Gymnastikverband *Junak* (Held), der über die sportliche Betätigung hinaus patriotische Ziele wie die Pflege des bulgarischen Brauchtums und die Förderung der Liebe zum Vaterland verfolgte[2]).

Die Anfänge der Arbeitersportbewegung wurden um die Jahrhundertwende mit der Gründung des Vereins *Borec* (Kämpfer) in Sofia gelegt. 1912 schlossen sich die Arbeitersportvereine im Bund der sozialdemokratischen Arbeiterjugend zusammen.

---

[1]) Enciklopedija Bălgarija (Enzyklopädie Bulgarien). Bd. 1. Sofia 1978, S. 454–457.
[2]) Kratka Bălgarska Enciklopedija (Kurze bulgarische Enzyklopädie). Bd. 1. Sofia 1963, S. 369.

Von diesem spaltete sich 1919 der kommunistische Teil ab. Neben dem kommunistischen Jugendbund entstanden Hunderte von Gymnastikgruppen unter dem Namen *Spartak*, die 1922 erste Sportwettkämpfe („Spartakiaden") durchführten. Nach dem Putsch vom 9.6.1923 wurde die Arbeitersportbewegung verboten. Wie die BKP wurde sie verfolgt und existierte nur noch illegal oder halblegal.

Der „offizielle" Sport hatte bereits in den 20er Jahren Auftrieb erhalten, als 1923 die verschiedenen Vereine und Clubs in der staatlichen Bulgarischen Nationalen Sportföderation (*Bălgarska nacionalna sportna federacija*, BNSF) zusammengefaßt wurden.

Mitte der 30er Jahre wurden alle Sportverbände in der Staatsjugendorganisation *Brannik* (Verteidiger) vereint, über die das autoritäre Regime des Zaren Boris III. sich mehr Rückhalt bei der Jugend zu verschaffen suchte[3]). – Die Sportverbände zählten einschließlich der Touristikvereine 1939 bereits 213 082 Mitglieder[4]).

Der bulgarische Sport der Zwischenkriegszeit erhielt von Deutschland und Ungarn wichtige Impulse. Nach dem Vorbild der beiden Länder wurde 1931 in Bulgarien das „Gesetz zur körperlichen Erziehung der bulgarischen Jugend" verabschiedet, das die Jugendlichen vom schulpflichtigen Alter bis zum 21. Lebensjahr zur sportlichen Betätigung verpflichtete. Träger der Ausbildung waren Schulen und Vereine. Nach ungarischem Vorbild mußten außerdem Fabriken mit mehr als 100 Arbeitern für eigene Sporteinrichtungen sorgen oder die Beitragskosten ihrer Belegschaft für Sportvereine übernehmen. Trotz der Gesetzgebung lag der Sport in Bulgarien mangels Einrichtungen und geeigneter Lehrkräfte auch in den 30er Jahren noch im Argen[5]).

III. Sportorganisation und Sportverbände

Nach dem Staatsstreich vom 9.9.1944 wurde der Sport in Bulgarien den Zielen des neuen Regimes (paramilitärische Ausbildung und kommunistische Erziehung) unterworfen und gleichgeschaltet – staatlich reglementiert und weitgehend zentralisiert. Mit dem „Gesetz für Körperkultur und Sport" von 1948 wurden staatliche Komitees zur Leitung und Kontrolle des Sports gegründet und die Eigenständigkeit der Sportorganisationen eingeschränkt. Der Sport wurde systematisch auch in den Betrieben eingeführt. Durch Sportkomitees und (freiwillige) Sportorganisationen sollten die „Werktätigen" in Stadt und Land über Sport und Körperkultur näher zusammengebracht, die „materielle Basis" verbessert und Sportkader für nationale und interna-

---

[3]) Enciklopedija Bălgarija (Anm. 1), Bd. 1, S. 454–456.
[4]) Nach anderen bulgarischen Statistiken hatten 1937 die Sportvereine 130 000 Mitglieder, das sind 2,5 % der Bevölkerung, verglichen mit 10 % bei den westeuropäischen Nationen. In der bulgarischen Zahl sind auch 34 000 Mitglieder des Jägerverbandes, in den viele nur zur Erwerbung des Jagdscheines eintraten, und 18 000 Mitglieder des Radfahrerverbandes enthalten, dem viele nur wegen Ermäßigung der Radsteuer beitraten. Nur ein geringer Teil der Mitglieder der Vereine betrieb plan- und regelmäßig Sport.
[5]) Diem, C.: Sport in Bulgarien, in: Jahrbuch der Deutsch-Bulgarischen Gesellschaft. 2 (1939), S. 152–165.

tionale Wettkämpfe vorbereitet werden. 1957 wurde der „Bulgarische Bund für Körperkultur und Sport" (*Bălgarski săjuz za fizičeska kultura i sport*, BSFS) als vorherrschende Organisation gegründet. Auch andere Verbände betreiben Sport und Körperkultur: der DKMS, der sich vor allem mit technischem und praktischem Sport (Flugzeugmodelle, Segelfliegen, Motorrad- und Wassermotorsport), die BPS, der Bulgarische Touristikverband (*Bălgarski turističeski săjuz*, BTS), der Jäger- und Anglerverband (*Bălgarski lovno-ribarski săjuz*, BLRS) und der Verband der bulgarischen Automobilisten (*Săjuz na bălgarskite avtomobilisti*, SBA). 1969 wurde die Massensportorganisation „Mehrkampf ‚Heimat'" (*Sporten mnogoboj ‚Rodina'*) nach dem Muster der sowjetischen paramilitärischen Bewegung „Bereit zur Arbeit und Verteidigung" (GTO) gegründet, die aber ebenso wie die „Freiwillige Organisation zur Unterstützung der Verteidigung" (*Dobrovolna organizacija za sădejstvie na otbranata*, DOSO) bei der Jugend wenig Anklang findet[6]).

Nach Angaben des SG hatten 1987 der BSFS 1,39 Mio. Mitglieder, der BTS 2,3 Mio., davon 96 694 aktive Sportler, der BLRS 209 959 Mitglieder, davon 37 744 Sportler, der SBA 788 363 Mitglieder, davon 248 226 Aktive, und die DOSO 2 848 Klubs mit 79 670 Sportlern. Insgesamt betreiben 1,5 Mio. Bulgaren Sport, davon 594 509 Sportspiele wie Fußball, Handball, Volleyball und Basketball, 273 993 Leichtathletik, 66 173 Schwimmen, 98 296 Schießen, 60 678 Ringen und 104 396 Tennis und Tischtennis. Mit Boxen befassen sich 4 484 Bulgaren und mit dem spektakulären Gewichtheben 4 215 Bulgaren[7]).

IV. Breitensport und Schulsport

Die Zahlen können nicht darüber hinwegtäuschen, daß die Bulgaren wenig Sport treiben und der Breitensport im Argen liegt. Die immer noch weit verbreitete körperliche Arbeit setzt dem Bedürfnis nach körperlicher Betätigung in der Freizeit Grenzen. Statt aktiv Sport zu betreiben, lassen sich viele Bulgaren lieber vom Fernsehen mit Sportsendungen überschwemmen[8]). Zwar werden bei Spartakiaden, Sportfesten, Sternstaffetten und Trimm-dich-Läufen *Bjagaj za zdrave!* (Lauf für die Gesundheit!) kurzzeitig erhebliche Massen für den Sport mobilisiert, doch fehlt den meisten Bulgaren die planmäßige und regelmäßige sportliche Betätigung. Immer wieder bemüht sich die Partei mit mäßigem Erfolg um Ankurbelung des Massensports. 1976/77 führte RD monatelang eine Leserdiskussion zum Thema „Massensport – lebensfähiges Volk" (*masov sport – žiznen narod*) durch. Der XI. Parteitag vom April 1976 und

---

[6]) Zu den Sportorganisationen siehe Kratka Bălgarska Enciklopedija (Anm. 2), Bd. 1, S. 369, und Enciklopedija Bălgarija (Anm. 1), Bd. 1, S. 455/456.
[7]) SG. 1988, S. 436.
[8]) Wegen seiner gesundheitsfördernden Wirkung wird in jüngster Zeit Yoga und Entspannungstraining in Bulgarien immer populärer. In Sofia und in fast allen wichtigen Städten haben sich Yoga-Gymnastik-Gruppen gebildet. Yoga soll inzwischen mehr als 200 000 Anhänger haben (Sofia News. 6.4.1988).
[8]) Oschlies, W.: Bulgarien – sportliches Entwicklungsland? Aktuelle Analyse, BIOST, Nr. 16/1980, 30.4.1980, S. 1–7.

das nachfolgende ZK-Plenum vom Juli sprachen sich für eine Förderung des Massensports aus und forderten, daß jeder Jugendliche schwimmen lernen und sich mindestens in einer Leichtathletikdisziplin üben sollte. Doch wurden Anfang 1978 auf einer gemeinsamen Sitzung des BSFS, des BTS, der Gewerkschaften, des Nationalrats der OF und des Ministeriums für Volksbildung fortbestehende Mängel im Sport festgestellt und ein umfassendes Programm des Breitensports für Schüler, Arbeiter, Angestellte und die Landbevölkerung aufgestellt[9]). Doch die Klagen bestehen bis heute fort: Es fehlt an Koordination zwischen Schulen, Vereinen und Behörden. Es mangelt an Trainern und Übungsleitern für den Breitensport. Die BPS, der DKMS, die Kommunen ziehen dem Breitensport „paradierende Prestigeveranstaltungen" vor. Und die Sportklubs sind lediglich an der selektiven Talentförderung interessiert. Die lokale Bürokratie torpediert teilweise die oberen Beschlüsse. Die sportliche Betätigung wird durch Formalismus und Fehlplanung behindert: So wurden z. B. in den Sofioter Parks nahezu alle Sport- und Erholungsmöglichkeiten beseitigt. Überall in Bulgarien fehlt es an Sportanlagen (Sportplätze, Turnhallen, Schwimmbäder etc.), und die vorhandenen sind unzureichend ausgestattet oder verfallen. Unerläßliche Sportgeräte werden vom Fachhandel entweder überhaupt nicht oder in unzureichender Menge und Qualität angeboten.

Wiederholt forderte Staats- und Parteichef Todor Živkov die gesellschaftlichen Organisationen und insbesondere den BSFS auf, im Interesse der Gesundheit und Schaffenskraft der Bevölkerung mehr für den Breitensport zu unternehmen. Auf dem XIII. Parteitag der BKP kam BSFS-Chef Trendafil Martinski am 3.4.1986 zu alarmierenden Feststellungen über den Gesundheitszustand der Jugend: Es steigt die Zahl der Berufserkrankungen, Erkrankungen der Atemwege, Neurosen, Hypertonie, Allergien, körperliche Anomalien und Übergewicht. Verbände und Kommunen sollten sich deshalb stärker um die Heranziehung aller Altersgruppen, insbesondere der Jugend, zu sportlicher Betätigung kümmern[10]).

Auch der Schulsport wird in Bulgarien vernachlässigt. Anders als in der Sowjetunion und in der DDR werden die bulgarischen Kinder in den Schulen nicht systematisch an den Sport herangeführt. In den Schulen wird zu wenig Sportunterricht erteilt – in den untersten Klassen drei Stunden wöchentlich, in den Klassen III bis V nur noch zwei. Forderungen nach mehr Sportunterricht wird entgegengehalten, daß für nur eine Stunde mehr Sport mehrere Tausend Lehrer, mehr Turnhallen und Sportgeräte benötigt würden. Auch wird der Sinn des Sportunterrichts oft nicht eingesehen. Eltern kritisieren, daß er oft demotivierend, zu streng und deshalb unbeliebt sei. Freude und Zufriedenheit fehlten. Zur Auflockerung seien mehr Leichtathletik, Aerobic, Ballspiele und eine bessere pädagogische Handhabung seitens der Lehrer nötig[11]).

---

[9]) Otečestven Front. 6.3.1978.
[10]) RD. 11.4.1986.
[11]) Siehe die Leserdiskussion in RD, Frühjahr und Sommer 1988: „Dava li učilišteto dostatăčno znanija, umenija i navici za sportuvane?" (Vermittelt die Schule genügend Kenntnisse, Fertigkeiten und Gewohnheiten für das Betreiben von Sport?).

V. Spitzen- und Hochleistungssport

Die Förderung des Breiten- und Schulsports dient auch dazu, die personelle Basis für den Spitzensport zu verbreitern und neue Talente systematisch aufzuspüren. Vorbild darin ist den Bulgaren die DDR mit ihrem fast lückenlosen Auslesesystem, mit der intensiven staatlichen Betreuung und hervorragenden Ausbildung der Sportler in Sportzentren und Fachschulen[12]). Auch in Bulgarien werden mögliche Talente schon im Kindesalter ausgesucht und gefördert. Doch ist die Kaderausbildung in Bulgarien nicht so breit angelegt wie in der DDR; sie beschränkt sich auf einige Sportarten wie Fußball, Volleyball, Basketball, dann Leichtathletik, Schwimmen, Rudern, auch Reitsport, und vor allem die traditionellen Kampfsportarten wie Ringen, Gewichtheben und Boxen. Die höchste Kaderausbildung sowie Forschung und Lehre finden an der Hochschule für Körperkultur „Georgi Dimitrov" und am Technikum für Körperkultur „Vasil Levski" in Sofia statt.

Große Popularität genießt bei den Bulgaren der Fußball: „Der Fußball ist in ihrem Hoffen tägliche Nahrung, durch ihn nehmen sie teil an der Welt jenseits der Zäune, und die Welt kommt zu ihnen", so ein Kommentator in den 60er Jahren[13]).

Der organisierte Fußball begann in Bulgarien in den frühen 20er Jahren. Das erste Länderspiel fand 1924 in Wien gegen Österreich statt. Im selben Jahr trat eine bulgarische Mannschaft bei den Olympischen Spielen in Paris an. Bis 1944 gab es vier führende Vereine, aus denen sich die Nationalmannschaft rekrutierte: Levski, Slavia, AC-23 und FK-13. Die Spiele um den Landespokal trugen in der Regel Levski „Die Blauen" und Slavia „Die Weißen" unter sich aus.

Nach dem 9.9.1944 wurden die Fußballvereine im Rahmen der Reorganisation des Sports staatlichen Behörden unterstellt. In den 50er Jahren verlagerte sich die Auseinandersetzung zwischen Anhängern und Gegnern des neuen Regimes auch auf das Fußballfeld – so bei Spielen des populären Vereins Levski (für kurze Zeit in Dynamo umbenannt) gegen die unbeliebten Parteifavoriten – die Armeemannschaft CDNA (*Centralen dom na Narodnata armija*/Zentrales Haus der Volksarmee) (früher AC-23) und das Milizteam Spartak (ehemals FK-13). Wenn in Stadien, Tavernen und auf den Straßen Sofias der Kampfruf „*Samo Levski!*" (Nur Levski allein!) erschallte, so hatte er bei den Levski-Fans auch einen politischen Akzent. Um den Club „Levski" politisch zu neutralisieren, wurde er mit dem Milizverein Spartak zum Club Levski/Spartak zusammengeschlossen. Die Popularität des Vereins erreichte Mitte der 60er Jahre ihren Höhepunkt mit dem Auftritt des begabten Fußballstars Georgi Asparuchov, im Volksmund „Gundi" genannt.

Durch intensive Talentsuche und Nachwuchsförderung (Aufbau von Jugendmannschaften) drang Bulgarien in den 60er Jahren in die Spitzengruppe des europäischen Fußballs ein. Von 1962 bis 1974 gelangte die bulgarische Nationalmannschaft viermal in die Endrunde der Fußballweltmeisterschaften. Doch bereits in den 70er Jahren wurde der bulgarische Fußball zum Dauerthema der Sportkritik: wegen seiner sinkenden Leistungen, unfairen Spiels, Rowdytums in den Stadien, der großen

---

[12]) Watch out for the GDR, in: Time. 19.9.1988.
[13]) Maier, M.: Ins Schwarze getroffen, in: Welt am Sontag. 2.12.1962.

Privilegien für die Fußballer und der Korruption bei Spielern und Funktionären. So wurden „schwarze Kassen" (*černi kasi*) aufgedeckt, aus denen Spielern und Trainern zusätzliche Prämien gezahlt und Spielresultate im voraus „gekauft" wurden[14]). Todor Živkov übte wiederholt harte Kritik am Zustand des bulgarischen Fußballs[15]). Und das ZK der BKP konstatierte im Juni 1979, daß die Auftritte der bulgarischen Mannschaften im In- und Ausland „das sportliche Prestige des sozialistischen Bulgarien aushöhlen"[16]). Zur Verbesserung des Fußballbetriebs wurde der alte Fußballverband aufgelöst und im Juni 1985 mit neuen Statuten und Gremien neu gegründet[17]). Die Vereine, bisher praktisch Abteilungen der Behörden, wurden in autonome Clubs innerhalb des Fußballvereins mit eigenem Budget und Management umgewandelt. Nur die Vereine der Hauptstadt blieben aus „Traditionsgründen" Ministerien unterstellt. Nach dem skandalösen Pokalendspiel zwischen Levski/Spartak und CSKA (*Centralen sporten klub na armijata*/Zentraler Armeesportklub) Sofia im Juni 1985, bei dem es zu Gewalttätigkeiten kam, wurden die beiden Sofioter Vereine aufgelöst und ihre Spieler mit drastischen Strafen belegt. Der Landespokal wurde 1985 nicht vergeben. Als Nachfolger der Sofioter Spitzenclubs wurden die Vereine CFKA Sredec und Vitoša Sofia gegründet, welche nicht mehr staatlichen Ministerien unterstellt sind.

Trotz dieser Veränderungen hat der bulgarische Fußball keine Spitzenqualität erlangt. Bei den Weltmeisterschaften 1978, 1982 und zuletzt 1986 in Mexiko war Bulgarien nicht mehr vertreten. Im September 1988 hieß es in der Sportkritik: „Der bulgarische Fußball nähert sich immer deutlicher der Schlußposition in Europa. Mit einzelnen guten Fußballern läßt sich noch lange keine gute Mannschaft aufbauen."[18]) Die *preustrojstvo* des bulgarischen Fußballs (in Richtung auf mehr Profitum) erfolge zu langsam, wie der Präsident der Fußballföderation Anton Trajkov beklagte[19]). Bei den Spielen um den Europapokal sind die Bulgaren schon im Herbst 1988 ausgeschieden.

Ein besseres Image hat der exklusive Tennissport, der in Bulgarien lange als snobistischer Diplomatensport („Konsulball") angesehen und nur von einigen Hundert Spielern, vornehmlich in Sofia, betrieben wurde. 1930 und abermals 1960 wurde diese Disziplin bei den Balkanspielen eingeführt. Ähnlich wie in der Bundesrepublik Deutschland der Tennissport durch die Spitzenstars Steffi Graf und Boris Becker populär wurde, sorgten in Bulgarien die Maleeva-Geschwister dafür, um die sich ein Fan-Club bildete[20]). Manuela Maleeva stand Ende 1988 auf Platz 9 der Weltrangliste. Bei den Herren sind noch keine bulgarischen Spieler an die Weltspitze gelangt. Und der Erfolg der Maleeva-Schwestern liegt wohl in erster Linie daran, daß sie von ihrer Mutter ausgebildet wurden, die in den USA trainierte.

---

[14]) Pogled. (1979) 25.
[15]) RD. 13.6.1970.
[16]) RD. 25.6.1979.
[17]) BTA Sofia. 23.6.1985; Trud. 28.6.1985; siehe auch Resolution des Politbüros des ZK der BKP vom Februar 1985 (RD. 9.2.1985).
[18]) Sofioter Nachrichten. 14.9.1988.
[19]) Radio Sofia. 28.4.1988.
[20]) Kooperativno Delo. 22.6.1987.

Bulgariens großer Stolz sind die Gewichtheber. In dieser (schon in der Osmanenzeit beliebten) Disziplin traten Bulgaren erstmals bei der Weltmeisterschaft in München 1955 auf. Zwei Jahre später gewann Ivan Abadžiev in Teheran die erste WM-Medaille (Silber) für sein Land. Seit den 60er Jahren wurden von Abadžiev (seit 1969 Cheftrainer) und weiteren 185 Trainern nach einer intensiven Talentsuche in den Städten und auf dem Lande 4000–5000 jüngere und ältere Gewichtheber entdeckt und nach einem besonders ausgeklügelten Trainingssystem (kombiniert mit Massage, spezieller Ernährung und wohl auch Doping) zu Spitzenleistungen hochgetrimmt. Der neuen Sportlergeneration gelang es, der Supermacht UdSSR mit ihren 340000 Gewichthebern und 2500 Vollzeittrainern immer mehr Weltrekorde abzutrotzen. Bei der Olympiade in München 1972 erfolgte der Durchbruch, als die Bulgaren im Gewichtheben drei Goldmedaillen erkämpften und die sieggewohnte Sowjetunion von der Spitze verdrängten.

Gewichtheben ist in Bulgarien inzwischen Bestandteil des Schulsports, und schon Kinder (Siebenjährige) läßt man mit Hanteln wie mit Spielzeug trainieren. Spätestens im Alter von 12 Jahren erfolgt die Auslese. Die ausgewählten Schüler verbringen ihre Jugend in Internaten, wo sie rund um die Uhr von Trainern, Masseuren und Medizinern betreut werden[21]. So war der Ausbildungsweg der neuen Stars im Gewichtheben wie Borislav Gidikov, Aleksandăr Vărbanov und Naim Sulejmanov, der, 1967 als Angehöriger der türkischen Minderheit geboren, mit 10 Jahren mit der Disziplin anfing, mit 15 Jahren bei der Jugendweltmeisterschaft in Brasilien den ersten Platz belegte (1982) und nach seiner Flucht aus Bulgarien (1986) bei der Olympiade in Seoul im September 1988 für die Türkei (unter dem Namen Naim Süleymanoğlu) die erste Goldmedaille holte[22].

Schonungslos legte Jurij Vlassov, sowjetischer Olympiasieger und Vorsitzender des Gewichtheberverbandes der UdSSR, die gesundheitlichen Schäden des Hochleistungssports im Ostblock, Anabolikamißbrauch und Korruption 1986 im sowjetischen Fernsehen und 1987 in der Deutschen Sporthochschule Köln offen. Und über das Training der Bulgaren soll er öffentlich erklärt haben, „daß im Lager der bulgarischen Gewichtheber etwas faul sei"[23].

Die schnellen Erfolge der Bulgaren im Hochleistungssport bei internationalen Wettbewerben weckten Bewunderung in der Öffentlichkeit. Doch manche Illusion über die Geheimnisse des bulgarischen Trainingssystems wurde durch Skandale und Affären im Spitzensport beseitigt. Und nach dem spektakulären Dopingskandal der Gewichtheber in Seoul scheint auch in Bulgarien ein Umdenken einzusetzen. Es stellt sich die Frage, ob im Sport alle Mittel recht sind, um Spitzensportler zu erzeugen, die mit ihren Leistungen die patriotischen Gefühle der Bevölkerung und das Prestige des Regimes fördern sollen.

---

[21] Todd, T.: Behold Bulgaria's vest pocket Hercules. In: Sports illustrated. 2.6.1984; Süddeutsche Zeitung. 10.11.1985.
[22] Gespräch mit Naim Süleymanoğlu am 26.10.1988 im Büro der Halter Federasyon in Ankara.
[23] Moskauer Nachrichten. 15.9.1988; Sofioter Nachrichten. 28.9.1988.

VI. Bulgarien und die Olympischen Spiele

1. Geschichtlicher Überblick

Das bedeutendste Weltspektakel zur Selbstdarstellung und Prestigehebung von Nationen und Staaten sind die Olympischen Spiele. Bulgarien war in der Olympischen Bewegung schon früh engagiert: Es gehört zu den 13 Gründerländern der modernen Olympischen Spiele auf dem Kongreß in Paris und nahm 1896 an den ersten Olympischen Spielen in Athen teil (mit einem Schweizer Turnlehrer in bulgarischen Diensten namens Šampov/Champo).

1923 wurde das Bulgarische Olympische Komitee (BOK) gegründet. Seit 1949 wurde das BOK mehrere Jahrzehnte ununterbrochen von Armeekommandeur a. D. Generaloberst Vladimir Stojčev geleitet[24]). Im Rahmen einer großen Wachablösung in der bulgarischen Führung mußte der 89-jährige 1982 demissionieren. Sein Nachfolger wurde der 42 Jahre alte Ehemann der ein Jahr zuvor verstorbenen Živkov-Tochter Ljudmila, Ivan Slavkov, Wasserballspieler und zuletzt Fernsehdirektor[25]).

Seit 1924 nimmt Bulgarien an Olympischen Sommerspielen teil, ausgenommen 1932 Los Angeles, 1948 London und 1984 Los Angeles.

Im Volkssport Ringen holte Bulgarien 1956 in Melbourne erstes Gold; weitere Medaillenerfolge verzeichnete es in Rom, Tokio und Mexiko. Nach München (1972) schickte Bulgarien bereits 127 Athleten in 16 Sportarten, die im Ringen, Gewichtheben, Volleyball, Kanusport und in der Frauenleichtathletik Medaillen errangen. Seitdem gehört Bulgarien zu den olympischen Spitzennationen. In München rangierte Bulgarien in der Länderwertung auf dem achten Platz, und in Moskau 1980 rückte es – wenn auch wegen des westlichen Olympiaboykotts mangels weiterer Konkurrenz – an die dritte Stelle auf, die es auch bis jetzt unter den Ostblockstaaten behalten hat. Dem Boykott der Olympischen Spiele in Los Angeles 1984 schloß sich Bulgarien nach der UdSSR als erstes der sozialistischen Länder an – wegen „der antisowjetischen und antisozialistischen Kampagnen" in den USA und angeblichen Verletzungen der Olympiacharta[26]). Doch um des Prestiges willen drängte es mit den anderen Bruderländern schnell auf das „olympische Parkett" zurück, um sich bei den Spielen in Seoul mit dem Westen und der Dritten Welt „friedlich" zu messen. Dabei spielte sicher auch die Kandidatur Sofias für die Winterspiele 1994 eine Rolle[27]).

---

[24]) Vladimir Stojčev, 1893 geboren, war Berufssoldat und diente bereits in den Balkankriegen, 1935 wurde er wegen antimonarchistischer Tätigkeit aus der Armee entlassen. Von Oktober 1944 bis Mai 1945 kämpfte er als Kommandeur der I. Bulgarischen Armee im „Vaterländischen Krieg" gegen die Deutschen, 1945 bis 1947 war er diplomatischer Repräsentant Bulgariens in den USA. 1949 BOK-Chef, wurde er 1952 Mitglied des IOC und war 1956 bis 1960 Mitglied des IOC-Präsidiums (vgl. Enciklopedija Bălgarija (Anm. 1), Bd. 1, S. 540; Kratka Bălgarska Enciklopedija (Anm. 2), Bd. 4, S. 640). Stojčev war vor dem II. Weltkrieg ein prominenter Kavallerieoffizier und Reiter.

[25]) Sport (Zürich). 2. 4. 1982.

[26]) AFP-Meldung. 9. 5. 1984. Der bulgarische Beschluß erfolgte am 9. 5. 1984.

[27]) Neue Zürcher Zeitung. 4. 10. 1988.

2. Die Olympischen Sommerspiele in Seoul 1988

Die Funktionäre und Sportplaner hatten sich 15 Goldmedaillen und Platz 4 für Bulgarien hinter UdSSR, DDR und USA bei der Olympiade in Seoul ausgerechnet. Doch durch den Gewichtheber-Skandal und enttäuschende Leistungen „sicherer" Kandidaten wurde dieses Ziel nicht erreicht. Immerhin errang Bulgarien (abgesehen von Moskau) in Seoul die bisher beste Position mit Platz 7. Dies ist eine beachtliche Leistung für das kleine Land, das im Ostblocksport auch in Seoul hinter der UdSSR und der DDR in der Gesamtwertung den dritten Platz behauptete[28]).

Tabelle 1: Bulgariens Medaillenerfolge bei den Olympischen Spielen 1952–1988

Olympische Spiele	Medaillen				Plazierung (Länder)
	Gold	Silber	Bronze	Total	
1952 Helsinki			1	1	49 (69)
1956 Melbourne	1	3	1	5	18 (67)
1960 Rom	1	3	3	7	17 (84)
1964 Tokio	3	5	2	10	15 (94)
1968 Mexiko	2	4	3	9	15 (113)
1972 München	6	10	5	21	8 (123)
1976 Montreal	6	9	7	22	8 (88)
1980 Moskau	8	16	17	41	3 (73)
1984 Los Angeles		boykottiert			
1988 Seoul	10	12	13	35	7 (160)

Quelle: RD. 4.10.1988.

Nach Seoul hat Bulgarien Sportler in 16 Sportarten entsandt, die in 8 Disziplinen Gold und in drei weiteren Silber- und Bronzemedaillen errangen. Nur im Tischtennis und im Fechten waren sie nicht unter den ersten sechs. Ausgerechnet in traditionellen heimischen Sportarten erlitten die Bulgaren u.a. durch unerwartete Konkurrenz Rückschläge: So erhielt im Ringen nur Atanas Komšev Gold (im griechisch-römischen Stil); das Freistilteam gewann nur zweimal Silber und eine Bronzemedaille. Die größte Enttäuschung bereitete das Gewichtheberteam – trotz zweier Gold-, einer Silber- und einer Bronzemedaille: Mitko Gräblev und Angel Genčev mußten ihre Goldmedaillen wegen Einnahme verbotener Diuretika zurückgeben. Die Blamage führte zur Zurückziehung des gesamten Gewichtheberteams[29]). Selbstgeschaffene

---

[28]) Siehe die ausführliche Bewertung der bulgarischen Leistungen in Seoul von Gatev, G.: Po pätja pod pette prepleteni kräga (Auf dem Weg unter den fünf verknüpften Ringen), in: RD. 17., 18. und 19.10.1988.

[29]) Die Bulgaren hatten offenbar doppeltes Doping praktiziert. Man hatte den Schwerathleten Gräblev und Genčev die üblichen Anabolika-Dosen über den normalen Zeitraum hinaus bis dicht vor dem Wettkampf in Seoul verabreicht. Um die Anabolika-Spuren zu verwischen, nahmen die Gewichtheber dann kurz vor ihrem Auftritt Diuretika ein (Welt am Sonntag. 2.10.1988).

Konkurrenz kam hinzu: Der ehemalige bulgarische Gewichtheberkönig und Nationalheld Naim Sulejmanov konnte gegen eine Ablösesumme von (umgerechnet) 1,8 Mio. DM in Seoul für die Türkei antreten und gewann für seine neue Heimat die erste Goldmedaille[30]. Mit Bedauern mußten die Bulgaren weitere Mißerfolge konstatieren: Erstmals seit 1980 verlor das Land seine Spitzenposition in Rhythmischer Sportgymnastik mit (nur) einer Silbermedaille. Auch im Luftgewehrschießen der Damen wurde nur ein zweiter Platz erreicht; die vielversprechende Damenrudermannschaft erhielt nur Bronze. Daneben stehen aber auch überraschende Erfolge, z. B. Gold im 100 m-Brustschwimmen der Damen und im Pistolenschießen der Damen und verschiedenen anderen Disziplinen.

3. Wintersport und Olympische Winterspiele

Während Bulgarien bei den Olympischen Sommerspielen zu den Spitzennationen gehört, wird es bei Winterspielen kaum erwähnt. Bei den 14. Olympischen Winterspielen in Sarajevo 1984 gab es fast nur Fehlschläge. Ivan Lebanov, der 1980 in Lake Placid mit Bronze erstmalig für Bulgarien eine Medaille gewonnen hat, war verletzt. Und der andere bulgarische Skiläufer von Rang, Petăr Popangelov, sorgte trotz Verletzung in Sarajevo beim Slalom mit dem 6. Platz dafür, daß Bulgarien überhaupt erwähnt wurde[31]. Bei den 15. Olympischen Winterspielen in Calgary 1988 konnte Bulgarien wiederum keine Medaille erlangen.

Vor 30 Jahren hatte Bulgarien einige gute Erfolge im Wintersport aufzuweisen, doch danach wurde er vernachlässigt zugunsten von Hochleistungen im „Sommersport". Noch immer ist der Wintersport in Bulgarien hauptsächlich Wochenend- und Freizeitbeschäftigung für wenige. Um so mutiger war die Bewerbung Sofias für die nächsten Winterspiele: Nachdem die Stadt bei der Wahl des Austragungsorts für die Winterspiele 1992 gegen Albertville knapp unterlegen war, meldete es in Lausanne im Februar 1988 erneut seine Kandidatur an – diesmal für die Olympischen Winterspiele 1994[32]. In ihrem Antrag wies die bulgarische Delegation auf die günstigen klimatischen und sportlichen Rahmenbedingungen hin, die Sofia und seine Umgebung zu bieten hätten: ähnlich wie Oslo 1952 die Vorteile einer Hauptstadt, die Nähe zum Vitoša-Gebirge und somit kurze Wege zu den Sportzentren. Mit dem Bau neuer Pisten, großzügiger Wintersportanlagen und eines Olympiadorfes für 18 000 Sportler sei bereits begonnen worden. Alle Anlagen sollten in einem Umkreis von 20 km untergebracht werden. Gegenüber der bulgarischen Öffentlichkeit rechtfertigte

---

[30] Um die bei einem Länderwechsel in der Olympiacharta vorgesehene dreijährige Sperre abzukürzen und Naim Süleymanoğlu die Teilnahme für die Türkei zu ermöglichen, benötigten die Türken die Zustimmung seiner ursprünglichen Heimat. Diese erhielten sie gegen eine Ablösesumme von 1 075 000 $ „zur Kompensierung der Ausgaben und des Aufwandes für Entdeckung, Förderung und Entwicklung Naims zum Sportler von Weltrang" und gegen Wiederaufnahme der wegen der Sofioter Minderheitenpolitik abgebrochenen Sportbeziehungen (Sofioter Nachrichten. 12.10.1988). Über diplomatische Kanäle wurde im Oktober 1988 die Ausreise von Naim Süleymanoğlus Familie in die Türkei ermöglicht (Hürriyet. 26.10.1988).

[31] RD. 20.2.1984.

[32] Sofia News. 17.2.1988.

BOK-Präsident Slavkov die Kandidatur Sofias – abgesehen von dem damit verbundenen Prestigegewinn – mit der Chance zur Verbesserung der Infrastruktur der Hauptstadt (Hotelwesen, Transport, Wirtschaft) und zur Erschließung des Vitoša-Gebirges als Sport- und Erholungsgebietes (Tourismus)[33]. Heftige Kritik wurde in Bulgarien bereits wegen der hohen Kosten – offiziell auf 300 Mio. Dollar geschätzt – und wegen der durch den Bau von Großanlagen möglichen Umweltschäden in einem der wenigen weitgehend unberührten Naturschutzgebieten Europas geübt[34]. Skeptiker im Ausland wiesen außerdem auf die geringe Erfahrung der Bulgaren auf dem Gebiet des Wintersports, auf die dortigen organisatorischen Schwächen und die besseren Sportbedingungen bei den Konkurrenten hin.

Am 15.9.1988, vor Beginn der Sommerspiele, wählte das IOC in Seoul überraschend den Außenseiter Lillehammer (Norwegen) als Austragungsort für die Winterspiele 1994. Sofia, der meistgenannte Favorit, schied mit 17 von 86 Stimmen des IOC schon im ersten Wahlgang aus. Möglicherweise haben nicht einmal alle IOC-Mitglieder des Ostblocks für Sofia gestimmt. Wahrscheinlich hat den Bulgaren auch die Spekulation geschadet, sie wollten für die Teilnahme in Seoul nach dem Boykott von Los Angeles belohnt werden[35]. Nach dieser Niederlage will sich Sofia künftig nicht mehr bewerben[36].

---

[33] Reuter-Meldungen vom 16.4.1988, 9.9.1988.
[34] Vgl. die Kritik von Ljubomir Ivanov, Dozent an der Universität Sofia, in: The Times. 15.10.1986 und 2.7.1987, sowie die Stellungnahme von BOK-Präsident Slavkov, in: Kooperativno Delo. 1.6.1987.
[35] Zur IOC-Entscheidung siehe Berichte in: FAZ. 16.9.1988 und NZZ. 16. und 17.9.1988.
[36] Reuter-Meldung vom 15.9.1988.

Zeittafel[1])

Lutz Häfner, Hamburg

1878
März	3.	Präliminarfriedensvertrag von San Stefano: Gründung eines großbulgarischen Staates.
Juli	13.	Vertrag von Berlin ersetzt San Stefano. Anstelle eines „Großbulgarien" Schaffung eines Fürstentums unter Suzeränität des Osmanischen Reiches.

1879
April	16.	Verfassung von Tărnovo.

1885
September	18.	Angliederung Ostrumeliens an Bulgarien.

1886
März	3.	Als Folge des serbisch-bulgarischen Krieges (Beginn 14.11.1885) Friede von Bukarest.

1912/13
Oktober –April	8. 14.	Erster Balkankrieg.

1913
Juni –August	29./30. 10.	Zweiter Balkankrieg. Friede von Bukarest: Bulgarien verliert die Süddobrudscha, Adrianopel und Makedonien wieder.

1915
Oktober	14.	Kriegseintritt Bulgariens auf seiten der Mittelmächte.

1919
Oktober	7.	1. Regierung unter Minpräs. A. Stambolijski (BZNS): Agrarrevolutionäre Tendenzen. BZNS bestimmt in mehreren Kabinetten die Innenpolitik bis zum 9.6.1923.
November	27.	Friede von Neuilly. Aufgrund der Friedensbedingungen revisionistische Außenpolitik Bulgariens.

1923
Juni	9.	Militärputsch: Am 10. Regierungsneubildung unter A. Cankov (*Demokratičeski sgovor* [Demokratische Eintracht]), am 14. Ermordung von A. Stambolijski.

---

[1]) Für die hier vorgelegte, aus Platzgründen sehr beschränkte Auswahl wichtiger Daten und Ereignisse wurden neben historischen Quellen und Darstellungen, der Tagespresse u. a. benutzt: Europa-Archiv. Halbmonatszeitschrift der deutschen Gesellschaft für Auswärtige Politik. 1 (1946) – 44 (1989); Osteuropa. Zeitschrift für Gegenwartsfragen des Ostens. 1 (1951) – 39 (1989); Terzijski, P.: Socialističeska Bălgarija v dati i săbitija. Chronika 1944–1984 (Das sozialistische Bulgarien in Daten und Ereignissen. Chronik). Sofia 1984.

Juli 24. Friede von Lausanne: Grenzregelung zwischen Bulgarien, Griechenland und der Türkei.

1924
April 3. Auflösung der BKP.

1925
März 16. Staatsschutzgesetz.
April 16. Bombenattentat in der Sofioter Sveta-Nedelja-Kathedrale (über 200 Tote).

1930
Januar 20. Begrenzung der Reparationslasten im Rahmen der Haager Schlußakte auf 171,6 Mio. Goldfrancs.

1934
Mai 19. Militärputsch: diktatorische Regierung von K. Georgiev, gestützt auf Teile des Zveno und der Militärliga (*Voenen săjuz*) (bis 22. 1. 1935).
Juni 12. Parteienverbot.

1935
Januar 22. Sturz Georgievs.
April 21. „Gegenputsch" von Zar Boris.

1940
September 7. Vertrag von Craiova: Abtretung der Süddobrudscha an Bulgarien.

1941
März 1. Beitritt zum Dreimächtepakt.
April 19. Einmarsch bulgarischer Truppen in Makedonien.
Mai 14. Annexion Westthrakiens und Griechisch-Makedoniens.
November 25. Beitritt zum Antikominternpakt.
Dezember 13. Kriegserklärung an Großbritannien und die USA.

1942
Juni 5. Kriegserklärung der USA.
August 26. Einrichtung eines „Kommissariats für Judenfragen".

1943
August 28. Tod von Zar Boris. Thronfolge seines minderjährigen Sohnes Simeon II.

1944
September 5. Kriegserklärung der UdSSR.
September 6. Abbruch der diplomatischen Beziehungen zu Deutschland.
September 8. Kriegserklärung an Deutschland. – Einmarsch sowjetischer Truppen.
September 9. Staatsstreich der kommunistisch gesteuerten OF gegen die am 2.9.1944 gebildete pro-westliche Regierung von K. Muraviev (BZNS). Neue Regierung unter K. Georgiev (Zveno).
September 17. Regierungsprogramm der OF.
Oktober 1. Gründungskongreß des Volksbundes Zveno.
Oktober 5. In Craiova Unterzeichnung eines Vertrages über die militärische Zusammenarbeit mit Jugoslawien gegen Deutschland (erster außenpolitischer Vertrag seit dem 9.9.1944).
Oktober 6. Einrichtung von Volksgerichten.
Oktober 9. „Prozentabkommen" zwischen J. V. Stalin und W. Churchill über die Interessensphären in Südosteuropa.

Oktober	14./15.	Nationalkonferenz des BZNS. Übergewicht des antikommunistischen Parteiflügels.
Oktober	28.	Unterzeichnung des Waffenstillstandes mit den USA, der UdSSR und Großbritannien in Moskau. Gemäß Art. 18 Errichtung der Alliierten Kontrollkommission (ACC) (bis 23.1.1947).
November	6.	Abbruch der diplomatischen Beziehungen zu Japan.

1945

Januar	3.	Aufnahme diplomatischer Beziehungen zu Italien.
Januar	10.	Unterzeichnung eines Handelsvertrages mit Rumänien.
Januar	20.	Gesetz über Einrichtung von Arbeitslagern.
Februar	2.	Hinrichtung der Regenten Filov, Kiril und Michov sowie zahlreicher Minister, Abgeordneter und Militärs.
Februar –März	27. 1.	VIII. erweitertes BRP(k)-Plenum.
März	9.–12.	I. Kongreß der OF. Wahl eines Nationalkomitees. Mitglieder u.a. N. Petkov (BZNS), G. Dimitrov, V. Kolarov und T. Kostov (alle BRP(k)).
März	14.	Handelsvertrag mit der UdSSR.
April	15.	Gesetz über die Errichtung der TKZS.
Mai	8./9.	Nationalkonferenz des BZNS.
Juli	26.	Forderung der bürgerlichen Oppositionsparteien nach Verschiebung der für den 26.8. anberaumten Wahlen zur XXVI. („regulären") NSb, Forderung ihrer Durchführung unter internationaler Kontrolle.
Juli	31.	Aufstellung von Einheitslisten für die Wahlen zur NSb. Rücktritt des stellv. Minpräs. N. Petkov (BZNS).
August	13.	Note der US-Regierung: Forderung der Verschiebung des Wahltermins.
August	16.	Aufnahme diplomatischer Beziehungen zur UdSSR.
August	24.	Aufnahme diplomatischer Beziehungen zu Polen. – Auf westalliierten Druck Aufschub der Wahlen zur NSb. Änderung des Wahlgesetzes: Zulassung aller Parteien, Einzelpersonen und Gruppen zur Wahl. – Akkreditierung von V. Stojčev als politischer Vertreter Bulgariens in den USA.
Oktober	10.	Aufnahme diplomatischer Beziehungen zur ČSR.
Oktober	17.	Gründung der DP unter Führung von N. Mušanov und A. Girginov.
November	4.	Nach 22-jähriger Abwesenheit Rückkehr von G. Dimitrov.
November	17.	Aufnahme diplomatischer Beziehungen zu Albanien.
November	18.	1. Nachkriegswahlen. Wahlbeteiligung: 88,23 %, Stimmenanteil der OF 88,18 %. Sitzverteilung (insg. 276): BRP(k) 94, BZNS 94, Zveno 45, BRSDP 31, RP 11, Unabhängige 1.
Dezember	15.	Zusammentreten der NSb. Wahl von V. Kolarov zum Vorsitzenden.

1946

Februar	22.	Memorandum des US-State Departments an die bulgarische Regierung: Forderung nach Vertretung der Oppositionsparteien in der Regierung.
März	12.	Bodenreformgesetz: Begrenzung des privaten Grundbesitzes auf max. 20 ha (30 ha in der Dobrudscha).
März	31.	Regierungsneubildung durch K. Georgiev; keine Ressorts für Oppositionsparteien.
April	19.	Pressegesetz: Verbot nichtkommunistischer Publikationen.
Juni	7.	Verurteilung des BRSDP-Führers K. Pastuchov zu 5 Jahren Haft (P. stirbt dort 1950).
Juli	2.	Gesetz über Führung und Kontrolle der Armee.
August	24.	Gesetz über Arbeitspflicht.
September	8.	Plebiszit: 95,63 % der Stimmen für Abschaffung der Monarchie.
September	15.	Proklamation der Volksrepublik. V. Kolarov (BRP(k)) Provisorischer Präsident.

Oktober	27.	Wahlen zur VNSb. Stimmenanteil der OF 70,1 %. Absolute Mehrheit der BRP(k) mit 53,16% (278 von 465 Sitzen) der Stimmen; trotz kommunistischen Terrors Stimmenanteil der Oppositionsparteien über 30%.
November	23.	G. Dimitrov neuer Minpräs.

1947

Februar	10.	Unterzeichnung des Pariser Friedensvertrages. Verbleib der Süddobrudscha bei Bulgarien. Gemäß den Beschlüssen der Außenministerkonferenz von New York (3.11.–12.12.1946) Reparationszahlungen an Jugoslawien ($ 25 Mio.) und an Griechenland ($ 45 Mio.).
Februar	12.	Aufnahme diplomatischer Beziehungen zu Großbritannien.
März	7.	Aufnahme diplomatischer Beziehungen zu Österreich.
März	10.–16.	Währungsreform.
April	1.	Beginn des 1. Zweijahresplanes.
April	4.	Einführung des staatlichen Außenhandelsmonopols.
Juni	6.	Verhaftung von N. Petkov wegen angeblichen Landesverrats.
Juli	8.	Ablehnung des Marshall-Plans (ERP).
August	5.	Prozeßbeginn gegen N. Petkov, am 16.8. Verurteilung zum Tode wegen Hochverrats, Hinrichtung am 23.9.1947.
August	28.	Auflösung des Petkovflügels des BZNS.
September	22.–27.	Errichtung des Kominform unter Beteiligung der BRP(k).
Oktober	1.	Aufnahme diplomatischer Beziehungen mit den USA. – Ablehnung des UNO-Aufnahmeantrages durch die UNO-Vollversammlung.
Oktober	8.	Prozeß gegen 39 Militärangehörige der Militärliga (*Voenen săjuz*).
November	25.–28.	Besuch von J. B. Tito in Evksinograd. Am 27. Unterzeichnung eines Vertrages über Freundschaft, Zusammenarbeit und gegenseitigen Beistand mit Jugoslawien.
Dezember	4.	Annahme der Dimitrov-Verfassung durch die NSb.
Dezember	10.	Wiederwahl von G. Dimitrov zum Minpräs.
Dezember	16.	Unterzeichnung eines Vertrages über Freundschaft, Zusammenarbeit und gegenseitigen Beistand mit Albanien in Sofia.
Dezember	24./26.	Gesetz über die Nationalisierung von Industrie (24.12.) und Banken.
Dezember	27.	XXVII. BZNS-Kongreß: Verneinung der Idee einer selbständigen Bauernmacht.

1948

Januar	16.	Unterzeichnung eines Vertrages über Freundschaft, Zusammenarbeit und gegenseitigen Beistand mit Rumänien.
Januar	18.	Interview mit G. Dimitrov auf der Reise von Bukarest nach Sofia: Grundlegung des Kominformkonflikts. Damit Scheitern einer Balkanföderation mit Jugoslawien.
Januar	25./26.	Tagung des höchsten Parteirats der BRSDP. Beschluß über Vereinigung mit der BRP(k).
Februar	2./3.	II. Kongreß der OF. Ausschluß der Nichtsozialisten; Annahme eines sozialistischen Programms.
Februar	10.	Moskauer Verhandlungen zwischen der UdSSR (Stalin), Bulgarien (Dimitrov) und Jugoslawien (Djilas) beenden die Pläne für eine Balkanföderation.
Februar	18.	Billigung der Nationalisierung aller Ländereien, landwirtschaftlichen Inventars sowie des Privatbesitzes an Häusern durch die NSb.
März	18.	Unterzeichnung eines Vertrages über Freundschaft, Zusammenarbeit und gegenseitigen Beistand mit der UdSSR.
März	25.	Gesetz über die Volksmiliz.
April	23.	Unterzeichnung eines Vertrages über Freundschaft, Zusammenarbeit und gegenseitigen Beistand mit der ČSR.
Mai	29.	Unterzeichnung eines Vertrages über Freundschaft, Zusammenarbeit und gegenseitigen Beistand mit Polen.

Juli	16.	Unterzeichnung eines Vertrages über Freundschaft, Zusammenarbeit und gegenseitigen Beistand mit Ungarn in Sofia.
August	11.	Anschluß der BRSDP an die BRP(k).
August	18.	Unterzeichnung einer neuen Donaukonvention in Belgrad.
Oktober –November	31.	BZNS-Konferenz. Annahme eines sozialistischen Programms. Anerkennung der Hegemonie der BRP(k) im gesellschaftlich-politischen Leben.
November	6.–15.	Prozeß gegen den sozialistischen Oppositionspolitiker K. Lulčev. Verurteilung zu lebenslanger Haft.
November	29.	Aufnahme diplomatischer Beziehungen zu Israel.
Dezember	18.–25.	V. Parteitag der BRP(k): Rückbenennung in BKP.

1949

Januar	1.	Beginn des (vorzeitig erfüllten) 1. Fünfjahresplanes (1949–1952).
Januar	25.	Gründung des RGW in Moskau unter Beteiligung Bulgariens.
Februar	19.	Aufgehen von Zveno in der OF.
März	1.	Religionsgesetz: Anerkennung der BPC als „traditionelle Kirche des bulgarischen Volkes"; staatliche Kontrolle über die Religionsausübung.
März	6.	XXIII. Kongreß der RP: Annahme des Aufgehens in der OF.
März	8.	Verurteilung von 15 protestantischen Pastoren zu langjährigen Haftstrafen wegen Spionage für die USA und Großbritannien.
Juli	2.	Tod von G. Dimitrov in Moskau.
Juli	20.	V. Kolarov neuer Minpräs., V. Červenkov stellv. Minpräs.
Oktober	3.	Kündigung des Vertrages über Freundschaft, Zusammenarbeit und gegenseitigen Beistand mit Jugoslawien. – Aufnahme diplomatischer Beziehungen zur VR China.
Oktober	17.	Aufnahme diplomatischer Beziehungen zur DDR.
Dezember	8.	Prozeßbeginn gegen T. Kostov (BKP) wegen „nationalistischer Abweichung, Konspiration und Titoismus". 16.12. Hinrichtung. (Rehabilitiert 14.4.1956).
Dezember	18.	Wahl zur I. NSb. Stimmenanteil der OF 97,66%.

1950

Januar	23.	Tod von Minpräs. V. Kolarov.
Februar	3.	V. Červenkov neuer Minpräs.
Februar	21.	Abbruch der diplomatischen Beziehungen durch die USA.
August	10.	Ankündigung der Übersiedlung von mehr als 250 000 in Bulgarien lebenden Türken.
September	10.	Schließung der bulgarisch-türkischen Grenze auf Initiative der Türkei.
Dezember	2.	Nach Einigung über den Übersiedlungsmodus Wiederöffnung der türkisch-bulgarischen Grenze.

1951

September	17.	Aufhebung aller Zollerleichterungen durch die USA.
November	20.	Aufhebung aller bis zum 9.9.1944 erlassenen Gesetze.

1952

Mai	12.	Währungsreform. 100 alte Leva = 4 neue Leva.
Mai	28.–30.	III. Kongreß der OF.
September		Prozeß gegen 40 katholische Priester wegen Spionage für den Vatikan. Verurteilung des Bischofs Bosilkov und dreier Priester zum Tode.

1953

Mai	10.	Wahl des Metropoliten von Plovdiv, Kiril, zum Patriarchen.
Oktober	23.	Parallele Aufwertung der diplomatischen Vertretungen Bulgariens und der DDR zu Botschaften.

Zeittafel 693

Dezember	5.	Unterzeichnung eines Handelsvertrages mit Griechenland.
Dezember	20.	Wahl zur II. NSb. Stimmenanteil der OF 99,8%.

1954

Februar –März	28. 3.	VI. Parteitag der BKP. Billigung des 2. Fünfjahresplanes (1953–1957). Einführung eines neuen Parteistatuts: Auflösung des Organisationsbüros bei gleichzeitiger Erweiterung der Kompetenzen des ZK. Ausarbeitung eines neuen Parteiprogramms. Wahl von T. Živkov zum 1. ZK-Sekretär.
Mai	22.	Aufnahme diplomatischer Beziehungen zu Griechenland.
Juni	2.–24.	37. Tagung der ILO: Erstmalige Teilnahme Bulgariens seit dem II. Weltkrieg.
Dezember	20.	Unterzeichnung eines Handelsvertrages mit Israel.

1955

Februar	23.	Unterzeichnung eines Handels- und Zahlungsvertrages mit der Türkei.
März	1.	Dekret der NSb: Beendigung des Kriegszustandes mit Deutschland.
Mai	14.	Unterzeichnung des Warschauer Vertrages. Bulgarien Gründungsmitglied (Ratifizierung am 28.5.).
Juli	27.	Abschuß eines israelischen Passagierflugzeuges nahe der griechischen Grenze. 58 Tote.
Dezember	14.	Aufnahme in die UNO.

1956

April	2.–6.	Aprilplenum des ZK der BKP. Einleitung der Entstalinisierung.
April	18.	Rücktritt von Minpräs. V. Červenkov. Nachfolger A. Jugov.
Mai	17.	Aufnahme in die UNESCO.
Mai	30.	Unterzeichnung eines Warenaustausch- und Zahlungsprotokolls mit der Bundesrepublik Deutschland.
September –Oktober	22. 7.	Besuch des 1. ZK-Sekretärs der BKP T. Živkov in Jugoslawien. Als Folge am 9.10. Wiederaufnahme der Beziehungen zwischen den KPen beider Länder.
Oktober	27.	Artikel in RD: Verurteilung der „konterrevolutionären Meuterei" in Budapest.
November	29.	Rundfunkansprache von T. Živkov: Keine Aufnahme von Nichtkommunisten in die Koalitionsregierung.

1957

Januar	1.–4.	Teilnahme von T. Živkov an der Konferenz der KP Ungarns, Rumäniens, der UdSSR und der ČSR in Budapest.
Februar	11./12.	IV. Kongreß der OF.
Februar	15.–20.	Besuch von A. Jugov und T. Živkov in der UdSSR. Gewährung eines sowjetischen Kredits in Höhe von 200 Mio. Rubeln.
Juli	11./12.	Plenartagung des ZK: Parteiausschluß des ehemaligen 1. stellv. Minpräs. G. Čankov sowie von J. Panov und D. Terpešev.
Dezember	22.	Wahl zur III. NSb. Stimmenanteil der OF 99,95%.

1958

Februar	14.	Gesetz über allgemeine Wehrpflicht.
April	4.	Tagung des ZK der BKP: Verabschiedung des (vorzeitig erfüllten) 3. Fünfjahresplanes (1958–1960).
Mai	20.–24.	Besuch von T. Živkov in Moskau. Am 23. Unterzeichnung eines Protokolls über wirtschaftliche Zusammenarbeit für die Jahre 1961–1965.
Juni	2.–7.	VII. Parteitag der BKP.
Juni	23.–28.	Besuch des 1. Sekretärs des ZK der USAP, J. Kádár. Am 27. Unterzeichnung eines Konsularabkommens und einer Konvention über Doppel-Staatsbürgerschaft.

September	22.	Erhebung schwerer Vorwürfe durch ZK-Sekretär D. Ganev gegen Jugoslawien wegen der Benachteiligung bulgarischer Bevölkerungsteile in Makedonien.
November	24.	Unterzeichnung eines Warenaustausch- und Kreditabkommens mit Albanien.
Dezember	1.	Wahl von D. Ganev zum Vorsitzenden des Präsidiums der NSb für den verstorbenen G. Damjanov.

1959

Januar	23.	Gebiets- und Verwaltungsreform: Reduktion von 30 auf 28 Regierungsbezirke.
März	24.	Wiederaufnahme diplomatischer Beziehungen mit den USA.
August	1.	Ablehnung des bulgarischen Vorschlages vom 22.7. zur Unterzeichnung eines auf 20 Jahre befristeten Nichtangriffspaktes durch Griechenland.
September	8.	Aufnahme diplomatischer Beziehungen zu Japan.
Oktober	8.–18.	Besuch von T. Živkov in Albanien.

1960

Januar	15.	Nach zehnjähriger Unterbrechung der diplomatischen Beziehungen Akkreditierung des neuen bulgarischen Botschafters durch US-Präsident D.D. Eisenhower.

1961

März	21.	Aufnahme der seit 1942 unterbrochenen diplomatischen Beziehungen zu Brasilien.
November	24.	Unterzeichnung eines langfristigen Handelsabkommens mit Italien.

1962

Januar	1.	Währungsreform. 10 alte Leva = 1 neuer.
Januar	20.	Absturz eines bulgarischen Düsenjägers bei Bari. Verhaftung des Piloten wegen Verdachts auf Luftspionage (3.1.1963: Entlassung des Piloten aus italienischer Haft).
Februar	25.	Wahl zur IV. NSb. Stimmenanteil der OF 99,9%.
März	16.	Regierungsneubildung unter Minpräs. A. Jugov.
Mai	14.–20.	Besuch von N.S. Chruščev.
Oktober	31.	Sitzung des ZK der BKP: Ausschluß von A. Kolčev, I. Rajkov, dem Minpräs. A. Jugov, der Botschafter in der DDR, der VR China und Japan, R. Christozov, G. Kumbiliev bzw. Ch. Boev aus dem ZK sowie des ehemaligen Minpräs. V. Červenkov aus der Partei.
November	5.–14.	VIII. Parteitag der BKP.
November	20.	Neuer Minpräs. T. Živkov, der 1. Sekretär des ZK der BKP.
Dezember	18.	Vertrag über die Entschädigung österreichischer Vermögenswerte in Bulgarien mit Österreich. Erster Vertrag Bulgariens dieser Art.

1963

März	14.–16.	V. Kongreß der OF.
Juli	4.–6.	Erster Besuch eines UN-Generalsekretärs (S. U Thant).
August	3.	Zurückweisung der Vorwürfe Chinas gegen die UdSSR durch das ZK der BKP: Akzeptanz des Primats der KPdSU in der kommunistischen Weltbewegung.

1964

März	6.	Unterzeichnung eines langfristigen Handelsabkommens mit der Bundesrepublik Deutschland (Handelsvolumen ca. 460 Mio. DM) durch den 1. stellv. Außenhandelsminister O. Tichomirov und den Staatssekretär im

		Auswärtigen Amt R. Lahr (gültig vom 15.7.1964–31.12.1966; automatische Verlängerung um je ein Jahr). Vereinbarung über die Errichtung von Handelsmissionen.
April	23.	Wahl von G. Trajkov zum Vorsitzenden des Präsidiums der NSb.
Juli	9.	Unterzeichnung von 12 Verträgen mit Griechenland in Athen.

1965

Februar	16.–21.	Besuch des stellv. Minpräs. S. Todorov in Großbritannien.
Februar	21.–24.	Besuch von S. Todorov in Frankreich.
April	14.	Aufdeckung eines für diesen Tag geplanten Militärputsches. In der Folge Dementis durch BTA.
Mai	8.	Rede von T. Živkov: Bestätigung der Aufdeckung einer Verschwörung gegen den Staat.
Juli	9.–13.	Besuch des österreichischen Außenministers B. Kreisky.
September	22.–27.	1. Besuch des jugoslawischen Staatspräsidenten J.B. Tito seit 1947. Abschluß eines Warenaustauschabkommens für die Jahre 1966–1970.
Oktober	25.	Protokoll über den Warenverkehr mit der Bundesrepublik Deutschland.

1966

Februar	27.	Wahl zur V. NSb. Stimmenanteil der OF 99,85 %.
August	16.–21.	Besuch von Außenminister I. Bašev in der Türkei. Unterzeichnung eines Protokolls über den Austausch auf den Gebieten Wissenschaft und Kunst.
September	1.–7.	Besuch des Schah von Iran, M. Reza Pahlevi.
September	19.–22.	Besuch des Generalsekretärs des ZK der KPdSU, L.I. Brežnev.
September	21.	Besuch des Staatssekretärs im Auswärtigen Amt der Bundesrepublik Deutschland, R. Lahr.
Oktober	10.–15.	Besuch von T. Živkov in Frankreich. Unterzeichnung eines Kulturabkommens und eines Abkommens über wissenschaftlich-technische Zusammenarbeit.
November	11.	Zweites Protokoll über den Warenverkehr mit der Bundesrepublik Deutschland.
November	14.–19.	IX. Parteitag der BKP. Annahme des 5. Fünfjahresplanes (1966–1970).
November	28.	Parallele Erhebung der diplomatischen Vertretungen Bulgariens und der USA in den Rang von Botschaften.

1967

April	3.–6.	Besuch des polnischen Minpräs. J. Cyrankiewicz, des 1. Sekretärs der PVAP W. Gomułka und des Außenministers A. Rapacki in Sofia. Am 6. Unterzeichnung eines neuen Vertrages über Freundschaft, Zusammenarbeit und gegenseitigen Beistand. (s. 29.5.1948).
Mai	10.–13.	Besuch des Generalsekretärs des ZK der KPdSU L.I. Brežnev. Am 12. Unterzeichnung eines neuen Vertrages über Freundschaft, Zusammenarbeit und gegenseitigen Beistand. (s. 18.3.1948).
Mai	15.–17.	VI. Kongreß der OF.
Mai	27.–31.	Besuch des türkischen Außenministers I. Çağlayangil.
Juni	5./6.	Besuch von T. Živkov in Jugoslawien. Erörterung der strittigen Makedonien-Frage.
Juni	10.	Abbruch der diplomatischen Beziehungen zu Israel.
Juli	18.–21.	Besuch von T. Živkov in der Mongolei. Am 21. Unterzeichnung eines Vertrages über Freundschaft, Zusammenarbeit und gegenseitigen Beistand.
August –September	31. 4.	Besuch des dänischen Minpräs. J.O. Krag. Aufhebung des Visumzwanges zwischen beiden Ländern; Abkommen über Zusammenarbeit auf wirtschaftlichem, kulturellem und wissenschaftlichem Gebiet.
September	6.–10.	Besuch des Staatsratsvorsitzenden der DDR W. Ulbricht und des Minpräs. W. Stoph in Sofia. Am 7. Unterzeichnung eines Vertrages über Freundschaft, Zusammenarbeit und gegenseitigen Beistand.

1968

März	16.	Einführung eines neuen Strafgesetzbuches.
März	20.–26.	Besuch von T. Živkov in der Türkei. Am 22. Unterzeichnung eines Vertrages über die Auswanderung türkischer Bulgaren in die Türkei, deren Verwandte vor 1952 in die Türkei emigriert waren.
April	23.–26.	Besuch von T. Živkov in Prag. Am 26. Unterzeichnung eines neuen Vertrages über Freundschaft, Zusammenarbeit und gegenseitigen Beistand mit der ČSSR. (s. 23.4.1948).
Juni –Juli	29. 2.	Besuch des UN-Generalsekretärs S. U Thant.
Juli	8.–10.	Besuch des Außenministers der ČSSR J. Hajek.
Juli	14./15.	Teilnahme von T. Živkov an der Konferenz der Partei- und Regierungschefs Ungarns, Polens, der DDR, der UdSSR und Bulgariens in Warschau. Scharfe Kritik an der KPČ.
Juli	22.	Ausweisung des albanischen Botschafters und sechs Botschaftsangehöriger wegen „subversiver Tätigkeit".
Juli	23.	Ausweisung des bulgarischen Botschafters und sechs Botschaftsangehöriger aus Tirana.
Juli	24.–26.	Tagung des ZK der BKP. Besorgnis über die „antisozialistischen Kräfte" in der ČSSR.
August	3.	Teilnahme der BKP an der Konferenz von Bratislava.
August	21.	Teilnahme bulgarischer Truppen an der Intervention in der ČSSR.

1969

Januar	22.–27.	Besuch von T. Živkov in Indien.
Juni	4.	Unterzeichnung eines Warenaustausch- und Zahlungsabkommens mit der VR China.
Juli	8.–11.	Besuch des 1. Sekretärs des ZK der USAP J. Kádár und des ungarischen Minpräs. J. Fock. Am 10. Unterzeichnung eines neuen Vertrages über Freundschaft, Zusammenarbeit und gegenseitigen Beistand. (s. 16.7.1948).
Oktober	20.–25.	Besuch des finnischen Minpräs. M. Koivisto in Sofia.
Dezember	8.–13.	Besuch von Außenminister I. Bašev in Belgrad. Klagen von J. B. Tito über antijugoslawische Berichterstattung der bulgarischen Presse.

1970

Januar	18.–22.	Besuch des niederländischen Außenministers J. Luns.
April	8./9.	Besuch von Außenminister I. Bašev in Griechenland. Betonung der gutnachbarlichen Beziehungen trotz unterschiedlicher sozialer und politischer Systeme.
April	26.–29.	Besuch des italienischen Außenministers A. Moro.
September	21.–30.	Besuch von T. Živkov in Norwegen, Island und Dänemark. Erklärung Živkovs: Voraussetzung für die Aufnahme diplomatischer Beziehungen zur Bundesrepublik Deutschland sei die Anerkennung der DDR durch alle NATO-Staaten.
Oktober	5.–9.	Besuch des türkischen Minpräs. S. Demirel.
November	18.–21.	Besuch des rumänischen Staats- und Regierungschefs N. Ceaușescu. Am 19. Unterzeichnung eines neuen Vertrages über Freundschaft, Zusammenarbeit und gegenseitigen Beistand. (s. 16.1.1948).

1971

Januar	29.	Abkommen über den visafreien grenzüberschreitenden Verkehr zwischen Bulgarien und der DDR.
Februar	12.	Unterzeichnung eines Abkommens über wirtschaftliche und technische Zusammenarbeit mit der Bundesrepublik Deutschland.
März	30.	Veröffentlichung des neuen Verfassungsentwurfes.

April	20.–25.	X. Parteitag der BKP. Verabschiedung des 6. Fünfjahresplanes (1971–1975); Billigung eines neuen Parteiprogrammes.
Mai	5.	Unterzeichnung eines Warenaustausch- und Zahlungsabkommens mit Albanien.
Mai	10.	Unterzeichnung eines Protokolls über Tourismus in makedonischer Sprache (Bedeutende Konzession Bulgariens, das seit 1966 die Unterzeichnung von Dokumenten in makedonischer Sprache abgelehnt hatte, weil damit eine Anerkennung einer separaten makedonischen Nationalität impliziert wurde).
Mai	16.	Volksabstimmung über den Verfassungsentwurf. Billigung mit 99,66% der Stimmen.
Mai	18.	Annahme der neuen Verfassung. Verfassungsmäßige Verankerung der führenden Rolle der BKP und die Bindung an die UdSSR. Konstituierung eines Staatsrates (DS) als höchstem Staatsorgan.
Juni	27.	Wahl zur VI. NSb. Stimmenanteil der OF 99,9%.
Juli	7.	Tagung der NSb. Wahl von T. Živkov in das neugeschaffene Amt des Staatsratsvorsitzenden.
November	22./23.	Besuch von Außenminister I. Bašev in Rom.
Dezember	16.	P. Mladenov neuer Außenminister anstelle des tödlich verunglückten I. Bašev.

1972

April	17.–19.	Besuch des 1. Sekretärs des ZK der SED E. Honecker. Unterzeichnung eines langfristigen Handelsabkommens und eines Abkommens über wirtschaftliche Zusammenarbeit.
April	20.–22.	VII. Kongreß der OF.
Juli	3.	Ernennung des Vorsitzenden der ideologischen Kommission der BKP, V. T. Kocev, zum stellv. Minpräs.
Juli	13.	V. T. Kocev verliert alle Parteiämter.
November	23.	Besuch von Außenminister P. Mladenov in der Türkei.

1973

Februar	7.–9.	Besuch des österreichischen Außenministers R. Kirchschläger. Am 9. Abschluß eines Abkommens über kulturelle und wissenschaftliche Zusammenarbeit.
Februar	20.–24.	Besuch des Sekretärs des Präsidiums des BKJ S. Dolanc in Sofia. Erörterung der Makedonien-Frage.
März	13.	Beschluß des Ministerrats und des Zentralrats der Gewerkschaften über die Einführung der Fünftagewoche und die Reduktion der Wochenarbeitszeit von 46 auf 42,5 Stunden.
April	5.	Schaffung einer einheitlichen Organisation des bulgarischen Tourismus: Ernennung von I. Vračev zum Vorsitzenden des neuen Komitees für Erholung und Tourismus.
April	6.	Ablösung von Innenminister A. Canev (ab 7.4. stellvertretender Vorsitzender der nationalen Verteidigungskommission) durch D. Stojanov.
Mai –Juni	29. 1.	Besuch von Außenminister P. Mladenov in Griechenland. Unterzeichnung einer Deklaration über die Prinzipien der guten Nachbarschaft, einer Konsularkonvention, eines Vertrages über kulturelle Zusammenarbeit und eines Vertrages über die Eröffnung von Generalkonsulaten in Plovdiv und Saloniki.
Juni	1.	Erhöhung der Benzinpreise um bis zu 35%.
Juni	27.	Tagung der NSb: Annahme eines neuen Wahlgesetzes.
Juli	16.–21.	Besuch des türkischen Außenministers H. Bayülken. Betonung des Interesses an der Repatriierung der in Bulgarien lebenden türkischen Minderheit.
Juli	20./21.	Besuch des französischen Premierministers P. Mesmer und von Außenminister M. Jobert.

August	2.–5.	Besuch von UN-Generalsekretär K. Waldheim.
September	18.–21.	Besuch des Generalsekretärs des ZK der KPdSU L.I. Brežnev.
September	22.	Abbruch der diplomatischen Beziehungen zu Chile.
Oktober	9.–13.	Besuch von T. Živkov in Österreich. Unterzeichnung einer Konsularkonvention und eines Abkommens über soziale Sicherheit.
November	21.–24.	Besuch von Außenminister P. Mladenov in Frankreich.
November	30.	Im Zusammenhang mit der Ölkrise drastische Reduktion des Öl- und Benzinverbrauchs. Einführung von Geschwindigkeitsbegrenzungen.
Dezember	21.	Aufnahme diplomatischer Beziehungen mit der Bundesrepublik Deutschland (als letzter der WP-Staaten). Umwandlung der bisherigen Handelsmissionen in Botschaften.

1974

März		Aufgrund schwerer Differenzen in der Makedonien-Frage Absage eines Jugoslawien-Besuches von T. Živkov.
März	25./26.	Besuch von Bundesaußenminister W. Scheel.
April	15.	Besuch von US-Handelsminister Dent in Sofia. Schaffung eines bilateralen Wirtschaftsrates. Unterzeichnung eines Konsularabkommens.
Mai	26.–28.	Besuch des italienischen Außenministers A. Moro. Unterzeichnung eines Zehnjahresabkommens über wirtschaftliche, wissenschaftliche, industrielle und technische Zusammenarbeit.
Juni	26.	Aufnahme diplomatischer Beziehungen zu Portugal.

1975

Januar	8.–10.	Besuch des griechischen Außenministers D. Bitsios. Erörterung des Zypern-Problems und eines Transitabkommens für Transporte von Bulgarien über Saloniki. (Nach dem Sturz der Militärregierung in Griechenland Intensivierung der bilateralen Beziehungen durch Bulgarien.)
März	4./5.	Besuch von Außenminister P. Mladenov in der Bundesrepublik Deutschland.
Mai	11.–14.	Besuch des österreichischen Bundeskanzlers B. Kreisky. Unterzeichnung eines Konsularabkommens.
Mai	14.	Unterzeichnung eines Abkommens über wirtschaftliche, industrielle und technische Zusammenarbeit mit der Bundesrepublik Deutschland.
Juni	2.–6.	Besuch von Außenminister P. Mladenov in Japan.
Juni	23.–27.	Besuch von T. Živkov in Italien und im Vatikan. Unterzeichnung eines Abkommens über wirtschaftliche Zusammenarbeit mit Italien für die Jahre 1975 bis 1979. Besuch bei Papst Paul VI.
Juli	2.–4.	Besuch des griechischen Minpräs. K. Karamanlis.
September	13.	Unterzeichnung eines Abkommens über wirtschaftliche, technische, industrielle und wissenschaftliche Zusammenarbeit mit der Türkei.
November	24.–28.	Besuch von T. Živkov in der Bundesrepublik Deutschland. Unterzeichnung eines Abkommens über kulturelle Zusammenarbeit mit einer Laufzeit von 5 Jahren.
Dezember	1.–3.	Besuch des türkischen Minpräs. S. Demirel. Unterzeichnung einer Erklärung über die Prinzipien der guten Nachbarschaft und Zusammenarbeit.

1976

März	9.	Tagung der NSb: Billigung des neuen Wahlgesetzes, des Gesetzes über das Gerichtswesen und der neuen Straßenverkehrsordnung. Vorverlegung der Wahlen auf den 30.5.
März –April	29. 2.	XI. Parteitag der BKP. Beschluß über den Umtausch der Parteibücher.
April	9.–11.	Besuch von T. Živkov in Griechenland.
April	14.	Billigung des 7. Fünfjahresplanes (1976–1980) durch den Ministerrat.

Mai	10.–13.	Besuch des Minpräs. S. Todorov in Österreich. Unterzeichnung eines Abkommens über die gegenseitige Anerkennung von Universitätsdiplomen und Ratifizierung eines Konsularabkommens (s. 11.–14.5.1975).
Mai	30.	Wahl zur VII. NSb. Wahlbeteiligung 99,93%, Stimmenanteil der OF 99,92%.
Juni	3.–6.	Besuch von T. Živkov in der Türkei.
Juni	7.	Empfang des CDU-Vorsitzenden H. Kohl bei T. Živkov in Sofia.
Juni	19.	Dekret des DS über die Bildung eines Komitees für Umweltschutz.
September	3.	Vermittlungsversuch Bulgariens im Ägaiskonflikt zwischen Griechenland und der Türkei.
November	3.–8.	Besuch des Sekretärs des Rats des Vatikans für Öffentliche Angelegenheiten der Kirche A. Casaroli.
November	16.–21.	Besuch von T. Živkov in Indien. Unterzeichnung eines Programms über den Kulturaustausch sowie eines Handels- und Zahlungsprotokolls für 1977.
Dezember	1.	Artikel von T. Živkov in der Zeitschrift „Probleme des Friedens und des Sozialismus": Verurteilung der Toleranz gegenüber dem Antisowjetismus als Abweichung vom Proletarischen Internationalismus sowie des Eurokommunismus als bürgerliche Propaganda.

1977

Januar	28.	Aufnahme diplomatischer Beziehungen zu Spanien.
Juni	14.	Unterzeichnung eines Abkommens über wissenschaftlich-technische und kulturelle Zusammenarbeit mit den USA.
Juni	14.–16.	VIII. Kongreß der OF.
September	13./14.	Besuch von DDR-Staats- und Parteichef E. Honecker. Am 14. Unterzeichnung eines neuen Vertrages über Freundschaft, Zusammenarbeit und gegenseitigen Beistand. (s. 7.9.1967).
Oktober	20./21.	Besuch von Bundesaußenminister H.-D. Genscher.

1978

Mai	3.–6.	Besuch des türkischen Minpräs. B. Ecevit.
Mai	16.–19.	Besuch des Schahs von Iran M. Reza Pahlevi.
Juni	7./8.	Besuch des SPD-Vorsitzenden W. Brandt.
Juni	24.	Erklärung über die Nichtexistenz einer makedonischen Minderheit in Bulgarien durch ZK-Sekretär D. Stanišev, den Leiter der BKP-Delegation auf dem XI. BKJ-Kongreß.
Juli	3./4.	Besuch von Außenminister P. Mladenov in der Bundesrepublik Deutschland.
Juli	24.	Stellungnahme des Außenministeriums gegen die „antibulgarische Kampagne" Jugoslawiens in der Makedonienfrage.
September	15.	BTA-Erklärung: Zurückweisung britischer Presseberichte über die Mitverantwortung am Tode des Emigranten G. Markov in Großbritannien.
Oktober	21.	Unterzeichnung eines Vertrages über Freundschaft und Zusammenarbeit mit Angola.
Oktober	24.	Unterzeichnung eines Vertrages über Freundschaft und Zusammenarbeit mit Moçambique.
November	27./28.	Besuch von Außenminister P. Mladenov in Belgien. Unterzeichnung eines Konsularabkommens.
Dezember	5.	Nach Angriffen durch die Bevölkerung Abberufung des bulgarischen Botschaftspersonals aus Ägypten.
Dezember	12./13.	Besuch von Außenminister P. Mladenov in Italien.
Dezember	14.	Privataudienz von Außenminister P. Mladenov bei Papst Paul VI. Wunsch Mladenovs nach Errichtung einer Diözese in Südbulgarien sowie der Ernennung eines Nachfolgers für den verstorbenen Bischof von Nordbulgarien.

1979

Januar	13.–17.	Besuch von L. I. Brežnev.
Januar	29.	Einführung des NIM in der Landwirtschaft auf der Basis der Selbstversorgung.
Mai	2.–4.	Besuch von Bundeskanzler H. Schmidt.
Mai	13.	Ernennung zweier neuer katholischer Bischöfe: B. D. Dobranov und S. S. Džundrin (dieser war 1952 als „Konterrevolutionär gegen die UdSSR" zu 12 Jahren Haft verurteilt worden).
Juli	9.–11.	Besuch von T. Živkov in der Türkei. Unterzeichnung eines Abkommens über die Aufhebung des Visumzwanges.
September –Oktober	29. 1.	Besuch von T. Živkov in Vietnam. Unterzeichnung eines Vertrages über Freundschaft und Zusammenarbeit.
Oktober	4.	Unterzeichnung eines Vertrages über Freundschaft und Zusammenarbeit mit Laos.
Oktober	22./23.	Besuch von Außenminister P. Mladenov in Frankreich.
Oktober	30./31.	Tagung der NSb. Annahme von Änderungen des Strafgesetzbuchs und des Gesetzes über die Volksmiliz.
November	1./2.	Besuch von Staats- und Parteichef E. Honecker.

1980

Oktober	12.–15.	Besuch des griechischen Minpräs. K. Karamanlis.
November	21.–25.	Besuch des kambodschanischen Minpräs. Heng Samrin. Am 25. Unterzeichnung eines Vertrages über Freundschaft und Zusammenarbeit mit einer Laufzeit von 25 Jahren.

1981

Januar	20.–23.	Besuch des Außenhandelsministers Ch. Christov in Italien.
März –April	31. 4.	XII. Parteitag der BKP. Annahme des 8. Fünfjahresplans (1981–1985).
Mai	12.–15.	Besuch des österreichischen Bundeskanzlers B. Kreisky.
Juni	7.	Wahlen zur VIII. NSb. Stimmenanteil der OF 99,93 %.
Juni	16.	Wahl von Minpräs. S. Todorov zum Vorsitzenden der NSb. Neuer Minpräs. G. Filipov.
Juli	7.	Amnestieerlaß der NSb anläßlich der 1300-Jahr-Feier der Staatsgründung.
Juli	8.–11.	Besuch von Bundesaußenminister H.-D. Genscher.
Oktober	20.	Rede von T. Živkov aus Anlaß des 1300. Jahrestages der Staatsgründung. Vorschlag zur Schaffung einer kernwaffenfreien Zone auf dem Balkan.
November	6.–9.	Besuch der indischen Premierministerin I. Gandhi.
November	9.–12.	Besuch des Staats- und Parteichefs der VR Jemen A. Nasir Muhammad. Am 11. Unterzeichnung eines Vertrages über Freundschaft und Zusammenarbeit.
Dezember	10./11.	Tagung der NSb. Erörterung des 8. Fünfjahresplanes (1981–1985).
Dezember	16.–23.	Besuch des afghanischen Staats- und Parteichefs B. Karmal. Am 22. Unterzeichnung eines Vertrages über Freundschaft und Zusammenarbeit.

1982

Januar	13.	Rede von Minpräs. G. Filipov. Erläuterung des seit 1.1. gültigen NIM. Selbstfinanzierung der Unternehmen, Arbeit nach dem Kosten-Nutzen-Prinzip. Gewährung staatlicher Subventionen nur in Ausnahmefällen.
Januar	27./28.	Besuch von Außenminister P. Mladenov in Bonn.
Februar	24.–27.	Besuch des türkischen Staatspräs. K. Evren.
März	10.–12.	Besuch von Minpräs. und NSb-Vorsitzenden S. Todorov in Jugoslawien. Fortbestehen des Makedonienkonflikts.
März	31.	Tagung der NSb. Änderung des Strafgesetzbuchs, der Strafprozeßordnung und des Strafvollzuges.
Juni	21.–23.	IX. Kongreß der OF.

Zeittafel 701

Juni	24.–26.	Besuch des griechischen Minpräs. A. Papandreou.
Juli	6.	Konsultationstreffen von Vertretern des bulgarischen und des bundesdeutschen Außenministeriums in Bonn.
September	7.	Erklärung der BTA: Zurückweisung westlicher Beschuldigungen, der Papstattentäter M. A. Agça habe im Auftrag des bulgarischen Geheimdienstes gehandelt.
November	9./10.	Sitzung der NSb. Beschluß über Änderung des Wahlgesetzes.
November	25.	Verhaftung des Vertreters der bulgarischen Fluggesellschaft „Balkan" in Rom, S. Antonov, in Zusammenhang mit dem Attentat auf Papst Johannes Paul II. (13. 5. 1981).
Dezember	22.	Prozeßbeginn in Sofia gegen zwei italienische Staatsbürger wegen Spionage. (Am 14. 4. 1983 Verurteilung zu hohen Freiheitsstrafen, Freilassung am 5. 9. 1984).

1983

Januar	17.–21.	Besuch des libyschen Staatschefs M. el-Khadafi. Am 21. Unterzeichnung eines Vertrages über Freundschaft und Zusammenarbeit.
April	25.–27.	Besuch des griechischen Präsidenten K. Karamanlis.
Mai	1.	Neue Visa-Bestimmungen. Aufhebung des seit 1967 gültigen visafreien Verkehrs für Touristen.
Mai	26./27.	Besuch von Akademiemitglied G. Bliznakov bei Papst Johannes Paul II. Überreichung der Kliment-Ochridski-Medaille im Auftrag von T. Živkov.
Mai	29.	Preiserhöhungen für Fleisch, Fleischprodukte und Obst um bis zu 23 %.
Juli	6.	Auslieferung des Entführers eines türkischen Verkehrsflugzeugs an die Türkei.
Juli	13.–17.	Besuch von Bundesaußenminister H.-D. Genscher.
August	5./6.	Besuch des japanischen Außenministers S. Abe.
Oktober	21.	Besuch von Bundeswirtschaftsminister O. Graf Lambsdorff.
Oktober	22.	Empfang von SPD-Präsidiumsmitglied H.-J. Wischnewski durch T. Živkov.
Dezember	12.–15.	Besuch von T. Živkov in Indien.

1984

Januar	3.	Tagung der NSb und des ZK der BKP. Umfangreiche Veränderungen in Partei und Regierung.
Februar	15.–17.	Besuch von Außenminister P. Mladenov in Finnland. Unterzeichnung eines Abkommens für gegenseitige Förderung und Schutz von Investitionen.
Februar	25.–27.	Besuch von UN-Generalsekretär J. Perez de Cuellar.
Mai	9.	Tagung des NOK. Beschluß über die Nichtteilnahme an den XXIII. Olympischen Sommerspielen in Los Angeles wegen mangelhafter Sicherheitsvorkehrungen.
Mai	10./11.	Besuch von Außenminister P. Mladenov in der Bundesrepublik Deutschland.
Mai	11.	Empfang des SPD-Präsidiumsmitglieds E. Bahr durch T. Živkov.
Juni	15.–17.	Besuch des nordkoreanischen Staats- und Parteichefs Kim Il Sung. Unterzeichnung eines Abkommens über Freundschaft und Zusammenarbeit mit einer Laufzeit von 20 Jahren.
Juni	22.–26.	Besuch des stellv. Außenministers der VR China, Qian Qichen.
September	1.	Erhöhung der Mindestlöhne, Renten und Stipendien.
September	7.–11.	Besuch des ZK-Sekretärs der KPdSU M. S. Gorbačev.
September	9.	Absage eines für Monatsende geplanten Besuchs von T. Živkov in der Bundesrepublik Deutschland aufgrund der Stationierung amerikanischer Mittelstreckenraketen.
September	15.	Besuch des chinesischen Ministers für Außenhandelsbeziehungen Chen Muhua. Unterzeichnung eines Abkommens über wirtschaftliche und technische Zusammenarbeit mit der VR China.

Oktober	26.	Würdigung des Patriarchen der BPC, Maksim, für seine Verdienste durch T. Živkov.
Oktober	27.	Protest der bulgarischen Regierung gegen die Anklageerhebung gegen S. Antonov u. a. (s. 27.11.1982).
Oktober –November	30. 1.	Besuch von Bundesjustizminister H. Engelhard.
November	20.	Eröffnung eines neuen Grenzübergangs nach Griechenland bei Svilengrad.
Dezember	1./2.	Besuch des SPD-Vorsitzenden W. Brandt.
Dezember	31.	Wiederaufnahme diplomatischer Beziehungen zu Ägypten.

1985

Januar	16.	Schriftliche Botschaft des türkischen Präsidenten K. Evren: Forderung nach Überprüfung der erzwungenen Bulgarisierung türkischer Namen, der Schließung türkischer Schulen und des Verbots des Gebrauchs der türkischen Sprache in der Öffentlichkeit.
Februar	10./11.	Besuch des britischen Außenministers Sir G. Howe.
Februar	19.	Abberufung des türkischen Botschafters zu Konsultationen nach Ankara.
März	7./8.	Besuch von Bundesaußenminister H.-D. Genscher.
März	8.	Verweigerung der Einreise eines türkischen Fernsehteams durch die bulgarischen Behörden.
April	22.–25.	Besuch des finnischen Präsidenten M. Koivisto. Unterzeichnung eines Abkommens zur Vermeidung der Doppelbesteuerung.
April	26.	Verlängerung des Warschauer Vertrages (s. 14.5.1955).
April	28.–30.	Besuch von T. Živkov in Syrien. Unterzeichnung eines Vertrages über Freundschaft und Zusammenarbeit.
Juni	7.	Ausweisung des BTA-Korrespondenten aus der Türkei.
Juli	26.	Erklärung einer Gruppe bulgarischer Intellektueller und Persönlichkeiten des öffentlichen Lebens über die Freiwilligkeit der Bulgarisierung türkischer Namen.
Oktober	22.–25.	Besuch des sowjetischen Parteichefs M. S. Gorbačev.

1986

März	21.	Ernennung von G. Atanasov zum neuen Minpräs.
März	31.	Freispruch von S. Antonov sowie der beiden bulgarischen Mitangeklagten.
April	2.–5.	XIII. Parteitag der BKP. Annahme des 9. Fünfjahresplanes (1986–1990).
April	12.	Unterzeichnung eines Investitionsförderungsvertrages mit der Bundesrepublik Deutschland in Hannover.
Mai	19.–21.	Besuch von Außenminister P. Mladenov in Bonn.
Juni	8.	Wahlen zur IX. NSb. Wahlbeteiligung 99,92%. Stimmenanteil der OF 99,91%.
Dezember	15./16.	Besuch von Bundesaußenminister H.-D. Genscher.

1987

Juni	2.–5.	Besuch von T. Živkov in der Bundesrepublik Deutschland. Unterzeichnung eines Abkommens über Vermeidung von Doppelbesteuerung.
Juli	6.	Einstellung der Störungen der Sendungen der Deutschen Welle in bulgarischer Sprache.
Juli	16./17.	Besuch von Bundesaußenminister H.-D. Genscher. Austausch von Militärattachés.
August	5.–9.	Besuch von Bundeswirtschaftsminister M. Bangemann.
August	17.	Rede des türkischen Minpräs. T. Özal in Bursa. Erneuerung des Angebots der Aufnahme aller türkischen Emigranten aus Bulgarien.
August	18.	Billigung einer radikalen Regierungsumbildung und Wirtschaftsreform durch die NSb. Abschaffung der erst im Vorjahr gebildeten 4 „Räte" für Wirtschaft, Sozialwesen, Landwirtschaft und intellektuelle Entwicklung. Entlassung von 9 Ministern. Verringerung der 28 Verwaltungsbezirke auf 9.

Zeittafel 703

1988

Januar	28./29.	Nationalkonferenz der BKP. Bestätigung des Wirtschaftsreformkurses: Erhöhung des Entscheidungsspielraums der Betriebe, Einführung der Selbstverwaltung in Gemeinden und Betrieben.
Februar	22./23.	Besuch des griechischen Minpräs. A. Papandreou.
Februar	24.–26.	Außenministerkonferenz der Balkanstaaten in Belgrad. Am Rande der Konferenz Unterzeichnung eines Protokolls über die „Förderung der Beziehungen der guten Nachbarschaft, Freundschaft und Zusammenarbeit" zwischen Bulgarien und der Türkei.
Februar	25.	Unterzeichnung eines Abkommens mit der Bundesrepublik Deutschland in Bonn über die Zusammenarbeit bei wissenschaftlicher Forschung und technologischer Entwicklung.
Juli	19./20.	Sondersitzung des ZK der BKP: Rücktritt von S. Todorov und Ausschluß des möglichen Nachfolgers von T. Živkov, Č. Aleksandrov, aus dem Politbüro.
November	21.–24.	R. v. Weizsäcker besucht als erster Bundespräsident Bulgarien. Unterzeichnung von Abkommen über Doppelbesteuerung und Kulturinstitute.
November	25.	Anerkennung des palästinensischen Staates durch Bulgarien.

1989

Januar	18.–20.	Vizeaußenminister I. Ganev nimmt an einer Konferenz der Vizeaußenminister der sechs Balkanstaaten in Tirana teil. – Als erster französischer Präsident besucht F. Mitterand Bulgarien und nimmt die Ehrendoktorwürde der Universität Sofia entgegen.
Januar	27.	DS und Regierung beschließen die Senkung der Verteidigungsausgaben für 1989 um 12 % sowie eine personelle und technische Reduzierung der Streitkräfte.
April	14.	Der Vorsitzende des Komitees für Umweltschutz beim Ministerrat, Nikolaj Djulgerov, unterzeichnet in Bonn ein Umweltschutzabkommen mit der Bundesrepublik Deutschland.
Mai		Proteste der türkischen Minderheit gegen Zwangsassimilierung werden gewaltsam niedergeschlagen.
Mai	29.	Živkov fordert in einer Fernsehansprache die Türkei auf, alle ausreisewilligen „muslimischen Bulgaren" aufzunehmen. Mit Hilfe neuer Paßbestimmungen wird eine Ausreise- und Aussiedlungswelle von Türken in die Türkei organisiert.
August		Bis zu diesem Monat haben ca. 310 000 Türken Bulgarien verlassen.
August	21.	Schließung der Grenzen zu Bulgarien durch die Türkei.
September	11.	Bericht des RD: Beschluß des Politbüros der BKP über die „vollständige politische Rehabilitierung" von ca. 1 000 Opfern des Massenterrors Stalins, ihre posthume Wiederaufnahme in die BKP sowie die Zahlung von Entschädigungen an die Hinterbliebenen.
November	10.	Das ZK stürzt Živkov und wählt P. Mladenov zum neuen Generalsekretär der BKP.
November	17.	Die NSb wählt Mladenov zum DS-Vorsitzenden.
Dezember	2.	A. Dimitrov löst P. Tančev als Sekretär des BZNS ab, der seine Unterordnung unter die BKP aufgibt.
November/ Dezember		Auf mehreren Tagungen von ZK und NSb verlieren Živkovs Anhänger ihre Positionen; Živkov, sein Sohn Vladimir u.a. werden aus der BKP ausgeschlossen. – Massendemonstrationen für demokratische Reformen. – Die neue Führung kündigt den Verzicht auf den Führungsanspruch der BKP, einen Parteitag und freie Wahlen im Frühjahr, eine neue Verfassung und eine Untersuchung von Korruption und Machtmißbrauch der Ära Živkov an. – Massenproteste gegen Änderungen der Minderheitenpolitik.

Oberste Organe

(Stand: 15.12.1989)

Götz Mavius †, Hamburg
Michael Schmidt-Neke, Hamburg

A. Staatsoberhäupter: I. Zar – II. Regentschaftsrat – III. Präsident des Provisorischen Präsidiums der NRB – IV. Präsidium der Nationalversammlung – V. Staatsrat – B. Vorsitzende der Nationalversammlung – C. Regierungen – D. Führungsorgane der BRP(k) bzw. BKP: I. Parteitage – II. Erste bzw. Generalsekretäre – III. Mitglieder des Sekretariats des ZK – IV. Mitglieder des Politbüros

Aus Platzgründen mußten die Kabinettslisten auf einen Kernbestand wichtiger Ministerien und Staatskomitees reduziert werden. Auch konnten die häufigen Umbenennungen, Teilungen, Fusionen usw. der Ressorts nicht berücksichtigt werden; es wurden einheitliche Kurzbezeichnungen gewählt. Es wurde nicht zwischen Vize-Ministerpräsidenten und Ersten Vize-Ministerpräsidenten unterschieden.
Die Parteizugehörigkeit der Regierungsmitglieder wurde nur bis 1950 angegeben, da durch den 2. Kongreß der OF (2./3.2.1948) das System konkurrierender Parteien zugunsten des Systems der OF aufgehoben wurde, in deren Rahmen neben der BKP (bis Dezember 1948: BRP(k)) nur noch der BZNS fortbesteht.
Quellen: für alle Staatsorgane: Bălgarskite dăržavni institucii 1879–1986 – enciklopedičen spravočnik (Die bulgarischen Staatsinstitutionen 1879–1986 – Enzyklopädisches Nachschlagewerk). Sofia 1987; für die Kabinette auch: Kaser, K.: Handbuch der Regierungen Südosteuropas (1833–1980). Bd. 1. Graz 1981; für die Parteiführungen: Bell, J.D.: The Bulgarian Communist Party from Blagoev to Zhivkov. Stanford 1986, die Protokolle der Parteitage sowie die Berichte von RFE/RL.

A. Staatsoberhäupter

I. Zar (Car)

28.8.1943–15.9.1946 Simeon II. (geb. 16.6.1937)

II. Regentschaftsrat (Regentstvo)

9.9.1944–15.9.1946 Todor Pavlov, Venelin Ganev, Cvetko Boboševski

III. Präsident des Provisorischen Präsidiums der NRB (Predsedatel na Vremennoto predsedatelstvo na NRB)

Nach der Abschaffung der Monarchie durch das Plebizit vom 8.9.1946 und der Ausrufung der NRB durch die 26. NSb (15.9.1946) amtierte das Präsidium der NSb als Provisorisches Präsidium der NRB unter Leitung seines Präsidenten:
15.9.1946–9.12.1947 Vasil Kolarov

Oberste Organe 705

IV. Präsidium der Nationalversammlung (Prezidium na Narodnoto săbranie)

Staatsoberhaupt aufgrund der Verfassung vom 6.12.1947

9.12.1947–20.1.1950
Vorsitzender: Minčo Nejčev
Vize-Vorsitzende: Dimităr Nejkov, Kiril Klisurski, Petăr Popivanov (ab 9.2.1948)
Sekretär: Jordan Čobanov (bis 11.2.1949), Damjan Popchristov (ab 11.2.1949)

20.1.1950–10.1.1954
Vorsitzender: Minčo Nejčev (bis 28.5.1950), Georgi Damjanov (ab 28.5.1950)
Vize-Vorsitzende: Kiril Klisurski, Peko Takov
Sekretär: Minčo Minčev

10.1.1954–15.1.1958
Vorsitzender: Georgi Damjanov
Vize-Vorsitzende: Georgi Kulišev, Kiril Klisurski
Sekretär: Minčo Minčev

15.1.1958–17.3.1962
Vorsitzender: Georgi Damjanov (bis 28.11.1958), Dimităr Ganev (ab 1.12.1958)
Vize-Vorsitzende: Georgi Kulišev, Nikolaj Georgiev
Sekretär Tačo Daskalov

17.3.1962–12.3.1966
Vorsitzender: Dimităr Ganev (bis 20.4.1964), Georgi Trajkov (ab 23.4.1964)
Vize-Vorsitzende: Georgi Kulišev, Nikolaj Georgiev
Sekretär: Apostol Kolčev (bis 28.11.1962), Minčo Minčev (ab 28.11.1962)

12.3.1966–18.5.1971
Vorsitzender: Georgi Trajkov
Vize-Vorsitzende: Dančo Dimitrov, Georgi Kulišev
Sekretär: Minčo Minčev

V. Staatsrat (Dăržaven săvet)

Staatsoberhaupt aufgrund der Verfassung vom 18.5.1971
I. (9.7.1971–15.6.1976), II. (16.6.1976–16.6.1981), III. (17.6.1981–18.6.1986), IV. (ab 19.6.1986)

Vorsitzender: Todor Živkov (9.7.1971–17.11.1989), Petăr Mladenov (ab 17.11.1989)
Erste Stellvertretende Vorsitzende: Krăstju Tričkov (bis 15.6.1976), Georgi Trajkov (bis 1.11.1974), Petăr Tančev (1.11.1974–8.12.1989), Angel Dimitrov (ab 8.12.1989)
Stellvertretende Vorsitzende: Georgi Andreev (bis 30.4.1973), Georgi Džagarov (bis 14.12.1989), Ivan Popov (1.11.1974–15.6.1976), Mitko Grigorov (ab 1.11.1974), Peko Takov (bis 18.6.1986), Georgi Atanasov (17.6.1981–4.1.1984), Jaroslav Radev (17.6.1981–17.11.1989), Vasil Mračkov (ab 14.12.1989)
Sekretär: Minčo Minčev (bis 15.6.1976), Nikola Manolov (ab 16.6.1976)

Mitglieder:	I.	II.	III.	IV.
Angel Balevski	x	x	x	x
Angel Šiškov	x	x	x	
Boris Velčev	x	x		
Bojan Bălgaranov	x			
Vladimir Videnov	bis 1.11.1974			
Griša Filipov	x	x		bis 17.11.1989
Evgeni Mateev	ab 1.11.1974	x		
Elena Lagadinova	x	x	x	x
Ivan Michajlov	x	x		
Ivanka Dikova	x	x	x	
Kostadin Gjaurov	bis 4.7.1974			
Mitko Grigorov	bis 1.11.1974			
Mišo Mišev	ab 1.11.1974	x		
Nadja Asparuchova	x	x	x	
Nikolaj Georgiev	bis 28.4.1972			
Pando Vančev	x			
Penčo Kubadinski	ab 2.7.1975	x	x	x
Radi Kuzmanov	x		x	
Stojan Tončev	x	x		
Todor Stojčev	x	x		
Jaroslav Radev	ab 4.7.1974	x		
Aleksandăr Lilov		x	x	
Draža Vălčeva		bis 21.12.1977		
Emil Christov		x	x	
Živko Živkov		x	x	x
Lalju Gančev		x		
Pantelej Zarev		ab 20.12.1979	x	x
Cola Dragojčeva		x	x	
Angel Dimitrov			x	x
Vladimir Bonev			x	x
Krăstju Tričkov			x	
Milko Balev			ab 4.1.1984	bis 17.11.1989
Načo Papazov			ab 4.1.1984	17.11.–8.12.1989
Nikolaj Žišev			x	x
Ognjan Dojnov			bis 4.1.1984	
Petăr Djulgerov			x	x
Stanka Šopova			x	
Andrej Bundžulov				bis 17.11.1989
Asja A. Emilova				x
Boril Orlinov Kosev				x
Gin'o Ganev				x
Dimităr J. Dimitrov				x
Emilija M. Kostova				x
Ivan Panev				x
Jordan Jotov				x
Kostadin Džatev				x
Čudomir Aleksandrov				x
Janko Markov				x
Andrej Lukanov				ab 17.11.1989

B. Vorsitzende der Nationalversammlung (Predsedateli na Narodnoto săbranie)

Vasil Kolarov	15.12.1945–6.11.1946	Georgi Trajkov	7.7.1971–27.4.1972
Ferdinand Kozovski	1.2.1950–12.9.1965	Vladimir Bonev	27.4.1972–7.4.1981
Sava Ganovski	6.12.1965–18.5.1971	Stanko Todorov	ab 16.6.1981

C. Regierungen

Regierung Kimon Georgiev 9.9.1944–31.3.1946
(Zveno, BRP(k), BRSDP, BZNS, RP)

Ministerpräsident:	Kimon Georgiev (Zveno)
Äußeres:	Petko Stajnov (Zveno)
Inneres:	Anton Jugov (BRP(k))
Bildung:	Stančo Čolakov (Zveno) (bis 29.9.1945), Stojan Kosturkov (RP) (ab 29.9.1945)
Finanzen:	Petko Stojanov (parteilos) (bis 17.8.1945), Stančo Čolakov (Zveno) (ab 17.8.1945)
Justiz:	Minčo Nejčev (BRP(k))
Krieg:	Damjan Velčev (Zveno)
Handel:	Dimităr Nejkov (BRSDP)
Landwirtschaft:	Asen Pavlov (BZNS) (bis 17.8.1945), Aleksandăr Obbov (vorl.) (BZNS) (17.8.–29.9.1945), Michail Genovski (BZNS) (ab 29.9.1945)

Regierung Kimon Georgiev 31.3.–23.11.1946
(Zveno, BRP(k), BRSDP, BZNS, RP)

Ministerpräsident:	Kimon Georgiev (Zveno)
Vize-Ministerpräsidenten:	Trajčo Kostov (BRP(k)), Aleksandăr Obbov (BZNS)
Äußeres:	Georgi Kulišev (Zveno)
Inneres:	Anton Jugov (BRP(k))
Bildung:	Stojan Kosturkov (RP)
Finanzen:	Ivan Stefanov (BRP(k))
Justiz:	Ljuben Kolarov (BZNS)
Krieg:	Damjan Velčev (Zveno) (bis 25.9.1946), Kimon Georgiev (Zveno) (ab 25.9.1946)
Handel:	Dimităr Nejkov (BRSDP)
Landwirtschaft:	Aleksandăr Obbov (BZNS)
Industrie:	Christo Lilkov (Zveno)

Regierung Georgi Dimitrov 23.11.1946–11.12.1947
(BRP(k), Zveno, BRSDP, BZNS)

Ministerpräsident:	Georgi Dimitrov (BRP(k))
Vize-Ministerpräsidenten:	Kimon Georgiev (Zveno), Aleksandăr Obbov (BZNS), Georgi Popov (BRSDP), Trajčo Kostov (BRP(k))
Äußeres:	Kimon Georgiev (Zveno)
Inneres:	Anton Jugov (BRP(k))
Bildung:	Minčo Nejčev (BRP(k))
Finanzen:	Ivan Stefanov (BRP(k))
Justiz:	Radi Najdenov (BZNS)
Krieg:	Georgi Damjanov (BRP(k))
Landwirtschaft:	Georgi Trajkov (BZNS)
Industrie:	Christo Lilkov (Zveno)
Handel:	Jordan Božilov (BRP(k))

Regierung Georgi Dimitrov 11.12.1947–20.7.1949
(BRP(k) (= ab Dezember 1948 BKP), BZNS, Zveno, BRSDP)

Ministerpräsident:	Georgi Dimitrov (BKP) (bis 2.7.1949), Vasil Kolarov (BKP) (vorl.) (ab 2.7.1949)
Vize-Ministerpräsidenten:	Trajčo Kostov (BKP) (bis 31.3.1949), Vasil Kolarov (BKP), Kimon Georgiev (Zveno), Georgi Trajkov (BZNS), Georgi Popov (BRSDP)
Äußeres:	Vasil Kolarov (BKP)
Inneres:	Anton Jugov (BKP)
Bildung:	Kiril Dramaliev (BKP)
Finanzen:	Ivan Stefanov (BKP)
Justiz:	Radi Najdenov (BZNS)
Verteidigung:	Georgi Damjanov (BKP)
Landwirtschaft:	Georgi Trajkov (BZNS)
Industrie:	Petko Kunin (BKP)
Außenhandel:	Dimităr Ganev (BKP) (ab 30.12.1948)
Plankomitee:	Dobri Terpešev (BKP)
Staatskontrollkomitee:	Georgi Čankov (BKP) (bis 9.2.1949), Dimo Dičev (BKP) (ab 9.2.1949)

Regierung Vasil Kolarov 20.7.1949–20.1.1950

Ministerpräsident:	Vasil Kolarov
Vize-Ministerpräsidenten:	Kimon Georgiev, Georgi Trajkov, Vălko Červenkov, Dobri Terpešev, Anton Jugov
Äußeres:	Vasil Kolarov (bis 6.8.1949), Vladimir Poptomov (ab 6.8.1949)
Inneres:	Anton Jugov (bis 6.8.1949), Rusi Christozov (ab 6.8.1949)
Bildung:	Kiril Dramaliev
Finanzen:	Ivan Stefanov (bis 6.8.1949), Petko Kunin (6.8.–8.10.1949), Kiril Lazarov (vorl.) (8.10.–5.12.1949), Kiril Lazarov (ab 5.12.1949)
Justiz:	Radi Najdenov
Verteidigung:	Georgi Damjanov
Landwirtschaft:	Georgi Trajkov
Industrie:	Petko Kunin (bis 6.8.1949), Vălko Gočev (ab 6.8.1949)
Außenhandel:	Dimităr Ganev
Plankomitee:	Dobri Terpešev (bis 6.8.1949), Kiril Lazarov (6.8.–5.12.1949), Karlo Lukanov (ab 5.12.1949)
Staatskontrollkomitee:	Dimo Dičev

Regierung Vasil Kolarov 20.1.–3.2.1950

Ministerpräsident:	Vasil Kolarov (bis 23.1.1950), Vălko Červenkov (vorl.) (ab 23.1.1950)
Vize-Ministerpräsidenten:	Vălko Červenkov, Vladimir Poptomov, Rajko Damjanov, Georgi Trajkov
Äußeres:	Vladimir Poptomov
Inneres:	Rusi Christozov
Bildung:	Kiril Dramaliev
Finanzen:	Kiril Lazarov
Justiz:	Radi Najdenov
Verteidigung:	Georgi Damjanov
Außenhandel:	Dimităr Ganev
Landwirtschaft:	Titko Černokolev
Industrie:	Anton Jugov
Plankomitee:	Karlo Lukanov
Staatskontrollkomitee:	Dimo Dičev

Regierung Vălko Červenkov 3.2.1950–16.1.1954

Ministerpräsident:	Vălko Červenkov
Vize-Ministerpräsidenten:	Vladimir Poptomov, Rajko Damjanov, Georgi Trajkov, Georgi Čankov (ab 13.11.1950), Ivan Michajlov (ab 4.1.1951), Anton Jugov (ab 20.8.1952), Karlo Lukanov (ab 28.2.1952)
Äußeres:	Vladimir Poptomov (bis 28.5.1950), Minčo Nejčev (ab 28.5.1950)
Inneres:	Rusi Christozov (bis 6.1.1951), Georgi Cankov (ab 6.1.1951)
Bildung:	Kiril Dramaliev (bis 4.2.1952), Demir Janev (ab 4.2.1952)
Finanzen:	Kiril Lazarov
Justiz:	Radi Najdenov
Verteidigung:	Georgi Damjanov (bis 28.5.1950), Petăr Pančevski (ab 28.5.1950)
Außenhandel:	Dimităr Ganev (bis 3.9.1952), Živko Živkov (ab 3.9.1952)
Landwirtschaft:	Titko Černokolev (bis 22.6.1951), Nikola Stojanov (22.6.1951–3.9.1952), Stanko Todorov (ab 3.9.1952)
Industrie:	Anton Jugov (bis 20.8.1952), Tano Colov (ab 20.8.1952)
Plankomitee:	Karlo Lukanov (bis 28.2.1952), Evgeni Mateev (28.2.–26.12.1952), Georgi Čankov (ab 26.12.1952)
Staatskontrollkomitee:	Dimo Dičev

Regierung Vălko Červenkov 16.1.1954–18.4.1956

Ministerpräsident:	Vălko Červenkov
Vize-Ministerpräsidenten:	Anton Jugov, Georgi Trajkov, Georgi Čankov, Ivan Michajlov, Rajko Damjanov
Äußeres:	Minčo Nejčev
Inneres:	Georgi Cankov
Justiz:	Radi Najdenov
Außenhandel:	Živko Živkov
Verteidigung:	Petăr Pančevski
Landwirtschaft:	Stanko Todorov
Industrie:	Tano Colov
Finanzen:	Kiril Lazarov
Bildung:	Demir Janev
Plankomitee:	Georgi Čankov
Staatskontrollkomitee:	Dimo Dičev

Regierung Anton Jugov 18.4.1956–15.1.1958

Ministerpräsident:	Anton Jugov
Vize-Ministerpräsidenten:	Georgi Trajkov, Georgi Čankov (bis 17.7.1957), Ivan Michajlov, Rajko Damjanov (bis 17.7.1957), Vălko Červenkov, Karlo Lukanov
Äußeres:	Minčo Nejčev (bis 11.8.1956), Karlo Lukanov (ab 20.8.1956)
Inneres:	Georgi Cankov
Justiz:	Radi Najdenov
Außenhandel:	Živko Živkov (bis 1.2.1957)
Handel:	Rajko Damjanov (1.2.–17.7.1957), Boris Taskov (ab 17.7.1957)
Verteidigung:	Petăr Pančevski
Landwirtschaft:	Stanko Todorov (bis 17.7.1957), Ivan Prămov (ab 17.7.1957)
Industrie:	Tano Colov
Finanzen:	Kiril Lazarov
Bildung:	Demir Janev (bis 1.2.1957), Vălko Červenkov (ab 1.2.1957)
Plankomitee:	Georgi Čankov (bis 30.12.1956), Rusi Christozov (ab 30.12.1956)
Staatskontrollkomitee:	Dimo Dičev (bis 1.2.1957)

Regierung Anton Jugov 15.1.1958–17.3.1962

Ministerpräsident:	Anton Jugov
Vize-Ministerpräsidenten:	Rajko Damjanov, Georgi Trajkov, Vălko Červenkov (bis 9.12.1961), Ivan Michajlov, Stanko Todorov (ab 25.12.1959), Živko Živkov, Kimon Georgiev
Äußeres:	Karlo Lukanov
Inneres:	Georgi Cankov
Finanzen:	Kiril Lazarov
Justiz:	Radi Najdenov
Bildung:	Vălko Červenkov (bis 9.6.1958), Živko Živkov (9.6.–25.12.1958), Načo Papazov (ab 25.12.1958)
Verteidigung:	Petăr Pančevski (bis 9.6.1958), Ivan Michajlov (ab 9.6.1958)
Handel:	Boris Taskov (bis 16.3.1959), Rajko Damjanov (16.3.–25.12.1959)
Außenhandel:	Georgi Kumbiliev (ab 25.12.1959)
Landwirtschaft:	Ivan Prămov
Plankomitee:	Rusi Christozov (bis 25.12.1959), Stanko Todorov (ab 25.12.1959)
Staatskontrollkomitee:	Ninko Stefanov (ab 16.3.1959)

Regierung Anton Jugov 17.3.–27.11.1962

Ministerpräsident:	Anton Jugov (bis 20.11.1962), Todor Živkov (vorl.) (ab 20.11.1962)
Vize-Ministerpräsidenten:	Rajko Damjanov, Georgi Trajkov, Ivan Michajlov, Georgi Cankov (bis 20.11.1962), Stanko Todorov, Živko Živkov
Äußeres:	Karlo Lukanov
Inneres:	Diko Dikov
Bildung:	Načo Papazov (bis 27.9.1962), Gančo Ganev (ab 27.9.1962)
Finanzen:	Kiril Lazarov
Justiz:	Petăr Tančev
Verteidigung:	Dobri Džurov
Außenhandel:	Lăčezar Avramov
Landwirtschaft:	Ivan Prămov
Plankomitee:	Stanko Todorov (bis 27.9.1962), Živko Živkov (ab 27.9.1962)
Staatskontrollkomitee:	Ninko Stefanov

Regierung Todor Živkov 27.11.1962–12.3.1966

Ministerpräsident:	Todor Živkov
Vize-Ministerpräsidenten:	Živko Živkov, Georgi Trajkov, Stanko Todorov, Tano Colov, Ivan Michajlov, Penčo Kubadinski
Äußeres:	Ivan Bašev
Inneres:	Diko Dikov
Verteidigung:	Dobri Džurov
Finanzen:	Dimităr Popov
Außenhandel:	Ivan Budinov
Justiz:	Petăr Tančev
Bildung:	Gančo Ganev
Plankomitee:	Apostol Pašev
Staatskontrollkomitee:	Boris Velčev (bis 22.7.1965), Ninko Stefanov (ab 22.7.1965)

Regierung Todor Živkov 12.3.1966–9.7.1971

Ministerpräsident:	Todor Živkov
Vize-Ministerpräsidenten:	Živko Živkov, Ivan Michajlov, Stanko Todorov (bis 22.11.1966), Lăčezar Avramov (22.11.1966–28.4.1971), Petăr Tančev, Tano Colov, Penčo Kubadinski

Oberste Organe

Äußeres:	Ivan Bašev
Inneres:	Diko Dikov (bis 27.12.1968), Angel Solakov (ab 27.12.1968)
Verteidigung:	Dobri Džurov
Finanzen:	Dimităr Popov
Außenhandel:	Ivan Budinov (bis 27.12.1968), Lăčezar Avramov (27.12.1968–28.4.1971), Ivan Nedev (ab 28.4.1971)
Justiz:	Svetla Daskalova
Bildung:	Gančo Ganev (bis 27.12.1968), Stefan Vasilev (ab 27.12.1968)
Landwirtschaft:	Nikola Palagačev (bis 27.12.1968), Vălkan Šopov (ab 27.12.1968)
Plankomitee:	Apostol Pašev (bis 27.12.1968), Tano Colov (ab 27.12.1968)
Staatskontrollkomitee:	Ninko Stefanov

Regierung Stanko Todorov 9.7.1971–15.6.1976
(Die Regierung blieb noch bis zur Neubildung des Ministerrats am 17.6.1976 geschäftsführend im Amt.)

Ministerpräsident:	Stanko Todorov
Vize-Ministerpräsidenten:	Tano Colov, Petăr Tančev (bis 1.11.1974), Penčo Kubadinski (bis 21.11.1974), Živko Živkov, Ivan Popov (bis 1.11.1974), Sava Dălbokov (bis 19.1.1973), Mako Dakov, Venelin Kocev (3.7.1972–4.7.1974), Ivan Iliev (ab 19.1.1973), Ognjan Dojnov (1.11.1974–23.4.1976), Kiril Zarev (ab 15.4.1975)
Äußeres:	Ivan Bašev (bis 13.12.1971), Petăr Mladenov (ab 17.12.1971)
Inneres:	Angel Canev (bis 7.4.1973), Dimităr Stojanov (ab 7.4.1973)
Finanzen:	Dimităr Popov
Verteidigung:	Dobri Džurov
Außenhandel:	Janko Markov
Justiz:	Svetla Daskalova
Bildung:	Stefan Vasilev (bis 19.1.1973), Nenčo Stanev (ab 19.1.1973)
Landwirtschaft:	Vălkan Šopov (bis 23.10.1973), Gančo Krăstev (ab 23.10.1973)
Plankomitee:	Sava Dălbokov (bis 19.1.1973), Ivan Iliev (19.1.1973–15.4.1975), Kiril Zarev (ab 15.4.1975)
Staatskontrollkomitee:	dem DS unterstellt

Regierung Stanko Todorov 17.6.1976–18.6.1981

Ministerpräsident:	Stanko Todorov
Vize-Ministerpräsidenten:	Tano Colov, Todor Božinov (ab 29.4.1979), Sava Dălbokov (28.9.1976–28.4.1978), Krăstju Tričkov, Kiril Zarev, Grigor Stoičkov (ab 12.5.1977), Mako Dakov (bis 28.4.1978), Andrej Lukanov, Georgi Jordanov (ab 29.4.1979), Stamen Stamenov (ab 26.2.1980), Draža Vălčeva (ab 28.12.1979)
Äußeres:	Petăr Mladenov
Inneres:	Dimităr Stojanov
Finanzen:	Belčo Belčev
Verteidigung:	Dobri Džurov
Bildung:	Nenčo Stanev (bis 15.11.1977), Draža Vălčeva (15.11.1977–28.12.1979), Aleksandăr Fol (ab 28.12.1979)
Landwirtschaft:	Gančo Krăstev (bis 28.4.1978), Grigor Stoičkov (28.4.1978–29.4.1979)
Außenhandel:	Ivan Nedev (bis 4.2.1977), Christo Christov (ab 4.2.1977)
Justiz:	Svetla Daskalova
Plankomitee:	Kiril Zarev
Staatskontrollkomitee:	Krăstju Tričkov

Regierung Griša Filipov 18.6.1981–24.3.1986

Ministerpräsident:	Griša Filipov
Vize-Ministerpräsidenten:	Todor Božinov (bis 28.1.1986), Čudomir Aleksandrov (4.1.1984–28.1.1986), Stojan Markov (ab 28.1.1986), Andrej Lukanov, Georgi Jordanov (bis 28.1. und ab 21.2.1986), Georgi Karamanev (19.7.1982–28.1.1986 und ab 21.2.1986), Grigor Stoičkov (bis 28.1.1986), Ivan Iliev (ab 18.10.1985), Kiril Zarev (bis 4.1.1984), Ognjan Dojnov (ab 21.2.1986), Stamen Stamenov (bis 26.8.1981), Staniš Bonev (bis 18.10.1985)
Äußeres:	Petăr Mladenov
Inneres:	Dimităr Stojanov
Verteidigung:	Dobri Džurov
Finanzen:	Belčo Belčev
Justiz:	Svetla Daskalova
Bildung:	Aleksandăr Fol
Außenhandel:	Christo Christov
Plankomitee:	Kiril Zarev (bis 19.7.1982), Staniš Bonev (19.7.1982–18.10.1985), Ivan Iliev (ab 18.10.1985)
Staatskontrollkomitee:	dem DS unterstellt

Regierung Georgi Atanasov 24.3.1986–19.6.1986

Ministerpräsident:	Georgi Atanasov
Vize-Ministerpräsidenten:	Stojan Markov, Andrej Lukanov, Georgi Jordanov, Georgi Karamanev, Ivan Iliev, Ognjan Dojnov
Äußeres:	Petăr Mladenov
Inneres:	Dimităr Stojanov
Verteidigung:	Dobri Džurov
Finanzen:	Belčo Belčev
Justiz:	Svetla Daskalova
Bildung:	Ilčo Dimitrov
Außenhandel:	Christo Christov
Landwirtschaft:	Aleksi Ivanov
Plankomitee:	Ivan Iliev
Staatskontrollkomitee:	Georgi Georgiev

Regierung Georgi Atanasov 19.6.1986 –

Ministerpräsident:	Georgi Atanasov
Vize-Ministerpräsidenten:	Andrej Lukanov (bis 18.8.1987), Stojan Markov (bis 18.8.1987), Grigor Stoičkov (bis 8.12.1989), Kiril Zarev (bis 18.8.1987 und ab 17.11.1989), Georgi Jordanov (4.7.–8.12.1989), Petko Dančev (4.7.–17.11.1989), Georgi Pirinski (ab 17.11.1989), Stojan Michajlov (ab 17.11.1989), Minčo Jovčev (ab 17.11.1989)
Vize-Ministerpräsident und Vorsitzender des Rates für	
– Wirtschaft:	Ognjan Dojnov (bis 18.8.1987)
– Soziales:	Georgi Karamanev (bis 18.8.1987)
– geistige Entwicklung:	Georgi Jordanov (bis 18.8.1987)
– Land- und Forstwirtschaft:	Aleksi Ivanov (25.12.1986–18.8.1987)
Äußeres:	Petăr Mladenov (bis 17.11.1989), Bojko Dimitrov (ab 17.11.1989)
Inneres:	Dimităr Stojanov (bis 15.12.1988), Georgi Tanev (ab 15.12.1988)
Verteidigung:	Dobri Džurov
Finanzen:	Belčo Belčev (bis 18.8.1987 und ab 17.11.1989)
Bildung:	Ilčo Dimitrov (bis 18.8.1987), Georgi Jordanov (bis 4.7.1989)
Justiz:	Svetla Daskalova, Asen Chadžiolov (ab 4.7.1989)

Oberste Organe

Landwirtschaft: Aleksi Ivanov (bis 25.12.1986 und 18.8.1987–15.12.1988), Georgi Menov (ab 15.12.1988)
Handel: Christo Christov (bis 18.8.1987), Ivan Špatov (ab 17.11.1989)
Außenhandel: Andrej Lukanov (18.8.1987–17.11.1989), Christo Christov (ab 17.11.1989)
Wirtschaft und Planung: Stojan Ovčarov (18.8.1987–17.11.1989), Kiril Zarev (ab 17.11.1989)
Plankomitee: Ivan Iliev (bis 18.8.1987)
Staatskontrollkomitee: Georgi Georgiev
Vorsitzender des Rats für Erziehung, Wissenschaft und Kultur: Aleksandăr Fol (4.7.–17.11.1989)

D. Führungsorgane der BRP(k) bzw. BKP

I. Parteitage

	Sekretäre des ZK (ohne den Ersten Sekretär)	Mitglieder des Sekretariats	Politbüro-Vollmitglieder	Politbüro-Kandidaten	ZK-Vollmitglieder	ZK-Kandidaten
8. ZK-Plenum (27.2.–1.3.1945)	2	/	13	3	39	11
V. Parteitag (18.–25.12.1948)	2	/	9	3		
VI. Parteitag (28.2.–3.3.1954)	2	/	9	2		
VII. Parteitag (2.–7.6.1958)	5	/	11	3	89	48
VIII. Parteitag (5.–14.11.1962)	5	/	9	3	110	
IX. Parteitag (14.–19.11.1966)	5	3	11	7		
X. Parteitag (20.–25.4.1971)	6	2	11	6	147	110
XI. Parteitag (29.3.–2.4.1976)	5	4	9	6	154	121
XII. Parteitag (31.3.–4.4.1981)	10	/	12	3	197	139
XIII. Parteitag (2.–5.4.1986)	9	/	11	6	195	145

II. Erste bzw. Generalsekretäre

Trajčo Kostov	Erster Sekretär 2.1945–12.1948
Georgi Dimitrov	Vorsitzender des ZK 3.1945–12.1948
	Generalsekretär 12.1948–7.1949
Vasil Kolarov	(vorl.) Generalsekretär 7.1949–1.1950
Vălko Červenkov	(vorl.) Generalsekretär 1.1950–11.1950
	Generalsekretär 11.1950–3.1954
Todor Živkov	Erster Sekretär 3.1954–4.1981
	Generalsekretär 4.1981–11.1989
Petăr Mladenov	Generalsekretär 11.1989–

III. Mitglieder des Sekretariats des ZK

	8. erw. Plenum 27.2.–1.3. 1945	5. PT 18.–25.12. 1948	6. PT 28.2.–3.3. 1954	7. PT 2.–7.6. 1958	8. PT 5.–14.11. 1962	9. PT 14.–19.11. 1966	10. PT 20.–26.4. 1971	11. PT 29.3.–2.4. 1976	12. PT 31.3.–4.4. 1981	13. PT 2.–5.4. 1986
Georgi Čankov	x									
Vălko Červenkov	x									
Georgi Damjanov	x 46									
Trajčo Kostov	x bis 2.45									
Nikola Pavlov	x ab 11.46									
Petko Kunin	x ab 11.46									
Dimităr Dimov		x bis 10.49								
Ruben Avramov		x								
Georgi Cankov		x 10.49–50								
Todor Živkov		x 50								
Ivan Rajkov		x ab 1.50								
Enčo Stajkov		x ab 1.50								
Dimităr Ganev		x ab 12.52	x 4.56–7.57							
Boris Taskov		x ab 4.52	x	x bis 59						
Bojan Bălgaranov			x bis 7.57							
Dančo Dimitrov			x ab 4.56	x bis 12.59						
Stanko Todorov			x ab 7.57	x	x	x bis 5.67, o ab 5.67				
Mitko Grigorov			x ab 7.57	x	x	x	x bis 7.71			
Penčo Kubadinski					x	x	x			
Lăčezar Avramov				x ab 12.59	x	x				
Načo Papazov				x ab 12.59	x		x bis 7.72	o ab 12.77		
Boris Velčev							x	x bis 5.77		
Tano Colov							x bis 7.72			
Venelin Kocev					x ab 11.62		x bis 7.72	x bis 7.78		
Ivan Prămov						o ab 12.68	x			
Georgi Bokov						o bis 12.68				
Stojan Gjurov						o ab 12.68				
Stefan Vasilev						o ab 67				
Roza Koritarova							o	o		
Vladimir Bonev							x bis 7.74			
Ivan Abadžiev							x ab 7.71	x		
Penju Kiracov								x	x bis 3.86	
Ognjan Dojnov							x ab 2.72	x	x bis 3.82	
Griša Filipov							x ab 7.72	x	x 3.86–11.89	
Konstantin Tellalov										
Aleksandăr Lilov									x bis 9.83	

	8. erw. Plenum 27.2.–1.3. 1945	5. PT 18.–25.12. 1948	6. PT 28.2.–3.3. 1954	7. PT 2.–7.6. 1958	8. PT 5.–14.11. 1962	9. PT 14.–19.11. 1966	10. PT 20.–26.4. 1971	11. PT 29.3.–2.4. 1976	12. PT 31.3.–4.4. 1981	13. PT 2.–5.4. 1986
Sava Dǎlbokov							o ab 1.73	o bis 10.76		
Mišo Mišev							o ab 9.74	o x ab 7.79	x bis 2.84	
Georgi Jordanov							o ab 7.72	o bis 7.79		
Dimitǎr Staniše v								x ab 5.77, x ab 12.77	x	
Petǎr Djulgerov								o ab 5.77, x ab 12.77		
Georgi Atanasov								x ab 12.77	x ab 3.86	x bis 7.88
Todor Božinov								x 7.78–7.79	x	x bis 11.89
Stojan Michajlov								x ab 7.78	x	x bis 7.88
Milko Balev								x ab 7.79	x bis 1.84, x ab 1.86	
Čudomir Aleksandrov									x	x bis 11.89
Vasil Canov										x bis 6.86
Kiril Zarev									x ab 3.82	x bis 11.89
Emil Christov									x ab 1.84	x bis 11.89
Jordan Jotov									x ab 3.86	x 12.88–11.89
Dimitǎr Stojanov										x ab 11.89
Andrej Lukanov										x 11.89–12.89
Načo Papazov										x ab 11.89
Prodan Stojanov										x ab 11.89
Dimo Uzunov										x ab 12.89

IV. Mitglieder des Politbüros

	8. erw. Plenum 27.2.–1.3. 1945	5. PT 18.–25.12. 1948	6. PT 28.2.–3.3. 1954	7. PT 2.–7.6. 1958	8. PT 5.–14.11. 1962	9. PT 14.–19.11. 1966	10. PT 20.–26.4. 1971	11. PT 29.3.–2.4. 1976	12. PT 31.3.–4.4. 1981	13. PT 2.–5.4. 1986
Georgi Čankov	x	x	x bis 7.57							
Rajko Damjanov	x	o, x ab 8.49 x bis 7.49	x	x						
Georgi Dimitrov	x									
Cola Dragojčeva	x	o ab 8.49	x ab 7.57	x						
Dimitǎr Ganev	x	x bis 1.50			x bis 4.64	x				
Vasil Kolarov	x						x		x bis 1.84	
Trajčo Kostov	x	x bis 3.49						x		
Petko Kunin	x									

IV. Mitglieder des Politbüros

	8. erw. Plenum 27.2.–1.3. 1945	5. PT 18.–25.12. 1948	6. PT 28.2.–3.3. 1954	7. PT 2.–7.6. 1958	8. PT 5.–14.11. 1962	9. PT 14.–19.11. 1966	10. PT 20.–26.4. 1971	11. PT 29.3.–2.4. 1976	12. PT 31.3.–4.4. 1981	13. PT 2.–5.4. 1986
Vălko Červenkov	x	x	x	x bis 11.61						
Georgi Damjanov	x	x	x	x bis 11.58						
Vladimir Poptomov	x	x bis 5.52								
Dobri Terpešev	x	x bis 1.50	x	x						
Anton Jugov	x	o, x 8.49–51								
Titko Černokolev	o	o ab 8.49								
Dimităr Dimov		o	o ab 8.49	o	o	o bis 2.68				
Gočo Grozev	o									
Minčo Nejčev	o	o, x ab 8.49								
Ivan Michajlov			x	x	x	x	x	x		
Enčo Stajkov		x ab 51	x	x	x					
Georgi Cankov		o ab 11.50, x ab 51	x	x	x	x	x	x	x	x bis 11.89
Todor Živkov			x	x	x	x	x	x	x	
Petăr Pančevski			o							
Todor Prachov			o							
Boris Taskov			x ab 7.57	x bis 4.59						
Bojan Bălgaranov			x ab 7.57	x	x	x	x bis 12.72			
Mladen Stojanov			o ab 7.57	o						
Mitko Grigorov				x ab 11.61	x	x	x			
Stanko Todorov				o ab 12.59, x 11.61–7.88	x	x	x	x	x	x bis 7.88
Boris Velčev					x	x	x	x bis 5.77		
Živko Živkov					x	x	x	x	x	x bis 12.89
Penčo Kubadinski					o	x	x	x	x	
Tano Colov					o	x	x			
Todor Pavlov						x	x			
Ivan Popov						x	x bis 7.74			
Ivan Abadžiev						o	o bis 7.74			
Lăčezar Avramov						o	x			
Kostadin Gjaurov						o	o bis 7.74	o, x ab 7.79	x bis 3.82	
Peko Takov								o		
Krăstju Tričkov						o	o bis 7.73			
Angel Canev						o	o bis 7.74			
Venelin Kocev										

Oberste Organe   717

Name				
Aleksandăr Lilov	x ab 7.74	x	x bis 9.83	x ab 12.89
Dobri Džurov	o ab 7.74			x
Petăr Mladenov		o, x ab 12.77	x	x
Draža Vălčeva	o ab 7.74	o, x ab 12.77		
Todor Stojčev	o ab 7.74	o		
Todor Božinov		o		
Ognjan Dojnov		x ab 7.79	x bis 1.86	
Ljudmila Živkova		x ab 12.79	x	
Petăr Djulgerov		x ab 7.79	x bis 7.81	
Andrej Lukanov			o	o, x ab 11.89
Georgi Jordanov		o ab 7.79	o	o bis 12.89
Milko Balev			o	x bis 11.89
Jordan Jotov			x ab 3.82	x bis 12.89
Čudomir Aleksandrov			x ab 1.84	x bis 7.88
Georgi Atanasov			x ab 1.84, o ab 1.84	x
Staniš Bonev			x ab 3.86	
Dimităr Stojanov			o 1.84–1.86, o ab 1.84	o, x 12.88–11.89
Grigor Stoičkov			o ab 1.84	o bis 12.89
Stojan Markov			o ab 1.86	o bis 12.88
Ivan Panev				x 12.88–12.89
Stojan Ovčarov				o 12.88–11.89
Petko Dančev				o 12.88–11.89
Načo Papazov				x 11.89–12.89
Pantelej Pačov				x ab 11.89
Minčo Jovčev				x ab 11.89
Dimităr Stanišev				o ab 11.89
Ivan Stanev				o ab 11.89
Ivan Ivanov				o ab 12.89
Petko Petkov				o ab 12.89
Belčo Belčev				x ab 12.89

Zeichen:
x = ZK-Sekretär bzw. Vollmitglied des Politbüros
o = Mitglied des ZK-Sekretariats bzw. Kandidat des Politbüros

Verträge

Christa Jessel-Holst, Hamburg

I. Vorbemerkung – II. Recht der völkerrechtlichen Verträge – III. Menschenrechte – IV. Internationale Organisationen: 1. Universale Organisationen: a) Vereinte Nationen – b) Sonderorganisationen der Vereinten Nationen – c) Sonstige Organisationen der „UN-Familie" – 2. Regionale Organisationen: a) RGW – b) Spezialorganisationen des RGW – V. Bündnisverträge: 1. Multilaterale Verträge – 2. Bilaterale Verträge – VI. Politische Kooperationsverträge – VII. Konsularabkommen – VIII. Rechtshilfeabkommen: 1. Universale Abkommen – 2. Regionale Abkommen – 3. Bilaterale Abkommen – IX. Staatsangehörigkeitsabkommen – X. Doppelbesteuerungsabkommen: 1. Multilaterale Abkommen – 2. Bilaterale Abkommen – XI. Investitionsschutzabkommen – XII. Grenz- und Visumabkommen

Abkürzungen

iK	– in Kraft
Izv.	– Izvestija na Prezidiuma na Narodnoto Săbranie (Mitteilungen des Präsidiums der NSb) (Gesetzblatt 1.12.1952–30.12.1962)
MS	– Ministerrat (Ministerski săvet)
o. A.	– ohne Angabe
unveröff.	– im Gesetzblatt nicht veröffentlicht
VO	– Verordnung

I. Vorbemerkung

Auskunft über Staatsverträge mit bulgarischer Beteiligung in bulgarischer Sprache gibt (neben dem Gesetzblatt DV) das periodisch erscheinende Werk *Spravočnik po zakonodatelstvoto na Narodna republika Bălgarija* (Handbuch der Gesetzgebung der NRB). Unter dem Stichwort *Meždunarodni dogovori* (Internationale Verträge) werden, nach Ländern geordnet, die bilateralen und anschließend für die jeweiligen Sachgruppen die multilateralen Abkommen mit Titel und Fundstelle im Gesetzblatt aufgeführt. Die Zeitschrift *WGO. Monatshefte für Osteuropäisches Recht* bringt einmal jährlich eine Zusammenstellung der internationalen Abkommen Bulgariens aus dem Vorjahr in deutscher Sprache. Ergänzend ist auch auf die in französisch von P. Dičeva verfaßte Übersicht *Accords multilatéraux et organisations intergouvernementales* hinzuweisen, die in dem Band: Droit international privé et public. Recueil d'études et de documentation, édité en collaboration avec l'Union des travailleurs scientifiques de Bulgarie. Hrsg. v. Association bulgare de droit international. Sofia 1978, S. 347–402, erschienen ist.

II. Recht der völkerrechtlichen Verträge[1])

Wiener Übereinkommen über das Recht der Verträge v. 23.5.1969, iK: 21.5.1987. DV. (1987) 14 u. 87.

Wiener Übereinkommen über das Recht der Verträge zwischen staatlichen und internationalen Organisationen oder zwischen internationalen Organisationen v. 21.3.1986. DV. (1987) 71.

III. Menschenrechte

Konvention über die Verhütung und Bestrafung des Völkermordes v. 9.12.1948, ik: 12.1.1951. DV. (1950) 153.

Übereinkommen von New York über die politischen Rechte der Frau v. 31.3.1953, iK: 7.7.1954 (unveröff.).

Zusatzübereinkommen über die Abschaffung der Sklaverei, des Sklavenhandels und sklavereiähnlicher Einrichtungen und Praktiken v. 7.9.1956, iK: 21.8.1958. Izv. (1958) 47 u. 64.

Übereinkommen über die Staatsangehörigkeit verheirateter Frauen v. 20.2.1957, iK: 20.9.1960. Izv. (1960) 37.

Übereinkommen Nr. 111 der ILO über die Diskriminierung in Beschäftigung und Beruf v. 25.6.1958, iK: 22.7.1961. Izv. (1960) 46.

Übereinkommen gegen Diskriminierung im Unterrichtswesen v. 14.12.1960, iK: 4.3.1963. DV. (1963) 6.

Internationales Übereinkommen zur Beseitigung jeder Form von Rassendiskriminierung v. 7.3.1966, iK: 4.1.1969. DV. (1966) 51.

Internationaler Pakt über bürgerliche und politische Rechte v. 19.12.1966, iK: 23.3.1976. DV. (1970) 60, (1976) 43.

Internationaler Pakt über wirtschaftliche, soziale und kulturelle Rechte v. 19.12.1966, iK: 3.1.1976. DV. (1970) 60, (1976) 43.

Konvention über die Nichtanwendbarkeit der Verjährungsfrist auf Kriegsverbrechen gegen die Menschlichkeit v. 26.11.1968. DV. (1969) 31.

Internationale Konvention über die Bekämpfung und Bestrafung des Apartheid-Verbrechens v. 30.11.1973, iK: 18.7.1976. DV. (1974) 46, (1977) 31.

Übereinkommen zur Beseitigung jeder Form von Diskriminierung der Frau v. 18.12.1979, iK: 10.3.1982. DV. (1981) 76.

Abkommen gegen Folter und andere grausame, unmenschliche oder erniedrigende Behandlung oder Bestrafung v. 10.12 1984, iK: 26.6.1987. DV. (1986) 80, (1988) 42.

Internationales Übereinkommen gegen die Apartheid im Sport v. 10.12.1985. DV. (1987) 56.

---

[1]) Vgl. im übrigen den Erlaß des DS Nr. 1496 v. 5.8.1975 über die Beteiligung der NRB an internationalen Verträgen (DV. (1975) 62).

IV. Internationale Organisationen

1. Universale Organisationen

a) Vereinte Nationen (UNO, gegr. 1945)
Charta v. 26.6.1945 mit Änderungen. Beitritt: 14.12.1955 (unveröff.).

b) Sonderorganisationen der Vereinten Nationen
Ernährungs- und Landwirtschaftsorganisation (FAO, gegr. 1946): Satzung v. 16.10.1945 mit Änderungen; seit 6.11.1967. (unveröff.).
Internationale Arbeitsorganisation (ILO, gegr. 1919): Verfassung v. 9.10.1946 mit Änderungen. Beitritt: 16.12.1920.
Internationale Zivilluftfahrtorganisation (ICAO, gegr. 1947): Abkommen v. 7.12.1944 mit Änderungen; seit 8.7.1976. DV. (1966) 62.
Internationaler Fernmeldeverein (ITU, gegr. 1866/1947): Internationaler Fernmeldevertrag v. 17.5.1865 in der Fassung v. 6.11.1982. DV. (1986) 36.
Organisation der Vereinten Nationen für Erziehung, Wissenschaft und Kultur (UNESCO, gegr. 1946): Satzung v. 16.11.1945 mit Änderungen. Beitritt: 17.5.1956. Izv. (1956) 31.
Organisation der Vereinten Nationen für industrielle Entwicklung (UNIDO, gegr. 1985): Satzung v. 8.4.1979. Gründungsmitglied (21.6.1985). DV. (1985) 37.
Weltgesundheitsorganisation (WHO, gegr. 1948): Satzung v. 22.7.1946 mit Änderungen. Beitritt: 9.6.1948. DV. (1948) 106.
Weltorganisation für geistiges Eigentum (WIPO, gegr. 1970): Übereinkommen v. 14.7.1967 mit Änderungen. Beitritt: 19.5.1970. DV. (1970) 5.
Weltorganisation für Meteorologie (WMO, gegr. 1951): Satzung v. 11.10.1947 in der Fassung v. 11./26.4.1967 mit Änderungen. Beitritt: 11.4.1952. (unveröff.).
Weltpostverein (UPU, gegr. 1875–1878): Satzung v. 9.10.1874 in der Fassung v. 10.7.1964 mit Ergänzungsprotokollen v. 14.11.1969, 5.7.1974 und 27.7.1984. DV. (1985) 87.
Internationale Seeschiffahrts-Organisation (IMO, gegr. 1958. Früher: Zwischenstaatliche Beratende Seeschiffahrts-Organisation (IMCO)), Übereinkommen v. 6.3.1948 in der Fassung v. 10.11.1984. Beitritt: 5.4.1960. Izv. (1960) 5.

c) Sonstige Organisationen der „UN-Familie"
Internationale Atomenergie-Behörde (IAEA, gegr. 1957): Satzung v. 26.10.1956 mit Änderungen. Beitritt: 17.8.1957. Izv. (1957) 34.
Wirtschaftskommission für Europa (ECE) v. 28.3.1947: Statuten in der Fassung v. 15.12.1955 und Geschäftsordnung v. 14.7.1947 in der Fassung v. 9.4.1956. Beitritt: 14.12.1955.

2. Regionale Organisationen

a) RGW (gegr. 1949)
Statut v. 14.12.1959 mit Änderungen v. 21.6.1974 u. 28.6.1979. Gründungsmitglied (25.1.1949). Izv. (1960) 16; DV. (1976) 30, (1979) 61. – Konvention über die Rechtsfähigkeit, Privilegien und Immunitäten des RGW v. 27.6.1985. DV. (1986) 58.

b) Spezialorganisationen des RGW
Gemeinsamer Güterwagenpark (OPW, gegr. 1964): Abkommen v. 21.12.1963. Gründungsmitglied (1.7.1964). VO MS Nr. 12/1964 (unveröff.).
Internationale Bank für Wirtschaftliche Zusammenarbeit (IBWZ, gegr. 1964): Abkommen über die mehrseitige Verrechnung in transferablen Rubeln und die Gründung der IBWZ v. 22.10.1963. Gründungsmitglied (18.5.1964). DV. (1963) 95, (1971) 20.

Internationale Industriezweigorganisation für die Zusammenarbeit auf dem Gebiet kleintonnagiger chemischer Erzeugnisse (Interchim, gegr. 1970): Gründungsabkommen v. 17.7.1969. Gründungsmitglied (20.7.1970). VO MS Nr. 298/1969 (unveröff.).

Internationale Investitionsbank (IIB, gegr. 1971): Gründungsabkommen v. 10.7.1970. Gründungsmitglied (1.1.1971). DV. (1970) 68.

Internationale Organisation für die Koordinierung der technischen Entwicklung und der Produktion von Landmaschinen für den Obst-, Gemüse- und Weinanbau (Agromasch, gegr. 1965): Gründungsabkommen v. 16.12.1964 mit Beitritts- und Änderungsabkommen. Gründungsmitglied (1965). VO MS Nr. 12/1965 (unveröff.).

Internationale Organisation für die ökonomische und wissenschaftlich-technische Zusammenarbeit auf dem Gebiet der elektrotechnischen Industrie (Interelektro, gegr. 1974): Gründungsabkommen v. 13.12.1973. Gründungsmitglied (1974). VO MS Nr. 265/1973 (unveröff.).

Internationales Zentrum für wissenschaftliche und technische Information (IZWTI, gegr. 1970): Gründungsabkommen v. 27.2.1969. Gründungsmitglied (3.4.1970). VO MS Nr. 116/1969 (unveröff.).

Organisation für die Zusammenarbeit in der Schwarzmetallurgie (Intermetall, gegr. 1964): Gründungsabkommen v. 15.7.1964. Gründungsmitglied (2.11.1964). VO MS Nr. 329/1964 (unveröff.).

Organisation für die Zusammenarbeit der Wälzlagerindustrie (OZWI, gegr. 1964): Gründungsabkommen v. 25.4.1964. Gründungsmitglied (13.11.1964). VO MS Nr. 218/1964 (unveröff.).

Rat für die gemeinsame Nutzung von Containern im internationalen Verkehr (SPC-Rat, gegr. 1974): Gründungsabkommen v. 29.6.1974. Gründungsmitglied (1974). VO MS Nr. 260/1974 (unveröff.).

Zentrale Dispatcherverwaltung der Vereinigten Energiesysteme (ZDV, gegr. 1962): Gründungsabkommen v. 25.7.1962. Gründungsmitglied (25.7.1962) (unveröff.).

V. Bündnisverträge

1. Multilaterale Verträge (WP)

Vertrag über Freundschaft, Zusammenarbeit und gegenseitigen Beistand zwischen Bulgarien, Ungarn, der DDR, Polen, Rumänien, der UdSSR und der Tschechoslowakei v. 14.5.1955 mit Verlängerungsprotokoll v. 26.4.1985, iK: 31.5.1985. Gründungsmitglied (4.6.1955). Izv. (1955) 44; DV. (1985) 41, (1986) 23.

Konvention über die Rechtsfähigkeit, die Privilegien und Immunitäten des Stabes und der anderen Führungsorgane der Vereinten Streitkräfte der Teilnehmerstaaten des Warschauer Vertrages v. 24.4.1973, iK: 3.12.1973. DV. (1973) 55, (1974) 44.

2. Bilaterale Verträge (Verträge über Freundschaft, Zusammenarbeit und gegenseitigen Beistand)

DDR: v. 14.9.1977, iK: 19.1.1978. DV. (1977) 88, (1978) 26.
(Vorgänger: Vertrag v. 7.9.1967, DV. (1968) 36).
Polen: v. 6.4.1967, iK: 24.8.1967. DV. (1967) 49 u. 79.
(Vorgänger: Vertrag v. 29.5.1948, DV. (1948) 152).
Rumänien: v. 19.11.1970, iK: 31.3.1970. DV. (1971) 10 u. 41.
(Vorgänger: Vertrag v. 16.1.1948, DV. (1948) 32).
Tschechoslowakei: v. 23.4.1968, iK: 30.4.1969. DV. (1968) 52, (1969) 50.
(Vorgänger: Vertrag v. 23.4.1948, DV. (1948) 152).

UdSSR: v. 12.5.1967, iK: 4.8.1967. DV. (1967) 49 u. 78.
(Vorgänger: Vertrag v. 18.3.1948, DV. (1948) 152).
Ungarn: v. 10.7.1969, iK: 8.9.1969. DV. (1969) 71 u. 81.
(Vorgänger: Vertrag v. 16.7.1948, DV. (1948) 258).

VI. Politische Kooperationsverträge
(Verträge über Freundschaft und Zusammenarbeit)

Äthiopien: v. 14.7.1980, iK: 11.7.1981. DV. (1980) 92, (1982) 99.
Afghanistan: v. 22.12.1981, iK: 6.9.1982. DV. (1982) 10 u. 90.
Angola: v. 21.10.1978, iK: 18.5.1981. DV. (1979) 32, (1981) 46.
Jemen, Demokratische VR: v. 11.11.1981, iK: 7.7.1982. DV. (1982) 10 u. 63.
Kamputschea, VR: v. 25.11.1980, iK: 19.6.1981. DV. (1981) 13, (1986) 23.
Korea, Demokratische VR: v. 17.6.1984, iK: 23.7.1984. DV. (1984) 59, (1986) 23.
Laos: v. 4.10.1979, iK. 31.3.1980. DV. (1979) 86, (1980) 40.
Libyen: v. 21.1.1983, iK. 8.3.1984. DV. (1984) 16 u. 28.
Mongolei: v. 12.6.1987, iK: 12.11.1987. DV. (1987) 80 u. 96.
Moçambique: v. 24.10.1978, iK: 24.3.1982. DV. (1979) 32, (1982) 39.
Syrien: v. 30.4.1985, iK: 23.10.1987. DV. (1986) 7, (1987) 90.
Vietnam: v. 1.10.1979, iK: 24.12.1979. DV. (1979) 86, (1980) 8.

VII. Konsularabkommen

1. Multilaterale Verträge

Wiener Übereinkommen über konsularische Beziehungen v. 24.4.1963 mit Fakultativ-Protokoll über den Erwerb der Staatsangehörigkeit und Fakultativ-Protokoll über die obligatorische Beilegung von Streitigkeiten. DV. (1989) 42.

2. Bilaterale Verträge

Äthiopien: v. 14.7.1980, iK: 10.8.1981. DV. (1981) 6, (1983) 2.
Afghanistan: v. 12.8.1979, iK: 21.8.1980. DV. (1979) 100, (1981) 32.
Belgien: v. 28.11.1978, iK: 1.3.1981. DV. (1979) 2, (1982) 7.
China, VR: v. 6.5.1987, iK: 2.1.1988. DV. (1987) 69, (1988) 12.
DDR: v. 1.6.1972, iK: 12.10.1972. DV. (1972) 57 u. 79 (Protokoll im Anhang).
Ecuador: v. 19.5.1987. DV. (1987) 63.
Frankreich: v. 22.7.1968, iK: 1.4.1970. DV. (1968) 93, (1970) 50.
Ghana: v. 28.8.1986, iK: 11.4.1987. DV. (1987) 12 u. 28.
Griechenland: v. 31.5.1973, iK: 22.1.1975. DV. (1973) 70, (1975) 34.
Irak: v. 7.9.1982, iK: 3.8.1983. DV. (1982) 97, (1983) 80.
Italien: v. 21.2.1968, iK: 26.6.1974. DV. (1968) 67, (1974) 51.
Jemen, Demokratische VR: v. 25.2.1980, iK: 11.12.1981. DV. (1980) 31, (1983) 14.
Jugoslawien: v. 21.3.1963, iK: 9.3.1964. DV. (1963) 41, (1964) 38.

Kamputschea, VR: v. 25.11.1980, iK: 19.7.1981. DV. (1981) 52 u. 72.
Korea, Demokratische VR: v. 27.6.1977, iK: 7.12.1977. DV. (1977) 95, (1978) 33.
Kuba: v. 31.7.1978, iK: 11.5.1979. DV. (1978) 98, (1979) 57.
Laos: v. 8.11.1983, iK: 7.4.1985. DV. (1984) 89, (1985) 81.
Libyen: v. 8.12.1981, iK: 20.2.1983. DV. (1982) 93, (1983) 15.
Mexiko: v. 1.10.1984, DV. (1985) 95.
Mongolei: v. 25.7.1972, iK: 24.11.1972. DV. (1972) 91.
Nicaragua: v. 22.11.1982, iK: 12.6.1983. DV. (1983) 9 u. 69.
Österreich: v. 14.5.1975, iK: 12.7.1975. DV. (1975) 59, (1977) 80.
Polen: v. 10.11.1972, iK: 20.6.1973. DV. (1973) 11 u. 79.
Portugal: v. 30.11.1977, DV. (1978) 13.
Rumänien: v. 18.1.1973, iK: 8.8.1973. DV. (1973) 23 u. 84.
Syrien: v. 12.6.1981, iK: 27.5.1982. DV. (1982) 11 u. 96.
Tschechoslowakei: v. 16.3.1972, iK: 23.3.1974. DV. (1972) 32, (1974) 28 (Protokoll im Anhang).
Türkei: v. 6.10.1970, iK: 30.9.1973. DV. (1970) 103, (1973) 95.
Tunesien: v. 16.10.1975, iK: 31.8.1976. DV. (1975) 98, (1976) 92.
UdSSR: v. 6.5.1971, iK: 25.11.1971. DV. (1971) 50, (1972) 15 (Protokoll im Anhang).
Ungarn: v. 26.11.1971, iK: 19.6.1972. DV. (1972) 30 u. 49 (Protokoll im Anhang).
USA: v. 1.10.1984, iK: 6.6.1986. DV. (1985) 95, (1986) 46.
Vereinigtes Königreich: v. 13.3.1968, iK: 21.12.1968. DV. (1968) 67, (1969) 38.
Vietnam: v. 1.10.1979, iK: 22.6.1980. DV. (1980) 13, (1983) 5.
Zypern: v. 24.3.1981, iK: 25.10.1986. DV. (1986) 36 u. 82.

VIII. Rechtshilfeabkommen

1. Universale Abkommen

Genfer Europäisches Übereinkommen über die internationale Handelsschiedsgerichtsbarkeit v. 21.4.1961. Beitritt: 11.8.1964. DV. (1964) 23 u. 57.

New Yorker Übereinkommen über die Anerkennung und Vollstreckung ausländischer Schiedssprüche v. 10.6.1958. Beitritt: 8.1.1962. Izv. (1961) 57; DV. (1965) 2.

2. Regionale Abkommen

Berliner Abkommen über die Übergabe von zu Freiheitsstrafe verurteilten Personen zum Zwecke der Strafvollstreckung an den Staat, dessen Bürger sie sind, v. 19.5.1978, iK: 26.8.1979. DV. (1979) 8, (1980) 9. Mitglieder: Bulgarien, DDR, Kuba, Mongolei, Polen, Tschechoslowakei, UdSSR, Ungarn.

3. Bilaterale Abkommen

Algerien: Vertrag v. 20.12.1975 über die gerichtliche und Rechtshilfe in Zivil-, Handels-, Familien- und Strafsachen, iK: 1.4.1985. DV. (1976) 13, (1985) 27.

DDR: Vertrag über den Rechtsverkehr in Zivil-, Familien- und Strafsachen v. 12.10.1978, iK: 12.10.1979. DV. (1978) 96, (1979) 92.

Frankreich: Vertrag über gegenseitige Rechtshilfe in Zivilsachen v. 18.1.1989, DV. (1989) 18.

Griechenland: Vertrag über Rechtshilfe in Zivil- und Strafsachen v. 10.4.1976, iK: 26.4.1980. DV. (1976) 68, (1980) 49.

Jemen, Demokratische VR: Vertrag über Rechtshilfe in Zivil- und Strafsachen v. 13.5.1988, iK: 22.1.1989. DV. (1988) 58, (1989) 11.

Jugoslawien: Vertrag über gegenseitige Rechtshilfe v. 23.3.1956, iK: o.A. Izv. (1957) 16.

Kuba: Vertrag über Rechtshilfe in Zivil-, Familien- und Strafsachen v. 11.4.1979, iK: 25.7.1980. DV. (1979) 90, (1980) 85.

Kuwait: Vertrag über gegenseitige Rechts- und gerichtliche Hilfe in Zivilsachen v. 26.12.1988, DV. (1989) 13.

Libyen: Vertrag über rechtliche Zusammenarbeit v. 8.3.1984, iK: 5.8.1985. DV. (1984) 33, (1985) 65.

Mongolei: Vertrag über gegenseitige Leistung von Rechtshilfe in Zivil-, Familien- und Strafsachen v. 27.11.1968, iK: 10.4.1969. DV. (1969) 2 und 88.

Österreich: Vertrag über Rechtshilfe in bürgerlichen Rechtssachen und über Urkundenwesen v. 20.10.1967, iK: 23.8.1969. DV. (1968) 12, (1969) 79 (Protokoll im Anhang).

Polen: Vertrag über Rechtshilfe und Rechtsbeziehungen in Zivil-, Familien- und Strafsachen v. 4.12.1961, iK: 20.4.1963. Izv. (1962) 31; DV. (1963) 37; mit Änderungsprotokoll v. 27.6.1980, iK: 25.2.1981. DV. (1980) 83, (1981) 20.

Rumänien: Vertrag über Rechtshilfe in Zivil-, Familien- und Strafsachen v. 3.12.1958, iK: 4.7.1959. Izv. (1959) 9, (1960) 18.

Syrien: Vertrag über Rechtshilfe in Familien-, Zivil- und Strafsachen v. 16.8.1976, iK: 5.12.1977. DV. (1976) 77, (1980) 53.

Tschechoslowakei: Vertrag über Rechtshilfe und Regelung der Beziehungen in Zivil-, Familien- und Strafsachen v. 25.11.1976, iK: 6.1.1978. DV. (1977) 34, (1978) 20.

Türkei: Vertrag über Rechtshilfe in Zivil- und Strafsachen v. 2.9.1975, iK: 27.10.1978. DV. (1976) 20, (1979) 16.

Tunesien: Vertrag über die Rechtshilfe in Zivil- und Strafsachen v. 16.10.1975, iK: 31.8.1976. DV. (1976) 3, (1978) 2 (Zusatzprotokoll im Anhang).

UdSSR: Vertrag über die Rechtshilfe in Zivil-, Familien- und Strafsachen v. 19.2.1975, iK: 18.1.1975. DV. (1975) 33, (1976) 12.

Ungarn: Vertrag über die Rechtshilfe in Zivil-, Familien- und Strafsachen v. 16.5.1966, iK: 10.3.1967. DV. (1966) 62, (1967) 29; mit Änderungsprotokoll v. 15.9.1981, iK: 29.9.1982. DV. (1982) 4 u. 76.

Vietnam: Vertrag über die Rechtshilfe in Zivil-, Familien- und Strafsachen v. 3.10.1986, iK: 5.7.1987. DV. (1986) 90, (1987) 69.

Zypern: Vertrag über Rechtshilfe in Zivil- und Strafsachen v. 29.4.1983, iK: 11.1.1985. DV. (1983) 49, (1985) 4.

IX. Staatsangehörigkeitsabkommen

DDR: Vertrag zur Regelung von Fragen der doppelten Staatsbürgerschaft v. 1.10.1971, iK: 11.5.1972. DV. (1971) 97, (1972) 39.

Mongolei: Vertrag zur Regelung der Fragen der doppelten Staatsbürgerschaft v. 21.11.1983, iK: 26.5.1984. DV. (1983) 101, (1984) 38.

Polen: Abkommen zur Regelung der doppelten Staatsangehörigkeit v. 7.2.1972, iK: 25.9.1972. DV. (1972) 21 u. 78.

Rumänien: Abkommen über die Regelung der Staatsangehörigkeit von Doppelstaatern v. 24.9.1959, iK: 24.12.1959. Izv. (1959) 90, (1960) 17.

Tschechoslowakei: Abkommen zur Regelung der doppelten Staatsbürgerschaft v. 31.5.1974, iK: 4.5.1975. DV. (1974) 53, (1975) 46.
UdSSR: Abkommen über die Regelung der Staatsangehörigkeit von Doppelstaatern v. 12.12.1957. Izv. (1958) 33.
UdSSR: Abkommen über die Verhinderung der Entstehung von Fällen der doppelten Staatsangehörigkeit v. 6.7.1966 mit Zusatzprotokoll, iK: 19.1.1967. DV. (1966) 66, (1967) 2.
Ungarn: Abkommen über die Regelung der Staatsangehörigkeit von Doppelstaatern v. 27.6.1958, iK: 3.7.1959. Izv. (1959) 81.

X. Doppelbesteuerungsabkommen

1. Multilaterale Abkommen (mit der DDR, Mongolei, Polen, Rumänien, Tschechoslowakei, UdSSR und Ungarn)

Abkommen zur Vermeidung der doppelten Einkommens- und Vermögensbesteuerung juristischer Personen v. 19.5.1978, iK: 1.1.1979. DV. (1978) 63.

2. Bilaterale Abkommen

Belgien: Abkommen zur Vermeidung der Doppelbesteuerung vom Einkommen und Vermögen v. 25.10.1988. DV. (1989) 3.
Bundesrepublik Deutschland: Abkommen zur Vermeidung der Doppelbesteuerung auf dem Gebiet der Steuern vom Einkommen und vom Vermögen v. 2.6.1987, iK: 21.12.1988. DV. (1987) 71, (1988) 98 (Protokoll im Anhang).
Dänemark: Abkommen zur Vermeidung der Doppelbesteuerung von Einkommen und Vermögen v. 2.12.1988, iK: 23.3.1989. DV. (1989) 21 u. 46.
Finnland: Abkommen zur Vermeidung der Doppelbesteuerung von Einkommen v. 25.4.1985, iK: 21.4.1986. DV. (1985) 71, (1986) 40.
Frankreich: Abkommen zur Vermeidung der Doppelbesteuerung und Verhütung der unterschiedlichen Einkommensbesteuerung v. 14.3.1987, iK: 1.6.1988. DV. (1987) 39, (1988) 41 (Protokoll im Anhang).
Italien: Abkommen zur Vermeidung der Doppelbesteuerung und Verhütung der unterschiedlichen Besteuerung von Einkommen und Vermögen v. 21.9.1988. DV. (1988) 89.
Malta: Abkommen zur Vermeidung der Doppelbesteuerung von Einkommen v. 23.7.1986, iK: 1.1.1988. DV. (1986) 74, (1988) 7.
Norwegen: Abkommen zur Vermeidung der Doppelbesteuerung von Einkommen und Vermögen v. 1.3.1988, iK: 1.4.1989. DV. (1988) 58, (1989) 48.
Österreich: Abkommen zur Vermeidung der Doppelbesteuerung auf dem Gebiete der Steuern vom Einkommen und vom Vermögen v. 20.4.1983, iK: 1.1.1985. DV. (1983) 56, (1985) 6.
Schweden: Abkommen zur Vermeidung der Doppelbesteuerung von Einkommen und Vermögen v. 21.6.1988, iK: 28.12.1988. DV. (1988) 78, (1989) 45.
Vereinigtes Königreich: Abkommen zur Vermeidung der Doppelbesteuerung von Einkommen und Gewinnen aus Vermögensübertragung v. 16.9.1987, iK: 1.1.1988. DV. (1987) 98, (1988) 8.
Zimbabwe: Abkommen zur Vermeidung der Doppelbesteuerung und Verhütung unterschiedlicher Besteuerung von Einkommen, Vermögen und Veräußerungsgewinnen v. 12.10.1988. DV. (1989) 3.
Zypern: Abkommen zur Vermeidung der Doppelbesteuerung von Einkommen und Vermögen v. 18.9.1985, iK: 27.8.1986. DV. (1986) 22 und 60.

XI. Investitionsschutzabkommen

Bundesrepublik Deutschland: Vertrag über die gegenseitige Förderung und den gegenseitigen Schutz von Kapitalanlagen v. 12.4.1986. DV. (1986) 48.

Finnland: Vertrag über gegenseitige Förderung und Schutz der Kapitalanlagen v. 16.2.1984. DV. (1984) 50.

Malta: Vertrag über gegenseitige Förderung und Schutz der Kapitalanlagen v. 12.6.1984. DV. (1984) 97.

XII. Grenz- und Visumabkommen

China, VR: Regierungsabkommen über visafreien Reiseverkehr und Reiseerleichterungen für die Bürger beider Länder v. 18.6.1987, iK: 18.7.1987. DV. (1987) 71.

Dänemark: Regierungsabkommen über die Abschaffung der Visa v. 2.9.1967, iK: 1.1.1968. DV. (1968) 9.

DDR: Regierungsvereinbarung über den visafreien Reiseverkehr der Bürger beider Staaten v. 29.1.1971. DV. (1971) 54.

Finnland: Abkommen über die Abschaffung der Visa v. 14.12.1967, iK: 1.1.1968. DV. (1968) 21.

Ghana: Regierungsabkommen über die Einführung eines erleichterten Visa-Regimes v. 29.6.1984, iK: 15.7.1986. DV. (1986) 59.

Griechenland: Beschluß über den Austausch von Flächen zwischen der NRB und dem Königreich Griechenland v. 21.10.1970. DV. (1970) 85. – Abkommen über die Kontrolle, Unterhaltung und Erneuerung der Grenzlinie an der bulgarisch-griechischen Grenze v. 4.9.1957, iK: 3.9.1959. Izv. (1960) 6. – Abkommen über Zusammenarbeit bei der Nutzung des Wassers der Flüsse, die durch die Territorien beider Länder fließen, v. 9.7.1964, iK: 9.7.1964. DV. (1964) 87. – Abkommen über die Schaffung einer neuen Straßenverbindung und Errichtung einer neuen Grenzkontroll- und Passierstelle zwischen beiden Ländern im Rayon Svilengrad-Ormenion v. 13.7.1979. DV. (1979) 90. – Abkommen über den Waren- und Passagierverkehr auf Straßen zwischen beiden Ländern sowie über den Transitverkehr v. 9.7.1964, iK: 9.7.1964. DV. (1964) 88.

Island: Abkommen über die Abschaffung der Visa v. 10.4.1968, iK: 1.7.1968. DV. (1968) 64.

Jugoslawien: Abkommen zur Erneuerung, Markierung und Erhaltung der Grenzlinie und der Grenzzeichen an der bulgarisch-jugoslawischen Staatsgrenze v. 9.10.1981. DV. (1982) 29. – Regierungsabkommen über die Regelung des Verkehrs von Grenzbewohnern in der Grenzzone v. 28.2.1972, iK: 6.8.1972. DV. (1972) 66. – Vereinbarung über das Verfahren der Untersuchung und Entscheidung von Grenzverletzungen, die an der bulgarisch-jugoslawischen Grenze vorgekommen sind, v. 6.10.1965 in der Fassung v. 23.4.1982. DV. (1965) 86, (1982) 70. – Vereinbarung über die teilweise Änderung der Grenzlinie am Fluß Timok v. 14.12.1961. DV. (1963) 1.

Libyen: Abkommen über ein erleichtertes Visaverfahren v. 8.3.1984, iK: 1.8.1985. DV. (1985) 78.

Malta: Regierungsabkommen zur Abschaffung der Visa v. 30.3.1984. DV. (1984) 73.

Mauretanien: Abkommen über die Abschaffung der Visa v. 29.7.1974. DV. (1975) 33.

Mongolei: Regierungsabkommen über die Bedingungen für den gegenseitigen visafreien Reiseverkehr der Bürger 25.12.1982, iK: 20.7.1983. DV. (1983) 76.

Nicaragua: Regierungsabkommen über ein erleichtertes Visa-Regime v. 22.11.1982, iK: 1.4.1983. DV. (1983) 76.

Norwegen: Regierungsabkommen über die Abschaffung der Visa v. 28.10.1967, iK: 1.1.1968. DV. (1968) 51.

Österreich: Abkommen über die Aufhebung der Sichtvermerkspflicht v. 21.4.1967, iK: 21.5.1967. DV. (1967) 46.

Polen: Regierungsabkommen über die Aufhebung des Visazwangs und die Entwicklung des Tourismus v. 8.6.1965. DV. (1965) 53 (mit Anlage).

Rumänien: Abkommen betreffend Erleichterungen für den Grenzübergang zwischen beiden Ländern v. 7.7.1948. DV. (1949) 31. – Regierungsabkommen über die Aufhebung der Ein- und Ausreisevisa für amtliche und private Reisende und Touristen sowie der Transitvisa v. 22.8.1967, iK: 10.12.1967. DV. (1967) 95. – Regierungsabkommen über Erleichterungen für Reisen der Bürger mit ständigem Wohnsitz in der Zone des kleinen Grenzverkehrs beider Staaten – mit drei Anlagen v. 11.3.1971, iK: 2.8.1971. DV. (1971) 65. – Abkommen über Schutz, Erhaltung und Instandsetzung der Grenzlinie und der Grenzzeichen des Landabschnitts der bulgarisch-rumänischen Staatsgrenze v. 27.5.1978. DV. (1978) 61. – Abkommen über das Verfahren für die Untersuchung und Entscheidung einiger Fragen der bulgarisch-rumänischen Staatsgrenze v. 9.3.1973. DV. (1973) 32.

Tschechoslowakei: Regierungsabkommen über die Aufhebung des Visazwangs und die Entwicklung des Tourismus v. 4.6.1965. DV. (1965) 53 (mit Anlage).

Türkei: Abkommen über die Verhütung und Lösung der Grenzzwischenfälle und Unterhaltung der staatlichen Grenzzeichen v. 28.12.1967. DV. (1968) 43. – Abkommen über die Zusammenarbeit bei der Nutzung des Wassers der durch die Territorien beider Länder fließenden Flüsse v. 23.10.1968. DV. (1968) 94.

UdSSR: Abkommen über das Verfahren für den gegenseitigen visafreien Reiseverkehr von Bürgern der NRB und Bürgern der UdSSR v. 3.11.1969, iK: 23.1.1970. DV. (1970) 29.

Zimbabwe: Regierungsabkommen über die Einführung eines erleichterten Visa-Regimes (Notenwechsel v. 7.7.1984/15.4.1985), iK: 31.5.1986. DV. (1986) 51.

Zypern: Abkommen über die Erleichterung des Visaregimes v. 10.8.1970. DV. (1970) 80.

Biographies of Prominent Public Figures

Stephen Ashley, München

Aleksandrov, Chudomir Asenov (* Sofia 26.7.1936) Working-class origins. *Kandidat* degree in technical sciences in the USSR. First worked in the Niproruda Institute for mining technology. 1972–77: (from 1973 1st) Secretary, Dimitrovski *Raĭon* BKP Committee in Sofia; 1977–79: 1st Deputy Head, BKP CC Organizational Department; 1979 (April-Oct.): 1st Secretary, Stara Zagora BKP District Committee; 1979–84: 1st Secretary, Sofia City BKP Committee; 1981–84: BKP CC Secretary; 1984–86: 1st Deputy Prime Minister; 1986–88: BKP CC Secretary (for organization and cadres); 1988–: Enterprise manager. BKP CC candidate member (1976–81), full member (1981–88); Politburo member (1984–88). Member of NSb since 1980, OF National Council since 1982 and DS since 1986. His demotion in 1988 was perhaps the result of his potential challenge to Todor Zhivkov's leadership.

Atanasov, Georgi Ivanov (* Pravoslaven, Plovdiv rgn. 25.7.1933) Peasant origins; father BKP member. Educated in Sofia University (History Faculty). BKP member since 1956. DKMS instructor in late 1950s. 1960–63: (from 1961 1st) Secretary, Sofia City DKMS Committee; 1962–68: (from 1965 1st) Secretary, DKMS CC Bureau; 1968–76: Head, BKP CC Science & Education Department; 1976–77: Head, BKP CC Records Department; 1977–86: BKP CC Secretary (for organization & cadres); 1980–81: 1st Deputy Chairman, State Planning Committee; 1981–84: DS Deputy Chairman; 1981–84: Chairman, Committee for State and People's Control; 1986–: Prime Minister. BKP CC candidate member in 1962 & full member in 1966; Politburo candidate member in 1984 & full member in 1986. Member of NSb since 1966 and OF National Council since 1967.

Balev, Milko Kalev (* Troĭan 14.8.1920) Poor artisan origins; father BKP activist. RMS member since 1936; BKP member since 1942. Educated in Sofia University (Law Faculty). Secretary of Troĭan RMS District Committee from 1941; arrested in 1943 & received death sentence (commuted to life imprisonment in 1944). 1944–50: RMS CC Secretary, then DKMS CC Department Deputy Head; 1950–65: BKP CC Propaganda and Agitation Department, later First Assistant in BKP General Secretary's Office; c. 1965–69 & c. 1973–81: Head of BKP General Secretary's Office; c. 1968–70: Head of Prime Minister's Office; c. 1978–81: Head of State President's Office; 1979–89: BKP CC Secretary. BKP CC candidate member in 1962 & full member in 1966; Politburo member 1982–89. Member of NSb 1971–89, OF National Council member 1972–89 and DS 1984–89. Considered one of Todor Zhivkov's closest allies, he fell together with him and was expelled from BKP.
Works: *Ogŭnĭat ne sveti za sebe si* (Fire Does Not Burn for Itself). Sofia 1986. [On Lîudmila Zhivkova].

Bozhinov, Todor Iliev (* Vŭrshets, Mikhaĭlovgrad rgn. 21.2.1931) RMS member since 1945; BKP member since 1960. Educated in Mining & Geology Institute, Sofia; worked 13 years in Svoge anthracite mines. Subsequently obtained *kandidat* degree in Economics; *dotsent* since 1977. BKP work since 1963. 1968–71: Secretary, Sofia BKP District Committee; 1972–?: Academic Secretary, Institute of Social Management; 1973–77: Secretary, Council for Management of Social Relations; 1977–78: 1st Deputy Chairman, State Committee for Planning; 1978–79: BKP CC Secretary; 1979–86: Politburo member; 1979–86: (until 1984 1st) Deputy Prime Minister; 1982–84: Minister of Metallurgy & Mineral Resources; 1984–85: Minister of Energy Resources; 1985–86: Minister of Supplies; 1986–87: Chairman, Committee for Protection of the Environment. Present post unknown. BKP CC member in 1977. Member of NSb since 1979 and OF National Council since 1987. Considered to have been supporter of Lîudmila Zhivkova & to have taken blame for economic failures in mid-1980s.

Bŭlgaranov, Boĩan Petkov (Shumen 20.10.1896–Sofia 26.12.1972) Father teacher & BKP CC candidate member (1948–54). Schooling only to secondary level; reserve officer in World War I. 1919–20: KMS Secretary in Shumen. Joined BKP in 1920. 1922–23: Military Staff Academy in Moscow; sent back to Bulgaria to assist preparations for September Uprising; imprisoned in Shumen but amnestied in 1924. Appointed Secretary of Shumen BKP District Committee & regional commander of BKP military organization in Varna, Ruse & Shumen (1924). Arrested in Nov. 1924 & given death sentence (commuted to life imprisonment); released under amnesty in 1933. 1933–34: Studied in Lenin International School, Moscow; 1934–36: Worked for KI in Moscow & Istanbul. Returned to Bulgaria in 1936 to support „Dimitrov line". In 1941 joined BKP CC Central Military Commission, taking command of operations in Ruse region. 1942–44: BKP representative on Supreme Command of Macedonian partisan forces; 1944: Commander of Sofia then Plovdiv Insurrectionary Operative Zones. After 9.9.1944 served as Deputy Commander in final phase of war. In 1945 became Deputy Head of Vasil Levski People's Military School; 1945–47: Commander of BNA 5th Infantry Division; 1947–48: Director of People's Militia; 1948–49: Chief of Political Directorate in Ministry of War. In disgrace accused of „Titoism" (1949–53). 1954–56: BKP CC Department Head; 1956–67: BKP CC Secretary; 1967–72: Chairman, Executive Committee of OF National Council. BKP CC member (1937–50 & 1954–72) & Politburo member (1957–72). Member of OF National Council (1948–53? & 1957–72), NSb (1953–72) & DS (1971–72).
Literature: Ianchev, V.: *General-leĩtenant Boĩan Bŭlgaranov*. Sofia 1984.

Chervenkov, Vŭlko Velev (Zlatitsa 6.9.1900–Sofia 21.10.1980) Father minor army officer. Educated in *gimnaziĩa* in Sofia. Joined BKP in 1919. In 1923 became Secretary of Sofia KMS; organized arms supplies for September 1923 Uprising. In 1924 elected to KMS CC; appointed as Head of its Agitprop Department, Editor of its newspaper *Bŭdeshte* (Future) & Organizer of KMS work in the army. 1925: On receiving death sentence *in absentia*, emigrated to USSR. Studied in Moscow Military Academy & Lenin International School. During exile, was variously Secretary of Central Emigres' Commission of BKP CC Foreign Bureau, a teacher and Secretary to Georgi Dimitrov. 1938–41: Worked in KI Propaganda Department; 1941–44: Chief Editor, „Khristo Botev" radio station in Moscow; 1941–44: Member, BKP CC Foreign Bureau. In Sept. 1944 appointed BKP Secretary for Agitation & Propaganda; 1947–49: Chairman, State Cultural Commission (later Committee for Science, Art & Culture); 1948–49: Chief Secretary, OF National Council; 1949–50: Deputy Prime Minister; 1950–54: BKP General Secretary; 1950–56: Prime Minister; 1950–57 Chairman, OF National Council; 1956–61: Deputy Prime Minister; 1957–58: Minister of Education & Culture; 1959–?: Chairman, State Council for Science. Denounced by Todor Zhivkov at Nov. 1961 & Nov. 1962 BKP CC plenums & 1962 BKP congress for enforcing a „cult of personality" during his period of supreme power (1950–54) and subsequently engaging in „antiparty plots". Expelled from party in 1962; his membership was restored in 1969. Lived on state pension until his death. BKP CC member (1944–62); Politburo member (1944–61). Member of NSb (1945–62), OF National Council (1944?–62?). m. Elena Dimitrova (sister of Dimitrov). Sometimes called Bulgaria's „Little Stalin".
Literature: Vŭlko Chervenkov-Bio-bibliografiĩa. Sofia 1950; Chervenkov, V.: *Po pŭtiĩa na Georgi Dimitrov* (On Georgi Dimitrov's Road) (Speeches). Sofia 1950.

Damĩanov, Georgi Pŭrvanov (Lopushna [now Georgi–Damĩanovo], Mikhaĩlovgrad rgn. 23.9.1892 – Sofia 28.11.1958) Poor peasant origins. Educated in Vratsa *gimnaziĩa* (1908–11). Worked as teacher & telegraphist. Joined BRSDP in 1912. During World War I, saw active service in Serbia & in Dobrudja where in 1916 he was seriously wounded & left an invalid. 1919–23: Active in Vratsa District BKP. 1923: Joint leader of September Uprising in Vratsa; after its defeat, took refuge in Yugoslavia until 1924. In 1925 emigrated to USSR. Studied in M.V. Frunze Military Academy (1926–29), served as Red Army commander (1929–32) and academy instructor (1932–34). In 1935 was sent back to Bulgaria with Stanke Dimitrov & Traĩcho Kostov to impose „Dimitrov line" on BKP; returned to USSR in 1936 or 1937 to work for KI & BKP Foreign Bureau. Came back to Bulgaria after 9.9.1944. 1944–45: headed BKP CC Military Department; 1946: BKP CC Secretary; 1946–50: Minister of War (from 1947, Defence); 1950–58: Chairman, NSb Presidium. BKP CC member (1935–58) & Politburo member (1936–? & 1945–58). Member of NSb (1945–58) & OF National Council (1948–58).
Literature: Krŭstina Stanilova, *Sŭdbata si izbirakhme sami, ili zhivotŭt na Georgi Damĩanov* (We Chose Our Own Fate, or the Life of G.D.). Sofia 1982; Mit'o Radukov, *Apostolŭt ot Lopushna* (The Apostle of Lopushna). Sofia 1982.

Dimitrov Mikhaĭlov, Georgi (Kovachevtsi, Sofia rgn. 18.6.1882 – Barvikha Sanatorium, near Moscow 2.7.1949) Poor artisan background; his mother was Protestant Macedonian; eldest of 8 children. Left school at 12 to become printer's apprentice. Joined BRSDP in 1903. 1904–05: Party Secretary in Sofia. 1909–23: Secretary-Treasurer, *Obshtiĭat Rabotnicheski Sindikalen Sŭiŭz* (General Workers' Trades Union Association). Elected to BRSDP CC in 1909 & NSb in 1913. Imprisoned briefly for antiwar activity (1918) and pro-Soviet agitation (1920). Lived in USSR (1921–23); returned to Bulgaria in 1923, but after defeat of Sept. 1923 Uprising returned to USSR to campaign for „united front" tactic within BKP & KI. Sentenced to death *in absentia* in 1926. Cofounder of BKP Foreign Bureau (1928); Secretary of Presidium (1923–25) & Executive Bureau (1929–33) of Balkan Communist Federation; Leader of West European Bureau of KI (1929–33). Acquitted of setting fire to German *Reichstag* in Leipzig Trial (1933). 1935–43: KI General Secretary. 1937–45: Deputy in Supreme Soviet of USSR. 1945–48: BKP CC Chairman. Returned to Bulgaria on 4.11.45. 1946–49: Prime Minister; 1948–49: OF National Council Chairman; 1948–49: BKP CC General Secretary. Left Bulgaria finally in April 1949 for medical treatment in USSR where he died. BKP CC member & Politburo member (1945–49). 1 m. Ljuba Ivošević († 1933), Yugoslav poet & journalist; 2 m. Roza Dimitrova († 1958).
Works: Sŭchineniĭa (Works). 14 vols. Sofia 1951–55; *Pisma 1905–49* (Letters). Sofia 1962. *Literature:* Blagoeva, S.: *Georgi Dimitrov: Biografichen ocherk* (Biographical Sketch). Sofia 1953; *Georgi Dimitrov 1882–1982*. Sofia 1982.

Dimitrov, Georgi Mikhov [Gemeto] (Yeni Çiftlik, Turkey 15.4.1903 – Washington DC. 29.11.72) Parents owned 50 acres; were evacuated to Doĭrentsi (Lovech rgn.) in 1913. Studies at Doĭrentsi *gimnaziĭa* (to 1921); in medicine at Sofia & Belgrade Universities (1924–29). 1921–23: Taught in Doĭrentsi & joined BZNS. Imprisoned in June 1923; amnestied in October but barred from teaching. After 1929 practised as doctor in Doĭrentsi & Sofia. Elected to NSb in 1931. Supported *Pladne* (Noon) group against BZNS leadership of Vergil Dimov & Dimitŭr Gichev; expelled from BZNS parliamentary group in 1932. For opposition to Tsar Boris, arrested & tortured in 1935 during consolidation of personal regime & in 1938. Drafted as military physician in 1939. In 1940 began to organize broad front to oppose Bulgarian adherence to Tripartite Pact. Fled to avoid arrest to Yugoslavia then Turkey. Sentenced to death *in absentia* (1941) after publishing democratic, pro-Western manifesto. During war, supported *Pladne* group's bid to lead the OF. Returned to Bulgaria in Sept. 1944 & began reorganizing BZNS (officially suppressed since 1934) as counter to BKP. Elected BZNS Secretary in Oct. 1944, but resigned under BKP pressure in 1945. Placed under house arrest, while BZNS (now led by Aleksandŭr Obbov) was purged of his supporters. Escaped from Bulgaria with US aid. Sentenced to life imprisonment *in absentia*. Settled in USA, where he founded the International Peasant Union, the Bulgarian National Committee & the newspaper *Svobodna i Nezavisima Bŭlgariĭa* (Free & Independent Bulgaria).
Literature: Moser, Ch. A.: *Dimitrov of Bulgaria*. Ottawa, Illinois 1979.

Doĭnov, Ognĭan Nakov (* Gara Bov, Sofia rgn. 15.10.1935) Parents were domestic servants. Educated at V. I. Lenin Higher Electrical Machine Technology Institute, Sofia; BKP member since 1962. Worked for Ministry of Transport (1959–60), Sofia City People's Council (1960–62) & Foreign Trade Ministry (1962–65). 1965–70: Deputy Trade Representative in Tokyo, Japan; 1970–73: Adviser to Ministerial & State Councils; 1974: BKP CC Industry & Transport Department Head; 1974–76: Deputy Prime Minister; 1976–86: BKP CC Secretary; 1981–84: DS member; 1984–86: Minister of Machine Building; 1986–87: Chairman, Economic Council; 1986–87: Deputy Prime Minister; 1987– : Chairman, Association for Heavy Machine Building. BKP CC member 1976–89; Politburo member (1977–1988). Member of NSb since 1974 & OF National Council since 1977.

Dragoĭcheva, Tsola Nincheva (* Bĭala Slatina 18.8.1898) Peasant origins. Educated in *gimnaziĭa* in Vratsa and Higher Pedagogical Institutes in Ruse & Sofia. BKP member since 1919. Took part in September 1923 Uprising in Bĭala Slatina, was arrested, imprisoned & permanently banned from teaching. On release in 1924, took up illegal work in BKP Military Organization in Ruse & Plovdiv regional leaderships. Rearrested in 1925 & given death sentence (commuted to life imprisonment on account of pregnancy); released under amnesty in 1932. 1933–35: Studied at Lenin International School in Moscow; 1935–36: Worked for KI International Women's Secretariat. In 1936 returned to Bulgaria, becoming Editor of RD & BRP Organizational Secretary in 1940. Interned in Sv. Nikola

camp in 1941; escaped to supervise nationwide foundation of OF. 1944–48: OF Chief Secretary, oversaw foundation of DSNM; 1945–50?: Chairwoman, BNZhS; 1947–57: Minister of Posts, Telegraphs & Telephones; 1957–67: Deputy Chairwoman, OF National Council; 1957–77: (from 1977 Honorary) Chairwoman, National Committee for Bulgarian-Soviet Friendship. BRP/BKP CC member since 1937; Politbüro member (1940–48 & 1966–84; retired in 1984 on account of her age). Member of NSb since 1945, OF National Council since 1967 and DS (1976–86). s. Chavdar (* 1925), heart surgeon.
Works: *Poveliã na dŭlga* (The Call of Duty). 3 vols. Sofia 1972–79 [Memoirs]; *Vseotdaĭnost na sotsializma, mira i bŭlgaro-sŭvetskata druzhba* (Dedication to Socialism, Peace and Bulgarian-Soviet Friendship). Sofia 1979.

Dzhurov, Dobri Marinov (*Vrabevo, Lovech rgn. 5.1.1916) Poor peasant origins. BKP member since 1938. Educated in commercial *gimnaziiã*, Sofia. Political prisoner (1937–38). Active in illegal party work in Bulgarian Army (1939–40). Interned in 1942 in Krŭsto Pole camp; escaped & helped found Chavdar partisan brigade, which he commanded from April 1944; wounded in combat at Ĭablanitsa, near Sofia. 1944–45: Worked for People's Court. Studied in USSR at M. V. Frunze Military Academy (c. 1947) & K. E. Voroshilov Higher Military Academy (c. 1959). Advanced from Colonel (1945) to Army General (1964). 1956–62: Deputy Minister of Defence; 1962– : Minister of Defence. BKP CC candidate member in 1958; full member in 1962. Politburo candidate member in 1974; full member since 1977. Member of NSb since 1962 and OF National Council since 1963. m. Elena. s. Chavdar († 14.6.1972); d. Aksiniiã, historian.
Works: [with Elena Dzh.] *Murgash.* Sofia 1966 [Memoirs]; [Co-Author] *Za voennata politika na BKP* (On the Military Policy of the BKP). Sofia 1977; *S viãra i mech prez godinite* (With Faith and a Sword through the Years). Sofia 1984.

Filipov, Georgi (Grisha) Stanchev (*Kadievka, USSR 13.7.1919) Father Bulgarian, mother Ukrainian or Russian, both of poor peasant origins. Lived in USSR until 1936, when family settled in Doĭrentsi (Lovech rgn.). Educated in Lovech (1936–38) & Sofia University (1938–?). Joined RMS in 1936, BKP in 1940; BKP Secretary in Doĭrentsi in 1940. Arrested in 1941 & sentenced to 15 years' prison; released on 9.9.1944. 1944–47: BKP work in Lovech & Pleven; 1947: Chief Inspector, Ministry of Industry; 1948–51: Studied economics in Moscow; 1951–58: Worked in State Planning Commission as Adviser, Department Head then Deputy Chairman (1957–58). *Kandidat* degree in Economics (1956); 1956–58: Chief Editor, *Planovo Stopanstvo* (Planned Economies). 1958–62: Deputy Head, BKP CC Department; 1962–66: Deputy Chairman, State Planning Committee; 1966–68: Chairman, Commission on the New Economic Management System; 1968–71: 1st Deputy Chairman, State Planning Committee (with ministerial rank); 1971–82: BKP CC Secretary; 1981–86: Prime Minister; 1986–89: BKP CC Secretary. BKP CC candidate member in 1962 & full member in 1966; Politburo member 1974–89. Member of NSb 1966–89, DS (1971–1981 & 1986–89) & OF National Council since 1972.
Works: *Po Leninski aprilski pŭt* (On the Leninist April Path) Sofia 1980.

Ganev Vŭrbanov, Dimitŭr (Gradets, Burgas rgn. 28.10.1898 – Sofia 20.4.1964) Poor peasant orgins. Educated in Sliven & Varna *gimnazii*; taught in Kotel area. Joined BKP in 1921. After Sept. 1923 Uprising, briefly imprisoned & banned from teaching; moved to Sofia as factory worker. 1924: Elected Secretary of Union of Industrial Workers & to central leadership of General Trade Union Alliance. 1929–35: Secretary, Dobrudjan Revolutionary Organization (BKP section in lands annexed by Romania in 1920); collaborated with RCP groups under Ana Pauker; elected to RCP CC & Secretariat in 1934; imprisoned (1930–32 & 1935–40). 1940–42: Secretary, Dobrich (Tolbukhin) BKP Municipal Committee; 1942–44: Secretary, Sofia District BKP Committee & Editor of RD. In Feb. 1944 assumed command of Varna & Ruse insurrectionary operative zones, returning to Sofia in July to help organize 9 September rising. After 9.9.1944, was Head of BKP CC Mass Organizations Department & RD Chief Editor. 1945–47: 1st Secretary, Sofia Region BKP Committee; 1946–47: NSb Deputy Chairman; 1947–48: Ambassador in Bucharest; 1948–52: Minister of Foreign Trade. In 1950 was strongly attacked & forced to make self-criticism at June BKP conference. 1952–53?: Ambassador in Prague; 1954–59: BKP CC Secretary; 1958–64: Chairman, NSb Presidium. BKP CC member (1929–64); Politburo member in 1942, later served as candidate member (1949–54) & full member (1957–64). Member of NSb (1945–64) & OF National Council (1952–64).

Georgiev Stoĩanov, Kimon (Pazardzhik 11.8.1882–Sofia 28.9.1969). Middle-class background. Educated at Sofia Military School. Became professional soldier; rose to rank of Major by end of World War I. Leading member of *Voenen Sŭĩuz* (Military League) responsible for overthrow of BZNS government of Aleksandŭr Stamboliĭski (1923). 1926–28: Minister of Railways, Posts & Telegraphs. Prominent in formation of *Zveno* in 1927 & in coup led by Officers' League in 1934. 1934–35: Prime Minister (resigned in opposition to Tsar Boris' foreign policy, urging alliance with USSR). Took part in foundation of OF in 1942 & in 9.9.1944 events. Sept. 1944–46: Prime Minister & Minister without Portfolio. Executive Committee Chairman of *Naroden Sŭĩuz Zveno* (*Zv.* People's Union) from Oct. 1944 until its dissolution into OF in Feb. 1949. 1946–50: Deputy Prime Minister; 1946–47: Foreign Minister; 1947–59: Minister for Electrification; 1957–69: OF Deputy Chairman; 1959–62: Deputy Prime Minister; 1962–69: NSb Presidium member. Member of NSb (1923–27, 1927–31 & 1945–69) & OF National Committee/Council (1945–69).
Works: Izbrani proizvedeniĩa (Selected Works). Sofia 1982.

Grigorov Dimitrov, Mitko (Ĩarlovtsi, Sofia rgn. 9.9.1920–Sofia 6.9.1987) Father teacher. Educated in a Sofia *gimnaziĩa* & Sofia University (Law Faculty); graduated finally in 1947. Joined BKP in 1940. Arrested in 1942 & sentenced to 15 years' prison; released on 9.9.1944. Worked for Sofia City BKP Committee until 1950. 1950–54 & 1957–58: BKP CC Propaganda & Agitation Department Head; 1954–57: 1st Secretary, Varna District BKP Committee; 1958–66: BKP CC Secretary; 1962–66: Minister without Portfolio; 1962–66?: Chairman, Commission on Cultural & Ideological Questions; 1966–69: Bulgarian Representative on Editorial Board, *Problemy Mira i Sotsializma* (Problems of Peace & Socialism); 1970–71: Ambassador in London; 1974–87: DS Deputy Chairman. BKP CC candidate member (1954–57) & full member (1957–87); Politburo member (1961–66). Member of NSb (1953–87), OF National Council (1963–87) & DS (1971–87). His potential rivalry to Todor Zhivkov seemed to cause his demotion in 1966.

Ĩordanov, Georgi Momchev (∗Tvurditsa, Burgas rgn. 29.5.1934) Educated at Sofia University (Law Faculty). BKP member since 1956. 1957–60: Prosecuting magistrate in Sliven; 1960–71: BKP work in Sliven, as District Committee Secretary (1965–67) & 1st Secretary (1967–71). 1971–79: 1st Secretary, Sofia City BKP Committee; 1972–79: CC Secretariat member; 1979–89: Deputy Prime Minister; 1982–87: Chairman, Committee on Culture; 1986–87: Chairman, Council for Intellectual Development; 1987–89: Minister of Culture, Science & Education. BKP CC candidate member in 1966; full member in 1971; Politburo candidate member 1979–89. Member of NSb since 1971 and OF National Council since 1977.

Ĩotov, Ĩordan Nikolov (∗Lipnitsa, Sofia rgn. 2.10.1920) RMS member since 1937; BKP member since 1944. In 1944 joined Chavdar partisan brigade & was Political Commissar of a battalion. Educated Sofia University (Law Faculty). Holds *kandidat* and *doktor* degrees and History professorship; Corresponding Member of BAN since 1981. 1955–77: (from 1962 Senior) Academic Assistant and (from 1969) Deputy Director, Institute for History of BKP; 1977–87: Chief Editor, RD; 1981–87: Deputy Chairman, Bulgarian Journalists' Union; 1986–89: BKP CC Secretary. BKP CC member in 1978; Politburo member 1984–89. Member of NSb since 1981 & OF National Council & DS in 1986.
Works: Pŭrviĩat kongres na BKP 1919 (The First BKP Congress: 1919). Sofia 1959; *Iz borbite na tesnite sotsialisti protiv oportũnizma na Vtoriĩa internatsional* (The ‚Narrow' Socialists' Struggles against the Opportunism of the 2nd International). Sofia 1964.

Ĩugov, Anton Tanev (∗Karasouli [now Polikastron], Greece 5.8.1904) Raised in extreme poverty after father died. Had minimal schooling. In 1919 moved to Plovdiv, becoming tobacco worker; participated in strikes of 1919 & 1922 and in September 1923 Uprising. Joined KMS in 1921, MFD (*Makedonskoto Federalno Dvizhenie* – Macedonian Federalist Movement, left-wing of VMRO) in 1922 & BKP in 1928. In 1930 became Chairman of BKP Minorities Committee and in 1932 MFD leader. 1934–36: Studied at Lenin International School in Moscow. 1936–41: BKP activist in trade unions and from 1938 Head of BKP CC Military & Mass Organizations Departments. In 1940 organized tobacco workers' strike in Plovdiv. Interned in Gonda Voda prison camp in 1941, but escaped; sentenced to death *in absentia* (1942). Elected BKP CC Secretary in 1942 and until 9.9.1944 led CC Military Section & served in insurrectionary forces' central command. 1944–49: Minister of Internal Affairs; 1949–50: Deputy Prime Minister. At January 1950 BKP CC plenum was accused by Chervenkov of direct personal responsibility for purge of Traĭcho Kostov; demoted to Minister of Industry (1950–51). 1951–52: Minister of Heavy Industry; 1952–56: (from 1954 1st) Deputy Prime Minister; 1956–62: Prime Minister. Attacked by Todor Zhivkov for „antiparty activities" at November 1962 BKP CC plenum and dismissed from all major posts. Said to live on generous state pension in Sofia. BKP CC member (1937–62) & Politburo member (1937–62). Member of NSb (1945–64) & OF National Council (1948–62?). Major figure of „home" communists who opposed rapprochement with Tito's Yugoslavia.

Patriarch Kiril [Konstantin Markov Konstantinov] (Sofia 3.1.1901–Sofia 7.3.1971) Father Macedonian; owned restaurant. Educated Sofia Spiritual Seminary; 1920–25: Studied Theology in Bĭalgrad & Chernovtsi, USSR; 1925–27: Doctorate in Theology in Bern; 1928–30: Studied Philosophy in Berlin. Took monastic vows while student. 1938–53: Metropolitan of Plovdiv; led Church mission to Bulgarian Army (1940–44), visiting occupying forces in Yugoslavia and Greece; imprisoned (1944–45). 1948–71: Deputy Chairman of Holy Synod; 1953–71: Bulgarian Patriarch & Metropolitan of Sofia; 1952–71: Deputy Chairman, National Peace Committee. In 1970 elected full member of BAN. In *gimnaziia* was class-mate of Vŭlko Chervenkov.
19 theological & historical *Works* incl.: *Paisiĭ Mitropolit Plovdivski v tsŭrkovno-narodnata borba* (Metropolitan Paisiĭ of Plovdiv in the Church-National Struggle). Plovdiv 1949; *Pŭt Gospoden* (God's Way). 5 vols. Sofia 1957–65.

Kolarov, Vasil Petrov (Shumen 3.7.1877–Sofia 23.1.1950) Father cobbler. Educated in Varna *gimnaziia*. 1895–97: Teacher in Nikopol. Joined BRSDP in 1897. 1897–1900: Studied Law in France & Switzerland (where he met G. Plekhanov). In USSR gained titles of *doktor* of Economic Sciences (1935) & professor; in 1946 elected BAN Academician. 1902–19: BRSDP Secretary in Shumen & Plovdiv, supporting Dimitŭr Blagoev against „broad" socialists; imprisoned in 1908; elected to NSb (1913–23). In 1919 elected BKP CC Secretary. Moved to Moscow in 1922 to become General Secretary of KI Executive Committee, but relinquished post in 1924 (remaining Committee member until 1943). In 1923 went back to Bulgaria to revise BKP line on June 1923 coup & co-organize September Uprising. 1923–45: Lived in USSR. 1926–28: Edited BKP scientific newspaper *Komunistichesko Zname* (Communist Banner); 1928–29: Head of Balkan Secretariat of KI; 1929–31: Worked for Peasant International; 1931–41: Director of International Agrarian Institute in Moscow; 1941–44: Worked for „Khristo Botev" radio station. 1936–44: Member of BKP CC Foreign Bureau. In 1945 was one of three BKP representatives on OF National Council; 1945–47; NSb Chairman. On declaration of republic in Sept. 1946, became Provisional President. 1947–49: Deputy Prime Minister; 1947–49: Foreign Minister; 1949–50: Prime Minister. (Was never appointed BKP General Secretary, but *de facto* held this post after Dimitrov's death on 2 July 1949.) BRSDP/BKP CC member (1905–50) & Politburo member (1945–50). Member of NSb (1945–50) & OF National council (1948–50).
Works: Izbrani proizvedeniia (Selected Works) 3 vols. Sofia 1954–55; *Detstvo, iunoshestvo, vŭzmŭzhavane* (Childhood, Youth, Manhood). Sofia 1966 [Memoirs].
Literature: Vasil Kolarov – Bio-bibliografiia. Sofia 1947.

Kostov Dzhunev, Traĭcho (Sofia 17.6.1897–? 17.12.1949) Father railway worker. Educated in classical *gimnaziia* & Sofia University, Law Faculty (did not graduate). 1915–18: Reserve officer. 1918–21: Stenographer in NSb & Sofia Municipal Council. Joined BKP in 1920. Member of KMS CC (1920–24). In Sept. 1923 helped prepare for uprising in Sofia that never materialized. 1924: Became BKP CC records keeper & deputy to Stanke Dimitrov; arrested & severely injured leaping from a 4th floor window during interrogation. Imprisoned until 1929. 1929–31, 1932–34, 1936–38: Worked for KI in USSR. Returned to Bulgaria periodically between 1931 & 1940 to edit legal & illegal BKP newspapers. 1938–40 & 1942–44: Interned; 1940–2: BKP CC Secretary. 1944–48: BKP CC (from 1945 1st) Secretary; 1946–49: Deputy Prime Minister; 1946: Minister for Electrification; 1947–49: Chairman, Committee on Economic & Financial Questions. Denounced at March & June 1949 BKP CC plenums, removed from all posts & expelled from BKP. 1949 (April–?): National Library Director. 1949 (Dec.): Tried (with 10 others) on charges of espionage & illegal contacts with

Yugoslav CP; executed. Rehabilitated by BKP CC in 1956 & posthumously awarded state decorations. BKP CC member (1931–49) & Politburo Member (1945–49). Member of OF National Council (1944–49) & NSb (1945–49).
Works: Izbrani statii, dokladi, rechi (Selected Articles, Lectures & Speeches). Sofia 1964; *Izbrani Poizvedeniia*. Sofia 1979.
Literature: Kostova, E.: *Spomeni za moia brat* (Memories of my Brother). Sofia 1967; Isusov, M. (ed.): *Traĭcho Kostov: Publitsistika, korespondentsiia, spomeni*. 2 vols. Sofia 1987.

Kubadinski, Pencho Penev (*Loznitsa, Razgrad rgn. 27.7.1918) Peasant origins. Attended *gimnaziia* in Tŭrgovishte & Kotel; frequently arrested for political activities. Joined RMS in 1934; BKP in 1940. Shumen RMS District Secretary (1942–1944). After illegal party work in Bulgarian Army (1941–42), helped establish partisans in Shumen district, becoming Deputy Political Commissar of 9th Insurrectionary Operations Zone (1943) and Commander of P. Volov detachment (1944). 1944: Regional Police Chief, Shumen; 1944: Secretary, Varna Region RMS Committee; 1945–48: RMS/DSNM CC Department Head; 1946–48: Leader, National Youth Construction Brigades; 1948–52: Chief Director, Dimitrovgrad State Construction Trust; c. 1952: Studied in Higher Party School; 1952–58: 1st Secretary, Ruse BKP District Committee; 1958–62: BKP CC Secretary; 1962–74: Deputy Prime Minister; 1962–66: Minister of Transport & Communications; 1966–71: Minister of Construction & Architecture; 1974–89: Chairman, OF National Council. BKP CC candidate member in 1954 & full member in 1957; Politburo candidate member in 1962 & full member 1966–89. Member of NSb since 1953, OF National Council since 1963 and DS since 1975.
Works: Otechestveniiat front i izgrazhdaneto na razvito sotsialistichesko obshtestvo (The OF and Building a Mature Socialist Society). Sofia 1982; *Surova i trevozhna prolet* (An Austere and Uneasy Spring). Sofia 1985 [Memoirs].

Lilov, Aleksandŭr Vasilev (*Granichak, Mikhaĭlovgrad rgn. 31.8.1933) Poor peasant origins. BKP member since 1954. Educated in Sofia University (Bulgarian Philology); 1966–69: *Kandidat* degree in Literature at KPSS CC Academy of Social Sciences, Moscow; 1981: *Doktor*'s degree. 1958–59: 1st Secretary, Belogradchik DKMS Municipal Committee; 1959–60: 1st Secretary, Vidin District DKMS Committee; 1960–66: Worked for DKMS CC; 1962–66: Member (from 1963 Secretary) DKMS CC Bureau; 1969–70: Deputy Head, BKP CC Propaganda & Agitation Department; 1970–72: Head, BKP CC Art & Culture Department; 1972–83: BKP CC Secretary (for ideology); 1974–83 and 1989–: Politburo member; 1983–: Director, Institute for Contemporary Social Theories at BAN. BKP CC candidate member (1971–72) & full member (1972–86). Member of NSb (1962–66 & 1971–86), DS (1976–86) and OF National Council since 1982.
Works: Kritika na sŭvremennite burzhoazno-esteticheski kontseptsii za prirodata na izkustvoto (A Critique of Contemporary Bourgeois Aesthetic Conceptions of the Nature of Art) Sofia 1971; *Kŭm prirodata na khudozhestvenoto tvorchestvo* (Towards the Nature of Artistic Creation) Sofia 1979.

Lukanov, Andreĭ Karlov (*Moscow 26.9.1938) Son of Karlo Lukanov, Deputy Prime Minister (1952–54) & Foreign Minister (1956–62). Educated in Moscow State Institute for International Relations. BKP member since 1965. 1963–65: Inspector in Foreign Ministry economic department; 1966–68: International Organizations Department Head, Foreign Ministry; 1968–72: 1st Secretary, Bulgarian Permanent UN Representation in Geneva; 1972–76: Deputy Minister of Foreign Trade; 1976–86: Deputy Prime Minister; 1976–86: Chairman, Commission for Economic, Scientific & Technical Cooperation; 1976–86: Bulgarian Permanent Representative on CMEA Executive Committee; 1986–87: 1st Deputy Prime Minister; 1987–: Minister of Foreign Economic Relations. BKP CC candidate member in 1976, full member in 1977; Politburo candidate member in 1979 & full member in 1989. Member of NSb in 1976, OF National Council in 1977 and DS in 1989.

Patriarch Maksim [Marin Naĭdenov Minkov] (*Oreshak, Lovech rgn. 29.10.1914) Artisan origins. Educated: 1929–36: Sofia Spiritual Seminary; 1938–42: Theology Faculty, Sofia University. 1936–38: Church clerk in Ruse. Took monastic vows & was ordained in 1941. 1942: Metropolitan Deacon in Lovech; 1942–47: Teacher in Sofia Spiritual Seminary; 1947–50: Metropolitan *protosingel* in Ruse; 1950–55: Bulgarian Orthodox Church Representative in Moscow; 1955–60: Chief Secretary of Holy Synod; 1960–71: Metropolitan of Lovech. Member of Holy Synod in 1965; its Deputy

Chairman, then Chairman in 1971. 1971– : Bulgarian Patriarch and Metropolitan of Sofia. 1971– : Deputy Chairman, National Peace Committee.
Works: *Na gospodnĭata niva* (In God's Field). 3 vols. Sofia 1985.

Mikhaĭlov Popov, Ivan (Ferdinand [now Mikhaĭlovgrad] 22. 2. 1897–Sofia 16. 5. 1982) Father clerical worker & "Narrow" Socialist; his brother Khristo, a BKP member, was executed by the police in 1944 (the town Mikhaĭlovgrad was named after him). Educated in Vratsa *gimnaziĭa* & Sofia University, Law Faculty (graduated in 1921). Joined BKP in 1919. 1921–23: Practised law in Lom & Ferdinand. Took part in Sept. 1923 Uprising, fleeing to Yugoslavia after defeat. 1924–25: BKP work in Ferdinand district; sentenced to death *in absentia*. In 1925 emigrated to USSR & joined CPSU. Studied at F. E. Dzerzhinsky Military Technical Academy in Leningrad; 1931–39: Military representative in factories in Gorki & Kiev; 1939–41: Taught in Artillery School in Tambov; 1941–45: Fought in war, attaining rank of colonel-engineer. In 1945 returned to Bulgaria to work in Defence Ministry; promoted to Commander of BNA Artillery (1947), Deputy Minister of Defence (1950) & army general. 1950–71: Deputy Prime Minister; 1957–58: Minister of Transport & Communications; 1958–62: Minister of Defence. BKP CC member (1954–82) & Politburo member (1954–81). Member of OF National Council (1952–82), NSb (1953–82) & DS (1971–81).
Works: *V stroĭa* (In Formation) Sofia 1973. [Memoirs].
Literature: *Voin i dŭrzhavnik* (A Soldier & Statesman). Sofia 1986. [Documents about I. M.]

Mladenov, Petŭr Toshev (∗Toshevtski, Mikhaĭlovgrad rgn. 22. 8. 36) Peasant origins. Parents BKP members; father political commissar of Georgi Benkovski partisan detachment, died in battle in 1944; mother partisans helper. BKP member since 1964. Educated in Suvorov School (USSR), Shumen Military School, Sofia University (Philosophy Faculty) & Moscow State Institute for International Relations. 1964–66: 1st Secretary, Vidin DKMS District Committee; 1966–69: DKMS CC Secretary and Bureau member; 1969–71: 1st Secretary, Vidin BKP District Committee; 1971–89: Foreign Minister. BKP CC member in 1972; Politburo candidate member in 1974 & full member in 1977. 1989–: BKP General Secretary; DS Chairman. Member of NSb in 1971 & OF National Council in 1972.

Panev, Ivan Dimitrov (∗Plovdiv 15. 12. 1933) Working-class origins. Father was pre-1944 BKP member. Educated at Karl Marx Higher Economic Institute, Sofia; *kandidat* degree in Economics. Joined RMS in 1947 & BKP in 1957. In early 1960s was DKMS 1st Secretary in Plovdiv. 1964–65: 1st Deputy Chairman, Plovdiv District People's Council; 1965–68: Chairman, Executive Committee of Plovdiv City People's Council; 1968–71: 1st Secretary, DKMS CC Bureau; 1968–71; Chairman, Ministerial Council Commission for Youth & Sport; 1971–77: Chairman, Executive Committee of Sofia City People's Council; 1977–87: 1st Secretary, Plovdiv District BKP Committee; 1987– : 1st Secretary, Sofia City BKP Committee. Elected BKP CC candidate member in 1966 & full member in 1971; Politburo member 1988–89. Member of NSb since 1971, DS since 1981 & OF National Council since 1982.

Pavlov, Todor Dimitrov (Štip, Macedonia 14. 2. 1890–Sofia 8. 5. 1977) Son of nationalist schoolteacher; family migrated to Sofia in 1900. Educated in classical *gimnaziĭa* & Sofia University (1908–10 & 1911–14). 1910–11, 1914–15, 1919 & 1921: Teacher in Lom, Kazanlŭk & elsewhere. During World War I worked for Red Cross on Dobrudjan front. Joined BKP in 1919. 1922–23: Chief Editor, *Mladezh* (Youth); arrested after June 1923 coup. After release, chaired illegal BKP conference on Mt. Vitosha (1924). Rearrested in 1925, imprisoned (1925–26 & 1927–29). 1929–32 & 1936–41: Active in BKP agitation & journalism. 1932–36: Sent to Moscow & held various academic posts in philosophy. Interned (1941–43). 1944–46: One of the three Regents of Bulgaria; 1945: Elected as academician in BAN; 1945–77: Chief Editor, *Filosofska Misŭl* (Philosophical Thought); 1946–48: Professor at Sofia University; 1946–51: Chairman, Bulgarian-Soviet Friendship Union. 1947–62: President of BAN (Honorary President of BAN since 1962 & Writers' Union since 1963). 1949–52 & 1960–77: Director, BAN Philosophy Institute. Elected BKP CC member in 1924, candidate member in 1954 & full member in 1957; Politburo member 1966–76. Member of NSb (1949–77), NSb Presidium (1947–54 & 1962–71) & OF National Council (1952–77).
Works: *Izbrani proizvedeniĭa* (Selected Works) 10 vols. Sofia 1957–71. *Smĭakh. Spomeni* (Laughter. Memoirs). Varna 1977.

Petkov, Nikola Dimitrov (Sofia 21.7.1893–? 23.9.1947) Son of Prime Minister Dimitŭr Petkov assassinated in 1907. Studied law in Paris. In 1923 worked briefly as secretary to his brother Petko, then a Foreign Ministry official in Sofia; returned to Paris as embassy attaché. After June coup remained in exile in France until 1931. Joined BZNS in 1930; became leading member of *Pladne* (Noon) group (although for a time in the mid-1930s he supported the rival *Vrabcha-1* faction); edited the newspapers *Zemiu* (Land) (1931–32) & *Zemedelsko Zname* (Agrarian Banner) (1932–33). Member of NSb from 1936 to 1939. Opposed Bulgarian alliance with Germany; member of OF National Committee from its foundation in 1942. Interned in Gonda Voda camp (1942–44). Sept. 1944-July 1945: Minister without Portfolio. BZNS Secretary after resignation of Dr. G.M. Dimitrov (Jan.–June 1945); edited *Narodno Zemedelsko Zname* (National Agrarian Banner) from 1945 to 1947. Served in NSb from 1946 as leader of pro-Western opposition; arrested in June 1947. Tried & hanged on bogus charge of espionage.
Literature: Padev, M.: *Dimitrov Wastes No Bullets*. London 1948.

Simeon II (*Sofia 16.6.1937) Son of Tsar Boris III and Tsaritsa Giovanna. Proclaimed Tsar on 28 August 1943 on his father's death, but never crowned. A three-man Council of Regents (Prince Kiril, former Prime Minister Bogdan Filov & former War Minister Nikola Mikhov) ruled until 9.9.1944, when three new pro-communist regents were appointed. After plebiscite 8 Sept. 1946 establishing People's Republic, Simeon took asylum in Spain, where he has since lived, now working in business.

Stoi͡anov, Dimitŭr Ivanov (*Strazhitsa 7.11.1928) Poor peasant origins. Father executed as partisans helper in 1944. Higher education in History; studied at KGB high school in USSR (1972–73). 1946–51: Active in DSNM in Gorna Ori͡akhovitsa and Sofia. 1955–58: 1st Secretary, Veliko Tŭrnovo DKMS District Committee; 1958–61: (from 1959 Deputy 1st) Secretary, DKMS CC Bureau; 1961–73: (from 1971 1st) Secretary, Veliko Tŭrnovo BKP District Committee; 1973–88: Minister of Internal Affairs; 1988–89: BKP CC Secretary. BKP CC candidate member in 1962; full member in 1976; Politburo candidate member (1984–88), full member (1988–89). Member of NSb 1971–89 & OF National Council 1977–89. Military rank of General-Colonel.

Tanchev, Petŭr Zhelev (*Gledka, Khaskovo rgn. 12.7.1920) Peasant origins. Higher education in Law. From 1935 to 1944 active in illegal Agrarian movement in Khaskovo region and Sofia, collaborating with RMS; interned in 1944. 1945–49: ZMS council Member (from 1946 Chairman); from 1949 worked as BZNS organizer, becoming council member in 1951. 1957–89: BZNS council Secretary; 1962–66: Minister of Justice; 1966–71: Deputy Prime Minister; 1971–74: 1st Deputy Prime Minister; 1974–89: DS 1st Deputy Chairman. Member of NSb since 1946 and OF National Council since 1948.

Todorov, Stanko Georgiev (*Klenovik, Sofia rgn. 10.12.1920) Father miner in Pernik. In youth worked in tailor's workshop. Joined RMS in 1936; BKP in 1943. Shot during arrest in Feb. 1944; escaped in March to join armed resistance in Pancharevo *rai͡on*; participated in 9.9.1944 seizure of power. 1945–47: Secretary, Sofia RMS Regional Committee; 1947–50: DSNM CC Secretary; 1950: Secretary, Sofia BKP District Committee; 1950–52: Secretary, Burgas BKP District Committee; 1952: CC Agricultural Department Head; 1952–57: Minister of Agriculture; 1957–59: BKP CC Secretary; 1959–66: Deputy Prime Minister; 1959–62: Chairman, State Planning Commission; 1962–66: Bulgarian Permanent Representative on CMEA Executive Committee; 1966–71: BKP CC Secretary; 1971–81: Prime Minister; 1981– : NSb Chairman. BKP CC member in 1954; Politburo candidate member in 1959 & full member 1961–88. Member of NSb since 1953, OF National Council since 1963. m. Soni͡a Bakish, journalist.
Works: Usilni godini (Strenuous Years). Sofia 1980 [Collected articles & speeches].

Traĭkov Girovski, Georgi (Vŭrbeni, near Florina, Macedonia 8.4.1898–Sofia 14.1.1975) Joined BZNS in 1919 & in 1921 became Varna District BZNS organizer & Editor of *Zemedelski Glas* (Agrarian Voice) [Varna]; 1922: Elected Executive Council member on foundation of ZMS. 1923: Joined resistance to June coup, arrested & imprisoned until 1924. In 1925 became ZMS Secretary. Insurance company agent in the 1930s. In 1934 became Assistant Mayor of Varna. Worked for united front with BKP & in 1942 joined OF; interned in 1944. 1944–c. 1945: Chairman, Varna OF Regional

Committee; in 1945 replaced Aleksandŭr Obbov as Secretary of OF National Committee. 1945–47: Chairman, BZNS Executive Council; 1946–50: Minister of Agriculture & State Holdings (from 1947, Agriculture & Forests); 1947–64: (from 1956 1st) Deputy Prime Minister; 1947–75: BZNS Secretary; 1962–64: Chairman, Agricultural Council; 1964–71: Chairman, NSb Presidium; 1971–72: NSb Chairman; 1971–74: DS 1st Deputy Chairman. Member of NSb (1945–75); OF National Council (1948–75: Deputy Chairman 1957–66; Chairman 1972–74; Honorary Chairman 1974–75) & State Council (?–1975).
Works: Izbrani sŭchineniia (Selected Works). Sofia 1986.

Velchev, Boris Lazarov (∗ Etropole, Sofia rgn. 23.7.1914) Artisan origins. Technical education to secondary level. Joined BKP in 1936; became secretary of a Sofia *raĭon* committee. 1941: Arrested, given death sentence (commuted to life imprisonment); released in Sept. 1944. After 1944 worked for Sofia region BKP & edited *Partien Rabotnik* (Party Worker); c. 1949–c. 1953: Deputy 1st Secretary, Sofia City BKP Committee; c. 1956–c. 1959: BKP CC Party & Youth Organs Department Head; 1959: 1st Secretary, Sofia BKP District Committee; 1959–77: BKP CC Secretary; 1962–65: Chairman, Committee for Party & State Control (with ministerial status); 1977–c. 1982: Enterprise manager in Tolbukhin district; 1982– : Chairman, Committee for Balkan Understanding & Cooperation. BKP CC candidate member (1954–58) & full member (1958–77); Politburo member (1962–77). Member of NSb (1962–81), OF National Council (1963–) & DS (1971–81). His potential rivalry to Todor Zhivkov seemed to cause his demotion in 1977.

Zhivkov, Todor Khristov (∗ Pravets 7.9.1911) Poor peasant origins. Educated in elementary school in Pravets & Polygraphical School, Sofia. From 1929 worked as printer in State Printing House (Sofia) & became involved in BKP agitation. Joined BKP in 1932. 1934–35 & 1941–42: Secretary, Sofia 3rd *Raĭon* BKP Committee. 1942–43: Helped organize publishing of illegal OF newspaper *Otechestven Front*. In 1942 joined leadership of Chavdar partisan detachment; sent by BKP to organize partisan movement in Botevgrad district in 1943. Became Deputy Commander of 1st Military Operative Zone (centred on Sofia) in July 1944; headed Operative Bureau to coordinate resistance forces in Sofia prior to 9.9.1944; led armed group in city park on 9.9.1944. After OF victory, became Chief of People's Militia in Sofia & 2nd Secretary of Sofia District BKP Committee. Promoted to colonel in 1945; to BKP Organizational Bureau in 1948. 1948–50: 1st Secretary, Sofia City BKP Committee (in 1949 also Chairman, Sofia City People's Council; in 1950 also 1st Secretary, Sofia District BKP Committee). 1950–54: BKP CC Secretary; 1954–89: BKP CC 1st Secretary (Secretary General from 1981). 1956–62: NSb Presidium Member; 1962–71: Prime Minister; 1971–89: DS Chairman. Elected BKP CC candidate member in 1945 & full member in 1948; Politburo candidate member in 1950 & full member 1951–89. Member of NSb 1945–89 & OF National Council 1952–89. Nov./Dec. 1989: dismissed from all functions and expelled from BKP. m. Mara Maleeva, physician. d. Lîudmila, s. *Vladimir* (∗ 5.6.1952) Director, Lîudmila Zhivkova International Foundation since 1982; Deputy Chairman, Committee of Culture since 1983; member of BKP CC 1986–89, NSb 1987–89 & OF National Council 1987–89; head of BKP CC culture department 1989. Lost positions after his father's downfall, was expelled from BKP. *Works: Izbrani sŭchineniia*. 38 vols. Sofia 1975–89.
Literature: BAN (Institute of History): *Todor Zhivkov – Biografichen Ocherk* (Biographical Outline). Sofia 1981.

Zhivkova, Lîudmila Todorova (Sofia 26.7.1942–21.7.1981) Daughter of Todor Zhivkov. Educated at Sofia University (History Faculty); Moscow University (in Art History) & Oxford (1969–70). From c. 1965 was Assistant in Institute of Balkan Studies. *Kandidat* degree in 1971. Joined BKP in 1967. Sustained serious head injuries in car accident (1973). 1971–75: (from 1972 1st) Deputy Chairwoman, Committee of Art & Culture; 1975–81: Chairwoman, Committee of Culture (with ministerial rank from 1976). Her initiatives included the Thracian exhibitions in Paris (1974), Vienna (1975) & London (1976); the *Zname na mira* (Banner of Peace) international children's festival (1979) & celebrations of 1300th anniversary of the Bulgarian state (1981). After her sudden death in 1981, the Lîudmila Zhivkova International Foundation was set up. BKP CC member (1976–81) & Politburo member (1979–81). Member of OF National Council (1972–81) & NSb (1976–81). 1m. Stefan Stoĭchev; 2m. Ivan Slavkov; d. Evgeniia (∗ c. 1965), s. Todor (∗ c. 1971).

Works: Anglo-turskite otnosheniĩa 1933–1939g. (Anglo-Turkish Relations 1933–39). Sofia 1971; *Das Grabmal von Kasanlak.* Recklinghausen 1973 & [in Bulgarian] Sofia 1974; *Das Tetraevangeliar des Zaren Ivan Alexandar.* Recklinghausen 1977 & Sofia 1979; *Za usŭvŭrshenstvuvane na choveka i obshtestvoto* (On the Perfection of Man & Society). Sofia 1980.
Literature: Mislete za mene kato za ogŭn (Think of Me as Fire). Ed. S. Mikhaĭlov. Sofia 1982; *Liudmila Zhivkova.* Oxford, 1982 & 1986.

Bibliographie

Jozo Džambo, München

Gliederung

I. Allgemeines
   a) Bibliographien
   b) Allgemeine Darstellungen und Nachschlagewerke
   c) Statistiken
   d) Zeitschriften und Jahrbücher
   e) Atlanten und Karten

II. Voraussetzungen
   a) Geographische Grundlagen
   b) Geschichte bis 1944

III. Politische Entwicklung; Politisches und Rechtssystem
   a) Politisches System
      1. Allgemeines
      2. Politische Parteien
         2.1. BKP
         2.2. BZNS
         2.3. Sonstige
      3. Massenorganisationen
      4. Politische Institutionen
      5. Politische Kultur
   b) Innenpolitik
   c) Außenpolitik
   d) Rechtssystem
      1. Allgemeines
      2. Staatsrecht
      3. Zivilrecht
      4. Zivilprozeßrecht
      5. Familienrecht
      6. Recht der Wirtschaft
      7. Arbeitsrecht
      8. Internationales Privatrecht
      9. Strafrecht
      10. Strafprozeßrecht
      11. Sonstiges
      12. Verträge
   e) Landesverteidigung

IV. Wirtschaft
   a) Wirtschaftssystem
   b) Industrie und Handwerk
   c) Land- und Forstwirtschaft
   d) Bergbau und Energiewirtschaft
   e) Handel, Versorgung und Verkehr; Tourismus
   f) Außenwirtschaft

V. Gesellschaft
   a) Raumplanung und Umweltschutz
   b) Bevölkerungsstruktur
   c) Sozialstruktur
   d) Nationale Minderheiten
   e) Schulwesen
   f) Hochschulen und Wissenschaft
   g) Kirchen und Religionsgemeinschaften
   h) Massenmedien und Sprachkultur

VI. Kultur
   a) Volkskultur
   b) Literatur
   c) Theater
   d) Film
   e) Bildende Kunst und Architektur
   f) Musik
   g) Sport und Körperkultur

I. Allgemeines

a) Bibliographien

Bălgarija v čuždata literatura 1964 [ff.] Bibliografski ukazatel (Bulgarien in der ausländischen Literatur 1964 ff. Bibliographisches Verzeichnis). Sofia 1966 ff.

Bălgarski bibliografski institut 1945-1955 (Bulgarisches Bibliographisches Institut 1945-1955). Sofia 1955.

Bălgarski disertacii 1974 – [...] (Bulgarische Dissertationen 1974 –). Sofia 1975 ff. (Nacionalna bibliografija na NR Bălgarija, Serija 2).

Bălgarski knigi. Mesečen katalog (Bulgarische Bücher. Monatskatalog). Sofia 1954 ff.

Bălgarski knigi 1878-1944. Bibliografski ukazatel. Azbučna poredica (Bulgarische Bücher 1878-1944. Bibliographische Serie. Alphabetischer Katalog). Bd. 1-6. Sofia 1978-1983.

Bălgarski knigopis. Godišen ukazatel na bălgarskite knigi, notni, grafičeski i kartografski izdanija (Bulgarische Bibliographie. Jahresanzeiger der bulgarischen Bücher, Noten-, graphischer und kartographischer Ausgaben). Sofia 1929 ff.

Bălgarski periodičen pečat. Bibliografski bjuletin... (Bulgarische Periodika. Bibliographisches Bulletin...). Sofia 1965 ff.

Bălgarski periodičen pečat. Tekušti vestnici, spisanija i bjuletini kăm 1 januari 1950 (Bulgarische Periodika. Laufende Zeitungen, Zeitschriften und Bulletins am 1. Januar 1950). Sofia 1950.

Bibliografija na bălgarskata bibliografija 1852-1944 (Bibliographie der bulgarischen Bibliographie 1852-1944). Sofia 1981.

Bibliografija na bălgarskata bibliografija, knigoznanie i bibliotečno delo 1963 – (Bibliographie der bulgarischen Bibliographie, der Buchkunde und des Bibliothekswesens 1963 –). Sofia 1965 ff. (Nacionalna bibliografija na NR Bălgarija, Serija 8).

Bibliografija na bălgarskata statističeska literatura 1878-1980 (Bibliographie der bulgarischen statistischen Literatur). I-II. Sofia 1981.

Bibliographie d'études balkaniques. 1 ff. Sofia 1966 ff.

Bulgaria: A Bibliographic Guide. Hrsg. M. V. Pundeff. Washington, D. C. 1965 (Repr. 1968).

Bulgarien im Buch. Eine Auswahl wichtiger Literatur zur Geschichte, Kultur und Gesellschaft Bulgariens. Veröffentlichungen, zur Verfügung gestellt durch die Botschaft der Volksrepublik Bulgarien in Bonn und aus den Beständen der Bibliothek des Instituts für Auslandsbeziehungen. Hrsg. v. Institut für Auslandsbeziehungen, Stuttgart. Auswahl und Red.: U. Rossbach. Stuttgart 1981 (Schriftenreihe des Instituts für Auslandsbeziehungen, Stuttgart; Reihe Dokumentation 16).

Čolov, P.: Bălgarski istorici. Biografično-bibliografski spravočnik (Bulgarische Historiker. Ein biographisch-bibliographisches Handbuch). Sofia 1981.

Cvetanov, C.: Bălgarska bibliografija. Istoričeski pregled i dnešno săstojanie (Bulgarische Bibliographie. Geschichtlicher Überblick und heutiger Stand). 2., überarb. Aufl. Sofia 1957.

Desev, B.: Spravočno-bibliografski izdanija (Bibliographische Nachschlagewerke). Sofia 1960.

Deutsch-bulgarische Kulturbeziehungen. Bibliographie. Bearb. v. F. Krause. Berlin 1970 (Deutsche Staatsbibliothek. Bibliographische Mitteilungen 23).

Gečeva, K.: Bălgarskata kultura prez văzraždaneto. Bibliografija. Bălgarska i čužda knižnina 1878-1983 (Bulgarische Kultur in der Wiedergeburtsepoche. Bibliographie. Bulgarische und ausländische Literatur 1878-1983). Sofia 1986.

Godišnik na Bălgarskija bibliografski institut (Jahrbuch des Bulgarischen Bibliographischen Instituts). I (1945-1946) ff. Sofia 1948 ff.

Haralampieff, K.: Bulgarische Bibliographie (1945-1950), in: Südostforschungen. 12 (1953), S. 419-442.

Haralampieff, K.; Schaller, H. W.: Bibliographie zur Bulgaristik in Deutschland (Ein Überblick). Sonderdruck aus: 1300 Jahre Bulgarien. Neuried 1981 (Bulgarische Sammlung 2/1; Südosteuropa-Studien 29), S. 433-470.

Ivanova, E.: Bibliografija na literaturata po žurnalistika, izdadena v Bălgarija prez perioda 1944-1969 g. (Bibliographie der Literatur über Journalistik, erschienen in Bulgarien 1944-1969). Sofia 1972.

Kănčev, S.; Radev, T.: Bălgarsko-nemski kulturni otnošenija 1806-1966. Bibliografija

(Bulgarisch-deutsche Kulturbeziehungen 1806–1966. Bibliographie). Sofia 1968.
Katalog na izdanijata na Bălgarskija bibliografski institut Elin Pelin (Katalog der Publikationen des Bulgarischen Bibliographischen Instituts Elin Pelin). Sofia 1957.
Katalog na izdanijata na BAN [1870–] (Katalog der Veröffentlichungen der BAN. (1870–). 1 ff. Sofia 1956 ff.
Lazarov, M.: Bălgarija na Balkanite 1944–1974. Bibliografija. [Parallelt.:] Bulgaria in the Balkans. Bibliography. Sofia 1975.
Lazarov, M.; Dančeva, J.: Disertacii, zaštiteni v čužbina ot Bălgari 1878– 1969. Bibliografski ukazatel (Die von den Bulgaren im Ausland verteidigten Dissertationen 1878–1968. Bibliographisches Verzeichnis). Sofia 1975.
Lazarov, M.; Dančeva, J.; Matakieva, M.: Disertacii s bălgarska tematika zaštiteni ot čuždestranni učeni 1878 [–] 1978 (Dissertationen zum Thema Bulgarien, verteidigt von ausländischen Wissenschaftlern). Sofia 1981.
Malčeva Petkova, Z.: Bibliografija na bălgarskata bibliografija 1944–1969 (Bibliographie der bulgarischen Bibliographie 1944–1969). Sofia 1971.
Novaja sovetskaja i inostrannaja literatura po obščestvennym naukam. Narodnaja Respublika Bolgarija. Bibliografičeskij ukazatel' (Neue sowjetische und ausländische Literatur über Gesellschaftswissenschaften. Volksrepublik Bulgarien. Ein bibliographisches Verzeichnis). Moskau 1976 ff.
Paprikoff, G.I.: Works of Bulgarian Emigrants. An Annotated Bibliography. Books, Booklets, Dissertations. Chicago 1985.
Plovdivski okrăg po pătja na socializma 1944–1964. Ukazatel na literatura v šest toma (Der Bezirk Plovdiv auf dem Wege des Sozialismus 1944–1964. Ein Literaturverzeichnis in sechs Bänden). Plovdiv 1972 ff.
Résumés des travaux publies par l'Academie des Sciences de Bulgarie en... 1944–1950 (Sofia 1960); 1951 et 1952 (Sofia 1958); 1953–1955 (Sofia 1960); 1956–1957 (Sofia 1961).
Ribarova, C.: Bălgarija pri socializma. Materiali za bibliografija. Publikacii na bălgarski učeni 1945–1980 (Bulgarien im Sozialismus. Materialien für eine Bibliographie. Veröffentlichungen der bulgarischen Wissenschaftler 1945–1980). Sofia 1980.
Săbeva, E.; Stančeva, M.: Opis na izdanijata na Bălgarskata akademija na naukite 1869–1953. [Parallelt.:] Bibliographie des publications de l'Académie des sciences de Bulgarie 1869–1953. Sofia 1956.
Slavčeva, C.: Istoričeskata bălgaristika v čužbina 1944–1980. Bibliografski spravočnik (Historische Bulgaristik im Ausland 1944–1980. Ein bibliographisches Handbuch). Sofia 1983.
Slavčeva-Ribarova, C.: Bălgarija prez epochata na socializma. Istoričeska bibliografija 1944–1984 (Bulgarien in der Epoche des Sozialismus. Historische Bibliographie 1944–1984). Sofia 1986.
Spasov, E. K.; Draganov, G.G.: Trinadeset veka Bălgarija. Istoričeska bibliografija (Dreizehn Jahrhunderte Bulgarien. Historische Bibliographie). Sofia 1980.
Spasova, M.V.: Bălgarski periodičen pečat 1944–1969. Bibliografski ukazatel (Bulgarische Periodika 1944–1969. Bibliographisches Verzeichnis). Bd. 1–3. Sofia 1975.
Staniševa, L.; Šopova, S.: Bibliografija na disertaciite, zaštiteni v Bălgarija 1929 – [...] [Parallelt.:] Bibliography of Dissertations, Defended in Bulgaria [...]. 2 Bde. Sofia 1969, 1979.
100 godini bălgarska bibliografija 1852–1952. Spomenna knižka (100 Jahre bulgarische Bibliographie 1852–1952. Ein Gedenkbuch). Sofia 1952.
Stojanov, P.; Djugmedžieva, P.; Veleva, N.; Karadžova, A.: 25 godini narodna vlast. Bibliografski ukazatel (25 Jahre Volksmacht. Ein bibliographisches Verzeichnis). Sofia 1969.
Südosteuropa-Bibliographie. Hrsg. v. Südost-Institut. Bd. 1 ff. München 1956 ff.
Trajkov, V.: Bălgarija v čuždata literatura 1954–1963. Bibliografski ukazatel (Bulgarien in der ausländischen Literatur 1954–1963. Bibliographisches Verzeichnis). Sofia 1965.
Trajkov, V.; Dančeva, J.; Lazarov, M.: Bălgarija v čuždata literatura 1944–1953. Bibliografski ukazatel (Bulgarien in der ausländischen Literatur 1944–1953. Bibliographisches Verzeichnis). Sofia 1968.
U.S. Bureau of the Census: Bibliography of Social Science Periodicals and Monograph Series: Bulgaria, 1944–1960. Washington 1961 (Foreign Social Science Bibliographies, Series P-92, No. 2).
Vasileva, Ju.: Bibliografija na izdanijata na Sofijskija universitet 1947–1955 (Bibliographie der Veröffentlichungen der Universität Sofia 1947–1955). Sofia 1956.

Vasileva, Ju.: Bibliografija na izdanijata na Sofijskija universitet „Kliment Ochridski" [1956–]. [Parallelt.:] Bibliographie der Veröffentlichungen der Universität zu Sofia „Kliment Ochridski" [1956–]. Sofia 1969 ff.

b) Allgemeine Darstellungen und Nachschlagewerke

Anastasoff, Ch.: The Bulgarians: From Their Arrival in the Balkans to Modern Times. Thirteen Centuries of History. Hickesville, NY 1977.
Andreev, M.; Angelov, D.: Istorija na bălgarskata feodalna dăržava i pravo (Geschichte des bulgarischen feudalen Staates und Feudalrechts). 3. Aufl. Sofia 1968.
Angelova, R. I.: 40 godini socialističeski văzchod na NR Bălgarija (40 Jahre sozialistischer Aufschwung in der NRB). Sofia 1984.
Bălgarija i Balkanite 681–1981. Naučna konferencija s meždunarodno učastie posvetena na 1300-godišninata ot săzdavaneto na bălgarska dăržava (Sofija 26–27 januari 1981) (Bulgarien und der Balkan 681–1981. Internationale Wissenschaftskonferenz zum 1300-jährigen Jahrestag der Gründung des bulgarischen Staates [Sofia, 26.–27. Januar 1981]). Sofia 1982.
Bălgarskata dăržavnost v aktove i dokumenti (Bulgarische Staatlichkeit in Akten und Dokumenten). Zusammengestellt v. V. Gjuzelev. Sofia 1981.
Bulgaria. Ed. by L. A. D. Dellin. New York 1957 (East-Central Europe Under the Communists).
Bulgaria Basic Handbook. 2 Vols. and Map Section. Ed. by British Government. London 1943.
Bulgaria: Past and Present. Studies in History, Literature, Economics, Music, Sociology, Folklore and Linguistics. Proceedings of the First International Conference of Bulgarian Studies Held at the University of Wisconsin, Madison – May 3–5, 1973. Hrsg. Th. Butler. Columbus, Ohio 1976.
Bulgarien heute. Geschichte, Politik, Wirtschaft, Kultur. (Red.: G. Bokow). Sofia 1982. – Engl. Ausgabe: Modern Bulgaria: History, Policy, Economy, Culture. Sofia 1981.
Bulgarische Sprache, Literatur und Geschichte. Neuried 1980 (Bulgarische Sammlung 1; Südosteuropa-Studien 27).
Četirideset godini socialističeska Bălgarija (Vierzig Jahre sozialistisches Bulgarien). Sofia 1984.
1300 godini bălgarska dăržava (1300 Jahre bulgarischer Staat). Sofia 1978.
Crampton, R. J.: A Short History of Modern Bulgaria. Cambridge 1987.
Enciklopedija „A – Ja" (Enzyklopädie „A – Ja"). Sofia 1974.
Enciklopedija Bălgarija (Enzyklopädie Bulgarien). Bd. 1 ff. Sofia 1978 ff.
Evans, S. G.: A Short History of Bulgaria. London 1960.
Fol, A. u. a.: Kratka istorija na Bălgarija (Kurze Geschichte Bulgariens). Hrsg. I. Dimitrov, M. Lalkov. Sofia 1981.
Georgiev, V.: Enciklopedija „Bălgarija" (Enzyklopädie „Bulgarien"). Sofia 1986.
Golub, V. I.: Bulgarija socialističeskaja (Das sozialistische Bulgarien). Kiev 1976.
Grigorova, Ž.: Balkanite sled Vtorata svetovna vojna (Der Balkan nach dem Zweiten Weltkrieg). 2 Bde. Sofia 1980.
Hacker, J.: Der Ostblock. Enstehung, Entwicklung und Struktur 1939–1980. Baden-Baden 1980.
Hartl, H.: Der „einige" und „unabhängige" Balkan. Zur Geschichte einer politischen Vision. München 1977.
Heß, G.: Bulgarien: Landeskundlicher Überblick. Leipzig 1985.
Information Bulgaria. A Short Encyclopaedia of the People's Republic of Bulgaria. Ed. by the Bulgarian Academy of Science. [Aus dem Bulgar. übers.] Oxford u. a. 1985 (Countries of the World Information Series).
Istorija Bolgarii v dvuch tomach (Geschichte Bulgariens in zwei Bänden). Red.: P. N. Tret'jakov, S. A. Nikitin, L. B. Valev. Moskau 1954–1955.
Istorija na Bălgarija (Geschichte Bulgariens). 2., überarb. Aufl. in 3 Bänden. Sofia 1961–1964.
Istorija na Bălgarija v četirnadeset toma (Geschichte Bulgariens in 14 Bänden). Sofia 1979 ff.
Kolarov, S.: Beležiti bălgari (Berühmte Bulgaren). Sofia 1981.
Kosev, D.; Christov, Ch.; Angelov, D.: Kratka istorija na Bălgarija (Kurze Geschichte Bulgariens). 2., überarb. Aufl. Sofia 1966. – Dt. Übers. der 1. Aufl. Sofia 1962: Bulgarische Geschichte. Sofia 1963.
Kratka bălgarska enciklopedija v 5 toma (Kleine bulgarische Enzyklopädie in 5 Bänden). Sofia 1963–1969.

Lendvai, P.: Der Rote Balkan zwischen Nationalismus und Kommunismus. Frankfurt a. M. 1969.
McIntyre, R. J.: Bulgaria: Politics, Economics and Society. London u. a. 1988 (Marxist Regimes Series).
Nikolova, V.; Kumanov, M.: Kratăk istoričeski spravočnik. Bălgarija (Kleines historisches Handbuch. Bulgarien). Sofia 1983.
Ognjanoff, Ch.: Bulgarien. Nürnberg 1967 (Kultur der Nationen. Geistige Länderkunde 22).
Săvremenna Bălgarija v 5 toma. Treta kompleksna meždunarodna naučna konferencija po bălgaristika, 1980 (Das moderne Bulgarien in 5 Bänden. Dritte komplexe internationale wissenschaftliche Konferenz über Bulgaristik, 1980). Sofia 1984, 1985.
Schaller, H.: Bulgaristik in Deutschland. Ihre Geschichte und gegenwärtige Situation, in: Südosteuropa-Mitteilungen. 27 (1987) 2, S. 135–142.
SIV 1949–1974. 25 Jahre Rat für Gegenseitige Wirtschaftshilfe. Sofia 1974.
Sovetskaja Bolgaristika. Itogi i perspektivy. Materialy konferencii posvjaščennoj 1300-letiju Bolgarskogo gosudarstva (Sowjetische Bulgaristik. Resultate und Perspektiven. Materialien der Konferenz zum 1300-jährigen Jahrestag der Gründung des bulgarischen Staates). Moskau 1983.
Stamenov, M.: Novata panorama na Bălgarija (Neues Panorama von Bulgarien). Sofia 1969.
Taschenlexikon Bulgarien. Leipzig 1983.
Terzijski, P.: Socialističeska Bălgarija v dati i săbitija. Chronika 1944–1984 (Das sozialistische Bulgarien in Daten und Ereignissen. Eine Chronik 1944–1984). Sofia 1984.
Todorov, N.: A Short History of Bulgaria. Sofia 1977.

c) Statistiken

Singh, Sh.: National Accounts Statistics and Exchange Rates for Bulgaria. Washington, D. C. 1985.
Statističeski danni 1939–1970 (Statistische Daten 1939–1970). Sofia 1971.
Statističeski danni 1950–1967 (Statistische Daten 1950–1967). Sofia 1968.
Statističeski godišnik na Narodna Republika Bălgarija (Statistisches Jahrbuch der NRB). Sofia.
Statističeski sbornik 1956–1962 (Statistischer Sammelband 1956–1962). Sofia 1963.
Statističeski spravočnik (Statistisches Handbuch). Sofia 1958.

d) Zeitschriften und Jahrbücher

Abstracts of Bulgarian Scientific Literature. [Verschiedene Ausgaben]. Sofia.
Aktualni problemi na naukata (Aktuelle wissenschaftliche Probleme). Sofia 1974 ff.
Architecture and Society – Architektura i obštestvo. Sofia 1954 ff.
Bălgaro-săvetska družba (Bulgarisch-sowjetische Freundschaft). Sofia 1945 ff.
Bălgarska etnografija (Bulgarische Ethnographie). Sofia 1975 ff.
Bălgarski ezik (Bulgarische Sprache). Sofia 1951 ff.
Bălgarski folklor (Bulgarische Folklore). Sofia 1975 ff.
Bălgarsko muzikoznanie. Sbornik (Bulgarische Musikwissenschaft. Sammelband). Sofia 1971 ff.
Balkanistika (Balkanistik). Sofia 1986 ff.
Balkansko ezikoznanie. Linguistique balkanique. Sofia 1959 ff.
Bulgarian Films. Sofia 1962 ff. - Früher: Films Bulgares.
Bulgarian Historical Review. Revue bulgare d'Histoire. Sofia 1973 ff.
Bulgarian Journal of Sociology. Sofia 1978 ff.
Bulgarische Gewerkschaften. Sofia 1959 ff. – Engl. Ausgabe: Bulgarian Trade Unions. Sofia 1953 ff.
Bulgarischer Außenhandel. Sofia 1952 ff. – Engl. Ausg.: Bulgarian Foreign Trade. Sofia 1952 ff.
Byzantinobulgarica. Sofia 1962 ff.
Dăržaven vestnik (Staatsanzeiger). Sofia 1897 ff.
Études Balkaniques. Sofia 1964 ff.
Études Historiques. Sofia 1960 ff.
Ezik i literatura (Sprache und Literatur). Sofia 1946 ff.
Ikonomičeska misăl (Ökonomischer Gedanke). Sofia 1956 ff.
Ikonomičeski život (Wirtschaftsleben). Sofia 1966 ff.
Ikonomika na selskoto stopanstvo (Agrarökonomie). Sofia 1964 ff.
Istoričeski pregled (Historische Zeitschrift) Sofia 1945 ff.
Izvestija na Bălgarskoto Istoričesko Družestvo. Bulletin de la Société Historique Bulgare. Sofia 1905 ff. – Bis 1944: Izvestija na Istoričeskoto družestvo v Sofija.

Izvestija na Etnografskija Institut (Mitteilungen des Ethnographischen Instituts). Sofia 1953 ff.
Izvestija na Instituta po istorija na BKP (Mitteilungen des Instituts für Geschichte der BKP). Sofia 1957 ff.
Izvestija na Visšija Institut za narodno stopanstvo (Mitteilungen des Hohen Instituts für Volkswirtschaft). Varna 1957 ff.
Letopis na statiite ot bălgarskite spisanija i sbornici. Articles from Bulgarian Journals and Collections. Sofia 1972 ff. – Früher: Letopis na periodičnija pečat... Sofia 1952 ff.
Literaturna istorija (Literaturgeschichte). Sofia 1977 ff.
Literaturna misăl. Spisanie za estetika, literaturna istorija i kritika (Literarischer Gedanke. Zeitschrift für Ästhetik, Literaturgeschichte und Kritik). Sofia 1957 ff.
Narodna kooperacija (Genossenschaft des Volkes). Sofia 1950 ff.
Narodni săveti (Die Volksräte). Sofia 1948 ff.
Narodnostopanski archiv. Visšija finansovostopanski institut „D.A. Cenov" (Volkswirtschaftliches Archiv. Hohes Institut für Finanz- und Wirtschaftswissenschaften „D.A. Cenov"). Sofia 1946 ff.
Naselenie (Bevölkerung). Sofia 1968 ff.
Novo vreme (Die Neue Zeit). Sofia 1925 ff.
Obzor (Übersicht). Revue bulgare de littérature et d'arts. Sofia 1967 ff.
Paleobulgarica. Starobălgaristika. Sofia 1977 ff.
Planovo stopanstvo (Planwirtschaft). Sofia 1946 ff.
Pravna misăl (Juristischer Gedanke). Sofia 1957 ff.
Problemi na bălgarskija folklor (Probleme der bulgarischen Folklore). 7 Bde. Sofia 1972 ff.
Problemi na geografijata (Probleme der Geographie). Sofia 1974 ff.
Problemi na izkustvoto (Probleme der Kunst). Sofia 1968 ff.
Rodopski sbornik (Rhodopen-Sammelband). Sofia 1965 ff.
Rudodobiv i metalurgija (Bergbau und Metallurgie). Sofia 1946 ff.
Săvremenni socialni teorii (Gegenwärtige Sozialtheorien). Sofia 1973 ff.
Săvremennik. Spisanie na SBP za săvremenna bălgarska i čužda literatura, kritika i publicistika (Zeitgenosse. Zeitschrift des SBP für zeitgenössische bulgarische und ausländische Literatur, Kritik und Publizistik). Sofia 1973 ff.
Sbornik za narodni umotvorenija, nauka i knižnina (Sammelband für Folklore, Wissenschaft und Literatur). Sofia 1889 ff.
Selskostopanska misăl (Landwirtschaftlicher Gedanke). Sofia 1956 ff.
Selskostopanska nauka (Landwirtschaftswissenschaft). Sofia 1962 ff.
Septemvri. Literatura. Kritika. Izkustvo (September. Literatur. Kritik. Kunst). Sofia 1948 ff.
Slavistični izsledvanija (Slavistische Studien). Sofia 1963 ff.
Sociologičeski problemi (Soziologische Probleme). Sofia 1969 ff.
Spisanie na Bălgarskata Akademija na Naukite i Izkustvata (Zeitschrift der Bulgarischen Akademie der Wissenschaften und der Künste). Sofia 1953 ff.
Statistika (Statistik). Sofia 1954 ff.
Stroitelstvo (Bau). Sofia 1954 ff.
Techničeska misăl (Technischer Gedanke). Sofia 1964 ff.
Trudove na Visšija Ikonomičeski Institut – Sofija (Arbeiten des Hohen Instituts für Wirtschaft – Sofia). Sofia 1952 ff.
Văprosi na fizičeskata kultura. Organ na Centralnija săvet na Bălgarskija săjuz za fizičeska kultura i sport (Fragen der Körperkultur. Organ des Zentralrates des Bulgarischen Bundes für Körperkultur und Sport). Sofia 1956 ff.
Vătrešna tărgovija (Der Binnenhandel). Sofia 1974 ff.
Wirtschaftsnachrichten aus Bulgarien. Bulgarische Handels- und Industriekammer. Sofia 1961 ff.
Zentralkomitee der Bulgarischen Kommunistischen Partei. Informationsbulletin. Sofia 1947 ff.

e) Atlanten und Karten

Atlas. Narodna Republika Bălgarija (Atlas. NRB). Red.: Ž. Gălăbov u.a. Sofia 1973.
Bălgarski dialekten atlas v 4 toma (Bulgarischer Dialekt-Atlas in 4 Bänden). Bearb. D. Vakarelska u.a. Sofia 1966 ff.
Bălgarski voenen atlas (Bulgarischer Kriegsatlas). Hrsg.: Kab – Glavno upravlenie po geodezija, kartografija i katastăr. Kompleksen institut za proučvane i proektirane po kartografija. Sofia 1979.
Kosev, D. u.a.: Atlas po bălgarska istorija (Atlas zur bulgarischen Geschichte). Sofia 1963.
Učeben geografski atlas (Geographischer Schulatlas). Sofia 1959.

II. Voraussetzungen

a) Geographische Grundlagen

Dimitrov, D.: Klimatologija na Bălgarija (Klimatologie Bulgariens). Sofia 1972.
Dinev, L.; Mišev, K.: Bălgarija. Kratka geografija (Bulgarien. Kurze Geographie). Sofia 1975.
Gălăbov, Ž.; Ivanov, I.; Penčev, P.; Mišev, K.; Nedelčeva, V.: Fizičeska geografija na Bălgarija (Physische Geographie Bulgariens). Sofia 1977.
Geografija na Bălgarija v dva toma (Geographie Bulgariens in zwei Bänden). Red.: I.P. Gerasimov u.a. Sofia 1966, 1961.
Geografija na Bălgarija v tri toma (Geographie Bulgariens in drei Bänden). Hrsg. T. Jordanov. Sofia 1981 ff.
Hoffman, G.W.: Transformation of Rural Settlement in Bulgaria, in: Geographical Review. 54 (1964), S. 45–64.
Ivanov, K.; Marinov, T.; Panajotov, T.; Petkov, A.: Chidrologija na Bălgarija (Hydrologie Bulgariens). Sofia 1961.
Keefe, E.: Area Handbook for Bulgaria. Washington D.C. 1974.
Koledarov, P.; Mičev, N.: Promenite v imenata i statuta na selištata v Bălgarija 1878–1972 g. (Namens- und Statusänderungen der Siedlungen in Bulgarien 1878–1972). Sofia 1973.
Mičev, N.; Michajlov, C.; Vapcarov, I.; Kiradžiev, S.: Geografski rečnik na Bălgarija (Geographisches Wörterbuch Bulgarien). Sofia 1980.
Penkoff, I.: Die Siedlungen Bulgariens, ihre Entwicklung, Veränderungen und Klassifizierung, in: Geographische Berichte. 5 (1960) 17, S. 211–227.
Penkov, I.; Christov, T.: Ikonomičeska geografija na Bălgarija (Wirtschaftsgeographie Bulgariens). Sofia 1978.
The People's Republic of Bulgaria, in: Economic Geography of the Socialist Countries of Europe. Hrsg. N. Alisov, E. Valev. Moskau 1985, S. 175–199.
Počvena karta na Bălgarija (Bodenkarte Bulgariens). Hrsg. V. Koinov. Sofia 1968.
Popov, P.: Geografijata v săvremenna Bălgarija (Die Geographie des gegenwärtigen Bulgariens). Sofia 1986.
Stojčev, K.: Vodnite resursi na zemjata (Wasserresourcen der Erde). Sofia 1986.
Subev, L.; Stanev, S.: Klimatičnite rajoni na Bălgarija i technijat klimat (Klimatische Regionen Bulgariens und ihr Klima). Bd. 1–5. Sofia 1959.

b) Geschichte bis 1944

Bell, J.D.: Peasants in Power. Alexander Stamboliski and the Bulgarian Agrarian National Union, 1899–1923. Princeton 1977.
Chary, F.B.: The Bulgarian Jews and the Final Solution. Pittsburg 1972.
Constant, S.: Foxy Ferdinand, Tsar of Bulgaria. London 1979.
Crampton, R.J.: Bulgaria, 1878–1918. A History. Boulder, Co. 1983 (East European Monographs 138).
Friedrich, W.-U.: Bulgarien und die Mächte 1913–1915. Ein Beitrag zur Weltkriegs- und Imperialismusgeschichte. Stuttgart 1985 (Quellen und Studien zur Geschichte des östlichen Europa 21).
Georgieva, C.: Dokumenti za istorijata na bălgarskija narod (XV–XIX vek) (Dokumente zur Geschichte des bulgarischen Volkes, 15.–19. Jh.). Sofia 1986.
Groueff, S.: Crown of Thorns: The Reign of King Boris III of Bulgaria, 1918–1943. Lanham, New York, London 1987.
Hoppe, H.-J.: Bulgarien – Hitlers eigenwilliger Verbündeter. Eine Fallstudie zur nationalsozialistischen Südosteuropapolitik. Stuttgart 1979.
Jireček, C.: Geschichte der Bulgaren. Prag 1876.
Jireček, C.: Das Fürstenthum Bulgarien. Wien 1891.
Kanitz, F.: Donau-Bulgarien und der Balkan. Bde. 1–3. 2. Aufl. Leipzig 1882.
Macdermott, M.: A History of Bulgaria 1393–1885. London 1962.
Milkova, F.: Istorija na bălgarskata buržoazna dăržava i pravo prez perioda 1918–1944 godina (Geschichte des bulgarischen bürgerlichen Staates und Rechts in der Periode 1918–1944). Sofia 1976.
Miller, M.L.: Bulgaria during the Second World War. Stanford, Calif. 1975.
Mitrovski, B. u.a.: Das bulgarische Heer in Jugoslawien 1941–1945. Belgrad 1971.
Oren, N.: Bulgarian Communism: The Road to Power, 1934–1944. New York 1971.
Otečestvenata vojna na Bălgarija 1944–1945. Dokumenti, materiali (Der Vaterländische

Krieg Bulgariens 1944–1945. Dokumente, Materialien). Bd. 1 ff. Sofia 1978 ff.
Političeski partii, organizacii i upravlenija v Bălgarija 1879–1944 g. (Politische Parteien, Organisationen und Regimes in Bulgarien 1879–1944). Hrsg. Ch. A. Christov u. a. Sofia 1983 (Izvestija na Instituta po istorija na Bălgarskata akademija na naukite 26).
Rothschild, J.: The Communist Party of Bulgaria. Origins and Development, 1883–1936. New York 1959.
Spasov, L.: Bălgaro-săvetski diplomatičeski otnošenija 1934–1944 (Die bulgarisch-sowjetischen diplomatischen Beziehungen 1934–1944). Sofia 1987.
Živković, N.: Ratna šteta koju je Bugarska učinila Jugoslaviji 1941–1944 (Der Kriegsschaden, den Bulgarien Jugoslawien 1941–1944 verursacht hat). Belgrad 1985.

III. Politische Entwicklung; Politisches und Rechtssystem

a) Politisches System

1. Allgemeines

Ajzenštat, J. I.: Gosudarstvennyj stroj Narodnoj Respubliki Bolgarii (Der staatliche Aufbau der NRB). Moskau 1951.
Aktualni problemi na izgraždaneto na razvitoto socialističesko obštestvo (Aktuelle Probleme beim Aufbau der entwickelten sozialistischen Gesellschaft). Sofia 1980.
Bojčev, G.: Săzdavane na formata na bălgarskata socialističeska dăržava (Entstehung der Form des sozialistischen bulgarischen Staates), in: Godišnik na Sofijskija universitet „Kliment Ochridski". Juridičeski fakultet. 72 (1982) 2, S. 319–351.
Brown, J. F.: Authoritarian Politics in Communist Europe. Berkeley 1976.
Costello, M.: Bulgaria, in: The Communist States in Disarray. Hrsg. Bromke, A.; Rakowska-Harmstone, T. Minneapolis 1972, S. 131–157.
Devedjiev, H. H.: Stalinization of the Bulgarian Society, 1949–1953. Philadelphia 1975.
Georgiev, K.: Izbrani proizvedenija (Ausgewählte Werke). Hrsg. G. Ganev, N. Nedev. Sofia 1982.
Isusov, M.: Političeskite partii v Bălgarija 1944–1948 (Die politischen Parteien in Bulgarien 1944–1948). Sofia 1978.
Jotov, K.: Političeskata organizacija na socialističesko obštestvo (Die politische Organisation der sozialistischen Gesellschaft). Sofia 1981.
Ostoič, P.: Văznikvane i utvărždavane na političeskata sistema na narodnata demokracija v Bălgarija (Das Entstehen und die Bekräftigung des politischen Systems der Volksdemokratie in Bulgarien), in: Političeska prosveta. (1983) 4, S. 50–61.
Petrov, K.: Bălgarija po pătja na razvitija socializăm (Bulgarien auf dem Weg zum entwickelten Sozialismus). Sofia 1981.
Petrova, S.: Devetoseptemvrijskata socialističeska revoljucija (Die Revolution vom 9. September). Sofia 1981.
Problems of the Transition from Capitalism to Socialism in Bulgaria. Sofia 1975.
Socialističeskata revoljucija v Bălgarija. (Die sozialistische Revolution in Bulgarien). Sofia 1965.
Ustanovjavane i ukrepvane na narodnodemokratičnata vlast. Sept. 1944–maj 1945. Sbornik dokumenti (Der Aufbau und die Festigung der volksdemokratischen Macht. Sept. 1944–Mai 1945. Dokumentensammlung). Sofia 1969.
Volksrepublik Bulgarien. Staat, Demokratie, Leitung. Dokumente. Ausgewählt, bearb. und eingel. v. W. Lungwitz. Berlin 1979.

2. Politische Parteien

2.1. BKP

Angelov, I.: Kačestvenijat săstav na partijata (Die qualitative Zusammensetzung der Partei). Sofia 1988.
Avramov, P.: Organizacionno izgraždane na BKP sled izlizaneto i ot nelegalnost (sept. 1944–fevr. 1945) (Der organisatorische Aufbau der BKP nach dem Verlassen der Illegalität), in: Istoričeski pregled. 21 (1965) 2, S. 3–31.
Bălgarska komunističeska partija. Kongres [...] Stenografski protokol (Die BKP. Parteitag. [...] Stenographisches Protokoll).
V. Sofia 1948. Sofia 1949;
VI. Sofia 1954. Sofia 1954;
VII. Sofia 1958. Sofia 1958;
VIII. Sofia 1962. Sofia 1963;

IX. Sofia 1966. Sofia 1967;
X. Sofia 1971. Sofia 1971;
XI. Sofia 1976. Sofia 1976;
XII. Sofia 1981. Sofia 1981;
XIII. Sofia 1986. Sofia 1986.
Bălgarskata komunističeska partija. Istoričeski spravočnik (Die BKP. Historisches Nachschlagewerk). Sofia 1985.
Bell, J.D.: The Bulgarian Communist Party from Blagoev to Zhivkov. Stanford, CA 1986 (Histories of Ruling Communist Parties).
BKP – răkovoditel i organizator na izgraždaneto na razvitoto socialističesko obštestvo (Die BKP – Führer und Organisator beim Aufbau der entwickelten sozialistischen Gesellschaft). Sofia 1974.
Červenkov, V.: Po pătja na Georgi Dimitrov. Izbrani dokladi i reči 1948–1950 g. (Auf dem Wege Georgi Dimitrovs. Ausgewählte Vorträge und Reden 1948–1950). Sofia 1950.
Costello, M.: Bulgarien, in: Die kommunistischen Parteien der Welt. Hrsg. C.D. Kernig. Freiburg u.a. 1969.
Dellin, L.A.D.: The Communist Party of Bulgaria, in: The Communist Parties of Eastern Europe. Hrsg. S. Fischer-Galati. New York 1979, S. 49–85.
Dimitroff, G.: Ausgewählte Werke. Bd. 1–3. Frankfurt a.M. 1976.
Dimitrov, G.: Izbrani proizvedenija (Ausgewählte Werke). 1–2. Sofia 1954.
Dimitrov, G.: Pisma 1905–1949 (Briefe 1905–1949). Zusammengestellt v. P. Radenkova u.a. Sofia 1962.
Dimitrov, G.: Reči, dokladi, statii (1942–1947) (Reden, Aufsätze, Beiträge). Bd. 1–3. Sofia 1947.
Dimitrov, G.: Săčinenija (Werke). Bd. 1–14 u. Register. Sofia 1951–1957. – 2. Ausgabe. Hrsg. J. Jotov u.a. Bd. 1 ff. Sofia 1981 ff.
Geschichte der Bulgarischen Kommunistischen Partei. Sofia 1986.
Hatschikjan, M.: „Weiße Flecken" in der bulgarischen Nachkriegsgeschichte – Der Fall Trajčo Kostov, in: Südosteuropa. 37 (1988) 9, S. 477–512.
Isusov, M.: Komunističeskata partija i revoljucionnijat proces v Bălgarija 1944/48 (Die Kommunistische Partei und der revolutionäre Prozeß in Bulgarien 1944/48). Sofia 1983.
Isusov, M.: Trajčo Kostov – Public Figure and Statesman, in: Bulgarian Historical Review. 16 (1988) 1, S. 3–15.

Kniga za partijnija sekretar (Das Buch für den Parteisekretär). Zusammengestellt von Z. Cvetanov, Z. Nikolova. Sofia 1987.
Kolarov, V.: Izbrani proizvedenija. 1944–1950 (Ausgewählte Werke. 1944–1950). Hrsg. B. Grigorov, P. Canev. Sofia 1977.
Kolarov, V.: Ausgewählte Werke. Sofia 1980.
Kosev, N.: Mestnite partijni organi. Funkcii, struktura, dejnost (Die örtlichen Parteiorgane. Funktionen, Struktur, Tätigkeit). Sofia 1988.
K'osev, Ch.: Bălgarskata Komunističeska Partija (Die BKP). Sofia 1985.
Kostov, T.: Izbrani proizvedenija 1944–1948. (Ausgewählte Werke 1944–1948). Sofia 1978.
Kostov, T.: Publicistika, korespondencija, spomeni za nego v dva toma (Publizistik, Korrespondenz, Erinnerungen an ihn, in 2 Bänden). Sofia 1987.
Kurze Geschichte der Bulgarischen Kommunistischen Partei. Sofia 1977.
Manev, I.: Partijna organizacija - proizvodstven kolektiv (Parteiorganisation – Produktionskollektiv). Sofia 1981.
Migev, V.: Aprilskijat plenum na CK na BKP i organizacionnoto razvitie na partijata (1956–1958 g.) (Das April-Plenum des ZK der BKP und die organisatorische Entwicklung der Partei 1956–1958), in: Istoričeski pregled. 42 (1986) 3, S. 3–19.
Nacionalna partijna konferencija. 22.–23.3.1984. Stenografski protokol (Nationale Parteikonferenz. 22.–23.3.1984. Stenographisches Protokoll). Sofia 1984.
Ognjanov, L.: Aprilskata politika na BKP. 1956–1980 (Die April-Politik der BKP. 1956–1980). Sofia 1981.
Ostoič, P.: BKP i izgraždaneto na narodnodemokratičeskata dăržava. 9. sept. 1944–dek. 1947 (Die BKP und der Aufbau der volksdemokratischen Macht. 9. Sept. 1944–Dez. 1947). Sofia 1967.
Pačev, T.: Socialno-ikonomičeskata politika na BKP (Die sozial-ökonomische Politik der BKP). Sofia 1984.
Pankova, V.J.: Partijnoto răkovodstvo na socialističeskata dăržava (Die Leitung des sozialistischen Staates durch die Partei). Sofia 1986.
Procesăt srešt u Trajčo Kostov i negovata grupa (Engl. Ed.: The Trial of Traicho Kostov and His Group.) Sofia 1949.
Programm der Bulgarischen Kommunistischen Partei. Sofia 1975.
Sabrutev, N.: Metodologičeski problemi na

partijnoto stroitelstvo (Methodologische Probleme des Parteiaufbaus). Sofia 1979.
Semerjeev, P.: The Trial of Traicho Kostov in Bulgaria (in Russian). The Hebrew University of Jerusalem. The Soviet and East European Center. Jerusalem 1980.
Shivkov, T.: Einheit auf der Grundlage des Marxismus-Leninismus. Reden, Berichte, Artikel. Sofia 1969.
Shivkov, T.: Für das moderne Bulgarien. Frankfurt a. M. 1975.
Socialnata politika na BKP i razvitieto na NRB (Die Sozialpolitik der BKP und die Entwicklung Bulgariens). Sofia 1980.
Stojkov, I.: Za partijnoto răkovodstvo na socialističeskoto obštestvo. Teoretiko-metodologičeski očerk (Über die Führung der sozialistischen Gesellschaft durch die Partei. Eine theoretisch-methodologische Skizze). Sofia 1984.
Tišev, D.: Sătrudničestvoto meždu BRP(k)i BZNS (9.9.1944-12.1.1947) (Die Zusammenarbeit zwischen BRP(k) und BZNS, 9.9.1944-12.1.1947). Sofia 1988.
Todor Zhivkov. Statesman and Builder of New Bulgaria. Oxford u. a. 1982.
Todorov, S.: Usilni godini. Izbrani proizvedenija 1949-1979 (Schwere Zeiten. Ausgewählte Werke 1949-1979). Sofia 1980.
Văprosi na ideologičeskata rabota na BKP. Sbornik dokumenti 1944-1975 (Fragen der ideologischen Arbeit der BKP. Sammlung von Dokumenten 1944-1975). Sofia 1975.
Zhivkov, T.: Modern Bulgaria: Problems and Tasks in Building an Advanced Socialist Society. New York 1974.
Živkov, T.: Izbrani săčinenija (Ausgewählte Werke). Bd. 1 ff. Sofia 1975 ff.
Živkov, T.: Sozialismus und Demokratie. Sofia 1986.
Živkov, T.: Über das neue Programm der Bulgarischen Kommunistischen Partei. Sofia 1975.
Živkov, T.: Za partijnoto stroitelstvo. Dokladi, reči, statii 1948-1977 (Über den Parteiaufbau. Vorträge, Reden, Aufsätze 1948-1977). Bd. 1-3. Sofia 1978 (2. Aufl. 1979).

2.2. BZNS

Bălgarskijat zemedelski naroden săjuz i socializmăt (Der BZNS und der Sozialismus). Sofia 1984.
Bălgarski zemedelski naroden săjuz. Kongres [...] (Der BZNS. Kongreß [...]). [Materialien].

XXVIII. Sofia 1952. Sofia 1952;
XXIX. Sofia 1957. Sofia 1957;
XXX. Sofia 1962. Sofia 1962;
XXXI. Sofia 1968. Sofia 1968;
XXXIV. Sofia 1981. Sofia 1982.
Černejko, G. A.: BZNS - vernyj sojuznik bolgarskich kommunistov (Der BZNS - ein wahrer Verbündeter der bulgarischen Kommunisten). Moskau 1979.
Hristov, H.: The Bulgarian Agrarian People's Union in the Political System of Socialist Bulgaria (1971-1986), in: Bulgarian Historical Review. 15 (1987) 1, S. 3-19.
Jotov, V.: Idejno-političeskata evoljucija na BZNS (Die Entwicklung der politischen Ideen des BZNS). Sofia 1966.
Jotov, V.: Prinosăt na BZNS za pobedata na kooperativnija stroj na selo (Der Beitrag des BZNS zum Sieg des kooperativen Aufbaus auf dem Dorfe). Sofia 1968.
Moser, Ch. A.: Dimitrov of Bulgaria: A Political Biography of Dr. Georgi M. Dimitrov. Thornwood, NY 1979.
Tančev, P.: BZNS i izgraždaneto na razvito socialističesko obštestvo. Izbrani proizvedenija (Der BZNS und der Aufbau der entwickelten sozialistischen Gesellschaft. Ausgewählte Werke). Hrsg. L. Božkov, S. Ninov. Sofia 1983.
Tančev, P.: Za edinodejstvieto meždu BKP i BZNS (Über die Aktionseinheit zwischen BKP und BZNS). Sofia 1983.
Tišev, D.: Săvmestnata rabota na BKP i BZNS v stroitelstvoto na socializma (Die gemeinsame Arbeit von BKP und BZNS beim Aufbau des Sozialismus). Sofia 1969.
Trajkov, G.: Izbrani proizvedenija 1944-1973 (Ausgewählte Werke 1944-1973). Hrsg. L. Božkov, S. Ninov. Vorw.: P. Tančev. Sofia 1980.
Zarčev, J.: BZNS i izgraždaneto na socializăm v Bălgarija 1944-1962 (Der BZNS und der Aufbau des Sozialismus in Bulgarien 1944-1962). Sofia 1984.

2.3. Sonstige

Dimitrov, I.: Naroden Săjuz 'Zveno'. 1.10.1944-19.2.1949 (Der Volksbund Zveno), in: Istoričeski pregled. 26 (1970) 5, S. 3-33.
Isusov, M.: Social'naja demokratija i narodno-demokratičeskaja revoljucija v Bolgarii (1944-1948) (Die Sozialdemokratie und die volksdemokratische Revolution in Bulgarien 1944-1948), in: Études balkaniques. (1972) 1, S. 41-62.

Ostoič, P.: Bǎlgarskata rabotničeska socialdemokratičeska partija. 9.9.1944–11.8.1948 (Die Bulgarische Sozialdemokratische Arbeiterpartei. 9.9.1944–11.8.1948). Sofia 1980.
Stefanova, Ch.: Bǎlgarskata radikalna partija 1906–1946 (Die Bulgarische Radikale Partei 1906–1946). Sofia 1984.

3. Massenorganisationen

Andreev, K.: Profsǎjuzite v političeskata sistema na socializma (Die Gewerkschaften im politischen System des Sozialismus). Sofia 1987.
Bǎlgarskite profesionalni sǎjuzi (1904–1984) (Die bulgarischen Gewerkschaften /1904–1984/). Zusammengestellt v. D. Mičev, B. Kalaora. Sofia 1984.
Dimitrov, I.; Genčev, N.: Izgraždaneto na edinen mladežki sǎjuz v Bǎlgarija (Der Aufbau des einheitlichen Jugendverbandes in Bulgarien). Sofia 1964.
Dimitrovskijat komunističeski mladežki sǎjuz v rezoljucii i rešenija na kongresite, konferenciite i plenumite na CK (Der DKMS in Resolutionen und Beschlüssen der Kongresse, Konferenzen und Vollversammlungen des ZK). T. 1–4. Sofia 1973–1977.
Genčev, N.: Političeskite borbi meždu Otečestvenija front i buržoaznata opozicija okolo sǎzdavaneto na Konstitucija na Narodna Republika Bǎlgarija ot 1947 (Die politischen Kämpfe zwischen der OF und der bürgerlichen Opposition um die Verabschiedung der Verfassung der NRB von 1947), in: Istoričeski pregled. 18 (1962) 5, S. 3–31.
Istorija na bǎlgarskoto profsǎjuzno dviženie (Geschichte der bulgarischen Gewerkschaftsbewegung). Hrsg. B. Kalaora. 2., erw. und überarb. Aufl. Sofia 1976.
Istorija na mladežkoto revoljucionno dviženie v Bǎlgarija (Geschichte der revolutionären Jugendbewegung in Bulgarien). Hrsg. D. Mičev u.a. Sofia 1971 (2., erw. Aufl. 1972).
Kalaora, B. (Red.): Partijata i profsǎjuzite v uslovijata na socialističeskoto stroitelstvo v Bǎlgarija (Die Partei und die Gewerkschaften unter den Bedingungen des sozialistischen Aufbaus in Bulgarien). Sofia 1978.
Kubadinski, P.: Otečestvenijat front – front na cjaloto otečestvo (Die OF – die Front des ganzen Vaterlandes). Sofia 1982.
Kubadinski, P.: Otečestvenijat front i izgraždaneto na razvito socialističesko obštestvo (Die OF und der Aufbau der entwickelten sozialistischen Gesellschaft). Sofia 1982.
Markov, M.: Socialističeskata demokracija i profsǎjuzite (Die sozialistische Demokratie und die Gewerkschaften). Sofia 1984.
Stojanov, K.: Roljata na RMS za utvǎrždavane na narodnodemokratičnata vlast (1944–1947g.) (Die Rolle des RMS bei der Festigung der volksdemokratischen Macht 1944–1947), in: Istoričeski pregled. 25 (1969) 2–3, S. 122–146.

4. Politische Institutionen

Dokov, D.: Charakter i rolja na narodnite sǎveti u nas (Charakter und Rolle der Volksräte bei uns), in: Novo vreme. 29 (1953) 5, S. 34–52.
Dokov, D.: Sozialistische Volksvertretung und Demokratie, in: Sozialismus und Demokratie. Berlin(Ost) 1977, S. 171–218.
Janev, Ja.; Kolev, Ž.: Vǎznikvane i razvitie na narodnite sǎveti v Narodna republika Bǎlgarija (Entstehung und Entwicklung der Volksräte in der NRB), in: Godišnik na Sofijskija universitet „Kliment Ochridski". Juridičeski fakultet. 70 (1979), S. 21–55.
Minčev, M.: Pǎrvoto pravitelstvo na Otečestvenija front (Die erste OF-Regierung). Sofia 1988.
Radev, J.: Dǎržavni predstavitelni organi v Bǎlgarija 1944–1947 (Die staatlichen Vertretungsorgane in Bulgarien 1944–1947). Sofia 1965.
Spasov, B.: Narodno sǎbranie (Die Volksversammlung). Sofia 1980.
Spasov, B.: Socialist Democracy in the People's Republic of Bulgaria. Sofia 1977.
Stojčev, S.: Izbiratelnata sistema na Narodna Republika Bǎlgarija (Das Wahlsystem der NRB). Sofia 1976.
Želev, G.: Narodnoto sǎbranie – vǎrchoven organ na dǎržavnata vlast v NR Bǎlgarija (Die Volksversammlung – das höchste Organ der Staatsmacht in der NRB). Sofia 1960.

5. Politische Kultur

Hadžinikolov, V.: Die sozialistische Lebensweise, in: Jahrbuch für Volkskunde und Kulturgeschichte. 22 (1979) NF 7, S. 27–48.
Iribadžakov, N.: Razvitoto socialističesko obštestvo (Die entwickelte sozialistische Gesellschaft). 2. Aufl., Sofia 1982.

Krăstev, K.: Religija i religioznost (Religion und Religiosität). Sofia 1974.
Mitev, P.-E.: Mladežta i socialnata promjana (Die Jugend und der soziale Wandel). Sofia 1988.
Mizov, N.: Praznici, obredi, rituali (Feiern, Sitten, Rituale). Sofia 1980.
Naučen ateizăm (Wissenschaftlicher Atheismus). Sofia 1987.
Osnovni nasoki za razvitie i usăvăršenstvuvane na praznično-obrednata sistema v NR Bălgarija (Die grundlegende Richtung der Entwicklung und Vervollkommnung des Feiern- und Ritualsystems in der NRB). Sofia 1978.
Sekerdžiev, K.: Razvitoto socialističesko obštestvo (Die entwickelte sozialistische Gesellschaft). Sofia 1972.
Socialističeskijat način na život – obekt na kompleksni izsledvanija (Die sozialistische Lebensweise – Objekt der komplexen Erforschung). Hrsg. BAN. Sofia 1980.
Socialističeskijat način na život. Teorija i praktika (Die sozialistische Lebensweise. Theorie und Praxis). Sofia 1985.
Tachirov, Š.: Socialističeskata obrednost i duchovno edinstvo (Sozialistischer Ritus und geistige Einheit). Sofia 1984.
Zagorov, O.: Obred i obštuvane (Ritus und Umgang). Sofia 1986.

b) Innenpolitik

Avramov, P.: Borbata na BKP protiv gemetovštinata i restavratorskata opozicija, za krepăk rabotničesko-selski săjuz, 1944–1947 g. (Der Kampf der BKP gegen die Gemeto-Anhänger und die restaurative Opposition, für einen starken Arbeiter-Bauernbund, 1944–1947), in: Izvestija na Visšata partijna škola „Stanke Dimitrov" pri CK na BKP: Otdel istorija. 4 (1959), S. 93–137.
Avramov, P.: Kulturnata revoljucija v Bălgarija (Die Kulturrevolution in Bulgarien). Sofia 1980.
Avramov, P.: Razvitie na văzgleda za Devetoseptemvrijskoto văstanie i narodnodemokratičnata vlast, 1944–1948 g. (Die Entwicklung der Interpretation des Aufstandes vom 9. September und der volksdemokratischen Macht, 1944–1948), in: Istoričeski pregled. 38 (1982) 3, S. 78–94.
Birjuzov, S.S.: Sovetskij soldat na Balkanach (Als sowjetischer Soldat auf dem Balkan). Moskau 1963.
Black, C.E.: The View from Bulgaria, in: Witnesses to the Origins of the Cold War. Hrsg. Th. Hammond. Seattle, Washington 1982, S. 60–97.
Bogdanova, R.: Overcoming the Ideological and Political Pluralism in Bulgarian Society (September 1947 – beginning of 1949), in: Bulgarian Historical Review. 14 (1986) 3, S. 3–22.
Božinov, V.: Zaštitata na nacionalnata nezavisimost na Bălgarija 1944–1947 (Der Schutz der nationalen Unabhängigkeit Bulgariens 1944–1947). Sofia 1962.
Brown, J.F.: Bulgaria Under Communist Rule. New York 1970.
Christov, F.: Deveti septemvri i bălgarskata narodna armija (Der 9. September und die BNA), in: Istoričeski pregled. 25 (1969) 2–3, S. 172–193.
Dragojčeva, C.: Povelja na dălga (Gebot der Pflicht). Sofia 1980; deutsche Ausgabe: Gebot der Pflicht. Erinnerungen. Berlin 1980.
Ganevič, I.V.: Dejatel'nost' Bolgarskoj kommunističeskoj partii po ukrepleniju diktatury proletariata, sentjabr' 1944–1948 gg. (Die Aktivität der BKP für die Stärkung der Diktatur des Proletariats, September 1944–1948). Kiev 1974.
Genčev, N.: Razgromăt na buržuaznata opozicija v Bălgarija prez 1947–1948 godina (Die Zerschlagung der bürgerlichen Opposition in Bulgarien von 1947–1948), in: Godišnik na Sofijskija universitet (ideologični katedri). 56 (1962), S. 181–273.
Georgiev, V.: Săzdavane i ukrepvane na obštija rabotničeski profesionalen săjuz prez perioda ot 9 septemvri do dekemvri 1947 g. (Bildung und Stärkung der allgemeinen Arbeitergewerkschaft in der Zeit vom 9. September bis Dezember 1947), in: Profsăjuzni letopisi. (1963) 2, S. 8–56.
Isusov, M.: Revoljucionnijat proces i političeskata sistema na narodnata demokracija v Bălgarija 1944–48 g. (Der revolutionäre Prozeß und das politische System der Volksdemokratie in Bulgarien 1944–48), in: Istoričeski pregled. 35 (1979) 4–5, S. 83–113.
Isusov, M.: Săzdavane na legalnite răkovodni organi na BRP(k) (Die Bildung der legalen Leitungsorgane der BRP(k)), in: Vekove. 11 (1982) 1–2, S. 43–52.
Ludžev, D.: Drebnata buržoazija v Bălgarija 1944–1958 (Das Kleinbürgertum in Bulgarien 1944–1958). Sofia 1985.
Markov, G.: Zadočni reportaži za Bălgarija (In absentia-Reportagen über Bulgarien). 2 Bde. Zürich 1980.

Migev, V.: Aprilskijat plenum na CK na BKP i organizacionnoto razvitie na partijata (1956–1958) (Das Aprilplenum des ZK der BKP und die organisatorische Entwicklung der Partei 1956–1958), in: Istoričeski pregled. 42 (1986) 3, S. 3–19.

Migev, V.: Izgraždane na razvitija socializăm v Bălgarija (Der Aufbau des entwickelten Sozialismus in Bulgarien), in: Istoričeski pregled. 37 (1981) 3–4, S. 3–21.

Migev, V.: Za etapite na kooperiraneto na selskoto stopanstvo v Bălgarija 1944–1959 g. (Über die Etappen der Organisierung der Landwirtschaft in Genossenschaften in Bulgarien 1944–1959), in: Vekove. 13 (1984) 1, S. 47–59.

Ognjanov, L.: Istoričeskite zavoevanija na socialističeska Bălgarija sled aprilskija plenum na CK na BKP, 1956 g. (Historische Errungenschaften des sozialistischen Bulgarien nach dem April-Plenum des ZK der BKP, 1956), in: Istoričeski pregled. 37 (1981) 2, S. 20–38.

Oren, N.: Revolution Administered: Agrarianism and Communism in Bulgaria. Baltimore 1973.

Oschlies, W.: Bulgariens Staats- und Parteichef – 75 Jahre alt. Skizzen zu einem Porträt Todor Shiwkows, in: Osteuropa. 36 (1986), S. 1015–1021.

Ostoič, P.: BKP i izgraždaneto na narodnodemokratičeska dăržava, 9 septemvri 1944–dekemvri 1947 (Die BKP und der Aufbau eines volksdemokratischen Staates, 9.9.1944–Dezember 1947). Sofia 1967.

Pejkov, I.: Podgotovka, provetždane i značenie na narodnija săd prez 1944–1945 g. (Die Vorbereitung, Durchführung und Bedeutung des Volksgerichts 1944–1945), in: Istoričeski pregled. 20 (1964) 2–3, S. 151–170.

Petkov, P.: Obštoto i specifičnoto v likvidiraneto na kapitalističeskata sobstvenost v promišlenostta v Bălgarija (Das Allgemeine und das Spezifische in der Liquidierung des kapitalistischen Eigentums in der bulgarischen Industrie), in: Izvestija na Instituta po istorija na BKP. 20 (1969), S. 5–50.

Petrov, K.: Bălgarija po pătja na razvitija socializăm (Bulgarien auf dem Weg des entwickelten Sozialismus). Sofia 1981.

Spasov, B.: Bălgarskite konstitucii (Die bulgarischen Verfassungen), in: Bălgarskata dăržava prez vekovete. Hrsg. V. Gjuzelev. Sofia 1982, Bd. 1, S. 477–491.

Živkova, L.: Za usăvăršenstvuvane na čoveka i obštestvoto (Für die Vervollkommnung der Menschen und der Gesellschaft). Sofia 1980.

Zlatev, Z.: Problemi na prechoda ot kapitalizma kăm socializma v Bălgarija (Probleme des Übergangs vom Kapitalismus zum Sozialismus in Bulgarien). Sofia 1982.

c) Außenpolitik

The American Military Mission in the Allied Control Commission for Bulgaria, 1944–1947. History and Transcripts. Ed. M. M. Boll. New York 1985 (East European Monographs 176).

Bălgaro-săvetski otnošenija. Dokumenti i materiali (Die bulgarisch-sowjetischen Beziehungen. Dokumente und Materialien). Mehrere Bde. Sofia 1974 ff.

Bălgarsko-germanski otnošenija i vrăzki (Bulgarisch-deutsche Beziehungen und Verbindungen). Red.: V. Chadžinikolov. Sofia 1981.

Balkanite i meždunarodnite otnošenija 1944–1948 (Der Balkan und die internationalen Beziehungen 1944–1948). Sofia 1984.

Boll, M. M.: Cold War in the Balkans. American Foreign Policy and the Emergence of Communist Bulgaria, 1943–1947. Lexington, Ken. 1984.

Bulgarien und der Frieden auf dem Balkan. Sofia 1987.

Charkov, D.: Balkanite v meždunarodnite otnošenija 1944–1948 (Der Balkan in den internationalen Beziehungen 1944–1948). Sofia 1984.

Cour Internationale de Justice. Mémoire, plaidoiries et documents. Interpretation des traités de paix conclus avec Bulgarie, la Hongrie et la Roumanie. Avis consultatifs des 30 mars et 18 juillet 1950. Leyde 1950.

DDR-VRB. Freundschaft und Zusammenarbeit. Berlin, Sofia 1979.

Dejanow, R.: Der kernwaffenfreie Balkan und das Streben nach allgemeiner Sicherheit. Sofia 1987.

Dobrijanov, T.: Overcoming Bulgaria's Isolation in Foreign Policy (1944–1947). Problems of the Transition from Capitalism to Socialism in Bulgaria. Sofia 1975.

Dokumente und Materialien der Zusammenarbeit zwischen der Sozialistischen Einheitspartei Deutschlands und der Bulgarischen Kommunistischen Partei 1977 bis 1984. Berlin, Sofia 1984.

Dokumente zur Entwicklung der Beziehungen zwischen der Bundesrepublik Deutschland und Bulgarien 1971–1974, in: Osteuropa. 24 (1974), S. A 548–555.

Dragoitschewa, Z.: Makedonien – kein Zankapfel, sondern Faktor der guten Nachbarschaft und der Zusammenarbeit. Erinnerungen und Gedanken. Sofia 1979.

From recognition to repudiation (Bulgarian attitude on the Macedonian question). Articles, speeches, documents. Sel. and red. V. Čašule. Skopje 1972.

Grigorova, Ž.: Balkanskata politika na socialističeska Bălgarija 1944–1970 (Die Balkanpolitik des sozialistischen Bulgarien 1944–1970). Sofia 1985.

Grothusen, K.-D.: Der Balkanpakt als Instrument der Friedenssicherung für Südosteuropa nach dem Zweiten Weltkrieg, in: Friedenssicherung in Südosteuropa. Föderationsprojekte und Allianzen seit dem Beginn der nationalen Eigenstaatlichkeit. Hrsg. M. Bernath, K. Nehring. Neuried 1985 (Südosteuropa-Studien 34), S. 179–190.

Grothusen, K.-D.: Zur „Sowjetisierung" der bulgarischen Außenpolitik nach dem Zweiten Weltkrieg, in: Kulturelle Traditionen in Bulgarien. Hrsg. R. Lauer, P. Schreiner. Göttingen 1989, S. 317–331.

Hatschikjan, M. A.: Tradition und Neuorientierung in der bulgarischen Außenpolitik 1944–1948. Die „nationale Außenpolitik" der Bulgarischen Arbeiterpartei (Kommunisten). München 1988 (Südosteuropäische Arbeiten 86).

Höpken, W.: Im Schatten der nationalen Frage: Die bulgarisch-türkischen Beziehungen, in: Südosteuropa. 36 (1987) 2/3, S. 75–95; 4, S. 178–194.

Jugoslovensko-bugarski odnosi u XX veku (Die jugoslawisch-bulgarischen Beziehungen im 20. Jh.). T. 1 ff. Belgrad 1980 ff.

Kerr, J. L.: Bulgaria and its Neighbours: A Hundred Years After Independance. RAD Background Report. 1 (Bulgaria). January 1978.

Lalkov, M.: Bălgaro-jugoslavski otnošenija i vrăzki (Die bulgarisch-jugoslawischen Beziehungen und Verbindungen). Sofia 1975.

Macédoine (Articles d'histoire). Hrsg. Institut d'Histoire Nationale. Skopje 1981.

Makedonien. Eine Dokumentensammlung. Hrsg. BAN. Sofia 1982.

Mateeva, M.: Diplomatičeski otnošenija na Bălgarija 1879–1974 (Die diplomatischen Beziehungen Bulgariens 1879–1974). Sofia 1976.

Meždunarodni otnošenija i vănšnata politika na Bălgarija sled Vtorata svetovna vojna. Sbornik ot studii i statii (Internationale Beziehungen und die bulgarische Außenpolitik nach dem Zweiten Weltkrieg. Studien und Aufsätze). Sofia 1982.

Mladenow, P.: Vier Jahrzehnte eine Außenpolitik des Friedens, in: Bulgarien – 40 Jahre auf dem Weg des Sozialismus. Sofia 1985.

Nakov, A.: Bălgaro-săvetskite otnošenija 1944–1948 (Die bulgarisch-sowjetischen Beziehungen 1944–1948). Sofia 1978.

Oschlies, W.: Bonn – Sofia. Vor und nach Aufnahme diplomatischer Beziehungen, in: Osteuropa. 24 (1974), S. 586–598.

Oschlies, W.: Bulgarien – nahe der Sowjetunion, fern dem Westen?, in: Der Sowjetblock zwischen Vormachtkontrolle und Autonomie. Hrsg. R. Löwenthal, B. Meissner. Köln 1984, S. 251–295.

Oschlies, W.: Bulgariens Stellung zur KSZE. Köln 1973 (Berichte des Bundesinstituts für Ostwissenschaftliche und Internationale Studien 24–1973).

Palaveev, Č.: Za preustrojstvo na meždunarodnite otnošenija (Für die Umgestaltung der internationalen Beziehungen). Sofia 1988.

Pismata na CK na BKP do Centralnija komitet na Jugoslavskata komunističeska partija (Briefe des ZK der BKP an das ZK der Kommunistischen Partei Jugoslawiens). Sofia 1948.

Resis, A.: The Churchill-Stalin Secret „Percentages" Agreement on the Balkans, Moscow, October 1944, in: The American Historical Review. 83 (1978), S. 368–387.

Reuter, J.: Die Außenministerkonferenz der Balkanländer in Belgrad, in: Südosteuropa. 37 (1988), S. 128–141.

Sander, O.: Turkish-Bulgarian Relations, in: Foreign Policy. 12 (1986) 3–4, S. 7–19.

Schönfeld, R.: Außen- und sicherheitspolitische Konzepte Bulgariens, in: Reform und Wandel in Südosteuropa. Hrsg. R. Schönfeld. München 1985 (Untersuchungen zur Gegenwartskunde Südosteuropas 26), S. 73–81.

Socialističeskata vănšna politika na Narodna Republika Bălgarija 1944/1974 (Die sozialistische Außenpolitik der NRB 1944/1974). Sofia 1974.

Sovetsko-bolgarskie otnošenija (1977–1982. Dokumenty i materialy) (Sowjetisch-bulga-

rische Beziehungen 1977–1982. Dokumente und Materialien). Moskau 1985.
Sovetsko-bolgarskie otnošenija. Dokumenty i materialy. 1983–1986gg. (Die sowjetisch-bulgarischen Beziehungen. Dokumente und Materialien. 1983–1986). Moskau 1988.
Stefanov, G.: Meždunarodni otnošenija i vănšna politika na Bălgarija 1879–1970 (Die internationalen Beziehungen und die Außenpolitik Bulgariens 1879–1970). Sofia 1977.
Stefanović, M.; Krstić, M.; Apostolski, M.: Velikobugarske pretenzije od San Stefana do danas (Die großbulgarischen Ansprüche von San Stefano bis heute). Belgrad 1978.
Todorova, R.: Meždunarodni otnošenija i vănšna politika na Bălgarija sled Vtorata svetovna vojna (Die internationalen Beziehungen und die Außenpolitik Bulgariens nach dem Zweiten Weltkrieg). Sofia 1982.
Tönnes, B.: Bulgariens balkanpolitisches Konzept, in: Südosteuropa. 33 (1984) 6, S. 313–326.
Tönnes, B.: Bulgariens Griechenlandpolitik, in: Südosteuropa. 33 (1984) 7/8, S. 417–428.
Troebst, S.: Die bulgarisch-jugoslawische Kontroverse um Makedonien 1967–1982. München 1983 (Untersuchungen zur Gegenwartskunde Südosteuropas 23).
Tuğlacı, P.: Bulgaristan ve türk-bulgar ilişkileri (Bulgarien und die türkisch-bulgarischen Beziehungen). Istanbul 1984.
Vănšna politika na Narodna Republika Bălgarija. Sbornik ot dokumenti i materiali (Die Außenpolitik der NRB. Dokumente und Materialien). T. 1 ff. Sofia 1970ff.

d) Rechtssystem

1. Allgemeines

Geilke, G.; Jessel, C.: Einführung in das Recht der Bulgarischen Volksrepublik. Darmstadt 1975.
Jolova, G.; Kiskinova, L.: Zakonodatelstvoto na Narodna republika Bălgarija 1944–1986 (Die Gesetzgebung der NRB 1944–1986). Sofia 1988.
Koschucharoff, A.: Bulgaria, in: International Encyclopedia of Comparative Law, Bd. 1: National Reports, B 59–B 76.
Razvitie na socialističeskoto pravo v Bălgarija (Entwicklung des sozialistischen Rechts in Bulgarien). Hrsg. J. Radev. Sofia 1984.
Schöndorf, F.: Einführung in das geltende slavische Recht (Privat- und Prozeßrecht) in rechtsvergleichender Darstellung, Bd. 1: Bulgarien. Leipzig und Berlin 1922.

2. Staatsrecht

Bălgarskite dăržavni institucii 1879–1986. Enciklopedičen spravočnik (Die bulgarischen Staatsinstitutionen 1879–1986. Enzyklopädisches Nachschlagewerk). Sofia 1987.
Dermendžiev, I.: Administrativen akt (Verwaltungsakt). Sofia 1985.
Dermendžiev, I.: Administrativen proces na NRB (Verwaltungsprozeß in der NRB). Sofia 1981.
Höpken, W.: Demokratisierung in kleinen Schritten: Die Kommunalwahlen in Bulgarien, in: Südosteuropa. 37 (1988), S. 208–218.
Jessel, Ch.: Die neuere Verfassungsentwicklung in Bulgarien, in: Verfassungs- und Verwaltungsreformen in den sozialistischen Staaten. Hrsg. F.-C. Schroeder und B. Meissner. Berlin 1978, S. 221–256.
Konstandinov, G., Dermendžiev, I.; Vodeničarov, A.: Administrativno pravo. Specialna čast (Verwaltungsrecht. Besonderer Teil). Sofia 1973.
Luchterhandt, O.: Bulgarien, in: Verfassungen der kommunistischen Staaten. Hrsg. G. Brunner und B. Meissner. Paderborn 1979, S. 45–49.
Menschenrechte in den Staaten des Warschauer Paktes. Bericht der unabhängigen Wissenschaftlerkommission. Bonn 1988.
Načeva, S.: Dăržavnopravni procesualni normi (Staatsrechtliche prozessuale Normen). Sofia 1983.
Narodnaja Respublika Bolgarija. Konstitucija i zakonodatel'nye akty (Die NRB. Verfassung und gesetzgebende Akte). Hrsg. B. A. Stašun, I. P. Il'inskij. Moskau 1981.
Narodnaja Respublika Bolgarija. Osnovy gosudarstvennogo stroja (Die NRB. Grundlagen des Staatssystems). Hrsg. Ja. G. Radev, B. N. Toporonin. Moskau 1974.
Schultz, L.: Die Verfassung der Volksrepublik Bulgarien vom 18. Mai 1971, in: Jahrbuch des öffentlichen Rechts der Gegenwart, N. F. Bd. 22 (1973), S. 203–248.
Sipkov, I.: The Bulgarian Communist Party and their Status under Law, in: The Party Statutes of the Communist World. Ed. W. B. Simons, St. White. The Hague, Boston, Lancaster 1984, S. 197–206.

Spasov, B.: Konstitucija i narodnoe predstavitel'stvo v Narodnoj Respublike Bolgarii (Verfassung und Volksvertretung in der NRB). Moskau 1977.
Spasov, B.: Tălkovatelnata dejnost na Dăržavnija săvet (Die Interpretationstätigkeit des DS). Sofia 1978.
Spasov, B.: Văprosi na novata konstitucija (Fragen der neuen Verfassung). Sofia 1973.
Spasov, B.; Angelov, A.: Dăržavno pravo na Narodna Republika Bălgarija (Staatsrecht der NRB). 2. Aufl. Sofia 1968.
Spasov, B.; Želev, G.: Dăržavno pravo na Narodna Republika Bălgarija (Staatsrecht der NRB). I–II. Sofia 1974.
Vălkanov, V.: Normativnite aktove na Ministerskija săvet (Die Normativakte des Ministerrats). Sofia 1979.
Vălkanov, V.: Pravnoto položenie na narodnija predstavitel (Die rechtliche Stellung des Volksvertreters). Sofia 1976.

3. Zivilrecht

Aktualni graždanskopravni problemi (Aktuelle Probleme des Zivilrechts). Hrsg. BAN. Institut po naukite za dăržavata i pravoto. Sofia 1983.
Cankova, C.: Zaveštanieto v bălgarskoto nasledstveno pravo (Das Testament im bulgarischen Erbrecht). Sofia 1985.
Čacev, L.: Zakon za sobstvenostta: Tekst, sădebna praktika, literatura (Sbornik) (Das Eigentumsgesetz: Text, Gerichtspraxis, Literatur (Sammelband)). Sofia 1982.
Garnefsky, A.: Bulgaria, in: The Law of Inheritance in Eastern Europe and in the People's Republic of China. Law in Eastern Europe. 5 (1961), S. 88–114.
Kožucharov, A.: Obligacionno pravo. Obšto učenie za obligacionnoto otnošenie (Schuldrecht. Allgemeine Lehren des Schuldverhältnisses). 3. Aufl. Sofia 1958.
Kožucharov, A.: Obligacionno pravo. Otdelni vidove obligacionni otnošenija (Schuldrecht. Einzelne Arten von Schuldverhältnissen). 3. Aufl. Sofia 1965.
Problemi na kodifikacijata na graždanskoto pravo v Narodna republika Bălgarija (Probleme der Zivilrechtskodifikation in der NRB). Hrsg. BAN. Edinen centăr za nauka i podgotovka na kadri po pravo. Sofia 1975.
Tadžer, V.: Graždansko pravo na NRB. Obšta čast (Zivilrecht der NRB. Allgemeiner Teil). Bd. 1–2. Sofia 1972, 1973.
Tasev, Ch.: Bălgarsko nasledstveno pravo (Bulgarisches Erbrecht). 4. Aufl. Sofia 1987.
Vasilev, L.: Graždansko pravo na Narodna republika Bălgarija. Obšta čast (Zivilrecht der NRB. Allgemeiner Teil). Sofia 1956.

4. Zivilprozeßrecht

Brajkov, S.: Osnovni văprosi na efektivnostta na graždanskoto procesualno pravo v NRB (Grundfragen der Effektivität des Zivilprozeßrechts in der NRB). Sofia 1987.
Čipev, T.: Meždunarodnata podvedomstvenost v sădebnija iskov proces (Die internationale Zuständigkeit in der streitigen Gerichtsbarkeit). Sofia 1987.
Jessel-Holst, Ch.: Anerkennung und Vollstreckung ausländischer Entscheidungen sowie Rechtshilfe in Zivilsachen nach dem bulgarischen Recht, in: WGO-Monatshefte für Osteuropäisches Recht. (1982), S. 255–267.
Stalev, Ž.: Bălgarsko graždansko procesualno pravo (Bulgarisches Zivilprozeßrecht). 3. Aufl. Sofia 1979.
Stalev, Z. S.: Besondere Rechtspflegeorgane in Bulgarien, in: Rabels Zeitschrift für ausländisches und internationales Privatrecht. 35 (1971), S. 698–713.

5. Familienrecht

Georgiev, Ch.; Palazov, I.; Beškov, P.; Damjanov, C.: Semeen kodeks. Komentar (Familienkodex. Kommentar). Sofia 1975.
Gocev, V.: Imuštestveni otnošenija meždu săpruzite po semejnija kodeks (Vermögensrechtliche Beziehungen der Ehegatten nach dem Familienkodex). Sofia 1988.
Jessel-Holst, Ch.: Bulgarien, in: Internationales Ehe- und Kindschaftsrecht. Hrsg. A. Bergmann, M. Ferid. 95. Lfg. Frankfurt a. M. 1988, S. 1–77.
Jessel-Holst, Ch.: Das Unterhaltsrecht in Bulgarien, in: Das Unterhaltsrecht in Osteuropa. Bonn 1989 (Studien des Instituts für Ostrecht München 36), S. 37–71.
Konstantinov, D.: Roditelskite prava sled razvod (Elternrechte nach der Scheidung). Sofia 1986.
Nenova, L.: Semejno pravo na Narodna republika Bălgarija (Familienrecht der NRB). Sofia 1977.
Pekov, J.: Zaštita na pravoto na izdrăžka (Schutz des Unterhaltsrechts). Sofia 1982.

6. Recht der Wirtschaft

Bulgarisches Wirtschaftskooperationsrecht. Aspekte des Erlasses Nr. 535 vom 25. März 1980 aus bulgarischer Sicht, in: Rabels Zeitschrift für ausländisches und internationales Privatrecht. 49 (1985), S. 678–733.

Goleminov, Č.: Plan i stopanski dogovor (Plan und Wirtschaftsvertrag). Sofia 1987.

Jessel-Holst, Ch.: Rechtsfragen der Wirtschaftsbeziehungen zu Bulgarien, in: Jahrbuch für Ostrecht. 19 (1978) 2, S. 87–109.

Jessel-Holst, Ch.: Reformen des Wirtschaftsrechts in Bulgarien, in: Sozialistisches Wirtschaftsrecht zwischen Wandel und Beharrung. Hrsg. K. Westen, G. Brunner, F.-Ch. Schroeder. Berlin 1988. S. 253–279.

Šiškov, A.: Pravni osnovi na ličnoto stopanstvo (Răkovodstvo) (Rechtliche Grundlagen der persönlichen Hofwirtschaft. Leitfaden). Sofia 1985.

Slavčev, M.: Zakonăt za kooperativnite organizacii. Tekst i komentar (Genossenschaftsgesetz. Text und Kommentar). Sofia 1985.

Tadsher, V.: Gemischte Gesellschaften in Bulgarien. Hrsg. Bulgarische Handels- und Industriekammer. Sofia 1986.

Tadžer, V.: Formi na stopansko sdružavane v NRB (Formen der Wirtschaftsgesellschaften in der NRB). Sofia 1987.

Valčev, N.; Pamikčiev, Ch.: Strukturno i organizacionno preustrojstvo na ličnoto stopanstvo na naselenieto (Strukturelle und organisatorische Umgestaltung der persönlichen Hofwirtschaft der Bevölkerung). Sofia 1988.

7. Arbeitsrecht

Danailov, D.: Văznikvane, izmenenija i prekratjavane na trudovoto pravootnošenie (Entstehung, Änderung und Beendigung des Arbeitsverhältnisses). Sofia 1986.

Kirčeva, E.: Das bulgarische Arbeitsgesetzbuch von 1986, in: WGO-Monatshefte für Osteuropäisches Recht. 30 (1988) 1/2, S. 59–84.

Mračkov, V.: Kontrol za spazvane na trudovoto zakonodatelstvo i otgovornost za negovoto narušavane (Kontrolle über die Einhaltung der Arbeitsgesetzgebung und Verantwortlichkeit für ihre Verletzung). Sofia 1985.

Nakov, G.: Trudovi sporove (Arbeitsstreitigkeiten). Sofia 1986.

8. Internationales Privatrecht

Cačev, L.: Sădebna praktika po graždanski sporove s meždunaroden element (Gerichtspraxis bei Zivilsachen mit internationalem Element). Sofia 1981.

Damjanov, C.: Priložnijat zakon po dogovora za vănšnotărgovskata pokupko-prodažba (Anwendbares Recht beim Außenhandelskaufvertrag). Sofia 1978.

Damjanov, C.: Stălknovitelnite normi po nasledstvenoto pravo na NR Bălgarija (Kollisionsnormen im Erbrecht der NRB). Sofia 1977.

Damjanov, C.: Stălknovitelni normi po obligacionnoto pravo na NR Bălgarija (Kollisionsnormen im Schuldrecht der NRB). Sofia 1972.

Damjanov, C.: Stălknovitelnite normi po semejnoto pravo na NR Bălgarija (Kollisionsnormen im Familienrecht der NRB). Sofia 1979.

Damjanov, C.; Aleksiev, S.: Nepozvolenoto uvreždane spored bălgarskoto meždunarodno častno pravo (Unerlaubte Handlung im bulgarischen internationalen Privatrecht). Sofia 1981.

Jessel-Holst, Ch.: Die Neuregelung des bulgarischen Internationalen Familienrechts im Familienkodex von 1985, in: Rabels Zeitschrift für ausländisches und internationales Privatrecht. 51 (1987), S. 35–59.

Kutikov, V.: Meždunarodno častno pravo na NR Bălgarija (Internationales Privatrecht der NRB). 3. Aufl. Sofia 1976.

Stalev, Ž.: Săštnost i funkcija na meždunarodnoto častno pravo (Wesen und Funktionen des internationalen Privatrechts). Sofia 1982.

Todorov, T.: Zakonăt na săda v bălgarskoto meždunarodno častno pravo (Das Recht des Gerichtsstands im bulgarischen internationalen Privatrecht). Sofia 1988.

Văprosi na meždunarodnoto častno pravo (Fragen des internationalen Privatrechts). Hrsg. BAN. Sofia 1983.

Zidarova, J.: Obštestvenijat red i meždunarodnoto častno pravo (Ordre public und das internationale Privatrecht). Sofia 1975.

9. Strafrecht

Dermendžiev, I.: Administrativni narušenija i nakazanija. Procesualnopraven režim (Administrative Übertretungen und Strafen. Prozeßrechtliche Regelung). Sofia 1981.

Georgiev, G. u. a.: Kriminologičeski problemi (Probleme der Kriminologie). Sofia 1988.
Guneva, M.: Amnistijata po nakazatelnoto pravo na NRB (Amnestie im Strafrecht der NRB). Sofia 1988.
Gunewa, M.: Bulgarien, in: Strafrechtsentwicklung in Europa 2, Teil 1. Landesberichte 1984/1986 über Gesetzgebung, Rechtsprechung und Literatur. Hrsg. A. Eser, B. Huber. Freiburg i. Br. 1988, S. 79–105.
Ljutov, K.: Prokurorskijat nadzor za zakonnost v NR Bălgarija (Staatsanwaltliche Gesetzlichkeitsaufsicht in der NRB). Sofia 1984.
Lyon, Th.; Lipowschek, A.: Das bulgarische Strafgesetzbuch vom 16. März 1968 (Nakazatelen kodeks) mit ergänzenden Vorschriften. Berlin 1973.
Nakazatelno pravo na NRB: Osobena čast (Strafrecht der NRB: Besonderer Teil). Bd. 1–2. Hrsg. K. Ljutov. Sofia 1987.
Našijat opit: Za dejnostta na drugarskite sădilišta (Unsere Erfahrung: Aus der Arbeit der Kameradschaftsgerichte). Hrsg. K. Kuzmanov, I. Kănčev. Sofia 1987.
Nenov, I.: Nakazatelno pravo na Narodna republika Bălgarija. Obšta čast (Strafrecht der NRB. Allgemeiner Teil). Sofia 1972.
Nenov, I.: Nakazatelno pravo na NRB (Osobena čast) (Strafrecht der NRB (Besonderer Teil)). 1. Folge, 3. Aufl. Sofia 1985.
Nenov, I.: Nakazatelno pravo. Osobena čast (Strafrecht. Besonderer Teil). Bd. 2. Sofia 1959.

10. Strafprozeßrecht

Pavlov, S.: Nakazatelen proces (Strafprozeß). Sofia 1985.
Pavlov, S.: Osigurjavane na graždanite pravo na zaštita v nakazatelnija proces na NRB (Gewährleistung des Rechts auf Verteidigung für die Bürger im Strafprozeß der NRB). Sofia 1986.
Radeva, R.: Pravoto na zaštita na obvinjaemija v nakazatelnija proces na NRB (Das Recht des Angeklagten auf Verteidigung im Strafprozeß der NRB). Sofia 1985.

11. Sonstiges

Goranov, N.: Bulgarisches Urheberrecht, in: Jahrbuch für Ostrecht. 24 (1983) 2, S. 299–321.
Jessel, Ch.: Die bulgarische Gerichtsverfassung, in: Jahrbuch für Ostrecht. 17 (1976) 2, S. 127–151.
Jessel-Holst, Ch.: Das Sozialversicherungs- und Versorgungsrecht Bulgariens, in: Jahrbuch für Ostrecht. 23 (1982), S. 201–243.
Popov, L.: Die Rechtsstellung des Ausländers in Bulgarien. Baden-Baden 1981.
Terziev, V.: Sădebnata zaštita i advokatura: Istoričeski pregled (Gerichtlicher Rechtsschutz und die Rechtsanwaltschaft: Historische Übersicht). Sofia 1987.
Vălkanov, V.: Bălgarskoto graždanstvo (Bulgarische Staatsangehörigkeit). Sofia 1978.
Waehler, J.-P.: Bulgarien, Länderbericht, in: Quellen des Urheberrechts. 11. Lfg. Hrsg. P. Möhring, E. Schulz u. a. Frankfurt a. M. 1981.

12. Verträge

Gendov, K. u. a.: Vizovi spogodbi na Narodna republika Bălgarija s drugi dăržavi (Visaabkommen der NRB mit anderen Staaten). Sofia 1987.
Höffken, H.: Übersicht über das deutsch-bulgarische Doppelbesteuerungsabkommen, in: Internationale Wirtschafts-Briefe. (1988) 23, S. 829/830.
Meždunarodni aktove po morsko pravo s učastieto na Narodna republika Bălgarija (Internationale Akte zum Seerecht mit Beteiligung der NRB). Hrsg. C. Damjanov. Sofia 1984.
Meždunarodni spogodbi po promišlenata sobstvenost, v koito učastvuva NR Bălgarija. (Za slediplomna kvalifikacija) (Internationale Abkommen über industrielles Eigentum unter Beteiligung der NRB. (Zur Qualifikation nach dem Diplom)). Hrsg. V. Vrana. Sofia 1980.
Nalbantov, B.; Kănčev, K.: Meždudăržavnite dogovori po socialnoto obezpečavane sključeni ot Narodna republika Bălgarija (Zwischenstaatliche Verträge über soziale Sicherheit unter Beteiligung der NRB). Sofia 1966.
Sbornik ot aktove po mnogostrannoto ikonomičesko sătrudničestvo meždu dăržavite – členki na SIV (Sammlung von Akten über die multilaterale ökonomische Zusammenarbeit zwischen den Mitgliedstaaten des RGW). Hrsg. M. Michajlov. Sofia 1979.
Zidarova, J.: Problemi na meždunarodnoto častno pravo v novite dogovori za pravna pomošt, sključeni ot NR Bălgarija (Proble-

me des internationalen Privatrechts in den neuen Rechtshilfeverträgen der NRB), in: Godišnik na Sofijskija universitet „Kliment Ochridski". Juridičeski fakultet. 75 (1982) 1, Sofia 1985, S. 117–171.

e) Landesverteidigung

The Warsaw Pact – Political Purpose and Military Means. Hrsg. R. W. Clawson, W. Kaplan, S. Lawrence. Wilmington Del. 1982.

Hines, J. G.; Petersen, P. A.: Sowjetische Führungskonzepte im Wandel – Schwerpunkt Operationsgebiet, in: Internationale Wehrrevue. 19 (1986) 3, S. 281–289.

Larrabee, S.: Balkan Security. London 1977 (Adelphi-Papers 135).

Nelson, D. N.: Alliance Behavior in the Warsaw Pact. Boulder Col. 1986.

Oschlies, W.: Volksrepublik Bulgarien, in: Reservesysteme des Warschauer Paktes. Hrsg. R. Woller. München 1978, S. 119–124.

Semerdshiew, A.: Die Verteidigungspolitik der Volksrepublik Bulgarien, in: Österreichische Militärische Zeitschrift. 26 (1988) 1, S. 11–17.

Semerdschiew, A.; Christow, F.; Penkow, S.: Geschichte der Bulgarischen Volksarmee. Berlin (Ost) 1977.

Simon, J.: Warsaw Pact Forces – Problems of Command and Control. Boulder Col. 1985.

Volgyes, I.: The Political Reliability of the Warsaw Pact Armies – The Southern Tier. Durham N. C. 1982.

IV. Wirtschaft

a) Wirtschaftssystem

The Agrarian Policy of the Bulgarian Communist Party Since 1944. Hrsg.: RFE. München 1958.

Angelov, I.: Novijat ikonomičeski mechanizăm trjabva da zaraboti (Der neue Wirtschaftsmechanismus muß zu wirken beginnen), in: Novo vreme. 63 (1987) 3, S. 44–61. – Dt. Übers. in: Südosteuropa. 36 (1987), S. 345–362.

Angelov, I.: Intenzifikacija. predpriemčivost i ikonomičesko sărevnovanie (Intensivierung, Unternehmertum und wirtschaftlicher Wettbewerb), in: Novo vreme. 62 (1986) 7, S. 36–50.

Arojo, Ž.: Ikonomičeskite protivorečija pri socializma (Die ökonomischen Gegensätze im Sozialismus). Sofia 1984.

Arojo, Ž.: Samoupravlenie i ikonomičesko regulirane (Selbstverwaltung und wirtschaftliche Regelung), in: Novo vreme. 63 (1987) 2, S. 27–39.

Barburski, G.: Aktuelle sozial-ökonomische Probleme in der VR Bulgarien. Sofia 1980.

Berov, L. B.: Bulgarien (Wirtschaftsgeographie im Überblick). Sofia 1984.

Berow, L.: Bulgariens ökonomische Entwicklung im Laufe der Jahrhunderte. Sofia 1980.

Bojčev, J.: Njakoi ikonomičeski problemi na razvitoto socialističesko obštestvo (Einige ökonomische Probleme der entwickelten sozialistischen Gesellschaft). Sofia 1975.

Bojčev, J.: Stokovo-paričnite otnošenija v sistemata na socialističeskite proizvodstveni otnošenija (Ware-Geldbeziehungen im System der sozialistischen Produktionsverhältnisse). Sofia 1984.

Bulgarien, Wirtschaftliche Entwicklung 1987. Hrsg. Bulgarische Handels- und Industriekammer. Sofia 1987.

Cankov, S.: Centralizacija, decentralizacija i efektivnost na socialnite dejnosti (Zentralisation, Dezentralisation und Effektivität der sozialen Tätigkeiten). Sofia 1987.

Dellin, L. A.: Bulgarien, in: Osteuropa. Wirtschaftsreformen. Hrsg. H. Gross. Bonn 1970, S. 75–89.

Detkov, G.: Ikonomičeska samostojatelnost i samoupravlenie v stopanskite sistemi (Die ökonomische Selbständigkeit und die Selbstverwaltung in den Wirtschaftssystemen). Sofia 1986.

Dimitrov, V.: Die neue Organisationsstruktur der Wirtschaft, in: Bulgarischer Außenhandel. 36 (1987) 3.

Dimitrov, V.: Neuregelung der Investitionen, in: Bulgarischer Außenhandel. 36 (1987) 6.

Dimitrova, N.: Cenite i cenoobrazuvaneto – dejstven regulator na intenzivnoto ikonomičesko razvitie (Preise und Preisbildung – ein effektiver Regulator der intensiven wirtschaftlichen Entwicklung), in: Ikonomika. 3 (1987) 12, S. 30–37.

Dobrin, B.: Bulgarian Economic Development Since World War II. New York 1973.

Dočev, I.: Stopanisvane na socialističeskata sobstvenost, kačestvo, ikonomičeski mechanizăm (Bewirtschaften des sozialistischen Eigentums, Qualität, Wirtschaftsmechanismus). Sofia 1985.

Efektivnost na narodnoto stopanstvo na Narodna republika Bălgarija (Effektivität der Volkswirtschaft der NRB). Sofia 1974.

Feiwel, G. R.: Economic Reform in Bulgaria, in: Osteuropa-Wirtschaft. 24 (1979) 2, S. 71–91.

Feiwel, G. R.: Growth and Reforms in Centrally Planned Economies. The Lessons of the Bulgarian Experience. New York 1977.

Gevrenov, S. P.: Realizacija na socialističeskata sobstvenost v investicionnija proces (Die Realisierung des sozialistischen Eigentums im Investitionsprozeß). Sofia 1985.

Gianaris, N. V.: The Economies of the Balkan Countries: Albania, Bulgaria, Greece, Romania, Turkey, and Yugoslavia. New York 1982.

Grosser, I.: Der neue ökonomische Mechanismus in Bulgarien. Wien 1984 (Forschungsberichte des Wiener Instituts für internationale Wirtschaftsvergleiche 98).

Grosser, I.: Bulgarien: Zwischenbilanz des „Neuen Wirtschaftsmechanismus". Köln 1984 (Berichte des Bundesinstituts für ostwissenschaftliche und internationale Studien 34).

Gumpel, W.: Sozialistische Wirtschaftssysteme. München 1983.

Gumpel, W.: Das Außenhandelssystem der sozialistischen Balkanstaaten in seinen Konsequenzen für deren internationale Wirtschaftsbeziehungen, in: Südosteuropa im Entwicklungsprozeß der Welt. Festschrift für Hermann Gross. Hrsg. W. Althammer, W. Gumpel. München 1979, S. 35–48.

Gumpel, W.: Agrarische Organisationsreform in Bulgarien, in: Wissenschaftlicher Dienst Südosteuropa. 29 (1980) 1–2, S. 23/24.

Höpken, W.: Bulgarien: Bilanz des ersten Wirtschaftshalbjahres, in: Südosteuropa. 35 (1986), S. 580–588.

Höpken, W.: Wirtschaftsreform in Bulgarien, in: Südosteuropa. 36 (1987), S. 45–57.

Ikonomičeska enciklopedija v dva toma (Wirtschaftsenzyklopädie in zwei Bänden). Sofia 1984.

Ikonomičeska geografija. Naselenie, selišta, stopanski otrasli (Wirtschaftsgeographie. Bevölkerung, Siedlungen, Wirtschaftszweige). Sofia 1981 (Geografija na Bălgarija v tri toma, t. 2).

Ikonomika na Bălgarija. V 6 toma (Die Wirtschaft Bulgariens. In sechs Bänden). Von N. Popov u. a. Sofia 1972–1980.

Intenzifikacija i efektivnost na obštestvenoto proizvodstvo (Intensivierung und Effektivität der gesellschaftlichen Produktion). Sofia 1984.

Jordanov, T.: Ikonomičeska geografija na NRB (Wirtschaftsgeographie der NRB). Sofia 1959.

Kalpošanov, S.: Osnovi na socialističeskata ikonomika (Grundlagen der sozialistischen Wirtschaft). Sofia 1984.

Kinov, D.; Stoilov, S. (Red.): Intenzifikacija i efektivnost na socialističeskoto văzproizvodstvo (Intensivierung und Effektivität der sozialistischen Reproduktion). Sofia 1986.

Kinov, D.: Mechanizăm za povišavane efektivnostta na obštestvenoto proizvodstvo (Mechanismus zur Erhöhung der Effektivität der gesellschaftlichen Produktion). Sofia 1984.

Kirov, T.: Metodika za planirane socialnoto razvitie na socialističeskite stopanski organizacii i trudovite kolektivi (Methoden der Planung der sozialen Entwicklung der sozialistischen Wirtschaftsorganisationen und Arbeitskollektive). Sofia 1985.

Kostov, M.: Finansova sistema i sistema na finansovopravno regulirane (Finanzsystem und das System der finanzrechtlichen Regelung). Sofia 1986.

Lampe, J. R.: The Bulgarian Economy in the Twentieth Century. London, Sydney 1986.

Lampe, J. R.; Jackson, M. R.: Balkan Economic History, 1550–1950. From Imperial Borderlands to Developing Nations. Bloomington 1982.

Lodahl, M.: Die wirtschaftliche Entwicklung in Bulgarien in den achtziger Jahren, in: Vierteljahrshefte zur Wirtschaftsforschung. (1987) 4, S. 340–349.

Lozanov, K. C.: Roljata na socialističeskata ikonomičeska integracija za povišavane kačestvoto na produkcijata v NRB (Die Rolle der sozialistischen ökonomischen Integration bei der Erhöhung der Qualität der Produktion in der NRB). Sofia 1985.

Markova, T. V.: Meždunarodnijat socialističeski pazar i strukturata na narodnoto stopanstvo na NRB (Der internationale sozialistische Markt und die Volkswirtschaft der NRB). Sofia 1984.

Minkov, M.: Bulgaria and the Economic Development of the Balkans. Sofia 1962.

Osteuropa. Wirtschaftsreformen. Hrsg. H.

Gross. Bonn 1970 (Dokumente und Kommentare zu Osteuropa-Fragen 8).
Perspektivi na ikonomičeskoto razvitie na NR Bălgarija (Perspektiven der Wirtschaftsentwicklung der NRB). Sofia 1980.
Planning in Eastern Europe. Hrsg. A. H. Dawson. London 1987.
Procesăt na socialističeskoto proizvodstvo (Der sozialistische Produktionsprozeß). Veliko Tărnovo 1983.
Reform und Wandel in Südosteuropa. Hrsg. R. Schönfeld. München 1985 (Untersuchungen zur Gegenwartskunde Südosteuropas 26).
Rochlin, R. D.: Die Wirtschaft Bulgariens seit 1945. Berlin 1957 (Deutsches Institut für Wirtschaftsforschung, Sonderhefte N. F. 38, Reihe A: Forschung).
Roussinov, S.: Economic Development of Bulgaria After the Second World War. Sofia o. J.
Socialno-ikonomičeskata politika na bălgarskata dăržava (681–1981) (Die sozial-ökonomische Politik des bulgarischen Staates 681–1981). Hrsg. L. Radulov. Varna 1981.
100 godini bălgarska ikonomika (100 Jahre bulgarischer Wirtschaft). Sofia 1978.
Stopanska istorija na Bălgarija 681–1981 (Wirtschaftsgeschichte Bulgariens 681–1981). Sofia 1981.
Tadžer, V.: Socialističeski stopanski organizacii (Sozialistische Wirtschaftsorganisationen). Sofia 1980.
Tuitz, G.: Wachstum und Strukturwandel in den weniger entwickelten europäischen Ländern Südwest- und Südeuropas. Wien 1982 (Forschungsberichte des Wiener Instituts für internationale Wirtschaftsvergleiche 73).
VR Bulgarien – Wirtschaftlicher Überblick 1984. Hrsg.: Bulgarische Handels- und Industriekammer. Sofia 1984.
Die Wirtschaftsordnungen Osteuropas im Wandel, Bd. 1: Länderberichte: Ausmaß und Bedeutung der institutionellen Veränderungen. Hrsg. H.-H. Höhmann, M. C. Kaser, K. C. Thalheim. Freiburg 1972.

b) Industrie und Handwerk

Antonov, V.: Proizvodstveni funkcii s obšteni faktori (Produktionsfunktionen mit Generalfaktoren), in: Ikonomičeska misăl. 30 (1985) 7, S. 106–118.
Business International: Bulgaria: High Goals for Electronic Growth, in: Business Eastern Europe. May 26, 1986.
Dočev, I.: Ikonomičeski problemi na modernizacijata i rekonstrukcijata v promišlenostta (v NRB). Izsledvane (Ökonomische Probleme der Modernisierung und der Rekonstruktion in der Industrie in der NRB. Eine Untersuchung). Sofia 1975.
Feiwel, G. R.: Industrialization in Postwar Bulgaria, in: Osteuropa-Wirtschaft. 23 (1978) 1, S. 1–17.
Ivanov, I.: Koncentracija na promišlenostta v NR Bălgarija i meždunarodnata socialističeska integracija. Izsledvane (Industriekonzentration in der NRB und die internationale sozialistische Integration. Eine Untersuchung). Sofia 1972.
Jackson, M.: Bulgaria's Attempt at „Radical Reform". Köln 1988 (Berichte des Bundesinstituts für Ostwissenschaftliche und Internationale Studien 2/1988).
Jackson, M.: Bulgaria's Economy in the 1970's: Adjusting Productivity to Structure, in: East European Economic Assessment, Part 1 – Country Studies, 1980. Papers submitted to the Joint Economic Committee, Congress of the United States. Washington 1981, S. 571–618.
Jackson, M.: Economic Development in the Balkans Since 1945 Compared to Southern and East-Central Europe, in: Eastern European Politics and Society. 1 (1987) 3, S. 393–455.
Jackson, M.: Recent Economic Performance and Policy in Bulgaria, in: Eastern European Economies: Slow Growth in the 1980's. Vol. 3 – Country Studies. Paper submitted to the Joint Economic Committee, Congress of the United States. Washington 1986, S. 23–58.
Keremidčiev, V.: Usăvăršenstvuvane strukturata na elektronnata i elektrotechničeskata promišlenost na NR Bălgarija v uslovijata na integracijata (Die Vervollkommnung der Struktur der Elektronik und der elektrotechnischen Industrie in der NRB unter den Bedingungen der Integration), in: Ikonomičeska misăl. 31 (1986) 6, S. 11–22.
Kovačeva, Z.: Bălgarskoto mašinostroene – rožba na aprilskata ikonomičeska politika na partijata (Bulgarischer Maschinenbau – Frucht der wirtschaftlichen April-Politik der BKP), in: Ikonomičeska misăl. 31 (1986) 4, S. 73–85.
Montias, J.: Industrial Policy and Foreign Trade in Bulgaria. Yale University – an unpublished paper. New Haven 1987.
Popov, N.; Miloševski, A.: Ot zanajatčijstvoto

do razvito promišleno proizvodstvo v Bălgarija (1878–1978) (Vom Handwerk zur entwickelten Industrieproduktion in Bulgarien (1878–1978), in: 100 godini bălgarska ikonomika. Sofia 1978, S. 45–112.

Spirkov, P.; Šapkarev, P.: Socialist Industrialization – the Basis of Building the Material and Technical Foundations of Socialism, in: Social and Economic Development of Bulgaria 1944–1964. Sofia 1964, S. 44–80.

Staller, G.: Bulgaria: A New Industrial Production Index, 1962–1972, with Extension for 1973 and 1974. Occasional Paper of the Research Project on National Income in East Central Europe, no. 47. New York 1975.

Zlatev, Z.: Socialist Industrialization in Bulgaria, in: Problems of the Transition from Capitalism to Socialism in Bulgaria. Sofia 1975, S. 173–200.

c) Land- und Forstwirtschaft

Agrarproduktion und Nahrungsverbrauch in Bulgarien, Rumänien und der Tschechoslowakei. Entwicklungen und Aussichten. Münster-Hiltrup 1982 (Schriftenreihe des Bundesministeriums für Ernährung, Landwirtschaft und Forsten C 14).

Bazala, R.: The Agricultural Economy and Trade of Bulgaria. Washington, DC 1969.

Beljaški, M.: Planirane na proizvodstvoto v TKZS (Die Produktionsplanung in der TKZS). Sofia 1968.

Brusarski, K. u. a.: Razvitie na selskostopanskoto proizvodstvo prez devetata petiletka na osnovata na naučno-techničeskija progres (Entwicklung der Landwirtschaftsproduktion im neunten Jahrfünft auf der Basis des wissenschaftlich-technischen Fortschritts), in: Ikonomika na selskoto stopanstvo. (1985) 6.

Cochrane, N.: The New Economic Mechanism in Bulgarian Agriculture. Washington, DC 1986 (ERS Staff Report 851121).

Cook, E.: Prospects for Bulgarian Agriculture in the 1980's, in: East European Economies: Slow Growth in the 1980's, vol. 3. Country Studies on Eastern Europe and Yugoslavia, Selected Papers submitted to the Joint Economic Committee, Congress of The United States. Washington 1986.

Cvetkov, G.: Tempove i proporcii na razširenoto văzproizvodstvo v selskoto stopanstvo (Tempi und Proportionen der erweiterten Reproduktion in der Landwirtschaft). Sofia 1972.

Devedžiev, M. S.: Teritorialno izpolzuvane na NRB (Die territoriale Ausnutzung der NRB). Sofia 1981.

Feiwel, G.: Growth and Reforms in Centrally Planned Economies – The Lessons of the Bulgarian Experience. New York, Washington, London 1977.

Filipov, V.: 25 godini socialističesko selsko stopanstvo v Bălgarija (25 Jahre sozialistische Landwirtschaft in Bulgarien). Sofia 1969.

Georgiev, N.: 15 godini narodna vlast i našeto selsko stopanstvo (15 Jahre Volksmacht und unsere Landwirtschaft). Sofia 1959.

Gregov, G.: Teritorialna struktura na selskoto stopanstvo v Bălgarija (Territorialstruktur der Landwirtschaft in Bulgarien). Sofia 1984.

Grosser, I.: Private Landwirtschaft in Bulgarien. Berlin 1988 (Giessener Abhandlungen zur Agrar- und Wirtschaftsforschung des Europäischen Ostens 154).

Höpken, W.: Bulgariens Landwirtschaft vor Problemen, in: Südosteuropa. 34 (1985) S. 611–628.

Ivanova, V.: Agroindustrial Complexes and Personal Holdings in Bulgaria – Does that Mean a „Mixed" Policy?, in: Industrial Policies and Structural Change. Hrsg. C. T. Saunders. New York 1987, S. 295–305.

Kostadinov, J.: Socialno-ikonomičeski problemi na agrarnopromišlenata integracija (Sozial-ökonomische Probleme der agrarindustriellen Integration). Sofia 1980.

Kuminev, Ch.: Aktualni problemi na socialističeskata organizacija na truda v selskoto stopanstvo (Aktuelle Probleme der sozialistischen Arbeitsorganisation in der Landwirtschaft). Sofia 1984.

Lucov, I.: Cooperatives and Agrarian Transformations in Bulgaria. Sofia 1984.

Lucov, I. u. a.: Planirane na selskostopanskoto proizvodstvo (Planung der Landwirtschaftsproduktion). Sofia 1983.

Ofer, G.: Growth Strategy, Specialization in Agriculture, and Trade: Bulgaria and Eastern Europe, in: East European Integration and East-West Trade. Hrsg. P. Marer, J. Montias. Bloomington 1980, S. 283–320.

Oren, N.: Revolution Administered: Agrarianism and Communism in Bulgaria. Baltimore 1973 (Integration and Community Building in Eastern Europe 8).

Petkov, D.: Socialističeskoto sărevnovanie v

selskoto stopanstvo (Sozialistischer Wettbewerb in der Landwirtschaft). Sofia 1978.
Petrov, K.: Agrarnata politika na partijata prez devetata petiletka (Die Agrarpolitik der Partei während des 9. Fünfjahresplanes). Sofia 1987.
Popov, T.: Haupttendenzen und charakteristische Merkmale der Entwicklung der Landwirtschaft Bulgariens in den sechziger und siebziger Jahren, in: Österreichische Osthefte. 26 (1984) 3, S. 500–512.
Popov, T.: Problemi na săvremennoto bălgarsko zemedelie (Probleme der modernen bulgarischen Landwirtschaft). Sofia 1985.
Pospelowa, G.; Fleiss, H.: Schlachttier- und Fleischproduktion in Osteuropa – Bulgarien. Berlin 1981 (Giessener Abhandlungen zur Agrar- und Wirtschaftsforschung des Europäischen Ostens 112).
Pouliquen, A.: Les „voies bulgare et est-allemande" en agriculture sont-elles purement soviétiques?, in: Revue d'études comparatives Est-Ouest. 16 (1985) 1, S. 67–84.
Prumov, I.: Bulgarian Agriculture Today. Sofia 1976.
Reiner, A.: Sammlung von ausgewählten Rechtsvorschriften zum LPG-Recht sozialistischer Länder. Potsdam-Babelsberg 1978.
Schopov, V.: Das bulgarische Dorf auf dem Weg des Sozialismus. Sofia 1972.
Selskostopanska enciklopedija (Landwirtschaftliche Enzyklopädie). Sofia 1984.
Syulemezov, S.: The Cooperative Movement in Bulgaria. Sofia 1976.
Tendencii v razvitieto na selskoto stopanstvo v Bălgarija (Tendenzen in der Entwicklung der Landwirtschaft in Bulgarien). Sofia 1976.
Trifonov, P. Ch.: Demokratičeskijat centralizăm v upravlenieto na selskoto stopanstvo (Der demokratische Zentralismus in der Landwirtschaftsverwaltung). Sofia 1980.
Trifonov, P.: Integracionni procesi v bălgarskoto selo (Integrationsprozesse im bulgarischen Dorf). Sofia 1981.
Trifonov, P.: Problemi na upravlenieto na APK (Probleme der Leitung von APK). Sofia 1973.
Valev, I.: Efektivnost na selskostopanskoto proizvodstvo (Effektivität der landwirtschaftlichen Produktion). Sofia 1979.
Vălkov, D. P.: Organizacija na socialističeskite selskostopanski predprijatija (Die Organisation der sozialistischen Agrarbetriebe). Sofia 1965.
Wiedemann, P.: Agricultural Development in Bulgaria: 1976–1985, in: Current Trends in the Soviet and East European Food Economy. Osteuropas Nahrungswirtschaft Gestern und Morgen. Berlin 1982 (Giessener Abhandlungen zur Agrar- und Wirtschaftsforschung des Europäischen Ostens 113).
Wiedemann, P.: The Origins and Development of Agro-Industrial Development in Bulgaria, in: Agricultural Policies in the USSR and Eastern Europe. Hrsg. R. A. Francisco, B. A. Laird, R. D. Laird. Boulder, Co. 1980, S. 97–135.
Wiedemann, P.: Probleme der Messung landwirtschaftlicher Produktion zum Zweck internationaler Vergleiche – dargestellt am Beispiel Bulgarien – Jugoslawien, in: Osteuropa-Wirtschaft. 21 (1976) 1, S. 63–76.
Wyzan, M.: Bulgarian Agriculture Since 1979: Sweeping Reform and Mediocre Performance (So Far), in: Farming Under Communism: New and Old Approaches. Ed. G. Grossman, R. Laird, K.-E. Wädekin. Routledge 1989.
Wyzan, M.: The Bulgarian Experience with Centrally-Planned Agriculture: Lessons for Soviet Reformers?, in: Contemporary Soviet Agriculture. Ed. K. R. Gray. Iowa State University Press 1989.
Zagorski, N.: Peasant Life in Bulgaria. Sofia 1964.
Zotschew, Th.: Bulgarien. Tübingen 1981 (Kieler Sonderdrucke 93). – Veröffentlicht in: Handwörterbuch des Agrarrechts. Bd. 1. Berlin 1981, Sp. 407–419.

d) Bergbau- und Energiewirtschaft

Bethkenhagen, J.: Die Energiewirtschaft der UdSSR und ihre Verflechtung mit dem RGW, in: Rat für gegenseitige Wirtschaftshilfe. Hrsg. Bundeszentrale für politische Bildung. Bonn 1987, S. 79 ff.
Bethkenhagen, J.: Nuclear Power in the USSR and Eastern Europe, Post Chernobyl, in: Eastern Europe and the USSR. Hrsg. The Economist Intelligence Unit. S. 27 ff.
25 godini bălgarski atomen reaktor (25 Jahre bulgarischer Atomreaktor). Sofia 1987.
Elman, J.: Uhelný průmysl v BLR (Kohlenindustrie in der NRB), in: Uhlí. (1985) 1, S. 35 ff.
Höpken, W.: Energiepolitik und Energieprobleme in Bulgarien, in: Südosteuropa. 37 (1988) 2–3, S. 73–94.
Popov, B.: Die Energiewirtschaft der Volksrepublik Bulgarien. Sofia 1979.

Steblez, W.: The Mineral Industry of Bulgaria, in: Bureau of Mines Minerales Yearbook. Washington, D.C. 1985.

e) Handel, Versorgung und Verkehr; Tourismus

Čaušev, A.: Socialističeskata tărgovija i razvitie na narodnoto stopanstvo (Der sozialistische Handel und die Entwicklung der Volkswirtschaft). Sofia 1962.
Dinev, L.: Tourismus und Infrastruktur am Beispiel der bulgarischen Schwarzmeerküste, in: Österreichische Osthefte. 26 (1984) 2, S. 304–312.
Georgiev, M.: Razvitieto na transporta v Bălgarija i meždunarodnoto razdelenie na truda. Izsledvane (Die Entwicklung des Transports in Bulgarien und die internationale Arbeitsteilung. Eine Untersuchung). Sofia 1970.
„Krăgla masa" po problemite na stopanskija turizăm v NR Bălgarija („Runder Tisch" über die Probleme des Tourismus in der NRB), in: Ikonomičeska misăl. 32 (1987) 4, S. 24–52.
Marinov, V.; Băčvarov, M.: Za integralen podchod kăm problemite na stopanskija turizăm (Für ein integrales Herangehen an die Probleme des Tourismus), in: Ikonomičeska misăl. 32 (1987) 12, S. 71–82.
Mieczkowski, B.: Transportation in Eastern Europe. Empirical Findings. New York 1978.
Razvitie na socialističeskata tărgovija i turizma (Die Entwicklung des sozialistischen Handels und des Tourismus), in: 30 godini socialističeska Bălgarija. Sofia 1974, S. 164–181.
Sălova, N.: Efektivnost na vătrešnata tărgovija v NRB (Die Effektivität des bulgarischen Binnenhandels). Varna 1978.
Stankov, G. u.a.: Geografija na otdicha i turizma v Bălgarija (Geographie des Erholungswesens und des Tourismus in Bulgarien). Sofia 1984.
Tončev, C.: Turističeskoto obslužvane – săstojanie, problemi i zadači (Das touristische Dienstleistungsangebot – Zustand, Probleme und Aufgaben), in: Ikonomičeska misăl. 32 (1987) 6, S. 35–44.
Traditionelle Transportmethoden in Ostmitteleuropa. Hrsg. A. Paládi-Kovács. Budapest 1981.

f) Außenwirtschaft

Aćimović, M.: Ekonomska suradnja pograničnih područja Jugoslavije sa susjednim zemljama (Wirtschaftliche Zusammenarbeit der grenznahen Gebiete Jugoslawiens mit den Nachbarländern). Zagreb 1984.
Agro-promyšlennaja integracija. Opyt sovetsko-bolgarskogo sotrudničestva (Agrarisch-industrielle Integration. Erfahrungen der sowjetisch-bulgarischen Zusammenarbeit). Moskau 1982.
Bašikarov, P.: Ikonomičeskata integracija i sbližavaneto săs SSSR (Ökonomische Integration und Annäherung an die UdSSR), in: 40 godini socialističeska vănšna tărgovija na NR Bălgarija. Bd. 1. Sofia 1985, S. 76–103.
Bulgarien als Handels- und Kooperationspartner. Hrsg. Industrie- und Handelskammer Berlin. Berlin 1983.
Bundesstelle für Außenhandelsinformation: Bulgarien: Ansprechpartner im Außenhandel. Zentrale Stellen, Außenhandelsorganisationen. Köln 1987.
Georgiev, G.: Bulgariens Außenhandel. Dreißig Jahre seit der sozialistischen Revolution in Bulgarien. Sofia 1974.
Georgiev, G.S.: Ikonomičeskite otnošenija meždu stranite-členki na SIV – meždunarodni otnošenija ot nov tip (Wirtschaftsbeziehungen zwischen den Mitgliedsländern des RGW – internationale Beziehungen von neuem Typ). Sofia 1984.
Georgiev, G.S.: Vănšnoikonomičeskata politika (săštnost, principi, realizacija) (Außenwirtschaftspolitik. Wesen, Prinzipien, Realisierung). Sofia 1985.
Glasmacher, P.: Möglichkeiten grenz- und systemüberschreitender Unternehmenskooperation durch westliche Beteiligungen an Unternehmen in Jugoslawien, Ungarn, Rumänien, Polen und Bulgarien. Frankfurt a.M. u.a. 1986 (Europäische Hochschulschriften; Reihe 2, 543).
Grosser, I.: Bulgarien 1987/88. Rege Reformaktivität. Hartwährungsposition nicht konsolidiert. in: Länder Osteuropas zur Jahreswende 1987/88. Hrsg. K. Bolz. Hamburg 1988.
Grosser, I.: Bulgarische Außenwirtschaftsreformen in den achtziger Jahren, in: Außenwirtschaftssysteme und Außenwirtschaftsreformen sozialistischer Länder. Ein intrasystematischer Vergleich. Hrsg. M. Haendeke-Hoppe. Berlin 1988.
Grozdanova, S.: Trade and Economic Rela-

tions Between Bulgaria and the Arab Countries, in: Soviet and Eastern European Foreign Trade. 21 (1985) 1/3, S. 120–128.

Gumpel, W.: Die bulgarisch-sowjetischen Wirtschaftsbeziehungen. Partnerschaft oder Bindung?, in: Osteuropa. 36 (1986), S. 261–276.

Ivanova, A.; West, B.: Bulgaria's Growing Technological Importance to the USSR, in: Radio Free Europe Research. Bulgaria SR/7 (29.7.1988).

Jackson, M. R.: Bulgarian Economic Reforms and the GATT, in: Südosteuropa. 36 (1987), S. 544–559.

Marinov, G.: Characteristics and Tendencies in the Economic Development of the Mongolian People's Republic, Cuba, and the People's Republic of Vietnam and Cooperation Between Them and Bulgaria, in: Soviet and Eastern European Foreign Trade. 21 (1985) 1/3, S. 191–203.

Marukjan, A. V.: Problemi na učastieto na stopanskite organizacii văv vănšnoikonomičeskite otnošenija na Bălgarija s razvitite kapitalističeski strani (Probleme der Beteiligung der Wirtschaftsorganisationen an den Außenwirtschaftsbeziehungen Bulgariens mit den entwickelten kapitalistischen Ländern). Sofia 1985.

Normative Acts of the Foreign-Economic Relations of the People's Republic of Bulgaria. Hrsg. P. M. Penkov. Sofia 1982.

Problemi na meždunarodnite ikonomičeski otnošenija (Probleme der internationalen Wirtschaftsbeziehungen). Red.: S. Šarenkov. Sofia 1986.

Schönfeld, R.: Die Balkanländer in der Weltwirtschaftskrise, in: Vierteljahrschrift für Sozial- und Wirtschaftsgeschichte. 62 (1975) 2, S. 179–213.

Schönfeld, R.: Probleme der Außenwirtschaft. Ungarn, Rumänien, Bulgarien, Jugoslawien, Albanien, in: Südosteuropa-Mitteilungen. 22 (1982) 3–4, S. 73–86.

Schönfeld, R.: Joint Ventures mit westlicher Kapitalbeteiligung in sozialistischen Ländern, in: Wirtschaftsrecht, Internationaler Handel und Friedliche Koexistenz aus osteuropäischer Sicht. Hrsg. G. Brunner. Berlin 1982 (Osteuropaforschung 7), S. 75–94.

Schönfeld, R.: Bulgariens Außenhandelspolitik und die Rolle der deutschen Wirtschaft, in: Südosteuropa. 31 (1982), S. 398–412.

Schönfeld, R.: Gemeinsame Investitionen im RGW und die Beteiligung der südosteuropäischen Mitgliedsländer, in: RGW-Integration und Südosteuropa. Hrsg. R. Schönfeld. München 1984 (Untersuchungen zur Gegenwartskunde Südosteuropas 24), S. 101–126.

Schönfeld, R.: Wirtschaftsentwicklung mit besonderer Berücksichtigung des Außenhandels in Bulgarien, in: Österreichisches Jahrbuch für internationale Politik. 3 (1986), S. 182–198.

Sotirova, R.; Gocheva, B.: Credit Relations in Bulgarian Imports from the Developed Capitalist Countries, in: Soviet and Eastern European Foreign Trade. 22 (1986) 1, S. 6–18.

Stankovsky, J.: Bulgaria as an Export Market for OECD and Developing Countries. [Vortrag anläßlich des Seminars „Bulgaria and the GATT", Graz, 7.–8. April 1987] Wien 1987 (Wifo-Vorträge 30).

Tönnes, B.: Bulgarien als RGW-Partner, in: RGW-Integration und Südosteuropa. Hrsg. R. Schönfeld. München 1984 (Untersuchungen zur Gegenwartskunde Südosteuropas 24), S. 163–187.

Vănšna tărgovija na NR Bălgarija s nesocialističeski strani (Außenhandel der NRB mit nichtsozialistischen Ländern). Hrsg. K. Nikolov. Sofia 1985.

Vănšna tărgovija na Narodna Republika Bălgarija. Statističeski danni 1939, 1945–1963 (Der Außenhandel der NRB. Statistische Daten 1939, 1945–1963). Sofia 1964.

Vănšna tărgovija na NRB. Statističeski danni 1939–1974 (Der Außenhandel der NRB. Statistische Daten 1939–1974). Sofia 1975.

Zlatev, Z. D.: Bălgaro-săvetski ikonomičeski otnošenija (1944–1958) (Die bulgarisch-sowjetischen Wirtschaftsbeziehungen, 1944–1958). Sofia 1986.

V. Gesellschaft

a) Raumplanung und Umweltschutz

Čačev, C. u. a.: Zamărsjavane na rekite v Bălgarija săs suspendirani veštestva (Verschmutzung der Flüsse in Bulgarien mit Abfallstoffen). Sofia 1973.
Oschlies, W.: Schwefelstaub auf Rosenblüten – Umweltsorgen in Bulgarien. Köln, Wien 1987.
Rizov, K.: Razvitie na prirodozaštitnoto delo v Bălgarija (Entwicklung des Naturschutzwesens in Bulgarien). Sofia 1987.

b) Bevölkerungsstruktur

Baldwin, G.: Population Estimates and Projections for Eastern Europe: 1950–2000, in: East European Economies: Slow Growth in the 1980's. Joint Economic Committee of Congress. Washington 1986, S. 263–297.
Charakteristika na bălgarskoto naselenie. Trudovi văzmožnosti i realizacija (Charakteristik der bulgarischen Bevölkerung. Arbeitskräfteressourcen und Realisierung). Hrsg. M. Minkov. Sofia 1984.
Demografija na Bălgarija (Demographie Bulgariens). Sofia 1974.
Demografska statistika (Demographische Statistik). Sofia 1966–1969.
Devedžiev, M.: Teritorialni aspekti na estestvenoto i mechaničnoto dviženie na naselenieto na NR Bălgarija (Territoriale Aspekte des natürlichen und mechanischen Bevölkerungswachstums in der NRB), in: Statistika. (1980) 1, S. 26–41.
Höpken, W.: Demographische Entwicklung und Bevölkerungspolitik in Bulgarien, in: Südosteuropa. 35 (1986), S. 88–99.
Jackson, M. R.: Comparing the Balkan Demographic Experience, 1860 to 1970, in: Journal of European Economic History. 14 (1985), S. 223–272.
Kiradžiev, S.: Tendencii v razvitieto na migracionnite potoci v Bălgarija (Tendenzen in der Entwicklung der Migrationsströme in Bulgarien), in: Izvestija na Bălgarskoto Geografsko Družestvo. 19 (1981), S. 75–82.
Kiradžiev, S.: Vlijanie na migraciite vărchu teritorialnoto razpredelenie na naselenieto v Bălgarija (Der Einfluß der Migrationen auf die territoriale Verteilung der Bevölkerung in Bulgarien), in: Izvestija na Bălgarskoto Geografsko Družestvo. 21 (1983), S. 101–109.
Kostanick, H.: Demographic Structure and Changes in Bulgaria, in: Bulgaria: Past and Present. Hrsg. Th. Butler. Columbus, Ohio 1976, S. 142–146.
Kostanick, H.: Turkish Resettlement of Bulgarian Turks: 1950–1953, in: University of California Publications in Geography. 8 (1957) 2, S. 65–146.
Kvočkin, M.: Bolgarija: Zbliženie goroda i derevni v uslovijach socialističeskogo sodružestva (Bulgarien: Annäherung von Stadt und Land unter den Bedingungen der sozialistischen Zusammenarbeit). Minsk 1982.
Mičev, N.: Naselenieto na Bălgarija (ikonomgeografsko izsledvane) (Bevölkerung Bulgariens. Eine wirtschaftsgeographische Untersuchung). Sofia 1978.
Minkov, M.: Demografskoto razvitie – tendencii i problemi (Demographische Entwicklung – Tendenzen und Probleme), in: Novo vreme. 63 (1987) 7, S. 27–38.
Minkov, M.: Migracija na naselenieto (Bevölkerungsmigration). Sofia 1972.
Minkov, M.: Naselenie i osnovni socialni strukturi (Bevölkerung und soziale Grundstrukturen). Sofia 1976.
Minkov, M.: Naselenieto i rabotnata sila v Bălgarija (Bevölkerung und Arbeitskräfte in Bulgarien). Sofia 1966.
Myers, P.: Demographic Trends in Eastern Europe, in: Economic Developments in Countries of Eastern Europe. Joint Economic Committee of Congress. Washington 1970, S. 68–148.
Naselenie (Bevölkerung). Sofia 1970–1988.
Oschlies, W.: Bulgariens Bevölkerung Mitte der 80er Jahre. Eine demographische und sozialpolitische Skizze, Köln 1986 (Berichte des Bundesinstituts für internationale und ostwissenschaftliche Studien 17–1986).
Şimşir, B. N.: Migrations from Bulgaria to Turkey: 1950–51 Exodus, in: Foreign Policy. 12 (1985) 3–4, S. 67–101.
Smărtnost na naselenieto v Bălgarija po pričini (Die Sterblichkeit der Bevölkerung in Bulgarien nach Ursachen). Sofia 1977.
Taaffe, R.: The Impact of Rural-Urban Migration on the Development of Communist Bulgaria, in: Population and Migration Trends in Eastern Europe. Hrsg. H. Kostanick. Boulder, Col. 1977, S. 157–179.

Taaffe, R.: Urbanization in Bulgaria, in: Études Balkaniques. (1974) 2/3, S. 50–63.
Totev, A. Iu.: Characteristic Demographic Features of Bulgaria, 1880–1980, in: Bulgaria: Past and Present. Hrsg. Th. Butler. Columbus, Ohio 1976, S. 132–141.
Zachariev, I.; Kožukorov, I.: Naselenie i trudovi resursi v teritorialnite edinici na NR Bălgarija (Bevölkerung und Arbeitsressourcen in den Territorialeinheiten der NRB). Sofia 1973.

c) Sozialstruktur

Aspaturian, V.-V.: The Soviet Impact on Development and Modernization in Eastern Europe, in: The Politics of Modernization in Eastern Europe: Testing the Soviet Model. Ed. C. Gati. New York 1974, S. 205–255.
Atanasov, A.: Rabotničeskata klasa v Bălgarija 1948–1958 (Die Arbeiterklasse in Bulgarien 1948–1958). Sofia 1987.
Dimitrov, K.: Character and Main Elements of the Socio-Class Structure of Developed Socialism, in: Bulgarian Journal of Sociology. 1 (1978), S. 72–80.
Dimitrov, K.: The Development of the Social-Class Structure of Socialist Society and the Changes Within the Working Class, in: Contemporary Sociology in Bulgaria. Sofia 1978, S. 319–333.
Dimitrov, K. V.: Socialnoklasovata struktura na săvremennoto bălgarsko obštestvo (Soziale Klassenstruktur der gegenwärtigen bulgarischen Gesellschaft). Sofia 1986.
Dobrianov, V.: Changes in the Socio-Class Structure of Bulgaria, in: Bulgaria: Past and Present. Ed. T. Butler. Columbus 1976, S. 147–163.
Draganov, M.: On the Social-Psychological Typology of the Patriarchal-Traditional Bulgarian Peasant, in: Contemporary Sociology in Bulgaria. Sofia 1978, S. 347–360.
Golemanov, H.; Popov, M.: Social Welfare in the People's Republic of Bulgaria. Sofia 1975.
Ivanov, V.: The Working Class in the Social Structure of a Developed Socialist Society, in: Bulgarian Journal of Sociology. 1 (1978), S. 81–89.
Kostanick, H.: Demographic Structure and Change in Bulgaria, in: Bulgaria Past and Present. Ed. T. Butler. Columbus 1976, S. 142–146.
Kyuranov, C.: On the Genesis of Social Stratification, in: Contemporary Sociology in Bulgaria. Sofia 1978, S. 211–222.
Kyuranov, C.: The Bulgarian Family Today. Sofia 1984.
Kyurkchiev, M.: Bulgarian Agriculture Today and Life in the Villages. Sofia 1974.
Mihailov, S.: Society as a Sociological System, in: Contemporary Sociology in Bulgaria. Sofia 1978, S. 53–68.
Minkov, M.: Development of the Social-Class Structure of the Socialist Society in Bulgaria, in: Contemporary Sociology in Bulgaria. Sofia 1978, S. 193–209.
Mironov, I.: Incomes and Socio-Class Structure in Bulgaria, in: Bulgarian Journal of Sociology. 1 (1978), S. 90–101.
Oshavkov, Z.: Sociological Structure and Socio-Class Composition of Society, in: Bulgarian Journal of Sociology. 1 (1978), S. 14–23.
Sanders, I.: Factors Influencing the Contemporary Bulgarian Family, in: Bulgaria: Past and Present. Ed. T. Butler. Columbus 1976, S. 164–170.
Sanders, I.; Whitaker, R.: Tradition and Modernization: The Case of Bulgaria, in: Tradition and Modernity. Ed. J. Lutz, S. El-Shakhs. Washington D. C. 1982, S. 147–163.
Socialnata politika na BKP i razvitieto na NR Bălgarija (Die Sozialpolitik der BKP und die Entwicklung der NRB). Sofia 1980.
Whitaker, R.: Continuity and Change in Two Bulgarian Communities: A Sociological Profile, in: Slavic Review. 38 (1979) 2, S. 259–271.
Whitaker, R.: Experiencing Revolutionary Change: The Role of Tradition, in: Bulgaria: Past and Present. Ed. Dimiter Kosev. Sofia 1982, S. 109–115.
Wiedemann, P.: The Distribution of Income and Earnings and Economic Welfare in Bulgaria and Yugoslavia, in: Southeastern Europe. 3 (1976) 1, S. 1–18.

d) Nationale Minderheiten

Amnesty International: Bulgaria: Imprisonment of Ethnic Turks. Human Rights Abuses during the Forced Assimilation of the Ethnic Turkish Minority. London 1986.
Bachmaier, P.: Assimilation oder Kulturautonomie. Das Schulwesen der nationalen Minderheiten in Bulgarien nach dem 9. September 1944, in: Österreichische Osthefte. 26 (1984), S. 391–404.

Baest, T. F.: Neues von der „einheitlichen sozialistischen Nation": Die VR Bulgarien und ihre türkische Minderheit (1944–1985), in: Neuer Nationalismus und nationale Minderheiten. Hamburg 1985 (Osteuropa-Info, Jg. 13, Nr. 61), S. 92–118.

Behar, N.: Izmenenija v socialnata struktura na bălgarskite evrei pri socializma (Veränderungen in der Sozialstruktur der bulgarischen Juden im Sozialismus), in: Proučvanija za istorijata na evrejskoto naselenie v bălgarskite zemi XV–XX vek. Sofia 1980, S. 208–214.

Boev, P.: Die Rassentypen der Balkanhalbinsel und der ostägäischen Inselwelt und deren Bedeutung für die Herkunft ihrer Bevölkerung. Sofia 1972.

Boev, P.; Schwidetzky, I.: Rassengeschichte von Bulgarien. München, Wien 1979 (Rassengeschichte der Menschheit 6).

Brunner, G.: Der Schutz ethnischer Minderheiten in Osteuropa, in: Jahrbuch für Ostrecht. 25 (1984), S. 9–41.

Brunner, G.: Die Rechtsstellung ethnischer Minderheiten in Südosteuropa, in: Nationalitätenprobleme in Südosteuropa. Hrsg. R. Schönfeld. München 1987 (Untersuchungen zur Gegenwartskunde Südosteuropas 25), S. 39–72.

Čingo, N.: The Macedonians and the First Population Census in Post-War Bulgaria, in: Socialist Thought and Practice. 16 (1976) 2, S. 56–76.

Dimitrov, G. V.: Za taka narečenata „kulturna avtonomija" v Blagoevgradski okrăg (Für die sog. „Kulturautonomie" im Kreis Blagoevgrad), in: Istoričeski pregled. 35 (1979) 6, S. 70–82.

Eminov, A.: The Education of Turkish Speakers in Bulgaria, in: Ethnic Groups. 5 (1983) 3, S. 129–149.

Georgeoff, J.: Ethnic Minorities in the People's Republic of Bulgaria, in: The Politics of Ethnicity in Eastern Europe. Hrsg. G. Klein, M. J. Reban. New York 1981, S. 49–84.

Georgeoff, J. P. (with the assistance of D. Crome): National Minorities in Bulgaria 1919–1980, in: Eastern European National Minorities 1919–1980. Hrsg. S. M. Horak. Littleton, Co. 1985, S. 274–308.

Georgieva, I.: Izsledvanija vărchu bita i kulturata na bălgarskite cigani v Sliven (Erforschung der Lebensweise und der Kultur der bulgarischen Zigeuner in Sliven), in: Izvestija na Etnografskija institut s muzej. 9 (1966), S. 25–49.

Holland, R.; Mondrova, G.: Bulgaria, in: World Minorities. Sunbury, Mddx. 1978, Bd. 2, S. 26–31.

Höpken, W.: Modernisierung und Nationalismus: Sozialgeschichtliche Aspekte der bulgarischen Minderheitenpolitik gegenüber den Türken, in: Nationalitätenprobleme in Südosteuropa. Hrsg. R. Schönfeld. München 1987 (Unters. zur Gegenwartskunde Südosteuropas 25), S. 255–280.

Hoppe, E. M.: Die Gagauzen, in: International Archives of Ethnography. 3 (1957), S. 119–129.

Human Rights and Documents on the Minority in the Western Thrace. Ankara 1987.

Izrael, S.: Bălgarskite evrei v godinite na narodnata vlast (Bulgarische Juden in den Jahren der Volksmacht), in: Godišnik na Obštestvenata kulturno-prosvetna organizacija na evreite v NR Bălgarija. 6 (1971), S. 113–139.

Iz minaloto na bălgarite-mochamedani v Rodopite (Aus der Geschichte der bulgarischen Muslime im Rodopengebiet). Sofia 1958.

Kenrick, D.: Notes on the Gypsies in Bulgaria, in: Journal of the Gypsy Lore Society. 45 (1966), S. 77–84.

Marinov, V.: Prinos za izučavaneto na bita i kulturata na Turcite i Gagauzite v Severoiztočna Bălgarija (Beitrag zur Erforschung der Lebensweise und Kultur der Türken und Gagauzen im nordöstlichen Bulgarien). Sofia 1956.

Marinov, V. A.: Prinos kăm izučavaneto na proizchoda, bita i kulturata na karakačanite v Bălgarija (Beitrag zur Untersuchung der Herkunft, Lebensweise und Kultur der Karakatschanen in Bulgarien). Sofia 1964.

Marinov, V.: Nabljudenija vărchu bita na cigani v Bălgarija (Betrachtungen über die Lebensweise der Zigeuner in Bulgarien), in: Izvestija na Etnografskija institut i muzej. 5 (1962) 1, S. 227–276.

Marinov, V.; Genov, D.; Tairov, T.: Siganskoto naselenie v Narodna republika Bălgarija po pătja na socializma (Die Zigeunerbevölkerung in der NRB auf dem Wege des Sozialismus). Sofia 1964.

Marinov, V.; Dimitrov, Z.; Koev, I.: Prinos kăm izučavaneto na bita i kulturata na turskoto naselenie v severoiztočna Bălgarija (Beitrag zur Erforschung der Lebensweise und Kultur der türkischen Bevölkerung im nordöstlichen Bulgarien), in: Izvestija na Etnografskija institut i muzej. 2 (1955), S. 95–216.

Meyer, P.: Bulgaria, in: The Jews in the Soviet Satellites. Hrsg. P. Meyer u.a. Syracuse 1953, S. 559–629.

Monov, C.: Prosvetnoto delo sred Bălgarite s mochamedanska vjara v Rodopskija kraj prez godinite na narodnata vlast (1944–1968) (Bildungstätigkeit unter den Bulgaren muslimischen Glaubens im Rhodopengebiet während der Jahre der Volksmacht 1944–1968), in: Rodopski sbornik. 3 (1972), S. 9–51.

Oppression and discrimination in Bulgaria. (The case of the Muslim Turkish minority). Facts and documents. Pref. K. Mackenzie. London, Nicosia, Istanbul 1986.

Oschlies, W.: The Jews in Bulgaria since 1944, in: Soviet Jewish Affairs. 14 (1984) 2, S. 41–54.

Penkov, M.: A bulgáriai „tatárok" (Rövid történéti áttekintés) ([Dt. Res.:] Die „Tataren" von Bulgarien), in: Ethnographia. 74 (1963), S. 418–434.

Popovic, A.: Problèmes d'approche de l'islam bulgare (1878–1978), in: Proceedings of the Ninth Congress of the Union Européene des Arabisants et des Islamisants, Amsterdam 1.–7. Sept. 1978. Hrsg. R. Peters. Leiden 1981, S. 241–247.

Popovic, A.: The Turks of Bulgaria (1878–1985), in: Central Asian Survey. 5 (1986) 2, S. 1–32.

Reuter, J.: Die Entnationalisierung der Türken in Bulgarien. Sofias Politik der Zwangsbulgarisierung aus jugoslawischer Sicht, in: Südosteuropa. 34 (1985) 3–4, S. 169–177.

Sačev, E.: Bălgarski turci i gagauzi (Etnogenetični problemi) (Bulgarische Türken und Gagauzen. Ethnogenetische Probleme), in: Izvestija na Narodnija muzej Varna. 19 (34) (1983), S. 52–63.

Sarides, E.: Ethnische Minderheit und zwischenstaatliches Streitobjekt. Die Pomaken in Nordgriechenland. Berlin (West) 1987. (Ethnizität und Gesellschaft. Probleme ethnischer Grenzziehung in Gesellschaften des Vorderen und Mittleren Orients. Occasional Papers 11).

Silverman, C.: Bulgarian Gypsies: Adaptation in a Socialist Context, in: Nomadic Peoples. 21/22 (1986), S. 51–62.

Silverman, C.: Pomaks, in: Muslim Peoples. A World Ethnographic Survey. Hrsg. R. V. Weekes. 2., rev. u. erw. Aufl. Westport, CT 1984, S. 612–616.

Şimşir, B. N.: The Legal Status of the Turkish Minority in Bulgaria Under Bilateral and Multilateral Treaties, in: Foreign Policy. 12 (1985) 3–4, S. 102–144.

Şimşir, B. N.: The Turkish Minority Press in Bulgaria. Its History and Tragedy 1865–1985. Ankara 1986.

Summary Record of the Debates Concerning the Turkish Minority in Bulgaria during the 761st and 762nd Meetings of the U. N. Committee of the Elimination of Racial Discrimination. New York, March 11, 1986.

Troebst, S.: Zum Verhältnis von Partei, Staat und türkischer Minderheit in Bulgarien 1956–1986, in: Nationalitätenprobleme in Südosteuropa. Hrsg. R. Schönfeld. München 1987 (Untersuchungen zur Gegenwartskunde Südosteuropas 25), S. 231–253.

Turkish Minority in Bulgaria. Foreign Press Coverage. Ankara 1986.

La vérité historique. L'opinion publique progressiste en Bulgarie et en Macédoine du Pirin sur la question nationale macédonienne. Documents, études, résolutions, appels et contributions de publicistes 1896–1956. Choix et réd. P. Korobar, O. Ivanoski. Skopje 1984.

Die Wahrheit über die bulgarischen Moslems. Sofia 1986.

Wer macht sich Sorgen um die Mohammedaner in Bulgarien und warum? Fakten, Dokumente, Fragen, Antworten, Reportagen. Sofia 1985.

e) Schulwesen

Aleksandrova, D.: Principi v politikata na partijata v oblastta na učilištnoto delo (Die Prinzipien in der Politik der Partei auf dem Gebiet des Schulwesens), in: Akademija za Obštestveni Nauki i Socialno Upravlenie na CK na BKP. Naučni trudove, br. 109: Serija Partijno stroitelstvo. Sofia 1979, S. 171–206.

Angelov, T.: Dălgosročna politika v oblastta na obrazovanieto (Langfristige Politik im Bereich des Bildungswesens). Sofia 1979.

Apanasewicz, N.; Rosen, S. M.: Education in Bulgaria. Washington, D.C. 1965 (U. S. Department of Health, Education and Welfare. Studies in Comparative Education).

Avramova, B.: Education in Bulgaria. Sofia 1971.

Bachmaier, P.: Bulgariens Weg zur neuen Schule. Die Bildungs- und Wissenschaftspolitik der Vaterländischen Front, 1944–1948. Wien 1984.

Bălgarskata komunističeska partijata i kulturata (Die BKP und die Kultur). Bd. 1: 1891–1944; Bd. 2: 1944–1981. Red.: A. Stojkov. Sofia 1983.
Bandoly, W.; Hegewald, H.: Das Bildungswesen in der Volksrepublik Bulgarien, in: Vergleichende Pädagogik. 20 (1984) 4, S. 377–390.
Bulgaria, in: International Handbook of Universities and Other Institutions of Higher Education. Paris 1981, S. 156–162.
Bulgaria, in: World of Learning, 1982–1983. London 1982, S. 218–231.
Čakărov, N.; Atanasov, Ž.: Istorija na obrazovanieto i pedagogičeskata misăl v Bălgarija (Geschichte des Bildungswesens und der Erziehung in Bulgarien). Sofia 1962.
Educational Policy and the Problems of Youth, in: Bulgaria Under Communist Rule. Hrsg. J. F. Brown. New York 1970, S. 215–239.
Fol, A.: Bulgaria: System of Education, in: The International Encyclopedia of Education. Hrsg. T. Husén. Oxford 1985, Bd. 1, S. 588–591.
Georgeoff, J.: Bulgaria, in: World Education Encyclopedia. Hrsg. G. Th. Kurian. New York 1988, Bd. 1, S. 165–178.
Georgioff, J.: The Educational System of Bulgaria. U.S. Department of Health, Education and Welfare. Education Around the World. Washington D.C. 1977.
Georgioff, J.: The Social Education of Bulgarian Youth. Minneapolis 1968.
Georgiev, G.: Istoričeskoto obrazovanie i săvremennoto političesko văzpitanie na učenicite (Die historische Bildung und die gegenwärtige politische Erziehung der Schüler), in: Bălgarija 1300. Institucii i dăržavna tradicija, Bd. 3. Sofia 1983, S. 629–634.
Grant, N.: Bulgaria, in: Society, Schools and Progress in Eastern Europe. Oxford 1969. Bd. 331–344.
Hegewald, H.: Zur Entwicklung des Bildungswesens in der Volksrepublik Bulgarien. Berlin (Ost) 1982 (Beiträge zur Schulpolitik und Pädagogik des Auslands 3).
Iskrov, K.: Partijno răkovodstvo na socialističeskata obrazovatelna sistema (1944–1985) (Die Leitung des sozialistischen Bildungssystems durch die Partei, 1944–1985). Sofia 1986.
Keefe, E. K. u. a.: Education, in: Area Handbook for Bulgaria. Washington, D.C. 1974, S. 93–122.
Mavrov, G.: Problemi na strategijata na obrazovanieto (Probleme der Strategie des Bildungswesens). Sofia 1986.
Oschlies, W.: Bulgariens Kulturentwicklung, 1944–1975. I–II. Köln 1976 (Berichte des Bundesinstituts für Ostwissenschaftliche und Internationale Studien 1/2–1976).
Oschlies, W.: Im Dienste zweier Kulturen. Aus der Vergangenheit deutsch-bulgarischer Zusammenarbeit im Bildungswesen. Köln 1980 (Sonderveröffentlichung des Bundesinstituts für Ostwissenschaftliche und Internationale Studien).
Oschlies, W.: Integrierung und Differenzierung im neuen bulgarischen Schulmodell. Köln 1972.
Pavlov, I.: Săvremenni problemi na politechničeskoto obrazovanie (Gegenwärtige Probleme der polytechnischen Bildung). Sofia 1986.
Samodumow, T.: Izbrani pedagogičeski proizvedenija (Ausgewählte pädagogische Werke). Bd. 1–2. Sofia 1959.
Shimoniak, W.: Communist Education. Its History, Philosophy and Politics. Chicago 1970.
Slavčeva, M.: Sociologičeski i ideologičeski aspekti na obrazovanieto (Soziologische und ideologische Aspekte der Bildung). Sofia 1986.

f) Hochschulen und Wissenschaft

Baka, B.; Georgiev, G.; Smiljanov, A.: Nasoki i văzmožnosti za usăvăršenstvuvane planiraneto na naučnata dejnost văv VUZ (Richtungen und Möglichkeiten zur Verbesserung der Wissenschaftsplanung an der Hochschule), in: Problemi na višeto obrazovanie. 25 (1987) 2, S. 9–15.
Balevski, A.: Problemi na naukata i obrazovanieto (Probleme der Wissenschaft und Bildung). Sofia 1974.
Brajnov, M.: Strukturni problemi na naučnata organizacija na višeto obrazovanie i na obrazovatelnata sistema (Strukturprobleme der wissenschaftlichen Organisation der Hochschulbildung und des Bildungssystems). Sofia 1971.
Bučkov, D.: Formirane na marksistko-leninski mirogled i komunističesko văzpitanie u studentite (Die Formung der marxistisch-leninistischen Weltanschauung und die kommunistische Erziehung der Studenten), in: Problemi na višeto obrazovanie. 25 (1987) 1, S. 8–13.
Cakova, V.: Izgraždaneto na novi strukturi na

naučna dejnost (Der Aufbau neuer Strukturen der wissenschaftlichen Arbeit), in: Problemi na visšeto obrazovanie. 25 (1987) 2, S. 16–20.
Christov, Ch. P.: Probleme der Hochschuldidaktik, in: Informationsdienst zum Bildungswesen in Osteuropa. (1973) 20/21, S. 72–78.
Dimitrov, I.: Usăvăršenstvuvane na visšeto obrazovanie v svetlinata na rešenijata na XIII kongres na BKP (Vervollkommnung der Hochschulbildung im Lichte der Beschlüsse des XIII. Parteitages der BKP), in: Problemi na visšeto obrazovanie. 25 (1987) 1, S. 3–7.
Jachiel, N.: Nauka i politika v uslovijach naučno-techničeskoj revoljucii (Wissenschaft und Politik unter den Bedingungen der wissenschaftlich-technischen Revolution). Sofia 1987.
Kačaunov, S.: Prognoznata dejnost v naukata (Prognostische Tätigkeit in der Wissenschaft). Sofia 1982.
Kostov, K.: Uvod u upravlenie na naučnoto izsledvane (Einführung in die Leitung wissenschaftlicher Forschung). Sofia 1982.
Maslarov, I. A.: Problemi na preustrojstvoto na sistemata za podgotovka na specialisti bez otkăsvane ot trudovata dejnost (Probleme der Umgestaltung des berufsbegleitenden Ausbildungssystems für Spezialisten), in: Problemi na visšeto obrazovanie. 25 (1987) 6, S. 3–10.
Naredba za izsledovatelskata i technologičnata dejnost (Verordnung über die Forschungs- und technologische Tätigkeit), in: DV. (1987) 17, S. 8–14.
Naučno-techničeskie programmy i upravlenie naučno-techničeskim progressom v socialističeskich stranach (Wissenschaftlich-technische Programme und die Leitung des wissenschaftlich-technischen Fortschritts in den sozialistischen Ländern). Moskau 1986.
Nikolov, P.; Nikolov, I.: Upravlenie na procesa izsledvane-vnedrjavane (Die Leitung des Prozesses Forschung-Anwendung). Sofia 1979.
Ninov, N.: Văzmožnosti za usăvăršenstvuvane na obučenieto bez otkăsvane ot proizvodstvoto (Möglichkeiten zur Vervollkommnung des berufsbegleitenden Studiums), in: Problemi na visšeto obrazovanie. 25 (1987) 2, S. 58.
Organizacija i upravlenie naukoj i technikoj (Organisation und Leitung im Bereich von Wissenschaft und Technik). Moskau 1987.

Oschlies, W.: Wissenschaft und Wissenschaftler in Bulgarien. Stand, Probleme, Perspektiven. Köln 1971 (Berichte des Bundesinstituts für Ostwissenschaftliche und Internationale Studien 32–1971).
Osnovni problemi na naukoznanieto (Grundprobleme der Wissenschaftswissenschaft). Sofia 1973.
Plovdivski universitet „Paisij Chilendarskij" 1961–1986 (Die „Paisij Chilendarskij" Universität Plovdiv 1961–1986). Plovdiv 1986.
Problemi na naučnata informacija (Probleme der Wissenschaftsinformation). Sofia 1976.
Proekt: Osnovni nasoki i zadači za preustrojstvoto na naučnija front (Projekt: Grundrichtungen und -aufgaben bei der Umgestaltung der Wissenschaftsfront), in: RD. 20. 5. 1988, S. 1–3.
Savov, M.: Osnovnye napravlenija sotrudničestva socialističeskich stran v oblasti vysšego obrazovanija (Grundrichtungen der Zusammenarbeit sozialistischer Länder im Bereich der Hochschulbildung), in: Sovremennaja vysšaja škola. 50 (1985) 2, S. 131–135.
Savov, M.; Nikolov, I.: Participation of Bulgarian higher education in international cooperation within the European region, in: Higher Eduation in Europe. 11 (1986) 1, S. 11–20.
Slavova, L.: Visšite učebni zavedenija – samoupravljavašti se organizacii (Hochschulen – selbstverwaltete Organisationen), in: Problemi na visšeto obrazovanie. 25 (1987) 6, S. 40–43.
Shiwkow, T.: Die Wissenschaft – eine wirksame Produktivkraft. Sofia 1986.
Sofijski Universitet „Kliment Ochridski" 9. IX. 1944–9. IX. 1974 (Universität „Kliment Ochridski" Sofia 9. 9. 1944–9. 9. 1974). Sofia 1974.
Sto godini Bălgarska Akademija na Naukite 1869–1969 (Hundert Jahre BAN 1869–1969). 3 Bde. Sofia 1969, 1972.
Stojanov, P.: Prelomen etap za razvitieto na obrazovatelnoto delo (Die Wende in der Entwicklung des Bildungswesens), in: Narodna prosveta. (1987) 12, S. 3–12.
Vasil'ev, G.: Pedagogičeskaja podgotovka prepodavatelej VUZOV (Die Pädagogische Vorbereitung der Hochschullehrer), in: Sovremennaja vysšaja škola. 60 (1987) 4, S. 159–166.
Vasilev, V.; Mavrova, R.; Nikolov, S.: Razrabotvane sistema za kontrol i ocenka na kačestvoto na prepodavatelskata rabota văv

VUZ (Beitrag zu einem System der Qualitätskontrolle und -bewertung der Unterrichtstätigkeit an der Hochschule), in: Naučni trudove na Plovdivskija universitet „Paisij Chilendarski". Plovdiv 1983, Bd. 20, Buch 1.
Virčev, L.: Didaktikata na visšeto obrazovanie – postiženija i problemi (Hochschuldidaktik – Ergebnisse und Probleme), in: Narodna prosveta. (1986) 3, S. 54–60.
Zakon za naučnite stepeni i naučnite zvanija (Gesetz über wissenschaftliche Grade und Titel), in: DV. (1972) 36, S. 1–2.

g) Kirchen und Religionsgemeinschaften

Babris, P. J.: Silent Churches. Persecution in the Soviet-Dominated Areas. Arlington Heights, Ill. 1978.
Bǎlgarskata Patriaršija prez vekovete (Das Bulgarische Patriarchat durch die Jahrhunderte). Hrsg. Ch. Kodov u. a. Sofia 1980.
Broun, J. A.: Religious survival in Bulgaria, in: America. 153 (1985), S. 323–327.
The Church and State under Communism. Vol. 1–9. Washington, DC 1964.
Church Within Socialism: Church and State in East European Socialist Republics. Hrsg. E. Weingartner. Rom 1976.
Johansen, A.: Theological study in the Russian and Bulgarian Orthodox Churches under Communist Rule. London 1963.
Mizov, N.: Isljamǎt v Bǎlgarija. Sǎštnost, modernizacija i preodoljavane (Der Islam in Bulgarien. Wesen, Modernisierung und Überwindung). Sofia 1965.
Mojzes, P. B.: A History of the Congregational and Methodist Churches in Bulgaria and Yugoslavia. Doctoral Diss. Boston Univ. 1965.
NR Bǎlgarija i religioznite izpovedanija v neja (Die NRB und die Religionsbekenntnisse in ihr). Sofia 1966.
Oschlies, W.: Bulgarien – Land ohne Antisemitismus. Erlangen 1976.
Oschlies, W.: Kirchen und religiöses Leben in Bulgarien. Köln 1983 (Berichte des Bundesinstituts für ostwissenschaftliche und internationale Studien 15–1983).
Pantschovski, I.: Patriarch Kyrill. Berlin (Ost) 1971.

Pravoslavieto v Bǎlgarija (Orthodoxie in Bulgarien). Hrsg. D. Angelov u. a. Sofia 1974.
Pundeff, M.: Church-State Relations in Bulgaria under Communism, in: Religion and Atheism in the USSR and Eastern Europe. Hrsg. B. Bociurkiw, J. Strong. London 1975, S. 328–350.
Raikin, S. T.: Nationalism and the Bulgarian Orthodox Church, in: Religion and Nationalism in Soviet and East European Politics. Hrsg. P. Ramet. Durham, N. C. 1984, S. 187–206.
Ramet, P.: Cross and Commissar. The Politics of Religion in Eastern Europe and the USSR. Bloomington 1987.
Slijepčević, Dj.: Die bulgarische orthodoxe Kirche 1944–1956. München 1957 (Untersuchungen zur Gegenwartskunde Südosteuropas 1).
Stupperich, R.: Kirche und Staat in Bulgarien und Jugoslawien. Witten 1971.
Turkish Muslims in Bulgaria, in: Religion in Communist Lands. 15 (1987) 2, S. 209–212.

h) Massenmedien und Sprachkultur

Jordanova, L.: Novite dumi v sǎvremennija bǎlgarski ezik (Die neuen Wörter in der bulgarischen Gegenwartssprache). Sofia 1980 (Rodna reč omajna 16).
Mišev, D.: Vǎzraždane črez pečata (Wiedergeburt durch die Presse), in: Bǎlgarija 1000 godini. Sofia 1927, S. 601–663.
Oschlies, W.: Lenins Enkeln aufs Maul geschaut – Jugend-Jargon in Osteuropa. Köln, Wien 1981.
Popov, K.: Po njakoi sporni i nerešeni vǎprosi na knižovnija pravogovor i pravopis (Zu einigen strittigen und ungeklärten Fragen der literarischen Aussprache und Rechtschreibung), in: Plamǎk. 14 (1970) 1, S. 55–63.
Popvasilev, S.: Bogat i zvučen – Besedi vǎrchu bǎlgarskija ezik (Reich und klangvoll – Unterhaltungen über die bulgarische Sprache). Sofia 1970.
Stojkov, S.: Sofijskijat učeničeski govor (Der Sofioter Schüler-Jargon), in: Godišnik na Sofijskija Universitet – Istoriko-filologičeski fakultet. 42 (1945/46).
Topenčarov, V.: Bǎlgarskata žurnalistika 1885–1903 (Die bulgarische Journalistik 1885–1903). Sofia 1963.

VI. Kultur

a) Volkskultur

Arnaudov, M.: Očerci po bălgarskija folklor (Skizzen zur bulgarischen Folklore). 2 Bde. Sofia 1968–1969.

Bălgarska narodna kultura. Istoriko-etnografski očerk (Bulgarische Volkskultur. Historisch-ethnographische Skizze). Hrsg. V. Chadžinikolov u. a. Sofia 1981.

Bălgarski junaški epos (Das bulgarische Heldenepos). Hrsg. C. Romanska. Sofia 1971 (Sbornik na narodni umotvorenija, nauka i knižnina 53).

Bălgarsko narodno tvorčestvo (Schöpfungen des bulgarischen Volkes). 13 Bde. Sofia 1961–1965.

Dinekov, P.: Bălgarski folklor (Bulgarische Folklore). Sofia 1972.

Dinekov, P.: The Development of Bulgarian Folklore Studies, in: International Folklore Review. 1 (1981), S. 43–47.

Etnografija i săvremennost (Ethnographie und Gegenwart). Hrsg. D. Todorov u. a. Sofia 1976.

Etnografija na Bălgarija (Ethnographie Bulgariens). Hrsg. V. Chadžinikolov u. a. 3 Bde. Sofia 1980–1985.

Ivanova, R.: Bălgarska folklorna svatba (Bulgarische Volkshochzeit). Sofia 1964.

Katzarova-Kukudova, R.; Djenev, K.: Bulgarian Folk Dances. Sofia 1958 (Nachdruck: Cambridge, Mass. 1976).

Kaufman, N.: Bălgarski gradski pesni (Bulgarische Stadtlieder). Sofia 1968.

Kaufman, N.: Pesni na bălgarite mochamedani ot Rodopite (Die Lieder der islamischen Bulgaren in den Rhodopen), in: Rodopski sbornik. 2 (1969), S. 41–130.

Kostov, S.; Peteva, E.: Selski bit i izkustvo v Sofijsko (Dorfleben und -kunst im Kreis Sofia). Sofia 1935.

Lane, Ch.: The Rites of Rulers. Cambridge, London 1981.

Matl, J.: Die patriarchale Altkultur und der Weg zur Neukultur, in: Aspects of the Balkans. Continuity and Change. Hrsg. H. Birnbaum u. a. Paris 1972, S. 355–369.

Nicoloff, A.: Bulgarian Folklore. Cleveland, Ohio 1983.

Nikolov, J.: Za tipologijata na socialističeskite rituali (Zur Typologie sozialistischer Rituale), in: Bălgarska etnografija. 10 (1985) 4, S. 37–46.

Obredi i obreden folklor (Bräuche und Brauchsvolkskunde). Hrsg. T. I. Živkov. Sofia 1981.

Osvoboždenieto na Bălgarija i razvitieto na bălgarskata narodna kultura (Die Befreiung Bulgariens und die Entwicklung der bulgarischen Volkskultur). Red.: V. Chadžinikolov, I. Georgieva. Sofia 1978.

Parpulova, L.: Bălgarskata socialističeska kultura i folklorăt (Die bulgarische sozialistische Kultur und die Folklore), in: Bălgarski folklor. 6 (1980) 4, S. 25–34.

Paskaleva, V.: Die Entwicklung des Handwerks und die kulturelle Vermittlungsfunktion von Handwerkern bei der „Europäisierung" Bulgariens im 19. Jh., in: Handwerk in Mittel- und Südosteuropa. Hrsg. K. Roth. München 1987 (Südosteuropa-Studien 38), S. 129–136.

Primovski, A.: Bit i kultura na rodopskite bălgari (Lebensweise und Kultur der Bulgaren in den Rhodopen). Sofia 1973 (Sbornik na narodni umotvorenija, nauka i knižnina 54).

Puntev, P.; Čerkezova, M.: Bulgarische Volkskunst. Sofia 1980.

Röhling, H.: Studien zur Geschichte der balkanslawischen Volkspoesie. Köln, Wien 1975.

Roth, J. u. K.: Gattungen und Inhalte der bulgarischen Popularliteratur, in: Bulgarien. Internationale Beziehungen in Geschichte, Kultur und Kunst. Hrsg. W. Gesemann, K. Haralampieff, H. Schaller. Neuried 1984 (Südosteuropa-Studien 35; Bulgarische Sammlung 4), S. 163–182.

Roth, K.: Der bulgarische Bänkelsang heute. Zum Wandel des Liederrepertoires eines Sängers, in: Festschrift für E. Klusen zum 75. Geburtstag. Hrsg. G. Noll u. a. Bonn 1984, S. 417–434.

Roth, K.: Die Pflege alter Handwerke im heutigen Bulgarien, in: Handwerk in Mittel- und Südosteuropa. Hrsg. K. Roth. München 1987 (Südosteuropa-Studien 38), S. 217–230.

Roth, K.; Wolf, G.: South Slavic Folk Culture. A Bibliography of Titles in English, German, and French. Südslavische Volkskultur. Bibliographie der Literatur in deutscher, englischer und französischer Sprache. Columbus, Ohio 1989 (im Druck).

Sanders, I.: Balkan Village. Lexington 1949; Westport (2. Aufl.) 1975.

Šapkarev, K. A.: Sbornik ot bălgarski narodni

umotvorenija (Sammlung des Geistesschaffens des bulgarischen Volkes). Sofia 1891.
Schmaus, A.: Südosteuropa, in: JRO-Volkskunde. Europäische Länder. München 1963, S. 221–240.
Silverman, C.: The Politics of Folklore in Bulgaria, in: Anthropological Quarterly. 56 (1983) 2, S. 55–61.
Stojkova, S.: Folklorät i kulturnite promeni (Die Folklore und die kulturellen Veränderungen), in: Folklor i obštestvo. Sofia 1977, S. 31–36.
Tachirov, Š.: Etnokulturni procesi sred bälgarskite turci (Ethnokulturelle Prozesse bei den bulgarischen Türken), in: Bălgarska etnografija. 5 (1980) 4, S. 3–16.
Todorov, T.: Săvremennost i narodna pesen (Gegenwart und Volkslied). Sofia 1978.
Vakarelski, Ch.: Altertümliche Elemente in Lebensweise und Kultur der bulgarischen Mohammedaner, in: Zeitschrift für Balkanologie. 4 (1966), S. 149–172.
Vakarelski, Ch.: Bulgarische Volkskunde. Berlin 1969.
Vakarelski, Ch.: Etnografija na Bălgarija (Ethnographie Bulgariens). Sofia 1974.
Wilhelmy, H.: Hochbulgarien. Bd. 1: Die ländlichen Siedlungen und die bäuerliche Wirtschaft. Bd. 2: Sofia. Wandlungen einer Großstadt zwischen Orient und Okzident. Kiel 1935, 1936 (Schriften des Geographischen Instituts der Universität Kiel 4, 5/3).
Živkov, T.I.: Folklor i săvremennost (Folklore und Gegenwart). Sofia 1981.

b) Literatur

Aprilska diskusija '80, '81, '82, '83, '84, '85 (Aprildiskussion 1980 ff.). Sofia 1985 ff.
A Biobibliographical Handbook of Bulgarian Authors. Hrsg. K.L. Black. Columbus, Ohio 1981.
Bliznakova, K.: Otvăd iljuzijata. Nabljudenija vărchu săvremennata bălgarska dramaturgija (Jenseits der Illusion. Beobachtungen zur zeitgenössischen bulgarischen Dramatik). Sofia 1984.
Čolakov, Z.: Debjutnata vălna. Problemi na mladata bălgarska poezija i proza (Die Welle der Debüts. Probleme der jungen bulgarischen Poesie und Prosa). Sofia 1974.
Delčev, B.: Măkite na realista. Literaturni văprosi (Die Leiden des Realisten. Literarische Probleme). Sofia 1954.
Dobrev, Č.: Lirična drama (Das lyrische Drama). Sofia 1973.
Formirane i razvitie na socialističeskata kultura v Bălgarija. Sbornik (Formierung und Entwicklung der sozialistischen Kultur in Bulgarien. Sammelband). Sofia 1971.
Georgiev, E.: Bălgarskata literatura v obštoevropejski kontekst (Die bulgarische Literatur im europäischen Kontext). Sofia 1984.
Georgiev, Lj.: Săvremennost i poezija. Estetičeski vzaimootnošenija (Gegenwart und Poesie. Ästhetische Wechselbeziehungen). Sofia 1979.
Gerlinghoff, P.: Bibliographische Einführung in das Studium der neueren bulgarischen Literatur (1850-1950). Meisenheim am Glan 1969.
Istorija na bălgarskata literatura. T. 4: Bălgarskata literatura ot kraja na părvata svetovna vojna do deveti septemvri 1944 godina (Geschichte der bulgarischen Literatur. Bd. 4: Die bulgarische Literatur vom Ende des Ersten Weltkrieges bis zum 9.9.1944). Hrsg. P. Zarev u.a. Sofia 1976.
Janev, S.: Tendencii v săvremennata proza (Tendenzen in der zeitgenössischen Prosa). Sofia 1977.
Kolevski, V.: Văprosi na săvremennata bălgarska literatura (Fragen der zeitgenössischen bulgarischen Literatur). Sofia 1969.
Konstantinov, G.; Minkov, C.; Velkov, S.: Bălgarski pisateli. Biografii. Bibliografija (Bulgarische Schriftsteller. Biographien. Bibliographie). Sofia 1961.
Konstantinova, E.: Bălgarskijat razkaz ot včera i dnes (Die bulgarische Erzählung von gestern und heute). Sofia 1987.
Kujumdžiev, K.: Raztvorena kniga. Tendencii v razvitieto na razkaza i povesta sled 9 septemvri 1944 g. (Das geöffnete Buch. Tendenzen der Entwicklung von Erzählung und Povest nach dem 9.9.1944). Sofia 1983.
Kulman, D.: Das Bild des bulgarischen Mittelalters in der neubulgarischen Erzählliteratur. München 1968.
Lauer, R.: Die deutsche Literatur in Bulgarien – Typologische und genetische Beziehungen, in: 1300 Jahre Bulgarien. Neuried 1981, Bd. 2, Teil 1, S. 247–269.
Lauer, R.: Einheit und Vielheit im Wechselspiel. Typologische Aspekte der Literaturen Südosteuropas, in: Südosteuropa-Mitteilungen. 17 (1977) 4, S. 20–34.
Lauer, R.: Tendenzen der bulgarischen Gegenwartsliteratur, in: Südosteuropa-Mitteilungen. 21 (1981) 3, S. 74–81.
Lauer, R.: Zur Frage der Fremdorientierung in

der bulgarischen Literatur, in: Kulturelle Traditionen in Bulgarien. Hrsg. R. Lauer und P. Schreiner. Göttingen 1989, S. 255–272.
Likova, R.: Razkazvačăt v săvremennata bălgarska beletristika (Der Erzähler in der zeitgenössischen bulgarischen Belletristik). Sofia 1978.
Literatur Bulgariens 1944 bis 1980. Einzeldarstellungen. Von einem bulgarischen Autorenkollektiv unter der Leitung von T. Shetschew und S. Stantschew sowie Bulgaristen der DDR. Berlin 1981.
Markov, G.: Die bulgarische Literatur seit 1944. Grundzüge und Tendenzen, in: Die zeitgenössischen Literaturen Südosteuropas. München 1978, S. 145–155.
Moser, Ch. A.: A History of Bulgarian Literature, 865–1944. The Hague 1972 (Slavistic Printings and Reprintings 112).
Ničev, B.: Săvremennijat bălgarski roman. Kăm istorija i teorija na epičnoto v săvremennata bălgarska chudožestvena proza (Der zeitgenössische bulgarische Roman. Zu Geschichte und Theorie des Epischen in der zeitgenössischen bulgarischen Kunstprosa). Sofia 1973, ²1981.
Očerci na bălgarskata literatura sled deveti septemvri 1944 godina v dve knigi (Skizzen zur Geschichte der bulgarischen Literatur nach dem 9.9.1944 in zwei Bänden). Hrsg. A. Guljaški, E. Karanfilov, B. Ničev. Sofia 1980. – [S. 410–471: ausführliche Bibliographie].
Panova, S.: Smjach i prisăda. Tendencii v razvitieto na săvremennata bălgarska komedija (Lachen und Urteil. Tendenzen in der Entwicklung der zeitgenössischen bulgarischen Komödie). Sofia 1977.
Ponomareva, N. N.: Sovremennaja bolgarskaja dramaturgija (Zeitgenössische bulgarische Dramatik). Moskau 1974.
Popivanov, I.: Săvremennata poezija. Estetičeski nasoki (Poesie der Gegenwart. Ästhetische Richtungen). Sofia 1986.
Problemi na săvremennata bălgarska poezija. Sbornik statii i studii (Probleme der bulgarischen Poesie der Gegenwart. Sammelband von Aufsätzen und Studien). Hrsg. E. Prochaskova und S. Chadžikosev. Sofia 1978.
Problemi na săvremennata bălgarska proza. Sbornik statii i studii (Probleme der bulgarischen Prosa der Gegenwart. Sammelband von Aufsätzen und Studien). Hrsg. M. Naimovič und Č. Dobrev. Sofia 1973.
Săvremennata bălgarska proza i evropejskite socijalističeski literaturi (Die bulgarische Prosa der Gegenwart und die europäischen sozialistischen Literaturen). Sofia 1986.
Slavov, A.: The „Taw" in Bulgarian Literature. Boulder, Co., New York 1981 (East European Monographs 74).
Spasov, I.: Černi ot săvremennata bălgarska literatura (Grundzüge der zeitgenössischen bulgarischen Literatur). Sofia 1980.
Trajkov, V.: Bălgarska chudožestvena literatura na čuždi ezici. 1823–1962 (Bulgarische schöne Literatur in fremden Sprachen. 1823–1962). Sofia 1964.
Văprosi na săvremennata bălgarska literatura (Fragen der zeitgenössischen bulgarischen Literatur). Sofia 1969.
Vasilev, M.: Bălgarskijat razkaz (1878–1970 (Die bulgarische Erzählung). Sofia 1987.
Vasilev, M.: Săvremennijat bălgarski razkaz (Die bulgarische Erzählung der Gegenwart). Sofia 1980.
Vtori meždunaroden kongres po bălgaristika. Dokladi 12 (Zweiter internationaler Bulgaristikkongreß. Referate 12). Sofia 1988.
Vučkov, Ju.: Bălgarskata dramaturgija 1944–1979. Nasoki i tendencii (Die bulgarische Dramatik 1944–1979. Richtungen und Tendenzen). Sofia 1981.
Das Wort – meine Waffe. 1878–1978. Hundert Jahre bulgarische revolutionäre Lyrik. Ausgewählt von H.-J. Neschtschenko. Berlin 1978.
Žečev, T.: Bălgarskijat roman sled Deveti Septemvri (Der bulgarische Roman nach dem 9. September). Sofia 1980.
Žečev, T.: Probleme des Humanismus im neuen bulgarischen Roman, in: Bulgarische Sprache, Literatur und Geschichte. Neuwied 1980, S. 157–168.

c) Theater

Beyer, B.: Zur Rezeption des deutschen Dramas in Bulgarien im 19. Jahrhundert, in: Bălgaro-nemski literaturni i kulturni vzaimootnošenija prez 18 i 19 vek. Sofia 1985, S. 201–215.
Bojadžiev, A.: Teatralnijăt proces. Preživjano i razmisăl (Der theatralische Prozeß. Erlebnisse und Reflexionen). Sofia 1985.
Bradistilova-Dobreva, M.: Văzroždenskata teatralna kultura v Bălgarija (Die Theaterkultur der Wiedergeburtszeit in Bulgarien). Sofia 1983.
Burkhart, D.: „Dr. Faustina" von Blaga Di-

mitrova. Ein Exempel der zeitgenössischen bulgarischen Dramenliteratur, in: Festschrift für Wolfgang Gesemann. Hrsg. H. B. Harder u. a. Bd. 1. Neuried 1986 (Typoskript-Edition Hieronymus; Slavische Sprachen und Literaturen 6), S. 25–44.
Deržavin, K.: Bolgarskij teatr (Das bulgarische Theater). Moskau, Leningrad 1950.
G'orova, S.: Bălgarskijat dramatičen teatăr (Das bulgarische dramatische Theater). Sofia 1979.
Hille, G.: Das bulgarische Kammertheater, in: Festschrift für Wolfgang Gesemann. Hrsg. H. B. Harder u. a. Bd. 1. Neuried 1986 (Typoskript-Edition Hieronymus; Slavische Sprachen und Literaturen 6), S. 103–110.
Javorov, P. u. a.: Bulgarische Dramen. Hrsg. W. Köppe. Berlin 1974.
Karakostov, S.: Bălgarskijat teatăr. Osnovi na socialističeskija realizăm 1881/1891/1945 (Das bulgarische Theater. Grundlagen des sozialistischen Realismus 1881/1891/1945). Sofia 1982.
Penev, P.: Istorija na bălgarskija dramatičen teatăr (Geschichte des bulgarischen dramatischen Theaters). Sofia 1975.
Popova, K.: Das bulgarische Theater. Sofia 1972.
Schaulov, I.: Das Theater in Bulgarien. Sofia 1964.
Teatărăt i estetičeskoto văzpitanie. Sbornik statii (Theater und ästhetische Erziehung. Ein Sammelband). Zusammengestellt A. Dunčev. Sofia 1984.
Veličkov, M.: Theater und Dramatik in Bulgarien, in: Südosteuropa-Mitteilungen. 20 (1980) 1, S. 73–78.
Vučkov, J.: Bălgarska dramaturgija (Bulgarische Dramatik). Bd. 1878–1944. Sofia 1983; Bd. 1944–1979. Sofia 1981.

d) Film

Bălgarskijat film i kritikata. Sbornik recenzii (Der bulgarische Film und die Kritik. Gesammelte Rezensionen). Hrsg. A. Grozev. Sofia 1974.
Brossard, J.-P.: Aspects nouveaux du cinéma bulgare. La Chaux-de-Fonds 1986.
The Bulgarian Art Feature Film. A Collection of Articles. Hrsg. M. Nikolova. Sofia 1971.
Bulgarian Cinema 1944–1984. Hrsg. I. Stojanovič. Sofia 1984.
The Bulgarian Cinema Today. Hrsg. I. Stojanovič. Sofia 1981.

Černokoleva, L. T.: Săvremennoto bălgarsko dokumentalno kino (Der zeitgenössische bulgarische Dokumentarfilm). Sofia 1977.
Cervoni, A.: Les écrans de Sofia. Voyage français dans le cinéma bulgare. Paris 1976.
Genčeva, G.: Bălgarski igralni filmi (Bulgarische Spielfilme). T. 2: 1950–1970. Sofia 1988.
Grenzüberschreitung – Bulgarien/Nouveau cinéma bulgare. Sondernummer der Zeitschrift Cinema (4/76). Zusammengestellt von J.-P. Brossard und B. Jäggi. Zürich 1976.
Holloway, R.: The Bulgarian Cinema. Cranbury u. a. 1986.
Markova, O.: Ot literaturata kăm ekrana (Von der Literatur auf die Leinwand). Sofia 1981.
Micheli, S.: Il Cinema Bulgaro. Padova 1971.
Micheli, S.: Cinema di animazione in Bulgaria. Bologna 1975.
Milev, N.: Bălgarskijat istoričeski film (Der bulgarische historische Film). Sofia 1982.
Ratscheva, M.: Bulgarische Filmkunst der Gegenwart. Sofia 1969. (Auch in englischer, französicher, russischer Ausgabe).
Ratschewa, M.; Eder, K.: Der bulgarische Film. Geschichte und Gegenwart einer Kinematografie. Frankfurt a. M. 1977.
Stanimirova, N.: Bălgarski kinorežis'ori (Bulgarische Kinoregisseure). Sofia 1984.
Stanimirova, N.: Kino i geroika. Gerojat v bălgarskite filmi za săprotivata (Kino und Heldentum. Der Held im bulgarischen Film über den Widerstand). Sofia 1973.
Stefanov, I.: Izkustvo i komunikacija v kinoto (Kunst und Kommunikation im Kino). Sofia 1976.

e) Bildende Kunst und Architektur

Architektura i gradoustrojstvo v socialističeskata Bălgarija 1944–1974 (Architektur und Städtebau im sozialistischen Bulgarien 1944–1974). Sofia 1984.
Aspekte bulgarischer Kunst heute. (Sammlung Ludwig, Aachen) [Ausstellungskatalog]. Wien o. J.
Berbenliev, P.: Kunstdenkmäler in Bulgarien. München, Berlin 1983.
Bildende Kunst in Bulgarien [Ausstellungskatalog]. Wien 1985.
Boschkov, A.: Bulgarische Volkskunst. Recklinghausen 1972.
Boškov, A.: Bălgarsko izobrazitelno izkustvo (Bulgarische bildende Kunst). Sofia 1988.

Bosilkov, S.: Bălgarskijat politiceski plakat (Das bulgarische politische Plakat). Sofia 1973.
Boškov, A.: Bălgarska revoljucionna grafika (Die bulgarische Revolutionsgrafik). Sofia 1958.
Die bulgarische Kunst, in: Allgemeine Geschichte der Kunst. Bd. 8. Leipzig o. J., S. 437–450.
Čuchovski, P.: Săvremenna bălgarska grafika (Die zeitgenössische bulgarische Grafik). Sofia 1971.
Enciklopedija na izobrazitelnite izkustva v Bălgarija v dva toma (Enzyklopädie der bildenden Künste in Bulgarien in zwei Bänden). Sofia 1980.
Erkundungen. Grafik und Plastik junger Künstler aus der VR Bulgarien und aus der DDR [Ausstellungskatalog]. Berlin 1988.
Ficker, F.: Bulgarische Kunst heute, in: Weltkunst. 57 (1987) 21, S. 31–72.
Goranov, K.: Izkustvoto kato proces (Kunst als Prozeß). Sofia 1977.
Ivanova, V.: Săvremenna bălgarska skulptura (Die zeitgenössische bulgarische Skulptur). Sofia 1971.
Kunsthandwerk aus der VR Bulgarien [Ausstellungskatalog]. Berlin 1972.
Malerei, Graphik, Kleinplastik aus Bulgarien [Ausstellungskatalog]. München 1982.
Michalčeva, I.: Săvremenna bălgarska živopis (Die zeitgenössische bulgarische Malerei). Sofia 1969.
Mladi bălgarski chudožnici (Junge bulgarische Künstler). Hrsg. M. Kirov. Sofia 1974.
Obretenov, A.: 20 godini bălgarsko izobrazitelno izkustvo (20 Jahre bulgarische bildende Kunst). Sofia 1964.
Ostoič, D.: Iz borbata za socialističeski realizăm v bălgarskoto izobrazitelno izkustvo (Aus dem Kampf um den sozialistischen Realismus in der bulgarischen bildenden Kunst). Sofia 1967.
Ostoič, D.: 15 godini izobrazitelno izkustvo (15 Jahre bildende Kunst). Sofia 1959.
Peneva, N.: Architektura i način na život (Architektur und Lebensweise). Sofia 1984.
Plastiken, Malereien, Graphiken aus Bulgarien [Ausstellungskatalog]. Konstanz 1986.
Praškov, L.: Bălgarski ikoni. Razvitie, technologija, restavracija (Bulgarische Ikonen. Entwicklung, Technologie, Restauration). Sofia 1985.
Rusev, S.: Družestvo na novite chudožnici 1931–1981 (Verein neuer Künstler). Sofia 1981.
Săvremenno bălgarsko izobrazitelno izkustvo. Živopis, grafika, skulptura (Bulgarische Bildende Kunst der Gegenwart. Malerei, Grafik, Skulptur). Hrsg. S. Rusev. Sofia 1982.
Săvremenno bălgarsko monumentalno izkustvo 1956–1986 (Die zeitgenössische bulgarische Monumentalkunst 1956–1986). Hrsg. Ch. Stefanov. Sofia 1986.
Šmirgela, N.: Za novo izkustvo (Für eine neue Kunst). Sofia 1962.
Stojkov, A.: Bălgarskata karikatura (Die bulgarische Karikatur). Sofia 1970.
Tomov, E.: Bălgarska grafika (Die bulgarische Grafik). Sofia 1958.
Zidarov, L.; Čavrăkov, G.: Săvremenna bălgarska iljustracija (Die zeitgenössische bulgarische Illustration). Sofia 1973.

f) Musik

Biks, R.: Bălgarski operen teatăr (Das bulgarische Opertheater). 2 Bde. Sofia 1976–1985.
Braschowanowa-Stantschewa, L.: Die mittelalterliche bulgarische Musik und Joan Kukuzel. Graz u. a. 1984 (Wiener musikwissenschaftliche Beiträge 12).
Chlebarov, I.: Istorija na bălgarskata muzikalna kultura (Geschichte der bulgarischen Musikkultur). Sofia 1984.
Cvetko, D.: Musikgeschichte der Südslaven. Kassel u. a. 1975.
Džudžev, S.: Bălgarska narodna muzika (Bulgarische Volksmusik). 2 Bde. Sofia 1970, 1975.
Džudžev, S.: Teorija na bălgarskata narodna pesen (Die Theorie des bulgarischen Volksliedes). 4 Bde. Sofia 1954–1961.
Enciklopedija na bălgarskata muzikalna kultura (Enzyklopädie der bulgarischen Musikkultur). Hrsg. V. Krăstev. Sofia 1967.
Iz istorijata na bălgarskata muzikalna kultura XIX i načaloto na XX v. Sbornik statii (Aus der Geschichte der bulgarischen Musikkultur des 19. und Anfang des 20. Jhs. Sammelband). Hrsg. V. Krăstev. Sofia 1979.
Kaufman, N.: Bălgarska narodna muzika (Bulgarische Volksmusik). Sofia 1970 (2. Aufl. 1977). – Dt. Übers.: Bulgarische Volksmusik. Sofia 1977.
Kaufmann, N.: Mehrstimmigkeit in der bulgarischen Volksmusik, in: Beiträge zur Musikwissenschaft. 6 (1964) 2, S. 101–128.
Krader, B.: Bulgarian Folk Music Research,

in: Ethnomusicology. 13 (1969) 2, S. 248–266.
Krăstev, V.: Bălgarska muzikalna kultura. Istoričeski očerk (Die bulgarische Musikkultur. Eine historische Skizze). Sofia 1974. – Engl. Übers.: Bulgarian Music. Sofia 1978.
Krăstev, V.: Bălgarskoto muzikoznanie i kritika – idei i problemi (Bulgarische Musikologie und Musikkritik. – Ideen und Probleme). Sofia 1972.
Krăstev, V.: Muzika (Musik). Sofia 1984.
Krăstev, V.: Očerci po istorija na bălgarskata muzika (Skizzen zur Geschichte der bulgarischen Musik). Sofia 1977.
Krăstev, V.: Očerci vărchu razvitieto na bălgarskata muzika (Essays über die Entwicklung der bulgarischen Musik). 2. Aufl. Sofia 1970.
Kremenliev, B.: Bulgarian Folk Music: Some Recent Trends, in: Bulgaria: Past and Present. Hrsg. T. Butler. Columbus, Ohio 1976, S. 373–393.
Kremenliev, B.: Bulgarian-Macedonian Folk Music. Berkeley, Los Angeles 1952.
Kuǹumdzhieva, S.: Die Forschungsarbeit auf dem Gebiet der alten bulgarischen Musik (aus dem Mittelalter und der frühen Renaissance) seit den 50er Jahren: Probleme, Errungenschaften und Perspektiven, in: Starobălgaristika. 6 (1982) 3, S. 59–72.
Messner, G. F.: Die Schwebungsdiaphonie. Tutzing 1980.
50-godini Săjuz na bălgarskite kompozitori (Fünfzig Jahre Bulgarischer Komponistenverband). Sofia 1983.
Petrov, S.; Kodov, Ch.: Starobălgarski muzikalni pametnici (Altbulgarische musikalische Denkmäler). Sofia 1973.
Petrov, S.; Kaufman, N.: Bulgaria. South-eastern European republic. I. Art Music; II. Folk Music, in: The New Grove Dictionary of Music and Musicians. Hrsg. S. Sadie. London 1980, Bd. 3, S. 420–438.
Sagaev, D.: Galerija ot obrazi-muzikalni tvorci na našeto vreme (Eine Galerie musikalischer Schöpfergestalten unserer Zeit). 2 Bde. Sofia 1981, 1985.
60 godini Bălgarska dăržavna konservatorija 1921–1981. Jubileen sbornik (60 Jahre Bulgarisches Staatskonservatorium. Jubiläumssammelband.) Sofia 1981.
Stoin, E.: Muzikalno-folklorni dialekti v Bălgarija (Die volksmusikalischen Dialekte in Bulgarien). Sofia 1981.
Stoykova, K.; Tsenkov, T.: Bulgarian Orchestral Music. Catalogue. Sofia o. J. [1976].

Tončeva, E.: Problemi na starata bălgarska muzika (Probleme der alten bulgarischen Musik). Sofia 1975.
Vitanova, L.; Gajtandžiev, G.: Muzikalnoto văzpitanie v bălgarskoto učilište (Die Musikerziehung in der bulgarischen Schule). Sofia 1975.
Živkov, T. I.: Narod i pesen (Volk und Lied). Sofia 1977.

g) Sport und Körperkultur

Alexandrova, N.; Sokolov, E.: Achievements of Bulgarian Sports. Sofia 1985.
Dzharov, T.: Volksrepublik Bulgarien. Höhepunkte des sozialistischen Sports. Sofia 1980.
Haralampiev, D.; Georgiev, N.: The Bulgarian Olympic Committee. Activities and Contribution. Within the Olympic Movement After 1951. Sofia 1985.
Kalev, Č.: Grižite na Partijata za fizičeskata kultura i sporta (Die Sorge der Partei für die physische Kultur und den Sport). Sofia 1968.
Kolew, N.; Exerow, M.: Bulgarien auf den Olympischen Spielen. Sofia 1980.
Merancov, Ch.; Georgiev, N.: Analiz na programata i učastieto na Bălgarija v olimpijskite igri (Analyse des Programms und der Teilnahme Bulgariens an den Olympischen Spielen). Sofia 1980.
Mišev, D.; Vasev, A.: Von Athen nach Melbourne. Sofia 1957.
Nonev, B.: Bulgarian Sport For a Peaceful World. Sofia 1984.
Oschlies, W.: Bulgarien – sportliches Entwicklungsland? Aktuelle Analyse des Bundesinstituts für Ostwissenschaftliche und Internationale Studien, Nr. 16/1980, Köln, 30. April 1980, S. 1–7.
Petrova, N.: 100 godini obštestveni fizkulturni organizacii v Bălgarija (100 Jahre öffentliche Körperkulturorganisationen in Bulgarien). Sofia 1978.
Popov, I.: Konzeptionelle Grundlagen der Sportlehrpläne in Bulgarien, in: Theorie und Praxis der Körperkultur. 34 (1985) 3, S. 184–186.
Popov, I.: Körperkultur, Sport und Touristik im neuen Schulsystem der VR Bulgarien, in: Theorie und Praxis der Körperkultur. 21 (1972) 4, S. 353–363.
Sladkova, O.: Vărchove na bălgarskija sport. Spravočnik (Höhepunkte des bulgarischen Sports. Handbuch). Sofia 1981.

Solakov, A.: Physical Culture and Sport in Bulgaria Through the Centuries. Sofia 1983.

Vasilčev, K.; Bankov, P.; Veličkov, K.: Mass Physical Education and Sport in Bulgaria. Sofia 1986.

Zonkov, V.: Bulgarien, in: Geschichte der Leibesübungen. Hrsg. H. Ueberhorst. Bd. 5, Berlin, München, Frankfurt a. M. 1976, S. 379–398.

Ortsnamenkonkordanz

Heutiger Name	Früherer Name	bis
Blagoevgrad	Gorna Džumaja	1950
Dimitrovgrad	Caribrod	1948
Georgi-Damjanovo	Lopušna	1958
Goce Delčev	Nevrokop	1950
Ivajlovgrad	Ortak'oj	1934
Michajlovgrad	Ferdinand	1945
Petrič	Srednogorec	1950–1966
Sandanski	Sveti Vrač	1949
Stanke Dimitrov	Dupnica	1949,
	Marek	1949/50
Šumen	Kolarovgrad	1950–1965
Tolbuchin	Dobrič	1949
Varna	Stalin	1949–1956
Velingrad	gebildet aus: Lă(d)žene, Kamenica und Čepino	1948

Abkürzungsverzeichnis

ACC	Allied Control Commission – Alliierte Kontrollkommission
APK	Agrarno-promišlen kompleks – Agrar-Industrieller Komplex – Agrarian-Industrial Complex
BAN	Bǎlgarska akademija na naukite – Bulgarische Akademie der Wissenschaften – Bulgarian Academy of Sciences
BDŽ	Bǎlgarski dǎržavni železnici – Bulgarische Staatsbahnen – Bulgarian State Railways
BKP	Bǎlgarska komunističeska partija – Bulgarische Kommunistische Partei – Bulgarian Communist Party
BNA	Bǎlgarska narodna armija – Bulgarische Volksarmee – Bulgarian People's Army
BNB	Bǎlgarska narodna banka – Bulgarische Nationalbank – Bulgarian National Bank
BNŽS	Bǎlgarski naroden ženski sǎjuz – Bulgarischer Frauenvolksbund – Bulgarian National Women Union
BOK	Bǎlgarski olimpijski komitet – Bulgarisches Olympisches Komitee – Bulgarian Olympic Committee
BPC (BPTs)	Bǎlgarska pravoslavna cǎrkva – Bulgarische Orthodoxe Kirche – Bulgarian Orthodox Church
BPS	Bǎlgarski profesionalni sǎjuzi – Bulgarische Gewerkschaften – Bulgarian Trade Unions
BRP	Bǎlgarska rabotničeska partija – Bulgarische Arbeiterpartei – Bulgarian Workers' Party
BRP(k)	BRP (komunisti) – Bulgarische Arbeiterpartei (Kommunisten) – Bulgarian Workers' Party (Communists)
BRSDP	Bǎlgarska rabotničeska socialdemokratičeska partija – Bulgarische Sozialdemokratische Arbeiterpartei – Bulgarian Workers' Social Democratic Party
BSFS	Bǎlgarski sǎjuz za fizičeska kultura i sport – Bulgarischer Bund für Körperkultur und Sport – Bulgarian Union for Physical Culture and Sport
BTA	Bǎlgarska telegrafna agencija – Bulgarische Nachrichtenagentur – Bulgarian News Agency
BZNS	Bǎlgarski zemedelski naroden sǎjuz – Bulgarischer Bauernvolksbund – Bulgarian National Agrarian Union
CC	Central Committee – Zentralkomitee
CMEA	Council of Mutual Economic Aid – Rat für gegenseitige Wirtschaftshilfe
CPSU	Communist Party of the Soviet Union - Kommunistische Partei der Sowjetunion
DKMS	Dimitrovski komunističeski mladežki sǎjuz – Dimitrov'scher Kommunistischer Jugendverband – Dimitrov Communist Youth League
DP	Demokratičeska partija – Demokratische Partei – Democratic Party
DS	Dǎržaven sǎjuz – Staatsrat – State Council
DSNM	Dimitrovski sǎjuz na narodnata mladež – Dimitrov'scher Volksjugendverband – Dimitrov People's Youth Union
DV	Dǎržaven vestnik – Staatsanzeiger – Official Gazette
EG	Europäische Gemeinschaft – European Community
FAO	Food and Agriculture Organization – Nahrungs- und Landwirtschaftsorganisation
GATT	General Agreement on Tariffs and Trade – Allgemeines Tarif- und Handelsabkommen
KI/Komintern	Kommunistische Internationale – Communist International
KMS	Kommunističeski mladežki sǎjuz – Kommunistischer Jugendverband – Communist Youth Union
KPdSU	Kommunistische Partei der Sowjetunion – Communist Party of the Soviet Union
KSZE	Konferenz für Sicherheit und Zusammenarbeit in Europa – Conference for Security and Cooperation in Europe

LP	Liberalna partija – Liberale Partei – Liberal Party
NAPS	Nacionalen agrarno-promišlen săjuz – Nationaler Agrar-Industrie-Verband – National Agrarian-Industrial League
NATO	North Atlantic Treaty Organization
NIM	Nov ikonomičeski mechanizăm – Neuer Ökonomischer Mechanismus – New Economic Mechanism
NLP	Nacionalliberalna partija – Nationalliberale Partei – National-Liberal Party
NP	Narodna partija – Nationalpartei – National Party
NPK	Naučno-proizvodstven kompleks – Wissenschaftlich-Produktiver Komplex – Scientific Production Complex
NRB	Narodna republika Bălgarija – Volksrepublik Bulgarien – People's Republic of Bulgaria
NSb	Narodno săbranie – Nationalversammlung – National Assembly
OECD	Organization for Economic and Cultural Development
OF	Otečestven front – Vaterländische Front – Fatherland Front
OKPOE	Obštestvena kulturno-prosvetna organizacija na evreite v NRB – Gesellschaftliche Kultur- und Bildungsorganisation der Juden in der NRB – Social Organization for Culture and Education of the Jews in the NRB
OPEC	Organization of Petroleum Exporting Countries – Organization Erdöl exportierender Länder
PAK	Promišleno-agrarno kompleks – Industriell-Agrarischer Komplex – Industrial-Agrarian Complex
PLO	Palestine Liberation Organization – Palästinensische Befreiungsorganisation
RD	Rabotničesko delo – Arbeitersache – Workers' Cause
RGW	Rat für gegenseitige Wirtschaftshilfe – Council of Mutual Economic Aid
RMS	Rabotničeski mladežki săjuz – Arbeiterjugendverband – Workers' Youth Union
RP	Radikalna partija – Radikale Partei – Radical Party
SBP	Săjuz na bălgarskite pisateli – Bulgarischer Schriftstellerverband – Union of Bulgarian Writers
SBŽ	Săjuz na bălgarskite žurnalisti – Bulgarischer Journalistenverband – Union of Bulgarian Journalists
SG	Statističeski godišnik na NRB – Statistisches Jahrbuch der NRB – Statistical Yearbook of the NRB
SKJ	Savez komunista Jugoslavije – Bund der Kommunisten Jugoslawiens – League of Communists of Yugoslavia
SNM	Săjuz na narodnata mladež – Bund der Volksjugend – People's Youth League
TKZS	Trudovo-kooperativno zemedelsko stopanstvo – Landwirtschaftliche Produktionsgenossenschaft – Agricultural Cooperative Farm
UdSSR	Union der Sozialistischen Sowjetrepubliken
USSR	Union of Socialist Soviet Republics
VITIZ	Visš institut za teatralno izkustvo „Krăstju Sarafov" – Hochschule für Theaterkunst „K.S." – Higher Institute of Performing Arts „K.S."
VMRO	Vătrešna makedonska revoljucionna organizacija – Innere Makedonische Revolutionäre Organisation – Internal Macedonian Revolutionary Organization
VNSb	Veliko narodno săbranie – Große Nationalversammlung – Grand National Assembly
WP	Warschauer Pakt – Warsaw Treaty Organization
ZK	Zentralkomitee – Central Committee
ZMS	Zemedelski mladežki săjuz – Bauernjugendverband – Peasant Youth League

Verzeichnis der Tabellen, Schaubilder und Karten

Transliteration (deutschsprachig)	2
Transliteration (englischsprachig)	3
Major Physiographic Regions (Karte)	9
Selected Climatic Data (Tabelle)	13
Major Energy and Metallic Mineral Resources (Karte)	16
Urban Settlements with over 50 000 Inhabitants (Karte)	22
Population By Mother Tongue, 1880–1934 (Tabelle)	31
Votes Cast in Bulgarian Elections, 1908–1923 (Tabelle)	40
Growth of State-Encouraged Enterprises, 1894–1937 (Tabelle)	54
Main Trading Partners, 1896–1939 (Tabelle)	54
Bulgariens territoriale Entwicklung 1878–1913 (Karte)	98
Bulgariens territoriale Entwicklung 1919–1947 (Karte)	99
Rechtsetzungstätigkeit der obersten Staatsorgane im Vergleich (Tabelle)	144
Neue territoriale Gliederung Bulgariens (Tabelle)	156
Entwicklung der Mitgliederzahlen der BKP (1944–1986) (Tabelle)	181
Sozialstruktur der BKP-Mitgliedschaft (1944–1986) (Tabelle)	183
Geschlechts- und Altersstruktur der BKP-Mitgliedschaft (1945–1986) (Tabelle)	185
Sozialstruktur des ZK der BKP (1958–1986) (Tabelle)	186
Personelle Erneuerung im ZK (1958–1986) (Tabelle)	188
Mitgliederentwicklung des BZNS (1944–1986) (Tabelle)	193
Sozialprofil der BZNS-Mitglieder (Tabelle)	200
Mitgliederentwicklung der Massenorganisationen (Tabelle)	204
Wahlergebnisse 1945 und 1946 (Tabelle)	212
Wahlen zur NSb und Mandatsverteilung 1949–1986 (Tabelle)	213
Mandatsverteilung in den lokalen Vertretungsorganen (1949–1986) (Tabelle)	216
Sozialprofil der Vertretungsorgane (1949–1986) (Tabelle)	217
Wehrpotential Bulgariens und der umliegenden Staaten (Tabelle)	267
Soldaten in der BNA und in den Teilstreitkräften (Tabelle)	271
Gliederung der bulgarischen Landstreitkräfte (Tabelle)	272
Entwicklung der bulgarischen Seestreitkräfte (Tabelle)	273
Estimates of Per Capita Industrial Output in the Socialist Countries as a Percent of the USSR (Tabelle)	306
The Shares of Industry in the Economies of the Socialist Countries (Tabelle)	307
Ratios of Actual to Calculated Normative Shares of Labor Force in Industry (Tabelle)	308
Indicators of Relative Over-industrialization in Bulgaria Compared to Other Socialist Countries (Tabelle)	309
Bulgarian Industrial Output Growth (Schaubild)	311
Comparison of Bulgarian Growth Rates of Industrial Production With Other Socialist Countries (Tabelle)	313
Regional Ranking of Industrialization in 1980 according to Share of NMP in Industry (Tabelle)	314
Bulgarian Regions By Relative Amounts of NMP Generated in Industry per Capita in 1980 and Relative Growth of Gross Industrial Output by Major Sub-periods from 1952 to 1983 (Tabelle)	315
Relative Growth of Branches By Periods (Tabelle)	317
The Branch Structure of Bulgarian Industry (Tabelle)	318
Allocation of Marginal Labor in Industry and Handicrafts (Tabelle)	319
East-West Differences in Industrial Structure (1964–1966) (Tabelle)	320
Deviations from Employment Shares (Schaubild)	321
Deviations of Bulgaria and Romania From Normal Socialist Industrial Structures (1950–1980) (Tabelle)	322

Industrial Output and Exports (Tabelle) 324
Evidence of Successful Industrial Policy in Branches of Bulgarian Machine-Building (Tabelle) 326
Bulgarian Exports of Some Industrial Commodities (Tabelle) 327
Bulgaria's Share of OECD Imports (Schaubild) 328
Share of „Intensively" Used Capital Investments in Bulgarian Industry (Tabelle) 330
Capital and Material Productivity in Bulgaria and Other Socialist Countries (Tabelle) 331
Growth and Output per Unit of Labor as a Percent of Industrial Output Growth (Tabelle) . 331
Volkswirtschaftliche Bedeutung der Land- und Forstwirtschaft (1948–1987) (Tabelle) 333
Bodennutzung (1960–1987) (Tabelle) 335
Wachstum und Struktur der Agrarproduktion (1966–1988) (Tabelle) 340
Pflanzenproduktion (1971–1988) (Tabelle) 342
Tierproduktion (1971–1987) (Tabelle) 344
Tierbestände (1971–1988) (Tabelle) 345
Außenhandel mit Waren agrarischen Ursprungs 1971–1987 (Tabelle) 348
Anteil des Bergbausektors an der Gesamtindustrie (Tabelle) 355
Produktion und Verbrauch von Nichteisen-Metallen (Tabelle) 356
Entwicklung der Eisen- und Stahlproduktion (1960–1987) (Tabelle) 357
Gewinnbare Kohlevorräte 1979 (Tabelle) 358
Wasserkraftwerke: Leistung und Stromproduktion (Tabelle) 359
Produktion von Primärenergie (Tabelle) 360
Die Förderung von Kohle (1960–1987) (Tabelle) 362
Stromproduktion nach Kraftwerksarten (Tabelle) 363
Stromaufkommen (Tabelle) 364
Stromverbrauch je Einwohner (Tabelle) 365
Kraftwerksleistung nach Kraftwerksarten (Tabelle) 366
Verbrauch von Primärenergie (Tabelle) 367
Primärenergieaufkommen (Tabelle) 368
Einrichtungen des Einzelhandels nach Warenarten und Eigentumsformen (Tabelle) 374
Entwicklung des nominalen Einzelhandelsumsatzes je Einwohner und der Einzelhandelspreise
  (Tabelle) 377
Entwicklung des nominalen Einzelhandelsumsatzes nach Eigentumsformen (Tabelle) 378
Leistungen des Waren- und Personenverkehrs, nach Verkehrsträgern gegliedert, 1987 (Tabelle) 382
Entwicklung des Reiseverkehrs von und nach Bulgarien (1960–1987) (Tabelle) 391
Zweck der Reisen von ausländischen Besuchern nach Bulgarien (Tabelle) 392
Warenstruktur des bulgarischen Außenhandels (Tabelle) 402
Exportwarenstruktur der RGW-Mitgliedsländer 1986 (Tabelle) 404
Wichtigste Handelspartner Bulgariens (Tabelle) 404
Länderstruktur des bulgarischen Außenhandels (Tabelle) 405
Regionalstruktur des Außenhandels der RGW-Mitgliedsländer (Tabelle) 407
Außenhandel Bulgariens mit der UdSSR (Tabelle) 410
Anteile sowjetischer Lieferungen an verschiedenen Rohstoffimporten Bulgariens (Tabelle) ... 412
Population Growth (1920–1988) and Sex Composition (Tabelle) 434
Average Annual Population Growth (1920–1988) (Tabelle) 434
Age-Sex Pyramid of Bulgarian Population (December 31, 1986) (Schaubild) 436
Births and Birth Rates (1920–1987) (Tabelle) 437
Net Fertility (1920–1987) (Tabelle) 437
Birth Rates, Death Rates, Natural Increase, and Marriage Rates (1920–1986) (Schaubild).. 438
Ideal Family Size among Bulgarian Married Couples under 40 (1977) (Tabelle) 439
Deaths and Death Rates (1920–1987) (Tabelle) 440
Life Expectancy (1921–1986) (Tabelle) 441
Natural Population Increase (1920–1987) (Tabelle) 442
International Comparisons of Demographic Rates (1985) (Tabelle) 443
Turkish Emigration from Bulgaria (1946–1985) (Tabelle) 444
Urban Growth (1920–1987) (Tabelle) 445
Rural-Urban Migrational Streams (1960–1985) (Tabelle) 446
Natural Urban Population Increases (1946–1987) (Tabelle) 447

Cities with a Population over 50000 (December 31, 1987) (Karte) 448
City-Size Distribution (1985) (Tabelle).. 449
Inter-Urban Migration (1965–1985) (Tabelle).. 449
Rural Population (1920–1987) (Tabelle).. 450
Natural Rural Population Change (1921–1987) (Tabelle) 450
Sources of Rural Population Change (1947–1985) (Tabelle)............................ 451
Rural Population Decline (1965–1986) (Karte)... 451
Rural Birth Rates, Death Rates, and Natural Increase (1986) (Karte).................... 452
Population Change (1965–1986) (Karte) 454
Population – Total, Urban, and Rural – (December 31, 1986) (Karte).................... 455
Population in Relation to Work-Force Age (1946–1985) (Karte) 456
Population by Census (1887–1946) (Tabelle).. 460
Collectivization of Agriculture (1945–1952) (Tabelle)................................... 462
Employed Population by Economic Sector (1980–1987) (Tabelle)....................... 463
Women Workers and Employees by Economic Sector (1980–1987) (Tabelle).............. 467
Birth-rates in Cities and Villages (1930–1987) (Tabelle)................................ 468
Ownership of Consumer Products (1980–1987) (Tabelle).............................. 470
Life Expectancy (1921–1986) (Tabelle) 471
Bulgaren und nationale Minderheiten in Bulgarien (1946–1965) (Tabelle) 475
Ethnisch-religiöse Gruppen in Bulgarien (1926–1973) (Tabelle)......................... 477
Schüler und Studierende unter den bulgarischen Türken (1957–1971) (Tabelle) 496
Kindergärten (Tabelle).. 499
Aufbau des bulgarischen Bildungssystems ab 1979 (Schaubild) 501
Allgemeinbildende Mittelschulen (Tabelle) 502
Unterrichtsstunden an allgemeinbildenden Mittelschulen (ESPU), I.–X. Klasse (Tabelle).... 503
Unterrichtsstunden an allgemeinbildenden Mittelschulen (ESPU), XI. Klasse (Tabelle)...... 504
Zahl der Schüler an Gymnasien, die den Unterricht in westlichen Fremdsprachen besuchten
  (Tabelle)... 505
Behindertenschulen (Tabelle) 506
Berufsschulen (Tabelle) 508
Fachmittelschulen (Tabelle).. 510
Studierende (Tabelle) 523
Studierende je 10000 der Bevölkerung (Tabelle) 523
Anzahl der Hochschulen und Fakultäten (Tabelle) 527
Lehrkräfte an den Hochschulen (Tabelle)... 528
Anzahl der wissenschaftlichen Mitarbeiter (Tabelle) 539
Einrichtungen für angewandte Forschung (Tabelle)..................................... 541
Bulgarische Presse bis 1877 (Tabelle) 567
Die Presse 1940 (Tabelle).. 568
Rundfunk vor dem II. Weltkrieg (Tabelle) 569
Entstehung der Parteipresse (Tabelle)... 570
Entstehung der Oppositionspresse 1944/45 (Tabelle)................................... 574
Mitgliedschaft der Parteien 1946 (Tabelle) 575
Auflagenzahlen in den 40er und 50er Jahren (Tabelle) 577
Presse in den 70er Jahren (Tabelle)... 582
Organisatorische Gliederung des SBP (Schaubild) 613
Vorsitzende des SBP (Tabelle) 614
Titelproduktion des Verlags „Bǎlgarski pisatel" (Tabelle) 615
Wichtige Literaturzeitschriften und Almanache (Tabelle)................................ 615
Zeittafel zur bulgarischen Nachkriegsliteratur......................................627–631
Anzahl der Theater (Tabelle) 642
Entwicklung des Sprechtheaters (Tabelle)... 642
Bulgariens Medaillenerfolge bei den Olympiaden (1952–1988) (Tabelle) 685
Parteitage der BKP (Tabelle) 713
Kartenbeilage am Schluß des Bandes

Verzeichnis der Autoren

Dr. Franz-Lothar Altmann
Südost-Institut, Abtlg. Gegenwartsforschung, Güllstraße 7, D-8000 München 2.

Dr. Stephen W. Ashley
Radio Free Europe/Radio Liberty, Oettingenstraße 67, Am Englischen Garten, D-8000 München 22.

Dr. Peter Bachmaier
Österreichisches Ost- und Südosteuropa-Institut, Zweigstelle Niederösterreich, Agnesstr. 51, A-3400 Klosterneuburg, Österreich.

Prof. Dr. John D. Bell
University of Maryland Baltimore County, Department of History, 5401 Wilkens Avenue, Baltimore/Maryland 21228, USA.

Dr. Milan Beneš
Freie Universität Berlin, Osteuropa-Institut, Sektion für Bildungswesen, Garystraße 55, D-1000 Berlin 33.

Dr. Jochen Bethkenhagen
Deutsches Institut für Wirtschaftsforschung (Institut für Konjunkturforschung), Königin-Luise-Straße 5, D-1000 Berlin 33.

Prof. Dr. Richard J. Crampton
The University of Canterbury, Rutherford College, Canterbury, Kent CT2 7NX, Großbritannien.

Dr. Jozo Džambo
Universität München, Institut für deutsche und vergleichende Volkskunde, Ludwigstraße 25/0, D-8000 München 22.

Klaus Eder
Schleißheimer Str. 83, D-8000 München 40.

Prof. Friedbert Ficker
Institut für Kunstgeschichte der Universität München, Georgenstr. 7, D-8000 München 40.

Ilse Grosser, M.A.
Wiener Institut für internationale Wirtschaftsvergleiche beim Österreichischen Institut für Wirtschaftsforschung, Arsenal Objekt 20, A-1103 Wien 3, Österreich.

Prof. Dr. Dr. h.c. Klaus-Detlev Grothusen
Univeristät Hamburg, Historisches Seminar, Von-Melle-Park 6/IX, D-2000 Hamburg 13.

Prof. Dr. Werner Gumpel
Universität München, Institut für Wirtschaft und Gesellschaft Ost- und Südosteuropas, Südosteuropa-Seminar, Akademiestraße 1/III, D-8000 München 40.

Lutz Häfner M. A.
Universität Hamburg, Historisches Seminar, Von-Melle-Park 6/IX, D-2000 Hamburg 13.

Dr. Magarditsch A. Hatschikjan
Forschungsinstitut der Konrad-Adenauer-Stiftung, Rathausallee 12, D-5205 Sankt Augustin 1.

Gunnar Hille
Auswärtiges Amt, Ref. 105, Sprachendienst, Adenauerallee 99–103, D-5300 Bonn 2.

Dr. Wolfgang Höpken
Südost-Institut, Abtlg. Gegenwartsforschung, Güllstraße 7, D-8000 München 2.

Dr. Hans-Joachim Hoppe
Universität zu Köln, Seminar für osteuropäische Geschichte, Kringsweg 6, D-5000 Köln 41.

Prof. Dr. Marvin A. Jackson
Arizona State University, Department of Economics, Tempe, Arizona 85287, USA.

Dr. Christa Jessel-Holst
Max-Planck-Institut für Ausländisches und Internationales Privatrecht, Mittelweg 187, D-2000 Hamburg 13.

Dr. Barbara Krader
Löhleinstr. 29, D-1000 Berlin 33.

Prof. Dr. Reinhard Lauer
Universität Göttingen, Seminar für Slavische Philologie, Platz der Göttinger Sieben 5, D-3400 Göttingen.

Priv.-Doz Otto Luchterhandt
Universität zu Köln, Institut für Ostrecht, Ubierring 53, D-5000 Köln 1.

Prof. Dr. Ian M. Matley
Michigan State University, Department of Geography, East Lansing, Michigan 48824, USA.

Dr. Götz Mavius †
Universität Hamburg, Historisches Seminar, Von-Melle-Park 6/IX, D-2000 Hamburg 13.

Prof. Dr. Gerald Florian Messner
Deakin University, c/o School of Humanities, Geelong/Victoria 3217, Australien.

Oberstleutnant Wilhelm Nolte
Führungsakademie der Bundeswehr, Fachzentrum Dokumentation, Manteuffelstr. 20, D-2000 Hamburg 55.

Priv.-Doz. Dr. Wolf Oschlies
Bundesinstitut für ostwissenschaftliche und internationale Studien, Lindenbornstraße 22, D-5000 Köln 30.

Prof. Dr. Marin Pundeff
California State University, Department of History, Northridge, California 91330, USA.

Prof. Dr. Klaus Roth
Universität München, Institut für deutsche und vergleichende Volkskunde, Ludwigsstraße 25/0, D-8000 München 22.

Dr. Michael Schmidt-Neke
Universität Hamburg, Historisches Seminar, Von-Melle-Park 6/IX, D-2000 Hamburg 13.

Dr. Roland Schönfeld
Südosteuropa-Gesellschaft, Widenmayerstraße 49, D-8000 München 22.

Prof. Dr. Robert N. Taaffe
Indiana University, Department of Geography, Kirkwood Hall, Bloomington, Indiana 47405, USA.

Dr. Stefan Troebst
Freie Universität Berlin, Osteuropa-Institut, Sektion für Osteuropäische Zeitgeschichte, Garystraße 55, D-1000 Berlin 33.

Prof. Dr. Roger Whitaker
Boston University, Metropolitan College, 755 Commonwealth Avenue, Boston, Massachusetts 02215, USA.

Register

Abadžiev, Ivan 682, 714, 716
Abakumov, V.S. 70
Abe, S. 701
Abrašev, Božidar 673
Abtreibung 81, 435, 439/40, 447
Adel 27
Adria 27
Adrianopel s. Edirne
Adženov, Ivan 568
Afanasieva-Koleva, A. 603
Afghanistan 121, 123, 700, 722
Afrika 50, 126
Ägäis 8, 12, 20, 27, 42, 49, 97–100, 106, 108/109, 129, 263/264, 381, 460, 480, 592, 699
Agça, Mehmed Ali 124, 701
Agrarpartei, Agrarier s. BZNS
Agura, A. 665
Ägypten 114, 699, 702
AIESEE 1
Ajdemir 483
Ajtos 272, 381
Akademien s.a. BAN 202, 275, 518/519, 523, 528, 535–541, 658/659, 661, 663, 674, 701, 729, 731, 735
Ak'ov, Vasil 653
Akron (Ohio) 561
Aktaseva, Irina 653/654
Aktien 299–301
Albaner 475, 486
Albanien 1, 39, 84/85, 87, 91, 103, 109, 114/115, 123/124, 127, 131/132, 258, 263, 331, 443, 475, 480, 690/91, 694, 696/97
Albena 24
Albertirsa 409
Albertville 686
Aleksandrov, Čudomir 83, 190, 703, 712, 715, 717, 728
Aleksandrovo 17
Aleksej, Patriarch von Moskau 546, 560
Alexander von Battenberg, Fürst 27, 32–36, 55
Alexander II., Zar von Rußland 33
Alexander III., Zar von Rußland 33/34
Algerien 369, 415, 723.
Alkoholismus s. Gesundheitswesen
Alliierte 20, 42/43, 50/51, 57, 59/60, 103–106, 204, 211
Alliierte Kontrollkommission (ACC) 59, 62, 92, 102, 104/105, 491, 545, 570, 690

Alpen 9
Altersstruktur s.a. Kinder, Jugend 74, 78, 170, 184–186, 188/189, 223, 433, 435–38, 440–442, 446, 450/51, 455–57, 460/61, 466, 471–73, 483, 500, 530, 590, 595, 680
Altkirchenslawisch 10, 28, 497, 589, 605, 621
Amerika s.a. USA 553, 625
Amnestie 60, 63, 73, 147
Amnesty International 130
Analphabetismus 206, 478/79, 482, 487, 492, 494, 515, 567, 593, 596
Anarchismus 574
Andonov, Ivan 649
Andonov, Metodi 637, 639, 649/650, 652/653
Andreev, Georgi 705
Andreev, Veselin 610, 627
Andrejkov, Todor 651
Andrić, Ivo 621
Andropov, Jurij Vladimìrovič 121
Angelov, A. 661
Angelov, I. 657
Angelušev, B. 660/61
Angestellte 181–184, 186, 199/200, 216–218, 223, 248, 337, 375, 379, 436, 464/65, 467, 479, 730
Angola 699, 722
Ankara 111
Anleihen s. Kredite
Antisemitismus 49–51, 109, 484, 549
Antonov, S. 701/702
Antonov, S.I. 124
APK 197–199, 288, 293, 333, 350/351, 353, 398, 522
Apostolov, G. 663
April-Plenum (des ZK der BKP) s. BKP
Arafat, Yassir 126
Arbanasi 430
Arbeit, Arbeitskraft 67, 72, 80/81, 160, 165, 170–172, 180, 184, 187, 206–209, 214/215, 221/222, 224, 228/229, 240–243, 247–249, 253–256, 283, 286, 291/292, 295, 298–300, 304, 306–310, 316–319, 322/323, 329–333, 336/337, 353/354, 369, 395, 409, 411/412, 421, 436, 440, 444–446, 455–473, 500, 502/503, 507, 509, 530–532, 609, 658/659, 661, 679/680, 697, 720
Arbeiter 18, 42, 44, 54, 58, 61, 68, 72, 75, 130, 138, 176–184, 194, 199/200, 216/217, 223, 248/249, 286–290, 318, 330, 337, 353, 355, 361, 375, 379, 409, 412, 436, 456, 459,

464/465, 467, 479, 492, 495, 497/498,
  506–508, 520, 530, 576, 593, 597/598, 616,
  633, 644, 650–652, 659, 677/678, 680, 728,
  732/733, 735, 737
Arbeitsdienst 43
Archäologie 385, 562
Architektur 426, 431/32, 527, 600/601, 656,
  664/65
Archive 91, 112, 134, 199, 540, 563, 646
Arda 11/12, 14, 25, 360
Armee s. Landesverteidigung
Armenien 483, 564
Armenier 52, 474/75, 482/83, 489, 492, 544,
  548/549, 558, 564, 566, 596
Aromunen 475, 596
Ärzte s. Gesundheitswesen
Asenov, Dragomir 623, 628, 630/631
Asenovgrad 25, 448
Asien 33, 263/264, 273, 384, 667
Askova, S. 664
Asparuchova, Nadja (Najde Ferchadova) 188,
  706
Assimilation 90/91, 120/121, 129–133, 171,
  187, 444, 475, 477–81, 487–89, 596/97, 703
Assoziationen s. Betriebe
Ästhetik 497, 503, 505, 517, 597, 599–601,
  606/07, 609, 612, 615, 626, 636, 639,
  647/648, 658/659
Atanasov, Georgi 189/190, 705, 712, 714, 717,
  728
Atanasov, Gerčo 630, 702
Atanasov, Žečo 513
Atheismus 206, 222/223, 543, 545, 548,
  558–560, 563, 565/566. 579
Athen 127/128, 684, 695
Äthiopien 722
Athos 561, 567, 605
Atomwaffen 90, 106, 121, 127, 273, 370
atom- und chemiewaffenfreie Zone 90, 116,
  127, 262, 266/267
Aufstände 29/30, 269, 423, 550, 572, 578
– Aprilaufstand 1876 30, 52
– Ilinden-Aufstand 1903 38, 654
– Septemberaufstand 1923 45/46, 55, 269,
  572, 616, 646–648, 678, 729/30, 732/33, 735
Ausländer 169–170, 225, 229/230, 232, 239,
  249, 260, 294, 298, 305, 377, 388–93, 397,
  400–411, 417, 493, 527, 550, 557, 559
Außenhandel 24, 36, 43, 49, 53/54, 69, 76, 87,
  91, 111, 114–117, 119, 121–123, 125, 130,
  245, 282–285, 299–302, 304/305, 310, 319,
  322–334, 341, 343, 345–348, 353, 355, 358,
  361–370, 394–418, 594, 691, 693–697, 699,
  703, 720
Außenhandelsbank s. Außenhandel, Bankenwesen

Außenpolitik 29–55, 58/59, 84–135, 143,
  147–149, 196/197, 218, 266, 488, 534, 538,
  540–542, 550, 568, 575, 582/83, 688–703,
  722/723, 732
Ausstellungen s. Museen
Australien 553
Auszeichnungen 151, 253, 530
Autobahnen s. Straßen
Autokephalie s. Kirche, Bulgarische Orthodoxe
Autonomie 29/30, 67, 110, 119, 139, 147, 209,
  220, 351, 520, 551, 645, 682
Autoritäres System 47–56, 59, 478, 510, 569,
  678
Avramov, Lăčezar 710/711, 714, 716
Avramov, P. 181
Avramov, Ruben 714
Azerbajdžan 494

Bačkovo-Kloster 555, 652
Badev, Jordan 634
Baev, G. 662
Bagrjana, Elizaveta 72, 609, 625–630
Bahr, Egon 701
Bajraktarević, Fehim 486
Bajuvi dupki 424
Bakadžici 11
Bakalov, Georgi 607, 633
Bakardžiev, G. 664
Bakiš (Todorova), Sonja 202, 736
Baku 494
Balčik 273/274
Balev, Milko 188–191, 706, 714, 717, 728
Balevski, Angel 706
Bălgaranov, Bojan 73, 78, 706, 714, 716, 729
Balkan 9/10, 19/20, 27, 29/30, 33/34, 39, 44,
  47–50, 53, 87–91, 97–100, 107–109,
  111–114, 116–121, 123, 126–134, 262–264,
  268, 270, 272, 276, 336, 340, 358, 380–382,
  388, 420, 423/424, 427, 436, 452, 475, 527,
  544/545, 555, 562, 564, 587, 590, 592, 595,
  602, 621, 628, 645, 667, 700, 703, 730, 733,
  737
Balkanbas 16, 25
Balkanbund 39, 47, 49
Balkanföderation 29, 44, 90, 96, 100, 103,
  107/108, 133, 492, 691
Balkankriege s. Krieg
Balkanski, N. 661
Bal'ozov, Rumen 674
BAN 74/75, 118, 424, 464/465, 485, 513/514,
  519–521, 525, 528, 535–541, 560, 565, 664,
  674, 676, 732–735
Bangemann, Martin 702
Banken 37, 47, 277, 279, 281–283, 287,
  289/90, 293, 295/96, 299–303, 399/400, 406,
  459, 485, 537, 691

Banken
- Bulgarische Nationalbank (BNB) 33, 53, 154, 281/282, 301/02, 396/97, 399
Bansko 383
Barakov, V. 659, 662
Barcelona 384
Bari 694
Barnes, Maynard 63
Barock 605/06
Barov, A. 665
Bartók, Bela 667
Bašev, Ivan 78, 128, 695–697, 710/711
Baševa, Mirjana 624
Basileios II. Boulgaroktonos, Kaiser von Byzanz 27
Battenberg, Alexander Prinz s. Alexander von Battenberg, Fürst
Bauern 32, 37, 43, 45, 47, 49, 52/53, 55, 68, 72, 75, 138, 176, 181–184, 192–201, 214, 223, 280, 337, 423, 458–466, 473, 479, 520, 530, 575, 578, 591, 594, 597, 605, 620, 623, 647/648, 652, 728–731, 734–737
Bauerninternationale 730, 733
Bauernvolksbund, Bauernpartei s. BZNS
Bauwesen 155, 158, 160, 294, 296, 302, 307, 330, 335, 354, 427, 463/464, 467, 507/508, 527, 563, 592, 664/665
Bayern 302
Bayülken, H. 697
BDŽ s. Eisenbahn
Beamte 37, 42, 44, 53, 59–61, 464/65, 493, 516
Becker, Boris 682
Beckett, Samuel 639
Befreiung 29/30, 44, 52, 88/89, 490, 554, 567/568, 591, 593, 598, 605/06, 647, 656, 660
Behinderte s. Gesundheitswesen
Belasica Planina 10
Belčev, Belčo 189, 191, 266, 711/712
Belene 12, 24, 365, 431, 553
Belev, Krăst'o 607, 627/628
Belgien 404, 547, 559, 575, 699, 722, 725
Belgrad 23, 29, 90, 104, 118, 123, 128, 381, 556, 696, 703, 730
Belgrader Außenministerkonferenz (24.–26.2.1988) 133, 136
Belletristik s. Literatur
Belmeken-Sestrimo 25
Belobrežk 358
Belovo 381
Benkovski, Georgi 30, 275, 735
Benzin 697/98
Bergbau 17–19, 23–25, 42, 296, 355–370, 423, 527, 728, 736
Bergson, Henri 519

Berija, Lavrentij 70
Berkeley, George 519
Berlin 41, 102, 122, 506, 556, 642, 644, 654, 672, 723, 733
Bern 733
Berufe, Berufsstruktur 172, 179, 182–184, 186/187, 216–218, 223, 241, 257, 371, 440, 458, 462–65, 469, 482, 484, 490, 492, 494–504, 506–10, 512–14, 516, 518, 528, 530–534, 537, 597, 624, 666, 670/71, 675/76, 719
Besatzung 50/51, 57
Beškov, I. 660/61
Betrieb 54, 57, 68, 73, 152, 157/158, 167, 198, 207/208, 219, 227/228, 238, 248/249, 255, 277–303, 333–335, 337, 344, 346/347, 349–351, 363/364, 372, 379, 389, 395–401, 411, 417/18, 425/26, 427–430, 432, 459, 462, 464, 495, 500, 506–8, 530, 540, 678, 703, 731
Bevölkerung 7, 19–21, 27, 52/53, 56, 59, 68, 75/76, 80/81, 90, 129, 155–158, 167, 400/401, 410, 419, 421/422, 426, 431, 433–489, 523, 536, 590/591, 594–596, 600, 602, 680
Bewässerung 12, 25, 335/336, 341, 354, 360
Bezirke s. Regionen
Bibel 551, 562, 564
Bibliotheken, 2, 43, 540, 572, 664
Bieber, Ute 625
Bilishti 480
Bildung, Bildungswesen 28/29, 43/44, 48, 59/60, 78, 80, 160, 167, 170, 182–184, 187, 293, 440, 446, 458, 460, 462/463, 467/468, 470/471, 478/479, 482, 484, 490–542, 571, 586, 589, 593, 606, 615, 632
Binnenhandel s. Handel
Biologie 540
Birjuzov, Sergej S. 59/60, 62/63, 104
Bischöfe s. Kirchen
Bitsios, D. 698
Bižkov, Georgi 515
Bjala 384
Bjala Slatina 730
Bjalgrad (UdSSR) 733
BKJ (KPJ) 101, 108, 118, 133
BKP 40, 42–48, 50, 52, 55–83, 86–89, 92, 100–103, 107/108, 119, 133, 136–139, 141–143, 147–151, 153, 159, 163/164, 166, 173–223, 262, 266, 270, 274–276, 279, 281, 291, 303–305, 334, 349, 396, 433, 441, 447, 450, 456–463, 479–481, 485, 487–489, 491/492, 494, 511, 516, 521, 525/526, 528, 533/534, 536/537, 545–547, 549, 551, 554, 558/559, 563, 565, 567, 569–580, 582/583, 585, 599, 607/608, 612, 616/617, 626, 634,

636/637, 658, 660, 662, 664, 673, 678–681, 688–704, 707/708, 713, 728–737
- Aprilplenum des ZK 1956 56, 73–75, 79, 112, 117, 174, 176, 195/196, 199, 206, 219, 488, 494/495, 520, 578, 605, 608, 616, 618/619, 621, 636, 659, 662, 664, 673, 693
- Parteiprogramm von 1954 693
- Parteiprogramm von 1971 86, 119, 173–177, 196, 697
- Fünfter Parteitag 1948 69, 92, 104, 107–109, 133, 176, 181, 183, 487, 519/520, 576, 608, 611, 627, 633, 659, 713
- Sechster Parteitag 1954 73, 112, 179, 693, 713
- Siebter Parteitag 1958 76, 113/114, 116, 118, 176, 187, 401, 508, 693, 713
- Achter Parteitag 1962 77, 112, 178, 184, 187, 286, 397, 694, 713
- Neunter Parteitag 1966 78, 116, 288, 695, 713
- Zehnter Parteitag 1971 79, 119, 121, 126/127, 289, 521, 697, 713
- Elfter Parteitag 1976 78, 679, 698, 713
- Zwölfter Parteitag 1981 78/79, 182, 188, 700, 713
- Dreizehnter Parteitag 1986 80, 86/87, 119, 121–123, 126–128, 132, 182, 188, 266, 297, 389, 522, 680, 702, 713
- Außerordentlicher Parteitag 1990 4
- Vierzehnter Parteitag 82
- Politbüro 57/58, 64, 69–74, 76–78, 80, 82/83, 136, 161, 177–180, 187–191, 209, 218/219, 276, 295, 352, 488, 494, 524, 526, 528/529, 536/537, 575, 578, 580, 583, 612, 617, 639, 703, 713, 715/716, 728–737
- Sekretariat des Zentralkomitees 57/58, 69, 76, 83, 136, 180, 187–191, 219, 275, 601, 704, 713–16, 728/29
- Statut 137/138, 177–180, 198
- ZK 58, 65, 69, 73–77, 80, 82/83, 86/87, 92, 107, 112, 137, 146, 151, 161, 163, 174–177, 179/180, 187/188, 202, 218, 266, 276, 281, 287, 291, 297, 350/351, 397, 479, 481/482, 488, 492, 494–498, 503–505, 509, 516, 521/522, 528, 530, 532, 572, 578, 607, 628, 639, 680, 682, 693/694, 696, 699, 701–704, 713, 728–737

Blagoev, Dimităr 617, 733
Blagoevgrad 18, 22/23, 132, 156, 272, 314/15, 383/84, 448, 451/52, 454/55, 480/81, 506, 511/12, 514, 527, 577, 581, 670, 777
Bled 107, 111
Bliznakov, G. 701
Blockfreie 2, 84, 126/127, 263, 421
Boboševski, Cvetko 704
Bobov Dol 17, 23, 358

Boden s. a. Umwelt 7, 14/15, 333–336, 338, 340–342, 349, 352/353, 419, 424, 426/427, 429, 432, 461/62, 465
Bodenschätze 7, 15–19, 279, 355–362, 386/87, 394, 412
- Erdgas 15–17, 358/359, 362, 366–369, 387, 394, 401/02, 404, 408/09, 412
- Erdöl 7, 15–17, 279, 324, 327, 358–360, 362, 366–369, 387, 394, 401/02, 404, 406, 408, 410, 412, 415, 698
- Kohle 7, 15–17, 23, 25, 358–363, 366–369, 386, 394, 401/402, 404, 408, 421, 428
- Metalle 16–19, 305, 355–358, 386, 394, 401/02, 404, 408/409, 412, 422
- Mineralien 7, 15–19, 279, 294, 327, 382, 394/395, 401, 404
Boev, Ch. 694
Bogdan (Berg) 10
Bogomilen 27, 550, 621
Bogorov, Ivan 567
Bojadžiev, Z. 662
Bojana 645, 654
Bokov, Georgi 714
Boljarovo 18
Bonev, Staniš 712, 717
Bonev, Vladimir 706/707, 714
Bonn 125/126, 700/01, 703
Borges, Jorge Luis 620
Boris I., Fürst 27, 543
Boris III., Zar 27, 36/37, 41, 48–51, 55/56, 60, 67, 101, 549, 678, 689, 730, 732, 736
Borisov, Lilčo 673
Borovec 13
Borozanov, Boris 647
Bosilkov, Evgenij 558, 692
Bosilov, Nikolaj 654
Bosnien 30
Bosporus 263/264
Boston 551
Botev (Berg) 9
Botev, Christo 29/30, 606/07, 612, 616, 630, 729
Botevgrad 10, 384, 737
Bourgeoisie s. Bürgertum
Boženci 601
Božilov, Božidar 618, 628, 630
Božilov, Dobri 51
Božilov, G. 662
Božilov, Jordan 707
Božinov, A. 661
Božinov, Rusi 630
Božinov, Todor 78, 80, 711/712, 714, 717, 728
Brandt, Willy 699, 702
Brasilien 404, 683, 694
Bratislava 112, 384, 386, 696
Brecht, Bertolt 618, 623, 637/638

Brežnev, Leonid Il'ič 85, 95, 112/113, 120/121, 132, 134, 159, 190, 695, 698, 700
Brežnev-Doktrin 95, 112–114, 121
Brown, J.F. 111, 117
BRP s. BKP
BRSDP 40, 42, 45, 57, 59, 61, 63–66, 181, 203/204, 209, 211/212, 214, 545, 569/570, 573–576, 677, 690–692, 707/708, 729/730, 733
Brunner, Georg 84
Brzezinski, Zbigniew K. 93
BTA (Nachrichtenagentur) 564, 569, 579, 695, 699, 701/02
Buch, Buchwesen 29, 72, 493/94, 500, 515, 518, 535, 540, 550, 559, 562, 567, 572, 594, 675/76
Büchner, Georg 623
Budapest 115, 384, 412, 561, 641, 693
Budevska, Adriana 633
Budinov, Ivan 710/11
Bukarest 28/29, 408, 558, 561, 564, 568, 691, 731
Buffalo 553
Bulgakov, Michail 620
Bulgarisches Reich, Erstes 20/21, 27, 81, 543
Bulgarisches Reich, Zweites 20/21, 27, 431, 543
Bulgarische Sprache 28/29, 481, 485, 487, 494, 503/04, 515, 552, 563, 567–589
Bulgarisierung 422, 562/563, 702
Bulgaristik 540
Bundesrepublik Deutschland 85, 93, 96, 115/116, 120, 125/126, 230, 239, 365, 367/368, 385, 390/391, 404, 416, 418, 430, 441, 443, 535, 541, 641/642, 645/646, 683, 693–696, 698–703, 725/726
Bundžulov, Andrej 706
Burgas 7/8, 11–13, 15, 17/18, 21/22, 25/26, 156–158, 265, 272–274, 314/15, 341, 357, 382–387, 413, 424, 432, 451–55, 481, 484/85, 511, 527, 568, 577, 614, 632, 637/638, 731/32, 736
Bürgertum 45–47, 55, 61, 71/72, 174/175, 177, 192, 204, 491, 571, 577, 579, 593, 602, 608–611, 616/617, 625, 635, 651, 699
Bürokratie 53, 80, 82, 157, 164, 209, 283, 296/97, 352, 420, 462, 491, 493, 517, 586, 623
Burov, Atanas 56, 63, 203
Bursa 702
Businci 656
Buzludža 424
Byrnes, James F. 64
Byzanz 21, 27, 240, 543, 605, 672
BZNS 37, 39–47, 52/53, 55–57, 59–66, 72, 79, 143, 173, 182, 191–201, 203–205, 207, 209, 211–214, 216, 219, 545, 569–571, 574–576, 688–692, 703/704, 707/708, 730, 732, 736/737

Çaglayangil, I. 695
Čajka 24
Čaira 25, 360
Calgary 686
Canev, Angel 697, 711, 716
Canev, Georgi 631
Canev, Stefan 630, 638
Cankov, Aleksandăr 45–47, 688
Cankov, Chrisan 633
Cankov, Dragan 32/33, 35
Cankov, Georgi 73, 76, 710, 714, 716
Čankov, Georgi 57/58, 73, 75, 693, 708/709, 713, 715
Cankov, Vili 637
Cannes 644, 654
Canov, Vasil 714
Cardenal, Ernesto 616
Casaroli, Agostino 699
CDU 699
Ceauşescu, Nicolae 4, 78, 91, 112, 116, 124, 696
Čechov, Anton 633
Cekov, C. 661
Čelopeč 18
Cem Sultan 621
Cenova, Julija 674
Čepelarska 11/12
Cepenkov, Marko 591
Čepinska 12
Čerepiš 554, 557
Čerkelov, Ivan 654
Černenko, Konstantin U. 131
Černobyl' 348, 365, 389, 426, 431, 583
Černokolev, Titko 708/09, 716
Černo More 358
Černovci 556, 733
Červenkov, Vălko 56, 58, 66, 69–74, 76–78, 88/89, 95, 110, 118, 174/175, 181, 189, 195, 199, 205/206, 208, 218/219, 493/494, 511, 520, 555, 692–694, 708–710, 713/714, 716, 729, 733
Češmedžiev, Grigor 61, 63/64
Chadžikosev, Simeon 625
Chadžiolov, Asen 712
Chajtov, Nikolaj 586/87, 589, 620/621, 623, 625/626, 629/630, 652
Champo (Šampov) 684
Chančev, Veselin 618, 628
Chaskovo 7, 21/22, 25/26, 156/157, 191, 272, 314–16, 340, 384, 386/387, 448, 451/52, 454/55, 476, 478, 481, 596, 671, 736
Chemie 402, 404, 429, 527, 540

Chen Muhua 701
Cheskija, Zako 645, 653
Chevetogne 559
Chile 698
China 75–77, 91, 109, 114/115, 121, 123/124, 406, 692, 694, 696, 701, 722, 726
Chranoiznos 47, 53
Chrelkov, Nikolaj 607, 627
Christentum 27/28, 171, 479, 487, 543/544, 547/548, 550/551, 558–561, 565, 595
Christov, Boris 624, 630
Christov, Christo 650, 652, 654, 700, 711–713
Christov, Dimităr 673, 675
Christov, Dobri 666, 672
Christov, Emil 706, 714
Christov, T. 21
Christova, Tanja 672
Christozov, Nikolaj 630
Christozov, Rusi 694, 708–710
Chruščev, Nikita Sergeevič 73, 76/77, 89, 95, 112/113, 159, 178, 187, 190, 220, 521, 532, 694
Churchill, Winston 88, 95, 101/102, 104, 689
Čiflik 17
Čiprovci 17/18, 656
Čiren 17
Čirpan 383
čitalište 29
Čobanov, Jordan 705
Cocev, Coco 431
Čolakov, Stančo 707
Colasuonno, Francesco (Erzbischof) 564
Colov, D. 664
Colov, Tano 76, 709–711, 714, 716
COMECON s. RGW
Computer 25, 413, 497/98, 532, 587
Končev, Dončo 631
Conev, K. 662
Conev, N. 662
Constanţa 381
Craiova 107
ČSR/ČSSR 87, 103, 112, 114/115, 118, 121/122, 124, 126, 132, 140, 182, 191, 201, 236, 306–309, 313, 325, 331, 338, 356, 364, 375, 382/83, 385/86, 392, 394, 396, 403/04, 407, 429, 432, 441, 443, 462, 626, 657, 690/91, 693, 696, 721, 723–25, 727
Čukurovo 358
Cyrankiewicz, J. 695

DAAD 535
Dăbova, Z. 661
Dăbovo 383
Dakov, Mako 711
Dakovski, Dako 647/648
Dălbokov, Sava 711, 714

Dalčev, Atanas 609, 626, 629
Dalčev, L. 663
Damjanov, Damjan P. 624, 626, 631
Damjanov, Georgi 58, 60/61, 73, 694, 705, 707–09, 714, 716, 729
Damjanov, Rajko 57, 73, 708–710, 715
Danailov, Juri (Yumer Dachilov) 188
Dančev, Penčo 631
Dančev, Petko 190, 712, 717
Dänemark 695/96, 725/26
Daniel, L. 636/637
Dănov, Petăr 565
Danovski, Bojan 633–635, 637, 639
Danzig 384
Dardanellen 264
Daskalov, Tačo 705
Daskalova, Svetla 239, 711/712
Davidkovo 18
Debelec 24
Debeljanov, Dimčo 606, 623
Debelt 357
Deggendorf 384
Delčev, Boris 618
Deli orman 476
Dellin, L. A. D. 93
Demirel, Süleyman 117, 696, 698
Demorgraphie s. Bevölkerung
Demokratičeski sgovor 40, 45/46, 55
Demokratie 2, 48, 62/63, 65, 75, 83, 104, 136, 139, 141–143, 152, 166, 169/170, 174/175, 201–203, 210/211, 215, 223, 268, 490/491, 524, 573, 584, 597, 608/609, 730
Den Haag 105, 689
Denkmäler 419, 430/31
Denkov, A. 661
Dent 698
Dernschwamm, Hans 423
Derventski 11
Deutsche 475, 486
Deutsche Demokratische Republik 7, 87, 92, 115–116, 122/123, 126, 140, 182, 190/191, 198, 200/201, 236, 252, 254/255, 262, 283, 286, 306–310, 313, 325, 327, 331/332, 338, 361, 365, 368, 374/75, 383, 386, 392, 394, 396, 403/04, 407, 429, 435, 441–43, 505/06, 512, 523, 535, 578, 649, 680/81, 685, 692, 695/96, 699/700, 721–726
Deutsche Forschungsgemeinschaft (DFG) 1, 5, 541
Deutsche Sprache 495, 505, 606
Deutschland 32, 36, 41, 49–51, 54–56, 60, 67, 88/89, 95, 99, 101–104, 120, 203, 224, 234, 263, 279, 395, 490, 493, 519, 549, 568/570, 606/07, 610–612, 640, 649, 678, 689, 693, 730, 736
Devetaki 17

Devisen s. Währungen
Devnja 24, 387, 421
Dezentralisierung 139, 297, 351/352, 398, 498, 517, 526
Dialekte 420, 584/85, 589, 592
Dičev, Dimo 59, 708/709
Dičeva, P. 718
Dichtung 586, 591/92, 613, 624–626, 730
Dienstleistungen 21, 158, 160, 285, 289/90, 293/94, 297/98, 310, 314, 379/380, 389/390, 396, 398, 417, 461/62, 502, 537
Dikov, Diko 76, 710/711
Dikova, Ivanka 706
Diktatur des Proletariats 175–177, 194
Dilova, Svetlana (Salicha Adilova) 188
Dimitrov, Angel 197, 200, 703, 705/706
Dimitrov, Bojko 712
Dimitrov, Dančo 705, 714
Dimitrov, Dimităr J. 706
Dimitrov, Georgi 46, 57/58, 62, 64/65, 69–71, 86, 88/89, 95, 100, 102–109, 113, 119, 133/134, 175/176, 181, 270, 435, 457, 527, 546–548, 552–555, 609, 616, 627, 629, 631, 634, 650, 664, 690–692, 707/708, 713, 715, 729, 733
Dimitrov, Georgi M. (Gemeto) 62–64, 192/193, 658, 730
Dimitrov, Ilčo 712
Dimitrov, Stanke 729, 733
Dimitrov-Majstora, V. 658, 662
Dimitrova, Blaga 202, 579, 586, 621, 623, 625–630, 649
Dimitrova, Elena 729
Dimitrova, Roza 730
Dimitrovgrad 17, 21/22, 25/26, 280, 361, 383, 387, 448, 637, 734, 777
Dimitrovo 413
Dimitrov-Verfassung s. Verfassung
Dimov, Dimităr 72, 610–612, 614, 616, 626–628, 650, 714/715
Dimov, Vergil 730
Dinev, Petăr 672
Dinov, Todor 651/652
Diplomatische Beziehungen 103–106, 109, 111, 115–117, 123, 125, 134, 147, 238, 550, 552, 557, 563, 684, 688–703, 722/723
Disraeli, Benjamin, Earl of Beaconsfield 30
Dissidenten s. Opposition
Djulgerov, Georgi 652–654, 703
Djulgerov, Petăr 209, 706, 714, 717
DKMS 46, 58/59, 67, 142/143, 145, 159, 179, 203/204, 209/210, 213, 275, 278, 494, 526, 533, 571, 576, 610, 679/680, 728/729, 731–736
Dnjepr 27
Dobranov, B.D. 700

Dobrev, Christo 276
Dobrinište 383
Dobrudscha 8, 11, 16/17, 30, 39, 42, 49, 52, 97–100, 106, 124, 409, 419/420, 484, 592, 595, 621, 625, 671, 688–691, 729, 731, 735
Dočev, P. 662
Dolanc, Stane 697
Dojrenci 730/31
Dojnov, Ognjan 78, 80, 190, 706, 711/712, 714, 717, 730
Dogmatismus 617, 634–638, 648, 650, 659
Dolna Mitropolija 24, 275
Dolni Dăbnik 17, 24, 359
Dolni Lukovit 17
Don 409
Donau 3, 8, 11–15, 17, 19–24, 30, 33, 49, 57, 104, 126, 202, 263–265, 273/274, 340, 365, 380/81, 383–385, 420, 425, 428, 430/431, 452/53, 484, 549/50, 553, 577, 592, 670, 692
Dončev, Anton 619, 629
Donev, Don'o 651
Dorf 19/20, 27, 32, 43, 155, 158, 197, 199, 255, 371, 433, 436, 445–61, 468, 472/73, 476, 484–487, 560, 563, 566, 576, 578, 589, 591, 593, 595/96, 598, 601/02, 620, 624, 626, 646–648, 652, 666, 668
Dospat 25
DP 40, 44, 56, 63, 66, 203, 211/212, 214, 574/575, 690
Draganov, D. 660/61
Dragojčev, Čavdar 731
Dragojčeva, Cola 57, 78, 133, 706, 715, 730
Dragoman 383
Dragostinov, Stefan 670, 674
Dragova, Nadežda 630
Dramaliev, Kiril 73, 492/93, 708/09
Dreibund 41
Dreimächtepakt 55/56, 689, 730
Dritte Welt s.a. Entwicklungsländer 115, 126, 197, 404, 414, 417, 535, 684
Drjanovo 24
Drumev, Vasil 632, 636
Družba 24
DS 33, 79, 82, 136, 141, 143–152, 154, 158, 160/161, 163, 165/166, 168, 174, 197, 200, 218–221, 255, 259, 267, 664, 697, 699, 703–706, 711/712, 719, 728–731, 734/735, 737
Dubno 541
Dubrovnik 380
Dürrenmatt, Friedrich 637
Džagarov, Georgi 74, 78, 81, 614, 618, 628, 630, 636, 705
Džakov, Emil 586
Džatev, Kostadin 706
Dženev, Kiril 671

Dzeržinskij, Feliks 735
DZS 200, 280, 286, 349, 495
Džindžirica 424
Džudžev, Stojan 667
Džundrin, Samuil 563, 700
Džurov, Čavdar 731
Džurov, Dobri 83, 189/190, 276, 710–712, 717, 731
Džurova, Aksinija 731

Ecevit, Bülent 699
Economic Commission for Europe (ECE) 320–322, 366, 720
Ecuador 722
Edirne 26, 39, 688
EG 2, 84, 326–28, 332, 365, 415/416
Ehen 81, 165, 170, 172, 224, 229, 231–233, 235–243, 438/39, 442, 456, 466, 470–72, 487, 545, 552, 566, 591, 594, 719
Eigentum 57, 68, 175/176, 194, 203, 225, 228–233, 277–280, 333, 349/350, 374/375, 417, 423, 465
– genossenschaftliches 57, 176, 228/229, 277–280, 298, 349/350, 374, 377/378, 465
– privates 56/57, 60, 132, 170, 172, 175, 192, 199, 228–233, 243, 253/254, 277–280, 298–300, 333, 335, 346/347, 349/350, 353, 371/372, 374/375, 377/378, 381, 421, 426, 459, 462, 468, 473, 571/572, 647, 656, 690/91
– sozialistisches 57, 158, 171, 176, 228/229, 238, 251, 277–280, 292, 298, 337, 346/347, 349/350, 372, 377/378, 395, 458, 462
Einkommen 195, 297, 467–469, 472, 725
Einzelhandel s. Handel
Eisenbahn s. a. Verkehr, Transport 21, 23/24, 26, 33, 35, 37, 53, 62, 160, 265, 293, 371, 381–84, 420, 733
Eisenhower, Dwight 694
Elacite 356
Elašica 24
Elbe 429
Elchovo 358, 484
Elektronik 294, 403, 407, 413, 498, 504, 542
Elektrotechnik 403, 407, 527, 530, 533, 578
Elena 10
Elin Pelin 606, 610, 646
Elite 32, 55, 61, 78, 173, 187–191, 505, 531, 539, 591, 593, 623
Elšica 18, 356
Emanuilova, V. 663
Emigration 43, 52, 62/63, 67/68, 70, 83, 91/92, 109, 111, 117, 131/132, 170, 354, 434/35, 443–45, 475, 479, 482–85, 550, 554, 557–559, 562, 625, 692, 702
Emilova, Asja A. 706

Energie 7, 15–19, 293/94, 296, 326, 329/330, 338, 355–370, 387, 394/95, 401, 408/409, 411–414, 427, 721
Energie, Atom- s. a. Kernkraftwerk 23, 154, 360, 364–370, 413, 419, 431, 521, 538, 541/542, 720
Energie, elektrische 12, 23–25, 281, 316, 338, 355, 359–366, 383, 409, 428, 508
Energie, Wasser- 359–361, 366/367
Engelhard, Hans 702
England s. Großbritannien
Englische Sprache 495, 505, 587
Engsozialisten s. BKP
Entspannung 78, 414
Entstalinisierung s. Stalinismus
Entwicklungsländer 407, 415
Erenburg, Il'ja 616
Erhard, Ludwig 116
Erziehung 599, 617, 728–737
Etăra 430, 601
Ethnisch-religiöse Gruppen s. a. Nationalitäten 422, 474, 477, 486/87, 548/549, 552, 566, 595–97, 600, 732
– Gagausen 474, 477/478, 487
– Pomaken 28, 30, 422, 474, 476–479, 486/87, 548, 558, 562/563, 595
Ethnische Zusammensetzung s. Nationalitäten
Ethnogenese 27, 589
Ethnographie 592, 595, 597/98, 601
Etropole 18, 737
Eumolpias 20
Europa 17, 20, 32, 41, 50, 53, 90, 100, 116, 264, 268, 273, 305, 333, 347, 364, 368, 419, 493, 605, 723
– Mittel- 3/4, 15, 49, 53, 101, 263, 394/95, 490, 590
– Ost- 3/4, 63, 84/85, 87, 89, 110, 174/175, 190, 201, 209/210, 277/278, 280, 292, 304–332, 336, 338/39, 344, 394–96, 429, 436, 439, 441–443, 462, 469, 523, 564, 580, 588/89, 677
– Süd- 262, 320
– Südost- 1–4, 18, 84, 87–89, 94, 101, 104, 107, 110, 264, 277/278, 280, 292, 355, 380, 394, 476, 593, 597, 656
– West- 18, 26, 130, 240, 320–22, 389, 391, 395, 441–443, 456, 490, 514/15, 551, 561, 617, 638, 657/58, 660, 663, 678, 730
Europarat 130
Evksinograd 691
Evren, Kenan 130, 700, 702
Evstatieva, Mariana 651
Evtimov, Evtim 89, 631
Evtušenko, Evgenij 624
Exarchat 28, 36, 544

Exekutive 38
Expressionismus 607

Fábri, Zoltán 648
Familie 81, 112, 117, 130, 165, 170/171, 222, 224–229, 231–233, 240–243, 278, 337, 346/347, 371, 392, 420, 438–440, 446/447, 456–461, 465–473, 476, 479, 513, 559, 583, 590, 594, 596/597, 602–605, 624, 657, 723/724
Familienrecht s. Familie
FAO 541, 720
Faschismus 47, 50, 60, 68, 78, 270, 491, 534, 547, 572, 585, 607–610. 612, 616, 625, 648/649, 653, 658, 662
Ferdinand, Fürst/Zar 27, 35–41, 55, 618
Fernmeldewesen 170, 413, 507, 510, 720, 729
Fernsehen, Fernsehgeräte 89, 325, 376, 379, 470, 510, 578, 581, 584, 588, 599, 679, 683, 702
Festivals 600, 646, 651/652, 654, 666, 671, 675/76, 737
Fičeto, Kol'o 431
Filipov, Griša 189/190, 700, 706, 712, 714, 716, 731
Film 594, 601, 613/14, 644–655
Filov, Bogdan 49, 51, 690, 736
Finanzwesen 160, 266, 527, 733
Finnland 105, 312, 470, 696, 701/02, 725/26
Firmen s. a. Betriebe 227, 230, 277, 296, 298–301, 352/353, 395, 397
Fischereiwirtschaft 21, 26, 379, 385, 423, 487
Flaker, Aleksandar 622
Fleisch 344–348, 352, 376, 379
Florina 736
Flüchtlinge s. Emigration
Flüsse 10–12, 385/86, 425, 428/29
Fo, Dario 637
Fock, Jenö 696
Fol, Aleksandăr 81, 711–713
Fol, Nikolaj 633, 637
Formalismus 607, 611, 614, 623, 627, 636, 659, 664
Forschung s. Wissenschaft
Forstwirtschaft 10, 14/15, 22–25, 52, 160, 333, 349, 424/425, 507, 527, 540, 712, 737
Fotinov, Konstantin 567
Franco, Francisco 610
Frankfurt/Main 651
Frankreich 51, 54, 106, 250, 364/65, 384, 418, 443, 470, 490, 493, 547, 550, 621, 649, 662, 695, 697/98, 700, 703, 722, 724/25, 733, 736
Französische Sprache 495, 505, 606
Frauen 29, 48, 170, 184–187, 199, 216/217, 222/223, 240–243, 318, 433–42, 458, 461, 463, 466–73, 486, 513, 523, 530, 534, 550, 554, 567, 582/83, 590, 598, 600, 623–626, 658, 670, 719, 731
Frauenverband (BNŽS) 203
Freimaurer 49
Freizeit s. a. Sport, Tourismus 208–210, 222, 513
Frenzke, D. 141
Freud, Sigmund 519
Fribourg (Schweiz) 545
Frisch, Max 637
Fučedžiev, Diko 622, 629–631
Fugger 423
Funev, I. 663
Fünfjahresplan 72, 75, 141, 258, 297, 339, 341/342, 345, 351, 358, 361, 368/369, 381, 396, 507/08, 536, 610, 691–93, 695, 698, 700, 702
Furmanov, Dmitrij 611
Furnadžiev, Nikola 618, 628

Gabe Dora 609, 618, 625, 629/630
Gabrovo 21/22, 24, 29, 156, 314–16, 384, 386/387, 448, 451–55, 512, 514, 527, 592, 601
Gačev, Georgi 605/06
Gagausen s. Ethnisch-religiöse Gruppen
Gallipoli s. Gelibolu
Galloni, Francesco 550
Gamzatov, Razul 616
Gančev, Lalju 706
Gandhi, Indira 700
Ganev, Christo 647–649
Ganev, Dimităr 57, 115, 694, 705–709, 714/715, 731
Ganev, Gančo 710/711
Ganev, Gin'o (oder: Ginju) 706
Ganev, Ivan 123, 128, 132
Ganev, Venelin 704
Ganovski, Sava 572, 707
Gara Bov 730
Gaststätten 372, 375–378
GATT 416
Gavazzi, M. 592
Gebirge 7–15, 20, 25, 263/264, 334/335, 341, 353/354, 388, 392, 421, 487, 592, 595
Geburtenrate 81, 433, 436–40, 442/43, 445, 447, 450–53, 456–458, 467–69
Gefängnisse 57, 59–61, 63, 70–72, 168, 261, 723, 728–732, 736
Geflügel s. Tierzucht
Geheimdienst 76
Geisteswissenschaften 537
Gelibolu 41
Gemeinden s. a. Territorialverwaltung, Städte, Dörfer 161–164, 166, 490
Genčev, Angel 685

Gendov, Vasil 646
Generationen s. Altersstruktur
Genf 559, 723, 734
Genkov, G. 662
Genossenschaften 43, 53, 167, 175/176, 192, 194–197, 227, 248, 255, 278/279, 294/95, 302, 318, 349/350, 371–373, 375, 381, 417, 459, 576
– landwirtschaftliche s. TKZS
Genov, Gavril 83
Genov, Todor 74, 617
Genovski, Michail 707
Genozid 118
Genscher, Hans-Dietrich 126, 699–702
Georgi-Damjanovo 729, 777
Georgiev, A. 689
Georgiev, Georgi 712/713
Georgiev, Kimon 47/48, 61, 64/65, 690, 707/708, 710, 732
Georgiev, Kollo 629
Georgiev, Marin 624, 630
Georgiev, Nikolaj 704, 706
Gerasimov, Gennadij 661
Gerasimov, Ivan 276
Gericht 60, 62–64, 66/67, 69–72, 77/78, 105, 136, 148, 162–168, 172, 181, 193, 197, 202, 224–261, 299, 353, 397, 427, 557/558, 601, 689, 698, 731
– Kollegengericht 168
– Oberstes 143, 145, 165, 168, 172, 234/235, 237, 259–261
– Schiedsgericht 723
Gerinska, Veselina 651
Gerov, Aleksandăr 628/629, 631
Geschichtswissenschaft 59, 80/81, 84, 88, 92, 94, 96, 102, 105, 107, 174, 204/205, 269, 503, 519, 540, 559/560, 562/563, 577, 728, 732, 736/737
Gesellschaft 32, 590/91, 595, 602, 619–621, 623, 626, 652/653, 658, 664
Gesetze s. a. Rechtsquellen 45/46, 49/50, 53, 57, 62, 67. 91, 131, 140, 143–151, 157–159, 166–168, 206–208, 214, 218/219, 224–261, 278/279, 294, 381, 423–426, 433, 435, 439/440, 447, 453, 461, 467, 469/470, 492, 494/495, 506, 519–521, 526, 529, 531, 544, 549, 551–553, 557, 559, 568, 572, 575, 678, 688–703, 718
Gesetzlichkeit 136, 139/40, 160, 163, 166, 172
Gesundheitswesen 43, 82, 151, 160, 170, 206, 257, 389, 392, 422, 430/31, 440/41, 462, 464, 466, 473, 500, 506, 508, 522/523, 539, 582/83, 598, 600, 602–604, 610, 680, 720, 730
Gewerkschaften (BPS) 42, 46–48, 56–58, 61, 64/65, 67, 143, 145, 151, 159, 202–204,
206–209, 248, 256, 275, 278, 299, 380, 392/393, 513, 525/526, 571, 576, 679/680, 697, 730–732
Ghana 115, 722, 726
Gheorghiu-Dej, Gheorghe 110
Gičev, Dimităr 56, 63/64, 730
Gidikov, Borislav 683
Gigen 17
Ginovski, V. 663
Giovanna, Zarin 736
Girginov, A. 690
Giurgiu 21, 430
Gjaurov, Kostadin 706, 716
Gjueševo 383/84
Gjulemetov, K. 661
Gjurov, Stojan 714
glasnost' 56, 79, 81–83, 178, 202, 432, 559, 567, 580–84, 586, 626
Gledka 736
Goce Delčev (Nevrokop) 481, 585, 777
Gočev, Vălko 708
Gogol', Nikolaj 620
Goljamo Kruševo 18
Gomułka, Władysław 695
Gondov, B. 663
Gorbačev, Michail Sergeevič 4, 85, 119–121, 131, 139, 174, 177, 190, 268, 411, 626, 701/02
Gor'kij, Maksim 611, 735
Gorna Banja 497
Gorna Orjachovica 24, 383, 386, 736
Gorni Dăbnik 17
Gorni Lom 18
Gorubso 18, 357
Göttingen 5
Grăbčeva, Ivanka 651
Grăblev, Mitko 685
Gradec 17, 731
Graf, Steffi 682
Grančarov, D. 662
Graničak 734
Graphik 656, 660/661
Gregory, P. 319/20
Grekov, Leonid 411
Grenzen 10–12, 14, 22/23, 26, 41/42, 44, 90/91, 106, 108/109, 111, 131, 134, 161, 264/265, 271, 354, 381, 384/385, 409, 419, 421/22, 429/30, 452, 530, 558, 670, 692/93, 696, 702/03, 718, 726/27
Grežov, Boris 646
Griechen 31, 34, 52, 422, 474/75, 484, 596
Griechenland, 1/2, 7/8, 10, 12, 20, 23, 28, 37–39, 41, 44, 47, 49–51, 63, 84, 89/90, 92, 96–100, 102, 104–106, 108/109, 111–113, 116/117, 119, 127–129, 134, 230, 263–267, 271, 308, 365, 377, 381, 383/384, 392, 404,

416, 421, 443, 475, 480, 484, 490, 543/544,
  548/549, 556, 584, 592, 604, 689, 691,
  693–703, 722, 724, 726, 732/33
Griechische Sprache 29, 31, 486, 492, 495,
  497, 506, 543, 606
Grigorov, Mitko 76, 78, 705/706, 714, 716,
  732
Großbritannien 30, 36, 46, 49, 51, 54, 57,
  63/64, 67, 70, 88, 101–105, 108, 404, 418,
  557, 559, 574, 576, 689–692, 695, 699, 702,
  725/726
Großmächte 29/30, 32, 35, 39, 49, 55, 97,
  100–106, 263
Grozev, Gočo 716
Grundbesitz s. Eigentum, privates
Grundpflichten s.a. Verfassung 136, 170/171
Grundrechte s.a. Verfassung 65, 68, 83, 136,
  143, 162, 168–172, 174, 202/203, 253,
  551/552, 557/558, 562, 626, 718/19
Guinea 115
Guljaški, Andrej 580, 607, 611, 625, 627–631

Hába, A. 673
Häfen 20/21, 25/26, 51, 265, 381, 385/86, 418
Hajduken 592, 647
Hajek, J. 696
Hamburg 535
Handel, Händler 20, 24, 36, 43, 68, 160, 175,
  224, 230, 233, 239, 284, 286, 288/289,
  293–295, 297/298, 301/302, 351, 371–380,
  385, 390, 394–418, 423, 427, 459, 463, 467,
  482, 508, 519, 527, 536, 592, 595, 601, 645,
  657, 680, 690, 693, 695, 698, 723
Handwerk, Handwerker 44, 68, 183, 228, 278,
  294, 304–332, 372, 482, 506, 592, 594, 597,
  601, 656/657, 661, 663/64
Hartl, Hans 93
Hatschikjan, Magarditsch A. 101
Haushalte s. Familien
Hebräische Sprache 31, 485
Heine, Heinrich 606
Helsinki 126, 685
Hermlin, Stefan 616
Hirsch, Baron 381
Hirten 486, 597, 668
Hitler, Adolf 49, 51, 88, 104, 174
Hochschulen 166, 184, 187, 203, 210, 255,
  275, 431, 478/79, 493–95, 497/98, 509,
  511–14, 516, 518–42, 577, 674
– Fachhochschulen 511
– Künstlerische Hochschulen 528, 640, 646,
  652, 658
– Landwirtschaftliche Hochschulen 525, 527,
  536, 541
– Medizinische Hochschulen 522/523, 525,
  527/528, 530, 534, 536, 540/541

– Militärhochschulen 60, 525, 528, 729
– Pädagogische Hochschulen 494/95, 506,
  511–14, 516, 527
– Sporthochschule 527, 681
– Technische Hochschulen 519, 523, 526/527,
  530, 534, 537, 578, 730
– Theologische Hochschulen 528, 545, 556,
  561, 564, 733/34
– Universitäten 50, 494, 505/506, 511/514,
  516, 518/519, 522, 526/527, 530, 533, 540,
  554, 560, 599, 699, 728, 730–732, 734/735,
  737
Hoher Bildungsrat 513, 525
Hoffmann, E.T.A. 620
Hollywood 646
Holz 386, 409
Honecker, Erich 125, 697, 699/700
Hotels 372, 391–393, 664, 686
Howe, Sir Geoffrey 702
Hoxha, Enver 123
Humanismus 605
Hutchings, R.L. 122

Ichtiman 668
Ideologie 78, 137/138, 169, 177, 192/193,
  195/196, 200–203, 205, 210, 221, 223, 346,
  392, 406, 459, 461, 496, 498, 502, 505, 514,
  524/525, 531–533, 535–537, 570/571, 573,
  577, 579, 589, 609, 612/613, 615, 617, 625,
  636, 645, 647, 734
Ignatievo 273
Il'ičevsk 24, 385
Iliev, Ivan 663, 711–713
Iliev, Konstantin 623/624, 630/631, 638, 673
ILO 693, 719/20
Immigration 50, 58, 132, 478, 484, 486, 549,
  553
Imperialismus 104, 114, 196, 266, 552, 571
IMRO s. VMRO
Indien 115, 126, 696, 699–701
Industrialisierung 72, 182, 200, 280, 285, 304,
  307–310, 314–317, 323, 328, 331/332, 334,
  336, 350, 355, 394/95, 401, 403, 406/07,
  412/413, 421/22, 424, 433, 437, 440/41, 458,
  461, 464/65, 506, 519, 589, 594/95, 597,
  602, 610, 652
Industrie 17–26, 37, 53–55, 58, 68, 75, 80,
  155/156, 160, 175, 183/184, 192/193, 274,
  278/279, 281, 285/286, 298, 304–332, 334,
  336, 355, 363, 371, 376, 383, 387, 394/395,
  398, 401–404, 407–410, 412/413, 416–422,
  425, 427/428, 435, 445, 456, 458–464, 467,
  479, 502, 506–508, 511, 515, 522–524, 537,
  540/541, 594, 601/602, 608, 645, 647, 691,
  698, 720/21, 730

Register

- Baustoff 19, 279, 284, 316-323, 327, 329, 409, 411, 508
- Chemie 23-25, 82, 286, 294, 316-323, 325-327, 329, 354, 407, 413, 427, 429/30, 508, 510, 721
- elektronische 23-25, 316-323, 325-327, 332, 376, 379, 416, 508, 510, 721
- Glas 23-25, 316-323
- keramische 23-25, 30, 316-323, 592
- Konsumgüter 23-25, 72, 280, 285/86, 294, 316-323, 325-327, 329, 376/377, 379/380, 416, 470
- Leicht- 23-25, 184, 316-323, 325-327
- Maschinenbau 23-25, 316-323, 325-327, 329, 332, 352, 354/355, 373, 380, 395, 401-04, 407, 411-416, 508, 527, 533, 721
- metallverarbeitende 17-19, 23-25, 316-323, 325-327, 329, 355-358, 409, 413, 422, 429, 508, 510, 592, 721
- Nahrungsmittel- 23-25, 198, 286, 325-327, 334, 344, 346, 348, 350/351, 354, 416, 527
- Schwer- 17-19, 23-25, 279/280, 285, 287, 297, 316-323, 332, 357/358, 508, 530, 721, 730
- Textil 23-25, 59, 316-323, 416, 428, 592
Inflation 42, 44, 379/380, 555
Informatik s.a. Computer 158, 515, 517
Infrastruktur s. Verkehr
Innenpolitik 1-4, 27-55, 56-83, 85, 94-96, 101/102, 105, 110, 112, 118, 134/135, 148, 218, 266, 488, 568, 688-703
Integration 558, 563
Intelligenz 32, 47, 55, 72, 74/75, 81-83, 138, 176, 182-184, 202, 464/65, 610/11
Internat s. Schulwesen
Internationaler Gerichtshof 105, 557
Internationalismus, Sozialistischer 84-136, 140/141, 161, 221
Investitionen 220, 246, 280, 282, 284, 287, 290, 293, 296/97, 303, 319, 329-331, 333, 337/338, 354/355, 361, 381, 389, 395, 398/99, 403, 408/09, 411, 413, 417, 426, 481, 702, 718, 726
Irak 369, 404, 415, 722
Iran 369, 415, 695, 699
Irkutsk 409
Isaev, Mladen 610, 627/628
Iskăr 9-12, 20, 360, 429
Islam 28, 52, 68, 130/131, 422, 478/79, 481, 484, 486-489, 544, 548, 558, 562/563, 591, 595/96, 668
Island 696, 726
Israel 67, 109, 115, 484, 557, 692/93, 695
Istanbul 23, 28, 30, 33, 37, 39, 380/81, 384, 551, 560/561, 568, 729
Italien 29, 47, 49, 51, 54, 105/106, 116, 124, 125, 224, 279, 365, 404, 443, 621, 690, 694, 696, 698-701, 722, 725
Ivajlovgrad 13, 486, 777
Ivan Rilski 546
Ivančev, I. 665
Ivanov, Aleksi 712/713
Ivanov, Ivan 191, 717
Ivanov, Miron 629
Ivošević, Ljuba 730
Iwaszkiewicz, Jarosław 616
Izdremec 18
Izmail 386
Izmir 567

Jablanica 731
Jagd 423
Jalta 62
Jalta, Konferenz von 91, 105, 108
Jambol 13, 17, 21/22, 25/26, 156, 272/273, 314-16, 383, 386/87, 448, 451/52, 454/55
Jamburg 369
Janev, Demir 70, 709
Jankov, Janko 647
Janev, St. 662
Jantra 12, 23/24, 429
Japan 413, 418, 690, 694, 698, 701, 730
Jaranov, A. 662
Javarov, Pejo 606, 623, 635
Jelavich, Barbara 93
Jemen 722, 724
Jesuiten 550
Jiddisch 548
Jobert, Michel 697
Johannes XXIII. 550
Johannes Paul II. 120, 124, 130, 161, 701
Joint Ventures 249, 279, 398, 417/418
Jončev, Z. 661
Jonkov, Nikola 607
Jordanov, Georgi 84, 190, 711/712, 714, 717, 732
Jordanov, L. 84, 661
Josif I., Exarch 544
Josifov, Veselin 631
Josifova, M. 664
Jotov, Jordan 189/190, 706, 714, 717, 732
Journalisten s. Presse, SBŽ
Jovčev, Georgi 564
Jovčev, Minčo 189, 191, 712, 717
Jovkov, Jordan 606, 637
Juč-bunar (Üç bunar) 484
Juden 31, 49-52, 67/68, 109, 441, 474/475, 483-485, 489, 492, 544,. 548/549, 556/557, 564-566, 596, 649, 689
Judenspanisch (Ladino) 31, 485, 548
Jugend 67, 160, 170, 179, 184/185, 209/210, 222, 252/253, 393, 409, 435, 446/47, 457,

463, 465, 471, 476, 483, 490–517, 530, 551,
  554, 558, 576/77, 587/88, 597, 629,
  648–650, 654, 677–81, 734/735
Jugendsprache 588, 603
Jugendverbände s.a. DKMS 46, 393, 525,
  554, 571, 574, 576, 619, 677–79, 734
Jugoslawien 1/2, 5, 7/8, 10/11, 42, 44, 47,
  49–51, 73, 84, 87, 89–93, 96/97, 100–103,
  105–109, 111, 113, 116–119, 127, 132–134,
  136, 176, 180, 205, 240, 246, 258, 263–267,
  269, 271, 291, 305/306, 308/309, 312, 314,
  320–322, 363, 365, 377, 381, 383–385, 390,
  392, 404, 421, 443, 475, 480, 486, 492, 529,
  547–549, 563, 574, 592, 604, 621–623,
  625/626, 670, 689, 691–695, 697–700, 722,
  724, 726, 729/730, 733–735
Jugov, Anton 58/59, 63, 72–74, 76/77, 189,
  694, 707–710, 716, 732
Jungtürken 38/39
Juristen s. Gerichte
Justiz 140, 147, 164–168, 170, 173, 205,
  224–261

Kac, M. 663
Kacarov, St. 662
Kádár, János 77, 88, 114, 693, 696
Kadievka (UdSSR) 731
Kairo 75
Kajlaš-Tal 429
Kalatozov, Michail 648/649
Kalčev, Kamen 607, 614, 619, 627–630
Kalinov, Kamen (Fachredin Chalilov) 188
Kalojan, Zar 27
Kalotina 383/84
Kalter Krieg 96, 102, 104, 109, 111/112,
  115–117, 129
Kamčija 12, 17
Kameno 387
Kamenov, S. 661
Kamputschea 700, 722/723
Kanada 76, 561
Kănčev, Angel 527
Kănčev, S. 661
Kandov, Aleksandăr 674
Kaneli, Radul 633
Kanitz, Felix Philipp 423
Kant, Immanuel 519, 606
Kapital 68, 279, 284, 292, 297, 299/300, 302,
  304, 306–308, 329–331, 333, 337/338, 353,
  355, 389/90, 394, 396, 408, 410/411, 414,
  417/418, 431, 726
Kapitalismus 67/68, 78, 176, 192, 194, 534,
  552, 557, 612
Kapitalistische Länder s.a. EG, Europa
  – Westeuropa 312/313, 318–322, 324, 328,

395/96, 398, 403/04, 406–408, 413–415,
  417/418, 535
Kara Tepe 17
Karadžić, Vuk 591
Karakatschanen 475, 485/86, 596
Karakostov, Stefan 630
Karalijčev, Angel 610, 629
Karamanev, Georgi 712
Karamanlis, Konstantinos 128/129, 698,
  700/701
Karamitev, Apostol 650
Karandaš s. Cekov, C.
Karanfilov, Efrem 630/631
Karaslavov, Georgi 607, 610/11, 614, 618,
  627/628
Karaslavov, Slav, Ch. 625, 631
Karasuli/Polikastron 732
Karavelov, Ljuben 29/30, 33, 606
Karavelov, Petko 33/34
Kărdžali 13, 18/19, 22, 25/26, 156, 280,
  314–316, 357, 384, 448, 451/52, 454/55,
  476, 478/79, 494
Karlovo 10, 25/26, 272/273, 383/384
Karlsbader Konferenz 116
Karmal, Babrak 700
Karnobat 26, 381, 383
Karpathen 9
Kăršovski, P. 661
Kaspičan 383
Katholizismus 28, 35/36, 493, 544, 547/548,
  550, 552, 557, 563, 595, 692, 699/700
Kaufman, Nikolaj 668, 675
Kaulbars, General Aleksandr 33
Kavarna 16, 487
Kazandžiev, Vasil 673/74
Kazanlăk 10, 21/22, 25, 272, 384/385, 448,
  484, 735
Kazasov, Dimo 61, 572
Kazaško 483
Kenarev, V. 662
Kerenskij, Aleksandr Fedorovič 42
Kernkraftwerk, 29/30, 409, 413, 583
KGB 59, 736
Khadafi, Muammar al 701
Kiembaev 409
Kiesinger, Kurt Georg 116
Kiev 545, 735
Kim Il Sung 701
Kinder 81, 171, 203, 224, 226/227, 229,
  231–233, 240–243, 250, 252/253, 435,
  437–43, 456/57, 460/61, 466–73, 483,
  490–517, 554, 571, 603, 613, 651, 737
Kindergärten 493, 499/500, 511, 516
Kinematographie s. Film
Kinos s.a. Film 43, 644–655
Kiracov, Pen'o (oder: Penju) 714

Kirche
s.a. Katholizismus, Protestantismus, Armenier 20, 27, 39, 56/57 59, 66/67, 105, 430/31, 490, 499, 543–566, 672
- Bulgarische Orthodoxe Kirche (BPC) 29, 34–37, 43, 50, 52, 57, 67, 240, 481, 483, 485–487, 510, 525, 543–566, 591, 605, 672, 699, 733–735
- Russische Orthodoxe Kirche (RPC) 545/546, 554, 556, 560
Kirchschläger, Rudolf 697
Kiril 518, 527, 543, 563/564, 654
Kiril, Patriarch 67, 559/560, 692, 733
Kiril, Prinz 51, 690, 736
Kiril von Plovdiv 556
Kirkov, Ljudmil 651/652
Kirkov, Vasil 633
Kirov, D. 662
Kiselov, Mladen 637
Kišelski, Ivan 29
Kjuljumov, Kostadin 629
Kjurkčijski, Krasimir 673
Kjustendil 18, 21–23, 44, 156, 314/15, 358, 383/8a4, 448, 451/52, 454/55, 484
Klassizismus 605/06
Klenovik 736
Klerus 543–566
Klima 7, 13–15, 334/335, 340/341, 363, 388, 427
Kliment von Ochrid 518/19, 526–528, 543/544
Kliment von Stara Zagora 555
Klimov, Elem 654
Kliniken s.a. Gesundheitswesen 441, 462, 485, 540, 553
Klisura 663
Klisurski, Kiril 705
Klöster s. Kirchen
KMS s. DKMS
Knjaževo 272
Kocev, Venelin 697, 711, 714, 716
Koexistenz, friedliche 84, 96, 119–134
Kohl, Helmut 131, 699
Koivisto, Mauno 696, 702
Kokanova, Nevena 649
Kolarov, Dimo 648, 653
Kolarov, Ljuben 707
Kolarov, Vasil 46, 58, 64/65, 69/70, 552, 554/555, 690, 692, 704, 707/708, 713, 715, 733
Kolarovgrad s. Šumen
Kolčev, Apostol 694, 705
Kolev, Aleksandăr (Ali Aliev) 188
Kollektive Führung 56, 73, 75–77
Kollektivierung s.a. TKZS 68, 175/176, 195–197, 199, 228, 333/334, 349, 421, 458, 462–64, 488, 506, 575, 578, 594, 597, 625

Köln 535, 683
Kombinate 398, 409, 413
Kominform 66, 90, 94, 96, 101, 103, 105, 107/108, 110/111, 117/118, 175, 180, 205, 691
Komintern 45, 71, 101, 730, 733
Komitee 152–154, 536, 704
- für Arbeit und Sozialwesen 292
- zum Schutze der natürlichen Umwelt 728
- staatliches Verteidigungs- 148, 161
- Staatliches Preiskomitee 281/282, 292
- für Wissenschaft und technischen Fortschritt 156, 281, 292, 536
Kommissionen 729
Kommunistische Partei, Kommunisten s. BKP
Komšev, Atanas 685
Konkordat 550, 552
Konservative 32–35
Konstantinopel (s. Istanbul)
Konstantinov, Aleko 424, 646
Konstantinovsk 409
Konsumgüter 401–04, 411, 413
Kontrolle 59, 61/62, 64, 67/68, 74, 79, 138/139, 145, 148, 151, 157–159, 164, 167, 172, 206–208, 212, 218–221, 278/279, 400
Konzentrationslager 50/51
Koprivštica 30, 430, 592, 600/01, 671, 675
Korabov, Nikola 650
Koritarova, Roza 714
Koralov, Emil 607, 628
Korruption 82/83, 167, 223, 703
Korudžiev, Dimităr 622, 624, 626, 630/631
Kosack, Hans-Peter 487
Kosaken 483
K'oseivanov, Georgi 48/49
Kosev, Boril Orlinov 706
Kosev, Kiril 587
Kosovo 592
Kostov, St. L. 637
Kostov, Trajčo 56–58, 62, 64, 69/70, 73/74, 105, 118, 181, 554, 690, 692, 707/708, 713–715, 729, 733
Kostova, Emilija M. 706
Kosturkov, Stojan 63, 707
Kosturkova, Ž. 661
Kotel 430, 592, 600/01, 731, 734
Kovačev, Christo 661
Kozloduj 23, 364–366, 369/70, 413, 431
Kozovski, Ferdinand 707
KPdSU 42, 69, 73, 76, 86, 94, 122/123, 178/179, 185, 268, 291, 504, 616, 695, 734/35
- XX. Parteitag 73, 112, 196, 636, 648, 701/02
Kraftwerke s. Energie
Krag, Jens Otto 695
Krakau 651

Krankheiten s. Gesundheitswesen
Krasen 18
Krăstev, Gančo 711
Krăstev, Krăst'o 606, 612, 623
Krăstev, Venelin 674/75
Kredite s.a. Verschuldung 36/37, 41, 46, 53, 281/282, 287, 290, 296, 301–303, 369, 396, 399, 406, 410–415, 537, 694
Kreisky, Bruno 695, 698, 700
Kremikovci 17–19, 23, 316, 357, 387, 413
Kresnenska 12
Kričim 25
Krieg 27, 38, 44, 256, 267, 274, 431, 544, 550, 730
– Erster Balkankrieg 39, 270, 684, 688
– Zweiter Balkankrieg 39, 55, 684, 688
– Krimkrieg 29, 550
– Russisch-Türkischer Krieg 263, 605
– Serbisch-Bulgarischer Krieg (1885) 40, 688
Kriegsverbrecher 60, 719
Krim 484
Kriminologie s. Recht
Krivoj Rog 409
Krleža, Miroslav 616
Kroaten 486
Krum, Chan der Bulgaren 423
Krumov, Krasimir 654
Krumovo 17/18
KSZE 115, 120–121, 124/125, 127, 202, 262
Kuba 375, 386, 404, 407/408, 723/24
Kubadinski, Penčo 82, 189/190, 706, 710, 711, 714, 716, 734
Kujumdžieva 672
Kukuzeles, Joannes 672
Kulata 384
Kulekov, P. 661
Kulišev, Georgi 705, 707
Kultur 2, 20, 27–29, 56, 67, 71/72, 78, 80/81, 88, 115, 117, 125, 151–153, 157/158, 168, 170, 173, 184–187, 197, 210, 221–223, 263, 420, 431, 466, 472/473, 476, 490, 695, 697–699, 703
Kulturorganisationen s. Verbändewesen
Kulturpolitik 149, 151/152, 597/98, 602, 608, 626, 632–639, 644/645, 648/649, 659/660
Kumbiliev, Georgi 694, 710
Kunin, Petko 58, 70, 708, 714/715
Kunst 71, 80/81, 153, 160, 202, 464, 495, 503, 506, 511, 513, 515, 525, 561, 568, 577, 579, 597, 601, 608, 617, 656, 695, 737
– Malerei 202, 592, 601, 654, 656
Künstler 464, 572, 652, 728, 730, 734, 737
Kursk 409
Kutev, Filip 670
Kuwait 724
Kuzmanov, Radi 706

KVAE – Folgekonferenz der KSZE 124, 262
Kyn, L. und O. 329

Lagadinova, Elena 706
Lahr, R. 695
Lăki 18
Lambsdorff, Otto Graf 701
Landesverteidigung 32, 34–36, 38/39, 41/42, 44–48, 50, 53, 55, 60–62, 64, 77, 81, 106, 115, 122, 129/130, 134, 140, 148/149, 160/161, 165, 167, 169, 171–173, 175, 180, 186/187, 189, 203, 239, 250/251, 254, 259, 262–276, 413, 480, 503, 525, 528, 531, 574–576k, 587, 598, 604, 623, 677–679, 681/682, 684, 690, 693, 700–703, 729–737
Ländliche Regionen 7, 19/20, 43–45, 51-53, 58, 62, 68, 72, 79, 155, 193, 353/54, 371, 421, 433, 445–457, 459–461, 463, 478, 481, 483/84, 499, 516, 549/50, 573, 576, 590/91, 594–597, 604, 606/07, 644, 652, 678, 680, 683
Landreform 43, 575, 690
Landwirtschaft 7, 15, 22–26, 43/44, 52/53, 72, 75/76, 80, 83, 155/56, 160, 175/76, 180, 182, 184, 192–201, 228, 245, 277–281, 285, 288/89, 294, 302, 325/26, 332–354, 371/72, 377, 380, 394/95, 401–403, 406, 412, 414, 416, 419, 421, 425, 427–429, 432/33, 446, 453, 456, 458–465, 467/68, 479, 487, 500, 502, 506–508, 511, 522, 530, 539–541, 574/75, 578, 594, 596, 602, 608, 625, 691, 700, 702, 720/21
Laos 700, 722/23
Latein 492, 495, 497, 506
Lausanne 686
Lazarov, I. 663
Lazarov, Kiril 708–10
Lebanov, Ivan 686
Lebensstandard 71, 75, 180, 185, 298, 467
Lebnica 18
Legislative s. NSb
Lehrer s. Schulwesen
Leipzig 567, 730
Leitung 88/89, 92, 108, 110, 113, 136–172, 178–180, 184, 187–191, 194, 200, 209, 218, 248, 282/283, 286/87, 289, 291–95, 299, 301, 330/31, 341, 350–53, 395, 397, 400/01, 414/415, 417, 458, 461/62, 464, 472, 518, 524–526, 528, 534, 536/37, 659, 678
Lenbach, Franz von 657
Lendvai, Paul 93
Lenin (Ul'janov), Vladimir Il'ič s.a. Marxismus-Leninismus 396, 527, 571, 612, 644
Leningrad 34, 37, 657, 735
Leonhard, Wolfgang 87
Levčev, Ljubomir 81, 614, 618, 624, 630

Levčev, Vladimir 626
Levski, Vasil 29/30, 275, 677
Liberale, Liberalismus 32–35, 40, 53, 55, 136, 174, 177, 196, 223
Liberman, Evsej Grigor'ovič 286
Libyen 369, 404, 415, 701, 722–24, 726
Lieder s. Musik, Volkskultur
Liliev, Nikolaj 606
Lilkov, Christo 707
Lillehammer 687
Lilov, Aleksandăr 78/79, 189–191, 706, 714, 717, 734
Limassol 384
Linksparteien 41/42, 55
Lipnica 732
Lisurov, Tan'o 624
Literatur 30, 71/72, 74/75, 78, 81, 202, 431, 504, 518/19, 540, 568, 577, 579–581, 585/86, 591–595, 598–601, 605–644
– Drama s. a. Theater 74, 613, 618/19, 621–24, 632–643
– Epik 619–24
– Lyrik 74, 610
– Roman 72, 74, 588, 610–12, 616, 619–21
Literaturkritik 72, 613
Literaturpreise 616
Ljapčev, Andrej 46
Ljubljana 118
Ljulin 10, 385
Löhne und Gehälter 88, 248, 253, 259, 275, 284, 287, 289/90, 303, 333, 336/37, 361, 371, 376–80, 432, 469, 513, 528, 537, 701
Lom 13, 23/24, 385/86, 632/33, 735
London 267, 684, 732, 737
Los Angeles 684/85, 687, 701
Loveč 7, 23/24, 156/57, 314/15, 340, 362, 384, 448, 451/52, 454/55, 495, 551, 601, 730/31, 734
Löwenthal, Richard 85
Lozanov, Georgi 515
Lozengrad 270
Loznica 734
Ludogorie 11, 14
Luftfahrt s. a. Verkehr
Luftverschmutzung s. Umwelt
Lukanov, Andrej 189/90, 706, 711–713, 715, 717, 734
Lukanov, Karlo 572, 708–10, 734
Lulčev, Kosta 61, 63–66, 211, 576, 692
Lundestad, G. 104
Luns, J. 696

Măcin 409
Madan 18
Madrid 610
Madžarovo 18

Mähren 543
Maillol, Aristide 663
Majakovskij, Vladimir 610/11
Makariopolski, Ilarion 28
Makedonien 10, 30, 34, 36–39, 41, 44–46, 48, 53, 55, 70, 90, 92/93, 97/100, 107, 117, 119, 132/33, 265, 420, 480/81, 492, 544, 550, 563, 578, 592, 611, 654, 670/71, 688/89, 694/95, 698/99, 729/30, 732/33, 735/36, 750/51
Makedonier 123, 422, 474/75, 480/81, 578, 596
Makedonische Sprache 481, 492, 581, 585, 589, 697
Maksim von Loveč 560/61, 702
Malakčiev, G. 663
Maleeva, Manuela 682
Maleeva (Živkova), Mara 682, 737
Malenkov, Georgij Maksimilianovič 66, 73
Mali 115
Malta 725/26
Manastirski 11
Mandov, I. 663
Mandrica 486
Manolov, Nikola 705
Manov, Emil 74, 610, 617, 622, 627, 630, 637
Manufaktur 21, 37, 53, 319
Mao Zedong 76/77
Marbas 16/17, 25
Marica 8, 11/12, 14, 20, 25/26, 263/64, 358, 361, 381, 427–29, 452, 487
Marie Louise von Bourbon-Parma 36/37
Marinov, Nikola 611, 627/28
Marinov, P. 661
Marinovič, Anton 647
Marko, Krali 592
Markov, Georgi 699
Markov, Janko 706, 711
Markov, M. 663
Markov, sowjet. General 381
Markov, Stojan 190, 712, 717
Markovski, Georgi 623, 630
Markovski, Venko 629/630
Marktwirtschaft 209, 286, 293, 298, 328, 352, 367–69, 371, 380, 400
Marmara-Meer 592
Marseille 384
Marshallplan 94, 96, 101, 103/104, 691
Martinovo 17/18
Martinski, Trendafil 680
Marx, Karl s. a. Marxismus-Leninismus 310, 459
Marxismus-Leninismus 42, 73, 108, 137/138, 169, 177, 179, 194, 199, 223, 314, 458/59, 467, 493/94, 502, 511, 514, 518–20, 531, 533, 545, 607, 613

Masalitinov, Nikolaj Osipovič 633
Massenmedien
s. Presse, Fernsehen, Rundfunk 80, 129, 153, 226, 425, 457, 567–589, 594, 599/600, 602/04, 639, 641
Mateev, Evgeni 706, 709
Matev, Pavel 614, 629
Mathematik 519, 540
Matnica 25
Matonica 360
Mauretanien 726
Maxim (Patriarch) 735
Mazedonien s. Makedonien
Mazzoli, Giuseppe 550
Medet 18, 356
Medizin s. Gesundheitswesen
Meere 382, 385/86
Meissner, Boris 85
Mekka 563
Melbourne 684/85
Melnik 430
Menov, Georgi 713
Menschenrechte s. Grundrechte
Meredith, William 616
Mesmer, Pierre 697
Messner, Gerald F. 667
Mesta 8, 10–12, 14/15
Metod 518, 543, 563, 654
Metodiev, Dimităr 628/29
Mexiko 547, 682, 684/85, 723
Meyerhold (Mejerchol'd) 633
Mezdra 10, 12, 383
Mičev, Georgi 620
Michail von Dorostol 555
Michajlov, Christo 735
Michajlov, Ivan 73, 78, 706, 709–11, 716, 735
Michajlov, N. 657
Michajlov, Stojan 83, 191, 712, 715
Michajlovgrad 7, 17, 21–23, 156/157, 314/15, 340, 448, 451–455, 728/29, 734/35, 777
Michov, A. 662
Michov, Nikola 51, 690, 736
Mićunović, Veljko 113
Mičurin 13
Miete s. Wohnungswesen
Migration 74, 353/54, 419–421, 433, 440, 443–54, 457, 460, 464, 594, 644, 652, 670
Miladinov, Dimităr 591
Miladinov, Konstantin 591
Milchwirtschaft 340/41, 344–48, 352, 379
Milev, Geo 607, 633
Mileva, Leda 631
Militärliga 44/45, 48, 689
Minčev, Georgi 673
Minčev, J. 661
Minčev, Minčo 705

Minderheiten s. Nationalitäten u. Ethnisch-religiöse Gruppen
Minderheitengarantien s. Nationalitäten
Minekov, V. 663
Ministerrat 33, 38, 41–51, 56–83, 87, 102, 107, 109, 127, 136, 138, 141, 143–155, 157–161, 163–165, 168, 173, 192/193, 200, 210, 214, 218, 221, 243, 246/247, 259, 281/282, 289, 291–294, 296, 298, 302/303, 350, 361, 372/373, 380, 388, 392, 398, 401, 410, 427, 430, 466, 469, 481/482, 484, 486–488, 491, 494, 506/507, 512, 521, 526, 531, 534, 536, 538, 540, 543/544, 549–556, 560, 562/563, 572–574, 633, 645, 664, 682, 697/698, 701–704, 707–713, 718
– Außenhandelsministerium 152, 283, 292, 373, 396, 398, 694, 700, 710–713, 730/31, 734
– Außenministerium 65, 84, 128, 132, 159/60, 164, 190, 262, 544, 553, 563, 695–699, 701, 703, 707–712, 732–735
– Bauministerium 152, 734
– Bildungsministerium 81, 152, 423, 491–93, 498, 506, 508, 512–15, 525/26, 530/31, 536, 580, 638, 680, 707–13, 729, 732
– Elektrifizierungsministerium 732/33
– Energieministerium 363, 728
– Finanzministerium 152, 191, 266, 282, 292, 707–12
– Gesundheitsministerium 540
– Handelsministerium 152, 292, 372/73, 707, 710, 713
– Industrieministerium 707–09, 731, 733
– Innenministerium 49, 57, 59, 63/64, 74, 76, 152, 160/161, 164, 257, 525, 528, 697, 707–12, 733, 736
– Justizministerium 57, 59/60, 64, 164, 239, 707–13, 736
– Komitee für Kunst und Kultur 153, 496, 520, 525, 640–642, 659, 675, 732, 734, 737
– Komitee für Staats- und Volkskontrolle 153, 163, 427, 708–13, 728
– Komitee für Wissenschaft, Kunst und Kultur 80, 152, 520, 525, 530, 536, 729
– Kulturministerium 74, 507, 525, 530, 645, 654
– Landwirtschaftsministerium 77, 152, 288, 292, 350–52, 707–13, 736/37
– Maschinenbauministerium 730
– Metallurgieministerium 728
– Ministerpräsident 32, 33, 35–37, 41, 44, 47/48, 51, 61/62, 65, 70/71, 74, 77, 79, 143, 147, 149/150, 189, 191, 200, 270, 546, 549, 554, 695/696, 699/700, 702, 707–11, 728–37
– NAPS 288, 294, 351/352
– Postministerium 382, 731

- Propagandaministerium 61, 572
- Räte beim Ministerrat 152, 292, 525, 712/713, 732
- Staatsplankommission 76, 152, 281/82, 292, 374, 507, 708–713, 728, 731
- Transportministerium 152, 271, 382, 730, 734/35
- Umweltministerium 425
- Verkehrsministerium 292, 382, 572
- Versorgungsministerium 152, 288, 373, 728
- Verteidigungsministerium 36, 38, 60/61, 64, 75, 84, 153, 161, 164, 189/190, 275/276, 431, 528, 697, 707–12, 729, 731, 735/36
- Wirtschaftsministerium 82, 152, 188, 229, 232, 292, 373, 376, 399, 536, 713

Minkov, Dimităr 647
Minkov, Svetoslav 607
Mirčev, Vasil 650/51
Mišev, Georgi 202, 629, 651/52
Mišev, Mišo 706, 715
Mittelalter 18, 20, 103, 543, 605, 621, 656, 666, 672
Mittelmächte 41, 688
Mittelmeer 13–15, 263, 267, 364
Mitterand, François 703
Mladenov, Petăr 78, 83, 91, 124, 131/132, 135, 174, 177/178, 189/190, 201, 215, 221, 563, 697–701, 703, 705, 711–714, 717, 735
Moçambique 699, 722
Modernisierung 20, 43, 53, 222, 281, 285, 330, 337, 341, 353/54, 381, 394, 399, 403, 406, 413, 419, 458, 472/73, 478, 498, 509, 521, 532, 589, 591, 593–96, 602–04
Moldau 381, 561
Molotov (Skrjabin), Vjačeslav 58, 64, 88, 102
Momčilgrad 18, 26
Momina 11/12
Monarchie 43, 57, 64/65, 210–212, 270, 544, 547, 569, 572, 607–11, 690, 704
Mongolei 375, 407/08, 695, 722–26
Monopole 278, 284/285, 287, 290, 298, 302/03, 372, 394, 396, 424
Montenegro 39
Montreal 685
Morava 8, 11, 30, 41
Moro, Aldo 696, 698
Moskau 45/46, 57/58, 62–64, 66, 69, 71, 76, 82, 101, 108, 114/115, 118, 112/123, 174, 176, 190, 263/264, 546, 561, 607, 633/634, 644, 652, 654/655, 684/685, 690–692, 729–735, 737
Moskov, Mosko 626
Mračkov, Vasil 705
Mramoren 17
Mrkvička, Jan V. 657
MTS (Maschinen-Traktoren-Station) 279, 349

München 49, 126, 625, 657, 659, 683–85
Munk, Andrzej 648
Muraviev, Konstantin 60, 689
Musala 10, 12/13
Mušanov, Nikola 56, 63, 203, 690
Museen 81, 423/24, 513, 540, 562, 601, 659/660
Musik 210, 482, 503, 511, 513, 519, 528, 581, 594/95, 597, 599–601, 603/04, 617/18, 643, 666–676
Muslime s. Islam
Mutafčieva, Vera 621, 629–31, 653
Mutkurov, Sava 35

Nachrichtenwesen 164, 381/382
Naher Osten 121, 126, 130, 262, 383, 527, 669
Nahrungsmittel 72, 76, 280, 294, 317, 327, 329, 332/33, 347/48, 350, 354, 374–77, 379, 395, 401–04, 406, 411, 413, 427, 431, 460, 472, 540, 602/03, 701
Najdenov, Radi 707–10
Nakovski, Atanas 622, 629, 631
Nalburov, Vasil 633
Nasir Muhammad, A. 700
Nation 28, 97, 130, 488/89, 496, 563, 581, 596–599
Nationaleinkommen 54, 156, 334, 368, 376
Nationalbewußtsein, Nationalismus 28–30, 34/35, 44, 69, 80/81, 110, 190, 221, 473, 478, 490/91, 510, 559, 591, 596/97, 599, 605, 609, 632, 656/57, 683
Nationalitäten 52, 125, 170/171, 184, 187/188, 216, 218, 419, 465, 474–89, 492, 495/96, 552, 558, 697, 703
Nationalitäten s.a. Ethnisch-religiöse Gruppen, Albaner, Armenier, Aromunen, Deutsche, Griechen, Juden, Karakatschanen, Kroaten, Makedonier, Montenegriner, Polen, Roma, Rumänen, Russen, Serben, Tataren, Tschechen, Türken, Ungarn
Nationalprodukt 290, 307–310, 313, 315/16, 323/24, 332
Nationalsozialismus 47, 61, 62, 546/47, 549, 569, 610
NATO 2, 84, 90, 114, 121, 127, 129/130, 262–265, 272, 421, 479, 696
Natur s. Umwelt
Naturalismus 607, 614
Naturwissenschaften 495, 503, 506, 517/20, 539
Nedelčev, R. 662
Nedev, Ivan 711
Nedkova, V. 662
Nejčev, Minčo 71, 705, 707, 709, 716
Nejkov, A. 661
Nejkov, Ch. 661

Nejkov, Dimităr 61, 63, 65/66, 705, 707
Nenov, Dimităr 673
Nenov, I. 662
Nesebăr 26, 430
Nešev, I. 663
Neškovci 17
Nestorov, Bončo 646
„Neuer Wirtschaftsmechanismus" s. NIM
Neutralität 41, 49, 51
New York 553, 691, 719, 723
Nicaragua 723, 726
Ničev, Bojan 620
Ničev, Ivan 654
Niederlande 250, 547, 696
Nikolaus I., Papst 543
Nikolčin, Ilija 630
Nikolov, Lazar 673
Nikopol 24, 67, 550, 563, 585, 733
NIM 56, 80, 244, 289, 296/97, 301, 351, 398, 400, 417, 700
Ninov, I. 661
Niš 20, 23, 44
Nišava 11
NLP 36, 40
Nomaden 482, 486, 596/97
Nordkorea 701, 722
Normandie 57
Norwegen 687, 696, 725/26
Novorosijsk 385
NP 37, 40, 56
NSb 32/33, 37–40, 44, 46–48, 50, 55, 60, 62–66, 68, 74, 79, 82, 136, 138, 140–154, 157, 159, 166, 168, 173/174, 193, 200, 202/203, 207, 210–221, 227, 244, 248, 255, 259, 267, 423/424, 466, 519/520, 549, 574, 616, 627, 690/691, 693–695, 697–705, 707, 718, 728–737

Obbov, Aleksandăr 63, 65, 193, 574, 707, 730, 737
Oberhausen 651
Oborište 424
Obročište 18
O'Casey, Sean 637
Odessa 24, 264/265, 381, 385
OF 51, 56/57, 59–66, 71, 74/75, 87, 105, 107, 141/142, 145, 159, 173–175, 192/193, 203–207, 210–216, 278, 380, 479, 482, 485, 488, 491, 519, 545, 549, 569/570, 572–575, 608/09, 611/12, 625, 633/34, 680, 689–95, 697, 699/700, 702, 704, 738–37
Ognjanov, Christo 625
Ognjanov, Sava 633
OECD 326–28
Ognjanova, J. 636/637
Ogosta 12, 429

Ogražden Planina 10, 19, 668
Ohio 7
Ökonomie s. Wirtschaft
Okudžava, Bulat 622
Olympische Spiele s. Sport
Ökologie s. Umwelt, Umweltschutz
Ончев, Nejčo 427
Oper 632, 672, 675
Opposition 35/36, 41–48, 51/52, 56/57, 61–68, 74/75, 82/83, 94, 173, 175, 191, 196, 201–204, 210–214, 218, 554, 573–576, 607/08, 626, 690–692, 736
Orenburg 369
Orešak 734
Organisationen und Verbände 57, 67, 74/75, 124, 137–140, 143/44, 151–153, 159, 163/64, 166/67, 170/71, 173/74, 186, 191, 201–210, 215/16, 219, 255, 278, 424–426, 430/31, 469, 476, 479, 481–485, 487/88, 494, 498, 513, 516, 519, 537, 540, 549, 554, 556, 564/65, 571–573, 599, 607, 612, 626, 633, 646, 655, 657/58, 666, 675–687
Orjachovo 19, 386
Ormenion 726
Orthodoxie s. Kirche
Orthographie s. Bulgarische Sprache
Osăm 12
Oschlies, Wolf 87
Oslo 686
Osmanisches Reich 19–21, 27–30, 34–36, 38/39, 41, 52, 55, 88/89, 263, 270, 380/381, 419/20, 423, 431, 478, 482, 484, 490, 518, 543/44, 548, 550, 559, 567/568, 590–93, 602, 605, 621, 632, 647, 652, 656, 683, 688
Osogovo 10, 18, 340
Ostblock 66, 69, 73, 84–135, 176, 179/180, 187, 189, 207, 228, 243, 250–252, 254, 256–258, 261, 263, 277/278, 280, 287, 296, 379, 386, 394, 396/97, 611, 625, 683/84, 687
Österreich 36, 54, 100, 103, 234, 381, 385, 404, 443, 490, 493, 505, 550, 667, 681, 691, 694/95, 697–700, 723–726
Ostrovski, Griša 649
Ostrumelien 30/31, 37, 98, 104, 477, 688
Ostsee 460
Ovčarov, G. 664
Ovčarov, Stojan 82, 188/89, 713, 717
Oxford 80, 564
Özal, Turgut 702

Pačov, Pantelej 189, 191, 717
Pädagogik 490–519, 525, 529, 532/33, 540, 680
Paisij Chilendarski 28, 527, 567, 605, 619
Paisij von Vraca 67, 555, 559
Palästina 126, 484, 703

Palagačev, Nikola 711
Panagjurište 18, 26, 663
Panajotov, P. 662
Panajotov, T. 661
Pančarevo 736
Pančevski, Petăr 709/10, 716
Pančovska, Rada 625
Panev, Ivan 190, 706, 717, 735
Panica, Konstantin 36
Panov, Janko 75, 693
Panova, Vera 616
Panslawismus 657
Papandreou, Andreas 90, 128/129, 701, 703
Papazov, Načo 706, 710, 714/715, 717
Papoulias, Karolos 129
Parangalica 424
Paraskevanov, L. 664
Paris 41, 96, 557, 646, 681, 684, 736/37
Parks/Reservate 422, 424, 432, 472, 680
Parlament s. NSb
Parteien 2, 38, 42–48, 55–57, 60–67, 79, 83, 112, 114/115, 122, 149, 159, 173–175, 177, 179, 182, 187, 191–193, 195, 197, 200–205, 207, 211–214, 406, 425, 510/511, 567–571, 573–576, 608, 612, 689–691, 704
Parteilichkeit 140, 166, 580, 626
Partisanen 50/51, 59/60, 75, 77, 189, 607, 610, 619, 649, 653, 659, 731/32, 734–737
Partizipation 208, 211, 214, 219/220, 288
Pašev, Apostol 710/11
Paskaleva, Katja 652
Pastuchov, Krăstju 61, 64, 575, 690
Patriarchat 543–46, 554–56, 702, 733
– von Konstantinopel 28, 543/44, 550, 560
– von Rußland 545/46
– von Sofia s. a. BPC 692, 733, 735
Pauker, Ana 731
Paul VI. 124, 698/99
Pavlikeni 485
Pavlov, Asen 707
Pavlov, Nikola 714
Pavlov, Todor 58, 74, 78, 607/08, 611, 634, 636, 704, 716, 735
Pazardžik 13, 21/22, 25, 156, 272, 314–316, 357, 383, 448, 451/52, 454/55, 511, 585, 633, 637, 668, 731
Peeva, Adela 654
Pejčev, Ivan 618, 628, 630
Pelin, Elin s. Elin Pelin
PEN-Zentrum 614
Penčev, G. 661
Penev, Krum 607
Penev, Pen'o 610, 628
Penkov, Bojan 515
Penkov, I. 21
perestrojka (russ. „Umgestaltung") 3/4, 56, 79, 81–83, 85, 95/96, 110, 121, 174, 190, 201/202, 208/209, 291, 626, 646
Perez de Cuellar, J. 701
Periodika s. Presse
Pernik 17, 21–23, 156, 158, 314–316, 357/58, 383–385, 387, 421, 428, 448, 451–55, 736
Personenkult s. Stalinismus
Peštera 486
Petkanov, Konstantin 609/10
Petkov, Dimităr 424, 736
Petkov, Ljuben 622
Petkov, Nikola 62–66, 72, 105, 192/93, 197, 199, 203, 211–214, 574–576, 690/91, 736
Petkov, Petko 191, 717
Petkov, Petko (Bruder von Nikola P.) 736
Petrič k 13, 23, 44, 481, 777
Petrov, Aleksi 424
Petrov, Dimităr 651
Petrov, Ivajlo 620, 621–622, 625, 628–31, 661/662
Petrov, Valeri 618, 626, 628/29, 637, 648–51, 662
Pferde s. Tierzucht
Pflanzenproduktion 22–25, 53, 333, 339–44, 351/52
– Futterpflanzen 22–25, 53, 335/36, 339, 343, 351/52, 401
– Gemüse 22–25, 53, 335–37, 340, 342/43, 346–48, 352, 376, 379, 406, 721
– Getreide 22–25, 43, 47, 53, 76, 334/35, 338, 340–43, 348, 351, 376, 379, 427
– Industriepflanzen 22–25, 53, 335/36, 340–42, 412
– Kartoffel 22, 53, 336, 340, 343, 347, 376
– Obst 22, 53, 335, 337, 340/41, 343, 346–48, 352, 354, 376, 379, 406, 721
– Reis 53, 340
– Saatgut 22–25, 53
– Mais 22–25, 53, 336, 340–43
– Sonnenblumen 22–25, 53, 340, 342, 352
– Tabak 22–25, 46, 53, 72, 278, 340, 342, 346–48, 401, 732
– Weinbau 22–25, 53, 340/41, 343, 346, 354, 487, 721
– Zuckerrüben 22–25, 53, 342, 354
Philipp von Makedonien 20
Philippopolis s. Plovdiv
Philosophie 74, 518–20, 547, 556, 561, 565, 577, 606/07, 612, 618, 621, 637, 733, 735
Physik 540, 730
Pidkov, Christo 654
Piloty, Karl von 657
Piłsudski, Jósef 47
Pimen von Nevrokop 561
Pipelines 382, 387, 408/09
Pipkov, Ljubomir 673

Pirdop 585
Pirin 8, 10/11, 17, 22, 90, 97, 107, 117/118, 133, 263, 358, 383, 388, 420, 422, 424, 480/81, 486, 492, 511, 577, 592, 595, 668, 670/71
Pirinski, Georgi 712
Pironkov, Simeon 648
Pisa 657
Pisarev, Pavel 645, 649
Piscator, Erwin 633
Piskov, Christo 649, 653
Pius XII. 558
Plankommission s. Ministerrat
Planung s. a. Fünfjahresplan 136, 138/139, 143, 149, 155, 157/158, 160, 207/208, 277–303, 330, 341, 351–54, 361, 365, 369, 374, 376, 381, 395, 397, 400, 406, 409, 411, 417, 419–422, 424, 426/27, 456, 458, 461, 463, 465/66, 472/73, 493, 518, 520/21, 524, 535, 537–39, 541, 552, 575, 583
Plechanov, Georgi 607, 733
Pleven 11, 13, 17, 21–24, 29/30, 156–158, 314/15, 359, 383–387, 448, 451/52, 454/55, 484–486, 511, 528, 568, 633, 636, 671, 731
Plovdiv 7, 13, 20–22, 25/26, 34, 69/70, 72, 156–158, 183/184, 191, 272/273, 280, 302, 314/315, 340, 357, 380/381, 383–385, 387, 428, 430, 432, 448, 451–55, 481, 483/84, 486, 511/12, 514, 527/28, 549/50, 554, 556/57, 564, 568, 576, 581, 593, 595, 599, 601, 614, 632, 646, 652, 657, 663, 671, 673, 692, 697, 728, 730, 732/33, 735
Pluralismus 56, 66/68, 173/174, 177, 191, 203, 207, 210, 223, 570, 573, 576, 584, 627
Podkova 26, 383
Polen (Land) 47, 51, 80, 87, 103, 112, 114/115, 121/122, 135, 141, 182, 200/201, 203, 207, 214, 224, 258, 305–310, 312/313, 331/32, 374/75, 377, 383, 386, 391, 396, 398, 403/04, 406/407, 414, 429, 432, 443, 462, 529, 626, 644, 648, 690/91, 695/96, 721, 723–26
Polen (Minderheit) 486
Polevoj, Boris 611
Polizei (Miliz) 48, 50, 59, 61/62, 69–71, 161, 167,. 175, 186/87, 189, 202/03, 205, 271, 464, 574, 691, 700, 734/35, 737
Polski Trămbeš 384
Polytechnische Bildung s. Schulwesen
Pomaken s. Ethnisch-religiöse Gruppen
Pomorie 26, 484
Popangelov, Petăr 686
Popchristov, Damjan 705
Popivanov, Petăr 705
Poplilov, A. 661
Popov, Dimităr 261, 710/11

Popov, Georgi 707/08
Popov, Ivan 705, 711, 716
Popov, Kiril 305
Popov, Konstantin 585
Popov, Ljubomir 564
Popov, Vasil 618, 620, 625, 629/30
Popova, Roza 633
Popovski 11
Poptomov, Vladimir 66, 71, 708/09, 716
Portugal 308, 416, 698, 723
Post 43, 160, 170, 720
Potsdam, Konferenz von 91, 102, 105
Prachov, Todor 716
Prag 370, 673, 697, 731
Prămov, Ivan 709/10, 714
Pravda 107, 286, 397
Pravec 737
Preise 69–71, 160, 195, 229, 277, 282, 285, 287–90, 296–98, 303, 305, 310, 324, 338, 340, 353/54, 361, 367–69, 371–73, 376–80, 397–399, 401, 406, 408/09, 410, 414/15, 427, 697, 701
Preslav 27
Presse 29, 36, 44, 47, 50, 58, 61, 63–65, 74–77, 82/83, 154, 167, 170/71, 188, 260, 261, 301, 411, 423, 425/26, 429, 431, 479, 482–486, 494, 513, 530, 540, 548–551, 553/54, 558/59, 561–565, 567–589, 606–608, 614/15, 630, 632, 638, 640, 646, 666, 674–676, 690, 696, 718, 729–733, 735–737
preustrojstvo (bulg. „Umgestaltung") 3, 79, 81–83, 180, 209, 214, 226, 248, 259, 277, 283, 291–303, 352, 505, 516, 524, 625, 640
Prizren 380
Prodev, Stefan 626
Produktionsmittel 228, 277/278, 298, 353, 380, 458
Produktivität 79/80, 156, 298, 304, 310, 312, 317, 329–31, 333, 338, 341, 343, 351, 354, 457
Propaganda 57, 75, 400, 493, 558/59, 571/572, 579, 699, 728, 30, 732, 734/35, 737
Provadijska 12, 19
Protestantismus 67, 493, 544, 548, 551/52, 557/58, 563–565, 692, 730
„Prozentabkommen" 51, 88, 95, 101/02, 104, 689
Prozeß s. Gerichte
Pryor, F. 312–314
Psychologie 524/25, 532/33, 612, 618, 620/21, 624, 633, 650–652
Puškarov, Nikola 424

Quian Quichen 701
Quellen, historische 84, 91/92, 102, 105, 108, 110, 119, 133, 354

Radev, Jaroslav 705/706
Radev, Milčo 628
Radev, Vălo 650, 653
Radevski, Christo 580, 618, 628
Radičkov, Jordan 619/620, 623, 625/626, 629–631, 637/638, 652
Radka 18
Radoev, Ivan 610, 618, 628, 637/638
Radomir 41, 383, 670
Radoslavov, Vasil 41
Rajčev, Aleksandăr 673
Rajkov, Ivan 694, 714
Rajnov, Bogomil 565, 619, 626, 628–631, 649, 651
Rákosi, Matyás 88, 110
Rakovski, Georgi 29, 275, 591
Ralin, Radoj 202, 579, 586, 629, 637
Rapacki, Adam 695
Rasputin, Valentin 620
Rassismus 126, 719
Raumplanung 155, 172, 419–432
Rauschgift 120, 125, 130, 251
Razgrad 7, 11, 156/157, 314–316, 340, 448, 494, 734
Razlog 23, 383, 481, 667
Realismus s.a. Sozialistischer Realismus 605, 620, 625, 633, 652/653, 661
Recht 60, 68, 81, 136–172, 209, 224–261, 300, 352, 426, 476, 505, 591, 618, 718–727
– Arbeitsrecht s.a. Arbeit 165, 224, 226, 233, 247–249
– Erbrecht 224/225, 231–233, 235, 241/242, 299
– Kirchenrecht s. BPC
– Strafrecht 141, 165, 191, 202, 224, 242, 250–261, 426, 428, 696, 723/724
– Verwaltungsrecht 59, 136–172
– Völkerrecht s.a. Verträge, internationale 107, 113, 141, 171, 718–727
– Wirtschaftsrecht 224, 226, 234, 244–247, 719
– Zivilrecht 165, 224–244, 246, 256, 466, 719, 723/724
Rechtsparteien 27, 45–48, 50, 55/56, 519
Rechtsprechung s. Gerichte
Rechtsquellen s.a. Gesetze 138, 144, 147–151, 158, 162, 167/168, 218/219, 224–261, 286, 288, 291, 298–301, 372, 377, 398, 400, 417/418, 424, 430, 482, 486, 493/494, 517, 526, 530, 536, 591, 609, 693, 699
Rechtswissenschaft 140, 164, 540, 728, 733, 736
Reformen 43, 56, 73–83, 138/139, 152, 155, 157, 180, 190/191, 201–203, 209, 218, 220, 224, 233–235, 268, 277/278, 281–284, 286–292, 301–303, 333, 350–354, 371, 374/375, 379/380, 394, 397–401, 417/418, 432, 490, 496–498, 500, 503/504, 507–509, 515/516, 518/519, 521–525, 532/533, 535, 555, 582, 584/585, 659/660, 694, 702/703
Regentschaftsrat 51, 58, 60, 62, 65, 704
Regierung s. Ministerrat
Regionen 7, 21–26, 58, 77/78, 82/83, 136, 146, 153–157, 187, 191, 198, 211, 214, 218, 220, 280, 314, 316, 332, 340/341, 350, 353/354, 419–422, 476, 487, 498, 500, 563, 571, 576/577, 582, 589, 592, 594–596, 620, 626, 668–671
Regisseur 632–655
Reinhardt, Max 633
Religion, Religionsgemeinschaften s.a. Kirchen, Islam, Juden 27, 44, 67/68, 73/74, 80, 170/171, 175, 179, 202, 221–223, 452–454, 461, 473, 485, 487, 489, 492/493, 543–566, 579, 591, 596, 600, 626, 632, 666, 692
Renaissance 605, 664
Reni 386
Rente, Rentner 160, 172, 299, 346, 446, 456, 471–473, 701
Reparationen 42/43, 102, 106, 108, 111, 117, 125, 689
Repressalien 60/61, 83, 105, 193/194, 202/203, 488, 553, 557, 575, 619, 650, 654, 719
Reservate s. Parks
Resnais, Alain 650
Ressourcen 409–411, 414, 458, 461/462
Revolution 29, 34, 41/42, 57, 66, 72, 162, 174/175, 204/205, 222, 269, 459, 521/522, 524, 532, 546, 578, 607, 619, 653
Reza Pahlevi, Mohammed 695, 699
Rezovska 12
RGW 2, 84, 87, 94, 96, 102/103, 110, 122, 135, 182, 282, 304–332, 330–334, 338, 340, 345, 347/348, 363–365, 367–370, 374–377, 379, 383/384, 394–418, 497, 538, 541/542, 692, 718, 720, 734, 736
Rhodopen 8, 10–12, 14/15, 18/19, 25, 263, 316, 340, 357, 380, 388, 420, 452, 476, 478, 548, 589, 592, 595, 620, 652/653, 665, 668/669
Riad 131
Ribarov, R. 664
Rice, Timothy F. 667
Richter s. Gerichte
Rila 10–12, 14/15, 19, 22, 263, 360, 388, 420, 424, 560, 592
Rinder s. Tierzucht
Rituale 596, 598–600
RMS s. DKMS
Robeva, Neška 202
Röhren 428
Rohrleitungen s. Pipelines, s. Transport

Rohstoffe 42, 281, 296–298, 312, 322, 328,
  330, 348, 355–362, 373, 382, 386/387,
  394/395, 401–404, 406, 408/409, 411/412,
  415/416, 431, 460
Rom 20/21, 124, 431, 543, 550, 563, 584,
  684/685, 697
Roma 31, 465, 474/475, 478, 481/482, 548,
  558, 562/563, 596/597, 669
Romani (Sprache) 31, 481/482
Romantik 605/606, 610, 634
Rosen (Ort) 18
Rosica 12, 23
Rote Armee s. UdSSR
Rožen 11
RP 63, 66, 203, 211/212, 214, 570, 574/575,
  690, 692, 707
Rudozem 25, 290, 357
Ruen 10, 18
Rumänien 1, 4, 7/8, 12, 21, 24, 29/30, 39,
  41/42, 47, 52, 57, 82, 84, 87–91, 97–101,
  104–107, 110, 112–116, 124, 126/127, 129,
  134, 141, 172, 182, 214, 224, 246, 255, 258,
  262–269, 271/272, 306–309, 312–314,
  319–323, 325/326, 329–331, 334, 338, 341,
  344, 365, 375, 377, 383–385, 387, 392, 394,
  396, 398, 404, 406, 409, 414, 429/430, 443,
  462, 475, 486, 523, 557/558, 570, 654,
  690/691, 693, 696, 721, 723–727, 731
Rumänen 475, 485
Rumänische Sprache 481, 486
Rundfunk 61, 63, 510, 569, 572/573, 578–579,
  581, 586, 594, 599, 693, 702, 729, 733
Ruse 20, 22, 24, 82, 156, 158, 202, 265,
  314/315, 381, 383–386, 430, 448, 451/452,
  454/455, 476, 478, 484/485, 511, 527, 534,
  549/550, 564, 577, 581, 596, 646, 673,
  729/730, 734
Rusenski Lom 12
Rusev, Charalan 610
Rusev, D. 662
Rusev, S. 202, 662
Ruseva, L. 662
Russen 44, 474/475, 483, 596, 633, 635
Rußland s.a. UdSSR 29–39, 42, 52, 55, 71,
  88/89, 100, 104, 234, 250, 259, 263, 266,
  269/270, 490, 578, 606, 613, 619, 622, 640,
  672
Russische Sprache 503, 505, 580, 585, 587

Saarland 535
Šabla 23
Săbranie s. NSb
Sachsen 18
Sakar 11, 14/15, 18, 25, 595
Salinger, J. D. 622
Saloniki 39, 47, 697/698

Salzburg 625
Samodumov, Todor 514
Samokov 12, 272, 380, 551, 565, 656, 670
Samrin, Heng 700
Samuil 383
Samuilovski 11
St. Petersburg s. Leningrad
Sandanski (Sveti Vrač) 481, 777
San Stefano, Vertrag von
  s. Verträge, internationale
Santov, Christo 649
Šapkarev, Kuzman 591
Sarafov, Krăstju 633, 640
Sarajevo 686
Šaraliev, Borislav 647/648, 650/651, 653
Šarlandžiev, Ljubomir 650, 654
Satire 579, 582
Šavelskij, Georgij 547
Savov, Stefan 628
Sazlijka 12
SBP 78, 605, 609–619, 625–631, 633, 638,
  641, 735
SBŽ (Journalistenverband) 429, 570, 582
Schafe s. Tierzucht
Schauspieler
  s.a. Film, Theater 513, 632–655
Scheel, Walter 125, 698
Scheidungen s. Ehe
Schematismus 611, 621, 634, 636, 647/648
Schiffahrt s. Verkehr
Schiller, Friedrich 633
Schmidt, Helmut 700
Schrift 2/3, 27, 543
Schriftsteller s. Literatur, SBP
Schulwesen 43/44, 59, 61, 67, 171, 187, 203,
  462–464, 472, 476, 479, 482/483, 485, 487,
  490–517, 521, 527, 530, 545, 547/548,
  550–553, 556/557, 566, 585, 598/599, 601,
  604, 615, 640, 677–681, 702, 719, 729–735
Schwarzes Meer 8/9, 11–14, 17, 24–27, 51,
  263–265, 271, 274, 341, 359, 381/382,
  384/385, 388/389, 392, 421, 425, 484, 487,
  577, 648, 650, 665, 670
Schweden 312, 470, 725
Schweine s. Tierzucht
Schweiz 71, 404, 418, 545, 547, 575, 733
Scott, Hilda 469
SED 115, 121, 123, 697
Sedmočislenici 18
Seen 12, 388
Selbstverwaltung 139, 154, 157, 159, 177, 219,
  277, 291–295, 299, 302/303, 352, 389, 398,
  417, 523–525, 536, 547, 552, 584, 639, 703
Selimovit, Meša 622
Semerdžiev, Atanas 269/270
Semov, Radi (Rafet Sejdaliev) 188

Sendov, Blagovest 515
Seoul 677, 683, 685–687
September-Aufstand s. Aufstände
Septemvri 383
Serben 475, 486
Serbien 20, 29/30, 34, 38/39, 89, 97, 107, 270, 480, 729
Serdica (Sofia) 26, 380, 426
Seton-Watson, H. 93
Sevlievo 10
Shakespeare, William 618, 633, 637
Siedlungen
  s. a. Dorf, Stadt 7, 19–21, 53, 159/160, 589
Siedlungssysteme 159, 350
Silistra 8, 21/22, 24, 156, 265, 314–316, 386, 448, 451/452, 454/455, 476, 483
Silkozija 424
Silverman, Carol 482
Simeon I., Zar 605
Simeon II., Zar 51, 65, 609, 689, 704, 736
Simeonovo 551
Singidunum (Belgrad) 380
Šipkapaß 9, 30, 270, 384, 424
Šipkovo 17
Široka Lăka 430, 600
Šiškov, Angel 706
Šišmanov, Dimităr 634
Šišmanov, Ivan 614, 634
Skopje 50, 380
Slănčev Brjag 26
Slavejkov, Penčo 606, 623
Slavejkov, Petko 591
Slavkov, Ivan 684, 687, 737
Slavov, Kiril 69
Slawen 2, 10, 19, 27, 88, 130, 420, 431, 475, 479, 486/487, 543, 546, 584/585, 590, 609, 672
Sliven 10, 16, 21/22, 25, 156, 158, 272, 314–316, 383–385, 387, 448, 451/452, 454/455, 482, 485, 511, 638, 731/732
Slivnica 34, 270
Šmirgela, N. 658, 663
Smirnenski, Christo 607, 612
Smoljan 18, 156, 314–316, 451/452, 454/455, 646
Smyrna s. Izmir
SNM (Jugendverband) s. DKMS
Sobolev, General Leonid 33
Sofia 3, 7/8, 10–13, 16/17, 19–26, 33, 36, 38, 41, 44, 46/47, 51, 53, 60, 62, 66, 69/70, 74, 81, 123, 125–129, 131, 155–158, 165, 183/184, 189, 202, 226/227, 229, 235, 239, 260, 263/264, 272/273, 275, 280, 302, 314–316, 340, 356–358, 380–384, 386–388, 406, 408, 412/413, 419/420, 422–424, 426–432, 448, 451–455, 480/481, 483–486, 497, 505/506, 510–515, 519, 521/522, 526–529, 532–535, 537, 540, 545, 548–551, 553–557, 560–562, 564/565, 568/569, 572/573, 577/578, 581, 585, 588, 592/593, 599, 601/602, 615, 623, 626, 630, 632, 637, 642, 645–648, 654, 657–659, 663/664, 672–674, 679–682, 686/687, 689, 691, 695, 698/699, 701, 703, 728–733, 735–737
Sofronij von Vraca 559
Solakov, Angel 711
Šolochov, Michail 611
Solouchin, Vladimir 620
Somovit 386
Šopen 592, 668–670
Šopov, Asen 652
Šopov, Vălkan 711
Šopova, Stanka 706
Souveränität 38/39, 84, 101, 106, 110, 136–138, 141
Sowjetisierung 84, 94–96, 101–110, 173, 175, 180, 205
Sowjetunion s. UdSSR
Sozialdemokraten s. BRSDP
Sozialismus 30, 41/42, 44, 66, 74, 79, 119, 137, 140, 152, 161/162, 165–167, 169, 171, 173–223, 396, 401, 413, 418–420, 424–427, 519, 521, 540, 571, 576, 581, 589, 596–600, 602, 608–612, 616, 618, 620, 623, 625, 633/634, 640, 647, 649, 659, 664, 673
Sozialistische Internationale 575
Sozialistische Länder
  s. a. RGW, Europa – Osteuropa, Ostblock 394, 396/397, 404–407, 414, 515, 534, 538, 541, 598, 610, 644
Sozialistischer Realismus 71/72, 579, 605–665
Sozialpolitik 81, 143, 149, 151/152, 155, 157/158, 160, 170, 180, 208/209, 392, 439/440, 457–473, 518
Sozialsystem 52–55, 167, 182–184, 186/187, 197, 199–201, 205, 216–218, 222, 458–573, 516, 615, 702
Sozialwissenschaften 137, 184, 221/222, 459, 464/465, 474, 477, 513, 518/519, 524, 527/528, 530, 539/540, 579, 581, 589, 734
Sozopol 26, 274, 485
Spanien 308, 312, 365, 384, 416, 548, 610, 699, 736
Spasov, Božidar 674
Spasov, Ivan 622
Špatov, Ivan 713
SPD 699, 701/702
Sport 121, 202, 278, 388/389, 495, 503/504, 506/507, 511, 528, 530/531, 534, 587, 665, 677–687, 701, 719, 735
Sprache 92, 420, 476, 478, 487, 503, 528, 537, 540, 567–589

Sredna Gora 9–11, 13–15, 18/19, 23, 25/26
Staatsangehörigkeit 136, 141, 169/170, 243,
  719, 722, 724
Staatsanwaltschaft s. Gerichte
Staatshaushalt 43, 47, 143, 149, 266, 282, 287,
  290, 296, 298, 300
Staatsoberhaupt
  s. a. Zar, DS 704–706, 728
Staatsrat s. DS
Staatssicherheitsdienst 59, 64, 70/71, 74,
  160/161, 167, 191
Staatsstreich 33/34, 45, 47/48, 56–59, 61, 66,
  68/69, 71, 95, 101–104, 154, 162, 173–175,
  177, 179–182, 189, 194, 204, 210, 269, 278,
  461, 465, 491, 510, 519, 570, 608, 612, 625,
  633, 640, 647, 658, 662, 678, 681, 688/689,
  692, 695, 732, 736
Stadt 7, 19–26, 28, 42, 44, 47, 52/53, 58, 68,
  76, 153, 155–158, 172, 192/193, 198, 214,
  255, 274, 309, 371, 385, 388, 421, 432/433,
  436, 440, 445–449, 456/457, 459, 461,
  463/464, 468, 471/472, 481, 483/484, 486,
  505, 553, 566, 573, 591, 593–596, 598,
  601–604, 620, 623, 624, 626, 652, 660, 665,
  678/679, 683
Stahl s. Metall, Industrie
Stajkov, Enčo 73, 714, 716
Stajkov, Ljudmil 650, 653/654
Stajnov, Petko 672, 674, 707
Stajkov, V. 660–661
Stalin, Iosif 56, 58, 64, 69–73, 85, 88, 94/95,
  101–104, 108, 110–113, 533, 545, 578, 611,
  616, 635–637, 659, 689
Stalin (s. Varna)
Stalingrad 51
Stalinismus 56, 66–74, 76, 84, 89, 92, 96,
  110–112, 139, 174, 178, 195/196, 205–207,
  277, 480, 490, 492–494, 520, 555, 578–580,
  610, 618/619, 647–650, 654, 693, 729
Stamatov, Vărban 630
Stambolijski, Aleksandăr 27, 39–45, 57, 72,
  100, 192, 194, 664, 732
Stambolijski, Asen 72, 688
Stambolov, Stefan 27, 35–37, 45
Stamenov, Stamen 711/712
Stančev, Ch. 657
Stanev, A. 663
Stanev, Emiljan 610, 616, 621, 627–629, 650
Stanev, Ivan 717
Stanev, Ljuben 631, 650
Stanev, Nenčo 711
Stanišev, Dimităr 699, 715, 717
Stanislavov, Filip 550
Stanislavskij, Konstantin 633–635, 637
Stanjanci 358
Stanke Dimitrov 23, 383, 484, 729, 777

Stara Planina 9–15, 17–19, 22/23, 25, 670
Stara Reka 360
Stara Zagora 19, 21/22, 24–26, 156, 158, 272,
  314/315, 383/384, 386, 428, 448, 451–455,
  511/512, 514, 527, 568, 581, 614, 673, 728
Starčev, V. 663
Staro Orjachovo 17
Statistik 59, 112, 118, 154, 172, 224, 258, 280,
  305, 310, 312–314, 317, 323, 329/330, 334,
  338, 347, 356, 366, 369, 375, 390/391, 453,
  457, 474/475, 480, 486, 559, 632, 641–643,
  645, 678
Stefan, Exarch 67, 545–549, 553/554, 556,
  560
Stefanov, Ivan 707/708
Stefanov, Kiril 670
Stefanov, Ninko 710/711
Stefanov, Părvan 630
Stefanova, Liljana 618, 628/629
Stefanova, Nevena 618
Sterblichkeitsrate 433, 440–443, 447,
  450–453, 457
Steuern 33, 37/38, 53, 68, 72, 81, 126, 158,
  171/172, 195, 233, 290, 296, 309, 353, 718,
  725
Štip 735
Stipendien 534/535, 701
Stoev, B. 661
Stoev, Genčo 629–631
Stoev, L. 661
Stoica, Chivu 90, 113, 116, 127
Stoičkov, Grigor 711/712, 717
Stoilov, Konstantin 37, 53
Stoilov, St. 661
Stoin, Vasil 666, 669
Stojanov, Dimităr 697, 711/712, 715, 717, 736
Stojanov, Georgi 190, 654
Stojanov, Ljudmil 72, 610, 618, 627–629
Stojanov, Mladen 716
Stojanov, Nikola 709
Stojanov, Penčo 673
Stojanov, Petko 707
Stojanov, Prodan 715
Stojanov, Todor 649
Stojanov, Zachari 587
Stojčev, Petăr 646
Stojčev, Stefan 737
Stojčev, Todor 706, 717
Stojčev, Vladimir 684, 690
Stojkov, Stojko 588
Stökl, Günther 95
Stoph, Willi 695
Strandža 11, 14/15, 18, 25, 592, 595
Strašimirov, Anton 606
Stratiev, Stanislav 623, 630/631, 637
Stražica 736

Streik 42, 45, 72
Strelkov, Lozan 579
Strindberg, August 624
Strjama 10–12
Struma 8, 10, 12–15, 17, 20, 22, 263, 381
Strumica 10
Studenten s. Hochschule
Subventionen 289, 299/300, 377, 419, 421, 440, 469, 547–549, 551–553, 555, 560, 562–564, 642, 700
Suchodol 424
Südosteuropa-Gesellschaft (SOG) 541
Südslawen 19, 92, 474
Sugarev, Edvin 626
Sülejmanoğlu (Sulejmanov, Šalamanov), Naim (Naum) 683, 686
Šumen 3, 13, 19–24, 156, 272, 314–316, 384, 448, 451/452, 454/455, 476, 478, 494, 511/512, 514, 527, 548, 563, 568, 581, 596, 632/633, 729, 733–735, 777
Surkov, Aleksej 616
Suzeränität 30, 32, 55
Sveta Nedelja (Kathedrale) 46, 55, 689
Svilengrad 26, 381, 383/384, 702, 726
Svištov 21, 24, 381, 386, 431, 519, 527, 550
Svoge 23, 358, 728
Symbolismus 606/607, 610, 612, 626, 634
Syrien 126, 384, 404, 702, 722–724
Szklarska Poręba (Schreiberhau) 175
Szondi, György 622

Tabakov, Emil 674
Tachirov, Š. 596
Takov, Peko 705, 716
Talev, Dimităr 611, 619, 627–629, 652
Tambov 735
Tančev, Petăr 79, 197, 200, 703, 705, 710/711, 736
Tanev, Georgi 712
Tantra 11
Tänze s. Musik, Volkskultur
Tărgovište 156, 314–316, 386, 451/452, 454/455, 481, 734
Tarkovskij, Andrej 644, 652
Tărnovo 18, 20–24, 27, 35, 156, 518, 543, 599, 601
Tărnovo-Verfassung vom 16.4.1879 s. Verfassung
Tartus 384
Taskov, Boris 709/710, 714, 716
Tataren 474/475, 484, 548, 562/563, 596
Tatarov, J. 665
Tatarova, Blaga (Elmaz Tatarova) 188
Technikum s. Schulwesen
Technologie 18, 79/80, 176/177, 180, 200, 246, 252, 281, 284/285, 290, 293, 295/296, 301, 316/317, 327, 329/330, 337/338, 341/342, 351–354, 394–397, 403, 406, 410–416, 418, 429, 432, 498, 515, 517–518, 523/524, 532, 536–540, 542, 546, 577, 601, 603, 645, 664, 696, 698/699, 703, 721, 728
Telefon 379, 470
Tellalov, Konstantin 714
Tenev, Ljubomir 631
Terpešev, Dobri 58, 72/73, 75, 189, 196, 693, 708, 716
Terror, Terrorismus 46, 66, 71, 125, 251
Terziev, Ivan 651
Terziev, N. 663
Thessaloniki 384
Theater 528, 572, 600, 621–624, 632–643
Theologie 457, 518, 521, 733
Thrakien 10–15, 19/20, 25, 30, 41, 50/51, 97–100, 103, 106, 109, 265, 484, 544, 550, 592, 652, 668–672, 689, 737
Tichomirov, O. 694
Tierzucht 22–25, 42, 68, 333, 336, 338–41, 344–48, 352, 401, 406, 527, 598, 600
– Geflügel 340, 341, 344–347
– Rinder 22–25, 336/337, 341, 344–347
– Schafe 22–25, 340/341, 344–347, 354
– Schweine 22–25, 336, 340/341, 344–347
– Ziegen 344–347
Timok 12, 429, 726
Tinčev, Stojan 564
Tirana 115, 128, 131, 696, 703
Tito, Josip Broz 69–71, 73, 96, 107/108, 118, 134, 691/692, 695/696, 729, 733
Tjulenovo 17, 359
TKZS 68, 72, 175/176, 182, 194–197, 200, 255, 280, 286, 289, 337, 347, 349/350, 353, 427, 429, 462, 464/465, 473, 495, 508, 690
Todesstrafe 60, 66/67, 70, 253/254, 728–730, 732, 735, 737
Todoriev, Nikola 363, 366
Todorov, Ljudmil 654
Todorov, P.J. 635, 637
Todorov, Stanko 76, 78/79, 83, 190, 202, 695, 699/700, 703, 707, 709–711, 714, 716, 736
Todorov, Todor 675
Todorov-Gorunja, Ivan 77
Tokio 684/685, 730
Tolbuchin 3, 8, 19, 21/22, 24, 156, 273, 314–316, 448, 451/452, 454/455, 511, 646, 671, 731, 737, 777
Tolbuchin, F.I. 269
Tomova, Ekaterina 625
Tončev, Stojan 706
Tončeva, Elena 672, 675
Tonev, Ljuben 432
Topenčarov, Vladimir 74/75, 572/573, 579
Töpfer, Klaus 126

Topolnica 10–12
Topolovgrad 487
Tošev, Andrej 48
Toševa, Nevena 651
Toševci 735
Toškov, Marin 425
Tourismus 24, 26, 115, 125, 230, 294, 377,
  388–393, 421, 424/425, 560, 587, 597, 599,
  665, 677, 687, 697, 701, 726/727
Tradition, Traditionalismus 67, 71, 80, 184,
  221–223, 433, 461, 467, 471–473, 478, 482,
  590–608, 644, 652/653, 656, 663, 664, 671
Trajanov, Teodor 606, 612, 623
Trajkov, Andon 682
Trajkov, Georgi 65/66, 79, 193, 200, 695, 705,
  707–710, 736
Transit s.a. Verkehr 230, 380, 390, 392, 698
Trănski, Slavčo 73
Transport s.a. Verkehr 20/21, 23/24, 34, 68,
  131, 160, 246, 265, 298, 302, 325, 354, 371,
  380–387, 396, 404, 408, 412, 463/464, 467,
  507, 687, 698, 720, 726
Tričkov, Krăstju 705/706, 711/712, 716
Trjavna 24, 592, 601, 656
Troebst, Stefan 93
Trojan 17, 24, 601, 728
Trojanovo 361
Trotzkismus 70
Truman-Doktrin 104/105
Tschechen 475, 486
Tschechoslowakei s. ČSR/ČSSR
Tscherkessen 484
Tulčansko (Eniköy) 677
Tuleškov, Krăst'o 424
Tundža 8, 10–16, 25
Tunesien 115, 723/724
Türkei 1, 8, 10–12, 25/26, 47, 49/50, 54, 62,
  68, 83/84, 89–92, 96, 105, 107, 109,
  111/112, 116–119, 124, 127–134, 230, 250,
  263–265, 271, 308, 354, 365, 381, 420/421,
  443–445, 478–480, 482, 549, 558, 683, 686,
  689, 692/693, 695–703, 723/724, 727, 730
Türken 31, 34, 52, 81, 83, 90/91, 109, 111/112,
  117, 120/121, 126, 129–133, 171, 184,
  187/188, 216, 218, 222, 316, 339, 354, 390,
  422, 434/435, 443–445, 452, 465, 474–480,
  492, 494–496, 511, 516, 548, 558, 562–563,
  566, 568, 596, 621, 654, 669, 683, 692, 697,
  703
Türkische Sprache 20, 479, 481, 487, 495/496,
  511, 581
Turnu Măgurele 24
Tvărdica 10, 732
Tvardovskij, Aleksandr 616

UdSSR 4, 24, 44/45, 47, 49–52, 55–60,
  62–64, 66–73, 75–79, 81/82, 84–141, 149,
  151/152, 154/155, 166, 170, 176–179, 182,
  188, 190, 193, 196, 201, 208, 221, 225, 234,
  247, 250, 254–259, 262–266, 268–270,
  272–280, 283, 286, 291, 301, 303, 306–309,
  313, 320, 322, 324, 329, 331/332, 334, 337,
  349, 357–360, 363, 365, 368–370, 375,
  381–383, 385/386, 392, 394–398, 403–416,
  424, 431, 436, 439, 443, 458/459, 462, 470,
  476, 482/483, 487, 491–495, 498, 506, 508,
  510, 512, 514, 518–520, 523, 534/535, 541,
  545, 547, 552, 554, 556, 558, 560/561,
  563/564, 566, 569/570, 572–574, 578/579,
  582/583, 587, 607, 609–611, 613, 616,
  619/620, 622, 624–626, 633/634, 636/637,
  642, 644, 646, 648/649, 655, 672, 679/680,
  683–685, 689–691, 693/694, 696/697,
  699/700, 702, 721–725, 727–733, 735/736
Ukraine 104, 269, 409, 561, 672, 731
Ukrainer 486
Ulbricht, Walter 695
Umgestaltung s. perestrojka, s. preustrojstvo
Umwelt, Umweltschutz 82, 126, 143, 154, 160,
  197, 202/203, 419–432, 536, 582, 587,
  624–626, 687, 699, 703
UN 105, 109, 111, 113, 115/116, 124,
  129–131, 168/169, 305, 366, 541, 557, 691,
  693/694, 696, 698, 701, 718, 720
UNESCO 1, 535, 541, 641, 693, 720
Ungarn 1–3, 51, 54, 74/75, 77, 84–88, 94, 96,
  100–101, 103–107, 110, 112–115, 118, 122,
  126, 135, 141/142, 168, 182, 201, 207, 209,
  214, 224, 228, 236, 240/241, 246, 250, 258,
  269, 302, 305–309, 313, 324, 327, 331/332,
  334, 338, 341, 355, 365, 374/375, 380–383,
  385/386, 391/392, 394, 396, 398, 400,
  403/404, 406/407, 409, 412, 414, 417, 435,
  441–443, 462, 523, 550, 557, 622, 641, 648,
  678, 692/693, 696, 721–725
Ungarn (Volk) 27, 475, 486
Unierte s. Katholizismus
Universitäten s. Hochschulwesen
Untergrundbahnen 385, 426, 582
Unternehmen s. Betriebe
Unterricht s. Schulwesen
Urbanisierung 20, 192, 310, 336, 422, 424,
  427, 432/433, 437, 440, 445–447, 454,
  593/594, 597, 602/603, 620
Urengoj 369
Urheberrecht 232/233
USA 49, 51, 57, 63–67, 70, 88, 92, 101–105,
  108, 111, 115, 418, 457, 470, 493, 495, 515,
  547, 551, 553, 557, 561, 565, 569, 574, 576,
  617, 625, 637, 645, 667, 682, 684/685,
  689–692, 694/695, 698/699, 701, 723, 730
Ust'-Ilimsk 409

Ustovo 656
U Thant, Sithu 694, 696
Uzunov, Dečko 662
Uzunov, Dimo 191, 715
Uzunov, Genčo 579, 657/658

Văca 11/12, 25, 448
Vachtangov, Evgeni 633
Vačkov, Grigor 652
Vagenštajn, Anžel 649, 653
Vakarelski, Ch. 592, 601
Vălčanov, Rangel 648, 650/651, 654
Vălčev, Jordan 627
Vălčeva, Draža 706, 711, 717
Vălčidol 487
Vălev, Dimităr 620
Vălkanov, Velko 151
Vălkov, P. 660/661
Vančev, Pando 706
Vapcarov, Nikola 275, 607, 610, 612, 616, 630, 647
Vărbanov, Aleksandăr 683
Vardar 8, 10, 480
Varna 7, 12/13, 17–26, 44, 79, 156, 158, 191, 265, 268, 274/275, 302, 314/315, 340, 381, 383–386, 427, 432, 448, 451–455, 476, 481, 483/484, 487, 512, 514, 519, 527/528, 581, 614, 633, 646, 651, 673, 729, 731–734, 736, 777
Văršec 728
Vasilev, Orlin 572, 627/628
Vasilev, Stefan 711, 714
Vasil'ov, J. 664
Vaterländische Front s. OF
Vatikan 67, 124, 550, 552, 558, 563/564, 692, 698/699
Vazov, Aleksandăr 646
Vazov, Ivan 423, 587, 606, 612, 635, 637, 639, 646/647
Vegetation 7, 14/15
Velčev, Boris 76–78, 190, 706, 710, 714, 716, 737
Velčev, Damjan 47/48, 60/61, 64/65, 707
Veleka 12
Velički, Andrej 553/554, 561
Veličkov, Georgi 630
Veličkov, Michail 623, 630, 636, 638
Veliko Tărnovo 27–30, 160, 275, 314/315, 383/384, 430/431, 448, 451/452, 454/455, 511, 514, 527, 736
Velimirović, M. 672
Velingrad (Lădžene) 486, 777
Venedig 657
Venev, St. 661
Verfassung, 4, 32, 48, 136, 161, 164, 218, 221, 226, 476, 489, 553, 555

- Tărnovo-Verfassung vom 16.4.1879 32–36, 38/39, 48, 55, 173/174, 211, 214, 544, 688
- Verfassung vom 4.12.1947 (Dimitrov-Verfassung) 64, 68, 79, 94, 136, 154, 259, 278, 476, 547, 552, 558, 575, 633, 691, 705
- Verfassung vom 16.5.1971 79, 83, 87, 112, 119, 136–172, 174, 191, 206, 220, 229, 266/267, 274, 277, 476, 496, 558/559, 696/697, 705
Verkehr 42, 155, 160, 172, 219/220, 265, 286, 296, 371, 380–393, 408, 418, 420, 426, 432, 467, 508, 593, 603, 698, 701, 721
- Luft- 124, 251, 279, 293, 371, 382, 386, 418, 701, 720
- Schienen- s. Eisenbahn
- Schiffs- 30, 109, 136, 233, 279, 296, 371, 381–382, 385/386, 720
- Straßen- 23, 26, 29, 51, 230, 265, 371, 380, 382, 384/385, 420, 430, 470, 593, 698
Verkovič, Stefan 591
Verlage 571/572, 614/615, 626/627, 640, 666, 675/676
Versicherungen 230, 247, 302, 396, 418
Versorgung 51, 75/76, 157/158, 219, 245, 280, 284–286, 288, 294, 298, 334, 347, 363/364, 371–380, 399/400, 408, 410, 413/414, 421, 427, 461, 472, 602, 635, 700
Verstaatlichung 33, 175, 228, 278/279, 295, 381, 458, 465, 555, 691
Verträge 166, 224, 228, 230, 242, 244–247, 249, 289, 295, 395, 398, 411, 413, 417, 508, 535, 640, 688–703, 718–727
Verträge, internationale 36, 39, 44, 49/50, 91–135, 140, 147, 149, 370, 479, 689, 718–727
- Vertrag von Berlin (1878) 33, 42, 89, 97/98, 544, 552, 688
- Bukarest, Friede von (1886) 688
- Vertrag von Bukarest (1913) 39, 97/98, 688
- Vertrag von Craiova (1940) 8, 49, 99/100, 106, 689
- Vertrag von Lausanne (1923) 8, 689
- Vertrag von Neuilly (1919) 41–43, 48, 99/100, 106, 688
- Kleine Entente (1933) 100
- Pariser Friedensvertrag (1947) 57, 63, 65/66, 90, 96, 99–102, 105–108, 110, 117, 127, 211, 395, 545, 551, 557, 691
Verträge
- Vertrag von San Stefano (1878) 30, 39, 97/98, 102, 133, 138, 688
Vertretungsorgane s.a. NSb 82/83, 138, 142/143, 153–162, 167/168, 173, 200, 205/206, 210, 215–220, 228/229, 238, 246, 350, 376, 512
Verwaltung 7/8, 20/21, 51, 58, 76, 78, 80, 82,

136–173, 180, 184, 193, 197/198, 204/205, 208, 218, 226/227, 235, 249, 254, 256–258, 279, 282–286, 289, 293, 296, 314, 351–353, 374, 379/380, 395/396, 420, 426, 432, 447, 458/459, 462, 490, 517/518, 520/521, 524–526, 534, 536/537, 591, 632, 639/640, 644–655, 681/682, 694, 702
Vešin, J. 657
Veterinärmedizin 344, 530, 540
Vežinov, Pavel 607, 619, 620–622, 625, 627–631
Videnov, Vladimir 706
Vidin 19, 21–23, 156, 274, 314–316, 383, 386, 448, 451/452, 454/455, 633, 734
Viehzucht s. Tierzucht
Vietnam 115, 375, 700, 722–724
Vinnica 409
Visa 701, 718, 726/727
Viskjar 10, 22
Vit 12
VITIZ (Film- und Theaterhochschule) 640, 646
Vitoša 10, 12, 14, 22, 422, 424, 648, 665, 686/687, 735
Vlachina Planina 10
Vladaja 269
Vladigerov, Pančo 672/673
Vladivostok 429
Vlassov, Jurij 683
VMRO 38, 44–46, 55
Vojnikov, Dobri 632
Vola 424
Volen, Ilija 629
Volev, Nikolaj 654
Volkelt, Johannes 606
Völkerbund 49
Völkermord s. Genozid
Volksabstimmung 148, 220, 690, 697, 704, 736
Volksbräuche 420, 562, 591, 593, 595, 598, 600, 604, 632, 656
Volksdemokratie 64/65, 136, 154, 173–177, 180, 194/195, 214, 279, 608
Volksfront s. OF
Volkskultur 2, 20, 28, 221, 473, 566, 590–605, 656, 666–676
Volkskunst 652, 663/664
Volksräte s. Vertretungsorgane
Volkszählung 31, 111, 118, 371, 433, 439, 457, 460, 475, 480/481, 550, 559
Volov, P. 734
Voznessenskij, Andrej 624
Vrabevo 731
Vraca 17/18, 22/23, 77/78, 156, 314–316, 383, 387, 451/452, 454/455, 485/486, 511, 568, 729/730, 735
Vracěv, I. 697

Vyšinskij, Andrej 64
Wachstum 78, 80, 285/286, 290, 303, 305, 310–314, 325, 327, 329–333, 339/340, 343, 345, 363, 377, 413, 458, 463, 465, 520
Waffen 44, 59, 120, 125, 130, 272–274, 413, 415
Waffenstillstand 60, 101/102, 104, 573, 690
Wahlen 37–42, 44–48, 62–65, 82, 137, 141–143, 148, 159, 166, 171, 173/174, 178–180, 191, 203, 206, 210–218, 221, 350/351, 526, 574, 690, 692–694, 697/698, 700–703
Währungen 67/68, 172, 229, 251, 301/302, 334, 346, 348, 367, 369, 390, 395–400, 408, 410, 414, 417/418, 691/692, 694, 720
Wajda, Andrzej 644, 648
Wald s. Forstwirtschaft
Waldheim, Kurt 698
Wallraff, Günther 616
Warschau 115, 693, 696
Warschauer Pakt 2, 84, 110, 113, 115, 122, 127, 135, 161, 262–276, 421, 698, 721
Washington, D.C. 10, 730
Wasser s.a. Umwelt 12, 359/360, 419, 426–429, 432, 726/727
Wasserwirtschaft 12, 25, 131
Weber, Max 164
Weideland 336, 340, 486
Weitsozialisten s. BRSDP
Weizen, s. Pflanzenproduktion
Weizsäcker, Richard von 125/126, 703
Weltkrieg, Erster 20, 41/42, 53, 55, 57, 60, 89, 99/100, 270, 424, 519, 550, 569, 611, 625, 633, 640, 650, 666, 688, 729, 732, 735
Weltkrieg, Zweiter 1, 3, 8, 20, 49–53, 55–57, 60, 67, 70–75, 78, 87–89, 93–96, 100–104, 106–110, 128, 133, 154, 174, 177, 180, 182, 189, 192/193, 195, 199, 210, 224. 263, 269/270, 278, 306, 333, 337, 339, 349, 355, 371, 381, 394–396, 401, 406, 420, 424, 436, 458–468, 472/473, 484, 492, 499, 506, 510, 514, 519, 548, 550/551, 565, 569, 571/572, 584, 587, 590, 594, 601, 606/607, 611/612, 618, 625, 633, 635, 637, 646/647, 649/650, 657, 659/660, 666, 684, 689, 693, 735
Weltmarkt s. Außenhandel
Westmächte 49–52, 57/58, 63–67, 84, 87/88, 91–97, 101–106, 110/111, 115/116, 124/125, 130, 134, 243, 285/286, 304, 326–328, 346, 352, 364, 367, 369, 518, 541, 587, 602, 604, 622/623, 626, 636, 651, 730, 736
Whitehead, John C. 125
WHO 541, 720
Wiedergeburt 28–30, 44, 490, 493, 516, 518, 544, 561, 567, 591, 601, 605, 652, 656/657

Wien 33, 35, 37, 49, 370, 556, 561, 657, 681, 719, 722, 737
Williams, E. V. 672
Wirtschaft 7–26, 32, 47, 49, 52–55, 69/70, 75/76, 78, 82/83, 87/88, 132, 136, 139/140, 148/149, 151/152, 155, 157/158, 161, 163–165, 167/168, 175, 179, 185–187, 190, 202/203, 208/209, 219/220, 224, 227–230, 252, 254, 258, 277–418, 380, 385, 389/390, 392, 394–421, 424, 435, 466–468, 472, 481, 487/488, 490, 498, 510, 519–524, 526, 531, 534, 536–538, 540, 552, 559, 568, 575, 583, 590, 592, 594/595, 597, 599, 601, 612, 646, 656, 658, 664/665, 687, 695/696, 698, 701–703, 720/721, 728, 731, 733–735
Wirtschaftsvereinigungen s. Betriebe
Wischnewski, Hans-Jürgen 701
Wissenschaft 1–5, 79–81, 87–89, 91–97, 106, 110/111, 134, 143, 153/154, 161, 170, 180, 186/187, 198/199, 203, 246, 252, 269/270, 288, 293, 329, 351/352, 379, 396, 411/412, 424/425, 431, 439, 468, 474, 477, 479, 485, 495/496, 498, 509, 513–542, 561, 566, 568, 577, 589, 595, 597, 600, 609/610, 650, 664, 666, 672, 674–676, 681, 695, 697, 698/699, 703, 728/729, 733
Wohnungswesen 72, 81, 170, 172, 180, 208, 225, 227, 229, 238, 241, 286, 290, 335, 430, 432, 440, 457, 460, 466–468, 471, 513, 534, 593, 596, 601, 615, 664
Wolf, Konrad 649
Wolff, R. L. 93

Yılmaz, Mesut 131
Zachariev, Eduard 651
Zachariev, I. 21
Zachariev, V. 660
Zachariev, Z. 661
zadruga 19, 590
Zagorčinov, Stojan 609, 627, 629
Zagreb 622
Žandov, Zachari 647, 654
Zar der Bulgaren 44/45, 704
Zarev, Kiril 711–713, 715
Zarev, Pantelej 612, 614, 627, 629, 706
Zarev, Vladimir 623, 630

Ždanov 385
Ždanov, Andrej Aleksandrovič 66, 71, 659
Žečev, Tončo 619, 631
Zeitschriften, Zeitungen s. Presse
Željaskova, Binka 648/49, 653/54
Žendov, A. 660/661
Zensur 45
Zentralisierung 522, 524
Zentralismus 143, 206, 341, 432, 461, 463, 465, 493/494, 517
Zentralismus, demokratischer 136, 138/139, 154, 158, 160, 178, 198, 205–207, 219
Žeravna 430, 601
Zidarov, Kamen 618, 627–629
Zidarov, L. 661
Ziegen s. Tierzucht
Zigeuner s. Roma
Zimbabwe 725, 727
Zionismus s. Judentum
Žišev, Nikolaj 706
Živkov, Todor 3/4, 56, 70, 73–86, 88–91, 95, 112–135, 146, 177, 188–191, 195, 197, 199–203, 209/210, 215, 218–220, 223, 283/284, 288/289, 291, 297, 352, 411, 489, 524, 538, 559, 562/563, 517, 628/629, 636, 680, 682, 693–703, 705, 710/711, 713/714, 716, 728/729, 732/733, 737
Živkov, Vladimir, 83, 188, 191, 703, 737
Živkov, Živko 77, 706, 709–711, 716
Živkova, Ljudmila 56, 78, 80/81, 496/497, 684, 717, 728, 737
Zjapkov, Vasil 557
ZK s. BKP
Zlatev, Penčo 48
Zlatev, Peco (Architekt) 664
Zlatica 10, 729
Zlatica-Pirdop 356
Zlatni Pjasăci 24
Zograf 561
Zoll 53, 327, 353, 377, 417/418, 692
Zveno 47/48, 55–57, 59–61, 65/66, 203/204, 209, 211/212, 545, 570, 575, 689/690, 707/708, 732
Zwangsbulgarisierung s. Nationalitätenpolitik
Zypern 1, 4, 84, 127, 129, 384, 698, 723–725, 727

Kulturelle Traditionen in Bulgarien

Bericht über das Kolloquium der Südosteuropa-Kommission 16.–18. Juni 1987. Einundzwanzig Beiträge. Herausgegeben von Reinhard Lauer und Peter Schreiner. 1989. 346 Seiten mit 6 Abbildungen und 8 Seiten Kunstdruck, kartoniert / Abhandlungen der Akademie der Wissenschaften in Göttingen, Philologisch-Historische Klasse, Dritte Folge, Band 177

Jugoslawien

Integrationsprobleme in Geschichte und Gegenwart.
Beiträge des Südosteuropa-Arbeitskreises der Deutschen Forschungsgemeinschaft zum V. Internationalen Südosteuropa-Kongreß der Association Internationale d'Études du Sud-Est Européen, Belgrad, 11.–17. September 1984. Herausgegeben von Klaus-Detlev Grothusen. 1984. 337 Seiten mit 57 Abbildungen, Leinen

Die Türkei in Europa

Beiträge des Südosteuropa-Arbeitskreises der Deutschen Forschungsgemeinschaft zum IV. Internationalen Südosteuropa-Kongreß der Association Internationale d'Études du Sud-Est Européen, Ankara, 13.–18. August 1979. Herausgegeben von Klaus-Detlev Grothusen. 1979. 271 Seiten mit zahlreichen Abbildungen im Text und 16 Tafeln, Leinen

Ethnogenese und Staatsbildung in Südosteuropa

Beiträge des Südosteuropa-Arbeitskreises der Deutschen Forschungsgemeinschaft zum III. Internationalen Südosteuropa-Kongreß der Association Internationale d'Études du Sud-Est Européen, Bukarest, 4.–10. September 1974. Herausgegeben von Klaus-Detlev Grothusen. 1974. 321 Seiten und 8 Tafeln, Leinen

Dankwart A. Rüstow
Die Türkei – Brücke zwischen Orient und Okzident

Aus dem Amerikanischen von Barbara Paulsen. Redaktionelle Bearbeitung von Johannes Fest. 1990. 186 Seiten mit 1 Karte, 1 Schaubild und 3 Tabellen, kartoniert / Kleine Vandenhoeck-Reihe 1549

Vandenhoeck & Ruprecht · Göttingen/Zürich